HISTORY

OF

Bond and Montgomery Counties,

ILLINOIS.

EDITED BY WILLIAM HENRY PERRIN.

ILLUSTRATED.

CHICAGO:
O. L. BASKIN & CO., HISTORICAL PUBLISHERS, LAKESIDE BUILDING.

Culver, Page, Hoyne & Co.
PRINTERS
118 & 120 Monroe St.

PREFACE.

THE history of Bond and Montgomery Counties, after months of persistent toil and research, is now completed, and it is believed that no subject of universal public importance or interest has been omitted, save where protracted effort failed to secure reliable results. We are well aware of our inability to furnish a perfect history from meager public documents and numberless conflicting traditions, but claim to have prepared a work fully up to the standard of our promises. Through the courtesy and assistance generously afforded by the residents of these counties, we have been enabled to trace out and put on record the greater portion of the important events that have transpired in Bond and Montgomery Counties up to the present time. And we feel assured that all thoughtful people in these counties, now and in future, will recognize and appreciate the importanee of the work and its permanent value.

A dry statement of facts has, as far as possible, been avoided, and incidents and anecdotes have been woven in with facts and statisties, forming a narrative at once instructive and interesting.

To those who have kindly assisted our corps of writers in gathering material, and furnished us data of historical value, we acknowledge our indebtedness; and to Williamson Plant, Esq., of Greenville; Judge A. N. Kingsbury, of Hillsboro; H. A. Coolidge, Esq., of Litchfield; and Rev. T. E. Spilman, of Nokomis, our thanks for able contributions are especially due.

AUGUST, 1882. THE PUBLISHERS.

CONTENTS.

PART I.

BOND COUNTY.

MONTGOMERY COUNTY.

PART I.

HISTORY

OF

BOND AND MONTGOMERY COUNTIES.

CHAPTER I.*

INTRODUCTION TO BOND COUNTY—GENERAL OBSERVATIONS—THE EARLY STATE OF THE COUNTRY—THE DIFFICULTIES OF OCCUPYING IT—COMING OF THE PIONEERS—HILL'S STATION AND JONES' FORT—PERILS OF THE WILDERNESS—TIMBER AND PRAIRIE—THE LATTER SHUNNED AS A DESERT—PRAIRIE FIRES—AN INCIDENT—HARD FARE OF THE SETTLERS—HOW THEY LIVED, ETC.

"Time though old is swift in flight,
And years go fleetly by."

THE advantages to be derived from the study of history are numerous and important. There is something in the breast of almost every individual which makes him desirous of examining the past, and ascertaining what has been, in relation to his own, as well as other countries. Man is anxious to look back and inquire into the transactions of the generation which immediately preceded him; this creates in his mind a desire to know something of the one preceding that, and so he goes on inquiring back from one generation to another, and from century to century, until he arrives at his origin—Adam—in the Garden of Eden, fresh from the hand of his Maker. Knowing this general desire of the human race, men have written histories, in every age of the world, from the time of Moses down to the present, in order to perpetuate the sayings and doings of their fellow-beings.

The words and actions of man, either for weal or woe, constitute the most important feature in all histories; there is no portion of the habitable earth that has not been made or ruined to a certain extent by his management. Christianity, the arts and sciences, peace and, as a consequence, civilization, render the earth

"One great garden of her God,
Bright with beauty and girt with power."

but when infidelity, ignorance, bigotry, superstition and war prevail, barbarism is the result and the earth becomes changed into a wilderness. Such has been the case in the past, and if it is any criterion by which to judge the future, it is certainly of great moment, that we become well acquainted with the history of all countries, more especially that of our own; when we peruse its pages and find there recorded the former errors and virtues of our

*By R. O. White.

race, whether considered as individuals, communities or states, or, in a political, social, or religious point of view, there are many instructive lessons to be learned. One of the first is to studiously avoid any course of action which has been fraught with evil consequences, and to earnestly strive for those principles that have been most productive of good, to all classes of society.

Among all grades of history, none is more instructive or sought after with a greater eagerness than that which truthfully delineates the rise and progress of the State, community, or even county in which we live. There is pleasure as well as profit to every well-educated and inquiring mind, in contemplating the struggles of the early settlers in all portions of the great West ; how they encountered and overcame every species of trial, hardship and danger to which human beings were ever subjected. But these things strike us more forcibly and fill our minds with more immediate interest when confined to our own little county of Bond, where we can yet occasionally meet with some of the now gray-haired actors in those early scenes, with whom life's rugged day is almost over, whose bravery in encountering the troubles and misfortunes incident to a frontier life has borne an important part toward making our county what it now is, and whose acts in connection with hundreds of others in the first settling of our vast domain, have compelled the civilized world to acknowledge that the Americans are an invincible people.

It may appear, to some, rather small and insignificant work to record the history of a diminutive county like Bond, but it will be remembered that our vast republic is comprised of States that are made up of counties, each of which contributes its share toward the general history of the country. Though occupying but a small portion of the State of Illinois, yet Bond County has a history that is fraught with interest to its own citizens, at least, besides many of those in adjoining counties.

How little do many of the present generation, when they behold the "old settler," as he is termed, either realize or appreciate the hardships through which he has passed, or the part he has performed in reclaiming our country from the rule of the wild and savage tribes that roamed at will over all parts of it. "Young America," as he passes the old settler by, without so much as nodding his head, little dreams that he has spent the bloom of his life in helping to make this country what it now is, or rather, in preparing it for the reception of all those modern improvements and business which surround us on every side. The old settler and his deeds should be remembered and appreciated by all. Every lover of self-sacrifice and undaunted energy cannot but admire that adventurous spirit, united with cool determination, which influenced the hardy pioneer to leave the civilization of the older States, and locate in this wild region, far removed from the influence of the schoolhouse and the church, driving back the savage, and paving the way for the great advantages we now so fully enjoy. And what must be the reflections of the old settler himself, as he looks upon this country and contrasts the present with the past—for he knows something of the past. He looks over the thriving county of Bond, which may be termed almost one vast farm, and calls to mind the time when all those prairies, now teeming with grain, fruits and vegetables, were thickly covered with grass six feet in height, where the deer and wolves held high carnival, undisturbed, save by the stealthy Indian, or the occasional appearance of a white hunter passing from one to another of the settlements or forts that were "few and far between." He views our elegant homes, telling of wealth, ease and comfort, and remembers the time when there was not a glass window in the whole county—not over two dozen dwellings, all of them log cabins with weight-pole roofs and wooden chimneys. He beholds neat churches, fine schoolhouses and colleges, and thinks of the time when there was not a church or schoolhouse in the county. He looks at our court house, provided with its comfortable rooms for the accommodation of various county officers, and remembers the holding of the first court that ever assembled in the county, which met in a rude log house, the jury room being in the woods. He contemplates with wonder and delight the railroad, one of the grandest achievements of human enterprise, and as he beholds the numerous trains of crowded cars rapidly conveying passengers and freight from one point to another, his mind reverts back to those early days when there were no railroads, and not even tolerable wagon roads in all this country, the means of transportation being ox teams, the only market St. Louis, then a small town, while in some portions of the year the mud was many feet in depth. He sees our fine flouring mills in all parts of the county, and thinks of the days when there were no mills here of any kind, and the inhabitants lived on hominy and bread made of pounded corn. He is delighted with our various agricultural implements, and recollects the hardships of farming, when there was not a seed-drill, corn-planter, reaper, mower, or thresher in the State, when scythes and sickles cut down the harvest and flails or horses' feet threshed or trod out the grain. He looks back to the first advances that were made here in improvement and civilization—the early schools, their teachers and many incidents connected with them; the singing-schools, where the young men brought their sweethearts behind them on the same horse; of camp-meetings in the olden time, and prominent individuals and circumstances connected therewith; of old-fashioned muster and election days, and the heroes of the various fights which there occurred, the result of old grudges and bad whisky. These, and a thousand other reflections must pass in review through his mind as he looks around upon the Bond County of to day in contrast with that of fifty years ago.

It will be the object of the following pages, to describe as accurately as possible the rise and progress of Bond County, and the incidents and characters pertaining thereto, from the first settlement within its limits down to the present time. In doing this, the great aim will be to present facts, so far as it is possible to obtain them. Many of these must necessarily be gleaned from individuals now living, who emigrated to the county in an early day, and either witnessed, or were actual participants in the scenes connected with its early history, there being no written account to which we can go for information.

The task will be a pleasant one, both to the reader and the writer, to go back to the period when this county, along with other portions of the State of Illinois, was a wilderness unmarked by the hand of man and note the advent of the first white families and contemplate the numerous and apparently insurmountable difficulties with which they were surrounded. But to give precise dates in all cases of the early history of Bond County will be almost impossible as there are but few of the old pioneers now living. The lapse of fifty-five or sixty years has not only swept from the theater of life most of those heroes of the old and perilous time, but has dimmed the memories of those who yet remain, so that some of them have forgotten the exact time when many events, appertaining to our history, transpired. However, by a careful comparison of the different statements and dates, they are given with sufficient accuracy for general utility, even in the instances where there is any lack of coincidence.

The first settlement made within the present limits of Bond County was at Hill's Station, or fort—(called also White's Fort)— about the year 1812. This fort was situated about eight miles, in a southwesterly direction, from where the town of Greenville now stands. One mile and a half south of this was another station, one called Jones' Fort built near the same time. These buildings were erected by the white inhabitants, as shelters not only to protect them from the inclemencies of the weather, but from the incursions of the Indians, with whom the county was infested, it being considered unsafe for one family to reside at a distance from others. These settlements were all made within a year or two of the same time, and during the last war with England.

When we view the present prosperous condition of the country, it seems scarcely credible to believe that no longer age than the period under consideration, the entire population of Bond County was comprised of only two feeble bands of adventurers, each containing but a few families, shut up within the walls of a fort, outside of which it was dangerous to venture any distance. These forts, stations or block-houses, as they were variously called, were located in the edge of the timber, and were constructed of hewed logs. They would not, it is true, present a very formidable resistance to the military arrangements of the present day, but when considered as a protection against the implements of savage warfare, they proved quite efficient

The only land cultivated was a few acres immediately surrounding or near the stations. These farms, or patches, as they would now be termed, were in the timber also, and planted in cotton, tobacco, corn, pumpkins, melons, potatoes and a few other vegetables. Wheat, for the first few years, was not cultivated, as there were no mills; hence, it would have been of little service. Most of the first settlers were from Kentucky, Virginia and North Carolina, where all the land is timbered, and the prairies, they viewed as uninhabitable deserts. The idea of hauling rails, fire-wood and building timber, several miles was not to be thought of by them. It was a current remark by the people then, that "the greatest drawback to this country was scarcity of timber."

In the autumn of 1816, a few families of emigrants were crossing the prairie east of Beaver Creek, in the southern part of this county. The grass had nearly all been burnt off, affording a fine opportunity for viewing the soil and situation of the country. An old gentleman belonging to the party was walking along behind the wagons, in company with a few others, who, like himself, had become fatigued with riding and got out to walk. The old man gazed with wonder and delight on the boundless expanse of prairie spread out before him in all its original beauty. Taking up handfuls of the rich, black soil, he would examine it minutely, then toss it aside with the exclamation, "Ah me, how rich it is; what a pity there's no timber to fence it." He greatly deplored the strange freak of nature, which deprived a vast extent of country of trees, otherwise so productive, evidently believing this arrangement one of the mysterious workings of an All-Wise Providence, in creating a soil where trees would not grow, and that it would be of no avail to ever plant them, for if the Almighty had so intended it, they would have been found growing there of their own accord.

It is stated by one who belonged to this party, that some of the old ladies felt afraid to enter the first prairie they ever beheld; fearful that the ground might give way and they be swallowed up as if in quicksand; or that night might overtake them before getting across, and they have to wait in the darkness without wood or water until morning.

It was the general opinion that, on account of the scarcity and inconvenience of timber, the prairies would remain as vast pastures, and hence the first farms were made in or near the edge of the timber. A heavy growth of coarse grass from four to eight feet high covered the prairies and all the upland portion of the timber, as well as much of the bottom land; its place in the woods is now supplied by scrubby underbrush. When the grass became dry in autumn, or killed by the frost it furnished material for vast conflagrations annually, sweeping over the country with destructive force, consuming everything of a dry nature in their pathway, and in some instances burning up wild animals overtaken by them in their devastating course. These fires broke out sometimes by accident, but were often put out on purpose to burn the grass off, so that people could see to hunt to better advantage. Farms or settlements being few this was not objected to. The neighbors united on a certain day agreed upon, and "burnt the woods," as it was termed, first making their farms or clearings secure by setting fire to the edge of the grass next to the farm and carefully watching it until a space was burnt all around it sufficiently wide to prevent the fire passing over. Fires were on some occasions set out by the Indians, many miles from the white settlements and, driven before the wind, spread over extensive tracts of country, destroying everything in their course. As may be imagined from the height of the grass, a fire on the prairie at that time was a grand and fearful spectacle, more particularly at night. When fanned by a strong wind, the flames rose to a height of thirty or forty feet, presenting in the large prairies an unbroken wall of flame several miles in extent, having the form of a semi-circle with the convex side in front and sending forth a roar that could be heard at a great distance. With a heavy wind, the flames advanced so rapidly that many instances occurred where persons, even on horseback barely escaped being overtaken before reaching a place of safety.

On one occasion, a party of hunters from the settlements near Greenville, returning home with a wagon load of honey and venison, when about a mile east of where Elm Point now is set fire to the grass, for amusement. As the wind was from the south and blew the flames in a direction opposite to the way they were going, no danger was apprehended. After enjoying the sight to their satisfaction, they started on, when, in a short time, the wind changed to a strong gale from the north, bringing the fire directly toward them in all its fury and so rapid was its advance, that they were forced to cut the horses loose from the wagon and, with all possible speed, escape for their lives. By great exertion they managed to outrun it, but the wagon, harness, venison and honey were consumed. Quite a number of marvelous adventures of this nature were related by the early backwoodsmen, detailing feats of horsemanship in comparison with which John Gilpin's perilous ride was mere child's play. In every public crowd would be found individuals who loved to hunt and tell of their adventures or listen to those of others. There was nothing wrong in this perhaps so long as the truth was kept in view, but as every such collection contained some "hard cases," especially when warmed up with whisky, they soon entered the regions of fancy, trying who could tell the "biggest tale," betting "drinks for the crowd" on the result. The narrators of these stories told them so often, that they grew into the belief that they were actually true.

One of these will be sufficient to give the reader. Its truth is not vouched for, but the substance of what the old hunter stated is here given. The hero of the adventure went by the name of "old Slaymush" and was acknowledged to be the "biggest liar" in Bond County at that time, with but one or two exceptions, which was saying much for him in that respect, for in those early times there were some heroes "hard to beat" on frontier incidents. The old fellow said he had been out hunting "in the fall of the year, over on the Okaw and there was a heap of bear and deer over thar," but it seemed like "luck was agin" him, having shot several deer, but failing to kill them instantly, or "drap them in their tracks," as he "ginerally done," they ran off and he lost them. He "snapped" six times at the "biggest bear that ever was seen," when the animal took fright and ran off. Attributing his bad luck to some newly-purchased powder, and expressing the modest desire that the individual who sold it to him might be safely domiciled in a region where powder would ignite without flint and steel, he started home, taking a westerly course through the prairie lying in the eastern part of this county. It was about 2 o'clock in the afternoon, and he was within two miles of the timber, on the west side of the "perara," when thick clouds of smoke appeared, stretching to some distance along the edge of the woods. At the first glance he "knowed the perara was a-fire, and that old Slaymush and his hoss would have to git out o' thar, or be roasted alive," and as there was a high wind from the west, something had to be done immediately. Putting whip to his horse he set out in a northern direction, hoping, by this flank movement, to get around the fire to a place of safety, but this was soon found to be unavailing, for the flames extended too far in that direction, and had already approached so close that the heat and smoke almost stifled him. The only remaining chance was to turn back and keep ahead of the fire to the Okaw timber—a distance of six miles. He said he never was as "nigh skeered" in his life as when he "seed" the race that was before him. Wheeling his horse, he took out his hickory rammer to urge him on, but his "hoss was the worst skeered of the two," and when he "sort o' leaned forred and fetched a big yell, the critter actually cum very nigh jumping from under" him, causing him to "drap his ramrod and lose his cap;" but holding on to his gun "like a possum to a simmon-tree limb," he sped on like the wind, with the fire advancing and roaring behind him like a hurricane. It often got so close that "great rolls of it, bigger than a kivered wagon, would bust loose" and run past him "roarin' like all natur," sometimes on one side and sometimes on the other. Occasionally one of these "big rolls" would rush "clean over" him, when he would throw himself forward on the neck of his horse till it passed over and then straighten up again. Fortunately, none of the fiery billows happened to envelop him entirely, and, with the jaws of destruction snapping at his heels, he flew onward, leaping gullies, one of which was "forty foot wide." In crossing this, he and the fire were side by side, and "jest the instant his hoss struck t'other bank, it was thar too." Thus he went on with his fearful race, anxiously looking ahead for the timber, near which the grass had been burnt some weeks before, knowing that there he would be in a place of safety. Though nearly blinded and suffocated with smoke, he thought of making one more desperate effort to increase the speed of his horse, although he seemed to be doing his very best already. So leaning forward and straining his voice to the utmost, he "fetched another big yell, when the animal "jumped clear from under" him. When he struck the ground, the momentum caused him to roll over two or three times and lose his gun, besides stunning him considerably. On rising to his feet, he found himself on the open, burnt ground, and, of course, safe. The fire having ceased in a few moments, he looked around a little, and found his gun, which had received no further damage than being discharged as the fire passed over it. He saw his horse standing at a distance of a hundred yards, gazing at him most intently; going up in front of the faithful animal and looking at him, he seemed unhurt—not a hair showed the least sign of having been in the proximity of fire; for this he was thankful, as also, his own preservation

—"there was not a har of his head even singed." He took his horse by the bridle and turned him round, when a sight presented itself that was horrible to behold. Every particle of hair and skin was burnt off his tail and hind legs, the tail itself being literally roasted. The hair was also burnt off his hips and back, as far forward as the loins, but no farther! The old man would relate this story whenever the subject of prairie fires was mentioned, evidently believing it to be the truth, for if any of his hearers showed any signs of incredulity he appeared much offended.

There being no mills in the country at the time the forts were occupied, and for several years afterward, the inhabitants used much less bread than at present; it was all made of corn meal, procured in the following manner: A large block of wood, two or three feet in length and from one to two feet in diameter, was set up endwise on the ground, the upper end being scooped out so as to make a hollow capable of holding from a peck to a half bushel of grain. The corn was put into this and pounded with a maul, or other heavy weight made on purpose. This was, in the fullest sense of the term, "earning bread by the sweat of the brow," but there being no other chance, it was better to procure it in that manner than to do without. These "machines," called "mortars," were sometimes made in the stump of a tree when conveniently situated. Hominy was much used, being considered a saving of bread.

The inhabitants, at first, depended mostly for meat on the game, with which the country abounded. Nearly every article of clothing worn by either male or female, was manufactured at home by the women, on the old-fashioned spinning-wheel, cards and loom. The man dressed buckskins, out of which were made pantaloons, hunting-shirts, moccasins, and occasionally pillow-cases, and dresses for the women.

They made shoes from leather tanned at home by themselves. To do this a tree, three or four feet in diameter, was cut down, and as large a trough as possible dug out of it; this constituted a kind of vat, into which the hides, after being duly prepared, were placed along with oak bark, broken to pieces, and pulverized a little by pounding, the whole being filled up with water. They were kept in this condition until tanned. Some of the leather manufactured in this way was very good, but most of it rather indifferent. These primitive tanners put no blacking on their leather, for the very good reason that lampblack could nowhere be obtained. Of course this kind of material made rather a rough shoe, but being the best that could be procured, the people were content. In fact, such shoes best suited the rough jaunts taken on foot by many of the pioneers, through brush, briers, swamps and grass, wet with dew and rain. Boots were seldom worn, except in the towns, and then only by professional men; no better evidence could be adduced of a man being a preacher, doctor or lawyer, than his appearing in public with boots on. This scarcity of boots continued for several years. Many old ladies seemed disposed to consider them as belonging especially to the legal fraternity, styling every man who wore them a "dandy lawyer."

Everything not manufactured at home was termed a "store" article, as "store shoes," "store hat," "store bonnet;" and any one wholly or even partially attired in "store" articles, excited envy in the breasts of the younger and more shallow-brained portion of the community, and many a young lass, when appearing in public, considered herself highly honored, if so fortunate as to secure the attentions of a "feller with store clothes on," furnishing an instance of that weakness in human nature, too common even yet, judging persons by external appearances.

The scarcity of the necessaries of life will not be wondered at, when we consider that St. Louis was the only market, and a very poor one at that, being then a small town of only a few thousand inhabitants, having but two ways of obtaining everything of foreign growth or manufacture, one by keel-boats rowed or pushed by poles up the Mississippi from New Orleans; the other from Philadelphia, by means of wagons across the Alleghany Mountains to Pittsburgh, thence down the Ohio River, in keel-boats, floating with the current to its mouth, and from this point, pushed up the Mississippi in the same manner as from New Orleans.

CHAPTER II.*

TRIALS AND HARDSHIPS OF THE PIONEERS—SKINS AS A CIRCULATING MEDIUM—THE WAR OF 1812—ITS EFFECT UPON THE SETTLEMENT OF THIS PORTION OF THE COUNTRY—MURDER OF COX AND HIS SON—THE BLESSINGS OF PEACE—PROGRESS OF EMIGRATION—BUILDING OF CABINS—EARLY MANNERS AND CUSTOMS—PIONEER COURTSHIPS AND OTHER SOCIAL EVENTS.

"Oh, the waves of life danced merrily
And had a joyous flow,
In the days when we were Pioneers,
Fifty years ago." — [illegible]

FROM the time the first settlements were made in what is now Bond County until the close of the war of 1812, money was scarcely ever seen. Skins of the mink, muskrat, raccoon and deer composed the circulating medium of the country. Tobacco, powder, lead and whisky were the principal articles purchased, and the merchant or grocery-keeper when asked the price of any of his goods replied by stating a certain number of skins per pound or gallon.

A story is told of a party of fellows on a Christmas spree, who, finding themselves about out of whisky, and not having the wherewith to replenish, hit upon the following expedient to obtain a supply: They went one night to a little grocery, having one raccoon skin with them. This paid for whisky enough to furnish them all a drink or two round, including the proprietor, who of course was fond of the article and imbibed rather freely, soon becoming quite hilarious from its effects. The party observed this, and each one, on placing the liquor to his lips, merely tasted it, but the grocery-keeper, whenever it came his turn, took a good drink; consequently objects soon began to assume a confused appearance to his vision. This was just what they wanted, and getting him "about right," as they expressed it, one of them slipped back where the pile of skins lay, took one and put it through a large crack in the wall of the hut to the outside, then going out at the door he went round, took up the skin, and after waiting a few minutes came in—being saluted by the others as a fresh arrival—and presented his raccoon skin in payment for a certain amount of whisky. This offer was readily accepted, the whisky measured out and the skin thrown back on the heap with the rest. This feat was repeated every few minutes till they obtained all the whisky they wanted, having actually sold the grocery keeper his own raccoon skin six or seven times in a few hours. After the close of the war money was brought into the country and gradually took the place of skins.

At one time during the war Hill's station and Jones' Fort were abandoned, on account of Indian hostilities, and all the white inhabitants left the country except one man named Kenson, generally called "Old Kenson." There is no account given of this man "showing whence he came or whither he went," but we are told he loved the spirit, but whether he was born of it or not is quite another question. He was as impervious to the angelic smiles and charms of the softer sex, and had never realized the truth, that

"The world was sad, the garden was a wild,
And man the hermit sighed till woman smiled."

but lived in the enjoyment of single blessed-

* By R. O. White.

ness, in a large hollow sycamore tree, situated in Shoal Creek Bottom, near where the Vandalia Railroad now crosses. "Old Henson" remained alone in this primitive residence to look after his hogs and hunt, returning to his tree each time by a different route, to avoid being tracked by the Indians. He stayed there unmolested until the rest of the people returned to the neighborhood, after which no further trace of him can be found. But the presumption is that he joined some band of Rocky Mountain trappers, spending his life in the wild seclusions of the land of sunset.

While the war of 1812 was in progress, but few emigrants came to the county, and these settled in the vicinity of the forts, or stations on account of the hostile incursions of the savages. Occasionally a settler erected his cabin, and made a "clearing" at quite a distance from the station, remaining there with his family as long as there were no signs of Indians about, but as soon as they made their appearance in the neighborhood, he would remove, with all his responsibilities and household goods, into the fort for safety, returning home when the danger had passed. Families thus situated moved to and from the forts, perhaps, several times in a year, and, while living at their homes, were in constant danger of being attacked by Indians; yet they appeared contented, and in the enjoyment of more happiness than seems possible, under the circumstances.

There was a man named Cox, who, in spite of the warnings and entreaties of others, persisted in staying at home instead of coming with his family, into Hill's Station, the savages being then encamped on Indian Creek, four miles nearly west from Greenville. His house was near Beaver Creek, a little below where Dudleyville is now situated, and several miles from the station, but he insisted there was no danger. As a result, however, of his imprudence, the Indians attacked his house one day during his absence, stole several articles of value, captured his daughter, Sally Cox, and carried her off with them. Intelligence of this melancholy event reached the station in a few hours. A party of men was instantly raised, the savages pursued, overtaken, and the girl rescued and brought back safe to her parents all within the space of twenty-four hours from the time of her capture. After this occurrence, Cox was willing to remove his family to the fort especially in times of imminent danger, but notwithstanding the remonstrances of others, he would go out to his house once or twice a week, "to see how things were getting along." On one of these occasions he was accompanied by his son, a small boy, both being on horseback.

When they came within a short distance of his residence, he sent the boy to water their horses at the creek, while he proceeded on foot to the house. As he approached he noticed Indian tracks, which aroused his suspicions, but being a brave man he went on, almost fearing to enter. The savages were concealed in the house, standing on both sides of the door with rifles cocked and presented, ready to shoot him the moment he entered. He came up to the door, and on opening it, was shot by an Indian and instantly killed. They then ran down to the creek where the boy was, and gave him to understand they would not hurt him, that they only wanted the horses. Being greatly frightened he endeavored to ride toward them, or hold the horses so that they could come near enough to take hold of the bridles, but the poor animals were so alarmed at the Indians he could not manage them. Hence, quite a struggle ensued; the Indians trying to get to the horses and they struggling away from them, while the boy was using every exertion to hold them, no doubt thinking his life depended on his efforts to do so. In this manner they gradually got farther from the creek, when, suddenly emerging into the prairie, the boy thought to escape, and started off at a rapid pace. The Indians perceiving this, one of them leveled his gun and shot the little fellow off his horse as he ran. The house in which this tragedy occurred was standing but a few years since.

The particulars of the murder of Cox and his son were related by the Indians themselves, at the treaty made near the close of the war. He was a large, powerful man, an experienced indian fighter, and had sent many a "brave" to the "happy hunting grounds." Had he certainly known they were concealed in the house, it would have cost them many lives to have taken his, for he was considered a match for two or three Indians at any time. Most of them knew him, and acknowledged that as they watched through a small crevice in the house, and perceived, from his looks and actions, that he had discovered their tracks, and yet was boldly approaching the door, they felt afraid of him, although ten to one in numbers.

An incident occurred at Jones' Fort, about the time Cox was killed, which is of interest in this connection. At a little distance from it stood a large elm tree, which at the height of several feet separated into three prongs, all branching out at the same distance from the ground. Each of these being very large afforded sufficient shelter to conceal a man standing in the space thus formed. An Indian, observing this, conceived the idea of climbing up into the ambuscade thus furnished and shooting at persons inside the fort. From this elevated position, he could see over the wall and fire on the people, which was impossible from the ground. One evening, near sunset, he ascended the tree and took his station; soon the report of a rifle was heard and one of the men in the fort fell dead. This was so sudden and unexpected that no one could tell from whence the firing proceeded, though all were satisfied it came from an Indian concealed somewhere outside the inclosure. This was repeated on several evenings until four or five white men had been shot down without any one being able to find out the whereabouts of the murderer. He was finally discovered, however, in his hiding place, and shot by a man watching for him.

Another attack by Indians took place at Hill's Station in the latter part of August, 1814. As there have been several versions of this fight already published it is but proper to mention that the following statement is in no particular derived from any of them, as they are not entirely correct. It coincides with them, however, in many of its details. It is obtained direct from persons now living who had the scene described to them by those residing in the station at the time of its occurrence, besides from the statement of the hero of the conflict himself, and may be considered reliable.

A few rangers, under the command of Maj. Journey, were stationed at the station in order to afford the settlers better protection against the savages. Benjamin Henson, a resident in the station, while out hunting one day saw an Indian, which circumstance he related on his return in the evening, adding that he believed they were in danger of an attack. This story was discredited by many, both officers and men, who believed he had manufactured the whole thing merely to get up an excitement and alarm. On the evening of the day in question some of the women found grains of parched corn scattered about the spring, situated a little distance from the station, and as none of the white people had been using any at that time, this was conclusive evidence that the "red skins" were about.

Strange as it may seem, however, some of the rangers still refused to believe that there was any danger. One Lieut. Boucher, on hearing Henson's statement, called him a liar to his face and treated with contempt every suggestion of danger.

After disputing and quarreling awhile over the matter, they decided to send out a squad of men on the following day to look for Indians.

Next morning Maj. Journey started out, taking all the men with him, thus leaving the fort in a defenseless condition, the gates all wide open and the women milking the cows, apparently unconscious of danger. The party of rangers proceeded along a narrow path leading down a narrow ravine, when they were suddenly fired upon by a large party of Indians concealed behind trees and in the grass on both sides of the path. Maj. Journey, Capt. Grotz and two of the privates, — — Lynn and William Pruitt, were instantly killed. The fifth man, — — Thomas Higgins, was shot in the thigh and fell from his horse, which ran off. The others, seeing danger ahead left the path immediately, scattering in different directions and taking positions at some distance from each other, managed to engage the enemy as best they could. Having seen Higgins fall from his horse with the other four they supposed him killed also, and took no further notice of him at that time. There was a small field of corn close to the fort, on the north side, in which several Indians had concealed themselves, for when the firing commenced the women saw three or four run out of this field and pass round to the scene of conflict. They had doubtless been watching the whites intending to commit some depredation as soon as the men all left. Immediately after Higgins fell from his horse he was attacked by three Indians armed only with spears, evidently believing him entirely within their power. His wound had disabled him so that it was with difficulty he could stand without support, but the knowledge that his life was at stake seemed to give him super-human strength. Cocking his rifle, he presented it whenever one approached nearer than the others, as if intending to shoot, determined, however, not to do so until he could make sure of his game. The Indians, being uncertain whether his gun was loaded or not, were afraid to rush on him. Thus he held them at bay for a short time; but they kept circling round trying to get on both sides of him, each time coming a little closer and closer, whirling about in various ways or falling down flat in the grass and weeds whenever he seemed likely to fire. Occasionally one gave him a thrust with his spear, when they would all laugh to see him dodge and writhe with the pain, but were afraid to advance near enough to take hold of him. He still reserved his fire knowing that his only chance for life was to kill one "dead" at the first and only shot he would get. He said that one of them was the biggest Injun he ever saw, and he thought if he could only kill him first his chance for life would be much better. At length feeling himself growing weaker, and receiving a severe wound in the mouth and jaw from the spear of the largest Indian, who also was the boldest, Higgins leveled his rifle at him as he pulled the spear from the wound and fired, killing him dead on the spot.

The other two, knowing that his gun was discharged, now advanced on him without fear. His success in killing the most formidable one inspired him with fresh courage, and not having time to reload his rifle, he seized it by the muzzle and as they rushed upon him with loud and triumphant yells, struck the foremost one with all his power over the head, knocking out his brains and killing him immediately. The force of the blow broke the gun off at the breach and the barrel flew out of his hands to some distance in the thick grass.

He now fell exhausted and being unable to rise to his feet commenced crawling toward the gun-barrel, his only means of defense, in order to obtain it before the remaining Indian, who had also started to search for it. The savage succeeded in getting it first and with a tremendous yell, came slowly up in front of him, brandishing the weapon in his hands, as if to give him all the anguish possible, before striking the final blow. Having reached a small tree, he raised himself by means of it to a standing position, leaning back against it for support, feeling that his time had come when, to his great joy, he beheld two white men—William Pursley and David White—on horseback, coming to his rescue. They were coming up behind the Indian, who was too much elated with the idea of capturing his victim to observe them. As soon as Higgins saw them he exclaimed, "Pursley, for God's sake, don't let him kill me."

The Indian still believing no one near, and that this was a cry of despair, laughed tauntingly in his face, and mimickingly repeated his cry in bad English. The words had scarcely passed his lips when the men were upon him with rifles leveled. Instantaneously he commenced a series of the most vigorous and ludicrous gymnastic exercises, but they finally succeeded in killing him.

A portion of this fight was witnessed by the women in the fort, and one of them—Mrs. White—when she saw Higgins likely to be overpowered, seized a gun, mounted a horse, and started to his assistance. She had not proceeded far, however, when, perceiving Pursley and her husband hastening to his relief, she returned to the fort. Higgins was taken to the station, where his wounds were dressed and cared for until his recovery. He died, a few years since, in Fayette County, having been a perfect specimen of a frontier man in his day. He was once assistant door-keeper of the House of Representatives of Illinois.

Such are the scenes through which some of the pioneers of Bond County passed during its first settlement. Our citizens should cherish the memory of those victims who fell at Hill's Station, Jones' Fort, and other places in the county. Their graves lie neglected, and some of them unknown. This ought not to be. They should all be found, if possible, neatly inclosed, and a monument erected to their memory.

At the close of our last war with England, a treaty of peace was made with the Indians as well as with the English, thus bringing peace to the pioneer. After the conclusion of this treaty, the forts in Bond County were abandoned, though with some misgivings on the part of the whites, lest the Indians should fail to observe the terms of peace. In a short time, however, the people becoming more satisfied of the peaceful intentions of the savages, "scattered out" from the different stations, forming settlements several miles apart.

Emigrants came to the country but slowly, so that by the year 1816, Bond County numbered not over twenty-five dwelling-houses, if their pole cabins could be called dwelling-houses. The people then managed to get along without nails, glass, sawed lumber or brick, for the reason they could not procure them. Their houses were small, consisting of one story, built of logs or poles, in many cases unhewed, with the ends projecting from six inches to two feet at the corners, the crevices between them being daubed with mud or clay, and the whole structure covered with clapboards, held on by heavy poles called "weight-poles." The same kind of boards, fastened to cross pieces by wooden pins driven into holes made with a gimlet, constituted the door shutters, generally constructed to open outwards. The floor, when they had any, was made of puncheons, pinned down or laid on loose. These, when carefully dressed and closely put together, constituted a very good floor, but some of them conveyed the idea that the settlers believed in ventilation, for they left cracks so wide that the children, in pursuit of their juvenile amusements, their little feet often slipped through those dangerous trap-doors, causing many squalls and bruises. A wooden latch, raised by a string, served as a fastening for their doors. This string had one end tied to the latch and the other passed through a small hole above it, and when the door, fastened on the inside, was left hanging out, the person wishing to enter having only to pull it, in order to raise the latch; hence, to leave the "latch-string hanging out," they considered synonymous with sociability and hospitality. They built wooden chimneys, plastering them inside with earth, making the jambs and hearths also of the same material—except when stone could be procured —beating the hearths with a maul to make them solid. The fire-places were from six to ten feet in width, and two rocks or billets of wood served instead of andirons. Though so wide, these fire-places were, nevertheless, quite convenient, furnishing a receptacle for most if not all the cooking utensils of the family, and when crowded the children, and in some families the dogs found accommodations on each side, in company with skillets, ovens and frying pans. But at one side or the other of these capacious hearths, one article always stood conspicuous, and that was the kettle of "blue dye," as the old ladies called it, in which they colored their "yarn" for weaving. This kettle being covered with an old barrel-head, or something of the kind, often did service as a seat for some member of the family, and even for visitors. Young fellows, when on courting expeditions, sometimes found it a very convenient seat, with the "idol of their heart" in close proximity. Some of the best men of our country wooed and won their brides, seated on a kettle of "blue dye" by the blazing fire of the backwoodsman's rude cabin. An incident is related of a youthful swain seated on a kettle of "blue dye," engaged in close conversation with a lass, whose love he hoped to win, when the covering gave way, precipitating him to the bottom of the vessel in a sitting position. As he wore white pantaloons, the results may be imagined.

Articles of household furniture were few and rude. With the exception of those brought from the States, chairs could not for several years be procured, their place being supplied by wooden stools, which, though answering very well the purpose of seats, were easily upset, a circumstance often causing much merriment.

The tables and bedsteads were rude, the former being constructed of the same kind of material as the doors, and many of the latter by boring two holes in the wall with a large auger, six or seven feet apart; into these, pieces of wood were driven having the opposite end of each inserted into an upright post, this constituting a kind of frame work, which, being covered with clap-boards, served as a receptacle for the beds. Sofas, rocking chairs, center-tables, bureaus and all such articles were not used except where some old lady or whimsical old maid had refused to part with these "household gods," and had them hauled out to this wild region, over mountains, hills and swamps, at much trouble and expense.

On the outside of the houses, it was no uncommon thing to see a goodly number of raccoon and deer skins stretched and hanging up against the wall to dry, and occasionally the skin of a wild cat, wolf or bear. The projecting ends of the logs at each corner of the cabin served as places to hang the various utensils used on the farm, such as hoes, rakes, bridles and harness.

CHAPTER III.

ORGANIZATION OF BOND COUNTY—THE TERRITORY FROM WHICH IT ORIGINATED—ACT OF THE LEGISLATURE—THE COUNTY AS NOW BOUNDED, WITH ITS DESCRIPTION AND TOPOGRAPHY—COURTS ORGANIZED—THE FIRST GRAND JURY AND COURT OFFICERS—COUNTY SEAT AT PERRYVILLE—JAIL BUILDING—A CASE OF LYNCHING—LAWYERS LOST ON THE PRAIRIE—PERMANENT LOCATION OF THE SEAT OF JUSTICE, ETC., ETC.

AS the country settled up and population increased, it became necessary to form the territory into smaller divisions for the purpose of convenience and the better administration of the laws. It may be of interest to the reader to give a few of the territorial changes of the country in which we now live. Illinois was taken from the British in 1778, by conquest of Gen. George Rogers Clark, and became a county of Virginia. It then embraced what is now the States of Ohio, Indiana, Illinois, Michigan and Wisconsin, with the seat of government at Kaskaskia.† In 1784, Virginia ceded it to the United States Government, and by the ordinance of 1787 it became the Northwestern Territory, with its capital first at Marietta and then at Cincinnati, Ohio. This continued until 1800, when it was made a part of the Indiana Territory, with the seat of government at Vincennes, Ind., and embraced the present States of Indiana, Illinois, Michigan and Wisconsin. In 1809, that portion now forming the States of Illinois and Wisconsin, became the Territory of Illinois, and in 1818, Illinois became a State of the Federal Union, with her capital at the ancient town of Kaskaskia. The Southern part of the State was settled long before the central and northern part, and here the first counties were formed, even before the State was admitted into the Union. The country within the boundaries of the present State of Illinois extending northward to the mouth of the Little Mackinaw Creek, was organized into a county in February, 1790, and named for His Excellency Gen. Arthur St. Clair, Governor of the Northwestern Territory. Other counties were formed, as population increased. In 1795, Randolph was created, and Madison in 1812. Bond County, comprising a large extent of territory, and from which several counties have since been formed, was organized in 1817. The following is the act of the Legislature, or that part of it pertaining to the subject, which gave it a legal existence.

An act forming a new county out of the county of Madison approved January 4, 1817:

Be it enacted by the Legislative Council and House of Representatives of Illinois Territory, and it is hereby enacted by authority of the same, that all that tract of country within the following boundaries to wit:

Beginning at the southwest corner of Township 3 north, Range 4 west; thence east to the southeast corner of Township 3 north, Range 1 east, to the third meridian line; thence north to the boundary line of the Territory; thence west with said boundary line so far that a south line will pass between Ranges 4 and 5 west; thence south with said line to the beginning. The same shall constitute a separate county to be called Bond, and the seat of justice for said county shall be at Hill's Fort until it shall be permanently established in the following manner, that is to say, there shall be five persons appointed, to wit: William Roberts, John Powers, Robert Gillespie, John Whitley, Sr., and John

*By R. O. White.

†Near Chester, the seat of the New Southern Penitentiary.

Laughlin, or a majority of them being duly sworn before some Judge or Justice of the Peace of this Territory to faithfully take into view the situation of the settlements, the geography of the county, the conveuience of the people and the eligibility of the place, shall meet on the first Monday in March, next, at Hill's Fort, on Shoal Creek, and proceed to examine and determine on the place for the permanent seat of justice and designate the same. Provided that the proprietor or proprietors of the land shall give to the said county, for the purpose of erecting public buildings, a quantity of land at the said place, not less than twenty acres, to be laid off in lots and sold for the above purpose. But should the proprietor or proprietors refuse or neglect to make the donation aforesaid, then, in that case, it shall be the duty of the Commissioners to fix upon some other place for the seat of justice as convenient as may be to the present and future settlements of said county, or should the said Commissioners fix it upon lands belonging to the United States, in that case, the Judges of the said county, or any two of them, may apply to the Register of the Land Office for that district, and in behalf of the county purchase one quarter section for the use of the county, and the seat of justice shall be established thereon, and the county shall be bound for the purchase money, which place, when fixed upon and determined, the said Commissioners shall certify under their hands and seals, and return their certificates of the same to the next County Court in the county aforesaid; and as a compensation for their services they shall each be allowed $2 for every day they may be necessarily employed in fixing the aforesaid seat of justice, to be paid out of the county levy, which said court shall cause an entry thereof to be made on the records, etc., etc.

The remainder of the act, which is a very long one is taken up with matters which have no reference to Bond County. It will be seen by this act that the county was much larger at the time of its formation than it is now. As at present constituted, it is bounded on the north by Montgomery, on the east by Fayette, on the south by Clinton, and on the west by Madison.

It contains nine entire townships, in a square, and five fractional ones on its northern and western sides, comprising about three hundred and seventy-eight square miles. The population is fourteen thousand, being thirty-seven to the square mile.

Shoal Creek and its tributaries water the western and central portions, and the Okaw River and Hurricane Creek the eastern part.

Shoal Creek rises in the northern part of Montgomery County, and crosses the line of Bond at the north half-mile corner of Section 28, Township 7, Range 4, and, flowing nearly south through the county, leaves it near the southwest corner of Section 30, Town 4, Range 4. It has on both sides a fine body of timber, varying in width from two to five miles. Its principal tributaries in Bond County are the Dry Fork, Indian Creek, East Fork, Locust Fork, Beaver Creek and the Lake Fork.

The largest of these streams is the East Fork, which rises in the northeastern part of Montgomery County, and, running southwest into Bond, empties into Shoal Creek, in the southwest quarter of Section 36. The timber on this stream is of a good quality, and several miles in width. Beaver Creek rises a few miles northeast of Greenville, and, flowing nearly south, crosses the line into Clinton County. The whole length of this creek is about twenty-five miles; it is a muddy, sluggish stream, and waters a fine portion of Bond County. When the Government Surveyors first came to this stream, they found a dead horse in it, and from this circumstance called it "Stinking Creek," a name which appears on some of the older maps. Lake Fork enters the county a few rods south of the northwest corner, flows in an easterly direction near the north line for a little over a mile; then, turning north and northeast, passes into Montgomery County and empties into Shoal Creek. It is noted for being a rapid, rocky, stream, furnishing numerous quarries of a good building stone, and for beds of coal along its banks at various points. Dry Fork rises in the southwestern part of Montgomery County, and, running southeast into Bond, empties into Shoal Creek. It is a rapid stream,

William S. Wait

and runs through a rough, broken tract of country. Indian Creek rises in the southwest part of Township 6, Range 3, and runs southwest into Shoal Creek. It was so named from the Indians having once been encamped on it during the first settling of the county. Locust Fork is a small stream in the the southern part of Township 4, Range 4, running southeast through a fine portion of country; coal, and extensive beds of the finest limestone in the county are found along this creek and its branches. It flows into Shoal Creek, a short distance north of the Clinton County line.

The Okaw or Kaskaskia River runs through the extreme southeastern part of the county. It rises in Champaign County, and, taking a southwestern course, empties into the Mississippi River, about one hundred and twenty miles above the mouth of the Ohio, passing through or bordering in its course the counties of Douglas, Coles, Moultrie, Shelby, Fayette, Bond, Clinton, Washington, St. Clair, Monroe and Randolph. A body of excellent timber, from two to ten miles wide, is found along this river, supplying the numerous and extensive farms on both sides of it with lumber. It is not navigable for any considerable distance, though a small steamboat once ascended as far as Carlyle in a time of high water. The Hurricane Fork and its tributaries water the eastern portion of Bond County, and are bordered with fine bodies of timber.

Bond County contains a due proportion of timber and prairie, and has a generally level or undulating surface, but no mountains nor very high hills. The general quality of the soil is second rate, though in certain localities there is excellent land. Some of the prairies are too level to answer well the purposes of cultivation without some artificial drainage, but most of the land is sufficiently undulating to drain well, and in fact some of the finest landscape views in the State are found in this county. The timber consists of white, black, Spanish, over-cup, water, black-jack, post and pin oak, hackberry, ash, hickory, walnut, elm, sycamore, cottonwood, sugar and white maple, locust, mulberry, sassafras, wild cherry and other kinds. Springs are not very numerous, but good wells can be obtained in all parts of the county. With but few exceptions the water is limestone. There are saline springs in Shoal Creek, a short distance above New Berlin, where, during the first settling of the country, salt was manufactured to a small extent, but, being down in the bed of the creek, they are inaccessible the greater part of the year, and have long since been abandoned.

In addition to the places already noted, good quarries of both sand and limestone are found in the western part of the county, at various points along the banks of the main fork of Shoal Creek, and many of the smaller streams running into it from the west. In the prairies are found, lying on or near the surface, large bowlders nearly round, weighing from five hundred to several thousand pounds. They are granite in formation, and have been broken from the parent quarry by some convulsion of nature, and removed to their present situation, probably through the agency of water, and seem to have been rounded by rolling over a hard surface. It is difficult to account for them on any reasonable ground. There is not, so far as is known, a quarry of granite in the State, and hence it is evident that these "lost rocks," as they are called, have been transported many miles.

As Bond County was organized in 1817, when Illinois was yet a Territory, it was one of the fifteen counties represented in the Constitutional Convention of 1818. Thomas Kirkpatrick and Samuel G. Morse represented this county in the Convention that formed the first State Constitution. Of the dimensions of Bond at the time of its formation, Rev. Thomas W. Hynes, in his address, July 4, 1876, says:

"Originally our county was of immense size, extending indefinitely northward and eastward; but in 1821 the formation of Montgomery and Fayette, and, in 1825, the county of Clinton reduced her extent on three sides till she was so small that an addition taken from Madison had to be made in 1843, to bring it up to the present extent of territory. This addition, two miles wide and nine miles long, leaves the county of respectable and convenient magnitude, though much below the average of the 102 counties in Illinois. Bond has 378 square miles, while the average for all the counties of Illinois is 544 square miles."

After the adoption of the act of the Legislature for the legal organization of the county, the next business in order was to establish the different departments, and set the political, civil and judicial machinery in motion. This was accomplished without any unnecessary delay. The first Circuit Court was held at Hill's Station, on Monday, May 30, 1817. The State being under a Territorial Government, all the offices were filled by appointment, and were as follows: The Hon. Jesse B. Thomas, Judge; Daniel Converse, Clerk; Samuel G. Morse, Sheriff; and Charles R. Matheny, State's Attorney. The following persons served as grand jurors: John Whitley, Sr., Foreman, Solomon Reavis, Fields Pruitt Conrod Hoosong, Samuel Davidson, Paul Beck, William Robinson, John Hopton, Robert Gillespie, Benjamin James, Charles Reavis, Charles Steel, Andrew Moody, Absalom Mathews, William McLane, John Whitley, Jr., Peter Hubbard, David White, Francis Kirkpatrick, William Burgess, John Samples, Elijah Powers, Thomas White.

The list of petit jurors cannot be given, for it does not appear in any of the old records of the county, and, so far as can be ascertained, John B. White, residing a short distance west of Greenville, is the only man now living who served on either jury at that court. The petit jury, on retiring to make up their verdict, instead of being shut up in a close room, went out and sat on a large log.

There was only one bill of indictment found, and but one case tried. Judge Thomas, alluding to this circumstance when dismissing the grand jury, remarked, "It speaks much for the morals of your community; long may such a state of things continue." In the foregoing list of grand jurors, quite a number of our citizens will recognize the names of ancestors and others with whom they have been familiar in former years.

Two or three terms of the Circuit Court were held at Hill's Station, after which it was held at Perryville, the first county seat, situated near the mouth of Hurricane Creek, in the southwestern part of what is now Fayette County. The following report of the Commissioners appointed to locate the seat of justice for Bond County, shows something of the extent of territory then under its jurisdiction, and also, the ideas entertained by the people in relation to the navigation of the small rivers and large creeks in this country:

SHOAL CREEK, April 15, 1817.
ILLINOIS TERRITORY, BOND COUNTY.

We, the Commissioners to fix the seat of justice for the county of Bond, being duly sworn, after reviewing different parts of said county for that purpose; we do nominate and appoint for that purpose, the bluff lying west of the Hurricane Fork of Okaw, being the southwest quarter of Section No. 5, of Range No. 1 west, of Township No ' north, now the property of Martin Jones, taking into view the *geographical center, the navigation*, the eligibility, and the common good of the people, as directed by law. Given under our hands and seals, the day and year first above written.

JOHN POWLES,
ROBERT GILLESPIE,
JOHN WHITLEY.

This town was laid out in the spring of 1818, and the plat recorded May 17 of the same year. Illinois having been in the meantime admitted into the Union, Bond County was regularly organized the following autumn, and named for Shadrach Bond, the first Governor of the State, who was elected in October, 1818, and filled a term of four years. The county then included a large scope of territory, extending to the north, east and south, which is now embodied in adjoining counties.

The first Justices' or County Commissioners' Court ever held in the county, met at Perryville in the month of October, 1818. The Justices were Thomas Kirkpatrick, Martin Jones and Isaac Price. Daniel Converse was Clerk, and Samuel G. Morse, Sheriff, Converse being Clerk of both Circuit and County Courts. The principal business of this first court at Perryville seems to have been rewarding persons for killing wolves, $2 being the amount paid for each scalp produced. There were thirty-five orders passed allowing pay for wolf-scalps, and it appears that fifty-one wolves had been killed. The whole amount of money expended by the county for the year previous, as stated by the Sheriff, was $97.75, which was probably mostly for wolf-scalps.

Among the orders passed at this term of the court was one for the erection of a jail at Perryville, giving plan and specifications of the building. It appears to be the only order of any importance passed after remunerating the wolf-killers; a jail, whether needed or not being evidently considered as a mark of civilization, or, at least, tending in that direction. After perusing this order, the reader can form his own conclusions as to the condition of the literature and architecture of Bond County at that time, and picture to himself the imposing appearance such a building would now present if located in the public square of Greenville. The following is the order, given word for word and letter for letter:

Ordered that Martin Jones be appointed and Empowered to let a Gail to the lowest Bidder to bee built in the following Manner; twelve by eighteen feet in the clear, to bee built of timber hewn squire 12 Inches, the log with a partition of the same kind of Timber, the partition to be 6 feet from one end, the corners to be dove-tailed together and also the partion walls, the outside door to be double, of two Inch plank, and sufficiently nailed with Strong nails and barred with two Iron barrs, half an inch thick and three inches wide, to answer for the hinges, to be hinged with steeples ¾ of an Inch in Diameter drove through the Logs and Clinched, and also steeples through the logs in the same manner on the other side of the door, with holes through the bolts to Lock the door with Pad Locks to each.

This jail was built, but not strictly in accordance with the above order, for if it had, it would have been without roof or floor. It is likely the architect, supplied with his inventive powers what was omitted in the specifications. The first man ever imprisoned in Bond County was incarcerated in this building during the first Circuit Court held at Perryville. He came into court not only a little "tight," but very drunk swearing and making quite a disturbance. The Judge ordered him to jail until he became sober, which order was promptly executed by the Sheriff. That worthy official, however, found it impossible to lock the door, for the reason that there had been no padlock provided, as stipulated in the building contract, but as the door opened to the outside, he closed it and placed fence rails and poles against it, making everything as he thought, secure. This was late in the afternoon, near sunset. The prisoner lay down and soon fell asleep. About midnight he awoke, duly sober, and finding himself in such a place, was at first much surprised, but after a little reflection, recollected his condition the day before, and imagined that somebody had put him in there for mischief. After groping around the walls awhile, he found the door, and by pushing kicking, swearing and yelling till almost daylight, succeeded in getting out. The next day he was going about trying to find the perpetrators of the outrage, swearing he could whip any man that helped to put him in there, never for a moment supposing that an order of court had anything to do with it.

Some idea of the sparseness of the settlements at that time may be obtained from the fact that a party of three or four lawyers, on their way to the above-named court, got lost in crossing the prairie between Shoal Creek and the Okaw. After wandering about for several hours, vainly endeavoring to discover some signs of a human habitation, night overtook them, and they were compelled to pass it in the tall grass near a pond, where, bitten by mosquitoes and gnats, and serenaded by hundreds of wolves and myriads of frogs, their meditations were anything but pleasant. They arrived at their destination the next forenoon, hungry and sleepy, where their acquaintances accused them of having been on a spree the night previous, judging from the reddened appearance of their countenances.

The courts continued to meet at Perryville for more than three years, and until Greenville was laid out and established as the permanent county seat, which occurred in 1821. In the chapters devoted to the history of Greenville, the erection of the public buildings will be fully given. For several years Bond County continued to exercise jurisdiction over a large extent of territory, as the following will serve to show: At one of the Justices' Courts, held at Perryville, an order was passed at a subsequent session, when a license was granted authorizing one Jones "to establish and keep in operation a ferry over the Okaw River at Vandalia." This large territory, however, was curtailed, as we have seen, in the organization, some years later, of Fayette, Montgomery and Clinton Counties. Notwithstanding the rough state of society then existing, and that the county contained some pretty "hard cases," yet the laws were, with few exceptions, strictly and promptly executed, without any serious resistance or attempts at lynching. The only case of the latter was that of a man named Baker, arrested on Big Shoal Creek for horse-stealing, where he was tied to a tree, whipped, and then driven from the county. He went to Vandalia, stole another horse, and started east, but was pursued, overtaken and shot near the Indiana line. The precise date of this occurrence is not known, but was probably about the year 1820.

Bond County, in its civil organization, differs from a majority of the counties in the State, in that it is not governed by township rule, or more properly speaking, is not under township organization. For civil purposes it is divided into ten election precincts, which do not correspond in territorial boundaries with the Congressional survey, but are laid off according to the best advantage, or to suit the will of the people. These precincts, which are more fully described in other chapters, devoted to each severally, are as follows: Greenville, Ripley, Cottonwood Grove, La Grange, Pocahontas, Beaver Creek, Okaw, Fairview, Mulberry Grove and Zion. These, as we have said, are more minutely described in chapters which are devoted exclusively to them, and in which everything of interest in regard to them are fully given.

CHAPTER IV.[1]

AGRICULTURE IN EARLY TIMES—THE FIRST PLOWS USED—HORSE COLLARS, HARNESS, TRACE CHAINS, ETC.—"GREEN HEADS"—WHEAT, AND THE MODE OF HARVESTING IT—AN INCIDENT—HOG RAISING—DIFFICULTIES OF TEAMING—ROADS TO ST. LOUIS AND SPRINGFIELD—A SERMON ON A LOAD OF APPLES—BUILDING MILLS AND OTHER MANUFACTORIES, ETC., ETC.

THE inhabitants of Bond County are an intelligent, industrious and enterprising people, and are engaged mainly in agricultural pursuits. In the early history of the country, when Southern Illinois was but sparsely settled, agriculture was in a very rude state, when compared to the science to which it is now reduced. The prime cause of this was the great lack of agricultural implements, which were few in number and of simple construction. Inventive genius and Yankee enterprise had not yet been employed in this direction to any great extent. The plows in common use when the first settlements were made within the present limits of the county of Bond were of a rude character, and of three kinds, viz., the "bar-shear," the "shovel" and the "bull-tongue." To attempt a description of the bar-shear plow would be useless, as those who never saw one could scarcely understand the description; like the alligator, it must be seen to be appreciated. It was constructed on about as simple a plan as could be imagined, having a heavy wooden mold-board to turn the soil. The shovel plow is yet in use and need not be described. The bull-tongue was like the shovel, though narrower and longer.

With such implements as these it was impossible to do good plowing, the ground being merely scratched over instead of broken up deep. The harrows then had wooden instead of iron teeth; but a heavy brush drawn by a pair of horses or oxen usually served in their place. As there were no seed drills of any kind the grain was all sown by hand, and covered by brushing or harrowing. Horse-collars were made by plaiting and sewing together corn-husks. They were constructed without opening at the upper end, and put on the horse by being pushed over his head, a feat sometimes difficult to accomplish, especially for boys. The hames were much heavier than those now used, and not plated with iron. A raw hide or buckskin strap fastened them together. When chains could not be procured for traces, raw-hide, hickory withes, bark ropes or dressed deer-skin served instead. These were held up in proper position by a strap or back-band made of the kind of material most convenient, a piece of rope passed over the back of the horse and tied to each trace, or a strap of leather or hide two or three inches in width and, in some cases, cloth obtained by taking strips of the best parts of worn-out pantaloons and other garments, sewing them together and forming a band of the required length and strength.

In addition to the lack of good plows and harness, the early farmers were much troubled and hindered by horse-flies, which annoyed their horses during the plowing season to such an extent that it was often impossible for them to work except during a small portion of each day—early in the morning and late in the even-

[1] By R. O. White.

ing. The flies were most numerous in the prairies and vicinity.

Some seasons, during "fly-time," it was impossible to ride across any of the prairies. In going a half-mile, or mile at farthest, the horse's neck and shoulders would be literally covered with flies, which would cause him to rear and jump about, or lie down and wallow to get rid of them, so that the rider could not maintain his seat. These flies were of a gray color, with green heads, by which they attained the name of "green-head flies." With the rude plows and harness of the time an acre was as much ground as one team would break up in an entire day; and hindered as they were by flies in the spring of the year, the amount plowed per day was much less. But, to compensate for this want of culture, the wild land was more productive than it is now, and the people raised the most abundant crops, in proportion to the ground cultivated.

Most of the early inhabitants of Bond County had emigrated from sections where corn was the principal grain, and continued its cultivation here as their main crop, raising but little wheat, notwithstanding it was of good quality and fair yield. But, little as they did raise, it was just about as much as could be harvested with the implements they then had. For several years after the first attempt at wheat-raising, the only means of harvesting was the old-fashioned sickle or "reap-hook," as some called it—a slow process—the man that could cut and bind one acre per day being considered an extra good hand. During harvest the people in a neighborhood would unite, on the principle that "many hands make light work," and beginning at the farm where the wheat was ripest, proceed to reap first one field and then another, till all the grain was cut. They looked upon harvest as a time of social enjoyment as well as profit when the neighbors, male and female, met together and had a good time generally. Sickles were succeeded by grain-cradles, which continued in use until superseded by reapers and mowers.

Wheat was threshed by beating it with flails, or laying the bundles down in a circle and tramping them out by horses. As barns were very scarce, the operation of threshing was performed mostly on the ground, scraped off and swept for the purpose. The grain was cleared by slowly pouring it from a half bushel, or sifting through a coarse riddle, in the wind, and when this proved insufficient, an artificial current of air was produced by two men holding a sheet or coverlet at each end, and bringing it round with a peculiar swing; this served to blow away the chaff and render the wheat tolerably clean. In consequence of the scarcity of wheat, flour bread was quite a rarity, some families having none at all, others enjoying the luxury of biscuits for breakfast only on Sunday morning.

The following incident will show the scarcity of wheat bread, and how highly it was prized by some persons: At a wedding party, the bridegroom, after the Justice had pronounced the words which bound two hearts together, for "weal or woe," called him to one side, and whether he gave him any money or not is unknown, but he took from his capacious coat-pocket six biscuits, with either of which one could knock a man down at a distance of twenty paces, and giving them to him, exclaimed, "Here, Squire, take these home with you, and keep them expressly for yourself and the old woman; hide them away somewhere, so the children can't get them, for you know what children are." The bridegroom is yet living in Bond County, and represents one type of the "old settler."

Some of the first apple and peach orchards in the State were planted in Bond County. For many years it was noted for producing more and better fruit than any of the adjoining counties, and at the present time, according to population, it produces more apples than any other, although the fruit is not as good as in former years, owing to the severe droughts.

As most of the early emigrants settled in the timber where nuts and acorns were plenty, they paid but little attention to the raising of any kind of stock except hogs. There was then but one breed, a lank, sharp-nosed, long-legged, ravenous hog, that ran in the woods at least three-fourths of the year. Near the commencement of winter, the settlers usually began to hunt up their hogs for the purpose of converting them into pork.

These hogs, when found in the fall, were more or less shy, many of them being half or entirely wild. After finding them, the first endeavor was to tame them in the woods, and when considered sufficiently gentle for the purpose, they were brought home and put into an inclosure, and afterward butchered.

Such was the commencement of hog-raising in this county. Great improvements have been made in this kind of stock in late years, both in the breeds now reared and in the taking care of them. Hog raising has become an extensive as well as a valuable industry with our farmers.

The same imperfection and rudeness of construction of other farm implements applied also to wagons, which were clumsily and heavily made, and drawn almost exclusively by oxen. Buggies, and the lighter kinds of carriages, were not used. When horses were worked to wagons, the harness was of but little better quality than that already described. Lines were ignored in those days; the driver rode the lead-horse, and either held the reins of the other in his hand or hung them on the hames of the leader. A wagon, team and driver fitted up in the style of fifty-five years ago, if now driven through the streets of Greenville, would present quite a grotesque and ludicrous appearance. When people first began to drive with lines some of the settlers ridiculed them, saying it was out of the question for a man to drive horses as accurately in that way as to ride one of them; that a horse could pull more, and with greater ease with a man on his back than without, and that it was all laziness, but notwithstanding their misgivings, the new way of driving soon became general, as everything always has done which tends to ameliorate, or to do away with any portion of manual labor.

The largest part of the hauling to and from St. Louis—our only market at that time—was done with ox teams. Wagons intended to be drawn by oxen, were much more stoutly made than others, in order to stand the rough usage on the road, for it was no uncommon thing to see six or seven yoke of oxen attached to one wagon going to market in the spring, when the mud was tough and almost bottomless. The business of teaming necessarily increased as the country became more populous, for this was the only way in which produce could be sent off, or merchandise procured. When people first began to haul to and from St. Louis, and for several years afterward, there were no bridges across the streams on the route; so the reader can imagine some of the difficulties attending those engaged in this business during the spring or breaking up of winter. Even after bridges were built over the larger streams it was, at certain seasons, a serious undertaking to perform the trip from Greenville to St. Louis and back, and usually occupied from two to four weeks, according to the state of the road. Persons were often under the necessity of unloading their wagons before going through a deep mud-hole, and after driving through reloading on the other side, carrying the load over by peacemeal on their shoulders; or worse than this, undertaking to go through loaded, the wagon would mire down, every wheel sinking to the axle in the tough mud, and they be compelled to wade through it knee deep or more and carry the loading out to solid ground.

After orchards were planted and apples became an article of produce, the settlers hauled them to other points besides St. Louis. Being scarce, they always commanded ready cash, and for several years it was not unusual to see teams from Bond County taking them to Springfield, a distance of eighty miles, over a worse road than that to St. Louis.

The writer heard a sermon delivered about twenty-seven years ago, by one of the primitive preachers of Bond County, wherein he related a case of miring down on the road with a load of apples, about the year 1836, in which he and another individual were the principal actors. As nearly as can be recollected, he described it in the following language:

"My dear brethring and sisters, I'm a going to tell you of a circumstance that happened to your poor, unworthy speaker on the road to Springfield with a load of apples. It is one that I love to tell to my dying hearers, whenever I'm called upon to stand up and try, in my stammering and imperfect manner, to preach about the mysterious workings of Providence toward the poor fallen sons and daughters of men and wimmin-ah. Oh, my hearers when I think of that awful winter night, when we lay out on the big prairie, with the wind and snow and sleet a pourin upon us-ah; and when we had no fire and only about a quart of whisky to keep us from freezing, I feel, my dying congregation, jest like the Lord had retched His hand down from the shinin canopits of heaven and jerked me right out from between the very jaws of death-ah. We were on the road to market, my dear brethring, with a load of apples. They were 'big Romanite' apples, put up in barrels, and were the finest apples I ever saw-ah. We had my big wagon and four yoke of oxens, and had on about forty hundred pounds; we had got along very well and were making great calculations on gettin a good price for our apples-ah. And right here, let me tell you, my dying hearers, I learnt what it is to feel disappointment and have all our calculations blasted-ah. Along in the evening, my brethring, it commenced raining a cold rain, that soon wet us from head to foot, and just about that time the wind turned to the north, and the first thing we knowed it was blowing and snowing and freezing, with all the combined fury of the elements-ah. Then, my congregation, we came to a big mud-hole, where the ground had froze a little on top, but not sufficient to hold up the wagon and team-ah. When we drove into it, my hearers, the wagon and oxens went in plumb up to the hub-ah, and the poor unworthy worm of the dust that stands before you to-day, my brethring, was soon in the same deplorable condition-ah. But, my dear friends, we believed we would get out safe, for we had a noble team—all except the off ox at the wheel. Sometimes he was a little tricky and wouldn't pull when it came to the pinch-ah; and now my dear brethring and sisters, when we needed all the help we could get it seemed as if Satan entered into that ox as he did into the swine of old, and he stopped stone still and wouldn't pull a pound-ah. So, my dear brethring, we had to unload and carry them barrels of apples about a hundred yards on our shoulders from the wagon to the dry ground and lay them down in the open prairie-ah; and my dear, dying hearers, as we carried them barrels through the mud, water, snow and ice, we sunk in up to our knees at every step-ah. Then, my dying congregation, we drove the wagon and team out, and crawled into it, wet, cold and hungry-ah; and wrapped up and kept ourselves alive with that little bottle of spirits till morning-ah. When morning came, my dear brethring and sisters, all our apples and two of the oxens' tails were froze hard and were fit only to be taken back and made into cider-ah. Thus you see, my dear congregation, that it is through the mysterious workings of a spiritual power that your unworthy servant stands before you to-day."

When the spring rains ceased and the roads

became dry, hauling was attended with fewer difficulties. One of the greatest troubles, however, was the failing of the water-courses, which became quite low in summer; some of them drying up entirely, and others having water standing only in holes. This being the only chance for watering teams, it was often a source of much inconvenience. After traveling many miles through the heat and dust, the oxen, of course, grew very hot and thirsty; in this condition, all who are acquainted with their nature, know that some of them are almost unmanageable when coming within sight of water. At such times, they would start with a rush, not stopping until the whole four or five yoke, wagon and all, were in the water, or mud and water, as deep as they could get, notwithstanding the driver used every exertion to prevent them from so doing. Sometimes they turned so abruptly out of the road into the stream as to upset the wagon in the operation, and sometimes the driver, fatigued with walking, would be carelessly seated on his wagon, when he would find himself suddenly roused by the sudden start of his team, and fearing an upset, would be forced to jump from his seat, alighting up to his knees, or coming down sprawling in mud and water.

Such scenes as teamsters passed through in the "olden times" until the building of railroads, may truly be termed the times that tried not only men's souls, but their temper and religion. The remark was often made, though perhaps intended as a joke, that any one, not even excepting a preacher of the Gospel, who could drive an ox team through the mud to St. Louis and back without swearing, would be regarded as one of the most remarkable men of the age.

The price of hauling varied with the condition of the roads and the distance; from Greenville to St. Louis it varied from 50 cents to a $1 or more per hundred; to Vandalia it was from $1 upward. This mode of transportation, although attended with so many inconveniences, was the only means of obtaining supplies for a large scope of territory, and as late as the year 1840, it was no uncommon thing to see ox teams, in gangs of five or six from Effingham County, passing through Greenville on their way to St. Louis. They were noted for offering venison hams for sale along the route; hence, some gave that county the appellation of "Venison Ham County," a name which it has long since lost the ability to sustain.

For several years after the first settlements were made in this county, the pioneers were compelled to do without mills of any kind. The sparsely settled country did not justify the expenditure required to erect mills even for grinding corn. The nearest place for having grain ground was at Edwardsville. For several years after corn-mills were first built in this section, the people had to take their wheat there to have it ground into what they called flour, though it would hardly be so considered at the present day. Most of the people were content if they had plenty of pork and corn bread, or "hog and hominy," as they called it. Warm corn "dodgers" and "johnny-cake," stewed pumpkins, fresh spare-ribs and backbones, with plenty of gravy, usually called "sop," varied occasionally by a dish of wild game, were considered the sum total of good eating by the early backwoodsmen.

In the year 1817, the first mill ever in Bond County was built by Paul Beck, on quite a primitive plan. It stood in the southwestern part of Greenville, near the cemetery, and is more particularly noticed in the history of Greenville. The fine spring near this mill was called "Beck's Spring." In a few years, other mills were built, some of which ground wheat, being supplied with a bolt turned by hand. The first water-mill in the county was put up on Shoal Creek, at Old Ripley, by Samuel Lee, about 1819 or 1820. E. R. Wheelock and Wyatt Stubblefield erected mills on the East

Fork of Shoal Creek shortly after. Both of these mills, together with their owners, have long since passed away.

Most of the mills for grinding, in Bond County, for a number of years, were horse-mills, similar to Beck's, with the improvement, however, of a large cog wheel instead of a raw hide band, but they ground very slowly. Every man had to hitch his own team to the machine and grind his own grain. The large wheel was furnished with two levers, so that either two or four horses could be worked to it. The work being much easier for four horses it was common for two neighbors to join teams, each putting in a span of horses, and grind both their grists. As an illustration of the inconveniences under which the people then labored to obtain meal, some of them carried their grain in sacks, on horseback, eight or ten miles to an old horse-mill, where they sometimes had to wait two or three days for their grinding.

Other manufactories were few in number and on a par with mills in quality and importance. The first settlers being mostly from the Southern States turned their attention early to cotton-growing, and hence establishments must necessarily be erected for its manufacture. So, in the year 1820, Thomas Long put up a cotton-gin not far from Stubblefield. A year or two afterward Samuel White and Moses Hinton put in operation a spinning-machine in Greenville. Neither of these establishments had a very extensive run, however, for their owners had built them with the expectation of obtaining supplies from the products of the surrounding country. But it was found impossible to supply them with material, as it was soon demonstrated that cotton would not grow to do any good upon the soil of Illinois. A tannery was started by Samuel White in 1820, at the spring west of Greenville, the first in the county. In 1822, James B. Rutherford commenced the manufacture of hats in Greenville, which he carried on for several years. Other establishments of the kind were started up from time to time. Somewhere about 1823-24, Milton Mills started a wool-carding machine in the county near Wisetown. Many other small manufacturing establishments were started, most of which, however, had but a brief existence.

In the years that have gone, since the first occupation of Bond County by the whites, rapid strides have been made in every department of life. Scarcely a trace now remains of the old customs of the people. We are surrounded by conveniences never dreamed of fifty years ago. Instead of Beck's primitive mill with its quaint "findings," we have a number of as fine mills as may be found anywhere. We no longer have to wade through mud, snow and rain with slow going ox-teams to St. Louis, but the iron-horse brings the best markets to our very doors. It is no longer necessary to go to Edwardsville for a physician; every community has one of its own, always ready to alleviate, so far as is possible, the ills of suffering humanity. Children are not compelled, as of yore, to sit all day in a close, ill-ventilated log-cabin, "to learn to cipher," but comfortable schoolhouses are found in every neighborhood. Churches, with their lofty spires pointing to heaven, dot the country everywhere. When we view all this, we are forced to acknowledge the Americans a progressive people, and the present an age of improvement.

CHAPTER V

THE STATE OF SOCIETY IN EARLY TIMES—DAILY USE AND MANUFACTURE OF WHISKY—DRUNKENNESS, FIGHTING, AND OTHER INNOCENT AMUSEMENTS—SHOOTING MATCHES—WORKING FROLICS—GOLD AND SILVER MINES OF THE COUNTY—GAYLORD'S SWINDLE—NEGRO SLAVERY—THE MAGOON KIDNAPING CASE—EARLY PHYSICIANS, ETC., ETC.

IN the early history of Bond County, whisky was considered as almost one of the necessaries of life, or at least "good in its place." This "place" was nearly everywhere, embracing all occasions and applying to nearly every condition of life. Of course, no one presumed to uphold or advocate drunkenness, but a *temperate* use of spirituous liquors, was not only considered harmless, but in many cases absolutely beneficial. Hence, distilleries were erected, and the manufacture of whisky begun soon after settlements were made in the country.

The first distillery in what is now Bond County, was put in operation, in 1819, by George Donnell, at a spring about two miles north of Greenville. Within a few years succeeding the erection of this one, several others were built in different portions of the county, one of which was at Beck's Spring, near the graveyard (a very appropriate place for a distillery). The manufacture of whisky at these distilleries was not carried on to a great extent, nor for any considerable *length of time*. And to the honor of Bond County be it recorded, that there is not now an establishment within its limits for the manufacture of ardent spirits. At the time these distilleries were in operation, and for several years after, intemperance prevailed to an almost alarming extent. It is not exaggerating to say, that whisky was in use, either moderately or otherwise, by more than one-half of the people in the county. On public occasions, drunken men were so common, that sober men seemed to be the exception. At any time between the years of 1830 and 1845, it was nothing unusual to see twenty or thirty men at one time, on election or muster day, in Greenville, drunk, swearing and yelling like Indians, the majority of them with coats off and sleeves rolled up, wanting to resent an insult which they fancied they had received from some one whom they were trying to find. Sometimes a fellow staggered against a tree, or post, or came in collision with another individual, and feeling the concussion, imagined that somebody had struck him. In an instant he would shed his coat and hat, and go rushing through the crowd, endeavoring to find his supposed enemy, and swearing that he was "a hoss," and could "whip his weight in wild cats." And woe be unto the luckless individual who was mistaken for the aggressor. Many an inoffensive, respectable citizen received rough treatment under such circumstances, and astonished his better-half by returning home from an election, or muster, with a smashed hat, black eye, or bloody nose, to satisfactorily account for which, required, in some instances, no ordinary amount of explanation.

By R. O. White

At the time of which we are writing, all the the voting at a general election was done in

Greenville. On these occasions the people from all portions of the county congregated together and proceeded to settle their old grudges. Quarrels were renewed, and fought out, under the exhilarating influence of whisky. People looked upon fights as inevitable on public days, especially at elections, and were disappointed if they did not occur. It was not uncommon to see two or three fights in progress at the same time on an election day in Greenville. These contests were conducted on the regular old-fashioned "fist and skull" style—knives and pistols being seldom used. Men prided themselves on their physical strength, and for one to declare himself the best man in the crowd was considered an insult to be resented by every one present. This expression, "best man," had no reference to anything further than mere bodily powers—the finer feelings and nobler qualities of the mind were not taken into consideration. It may with safety be said that Main street, in the old part of Greenville, has been the scene of more hotly-contested fist-fights, louder yells and oaths, and more brutal, as well as ludicrous drinking revels, than all other places in the county put together. On that street were located the dram-shops where liquid ruin, dealt out by glasses, quarts and gallons, sent misery and destitution to all portions of the community.

Other amusements, not quite so rough as fighting, were engaged in by the inhabitants on public days, such as wrestling, jumping, running foot-races and shooting with the rifle. Main street was, chiefly, the theater of these sports, except shooting. The scenes connected with them were more interesting, and occasionally somewhat ludicrous, and numerous incidents of the latter might be given, but space will not permit.

Shooting with the rifle was practiced just outside of the town, that there might be no danger attending it. Certain individuals spent the greater portion of every public day in this exercise; and many of them became expert marksmen, and very proud of their skill. Shooting-matches were then of frequent occurrence. A beef was "put up," at a certain price, to be shot for, each man paying a stipulated amount—usually 25 cents—for every shot. The best shots took the first choice of the beef, the next best, the second choice, and so on. About Christmas times, a live turkey, fastened on a stump or fence at the distance of a hundred yards, was sometimes put up and shot at, the first man that drew blood taking the turkey.

Bond County, as we have already stated, at the time of its early settlement abounded in all of the wild animals common in this latitude—bears, panthers, lynxes, wolves, catamounts, wild cats, deer, and many kinds of smaller game. Bears and panthers, however, were not very numerous, and soon became extinct. A bear was killed in 1821, on Shoal Creek, in the northwestern portion of the county, which is the last account we have of Bruin in this part of the State. But many of the other animals remaining until a much later date, gradually leaving the country, however, as the settlements increased. A few deer and turkeys are yet found in two or three localities on Shoal Creek, where there are large bodies of timber. As the wild animals disappeared before the advance of the pioneer, a certain class of people left also, or changed their mode of living to the greater credit of the community.

The inhabitants were, for several years, annoyed by the ravages of wolves, which destroyed many of their sheep and pigs. Wildcats and catamounts were also troublesome—killing many young pigs and lambs. Wolves continued so destructive that, as late as the year 1842, wolf-hunts were organized, in order to rid the country of these troublesome marauders. The writer attended one about that time, in the prairie northwest of Greenville, a description of which we will give as a sample. The people assembled on horseback, and formed a circle six or eight miles in diameter. At a certain hour, all commenced moving toward the center, and as the circle contracted, their line became more compact.

The plan did not succeed well, only one wolf being killed during the hunt. Wolves are very suspicious of danger, and in nearly every case, before the hunters got close enough together to prevent it, they broke through the circle to the outside, and escaped. This sport was both exciting and amusing, and was often indulged in by the early settlers.

In those early times, the people were more dependent on each other than at the present day, and, as a consequence, more social and accommodating. It was the general custom for the neighbors all to meet and assist each other in performing their heaviest work, such as harvesting, log-rolling, house-raising, corn-husking, etc., etc. In opening a farm, a great many logs had to be burned, or taken off the ground, before it could be plowed, hence log-rollings were common. At these annual gatherings, the logs were collected in large heaps suitable for burning, and men took special pride in testing their manhood at the end of a handspike.

At corn-huskings and various other gatherings common in those early days, lively, social times were experienced by both sexes. Whenever men met to roll logs, husk corn, or raise a house, the ladies would have a quilting, "sewing-bee," or something of the kind at the same place. When night came, it was not uncommon for the youngsters to have a dance or play. The dances were old-fashioned reels, and were sometimes continued till a late hour, and occasionally they

"Danced all night till broad day light,"

when the young swains, with love-stricken hearts, and warmly-beaming affections, deemed it their duty to

"Go home with the girls in the morning."

Plays of various kinds, were as much in vogue as dancing, but they have long since become obsolete. Many persons, however, now living, can look back to the scenes of those old plays with pleasant memories. Who can think of the old lines,

"Oh, sister Phebe, how merry were we,
When we sat under yon juniper tree."

Or,

"We're marching down to Quebectown,
And the drums are loudly beating,
The Americans have gained the day,
And the British are retreating,"

without thinking also of the "lads and lasses" assembled on such occasions. Many delightful reminiscences are connected with those scenes, when memory calls them up from the far distant past.

A great excitement was created here many years ago from a belief in the existence of the precious metals in Bond County. Both silver and gold were believed to be deposited at various points in the middle, western and south-western parts. Tales were related by some of the old settlers, giving accounts of fabulous quantities of silver ore being obtained here by the French and Indians, more than a hundred years before. The people credited these stories and dreamed of future wealth and luxury.

Robert Gillespie, living on Shoal Creek, a few miles above Pocahontas, found shining particles in the sand of a spring near his house, and washing out a quantity, showed it to some fellow in St. Louis, who pronounced it pure gold. This was enough; the demand for Gillespie's "dust" was such, that small quantities of it were in the possession of various persons, in order to compare it with such as might be found on their own premises. About this time, a man by the name of Gaylor, who was supposed to know something about minerals, being a "water witch," astonished the neighborhood by announcing that he had discovered an inexhaustible mine of silver on the land of Samuel Hunter, near Indian Creek, about four miles from Greenville.

A furnace was erected at the expense of Mr. Hunter, and Gaylor went to work manufacturing silver. The business was carried on for some weeks, producing but little silver, however, in proportion to the amount of ore smelted. Specimens of the metal had been tested by competent judges, and found to be silver, and men became almost insane with excitement, as they beheld the treasure issue from Gaylor's crucible. Some individuals actually neglected their business, spending days in wandering up and down creeks, branches and ravines, and returning at night with their pockets crammed full of little pieces of the substance known as "hornblende," the shining particles of which they believed to be gold and silver.

Several of Hunter's neighbors, believing the whole thing to be a deception, went, one afternoon, to the furnace, where Gaylor was at work, expressing a desire to see him smelt some ore taken from the mine in question. He did so, producing a small quantity of metal which was pronounced silver by all present. But while stirring the mass of pulverized ore, one of the men saw him drop a piece of silver coin into the crucible, which fact he communicated to the others. They then filled the crucible themselves with precisely the same kind of ore, and placing it in the furnace, told him that, after being thoroughly searched, he should smelt it, with his coat off and sleeves rolled up. He refused to do so, when they took him into custody and proceeded to melt it themselves. After heating and stirring the precious mass as he had done, they poured it out, but no silver was found.

Gaylor was taken to Greenville and lodged in jail on a charge of swindling, but was soon after released. He left the country, and thus ended the gold and silver excitement in Bond County.

Strange as it may appear to the reader, slavery existed in Bond County in the early period of its history. A man named Houston, from Kentucky, emigrated to this county and purchased a farm three miles west of Greenville, the place first settled and owned by Dr. Perrine. He brought with him a number of slaves, among whom were a woman named Fanny and her two children, a boy and girl, Stephen and Charity. His family soon became dissatisfied, and he returned to Kentucky, taking all his negroes with him except Fanny and her children—she not being able at the time to travel. They were left at the residence of Thomas White, two miles west of town, until her recovery, when she went to Greenville and hired to work.

According to the laws of Illinois then in force she and her children were free, having been in the State longer than the time specified, sixty days. About this time, one Magoon came to Greenville and stated that he had purchased those negroes from Houston. He was informed that they were free and could not be removed without a violation of law. He then formed a conspiracy with two citizens of Bond County to kidnap them, which they carried into effect one Sunday while the people were at church. They were pursued and captured at Pearce's, on Silver Creek, in Madison County. After being all brought back, the negroes were released and the kidnappers placed under bonds for trial, but it appears were never brought into court.

Magoon left the country, and remained away until the excitement subsided a little, when he returned and arranged with one of the Batemans, living on the Okaw, to steal the boy, Stephen, from a place north of Greenville, where he had gone to live. Bateman succeeded in kidnapping him, and carried him down into the neighborhood where he lived. He was kept concealed in the Okaw bottom until Magoon found an opportunity to escape with him.

The excitement was intense, and a crowd of resolute men soon started in pursuit. They followed on to the neighborhood of the Batemans, and spent several days searching in the woods. Failing, however, to find the boy, the pursuit was abandoned and the party returned home.

Magoon succeeded in escaping south with the boy, where he sold him into slavery, in which condition he remained until liberated by the late war between the States. He was never heard from until near the close of the rebellion, when he was found in the southern part of Georgia, by a Bond County soldier, to whom he related the particulars of his capture and abduction. Bateman was one of the Okaw desperadoes and drunkards, who were wont to assemble in Greenville in the early history of Bond County, on public days, to drink and fight. He died not many years since, in a state of intoxication, uttering with his last breath the most horrible blasphemies.

Old Fanny's husband, Stephen Hudley, was a slave in Missouri, and she, after years of toil, saved money enough cooking, washing and selling ginger cakes, to purchase his freedom, and thus had the proud satisfaction of re-uniting those sacred ties which had been sundered by the curse of slavery. An attempt, as we have seen, had been made to kidnap her and her little children, not by slaveholders, from whom nothing better could have been expected, but by citizens of a *free State*—the last men it would be supposed, who would commit such a dastardly act. But who can account for human depravity?

The health of the people of Bond County is much better now than in former years. This is attributable to the fact that there is less rain, less decaying vegetation, fewer marshes and stagnant pools, and a consequent diminution of the vapors thus generated, which have proved, in so many cases, fatal to the human family. In addition to all this, we live in more comfortable houses, are better clothed, and expose ourselves less to the inclemencies of the weather.

The first physicians who located here were Drs. William Perrine and J. B. Drake, from New Jersey. Before this, when people became sick, they had to send to Edwardsville for a doctor. Both Dr. Perrine and Dr. Drake were young men of talent and education, and well versed in their profession. They soon got a good practice, and became noted physicians.

Dr. Perrine married a Miss Townsend—the daughter of a Presbyterian preacher, residing in the northwestern part of the county, and a few years later removed with his family to Florida. During the Seminole war, he was murdered by Indians at his own house. Dr. Drake removed to Greenville, where he continued the practice of medicine for many years. He then engaged in the mercantile business, and, still later, married, residing in Greenville until his death.

As the county became more populous, other physicians of eminence located here and acquired considerable note as medical practitioners. During some of the sickly seasons, there were not enough well persons to take care of the sick. This state of affairs was not confined to Bond County alone, but extended over the southern part of the State. The year 1841 was, perhaps, the most unhealthy one ever experienced in this part of Illinois. Then, all the physicians of this county resided in Greenville, and, of course, their practice extended many miles. They were kept going night and day during the sickliest portion, not only of 1841, but of several years preceding, and after that time.

There was much sickness then of a serious and fatal character, yet there were some persons who would send for a physician for every trifling illness. When an individual mounted a horse to go for a doctor, he generally "put him through," no matter what the distance, nor what the disease, whether a sprained ankle, or congestion of the brain; the speed was about the same. A man living ten or twelve miles from Greenville was seen one day riding at a fearful rate toward town, his horse in a foam of sweat, and evidently going for a doctor in a desperate case. He was hailed on the way, when the following dialogue ensued: "Who's sick?" "My brother." "What's the matter with him?" "He's bleeding." By this time he had got so far off as to render further questions impracticable. It was afterwards ascertained that his brother had only taken a spell of bleeding at the nose, from which he soon recovered.

A G Henry

CHAPTER VI.*

RELIGIOUS HISTORY OF BOND COUNTY—THE FIRST PREACHERS AND THE FIRST CHURCHES—THE METHODISTS AND PRESBYTERIANS—MOODY'S CAMP GROUND—SUNDAY SCHOOLS—THE "JERKS"—TEMPERANCE—EDUCATIONAL FACILITIES—IMPROVEMENT IN SCHOOLS—STATISTICS—THE PEOPLE AND THE STATE DEBT—WAR HISTORY, ETC., ETC.

"Many things of many kinds."

THERE is no better evidence of moral advancement and Christian civilization in a newly-settled community than the establishment of churches. The history of Christianity in Bond County may be termed coeval with its settlement by white people. The first preacher of whom there is any authentic account made his appearance in the county in the year 1816, and was of the Methodist denomination, among which were found those pioneer soldiers of the cross, who preceded or followed close in the wake of civilization in the West. Rev. Jesse Hale, the pioneer minister of Bond County, preached his first sermon at the house of Robert Gillespie, who lived two miles southwest of Greenville, in the year mentioned (1816), and where he continued preaching at intervals, during that and part of the ensuing year. A church, the first established in the county, was organized in that neighborhood during the two years of his ministration. What State he was from, or where he went after this, cannot now be ascertained.

The next preacher was Salmon P. Giddings of St. Louis, a Presbyterian, who preached occasionally at private houses, and in 1818 or 1819, organized a church at "Moody's Spring," about a mile southwest of Greenville. This spring was so named for Andrew Moody, who lived there several years, though the place was first settled by Thomas Kirkpatrick. Here the first church in Bond County was erected during the year 1817, by the Methodist denomination. It was built of hewed logs, and thirty feet long by twenty-five feet in width. We have not been able to ascertain the precise dates when the first ministers belonging to each of the denominations now in the county came here, but those of the Baptists and Cumberland Presbyterians arrived soon after the two already mentioned, and those of the others at a still later day.

At "Moody's Spring" the Methodists held the first camp-meeting in the county, and for a series of years these meetings were annually held there, so that it afterward became generally known as "Moody's Camp-ground." As the county became more thickly settled, the number of "camp-grounds" increased, and, for many years, camp-meetings were annually held in various portions by the Methodists and Cumberland Presbyterians. These gatherings of the people for religious purposes took place in July, August or September, when fruits and vegetables were the most abundant, and provisions to "feed the multitude" could most easily be procured.

One of the most noted places in the county for holding camp-meetings was situated near the town of Newport, and called "Zion Camp-ground," a brief description of which may not be uninteresting to the reader. Many of us can

*By R. O. White.

well remember its cool, shady arbor in the green forest, with its primitive seats, the temporary pulpit or "stand," in front of which, on a nail driven in the trunk of a tree, was suspended the tin trumpet or horn, by which the people were called together for religious services; the tents with their straw-covered floors, forming three sides of a square around the seated area, at a distance of thirty or forty yards; back of these the cooking operations presided over by old ladies with caps on their heads, and young maidens with bright eyes, rosy cheeks and glossy curls; the space reserved for "anxious seats," called the "altar," immediately in front of the stand and covered with straw; the shady and well-beaten path to the cool spring, trickling from its moss-grown sycamore gum, the tables spread with the choicest viands of the country, of which all were invited freely to partake freely, "without money and without price;" and the groups of singers in the tents, composed mainly of young gentlemen and ladies, assembled for the ostensible purpose of singing. All these, and many other associations of these old camp-meetings, will long remain fresh in the memory of those who witnessed them.

Preaching then was very different from what it is now being generally of the noisy order. Society, too, was in a rough state, and the preaching, in order to rivet attention and be effective, had to correspond with the times. For, unless a speaker can gain the attention of his audience and hold it, he may preach till doomsday and then find that his time and breath have been spent in vain. Thus the style of preaching, as well as any other public speaking, changes with the manners of the people. In those early days, the preacher who had the strongest voice and exercised it most; who could give the most extravagant and over-wrought descriptions of heaven, hell and the day of judgment, and could slash the air with his hands and arms in the wildest manner, was considered the greatest man by the majority of the people. The singing partook of the same noisy character as the preaching and at night, with favorable wind, both the singing and preaching might be easily heard three miles.

With the rude state of society then existing in the community, the behavior of some at camp-meetings was not always of the best and ministers and members had much difficulty some times in maintaining good order, especially at night. Notwithstanding their best endeavors, frequent disturbances occurred after dark, such as shaving off horses' manes and tails, smearing tar over the seats of saddles, and throwing watermelon rinds, empty whisky bottles, etc., into the altar among the mourners. Taking all things into consideration however, the general behavior was as good as could have been expected at that time; and much as we may now pride ourselves on our superior refinement and deplore such conduct, we have, nevertheless, in our community at this day individuals who are only restrained from committing such disgraceful acts by the force of public opinion and the laws of the land.

Though the religious exercises partook, to a great extent, of this noisy character, and the preachers were less polished in their phraseology than at this time, yet the people were as sincere in their profession of Christianity as they are now. In proportion to number there were, doubtless, as few hypocrites among religious people and as much true piety as at the present day. The pioneer ministers were not all of the above type, but many possessed talent and learning, used the best of language, and were graceful and dignified in their preaching. These backwoods preachers contributed largely in their day to the morals of the community, and were mainly instrumental in laying the foundation of the various religious denominations in our county. They were not ashamed to be seen traveling on foot or on horseback many miles to meet their appointments, often encountering hunger and thirst and exposing themselves to the inclemencies of the weather.

The first Sunday school in the county was organized in the year 1818, at the residence of William Robinson, about one and a half miles northwest of Greenville. It was under the supervision of the Presbyterian Church, which we have already mentioned. It was composed of grown people and children, and was termed a Bible class or society. This school has been kept up by that denomination ever since, and meets now in Greenville, at the Old Presbyterian Church, and is very justly entitled the pioneer Sunday school of Bond County. After its organization, others, under the control of the different religious denominations, were established in various portions of the county, as new churches were organized. The progress of these schools was at first slow, but they gradually gained in strength and popular favor, keeping pace with the various religious denominations, until there are now in every neighborhood, not only neat commodious churches, but well-attended and flourishing Sunday schools.

Among the ministers of the Gospel who labored here at an early day, may be mentioned Bishop Ames, Peter Cartwright and James B. Woollard, of the Methodist; Peter Long, of the Baptist, and Joel Knight, of the Cumberland Presbyterian Church. These, with the exception of Peter Cartwright, have preached in nearly all parts of the county. J. B. Woollard and Peter Long have doubtless performed more marriage ceremonies and preached more funerals than any other two ministers in this portion of the State. Of the early preachers of this county long since dead, were Revs. John Dew, John M. Peck, William K. Stewart, and many others of the various denominations, whom the old settlers can call to mind.

It is not inappropriate, in concluding this sketch of the religious denominations of the county, to notice briefly what was termed in those early times "the jerks." Although not so common here as in many other localities of the Western country, yet they were of frequent enough occurrence as to excite considerable speculation as to their origin. There is little doubt now, perhaps, that they were a species of religious excitement, though many believed then that they originated from witchcraft or were the direct work of Satan. Persons having them were affected with violent convulsions, their heads, necks and limbs being involuntarily and forcibly jerked in every possible direction, their hands clenched, and their jaws tightly set.

A young lady took the jerks one evening at a camp-meeting at Mount Gilead, four miles west of Greenville, about thirty-five years ago, and so violent and rapid were her motions that four men who attempted to hold her, to prevent her being thrown against the benches or trees, were unable to do so. Her hands were shut more firmly than her natural strength seemed to warrant. Attacks of this kind came on suddenly, lasting generally only a few minutes, though sometimes longer, and occurred only at camp meetings when the religious excitement was at its greatest strain. There was another phase or modification of the jerks, termed "the falling down exercise," in which the persons affected suddenly fell down and lay perfectly helpless. Sometimes they remained in this condition for several hours, but usually only a short time, when they would rise to their feet and in most instances commence running and jumping about, throwing their arms in every direction, manifesting all the symptoms of the first form of the disease, with the exception that in the former cases they seldom spoke a word, but in the latter, after rising from the ground, they often screamed, sang or laughed in the wildest manner. Persons after recovering from one of these attacks appeared listless and dull for awhile, having little or nothing to say to anyone, and utterly incapable of being excited in any way whatever, until the return of the paroxysm, which to some came every night of the meeting, when the mourners were called to the "altar,' and the excitement again became great.

From what has been said in a preceding chapter of the prevalence of whisky-drinking among the early settlers, and the general belief that ardent spirits "were good in their place," it will not be supposed that Bond County was a fruitful field for temperance organizations in old times. Temperance societies were formed, however, at different periods, between the years 1830 and 1840, though with but little permanent success. A man would come along, deliver a lecture, organize a society, and, for a while, all would go well; but in the course of a year or two, the whole thing went to naught and those of the members who had been in the habit of drinking, like the Biblical sow, "returned to their wallow."

As late as 1846, when the company for the Mexican war from Bond County was organized at Greenville, after the requisite number had volunteered, the men were drawn up in line, on the public square, and a bucket-full of whisky brought out and distributed as a "treat." of which most of them partook, drinking it out of a tin dipper. It was not many years after this, however, before the temperance cause began to gain ground, encountering more or less opposition, until at present no one who is an habitual drinker is admitted into the best society, and no young lady of the community will tolerate the addresses of a regular and known dram-drinker. This state of things is not so much attributable to the influence of temperance organizations, perhaps, as to the better training and education of the present generation.

The schools and educational facilities of the county now claim our attention, and follow very appropriately the history of the churches. Both possess refining influences, and furnish the highest standard of the civilization of all communities. It is a characteristic feature of all American settlements that among their first efforts of a public nature is the establishment of churches and schools. The early schoolhouses in Illinois were rude, and constructed upon a primitive plan.

The first school in the county was taught, in the year 1819, by Thomas White, in a little log cabin, on the hill west of Greenville, between the residence of Mrs. Black and where Samuel White's tanyard was situated. This school was small, as the inhabitants were few, some of whom had no education themselves, and did not care whether their children ever received any or not. But as the population increased, schools sprang up in various parts of the county, whenever a neighborhood became strong enough to sustain one. In some instances, where but two or three families lived near each other, they sent off several miles to those similarly situated, took in children and boarded them free, in order to have a school that would justify the paying of a teacher.

There being no school fund then, every man paid for the tuition of his children out of his own pocket. The price of teaching was from \$1.50 to \$2 per scholar per quarter—equivalent to \$12 or \$15 a month, for a school of twenty-five pupils, which was more than any school in the county averaged for many years.

The schoolhouses, for many years, were built of logs with puncheon floors, weight-pole roofs, and wide chimneys of wood and clay, on a par with the dwellings of the settlers themselves. The seats were long benches made of puncheons or slabs, without backs, and frequently so high that the feet of the smaller pupils could not touch the floor, and it was quite an irksome task for the little fellows to sit from early in the morning till late in the evening, with nothing to support their backs, and their legs dangling from the rough seats. It is no wonder, then, that some scholars, instead of going on to school when they left home in the morning, often played truant all day, concealing themselves in the bushes till the usual time to return in the evening. This trick the writer remembers having been guilty of several times. He once lay all day in a field of tall rye, near harvest, when the heat of the sun and his thirst were far more intolerable than sitting on a bench at school.

The schools were conducted on the most noisy plan imaginable. They received the appellation of "vocal schools," that is, the scholars spelled, read and "ciphered" aloud while studying their lessons, as well as when reciting, and such another jargon of unintelligible sounds as one of those schools presented has never been witnessed, perhaps, since the confusion at Babel. Some of the pupils tried to study, others gabbled away with all their might without uttering an intelligible sound, and the noise made rendered it almost impossible for the instructor to tell who were studying and who were not. But the culminating point came, when they were told to study the "spelling lesson," which was the last one recited before school "turned out" at noon and in the evening, and was participated in by all the scholars. The noise then produced has been often heard at the distance of more than a mile. When the teacher wished the class to recite, he brought his foot to the floor with a loud and vigorous stamp, which shook the whole house, and had the effect of stilling the noise for a moment, similar to the throwing of a billet of wood into a pond of croaking frogs. The whole school would instantly rise to their feet and make an unceremonious rush for "their places," recklessly running against or over each other.

Occasionally, a "downy-chinned" lad, under the influence of "puppy love," took advantage of the confusion to imprint or, rather, daub a kiss on the cheek of some fair damsel, whom he imagined as far gone in the tender passions as himself.*

The teacher of one of these noisy schools once gave his usual stamp to call up the class, when his foot came down upon the end of a loose puncheon, which fell beneath his weight, letting him through as far as he could go, and tearing one leg of his pantaloons from the ankle to the knee on a nail. The effect upon the school, of course, was a serious and melancholy one. Some of the teachers, when pronouncing the words to the class, or "giving out" the lesson, as it was called, spoke as though they intended not only their pupils, but many of the neighbors to hear them.

When schools prohibiting pupils from studying aloud first began to be taught, they were called "silent schools," and such was the prejudice in favor of the old, noisy system that in some neighborhoods it was made the test of qualification of teachers. School books then were scarce. Webster's Spelling book the English Reader, New Testament and Pike's Arithmetic constituted the list of books used for many years.

Male teachers only were employed for several decades after the first organization of schools in this county. Female teachers were so scarce that none offered their services, and had they done so, the prejudice against them was so great that no neighborhood would have employed them. So great was the opposition to female education, many of the first settlers of the county held that all the education a girl required was to be able to read the Bible and Testament and write well enough to sign her own name. Some would not even go this far, but allowed her only the privilege of learning to read. When speaking of the literary attainments of a girl, it was a common remark "she has education enough for a woman!"

Our educational interests and facilities,

*This was a part [illegible] the performance, [illegible] that was left off the [illegible]gramme [illegible]d.

though at first so inferior, have gradually kept improving as the county increased in population and wealth, aided by wise legislation, until we have arrived at our present system of free schools, of which all may feel justly proud. Below we present the following condensed school statistics of Bond County, as a matter of interest:

Number of white persons in the county between the ages of six and twenty-one years	4,618
Number of colored persons in the county between the ages of six and twenty-one years	[illegible]
Total	4,650
Number of schools in the county	69
Number of districts in the county	69
Number of scholars attending school	3,6[illegible]
Number of teachers	111
Number of male teachers	6[illegible]
Number of female teachers	[illegible]
Number of brick school houses	12
Number of frame school houses	57
Number of log school houses	2
Amount of [illegible] fund [illegible]	$14,[illegible]01.64
Amount [illegible]	[illegible]512.98
Highest monthly wages paid any male teacher	1[illegible]5
Lowest monthly wages paid any male teacher	[illegible]
Highest monthly wages paid any female teacher	50
Lowest monthly wages paid any female teacher	20

The highest monthly wages paid to male teachers are in Township 5, Range 3, $165; Township 4, Range 1, $65; Township 4, Range 3, $60. The lowest wages paid to males are in Township 7, Range 3, $25; Township 4, Range 2, $[illegible]. The highest monthly wages paid to females are in Township 5, Range 3, $50; Township [illegible], Range 4, $45; Township 7, Range 3, $40. The lowest are in Township 4, Range 2 and Township 6, Range 3, Township 4, Range 4, and Township 7, Range 4, each $20 per month.

Almira Female College, beautifully situated in Greenville, is an educational institution of which Bond County may well feel proud. It was founded in 1857, and is in a very flourishing state. A full history of it, however, will be found in the chapters devoted to the history of Greenville.

The citizens of Bond County have not been behind those in any other portion of the State in asserting their opinions, demanding their rights, or responding to the calls of patriotism. As an instance of their readiness to make a public declaration of opinion, they were the first in the county to oppose what was called the "internal improvement bill," passed many years ago by the Legislature, the following notice of which appears in Ford's History of Illinois, page 291:

"The people of Bond County, as soon as the internal improvement system passed, had declared in a public meeting that the system must lead to taxation and utter ruin; that the people were not bound to pay any of the debt to be contracted for it; and that Bond County would never assist in paying a cent of it. Accordingly, they refused to pay taxes for several years." The citizens of the county were correct in their conclusions, for in a few years the system went down, and left the State in the almost bankrupt condition they had foretold, with a debt of $14,000,000 hanging over it. When the subject of paying this debt by increased taxation came up in 1844, William S. Wait addressed a very able letter to Thomas Ford, Governor of the State, in opposition to the plan.

In patriotism the county has been equally prompt in maintaining her position. When the State of Illinois was called upon for four regiments of volunteers for the Mexican war, in 1846, Bond County furnished one company of ninety-three men. This company had the following officers: Benjamin E. Sellers, Captain; J. M. Hubbard, First Lieutenant; S. G. McAdams, Second Lieutenant, and I. N. Redfearn, Third Lieutenant. Of this number only about forty men returned at the close of the campaign, the remainder having died or been discharged on account of sickness. But few of them are now living in the county.

During the late rebellion, the county, small as it is, furnished five companies of cavalry, besides several companies of infantry.

Notwithstanding so many companies went from this county into the late war, many of the citizens strongly opposed it. In consequence of their opposition, much excitement prevailed during a portion of the time, resulting, however, in no very serious trouble, except in a few instances. Many occurrences, both ludicrous and otherwise, might be related, but lest they stir up and keep alive old prejudices and differences, they will be passed over in silence. Suffice it to say, in conclusion of the county's war record, that those who went forth to battle for their country's honor acquitted themselves as became American soldiers, and their history in the long and dreadful four years' struggle was that of all the soldiers from Illinois—noble and honorable. Those who met a soldier's death fell in a high and holy cause; those who survived the struggle and returned home enjoy the proud consciousness that the Union was preserved—the government unshaken.

CHAPTER VII.*

RAILROAD HISTORY—THE INTERNAL IMPROVEMENT SYSTEM—OLD NATIONAL OR CUMBERLAND ROAD—MISSISSIPPI AND ATLANTIC RAILROAD—THE EARLY DIFFICULTIES IN ITS CONSTRUCTION—FINAL COMPLETION—THE PRESENT VANDALIA LINE—OFFICERS OF THE ROAD, ETC.—THE PRESS OF BOND COUNTY—EARLY NEWSPAPERS—"ADVOCATE" AND ITS ANTECEDENTS—THE "SUN," ETC.

ALL who are acquainted with the history of Illinois, will remember the old Internal Improvement System, which well-nigh wrecked the Commonwealth. For a time it seemed as if the whole country had gone wild upon the subject of internal improvements, and railroads and canals were chartered without regard to cost or eligibility of location. Illinois took a front rank in this reckless expenditure, and voted away millions of money for internal improvements. But it is not our intention to go into details upon the subject—a subject that many still living in Bond County are familiar with. It is merely alluded to by way of introduction to the internal improvements of the county.

The old National road was the first internal improvement in which Bond County took an active interest. Perhaps no work has ever taken place in the United States, of a public character, which excited so much interest throughout the country as the "National, or Cumberland road" from Washington City to St. Louis, with a branch diverging at Zanesville, Ohio, passing through Kentucky, Tennessee, and on to New Orleans. Not even the Union Pacific Railroad excelled in magnitude the enterprise of the Old National road in its day, and which passed through Vandalia and Greenville on to St. Louis. For years it was the great question in the National Congress, as the Mississippi River Improvement is now the all-absorbing theme in that august body. Our space, however, will not allow a sketch of this great project, and the reader is referred to other publications for its history. The remarks upon this road, as well as the old internal improvement system, are but prefatory to the subjoined sketch of the Mississippi & Atlantic Railroad, now so extensively and favorably know everywhere as the "Vandalia Line." The history of this famous railroad thoroughfare is written by Mr. Williamson Plant, who has been connected with it from the very inception of the enterprise, and is perfectly familiar with its career from the original survey to the present time. He has written it up fully, and the article will be found interesting to all the friends of the road. It is as follows:

The first railroad that gave any assurance to the people of being built through Bond County was the Mississippi & Atlantic Railroad from St. Louis through Greenville, Vandalia, Terre Haute, connecting with lines to New York.

One of the most earnest workers for that road was the Hon. William S. Wait, who was one of Bond County's oldest and most respected citizens. His letter written in June, 1863, to ex-Gov. B. Gratz Brown, of St. Louis, will fully explain the difficulties that surrounded, and finally overcame that road:

"The railroad projected so early as 1835 to

* By W. H. Perrin.

run from St. Louis to Terre Haute was intended as the commencement of a direct line of railway to the Atlantic cities, and its first survey (of which a copy is inclosed) was taken over the exact line of the great 'Cumberland' road. We applied to the Illinois Legislature for a charter in 1846, but were opposed by rival interests, that finally succeeded in establishing two lines of railroad connecting St. Louis with the Wabash—one by a line running north, and the other by a line running south of our survey, thus demonstrating by the unfailing test of physical geography that our line is the central and true one. The two rival lines alluded to, viz., Terre Haute & Alton and Ohio & Mississippi. We organized our company with the name of the 'Mississippi & Atlantic Railroad,' in 1850, by virtue of a General Railroad Law passed the year previous, and immediately accomplished a survey. An adverse decision of our Supreme Court led us to accept the offer of Eastern capitalists to help us through, who immediately took nine-tenths of the stock, and gave us John Brough for President. Our right to construct was finally confirmed in February, 1854; the road put under contract, and the work commenced. The shock given to all railroad enterprise by the "Schuyler fraud" suspended operations, and before confidence was restored, the controlling power, which was enthroned in Wall street, had arrived at the conclusion, as we afterward discovered, to proceed no further in the construction of the Mississippi & Atlantic Railroad. For purposes best understood by themselves, the Eastern managers amused us for several years with the hope that they were still determined to prosecute the work. When we were finally convinced of the intentional deception, we abandoned the old charter and instituted a new company under the name of the 'Highland & St. Louis Railroad Company' with power to build and complete by sections the entire road from St. Louis to Terre Haute. The charter was obtained in February 1859, with the determination on the part of the Highland corporators to make no delay in constructing the section connecting them with St. Louis, but were prevented at the outset by difficulties, since overcome, and afterward by the existing rebellion."

The foregoing letter portrays truthfully some of the prominent difficulties with which Bond and other counties on the central line had to contend. State policy was openly urged by many of the leading men north and south of the "Brough road," as it was generally called. Hon. Sidney Breeze, a long resident of Carlisle, on the line of the Ohio & Mississippi Railroad, publicly declared for that doctrine, "that it was to the interest of the State to encourage the policy that would build the most roads through the State; that the north and south roads (alluded to in Mr. Wait's letter) should first be allowed to get into successful operation, when the central line should then be chartered, as the merits of that line would insure the building the road on that line at once, giving to Middle Illinois three roads instead of one, as the chartering of the central line first would be a death blow to the other two, at least for many long years to come." Mr. Wait replied immediately, saying it was the first instance he had ever known where the merits of a railroad line had been urged as a reason why it should not meet with merited encouragement, and after more than $100,000 was expended on the "Brough" road, further work on it was, of the necessity before referred to, suspended.

In February, 1865, the rebellion nearing its close, the people along the "Central Line" or "Brough" survey, again renewed their petition to the Illinois Legislature for a negotiation of their right to build their railroad on their long-cherished route.

On the 10th of February, 1865, a liberal charter was granted for building the present St. Louis, Vandalia & Terre Haute Railroad. The line was designated in the charter as "commencing on the left bank of the Mississippi River, opposite St. Louis, running thence eastwardly through Greenville, the county seat of Bond County and through Vandalia, by the most eligible route, to a point on the River Wabash. The persons named therein as incorporators were Henry Wing, T. W. Little, John S. Dewy, Andrew Mills, Solomon Koepfli, Garritt Crownover, Curtis Blakeman, William S. Smith, Charles Hoiles William S. Wait, John B. Hunter, Williamson Plant, Andrew G. Henry, Jediah F. Alexander, Nathaniel M. McCurdy, August H. Dieckmann, Ebenezer Capps, Frederick Remann, Mathias Lehren, Michael Lynch, Thomas L. Vest, J. F. Weschfort, Samuel W. Quinn, Chauncey Rose and Joseph H. Morgan. The citizens of Bond County led in the enterprise of building the road, not only by words, but by liberal individual and county subscriptions. The county, small in territory, made the liberal subscription of $100,000, payable in fifteen annual installments with 10 per cent annual interest, all of which has been met promptly, and at this date only $16,000 remain due, all of which will be paid this year, the tax being already collected for that purpose, and Bond County will be free from debt, but the advantages in the use of the road to the people and the yearly tax paid by the railroad company will continue as long as taxes are levied and collected. The railroad tax paid in Bond County for 1881 amounted to $4,274.29. The individual subscriptions in Bond County were some $46,000 at Greenville and $24,000 at Pocahontas were not only promptly paid as called for but some half dozen citizens of Greenville viz., W. S. Smith, J. F. Alexander, Williamson Plant, Andrew G. Henry and others, gave to the Highland subscribers their individual guaranty to refund their $65,000 subscribed by them and being if the road was not finished to Highland by July 1, 1868, as per condition in their subscriptions.

The road was completed to that point at the date agreed upon, and the Highland subscribers finished the payment of their subscription promptly. And although of the citizens of Bond County it may be said they led in starting this great railroad enterprise, which has led to the building one of the most popular lines across the State of Illinois, the fact should not be overlooked that Collinsville, Highland, Vandalia, Effingham and Clark County did their duty nobly. The entire subscription list along the line amounting to $500,000, and was divided as follows:

Collinsville and vicinity, individual.......	$ 9,600
Highland, individual, and about $10,000 from St Louis	75,000
Highland City	10,000
Pocahontas, in Bond County, individual....	24,100
Greenville, in Bond County, individual	46,000
Greenville City in Bond County, for depot building	2,000
Bond County.........	100,000
Vandalia, in Fayette County..............	50,000
Douglas Township, in Effingham County...	50,000
Teutopolis in Effingham County..	15,000
Mason in Effingham County	5,000
Summit in Effingham County.............	10,000
Clark County.	100,000
Individual subscriptions in Clark County...	2,700
Individual subscriptions in Cumberland County....	600
Total.....	$500,000

The first meeting of the Board of Corporators was held at Vandalia Ill., on the 14th day of November, 1865, for the purpose of organizing and electing a Board of nine Directors, with following result: John Scholfield, and Charles Duncan, Clark County, Ill.; Samuel Quinn Cumberland County, Ill.; J. P. M. Howard and L. W. Little Effingham County Ill.; C. Floyd Jones and F. Remann, Fayette County, Ill.; William S. Smith and Williamson Plant,

At the first meeting of the Board of Directors held at Effingham on the 22d day of November, 1865, for the purpose of electing the first officers of the company, H. P. M. Howard was elected President, and Williamson Plant Secretary.

Through the influence of E. C. Rice, who was chief engineer of the "Brough" survey, and had made estimates for the work under the same Gen. E. F. Winslow, a gentleman of great energy and considerable railroad experience, after various propositions being made to build part of the line, or parts of the road, contracted, August 22, 1866, to build the entire line from the west bank of the Wabash, to the east end of the dyke at Illinoistown. The contract was finally ratified at a meeting of the Board of Directors held at Vandalia November 14, 1866. An additional agreement was entered into November 28, 1866, and made part of the original.

The first shock received by the Railroad Company in the outset was the lamented death of its earnest leader and judicious friend, Hon. William S. Wait, July 17, 1865, thereby depriving them of his mature judgment and wise counsel in making and carrying out the contract about to be entered into for the building of the road under the charter so recently obtained from the Legislature.

In 1867, first mortgage bonds were put on the property, rights, franchises, leases and estate, etc., of the company to amount of $1,90[illegible],000. When the property was leased in February, 1868, a second mortgage was put on the same to amount of $2,600,000, each mortgage bearing 7 per cent interest, payable semi-annually. For the purpose of further equipment of the road, preferred stock has been issued to the amount of $1,511,700, bearing 7 per cent interest. The issue of $2,000,000 has been authorized. This stock will take precedence over the common stock of the company in receiving dividends, and as the interest on the preferred stock may accumulate before any payment thereof, the prospect for dividends on common stock is remote.

By mutual understanding between the contractor and the company, E. C. Rice was engaged as Chief Engineer of the company January 18, 1867, and he commenced the first survey on the west end of the line in March, and the grading was begun as soon as the line was fixed at the west end, in April following. At the same meeting a code of by-laws was adopted, and Greenville was designated as the general office of the company.

At the annual election held in January, 1867, J. P. M. Howard was re-elected President, Williamson Plant, Secretary, and W. S. Smith, Treasurer. April 3, 1867, Mr. Howard gave up the position, on request and J. F. Alexander was chosen President of the Company in his place. This gave to Bond County all the officers of the company, and at the same annual election Bond County had three of the nine Directors. By the charter the company was authorized to issue first mortgage bonds not to exceed $12,000 per mile. The capital stock was made $3,000,000, which could be increased at an annual meeting by a majority of stockholders in interest, as they should direct.

At the annual election in January, 1868, five Directors from Bond County were chosen out of the nine, viz: J. F. Alexander, W. S. Smith, Andrew G. Henry, William S. Wait Jr. and Francis Dressor. The same officers, J. F. Alexander, President, Williamson Plant, Secretary, and William S. Smith, all from Bond County, were re-elected, giving to Bond County again all its officers and a majority of the Directors. Mention is made of these facts only to show that in the building of the road Bond County citizens were considered and acknowledged as leading in the enterprise. This may be owing in some degree, to the geographical position of the county, being twenty miles from Greenville north, south or east to any railroad, advantages. It is not the intention of this article to detract in any way from the many persons and places along the line that responded with their liberal subscriptions. Highland, and the country around it in particular, by their heavy individual, though conditional, subscriptions, are deserving special recognition for the same. The road was completed to Highland by July 1, 1868, and the stock was issued to the subscribers and they paid up in full as specified in their subscriptions. The first regular passenger train did not run, however, until August 20, 1868, from Highland to St. Louis.

By the consent of the railroad, company Gen. Winslow as contractor was paid $120,000 for labor expended on the line to the 10th day of February, 1868, and at his request was released from his contracts. The same was ratified and accepted by the company at their meeting March 13, 1868. The railroad company entered into a contract February 10, 1868, with Thomas L. Jewett and B. E. Smith, of Ohio; George B. Roberts of Philadelphia, and W. R. McKeen, of Terre Haute, in the firm name of McKeen, Smith & Co., to complete the road at an early day. At the same time and place an agreement was entered into, leasing the St. Louis Vandalia & Terre Haute Railroad to the Terre Haute & Indianapolis Railroad Company. In the report of the President of the Vandalia Company made to the stockholders at their annual meeting held at Greenville, Ill., January 6, 1872, he says:

"When, on the 10th day of February, 1868, the contract was made insuring the completion of your road, another contract was also made, providing for its forming a part of a continuous railroad line from St. Louis (via Indianapolis) to Pittsburgh; and for perfecting this object your line was leased for a period of 999 years to the Terre Haute & Indianapolis Railroad Company, for the joint interest of this company and the several railroad companies forming the said line. Under this lease the lessees were to work your road at their own cost and expense, and to pay to your company thirty-five (35) per cent of the gross earnings, first paying therefrom all the interest due on the bonds of the company, and all taxes assessed against the property of the company, advancing any deficit in the amount needed to meet these liabilities and paying the surplus (if any remained) of the thirty-five (35) per cent to your company. Your board, in view of the light traffic usually done upon a new line, reduced the proportion due your company of the gross earnings to thirty (30) per cent, provided, that after payment by the lessee of the cost and expense of working your road out of the seventy (70) per cent received for that purpose, if any surplus remained it should go to your company."

From small earnings from the time the road was opened, first to Highland and Greenville in 1868 and finally through to Terre Haute, July 1, 1870, it has developed a marvelous increase of business, not only to the road, but to the farming and all other industries along the line. The whole cost of the road and equipment of the same to July 1, 1868, when the contractors turned the road over to the lessee, was $7,171,355.89, which has increased steadily as the line is more fully developed by "rolling stock" and "betterments," etc., on the road, until the last report of Treasurer W. H. Barnes, made the total cost of road and equipment to October 1, 1880, $8,330,410.75. The amount of business over this line, for the past year, aggregates $1,565,515.04; and the rental due to the company from the lessee for the year ending October 31, 1881, was $469,654.50; and for the same time, $424,827.04 was earned in carrying passengers, $43,490.57 for express, and $96,835.98 for mail services.

Under the management of McKeen, Smith & Co., the line was completed to Greenville on the 5th of December, 1868; the first passenger train reached Greenville on the night of December 7, and the first regular passenger train on schedule time, from Greenville to St. Louis, was on the morning of December 8, 1868.

The first train ran into Effingham April 26, 1870. On the 8th of June, 1870, an excursion train was run through from Indianapolis to St. Louis, over the St. Louis, Vandalia & Terre Haute Railroad; and the first regular passenger train, over the whole line on schedule time, was on the 12th day of June, 1870; and, as mentioned before, the contractors turned over the road as per contract to the Terre Haute & Indianapolis Railroad Company, July 1, 1870.

At first, one passenger train each way was started, but soon found necessary for two; and now four regular trains each way for passengers, and twice as many freights, are needed to keep up with the increasing business. Bond County furnishes its full share of the heavy business of the road as it passes through the county from west to east, passing through Oakdale, Pocahontas, Stubblefield, Greenville, Smithboro and Mulberry Grove.

The St. Louis, Vandalia & Terre Haute Railroad is 158 miles from East St. Louis to eastern line of the State, and seven miles from State line to Wabash River at Terre Haute.

The interest of the people of Bond County in the Vandalia Railroad is such that the history of the county would be incomplete without, not only a history of the road, but a detailed history or record so far as can be given of those who have been and now are connected with the same, probably made more appropriate as the general office of the company is located at Greenville, where the annual meetings of the stockholders and directors are held.

Presidents—J. P. M. Howard, Effingham, Ill., November 22, 1865, to April 3, 1867; J. F. Alexander, Greenville, Ill., April 3, 1867, to February 15, 1871; George B. Roberts, Philadelphia, February 15, 1871, to January 11, 1876; Thomas D. Messler, Pittsburgh, January 11, 1876, to present time.

Treasurers—William S. Smith, Greenville, Ill., January 18, 1867, to April 14, 1869; Williamson Plant, Greenville, Ill., April 14, 1869, to February 15, 1871; Albert Hewson, Philadelphia, February 15, 1871, to June 26, 1871; William P. Shinn, Pittsburgh, June 26, 1871, to January 11, 1876; W. H. Barnes, Pittsburgh, January 11, 1876, to present time.

Secretary, Williamson Plant, Greenville, Ill., November 22, 1865, to present time.

Superintendents and General Managers R. B. Lewis, first Superintendent in 1868 J. W. Conlogue, second Superintendent, 1869 and 1870; Charles R. Peddle, third Superintendent, 1869, 1870 and 1871; Maj. John E. Simpson, General Superintendent, from 1870 to 1876, and General Manager from 1876 to the time of his death in August, 1880; Joshua Staples, Superintendent, 1877 to 1880; D. W. Caldwell, General Manager, after the death of Maj. Simpson, August, 1880, to May 1, 1882; Joseph Hill, General Superintendent from January 1, 1881, to the present time, and since the resignation of Mr. Caldwell, May 1, 1882, has the entire management of the Vandalia line from St. Louis to Indianapolis.

H. W. Hibbard has very acceptably filled the responsible position of General Freight Agent of the Vandalia line to Indianapolis for the past ten years or more. C. R. Peddle has been Master Machinist and Superintendent of Machinery, etc., since 1870 to present time; and held the same position with the Terre Haute & Indianapolis Railroad, for fourteen years continuously before 1870. H. W. Billings was the first General Solicitor of the company. John Scholfield was General Solicitor for the company from May 1, 1870, until he resigned to accept the Supreme Judgeship to which he had been elected in the latter part of 1873. R. W. Thompson, of Terre Haute, was appointed January 13, 1874. Mr. Thompson held that position until he was selected by President Hayes, in 1877, as one of his Cabinet (Secretary of the Navy). John G. Williams, the present General

Solicitor of the company, was appointed in 1877.

The interest of the St. Louis, Vandalia & Terre Haute Railroad and the Terre Haute & Indianapolis, as lessee, being almost identical, a history of one road necessarily includes much that belongs to both, and whilst their organization are entirely separate—each having a Board of Directors, a President, Treasurer and Secretary—many of the other officers and employes besides the General Manager, General Superintendent, General Freight Agent and General Solicitors as given above are covered in both roads, under the latter head the names of F. M. Colburn, General Ticket Agent, St. Louis; W. S. Roney, Auditor; N. K. Elliott, Master of Transportation, and many others will be readily recalled.

The intelligent traveler will soon make the acquaintance of the many gentlemanly conductors on this line, who vie with each other to make the passengers feel at home whilst riding in the "Vandalia" cars. In his memory he will carry the names of John Wise, John McMahon, John Trindle, Samuel Trindle, L. D. Hibbard, Joseph Haselton, Richard Cornell, D. T. Conway, Curtis Paddock, John T. Elliott and A. E. Robbins. The station agents at Greenville have been: First, S. B. Hynes; second, J. E. Hunt; third, M. W. Van Valkenburg, and fourth, our present efficient and affable agent, W. S. Ogden. Pocahontas has had, among others, P. Powell, Mr. Record and W. H. Spradling present incumbent. Mulberry Grove, among others, Pitts Powell; M. J. Robinson, present incumbent. W. D. Hynes, mail agent since the road started from Greenville, having held his place until the present, is worthy of mention, a period of nearly fourteen years.

The general management of the St. Louis, Vandalia & Terre Haute Railroad is in the hands of W. R. McKeen, President of the Terre Haute & Indianapolis Railroad Company, as lessee, who has, by his judicious management, and the management of those acting under and in harmony with him, made it one of the most popular lines in the United States.

Col. J. Hill, a gentleman of large railroad experience, has been General Superintendent since January 1, 1881, and has had full control of the line as General Superintendent since the resignation of General Manager D. W. Caldwell, May 1, 1882. Col. Hill, since assuming full control of the line, has shown a determination to keep the good name of the Vandalia in the lead by putting on an extra fast express train for the Eastern cities, and also by extending the Highland accommodation to Effingham, where the company have proper accommodation for their engines and cars, and make an extra connection with trains of the Illinois Central at that place. This last change will greatly encourage the small stations along the road, and will aid in developing the whole line. But a few years will elapse before the growing demands of trade and travel will require the company to make a double track the whole line. Already steel rails are being laid as fast as the finances of the company will allow, and at the rate they are now being placed, will soon be laid on the entire road.

The Jacksonville & Southeastern Railroad is a project now, not only in agitation, but in the course of construction through Bond County. Its history, however, will be more fully given in the part of this work devoted to Montgomery County.

The Press.—If journalism does not come under the head of internal improvements, there can be no denying of the fact that it is a staunch advocate of all legitimate public improvements, and that the press of the country is ever ready to lend its influence to promote all honest enterprises for the common good, and for the welfare of the people. The fact is, the people themselves do not appreciate the press as it deserves. It is a power for good in the country, and should be honestly supported by all enterprising and wide-awake people. The press of Bond County merits an extended notice in this work, and the following sketch of the Greenville *Advocate* is compiled from an article published in its columns, January 19, 1882:

With this issue the *Advocate* goes to its many readers as No. 1 of Vol. XXV. In other words, it enters upon its twenty-fifth year, or quarter of a century of service. As with individuals and nations, so with newspaper proprietors there is a pleasure in looking back over the past history on special occasions. Inasmuch as readers have as much, though not exactly the same, interest in their paper that its editor has, it is quite appropriate that this historical review should not be confined to the editor's easy chair, but given to the public through the columns which all read—especially since about all the day-dreaming an editor finds time to indulge in must flow from the nib of his pen. Though the *Advocate* proper, and by that name, is scarcely yet twenty-five years old, it is really a continuation of previous journalism, which only the oldest settlers will remember. It seems that in this review a brief notice of that and cotemporaneous journalism will not be out of place, and that it should come in the order of the respective papers.

Of *The Barn-Burner*, nothing is preserved, and the memory of the men of that time has been resorted to in order to get even a trace of its existence. Since then, however, everything has been preserved, and all the back numbers that could be obtained have been securely bound, and are kept in a convenient place for reference. The first that is accessible of the above is No. 30 of Volume I of the *Protestant Monitor*. This was the first paper ever issued in Bond County. As its name indicates, it was a religious paper. By counting the numbers backward from the number just mentioned, which bears the date of Wednesday, January 6, 1846, it will appear that the first number was issued about the 16th of June, 1845, or more than thirty six years ago—over a third of a century ago. It was owned and published by Mr. E. M. Lathrap. The subscription price was $2 per annum, in advance; $2.50 at the end of three months, and $3, if payment was delayed to the end of the year; single copies, 6¼ cents. So far as its denominational views gave color to its columns, it was a Protestant Methodist paper, and had a circulation and list of contributors reaching over an area of more than a hundred miles in every direction, including Springfield, Jacksonville, Alton and even St. Louis. Though a religious journal, it mingled secular affairs in its columns quite freely, after the fashion of day. There was but little local news, for in those days of little, and at best slow and tedious travel, people wished to hear from the outside world, a want which is now supplied by the dailies and large city weeklies which few could take at the then high prices. The last *Protestant Monitor* that is preserved in this office is dated May 24, 1848, and is two inches larger each way than the first issue.

On Friday, September 13, 1850, the Greenville *Journal* issued No. 37, Vol. 3. This was a four page paper about the size of the first *Monitor*. J. F. Alexander appears as its editor at this time though in the absence of other back files we are obliged to rely on the recollection of O. Buchanan, that it was first owned by John Waite. According to Messrs. O. Buchanan and J. Harvey Alexander, J. F. Alexander was in partnership with Mr. Waite for a short time, when he bought out his interest, but subsequently re-sold the entire concern back again to Mr. Waite. Mr. Waite again sold out this time to Alexander Brothers, Harvey and Cal. who had been working in the office. These two sold to another brother, D. W. Alexander and he in turn to Dr. Smith, whose widow, Mrs. Mary Smith, Greenville citizens remember as a resident of this city only a few years since. Mr. John Harper also owned the paper, but whether he sold out to J. F. Alexander the records do not show.

It should here be noticed that while Mr. Waite had the *Journal*, J. F. Alexander started and conducted for about one year the "*Barn-Burner*," as an organ of the extreme, or as we would now say, Stalwart Free-Soilers, who in New York had acquired the name of "barn burners" and who were for Martin Van Buren. This was the first journalistic venture of Mr. Alexander, and died out soon after the election. It was printed in the *Journal* office. A copy of the first issue was sent to Martin Van Buren, who soon acknowledged the receipt of it in a letter of thanks to the editor, enclosing also a five-dollar bill. Mr. Charles Hoiles remembers having the bill shown to him and further says that it was considered a big thing in those times. This change was without material difference in the paper or its management, except that J. F. Alexander was left to give his time to editing the paper by D. W. Alexander's entering the office as publisher. The *Journal*, as has since been the record of the paper, supported what are now distinctive Republican principles either settled or undergoing that process. Beneath the picture of a hand holding a pen, are the Fremont and Dayton tickets, followed by the State ticket.

Next we find the *American Courier*, of which No. 47, of Vol. I, bears the date of May 21, 1857. Othniel Buchanan was editor and proprietor. The entire outfit for this paper was purchased new at St. Louis, by Thomas Russell and Othniel Buchanan. Mr. Russell, however, retired in about a year, leaving Mr. Buchanan alone. This outfit was the nucleus from which the present *Advocate* equipment has been developed. That identical hand press is still in this office. This outfit, press and all, cost $800 in St. Louis, whence it was ordered shipped to Carlyle. About the time it was expected at Carlyle, a wagon was driven over after it. Failing to find it at Carlyle, it was thought that the shipment had been made to Hillsboro. At the latter place some one told the "office-seeker" that he had seen a printing press traveling toward Vandalia, where the searchers were fortunate enough to find it. So the *Courier* continued a very readable paper of the dimensions of the present *Advocate*, only that it was a single instead of a double sheet. It should be stated that O. Buchanan purchased of J. F. Alexander the *Journal* office, and subsequently sold both the *Journal* and the *Courier* to Alexander & Bro., consisting of J. F. and J. H. Alexander, who, after a while, disposed of the *Journal* outfit to a Scotchman named Parson Percy, who took it to Stanton, Macoupin Co. Thus it will be seen that none of the *Monitor* or *Journal* material is now in Greenville.

Next the paper became the Greenville *Advocate*. Under this name, which it has ever since retained, the paper began its first volume February 11, 1858. In size the paper was what the *Advocate* of to-day would be without the inside pages Its editorial management continued to be conducted by J. F. Alexander, who was also proprietor. All know that those times were eras of terrible earnestness. The old and the middle-aged remember, and the young have since learned of the situation of that day. The columns of the *Advocate* from that day to this have been true to the great principles of Republicanism, freedom and human right.

It might be well enough to state here, that John H. Hawley, who is now, and has been for three years, one of the *Advocate* force, worked on the Greenville *Advocate* in 1860–61, commencing the 14th day of November, 1860. J. F. Alexander was editor, and Thomas Russell foreman. The paper at that time being less than half its present size, about one good man, and a country boy like Mr. Hawley, was then all that was necessary to do the work. The only machinery about the office was the old hand-press, now in use. On the editorial page an

Williamson Plant

"Educational Department" was conducted by Thomas W. Hynes, who still continues a warm friend and occasional contributor to the *Advocate*. An article from his pen on "Our Early Local History" urged the formation of an old settlers' society, that the early incidents might not be forgotten, and that memories of the past might be preserved.

During the late rebellion, J. F. Alexander was succeeded as publisher and proprietor of the *Advocate* by his brother, E. J. C. Alexander, who continued the paper until August, 1865, when his interest was transferred to S. C. Mace, who managed the paper alone until April of 1866, when he associated with him T. O. Shenick, as publisher, who combined his energy with Mr. Mace, giving the public the only local reading in the county, till March, 1869, when Mr. Mace was again left alone. In November, 1871, Mr. Mace sold out to Samuel B. Hynes, under whose proprietorship, his father, Rev. Thomas W. Hynes, had the editorial and general management of the *Advocate*, which, with the beginning of the year 1872, they had changed from a four page with eight columns to an eight-page paper of six columns each, considerably smaller than its present size. This form was retained for two years, when the former dimensions were again adopted. From Mr. Hynes the *Advocate* was purchased by George M Tatham, the present proprietor and editor. This was October 1, 1873. Since that time the *Advocate* has steadily increased in size, never decreasing, and often requiring large supplements, so that readers might not be stinted by the pressure of advertisements. From a subscription list of about five hundred, many for wood and produce, which often never came, the present editor acknowledges the appreciation of the reading community to the extent of over twelve hundred subscriptions, all settled for, and an influence extending over the entire county, and not unnoticed in neighboring counties, States and cities.

Also from a paper treating almost entirely of general principles, and news from the outside world alone, with rarely a word from different parts of the county, except a special letter now and then on some mooted question, the *Advocate* keeping up with the demands of the age, has become a real news paper, with such an array of correspondents from every part of the county, that "Widow Bond" is no longer lonesome, but every week her children learn how the rest of the family are prospering.

The *Sun*, published by William Boll and Fordyce C. Clark, at Greenville, is the successor of the *Bond County Democrat*, which was started by J. B. Anderson, June 2, 1876. On the 25th of January, 1877, Boll & Clark bought the paper, and changed its name from *Bond County Democrat* to the *Sun*. They worked up the circulation from 400 pay-as-you-please subscribers in 1877, to an edition of 1,280, on the cash-in-advance rule, reaching that circulation during the campaign of 1880.

The *Sun* is an eight-page paper, with six columns to a page, being considerably larger than the average country paper. It is cut and pasted in pamphlet form by a machine invented by the senior proprietor. Its publishers are both practical printers, and spare no effort to get up a good looking paper. It is credited by newspaper men with being one of the neatest and newsiest country journals in the State; its particular specialty is home news. A page is given every week to Greenville happenings, including court house news, real estate transfers, circuit and county proceedings, doings of the County Board, City Council proceedings, school and college notes, church and Sunday school news, local personals, home markets, etc. etc. Besides this, the paper has a reporter in almost every school district in the county, and gives from three to five columns of news items from these county neighborhoods regularly. News from neighboring counties is faithfully gleaned also, as well as State news and a good sum-

D

ming up of general news. Its editorial comment is on topics relating to home matters, and its opinions are stated clearly, forcibly and fearlessly, a proper respect of the right of opinion in others being observed. The *Sun* is popular, and while it has many friends, like all papers of influence, it also has enemies. Politically, it is independent, leaning toward Democracy, but not controlled by party caucus or office-seekers' cliques. Its opinions in politics as well as on other topics are the expression of the convictions of its editors after study, and are not dictated or suggested by outsiders.

The foregoing is a brief sketch of the press of Bond County, as there never has, we believe, been a paper published outside of Greenville none at least, of especial note.

CHAPTER VIII.*

GREENVILLE PRECINCT—INTRODUCTION—BOUNDARIES, AREA AND GENERAL CONFIGURATION—EARLY SETTLEMENT—[illegible] HARDSHIPS [illegible] PIONEER INDUSTRIES AND IMPROVEMENTS—[illegible] OF WILLIAM [illegible] VILLAGES—GOLD AND SILVER MINES—[illegible] [illegible] THE [illegible] CHURCHES ESTABLISHED IN THE [illegible]

"Where nothing dwelt but beasts of prey,
Or men as fierce and wild as they."

THE history of Greenville Precinct commences more than sixty years ago, and dates back prior to the departure of the savages for the land of the setting sun. It is the story of a community planted in the wilderness amid the murderous raids of prowling Indians—of camp-fires that grew into block houses, forts, and then into log cabins, and finally into wealthy and prosperous homes. There is a page which should come before this history, and, like the prologue to a drama be recited first, but space forbids it, and the page which calls to mind the Indian occupation of the country will be found in other chapters of this work. Our narrative will begin with the settlement of the whites among wild, ferocious beasts and savage men, and will recount their trials and hardships, their perils and hazards in subduing the country.

Greenville Precinct comprises a large territory lying in the central part of Bond County. It is irregular in shape, and embraces portions of Township 5 north, Ranges 2, 3 and 4 west, with one tier of sections in Township 6, and same ranges. The land is diversified between hill and prairie, the latter predominating; the rough and broken country being confined to the vicinity of the water courses. The principal streams are the east and west forks of Shoal Creek. The east fork flows nearly through the center of the precinct in a rather southwesterly direction, while the west fork makes its tortuous course almost southeast and unites with the east fork at the southern line of the precinct. Beaver Creek rises in the vicinity of Greenville, flows southwest and passes out through Section 34 into Beaver Creek Precinct. Indian Creek touches the northwest corner of the precinct, and a few other small and nameless streams intersect it. The timber consists of oak, hickory, walnut, elm, sycamore, cottonwood and other species common in this section. This precinct is noted for containing the capital of the county, and hence, much of the history of the surrounding community centers in the town of Greenville. Two or three small villages have sprung up along the railroad since its completion, which will receive notice further along in this chapter. Upon the whole Greenville Precinct is a fine agricultural region, and contains many excellent farms.

The settlement of Greenville Precinct dates back to the days of forts and block-houses. Says a pioneer of the town: "Wyatt Stubblefield, George Davidson and the Kirkpatricks all came prior to the war of 1812, and when the war came on they left through fear of the Indians, but when peace was declared, they returned to their former settlements." Thomas White and William Robinson came into the precinct in 1816. They lived one year in [illegible]

*By W. H. Perrin.

ley's Fort, and in the fall of 1817 settled one and a half miles from where Greenville now stands. William S. Wait and his brother settled a little east of the present village of Ripley (just over the line in what is now Ripley Precinct), in 1820-21. They went back East in a short time, but in a few years returned and settled permanently. William S. Wait was so long prominently known in the county, that a few words of him are not out of place in this connection, although he is extensively mentioned in the railroad history. He will be remembered as an early friend and supporter of the Mississippi & Atlantic Railroad, now the famous Vandalia Line. He wrote many articles in the Illinois papers, the St. Louis *Republican*, New York *Evening Post*, the New York *Tribune*, and other prominent newspapers, in earnest support of the enterprise. He was a constant worker for the road, from 1847, the time of the first agitation of the question, to 1865, and a large portion of his time was spent in procuring the charter, right of way, stock, attending meetings in its interest, etc., and in discharging the duties of the different offices, viz., President, Vice President, Secretary and Treasurer, which he successively held in the company. He was a thorough student, an investigator of all new subjects and theories, and a voluminous writer on political, educational, agricultural and reformatory questions, and always took the side of progress and improvement. A regular contributor to the press and in constant communication with many of the leading minds of the United States, he was fully familiar with all topics of interest, and versed in all questions pertaining to the public good.

Mr. Wait was Chairman of the National Industrial Convention, held in New York in October, 1845, and delivered an able address. He was nominated for Vice President of the United States on the ticket with Hon. Gerritt Smith (on National Reform Ticket) in 1848, but respectfully declined the exalted position. He wrote numerous newspaper articles, and able letters on the Constitution of Illinois adopted in 1848, and many portions of which were from his pen. In county and State agricultural societies he took an active interest, and was a zealous friend to the public schools; an active and valuable citizen, honored and admired by the people of the country at large.

Joseph Lindley built the first house in the forks of the creek southwest of Greenville in 1817, and was the first white settler in that locality. Hezekiah Archer settled just below him soon after, and in 1818-19, the Hunters settled in the same neighborhood. John Pickett settled six miles west of Greenville about the same time as the Hunters. George Nelson in 1819 settled one mile east of Pickett. Samuel White settled in the neighborhood very early, and Thomas Long in the vicinity of Stubblefield. Mrs. Morse, in a letter to Rev. Mr. Hynes, says: "One of the early settlers was Mr. Seth Blanchard, who arrived in 1820. He came out from New York expecting to settle in St. Louis, but, disgusted with the Frenchy look of that place, bought land of Mr. Wyatt Stubblefield, east of town, and opened a store and tavern in town, just laid out by Green P. Rice. Samuel G. Blanchard assisted in laying off the public square. The principal families there were the Kirkpatricks, Messrs. Camp, Goss, Leonard, Rutherford, Fergueson, White, old Father Elam, the Birges, and Drs. Drake, Newhall and Perrine." Andrew Moody was an early settler, and occupied a place originally settled by Thomas Kirkpatrick, about one mile southwest of Greenville. The famous spring at this place took its name from Mr. Moody, and was known far and wide as "Moody's Spring," a famous place for holding religious meetings, and the site of the first church built in Bond County. William Perrine and J. B. Drake might be termed early settlers, though they were young men and single when they came here. They boarded at Richard White's, two and a half miles west of Greenville and were physicians.

It is not possible, however, at the present day, to give the names of all the early settlers in as large a district as the precinct of Greenville is, as at present laid off. As the settlement of the country progressed, people scattered out on to the prairies, opening farms first near the timber, but gradually extending farther and farther from it. Thus large farming communities sprang up in different portions of the precinct, and at considerable distances from Greenville. Especially was this the case after all danger from the Indians had passed away, and the more savage of the wild beasts had been driven from the vicinity. Even then, however, the lives of the pioneers were not all sunshine and prosperity but many hardships mingled with their every-day experiences. Their implements of agriculture would be considered the most extreme hardships by the farmers of the present day, if they had to work with them, and the mode of obtaining bread and other needed supplies, would be deemed by us among the impossibilities, and beyond human power to overcome. The Rev. Thomas W. Hynes, in a historical address on Bond County, delivered July 4, 1876, says

"We look back from our present position to the time when the brave and enterprising pioneers left their homes and friends and came to this wild and unsubdued land to make their residence here. They faced danger, for up to 1816 the country was the frequent resort of hostile and predatory savages. They endured toil —for houses, orchards, farms, implements of husbandry, mills and shops, schools and churches, in short, all that men need in civilized society, were to be provided here out of the rough material. They bore self-denial —for they left behind them the comforts and abundance of their old homes. They were few at first in their numbers, but strong in their faith and courage. They developed a character of which we, their descendants and successors, need not feel ashamed. Their necessities made them ingenious. Their perils made them brave. Their fewness made them sociable. Their community of wants and dangers made them sympathetic and helpful of each other. However scanty their board, it was shared with the neighbor or stranger with a free-heartedness that gave a relish to the plain repast. However small and unsightly their cabin, its room and bed and genial warmth were divided with a cordiality that sweetened your welcome. Their social life was adorned with the graces of liberality and true friendship. They did wisely and well their peculiar work of laying the foundations that we might build upon them. They established schools and churches, and organized society and civil government, and left us a heritage of freedom and a home of peace and comfort. Let us honor their names, cherish their memory, record their virtues, and, thankfully recognizing our obligations to them, see to it that we hand down to our successors an untarnished inheritance of manly independence, wholesome liberty, free intelligence and pure religion."

As the community increased in wealth and importance, the people enlarged the facilities for living more comfortably, and with less toil and privation. Mills were built, and roads leading to them were laid out. Probably the first mills in the precinct were those of Wyatt Stubblefield and Beck, erected prior to 1825. Stubblefield's stood a little northwest of Greenville, on Shoal Creek, near where the Hillsboro road now crosses. A notice of Beck's will be found in the history of Greenville. Stubblefield's was constructed for sawing as well as for grinding, and was a great convenience to the neighborhood. The Waits built an ox-mill very early. The power was received from a "tread-wheel" —that is, a large inclined wheel, trod by oxen, was used, which, when put in motion, operated the machinery of the mill. They added a distillery, and for several years carried on both distillery and mill. Samuel White started a tan-yard at the spring west of Greenville in 1820, where he manufactured leather for the purpose of contributing to the "understanding" of the community. Thomas Long put up a cotton gin the same year, near where Stubblefield now stands. The cultivation of cotton having been attempted by the early settlers, led Mr. Long to that enterprise, but cotton growing in Southern Illinois proved a failure, and gins turned out to be poor investments.

It is a characteristic of the human race to be easily duped, and it has been said that the American people are more easily humbugged than any other race of beings below the sun. The settlers in this section of the country were no exception, and when reports were circulated that gold and silver ore was hidden in the Shoal Creek bluffs and ravines the most intense excitement prevailed in every home. People spent days and weeks in search of the precious metals roaming through the swamps of Shoal Creek bottom, digging in the hills, and scratching in the sands of the ravines, filling their pockets with glittering rocks, and accumulating stuff that in the end proved utterly worthless. A silver mine was once supposed to be found on Samuel Hunter's place by a man named Gaylor. Hunter lived on Indian Creek, four miles from Greenville. A close investigation showed that neither gold nor silver were native in that region, but that Gaylor was a good-sized fraud. He was arrested for an attempt to swindle but finally succeeded in making his escape from the country. This put a damper upon the idea of digging out fabulous wealth from the creek hills and had a tendency to shake the confidence of some of the wiser heads but the excitement continued quite a time before the people settled down quietly again to their every-day duties.

The first physicians in Greenville Precinct to, and practiced the healing art for some time among the pioneers. Malarial diseases prevailed in the first settling of the country, some years to a fearful extent, and before the coming of Perrine and Drake, the people of this section had to go to Edwardsville for a physician. Although doctors were often actually needed when their services could not be obtained, yet many people sent for them for the simplest cases. Mr. White relates the following, which is illustrative: "One morning," says he, "we saw a fellow coming down the road on a gallop, whom we had seen pass my father's every day for a week or more, going for a doctor for his sick wife. This time he was riding faster than usual, without a saddle, the bottom of his breeches' legs slipped up nearly to his knees, showing his bare legs although he had on coarse shoes; and the rim of his old wool hat blown back in front. He was urging his horse along by the repeated strokes of a hickory sprout four or five feet long. As he passed the house, some one screamed out 'How's your wife?' 'She's worse, git up!' was the reply, the last part of which was addressed to his horse, at the same time he gave him a cut round the flank with the hickory which might have been heard at the distance of a hundred yards." Such scenes were common in those days, as though the pioneers were determined that the doctors should earn their money. Dr. Newhall was also an early physician in this neighborhood. These early practitioners, however, are more particularly mentioned in a preceding chapter.

Schools were established and schoolhouses were built as soon as the population of the precinct would permit. Just where, when and by whom the first school was taught outside of the town of Greenville we cannot say. The early education of the surrounding country centered in the town, and the first schools were taught there, and will be alluded to more fully in the chapters on Greenville. There is now, in the more excellent schoolhouses, where good schools are taught, and the rising generation can be educated "without money and without price," an advantage not possessed by their ancestors.

Two small villages are located in the precinct, in addition to the city of Greenville, viz., Smithboro and Stubblefield. Smithboro, or Henderson Station, was laid out by H. H. Smith in 1870, and is on the Vandalia Railroad, about three miles from Greenville. It is called Henderson Station, but the post office is named Smithboro, and was established in 1871, with H. H. Smith as Postmaster. There is a grain elevator operated by Hoffman & Hinkle, who ordinarily ship a large quantity of wheat. A cheese factory or creamery was started in 1879. H. H. Smith was the first President of the Company. The establishment is doing an extensive business, and makes up the milk of about five hundred cows. A store is kept by T. L. Miner, the only one in the place. The Jacksonville & Southeastern Railroad is laid out through this village, and, when built, will add considerably to its importance.

Stubblefield is merely a station on the Vandalia Railroad, about four miles west of Greenville. It consists of but half a dozen or so of houses, a water tank of the railroad, and a shipping place for farm products.

A place was laid out, probably about 1840, some three or four miles northwest of Greenville, on the Hillsboro road, called Elizabeth City. "This famous city," says Mr. White, "was to occupy ground little better than a frog-pond, and yet five plats of it were made and sent back East on which appeared in high-sounding names, its streets, avenues and squares. Flaming notices of it were published in the newspapers, in which it was represented as being eligibly situated on 'Shoal River,' and in the midst of a country which, with comparatively little labor, could be transformed into an earthly paradise." These flattering representations, or more properly speaking, misrepresentations, led many persons in the older settled States to invest in this "city on paper," all of whom, it is needless to say, were "taken in," as Elizabeth City never had any existence other than fancy plats and flaming advertisements.

The first churches organized in Bond were in Greenville Precinct, by the Methodists and Presbyterians, and are fully noticed in a preceding chapter. There are now, so far as we are able to learn, three churches in the precinct, outside of the city of Greenville, viz.: Methodist, Baptist and Cumberland Presbyterian. The Methodists and Presbyterians are about four miles west of Greenville, and are but a short distance from each other, while the Baptist stands near Stubblefield.

The Centenary Methodist Episcopal Church, one of those mentioned above, is a very old church, and is believed to have been originally organized some time about 1820. William Hunter states that when he came here in 1821, the society was then in existence. The families forming it were those of Allen Conner, Aquilla Suggs, Richard White, John Hunter, Samuel Hunter, McHenry Nesbit, etc. The first minister was Rev. Samuel Thompson; Rev. Jesse Hale also preached here, and Rev. Joshua Raines. The society met at private residences at first. Allen Connor was a zealous Methodist, and his house was long used as a place of worship, and a home of the preachers, who frequently stayed with him a month at a time, and preached as often on week days as on Sundays. The name of the society was finally decided as "Sinai," and they met in a schoolhouse which was dedicated to worship. The present society is called the "Centenary Methodist Episcopal Church," and was formed from the Mt. Horeb and Sinai societies as early as 1825. The church was built in the Centennial year of Methodism, and is thirty-four by forty-six feet—a frame building, costing $2,300. The present minister is Rev. J. H. McGriff. The Trustees are Wesley White, W. B. Sibert, W. C. Nelson, James C. Causay, John Ward, John W. Plant and William Hunter; has about sixty members. A Sunday school was organized early, of which Allen Conner was first Superintendent; Conner was also the first class-leader; the next, John, and then Samuel Hunter.

Mount Gilead Cumberland Presbyterian Church was formed, or the society from which it originated, was formed about 1850-21. Among the first members were James Johnson, John Edwards, James Hunter, Thomas Hunter and their families, Mrs Mary Nelson, etc.—about a dozen in all. The church was organized by Rev. Joel Knight, and among the first preachers were Rev. John Berry, David Foster and G. P. Rice. Soon after the formation of this society, the members joined together and built a log church. Some years afterward, a frame house was built. The present church was built in 1860, and cost about $1,500. There are at present about sixty members. The first Elders were James Johnson and Thomas Hunter; the present Elders are Macklin Hunter, William King and Alvin Jackson; Trustees, Robert Mackey and Larkin Jackson. Sunday school has been in existence nearly ever since the organization of the church, and now averages about fifty children in regular attendance.

The Smith's Grove Baptist Church was organized less than twenty years ago. Prior to this organization, however, there was a society formed, perhaps as far back as 1828 and was under the ministrations of Elders John Crouch and James Long. They put up a large log building, which was used both as church and school-house, and was located but a short distance from the present church. The society prospered for that early day, but dissensions finally sprang up, which injured its usefulness, and it after awhile became extinct. Through the instrumentality of the ladies of the old society, a new church was organized with the following members: Henry Harris and wife, John J. Smith and wife, John Leverton and wife, James Harris and wife, John Hagin and wife, Monroe Ditch and wife, and Mrs. Hillard. The church was organized July 23, 1869. Elder F. M. Long was chosen Pastor, and John J. Smith, Clerk. They decided the church should be called "Smith's Grove Church," to belong to the Apple Creek association. Elder W. C. Harvey is the present minister, and J. M. Harris, Clerk. The church is a frame building and cost about $2,000. Preaching every two weeks.

This comprises the history, so far as we have been able to obtain it, of Greenville Precinct, and with its conclusion we end the chapter, leaving the history of Greenville to be treated of in a new chapter, by Mr. Williamson Plant, from whose pen we have no doubt that it will receive justice, and all the importance it merits.

CHAPTER IX.

CITY OF GREENVILLE—LOCATING THE COUNTY SEAT AT PERRYVILLE—ITS REMOVAL TO GREENVILLE—LAYING OUT OF THE LATTER PLACE—THE NAME GREENVILLE—EARLY SETTLERS OF THE TOWN—THE KIRKPATRICKS AND OTHERS—FIRST BUSINESS MEN AND PROMINENT CITIZENS—THE ROLL OF PIONEERS—MISCELLANEOUS MATTERS, ETC.

AS has been heretofore noticed in this work under that part covering the county history, the act of the Legislature approved January 4, 1817, forming a new county out of Madison County, to be called Bond, in honor of Shadrack Bond, afterward elected first Governor of the State of Illinois, also appointed William Roberts, John Powers, Robert Gillespie, John Whitley, Sr., and John Laughton, Commissioners to locate and establish a permanent seat of justice for Bond County, and that their first meeting should be held at the house of David White, at Hill's Fort on Shoal Creek, on the first Monday of March, 1817, and the act further provided that Hill's Fort should be the county seat of justice for Bond County until the same was located by said Commissioners or a majority of them, and that the County Court should be held on the first Mondays in February, June and October.

The first County Court for Bond County was held June 2, 1817. The following copy of their record at this first meeting, and the report of the said Commissioners to that court will be interesting:

Be it remembered that on the 2d day of June, 1817, at a County Court held for Bond County, began and held at Hills Station, in pursuance of an Act of the Legislature of the Illinois Territory, passed in the year 1817 [January 4], Thomas Kirkpatrick, John Powers and Martin Jones produced commissions from His Excellency, Ninian Edwards, Governor of said Territory, appointing them Judges of said County Court, who, having taken the several oaths prescribed by law, and thereupon took their seats. Present Thomas Kirkpatrick, John Powers and Martin Jones, Judges. Samuel G. Morse produced in court from His Excellency Ninian Edwards, a commission appointing him Sheriff of the said county of Bond, and also a certificate that he had taken the several oaths (before His Excellency) prescribed by law. Daniel Converse produced in court a commission from His Excellency Ninian Edwards, appointing him Clerk of the said court, and also a certificate of his having taken the several oaths prescribed by law. The court then proceeded to business.

The Commissioners made the following report to the court:

A majority of the Commissioners appointed to fix and establish the permanent seat of justice for this county, this day present the following report: "We the Commissioners to fix the permanent seat of justice for the county of Bond, met according to appointment, on the west side of the Hurricane Fork of the Kaskaskia River, on the southwest quarter of Section No. 5, of Town No. 4 north, of Range No. ' west, and stuck a stake for the center of the public square, as may be at any time when necessary.

"May 16, Anno 1817.

"JOHN POWERS.
"ROBERT GILLESPIE.
"JOHN WHITLEY.

ILLINOIS TERRITORY, BOND COUNTY:

We, the Commissioners to fix the seat of justice for the county of Bond, being duly sworn, after veiwing different parts of said county for that purpose, we do nominate and appoint for that purpose the bluff lying west of the Hurricane Fork of Okaw, being the southwest quarter of Section No. 5, [illegible]

Range No. 1 west, of Township No. 4 north, now the property of Martin Jones, taking into view the geographical center, the navigation, the eligibility, and the common good of the people as directed by law.

Given under our hands and seals the day and year first above written.

JOHN POWERS.
ROBERT GILLESPIE.
JOHN WHITLEY.

The Commissioners were not authorized to locate the county seat on the land of any person, unless the owner or owners should first donate to the county at least twenty acres of land where the location was made, to be laid off in town lots, to be sold, and the proceeds to be applied toward erecting county buildings.

The land designated by the Commissioners was deeded to the county by Martin Jones, who also surveyed and platted the same, and named it Perryville. The County Court "ordered that the lots be exposed to public sale for the use of the county, on the 28th day of October, inst., [1817] and it is further ordered that an advertisement describing the place be inserted two weeks successively in both the *Illinois Herald* and the *Missouri Gazette* [now the *Missouri Republican*]; and it is further ordered that money be lodged in the hands of the Postmaster at Edwardsville, for the payment of the advertising of the same."

William M. Crisp, the first Constable appointed by the County Court, cried the sale of the town lots sold in Perryville, for which he was allowed $2.

The first County Court held at Perryville, and being the third held in the county, was on the 20th day of July, 1818, and was called a "Justice's Court," three Justices of the county acting, viz., Thomas Kirkpatrick, Martin Jones and Isaac Price; Samuel G. Morse was Sheriff, and Daniel Converse had again been appointed Clerk of said court. The principal business transacted by the County and Justice's Courts for several years after the organization of the county, was the laying-out the various county roads needed by the inhabitants, the hearing petitions from those desiring to erect water grist-mills on the numerous streams in the then large though not populous county. To that end the appointment and the summoning for each applicant "twelve discreet householders of the vicinage," to assess any damage that may accrue to the owner or owners of adjoining lands by overflow or otherwise, by the erection of a mill dam at the place stated in the petition, and to report whether in their opinion the health of the neighborhood would thereby be endangered, and the height of dam that the petitioner may erect, etc., and also granting license to those persons desiring to keep tavern and to sell spirituous liquors, and grant orders to those entitled to pay for various services performed, a large number of which were for wolf scalp premiums. Every age has its day; much of the time of courts and citizens of fifty or sixty years ago was taken up in harmony with the surroundings of that time, much of which would be inappropriate for the present day and generation.

Before closing the history and events connected with the County Court whilst being held at Perryville, it would be interesting to know that the court at its session July 20, 1818, empowered Martin Jones "to let the contract for building a jail, provided the bids did not exceed $200. The building was to be 12x18 feet in the clear, to be built of hewed timber, squared one foot at each side, and laid up and dovetailed at the corners; the floors, both upper and under, to be of hewed timber one foot square, and laid close together with a partition of timber neatly hewed eight inches thick, and laid close together; the roof to be made by laying ribs or straight timber in the form of a common cabin roof, and clapboards nailed on, so as to be perfectly tight and secure from storms, the outside door to be made of plank two inches thick, doubled and riveted together, or nailed with large nails, and hung with two [illegible]ers of iron, half an inch thick and three inches broad hung on staples at one side, and the [illegible]er the staples through the bar, so as to receive a padlock at each end, the steeples to [illegible] or drove in through the log and clinched. And the wires to be three-fourths of an inch in diameter, and the inside door to be made of one inch plank, double, and riveted or nailed, and hung with strong iron hinges, with a good padlock, with sufficient clasp and staples.

In 1820, Francis Brown and Eleazer M. Townsend were the only acting County Commissioners. James Jones was Clerk of said Court; the Clerks at this time were appointed by the County Courts; the Justices of the Peace were appointed by the Governor on recommendation from the County Court.

[illegible] day a second term of the Circuit Court was held at Perryville. Only five indictments were presented at this court. It does not appear that any other business was acted upon.

The last County Court, and being the eleventh [illegible] at Perryville was held October 9, 1820. For some time prior to this date it was apparent that a new county seat for Bond County must be chosen.

The county was large, and the settlements were being scattered over a large district of country, generally in the timber, near some water course; always near any spring found, no matter how rough the surrounding country [illegible] as the inhabitants found it necessary to make division of the county, necessarily the county seat must be removed. The act of the Illinois Legislature, at its session February 14, 1821, passed the following act:

SECTION 1. Be it enacted, etc., That all that tract of country lying north of a line beginning at the southwest corner of Township No. 5 north, Range No. 1 west, extending east to the southeast corner of Township No. 3 north, of Range No. 6 east of the Third Principal Meridian, shall constitute a new county, to be called Fayette, the county seat of which shall be Vandalia.

SEC. 2. Be it further enacted, That for the purpose of fixing a permanent seat of justice for the county of Bond, the following persons, to wit: James B. Moore, Abraham Eyman, Joshua Oglesby, Samuel Whiteside and John Howard be, and they are hereby appointed Commissioners, which said Commissioners, or a majority of them, being duly sworn before some Judge or Justice of the Peace of this State, to faithfully take into view the convenience of the people, the situation of the settlement, with an eye to future population, the eligibility of the place, and the preservation of the boundaries of counties the limits of which have been heretofore established, shall meet on the first Monday of April next, or at such other time thereafter as they may agree upon, at the house of Thomas White, in said county, and proceed to examine and determine on the place for the permanent seat of justice, and designate the same. Provided, That the proprietor, or proprietors of the land shall give to the county, for the purpose of erecting county buildings, a quantity of land, not less than twenty acres, to be laid out in lots and sold for that purpose. Or should the proprietor, or proprietors prefer paying the donation in money, in lieu of land, then and in that case the Commissioners are authorized to receive the bond of the proprietor, or proprietors, with good and sufficient security, for such sum as in their opinion will be sufficient to defray the expense of the public buildings of the county, the same to be paid in three equal semi annual installments. And should the proprietor, or proprietors, refuse or neglect to make the donation aforesaid, then and in that case it shall be the duty of the Commissioners to fix on some other place for the seat of justice, as convenient as may be to the inhabitants of said county, which place fixed and determined upon, the said Commissioners shall certify under their hands and seals, and return the same to the next Commissioners' Court in the county aforesaid, which court shall cause an entry thereof to be made in their book of record, which place so designated shall be the permanent seat of justice for Bond County.

And until the public buildings shall be erected, the courts shall be held at Greenville, in said county. And it shall be the further duty of said Commissioners, or a majority of them, within three days after they shall have established the seat of justice of Bond County, to repair to Perryville, in the county of Fayette, and proceed to appraise and ascertain the damages sustained by the proprietor or proprietors of said town in consequence of the removal of the seat of justice therefrom, [illegible] shall certify the amout to the County Commissioners' Court of Fayette and Bond Counties. Provided, however, That the Commissioners, before they proceed to ascertain the said damages, shall be sworn before some Judge or Justice of the Peace of either of said counties faithfully and to the best of their judgment to ascertain the damage as aforesaid: and when the damages assessed as aforesaid shall have been certified as aforesaid the said County Commissioners of the said counties respectively, shall allow and direct the same to be paid out of the County Treasuries in proportion to the number of taxable inhabitants of each county.

The compensation allowed said Commissioners for the time necessarily employed in fixing the county seat, and assessing the damages heretofore referred to, were to be paid $2 per day out of the treasury of Bond County, by order of the Commissioners Court. The said court in Bond, Fayette and Edwards Counties were authorized and required to levy a tax, not exceeding one-half per centum per annum, on all taxable property within their respective counties, to pay the damages which may be adjudged by the removal of the county seats of Bond and Edwards Counties, which shall continue until a sufficient sum shall be raised to pay all the damages which shall be allowed by said removals.

In accordance with the act just recited, the first Commissioners' Court for Bond County was held in Greenville, April 16, 1821. The Commissioners appointed to locate the county seat for Bond County made their report to said court fixing upon twenty acres of land in the northeast quarter of Section 10, Township 5 north, Range 3 west, of Third Principal Meridian, and near the center of which the said Commissioners fixed a stake for the public square. The court made the demand upon Samuel Davidson, the owner of the land upon which the location had been made, as appears by their record, to wit:

Wednesday, 18th April 1821. The court met according to adjournment; present William Russell, John Kirkpatrick and Rob[illegible] McCord, Judges.

This day a demand was made by the court upon George Davidson, for twenty acres of land immediately around and contiguous to a stake fixed by the Commissioners authorized to locate the seat of justice for Bond County, which demand was declined [illegible] words hereafter inserted. It is considered by [illegible] court that the statute authorizing the location of [illegible] seat of justice required the donation of twenty [illegible] of land to lie in a body, and the court indulging [illegible] construction of the statute, had made the d[illegible] above set forth, in consequence thereof. John Kirkpatrick, one of the Judges dissenting in [illegible] from the court with regard to the demand.

To which Mr. Davidson made the foll[illegible] answer:

"I, George Davidson, in answer to a dem[illegible] day made upon me by the County Commiss[illegible] for a quantity of land around the stake [illegible] twenty acres, to be laid off in lots and [illegible] benefit of the county, present to the Hon[illegible] Court the following for my reply to the d[illegible]mand (to wit) that in order fully and entirely [illegible] isfy the requisitions of an act entitled an ac[illegible] ing a new county out of the parts of counti[illegible] mentioned, I duly executed to the Commis[illegible] therein named a bond with sufficient securi[illegible] the gift or grant to the County Commissio[illegible] the county of Bond, which said obligation [illegible] the files of the County Commissioners' Cou[illegible] county of a quantity of land equal to twent[illegible] the terms and conditions of which said writi[illegible] ligatory I am now perfectly ready and will[illegible] fulfill. GEORGE DAVIDSON.

April 18, 1821.

Mr. Benjamin Mills, a lawyer of some [illegible] and Probate Judge in 1822, etc., acted as [illegible]torney for Mr. Davidson.

An examination of the records and papers pertaining to the location, shows that Mr. Davidson had previously sold a small portion of the land (on the north side) included in [illegible] twenty acres fixed upon by the said Com[illegible]sioners for the county seat of Bond Coun[illegible] one Samuel Whitcomb, and was thereby un[illegible] to comply with the demand for the dona[illegible]. Two members of the court, Russell and McCord, believing that the donation should [illegible] in a square around the stake fixed for the ce[illegible]er of the public square; John Kirkpatrick [illegible] other member, believing that the statute would be fully complied with if the land was adjoining. The court met again on the 4th of June, 1821 same Judges as last term. Samuel Davidson was allowed to withdraw his bond given for the twenty acres of land, and substitute for the bond given April 18, 1821, a bond for that amount of land

"* * * in the form of a square as near as may be, of which said square the stake fixed by the commissioners appointed by the last General Assembly to locate a permanent seat of justice for the county of Bond, shall be the center, by or before the first Monday in December next, then this obligation to be void, otherwise to remain in full force. Provided, nevertheless, that this obligation shall not be held to obligate the above bound George Davidson to make a title to any land at present comprised within a tract for the conveyance of which the said George Davidson has given his bond to Samuel Whitcomb.

Witness our hands and seals this 5th day of June, in the year of our Lord, Eighteen Hundred and Twenty-one.

"GEORGE DAVIDSON, [SEAL.]
"SAMUEL G. BLANCHARD, [SEAL.]
"ROBERT G. WHITE, [SEAL.]
"SAMUEL WHITCOMB, [SEAL.]
his
"DANIEL X FERGUSON, [SEAL.]
mark
"MILO WOOD, [SEAL.]
"SAMUEL HOUSTON, [SEAL.]

Witness, BENJAMIN MILLS."

More than two-thirds of a century has elapsed since the first white settler made his "clearing" and built his first log cabin in what was for many years called "East Fork," now Greenville Precinct, near the center of which, nestling on the brow of the highest point of land between Terre Haute and St. Louis, sloping gently to the south, is situated the beautiful city of Greenville. Few are now living who can recall the time and the occasion of the settler, his clearing and his cabin.

That settler has long since passed from the active duties of this life, his cabin is no more but his clearing then commenced, is now widespread, and truly may it be said of him, 'his works do follow him.'

And afterward, whilst he lived, though far removed from his early home, it has been said by those who occasionally met him, that he spoke of Greenville as a fond parent would of his absent child to whom he was devotedly attached. It was to him, as the childhood home is to us all, to be recalled with grateful and joyous recollections.

That first cabin built on the primitive style of logs, with clapboard roof, weight-poles on same to hold them in place, with puncheon floor made of split and hewed slabs, the entire structure without nails or glass was situated on the hillside, between the present residence of the family of J. H. Black, in the extreme western part of the present town, and the "tan-yard," was the first home of George Davidson in 1815 or 1816, the first known settler and owner of the land upon which Greenville has since been built.

Mr. Davidson's family consisted of himself, wife, two sons and two daughters. Mrs. George Davidson was regarded as a most estimable woman, and an excellent nurse for the sick. One of the sons, Samuel Davidson, married Miss Violet Enloe, sister of James and Isaac Enloe, and died in 1820. He was taken to his father's house shortly before his death, that he might in his last days have his mother's care and sympathy. The widow of Samuel Davidson married Thomas L. Waddle, County Treasurer, in 1827. Vance L. Davidson, the other son, married Miss Purse, one of the daughters, Sally, was blind, and Caroline, the other daughter, married William Blundell. Mrs. Blundell now resides in California; letters have been received from her within the past three years, in which she speaks with happy recollection of her early home and friends at Greenville. Mr George Davidson laid off some of his land in Section 10, Town 5 north, Range 3 west, in 1819, into lots, but by some neglect the plat of the town was not recorded, which occasioned much trouble to those who purchased lots in the first laid out town.

Some diversity of opinion exists as to how or by whom Greenville was named. The descendents of Mr. Thomas White (R. O. and Sprague White), affirm that when the town was first surveyed, the question of name for same came up, and the bystanders said "we will leave it to Mr. Thomas White for a name, as he is the oldest man present" and Mr. White responded as he cast his eyes over the green woods and prairie around "everything looks so nice and green we will call it Greenville." Rev. Peter Long who came to Greenville in 1821, and still lives to recount the incidents of early life in the county, heard Mr. John Ellis (who came here earlier than Mr. Long), say that his understanding of the name was, that Mr. Thomas White named it in honor of Greenville in North Carolina, a State from which Mr. White had recently emigrated.

Mr. James Enloe who came to Greenville in February, 1818, when he was over fourteen years old, and more than a year before the town was first laid out, says that Greenville was named in honor of Green P. Rice, a Cumberland Presbyterian preacher, who resided here at an early day and kept the first store ever kept in the place and was Clerk of the Commissioners Court of Bond County from August 15, 1822, to March 3, 1823. For a number of years Mr. Rice lived on the old Stafford property, where Mr. William Morris now resides. Be the question or problem of the origin of the name as it may be, neither of the gentlemen to whom the honor is credited, could they see it to-day, would recognize the village then laid off in the wilderness now sixty-three years ago.

George Davidson is recognized as the pioneer settler of the land upon which Greenville has since been built. His son Samuel Davidson, [illegible]

west corner of Sixth and South streets; his health failed him, and he sold his stock of goods to Elisha Blanchard, and he sold to Thomas Long, brother of Rev. Peter Long, who kept the store for his brother until he sold to Drake & Durley.

George Davidson "moved up into town," as they termed it, from his residence at or near the west end of Main street, to a lot just south of northwest corner of Sixth and Main streets, and kept what was then known as a tavern in 1819–20, and until September, 1821, when Seth Blanchard became his successor, and kept and enlarged tavern for many years, who was in turn succeeded by David Berry January [illegible], 1828, to March 1, 1829, when he moved, and Thomas Dakin took the place for many years, and was well known by traveling men who made long and tedious journeys on horseback, crossing the State and going to and from St. Louis. Mr. Berry removed to the lot just west of Birges store (No. 7), where he kept an excellent hotel, which was headquarters for the stage stand for a great many years. His table was well supplied with the best the country afforded.

Among the early settlers of Greenville and vicinity may be mentioned the Kirkpatricks, who came at least as early as 1817. Thomas Kirkpatrick lived about one and half miles southeast of Greenville in the hewed log house in which uncle Tommy Brown lived for many years afterward and died. He was, as has been stated before in this work, a member of the first County Court held in the county at Hills Station June 2, 1817, and also a member of Constitutional Convention for Bond County in 1818. John Kirkpatrick, a Methodist preacher, lived northeast of Greenville, near where Madison Allen now resides about half mile north of Almira College. He was one of the members of the first Commissioners' Court held at Greenville April 16, 1821. His associate members of that court were

Francis Kirkpatrick, brother of John and Thomas, above mentioned, lived about half mile northeast of John Kirkpatrick. The Kirkpatrick family were Methodists. Capt. Paul Beck whilst he held the office of Captain, and was duly qualified as such May. 12, 1817, also had a little band horse-mill situated some forty rods south of the old cemetery, and nearly west of the present cheese factory. His mill ground wheat and corn. The bolt for the flour was turned by hand, as was common for many years at the horse-mills in operation throughout the county. Asahel Enloe settled in 1818, on the highest point in what is now the old cemetery, west of Greenville. A short time afterward, Asahel Enloe and his son, Ezekiel, lived just southeast of the passenger depot at Greenville, about eighty rods therefrom—the first about where the old Lansing House was situated, and the latter (Ezekiel) a few rods north of his father; whilst James Enloe's house was on the north side of southeast quarter of northeast quarter Section 15, Township 5 north, Range 3 west, about fifty rods southwest of his father's house. He sold the land to Daniel Ferguson a few years afterward. Isaac Enloe, brother of James and Ezekiel, is at present a resident of the county. Ezekiel Enloe died about twenty years ago. Mr. A Enloe and his sons cleared off a tract of land near the court house square, and planted the same in corn in the year 1819. Wyatt Stubblefield entered land east and adjoining Greenville in 1817, and remained on same until the time of his death somewhere near 1851. He had a horse-mill and a cotton-gin in operation many years near his residence. Mr. Stubblefield was very generously disposed toward those who came from a distance to his mills. He had three brothers, John, William and Jeremiah, who lived much of their time within a few miles of Fairview in Bond County.

Thomas White and his sons, John B., James, Hugh Alexander and Thomas White (tanner) came into the county about the year 1818. Only one, James White, is still living. Samuel and Eleazur White, sons of John B. White live on the old White homestead. R. O. and Sprague White, sons of James White (who is also alive), live in Bond County.

Of the early settlers near Greenville, none are more worthy of mention than Mr. George Donnell, who moved into the county, from North Carolina, about 1819, and after living on Shoal Creek, near Bilyew's Mill (northwest quarter Section 23, Town 5, Range 4), a few years, settled on a farm about three miles north of Greenville, where he lived many years, until the burdens of farm work, the privations of church privileges and advanced age admonished him that he must retire from the farm. He sold his farm, came to Greenville, where he spent the last dozen years of his life. He died about 1874. Mr. Donnell was an active man, in not only the Presbyterian Church, to which he belonged—an account of which is given in this history, under proper headings—but he was a co worker in the cause of religion and temperance with all denominations. He was also the leader in the first Sunday school ever taught in the county, and scholars came often eight or ten miles to attend. The writer of this article heard Mr. L. D. Plant say that, in his lifetime, he was under lasting obligation to Mr. Donnell for the Sunday schools he organized and taught, as a large part of his education was received from those schools. Mr. Donnell displayed more than ordinary wisdom in providing homes and farms for his large family of sons. His family consisted of Joseph M., John D., William N., Mary J., James M., Thomas S., George W., Henry C. and Emily R.

His sons worked well when young and their father secured for himself a good farm of good proportions, and, as the sons reached the period when they would need a farm, he bent his energies, with the help of the sons at home and the savings of the home farm soon secured the needed farm. Commencing at an earl day, as he did, with the low price of land and his good judgment, he was enabled to locate his family around him with but little trouble. To those who did not want land, he gave money and his own notes, as a matter of business. He lived to see the largest part of his family settled around him, happy and contented.

Samuel G. Morse was also an early settler. He was one of the delegates from Bond County to Kaskaskia that made for Illinois the old Constitution, adopted August 26, 1818, as has been stated before. He was the first Sheriff of Bond County, in 1817 and 1818; was fond of music, and taught singing schools occasionally.

The following persons were in the county more than fifty years ago, and their faces were familiar in the streets of Greenville whilst they lived, or were in the county, viz.:

Daniel Converse, first County Clerk, and half owner of water-mill of Converse & Lee, where Brown's Mill now stands.

Samuel Houston, first Deputy Sheriff and member County Court, August, 1826, to April 10, 1827.

James B. Rutherford, first hatter in Greenville.

Samuel Whitcomb owned land in Davidson tract before county seat located.

James B. McCord, a cabinet-maker in McCord settlement.

Andrew Finley, a good farmer and cooper in the northwest part of county; kept a store in 1835–36 at his home.

James Wafer came to the county in 1818; was anti-slavery; Presbyterian; died February 8, 1873, aged more than eighty-seven years.

David White lived in the fort near the center of Section 6, Town 4, Range 3, southwest of Mr. Patrick Byrne's residence, as early as 1816- and from David White took the name of "White Fort" sometimes called Hill's Station or Fort —and at this place the first two County Courts were held, before the county seat was established at Perryville. And it was at this fort Tom Higgins was so terribly wounded, and William Burgess surprised and cut off from communications by the Indians, as they were out for water. Mrs. Pursley, seeing the danger which surrounded them, seized a gun and shot the Indian who was leader in the attack, and then succeeded in getting them into the fort alive. Tom Higgins lived to relate the adventure and thank his deliverer, for more than fifty years, and died near Vandalia about 1872. Mr. Burgess lived more than forty years afterward, and died at his home, near Millersburg, in this county. Benjamin Henson was out of the fort on horseback at the time, but by good luck he escaped the Indian bullet. Mr. White had a little band horse-mill to grind for those stopping in the fort during the war. This was the first mill in the county. Mr. White was a Methodist.

John Powers, a Methodist preacher, and preached at Jones Station, near Andrew Green's, in February, 1816, and at White's Fort in March of the same year. These were his regular preaching places. The company who came with the Rev. Powers were his three sons, Thomas, Elijah and Samuel, all heads of families, Rev. William Hunter, son-in-law of John Powers, John Hunter and James Bolds.

William M. Crisp, first Constable in 1817, lived in Locust Fork Precinct.

Henry Rule, appointed Constable same time in "East Shoal," now Greenville Precinct.

Francis Travis, first Treasurer Bond County, July 5, 1819. No record of any Treasurer before that date.

Martin Jones, one of first Judges of County Court, member of Legislature, owner of Perryville.

James Jones (brother of Martin) appointed County Clerk June 6 and October 5, 1820; was Circuit Clerk same time.

John D. Alexander, Constable in 1821; Tax

Collector afterward; now lives near Bethel, with his son.

Elezarum Ripley Wheelock, laid out Ripley; named same in honor of his uncle, Gen. Ripley.

John Powers, a Methodist preacher and one of the first County Judges of Bond County; built water-mill, east of Millersburg, in 1818. Thomas Powers (son of above), built the water-mill near John A. Smith's old residence, in Section 25, Town 5, Range 4.

Francis Brown, member of the County Court in 1820.

Eleazur M. Townsend, member of the County Court in 1820; was an Eastern man; his sister married Dr. Perrine.

Green P. Rice, Cumberland Presbyterian preacher; kept first store in Greenville.

Samuel Hill, near Ripley, was father of Anderson Hill.

Hezekiah Archer, had water grist-mill on Shoal Creek, near Brown's present mill.

John and Hubbard Short, intelligent men. John married Robert McCord's daughter.

Evan Hinton, first wife, sister of Rev. Peter Long's mother; second wife, mother of James Bradford.

David Smith lived about six miles southwest of Greenville, near Hill's Station.

Jonathan Berry, from Tennessee, lived in southwest quarter of Section 6, Town 6, Range 3.

Williamson Plant, Sr., from Tennessee in 1818; lived and died on his farm, one mile northwest of Pocahontas.

Charles Johnson, from Tennessee, settled on land now laid out as Pocahontas in 1817. He was a member of the County Court at Perryville from July 5, 1819, to June 5, 1820.

Benjamin Johnson, son of the above, brought the first drove of cattle to the county; was an energetic, thoughtful man; was a member of the Illinois Legislature, and was generally consulted in the neighborhood where he lived for fifty years. He built Pocahontas Academy, and laid out Pocahontas; his home adjoined Pocahontas on the north; he died April 6, 1862.

John Leeper, Presbyterian, was a member of County Court, July 5, 1819, to June 5, 1820, also from August 15, 1822, to September 2, 1823; he built a horse grist-mill about four miles south of Greenville, near James McAdams' old farm.

Robert Gillespie, one of the Commissioners who located county seat, Bond County, at Perryville.

James and Andrew, sons of the above, lived ten miles west of Greenville; James having trouble with his eyesight from infancy, became quite famous for his remarkable memory; he had a clear head, and was often consulted on points of law.

John Laughlin, one of the Commissioners who located County seat Bond County, at Perryville.

John Whitley, Sr., one of the Commissioners who located county seat Bond County, at Perryville.

Hugh Kirkpatrick brought Titus, Jack, Bob and Haley, respectively ten, six, five and two years old, colored children, December 18, 1817, and had them registered, agreeable to the act of the Illinois Territory of September 17, 1807, to serve the said Kirkpatrick, the males until they are——— years of age, and the girl until she is———. Mr. Kirkpatrick brought two colored women and had them indentured by "their consent" for a period of ninety-nine years—should they not consent to the indenture, Mr. Kirkpatrick had the privilege, under the law, to remove them to a Slave State at any time within sixty days.

William Vollentine, son of Hardy Vollentine, an energetic and successful farmer, living twelve miles northwest of Greenville; he died about sixteen years ago; on the 17th day of June, 1817, he had Silas, a colored boy, registered under the law of 1807; Silas was registered as five years old, but as he had the appearance of being at least five or six years older, he probably served longer than otherwise would have served, had his age been certainly known; Silas took the name of Register from the fact or his being registered, as before stated. The sons of William Vollentine, W. P., in his lifetime, George and James M. Vollentine, have furnished many substantial comforts for old "uncle Si," as he has been called for the past thirty-five years; Mr. James M. Vollentine, son of William, as before said, has cared for the wants of Silas almost as his own family. Silas was the last survivor of all the ten colored persons "registered" and "indentured" in the county so far as known. He was taken sick some two weeks before his death, which occurred on Thursday, June 22, 1882; he was about seventy-six years old at his death; he was an exemplary Christian, had been a member of the Methodist Episcopal Church more than forty years.

Hardy Vollentine (father of William), registered a colored girl fourteen years old, on June 30, 1817, named Tisby.

Isaac Hill, of Okaw Township, indentured his colored man, named Peter, to serve him ten years.

John Hapton, Sr., was a farmer living six miles southwest of Greenville.

John Hapton, Jr., inherited a competency from his father, and kept it. He lived many years, before moving to Missouri, on the farm of W Barker.

Wilson Brown was an early settler and good citizen living near White Fort, the fort being a few rods south; he acquired considerable property, which he left by will, to his children.

Stringer Potts was neighbor to Hapton, Sr., and Wilson Brown.

Henry Williams, an intelligent farmer for many years two miles northwest of Pocahontas, and for several years before his death twelve miles southeast of Greenville; was a member of the County Court August 15, 1822 to 1824; he served in later years in the same capacity.

A. C. MacKay was for considerable part of his life in some official capacity; was Justice of the Peace, and was member of the Commissioners' Court in 1834 and 1835, and also in later years held same position.

James M. Davis, always characterized himself as "old settler;" he was an active Whig; member of County Court in 1834 and 1835; was engaged in merchandising in Greenville.

Thomas M. Davis, brother of above, now living seven miles north of Greenville, was a Captain in the civil war, from Bond County; resides on his farm.

Richard Bentley was a member of the County Court in 1835 and 1836; was also a member of the Legislature at a later period; many anecdotes were related bearing on his official position.

Samuel White and Thomas White (brothers). Samuel had the first tannery just west of Greenville; he sold the same to J. Harvey Black, who manufactured leather for many years; he kept store in the brick building on the northeast corner of Main and Sixth streets, in 1829. Mr. White retired to his farm adjoining Greenville on the east, more than forty years ago, where he amassed a handsome fortune, and died much respected about twelve years ago; his sons were Edward B., John B. O., James W. Samuel G. and William C. White.

William and John Russell (brothers). William was a member of the County Court from April 16, 1821, to June 4, 1822; John was a member of the County Court from August 7, 1827 to 1833; John Russell was the surveyor who laid out Greenville, June, 1821.

Rev. Peter Long, now living on his old farm on southeast quarter of northeast quarter of Section 35, Town 6, Range 4, some four miles northeast of Old Ripley. He and his brother, Thomas, came with their father, James Long, a Baptist minister, from Indiana; the family were orginally from Virginia. Peter Long taught school soon after coming to the county, near the house of Bonham Harlan (father of William and Abner Harlan), he also clerked in his brother, Thomas Long's, store, who had bought the stock of goods of Blanchard, on the corner of Main and Sixth streets, Greenville. Mr. Long did not continue in the business but a few months when he sold his goods on hand to Dr. J. B. Drake and William Durley, who continued the business for a few years, when Dr. Drake purchased the interest of Durley and carried on the same for more than twenty-five years. Rev. Peter Long, now nearly fourscore years of age, has been a faithful and consistent Baptist minister of the Gospel for nearly sixty years; continues to preach within the circuit of his near friends once each week, without compensation from his hearers; he has never used tobacco in any manner.

Ransom Gaer, a member of the County Court, from August, 1824, to August, 1825.

Robert W. Denny, a member of the County Court from August, 1826, to August, 1832.

Cyrus Birge kept store on Lot 8, Davidson's Addition to Greenville, in 1819 to 1824.

Ansel Birge bought his brother's (Cyrus) stock of goods early in 1825, and kept same stand for at least eight years; he removed afterward to his beautiful farm one and a quarter miles south of Greenville. He died over twenty years ago.

Williard Twiss, a brother-in-law of Ansel Birge, continued the sale of goods from same stand, having purchased the stock of Mr. A. Birge. Mr. Twiss was also clerk of the County Court in 1831, to March 9, 1836, when he resigned.

William S. and Thomas W. Smith (brothers) had a store, for some years in name of W. S. Smith, in 1833, on the corner of Main and Sixth street, and after some twenty years of success as partners they removed to the corner of Main and Fourth street, northeast corner, and after enlarging to suit their trade carried on a heavy business. Mr. W. S. Smith carried on the mercantile business after the death of his brother in 1862, to 1876; was County School Treasurer for a number of years, and served one term in the Legislature of Illinois; he also was President of the First National Bank of Greenville several years, at present holding the place of Director; he is also one of the Directors in the St. Louis, Vandalia & Terre Haute Railroad Company. Thomas W. died about twenty years ago.

J. E. Rankin was appointed Clerk of the County Court, in place of Isaac Murphy, who, by non-attendance, the court declared out of office, June 1, 1829. Mr. Rankin has filled several important trusts during his long residence in the county; he is quietly living on his farm, at present, in Pleasant Prairie, at a ripe old age, much respected.

Space cannot be allowed to give further detailed history individually of "old settlers," but we will give a concise list of those whose names or faces are familiar to those who have lived in the county for the past forty years, with occasionally some repetition of previous mention:

Anderson, Ignatius, Beaver Creek.

Anderson, James, Beaver Creek.

Allen, Benjamin, large farmer, Beaver Creek.

Armstrong, Joseph, father of Wesley and William.

Armstrong, Wesley, died in Iowa.

Armstrong, William, died in Bond County.

Armstrong, Robert, strong Democrat and Presbyterian, died in Bond County.

Armstrong, Thomas, died in Missouri.

Armstrong, Joseph.

Armstrong, Mid. These four—Robert, Thomas, Joseph and Mid., being sons of one man and cousins of Wesley and William.

Alexander, Josiah N.

Alexander, Jediah F., State Senator; President Vandalia Railroad, Receiver St. L. & S. E. Railroad, etc., died in Greenville in 1876.

Alexander, E. J. C., State Representative and editor.

Alexander, J. H., farmer. These three—Jediah F., E. J. C. and J. H., were brothers.

Allen, Albert, merchant, Greenville.

Adams, John and James I., brothers, Zion.

Alexander, John, early settler in Bond County.

Alexander, M. H., son of John.

Allen, Hector.

Allen, William, Allery, J. M., A. J., Daniel, Jerry and George, sons of Hector, and the first four Whigs.

Adney, William D., peddler.

Abbott, Thomas J., Hurricane, father of John B., Samuel W. and William H.

Abbott, John.

Abbott, Samuel W., died in the army, at St. Louis, during the war.

Abbott, William H., cabinet-maker and merchant, Fairview.

Abbott, John B., brother of Thomas J.

Andrews, John, Beaver Creek.

Austin, Josiah, Okaw.

Aldeman, Henry, pump-maker.

Aldeman, William P. and James W., brothers.

Austin, William M., Zion.

Alexander, H. B. and John, brothers, Greenville; the former a druggist, latter a carpenter.

Allen, W. A., physician, Greenville.

Abell, J. H., North Zion.

Brown, Tommy, model Christian, near Greenville.

Berry, David, kept hotel at Greenville and died there.

Berry, James W., David P., George F. and Franklin, sons of David, Greenville, the first named dying at Greenville.

Beech, Rufus.

Bryant Thomas, southwest of Pocahontas.

Blizzard, ———

Blizzard, James and William, sons of above.

Blizzard, J. J., son of James.

Blanchard, Samuel G., Elisha, Seth and Lemuel, the first three being merchants; Seth, a hotel-keeper; Lemuel, a farmer.

Brown, Wilson.

Brown, Calvin, Marion, Charles, Robert and Kerney, all sons of Wilson.

Bilyew, Joseph, who had a horse-mill south of Pocahontas.

Bilyew, Jesse, Joseph, Isaac S. and John, sons of Joseph, the two latter being twins.

Bilyew, Louis G., son of John.

Bilyew, W. A. and Finis, sons of Joseph, Sr.

Balch, Amos P., La Grange.

Balch, Calvin, son of Amos P.

Barr, Isaac G., S. N. and W. H., Isaac a farmer, La Grange S. N., La Grange; W. H., a blacksmith, Fairview.

Bird, John H., Beaver Creek.

Birge, Cyrus, Ansel and James, brothers.

Birge, Cyrus, Edwin and William, sons of Ansel.

Birge, J. H., son of Cyrus, Sr.

Barlow, J. N., Town 7, Range 4.

Barlow, W. Carroll, son of J. N.

Buchanan, Welsheir.

Buchanan, Othniel, son of Welsheir.

Buchanan, John, cousin of Othniel.

Bunch, Lambert.

Baker, Hiram.

Booth, James.

Baldridge, D. C.

Brown, Simon.

Brown, Thomas M., W. W. and McCune, sons of Simon.

Brown, Benjamin, William, Matthias and Henry, brothers; the first three farmers; Benjamin, formerly a miller; Henry, near Old Ripley.

Brown, Thomas, southeast quarter of Section 12, Township 6, Range 4.

Bine, Alexander, merchant, Greenville.

Baits, Anson, Josiah, Samuel J. and Eliphalet, brothers; the first two were farmers, the last two carpenters, as well as Anson.

Baldwin, Samuel.

Baldwin, William T., S. F., J. P., John and Charles, all sons of Samuel, and farmers.

Brown, J. M., Zion.

Brown, J. H.

Bradford, James, County Treasurer, Clerk Circuit and County Courts, and County Judge.

Badoux, J., Beaver Creek.

Blankenship, James and John, brothers.

Bass, Henry and William, brothers; the first a stock-dealer and large farmer, the latter also a farmer.

Barth, Jacob, Okaw.

Barth, Joseph, Millersburg.

Bulkley, Samuel B., merchant, 1843, Greenville.

Barber, Rev. John, Cumberland Presbyterian clergyman.

Badoux, F. E., Beaver Creek.

Barber, Rev. D. K., Cumberland Presbyterian clergyman, son of John.

Barr, John T., Sr., merchant, Greenville.

Byrnes, Patrick O., large land owner and farmer, died about ten years ago.

Barker, Joshua and Jordan, sons of William, deceased.

Barker, Williamson, son of Jordan.

Briggs, Henry.

Briggs, Kendall, son of Henry.

Briggs, Richard, brother of Henry.

Brookman, Garrett, hatter in Greenville in 1836.

Brooks, Dr. T. S., died of suffocation in fire at Greenville.

Brown, W. P., physician.

Brown, J. M., Mulberry Grove.

Blaze, William, Beaver Creek.

Coyle, John and James, brothers.

Coyle, Jeremiah, son of James.

Chisenhall, Alexander, Pocahontas.

Cormack, William.

Cormack, T. Jeff, son of William.

Castle, John T., son of J. H.

Castle, John H.

Comer, Allen and James, brothers; the former a Methodist, who settled in the county in 1817.

Comer, Thomas F., Samuel B. and Johnson sons of Allen.

Coleman, Isaac.

Casey, Green.

Cochrane, Henry M.

Clarage, John.

Cock, Robert, Constable in 1826.

Cawvey, Conrad and Martin, brothers.

Cheesman, William, Mulberry Grove.

Curlee, J. W., Zion.

Cushing, Roswell, died in Indianapolis.

Cushing, Charles and Henry, sons of Roswell.

Callihan, Alexander, Greenville.

Cole, Rev. A. J., Methodist clergyman, Okaw.

Coal, C. C., brother of A. J., merchant at Keysport.

Crosbie, House.

Corie, Joseph.

Corie, Joseph T. and Horatio, sons of Joseph.

Clark, Solomon, son-in-law of Isaac Reed.

Carson, William and John W., sons of Andrew.

Carson, Andrew.

Cruthis, James and John, brothers.

Cruthis, Vincent, William and Henry, brothers.

Cruthis, Neely, son of John.

Clanton, James.

Clanton, Wesley, Chap., John and Alfred, sons of James.

Camp, Hosea T., was Sheriff and Clerk; lived on home farm of Williamson Plant.

Clouse, William and John, brothers.

Colcord, Samuel, William S. and Otis B., brothers.

Carroll, Mac.

Carroll, Tillman, son of Mac.

Clark, William.

Crichfield, Joseph and James, brothers.

Crichfield, William.

Causey, James E., blacksmith and farmer, northwest quarter of the southeast quarter of Section 33, Town 5, Range 4.

Comeitus, Zachariah, exhorter.
Chittenden, M. B., Police Magistrate.
Challis, S. H., Representative in Legislature and merchant at Pocahontas.
Combs, J. A., Justice of Peace, Mulberry Grove.
Crutchley, M. W. and Samuel E., brothers.
Coburn, Reuben, Fairview.
Dove, David.
Duckworth, Thomas, Okaw.
Daniels, Eli E., carpenter, Pocahontas.
Dorman, L. D., blacksmith, Bethel.
Davis, Joel M.
Durham, Kindrick and Baldy, brothers.
Durham, Gideon L., son of Baldy.
Der, John.
Der, Fred, son of John, Zion.
Dunsmore, S. L.
Davis, James M., Thomas M. and William, brothers; James died at Hillsboro.
Davis, Robert W., son of J. M., died at Hillsboro.
Drake, J. B., physician and merchant at Greenville.
Denny, Robert W.
Denny, George, father of Jesse Denny.
Denny, Samuel.
Denny, James.
Denny, John.
Denny, J. S. and A. S., sons of John; the former Treasurer and County Clerk many years.
Denny, M. V., son of Samuel, Cashier First National Bank.
Denny, Imbert H.
Denny, J B.
Drake, William and John, brothers.
Denny, Alexander.
Douglas, Nathaniel and James M., brothers—Bethel.
Diamond, Robert.
Diamond, Samuel.
Duncan, Robert.
Duncan, Elisha, James Riley and Abraham, sons of Robert; Elisha in Colorado; James died in Okaw.
Dulaney, Aaron, Dudleyville.
Dowler, John Q. A., shoemaker (lame).
Dixon, Walton B., Bethel.
Downing, James, Beaver Creek.
Duckworth, Paden, lived northwest of Pocahontas.
Duckworth, Thomas, son of Paden.
Denson, Joseph, Constable in 1827.
Dwelly, Alexander, merchant, Beaver Creek.
Donnell, George.
Donnell, T. Carson, S. Rankin and John P., sons of George.
Dressor, Rufus, member of Circuit Court several years.
Dressor, Nathaniel, Hiram and Joshua P., sons of Rufus; Nathaniel is President First National Bank of Greenville; Hiram was member of Legislature; Joshua a farmer.
Douglas, H. B., son of James, Sunday school worker.
Douglas, A. B., son of Nathaniel.
Davis, Ira B., died at Bethel.
Dixon, William, died northwest of Greenville.
Dixon, James I. and William A., sons of William; southwest quarter Section 6, Town 5, Range 3.
Durley, William and James, brothers; the former of firm of Drake & Durley; the latter Clerk of County Court in 1831, also County Treasurer.
Donnell, George, a Presbyterian and Sunday school worker.
Donnell, Joseph M., John D., William N., James, Thomas S. and George W., all sons of George Donnell.
Dale, G., member of Constitutional Convention in 1848, County Judge, etc.
Dakin, Thomas, hotel keeper at Greenville in 1836, etc.
Dewy, R. K., Greenville.
Dugger, Alfred.
Dugger, James A.
Davis, William, Jr., son of Major Davis, southeast quarter of the southeast quarter of Section 22, Town 5, Range 2.

Davis, Major William, Greenville, died in 1882.

Dechenne, Phillibert, southeast quarter of the southwest quarter of Section 21, Town 6, Range 2.

Dewy, Nelson, Yankee farmer.

Dewy, H. C. and Theron, sons of Nelson, southwest quarter of the northwest quarter of Section 13, Town 4, Range 3.

Driskill, William, Pleasant Prairie.

Dixon, Bluford.

Daggett, Daniel.

Edwards, William M. and John N., old settlers.

Evans, Edward, large land-owner, Zion.

Etchison, W. H. southeast quarter of Section 1, Town 6, Range 2.

Elam, Alexander.

Elam, Josephus, farmer.

Elam, Samuel.

Elam, James N., Sr.

Elam, F. M., large farmer.

Elam, David.

Elam, Moses.

Elam, James N., Jr.

Elam, Edward, blacksmith, Greenville, 1819.

Elam, Joel, brother of Edward.

Elmore, Hiram.

Elmore, Hardin, son of Hiram.

Elsworth, George, Wesley and Jerry, brothers.

Eldridge, C. L., Greenville.

Edwards, Charles.

Etheridge, Henry.

Etheridge, N. B.

Enloe, Asahel, settled at Greenville, 1818.

Enloe, Ezekiel.

Enloe, James.

Enloe, Isaac.

Etzler, John.

Etzler, George B., son of John.

Ellison, Price.

Etheridge, Burrell.

Elligood, Elijah.

Essenpries, Les, large farmer, north half of Section 18, Town 4, Range 4.

Ellis, Ed., large land-owner.

Eblin, Samuel.

Elder, John.

Ellis, John, old settler.

Ellis, Noah A., son of John.

Ellis, Joel, Hurricane.

Eyman, Henry.

Ewing, Thomas, Town 6, Range 3.

Ewing, John H., son of Thomas.

Eakin, James, son of Samuel.

Eakin, Ichabod and Samuel, brothers and farmers near Fairview.

Fitch, J. W., physician, Greenville, 1835–1849.

File, Henry, old settler.

File, Daniel, Moses, Tobias, George, J. Nelson, Jacob and William, sons of Henry.

File, John N. and Thomas B., sons of Moses; the former southeast quarter of the southwest quarter of Section 16, Town 5, Range 4.

File, Ed B. and E. J., sons of Daniel.

Fisher, Charles, cabinet-maker, Greenville.

Fuller, Seth, surveyor and carpenter, Greenville.

Fuller, H. Lyman, son of Seth, died in Greenville in 1881.

Fuller, Lucius, hotel-keeper, died in Mulberry Grove.

Floyd, John W. and C. Stewart, brothers; former a Methodist, and died in Beaver Creek.

Floyd, George, J., Wesley, John S. and Dr. Thomas W., sons of John W.; George, of Greenville; J. Wesley, north of Greenville; John S. died on Beaver Creek; Thomas W. died at Gillespie, Ill.

Foster, Edwin, carpenter and farmer, dead.

Foster, Charles, son of Edwin.

Fenton, William, dead.

Foster, Elijah, Okaw.

Ferguson, Daniel, settled at Greenville, 1819.

Ferguson, William, George and Horatio N., sons of Daniel.

Floyd, Jonathan C.—Okaw.

Finley, Michael—Pleasant Prairie.

Fouke, Joseph T., old settler, Greenville.

Garland, B. F. and John P., brothers; former died at Patoka, latter resides at Greenville.

Gossage, ——.

Gwyn, Elisha, died near Elm Point.

Gwyn, H. B., R. H., Thomas C. and John, sons of Elisha; the first two live at Elm Point, the last one in Kansas.

Graff, Daniel and Peter, brothers, Beaver Creek.

Gross, Gustave, northwest quarter of Section 25, Town 5, Range 3.

Gill, Francis, early settler, Mulberry Grove.

Grigg, Daniel, Frederick, Bowlin, Samuel, Jesse, J. R., John T. and Richardson—all Zion.

Goodson, John, Spencer M. and Urban, brothers; first-named died south Greenville; last one died west Beaver Creek.

Goodson, Preston.

Goodson, James M. and J. K., sons of Urban; James M., Beaver Creek.

Goodson, S. Monroe and John, sons of John.

Gaskins, E., County Judge and County Clerk many years.

Gaskins, E. V., son of E. Gaskins.

Gall, J., southeast quarter of southwest quarter of Section 32, Town 4, Range 4.

Greenwood, John, cabinet-maker and farmer.

Greenwood, John K. and A. W., sons of John.

Goddard, John and Alexander.

Gillespie, Samuel.

Gillespie, Robert, settled in Bond County in 1816.

Gillespie, James Mc., Andrew, Robert and John.

Gillispie, Nathaniel.

Gilley, James C.

Grotts, Joseph and George F., brothers, Okaw.

Glaze, William—Beaver Creek.

Gum, Henry, Isaac J., Riley and J. Finley, brothers; first named died northwest Greenville, the second died at Okaw.

Gill, W. R. and James, brothers; former a farmer, latter a stage-driver.

George, Aaron—Hurricane.

Gardenhire, J. M.—Mulberry Grove.

Gilliland, S. M.—Beaver Creek.

Gower, A. V. S. M.—Dudleyville.

Gaston, John.

Green, William, Andrew, George and Royal.

Gracy, Joseph and William.

Gilmore, John, Treasurer and County Judge.

Gilmore, J. Mc. son of John.

Goodin, Hezekiah and John, brothers, Okaw.

Gullick, A. J., Sheriff Bond County eight years.

Harkey, William, Town 7, Range 3.

Helms, Thomas, second County Clerk.

Herrin, Moses, Section 8, Town 4, Range 4.

Huffstedler, John, Town 5, Range 4.

Hill, Nathan, colored, originally slave of Samuel Hill.

Henry, John, farmer, Beaver Creek, died in Texas.

Henry, Andrew G., William D., Samuel T. and P. C., sons of John; the first, a member of Legislature and County Judge, Greenville; second, a farmer; the third, a farmer and stock-dealer; the last, a money-lender, Terre Haute.

Hug, Martin, farmer, Town 4, Range 4.

Howell, Joseph, farmer and Presbyterian, Town 5, Range 3.

Howell, J. S., son of Joseph, Presbyterian minister, Elm Point.

Haisley, Alexander, Greenville.

Hastings, Sutton, early settler—Zion.

Hastings, Joseph W. and William, sons of Sutton.

Harper, Robert, farmer, Zion.

Harper, James R., Isaac and Samuel W., sons of Robert; James died in Montgomery County; Isaac lives near Fairview, and Samuel near Zion.

Hawks, Solomon and Drewry—Okaw.

Hundley, James—Hurricane.

Hays, W. T., southwest Mulberry Grove.

Harper, Peter, south half Section 10, Town 5, Range 2.

Harper, J., Madison, northwest quarter Section 22, Town 5, Range 2.

Hameteaux, Louis, southwest quarter Section 33, Town 4, Range 3.

Harrison, Daniel—north Bethel.

Hill, Anthony—north Elm Point.

Hill, D. W. and Joseph S., sons of Anthony, north Elm Point.

Huffman, B., southwest part of county.

Hubbard, David, Peter and Philip, brothers; the first, Mulberry Grove; second, east Greenville; last, west Greenville.

Hubbard, T. S., L. B. and George W., sons of Peter; first two, east Greenville.

Hubbard, Simeon W. and John, sons of Philip; Simeon, west Greenville; John, killed in Texas during the war.

Henry, Matthew, old settler.

Henry, Johnson, son of Matthew.

Hull, William T. and S. V. R., brothers; former died in St. Louis during the war; latter moved to Kansas.

Harned, William, died on return from California.

Harned, John W. and D. B., sons of William.

Hawley, Milton, lawyer and farmer.

Hawley, R. M., Delavan B. and Luther C., sons of Milton; R. M., in Northern Illinois; Delavan, southeast of Greenville; Luther, attorney, in California.

Hittle, William and Jacob, brothers, Town 7, Range 2.

Harris, U. B. and W. C., brothers; former member of County Court; latter a Cumberland Presbyterian minister.

Hill, George W., merchant, Greenville.

Hurley, Isaac.

Hoffman, Nicholas.

Harlan, Bonum—Beaver Creek.

Harlan, William and Abner, sons of Bonum.

Hull, Benjamin, farmer, Beaver Creek.

Hudson, R. H., farmer, Mulberry Grove.

Hunter, David.

Hunter, William, Methodist clergyman.

Hunter, Samuel, John P., William M., Marshall, W. Mc., Samuel J., James B. and D. N.

Hunter, John B., Thomas N. and T. J., sons of David; the first, a large stock-dealer; the last, gone West.

Hutchinson, Z. K., of singing family.

Hazler, V. W.—Okaw.

Hadley, S. P.—Okaw.

Holsberry, John—Okaw.

Holcomb, P. J.—Greenville.

Holcomb, S. B. and P. E., sons of P. J.

Hunt, Charles W.

Hagan, John T.

Hutchinson, W. T., Cumberland Presbyterian minister.

Hoiles, Charles, banker and merchant, Greenville.

Harmon, Anderson and William.

Hampton, John M.—Pleasant Prairie.

Holbrook, Amos, farmer and old settler.

Holbrook, Jacob, Methodist and great hunter.

Hilliard, J. C., farmer.

Harris, James H.

Harris, James W., Charles D., Patrick H. and Jacob, sons of James H.; James, Patrick and Jacob, farmers; Charles D., lumber-dealer.

Hynes, Thomas W., Presbyterian minister, Old Ripley, and Superintendent of Public Instruction.

Hynes, A. W., merchant, Greenville, brother of Thomas W.

Hess, H. W., northwest quarter of northeast quarter of Section 32, Town 4, Range 4.

Hugg, S., southwest quarter of the southeast quarter of Section 32, Town 4, Range 4.

Isley, Stanford--Zion.

Ives, Myron, farmer.

Ives, Charles, son of Myron.

Jackson, Larkin, James W., John C. and George W., brothers.

Jones, James, second County Clerk, 1819.

Johnston, James.

Jandt, H. G., merchant, Old Ripley.

Jandt, H. A., merchant, son of H. G.

Jett, John, had large family, died in La Grange.

Jett, Thomas, Francis and Humphrey, all died north Zion.

Jett, Thomas A.

Jett, William A. and Stephen J., sons of Thomas.

Jett, J. Madison, north part of Section 4, Town 6, Range 3.

Jett, T. Jefferson.

Jett, Jacob H., died in La Grange.

Jett, B. F. and James W., live in La Grange.

Jett, John H. and Gabriel, sons of Francis; the former on northeast quarter of Section 31, Town 5, Range 2.

Jett, Stark N. and Thos N., sons of Humphrey.

Jackson, John.

Jackson, James T., Jonathan, W. H. and Freling, sons of John.

Joy, Samuel N. and Sylvester.

Jones, Nathaniel C. and Daniel D., brothers and twins; the former died in the army.

Jarrard, Abram, runs saw-mill.

Jewett, Benjamin, near Fairview.

Johnson, Israel, died north Bethel.

Jennings, B., died east Greenville.

Jennings, W. E. and C. W., brothers; former died north Bethel.

Jay, J. A., blacksmith.

Jones, William, north Bethel.

Johnson, Charles, member County Court, 1820, etc.

Johnson, Benjamin, member Legislature, Pocahontas.

Johnson, Charles, died in Bond County.

Johnson, Duncan, died at Vandalia.

Johnson, J. P., banker, Highland, Kan.

Johnson, Hugh, killed at the South.

Johnson, James, died in California.

Kershner, Isaac, died in Bond County.

Kirkpatrick, William.

Koonce, Nicholas, died in Bond County.

Koonce, George, Jacob, Christ H. and Joseph L., sons of Nicholas; George moved to Harper's Ferry; Jacob, Sheriff of Bond County, 1852, etc.; Joseph a farmer.

Kelsoe, Alexander, Clerk Circuit Court.

Kizer, Henry, Okaw.

Kimbro, Frederick, Zion.

Kirkham, Jesse, Pocahontas.

Kirkland, John.

King, John B., Okaw.

Kesner, Jacob, William C. and Josiah, Okaw.

Kesterson, Robert, Okaw.

Kuykendall, Simon, runs saw-mill and farm.

Kingsbury, Ira, farmer and surveyor.

Kingsbury, A. N., Daviess, A. N. and John, sons of Ira; all attorneys, and the latter, A. N., Judge of Montgomery County Court.

Kerr, Lewis, Zion.

Keys, Thomas, merchant, Keysport.

Long, James, Baptist clergyman; came in 1822.

Long, Peter, Baptist clergyman, son of James.

Long, Thomas, son of James, merchant and had a wool factory.

Long, James, Lemuel B., Isham V. and Peter, sons of Peter; James, a farmer, and Lemuel a merchant at Old Ripley.

Lindley, Jacob, an old settler.

Lindley, Elisha, Town 7, Range 4.
Lindley, Urias, Town 4, Range 3.
Lindley, Joseph, an old settler.
Libbey, W. P., near Elm Point.
Libbey, W. A., S. H. and John, sons of W. P.
Little, James.
Leaverton, Noah, Methodist minister, died in Kansas.
Leaverton, John A. and Wilson, sons of Noah; former died in Sangamon County, a large land owner; the latter lives at
Chatham, Ill., a farmer.
Lyttaker, Moses, a brave soldier.
Lynch, Henry.
Lynch, Henry F., son of Henry.
Lookinbill. J. H.
Lucas, William, old settler.
Lister, W. W.
Laws, Fielding, and John A, brothers, north of La Grange.
Laws, Thomas A., James and Newman, sons of Fielding.
Lawson, Joseph, Beaver Creek.
Lampkin, P. W., merchant and farmer, Pocahontas.
Lampkin, Benjamin and George, sons of P. W.; former died at Pocahontas.
Lansing, J. D., died at Greenville.
Littlefield, L. P., gone West.
Lester, J. L. D.
Lovet, John G., farmer.
Lovet, John C., son of John G.
Mains, James, died near Greenville.
Moore, Albert, died near Beaver Creek.
Mills, George S., son of David.
Miles, David, son of William.
Miles, William, Methodist minister, Pocahontas.
Miles, James, Elijah and Morris, brothers.
Miles, Irving, Jonathan and William, sons of Elijah; the first named died at home, Beaver Creek.
Moss, W. W., died near Woburn.
Moss, Lemuel S. and James H., sons of W. W.
Malone, John M., harnessmaker, Greenville.
Moore, Emery, farmer, Okaw.
Meritt, Isaac N., farmer, Okaw.
Murray, Jordan, farmer, Okaw.
Moore, Joseph, farmer, Beaver Creek.
Moore, William, farmer, son of Joseph.
Metcalf, Balaam, died on Beaver Creek.
Metcalf, William and Henry H., sons of Balaam, and farmers.
Mason, Haywood,—Gillham Creek.
Mayfield, William and James, brothers, Gillham Creek.
Miller, George W., Mayor of Greenville.
Mattinly, J., eye doctor, Mulberry Grove.
Miller, Rufus, —Mulberry Grove.
Maxey, Joel, Fairview.
Mathews, Elisha, north of Fairview.
Mathews, J. J., John F. and E. P., sons of Elisha; J. J. moved to Fayette.
Moore, Daniel and Philip, brothers, early settlers; the former a brother-in-law of Ned Elam.
McClung, James, north of Greenville.
Mills, Jonathan and Thomas J., sons of Rev. William Mills; former died in Texas.
Mills, W. J., harness-dealer, Greenville.
May, John,—north of Zion.
Maxey, William O.
Merry, Prettyman, David, Robert, Samuel, James C., Andrew B. and David W., brothers, sons of David; Robert keeps livery-stable; Samuel southeast quarter of the southeast quarter of Section 33, Town 6, Range 3; James, northeast quarter Section 20, Town 6, Range 3; Andrew, northeast quarter Section 31, Town 6, Range 3; David, northwest quarter Section 32, Town 6, Range 3.
McAdow, S. N. and David K., brothers; former County Judge and member of County Court.

McAdow, John and William, sons of S. N.
Miller, Lewis, near Ripley.
Miller, Charles, founder of Millersburg.
May, Morris, southeast part of Pleasant Prairie.
May, Robert, Isaac J. and M. V., sons of Morris.
McCulley, Clinton and Clement, brothers.
McLean, James K., Captain in late war.
McManus, B. P.
McVey, Nathan, died at Greenville.
McVey, Peter, Cleaveland and Thomas, sons of Nathan.
McAdoo, D. C., farmer, near Fairview.
McCollum, William, south of Pocahontas.
McCollum, Aaron, A. W. and Henry, sons of William; A. W. lives in Pocahontas.
McShawt, William, southwest quarter Section 5, Town 5, Range 3.
McKenzie, George,—Bethel.
McDonald, F. R.,—Okaw.
McLearen, John,—Okaw.
McCaslin, J. O. and Hugh, brothers; former Beaver Creek.
McCaslin, William G. and Williamson, sons of J. O.
McAdams, Jesse, Robert, James, Sloss and John, brothers; first three farmers; Sloss for many years Sheriff; John member of County Court.
McAdams, Jesse and Hiram, sons of Jesse.
McAdams, Henry, son of James.
McLenny, John H.
McAlilly, James J.
Murphy, John and Thomas.
Morey, Hiram, Mulberry Grove.
Mayo, Benjamin F., Henry and Charles, brothers: Benjamin north of Fairview.
Myatt, Alexander, member County Court.
Myatt, Wesley, Alexander B., W. C. and J. B., sons of Alexander; Wesley, killed; Alexander and W. C. farmers, Okaw.
McNeill, Neilly, father of Abe and William.
McNeill, Abe, large land owner.
McNeill, William, farmer.
Mills, Andrew G., old settler, Beaver Creek.
Mills, Milton, son of A. G.
Mackay, A. C., member of County Court several years.
Mackay, Robert, son of A. C.; also member of County Court.
McCaslin, John M., Sheriff, 1879–80.
McCaslin, Younger, early settler.
McCracken, James, Nathan and John P., brothers; the two first near Bethel; John southeast quarter of southeast quarter Section 30, Town 7, Range 4.
McCord, John H., Robert E. and James S., Bethel.
McCord, Elihu R., hotel-keeper, Greenville.
Morgan, Thomas, Circuit Clerk, 1833, etc.
Morgan, W. T., farmer.
McFarland, Robert, died near Bethel.
McFarland, C. C. and John V., farmers, sons of Robert.
McCulley, James I. and Joseph, brothers, the former gone to Kansas; the latter a farmer.
McCracken, Eli, Methodist minister.
McCurley, Abraham.
McCurley, Hartwell, son of Abraham.
McCann, William, and Joseph, brothers, Pleasant Prairie.
Murray, William B., member County Court, Pocahontas.
McReynolds, John.
Margrave, John, farmer and Presbyterian.
Margrave, Felix, Treasurer of Bond County.
Mears, Edward A.
Moody, Richard.
Moody, Andrew, son of Richard.
McLain, John A., and J. Thomas, brothers.
McLain, N. W., C. D., Thomas R., A. H. and Milton J., sons of John A.; N. W. a machinist; C. D. and Thomas, farmers; A. H. and Milton, in Kansas.
Myres, Joseph,—Beaver Creek.

McAdams, William.

McAdams, Samuel G., son of William, Captain Company E, Twenty-second Regiment Illinois Volunteer Infantry, a brave soldier, killed while searching for deserters.

McAdams, J. M., son of Captain S. G., Treasurer of the county.

McCaslin, W. R., northwest quarter Section 29, Town 7, Range 3.

Montgomery, John.

Newhall, Horatio, Greenville, 1824.

Nowlin, David, Circuit Clerk in 1825.

Nowlin, John.

Neathery, G. W., northeast quarter Section 35, and northwest quarter Section 36, Town 7, Range 2.

Nesbit, Robert, north of Fairview.

Nance, Berick, north of Old Ripley.

Neidhammer, John, east of Old Ripley.

Neifardt, Jacob, north of Old Ripley.

Near, Alfred,—Greenville.

Nicholson, J. F. and George W., brothers; J. F., Pleasant Prairie.

Ormsby, Martin P., Presbyterian clergyman.

Oates, W. S., east Greenville.

Overstreet, William—Kansas.

Pritchett, Thomas J.—Fairview.

Potts, Stringer, Amos, Daniel; F. G., northwest quarter Section 7, Town 4, Range 3; Henry and Robert.

Potter, J. M.—Elm Point.

Pender, Andrew.

Pugh, William H., east Fairview.

Price, Jonathan, Isaac H., Oliver and Thomas.

Powell, Benjamin E. and W. C., brothers.

Page, R. G. and Jesse, Town 7, Range 4.

Pierson, Aaron, Town 4, Range 2.

Purveyear, James A., Town 4, Range 3.

Pettijohn, Reuben, an early Justice of Peace.

Perry, Joseph, east Elm Point.

Paine, Elisha and William, brothers, Town 5, Range 4.

Paine, William R., Thomas and John B., sons of Elisha.

Plant, Williamson, settled in county 1818, died 183–.

Plant, John, William, Robert, Williamson, Lorenzo D. and James, sons of Williamson; John died in 1865; William, at New Orleans; Robert died July 4, 1852; Williamson died of cholera May 12, 1833; Lorenzo died May 21, 1861; James died March 22, 1850.

Plant, L. B., son of Robert.

Plant, Lemuel H. and Williamson, sons of L. D.; former died on the way to California in 1852; latter, Sheriff of Bond County many years, and Secretary of Vandalia Railroad Company.

Plant, W. L., James D. and George F., sons of James; W. L., Town 5, Range 4; George, Town 5, Range 3.

Pool, John, settled afterward in Putnam County.

Perkins, John, north Fairview.

Perkins, Ephraim, Henry, William C. and Thomas, sons of John; Ephraim—Fairview; William and Thomas, Town 5, Range 2.

Prater, Brice and Samuel, brothers, north Zion; Brice, Town 6, Range 2.

Prater, John W., son of Samuel.

Plant, John W. and Charles B., sons of John; John, Section 1, Town 5, Range 4; Charles, Section 33, Town 5, Range 4.

Page, William—Mulberry Grove.

Pigg, Elijah—Mulberry Grove.

Pollitt, John W., drowned in Shoal Creek, near Pocahontas.

Peterson, Alexander, northwest part of Old Ripley.

Plog, Charles F., died near Old Ripley.

Plog, John and Peter, sons of Charles F.

Phelps, S. A., attorney, Greenville.

Paisley, William and Robert, brothers; former died at Elm Point; latter died of hydrophobia.

Paisley, Robert C. and William F., sons of William; Robert, southeast quarter of northeast quarter Section —, Town 6, Range 3; William, on old homestead.

Parr, Samuel, had a water grist-mill, east Shoal Creek.

Pruitt, Solomon, early settler.

Pursley, William.

Peter, W.

Pruitt, Fields, came to county in 1816.

Ridgeway, William, northwest Pocahontas.

Ridgeway, J. S. and George W., sons of William.

Rosebrough, James.

Rutherford, James B., first hatter in Greenville.

Redfearn, James and Ira.

Ross, J. Milton, Andrew B., Thomas and William B., brothers.

Rea, Andrew.

Rhea, Henry D., County Commissioner and farmer.

Reavis, Isham, early settler.

Reavis, Hiram, Isham T. and Ewing, sons of Isham.

Redding, Andrew J.—Mulberry Grove.

Redding, William M. and James, sons of Andrew.

Robinson, James W. and Isaac, sons of Alexander.

Robinson, Alexander.

Rench, Joseph.

Rench, David, William, John and Peter, sons of Joseph.

Reeves, John, farmer, north Fairview.

Reeves, W. B., George W. and James, sons of John.

Rushton, Gaius.

Riley, Barnabas, farmer, near Mulberry Grove.

Riley, James, John and William, sons of Barnabas; James, a farmer; John, member of County Court.

Robinson, Gideon, married in Bond County, 1817.

Robinson, Lawson H., Sheriff in 1828–29.

Rodgers, James, farmer.

Rodgers, William M. and F. M., sons of James.

Reams, William, farmer, Locust Fork, a great hunter.

Stout, Samuel and Thomas, brothers; the latter a miller and hotel-keeper.

Stout, H. E., son of Thomas.

Senn, John, merchant, Pocahontas.

Stewart, Robert, Presbyterian minister, and W. M., brothers.

Stroube, Jacob, north Zion.

Snow, James and William, north Zion.

Seybert, Henry, west Greenville.

Seybert, Morgan, H. V., Jacob and W. B., sons of Henry; first two, west Greenville; Jacob, north Pocahontas.

Sugg, Aquila, Josiah, William and Lemuel, sons of Noah; the first a Methodist clergyman, west Greenville; the second, a farmer near Pocahontas.

Sugg, Howell and Noah, sons of William.

Sugg, Noah A., Thomas W., W. Fletcher and Foushe T., sons of Aquila; Noah, a Methodist clergyman; Foushe, noted for a great memory.

Sugg, William T. and Josiah F., sons of Josiah; latter was Treasurer of Bond County 1853–56, and Sheriff 1856–58.

Sherrod, Joel.

Stoneburner, Samuel and William, brothers, near Dudleyville.

Stone, James.

Sellers, Benjamin E., Captain in Mexican war.

Sellers, L. J., Sr.—Mulberry Grove.

Spradling, James—Mulberry Grove.

Spradling, James H., son of James.

Sturgis, Dr. D. B., laid out New Hamburg.

Scott, John, south New Hamburg.

Segraves, Bennett, south Mulberry Grove.

Segraves, L. J., son of Bennett.

Stubblefield, Wyatt, William, Jeremiah and John, brothers and early settlers; Wyatt—east Greenville.

Stubblefield, John M., W. H. and A. H., sons of Wyatt; John, at Stubblefield Station; others, Greenville.

Skelton, John, early settler.

Scott, Moses, southeast Fairview.

Spratt, William.

Sargeant, James W.—Okaw.

Sturgenhofecker, G. L., peddler.

Snodgrass, Isaac, member of County Court.

Stallard, Samuel D.—Pocahontas.

Stallard, Rawley E., son of Samuel D.

Shields, Thomas -Okaw.

Savage, Richard.

Scott, A. E., carpenter and cabinet-maker.

Stephens, Cyrus H. and Alvan, brothers.

Smith, John and James, brothers; the former a nurseryman.

Smith, J. J., son of James.

Smith, C. J., T. N. and James M., sons of J. J.

Schneider, Theodore, member of County Court; south half Section 19, Town 5.

Smith, Elisha, on Hurricane.

Smith, C. T., George M., Sowell and Merit, sons of Elisha.

Sharp, Henry.

Sharp, Milton, Treasurer of Bond County 1877 80.

Smith, Peter and Andrew.

Stoker, Joseph.

Sherwood, David.

Tatum, Richard.

Teasly, Jonathan.

Teasly, William, son of Jonathan.

Tedrick, Alvin—Hurricane.

Tate, Charles F.

Taylor, John H.

Thompson, James W. and Williamson, brothers.

Thacker, Abner, Martin, W. H., Allen and Elijah.

Tabor, D. N., removed to Litchfield.

Tabor, S. M., Captain in the late war.

Travis, John E.

Toler, Reuben.

Ulmer, Martin, father of George, Casper and Martin, Jr.

Vanlaningham, Zimri.

Van Grundy, John.

Vaughn, Newman, John, David C., William, Samuel, Sr., and Samuel, Jr., member County Court.

Vollentine, Hardy.

Vollentine, William, son of Hardy.

Vollentine, J. O., W. P., George W., Hardy, James M., Benjamin, John J. and C. C., sons of William; J. O., killed by falling of a house; W. P., deceased; George, in Christian County; Hardy, in Northern Illinois; remaining four Methodists.

Vest, James, Mulberry Grove.

Vest, Thomas L. and J. E., sons of James.

Vawter, Presley G.

Watson, Matthew, carpenter and farmer.

Wood, Charles, large farmer, Town 7, Range 3.

Wood, Eli, Ezra and John, sons of Charles, and farmers.

Webster, F. M., George, A. J. and Levi.

Willey, John F., Wilson W. and James W., brothers.

Watson, Fielding.

Widger, James D.

Williams, Henry, member of County Court several years.

Williams, Henry M.

Walker, Andrew, north Zion.

Wightman, Charles.

Washburn, John A., Nevils, Lemuel, Martin and J. S.

White, Thomas, Commissioner to locate Greenville as county seat; they met at his house in 1821.

White, Hugh T., John B., James, Thomas (a tanner), and Alexander, sons of Thomas, and Presbyterians.

White, Robert G. and William, brothers; north Greenville; Presbyterians.

White, S. D., killed by falling of Shoal Creek bridge.

Wood, Frederick, shoemaker, Greenville.

Weathers, Wilson, west Zion.

Walker, Richard, north Zion.

Wright, J. J., north Zion.

Wollard, James B., Methodist minister.

White, J. C. Stephen and Ambrose B.

Wilmarth, Joel, son of William.

Watson, Isaac and Joab, brothers.

White, Richard, a Methodist.

White, Wesley and Thomas M., sons of Richard; former a farmer; latter a Methodist minister.

Williams, Henry, son of Henry.

Wishon, Ralph,—Okaw.

Williamson, William.

Whitsides, John, Town 7, Range 4.

Wilson, Samuel, south Greenville.

West, Alexander, cabinet-maker.

Williford, James.

Williford, Robert, J. H. and Willis, sons of James; Robert, west Old Ripley; Willis, east Old Ripley.

Williford, James M.—Greenville.

White, Samuel, east Greenville.

White, Ed B., Samuel G., John B. O., James W. and W. C., sons of Samuel; E. B.,—Greenville; Samuel,—Beaver Creek; James died in the army; W. C., east Greenville.

White, Thomas, brother of Samuel.

White, John,—Beaver Creek, northwest quarter Section 36, Town 4, Range 3.

Wafer, William, Thomas, Sr., and James, brothers; latter came to the county in 1819.

Wafer, Thomas, James E, and John F., sons of James; Thomas a miller and farmer; James, a machinist; John, Sheriff of Bond County 1869-70, now Sheriff in Kansas.

Wait, Silas Lee and William S., brothers; latter a large farmer, died July 17, 1865.

Wait, William S., Richard S., Henry W. and Foster F., brothers; William,—Pocahontas; Richard in California; Henry, east of Greenville; Foster, southwest Greenville.

Watson, Hugh, had a horse-mill, Zion.

Watson, A. W. and W. P., sons of Hugh.

Wait, Stephen, farmer.

White, Thomas D., north Greenville.

Wait, Lee, son of S. L.

Young, Tapley, a Methodist.

Young, William M., Methodist minister.

There may be omissions in the foregoing list, but it is as nearly correct as can now be given.

George Donnell,

CHAPTER X.

GREENVILLE—THE SALE OF LOTS—BUILDING A COURT HOUSE—PUBLIC BUILDINGS OF THE COUNTY—TAVERNS AND THEIR CHANGES—UNCLE JIMMY'S GROCERY—COUNTY OFFICERS—THE WATER SUPPLY—WAR HISTORY OF GREENVILLE AND BOND COUNTY—THE DIFFERENT REGIMENTS IN WHICH THEY WERE REPRESENTED—THE HILLIARD RIFLES, ETC., ETC.

AS has been referred to heretofore, Greenville was surveyed and platted by John Russell, in June, 1821. The court ordered June 5, 1821, "that thirty lots be sold in the town of Greenville on the first Monday in July, on a credit of six, twelve and eighteen months, payable in three equal installments, for the benefit of the county;" and it was further "ordered that the Clerk procure the insertion of the foregoing advertisement in the Edwardsville *Spectator* and the *Illinois Intelligencer*, for three weeks successively." The proceeds of the sale of the lots to be applied toward erecting public buildings for the county.

At a court held September 4, 1821, it was "ordered that the court house of Bond County be let to the lowest bidder on Wednesday, the 19th inst., and that the Clerk give due notice by advertisement of the same." The court met on the 19th of September, 1821. When the bids were opened, it was found that Robert G. White was the successful bidder, for the sum of $2,135, and he immediately entered into bond for the fulfillment of the contract, with Andrew Moody, Samuel Houston and Elisha Blanchard his securities, payment of same to be notes of purchasers of town lots. At a court held December 3, 1821, the Commissioners delivered notes from sale of lots to R. G. White on his contract to the amount of $1,338. The lots sold for average price of $44.60 per lot, provided the thirty lots were sold; if a less number sold, the average would be larger. Other lots were sold at various prices at private sale. By agreement between the court and the contractor, some change was made in the number of lights to be put in the windows; those below, twenty-four lights instead of twenty, and those above, twenty in place of sixteen, as per contract, and only to have two windows in each end to correspond with those on the sides in size. The glass in the windows were 8x10 inches, and to have but one chimney in place of two, as first designed, and that one in the end opposite the Judge's seat. At this time, and for several years after, there was not a stove in the county, the old-fashioned fire-place, that which yet brings to our minds the comforts of other days, was in use in every house, many of them being from four to six feet in length, and when a good fire was made in the same, resembled the burning of a log heap, such as are made when clearing timber fields for the plow. This house, made of a poor quality of bricks, was badly damaged by storms, wind and rain before it was completed. In fact, it can hardly be said to have ever been completed. Commenced in 1821, it was so nearly completed on June 4, 1822, that the court paid to Robert G. White, the contractor, nearly the balance due.

At this time the center of business of Greenville was at the crossing of Main and Sixth streets, in the west end of the present town. And the bad boy, of which there is sufficient evidence, was fully represented in this new town, would, for pastime and comfort, only understood by himself, gravitate, when his convenience was suited, near that public institution of justice, and, with his sling in hand, under cover of the surrounding bushes, would watch the falling stone drop on those coveted 8x10 lights. The building, only half built at first, greatly perplexed the court to get and keep it in repair for the few years that it stood. They made at least two orders appointing agents at different times, to prosecute those who broke the glass, smashed in the sash, and defaced the house generally. Nothing appears on the record to show that any guilty parties were brought to justice. In the building of the next court house, which was commenced in 1829, and not completed until about 1835 or 1836, the court had the benefit of the experience of the court who superintended the building of the first one. On consultation, they thought best to try a frame building this time. Instead of the letting of the whole contract to one man, they let it out in parts. Thomas Stout furnished most of the lumber, others hewed the timbers, some furnished the shingles. Hosea T. Camp engaged to haul a large part of the lumber from Stout's Mill, and James McGahey contracted to "lay the floor, partition the upper story into four rooms, run up stairs, make Judge's seat and bar agreeable to the draft, previously season the plank in a suitable manner, furnish and put in such joists as may be necessary, make suitable steps of hewn timber at the outside doors, and have the same completed on or before the 1st day of September next (this was April 6, 1829), for which he is to be paid such sums of money as may be ascertained and fixed by three disinterested workmen, chosen by the County Commissioners, to be paid on or before the first Monday of December next." The house was several years under contract before it was called completed, as a sale of window sash, with glass, paints and oils, was made at public sale on the 25th day of June, 1836.

This building served the people until 1853, when a contract was made in April, 1853, with Mr. Daniel W. Norris, to build the present court house of brick, at a contract price of $10,000. Some improvements have been added, making the total cost about $12,-000. Those who witnessed its erection can hardly realize that it is now more than a quarter of a century since it was completed. Could the court have fully comprehended the growth and prosperity of Bond County at that time, they would have built more with reference to fifty than twenty-seven years. The present building is 40x60 feet, two stories high, with two jury rooms, which are used outside of court for the State's Attorney and Surveyor, two rooms for the use of the County Clerk, Circuit Clerk's office, with vault for records, Sheriff's office, and one for the County Judge, and for the holding of County Courts.

Let us go back again in this history for a moment. Although the village of Greenville contained but few inhabitants, and the county was sparsely settled from the time of its organization of the latter, until twenty years had rolled by, yet we find that the number of "taverns" licensed should have only been called for if the necessity for such could be admitted in a county containing many times the number of people in Bond County.

The tavern licenses were more designed for the sale of liquors than for the accommodation of "man and beast;" but, with the granting of such license, a lists of charges that the landlord may make were attached to each permit. We give the rates made by the County Court, March term, 1827. These rates varied slightly from year to year:

For breakfast, dinner or supper......	25 cents.
Bedding, per night..................	12½ cents.
Feed for horse.....................	12½ cents.
Stable and forage, per night.........	50 cents.
Whisky peach or apple brandy, per half pint........................	12½ cents.
Run, French brandy or wine, per half pint............................	25 cents.
Gin, per half pint..................	18¾ cents.

Whilst but few can be found who can go back to the first days of the county, when we step forward fifteen or twenty years we find many who, if fifty five years old or more, and here at that time, cannot forget the excitement generally that attended "court week," "election" and "muster" days. The men of muscle were the heroes of that day. Each militia company had one particular man who could whip any man in any other similar company. Each neighborhood had within its borders a man who could and would, on any suitable occasion, whip any man in some other neighborhood; and last, though by no means least, one political party had each a particular man who could and would, on any pretext, whip any other man or particular man belonging to that other party.

The writer of this article, when a boy, say in 1835-36, so well understood these matters, that on public occasions referred to, or on Saturdays, he would station himself upon the fence across the street in good season opposite "Uncle Jimmy Clark's" "grocery," as such places were then called, about 1 or 2 o'clock in the afternoon, and await the milling fun that was sure to come, especially if Chap Clanton, Cob Coffee, Allery Allen, the Adamses, Washburnes, Will Coyle, Henry Harmon, the Albertses, Batemans or Dowds, or many others that might be named, were patronizing Uncle Jimmy. When all got ripe, the first intimation of what was certain to follow would be first, a quick, rumbling sound, "like a small earthquake in close proximity," then out they would come, piling over each other as they came out of the door, with their coats flying thick and fast in the air, only likened by coming out of bees from their hives to swarm. As soon as a ring could be formed, they raised or lowered their names with their friends, as the tide of battle turned. If any "foul" was called, then the fight became general, and, under such circumstances, the high fence upon which the writer was perched as a witness, would have to be abandoned in haste to some more distant place of safety. In later years, in 1844, in the high political excitement, when Clay and Polk were candidates, the Democrats thought they had a man, Mr. James Adams, who could whip any Whig in the county. Of course, the Whigs could not stand such a challenge, or, perhaps, the challenge came from the Whigs to the Democrats. With many, this was the biggest issue in the campaign, when and where would it take place? The mere mention of the subject in any crowd was enough to start excitement. On a hot, sultry day, when a great gathering of people was in the city of Greenville, these two giants were in the crowd with their friends. They seemed slow to meet each other from the fact that both kept reasonably clear of that which both knew might put them out of condition; but suddenly they came together, in the cross of Main and Second streets (between Justice's store and the southeast corner of the public square), they struck (as a bystander said), like "horses kicking." They were both powerful men. When the fight was over, the animosity was gone, and they became better friends. Of all this long list of men whose names are mentioned, most of them were as honorable men as the community afforded, and only acted in harmony with their surroundings of the times in which they lived. Those who have lived on to the present time find no satisfaction in allowing a stronger man than they to whip him, or for themselves to find some man not so powerful as themselves, and turn upon him and force him to cry "enough."

Liquor was common at almost every house, and a store without it would be as hard to find as the average retail store in Greenville at the present day without sugar and coffee. One thing may be said in its favor then, it was pure, and not the poisonous compound made at present under the name of liquor.

As we have said, Daniel Converse was the first County Clerk for Bond County in 1817–18; Thomas Helms in 1819-20; James Jones, June 6, 1820; Jonathan H. Pugh, March 5, 1822; Green P. Rice, August 15, 1822; James M. Johnson, March 23, 1823; Asahel Enloe, March, 1825; Joseph M. Nelson, April 10, 1827; Isaac Murphy, March 2, 1829; James E. Rankin, June 1, 1829; James Durley, June 30, 1830; Willard Twiss, December 31, 1831; James Bradford, March 9, 1836; Enrico Gaskins, September 7, 1846; J. S. Denny, November, 1865; Robert L. Mudd, November, 1874, the present County Clerk.

James Jones was the first Circuit Clerk, in 1819. His successor was James M. Johnson, March 2, 1821, Clerk at the first court held in Greenville, on that date; next, David Nowlin, September 19, 1825; Thomas Morgan, June, 1833; James Bradford, October, 1836; Alexander Kelsoe, 1848; John B. Reid, November, 1860; J. A. Cooper, November, 1868; George S. Phelps, September, 1872; T. P. Morey, November, 1876, the present incumbent.

First Sheriff, Samuel G. Morse, 1817–18; second, Samuel Houston, 1819 and 1824; Hosea T. Camp, 1824 to 1827; Lawson H. Robinson, 1828-29; Sloss McAdams, 1830 to 1846; W. K. Mastin, 1846, and part of 1848; S. H. Crocker, balance of 1848; Richard Bentley, 1848 and 1850; Samuel H. Crocker, 1850, and 1852; Jacob Koonce, 1852, and 1854; Williamson Plant, 1854, and 1856; Josiah F. Sugg, 1856, and 1858; Samuel H. Crocker, 1858, and 1860; William Watkins, 1860, and 1862; Williamson Plant, 1862, and 1864; James L. Buchanan, 1864, and 1866; John Fisher, 1866, and 1868; John F. Wafer, 1868, and 1870; Williamson Plant, 1870, and 1872; Andrew J. Gullick, 1872 to 1878; John M. McCasland, 1878, and 1880; Andrew J. Gullick, 1880, and 1882.

Mr. Francis Travis was first County Treasurer, appointed June 5, 1819; next, James Galloway, June 6, 1820; James Durley, June 5, 1821; Felix Margrave, March 2, 1824; Leonard Goss, March 11, 1825; Thomas S. Waddle, April 10, 1827; John Gilmore, March 5, 1828; James Bradford, March 9, 1831; Peter Hubbard, March, 1836.

Peter Larrabe, Treasurer, 1845; John M. Smith, November, 1851; J. F. Sugg, November, 1853 to 1854; J. F. Alexander, 1854 to 1856; J. K. McLean, 1856 to 1858, J. S. Denny, 1858 to 1864; Milton Mills, 1864 to 1866; Cyrus Birge, 1866 to 1870; R. L. Mudd, 1870 to 1876; M. J. Sharp, 1876 to 1880; J. M. McAdams, 1880 to 1882.

One of the first difficulties met by the people of Greenville was the supply of water needed. The first settlers, Mr. Samuel Davidson, Capt. Paul Beck, Asahel Enloe, with their families, settled near the spring on the west of the present town to obviate any trouble for water. But those settling up in the town carried all the water they used from the springs, except for washing clothes, and for that purpose went to Wash Lake, just west of town; but they found it too much labor for so small return. About March, 1822, the subject of public wells was discussed. Some attempts had been made, and failed to find water within a reasonable depth. The depth necessary to find water was found to be from ninety to one hundred feet. Three wells were finally dug and curbed with wood puncheon or plank, the part under water was mulberry, "charred by fire" before using, to add, as was supposed, to its lasting qualities. The first well was dug in the middle of the street, where Main and Sixth streets cross each other, in the west end of town. The next one was in the middle of the street, where Third and College streets cross, the other at the crossing of Second and Main streets. The mode of drawing water was with the old-fashioned windlass, a brake to hold on the same while the bucket was sent down. There was a frame around each well above the ground some three feet, which made it dangerous for the many boys of ten or twelve years that often had to draw from them. In 1836, whilst a son of Mr. Hildreth, some twelve or fourteen years old, was looking over the curb into the well, when his feet slipped out, and down he went head first. It was never known whether he ever drew breath after striking the bottom. An accident also occurred at the well in the middle of the street, near the southeast corner of the public square. A Mr. William Gray, an experienced well-digger, was employed to clean out the well. Two men were at the windlass. He was warned by some bystanders of their fears of the safety of the rope, but he fearlessly stepped into the bucket, holding to the rope or chain above, and had only made a start when the upper part of the rope or chain broke, and he was precipitated to the bottom, a distance of over ninety feet. He received internal injuries, beside dislocation of the ankle. He lived about twenty-four hours, and died in great pain. In time, these wells gave evidence of caving in, and were filled up to prevent accidents. A few months ago, the filling that had been put in this well more than twenty five years before sunk, leaving a hole the size of the well, eight or ten feet deep.

Cisterns have since become plentiful, and the water is so much preferred to the limestone water contained in the former wells, that no complaint is made on the question of water, except in excessive dry seasons, or when by some cause the cistern is out of order. Some of the best natural springs immediately north and west of the town are found, and the day is not far distant when they will be utilized by water-works in furnishing the town with a bountiful supply of water.

The St. Louis, Vandalia & Terre Haute Railroad is supplied with water from two of these strong springs. Nearly all trains take water at Greenville, the water giving the least trouble to their boilers of any other along the line of the road. The railroad company have made some very substantial engine houses, tanks and dams to secure the water.

In the year 1825, the Legislature appropriated $200 to aid in constructing a bridge across Shoal Creek, on the St. Louis wagon road. Before this bridge was built, Benjamin Henson had a primitive boat at his house, a short distance below the present bridge, that was used in cases of high water. It has been stated in a preceding chapter in this book, that Mr. Henson was thought to have been the first white settler in Bond County, having been here in 1812 or 1813, and for a considerable time his house was a large, hollow sycamore tree, not far from the cabin he afterward built and lived in until his death, about 1848. When he first came into the county the Indians were in some parts of the then large county.

At a session of the County Court held June 3, 1822, an order was made for the erection of a "stray pen in Greenville, forty feet square, to be made of posts and railing, each panel six feet high above the surface of the ground, and the posts let into the ground two feet and a half." In this "stray pen," the estray stock of the county was brought during the sessions of the Circuit Courts, and, perhaps, muster and other public occasions in Greenville, and any one having lost stock would go to the estray pen on these days and examine for his missing animal.

When the county was first formed, not many years had elapsed since the struggle of the Revolution, and the war of 1812 and 1814 had only just preceded the first settlement.

It would be but natural for a people who had so signally in the first and latter struggle achieved and maintained their independence, to call together their comrades in arms, with their neighbors and friends at stated periods, and refight those battles, and thereby infuse into the rising generations, who are always the hope of a country, the spirit of their fathers. Actuated by a spirit of patriotism, the people held the election of military officers, their drills and muster, as their highest privileges. The first election of military officers was held as other elections for county officers, but in later years the mode adopted was for the candidates for whatever office they desired to elect, to step out of the crowd assembled and call out, "All who will join — Company fall into line." This often led to much excitement, but was always kept within the bounds of good humor. Paul Beck was made a Captain as early as May 12, 1817, and Samuel Davidson, Ensign, same date. John Laughlin was elected Captain June 14, 1817, and John Hopton, Lieutenant, and John Whitley, Jr., Ensign, same date. The troubles with the Indians in some of the northern counties, and anticipated trouble within the borders of the county, followed soon after by the Black Hawk war of 1831–32, kept the military companies throughout the county well organized until about 1840. Since that time it declined rapidly, until a Captain, Major or a Colonel was only a thing of the past, until revived by the active military movements in this country during the late civil war.* This civil war in a land so peculiarly blessed, between a people so enlightned and refined, this fratricidal war, now as we review it when it is passed, having seen its commencement, its continuance and its close, seems only as a dream of the past; yet it was to many hundred thousands a fatal dream.

Bond County was in the front in furnishing her full quota of brave and patriotic soldiers to defend and uphold the flag and honor of our whole country. They went promptly at every call for volunteers, carrying with them the prayers of sympathizing friends and relatives, many of whom never returned, some returning with lost or shattered limbs, or a diseased body, as can be attested by the large pension roll in our Bond County.

The volunteer companies, with their commissioned officers for Bond County, may be mentioned as follows:

Company D, Twenty-second Regiment Illinois Volunteers.—Captains, James A. Hubbard, John H. Phillips; First Lieutenants, E. J. C. Alexander, Lemuel Adams, John H. Phillips, Enoch J. File; Second Lieutenants, Lemuel Adams, Edward Stearns, J. H. Phillips, Cyrus M. Galloway, Enoch J. File, Joel B. Paisley.

Company E, Twenty-second Regiment Illinois Volunteers.—Captains, Samuel G. McAdams, George Gibson; First Lieutenants, James M. Hamilton, George Gibson, J. M. McAdams; Second Lieutenants, George Gibson, J. M. McAdams.

* For convenience the war history of Bond County is given in connection with the city of Greenville.—Ed.

Company C, Twenty-sixth Regiment Illinois Volunteers.—Captains, George M. Keener, James A. Dugger, Owen W. Walls, Isaac N. Enloe; First Lieutenants, Thomas L. Vest, J. A. Dugger, Owen W. Walls, James Manes, John McCallister; Second Lieutenants, J. A. Dugger, E. B. Wise.

Company E, One Hundred and Thirtieth Regiment Illinois Volunteers.—Captains, U. B. Harris, W. C. Harned; First Lieutenants, William Harlan, William C. Harned, Charles W. Johnson; Second Lieutenants, W. C. Harned, Charles W. Johnson.

Company F, One Hundred and Thirtieth Regiment Illinois Volunteers.—Captains, William M. Colby, John D. Donnell, F. D. Phillips; First Lieutenants, John D. Donnell, Charles Ives, Fielden D. Phillips, John Murdock; Second Lieutenants, Charles Ives, F. D. Phillips.

Company F, One Hundred and Thirty-fifth Regiment Illinois Volunteers.—Captain, Samuel G. McAdams; First Lieutenant, James A. Hubbard; Second Lieutenant, Edward Stearns.

Company F, One Hundred and Thirty-fifth Regiment, enlisted June 6, 1864, and discharged September 28, 1864; served one hundred days; only one man died during the time, viz.: James McCann, at Ironton, Mo., July 25, 1864.

The Twenty-second Infantry Illinois Volunteers was organized at Belleville, Ill., May 11, 1861, and was mustered into service for three years at Caseyville, Ill., June 25, 1861, by Capt. T. G. Pitcher, U. S. A. July 11, they moved to Bird's Point, Mo. November 7, seven companies engaged in battle at Belmont, three being left to guard the transports; loss, 144 killed and missing. At Stone River, December 31, 1862, and January 1, 1863, they lost 199 men out of 342 going into action. At Chickamauga, September 19 and 20, they lost 135 officers and men out of an aggregate of less than 300 men. The severity of the battle was such on the 19th they lost ninety-six men in less than ten minutes. They were engaged in many hard-fought battles during the three years of their service, including the storming of Mission Ridge, Resaca, battle of Farmington, Chickamauga, etc. Among the many brave officers and men who had their names inscribed on the roll of honor in Company E, may be mentioned that of our lamented Capt. Samuel G. McAdams.

The history of the Twenty-sixth Infantry of Volunteers would be almost a history of the war. They were mustered into service at Camp Butler, Ill., August 31, 1861, and, after serving four years, were discharged or mustered out of service at Louisville, Ky., July 20, 1865. The company was paid off at Springfield, Ill., July 28, 1865. The commanding General ordered the placing on their banners "New Madrid," "Island No. 10," "Farmington," "Siege of Corinth," "Iuka," "Holly Springs," "Vicksburg," "Mission Ridge," "Kenesaw," "Ezra Church," "Atlanta," "Savannah," "Columbia," etc., etc., as recognition of the many hard-fought battles in which they had been engaged. The One Hundred and Thirtieth Regiment of Infantry Illinois Volunteers was especially noted for bravery, of which Companies E and F, from Bond County, whilst in the service, discharged their duty nobly. They were engaged in the battles at Port Gibson, siege of Vicksburg, siege at Jackson, Miss., battle at Sabine Cross Roads, or Mansfield, where Col. J. B. Reid was seriously wounded, siege of Blakely, Spanish Fort, Ala., and Mobile. Maj. J. B. Reid was promoted to that of Lieutenant Colonel in this regiment for meritorious services. Dr. David Wilkins was First Assistant Surgeon, and Rev. W. D. H. Johnson, of Greenville, Chaplain of the regiment.

The Third Cavalry was organized at Camp Butler by Col. E. A. Carr, in August, 1861. The regiment moved to St. Louis September 25; October 1, moved up the Missouri River to Jefferson City, and thence marched to Warsaw, where they arrived October 11; on the 23d, marched toward Springfield, Mo., in Col. Carr's Brigade, Brig. Gen. Ashboth's

Division. On November 2, Gen. Hunter took command of the army. November 13, the First and Second Battalions moved with the army on Rolla, Mo. The Third Battalion, Maj. Ruggles commanding, remained with Sigel's Division, and was the last to leave Springfield.

On the 18th of February, 1862, the Third Battalion participated in a calvary charge, routing the enemy. The regiment moved rapidly from point to point as ordered and the interest of the service required, and were engaged in many skirmishes and battles during the three years they were in the service. Their active duty was at Pea Ridge, Huntsville, Grenada, Vicksburg, Chickasaw Bayou, Port Gibson, Tupelo, Okolona and Gun Town, Miss. September 27, 1864, six companies crossed the Tennessee at Clifton, and confronted Hood's army; fell back skirmishing, and took part in the battles of Lawrenceburg, Spring Hill, Campbellsville and Franklin. They were also engaged in an expedition after the Indians in 1865. Capts. Thomas M. Davis, J. K. McLean and S. M. Tabor, all belonging to Bond County, made for themselves a noble record. The regiment was mustered out of service at Springfield, Ill., October 13, 1865. During the time of service, a large number of the regiment re-enlisted as veterans.

Hilliard Rifles.—The company was first organized with a view of entering the State militia, entitled the National Guards of Illinois. Charles H. Beatty was one of the most active in securing the names that formed the first organization, effected December 30, 1878. At a meeting held at the county court house the above date, and presided over by Lieut. Col. James T. Cooper, of Alton, Ill., the following list of officers was elected: Captain, P. E. Holcomb, a retired Major of the regular army; First Lieutenant, S. M. Inglis; Second Lieutenant, Charles H. Beatty. The number enrolled in this first company was seventy-one. Maj. Holcomb, being a retired army officer, consequently skilled in millitary science, the company, under his command, became one of the best drilled companies in Southern Illinois, and enjoyed general prosperity. In December, 1878, it received the title of Company G, Fifteenth Battalion, I. N. G., and was assigned to the Second Brigade, under command of Brig. Gen. J. N. Reece, and in September, 1879, entered encampment at Camp Cullom, near Springfield. The company at this time had been recruited to the number of forty-five members, with three commissioned officers. The Hilliard Rifles, as a social organization, by this time had gained some local prominence. In November, 1880, they leased and established themselves in their commodious and well-equipped armory (hall), in which, from time to time, under their auspicies, the public was treated to first-class lectures, musical and other entertainments, festivals, etc. In the fall of 1881, they again went into encampment near Bloomington, Ill., where they made a reputation and an excellent record in target practice, Lieut. Elam representing his battalion, and doing excellent work. February 18, 1882, the company was re-organized by a new election of officers, the term of service of the first elected having expired. Col. George C. McCord, of Gov. Cullom's staff, and a resident of Greenville, presided at this meeting, and Lieut. S. M. Inglis was elected Captain, C. F. Thraner, First Lieutenant, John A. Elam, Second Lieutenant. About this time the State militia was also re-organized into ten regiments, and the Hilliard Rifles, Company G, Fifteenth Battalion, was assigned to the Eighth Infantry as Company F. It has been recruited to fifty-three men, with three commissioned officers, and in all essential respects is enjoying prosperity.

CHAPTER XI.

GREENVILLE—EDUCATIONAL HISTORY—COMMON SCHOOLS—ALMIRA COLLEGE—RELIGIOUS—ORGANIZATION OF CHURCHES—THE PRESBYTERIANS AND METHODISTS—THE ERECTION OF CHURCH BUILDINGS—SECRET AND BENEVOLENT ORDERS—MASONS AND ODD FELLOWS—OTHER ORGANIZATIONS, ETC., ETC.

"The Church and State, that long had held
Unholy intercourse, now divorced
She who, on the breast of civil power,' etc., etc.

THE education of children at an early day, all over the country, was much the same. and many were to be found who would recognize the necessity of any special effort to educate the females. They were quite unanimous forty years ago in believing that, at most, they might learn to read and write. Arithmetic and grammar were thought to be quite useless. But however much the parents may have desired to give their children a good education at that time, they would have found it often very difficult to find teachers with the requisite qualifications to teach the required branches to enable them to draw the small school-fund distributed annually by the State.

The first schools taught at Greenville, so far as can now be known, was by Mr. Enloe, a Mr. Beeman and White. Miss Elizabeth Norton (afterward Mrs. Foster) taught a school in 1835, in a cabin on part of Lot 22, Greenville, nearly in front of Mrs. Larrabee's present residence. A number of teachers were at different times employed with varying success, until under the free-school system the present brick school building was erected about 1859. The first teachers in the new building as principals, have been Messrs. Cunningham, Clark, Hynes, Taylor, Mudd, Dean and Inglis.

August 8, 1868, the School Directors of Greenville District employed Samuel M. Inglis, at a salary of $100 per month, and who has also been employed from time to time since, and at the end of the fifth year as Principal of the school he had the pleasure of having seven graduates. The sixth year, 1874, seven more graduated; in 1875, nine graduated; in 1876, eight; in 1877, eleven; in 1878, six; in 1879, nine; in 1880, fourteen; in 1881, eleven; in 1882, twelve, making a total graduation of ninety-four for the ten years after the school was brought up to the present graded system. The same Principal is employed for the coming school year, making fifteen years of continuous principalship. Ten assistants are now necessary to aid in giving instructions in the different departments.

This school is very popular at home and enjoys a high reputation abroad.

Almira College.—In 1827, two lads, Stephen Morse and John B. White, attended school together at a public institution in New Hampton, N. H. One year later they entered Brown University, Rhode Island, where they were class and room mates during their collegiate course. After a few years, one devoted himself to teaching, and the other engaged in the mercantile business. These boys were raised by unusually intelligent, devoted, Christian parents, and each sought the path in life that seemingly would promise the most useful and lasting results.

Mr. Morse was prospered in his business,

* By Williamson Plant

and accumulated wealth. Occasional letters passed between these old friends and classmates, in which the subject of education was frequently discussed. Nothing of unusual interest occurred, however, until 1854, when they arranged to meet in Greenville, Ill., which meeting resulted in the initiatory steps for founding the much-talked-of institution. After some days of consultation and study, it was decided that the institution should be for the higher education of young women. That it should not be engaged in as a private enterprise, but that an act of incorporation should be secured, so that the contributions could be held in perpetuity for educational purposes. Mrs. Almira B. Morse, a lady of thorough and accomplished education, was fully in sympathy with her husband, and seconded every effort of his for the advancement of the worthy enterprise, aiding not only by words of encouragement and cheer, but with a generous personal money gift; and thus the institution was founded in 1855-56, a charter being obtained in 1857. The work of erecting the building was immediately begun, and one wing completed and occupied in May, 1858. Work was gradually carried on and the main structure was finished in 1864. It presents a frontage of 160 feet; width, forty-eight feet; is four stories high, and contains seventy-two large and elegant rooms. The college grounds contain twelve acres, consisting of a park, a yard front of the building, and land in the rear for domestic and ornamental purposes. In honor of the lady, Mrs. Almira Blanchard Morse, who endowed it with her little fortune of $6,000, this college was appropriately named Almira.

From its foundation, the institution has been under the instruction and general management of Prof. White, and his wife as assistant, except for three years during the rebellion, during which time the Rev. D. P. French and Mr. Morse assumed control. Prof. White severed his connection with the institution in 1879, when Prof. J. B. Slade, of Springfield, took control.

Mrs. Almira B. Morse died at her home in Palva, Kan., in August, 1881. Her remains were returned to Greenville and interred in Mt. Rose Cemetery.

The ladies of Greenville and vicinity, desirous of promoting social intercourse and of aiding in the intellectual and moral elevation of society, met on the 19th of January, 1856, and organized a society for the aforesaid purpose and adopted a constitution and by-laws. It was called the Social Circle, and its object was the purchase of a library. The ladies present at the meeting for organization were Mrs. A. Morse, Mrs. M. Shields, Mrs. L. Stewart, Mrs. E. Hutchinson, Mrs. S. Morse, Mrs. E. G Smith, Mrs. S. Sprague, Miss J. Merriam and Miss E. M. White.

The meetings were held once a week. In the afternoon, the ladies sewed, and, in the evening gentlemen came in and some literary entertainment was given. An idea of the energy and labor bestowed upon the project may be seen from a single quotation from the records: "Work on hand for January 28—Knitting, a cradle quilt, three sun-bonnets, two pairs of pantalets, infants' dresses, caps and aprons, three shirts finished and price for making the same $2.25.

An attractive feature in the evening entertainments for years was the reading of *The Gazette*, a collection of articles and essays written by the members of the society. Many of the papers contained productions that reflected no discredit upon their composers, indeed some evinced more real literary merit than much that appears in the leading periodicals of to-day.

Besides the labor thus bestowed, we note a supper given April 25, 1858, at which $61.88 were realized; also, June 25, a concert, the proceeds of which were $21. The first purchase of books was made August 26, 1856; the amount invested, $100. October 22 of the same year, by vote, the name was changed to Ladies' Library Association. Thus we find the little germ, planted and nurtured by the ladies, and supported by the good wishes and patronage of the gentlemen, steadily growing.

In the year 1867, through the instrumentality of Hon. J. F. Alexander, a charter was obtained. About this time, the need of a town hall being greatly felt in Greenville, a number of ladies, many of them being also members of the Library Association, determined to raise money to build one and connect with it a room for the public library, which had been kept at the residence of some member of the society. After nearly $1,000 had been obtained, the project was abandoned, and a donation of $712.40 was made to the Library Association on the 13th of February, 1873.

The interest of this fund is annually expended in the purchase of books. The services of librarian having always been gratuitous, the institution is self-supporting, and has added some to the permanent fund.

The twenty-fifth anniversary was celebrated on the 19th of January, 1881, at the residence of Dr. William Allen. The event proved an important epoch, in that it revived much of its history that had never been put on record, and awakened new zeal in the work. Letters were read from absent members, an historical sketch of the society was given, some poems of merit, good music and an elegant repast, combined to form a delightful re-union.

At present the library consists of 1,500 volumes. Seventy-five or one hundred new books are added yearly, and it furnishes patrons the best magazines of the day. The library room is large, pleasantly situated in Bennett's Block, well furnished, and kept open every Saturday afternoon.

The following is a list of the officers at the present time:

Mrs. F. C. Mudd, President; Mrs. E. Denny, Vice President; Mrs. J. W. Hoiles, Secretary, Miss A. E. White, Treasurer and Librarian; Misses E. Birge and G. Blanchard, Assistant Librarians.

Presbyterian Church.—On the 10th day of March, 1819, a church was formed in Bond County, called the "Shoal Creek" Church, embracing all the Presbyterians in the county at that time, with thirty-three members enrolled. On the 15th of September, 1825, the committee appointed by the Presbytery of Missouri, at a meeting held for that purpose, divided this church into three separate churches, known as the Bethel, Shoal Creek and Greenville; and the following list of male members was assigned to Greenville at that time: John Gilmore, Hugh T. White, James White, John B. White, Samuel White, John Russell, John Short, George Donnell, Robert G. White, John White, Joseph Howell and William Nelson.

The location of Shoal Creek Church was in what was then known as the Ohio Settlement, some four or five miles northwest of Greenville, where the Union Grove Church now stands. The Bethel Church was about ten miles northwest of Greenville. These churches maintained a separate existence until April 7, 1832. At this time, the Shoal Creek Church had become so enfeebled by removals and deaths, it seemed necessary for them to unite with the Greenville Church. The Greenville Church was organized by Messrs. Giddings and Lacy and Elder Collins, of Collinsville, September 15, 1825, with twenty-nine members. As before stated, the two branches of the church were consolidated April 7, 1832. Up to this time, no house of worship had been built at Greenville, but soon after the churches had united they built a house about two miles northwest of Greenville, as a more central and convenient point for all the members. The members of the united church hauled and hewed the logs, sawed the timber, split the boards and shingles, and did all the work for the completion of the same within the membership. From 1825 to 1829, the church had no stated pastor, but was served from time to time by transient ministers whose names are unknown. From 1829 to 1831, Rev. Solomon Hardy was the minister in charge; in 1832, Rev. W. J. Fraser; then followed the labors of Revs. A. Ewing, T. A. Spillman, W. K. Stewart; Rev. J. Stafford, from 1837 to 1838, and again from 1840 to 1850. In 1847, the pastor was absent, and P. D. Young supplied the place for six months. In 1851 and 1852, Rev. William Hamilton, and from 1852 to 1867, Rev. Thomas W. Hynes were the stated supply; 1867 to 1868, Rev. Arthur Rose, 1869 to 1872, Prof. George Frazier, were the ministers in charge. About this time, eighteen members withdrew from the New School or Congregational Church, and joined the Presbyterian Church of Greenville. Rev. N. S. Dickey was the stated supply from 1873 to 1880, since which time the Rev. Hillis has been their very acceptable minister of the Greenville Presbyterian Church. In 1873, the building of the church had become so dilapidated, having been built and occupied since about 1845, that the members and friends enlarged the same with cupola, at a cost of about $2,000. It was rededicated July 13, 1873, free from debt. And now to day it stands, as it has stood for more than fifty-seven years, like a city set upon a hill, radiating its light, shedding its beneficent influence on all around, in harmony with the community for good, and in fellowship with its sister churches. Its large membership and its admirable Sunday school speak well for its continued usefulness in the future.

Congregational Church.—The origin of the Congregational Church was with the division of the Presbyterian Church about 1836, into the old and the new school churches. Dr. Lansing from New York came to Greenville in 1839, and through his influence a house of worship was commenced soon after, which was not, however, completed and dedicated until January 1, 1843. Rev. Thomas Lippincott preached the dedicatory sermon.

Up to this time no Presbyterian Church for the old division of the church had been built at Greenville, and many of both branches of the church held their membership together with a number of Congregationalists. By an act of the Legislature of Illinois in 1844, the worshipers of the new building were afterward known as the Congregational Church of Greenville. About this time the old Presbyterian branch had built for themselves a house of worship, and the churches exchanged and withdrew from time to time according to their peculiar ideas—the Congregational society making some payment to the Presbyterians withdrawing from their church for their interest, and aid in building the Congregational Church. Considering the early period in which it was built, the Congregational Church to-day is quite an imposing structure, standing as it does on Lots No. 27 and 28, Davidson's Addition to Greenville.

The church was for many years prosperous, especially so during the time Rev. Robert Stewart, Rev. George C. Wood and Rev. M. M. Longley were pastors, since which time the church has so often been without a regular pastor that its spiritual interests have not advanced as it otherwise would. Rev. John Ingersoll, father of Robert G. Ingersoll, of infidel notoriety, preached to this church about six months about the year 1852. Since that time Rev. Longley was for a time a stated supply, as also have Rev. Isaac Godell and Rev. M. A. Crawford not labored in vain for the short time they each occupied the pulpit. The present pastor, Rev. Joseph Wolfe, sustains well the position assigned him, and the outlook of the church is brightening.

Methodist Episcopal Church.—It is impossible to give anything like a complete history of the Methodist Episcopal Church in Greenville, because, as its present pastor,

Rev. E. A. Hoyt, states, Methodism sets little value on the formalities of organization. Its methods are simple; those who desire a home in her communion are enrolled as a class, and one of the number appointed her leader. No official minutes of the transactions are kept or recorded, except incidentally on the class books. The first sermon perhaps preached in the county by the minister of any denomination was that by Rev. John Powers, a Methodist minister at Jones Fort, in February, 1816. His next appointment was at White's Fort or Hill's Station in March, 1816, and for a time these two forts or stations were his regular preaching places. Jones Fort was in the Green neighborhood, and White's Fort was a few rods southeast of the old residence of Wilson Brown in Section 6, Town 4, Range 3. The first Methodist meetings at Greenville were conducted by Rev. John Kirkpatrick, assisted occasionally by Rev. John Powers, Joshua Barnes, John Dew and others. The several Kirkpatrick families were Methodists. The first Methodist Church was built about a mile and a half southwest of Greenville where camp-meetings were held for several years, at which an old neglected burying ground some eight or ten rods northwest of the southeast corner of north half of northwest quarter of southeast quarter of Section 16, Town 5, Range 3, is yet visable. For more than twenty years after the first settlement of the county, Methodist services were very irregular. Mr. J. E. Travis, now living in Greenville, remembers of Methodist preaching at the house of his grandfather, Tapley Young, where the old cemetery is now located, and heard their family relate of those attending church bringing their guns and stacking them at the door whilst two sentinels stood watch outside the door to give the alarm, if any Indians made their appearance. His first recollection was associated with class meeting, being held at the house of one Knapp, in Greenville, by Rev. John H. Benson, an early circuit rider of Carlisle Circuit in 1839. His appointment at Greenville was once in four weeks, and continued one year; only four of that class are obtainable. Knapp and wife, Elizabeth Drake and Elizabeth Stubblefield. The Rev. Thomas Brown was the next to take up the work, just at what date cannot be stated, but he held services once in four weeks until the fall of 1844, when he died, having left a good name. For the next three or four years services were only held by transient preachers. The first Methodist Episcopal Church built in Greenville on Lot No. 15, Davidson's Addition to Greenville, in the years 1848 and 1849. For several years previously meetings were held in the old court house, and in the Odd Fellows hall, which was the upper story of the present residence of William Evans.

Before the building was erected, the "circuit riders" were unceasing in their labors to increase the membership of the church, and to that end, one of them, a Mr. Falkner, would at the close of every service, "open the doors of the church." On one occasion, after the usual services in the Odd Fellows hall, whilst the brethren were singing a familiar hymn, the minister calling loudly and earnestly for any "who desired to unite with the church to manifest the same by coming forward, and give to him their hand, and God their hearts." As they were singing the chorus of the second verse, and manifestly a deep feeling prevailing through the audience, two well-known females of not the most unblemished character came forward, and gave to the minister their hands, who took them, but without that cordiality sometimes discernible, and with a queer and much-puzzled expression on his countenance, remarked, as he released that slight grasp: "Occasionally, when the fisherman casts in his net he brings in a gar." It is unnecessary to add, that the records of the church next day did not show any increase of membership for the meeting of the previous night to the Methodist society in Greenville

For more than thirty years past the Methodist Episcopal Church in Greenville has enjoyed a reasonable degree of prosperity under the charge of the many preachers sent by the conference of the church to minister to her people. A few familiar names of some of those worthy men are called to the mind of those acquainted with the church for half of a century or more, such as Kirkpatrick, Powers, Barnes, Benson. Johnston, Falkner, Lingenfelter, Munson, Moore, Vancleve. Morrison, Taylor, Waggoner, House, Massey, Van Treese, Gibson, Robinson, down to the present minister, E. A. Hoyt.

Some six years ago. the old church was sold, the title to the property being made to some of the members of the Christian Church, and the Methodists by the aid of many friends outside the church, have built a handsome brick edifice on Lot No. 50, on Second and Sumer streets, which was finished and dedicated some five years since. The membership of this church is steadily increasing, and their congregations and Sunday schools rank with the first in the city.

Greenville Baptist Church—Was organized September 18. 1836. by Revs. James Lemen Elijah Dodson, Joseph Taylor, Joseph Lemen and A. W. Cooley. The church comprised six members. namely, Lemuel Blanchard, Charles, Eunice, A. N. and Elizabeth C. Norton and Sibbel Blanchard. Within a year of its organizing. although without a pastor, and having preaching only occasionally, the number of members had increased to twenty, and up to 1842 twenty-two had been received by experience and baptism. and fourteen by letter, making the total membership forty-two. From this date, July. 1842. no additions were made, but on the contrary the church declined in numerical strength, until in May, 1847, the church relations were dissolved. This was done at a meeting held by the Rev. Ebenezer Rogers, who acted as moderator. At a meeting held in July, 1847, a new organization was effected, under the title of the Baptist Church of Christ of Greenville. The Revs. E. Rogers and I. D. Newell assisted, and the following persons signed the roll: K. P. and Elizabeth Morse, Sibbel Blanchard, Elizabeth Foster and others. During the year, seven others were added. making in all twenty-two. Like most churches organized in early days, this one had to depend for preaching for years on such occasional supplies as could be obtained. Among those who occupied the pulpit from time to time were Revs. John M. Peck, James and Joseph Lemen, Joel Sweet, Elijah Dodson, Joseph Taylor, Eben Rogers and Jonathan Merriman, all now deceased.

The first regular pastor was the Rev. Thomas W. Hynes. He served two months, from June to August 1838, and was succeeded by Rev. E. Dodson, et. al.

Lemuel Blanchard and M. P. Ormsby were ordained the first Deacons, and served until their deaths, 1838 and 1845. respectively. Benjamin Floyd and K. P. Morse succeeded them. Prior to April, 1854, meetings of the church were held in private houses or in the Presbyterian Church. In 1839. the subject of erecting a Baptist meeting-house in Greenville was agitated, but nothing was accomplished. and the courtesies of the Presbyterian Society were gladly extended and accepted, until the present church. 32x50, was completed in April. 1854, at a cost of $2,500. In the summer of 1856, Mr. Charles Perry donated $200, to be used in procuring a bell. The sum was made sufficient by additions. and the present bell, weighing 1,500 pounds. was cast in St. Louis. Much more might be said of this flourishing Christian organization, but space forbids more than that it is firmly established, and is now doing a good work.

Catholic Church of Greenville—Was organized in April, 1877. First mass was celebrated on Sunday. May 6, following, Rev. Father Quitter, of Vandalia, officiating. There were but a few Catholics in the Greenville district, and those living remote from Catholic divine service had become lukewarm in the faith. A few of the faithful, feeling the need of religious culture and a strengthened faith, had accustomed themselves to meet in a small hall on the third floor of the First National Bank building. In this room services were conducted for about three years. The subject of a more suitable place of worship was from time to time discussed and a building fund started. The citizens of Greenville were all afforded an opportunity, and many responded with liberal donations, Protestants not excepted. In November, 1879, a contract for the building of their present commodious edifice, situated in the eastern portion of the city, was awarded, the good work pushed to completion. On the first Sunday in June, 1880, Father Quitter, assisted by Mr. James Henry and others from Vandalia, celebrated the first High Mass. This congregation was made up of Catholics of many nationalities, but all met upon the one religious plane for one and the same purpose. The same harmony and true fellowship still prevail, and while the church is still in its infancy, it is thought that a permanent pastor will in the near future be engaged and a larger church needed.

Protestant Episcopal Church.—Up to the year 1878, the Protestant Episcopal Church had not been known in Bond County. There had been several Episcopalians in Greenville for years past, but no effort had been made to secure the services of the church. Feeling the importance of a Christian education for their families they had worshiped with other religious societies.

July 20, 1878, Messrs. C. K. Denny, M. B. Chittenden, W. S. Ogden, Henry Howard and Henry Chittenden met at Squire Howard's office, and there decided to organize a parish to be known as Grace Church. To the above list the names of about seventeen persons were added, who had been baptized in the Episcopal Church, also names of twelve others who were not connected with any church, and seemed inclined to aid in sustaining this. The Rev. Mr. Van Duzen, then officiating at Paris, Edgar Co., Ill., heard of this movement and visited Greenville, and about the 1st of August, 1878, and for the first time, services of the Protestant Episcopal Church were held in Greenville, at the Congregational Church. It was found that the Canons of the Diocese did not permit the organization of a parish to so limited a number of communicants. W. S. Ogden was sent to attend the annual Diocesan Convention of 1879, at Springfield, Ill., and to confer with Bishop McLaren, Bishop of the Diocese. He carried with him a petition embracing some thirty-odd names. The petition was favorably acted upon, and Messrs. Ogden and Denny appointed Senior and Junior Wardens; M. B. Chittenden, Treasurer, and H. A. Stephens Clerk, with Henry Chittenden Licensed Recorder. In July, 1879, Rev. R. E. G. Huntington was called as Rector of Christ's Church, Collinsville, and as Missionary to Grace Mission, Greenville, and thereafter, fortnightly, services were held until May, 1881, when Mr. H. resigned and removed to Kansas. During these two years, quite a number were added by baptism and confirmation. The church, however, lost by death and removals, more than she had gained. For about one year, the church was without a rector; but April 1, 1882, the Rev. Joseph G. Wright, of Altamont, took charge of the Mission, and the life of the church much revived. Measures have been taken looking toward the erection of a church edifice, and it is now believed that a pretty Gothic structure, sufficiently large to seat some two hundred worshipers, will be built at a cost not to exceed $2,000, and completed this coming fall of 1882. Everything connected with the Mission, owing to the zeal and energy of the rector, is in a flourishing condition, and no doubt but that a bright future is before it.

The Plymouth Brethren (so called). *By one of the Brethren.*—Those people who, for about twenty-eight years, have met together in this city as Christians, are not connected in any way with any of the other denominations of Christians, as they meet on quite different ground than they do. First of all, they have no creed; (and as one of them expressed) our creed is the word of God. They take into fellowship any believer in the Lord Jesus Christ, whose doctrine is sound according to God's word, and whose walk in the world is in accordance with the teachings of God's word, as to how a believer should behave himself, who has been redeemed by the precious blood of Christ. As to their ground of meeting together, they do so as the disciples of the Lord, after he had left them to go in the glory; that is, meeting every Lord's Day morning to break bread in remembrance of their Lord, as He told them, before He departed, "Do this in remembrance of me." They do not believe in ordination, accepting only the word of God, which says that He has given the church gifts, some apostles, some doctors, evangelist teachers, etc.; not educated by man, but by God alone. They meet without preachers, and any member of the body, led by the spirit, is free to offer a prayer or give a word of exhortation, or words of thanks to the Lord. If the Lord sends them one of His gifted servants from time to time, they gladly receive him, as from the Lord, to either teach, exhort or comfort, or preach the Gospel to sinners. Those gifted servants receive no fixed salary, but depend entirely on the Lord, thus walking by faith, and they are generally better cared for than those who are depending on man for support, though surely man is the instrument that God uses. This is, in short, the history of those people, so called, Plymouth Brethren. The building in which they meet was built by Mr. George Rutchley, for the purpose, and the assembly pays rent for it to him with money put in a box every Lord's Day morning, by those whose heart is opened, and are able to thus contribute not only to expenses of rent, light, and so on, but also for the servants of the Lord, who are traveling from place to place, working for the Master.

A., F. & A. M., Greenville Lodge, No. 245, received a dispensation October 28, 1866, and the following list of officers were elected: W. H. Collins, W. M.; T. W. Hutchinson, S. W.; W. T. White, J. W.; W. A. Allen, Secretary; J. Burchsted, Treasurer; Neely McNeely, Tiler. Charter for this lodge was issued October 7, 1857, and was signed by J. H. Hibbard, G. M.; William Lane, D. G. M.; Harrison Dills, S. G. W.; F. M. Blair, J. G. W.; Harman G. Reynolds, Grand Secretary. Charter members were: W. H. Collins, P. W. Hutchinson, W. T. White, John Burchsted, W. A. Allen and Neely McNeely. According to last report, the lodge contained sixty-five members.

I. O. O. F., Clark Lodge, No. 3, was instituted January 10, 1839; chartered August 1, same year. The following were the charter members, of whom only one, James E. Star, of Elsah, Jersey County, Ill., is now living. James Clark, Patrick O'Byrne, David P. Berry, George Files, Thomas Dakin. Charter was signed by S. C. Pierce, M. W. G. M.; M. Botkin, D. G. M.; Daniel Ward, G. W.; John M. Krum, G. T.; Alfred Shannon, G. S.; J. R. Woods, P. G.; James E. Star, P. G.; A. W. Chenoweth, P. G.; John R. Batterton, P. G. Original officers were; James Clark, N. G.; Patrick O'Byrne, V. G.; James Bradford, Secretary; R. F. White, Treasurer. Present number of members of the lodge is fifty-three.

I. O. O. F., Greenville Encampment, No. 39, was instituted February 5, 1869. First officers were: Henry Howard, C. P.; C. W. Holden, H. P.; L. Adams, S. W.; J. F. Bowman, J. W.; G. A. Collins, Scribe; E. Reidemann, Treasurer.

Alfred Blackwelder

Charter was issued October 12, 1869, and was signed by J. J. Tichner, Grand Patriarch; N. C. Nason, Grand Scribe. Present number of members, twenty-five.

Independent Order of Good Templars, Greenville Lodge No. 440, chartered May 2, 1870, with the following members and officers: C. W. Moore, Wyatt Cansey, J. H. Hallam and thirty-one others signed the call. First officers elected: S. French, W. C. T.; Mrs. E. C. Smith, W. V. T.; Rev. M. N. Powers, W. C.; J. J. Clarkson, W. S.; George Perryman, W. A. S.; W. C. Brown, W. F. S.; Mrs. Alice Phelp, W. T. R. E. A.; Munroe McAdams, W. M.; Miss Alice Alexander, W. D. M.; Mrs. C. Larabee, W. I. G.; H. H. Hughes, W. D. G.; Miss Kate Kelso, W. R. H. S.; Miss Flora Larabee, W. L. H. S.; H. H. Smith, P. W. C. T. Original number of members in good standing was forty-six, and present number is sixty. The lodge is in a prosperous condition, and accomplishing much good.

The title, Women's Christian Temperance Union, is strikingly suggestive of the laudable object of the society. A union of Christian women representing the different evangelical churches, organized so as to systematically, and with the blessings of God, aid in the suppression of intemperance in their midst, working in harmony with the State and National organizations of their order. The Greenville Union was constituted April 1, 1879, with officers as follows:

Mrs. E. W. Dewey, President at Large; Mrs. Dr. R. C. Sprague, Vice President at Large; Mrs. A. B. Byram, from the Presbyterian Church; Mrs. S. Perry, from the Baptist Church; Mrs. W. S. Dann, from the Methodist Church; Mrs. Charles Clark, from the Congregational Church; Caroline Phelps, Corresponding Secretary; Mrs. Samuel Colcord, Recording Secretary; Miss Allie Robinson, Treasurer. The Union is in a prosperous condition and accomplishing much good, and at their last election, April 11, 1882, the following officers were elected: Mrs. A. E. Haven, President; Mrs. P. C. Reed, Vice President; Mrs. N. H. Jackson, Recording Secretary; Mrs. Mary Murdock, Treasurer. The Union has about thirty enrolled members.

A temperance society that accomplished much good was organized April 6, 1848, by J. R. Woods, A. D. G. W. P. of the State of Illinois, with the following charter members: Robert F. White, John Burchsted, John T. Barr, Otis B. Colcord, Daniel Detrick, John Waite, Franklin Berry, John A. Dowler, S. B. Holcomb, George Ferguson, Nathaniel Maddux, Lonson Lane, Joseph T. Fouke, Samuel H. Crocker, E. Gaskins and James Stafford. The following officers were elected and installed: Franklin Berry, W. P.; John T. Barr, W. A.; John Waite, R. S.; S. B. Holcomb, A. R. S.; Joseph T. Fouke, F. S.; Daniel Detrick, F.; R. F. White, C.; George Ferguson, A. C.; Nathaniel Maddux, I. S.; O. B. Colcord, O. S.; E. Gaskins, P. W. P. James Stafford was appointed Chaplain, and John Waite alternate. During the remainder of April sixteen more were added to the membership, making thirty-two. This number increased rapidly, and the prosperity of the order was unbounded. Many men joined who had been for years habitual drunkards, came for miles to attend the meetings, and in most cases were prosperous in their business whilst they were members, and often testified to their enjoyment during those several years of their membership. It gave way to other temperance societies, its last meeting being April 29, 1853. Its enrollment was over 200 members.

Integrity Lodge, No. 72, A. O. U. W., was instituted April 28, 1877, with the following officers: S. M. Inglis, P. M. W.; George S. Phelps, M. W.; Henry Howard, F.; William Ballard, O.; Cyrus Birge, Recorder; George C. Scipio, Financier; M. V. Denny, Receiver, C. W. Holden, G.; Samuel Werner, I. W.; S. M.

Tabor, O. W. Henry Howard was the first representative to the meeting of the Grand Lodge at Ottawa, Ill., February, 1878. The lodge now has sixty-three members, and is in a prosperous condition.

I. O. M. A. was organized September 20, 1880, with the following officers: J. J. Clarkson, P.; C. W. Sawall, P. P.; John Kingsbery, V. P.; Henry Rammel, R. S.; J. M. McAdams, F. S.; H. T. Powell, T.; E. C. Stearns, J. J. Clarkson, H. T. Powell, Trustees; A. T. Reed, C.; C. H. Beatty, I. G.; O. L. Lupton, O. G.

The I. O. M. A. is a State organization, and the Greenville branch contains twenty-seven members.

The Greenville Band consists of thirteen public-spirited and enterprising young men of esthetic musical tastes, who have, by enduring perseverance, accomplished much in the way of musical culture, and rendered themselves a credit to their city, county and State.

The band was organized October 10, 1879; chartered November 12, 1880, with John A. Elam as their leader; Adel Albright, first E flat cornet; Ward Reid, second E flat cornet; Will E. Robinson, clarionet; Charles Thraner, piccolo; Wallace Barr, first B flat cornet; Will Johnson, second B flat cornet; Will Donnell, third B flat cornet; Robert Johnson, first solo alto; Jesse Watson, second solo alto; Walter Powell, third solo alto; Rome Sprague, first tenor; Jesse Smith, second tenor; Frank Shaw, baritone; Louis Derleth, tuba bass; Frank Boughman, tenor drum; Will White, bass drum and cymbals.

Of the above only five were, according to law, old enough to have their names appear on the charter, namely, Leader Elam, Messrs. Albright, Johnson, Shaw and Boughman. Messrs. Reid, Robinson, Albright and Smith have resigned and their instruments are at present silent, but a movement is on foot that will undoubtedly result in filling their places.

On the evening of September 20, 1880, the band was treated to a most happy and appropriate surprise by the loyal ladies of Greenville, who presented them with an elegant flag of our country, twelve feet long and six feet wide, mounted on a substantial staff, and surmounted with a gold gilt American eagle with extended pinions. The stars are worked in silk floss, and among them appear the letters G. B. The cost of this flag was $50. The band is in constant practice, and bids fair to soon become one of the best in Illinois.

CHAPTER XII.

GREENVILLE—A RETROSPECTION—BUILDING OF JAILS—SITUATION OF THE CITY—MORE OF THE EARLY BUSINESS AND BUSINESS MEN, STORES, ETC.—GRIGG, BARR, DAVIS, ELLIOTT AND OTHERS—AGRICULTURAL WAREHOUSES—THE BANKING BUSINESS—SHOPS AND MECHANICS—SUMMARY, ETC., ETC.

TO what extent the early settlers of Bond County believed in the existence of ghosts, no official record has been left: but they have recorded their belief in that mysterious healing art where faith is the active agent as late as June 2, 1829. In that record is found that Polly Harness, "in consequence of a canser or ulser is unable to earn a livelihood;" whereupon the court makes the following order: "Ordered, that Thomas Hunter be appointed Agent to convey Polly Harness to a Dutch Doctor, living about ten miles below Herculanium, in Missouri, and that the sum of $30 be paid to said Thomas Hunter to defray said expenses." The record in due time shows that the said Thomas Hunter reported to the court the delivery of the said Polly Harness to one "William Neill, and took his receipt for the cure and maintanence" of the said Harness "near Harkalenaum," and that the $30 was duly expended; after that announcement the record is silent.

At least two jails have been built in Greenville before the one now in use, which was built in 1859. The first was built by Andrew Moody and Thomas Stout, of square logs, according to specifications, at a cost of $244.50, in State paper. It was built somewhere near the present house of Samuel Bradford. The contract is dated July 4, 1829, to be completed by the first Monday in December following. The second jail was built by Richard Tatom, on the public square, for $321.74, payment made for same July 4, 1835, that probably being the date of receiving the building. The present jail is a very respectable building, having none of the forbidding outward appearances often attending that class of buildings. It was built at a cost of about $5,000, with the cells since fitted up on the west side. But few persons have escaped from the same since it was finished.

The city of Greenville, containing a population of 2,500 inhabitants, is located on the highest point of land on the line of the St. Louis, Vandalia & Terre Haute Railroad, fifty miles from St. Louis, gently sloping to the south, with woodland in close proximity on the north and west, through which numerous springs of pure water flow continuously, giving early promise of furnishing for the city and manufactories, to be established, a bountiful supply of water.

Beginning as the town did in 1819, with one small building made of unhewed logs, in which Green P. Rice measured his first yard of cotton goods to the early settler; next, to the time when it was made the county seat, in 1821, when he had retired from the trade, and his successor, Samuel Davidson, was no more; then the erection of county buildings, and, within the next ten years, the increased number of stores in the hands of Blanchard,

* By Williamson Plant.

Birge, Long, Durley, Drake and White, although frequently changing in the time. Then George Davidson with his small cabin entertains, as best he can, man and beast. Next, Seth Blanchard, his successor, and David Berry, each with enlarged cabins, gave ample accommodations for shelter, and their ever well loaded tables (of which tradition speaks in praise), fed the weary traveler as he wended his way on horseback through the new country to the West. The next ten years bring an increased population, more extensive business in every department. The first old court house had returned to the ground if not to the dust. The old jail failed of its purpose, and both were condemned as unsuitable longer for usefulness.

We have now reached 1841. The business houses have increased not only in number, but their stocks of merchandise have been greatly enlarged. Within this last ten years we find Seth Blanchard, J. B. Drake, Ansel Birge, Williard Twiss, W. S. Smith, L. D. Plant, William Davis, Gooding, Morse & Bros. and James M. Davis have been selling goods, not all at one time, for many changes were made within that time. The hotels in the meantime had made further improvements under the management of Blanchard; then his successor, Thomas Dakin, and David Berry at his old stand, second house west of Drake's. A new court house has also been built, of wood, in place of the old crumbled brick, and a new jail on the southeast corner of the public square.

During all these years, many times without building for Clerk's offices and places for holding courts, among the first places for holding the courts was in a building west of Elam's old blacksmith shop, southwest of Joel Elam's present residence; then in the house of Wyatt Stubblefield; then in the old Berry Tavern, where the difficulty between two lawyers occurred during session of court. One twisted the nose of the other, which he resented with his cane. If we move up ten years more, to 1851, living witnesses are numerous who know of the changes. We have some of the old merchants, with many that are new. The list now is covered by W. S. & Thomas W. Smith, J. B. Drake, Morse & Bros., Charles Hoiles, George W. Hill, S. B. Bulkley, P. J. Holcomb and L. D. & W. Plant.

The hotels, by David Berry, Thomas Stout, J. B. O. White, the latter where Mrs. McCord's hotel is now kept, and who that lived within the last period named does not remember the private boarding house of Mr. and Mrs. John Ackerige, next house east of Dr. Drake's? what nice meals at "moderate prices" they prepared! During court week, their table was always crowded by jurors, witnesses and those interested in court, living in the county, whilst the Judge and most of the members of the bar from abroad stopped at the Berry House. The tables of these houses were abundantly supplied with wild game, such as venison, prairie chickens, quail, etc., which were plentiful and very cheap. The common price for "venison saddle" (the hind quarters with the loin), would sell for 37½ cents per pair. The average weight would be from thirty to fifty pounds each, making the meat average about 1 cent per pound. What boy now living that was in Greenville during this time does not remember the ginger cakes made by old Mother Allred? The next ten years takes us to 1861. Increased business on every hand. We find during this time that the merchants are covered by the following list: W. S. & T. W. Smith, Morse & Bros., Charles Hoiles, E. A. Floyd, Alexander Buie, G. W. Hill, Samuel A. Blanchard, Elliott & Kershner, A. W. Hynes, and Barr & Elliott.

The hotels are now all removed to near the public square. The St. Charles Hotel, by E. R. McCord, Franklin House, by Franklin G. Morse, from whom it took its name. Within this last period a new jail has been built, of brick, where it now stands on Third street, and the present court house completed in 1855.

Now let us pass from 1861 to the present, 1882, covering a period of twenty-one years, as the town has grown until it would be impossible to make mention in detail of many changes and occurrences. The greatest impetus given to Greenville since it was first named, was the building and completion of the St. Louis, Vandalia & Terre Haute Railroad through the southern line of the city. The first passenger train from Greenville to St. Louis was on the morning of December 8, 1868, and from that date we mark the first march of improvement. As has been shown by an article in this book covering a history of the Vandalia Railroad that the citizens of Greenville and Bond County have more than ordinary interest in the success of this road.

The stores that have been in operation in that time, but have closed out, are as follows: W. S. Smith & Co., J. M. Smith, Morse & Bros., C. Hoiles, G. W. Hill, A. Buie, William M. Evans & Co., J. G. Sprague, H. Y. Schell, J. W. Elliott, P. C. Reed, McLain & Wafer, John B. Reid, Samuel B. Hynes, E. V. Buchanan, George F. Salisbury.

If a stranger visiting Greenville for the first time should desire detailed information in regard to the business transacted in the city at the present time, and ask to be shown first the merchant longest in the trade, any one of whom the request was made would conduct him to the well filled "U. S." store of John T. Barr, successor of Messrs. Barr & Elliott, on Main street, south side of the public square. This house has always had a good, regular trade.

He would next be shown the store of Daniel R. Grigg, on Lot 31, corner of College and Second streets. Mr. Grigg has well proved the old adage to be correct, that "He who by the plow would thrive, himself must either hold or drive." Mr. Grigg has succeeded well by his personal attention to his business. He would next be shown north across the street to the large, well-filled house of W. S. Dann & Co. This house speaks for itself, the proprietors having the happy faculty of pleasing their numerous customers, and to meet the requirements of their trade have recently enlarged their already commodious building.

The firm of Berry & Davis, Third street, west side of the public square, would claim his attention next. The business of this firm has increased until they now stand in the front ranks with their worthy competitors; the range of their trade is varied, keeping a general stock of dry goods; they have bought and sold grain, wool, etc. Adjoining their store on the north is the well and favorably known house of Jandt & Weise, successors to Jandt & Reed. This house is connected in some degree with the house at Pocahontas, under the name of H. A. Jandt & Co., and, by concert of action by the two houses, have now a lucrative business.

These five stores of general merchandise are all in a prosperous condition, each house having their friends, makes a good division in the trade, and, the competition being close, each stands as a guard on prices, to keep them within proper bounds.

Only three clothing houses are in operation at present; a fourth, however, is in prospect.

The New York Clothing House, on Lot 42, corner of Third and Main streets, first made its bow to the public some fifteen years ago, with Mr. S. Stearn as proprietor. Mr. Stearn was lost whilst crossing the Atlantic on the steamer Schiller, in company with Mr. John Suppiger and family. Soon after, Mr. Louis Kaufman took charge of the store and conducted it successfully until recently. Mr. E. B. Wise became associated with him under the name of Kaufman & Wise. They have always had a good trade.

The store of A. Abrams, on Lot 41, corner of Main and Second streets, under the name of "Golden Eagle," though not one of the largest, is well assorted for the trade. This store was broken into one night a few months since by two tramps, strangers to the town, and several hundred dollars' worth of goods taken. The thieves were captured soon after, the goods recovered, and are now serving out their sentence in the Chester Penitentiary.

Theodore W. Coverdale is proprietor of the "Elephant" clothing, boot and shoe house on Lot 61, corner of Second and South streets. Commencing some eight years ago with a small stock of boots and shoes, he now enjoys a large, prosperous trade from his new stand with his large stock of clothing, as well as boots, shoes, etc.

Mr. H. T. Powell is just fitting up his building on the northwest corner of Lot 47, on Main street, with a new stock of ready-made clothing. He has been a successful business man in the past, which argues well for him in the future.

Of the grocery stores there are five, all apparently doing a flourishing business. The oldest is that of Mr. E. P. Justice, on Lot 48, corner of Main and Second streets; has held a good trade for many years past. Mr. John Perryman's comes next. Mr. Perryman's business has been conducted for several years by his son George, who has made a first-class grocery house of it. It is situated in his new building, built recently on his lot for the business for which they are so successfully using it. It is located on the south side of the public square. Robinson & Son, just north of Abram's clothing store, have had their share of the grocery business during the several years they have been in business, always keeping reliable goods.

The firm of Watson & Jett, although only some two years in business, have a trade that often takes many years to secure its equal. They were not new men in the trade, but had had several years' experience in business at another point. Their trade is all they should desire.

Mr. Warren B. Beedle, successor to E. V. Buchanan, on the west side of the public square, enjoys his share of the grocery trade. He is well located, and his pleasant address will not fail to add to his already increasing business.

Four drug stores adorn the town. The health of the county and city is so good that did they depend on the sale of medicines alone for a support, one would easily satisfy every demand; but these stores include, besides their drugs and medicines, a great variety of fancy and toilet goods, cutlery, paints, oils, dye stuffs and some medicinal liquors, to which they add the soda fount, etc., etc., and with a full line of these, each establishment, although of good proportions, find a paying business throughout the year.

C. R. Bennett may be found at his old stand, on Lot 23, corner of Third and College streets. Mr. M. Ouyden, with a comparatively new stock of goods, just south, across the street, on the opposite corner. C. W. Watson & Co., successors of H. T. Powell, one door east of the First National Bank, and George W. Seaman, on the corner of Lot 47, corner of Main and Second streets. These four drug houses are all first-class.

Only two tin and hardware shops are located in Greenville, but they have ample facilities to meet the requirements that may be made upon them. Mr. Theodore Smith has been in business more than twenty-five years; is proprietor of one of the shops. He is now located on Lot 45, on Third street, in a large, commodious room, well suited to his business. The other is owned and conducted by Messrs. F. Seewald & Co., on Lot 49, Greenville, on Main street. A double building was found necessary to give sufficient room for their work and trade.

There are two furniture stores, one kept by Gerichs & Norman, on Third street, who also keep undertakers' goods. The other, in charge of Mr. Gus Tripod, on Second street; besides which there is the cabinet shop of Mr. Barbey, who includes in his stock picture frames, undertakers' goods, etc.

Three regular agricultural warehouses, with partial hardware stores attached, are to be found in the city—one on the corner of Main and Third streets, kept by Messrs. J. J. Clarkson and G. W. Lowrance, under the name of Clarkson & Lowrance. They handle many manufactures of plows, several self binders, and keep a good stock of hardware, seeds, etc. Another, and quite similar establishment, is first door north of the Presbyterian Church, kept by Jonathan Seaman and Hubbard, under the style of Seaman & Hubbard. The third agricultural house is kept by William Leidel. He keeps everything belonging to a first-class agricultural establishment, and is located across the street, west from his residence, near the railroad depot. Other agricultural implements are sold by parties who have no regular house for their sale.

Three millinery and fancy stores may be named. McLain & Co., on Lot 49, Main street, is a house that has been established a number of years, and has always had the confidence of the public. The millinery parlors kept by Misses Jennie F. and May Barr, on Second street, one door south of the Thomas House, is well filled with fashionable goods; and the St. Louis Bazaar, by Mr. A. W. Hynes, one door east of E. P. Justice's grocery store. This last is more of a fancy store, with rare fruits, than to be called a millinery establishment. These houses have careful attendants, and are getting good trade.

Five blacksmiths are scattered through the town. John Schlup, who also makes a specialty of manufacturing wagons, has his shop on Third and Summer streets, T. B. Savage, aid to N. W. McLain's machine shop, is also, on Third street; J. E. Travis' shop is on Summer street, and W. W. Williams is located on Main, on Lot 50. J. D. Dorsey, "the village smith," makes a specialty of horseshoeing, on what is claimed to be an improved system; is located between the Baptist and Christian Churches.

Three banks have been in successful operation from fifteen to twenty years each. The first was under the style of W. S. Smith & Co., which was succeeded by the First National Bank of Greenville, located on the northwest corner of Lot 46, Main and Third streets, with a capital of $100,000, which has since been reduced about one-third. Its officers are: Nathaniel Dressor, President; Abe McNeil, Vice President; M. V. Denny, Cashier.

Mr. Charles Hoiles having retired from the bank bearing his name some two years ago, the same is now very successfully conducted by his two sons, C. D. and S. M. Hoiles, under the old firm name of Hoiles & Sons. Their bank is located on the southeast corner of Lot 47, on Second street. The bank of James Bradford and Samuel Bradford, under the style of Bradford & Son, is situated on the southwest corner of Lot 31, Second street. Each of the banks has the confidence of the people as regards their solvency.

Two large lumber yards are located within

the corporation, that of Messrs. G. W. Flint & Co., successors to Gerichs & Koch, on Fourth and Washington streets, and that of C. D. Harris & Co., successors to Mudd & Harris, opposite the public school buildings. The lumber trade of Greenville is very large. The hotels should not be overlooked. The Franklin House, by L. Silverman, is well located on College and Third streets. The house was built in 1840, by L. D. Plant, for a hotel, but was not used as such for many years after. It has undergone considerable repairs and additions since building. The hotel on the east side of the public square, by Mrs Elizabeth McCord, is the same building in which J. B. O. White kept hotel over twenty-five years since. Mrs. McCord has attended closely to her duties, and has kept up the name of her house. She has many old traveling friends.

The Thomas House, kept by Mrs. Mary A. Thomas, deserves special notice. She commenced some ten years since, keeping her first hotel in the old Sergeant House; then the Franklin; next the new Empire. Her success in these houses enabled her to purchase the house she now occupies, which she has been keeping for the past three years, under the name of the Thomas House. She has shown more than ordinary executive ability in conducting her hotel business in the past, which is a sure guaranty for success in the future. Her table is loaded with the delicacies of the season, as the market affords.

Three jewelry stores are at present in Greenville. That of G. S. Haven, on Lot 32, northwest corner of court house square, is the oldest, Mr. Haven having been in the business about thirteen years. The other two stores are situated side by side on Lot 47, southeast corner of the square, one kept by Mr. Charles Derleth, the other by Mr Phillip Frech. Both make attractive exhibits of their wares. There is but one machine shop in the city, and is kept on Lot 11, Third street, where ordinary repairs to machines needing experts are repaired.

A number of shops for the manufacture of boots and shoes can be found by walking through the town. Across the street, on the north side of the square, may be seen the shop of Messrs. Flaharty & Sala. Just south of Mr. Justice's store the shop of Mr. Jacot, and south, on the same street, on Lot 53, the well-known shop of August Brunning: and the shop of Louis Derleth, in the basement of Hoiles Block, has had a good run of trade since he has been conducting the same. Mr. James Lyon's, two doors west of the Baptist Church, is the convenient shop for those living at the west end of the city. He has not been known to refuse to sell or work for those living in any other part of Greenville.

For a number of years three elevators have been in operation in Greenville, buying and shipping grain, besides the mill of Plant & Wafer. The proprietors of the largest of these elevators have recently retired from the business, but the business will probably continue under another management.

Adolphe Breuchand and his brother Mark Breuchand have each an elevator on the line of the railroad, some forty rods distant from each other. The buying of wheat for shipping and grinding at Greenville annually amounts to more than two hundred thousand bushels, in good seasons.

There are three steam flouring-mills at Greenville—one situated half a mile north of the city, near the creek, from which the supply of water needed in running the mill is taken. A similar mill, though not so large, was burned on the spot where the present one stands, by one Page, some forty years ago, for which he suffered the penalty of the law. Mr. W. S. Smith is the owner of the property at present. On account of its having been built on the ashes of the old mill, it was for years known as the Phœnix Mills. The small mill immediately north of the railroad, known as the Star Mills, was built some ten years ago by J. E. Walls and W. M. Evans. It was designed for a custom or exchange mill. Mr. E. Tinkey, its present proprietor, has made some improvements in the same during the past two years he has owned it, and he runs it to the extent that business justifies.

The mill on the south side of the railroad, known as the Greenville City Mills, was built some fourteen years ago by N. W. McLain and James E. Wafer, who ran it for a number of years, when John B. Reid became their successor, added some improvements, and sold it to its present owners, Williamson Plant and Thomas Wafer, who have recently expended several thousand dollars putting in improved machinery to enable them to manufacture a superior grade of flour for their large and growing trade. They have opened up a good shipping trade within the past two years with Belfast, Ireland, Glasgow, Scotland, Liverpool and London, having shipped to those points within that time over thirty car loads of flour, at prices in advance of any market in the United States. This mill also does a general exchange business with farmers the same as the other two mills before referred to. The water for running this mill is abundant in a good well in the mill. In addition to the above, Messrs. Elam & Sons are putting up a mill on the railroad near the stock pens for sawing walnut blocks into legs for tables, and hickory butts into carriage and wagon spokes, etc.

The perplexities and uncertainties of the law in Greenville is explained and argued if necessary, for a proper fee, by Messrs. S. A. Phelps, D. H. Kingsbury, A. G. Henry, W. H. Dawdy, John Kingsbury, W. A. Northcott (Mr. Northcott at present being State's Attorney), and L. H. Craig. Robinson & Reid, over the post office, are engaged in an abstract, loan and insurance business.

The citizens of Greenville claim that the health of their city and surrounding country has been so good that they will need, if such continues, a list of the names of their resident physicians placed in some conspicuous place that they may not forget them. If such a list was posted in the order in which they came to the city, it would be in the following order: Drs. W. P. Brown, R. C. Sprague, J. A. Slaughter, David Wilkins, James Gordon, D. R. Wilkins, Frank Brown, W. H. H. Beeson and Miss Florence B. Holden.

The above list will not need to have the name of our excellent dentist, Dr. N. H. Jackson, inscribed on it for fear we may forget him, as each one, sooner or later, will have occasion to know of him or his brethren in the profession elsewhere. He is at present located pleasantly in rooms above the Elephant Clothing House.

The three harness shops will not be overlooked by the farmer, or those in need of their goods. That of T. B. Wood, one door south of Bradford's Bank, of W. J. Mills, on Lot 25, northwest corner of the public square, and last, but not least, that of Will Holdzkom, on Lot 32, west side of the square. All these men give personal attention to their business.

The pleasure-seekers will always be glad to make the acquaintance of the good natured livery stable man. When you step out of the Thomas House, on the first lot to your left you will find the Empire Stable, kept by Mr. James W. Whittaker, and he keeps many new buggies to sell to those who do not want to ride in his.

Capt. S. M. Tabor, in the Francisco Stables, has had an excellent run of business. Capt.

Tabor's friends are loud in praise of the speed of some of his horses.

Mr. Robert Merry, successor to Wood & Merry, has found it necessary to own two stables to enable him to carry on his large and growing business—one just west from Capt. Tabor's, and the other across the street north. Mr. Merry has some good rigs for the business. All seem to do a good business.

The tonsorial art, in the hands of Messrs. C. R. Jones, Thomas Barbee, Mr. Kepler and Joseph Jones has had the tendency of smoothing the faces and shortening the locks of their numerous visitors, adding largely to their personal appearance in proportion as they remove this surplus growth.

No one should shun Messrs. Hurley & Co., on Third street, below the First National Bank, because their home and business is among the tombstones. A call upon them will give some idea of the work that may stand as a sentinel at your last resting-place.

No business list of Greenville would be complete that did not include the bakeries of Messrs. Frank Parent and Nicholas Faust; and they know how to make a good lunch or square meal.

Mr. C. R. Brenning makes a specialty of his restaurant, and knows how to please his patrons by keeping a nice, clean house. The ice cream saloon and fancy bakery of Mrs. Heffer & Sons commands the attention of not only the young man and his girl, but older people find real comfort in those dishes they know so well how to serve. In closing our Greenville notes, mention must be made of the "boy merchant," Lincoln Reid, son of Col. J. B. Reid, a mere lad, yet he has been in business about three years, beginning at first selling stationery on a small scale from a counter in the corner of the post office in Greenville. His business is steadily increasing, until now it is developing into a business of larger proportions. Such enterprise gives hopeful promise in the future.

To write of incidents of a foreign land as they fall under our observation or related to us by others, is largely of the nature of machine work. But to write of one's home, early associations and recollections, of incidents of days that are passed never to return and bring back those happy inspirations of youth, cannot but bring its share of sadness. But let these be as they may, the writer has honestly, but perhaps too hurriedly, given in the preceeding pages (or at least that part allotted to him), which came under his personal knowledge, or was derived from official records of the different events as they occurred, faithfully and impartially, knowing full well that some errors may have crept in unobserved, for which great care has been used to make the number of such as few as possible.

CHAPTER XIII.

RIPLEY PRECINCT—TOPOGRAPHICAL AND DESCRIPTIVE—EARLY SETTLEMENT—PIONEER LIFE AND HARDSHIPS—THE WHEELOCKS—THE ANCIENT TOWN OF "OLD RIPLEY"—OLD SPANISH TRADITION—CHURCHES—SCHOOLS—VILLAGES, ETC.

"The past and present as herein told,
Form topics of thought for young and old."
—*Riley.*

NATURE in her green mantle is nowhere more lovely than in that portion of Bond County set aside by survey and known as "Ripley Precinct." Cozy farmhouses nestle in somber quietude amid the green orchards which dot the landscape in every direction. Though it has every appearance of newness, this country has been settled for many years. Scenes, familiar to many of the older residents, are fast passing from view, and the old landmarks are disappearing with those to whom they owe their existence, and mention must be made of them before the places which once knew them shall know them no more. Only too frequently it is the case, that people do not see beyond the narrow limits of their own lives, and items of private and public interest are neglected and allowed to drift into the channel of the forgotten past. A great many important facts connected with the earlier history of Ripley Precinct are irrecoverably lost, but a few have been found by careful research, which will be appropriately mentioned.

Ripley Precinct lies almost directly west of Greenville, and is somewhat irregular in shape, very much resembling in form an inverted L. It extends from the western limits of Greenville Precinct to the Madison County line, with Cottonwood Precinct extending along its northern boundary and Pocahontas Precinct bounding it on the south. The entire surface is sufficiently rolling, so that artificial means of drainage is unnecessary. Some of the land, however, along the creeks is low, or so very rugged that it can only be used for grazing purposes, and is not susceptible of cultivation, but the farming lands are nearly level, or but slightly undulating. The soil is of the finest quality, and yields abundant harvests of all crops usually grown in this latitude. The principal products are wheat, corn and oats, which indeed are almost the *only* products.

The residences throughout this precinct are mostly good, substantial buildings, though very little attempt is made at the elegance displayed in older and longer settled countries, but the finely cultivated farms bespeak the success which has attended those who were fortunate enough to secure a footing here, when land was much cheaper. The original timber consisted of hickory, oak, ash, poplar, walnut, sugar maple, and the present growth is much the same, though a great deal of the original timber has fallen before the industrious hand of the settlers. The water-courses flowing through Ripley Precinct are Shoal Creek, the only one of any importance which enters from the north and flows across the precinct in a southeasterly direction. There are also two small creeks, both known as Dry Fork, one coming from the south and the other from the north, and, uniting, flow about three-quarters of a mile into Shoal Creek. Shoal Creek has a number of other small tributaries, hardly worth mentioning.

The early settlement of Ripley Precinct is

By Taylor J. Riley

somewhat involved in obscurity, but prominent among those of whom anything is known was Anderson Hill, who came from South Carolina, in the time of the Indians, and settled upon the farm now owned by John Davis. His son, Anderson Hill, Jr., then but a child, came with his father and afterward settled upon the farm now owned by William Brown, where he lived until his death, which occurred in 1853. Moses File was also among the early settlers, coming from North Carolina and settling about seven miles west of Greenville in 1818. His son, John N. File, now owns the old home farm. The Wheelock Brothers came from the East, in 1812, and founded the town known as "Old Ripley," which in early times was quite a trading post, people coming from within a radius of fifty miles to do their trading. The town was founded upon a farm belonging to a Mr. Lust, of Edwardsville, now owned by William Brown, and numerous signs are still visible, though the buildings have long since been torn down or moved away, the ruins of old blacksmith shops and several old wells alone remaining to mark the site of this once prosperous village. Dr. Baker came about this time, and occupied the house now owned by the Widow Jandt. He was the first person buried in the old Brown Graveyard, where many weary mortals are now resting. Numerous descendants of the above-named early settlers still live in this precinct, and the farms of their forefathers, which were then a wilderness, have indeed been made to "blossom as the rose." Other families continued to move into the community just described, until the war of 1812 put a slight check on immigration for a time, but after its close it commenced again with renewed vigor. Glowing accounts were carried back to the older settlements of the richness and fertility of this new country, which brought many of the sturdy backwoodsman of Virginia and North Carolina, accustomed from their earliest childhood to lives of self-dependence, and in whom had been generated a contempt of danger and a love for the wild excitement of an adventurous life. "We of the present day, accustomed to the luxuries and conveniences of a highly civilized state of society, lapped in the soft indolence of a fearless security, accustomed to shiver at every blast of winter's wind, and to tremble at every noise, the origin of which is not perfectly understood, can form but an imperfect idea of the motives and influences which could induce the early pioneers of the West to forsake the safe and peaceful settlements of their native States and brave the unknown perils and undergo the dreadful privations of a savage and unreclaimed wilderness."

In early times, the procuring of bread was a source of great anxiety to the settlers, and when the first white people came to this country they found none of the conveniences of to-day. An enterprising settler named Lee was the first to erect a mill. It was built on Shoal Creek, where Brown's Mill now stands, over sixty years ago, and for many years supplied the settlers of Ripley Precinct with corn meal and a scanty supply of flour. All signs of this mill have entirely succumbed to the lapse of time, and where it once was there now stands a thriving grist-mill, which was erected in the year 1840, by Benjamin and Henry Brown. When this mill was first built, it was used only for sawing lumber, but in 1847 William Brown purchased the interest of Henry Brown (his cousin), and he and Benjamin Brown put in machinery for grinding grain, and for thirty-five years this vicinity has been filled with the merry din of the wheels of "Brown's Mill." A few years later a saw and grist mill was built on Shoal Creek, about three and one-half miles below Brown's Mill, by William Hunter, which was afterward purchased by Wesley Bilyew who ran it for several years. No traces of this mill at present remain. At an early date a tannery was built on the farm now owned by William Brown, though the builder's name could not be ascertained, and only an old vat, or two remain to mark the place where it once stood. A distillery, supposed to have been built by the Wheelocks about 1813, once stood near where Brown's Mill now stands, though one looking at the place to-day would scarcely imagine it ever to have been the scene of an active industry.

One particular in which Ripley Precinct is sadly deficient is its roads, which are very little superior to the early day "trails" or "traces." The first road of any importance was the old "Vandalia road," which is but little better now than it was then, being the same old, unimproved dirt road, and in the spring becomes almost impassable. It is an old road, and as there are no pikes in the precinct, it is very much used. Another road which has been used as a highway since an early date, is the "Pocahontas and Ripley road," but its unimproved condition renders travel upon it anything but comfortable.

The first bridge constructed in this precinct was over Shoal Creek, on the "Vandalia road," and was made of wood. It has been washed away twice and rebuilt of wood, and it was washed away the third time in 1875, and rebuilt of iron, the same year. In April of the present year (1882), this iron bridge was washed away, but was caught and replaced in June, without any material damage having been done. This bridge is the only one ever built in the precinct.

For many years, an old tradition has been going the rounds in this vicinity to the effect that the Spanish, who lived here at a very early date, had buried three barrels of silver dollars in that portion of Ripley Precinct known as "Shoal Creek bottom," on land now owned by Thomas B. File. So much credit has been placed in this tale that the three barrels of Spanish dollars have been often sought for, and numerous places give evidence of having been dug up, in the vigorous search for this mythical fortune. An old gentleman named Bates living near New Berlin, claims to know where this "hoard" is located, but the thinking portion of the inhabitants place no credit in it. It is also stated that the Indians who inhabited this region in an early day have been heard to say that "if the people of Shoal Creek bottom knew what *they* did, they could shoe their horses with silver."

The precinct of Ripley cannot boast of many churches. The first one erected was "Mount Nebo," built by the Baptists, in 1835. The church was organized on the 9th of February, 1832, at the residence of John Coyle, on Round Prairie, by Rev. Peter Long, assisted by Thomas Smith, of Madison County, and with twenty-three members, several of whom were subsequently turned out for unfaithfulness. At a meeting in March of the same year, Rev. Peter Long was chosen pastor, in which capacity he served for over forty years, and, in 1874, in his seventieth year of age, on account of his enfeebled condition, he resigned his pastorate, though he is still a member of the same church. Since its organization, the membership has run up as high as 130, and during this time two other churches have been organized out of it. Since the resignation of Rev. Peter Long, the pastors have been: Rev. W. C. Harvey, A. J. Sitton, John H. Jones, who filled the pulpit for about three years, and J. B. White, who is the present pastor, with a membership of about sixty. Their first church building was constructed of hewn logs, and was an enormous affair, said to have been the largest log building ever built in the county. About 1850, it was replaced by a frame house, which was destroyed by fire in 1852, by ashes being put in a keg and igniting. Late the same year the frame edifice, which at present occupies the site, was erected. No other churches have been built in Ripley Precinct until the present year (1882), when the Presbyterians led by Rev Thomas Hynes, erected a beautiful little church of brick in the village of New Berlin. The organization is as yet quite small, but supports a very good Sunday school, and is in a flourishing condition. Quite recently, also, the Regular Baptists have built a frame church on the "Vandalia road," about two miles east of New Berlin. Their membership only numbers about twenty souls, and their church is presided over by no regular pastor. For nearly twenty years the African Baptists, numbering about twenty members, have been worshiping in a little log church on "Shoal Creek Hill," near New Berlin, but have never had a regular pastor.

The subject of education and the building of schoolhouses were paid very little attention to by the early settlers in Ripley Precinct. For many years school was had in a small way around at the houses of the settlers. The first schoolhouse erected in this precinct was built on the old "Lee Wait farm," in 1830. For some time, it was taught by Thomas Armstrong, and afterward, the tutorship was assumed by Peter Long. At present, nothing remains to show where this old pioneer schoolhouse was located. The instruction given the pupils at this time was of the most primitive character, embracing only the most common of the school branches, such as reading, writing, spelling and a knowledge of the rudimentary principles of mathematics. There are at present six schoolhouses in Ripley Precinct, namely: Round Prairie Schoolhouse, present teacher, F. W. Fritz; Ray's Schoolhouse, present teacher, Henry Dixon: the Baker Schoolhouse, presided over by Miss Bunn; the Ripley Schoolhouse, teacher, George H. Donnell; the Mount Vernon Schoolhouse, teacher, R. O. White, and the Terrapin Ridge Schoolhouse, presided over by Millard Dixon. Of late years, the subject of education has received much more attention than it did in an earlier day; efficient teachers are employed at reasonable salaries and many of the higher branches are taught.

New Berlin, the post office name of which is Old Ripley, is the only village in this precinct. It was founded in September, 1850, by Charles Plog and Mathias Brown, and is located on a part of the south half of Section No. 8, Town 5 north, of Range 4 west, of the Third Principal meridian, near the old "Vandalia road." The originial plat contained twenty-four lots, 50x120 feet in dimensions, and, in June, 1866, H. G. Jandt made an addition of sixteen lots, of the same dimensions as those in the original plat. Mr. Jandt was among the first residents in New Berlin, and for probably twenty years kept a general merchandise store. I. V. Long also was engaged in the general merchandising business about this time. William Lytle built and ran the first tavern, and kept in connection with it a small stock of groceries, and retailed liquors. The monotonous quiet, which always exists about a small village, was relieved in New Berlin by the merry clanging of the hammer of Ferdinand Gauzer, the first village blacksmith, and every Sunday divine service was held in his shop, led by the Rev. Thomas Hynes. H. G. Jandt kept the first post office in the rear end of his store. The present Postmaster is R. O. White, who is also engaged in teaching the "young idea how to shoot" at the Mount Vernon Schoolhouse. At present, New Berlin is a thriving little hamlet of about one hundred and fifty inhabitants, mostly Germans, and is considerable of a trading-point, the business enterprises consisting of two general merchandise stores, one brick drug store, two blacksmith-shops, two wagon-makers' shops, two shoe shops, two saloons, a steam grist and saw mill, owned by Mrs. Cox, and a neat, comfortable hotel, owned by Mrs. Mary Arnold. No secret societies exist in New Berlin as yet, though a number of the inhabitants are members of organizations in the neighboring towns.

CHAPTER XIV.*

MULBERRY GROVE PRECINCT—PHYSICAL, TOPOGRAPHICAL AND DESCRIPTIVE—EARLY SETTLEMENT—REV J. B. WOOLARD AND OTHER PIONEERS—FIRST BIRTH, MARRIAGE, ETC.—THE BEGINNING OF ALL THINGS—CHURCHES AND SCHOOLS—VILLAGE OF MULBERRY GROVE—WHEN LAID OUT—GROWTH, DEVELOPMENT, ETC., ETC.

"A song for the early times out West,
And our green old forest home."
—*The Old Pioneer*.

MULBERRY GROVE PRECINCT is rather diminutive in size, and its citizens, as has been said of those of the State of Rhode Island, when they want to communicate with each other, do not write letters or send messages, but go out in the yard and call to them. Though small in extent, it is fine land, well adapted to cultivation, and numbers some excellent farms. It is mostly level prairie, with a few hills along the small water-courses which intersect it. It contains a fractional part of two townships; a portion lying in Township 5, the remainder in Township 6, Range 2 west, and is bounded on the north by Zion Precinct, on the east by Fayette County, on the south by Fairview Precinct, and on the west by Greenville and Zion Precincts. The land is watered and drained by Owl Creek, Lick Creek, Town Branch, Seagraves' Branch, and a few smaller streams that are nameless on the maps. The streams drain the land sufficiently, without the farmers having to resort to artificial means. More or less timber bordered the water-courses, consisting of the species common to this section. The precinct has the advantage of the Vandalia Railroad, which passes nearly across the center, with a station at the village of Mulberry Grove, whence large shipments are made of the surplus products of the surrounding country. Upon the whole, this little division, called Mulberry Grove Precinct, ranks among the best and most prosperous portion of Bond County.

The first settlement or improvement made in what is now known as Mulberry Grove Precinct was made about the year 1826 by Zopher Foster, on the place now occupied by Rev. James B. Woolard. The next settlers after Foster were John Bilyew and Duncan Johnson, who came in about 1829-30, and were from Tennessee. Rev. James B. Woolard, from North Carolina, was the next permanent settler. He came to the country in 1831, and purchased the improvements of Zopher Foster, where he has resided ever since—a period of more than fifty years.

Mr. Woolard has lived an active life, and been closely identified with Bond County throughout a long period of time. From a published sketch of his life, we extract a few facts and incidents that will probably interest the reader, and without which a history of Bond County would scarcely be complete. He was born in North Carolina, but brought up principally in Tennessee, and, as we have said, came to Bond County in 1831, locating upon the place where he still lives. In the spring of 1832, the next year after he came here, upon the call of Gov. Reynolds for volunteers for the Black Hawk war, he enlisted as one of the fifty men comprising the quota of Bond County. For the money received for his services in the

*By W. H. Perrin.

campaign, he entered his first forty acres of land, being that upon which he lives, and to which, in a few years, by industry and economy, he was enabled to add, until he was the owner of 600 acres in a body. He was one of the Judges of the first election held in his part of the county, and when a post office was established in 1834–35, he was appointed Postmaster.

Of his religious life, much might be said which space will not permit. In the summer of 1823, he made a profession of religion, joined the Methodist Episcopal Church, served as class leader and licensed exhorter. In the fall of 1829, was licensed a local preacher; his first license was signed by Rev. Peter Cartwright, Presiding Elder. In 1834, was ordained Deacon by Bishop R. R. Roberts. In the fall of 1836, was received as an itinerant in the Illinois Conference, and was appointed to the Carlyle Circuit, in the bounds of which he lived. In 1837, to Grafton Circuit, and in 1838 to Carlinville. In 1839, was ordained Elder by Bishop Morris, and appointed to the Carlinville Station; 1840, to Staunton; 1841 again to Carlyle, 1842 to Shelbyville, 1843, to Sharon. On account of his aged and feeble parents and young family depending upon him, in 1844 he asked and obtained a location from the annual conference. He continued laboring diligently as a local preacher until the fall of 1853; after he had buried his aged father, who died in his eighty-fifth year, and made comfortable provision for his mother, he again entered the itinerancy in the Southern Illinois Conference, was appointed agent for McKendree College, and removed to Lebanon. In the fall of the same year, was appointed to Trenton Circuit; 1854 to Shiloh, and again, in 1855, to Shiloh. In 1856, to Fillmore; 1857 and 1858, to Salem; 1859 and 1860, to Middleton. In 1862, was appointed Chaplain in the One Hundred and Eleventh Illinois Volunteers. J. S. Martin, Colonel, in which capacity he served three years, but through exposure and fatigue of camp life, his health failed, and he came home at the close of the war with a broken constitution, not able to perform the labors of an itinerant minister. Yet his friends of the Conference continued him on the itinerant list as a superannuated member of the Southern Illinois Conference, and now, in the seventy-eighth year of his age, his voice still clear and strong, he frequently preaches and attends funerals.

Since his first settlement in the county, his home has been a welcome stopping-place for friends, and especially for ministers; none were ever turned away from his door. And now, full of years and full of honors, the hero of two wars, he is calmly awaiting the summons, "Well done, thou good and faithful servant," etc.

Other early settlers in Mulberry Grove Precinct were Richard Moody, James Dunaway, James Spradling, Mark Dunaway, Joseph Armstrong, Bennett Seagraves, Arthur Sherard, Drury Petty, Durham, Henry Inman, John Perkins and others. Durham settled on Section 12, and was from Tennessee. He has a son and a daughter living in Fayette County. Inman settled on Section 1, about the year 1830; Perkins, about the same year, settled on Section 10, and has several sons living in the county. Moody settled on Owl Creek, and was from the southern part of the State; the Dunaways settled east of Moody; also, Petty. The latter sold out to Spradling about 1830. Armstrong was a Tennesseean, and bought out Mark Dunaway. Sherard was also from Tennessee, and settled on Section 36, in 1833. In illustration of the healthfulness of the neighborhood, Mr. Woolard says that the first fifteen years he lived there, he did not pay $15 in doctors' bills, and although more than twenty different families have lived on the farm at different times, there has never been but one death on it since it was settled.

This comprises the sum and substance of

William Chapman

what we have obtained of the early settlement of this portion of Bond County. The story of the early trials of the pioneers may be found in other chapters of this work. What applies to them in one section of Southern Illinois is common in all parts of the State. Their life for years was hard, and beset with dangers and difficulties, but patience and perseverance, coupled with an indomitable will, carried them over safe, and wafted them on to wealth and prosperity.

John Bilyew, who is mentioned as one of the first settlers of the precinct, and who built his cabin near where the village of Mulberry Grove now stands, erected a horse mill at a very early day, upon or near the site of the present Methodist Church, which he operated for a good many years. It was a great benefit to the neighborhood, and continued to do good service until enfeebled by age, and it had became so frail and rickety that the customers had to withe in the cogs with hickory withes so that they could grind their corn. But it finally went "the way of all the earth," and a good steam mill now occupies its place in the business of the community.

Everything must have a beginning, and in Mulberry Grove Precinct, the increase of population began by the birth of a daughter to the wife of Zopher Foster, the first settler, and was the first birth in the precinct. The first marriage was a daughter of Arthur Sherard. She was married by Duncan Johnson, who was the first Justice of the Peace, but who she married we did not learn. The first election was held in the neighborhood under a tree near the dwelling of Bennett Seagraves, about 1833–34. Rev. J. B. Woolard and Drury Petty were the Judges of this election, and John Russell and William Hunter were candidates for the Legislature. The first sermon preached was by Rev. E. R. Ames, afterward Bishop Ames. The first post office was established about the year 1834–35, and J. B. Woolard was appointed Postmaster. From the great number of mulberry trees standing around his cabin in which the post office was held, he gave it the name of Mulberry Grove, a name it still bears, and which has been given both to the village and precinct.

As soon as a sufficient number of people had settled in the neighborhood, a schoolhouse was built and a school established. This schoolhouse was of the regular pioneer type, being of the rudest architecture, and having the usual puncheon floor, stick chimney, and great, wide fire-place. The school was taught on the subscription plan, as was the custom then, but the name of the first teacher was not obtained. On Sunday, the building was used as a temple of worship, where the pioneers gathered to hear the word. Near this house a cemetery was laid out, and the first person who died in the precinct (Mrs. Margaret Riley) was buried in it. Since then, many of the pioneers have been buried there. Arthur Sherard was one of the early school teachers, but we do not know if he was the first one. There are now three schoolhouses in the precinct, besides that in the village of Mulberry Grove. Education has advanced considerably since the building of the rude schoolhouse described above, as the present handsome and comfortable houses now in use, and the excellent schools taught annually in them truthfully attest.

Bethlehem Baptist Church was originally organized July 10, 1830, on Hurricane Creek, in Fayette County. Among the first members were D. E. Deane, James Street, Willis Dodson, Larkin Cragg and Henry Sears. In a few years, a great many others united and it became strong in numbers. Elder Dodson preached the first sermon; the first Clerks were Joseph Williams and James Ferrell. The first meetings were held at the houses of the brethren alternately. The church was "dissolved" in Fayette County, June 11, 1835, and in 1837 the first meeting of the congregation was held in Bond County, the church to be called Bethlehem. The church house was built in the fall of the same year. Elder John Crouch was the first minister; the present, Elder John Lawler, and the present Clerk, J. H. Taylor; meetings, the second Saturday of each month.

The village of Mulberry Grove was surveyed and laid out April 28, 1841, by Asahel Enloe, for Francis Gill, the proprietor of the land upon which it stands. It is the second largest town in the county, and from the records seems to have been first called Houston, but afterward changed to Mulberry Grove. It is situated on the Vandalia Railroad, about eight and a half miles from Greenville. Contiguous to it on the east (in Fayette County), and lying on Hurricane Creek, is a fine body of timber, while north, west and south is a thickly settled country, in a fine state of cultivation, rendering this an excellent shipping point for grain, stock and other products of the farmers.

The first house in Mulberry Grove was built by David Hubbard, several years prior to the laying-out of the town. In this house, he and a man named Dewelly kept a store, the first in this part of the county. Hubbard also built a steam mill in the fall of 1837, which succeeded Bilyew's old horse-mill, already described. It was a custom mill, and did a good business. A saw-mill was added, and the two were carried on until about 1850. In April, 1869, the present mill was built It was first started as a saw-mill by E. W. and C. E. Dee, brothers. The saw-mill was sold in 1872, and moved to Fairview, flour-mill machinery having been put in by the Dees in 1870. C. E. Dee is the present proprietor, having bought the remaining half-interest in 1873. The mill is operated by a twenty-five horse-power engine, has two run of buhrs, and makes "straight grade" flour only. The first blacksmith was David Elam, just across the line. He did all the work for this neighborhood, as well as a large portion of Fayette County. The first school in the village was taught by Arthur Sherard, and the first church society was that of the Methodists. The town at present shows the following business: Three or four general stores, grocery stores and drug stores, blacksmith, wagon, carpenter and shoe shops, flour and saw-mill, several physicians, two churches, and an excellent school. The population is about 500 souls

The Methodist Episcopal Church at Mulberry Grove was organized by Rev. J. B. Woolard, about the year 1830, with a membership of six, besides himself and wife; the others were Duncan Johnson and wife, John Bilyew and wife and Zopher Foster and wife; Duncan Johnson was the first class-leader, and Revs. William Chambers and Wilson Pitman the first ministers. This church has since grown to a large congregation from which several other churches have been formed. The old log schoolhouse, already mentioned, was the first place of worship, and served as a church for several years. The first church building was erected in 1841, on the site of the present church, and occupied by the congregation until 1866, when the present brick church was built at a cost of about $3,000. The present pastor is Rev. J. W. McGriff, and John Riley, class-leader. The first Sunday school was organized by Duncan Johnson in 1834, and has been kept up pretty nearly ever since: the present superintendent is John Riley the school is well attended, and both it and the church are prosperous and healthy. This church was included in the first circuit ever traveled by Rev. E. R. Ames, afterward Bishop Ames, of the Methodist Episcopal Church.

The Christian Church, or "Church of Christ," as it is called, was organized in the year 1865, by Elder John A. Williams of Salem, Ill. The only two members living here at the time of the formation of the church were A. J. Leigh and Elizabeth Hensley, but this did not deter them from organizing a society, on the Bible principle perhaps, that "where two or three are gathered together in my name' etc. Elder Williams preached for the church about seven years after it was formed, and is now preaching for it. The membership is about eighty, with a good attendance. A large and flourishing Sunday school is maintained, of which J. B. Rodecker is Superintendent.

Charity Lodge, No. 1,733, Knights of Honor, was organized in August, 1879, and has been in operation ever since. The meetings are held in Prather's Hall on the first and third Saturdays of each month. The present officers are: C. Ormsworthy, Dictator; C. A. Ragland, Past Dictator; W. B. Hutchison, Financial Reporter; S. G. Gillian, Guide; C. C. Simmons, Vice Dictator; have about twenty-six members.

Mulberry Grove village is provided with excellent schools. The school has been graded for the past eight years. There are two school buildings—one brick and the other a modern frame, two stories high, costing about $2,600. Three teachers are employed, and the average general attendance is about one hundred and fifty children.

CHAPTER XV.*

POCAHONTAS PRECINCT—TOPOGRAPHY AND DESCRIPTION—ITS EARLY SETTLEMENT—FIRST PIONEERS—THE PLANTS AND JOHNSONS—THE OLD METHODIST CHURCH—THE TOWN OF POCAHONTAS—OTHER VILLAGES—SCHOOLS, CHURCHES, ETC.

"O sprecht! warum zogt ihr von donnen?
Das Neckarthal hat Wein und Korn;
Der Schwarzwald steht voll finstres Tannen,
Im Spessart klingt des Alplers Horn."

THE Precinct of Pocahontas lies in the southwest corner of Bond County, and is bounded on the north by Ripley Precinct, on the east by Beaver Creek Precinct, on the south by Clinton County, and on the west by Madison County. Most of the surface of this precinct is level prairie land, especially the western half. The eastern portion, however, is somewhat higher and more rolling, and well adapted to agriculture. The only broken or rough land is found along the borders of the creeks and water courses, and is mostly devoted to grazing.

The timber consists of oak, ash, elm, walnut, hickory, etc. The original timber has been mostly cut down for building and various other purposes, and the present timber is a younger growth. The water-courses of Pocahontas Precinct are all small. The most important stream is Shoal Creek, which flows in rather a southerly direction across the precinct, near its center. It has a number of branches and tributaries, all of which are small and of but little importance. A small stream called Locust Fork flows through the southern part, and near it is Dry Branch; both of these are very small.

Prominent among the pioneers who first located in this precinct was William Burgess, who came in shortly after the war of 1812, and settled just south of where Millersburg now is, on Sections 22 and 27. He was a volunteer in this war, and has no descendants living here at present. Joseph Critchfield, another very early settler, came in about the same time, and located on Section 25. His wife was for some time an inmate of the old fort (in Beaver Creek Precinct, and referred to elsewhere). He has still one descendant, Mrs. Prichett, living in the county. Joseph Bilyew, another early pioneer, came to this State prior to the war of 1812, and settled in Madison County. In 1817, he moved to this precinct and settled on Section 10. He has several great-grandchildren, at present residing in this county. A family named Coles settled east of where Millersburg now is, about 1820. John Bilyew came in as early as 1822, and settled on the land where Frank Meyers now lives (near Pocahontas). He afterwards sold this farm to William Mills. James Nance settled on Section 27, in 1820. Samuel Lee came in prior to Nance, and located in the same neighborhood. William Reams came in 1830, and settled in Section 28. A man named Rolten settled southwest of where Millersburg now is, about 1822, but on account of ill health he soon after moved away. John Powers settled on Section 25 in 1820, but at present has no descendants living here.

About this time three brothers, Andrew George and James Green, located on Shoal Creek a little above Powers. David White, after whom White's Fort received its name, settled near them late in the same year. Isaac

* By F. J. Riley

Reed settled a little farther up the creek on Section 10 in 1820. The Johnsons and Williamson Plant settled near where Pocahontas now is during the same year.

About 1833, Benjamin Johnson, accompanied by five brothers, Duncan, Charles, James P., Hugh and John P., came in and located near where the town of Pocahontas now stands. Benjamin was a large land owner, and at one time was a member of the Legislature from this district. He lived here until his death, which occurred in 1861. There are a number of the descendants of the Johnsons living here at present. About this time, came the Sugg family and the Gillespie family, from Tennessee, and the Ridgeways from Ohio. Two men, named Weise and Stoekley, settled in the southwest part of the precinct in 1833. Josiah File came in 1837, and was followed, in 1840, by Edward Ellis, who is now the largest land owner in the precinct.

The early industries in Pocahontas Precinct were of the most primitive pattern. Among the first was a mill, built on Shoal Creek by Thomas Stout about the year 1831. It was a saw-mill, run by water-power, but a small attachment for grinding purposes was afterward put in, which did not prove much of a success. The mill ceased operations in 1870, and has done nothing since. William Burgess ran a small copper still on a spring branch on Section 26, but it ceased to live in 1828. About the time the town of Pocahontas was laid out, Duncan Johnson built a mill on Shoal Creek, but it has long since ceased to exist.

In early times, a great excitement was created on account of a belief that gold and silver was to be found in Bond County. To add to this excitement, Robert Gillespie, a settler who lived on Shoal Creek, a few miles above where the town of Pocahontas now stands, found some shining particles in a spring near his house and gathering them carefully together, he took them to St. Louis, and showed them to a fellow who pronounced them gold. For some time after this the fever ran high, but as time gradually elapsed and no more was found, the search was finally abandoned.

The Methodist Episcopal denomination organized a church at the house of Charles Johnson about the year 1820. Among the early members were Charles Johnson, the Plant family, the Williams family, Harley Valentine and wife, and a part of the Bilyew family. Among the first class leaders was Henry Williams. The first church was built south of where the town of Pocahontas is now located, near where the depot now stands, sometime during the year 1826. It was a log building of the most primitive structure. About 1835, this organization erected a new frame church three and one-quarter miles west of the old log church. The next church was built in the village, in 1854. It was a frame building, 50 feet long and 34 feet in width, and cost about $1,500. The ground was donated by Benjamin Johnson, with the proviso that it should be open to all denominations, except Catholics and Mormons.

The town of Pocahontas was surveyed on the 21st day of March, 1838, by T. S. Hubbard, for Benjamin Johnson, the proprietor. It is located in Section 3, Township 4 north, Range 4 west, nine miles southwest of Greenville, on the Vandalia Railroad. The town was first called Amity, and the post-office name was Hickory Grove. When this town was laid out Mr. Johnson (the founder) made provision that no lots were to be sold to any one unless they would agree not to handle liquors of any kind in any way. It is a well-known fact, that the Germans like their beer, and as most of the settlers were Germans, instead of locating in Pocahontas, they went to Highland, a neighboring village, and settled there. The plan proved to be a bad one, and after a few years it was abandoned.

Benjamin Johnson was the first Postmaster, and the first hotel was run by P. W. Lampkins in 1837. Benjamin Johnson owned the first blacksmith shop, and it was run by a smith named Herron. The first store was a general merchandise establishment owned by Benjamin Johnson and Dr. Fitch, in 1836. Dr. Griffith was the first physician, about 1843, and the first church building was erected in 1852 by the Methodist denomination.

At present Pocahontas is a flourishing village of a little over four hundred inhabitants. It contains three churches, a flouring mill, owned by W. S. Wait, one furniture store, one agricultural implement store, the Union Hotel, kept by William Justi, and the Western Hotel, kept by Henry Idler, three blacksmith shops, two wagon-maker's shops, one harness shop run by Frank Senn, two millinery establishments, one barber shop. Leopold Knobel and Joseph Leibler buy grain, and John Snyder and John Meyers deal in stock. There are also two dry-goods stores and one grocery store. A. A. Simms is the Justice of the Peace, and Drs. John Gordon and J. R. Clinton represent the medical fraternity. The present Postmaster is H. C. Challis.

But little need be said concerning the schools of Pocahontas. The land on which the first school building was erected was donated by Benjamin Johnson for the purpose of building an academy thereon. At its completion, in 1854, it was put in the charge of Prof. Cavanaugh (a minister), of Lebanon.

The first Trustees were Benjamin Johnson, N. Leaverton, W. Mills, B. Kavanaugh, P. Lampkins, D. Johnson and L. D. Plant, who gave it the name of Amity Academy. The academy was run according to the original plan for some time, but on account of its being so far in advance of the times, it was not sufficiently patronized to warrant the management in continuing it as an academy, and finally the project was given up. At present the building is used as the public school in District No. 4, and is the only school in the village of Pocahontas.

The "Gordon Lodge," of A., F. & A. M., was organized at Millersburg October 3, 1866, by Grand Master Bromwell, but in 1867 was moved to Pocahontas. The first officers were: James Gordon, W. M.; Edward Teter, S. W.; Robert Elegood, J. W.; R. J. Collin, Treasurer, and A. J. Gullick, Secretary. The charter members were: Sidney and Harvey Cole, William Casey, Robert Elegood, Bellfield Featherston, James Gordon, A. J. Gullick, Edward Teter, John C. Gordon, Isaac Howell, Jacob Lindley, J. M. Lucas, James Pigg, Franklin Pressgrove and P. C. Reed. The present officers are. S. H. Challis, W. M.; Joseph Dever, S. W.; J. M. Minor, J. W.; George Powell, Secretary; John Gordon, Treasurer; Morris Margood, S. D., and Joseph Hunter, J. D. The lodge at present has a membership of about twenty, is in a flourishing, prosperous condition, and has about $800 in the treasury. For some time after the removal of the lodge from Millersburg to Pocahontas, they held their meetings in the the schoolhouse, but since 1873 they have occupied a large, convenient lodge room of their own.

Lodge No. 177, of the Independent Order of Odd Fellows, was organized on the 12th day of October, 1855, by James Starr, the Grand Master of the State. The charter members were: R. K. Dewey, George H. Dewey, A. W. Greenwood, R. T. Sprague and J. F. Sugg. The first officers were: R. K. Dewey, N. G.; R. C. Sprague, V. G.; A. W. Greenwood, Secretary; and J. F. Sugg, Treasurer. The lodge held their meetings in the schoolhouse, until in the fall of 1873, when they moved into the hall they now occupy. The lodge is at present in good condition, having about twenty-two members, and $700 in the hands of their Treasurer. They built their hall in 1873, at a cost of about $3,000, but the building has since been purchased by S. H. Challis. The present officers are: H. E. Reed, N. G.; Joseph Noathammer, V. G.; John Robinson, Treasurer, and W. S. Wait, Secretary.

The A. O. of U. W. was organized by C. W. Sewell, District Deputy, in June, 1880. The charter members were: W. M. Hays, F. E Jandt, William Justi, Frank Meyer, James, Chiswell, J. M. Minor, Joseph Lawrence and John Neathammer, L. B. Long, William Bolt, Jacob Segar, Harmon Treadbar, Hartman Gruner, Perry Reed, Fred File, Philip Leibler, Frank Hochdafer, H. E. Reed, W. E. Smith, D. C. Heston and J. A. Hampton. The officers who have filled the places since the organization of the lodge are: W. M. Hays, M. W.; F. E. Jandt, Recorder; J. M. Minor, Financier; H. E. Reed, Receiver; W. E. Smith, P. M. W.; Fred File, Overseer, and William Justi, Foreman. At present, the lodge is in a thriving condition, and is growing steadily in popularity and members. They hold their meetings in the Odd Fellows hall, and have a regular attendance of about twenty-two members.

The Good Templar Lodge was organized February 9, 1881, with ninety charter members. The first officers were: Z. T. Hendricks, Worthy Chief; Miss Laura Stevens, Vice Worthy Chief; E. Balch, P. W.; H. Hatchet, Secretary; Miss Jennie Harned, Assistant; C. Phelps, Financial Secretary; Joseph Dever, Chaplain; E. Alderman, Marshal; Fannie Savage, assistant; John Savage, Outside Guard, and Miss Hannah Challis, Inside Guard. The lodge has at present a membership of about forty-five, and meetings are held regularly every Thursday evening in Remick's Hall. John Jett is the present Worthy Chief; E. Alderman acts as Secretary, and Mrs. Bridgewater is Treasurer.

The Catholic Church was organized in the spring of 1869, by Father Peter Peters. Among the first members were: John M. Gilmore and wife, Louis Loux and wife, Mr. Schwedenman and wife, George Hochdefer and wife, George Arnold and wife, George Hansilman and wife, father and two sons; Charles Kuebel and wife, Tom Ryan and wife, Charles Rovolt and Frank Rudolph and wife. The society worshiped in a private house, which they purchased and used as a place of worship until the erection of their present church building in 1872. It is a frame building fifty feet long and twenty-six feet in width, and cost about $2,400. It was dedicated by Bishop Battles. For some time after the organization of this church, it was under the care of the Franciscan priests of Teutopolis, Ill., but of late years it has been under the pastorate of regular priests. The first Trustees were Leo Eisenpris and John Senn. The present Trustees are Baptist Eisenpris, Timothy Coffee, Frank Senn and Fred Eisenpris. The Treasurer is Frank Senn, and the priest now in charge is Rev. A. Kersting. About forty families now belong to the church.

The United Baptist Church was organized on the 10th day of January, 1873, by Peter Long. The church was formed from members of the old Mount Nebo Church in Ripley Precinct. The first members were Albert Ray and wife, S. N. Jett, Agnes E. Jett, Mildred Wait, Mary Bridgewater, Catharine Harvey and W. C. Harvey. Albert Ray and S N. Jett were the first Deacons, and W. C. Harvey was the first clerk. The society worshiped at the houses of the members until in the spring of 1874; a church fifty feet long and thirty feet wide was erected at a cost of about $1,400. The first Trustees were Lee Wait, J. G. Scott and S. N. Jett. The present Trustees are N. Bridgewater and Louisa C. Gilmore. The church at present is under the pastorate of Rev. J. H. Jones, has about twenty-five members, and is in good running order. It belongs to the Apple Creek Association, over which Peter Long is Moderator. A flourishing Sunday-school is conducted in connection with the church, under the superintendency of Lawrence Stevens. An interesting Bible school of about fifty scholars is also taught regularly every Sunday.

Millersburg is a small village situated in the southern part of the precinct. It was laid off by William Burgess from Kentucky and received its name from a man named Charles Miller, who built the first mill. The first store was run by David C. Baldridge, who built the first house erected in the village. Fritz Hackick was the first blacksmith. At present it is a flourishing little hamlet of between one and two hundred inhabitants. It contains one store run by Peter Minges, three blacksmith shops, one wagon shop, run by John Dishouser; one schoolhouse and one saloon. The postoffice name is "Baden Baden," and Clem Williams is the present Postmaster. Only three mails are received each week. The mill is run at present by Peter Strife, and is doing only a moderate business. There are no churches in the town. Recently, for the convenience of citizens living in the southern part of the precinct, a sub-voting place has been established at Millersburg. This sub-voting precinct includes a part of the southern portion of Pocahontas Precinct, and a couple of tiers of sections off the western side of Beaver Creek Precinct, but as yet no lines have been made on our maps to indicate it, and it was doubtless made more for convenience than anything else.

Pierron, a small village of about one hundred inhabitants, is situated near the midway of the western boundary line of the county, a part of it lying in Bond County and a part in Madison County, though most of the business portion lies in this county. It was laid off in 1868, by J. Pierron, who built and ran the first store. August Pierron was the first Postmaster. At present the town is in a prosperous condition, and contains one store run by Suppiger & Utiger; two blacksmith shops, one on each side of the county line; two wagon shops; one elevator owned by Kuebel & Co.; three hotels, only one of which is in this county, namely, the "Oak Dale House." A. A. Pierron and Louis Schnert handle agricultural implements, and A. A. Suppiger is the present Postmaster.

CHAPTER XVI.

BEAVER CREEK PRECINCT—DESCRIPTION AND GENERAL TOPOGRAPHY—TIMBER AND WATER COURSES—EARLY SETTLEMENT—MANNERS AND CUSTOMS OF THE PIONEER TIMES—THE FIRST POST OFFICE, BLACKSMITH, STORES, ETC.—MILLS AND CARDING MACHINES—VILLAGES—EDUCATIONAL AND RELIGIOUS—CHURCHES, ETC.

THE precinct of Beaver Creek, to which this chapter is devoted, lies in the southern part of Bond County, directly south of Greenville, and comprises Township 4 north, Range 3 west, together with a tier of fractional sections along Shoal Creek on the western side of the precinct; thus giving it these fractional sections more than a regular Congressional township. The surface of the land is generally level, much of it originally being prairie. Along the margin of the streams it is somewhat hilly and broken, and was covered with timber when the country was first settled. The timber, which was that common in this section, has been considerably thinned out, and that planted by the settlers themselves now makes nearly as much show as the original growth. The precinct is drained by Shoal and Beaver Creeks, and their tributaries. Beaver Creek flows through the eastern part in a southerly direction, receiving numerous small streams in its course, while Shoal Creek drains the western portion. The precinct, as at present laid off, is bounded on the north by Greenville Precinct, on the east by Okaw, on the south by Clinton County and on the west by Pocahontas Precinct. It is as fine an agricultural district as can be found in this section; the people are an intelligent and industrious class, well educated, and rank among the best citizens of the county. The surplus products of the precinct find a market over the Vandalia Railroad, which passes near the northwest corner, but does not come within the limits. It has no lack of churches, schoolhouses and villages.

Settlements were made very early in the present precinct of Beaver Creek. The first white man of whom we have any account of making a settlement here was James Blizzard, in the winter of 1817-18, unless we except "Old Kenson," as he was called, and Cox, who was murdered by the Indians near the present town of Dudleyville. Of Old Kenson there is nothing but a vague tradition. It is said that he lived in a hollow sycamore tree in Shoal Creek bottom, near where the Vandalia Railroad now crosses (whether the "hollow sycamore" stood in this precinct or not we are unable to say), and that he was there during the war of 1812. When the few people then living in Bond County fled to the forts for safety from the Indians, "Old Kenson" remained in his "den," looking after his hogs, and hunting. When the war closed, and the people returned to their cabins, "Old Kenson," like the Arab, pulled up his hollow sycamore, or his tent—

"And as silently stole away,"

leaving no trace behind. What became of him or whither he went no one ever knew. He utterly refused to go into the fort with the other whites, alleging there was no real danger, and that the Indians would not molest him.

Mr. Blizzard made the first permanent set-

*By W. H. Perrin.

tlement, as we have said, in the winter of 1817–18. He settled on the northwest part of Section 7, near where the schoolhouse now stands. He has two sons living here, J. J. and William M. Blizzard; a daughter, Mrs. Harriet A. Gower, lives in Missouri. A Mr. James settled on Section 3, about 1825, and a man named Harlan settled near Dudleyville, on a place since owned by his son. A Mr. Hoffman, John Henry and A. G. Mills also settled near. Wilson Brown came in soon after Blizzard and settled on Section 6. Abraham McCurley and family settled on Section 3, in 1830. Richard Briggs came in with Wilson Brown and settled in the same neighborhood. McCurley has a daughter still living in Bond County—Mrs. Mary Woolard, wife of Rev. J. B. Woolard, of Mulberry Grove. Wilson Brown has two sons, Charles and Marion, living in the county. Andrew Green settled on Section 18, and was a blacksmith—the first perhaps in the precinct. James Kirkpatrick and Samuel G. Morse settled a little south of Harlan, and William Burgess settled on the west side of Beaver Creek, near the county line. As early as 1826, the Crutchfield brothers, Joseph and Jacob, settled on Section 30; they have descendants still living here. The Drake family, who were from Tennessee, settled on the same section. Durham and Phipps came in about 1826; Phipps has a daughter, Mrs. Goodson, and Durham a son, Gideon Durham, living in the neighborhood. John Henry was an early settler, and the first Postmaster in the precinct. The "old fort,' mentioned so extensively in preceding chapters of this work, stood on Section 7, the land now owned by the Byrnes heirs.

About the year 1826 or 1827, the McCaslands, James McCasland, and his sons, John and Hugh, came into the precinct. They were from Kentucky, and John settled on Section 11; Hugh settled on Section 23, but afterward moved on to Section 11. He finally moved to Montgomery County, where he now lives. A Mr. Harlan settled on Section 15 in 1825 and 1826. Andrew Mills and family, from Tennessee, settled on Section 14. Joseph Mills, a descendant, still lives in the precinct. A family of Browns came in early and settled on the same section with Mills. Balaam Metcalf, from Tennessee, settled on Section 14 about the year 1828. He has a son, Henry Metcalf, still living in the precinct. William Downing settled on Section 24, and afterward sold out to Allen. Joseph Meyers settled on Section 22. This comprises a list of the early settlers so far as we have been able to learn anything concerning them.

The first years in a new country are years of toil and hardship. It was particularly so in the early settling of Southern Illinois. There were no railroads then; no improved agricultural implements; no mills deserving of the name, and, indeed, no luxuries, and very few of the necessaries of life. Log cabins with puncheon floors; "hog and hominy;" the bar-shear plow, reaping-hook, and scythe and cradle were things with which the pioneers were altogether familiar fifty years ago in Bond County. We in this age of civilization and refinement and of peace and plenty, know little of what the early settlers had to contend with. The following incident will illustrate, to some extent, the dangers they were exposed to in the early days of this country: A man named Cox, who had built a cabin, near or a little below where the village of Dudleyville now stands, notwithstanding the remonstrances of the people, refused to take refuge in the forts during the war of 1812, but remained at his cabin several miles distant. He was a brave man, a celebrated Indian fighter (considering himself a match at any time for half a dozen "red skins"), and a thorough frontiersman. One day, during his absence, a party of Indians attacked his cabin, and, among other depredations, carried off his daughter a captive. She was rescued, however, a few hours later, without injury other than a severe fright. After this, he deemed it prudent to remove his family to the fort, but he persisted in visiting his cabin every day "to look after things," until the Indians finally looked after him. Going to his cabin one day as usual, accompanied by his little son, they were fired upon by a party of Indians, who had concealed themselves in the house, and were both killed. Their fate was a sad one, but was nothing more than had been anticipated and predicted by his friends. The incident, with its attending circumstances, is more particularly noticed in a preceding chapter.

The first settlers in this section had to go to Edwardsville to mill, an undertaking that sometimes occupied several days or weeks. The first mill in this precinct, of which we have any account, was a horse-mill built by William Downing, and was one of the early institutions of the community. For a number of years, it did good service, and was a great accommodation to the people. A carding-mill, or carding-machine, as they were more commonly called, was built by Milton Mills on Section 13, about 1823 and 1824, and was the first, not only in this precinct, but the first in the county. Before it was put in operation, the people carded their wool themselves on hand cards, or took it to Edwardsville. This mill was shipped here from Kentucky, and was successfully operated for a great many years. Other pioneer industries were confined to blacksmith shops, stores, and such other business as the wants of the time demanded. As the country settled up and improved, roads were laid out through the precinct to the different towns, bridges were built over the largest water-courses, which combined very materially to facilitate locomotion and transportation. The latter, in those days, was a very serious undertaking, as everything had to be transported by teams, and ox-teams at that, and several weeks, according to the state of the roads, were required to make a trip to St. Louis, then the principal market.

In 1869, a circumstance occurred near the little village of Dudleyville, which cast a gloom over the entire community. We allude to the brutal murder of Mrs. Louisa McAdams, in July of that year, by John Moore, a near neighbor. He went to her residence in the absence of her husband, grossly insulted her, and when she attempted to escape from him, he pursued her and cruelly murdered her by cutting her throat from ear to ear. For this crime, he was arrested, tried, convicted, and sentenced to be hanged by Judge Gillespie. He made a full confession of his guilt, which was afterward published, and, on the 23d of October, 1869, he expiated his crime upon the gallows, under the sentence of the court—the only execution that has ever taken place in Bond County.

There are two villages in Beaver Creek Precinct, viz.: Dudleyville and Wisetown. The former was surveyed and laid out by R. K. Dewey, for John Dudley, the proprietor of the land, March 14, 1857. It is situated on Section 3 of Township 4, Range 3, and is five miles from Greenville on the Carlyle road, surrounded by an excellent farming region. It bears the name of Dudleyville, for its founder and proprietor, and, for a small place does considerable business. Mr. Dudley inherited the land upon which the town stands, through his marriage with Fanny Blizzard, daughter of one of the early settlers of the precinct. He kept the first store opened in Dudleyville. Fred Kahn was the first blacksmith; H. C. Dunham was probably the first physician of the place, and F. Thraner was the first Postmaster. Thraner was among the very first settlers in Dudleyville, and built the best storehouse in the place, and which is still in use by W. D. Rockwell, the present merchant. About this time, a number of German families settled in the village, and opened shops of different kinds. F. Geries built a cooper shop, and John Schlup, a wagon shop. R. W. Chapman and brother came in soon after Kahn, and remained several years. There are now two blacksmith shops kept by Albert Keagy and A. W. Reed. The town now has about twelve families comprising some fifty inhabitants.

The Methodist Episcopal Church of Dudleyville was organized so long ago (about 1820 it is believed) that no one now can give the names of the original members, except James Blizzard and several members of his family. The church was originally organized at his house by (it is believed) Rev. Simeon Walker. Services were held at the house of Mr. Blizzard for several years, then at Rebecca Hoffman's, his daughter, and subsequently at schoolhouses. The church building was erected about 1856–57, and was a frame 26x40 feet. It cost $900, and was built upon land donated by John Dudley for the purpose. There were about fifty members when the church was built at Dudleyville, and the Rev. Daniel Oglesby was the minister, and J. J. Blizzard the class-leader. The membership is still about fifty; the Trustees, J. J. Blizzard, Thomas Harlan, Jesse McAdams and H. W. Blizzard; and the pastor, Rev. J. H. McGriff. A Sunday school continues the year round, of which J. J. Blizzard is Superintendent, and which has a regular attendance of about sixty persons.

The Free Methodist Church of Dudleyville was organized in the fall of 1880 by Rev. F. M. Ashcraft, and was originally composed of eight members as follows: P. M. Rogers and wife, Wilford Hockett, Ellen Upchurch, Charles Mayfield and wife, John Upchurch and James Garrett. The church edifice was built in the summer of 1881, is a frame 28x40 feet in size, and cost about $800. The first class-leader was Wilford Hockett; Trustees, P. M. Rogers, Wilford Hockett and James Garrett. The church has a membership at present of about twenty-five, under the pastorate of Rev. C. C. Bruner. Sunday school organized when the church was built; the first Superintendent was James Garrett; the present one, P. M. Rogers; attendance good.

The village of Wisetown, or Beaver Creek, as it is sometimes called, was surveyed and laid out March 14, 1860, by R. K. Dewey, for David W. Wise, the proprietor and founder. It is located on Section 26, about ten miles nearly south from Greenville, and five miles from Dudleyville. Although christened Wisetown for its founder, the post office is called Beaver Creek, after the name of the precinct, and first one name and then the other is applied to the village. It is quite a business little place, and is surrounded by a class of enterprising farmers. No saloon has ever been opened, which speaks well for its morals. There were a few houses here long before it was laid out as a town. A post office was early established, with John Henry as Postmaster; Samuel Avis was the first blacksmith, Peter Bostock the first wagon-maker, and —— Delkhaus the first shoemaker. Dr. O. E. Hornedy was the first physician of the village, and the first drug store was opened by Dr. Powell Gordon. The next physician of the place was Dr. D. A. Bailey, then came Dr. J. A. Warren, still here in practice. The place now has one store, kept by N. B. Harnes & Company; two blacksmith shops, A. J. Sapp and T. J. Sapp, each running a separate establishment; W. A. McNeil, undertaker, and also wagon-maker; drug store, kept by J. M. Harlan, and an excellent schoolhouse. The place consists of some twenty-five houses, and has about one hundred and fifty inhabitants.

Union Church, in the village of Wisetown, is composed of the following denominations, viz.: Methodist, Cumberland Presbyterian and Missionary Baptist, members of which had belonged to no organized body until the formation of this church, except the Methodists, who worshiped at a schoolhouse. The church building was erected in the summer of 1878, and is

32x48 feet. The ground upon which it stands was donated and deeded by Dr. J. A. Warren, on the following conditions: That the Methodists have it the first and third Sundays of each month, commencing at 6 o'clock P. M., preceding, and ending at 6 o'clock P. M. on Friday following these Sundays; the Baptists to have the same privilege, including the second Sunday, and the Presbyterians the fourth. The four extra Sundays in each year are divided up on the same principle. This plan was adopted by the donor of the land that no discord might arise as to the ownership of the church. The building cost $1,200; the Trustees are N. B. Harnes, D. C. Baldridge, J. M. Myers, A. J. Miller, E. B. Wise, J. A. Warren and Jesse Burch. A good Sunday school is kept up all the year round.

The precinct paid early attention to matters of education, and schools were established as soon as the country was sufficiently settled to justify the expense of paying teachers. The first schoolhouse of which we have any account was built on the present site of the town of Dudleyville, just in the rear of the old Methodist Church. It was a log building of the pioneer pattern, with puncheon floor, and the first school taught in it was by a man named Babcock. Another of the early schoolhouses was built on Section 26, a little south of the spring of the old camp-ground. The first school in it was taught by a man named P. G. Vawter. A school was taught about three miles west of Wisetown, in 1835, by a man named Tobey. There are now seven schoolhouses in the precinct, all of which are comfortable and commodious buildings, well-furnished and ventilated, and in which good schools are taught for the usual term each year by competent teachers.

The people of Beaver Creek Precinct are a religious people, if one may judge from its number of handsome churches, of which there are several in the precinct, outside of the villages of Dudleyville and Wisetown.

The first house in the precinct built exclusively for church purposes, and used also for a schoolhouse, was built at the old camp-ground on Section 26. The Baptists organized a church society here very early, and their church for some time had no floor except the ground; the pulpit was 6x8 feet in size, raised (the platform) about a foot above the ground, and the whole thing boarded up about to the preacher's shoulders, so that while speaking, only his head and arms could be seen. The people attended this church for miles and miles away. Camp-meetings were held here, when the worshipers came and camped upon the grounds until the meetings closed. Among the first ministers at this church were Revs. Arnot, Joseph Taylor, Semons, Jesse Ford, etc. The congregation worshiped here for many years, and then moved into a schoolhouse. Several denominations worshiped here also, but about 1866, religious services were discontinued, and the house was removed to Wisetown, where it is yet standing, being used for a dwelling. The members went elsewhere to worship, and joined themselves to other churches.

The German Methodist Church was built in 1865, and cost about $1,400. The society was first organized in 1850, and consisted of the following original members, viz.: George Ulmer and wife, John Hilde and wife, Elizabeth Dollanbach, Charles Dollanbach, Elizabeth Tishruser, Mary Dollanbach, John Danler and wife, Mathias Huffman, Elizabeth Barnridher and Conrad Peters. The first Trustees of the church were John Thoman, Henry Garke, Frederick Schubert, George Barnridher and Christian Dollanbach. The first minister was Rev W. Fiegenbaum, who organized the church; the membership is now about twenty-eight. A Sunday school was organized in 1870, of which George Ulmer was the first Superintendent. It continues the year round, and is at present under the superintendence of Henry Garke and Mr. Thoman.

Mount Carmel Methodist Episcopal Church stands on the southwest quarter of Section 20, and was organized in the early part of 1862, by J. J. Blizzard. The first regular minister was the Rev. Simeon Walker. Among the first members were J. J. Blizzard, Samuel J. Gilleland (class-leader), and others, amounting in all to about fifteen. The church edifice was erected in the fall of 1866, and was built of brick, costing about $960, and is a handsome little church building.

The Camp Ground Cumberland Presbyterian Church was quite early in the field—believed by some to have had a society here about 1826. Among the first members were the McAdamses, Goodsons, John Harris, William Harlan, etc. Early ministers were William Finley, Joel Knight, John Barber and Joseph Barlow. The society first worshiped in a log cabin, purchased of one of the first settlers named Durham. This house was used for several years, when the present house was built, probably about 1835, and is 24x30 feet in size. The organization is still kept up. The church property is deeded to the Board of County Commissioners for the benefit of the Cumberland Presbyterians. The present minister is Rev. Allison Hunter; the Sabbath school is kept up all the year.

CHAPTER XVII.

FAIRVIEW PRECINCT—INTRODUCTORY AND DESCRIPTIVE—THE NAME "FAIRVIEW"—TOPOGRAPHY AND PHYSICAL FEATURES—SETTLEMENT—ISAM REAVES AND OTHER PIONEERS—THE FIRST ELECTION—EARLY SCHOOLS AND SCHOOLHOUSES—RELIGIOUS—"OLD HURRICANE" AND OTHER CHURCHES—VILLAGE OF FAIRVIEW, ETC.

"The fairest among ten thousand,
And altogether lovely."

ONE in traveling through that part of Bond County known as Fairview Precinct, would scarcely realize that, less than a century ago, over these same rolling prairies, the red man roamed in all his savage glory, undisturbed save by rival tribes of his own race. That where now may be seen in every direction beautiful and well-improved farms, he hunted the buffalo, chased the deer, and shouted his blood-curdling war-whoop as he dashed in pursuit of his fleeing enemy. Since that time, the light of civilization has spread o'er the land. The "wigwam blaze" has been extinguished, and the red man has folded up his "tepee" and followed after the retreating herds of buffalo. This precinct as well as the other precincts of Bond County, partook of the change, and the vast prairie was transformed into blooming fields, and beautiful homes. Because of the beautiful view this precinct presents, it received the name of "Fairview," which appellation it rightfully deserves, being without doubt one of the prettiest landscapes in this portion of the "Sucker State."

Fairview Precinct comprises sixteen sections in the southeast corner of Township 5, Range 2 west, and is bounded on the north by Greenville and Mulberry Grove Precincts, on the east by Fayette County, on the south by Okaw Precinct, and on the west by Greenville Precinct. Its surface is mostly prairie, being gently rolling or undulating, except that portion which borders the water-courses, it being quite broken and very rugged in places. In some portions of the precinct, however, artificial means of drainage is necessary, but it is as fine an agricultural region as any part of Bond County, the land being rich and fertile and growing in value yearly. There is more timber in this section than there was originally, considerable having been planted by the early settlers. The original timber, very little of which is now left standing, is found almost exclusively along the numerous streams throughout the precinct, and consists principally of oak, ash, hickory, walnut, etc. Most of the precinct is devoted to agriculture and grazing, the principal crops produced being corn, oats and wheat.

Until recently, very little attention has been paid to stock-raising in this section, but the fine grazing facilities of the country induced some of the more enterprising residents to embark in this branch of farming, and of late years the stock has been very much improved.

Numerous small streams contribute to the productiveness of the soil of this precinct the most important of which is Sanders' Branch, which rises in the northwestern corner of the precinct and flowing a little south, and then directly east leaves the precinct near the section line dividing Sections 13 and 24. Its strongest tributary is Booker's Branch, which

By W. H. Perrin.

rising in the northern part of Section 10, of Greenville Precinct, flows in a southeasterly direction into Sanders' Branch, which it enters in the southeast corner of Section 14 of Fairview Precinct. Several other streams flow through various parts of the precinct, but they are so small as to scarcely deserve being named.

The settlement by white people of Fairview Precinct extends so far back into the past that it is somewhat difficult to obtain reliable data in regard to the original pioneers. Among the first white men to locate here, probably, was Isam Reaves, who came here from Maryland with his family prior to the war of 1812. Some time after this the Reaves family removed to Kentucky, near Bowling Green, and, after remaining there for awhile, again moved to this State and settled in Madison County, near Collinsville. In 1832, Isam Reaves again moved to this county and settled in what is now Fairview Precinct. He died on the old Reaves farm, which he entered at a cost of 50 cents per acre. He participated in the war of 1812, on the Beaver Creek side. In one of the battles, two of his comrades named Prewitt and Gratts were killed by the Indians, and Joseph Gratts' father, Thomas Higgins and William Burgess were wounded. Gen. Whitesides was also wounded at the same time. This occurred about the close of the war. Hiram Reaves, the son of Isam Reaves, was born in this county, four miles south of Greenville, and within one mile of the old fort on Shoal Creek, on the 10th of June, 1816, and is probably the oldest resident now living in the county who was born in it. He resides in the southeast corner of Fairview Precinct, and is totally blind. Some time after the advent of Isam Reaves, in 1829, came William Harper, Thomas L. Harper, Elisha Mathews and John Reaves, all from Tennessee. John Reaves settled on Section 11, on the farm now owned by Mrs. Booker. William Harper settled on the northeast quarter of Section 22, where J. M. Harper now resides. John Reaves and William Harper both died in this township, and both have descendants now living here. Reaves has two sons and two daughters at present residing in this county. Among the early settlers were also Jerry Stubblefield, Henry Brown and three brothers named Jordan, Morgan and William Murray. About this time came the Long family. There were three brothers of them, namely, Abner, Joseph and John, who settled on the northeast quarter of Section 22. They afterward separated, Joseph settling on Section 15 on land now owned by J. M. Harper, and John settling on the land now owned by D. Cable. Abner being a "potter" and a maker of earthenware, floated about from place to place, plying his trade, until 1840, when they all "pulled up stakes" and moved to Missouri, leaving no descendants in this county.

Isaac Snodgrass came in with the Longs and located on Section 15, on land now owned by Charles Bowman. He was a Justice of the Peace, and was probably the first Justice in this section of the county, but he has no descendants living here now. In the spring of 1832, the Bates family, headed by Anson, came and settled on Section 22. He had a brother Samuel, who came shortly after him, and settled on the same section. John Crouch, a Baptist minister, also came at an early day and settled on the northeast quarter of Section 23, on the land now owned by E. Perkins. He was followed soon afterward by James Clark and Maj. William Davis, who settled on Section 22, and John H. Taylor, who settled on the east half of Section 13. In the spring of 1830, two men named Fisher and McKee came in and settled on Section 22. Ben Jewett entered Section 27, and Andy and John Williams settled on Sections 36 and 25, respectively. In 1820, Isaac Jones and John Williams came with their families from Virginia, the former settling near the Fayette County line,

Jacob Gress

on the east half of Section 24, and the latter settled on Section 13. They have no descendants in this county now, except one nephew named Winslow Taylor. Then, in 1827, John Lockhart came from Maury County, Tenn., and settled on Section 11, on the farm where L. J. Segraves now lives, where he resided until 1841, when he removed to Arkansas. He has one daughter, Nancy, the wife of L. J. Sellers, residing at Mulberry Grove, this county Then came Bennett Segraves, from Georgia, in the spring of 1829, and located in the northeast corner of Section 11, where he remained until his death, which occurred in 1868. His son, Lockhart J. Segraves, succeeded him, and now lives on the old home farm.

The first election ever held in Township 5, Range 2, was held in the brush, near the cabin of Bennett Segraves, in August of 1835. The people cast their votes in the old-fashioned manner, by calling out the name of the candidate whom they desired to vote for, and their own name, a register of the same being kept by a clerk, appointed for that purpose.

It is not known at this day who taught the first school in Fairview Precinct, but the one said to have been the first, was taught by Joseph Williams, the schoolhouse built about 1831, on the northwest quarter of Section 13. It was a log building, the crevices between the logs being plastered up with mud, and the pupils were accommodated with seats upon a slab, the ends of which were stuck into chinks between the logs on either side of the building. The school was taught on the subscription plan the teacher receiving a small remuneration (usually from $1 to $1.50 per term of three months) for each pupil placed in his charge.

The first minister, of whom anything authentic can be learned, was a Methodist Episcopal minister named Rev. James B. Woolard, who came to Fairview Precinct about the year 1830, perhaps sooner. Usually divine services were held at the house of John Reaves, on Section 14 and it was his custom to gather up his congregation on his road to the meeting, as they were generally to be found in the woods engaged in hunting or fishing.

Another church which figured quite prominently in the early church history of Fairview Precinct, is the one known as "Hurricane Church." It is of the German Baptist order, and the present organization was established in 1858. For a number of years after the organization of this church, meetings were held in schoolhouses, in barns, and at the residences of the different members, and the first minister was the Rev. D. B. Sturges, who was assisted in his ministerial duties by George Beanblossom. Rev. Sturgis was some time after this made a bishop, and the Rev. John Heckman succeeded him as pastor of Hurricane Church, and he was, in turn, succeeded by Rev. William Elam. After this, the church was taken charge of by Elder John Metzsger, after whom Elder John Wise assumed the pastorate. The first Deacons of this church were William and Edward Elam and Jacob Cripe. In 1874, this organization built a neat frame church building, at a cost of about $1,500, on land donated for that purpose by Henry Jones, who is the present minister. The present Deacons are Jacob Root, Daniel Noffsinger and Cornelius Kessler. The church has at present a membership of about seventy, is in a highly prosperous condition, and regular meetings are held every first and third Sunday in each month.

In 1833, a number of the old, original "Hard-Shell" Baptist denomination organized a congregation, and built a log church on Section 12, and Rev. Crouch was installed as pastor. This building still remains standing, and at present is occasionally used as a place for holding divine service. Among the first members of this organization were John Crouch and wife, Mrs. Mary Rushton, Polly Rushton and her daughter Susie, Elisha Mathews, John Taylor, etc.

Another church of the German Baptist denomination, and probably the first church of this kind in Fairview Precinct was organized by Joseph Rench and George Beanblossom, prior to the establishment of "Hurricane Church," in 1858 and the teachings of the Bible were explained by Rev. Isam Gibson. Its early membership was, of course, very small, but among those who were the first to join, were: George Beanblossom and wife William Rench and wife, John Rench and wife, Aaron Rench and wife, Joseph Rench and his daughter, Mrs. Rhoda Sutton Hiram Reaves and wife, Jacob Cripe and wife Charles Edwards and wife, etc. This church gradually drifted out of existence and most of its old members, now living have united themselves with "Hurricane Church."

About 1848, a Pennsylvanian named Dr. Daniel B. Sturgis, laid off a town near the section line between Sections 23 and 24, and gave to it the name of Hamburg, his idea being that the name would induce German emigrants to come there and locate. It, however, being located on low ground, those came who did not take to it readily, and pointed to the hill near by, significant of its superiority as a place of settlement. The first store and dwelling house in this village was erected by the Perkins Brothers, in 1854. They also ran a blacksmith shop. This little hamlet had only about five families in it and all the dwellings, excepting one, were rudely constructed of logs.

In 1856, the Perkins Brothers accepting an offer of four lots to build upon if they would come, removed to what is now the village of Fairview and Hamburg virtually met its death, most of the inhabitants removing to Fairview.

The town of "Fairview" lies eight miles nearly east of Greenville, in Section 23, Township 5, Range 2. It was surveyed by R. K. Dewey for the proprietors, E. P. Mathews and John Reaves on the 28th day of January, 1857. It is situated on a high ridge, affording a magnificent view in every direction, and surrounded by the best and most beautiful portion of Bond County. (Hence its name.) In 1857, the Perkins Bros. traded their store to J. F. Mathews, for land on Section 28. He continued the business for one year, when he died, and his brother, J. J. Mathews, succeeded him, and run the store for about two years when he sold out to Elisha Matthews and Ephraim Perkins, who were succeeded by W. C. Perkins and J. H. Perkins (brothers). These gentlemen finally sold out to Owen Walls, who soon afterward sold out to J. H. Pahlman. He ran the store some time, when he was bought out by J. S. Gorline, who continued the business about one year, when Elisha Mathews again purchased it, and after running it some time it was repurchased by J. H. Pahlman, who is the present incumbent. The first blacksmith shop was owned by the Perkins Bros., and was run by a German named Fred Kahn. Emmet Roberts was the first wagon maker. The first mill was run by Stephen D. Bourner and Daniel Faulkner. It was a wind-mill and ground mostly corn, and some little wheat. This mill was not a success, and as a wind-mill it was run about one year, when steam power was put in. It has made several changes of ownership, and at present is run by Hammond & Tompkins, who have attached a saw mill to the grist or grinding part, but as it is behind in the way of improvements, it is doing only a moderate business.

There were at one time two stores in the village, but in 1879, the second one, run by Wellington Bourner, was closed out, and since that time no goods have been kept there. The first shoemaker was William Rench. Allen Caylor ran the first drug store in 1876, and the present drug store is run by S. D. Bourner. The first Postmaster was Reuben Coburn, in 1862, and the present Postmaster is J. H. Pahlman. There are two churches in Fairview, the United Baptists and the Cumberland Presbyterians.

The latter-named church was founded about 1840, and their first minister was Rev. Barber. Meetings were held around at the houses of the members, until in 1849 a schoolhouse was built on Section 23 on land owned by John Reaves, and meetings were held in it from that time forward, under the spiritual guidance of Rev. William Hutchinson. The church was re-organized in April of 1866 and a frame building was erected at a cost of about $1,300, and Rev. William Turner was installed as minister. The first *regular* minister, however, was the Rev. William B. Poland. The first Elders were George F. Berry, John H. Minor and William Davis, Jr. The first Trustees were John H. Minor, D. H. McAdoo and Thomas L. Reaves. At the time of its re-organization in 1866, the membership of the church numbered about thirty, and they have had preaching regularly ever since until within the past year (1882). At present there is a Sunday school conducted in the church, under the superintendency of G. S. Duff. It is a recent affair, having been organized in April of this year (1882), and as yet they have no library.

The United Baptist Church was first organized December 30, 1869. The first members were E. P. Mathews, Mary J. Mathews, W. C. Perkins, John H. Perkins, Martha A. Perkins, Amanda Perkins, Amanda Stubblefield, Anna Perkins and Catharine Shipby. Their first minister was Rev. R. B. Reaves and the first Clerk was W. C. Perkins. The Deacons in February of 1870 were E. P. Mathews and John Perkins. At this time they worshiped in the building of the Presbyterian Church, and afterward in an old dwelling-house belonging to J. H. Perkins, where they continued to worship until the erection of their own church building in 1877.

CHAPTER XVIII.

LA GRANGE PRECINCT—TOPOGRAPHY BOUNDARIES AND PHYSICAL FEATURES—SETTLEMENT BY WHITE PEOPLE—THEIR TRIALS, TROUBLES AND TRIBULATIONS—AN INCIDENT WITH WILD HOGS—NO TOWNS, VILLAGES NOR MILLS—BUT PLENTY OF CHURCHES AND SCHOOLS—A PRIMITIVE SCHOOLHOUSE—THE DIFFERENT CHURCH ORGANIZATIONS, ETC.

LA GRANGE PRECINCT, the subject of the following pages, is situated in the northern part of the county, adjoining the Montgomery line, and is comprised of fractional portions of Townships 6 and 7 north, in Range 3 west. It has something like about thirty-two sections of land, which are well watered and drained by the East Fork of Shoal Creek, Indian Creek and Panther Branch. East Fork flows through the eastern part a little west of south, receiving a few small tributaries within the precinct, while Indian Creek and Panther Branch drain the southwestern portion. The land is diversified with hills and prairie, the latter predominating, the hills being contiguous to the water-courses, and were originally well timbered. As now formed, it is bounded on the north by Montgomery County, on the East by Zion Precinct, on the south by Greenville Precinct, and on the west by Cottonwood Grove Precinct. It has no towns, villages, railroads nor manufacturing establishments, but is dotted here and there with churches and schoolhouses affording to the people excellent religious and educational facilities.

Settlements were not made in what is now La Grange Precinct as early as in some other portions of Bond County. Among the pioneers of the precinct may be mentioned John Berneathy, Jonathan Teasley, John A. Laws and Fielding Laws Abner and Allen Thacker. Richard Savage. Elizabeth Mallard. John and George Denny, T. G. McCasland, James White, Thomas Wafer, C. D. McLean, Charles Wood, a Mr. Parr, Humphrey Jett and others. Who of these are entitled to the honor of being the first settler we do not know; most of them settled prior to 1830. Bernеathy, Teasley, the Laws, Thackers, Savage and Elizabeth Mallard were from Kentucky, and some of them still have descendants in the county. The Dennys came from North Carolina and settled on Section 33; McCasland settled on the northeast quarter of Section 29; Wood settled also on the same section in the fall of 1828; Wafer and McLean settled on Section 30, and Parr on Section 35. Settlers were now coming in too rapidly to keep track of them. And after this long lapse of time, it is not strange if names have been overlooked that are entitled to mention in the list of early settlers.

The first decade or two after the whites occupied this country they lived in constant danger, exposed to marauding bands of Indians and the depredations of wild beasts. Incidents are related in other parts of this work, of persons slain in what is now Bond County, by the savages, before they were finally removed to distant reservations in the West. Other dangers, as well as from savage foes, surrounded the early settlers. Wolves panthers bears and other wild beasts were numerous, that, when made furious by hunger, did not hesitate to at-

*By W. H. Perrin

tack human beings. Add to these actual dangers the troubles and annoyances that the people were exposed to from the "ager" and other malarial diseases; from mosquitoes buffalo-gnats, "greenhead" flies; the difficulty of procuring supplies, and a hundred other drawbacks which stood in the way as large and bold as Don Quixote's windmills, and we conclude that the pioneer's lot was not cast

"On flowery beds of ease."

But little stock was kept for many years except cattle and hogs, and the latter were reared principally in the woods where they lived on the "mast" otherwise nuts and acorns. By the time they were wanted for meat they were almost as wild as the native animals of the forest, and quite as fierce and dangerous when a little angered and excited. Mr. White relates an incident illustrative of their savage nature when half wild and provoked to anger by a restriction of their liberty, which, although it was quite dangerous, was ludicrous in the extreme. A drove of large, half-wild hogs had been driven into an inclosure in the spring of the year for some purpose, when the sap was running and the bark peeled easily from the trees. Several men were present with dogs by which the wildest of the hogs had been caught in order to get them in the inclosure, and this had served to madden the entire drove to quite a degree. The inclosure contained several acres, in which stood a number of trees. The men were all inside endeavoring to drive the hogs through a gap into another lot, but the more they tried to drive them the more they, hog-like, wouldn't drive, while all were more or less afraid of them. At last, one fellow who had made much sport of the others on account of their timidity, swore he was not afraid of any hog "that ever wore har," and so boldly started toward the gang, waving his hat at the excited porkers. Not one moved until he was in twenty paces of them, when a large male started right at him with an angry snort, displaying an array of long white tusks that did not look at all pleasant. Quick as thought the brave man dropped his hat, turned tail and made for the nearest tree which chanced to be a small elm, not over six inches in diameter and from which the bark had lately been peeled, rendering it about as sleek as if it had been smeared with soft soap. The sapling was perfectly straight and it was fifteen or twenty feet up to the first limb, and when the luckless individual reached it the hog was in ten feet of him. The exertions he put forth in trying to climb that tree was probably never excelled by mortal man. He gave a bound and sprang as far up the tree as possible clasping it with his arms, legs and feet and clinging for dear life tried to hold fast but despite his efforts down he went to the ground. But the hog, as it happened, passed the tree while he was up out of reach, and, missing its enemy, kept on beyond. The man, however, unaware of that fact, continued his efforts to climb the tree, believing that his life depended upon his accomplishing it until he fell exhausted. His companions were in convulsions of laughter, but he, even after he discovered the danger was past failed to see the least bit of fun in the matter. It cured him effectually, however, of his boasted bravery among wild hogs.

This precinct, as we have said, has no villages nor manufacturing enterprises. It is an agricultural region, and is devoted wholly to that calling. The early settlers went to other neighborhoods to do their milling, and even follow the same example to the present day. The first roads through the precinct were but trails, which were improved as the country settled up, and finally made into good roads. In later years, these have been further improved by bridges over the largest streams, which tend to facilitate travel. The people go to the neighboring villages and to Greenville to do their trading, and to purchase their supplies.

The pioneers of La Grange were alive to the

value of education, and established schools at an early day. The first school of which we have any reliable account was taught in a small log cabin on Section 28. This primitive temple of learning was without floor other than the ground and had a chimney of mud and sticks. When the pupils practiced writing, it is said, they sat on a sycamore pole, the ends of which were placed in the cracks between the logs. The first teacher in this cabin was McCasland, and he taught at $1 and $1.25 per scholar for three months. If the youth of the present day deserve credit for educating themselves what did they not deserve in those days for obtaining an education under the circumstances such as described above?

Another of the early schools of this precinct was taught by Rev. John Barber on Jett Prairie. It was also taught in a small log house, which has disappeared with other pioneer landmarks. To note the advancement in educational matters, we have but to look around us at the neat schoolhouses to be found in every neighborhood, which afford ample evidence of the present perfect school system. There are about nine schoolhouses in the precinct as at present laid off. These are comfortable houses well furnished in which good schools are maintained during the school year.

On the land of Thomas Booker in this precinct is a mound, supposed to have been made by the pre-historic races. Bones, it is said, have been dug up, which show their owners to have been of extraordinary large size. This corresponds with many writers upon the Mound Builders who are represented as a race large in stature.

If the citizens of La Grange Precinct are not a God fearing people it is certainly their own fault and not for any lack of church facilities. There seem to be almost as many churches in the precinct as schoolhouses. Nothing speaks more loudly for the civilization of a community than its churches and schoolhouses. Where plenty of these evidences of enlightenment exist, the people cannot be very bad or very ignorant. One of the first churches organized in the north part of Bond County was by the Old School Presbyterians in this precinct in 1825. Among the principal members of this pioneer organization were George Donnell, Newton and Joseph Laughlin, Robert Stewart and John Denny. These were from Ohio. Denny was a prominent member of the church from its organization, an Elder, and an upright and zealous Christian. Robert Stewart's remains lie buried in the cemetery adjacent. He was the first person buried there about 1826; one of the Laughlins is also buried there. This was an old log building, and stood upon the site of the present Union Grove Church. It was heated by a charcoal fire in the center of the building, and the floor and "loft" were laid with broad puncheons. A Sunday school was organized about the time the church was, which was kept up for a number of years. Services were finally discontinued at the church about 1831, when the building, grounds, etc., were vacated until the organization of Union Grove Church.

The church originally known as "Union Grove Church" was organized January 12, 1855, under the superintending care of the Vandalia Presbytery of the Cumberland Presbyterian Church. The minister at this time was Rev. William T. Hutchinson; the Elders were Thomas Cline, S. N. Jett and Thomas M. Davis. The members were William T. and M. C. Hutchinson, Thomas N. and Jane Davis, Thomas and Sarah Cline, S. N. and Agnes E. Jett, John M. and Sarah Johnson, Thomas and Elizabeth Scott, Henry C., Elizabeth and Patty Hutchinson, James Hunter, Isaac and Minerva Kershner, Caroline Crocker, Newton Barr, J. L. and Martha Matherson, Mary Enloe, Maria Balch, and William and Lucy Davis. The society occupied the house known as the Union Grove Church and grounds, which had been [illegible] by William T. Hutchinson to found the

nominations, viz.: The Old School Presbyterians, United Baptists, Cumberland Presbyterians and the Methodists. This organization continued until the formation of Maple Grove Church, since which time the other three denominations have occupied Union Grove until recently. It is now occupied by the Free Methodists. The church is a frame structure, about 20x30 feet, and was built in 1854-55 by voluntary labor of the people.

Maple Grove Church alluded to in the above sketch, was organized by Rev. William T. Hutchinson, and worshiped at Union Grove until their church here was built in 1868. It is a frame building, 30x40 feet, and cost about $800. The present officers are N. A. Hughey, Wm. Smith, D. D. Jones and J. M. Jett Elders; Madison Jett, D. D. Jones and W. H. Vaughn, Trustees. Rev. Thomas McDavid is the present minister, who preaches twice a month, and has a membership of about sixty-five. A Sunday school was organized at the same time of the church, and it is still maintained.

Hopewell Christian Church was organized in 1869, of scattering members—some from Walnut Grove Church and some from other points. Among the original members were Jacob Young and wife, James Baker and wife, Charles Baker and wife, John Davis and wife, Mrs. Rahm, William T. Gwinn and wife, Mrs. Caroline Jett, William Clouse and wife, Miss Mary Oaks, Mrs. Eliza Harris, Miss Caroline Laughlin, Miss Jennie East, Mrs. Sarah A. Sharp, Mrs. Nancy J. White and John Haley. The society first worshiped in the brick schoolhouse at Elm Point, then at the schoolhouse on Section 33, where they remained until they built their church in 1870. The first minister was Elder O. Hulen, J. G. Baker and W. T. Gwinn, Elders; present Elders, Ezra Wood, Hiram Crocker and William Vaughn. The Sunday school was organized since the church was built, and is flourishing at present

The Mount Carmel congregation of the Cumberland Presbyterian Church was first organized by Rev. Joel Knight, in Montgomery County Ill., February 24, 1868, and after one or two changes in reference to name and place of worship, said congregation having erected a house of worship in Pleasant Prairie, Bond County, they therefore petitioned Vandalia Presbytery at the regular session at Blue Mound (in Bond County) in the fall of 1868, to change the name of the congregation, so that it should be known as the Pleasant Prairie Congregation of the Cumberland Presbyterian Church.*

After leaving Mount Carmel, the church worshiped at Willow Spring Schoolhouse until the erection of their house of worship. The trustees of the Pleasant Prairie Church are Jas. E. Rankin, James F. Nicholson and Imbert H. Denny. The church is in a goodcondition.

Mount Tabor Baptist Church was organized about the year 1857 by Richardson Grigg. J. G. Davis, Gabriel Jett and Kinley Hittle were the first Deacons, Robert Horton, Clerk. Among the original members were J. G. Davis and wife, Gabriel Jett and wife and daughters, Kinley Hittle and two sisters Richard Savage and wife, Parmela and Mary Teasley and others. The church was built by the voluntary labor of the neighbors, and was 30x40 feet in size. It has prospered since organization, and at present has some sixty-five members under the pastorate of Rev. Mr. Duff. The present Trustees are Thomas Jett, James T. Davis and George Sharp; Deacons, John G. Davis and Martin Nelson, and Robert Savage, Clerk. A Sunday school has been in existence for a number of years, the first Superintendent was Elijah Thacker; the present Superintendent is Jesse Denny, and the school is in a flourishing state. This church was built by three denominations, viz.: Baptist Methodist and Presbyterian; but is now only used by the Baptists.

Thus we see from the foregoing that the people of La Grange Precinct have no lack of religious facilities and if they are not good Christians it can certainly be the fault of none but themselves.

* From the Church Records.

CHAPTER XIX.

ZION PRECINCT—TOPOGRAPHICAL AND DESCRIPTIVE—EARLY SETTLEMENT—EARLY PIONEERS—[illegible] ON THE [illegible] HOSTILE—PIONEER INDUSTRIES—OLD ZION CAMP GROUND—VILLAGE OF WOBURN—SCHOOLS, CHURCHES, ETC.

WHEN that section of Bond County known as Zion Precinct was first settled, the brave men who undertook its subjection were exposed to cold, hunger and savage brutality. They commenced clearing the wilderness and thus laid the foundation of the beautiful country thickly dotted over with comfortable luxurious homes that we find there to-day. The pioneers of fifty years ago are gone and "Old Time" with his scythe has made sad havoc among the children of men. They sleep in the quiet graveyard, beneath the sighing elms and weeping willows, where the balmy breath of summer brings beautiful blossoms and luxuriant verdure. We know comparatively little of their trials except as they are handed down to us through family traditions. To the early settlement and to the pioneers of that portion of Bond County now forming Zion Precinct, this chapter will be devoted.

It lies in the northeast corner of Bond County and is bounded on the north by La Grange Precinct and Montgomery County, on the east by Fayette County and Mulberry Grove Precinct, on the south by Mulberry Grove Precinct and Greenville Precinct, and on the west by La Grange Precinct. It is well watered by numerous small streams, the most important of which probably is Zion Creek, which rises in the northern part of Section 10, and flowing first south and then directly west leaves the precinct in the southwest corner of Section 19. Its most important tributary is the Dry Creek, which, rising near the center of Section 30, Township 7, takes its course a little west of south and enters Zion Creek in the southern part of Section 19, uniting with it about a mile from where it leaves the precinct. A number of other small brooks and rivulets flow through various parts of the precinct, rendering the rich soil still more productive and very little artificial drainage necessary.

At one time this precinct was known as "Dry Fork" Precinct, but in 1857 or 1858 the voting place was changed from Sutton Hastings's, where elections had previously been held, to what is now Newport, and at the same time the name of the precinct was changed to "Zion," in honor of the old Zion Church and camp ground.

The early settlement of Zion Precinct is very interesting, it being one of the first-settled precincts in Bond County. Sutton Hastings came in from North Carolina early in the year 1818, the same year that Illinois was admitted into the Union as a State. Two years later (in 1820), Daniel Moore and family, also from North Carolina, came and settled in Section 19. His father, Philip Moore came at the same time. He raised a large family of boys, all of whom are either dead or have left the precinct. In 1817, Horatio Durley came from Kentucky, and in 1819 he entered about one thousand acres of land, a part of which is the farm now owned by James H. Moss. Mr. Durley was considered a very wealthy man. He ran the first horse-mill in the precinct, about 1820. It

by T. J. [illegible]

was a grist-mill, but at that time was used mostly for grinding corn; it was located near where the old Enloe place now is. A family named Stubblefield came in 1818 and in August of 1819 John Stubblefield entered the farm now owned by John Griggs. Daniel Griggs came from North Carolina in 1825, and settled in Section 31. He was accompanied by his brothers Samuel and Richardson, both Baptist ministers, and Bolin Griggs, another brother, who at present resides in Section 4, and is the oldest man in the precinct (ninety-two years old). There was a large family of Griggs and numerous descendants at present reside in Bond County. Prior to the war of 1812 a man named Truitt came from Kentucky and settled on what is now known as the "Old Kline place," but about the time of the war the Indians became so bad that he was compelled to leave and he returned to Kentucky. He afterwards returned to Illinois, and lived until his death near Edwardsville in Madison County, where he became quite a prominent man, and accumulated considerable wealth.

The Diamond family came from South Carolina in 1820, about the time the Watsons came. The father, John Diamond, was a very old man, and deserves especial mention, from the fact of his having been a soldier in the Revolutionary war. He died soon after removing to this precinct, and was buried in the "Old Diamond Graveyard," near Zion Spring, in the northwest corner of Section 29. His son Robert lived in the precinct until his death, which occurred in 1850. He was a very old man, and has three brothers still living in Arkansas. William W. Moss came in 1835, and located in Section 21. His son, James H. Moss, came with his father, and also settled in same section. He at present resides in Section 30, and is considered one of the best, most industrious and responsible citizens in Zion Precinct.

On the "Old Kline place" there is an immense spring, known as "Zion Spring," and when the earliest settlers came to this region, a widow named "Clarey," and her sons, occupied a cabin near this spring. She is said to have come from Kentucky though nothing definite concerning her can be learned. She must have been a courageous woman, however, to brave alone the dangers and perils of the wilderness. Alex Glenn came from North Carolina about 1828 and located in Section 17. He was, for many years, a Justice of the Peace appointed by common consent, to settle the grievances of the settlers of this region. Thomas Kline came with Glenn, and settled in Section 30. His widow at present resides in the village of Newport. William Hunter settled near the Cross Roads, in 1820. He was the first Methodist minister in this section of the county, and was a very popular and good man and very highly respected. Hugh Watson also came in 1820, from North Carolina and entered the land on which the village of Newport now stands. His son Wilson, who died last summer, was about the first merchant in that town. Daniel Moore came from North Carolina in 1825, and settled in Section 31. His widow, Jennie Moore, who is now more than eighty years of age, at present resides with her daughter, Mrs. Henry Hill, about four miles west of the town of Greenville. It was at her residence and at the residence of Sutton Hastings that the first Methodist preaching in Zion Precinct was held. Asa Oliver came from Tennessee about the year 1830, and settled on Section 29. John Griggs came from North Carolina in 1829, and located on Section 30. Lemuel Scroggins came from the same State in 1833, and settled in Section 17. Three or four miles north of the village of Mulberry Grove, a Frenchman, named St. John, kept a trading post, which was established prior to the year 1816. Some of the first white settlers used to haul furs and skins from that place to Cahokia. Another Frenchman, named La Croix, lived near St. John, and also dealt in furs. When horses belonging to any of the settlers strayed away they were sometimes taken up by the Indians. In such cases the settlers would employ these Frenchmen to recover them, by giving such rewards as they could afford. A few years subsequent to this time, settlers came in so fast that it is difficult to keep trace of them.

The first church built in this precinct was the "Old Zion Church," reference to which is made elsewhere. It was built on Section 19, about the year 1828; was a log building twenty-four feet in length, by twenty feet wide. It was built facing the south, and on the west side was an immense fire-place. The only window in the building was on the east side, and was sixteen feet feet long, and two panes of glass in width. It had puncheon floors, and the congregation was accommodated with seats upon slab benches, made by splitting a log in two and putting peg legs in each end. In 1833, the camp ground was cleared off, and regular camp meetings were held there until late years. About 1840, the old log building was torn down and a neat frame church, twenty-four by thirty-six feet was built in its stead, at a cost of about $500. In 1861, the society, which was of the Methodist denomination, removed to Newport, the Zion Church was torn down, and a new edifice erected in that village, which they now occupy. Among the original members of this church were Robert Stewart and wife, Philip Moore and wife, Rev. William Hunter and wife, Arthur Sherrad, Asa Oliver, Jane McCracken, Eli McCracken, Ephraim McCracken, and Daniel and Jane Moore.

In 1881 the Free Methodists built a church on the camp ground, on the site of the "Old Zion" Church. It is a frame building, forty-two feet in length and twenty-eight feet in width. On the site of the Zion Camp Ground, there is at present a cemetery where repose the last remains of many of those who, in an early day attended meeting on that same spot.

Schools were taught in the precinct as soon as there was sufficient population to support them, but where, when and by whom the first schools were taught, we are now unable to state. They were of the primitive pioneer pattern, being constructed of logs and having either puncheon floors or no floors at all. The advancement made in the schools in this precinct is observable, however, in the number of good, comfortable, commodious school-buildings which may be seen there to-day, in which schools are taught for the usual term each year.

The village of Woburn was first called Newport, but on account of there being another post office of the same name in the State, the name was changed to Woburn. In this section, it is more generally known as the Cross Roads, the name it bore in early days. It was laid out by John Hughes, of Virginia, who owned the land, about the year 1856. The first store was built and run by William Harper. The first Postmaster was A. W. Watson. His father, Hugh Watson, ran the first blacksmith shop. John Hughes was the first miller, and Abraham Jarred was the first wogon-maker. Dr. Harnady first administered to the ailments of the settlers in this precinct. The first mill of any importance in the precinct, was erected here in 1866. It was a saw-mill, but was afterward purchased by the Moss Brothers, who took out the saw-mill and put in two run of buhrs for grinding purposes. These brothers run the mill for several years and finally sold out to Porter McKay, who, after running it about one year, sold out to J. W. Daniels and William Davidson. These gentlemen, after continuing the business for some time, sold the mill to its present owner, George Force, and at present it is doing a fair business. Melton Phillips was the first shoemaker. At present there are about 150 inhabitants in the village; two stores, one run by Joseph Isley and the other by Eugene Enloe, who is also the present Postmaster; three blacksmith shops, doing a good business, though Thomas White has the best trade. Dr. Poindexter is the present doctor, and has the best practice of any physician who ever did business here.

The Protestant Methodist Episcopal Church was organized here about the time of the laying-out of the village, through the influence of Samuel Glenn, of North Carolina. He and his wife had been members of this church in North Carolina. His family formed the nucleus around which this organization formed. Their first minister was Rev. William H. Collins. Among the first members were Samuel Glenn, wife and two daughters; Thomas Kline, wife and two daughters; Mrs. Thomas Enloe and Mrs. Joseph Washburn. The society at first had no church, and for several years worshiped at the houses of the members, and afterward in the schoolhouse. In 1871, a church building, forty feet in length and twenty-eight feet in width, was erected, at a cost of about $1,400. At present the membership, which has been as high as forty numbers but nineteen. The present minister is Rev Edward Bache, and services are held semi-monthly. A flourishing Sunday school is at present held in the church under the Superintendency of Saburn Middleton.

The United Baptist Church, commonly called "Liberty Church," was established about 1856. The first minister was Richard Keel. Among the first members were Richardson, Samuel and Bolin Griggs, James Elam, Gabriel Jett and wife, and Charles Messenger and wife. At that time there were only eight members, all told. Samuel Griggs and James Elam were the first Deacons. Their first meeting was held at the house of Gabriel Jett and afterward at the residences of the several members, until in 1859, when they erected their present church, which is a frame building thirty-six feet long and twenty-six feet in width, and cost about $600. In this building, Richardson Griggs preached the first sermon, and was succeeded by Samuel Griggs, who is the present minister. The Deacons are R. S. D. Roberts, Joseph Bigham and Anderson Elam, and the Clerk is R. B. Griggs. The membership is at present 215. Regular services are held every third and fourth Sabbath, and prayer meetings on the first and second Sabbaths in each month. The first Sunday school was established in 1860, with John Fisher as Superintendent, and at present a large and flourishing Sunday school is conducted here.

The Church of God in Christ, or Christian Church, was organized at Newport in 1859. They experienced considerable difficulty in establishing a church but through the exertions of Jonathan Skates who located here in the spring of 1858 they finally succeeded. Among the early members were Jonathan Skates and wife, Miranda Lemert, Henry Allen, Daniel Tabor, James Adams, John Curlee, etc. In August 1860, by vigorous efforts, they succeeded in erecting a church, and Brothers Adams, Skates and Tabor were chosen Deacons. At present the church is in a very prosperous and thrifty condition, having a good membership, regular services and maintaining a good Sunday school. From the foregoing church history, it will be seen that Zion Precinct is well supplied with religious instruction. That it is not only well supplied at present, but ever since the settlement of the country it has had no lack of church facilities. If the people are not moral and religious, it is certainly nobody's fault but their own, and nobody but themselves, perhaps, will be held to account for their shortcomings. With this finale on the moral influence of this favored section, we close our chapter on Zion Precinct

CHAPTER XX.

COTTONWOOD GROVE PRECINCT—ITS EARLY HISTORY—WHITE SETTLEMENT—THE McCORDS AND ROBINSONS—OLD SHOAL CREEK CHURCH—THE VILLAGE OF [illegible]—SCHOOLS, CHURCHES, ETC.

THE early pioneers of "Cottonwood Grove Precinct"* notwithstanding all the uncomfortable circumstances by which they were surrounded, were contented, and enjoyed life to its utmost. They knew nothing of railroads, and had never heard the whistle of a locomotive. The present improved mode of farming was far beyond their most extravagant expectations. To chronicle the changes and note the vast improvements made within the past fifty years, is the most interesting part of the historian's work. Notwithstanding these vast changes, numerous indications and landmarks remain to mark the primitiveness of the early pioneers in this section.

Cottonwood Grove Precinct, to which this chapter is devoted, lies in a northwesterly direction from the town of Greenville in the northwest corner of Bond County, and well adapted to agriculture. It is bounded on the north by Montgomery County, on the east by the precinct of La Grange, on the south by La Grange and Ripley Precincts, and on the west by counties of Madison and Montgomery. It is well watered by numerous small streams. The most important of which is "Shoal Creek," which entering near the middle of the northern line of Section 3, winds its tortuous course entirely across the precinct near its center. Another stream of considerable importance is Dorris Creek, which enters the precinct near the southeast corner of Section 12, and, taking first a westerly course and then directly south, leaves the precinct at the southern boundary line of Section 34. These streams have several small branches or tributaries, most of them of such diminutive size as to be considered scarcely worthy of mention.

The early settlement of what is now Cottonwood Grove Precinct cannot be given with perfect correctness. The precise date of the building of the first cabin by a white man within its limits is obscured in the shadows of half a century, and we are left to conjecture to a certain extent as to the commencement of its settlement by white people. Alexander Robinson, from Tennessee, settled here about the year 1816, and still has descendants living in the precinct. He was accompanied by Robert and Daniel McCord from Virginia. These men came together from Tennessee to Bond County and made a settlement in Cottonwood Grove Precinct, in the spring of 1816. They made their first camping ground where the cemetery now is, and kneeling upon the ground dedicated the land to the service of the Lord, and called the place "Bethel." In later years, about 1825, a church was built here, which still remains. It was a log structure, with no fire-place or stove. The only warmth was afforded by means of a raised place of dirt in the center of the room on which charcoal, which the members were required to furnish, was burned, the only escape for the smoke being a hole in the roof immediately above the mound. Robert McCord settled on the northwest quarter of Section 11. He has one daughter, Mrs. Mary Mears, living

* By T. J. Riley

in Greenville, and a son, Blackburn, living in Iowa. David McCord settled on the east half of Section 11, where J. T. McCracken now lives, in 1820. James Water was an early pioneer in this section. He located northwest of Bethel in 1817. James Denny settled on Pleasant Prairie, about 1819. During the same year, George Donnell settled near the mouth of Indian Creek. George and John Denny, sons of James Denny, settled on the east side of Shoal Creek, in the north part of the precinct, in 1820 or 1821, and about the same time the Jetts, Vaughns and Thackers settled in the same neighborhood, on both sides of the creek. William and Lawrence Stewart settled on the west side of Shoal Creek about 1821. Jesse Margraves and others also located along the west side of Shoal Creek about this same time. In 1819, Newton Coffee came in and settled on Jett's Prairie.

In February of 1880, a church was organized in this precinct by the Free Methodist denomination. The first minister chosen by them was the Rev. J. B. Colt. Among the first members were James Robb, J. F. Nicholson, John Parmalee, John McCracken, Daniel F. Justice, John F. Humphrey and Winnie Singleton. James Robb was chosen Class-Leader, and John Parmalee was chosen Steward. Early in the spring of the present year (1882), a neat frame church, thirty-six feet long and twenty-eight wide, was erected on Section 31, at a cost of about $700, and John Parmalee, James Robb and J. F. Nicholson, were appointed as Trustees. This organization has grown in strength from the beginning, and at present has a membership of about thirty-five, and maintains a good Sunday school.

In noticing the early churches of Cottonwood Grove Precinct, one church stands out prominently, and seems to be to a great extent the "mother" of all the Presbyterian Churches in this section. We refer to the "Old Shoal Creek Church." The original church was organized by Rev. Solomon Gidings, of St. Louis, Mo., on the 10th of March, 1819, and is more particularly referred to in a preceding chapter.

The "Pleasant Prairie Presbyterian Church" in Township 7, Range 4, was formed from the Mt. Carmel society of the same denomination, then existing in Montgomery County, on the 24th day of February, 1828. Through the exertions of Rev. Joel Knight, Andrew Finley and Joseph Barlow were chosen Elders, at its organization, and C. G. Keown was their first regular pastor. The first Clerk was Andrew J. Finley. Among the first members were William, Elizabeth, Andrew and Rebecca Finley; Joseph and Harriet Barlow; Elizabeth, Sarah, Emily and Polly Barlow; Sarah Keown; William and Polly Pitman; William and Jane Kline; Nelly Breance; Catharine, Polly and Joseph Buck; Michael, Elanor, Sinah, Catharine, Polly and Palsey Finley; Andrew Keown, James E. Rankin, Eli Cowdon and James Driscol. They have at present a good frame church building sixty feet long by forty feet wide, which was erected at a cost of about $2,200, and the present membership is about thirty in all. James E Rankan, the first Superintendent, organized a good Sunday school, which has been conducted here for many years.

In an early day, some of the pioneers of this section built a "sod fence" for some purpose, out of which sprouted a beautiful grove of cottonwood trees. It is from this grove that the village of "Bethel, or Cottonwood Grove," obtained its name. It was originally called "Augusta," but the name was afterward changed to "Cottonwood Grove, or Bethel." It was surveyed on the 9th day of June, 1836, by Asahel Enloe, for John Mitchell & Co., the proprietors, and is located in Section 11, Township 6 north, Range 4 west, about eight miles northwest of the county seat (Greenville). It is a flourishing little village, and is surrounded by an intelligent and industrious community.

The Bethel Presbyterian Church was established here on the 15th day of September, 1826, several years prior to the laying-out of the town. It was the outgrowth of the church already alluded to, as the first church in the county, called Shoal Creek Church. The original church was in 1825 divided into three churches—Shoal Creek Church, Bethel Church and Greenville Church. Of these three the two last named still exist. The Bethel Church was organized with sixty-two members, and their first house of worship was a log building 20x26 feet. It was heated in a novel manner. A space about six feet in diameter in the middle of the house was left without flooring, thus securing an earthen hearth. A bushel of charcoal was laid there and then set on fire, rendering the house quite comfortable. Among the ministers in Bethel Church for the past fifty years are the following: Thomas A. Spillman, Albert Hale, E. L. Huntington, Thomas Lippincott, Samuel Foster, Charles L. Adams, Charles Barton, E. B. Olmstead, N. A. Hunt, Robert Stewart, William Rankin, William H. Bird, J. S. Davis, Charles Barton (a second term), James H. Spillman, etc. Some years later, when the church had become strong in numbers and wealth, a new church was built a few rods from the old one. It was a frame building well adapted to the wants of the church and the times. A large volume might be written of this pioneer church, but our space is limited and only this brief sketch can be given. A large and interesting Sunday school of both young and old has always been maintained in old Bethel Church.

In 1838, the town of Harrisonville was surveyed by T. S. Hubbard, for Andrew Finley, proprietor. It was situated on Section 32, Township 7 north, Range 4 west, on Pleasant Prairie, about twelve miles northwest of Greenville. For some time this village gave considerable promise, but it gradually died out until nothing now remains of it except the records of the platt.

On the 17th of May, 1856, the town of Elm Point was laid out by Anthony Hill, for William P. Libby. It is located on Section 31, Town 7, Range 3, about nine miles in a northwesterly direction from the town of Greenville. It is on the prairie, and is surrounded by a well cultivated country, but has never made much improvement, and at present there is scarcely what might be called a town remaining.

CHAPTER XXI.

OKAW PRECINCT—DESCRIPTION AND TOPOGRAPHY—EARLY SETTLEMENTS—THE FIRST PIONEERS—THEIR EARLY LIFE AND HABITS—SCHOOLS, SCHOOLHOUSES, CHURCHES, ETC.

IN giving the history of Okaw Precinct there is probably less to tell than of any other precinct in Bond County, from the fact that it was settled at a much later day than any other portion of the county. For many years the land was held almost exclusively by large land-owners, and this is still the case to a considerable extent. These land-owners would not sell, except at such exorbitant prices as deterred settlers from purchasing, especially as other lands at that time were sold at a very low figure. Thus it was that settlers who might have located here purchased elsewhere, and at present we find that, though there are a number of good farmers in this locality, it is settled mainly by squatters, or farmers on a small scale, who have come in at a comparatively late day and purchased small tracts of land.

Okaw Precinct lies in a southeasterly direction from the county seat (Greenville), and comprises thirty-six sections in the southeast corner of the county. It is bounded on the north by the precincts of Greenville and Fairview; on the east by Fayette County; on the south by Clinton County and on the west by Beaver Creek Precinct. Almost the entire surface of the land is very low and level, so that artificial drainage is largely resorted to. The low flat nature of the most of the land is another reason why it was not settled sooner. In the southern part however, near the Clinton County line, it rises into nice rolling land, well adapted to agriculture, and it was here that the earliest settlers located. There is very little of the land but is susceptible of cultivation, the soil is of the richest quality, and yields abundant harvests of all the crops usually grown in this section. The principal crops are corn, wheat and oats. This precinct is not very thickly wooded, though along the creeks may be found an abundance of hickory, ash, maple, walnut, etc.

Numerous small streams flow through Okaw Precinct, and among them is one of considerable importance, namely, the "Kaskaskia," commonly known as the "Okaw," which flows just across the southeastern corner, through Section 36. This stream abounds in large numbers of the finny tribe, and is a great resort for fishing parties. Another stream is "Flat Creek," which takes its rise in "Calamus Lake," a small body of water in the northwest corner of Section 16, and, flowing a little west of south, leaves the precinct near the line, between Sections 31 and 32. Little Beaver Creek, another small stream, flows across the northwest corner, through Sections 5 and 6. Another stream deserving of mention is "Keysport Creek," which, rising in the northern part of Section 14, flows directly south and leaves the precinct at the southern boundary line of Section 35.

It is sweet, yet sad, to recall the scenes of the past; sweet, because we see the faces of dear ones; sad, because the picture is unreal, and will vanish like the mists of the morning. Though the early settlement of Okaw Precinct is not so remote, still most of the earliest settlers have been laid away in the quiet graveyards and, though lost to sight are to memory

* by F. J. Kuey

dear." Among the first settlers who located in Okaw Precinct was Josiah Austin, who came in 1833, and located in the southern part, on Section 32. Two men, one named Bateman and the other named Martin, settled near him about the same time.

John Butler came in prior to the coming of Josiah Austin, and located in the southern part of the precinct. Alexander Myatt came in an early day, and settled in the west half of Section 33, and about the same time a man, named Fix, settled in the southeast part of the precinct. Among the earliest settlers in this section was Mathew Henry, who first settled in Greenville Precinct, about four miles west of the county seat, and after remaining there some time, located in this precinct, where, at present, a number of his descendants reside. On his way to Bond County, Mr. Henry came through St. Louis, and it is said that, while there, he was offered five lots where the Southern Hotel now stands for a little pony mare, which he refused. Mr. Henry also was the possessor of one of the first "cook stoves" in this county.

But little can be said of the early schools in Okaw Precinct, and for many years after its settlement but little attention was given to the subject of education, but of late years a great improvement has been made in this direction, and at present there are several schoolhouses in the precinct, in which school is taught by efficient instructors for the usual term each year.

At present, there are two churches in this precinct, the Methodist Episcopal and the Evangelical Lutheran. The former was established early in the year 1842. For some time after the organization of this church, meetings were held at the residence of Alexander Myatt. Among the first members were Alexander Myatt and wife, Joshua Sharp and wife, Micajah Bowen, Mr. Zimmerman, Mrs. Rainey, Mrs. Gillespie, Robert Tucker, wife and mother and the Rev. Joshua Barnes. Their present church building was erected about the year 1856, on the southwest quarter of Section 33. It is a frame building forty-four feet long and thirty-four feet wide, and was built at a cost of about $1,000. The first minister who assumed the pastorate, after the building of this new church, was the Rev. J. W. Low. The Trustees were A. L. Cole, William Hoppock, B. F. Taylor and A. J. Cole, and the first Class-Leader was A. L. Cole. Alexander Myatt was chosen the first Steward. The church is now in a highly, prosperous and flourishing condition, and the present Class-Leader is J. D. Blackwell, and J. B. Myatt and D. L. Reynolds are acting as Stewards. A good Sunday school is and has been maintained ever since the organization of this church.

The last named, the Evangelical Lutheran, or St. Peter's Church, was built in the fall of 1874, on the southeast quarter of Section 33. Among the men who were instrumental in getting the church built were, Frederick Meyer, J. H. Pahman, Julius Meyer, Conrad Kromer, Henry Shumaker, Henry Brauchmiller, etc. Their first minister was Rev. Kornbeaun. Prior to the erection of their church building, the society worshiped at the private residences of its members, and continued thus until their present church was built. It is a frame building, thirty feet long and twenty-four feet wide, and was built at a cost of about $600.

No regular meetings were held here until in 1880, but before this time, Rev. H. Wolfman, who had dedicated the church, preached at intervals. Since November, 1880, they have been having meetings every Sunday, and Rev. H. Baker, the present minister, is employed at a yearly salary of $300, which, it may be said to their credit, is always promptly paid. At present the church is in a prosperous, thriving condition, and maintains a large and very interesting Sunday school. The Trustees at present are Julius T. Brauchmiller and John Tureuck.

Solomon Hartley

HISTORY OF MONTGOMERY COUNTY.

CHAPTER I.

MONTGOMERY COUNTY—INTRODUCTORY—DESCRIPTION AND GENERAL TOPOGRAPHY—THE VARIETIES OF TIMBER—GEOLOGICAL FEATURES—LIMESTONE AND SANDSTONE—COAL MEASURES—QUALITY OF THE COAL—QUARRIES OF BUILDING STONES—OBSERVATIONS—CLIMATOLOGY—THE CHANGES OF SEASONS—NOW, AND FIFTY YEARS AGO.

"When rust shall eat her brass, when Time's strong hand
Shall bruise to dust her marble palaces,
Triumphant arches, pillars, obelisks;
When Julius' temple, Claudius' aqueducts,
Agrippa's baths, and Pompey's theater;
Nay, Rome itself shall not be found at all,
Historians' books shall live."

THE annals of time are marked by various ages under different denominations. The ancients had their fabled ages of iron and of gold. To the downfall of the Roman Empire succeeded the Dark Ages, with their dismal concomitants of superstition and crime. Next came the age of the Revival of Letters, which was followed by that of the Reformation of Religion. Great men have also stamped their names on ages, as their likenesses have been perpetuated by statues and medals. Egypt had her age of Sesostris, Greece of Pericles, and Rome of Cæsar, Pompey and Cicero. Britain boasts of her age of Alfred the Great, and France that of Henry the Fourth. History will yet speak of the age of Washington, Franklin and Jefferson, and that of Napoleon will also be commemorated. In splendor, usefulness, the wonders of science and the power of art, the present age far surpasses all that have preceded it, and may be fitly denominated the age of improvement. Instead of the monk laboring to ameliorate the condition of man by the dreams of his dusky and secluded closet, the real philosopher now walks abroad in open day, looks at things around him as they are, consults nature as his oracle, receives her responses as pure emanations from the fountain of truth, and employs them successfully for the benefit of his race.

In the wonderful changes which the present age has witnessed, the period of vision and hypothesis has gone by. Fact has assumed the place of abstract theory, and practice has ejected speculation from her seat. All this and much more has been accomplished, but we will not follow up the subject. In nothing are the changes of the present age more strikingly illustrated than in the wonderful improvement and advancement of our country, and especially the great West. But a few decades ago and this country was the home of the red man and his kindred; these broad prairies his hunting grounds, where he chased the buffalo and deer. Less than a century has passed; the Indian of the haughty bearing and the falcon glance has disappeared, and Cooper's "Last of the Mohicans," preserves in romance a story of the [illegible]

From a wilderness, infested with savages and wild beasts, the country has been reclaimed, and transformed into an Eden of loveliness, unsurpassed in glory and beauty, nowithstanding the poet has sung of

"——— a clime more delightful than this;
The land of the orange, the myrtle and vine."

The history which attaches to every portion of our country increases in interest as time rolls on. Its wonderful development and advancement are more like magic tales than actual occurrences, and its vast resources the wonder of all nations. No section but has its traditions and memories: no spot, however small, but is more or less historical. Montgomery County, which forms the subject matter of the pages following, bears no mean part in the history or the importance of the State of Illinois, as she bears no inconsiderable part in the history of our common country.

Topography.—The county of Montgomery, as formed at present, is bounded on the north by Sangamon and Christian Counties, on the east by Christian, Shelby and Fayette, on the south by Fayette, Bond and Madison, on the west by Macoupin, and has an area of 702 square miles. Of its topography, timber growth, prairies and general surface features, the following has been published, which we give entire for the benefit of our readers: "On Ramsey Creek, the hills are low and the country gently undulating; near Nokomis there are several mounds, with long, gentle depressions between, stretching off into rich plains. Westwardly, across the country, through Townships 10, 11 and 12 north, the country is for the most part rather flat. Near the East Fork of Shoal Creek, the hills are generally low, becoming higher as we descend the stream; in the south part of Township 8 north, they are forty to fifty feet high. On Shoal Creek and Middle Fork, the hills are forty to fifty feet high, and rise by long, gentle ascents. On the West Fork of Shoal Creek the country is generally broken for a few miles from the stream, and the hills sixty to seventy feet high; near Lake Fork, the hills are not very high. In the south half of the county, between the main streams, there are occasional mounds, often a mile or more across their base, and about fifty feet above the adjacent plain, with which they are connected by a long descent.

"A little less than two-thirds of the area of this county is probably prairie. The northern part is mostly prairie; the southern has a large proportion of timber. Near Hurricane Creek, there are post oak flats, changing to large white-oak hills near the creek. At the edge of the prairie, the growth is mostly laurel oak, sumac, hazel, plum, etc. Near Ramsey Creek, the upland growth consists of white-oak, black-oak, post-oak, laurel oak, hazel and sassafras. The East Fork hills have mostly pin oak, black-oak and post-oak, changing near the prairie to laurel oak, black-oak and hazel. Shoal Creek hills have mostly white-oak, black-oak, sassafras and hickory, often extending to the prairies. Near Hillsboro, the growth is principally black-oak, with some white-oak, hickory, sassafras and hazel. Near Walshville and Lake Fork, the country is gently undulating, with a growth principally of plum, black walnut, honey-locust, wild-cherry and grapevines. Wild vines loaded with grapes are observed nearly everywhere in the woods, proving the soil to be naturally well adapted to the grape. Post-oak flats occur near West Fork, as far as Township 10 north. Sugar trees are occasionally found along the Middle and West Forks, and some extensive groves are found on the bottoms of main Shoal Creek.

"The following comprises a list of such trees and shrubs as were observed occurring in this county: Crabapple, ash, prickly ash, red birch, buckeye, box-elder, button bush, bittersweet, blackberry, coralberry, chokecherry, common cherry, coffee tree, *cornus* (two species); cottonwood, *Clematis Virginiana:* elder, grape (four or five species), gooseberry, black haw, hackberry, honey-locust, *hop tree*; hazel, shellbark and thick shellbark hickory, pig-nut hickory, black hickory and common hickory, iron-wood, linden, white maple, sugar tree, red mulberry, papaw persimmon, plum; black, red, white, post, laurel, pin, chestnut, black-jack, burr and swamp white-oak; red and American elm, red-bud, raspberry, rose, red-root, poison oak, sassafras, service berry, sarsaparilla, sumac, trumpet creeper, Virginia creeper, willow (several species), and black and white walnut."

Geology.—The geological formations of a country are the most important part of its history. By the science of geology, the history of the earth is traced back through successive ages to its rudimental condition. It is not inappropriate then to introduce the history of this county with a brief sketch of its geological structure, as compiled from the official survey of the State. A familiarity with the subject should be of interest to all citizens, for we are told by men of science that upon the "geological structure of a country depend the pursuits of its inhabitants and the genius of its civilization. That agriculture is the outgrowth of a fertile soil; mining results from mineral resources," etc., etc. Hence, for the benefit of our readers, a few pages will be devoted to the geology of Montgomery County, as reported in the geological survey. "Along the various streams," says this authority, "are occasional exposures of sand and pebbles, with some beds of brownish-yellow clay. Five miles northeast of Litchfield forty-five feet of drift is exposed, the lower part a compact bed of dark clay, with some sand and pebbles. The following description is given of the various clays passed through in well-digging in the vicinity of Hillsboro: First, soil; second, yellow clay or hardpan: at twenty-four feet, reached a three-foot bed of sand, then soft, moist clay. Seventy-five yards from this, another well was dug, showing in the upper part brownish-yellow clay at twenty feet, and at thirty-eight feet was a two-foot bed of sand, and, at forty-two feet, specimens of wood.

"On the head-waters of the Ramsey, there are many springs slightly chalybeate, and some containing sulphate of iron, issuing from beds of drift, sand and pebbles. There is certainly evidence that at some former period of time the whole surface of the county was fifty to seventy-five feet higher than at present; that since the original drift deposition (it may have been just at the close of the drift period), large masses of these deposits were washed off, leaving occasional mound-like elevations several of which may be seen near Nokomis, a few between the East and West Forks, and the hills between Hillsboro and Butler.

"The upper coal measures appear in part in this county, and underly all the superficial deposits, and include coal beds No. 11 and No. 13, and a trace of No. 12, and embrace 150 feet of rock, reaching from the base of No. 33 to No. 20 of the upper coal measure section. Nos. 20 and 21, in Section 12, Township 10 north, Range 1 west, there crops out along the creek eight feet of sandy shale and blue limestone; close by is an outcrop of brown, shaly soft limestone, containing *Hemipronites crassus* and crinoid stems; *Macrocheilus* and *Spirifer cameratus* were also found. The exact thickness between 21 and 22 is unknown; the outcrops are ten miles apart, with no evidence of a continuous easterly dip, but it is probable that twenty-five or even fifty feet may intevene.

"Northeast of Irving on East Fork, and down stream for a mile, there are occasional outcrops of an ash-blue hard shelly limestone, abounding in a large variety of *Productus Prattenianus*. It also contains *P. costatus*, *P. punctatus*, *P. Nebrascensis*, *Spirifer cameratus*, *Aviculopecten carboniferous*, *Chonetes*, *Verneuilianus*, *Ch. Flemingii*, and a branching coral. A quarter of a mile up stream, the limestone appears in a regular layer, stretching across the bed of a small branch. Three miles up stream, many fossils were collected, weathered out of the shale beds in a fine state of preservation, including beautiful specimens of *Pleurotomaria*, *sphærulata*, *P. tabulata*, *Orthoceras*, *Macrocheilus paludinaformis*. and one like the *M. primigenius*, but with body, whorl and spire more elongated; *Goniatites globulosus*, *Bellerophon carbonarius*, *Leda bella-striata*, *Nucula ventricosa*, *Astartella vera*, *Conularia*, *Leda Oweni*, *Euomphalus*, *subrugosus* and *Polyphemopsis peracuta*. These shales contain round and oblong clay and ironstone concretions. In Section 28, Township 10 north, Range 3 west, a few fossils were obtained, indicating the presence of the same beds as those last named. The upper blue limestone, named above, undulates along East Fork for about eight miles, which is regarded as equivalent to No. 22 of general section. Near Section 36, Township 8 north, Range 3 west, on the East Fork of Shoal Creek, there crops out eight feet of sandy shale and sandstone. On West Fork, at the bridge on the Hillsboro and Walshville road, there is a bluff of thirty-five feet of bluish-gray sandy shales with a thin bed showing markings resembling those of *Fucoides cauda galli*, and containing one *Bellerophon*. East of Litchfield, at the creek bluffs. is seen thirty feet of sandy, shale, and below that ten feet of thick-bedded sandstone resting on limestone. Four miles up stream this sandstone is quite ferruginous at the base. and contain many remains of plants. *Calamites*, *Sigilaræ*, *etc*. One mile farther up stream, there were observed forty-eight feet of darkish micaceous sandy shale. On Five-Mile Creek in Section 26. Township 10 north, Range 5 west. there are twelve feet of sandy shales, with a thin bed of partially carbonized wood, containing a fossil fern. A quarter of a mile up the creek there is an exposure of sixteen feet of this olive-drab clay shales, with ironstone nodules These shales are evidently continuations of the same beds. and make the total thickness of No. 26 not less than eighty-five feet. The best exposures of Nos. 27 to 33 inclusive are on Lake Fork and at Litchfield. The section on Lake Fork, at the Bond County line, near McCracken's, coal, is as follows:

	Ft.	In.
Drift slope	20	0
No. 27—Lead blue limestone, with crinoid stems, and *Athyris subtilita*	2	0
No. 28—Coal	0	2
No. 29—Blue clay shales	10	0
No. 30—Shale and shaly limestone abounding in fossils, but many are much crushed including *Spirifer cameratus*, *Productus punctatus*, *P. Nebrascensis*, *Spiriferina Kentuckensis*, *Hemipronites crassus* *Productus*, *Prattenianus*, *Athyris subtilita* *Terebratula bovidens*, *Myalina subquadrata*, a *Macrocheilus*, a *Pleurotomaria*, and one in fish tooth	4	0
No. 31—Ash-gray limestone; in the lower part there is from one to one and a half feet of dark ash-colored limestone, often traversed by fine lines of calc spar; fossils not abundant contains *Productus longispinus*	13	0
Bituminous shale	4	0
No. 33—Coal No. 11	1	5

"Part of No. 27 appears two and one-half miles northwest in the bed of the creek, containing *Spirifer cameratus*, *Fistulipora*, *Productus costatus*, *P. Nebrascensis*, *P. Prattenianus* and *Myalina subquadrata*. The fossils here have a well preserved and nacreons appearance. One and a half miles southwest of Bethel. part of No. 31 crops out along the creek; the upper portion is an even bedded bluish-gray sub-crystalline limestone; but below it is more irregularly bedded. *Productus longispinus* abounds, associated with *Aviculopecten carboniferus*. Four miles northeast of Litchfield. the upper part of No. 31 is a thick bedded brownish-gray limestone, abounding in *Rhynchonella Uta*.

Coal.—"On J. Wilson's land, Section 7, Township 8 north. Range 2 west. coal No. 13 (No. 24 of upper coal measures section) has been mined; that used was from near the out crop, and does not appear very favorable; the quality and thickness might improve by thorough opening. The same coal has also been taken out on the land of John L. Newsman, in Section 28, Township 10 north, Range 3 west, some eighteen inches thick, but could not be thoroughly examined on account of the overlying *débris*. On the land of Mr. McCracken, near the south county line (probably in Bond County) Coal 13 is seventeen inches thick. Occurring as it does below the bed of the creek, it can only be reached at low water, and even then the labor of one man is required most of the time to keep the pit sufficiently dry for two others to work; but with this trouble it will repay very well to work for neighborhood purposes. The same bed has also been worked at Ross' old mill, on Shoal Creek, at the south county line, and may also be reached just below the surface of the water on Shoal Creek above Long bridge. At the limestone quarries on the creek near Butler, it may be reached at about ten to fourteen feet beneath the bed of the creek; also about four feet beneath the darker colored limestone at the base of Michael Cleary's quarry east of Litchfield.

Building Rock.—"On East Fork, about Section 26, Township 8 north, Range 3 west, there is a tolerably good bed of hard bluish limestone. On Rocky Branch, east of Litchfield, there are extensive quarries of pretty good limestone; the beds are rather irregular, but the rock is very extensively used for ordinary stone work, and makes very good lime. North of the railroad on the West Fork, there are several outcrops of a brown and gray limestone in three-foot beds. The same rock is also found four miles farther up stream. At the latter place, part of it presents a beautiful bluish-gray variegated appearance. This limestone possesses much durability, and being in a thick even bed, may become in time very useful for large columns. It is believed to be equivalent to that used in the construction of the old State House at Springfield. West of Butler, there are good quarries of limestone for lime, and it is also much used in the neighborhood for ordinary building purposes."

The foregoing presents a pretty good digest of the geology of Montgomery County and its wealth of coal measures, building rocks, etc., and will be found of interest to land-owners at least.

The climate of Montgomery County, in common with Southern and Central Illinois, is variable. No one who has lived here long needs to be told this; it very soon becomes an established fact in his own personal experience. Of the temperature, climate and the various changes of Southern Illinois weather generally, Foster's Physical Geography has the following: "The melting snows of winter, generally attended by rains, convert the rich soil of the prairies into mud, and render early spring the most unpleasant part of the year. The heat of summer, although more intense than in the same latitude on the Atlantic, is greatly relieved by the constant breezes which fan the prairies. Autumn, with its slowly diminishing heat terminates in the serene and beautiful season known as Indian Summer. Its mild and uniform temperature, soft and hazy atmosphere, and forests beautifully tinted with the hues of dying foliage, all conspire to render it the pleasant part of the year. Next comes the boreal blasts of winter, with its social firesides, and tinkling bells in the mystic light of the moon, as merry sleighs skim over the level snow-clad prairies. The winter has its sudden change of temperature, causing colds and other diseases arising from extreme vicissitudes of weather. This is the most unfavorable feature of the climate, which in other respects is salubrious." These sudden changes seem to increase both in number and in extremes, a fact doubtless attributable to natural causes—the settling-up and cultivation of the country. It is very common to hear old citizens who have lived in the State forty or fifty years, tell how different the seasons are now and when they first came here. There is more or less snow or rain, the seasons are less favorable for farming, the springs more backward, etc., etc., just as their fancy happens to get the start of them.

The following extract from an article in the old Illinois *Gazetteer*, published in 1834, would indicate that there had been considerable atmospherical changes within the last half-century: "There are a great proportion of clear, pleasant days throughout the year. Dr. Beck, who resided at St. Louis during the year 1820, made observations upon the changes of the weather, and produced the following results: 'Clear days, 245; cloudy, including all the variable days, 110.' The results of my own observations, kept for twelve years, with the exception of 1826, and with some irregularity from traveling into different parts of Illinois during the time, do not vary in any material degree from the above statement." Taking the present year of grace (1882) as a sample of cool, cloudy, disagreeable weather, it presents a striking contrast to the observations of Dr. Beck quoted above, and proves conclusively that changes are taking place in the climate and seasons.

CHAPTER II.[*]

EARLY OCCUPATION OF THE COUNTRY—THE MOUND-BUILDERS—THEIR REMAINS AND FORTIFICATIONS—THE INDIANS—TRACES OF THEM IN MONTGOMERY COUNTY—THEIR SUCCESSORS, THE WHITES—DIFFICULTIES ENCOUNTERED BY THE EMIGRANTS ON THEIR WAY TO NEW HOMES—INCIDENTS OF THE PIONEER PERIOD—GROWTH AND DEVELOPMENT OF THE COUNTRY.

PRE-HISTORIC research has evolved the fact that, at a period lying wholly within the province of conjecture, a semi-civilized people, whose origin and final fate, as well as their habits and customs, are enshrouded in comparative mystery, inhabited, not only this country, but most of the Western Continent. All attempts to unravel the mystery enveloping their peculiar lives meet with failure, save where their fast-decaying works cast a feeble ray of light on the otherwise impenetrable darkness. From the northern lakes through the Mississippi Valley into Mexico, and thence into South America these relics of a lost race extend. Many archæologists believe that their occupation of this country was anterior to that of the Eastern Hemisphere, and that this continent is really the Old instead of the New World. However extravagant this opinion may be, there is no longer any doubt in the mind of the archæologist that this country was occupied by a race of people, of whose origin the Indians, found in possession of the country by the Europeans, knew absolutely nothing. The mounds and fortifications left by them form by far the most interesting relics of American antiquity. Some of the most extensive mounds in the United States are in Illinois, and are located contiguous to the Mississippi River. But our limited space will not admit of a detailed account of this lost race of people. Their name, language and history have utterly perished from the earth, and their very existence even would never have been known but for the almost obliterated remains which still show the work of their hands. That they did exist, such writers as Rafinesque, Foster, Lubbock and others, who have spent years in pre-historic research, stoutly maintained. No traces, however, of the "lost race" are found in Montgomery County so as we can learn. Fortifications, camps, burying-grounds, etc., which some have attributed to the Mound-Builders', and which are located in different sections of the county, are believed by others, better informed, to be but the works of the American Indians. The latter theory is, doubtless, the correct one.

Following the Mound-Builders, and supposed by writers upon the subject to have been their conquerors, came the Indians, the red sons of the forest. They next occupied this country and resisted the encroachments of the whites to the bitter end. From the Atlantic coast, they were pressed backward toward the setting sun, strewing their path with the bones and skeletons of their martyred warriors. They crossed the Alleghanies, and, descending its western slope, chanted their death songs as they moved slowly and mournfully away from the land of their fathers, before the ever-advancing tide of pale-faces. Halting upon the plains of the "Illini, amid the forests that bounded its streams they made the last home of their own choosing.

[*] W. H. Perrin.

But here they were not allowed to remain in peace. The handful of whites, who had dropped upon the western shore of the Atlantic, had grown into a great multitude, and like the little stone cut out of the mountains by unseen hands, were rolling on, as a mighty avalanche, crushing all that opposed. In the early dawn of the nineteenth century, the red man was again forced to take up his line of march from Southern Illinois, nor allowed to rest until he reached his promised land, the great plains of the far West. His foot-prints are still visible in what now forms Montgomery County, in fortifications, burying-grounds, etc.

The Indians occupying this portion of Illinois, were the Kickapoos. The following extract will be found of interest to our readers: "The Kickapoos, in 1763, occupied the country southwest of the southern extremity of Lake Michigan. They subsequently moved southward, and at a more recent date dwelt in portions of the territory on the Mackinaw and Sangamon Rivers, and had a village on Kickapoo Creek, and at Elkhart Grove. They were more civilized, industrious, energetic and cleanly than the neighboring tribes, and it may also be added, more implacable in their hatred to the Americans. They were among the first to commence battle and the last to submit and enter into treaties; unappeasable enmity led them into the field against Gens. Harmar, St. Clair and Wayne and to be the first in all the bloody charges on the field of Tippecanoe. They were prominent among the Northern nations, which, for more than a century, waged an exterminating war against the Illinois Confederacy. Their last hostile act of this kind was perpetrated in 1805, against some poor Kaskaskia children, whom they found gathering strawberries on the prairie above the town which bears the name of their tribe. Seizing a considerable number of them, they fled to their villages before the enraged Kaskaskias could overtake them and rescue their offspring. During the years of 1810 and 1811, in conjunction with the Chippewas, Pottawatomies and Ottawas, they committed so many thefts and murders on the frontier settlements that Gov. Edwards was compelled to employ military force to suppress them. They claimed relationship with the Pottawatomies, and perhaps with the Sacs and Foxes and Shawnees. When removed from Illinois, they still retained their old animosities against the Americans, and went to Texas, then a province of Mexico, to get beyond the jurisdiction of the United States. There were other tribes, also, who roamed through this part of the State. The Foxes sometimes made incursions into this immediate section, and if they did not live here permanently, they remained at least temporarily. In what is now East Fork Township, on McDavid's Branch, in Section 34, at a fine spring, the Foxes once had a village or camp. Of this, however, we have but little that is definite, as none now living remember the event from their own personal knowledge.

There is a tradition, but how true we do not know, that Capt. Whiteside, the celebrated pioneer and Indian fighter, once, in company with a few kindred spirits, fought a battle with the Indians on Shoal Creek, in the southeast part of North Litchfield Township; but of this battle there remains no record, other than tradition. Many other traditions may be gathered of the occupation of the county by the aborigines, but none of them are particularly reliable. In many parts of the county there are remains of camps some of them fortified with something of military order. One of these near Hillsboro still shows the old fortifications very plainly, and has been examined by military men, who recognized its situation for a successful defense. Nothing, however, has been published in regard to it, and few people in the county know the place of its location.

As the white settlement increased, the Indians left the neighborhood, falling back, as has ever been their fate, before the advancing tide of immigration. Their camp fires paled in the sunlight of civilization, and then went out on the prairies of Illinois forever.

The first white people who traversed this country, and claimed it by the right of discovery, were the French explorers and travelers. More than two hundred years ago, such men as La Salle, Marquette, Hennepin, Joliet and other Frenchmen, had traversed the State of Illinois, or what now forms this great State, and made settlements along the Mississippi River. Many trees and stones bore the impress of the *fleur de lis* of France, and Kaskaskia Cahokia and Vincennes became enterprising French towns surrounded by flourishing settlements. Marquette discovered the Mississippi River, and spent years of toil in explorations and Christianizing the natives of the great West, then died, with none to soothe him in his last moments save his faithful Indian converts. La Salle penetrated to the mouth of the "Great Father of Waters," and after planting the standard, and claiming the country in the name of his king, was treacherously murdered by his own followers. But time passed on, and eventually the lilies of France drooped and withered before the majestic tread of the British lion, who, in his turn, quailed and cowered beneath the scream of the American eagle. The conquest of Gen. George Rogers Clark made Illinois a county of Virginia, and wrested it forever from foreign rule. But few decades after Clark captured Kaskaskia and Vincennes, white people from the Eastern States began to cross the Wabash into the present State of Illinois. The first settlements were made in the southern part of the State, and not until about the years 1816-17 was there a settlement made by the whites in what is now Montgomery County.

It was in the latter part of 1816 or early in 1817 that the first white settlement was effected in the county. This pioneer settlement was made in the extreme southern part, on Hurricane Creek. Among the settlers forming it were Joseph Williams, Henry Pyatt William McDavid, John and Henry Hill, Jesse Johnson, Henry Sears, Aaron Case, Harris Reavis, Joseph and Charles Wright, Easton Whitten, John Kirkpatrick Henry Rowe, John Russell, David Bradford, E. Gwinn and others. In what is now Hillsboro Township, on Shoal Creek, the next settlement was made by an importation of Kentuckians and Tennesseans in 1817-18, among whom were the following, viz.: Alexander McWilliams, Solomon Prewitt, John Norton, Roland Shepherd, Jarvis Forehand, Gordon Crandall, William Clark, David McCoy, Nicholas Lockerman, Hugh Kirkpatrick, Melcher Fogleman, William Griffith, Joseph McAdams, Israel Seward, James Street, Luke Steed, John McPhail, Joel Smith, David Kirkpatrick, Jesse Townsend, Jacob Cress, Israel Butler, the Harkeys, and a number of others now forgotten. Hiram Rountree, one of the prominent men of the county, who is noticed fully elsewhere, settled in this neighborhood in 1821, and spent the remainder of his life here.

These settlements were made in the timber bordering the water-courses. The people who composed the original settlements came from timbered countries, abounding in springs and streams of running water. To them, the broad prairies of waving grass, overtopped with innumerable blossoms and fragrant flowers (in summer), presented all the monotony if not the dreariness of sandy deserts, and the groves of timber were as welcome as the "shadow of a great rock in a weary land." It was not for years after the first settlements were made in the timber that people ventured out on the prairies. The prairies, they believed, would never be utilized, except for pasture, as the country afforded an insufficiency of timber to fence them, and "if God Almighty did not make timber grow on the prairies, they argued, "it was no use for man to attempt it."

Hence, the prairies would never be fit for anything but pasturage.

Settlements were made in other portions of the county soon after those already mentioned. Some of the people composing these early settlements, after a temporary rest, made other settlements. Melchoir Fogleman, with Nicholas Voylis and William Stephens, settled in what is now Walshville Township some time in 1818. A little later, Austin Grisham, James Baker and John Jordan settled in the same neighborhood. In what is now Butler Grove Township, Jacob Cress and family, already mentioned, settled in 1818. The present township of Fillmore was invaded by a colony from Kentucky about 1820, among whom were James Card, Thomas J. Todd, John Alexander, Henry and Peter Hill, M. Mason and others. Thus settlers came in every year, and settlements were made in every body of timber in what is now Montgomery County. As the population increased, and the timbered land was occupied, settlers began to branch out on the prairies. Slowly at first, and with many misgivings, but as the first venturesome ones did not starve to death, others soon followed them, until all the prairie land was either settled or taken up. It is not our purpose to minutely describe the settlements made in different parts of the county in this connection, but will leave it to chapters devoted to each individual township.

For a number of years after the first settlements were made in the wilderness, life possessed few pleasures and comforts, and was hard in the extreme and often dangerous. The people were exposed to danger, and were forced to undergo the most arduous toil to maintain life. The following extract from an article by Mr. Coolidge will give the reader some idea of the life led by the early settlers until civilization and prosperity improved the times. The article referred to says: "The earliest houses or cabins were of logs, one story high, and usually of one room. The door was frequently made of split stuff, and the openings for light sometimes were defended by a frame or rude sash, with oiled paper for glass, but more usually the opening was closed only by a solid shutter. In the summer, this was left unclosed; in the winter, the cabin was lighted down the chimney or through an open door. In such a residence we have seen the entire family of father and mother and well grown boys and girls and the occasional guest sleeping on the floor, and heard Senator Douglas repeat the ludicrous comments of the grown-up daughters on the 'right small chance of legs' he was forced to exhibit when dressing in the morning after a night's rest *en famille*. The kitchen utensils were a pot for boiling potatoes, a bake-kettle for bread and a skillet for frying meat. Twenty-five dollars would buy the entire domestic outfit of a family, the coveted feather-bed representing a moiety of the same. Chairs or seats were made at home, strong, durable and weighty, but not luxurious. The pantry was a rustic shelf or two in a corner, with a bit of cloth before them. We are dubious as to the cradles, but the crop of children was sure and large. They grew up stout, rosy-cheeked, and shy as untamed colts. As for pocket-money, nobody seems to remember if they had any. The writer's allowance, when sixteen, was but 5 cents a year. A tea-kettle was a superfluity and irons were supplied by a couple of flat stones. The hearth was the naked earth; the chimney was outside the house. A bank of clay and stone was raised up several feet; about four feet from the general level, two stout pieces of timber were fastened on each side of the fire-seat the upper ends inclining toward each other, and resting against a loft-beam, a yard and a half from the wall of the house. The angular space thus inclosed was filled with split sticks and clay mortar. At a convenient height on each side, a hole was left into which was thrust a pole from which depended a log chain, into which pot-hooks could be inserted to sustain a pot or kettle. If the owner was forehanded, he substituted a trammel for the chain; this was usually a flat bar of iron, the upper part bent to grip the pole easily, and the lower portion pierced with numerous holes for the insertion of pot-hooks.

"After 1830, wagons began to be seen. Prior to this, the ox-cart was the universal vehicle of transportation. Judge Rountree brought his wife and worldly possessions to the county, drawn by a yoke of two-year-old steers. Thomas C. Hughes brought his family here in a similar vehicle. These carts were not built for rapid movement. A yoke of oxen usually lounged onward at the rate of a mile and a half an hour, and five days was the usual time for a trip to St. Louis. With the use of wagons horses began to be employed to draw them. Mules were not seen here until well on in the thirties. If a stranger noticed a house a furlong or half a mile from a highway, and approached only through several gates, he knew he was gazing on the site of a pioneer home.

"The plague of insects was intolerable to man and beast. A green-headed fly was the most formidable pest. In the heat of the day, horses were frantic and for safety were put in stables. Cattle would dash through thickets of hazel brush to dislodge their tormentors or stand midside deep in pools of water. The people would at times maintain 'smudges' to drive away mosquitoes, and cattle would seek and stand in the smoke for hours for relief. With the increase of land cultivation, these pests have disappeared."

In further illustration of the pioneer period, we quote the following from the "Rountree Letters" published a few years ago in the Hillsboro *Democrat*: "Biscuits and corn-dodgers baked in an oven over and under glowing coals at the fire-place, and johnny-cakes baked on a board in front of the fire, are among the pleasantest memories. The big pot of [illegible] was also one of our earliest delights. Game was so plenty that it rarely happened that meats were scarce. But the means of obtaining meal and flour for bread were scarce. Mills for flour came after awhile, but hand-mills, run not by steam, horses nor oxen, but by women and children, were occasionally seen; new corn was often grated by hand for immediate use. * * Instead of our gay chandeliers and coal oil lamps, were candles of tallow or wax, and an old-fashioned affair, dignified by the name of lamp, that was stuck in a crack in the wall and held lard in a heart-shaped sheet-iron basin, in which was a wick which burned well and gave a torch-like glare. Those who had brass or silver or even iron candle-sticks strove to keep them as bright as their pewter and tinware.

"The clothing for both sexes was made at home. If of cotton, the cotton was raised, picked, ginned, carded, spun, woven, colored and cut and made at home. If of wool, the sheep were raised, the wool clipped, picked by hand, carded, spun, colored, woven and made up at home. All members of the household, male and female, men, women and children were usually employed in some part, if not in all parts, of the manufacture. It is true that the men and boys frequently wore clothing either made entire of the dressed skins of animals or had their clothes 'foxed' with them. There are no doubt many now living in our old county who can tell of the long linen shirts, home-made, that were the only summer garments worn by children and of the moccasins and the buckskin clothing. Boots were nearly unknown, and shoes were indulged in as a luxury

[illegible] following [illegible] of Judge [illegible] in [illegible]: A settler was at work upon his [illegible] the south end of the present town, when he heard a [illegible] which he was wholly unable to comprehend, and which [illegible] growing as to make every particular hair [illegible] stand on end. Stories of Indian outrages were rife in the [illegible] and he imagined it was some Indian device to draw the [illegible] and with the greatest caution, he set out to [illegible]. When he reached a point commanding a view of the [illegible] the Vandalia road—he saw Judge Rountree coming up the [illegible] driving an ox-cart, the creaking and [illegible] which had produced the horrible sounds so alarming [illegible] ear, [illegible] the alert for danger.—Ed.

only by the grown people, while moccasins made at home sufficed for the smaller members. However, as soon as tanning could be done, and it was also often done at home, it was not unfrequent that the shoe-maker went from house to house with his implements, and made the shoes for the family. There are no doubt many now living in the county who never wore boots until they were nearly grown, and, perhaps, never saw any until nearly grown. Yet while there were days of self-denial, they were days of sincere happiness; and though the memories are pleasant, would we go back to them? Would we be willing to live as our fathers lived? Would those who grew up thus, like to try it again? Times have changed, and with the times our people, and their notions and tastes; and no doubt it is all right. But the memory is pleasant."

Such were some of the experiences, and the hardships with which the early settlers of this county had to contend in reclaiming it from a wilderness. In the grand march of civilization the great changes that have taken place within the last half-century is almost beyond the power of the mind to comprehend. When we look around us at the enterprising cities and towns, the magnificent residences and broad, productive fields, the manufactories of various kinds, and the improved machinery in use, thus facilitating men's work and giving employment to hundreds and thousands of human beings, we are startled at the fact that fifty or sixty years ago these fertile plains were the abode of savages and wild beasts; and the few whites, scattered here and there, as little dreamed of the results of to-day, as we dare predict what the next fifty years may bring forth. The pioneer's cabin "rude in its simplicity and simple in its rudeness" has given place to comfortable homes; the rude implements of agriculture have disappeared before improvements and inventions that have made farming not a labor but a science; while the patient ox has been supplanted by the iron-horse.

Additional to other troubles and trials of the pioneers in the early period of the country were prairie fires. These fires have always been a source of terror to people living in a prairie country, and much damage and loss of property and even of life have resulted from them. The tall prairie grass, from four to six feet high, when dry, with strong winds prevailing, presented combustible matter only surpassed by kerosene, gunpowder, etc. "In time of peace prepare for war," is an adage that was very generally observed by the settlers living on the verge of the prairies and later in the prairies themselves. As soon as the grass began to die and dry up in the fall of the year, preparations against fire were made by burning or plowing roads around fields and farms. But even these barriers were sometimes overleaped, and distressing consequences followed to the poor man, who had but little to begin with, and lost that almost in the twinkling of an eye. The early inhabitants were often melancholy witnesses to these great conflagrations—so glorious in their grandeur, and gloomy in their ruin and waste. The dense smoke arising from them in the days of Indian summer, often enveloped the land in the "shades of evening," recalling the lines of Milton—

> "The sun,
> In dim eclipse, disastrous twilight
> Shed o'er half the nations."

In the natural course of events everything must have a beginning. As the county settled up and population increased, mills were built, shops and stores established to supply the wants of the community, and highways opened to the markets of the outside world. The first store in the county was kept by John Tilson, a man prominent in the early history of the county. He was from Boston, and located on the farm afterward known as the "Scherer place," about three miles southwest of Hillsboro. He opened a store about the year 1820–21, where he lived, and when the county seat was established at Hillsboro, moved his store to town. He built the first brick house in Hillsboro, and kept the first store in the town as well as in the county. When the post office was established, he became the first Postmaster. Melchoir Fogleman is believed to have been the first blacksmith, and had a shop in the west part of the county. The first mills, manufactories, etc., will be found in other chapters of the work. We are informed by a local authority, that N. Lockerman was the first man married, and that he was married by Rev. James Street, while hoeing corn, but whether it was Mr. Street or Mr. Lockerman hoeing corn, deponent saith not. It is said there is a woman in everything, whether for good or ill, but there is none mentioned in connection with the marriage of Mr. Lockerman, and it may be that he was married by Mr. Street to the corn he was hoeing. We would be glad to describe the toilettes and bridal presents of this pioneer wedding, for the benefit of our lady readers, who are always interested in such things, but, owing to circumstances, are unable to do so. We doubt not, however, but that they were in accordance with the customs of the time. As to the truth of the assertions that

> "Full many cares are on the wreath,
> That binds the bridal veil,"

we cannot say, but presume that Mr. Lockerman and his bride—if he had one—lived as happily as the common lot. The second marriage celebrated in the county was David McCoy to Miss Kirkpatrick, and the third, William H. Brown to Miss Harriet Seward. The license of the latter couple were the first returned to the Clerk's office of Montgomery County.

Apropos of "marrying and giving in marriage," the following incident comes in place: In the early years of the county, Judge Rountree was the engineer that ran pretty much all of its machinery. He was Probate Judge, Recorder, County and Circuit Clerk, Justice of the Peace, legislator, and held a dozen or two [illegible]

Once, while at Springfield on legislative business, a couple came to town to get married, and when they found him gone, they seemed greatly troubled in "body and mind." But somebody sent them to Mrs. Rountree, who told them that she could issue the license if she could get in the office, but that Mr. Rountree had carried off the key with him to Springfield. They went to the office, however, when the bridegroom elect set up a lot of fence-rails against the window and finally succeeded in forcing it open. He then entered and opened the door from the inside, and Mrs. Rountree went in where she found a license signed by Judge Rountree, which she filled up for the happy couple, and sent them on their road to Hymen rejoicing. Since then, many couples have gone and done likewise; the old, old story, and yet forever new, has been told over and over again, and still the work goes on. The date of the first birth is forgotten, but as Mr. Coolidge says, the crop of children was sure and large; there *was* a first birth, and, perhaps, at an early day. The present population of the county indicates their frequency.

The first death which occurred is not now remembered. Sixty-five years have come and gone since the first white people came here, and now most of them have passed to that bourn whence no traveler returns.

> "Long years have flown o'er the scenes of the past,
> And many turned gray in the winter's cold blast;
> While others but dream of the time that is gone
> They are bent by the years that are fast rolling on."

It was appointed unto all men to die, says Holy Writ, and pretty faithfully have the pioneers of Montgomery County obeyed the summons. The grass has grown over their graves in the old churchyard, the flowers have bloomed and withered with the coming and waning years and a new generation now fill their places upon the stage of action.

CHAPTER III.

ORGANIZATION OF MONTGOMERY COUNTY—THE ACT OF THE LEGISLATURE CREATING IT—EARLY OFFICERS AND COURTS—LOCATION OF THE COUNTY SEAT—COURT HOUSES AND PUBLIC BUILDINGS—DIVISION OF THE COUNTY INTO PRECINCTS AND TOWNSHIPS—CONVENIENCE OF TOWNSHIP ORGANIZATION—THE POOR FARM, ETC.—POLITICS AND POLITICAL PARTIES.

THE American people tend naturally to self-government. Hence, the formation of States and counties as soon as the number of inhabitants will allow. Under the history of Bond County, we have seen how Illinois formed, first a county of Virginia, then a portion of the Northwestern Territory, then of the Indiana Territory, later a territory of itself, and finally, a State of the American Union. Its first division into counties is there noted, and the manner in which Bond was created while the State was still a Territory, and embraced a vast extent of country now divided into a number of counties. This tendency to independence and self-government led to the formation of Montgomery County, when there were but a few hundred people within its present circumscribed limits. It was set off from Bond County, by act of the Legislature, passed at the session of 1820–21, and approved on the 12th of February of the latter year. That portion of the act pertaining to the organization of Montgomery County, or the main point of it, were as follows: "Be it enacted by the General Assembly of Illinois, and it is hereby enacted by authority of the same, that all that tract of country lying within the following prescribed boundaries, to wit:

"Beginning at the southeast corner of Section 24, in Township 7 north, and Range 2 west, of the Third Principal Meridian; thence west eighteen miles to the southwest corner of Section 19, in Township 7 north, and Range 5 west; thence south to the line of said township, thence west to the southwest corner, and thence north to the northwest corner of Township 12 north; thence east twenty-four miles to the northeast corner of Township 12 north, and Range 2 west, thence south to the beginning, to be known as Montgomery County, and that Melchoir Fogleman, James Street and Joseph Wright, be appointed Commissioners to locate the seat of justice of said county, etc., etc." The remainder of the act, with a number of "whereases" and "enactments," has no particular reference to this county and is omitted. The newly created county was named, it is said, in honor of Gen. Montgomery, a Revolutionary officer, while others are dubious as to whence it received its name. In the absence, however, of certainty, we will leave the honor with the old soldier mentioned above.

Montgomery County retained its original boundaries until the formation of Dane County, now called Christian, the act of which was approved February 15, 1839, when a large mouthful was taken out of the northeast corner of Montgomery, leaving it in its present irregular shape. The Commissioners, appointed to locate the county seat, met at the house of Joseph McAdams, to determine the matter, and to decide upon an eligible site. According to the act creating the county, the owner of the land selected for the county seat was to donate twenty acres for public buildings, as an inducement for his land being accepted for the pur-

By W. H. Perrin.

pose. After mature deliberation, the Commissioners made selection of a site, known since as the "McAdams place," and which is about three miles southwest of Hillsboro. A town was laid out and called Hamilton, lots were sold, streets surveyed, and contracts let for public buildings, and every effort made to start a town. In the meantime, however, there was much dissatisfaction as to the place selected, and strong objections raised to the erection of a court house and a jail at Hamilton. Joseph Wright, one of the Commissioners appointed to locate the county seat, refused to sign the report of the Commissioners, and made a kind of minority report on the question, urging as a reason for his course, that Hamilton was neither the geographical center of the county or of population. So great was the controversy over the matter that, by another act of the Legislature, passed early in the year 1823, new Commissioners were appointed to relocate the county seat. This new board consisted of Elijah C. Berry, Silas L. Wait and Aaron Armstrong, and in accordance with the provisions of the act they met and, after considering the different points contesting for the honor, they chose the present site of Hillsboro. The name is said to have been given by a North Carolinian, many of whom were among the early settlers of this section, in honor of his native place, Hillsboro, N. C. But it is quite as probable that the name was attained from the numerous hills, upon which the little city now sits as majestically as did ancient Rome upon her seven hills.

The following incident is related in connection with the location of the county seat at Hillsboro. The land upon which the town stands, and which had been selected for the capital, had not been entered at the time. The Commissioners had heard of a man living in the southern part of the county, of the name of Newton Coffey, who was said to have fifty dollars in money, something very unusual for a pioneer citizen of Illinois at that day. So they sent for him and prevailed upon him to enter the land, as none else had money enough to do so. Coffey entered the land, made a donation of the usual twenty acres for public buildings, and proceeded to lay out the town of Hillsboro as will be fully detailed in succeeding chapters of this work.

The Courts.—No public buildings as we have said, were erected at Hamilton and the first court of the newly-organized county was held at the house of Joseph McAdams and after the relocation of the county seat at the house of Luke Steel, until a building of a court house at Hillsboro. The first term of the Circuit Court, as well as the County Commissioners Court, was held at McAdams', and was presided over by Hon. John Reynolds Judge Hiram Rountree was Clerk, and Joel Wright Sheriff. The grand jury were as follows: John Seward, James Black, George W. Shipman, David Bradford, William McDavid, John Beck, James Card, George Davis, Elisha Freeman, Henry Hill, Lewis Scribner, Hiram Reavis, James Walker, Newton Coffey, Jarvis Forehand, John Yoakum, John Elder and Thomas Robinson. The first County Commissioners' Court was held April 7, 1821, the Commissioners being John Beck, John McAdams and John Seward The following county officers were appointed at this term of courts, viz.: Hiram Rountree, Clerk; John Tilson, Treasurer; Joel Wright Sheriff, and E. M. Townsend, Probate Judge: James Wright and Daniel Meredith were appointed first Constables of the county. Thus was the civil machinery of the county set in motion, by the organization of the different branches of the court, and the appointment of the requisite officers to properly administer the same. Some of these early officers were men of ability, and left their impress upon the history of the county as will be seen from sketches of their lives in different departments of this work.

As population increased, the county was laid

off into districts for the greater convenience of the people and the better administration of the laws. It was first divided into election precincts, and subdivided as occasion required. The election precincts were continued until within the last decade, when the county adopted township organization, and the precincts were changed into civil townships. There are now eighteen townships in the county, viz.: Hillsboro, North and South Litchfield, Zanesville, Harvel, Pitman, Raymond, Bois D'Arc, Rountree, Nokomis, Audubon, Witt, Fillmore, East Fork, Irving, Butler Grove, Walshville and Grisham. These are all full Congressional townships, that is, comprise thirty-six sections, except Harvel, Bois D'Arc, Audubon, Fillmore, East Fork and Grisham. Some of these have been divided for election purposes, but otherwise remain subject to the same township government. Under the old precinct system, the court consisted of three Commissioners, elected by the people, and all business relating to the county was transacted by this court as it is now done by the Board of Supervisors. The system of township organization had its origin in the United States, in the early history and settlement of New England. "The root of this form of local government," says a late writer, "may be traced to the districting of England into tithings by King Alfred, in the ninth century, to crush the widespread local disorders which disturbed his realms." Upon this ancient idea of tithing districts, the Puritans grafted their great improved township system. The county system originated in this country, in Virginia, and is also of English origin. The tobacco planters of the Old Dominion, owning their laborers more completely than did the Barons of England their vassals, lived isolated and independent upon their large landed estates, in imitation of the aristocracy of the mother country. They also modeled their county and municipal institutions with certain modifications suitable to the condition of the new country, after the same prototype; whence has spread the county system into all the Southern and many of the Northern States. All the Northwest Territory, now constituting five States, after the conquest of Clark, was, by Virginia, in 1778, formed into one county under jurisdiction (as already mentioned), called Illinois. The county feature was after retained in all the States carved out of this territory. The county business in Illinois was transacted by these Commissioners, in the respective counties, who constituted a County Court, which, besides the management of county affairs, had usually other jurisdiction conferred upon it, such as that of Justice of the Peace and Probate business. By the constitution of 1848, owing to Eastern or New England settlers in the northern part of the State, township organization was authorized, leaving it optional for any county to adopt or not the law to be enacted. In accordance with the provision of that constitution, and in obedience to a demand from the people in the northern part of the State, who had observed its practical workings in the Eastern States, the first township organization act was passed by the Legislature. But the law, in attempting to put it into practical operation, disclosed radical defects. It was revised and amended at the session of 1851, substantially as it has existed until the recent revision in 1871. The adoption of the township system marks an era in the management of fiscal affairs in many of the counties of the State. Our township system is not, however, closely modeled after the New England States. There a Representative is sent directly from each town to the Lower House of the Legislature. In New York, owing to her vast extent of territory, this was found to be impracticable and a county assembly denominated a Board of Supervisors composed of a member from each town, was then established. This modified system we have copied, almost exactly, in Illinois.

"Townships are often compared to petty re-

A. N. Kingsbury

publics, possessing unlimited sovereignty in matters of local concern; and Boards of Supervisors are often popularly supposed to be vested with certain limited legislative powers. Neither is the case. Both the County and the Township Boards are the mere fiscal agents. They hold the purse-strings of the counties; they may contract, incur debts, or create liabilities—very great powers, it is true—but they cannot prescribe or vary the duties, nor control in any manner the county or township officers authorized by law. While the County Court of three members is a smaller, and, therefore, as a rule, more manageable, or controllable body by outside influences, there is little doubt that a Board of Supervisors is not only more directly expressive, but also that a thousand and one petty claims of every conceivable character, having no foundation in law or justice, are constantly presented, and, being loosely investigated and tacitly allowed, aggregate no insignificant sum. A Board of Supervisors also acts or is controlled more by partisan feelings. There ought to be uniformity throughout the State in the management of county affairs. No little confusion seems to pervade the laws at the present time relating to our two classes of counties."

Whatever may be the opinion of the writer of the foregoing, the system of township organization now in vogue in a majority of the counties of Illinois, is not without its merits. The fact—a very potent one, too—is that when once adopted by any county, it is never changed. None have been known, as far as we have been able to learn, though the attempt has often been made to recede from the position and return to the old system. And, slowly as some of the counties were to enter into it, yet when they did finally adopt it, they have continued to cling perseveringly to it. Montgomery, as we have said, was late in adopting township organization, remaining under the old precinct organization until 1873, when the new order of local government was inaugurated. The most important township officers are a Supervisor, Township Clerk, Assessor, Treasurer, etc. The number and names of the townships of Montgomery County have already been given in this chapter.

The Poor Farm.—This is a county institution and deserves some mention in this connection. It is located in East Fork Township, about three miles south of Hillsboro. The costs of pauperage in this county are but small compared to those borne by the people of England and some other European nations. The local communities of Illinois give equally good care to a few unfortunates who, by constantly recurring misfortunes, are at last brought to live upon the county.

The first Poor Farm was in Irving Township, and was known as "swamp land," which was set apart for the purpose of a Poor Farm, but was never used nor improved as such. It was selected December 6, 1873, and was the northeast quarter of Section 1, Township 9 (Irving), Range 3. A committee was appointed to prepare a place for erecting buildings, etc., and March 27, 1874, a contract was let for $3,900 for that purpose, but on the 29th of April, before work commenced, the site was changed to the Blackman farm, in East Fork Township. The contractor was to put up the same buildings as those designed in Irving Township. May 1, 1874, the east half of the northeast quarter of Section 24 (eighty acres), and part of the east half of the southeast quarter of the same section (sixteen acres); west half of northwest quarter of Section 19, and part of the west half of the southwest quarter of same section, 172 acres, was purchased of O. Blackman, at $35 per acre, and a deed made to the Board of Supervisors of Montgomery County. The buildings as originally designed, were completed and accepted September 9, 1874, by the Board of Supervisors.

In a recent article upon the institution, Mr.

Springer says: "The Poor House is shaded by handsome forest trees, and flanked on the left with a well-trained and productive orchard. The care and comfort which its inmates, who have in most instances some mental or physical defects, and often both, is far better than they had met in earlier parts of their friendless lives, and here they seem actually to enjoy an existence, which to the rational visitor appears unenviable. The establishment has been satisfactorily conducted ever since its removal here from its first location in Irving Township, and at an expense (under the management of Mr. Staub) to the county, comparatively light. It is part self-sustaining, the soil of the farm being productive under careful cultivation."

Political.—In the early history of Montgomery County, there was but little strife among political parties as compared to that of a later day. The war of 1812, and the accompanying events, wiped out the old Federal party that had so bitterly opposed Mr. Jefferson, and for some years politics ran on smoothly. The scramble for office in the early period of the county was almost nothing to what it is at present. The office sought the man and not the man the office; and an unfaithful "steward" was rarely heard of. The most lucrative offices were filled by appointment and not by popular election, and as a general thing by faithful and competent men, who discharged their duties without fear or favor. Thus, Judge Rountree held several important offices at the same time, for more than twenty years—a pretty good proof that he discharged his duties faithfully.

The appointing power, conferred by the Legislature upon the court, although anti-republican in principle, is believed by many to be the best calculated to secure efficiency and competency in office. Experience has proven, in many instances, that the less frequently changes are made, the better it is for the public service. The early records of the County show, under the appointing power, but few changes—the case of Judge Rountree being an example in point.

The Presidential election of 1824 was attended with unusual excitement. The candidates for President were Henry Clay, Gen. Jackson, John Quincy Adams, and William H. Crawford. Mr. Clay carried his own State but was overwhelmingly defeated. Neither of the candidates had a majority of the votes in the Electoral College, according to the Constitutional rule, and upon the House of Representatives devolved the duty of making choice of President. Each State, by its Representatives in Congress, cast one vote. Mr. Clay was Speaker of the House of Representatives, and it is supposed that, through his influence, the Kentucky delegation cast the vote of that State for Mr. Adams instead of for Gen. Jackson. By this *coup d'etat* Mr. Clay was instrumental in organizing political parties that survived the generation in which he lived, and ruled in turn the destines of the Republic for more than a quarter of a century.

For several years after the political power and official patronage had passed into the hands of Old Hickory, parties were known throughout the country as the Jackson and anti-Jackson parties. These finally became the Whig and Democratic parties, the latter of which has retained its party organization down to the present day, and is still one of the great political parties of the time, and has ever been the dominant party in Montgomery County. During the existence of the Whig party, the Democrats usually carried off the spoils of office in the county; and when the Whig party died and was resurrected under the title of Republican party, the ghost of Andrew Jackson still led the old hero's adherents on to victory, as he himself had led his ragged militia to victory at New Orleans. It is sometimes told of them, by way of derision that many Democrats are still voting for him, particularly in the south end of the county. We were informed, however, by a gentleman whose party predilections do not coincide with them, that, from the amount of mail matter which goes to that section, they have doubtless learned of his death ere this. But, with all the slurs cast at the party, it is a significant fact that the Democratic party, inaugurated during the political career of Gen. Jackson, still exists, and was never stronger or in a more flourishing condition, with better show of success, than at the present day.

CHAPTER IV.[*]

EARLY RELIGIOUS HISTORY — PIONEER PREACHERS — ORGANIZATION OF CHURCHES — EDUCATIONAL—THE FIRST SCHOOLS AND TEACHERS—THE PIONEER SCHOOLHOUSES—PRESENT EDUCATIONAL FACILITIES OF THE COUNTY — STATISTICS — COMPULSORY EDUCATION AND ITS GENERAL EFFECTS—THE PRESS OF THE COUNTY, ETC., ETC.

EDUCATION and religion received the early attention of the pioneers of Montgomery County. It is a fact highly commendable to them that churches were established while yet there was but a handful of residents in the newly-settled community. People in those early days seem really to have been more religious, more zealously devoted to their church and the cause of their Master than at the present day. Whether this resulted from their lonely life in the wilderness, beset with toil and with danger as it was, or whether they were more zealous Christians, we will not attempt to say. But since we heard a minister of the Gospel recently declare in a sermon that some of the heathen countries of the Globe, who, fifty years ago, had never seen a Bible nor heard the story of the Cross, now had more Christians in proportion to their population than this enlightened country of ours, we are forced to believe the pioneers were more religious than their descendents. Their religion was more simple, earnest, and sincere, and possessed fewer forms and ceremonies than that now in vogue. Religion, like everything else, has kept up with the marvelous march of civilization, and the genuine old article, given us by "Him who spake as never man spake," has been wonderfully improved to adapt it to the lively wants of the nineteenth century.

The introduction of the Gospel into Montgomery County was coeval with its settlement by white people. The preachers came in reality "as one crying in the wilderness," and whereever they could collect a few of the pioneers together, they proclaimed the glad tidings of salvation "without money and without price." The first sermon preached within the present limits of the county, is believed to have been preached by Rev. James Street, in 1817, at the house of David McCoy, one of the early settlers of what is now Hillsboro Township. A church was organized in 1820, the first Christian organization in the county, and in 1821 a church edifice was erected. It was of the pioneer type, built of logs, the cracks daubed with mud and split logs formed the "pews," or, in backwoods parlance, the "benches." A Baptist Church was built in 1823, which was also a rude log structure. Although Rev. Street preached the first sermon, Rev. Henry Sears, it is claimed, was the first resident minister. The first resident Presbyterian minister was Rev. Jesse Townsend. Rev. Daniel Scherer organized the first Lutheran Church; the Presbyterians organized a church in East Fork in 1830, of which Rev. Joel Knight and Rev. John Barber were the first ministers.

Thus churches were organized and temples of worship erected in the different settlements as soon as the number of inhabitants would permit. In the chapter devoted to the individual townships, villages and cities, the history of all the different denominations and churches

[*] By W. H. Perrin.

will be written. The subject is alluded to here, merely to show the zeal of the early settlers of the county in religious matters and their devotion to the cause of Christianity.

Education.—The pioneers were quite as energetic in matters of education as in religion, and schools were established as soon as the settlements produced children enough to form a school or pay for the employment of a teacher. The first schools were taught on the subscription plan and were as primitive as the cabins in which they were held. The first school of which we have any account was taught by a man named Brazleton, in the winter of 1818-19, in the present township of Hillsboro. It was taught in a little cabin on Mr. Griffith's place, and was a subscription school, each patron paying at the rate of from $1.50 to $2 per scholar, for a term of three months. During the progress of this school Indian boys and young squaws used to come and play with the children at noon and at recess from their camps in the vicinity. The first regular schoolhouse built in this neighborhood was on Section 9, in 1822, and was the usual small log cabin. In 1825, a schoolhouse was built in what is now Fillmore Township, and in 1828 the first temple of worship was built in what is at present East Fork Township. Mrs. Townsend taught school in 1823, in the present township of Butler Grove, in a small log cabin which stood on Section 31, and which was the first school in that neighborhood. The first schoolhouse built in Irving Township was in the southwest corner in 1827, and the first school taught in it by a man named McIntire, then seventy years of age. Henry Lower was an early teacher of the county, and taught in a room of his own house. John King and Charles Turner were also early teachers. Martha B. Cass was an early teacher in the Raymond settlement, and taught in her own house. The first schoolhouse was built there in 1832, a small log building. A schoolhouse—the first in Walshville Township—was built in 1834, and a Mr. Clowson was the first teacher to occupy it. Other neighborhoods and settlements inaugurated schools as soon as their population required them.

The children now in school know little of the school facilities their parents and grandparents enjoyed. The schoolhouses of fifty years ago were log cabins—some with puncheon floors and some with no other floor than the ground. They were built mostly of round logs, the cracks filled in with mud, a log taken out across one end and the space filled with greased paper. This served as a window and under it was placed the "writing bench," where the entire school would repair to practice their writing lesson, which was done with pens made of goose-quills, and ink of home manufacture. The books used in the schools were as primitive as the houses wherein the schools were taught. The New Testament was the usual reader; a few had the "Pleasant Companion," the "Columbian Orator," and the "English Reader." Kirkham's grammar and Pike's arithmetic served to enlighten the pupil in those branches, and the boy who could "cipher" to the "rule of three" was considered a prodigy in figures. There are hundreds now living in Montgomery County to whom these reflections will vividly recall their school days—days when they sat ten hours out of each twenty-four, on a split log for a seat, and studied hard, with but an hour's intermission during the day. To them the log schoolhouse with its wide fire-place, its puncheon floors and uneasy benches recall few pleasant memories.

School facilities have improved wonderfully, however, since the period of which we write. The log-cabin schoolhouse, with its rude furnishing is a thing of the past, and the most liberal schools and comfortable houses are now the order of the time. The basis of the school system of Illinois and the northwest was the act of Congress, by which one thirty-sixth of the public lands were donated to the several Northwestern States for the purpose of aiding a system of public free education. In the survey of the lands, thirty-six square miles or sections, constituted a township, and the sixteenth section of each township was designated as the "school section." By the law of the State of Illinois, each Congressional Township was made to constitute a school township, without regard to either county or other division lines. In many of the counties, especially in Northern Illinois, the county authorities have made the lines of political townships identical with the Congressional or school townships, while in the central and southern portions of the State many are smaller and others larger. In many townships, the land was sold at a comparatively early date, when land was cheap, and therefore but little was realized, the whole section in some instances being sold at the Government price. The land would now sell, perhaps, for $40 or $50 per acre. To say that any great mistake was made in thus disposing of the lands at so early a date would be to cast a reflection on those having charge of the same. In the early history of the county the people were poor and were sadly in need of the little revenue arising from so small a principal. With schoolhouses to build and teachers to pay, they found it no small burden to make provision for the education of their children. And then, again, it would have taken no less than a prophet to predict that within half a century this land would double in value five times over. Indeed, it was almost universally conceded that the prairie lands would never be occupied. The fund realized from the sale of these lands is irreducible, being loaned by law to responsible parties, the interest only being used for the purpose of paying teachers' salaries.

The Legislature of the State, in 1855, passed a law levying an annual school tax of 2 mills on the dollar on all taxable property in the State. This revenue is somewhat variable with different years and different assessments, increasing as the country grows wealthier. These two funds constitute the nucleus of the school system in this, as in the other counties of the State. By the law making these generous provisions for the education of the youth, a provision was enacted making it obligatory on the part of a district to support a school a certain number of months in the year (formerly six, but at present five), otherwise the district receives no benefit from either fund.

This provision insures the co-operation of district authorities in the support of schools; and as a consequence, none of the districts in the county are without the benefit of school instruction. Under the old system, every community claimed the privilege of managing the schools without interference of other parties or modification by general laws. Teachers were accountable only to their employers, and no particular standard of qualification was required. Schools were kept open only for such a length of time, or not at all, as the whims or prejudices of the people might dictate. Consequently, while some of the more wealthy and intelligent neighborhoods were well supplied with school facilities, others were almost wholly without them. The following facts, furnished by Mr. Thomas E. Harris, County Superintendent of Schools, show the present state of the common school system for 1881, in Montgomery County:

Number of persons in the county under twenty-one	14,274
Number of persons between six and twenty-one	9,544
Number of school districts in the county	136
Number of schoolhouses in the county	135
Number of districts having school five months or more	132
Whole number of months school	1,155
Whole number of pupils	7,157
Male teachers employed	88
Female teachers employed	131
Number of ungraded schools	127

Number of graded schools..............	7
Number of private schools..............	1
Whole amount paid teachers.............	$39,727 68
Estimated value of school property......	162,275 00

In conclusion of the educational history of the county, a word upon compulsory education, a subject attracting more or less attention now in nearly every State of the Union, may not be uninteresting to our readers. Concerning the right of State or Government to pass and carry into effect what are known as compulsory laws, and require parents and guardians, even against their will to send their children to school, there does not appear to be much diversity of opinion. But concerning such a policy, dependent upon so many known and unknown conditions there is the widest diversity. That a great good would be wrought is indisputable, if the wisdom of State government could devise some means to strengthen and supplement the powers of Boards of Education, and enable them to prevent truancy, even if only in cases where parents desire their children to attend school regularly, but their authority is too weak to secure that end. The instances are not few in which parents would welcome aid in this matter, knowing that truancy is often the first step in a path which finally ends in vagabondage and crimes. It is our liberal system of free education that has preserved our Government so far, and its perpetuation depends upon the education and enlightenment of the masses. With the most scrupulous care, England fosters her great universities, that the sons of her nobility may be properly trained for their places in the House of Lords, in the army, navy and church. Then, the character of citizenship should be high indeed, where every man is born a king and sovereign heir to all the franchises and trusts of the State and Republic. An ignorant people can be governed but only an intelligent people can govern themselves; and that is the experiment we are trying to solve in these United States. "The growth of agrarianism and communism has appalled statesmenship, and alarmed the dull ears of the people, who see in these twin brothers of ignorance impending ruin. The great army of tramps marching through the land, disturbing our domestic tranquillity and moral safety, furnish another element to the problem confronting those who yearn for a solid and stable peace, and seek for the security assured by a permanent government. Intelligence wedded to virtue constitute the palladium of the union. Relaxation of vigor in the effort to improve the quality of our citizenship, will result in certain ruin. From all the towers of the Republic the watchmen cry, 'Educate! Educate! Educate!'"[*]

Viewing the subject from the above standpoint, is one of the strongest arguments in favor of compulsory education. Whatever may be said to the contrary, or in opposition to compulsory education, it is a fact apparent to all, that the youthful idlers upon the streets of towns and cities should be gathered up by somebody and compelled to do something. If they learn nothing else, there will be at least this salutary lesson, that society is stronger than they, and without injuring them, will use its strength to protect itself. While reform schools are being established for those who have already started on the downward road, it would be well to provide some way to rescue those lingering upon the brink of ruin, and there is no better way, perhaps, than by compulsory education.

The Press.—The newspaper and the printing press of the present day constitute one of the most important features of the time and of the country, and a chronicle that said nothing of their power and influence would be, and justly, too, considered very incomplete. The daily paper, by the aid of the telegraph, gives us to-day all the news that transpired yester-

[*] Kentucky State Superintendent of Public Instruction.

day in the uttermost parts of the earth. And the county press, the faithful exponent of the county's interest, is the intellectual criterion for the masses, and the most popular channel for general information. It is furthermore a true record of the county's history; the very advertisements in local papers eventually become historical facts, and it is to be regretted that so few persons seem to appreciate the value and importance of their county papers.

Montgomery County is well supplied with local newspapers. In Hillsboro, Litchfield, Nokomis and Raymond, papers are published weekly, and it is but justice to them to say that they are above the medium standard of newspapers published in country towns. The papers of each city and town will be fully written up, as a part of the history of their respective places, and are only referred to here in a general way.

CHAPTER V.

AGRICULTURE—ITS GROWTH AND DEVELOPMENT AS A SCIENCE—THE WAY OUR FATHERS FARMED—IMPROVED METHODS AND IMPLEMENTS—COUNTY AGRICULTURAL ASSOCIATION—OFFICES, FAIRGROUNDS, ETC—RAILROAD HISTORY—THE INDIANAPOLIS & ST. LOUIS RAILROAD—DIFFICULTIES ATTENDING ITS CONSTRUCTION—OTHER RAILROAD ENTERPRISES.

MONTGOMERY COUNTY has the reputation of being a fine farming section, and without doubt its claim in this regard is well founded. While some counties may show more of rich soil, and while others may be better adapted to some specialty, yet we believe not a county in the State can lay claim to all the advantages in climate, soil, water, timber and healthfulness that are justly claimed for this. While in some sections a certain advantage may, with propriety, be claimed as peculiar, we believe no other county combines so many natural advantages. In some of the more northern counties we find larger crops of corn, and in some of the more southern, a greater amount of fruit; but these specialties, even in the localities named, are not always a certain crop. The farmer's safest course is a diversity of products, and Montgomery County furnishes an example of soil and climate which make it in an eminent degree fitted for such pursuits.

For a number of years the natural advantages of this region were scarcely appreciated, as the farming was carried on in such a manner as to obtain results far below those now realized. Better farm machinery, better methods of planting and cultivation, and the adoption of crops better suited to the soil have wrought great changes. In an especial manner is this true in regard to methods of planting, cultivating harvesting and taking care of products. The way that our fathers performed their farming operations is so little known to the present generation who depend much upon farm machinery, and require the horses to do all the work which men, women and children formerly did, that a description of the old way, gathered from conversations with those who know whereof they speak, cannot but prove interesting to the young farmer of the present day. Banish all such modern implements as reapers, mowers, corn-planters, sulky plows horse hay-rakes, threshing machines, riding-cultivators, and some conception may be formed of the primitive way of farming. The following was the mode of planting corn. After the ground had been plowed with a wooden mold-board plow (which had to be cleaned every few rods with a paddle carried for the purpose), and had been scratched over with a harrow in which wooden pins were used for teeth, the little shovel plow and a single horse were used for marking out both ways. After the marking was done, the children, big and little, the men and the women went into the field, and while the children with tin pails or small baskets dropped the grains of corn in the crossings the others, with great heavy iron hoes covered or "kivered" it with dirt. After the planting came the hoeing, now superseded by the improved cultivators. The tending by the single-shovel plow was common until a few years ago. But the single shovel plow has had to take its

By W. H. Perrin.

place with the old spinning wheel and loom, and they are now considered as relicts of a past age.

Harvesting wheat, oats, rye and grass was formerly a laborious process. Even within the recollection of comparatively young men of the county, the scythe and cradle were counted as improved implements of husbandry; but the reaper and mower, now in use, not only do a better job, but transfer the hardest of the labor to the horses. The manner of cleaning the wheat from the chaff, after it had been tramped out by horses or oxen, was by pouring it slowly out of a bucket or half-bushel measure, for the wind to blow the chaff away. Next came the old "fan-mill," turned by hand. But now the perfected thresher not only cleans and separates the wheat from the chaff and traw, but sacks and counts the number of bushels.

With corn at from 6 to 10 cents per bushel, oats but little more, wheat at but 25 to 50 cents, and other products in proportion, with the market at Chicago and St Louis it is a matter of wonder that a farmer succeeded in obtaining enough for his labor to pay for saving his crops. It is not difficult to understand why so much of the county lay for so many years without occupants. Of course the farmer in those days did not ride in carriages, pay heavy taxes, wear fine clothes, or indulge in many luxuries; but they rode to meeting on horseback or in the farm-wagon, wearing their every day apparel done up clean for Sunday, and paid the preacher with a bag of corn or potatoes, or not at all, as they felt able. Yet, to say that they did not live comfortably and independently would be a great mistake. The rifle supplied venison and other game, and the actual needs of life were all furnished, though it would seem a great hardship to go back to what some are pleased to call the good old times.

Fairs.—The farmers of the county turned their attention to the improvement of agriculture and stock very early. To this end an agricultural association was formed about the year 1850, as nearly as can now be ascertained, but as the records of this association have been lost or destroyed, but little of it is known beyond the fact that such an association existed, and was superseded by the present society in 1857. Of the latter, the facts given herewith are furnished by Mr. William K. Jackson, Secretary of the association.

The Montgomery County Agricultural Society, as it is now known, was organized on Friday, July 3, 1857, at a meeting of a requisite number of the legal voters of the county, all of whom have a voice in the affairs of the society. Of this meeting, Hiram Rountree was Chairman, and John W. Kitchell, Secretary. A committee was appointed, consisting of Benjamin Sammons, A. S. Haskell and Austin Whitten, to frame a constitution and code of by-laws. The following gentlemen were elected officers of the Society, to wit: Morgan Blair, President; J. W. Kitchell, Recording Secretary; Solomon Harkey, Treasurer; J. A. Kolston, Corresponding Secretary, and the following Vice Presidents: Thomas Standing, Hillsboro; Robert Little, Audubon, James Kirk, Hurricane, Easton Whitten, Jr., East Fork; James McDavid, Bear Creek; C. V. Seymour, Walshville and John A. Crabtree Litchfield. The following General Committee was appointed: Henry Philips, William C. Miller, Henry Richmond, Harrison Brown, Hillsboro; William Wright, Daniel Easterday, Audubon; Cleveland Coffey, Thomas L. Harvey, Hurricane; Austin Whitten, Ezekiel Bogart, East Fork; John Price, William Cannon, Bear Creek, William Kingston, Joseph Price, Walshville; Elihu Boan, Thomas Hughes, Litchfield; Edgar Smith, Benjamin Rogers, Zanesville; L. H. Thomas, P. De Witt, Bois D'Arc. The following resolution was adopted by the Executive Committee: "*Resolved*, That we adopt and indorse as our own, all the proceedings of the incorporated association heretofore known as the 'Montgomery County Agricultural Society,' and are responsible for all debts heretofore contracted by the same.' A committee, consisting of Henry Richmond, J. A. Watson and J. W. Kitchell, were appointed to select and purchase suitable fair grounds for the use of the society.

The fortune of the society has been somewhat checkered, and from the records it appears never to have been attended with very great prosperity as an agricultural association. It owns very fine grounds southwest of town, and which, with slight expense, could be so improved, as to render them very beautiful, and at the same time valuable to the society. But the grounds and buildings have now a rather dilapidated appearance, as though little attention was bestowed upon them.

The present officers are as follows: Moses Berry, President; Robert Morell and A. G. Butler, Vice Presidents; William K. Jackson, Secretary and Treasurer; Directors—W. L. Blackburn, William Brewer, Hillsboro; A. T. Withers, Walshville; Miner S. Goring, Morrisonville, and James Young, Nokomis.

The Litchfield Fair.—Mr. Coolidge furnishes us the following of the Litchfield Agricultural and Mechanical Association: When, in 1857, the permanent location of the County Fair was in suspense, it was officially announced that the question would be decided by the town offering the largest contribution to its funds. At the specified time Litchfield offered a sum at least double any competing town. But the authorities delayed their award and a recess was taken. Before re-assembling, a pledge, which it was well understood would subsequently be released, was made by James M. Davis, of Hillsboro, to carry his town to the top of the list. It was an accommodation pledge, and was used to secure the location of the fair at the county seat. The trick, to which the fair authorities were parties, was remembered when in 1867 68, Litchfield was reproached by a Hillsboro journal in coarse scurrilous terms, for not raising a large sum as a gift to the County Agricultural Society. The citizens, thus censured, gave reins to their indignation by organizing the Litchfield Agricultural and Mechanical Association. An eligible tract of land was bought, near the southeast corner of the town, and inclosed. Cattle-pens and stalls were constructed, a half mile speed-ring prepared, and an amphitheater for a thousand persons erected, and in October, 1868, the first fair was held. John W. Davenport was President, P. B. Updike, Treasurer, and H. A. Coolidge, Secretary. The weather was of a rigorous character. The wind and cold had a February ancestry, yet the attendance was large and the fair was a success. The premium list was liberal, and the awards were paid. But the cost of the ground and fencing and buildings remained a dead loss. The association passed into the hands of thirteen joint proprietors, who assumed the debts and went forward in their improvements. Fairs were held each year until 1875, when a fair was omitted. But the next year the last one was held, and the association went into liquidation and the losses were paid by the proprietors. The property was sold, and the concern became a thing of the past. A succession of vile weather Fair weeks, and the wearing off of the novelty and the hard times ate out its prosperity. But its existence brought its compensations. It advanced the reputation of the city for enterprise and courage, and the money sunk gained for the community character worth many times the sum swallowed up.

Railroads.—The earliest attempts to construct railroads in the West originated in the insane desire to enrich that great empire, as it might be called, by the system of "internal improvements." This fever of speculation broke out in different parts of the United States about the year 1835, and soon after it appeared in

Pennsylvania. Ohio. Indiana and Illinois. leaving, when past. an enormous debt upon each municipality or State Government. In Illinois it amounted to nearly $15,000,000. while in Pennsylvania it was more than double that amount, and in Ohio and Indiana did not vary far from it. Examination of the legislative acts of the Prairie State, at that period. discloses an almost unbroken line of acts for the construction of some highway. which was destined to only partially see the light of day in detached parcels, some of which still remain as silent monuments of a supreme legislative and popular folly. When the collapse came in 1837, and work on all was entirely suspended, only the old "Northern Cross Railroad," as it was called, now the Wabash, was found in a condition fit to warrant completion, and that only a short distance. It was originally intended to extend from Meredosia through Jacksonville to Springfield, Decatur and Danville to the Eastern State line, where it was expected it would be joined to some road in Indiana, and be continued eastward. A vast quantity of old flat-bar rails had been purchased in England by the agents of the State, at an enormous expense, too: and quite a quantity had been brought to Meredosia, preparatory to being laid on the track. In the spring of 1838, some eight miles of this old track were laid, and on the 8th day of November of that year, a small locomotive, the "Rogers," made in England, and shipped here in pieces, was put together, and made a trial trip on the road. It was the first that ever turned a wheel in the Mississippi Valley. The first rail on this road had been laid, with imposing ceremonies, on the 9th of May preceding, and on through the summer the work progressed slowly, until the locomotive made the pioneer trial trip above described. Only twelve years before had the first railroad train made a trip in the new continent, and only a year or two before this had the first application of steam been successfully made in this manner

This pioneer railroad, as stated, is now a part of the Wabash system, a division of which diverges from the main line at Decatur, and extends to St. Louis, passing through the western part of this county, intersecting the townships of Harvel, Raymond, Zanesville and North and South Litchfield. It was completed through in 1870, giving that portion of the county through which it passes increased railroad facilities, and forming a valuable improvement in that section. Further particulars of it will be found in the chapters on Litchfield.

The oldest railroad in Montgomery County is the present Indianapolis & St. Louis Railroad, whose earliest inception may be traced to the speculative fever of 1835. When the appropriations for different roads were made, a route from Terre Haute to Alton was one designated, and work performed on it in many places. Contracts were let, portions of the road were graded, and the workmen were paid in State paper, which, when the internal improvement system began to decline, partook of a downward tendency and left the creditors in rather a sad plight. The work dragged for a time, and was at last wholly suspended as a result of the hard times following the panic of 1837. It was not until about 1849, that the country was aroused from its dormant condition, when the Baltimore & Ohio Railroad reached the east line of Illinois, and craved permission to come in and cross the State on its way to St. Louis, its western terminus. At this point, however, it met with a check which took it years to overcome. A "State Policy" party sprang up, denying the right of any foreign corporation to cross the State, especially when the effect would be to enrich the neighboring city of St. Louis, a city Alton was vainly endeavoring to outstrip in the march of progress, and which she then vainly expected to do. The "State Policy" party held several rousing meetings in furtherance of their scheme, a scheme delusive in its effects upon the State at large, and confined mainly to the Alton interest. Counter influences were aroused, meetings were held, and an antagonistic party, much the inferior at first, began to appear. The culmination came when the Terre Haute, Vandalia & St. Louis road asked for a charter. The Baltimore & Ohio road had succeeded in their endeavor to build their track across the State mainly brought about by the press foreign to the State. It had, with one voice, denounced the "policy" as narrow, selfish, mean, contemptible and invidious. It was sustained by the press in the northern parts of Illinois, and had already begun to open the eyes of many influential persons belonging to the policy party. When the Vandalia road asked for their charter, the policy party exerted themselves to the utmost to defeat that, and for a time prevailed.

While these affairs were agitating the State, Congress had passed an act granting a magnificent domain of land in aid of the Illinois Central Railroad. The Senators in Congress from Illinois wrote letters to many influential men at home, urging upon them the necessity of being more liberal in their acts to foreign corporations, and not attempt to arrogate to the State a right she could not expect to possess. They further urged that the donation from the General Government could not have been secured had they not pledged their earnest effort to wipe out this disgraceful policy. These influences had their effect. The "Brough" road, so called from its principal projector, afterward Governor of Ohio, gained a charter, and were enabled to begin work on their proposed Vandalia Line. In the meanwhile, influences were working to build anew the projected roads of the internal improvement period. The grade on the old route from Terre Haute to Alton, was, in many places, in a tolerably good condition and only needed energy to push it to a conclusion. A company was formed, the name Terre Haute & Alton Railroad adopted, and work began. Montgomery, in common with other counties on the route subscribed aid to the enterprise. The road was completed from the west end eastward some distance, and from Terre Haute west to Mattoon, where it intersected the Chicago Division of the Illinois Central, then uncompleted, and in January following the breach was closed, and a passenger train made the entire trip from Terre Haute to Alton. For awhile, it transferred freight and passengers here to boats, and sent them to St. Louis, so strong was the Alton interest against that city. This, however, could not always endure, and the coal road from one city to the other was purchased, and trains run down on that. That changed the name to the Terre Haute, Alton & St. Louis Railroad. When the route was extended eastward from Terre Haute to Indianapolis, the name was again changed to the Indianapolis & St. Louis Railroad, by which it is now known.

Montgomery County subscribed $50,000 stock in this road, while the city of Hillsboro also took an active interest in it, as will be found in a subsequent chapter. The county has sold her stock to Eastern capitalists, the sale of the last $25,000 having been recently made. The road has become involved in late years, and is at the present writing, we have been informed, upon the eve of being sold. It has been for some time controlled by the Bee Line—an Ohio road—by which the latter makes its connections with roads diverging from St. Louis for the West, and of which system it will in all probability eventually become a permanent division.

Another Montgomery County road, now in course of construction, is the Jacksonville Southeastern Railway. This project has been in process of agitation some twelve or fifteen years, and is now completed, and trains are running from Jacksonville to Litchfield. The original intention was to extend the road from Jacksonville in a southeastern direction to Centralia, or Mount Vernon, or some eligible point either on the Illinois Central Railroad, or in that section of the State. Several routes have been laid out and surveys made through this and Bond Counties. Through some lukewarmness or indifference on the part of the people or cities, both Hillsboro and Greenville have failed in obtaining this road, it passing a little west of Hillsboro and crossing the Vandalia line at Smithboro, some three miles west of Greenville. The road will, probably, be completed though at no distant day, and if it does no more, will become a valuable feeder to the East and West roads which it crosses. The cities which sat still and let it pass around them, perhaps, know what they are doing, but to an outside looker on, their acts seem scarcely up to the present standard of railroad enterprise.

A narrow-guage railroad is also in course of construction through Bond and Montgomery, passing near the line between the two counties. But in this day of railroads and railroad enterprise, a narrow-guage road is hardly looked upon as of sufficient importance to create even a small ripple of excitement. Of this road we learned but little, except that there is such an enterprise in existence.

CHAPTER VI.

WAR HISTORY—MONTGOMERY COUNTY IN THE BLACK HAWK WAR—MUSTER ROLLS OF COMPANIES—THE MEXICAN WAR—SOLDIERS FROM THE COUNTY—THE GREAT CIVIL WAR OF 1861—THE DIFFERENT REGIMENTS, OFFICERS, ETC.—LITCHFIELD'S PARTICIPATION—INCIDENTS, ETC., ETC.

"Dulce et decorum est pro patria mori."

ALL readers of American history are familiar with the questions that led to our Revolutionary struggle, and eventually culminated in the independence of the original thirteen colonies. The results of that war secured to us the liberty and freedom we to-day enjoy. Smarting under the humiliation of defeat, the mother country lost few opportunities to oppress and insult her former colonies and their people. In resentment of these oft-repeated insults, followed, what is known in our history, as the "War of 1812," and another chastisement of the British Lion. These wars occurred before there were any white settlements made in the present county of Montgomery. Many of the pioneers, however, of the county, had participated in one or the other of these wars, and in the Indian wars of the frontier. As boys, they had fought savages with their mothers and sisters in their cabins; in youth and ripe manhood they had fought them in ambuscade and in open fields, and felt themselves a match for any foe, white or red. But it was several years after the close of the war of 1812 before the whites took possession of what is now Montgomery County, and hence it cannot be said that the county participated in our last war with Great Britain.

The Black Hawk.—This was the first conflict in which the people of Montgomery County were called upon the take part. As soon as the war had assumed a serious aspect, Col. Stillman led a small force against the savages, but was signally defeated by overwhelming numbers. Upon the defeat of Stillman, Gov. Reynolds deemed it expedient to call out troops to defend the more exposed settlements of his State, and at the same time check the operation of Black Hawk. He called for volunteers to rendezvous at Peru, in La Salle County, and in response, Dr. Levi D. Boone, a scion of the old Daniel Boone stock, recruited a company in Montgomery County, and was sworn into service April 20, 1832. From the "Rountree Letters" published in the Hillsboro *Democrat*, we copy the muster-roll of this company, and of a company made up subsequently by Capt. Rountree. The roll of Boone's company is as follows:

Levi D. Boone, Captain; James G. Human, First Lieutenant; Absalom Cress, Second Lieutenant; C. B. Blockberger, First Sergeant; M. H. Walker, Second Sergeant; Israel Fogleman, Third Sergeant; William McDavid, Fourth Sergeant; J. Prater, First Corporal; A. T. Williams, Second Corporal; C. S. Coffey, Third Corporal; Newton Street, Fourth Corporal.

Privates—William D. Shirley, Peter Cress, George E. Ludwick, George W. Conyers, A. H. Knapp, J. B. Williams, John Crabtree, Eastin Whitten, Samuel Peacock, Michael Ternan, Robert A. Long, E. Kilpatrick, Daniel Steel, Thomas J. Todd, Johnson Hampton, Stephen Killingworth, McKenzie Turner, Samuel Ish-

* By W. H. Perrin.

mael, James Brown, Samuel Briggs, James Hawkins, Harrison Brown, Benjamin R. Williams, Eli Robb, James Young, John K. McWilliams, James M. Rutledge, Thomas Mansfield, William Griffith, James Grisham, Benjamin Holbrook, William Jordon, William Roberts, Barnabas Michaels, Joshua Hunt and Hiram C. Bennett. They served through the campaign for which they volunteered (one month) and were mustered out May 28, 1832, at the mouth of Fox River. The Indians being still far from subdued, the Governor made another call for troops, and under this second call, Hiram Rountree raised a company in this county, of which the following is the roll:

Hiram Roundtree, Captain; John Kirkpatrick, First Lieutenant; Thomas Philips, Second Lieutenant; A. K. Gray, First Sergeant, John Stine, Second Sergeant; Samuel Jackson, Third Sergeant; ——— ——— Fourth Sergeant; Spartan Grisham, First Corporal; Malachi Smith, Second Corporal; Thomas McAdams, Third Corporal; Thomas Edwards, Fourth Corporal.

Privates—Luke Lee Steel, Thomas Sturtevant, George Harkey, Jacob Rhodes, John McCurry, Malcom McPhail, A. Forehand, John M. Holmes, John K. Long, Joseph Burke, William Harkey, Alfred Johnson, David T. McCullock, Samuel Paisley, William Young, William Jones, Thomas Evans, J. M. McWilliams, John Hanna, John Brown, Jesse Johnson, Samuel Bennett, (Quartermaster), C. C. Aydelot, Thomas Wood, Thomas Johnson, A. McCullock, James Cardwell, Thos. Early, Willis Rose, Zeb. Shirley, W. S. Williams, Thomas C. Hughes, John Hart, S. W. Booher, Alexander Gray, Thomas W. Heady, John Corlew, Harace Mansfield, Thomas Potter, John Briggs, J. W. Wilson, D. M. Williams, David Copeland, James Potter, James Wilson, Thomas Gray, James M. Berry, John Slater, Thomas Williford, James Lockerman, Robert McCullock, John Duncan, Levi D. Boone (Surgeon), McDavid. The men, so far as they were able furnished their own arms, horses and other accouterments, and marched to the place of rendezvous near Peru, where they arrived about the 20th of June, 1832. The company continued in the service until the defeat of Black Hawk, at Bad Ax, which terminated the war.

The Mexican War.—After the close of the Black Hawk war, Montgomery County remained at peace with all mankind until Mexico ruffled the feathers of the American Eagle. The war with Mexico grew out of the annexation of Texas, formerly a province of Mexico, to the United States. Texas had revolted from Mexico, and at the battle of San Jacinto, where her army had captured Santa Anna, then Commander-in-chief of Mexico, and most of his army had forced him to acknowledge her independence. Mexico, however, paid no attention to this acknowledgment, but continued the guerrilla warfare, and used every means to annoy the Texans. Many people from the States had settled in Texas, and propositions from this time on were made by them to admit Texas into the Union. These propositions were favored by the Democratic party, but strongly opposed by the Whigs. In the Presidential campaign of 1844, the annexation of Texas was made one of the chief issues of the contest, and Mr. Polk, the Democratic Candidate, was elected. This was taken as an endorsement of the question by the people, and early in the year 1845, Texas was admitted into the sisterhood of States. Mexico at once broke off all diplomatic relations with the United States, called home her minister and prepared for war, which soon followed.

Illinois, with that spirit of patriotism that has always characterized her, responded heartily to the call for troops. Under an act of Congress, the President was authorized to order out 50,000 men, and Illinois was required to furnish three regiments. These were made up without delay, and rendezvoused at Alton.

T. C. Kirkland

brave Col. John J. Hardin, of Jacksonville, who fell in the battle of Buena Vista, in the same charge with the lamented Clay and McKee, of Kentucky. The Second regiment was commanded by Col. Bissell of the southern part of the State, and contained a large proportion of Germans, while the Third regiment was commanded by Col. Foreman, of Vandalia. It contained a Company from Montgomery County ninety-six strong, under the following commissioned officers: James C. McAdams, Captain; Thomas Rhodes, First Lieutenant; John Burk, Second Lieutenant; and John Curlew, Third Lieutenant. The names of the private and non-commissioned officers cannot now be given. Many of them are dead, and others have moved away and are forgotten. Under the second call for troops, Illinois furnished another regiment, which was commanded by Col. Baker, of Cairo. These four regiments comprise the quota of Illinois in the Mexican war, and formed the starting point for the numbering of her regiments in the late civil war—her first regiment being known as the Fifth Infantry.

As stated, it is impossible now to give the names of all those who went into the Mexican war from Montgomery County Many are now dead, and others have moved away and are forgotten. Many have also moved into the county, who went into the service from other States, and other counties of this State. Suffice it, they did their duty as Illinois soldiers always have done, before, as well as since.

The Civil War.—After the close of the Mexican war, the country remained in comparative peace for more than a decade.

A storm, however, had been gathering, and more than once had threatened to burst in fury upon the country, but after spending itself in low-muttered thunder, had passed over. But the political atmosphere was still heavy and oppressive, and it required no prophet to foresee the approaching tempest. The great question of slavery, which had been in agitation for a quarter of a century, culminated in the election of Abraham Lincoln to the Presidency in 1860, by a party supposed to be hostile to Southern institutions, and the result was the "Great Rebellion"—a civil war without parallel in the annals of history. To go into the details of this war, would be to open afresh wounds now rapidly healing; but a history of a county, which said nothing of its war history, would, at least, be incomplete, and hence, a brief space in this chapter will be devoted to the part taken by Montgomery County in the late war between the States. Upon the fall of Fort Sumter, a blaze of excitement swept over the loyal States, and aroused the people to instant action. The roll of the drum was heard in every city, town and hamlet, and the sturdy yeomanry rushed to the defense of their country.

> "The herds without a keeper strayed.
> The plow was in mid-furrow stayed,"

while the men, imbued with the spirit of their Revolutionary sires, gave themselves to the service of the Government.

The Ninth Illinois Infantry, was the first regiment that drew on Montgomery for troops. Company C, of the Ninth, was made up almost entirely in this county, and the Lieutenant Colonel of the regiment, Judge J. J. Philips, is too well known to our readers to require any eulogy here. The commissioned officers of Company C were Jacob Miller, Captain; A. J. Sheldon, First Lieutenant; and George Short, Second Lieutenant The latter was killed in battle November 23, 1864, and John Droesch promoted to Second Lieutenant. Capt. Miller, Lieut. Sheldon and Droesch, were mustered out with the regiment July 9, 1865.

The Ninth Infantry was one of the six regiments which was allotted to Illinois under the President's first call for 75,000 men for three months.* It was organized at Springfield, and mustered into the service April 28, 1861, when it was ordered to Cairo, and brigaded under Gen. B. M. Prentiss. At the end of its three-months' service, about five hundred of its men re-enlisted for three years, and on the 26th of July, 1861, was mustered into the United States' service. The zeal with which recruiting was kept up during the summer of 1861 enabled the Ninth to number 1,040 men by the 1st of September. The regiment was ordered to Paducah, Ky., where it passed the winter, engaging in numerous expeditions in Western and Southern Kentucky. In February, it moved up the Tennessee River, and, as a part of Col. McArthur's brigade, participated in the battle of Fort Donelson, in which it lost thirty-five men killed, and had 166 wounded. March 6, 1862, it embarked for Paducah, from Nashville, where it had been for some time, and proceeded to Pittsburg Landing. It engaged in the battle of Shiloh April 6, and sustained a loss of sixty-one killed and 287 wounded. Out of the twenty-six commissioned officers who went into action, twenty-one were either killed or wounded.

The Ninth, during the advance on Corinth, formed a part of the brigade commanded by Brig. Gen. R. J. Oglesby, and on the evacuation of Corinth, was attached to the Third Army Corps, under the command of Maj. Gen. John Pope, and pursued the retreating enemy to Booneville. In the battle of Corinth, October 3 and 4, it lost nineteen killed and eighty-two wounded and fifty-two prisoners. After this the regiment served mostly in Mississippi, where it performed the most arduous service. The Adjutant General's report of the State, from which these facts are gleaned, sets down the number of battles and skirmishes, in which the Ninth participated, at 110, beginning with Saratoga, Ky., October 15, 1861, and ending with "near" Neuse River, N. C., April 10, 1865. The regiment was mustered out of the service July 9, 1865, and discharged.

The One Hundred and Seventeenth Illinois Infantry received a company from the county, principally from Hillsboro, and the immediate vicinity. This was Company B, and was officered as follows: Robert McWilliams, Captain; Frank H. Gillmore, First Lieutenant, and George W. Potter, Second Lieutenant. McWilliams was promoted to Major, and resigned January 29, 1865. Gillmore was promoted to Captain, Potter to first Lieutenant, James M. Truitt to Second Lieutenant, and all mustered out with the regiment August 5, 1865.

The One Hundred and Seventeenth was organized at Camp Butler, in September, 1862, by Col. R. M. Moore, and mustered into the service by Capt. Washington, of the United States Army, on the 19th of the same month. It left Camp Butler on the 11th of November for Memphis, Tenn., where it arrived on the 17th, and where it remained until July, 1863, when it was sent to Helena, Ark., but soon after returned. It was next (in December) sent against Gen. Forrest in Western Tennessee, and, in a skirmish with him at La Fayette, lost three men killed. It was engaged in the operations around Vicksburg, and served in Mississippi, Louisana and Arkansas, and September 19, 1864, arrived at Jefferson Barracks. For two months it operated in Missouri, returning to St. Louis November 19, when it embarked for Nashville, Tenn., and took position in the works there December 1, 1864. It was engaged in the battle of Nashville December 15 and 16, and took part in the pursuit of Hood's army. Afterward it proceeded to New Orleans, where it arrived January 17, 1865. It participated in a number of battles and skirmishes, ending in the capture of Blakely on the 9th of April.

*Under the three months' service, the Montgomery County Company was H, and was officered as follows: J. J. Philips, Captain; J. W. Kitchell, First Lieutenant, and William F. Armstrong, Second Lieutenant. Philips was promoted to Major, during its three months' service, and, on its organization for three years, to Lieutenant Colonel. Kitchell was promoted Captain in the place of Philips and James Munn became First Lieutenant. Armstrong entered another regiment at the close of the three-months' service, where he served faithfully, and rose to the rank of Major.

It marched for Montgomery April 13, and then to Camp Butler, Ill., where it was mustered out of service August 3, 1865, by Capt. James A. Hall.

The regiment during its term of service traveled by rail 778 miles, by water, 6,191 miles, and marched 2,307 miles.

The One Hundred and Twenty-sixth Illinois Infantry had also a company from this county. David W. Munn, of Hillsboro, was Adjutant of the regiment, and Company D was from Montgomery County, and went out with the following commissioned officers: L. R. Slaughter, Captain; E. T. Somers, First Lieutenant, and J. W. Newberry, Second Lieutenant. Slaughter resigned July 23, 1864, and Somers was promoted to Captain in his place and as such mustered out with the regiment July 12, 1865. Louis Wagner was promoted to First Lieutenant in the place of Somers, and mustered out as such. Second Lieut. Newberry died September 3, 1863, when James M. Boone became Second Lieutenant, and was mustered out with the regiment.

This regiment was organized at Alton, and mustered into service September 4, 1862, by Col. Richmond, who served as its Colonel until March 3, 1864, when he resigned. It served in Tennessee, Arkansas and Mississippi, and participated in the siege of Vicksburg. It took part in the capture of Little Rock, Ark., and in the fight at Clarendon, Ark., June 26, 1864. It was in active service from the time of its enlistment until the close of the war, and on the 12th of July, 1865, it was mustered out and discharged.

The One Hundred and Forty-third Infantry, enlisted for one hundred days, contained a company (H) from Montgomery, which was officered as follows: James G. Seward, Captain; William R. Truesdell, First Lieutenant, and George P. Fowler, Second Lieutenant. The regiment was organized at Mattoon, and mustered into service June 11, 1864, for one hundred days, under the command of Col. D. C. Smith. It served in Tennessee and Arkansas, and on the 14th of September returned to Mattoon, where, on the 26th, it was mustered out of service.

The First Illinois Cavalry was represented by a company from this county, viz.: Company E. The commissioned officers were as follows: Paul Walter, Captain; Isaac Skillman, First Lieutenant, and Morgan Blair, Second Lieutenant, all of whom were mustered out with the [illegible]. The First Cavalry was organized [illegible] 1861, and entered the service for one year. Of its operations we [illegible] no account in the Adjutant General's Report of the State, [illegible] beyond its muster-roll, and that it was mustered out July 12, 1862, at the [illegible] of its term of service.

Additional to the foregoing, Mr. Coolidge furnishes us the following as the war history of Hillsboro and immediate vicinity.

[illegible] of the firing on Fort Sumter was [illegible] from the wires on Sunday evening, and the fuller details came the next day in the morning dailies. A call was instantly issued for a public meeting in the evening at Empire Hall. The hall was crowded with men. Speaker after speaker was called to address his fellow-citizens and declare his sentiments as to the republic. There was but one opinion. War had begun. Force must be repelled by force, and forty men responded that evening to the call for 75,000 troops to preserve the Union. In three days, the company had a hundred and twenty rank and file, and with B. M. Munn as Captain, and E. Southworth and M. P. Miller as Lieutenants, had departed to Springfield to become a part of the first Illinois regiment raised. For a few weeks the regiment was quartered at Alton, then ordered to Cairo, where Gen. Grant was in command. It completed its extended period of enlistment at Mound City. The company saw no hostile flag, and heard no hostile bullet. Only the

Captain and a few of his men re-enlisted for three years. The first exaltation of feeling was over, and the soldiers came home, some to enter other organizations, and the most to labor for daily bread, for no county can long keep on the field over four per cent of its population.

"The three months' volunteers being in the field, steps were taken to enlist a company for three years. The attempt was speedily successful, and under Delos Van Deuzen, Captain, and L. G. Perley and P. G. Galvin, Lieutenants, and R. W. Short, First Sergeant, the company was mustered into service at St. Louis June 16, 1861, as Company H, Sixth Missouri Volunteers, Col. Blood commanding. No regiment was then forming in Illinois. This Litchfield preferred to go into a foreign regiment, if it was necessary, in order to gain a recognized military status. Guarding Pilot Knob until November, the regiment then proceeded to Springfield, via St. Louis and Tipton, forming a part of the army under Fremont, which this leader marched to fight Gen. Price, but which Hunter led into pacific quarters, under the shelter of St. Louis. Wintering at Otterville, the Sixth, in April, departed for Pittsburg Landing, and joined the army before Corinth, being the First of the First Brigade, Second Division, Fifteenth Army Corps, commanded in succession by Sherman, Blair and Logan, went down the railroad to Memphis. The regiment preserved this position through its campaigns.

"In December, 1862, the Sixth bore a bloody part in the assault on Chickasaw Bayou, leaving eighty men dead before the walls. This was the first sharp affair in which it participated. Then it assisted at the capture of Arkansas Post, and, returning, was detained by high water at Young's Point, opposite Vicksburg, until May, 1863, when it crossed the Mississippi thirty miles below, and advanced on Jackson. That town taken, the regiment bore its flag through the battles which sent Johnson whirling to the rear, and cleared the way to the successful investment of Pemberton in his stronghold. When Vicksburg surrendered, the regiment assisted in the recapture of Jackson, and it was stationed in winter quarters on Black River until ordered to move to the relief of Chattanooga. The Sixth was the first regiment to cross the river against Mission Ridge, and was on picket duty for sixty consecutive hours. In November, the regiment marched to the aid of Burnside, beleaguered at Knoxville, going light, without baggage or provisions, and foraging for food while advancing forty miles a day. In the spring of 1864, it re-enlisted as veterans, and were furloughed home for sixty days, and Capt. Van Deuzen went back as Lieutenant Colonel, commanding the regiment. Lieut. Galvin was promoted to Major, and Sergeant R. M. Short was made Captain of his company. A portion of the winter, the regiment lay at Huntsville. In May, 1864, the advance on Atlanta began, and Company H saw bloody service at Resaca, Dallas and Kenesaw Mountain. July 22, 1864, its depleted ranks fought on the field where McPherson fell, and six days later burnt powder at Jonesboro, and Atlanta was fairly taken. Hood, throwing himself on Sherman's communications, the latter marched to the north until his antagonist was beyond the Tennessee, and too far from his base of supplies to be troublesome. Then leaving him to the stern mercies of Gen. Thomas, Sherman disappeared in the direction of the sea, to reach tide-water about Christmas. The Sixth led the sharp assault of Fort McAllister, whose capture restored the connection between the army and the fleet sent to meet it with indispensable supplies.

"The regiment was a Columbia, and winning fields by rapid marching even more than by fighting, fired its last shot on Goldsboro, and was present at the surrender of Johnston at Raleigh; having kept step to the music of the Union in a hundred fights in nine States, and marched in proud triumph in the grand review at Washington, the regiment was honorably mustered out of service at St. Louis, in September, 1865, only a remnant having survived the perils of battle and the more deadly camp.

"Many Litchfield men enlisted in companies recruited elsewhere. Some of them were with Zagonyi in his mad charge at Springfield, one against ten—a dash indefensible by military rules, but in its consequences hardly less valuable than a battle gained. Others were surrendered at Lexington. They fought at Pea Ridge; they did Garrison duty at St. Louis and Camp Butler; they were in the gunboat service; they bled at Fort Donelson and suffered and lived through the horrors of Andersonville.

"In August, 1861, half a company of cavalry was enlisted here, and being refused admission to an Illinois regiment, completed an informal organization and became Company C, First Missouri Cavalry. While at St. Louis, the company received recruits from home until the ranks were full. James Barrett was elected Captain, a position from which he retired in a few months, on account of deafness. The regiment took possession of Lexington on Gen. Price's retreat to avoid Fremont, and joined the latter's army at Warsaw. His body guard and two companies of the First Regiment were sent forward to disperse a small force at Springfield, and Company C in Zagonyi's famous charge learned they were one against ten. The company wintered at Leavenworth, and for two years were fighting Quantrell and the guerrillas. At Pleasant Hill, Quantrell lost seventy-five men, while the Federals were weakened by about a dozen killed and wounded. In 1863, the regiment entered Davidson's Division at Clarendon, back of Helena, and slowly approached Little Rock, which was captured with slight loss. In 1864, the regiment then dismounted, formed the advance guard of Steele's army to co-operate with Banks' Red River expedition. The First Missouri was under fire forty days of the forty-one, while absent; on five days in severe battles. At the last one, at the crossing of the Saline, Kirby Smith lost his artillery, and Steele sacrificed 1,200 wagons on his retreat. In August, 1864, the regiment was discharged on the expiration of its term of enlistment. There reremained in the city and its neighborhood only four or five of the riders who fought Quantrell.

"In 1862, E. Southworth began to raise the fourth entire company in the city. Isaac Skillman soon co-operated with him, and when the ranks were full, was elected Captain; M. Pack and J. Reubart, Lieutenants. The company was assigned the post of honor in the Ninety-first Illinois Volunteer Infantry, Col. Day commanding, and being ordered to Kentucky, was captured by John Morgan, at Elizabethtown, and paroled and sent home. Being at length exchanged, the regiment was sent South and put on outpost duty near Galveston. Thence, in 1865, it was ordered to New Orleans, and saw active service at Mobile, where it bore an honorable part in the capture of Fort Blakely.

"Three entire companies raised here were incorporated in Missouri regiments, in addition to several detachments enlisted here, by Lieutenants Gurney, Henderson, Perkins and others. Lieut. Perley was promoted to the Captaincy of Company K, and was killed by falling from a window in Memphis. Lieutenants White and Henderson, Pack and Reubart, and Sergeants Short, V. Hoffman, and private W. Edgar, rose to Captaincies.

"While the city thus sent her hundreds into the field, the men who could not go had an onerous duty to perform at home. A member of the Golden Circle visited a friend here in the critical time when trouble was apprehended in this county. 'I understand,' said he, 'that you have 4,000 stand of arms at the service of the Union League.' 'Certainly. I will show you a specimen of our guns,' and going to a neighbor he borrowed his Ballard rifle. 'This,' said he, 'is a specimen of one-half our supply,' and producing a sixteen-shooter Henry rifle and explaining its construction and efficiency, 'this is the pattern of the other half.' The emissary of the Golden Circle was dismayed, and his report to the Order was instructive, and bore an obvious moral. Before this incident, parts of the Circle had been established in this county, and for a short time one met in the city. Military reviews or drills were held in the close neighborhood. At least three public addresses were made here by its orators, usually by way of a surprise, and the local speakers still live under an immeasurable weight of public odium. A Democratic Club was formed, which met each evening to hear read the latest war news, and an invitation was sought to address it by the Colonel of the Golden Circle regiment, which, in military array, had stalked through Hillsboro. The invitation was refused, and only by an abuse of authority and courtesy was he permitted to ascend its platform. The club was so deeply offended that it never met again. It was about this date that no one was permitted to call himself a Democrat unless he was hostile to the further prosecution of the war. The writer saw and suffered from the zeal and malevolence of the disloyal element. But it is true that in proportion to their numbers, as many Democrats enlisted and served in the war as Republicans. Three of the four captains who raised companies here were Democrats, as were a majority of the rank and file.

'Isaac Skillman, in the spring of 1861, enlisted half a company of cavalry which became a part of an Illinois regiment. The command was taken prisoners at Lexington, paroled and sent home. D. W. Henderson, Belmont Perkins, Al Gurnee and others enlisted men here who were mustered into Missouri regiments. For a time the fervor for enlisting was such that volunteers, being refused in Illinois, went into Missouri regiments. At least 600 men were raised here, quite one-half the entire force supplied by the county, and the city, in draft times, received no credit for its sons fighting under the flags of other States.

"Litchfield responded promptly to each call for troops, and what sort of men she furnished can be seen in her record of pensioners, and on the headstones of national cemeteries. She did her duty—no town could do more—and the Divine thing, which is duty, is always great, and always equally great. It is as great in the sentinel, pacing at midnight his narrow round, as in the General who gains his fame by hurling redoubtable squadrons against intrepid foes to whom the day of battle is a time of of joy.'

This comprises a very brief, and, perhaps, imperfect sketch of Montgomery County's war history—a history that runs through three wars. How many men the county furnished to the national armies, in the late civil war, it is impossible to say, as many enlisted in regiments organized in other States, and for whom Montgomery County received no credit. Those who survived the conflict, have their reward in the knowledge that the old flag still floats over *all* the States; those who fell in the fight, and rest in soldier's graves, are embalmed in the nation's history.

CHAPTER VII.

HILLSBORO TOWNSHIP—DESCRIPTION, BOUNDARIES AND TOPOGRAPHY—ITS EARLY SETTLEMENT—THE McADAMSES, RUTLEDGES, BOONES, AND OTHER PIONEERS—HARD LIFE OF THE PEOPLE—THEIR ROUGH HABITS—COARSE FARE AND SEVERE DUTY—THE PRIMITIVE CABIN AND ITS COMFORTS—MILLS, ROADS AND BRIDGES—EARLY SCHOOLS, CHURCHES, ETC., ETC.

"Our grandmothers long have reposed in the tomb;
With a strong, healthy race they have peopled the land;
They worked with the spindle, they toiled at the loom,
Nor lazily brought up their babies by hand."
—*Eugene Hall.*

FAR across the dense woodlands of Indiana, beyond where Ohio's placid waters roll onward toward the Mississippi, and yet still farther on, among the grand old forests and gushing springs and fertile plains of Kentucky, Tennessee and North Carolina, came the pioneers of this section of the county. Many of them left homes of comfort behind them, others but a small farm upon which they lived and rented by the year, and which barely gave them a support. All came to better their condition, to secure cheap lands, and to finally enable them to give their children a start in the world. Their journey hither was a hard one, and well calculated to discourage men of lesser energy. To those who settled the territory, now embraced in Hillsboro Township, their trials and hardships their toils and dangers, the pages following are inscribed.

The township of Hillsboro occupies a position a little south of the center of the county, and is bounded on the north by Butler Grove Township, on the east by East Fork Township on the south by Grisham Township, and on the west by South Litchfield Township. It is mostly of uneven surface, rolling and somewhat hilly along the water-courses, breaking, in places, into bluffs, and when first seen by white men the larger portion was covered with timber. Nearly all of it, however, is susceptible of cultivation, and produces fine crops of corn, oats and wheat. The timber is principally oak, sugar-maple, cottonwood, elm, walnut, ash, pecan, hickory, etc., etc. The land is drained by Shoal Creek and its tributaries. Middle Fork of Shoal Creek passes nearly through the center of the township in an almost southwest direction, while the West Fork flows through the western part to the southward, and unites with Middle Fork near the south line. Brush Creek is a small stream in the northwest corner and empties into the West Fork, while there are several other insignificant streams that are nameless on the maps. Hillsboro, since the date of township organization (1873) has corresponded in size with the Congressional survey, embracing within its limits thirty-six sections of land lying in a square.

The settlement of Hillsboro Township dates back to 1817 or 1818, and was among the first settlements made in the county. Look at the dates, 1817—1882! Sixty-five years stands between these milestones. Half that number is the average of a generation's lifetime, and hence, two generations have come and gone since the beginning of the settlement in what now forms Hillsboro Township. Among its early pioneers we may mention the names of

* By W. H. Perrin.

the Killpatricks, Joseph McAdams, Jarvis Forehand, William Clark, Dr. Levi D. Boone James Rutledge, Solomon Prewitt, John Tillson, David McCoy, Nicholas Lockerman, the Wrights, Benjamin Rose, Hiram Rountree, Alexander McWilliams, Roland Shepherd, John Norton, D. B. Jackson, Gordon B. Crandall, Joel Smith and a number of others whose names cannot be recalled.

Joseph McAdams, the progenitor of the McAdams family, at whose house the first courts were held, settled some three miles southwest of the present town of Hillsboro. The McAdams family was a prominent one, and many descendants of the patriarch, whose name is mentioned above, still reside in the county, and are useful and worthy citizens. Joseph McAdams raised a family of nine sons and three daughters, and it is a remarkable fact that not one of them—father, mother, sons and daughters—but are dead, and, with perhaps, a single exception, the husbands and wives are also dead.

"The mother that infant's affection approved,
The husband that mother and infant who blessed,
Each, all, are away to their dwellings of rest.

All were prominent citizens, but John only held office, and was one of the first County Commissioners. Joseph, the patriarch of the family, died many years ago, leaving a name untarnished. He was the first Coroner of Montgomery County, but never aspired to office; one of his sons died on a place settled by William Clark, mentioned above as one of the early settlers of the township. But our space will not admit of a detailed sketch of this large family.

About two miles west of Hillsboro, and near where the first county seat (Hamilton) was laid out, David Killpatrick settled. He was of Irish descent, well educated, and said to be one of the finest mathematicians of his day in the county. A man of stern integrity, useful and intelligent, he was often elected to the office of the Justice of the Peace. He, too, raised a large family, and has many descendants living in the county. It was a daughter of his, Martha Killpatrick, who married Dr. Garner, the first doctor that ever practiced medicine in the county. Near Killpatrick, Joel Smith settled. He was the step-father of David B. Starr, who is prominently mentioned elsewhere in this work. David B. Jackson and James Rutledge settled where Hillsboro now stands, and were early hotel-keepers. They are more especially noticed in connection with the early history of the city. Of Mr. Rutledge we extract the following from the Rountree Letters: "In an early day, he cut a conspicuous figure in our county, having served as Constable for many years, and incidentally as Deputy Sheriff, and many times have we seen him 'cheek by jowl' with some horse-thief or other violator of the law, We remember one fact of him, that he put in our old log jail the first prisoners we ever saw go to jail, a couple of horse thieves, by the names of Parks and Means. 'Uncle Jimmy' also served in the Legislature as a Representative from this county. Indeed it may be remarked of him that he always took a large interest in the welfare of our county and our people. He was always at their service, and ever free to express his opinions on all subjects."

Benjamin Rose was an early settler south of Hillsboro, near where the old woolen factory stands. He married a widow, who had two children by a former husband, William and Charles Linxwiler, whom he raised, and who became well-known citizens. He afterward settled a place known as the "Linn Knoll," near Brush Creek. He had two brothers, who were also early settlers, and both of whom are now dead. Other settlers soon flocked around "Linn Knoll," among whom were George H. Anderson, Robert Mann, Mark Rutledge, William Knight, John Bostick, James Grantham, James Wiley, etc., etc., all excellent men and citizens. Anderson had a large family; most of those living reside in Christian County. His wife was a daughter of Robert Mann, who is long since dead. Knight and his wife and most of their family are dead. John Bostick and his aged father, Ezra, a soldier of the Revolutionary war, have likewise gone to that land, "whose sands bear the marks of no returning footprints." James Wiley and his good old father, Aquilla Wiley, have followed them. Thus the pioneers have passed away, leaving but few of their number who stand "like the scattered stalks that remain in the field when the tempest has swept over it."

Dr. Boone was one of the early physicians, a contemporary of Dr. Garner, believed to be the first physician in the county. He was a man of intelligence, of the old Daniel Boone stock, and personally very popular. He commanded a company of Montgomery County boys in the Black Hawk war, and when he served out his term re-enlisted as Surgeon in Capt. Rountree's company, and served to the close of the war. Afterward he removed to Chicago, grew rich, became President of a bank, was elected Mayor, and was a man of much prominence. During the late war, he got into trouble, because his whole-souled generosity prompted him to provide comforts for the Confederate prisoners confined in Camp Douglas, and he was arrested by the Federals for thus succoring those upon whom the fortune of war had frowned, and many of whom were sons of his old Kentucky friends. Hiram Rountree and John Tillson, two men, perhaps, more prominently connected with the county than any others, will receive further mention in the chapters devoted to the town and city. Alexander McWilliams settled about four miles west of Hillsboro, on what was afterward known as the Zimmerman place. John McWilliams was a son, a man of excellent qualities, and one of the early business men of Litchfield. Lockerman settled in the western part of the present township. C. B. Blockberger settled in Hillsboro when it consisted of but a few log houses. He was a tinsmith, and opened the first tin shop in the county. He was a public-spirited man, made himself very useful to the early settlers, kept a general store; made brick; kept a hotel, and was several times elected to the Legislature. He was Deputy United States Marshal in 1840, afterward Postmaster, also served as Probate Judge, and held several military offices. He was chiefly instrumental in organizing the first Masonic lodge in Hillsboro, and the first in the county, to which he was greatly devoted. When he died he was buried with Masonic honors, Gen. Shields officiating.

The Cannons were early settlers, locating here as early as 1824. There were three brothers—William, John and Charles—all of whom settled near Hillsboro, and some of them in the town. William raised thirteen children out of fifteen born to him. Says Mr. Rountree in his sketches: "He is now nearly threescore and ten, and is quite a patriarch. He counts his descendants as follows: Children, 15, of whom are living, 13; grandchildren, 99, of whom are living, 90; great-grand children, all living, 13, making 127 descendants, of whom 116 are now living." But our space will not admit of further details of the early settlement of the township. We have endeavored to trace its settlement from the beginning down to a period within the memory of those still living, giving the names and facts of the early history of the more prominent of its pioneers. Though doubtless the names of many are overlooked who are entitled to honorable mention among these pioneer fathers, yet no pains have been spared to make the list full and complete.

The early life of the pioneers was one not to be envied, and one that could scarcely be endured or borne by their more tenderly-nurtured descendants. The early settlers as we have said came here to better their condition, and make homes for themselves and families. Their first duty was to provide shelter, and their cabins were hastily built, the cracks between the logs rudely daubed with mud; the floors were often mother earth, or of rough puncheons, and the bedsteads and tables, with a chair or two, were almost the sole furniture. Pewter plates were common, and the big fire-places surrounded by pots, skillets, ovens, pans, etc., were used for cooking instead of stoves. Biscuits and corn-dodgers baked in an oven or skillet, and "johnny cake" baked on a board before the fire, were considered diet fit for the gods. Game was plenty and hence meat was never scarce but the facilities for obtaining meal and flour were very limited. Mills for flour came after years with other improvements, but hand-mills, run not by steam, horses or oxen, but by the women and children, were the chief means of getting meal. New corn was often grated by hand for immediate use. Fruit could only be obtained from abroad, and with great difficulty, except such as grew wild. Honey was abundant, and could be had for the simple cutting down of the bee trees, so common in the woods.

The clothing was cheap and primitive as that of the cabin and its surroundings. That for both sexes was made at home, going through all the processes from the time of leaving the sheep's back until placed upon the back of the wearer. All the members of the household, male and female, men, women and children, were usually employed in some parts, if not in all parts of its manufacture. The men and boys often wore clothing made of the dressed skins of animals; boots were unknown, and shoes indulged in only as a luxury by the grown people while moccasins made at home sufficed for the smaller members of the family. Says Mr. Rountree: "We wonder if the boys of our day are curious to know what kind of hair oil and neck-ties, what shaped collars and cuffs were the fashion then? We wonder if our girls are curious to know what sort of dress trimmings, what shape were the bonnets and hats, and if they wore paniers and bustles, sacks and overskirts, and whether they wore furs, muffs, cuffs, etc., etc., and when fully informed upon the subject no doubt their looks of incredulity would be refreshing. There are doubtless many now living in the county who can tell of the long linen shirts home-made, that were the only summer garments worn by boys and children, and of the moccasins and buckskin clothing. There were many who never wore a pair of boots until they were men, and others who never even saw a pair until nearly grown." It is still a mystery how the people lived and prospered in those early days. The manner of cultivating the crops was so simple, the tools so different and rude, and the distance to market so great and the prices so incredibly low, that we wonder how any one, even with the strictest economy, could prosper at all. The farmers of to-day, who have reduced agriculture to a science, and cultivate their lands almost wholly with machinery, know little of what that same work required here fifty or sixty years ago. But times have changed, and the world, or the people have grown wiser as they have grown older.

Among the amusements of the early citizens of the community, was that of fishing in the classic waters of Shoal Creek. The numerous Shoal Creeks, East, West and Middle Forks, afforded ample "fishing grounds" for the pioneer fathers. A rural bard thus sings of its glory, and of those who fished and swam in its tranquil waters "forty years ago." He says, or sings:

"How many times I wander back
In pensive mood, on memory's track
To thy green banks thou dear old stream,
Where in my youth, so like a dream
My days were passed, that toil and strife,
No shadow cast upon my life.

"E'en now with memory's eye I see
Thy waters gliding bright and free

O'er shining sands and pebbly beds,
Where bass and perch, and knotty heads,
Pursued the minnows, that essayed
To steal the eggs that they had laid
On pebbly heaps. With crooked pin,
Tied on a thread, I've waded in,
And coaxed, and coaxed, with all my might,
Those finny ones to take a bite—
One little bite of angling worm,
That on my hook did twist and squirm.

"As dear as Jordan to the Jew,
Or Ganges to the grave Hindoo,
Has ever been thy name to me:
And this my sole excuse must be,
For pouring out this flood of rhymes,
In mem'ry of those happy times
I've spent, in angling on thy shores,
Or 'mong thy hills in gathering stores
Of nuts to crack in winter nights;
An entertainment whose delights
No boy or girl can e'er forget
Till mem'ry's sun in death has set.

"How often I in mem'ry meet,
And with a hearty welcome greet
The friends of yore who roamed with me
Along thy banks in mirth and glee,
* * * * * * * *

"But, oh! what changes time has brought!
What havoc has that monster wrought,
Whose hungry jaws still cry for more,
Devouring alike the rich and poor.
Upon the brow of yonder bluff,
With face so jagged and so rough,
I see e'en now the resting place
Of many, who began the race
Of life with me who fished and swam,
From Wiley's ford to Lemon's dam;
And gained with me their stock of lore,
In log schoolhouses, where the floor
Was naked earth, with weight-pole roof,
That seldom proved quite water-proof;
With slabs for seats, with rough split-pegs,
In two-inch auger holes, for legs.
I see with retrospection's eye,
Upon yon hill so steep and high
[Where J. M. Rutledge now resides],
A cabin rude, where many a day
I passed the tedious hours away
In picking up the little store
That I possess of useful lore;
Exciting many times the ire

A native of the Emerald Sod,
Whose scepter was the hazel rod.
How often in Hibernian brogue,
He called me 'spalpeen,' or a rogue!
And cowed when I some mischief did,
That he would *cut* [illegible] *to the rid.*
At noon we often truant played,
In thy cool flood to swim or wade,
Forgetting how the moments sped,
Until the time for books had fled,
And then crept back with some excuse,
Though poor, intended to induce
The auld Hibernian to forget
The punishment we dreaded so.
* * * * *

"I sometimes meet those Nimrods here
Who once pursued the wolf and deer
Among thy hills, or traced the bee
To where, in some old hollow tree,
Its luscious stores were hoarded up
In many a little waxen cup.
Of all those Nimrods none remain
With gun in hand to scour the plain.
The wolf and deer are seen no more
Among the woods along the shore;
And where now we heard the panther's scream,
The farmer drives his patient team.
Where once the Indian wigwam stood
Upon the border of some wood
The stately mansion now is seen
Amid broad fields and pastures green.

"But I have neither space nor time
To put the feelings into rhyme,
That rise, while I, in mem'ry roam,
O'er scenes about my childhood's home.
Then, dear old stream, you'll pardon me
For thus apostrophizing thee,
And grant me leave at any time,
To talk to thee in rambling rhyme."

The foregoing lines, from the pen of J. N Wilson, of Springfield, contain quite a little history in themselves, and will doubtless call up pleasant reminiscences in the minds of many of our readers. Shoal Creek was early utilized for mills, as well as for "fishing and swimming" purposes. These are mentioned more fully however, in subsequent chapters. The "Pepper" mill, as it was called, was an early institution, and was southwest of Hillsboro some three or four miles. But it has long since gone to decay, and few people in Hillsboro remember anything about it.

The early roads were trails over the country, many originally made by the Indians, and afterward improved by the people and made into roads. One of the first in the township—and but very little of it was in the present township of Hillsboro—was the Hillsboro & Springfield road. Another was the Hillsboro & St. Louis road, which runs out by the Fair Grounds. When first laid out, there were no bridges where these roads cross the streams, and hence, in time of high water, travel was suspended. Now there are substantial bridges where all the principal roads cross the streams, so that high waters are no impediment now to travel.

The first school taught in the township was in Hillsboro, and will be more especially noticed under the head of the city. There are now six schoolhouses, all comfortable buildings, in the township, outside of Hillsboro, which afford ample facilities to the people for the education of their children.

Hamilton, the first county seat, was in Hillsboro Township, some three miles southwest of Hillsboro. It was laid out as a town after being selected for the seat of justice. Lots were sold, and a few houses built, though no court house or other public buildings were erected. John Tillson opened a store there, but as soon as Hillsboro was selected as the county seat, he moved to the new town. The changing of the location of the county seat, of course, was the death-knell of Hamilton, and it soon became another "Goldsmith's Deserted Village." From its ruins, however, arose eventually, the village of Woodsboro, which was laid out very near if not at the same place where Hamilton had formerly stood.

Woodsboro was laid out about 1848, by William Wood, a man of the most untiring energy and industry. He first settled six miles southwest of Hillsboro, where he opened a store, and about 1837 he commenced improvements on the "Woodsboro farm," and removed his store there. He succeeded, in 1848, in getting a post office, of which he was Postmaster. He laid out the town where the Springfield & Greenville road crossed the Hillsboro & St. Louis road, and, as we have said, it was some three miles southwest of Hillsboro. It was at one time a place of considerable business. Mr. Wood, in addition to his store, was instrumental in having a wagon shop, blacksmith shop, cooper shop and tin shop opened in his town, and, in 1851, he built a steam saw and grist mill, which he ran for several years. So Woodsboro flourished until the completion of the Indianapolis & St. Louis Railroad, when most of the town went to Butler, Mr. Wood, himself, having moved to that place, and took an active part in building it up. He continued an active business man until his death, which occurred in 1873. A church of the Methodist denomination was built at Woodsboro, which is still in use, and comprises about all of the town there is left.

Some two miles south of Woodsboro stands the Presbyterian Church of Waveland, an offshoot of the Presbyterian Church of Woodsboro. This and the Methodist Church at Hillsboro are the only churches, we believe, in the township, outside of the city.

CHAPTER VIII.*

CITY OF HILLSBORO—LAID OUT AS THE COUNTY SEAT—ITS LOCATION, ETC.—FIRST SALE OF LOTS—STREETS AND ADDITIONS—THE FIRST INHABITANT—JUDGE ROUNTREE—OTHER PIONEERS—FIRST FRAME AND FIRST BRICK HOUSE—STORES, SHOPS, MILLS, ETC.—AN INCIDENT—MANUFACTURING INDUSTRIES—THE GRAIN TRADE AND RAILROAD—COURT HOUSES AND JAILS—INCORPORATION OF THE CITY, ETC.

"Full sixty years have come and gone
Since we commenced life's rugged way—
Facing December's fleecy snows,
And plucking flowers that grew in May."

THE events which led to the birth of Hillsboro originated in the general dissatisfaction of the people of the first seat of justice of Montgomery County, as noted in a preceding chapter. Hence, an act was passed by the Legislature, January 30, 1823, authorizing the relocation of the county seat, and appointing three Commissioners, viz.: Newton Coffey, Maj. James Wilson and Harris Reavis, for that purpose. The site selected by them was that of the present city of Hillsboro, the land of which was at the time owned by Newton Coffey, one of the Commissioners. In conformity with the provisions of the act, he executed a deed for twenty acres of land, June 30, 1823, for the purpose of defraying the expense of erecting public buildings. Upon this twenty acres, the original town of Hillsboro was laid out, and the sale of lots took place August 12, 1823. In another twelve months, the city may celebrate its three score years.

Hillsboro is beautifully situated on high rolling ground, commanding a fine view of the surrounding country, and on the Indianapolis & St. Louis Railroad, some sixty-five miles nearly northeast of St. Louis, and about two hundred miles southwest of Chicago, the great commercial metropolis of Illinois and the Northwest. It is a city of about two thousand inhabitants, and is noted for its intelligent and enterprising inhabitants, for its excellent schools and handsome and spacious churches. It is a healthy place—what might be termed by enterprising physicians "distressingly healthy"—its high and dry location being a safeguard against the malarial fevers prevalent in early times in the lower lands.

The area embraced within the limits of the present city of Hillsboro is sufficient for a place of 20,000 inhabitants. To the stranger it would appear that the town was laid out without shape or design, and this, we learn, is to some extent true. Says Mr. Rountree: "The territory was of such shape, being filled up with hills and hollows, springs and running streams, it was deemed almost impossible that the streets could ever become harmonious by labor, the hollows filled up and the space economized, and, even if it could, there would never be no necessity for it, the original town being only north of Col. Walters' hotel (now the American House) on each side of Main street, and ending south of the public schoolhouse. The distance east and west being from the section line to Hamilton

*By W. H. Perrin.

street, and this embraced almost all the level land; and even then there was a deep hollow running southwardly from George Brown's house through the Seward and Col. Walters' property; also, there was, and still is in part, a series of hollows along Hamilton street. To avoid one hollow, John Tillson, in making his addition east and south of Col. Walters' hotel, made a jog seemingly necessary then to find good ground for streets. Cress and Wright afterward laid out a few lots south and west of Solomon Harkey's property, running the lots far down the hill, while Hiram Rountree made an addition on the north, which was laid out by Harry Wilton. The other additions were made many years later."

The first settler upon the site of Hillsboro was a German, named John Nussman. The land was owned, or, rather, was entered for the purpose of laying out a town, by Newton Coffey, who had first settled in the southern part of the county. Previously, however, Nussman, who had emigrated from North Carolina, had settled upon it. His cabin stood upon the ground occupied by the residence of the late A. H. H. Rountree, and where Mrs. Rountree now lives. Mr. Nussman raised a large family of children, some of whom are, we believe, still citizens of the city and county. He was also one of Hillsboro's early mechanics, and carried on a wagon shop—the first, perhaps, in Montgomery County. Among other early settlers of the town of Hillsboro were the Wrights, Joseph Miller, John Tillson, Lloyd Martin, David B. Jackson, Hiram Rountree, James Rutledge, and others now forgotten. Jackson built the first frame house in Hillsboro, which is now a portion of the old American House. He was quite an enterprising man in his day—an early merchant, a tavern-keeper, surveyor, saw mill, etc., etc., and an energetic business man generally. He has a son, William K. Jackson, still living in the town.

Judge Hiram Rountree was a ruling spirit in Hillsboro for many years, exerting a greater influence than any man, perhaps, that has ever lived in the place, and deserves more than a mere passing notice in these pages. He was a native of North Carolina, where he was born December 22, 1794, but his early life was spent mostly in Kentucky. He was a soldier in the war of 1812, under Gen. Shelby, the first Governor of Kentucky, and who was a Revolutionary officer, and the hero of King's Mountain. He studied law in Bowling Green, Ky., and, in 1817, removed to Edwardsville, Ill., where he taught school for two years. He afterward removed to Fayette County, when the capital of the State was at Vandalia, and for several sessions was Enrolling Clerk of the House of Representatives. In 1821, he removed to Montgomery County, and, as Circuit Clerk, organized it. The remainder of his life was spent in the county, and there were few positions of importance but what he held at some time during his long and useful life. His official career has been so often alluded to in these pages that it is unnecessary to repeat it here. Suffice it, for forty-eight years in succession he served the county in an official capacity. He was a zealous member of the Methodist Church from the year 1818 to the time of his death, March 5, 1873, and his Christian life is still familiar to many residents of the city and county.

Joel Wright was the first Sheriff of the county, and was from one of the Eastern States. He served as Sheriff from 1821 until 1826. James Wright was the son of a widow lady, known as "Granny" Wright, who lived in a cabin in Hillsboro, on the place recently occupied by Henry Haller. The following incident is related of "Granny" Wright, who is described as an "estimable woman, of strong, good sense and ardent friendships." She, it is said, always had corn to sell, and would demand a very high price for it. In measuring it, however, she always told them to "heap it up, to heap it up as long as it would lie on; that if the old boy ever got her, it should be for high prices, and not for scant measure." The manner of measurement she intended, should bring the price down about fair.

John Tillson, prominently mentioned in connection with the church and school history, was the first Treasurer of Montgomery County. He first settled on the Scherer place, some three miles southwest of Hillsboro, and was originally from Boston, Mass., but emigrated West while still a bachelor. He went back to Boston and married, brought his wife to his new settlement, where he resided till after Hillsboro was made the county seat when he removed to the town and built the first brick house ever erected in Hillsboro. The house was a large, massive, two-story edifice, and was built under the supervision of John Nickerson and David Eddy. Nickerson also made the brick, but they were not of a good quality, and hence the house was not thought to be a success. It stood for many years, however, and was finally torn down, and the brick used in buildings erected down near the railroad.

Mr. Tillson was also the first Postmaster of Hillsboro, likewise the first merchant, and one of Hillsboro's most energetic and useful citizens. He engaged largely in land speculations in this as well as in other counties, and handled large sums of money. In the early struggles of the State to build railroads, which proved so disastrous to Illinois finances, he was one of the Fund Commissioners, and prospered well until the great crash of 1837, from which he never fully recovered financially. By that he lost largely and soon after disposed of his landed property here, and was no more identified with the county. He raised quite a large family of children, none of whom live here now. Gen. Tillson, of Quincy, who attained considerable distinction in the late civil war, was his son. Mr. Tillson died suddenly, of apoplexy in Peoria.

James Rutledge came to Hillsboro about the year 1825, and settled on a lot recently occupied by George Paisley. He was one of the first, if not the first, tavern-keeper in the town. He raised a large family of children among whom may be mentioned Thomas J. Rutledge, an attorney, and Dr. H. E. Rutledge, dentist, both now of Hillsboro.

Our space, however, will not admit of extended sketches of the early settlers and business men of Hillsboro, but in the biographical department of this volume, such sketches will be more fully given. We might fill many chapters with sketches and incidents of the pioneers of the town, but must confine our work to historical facts.

The village was now laid out and permanently established, as we might say. It was the county seat, and the commercial center of a rich area of country. This brought merchants, mechanics and trades-men to the place, with the intention of entering into active business life. We have stated already that John Tillson opened the first store in Hillsboro, and that he was the first merchant in the county, having first opened a store at his residence before Hillsboro was laid out, and then removing it to the town.

The second store in Hillsboro is believed to have been opened by John Prentice, about the year 1825. He came from St. Clair County to Hillsboro and lived in the "Granny Wright cabin," as it was called.

There were but few houses in the town at that time, and Mr. Prentice opened his store in a log cabin which stood near the present Ralston brick storehouse. The following is told of his settlement in Hillsboro. Before moving here, he came on a prospecting tour, and for the purpose of consulting with the citizens as to the propriety of locating here. He asked them if they thought he could sell on an average $5 worth of goods a day, to which he received a most decided "No" in response. He then asked if he could sell an average of $4 worth a day. Upon this proposition, the testimony was divided, when he asked if he could sell an average of $3 a day. They believed unanimously that he could. With this encouraging prospect ahead of him—the selling of $3 worth of goods per day on an average—he decided to locate in Hillsboro. His store was a general country store, and contained iron, nails, salt, sugar, molasses, whisky, dry goods, axes, common cutlery, dye stuffs, etc., etc. He brought on a few hundred dollars' worth of goods and opened out his store in full blast, but made no grand display, such as now attends the opening of a new mercantile establishment, such as flaming posters, newspaper puffs, fine show windows, etc. Mr. Prentice kept his goods on his shelves, behind and under his counters, and in front, but inside the building. He continued long in the business in Hillsboro, but his family all scattered off to other localities, and none now live even in this county.

Another of the early mercantile establishments of Hillsboro was that of Charles Holmes. He opened his first stock of goods in a log house where Union Block now stands, about 1832 or 1833. John S. Hayward, from Boston, became a partner. Mr. Tillson was also a silent partner for a time. About 1842, they dissolved, and Holmes and Tillson retired. Holmes went to St. Louis, amassed a fortune and died there. Tillson had embarrassed himself in his land speculations, and with him Mr. Hayward. The crash of 1837 had paralyzed all enterprises, and the holding and paying taxes on land became burdensome. Hayward by some means released himself from his entanglements with Mr. Tillson, and, seeing his way clear, and, by years of residence in Illinois, became satisfied that lands would eventually be valuable, he sold out his store and engaged in land agencies. He commenced the purchase of the lands held by Eastern land companies at very low figures, and, through his friends in the East, was enabled to hold them until the real prosperity returned, when he sold them at advanced prices, re-invested his funds and finally became very wealthy. He was a discreet man, public-spirited, and took an active part in securing the railroad to Hillsboro. Somewhat late in life, he married Miss Harriet F. Comstock, a daughter of Deacon Comstock, of whom Mr. Rountree, in his reminiscences, relates the following incident:

Deacon Comstock had an exceptionally long nose, and, having the end of his nose skinned on one occasion, he applied a circular piece of black court plaster to it. While officiating in church one day in that condition, he saw on the floor what he thought was the court plaster, and, picking it up, moistened it and placed it upon his nose, quietly took his seat and engaged in pious meditation. But smiles and nudges, nods and winks all around him convinced him that his neighbors were otherwise engaged. All of his pious frowns and dignity could not reduce them to order. Merriment and fun had possessed them, even of his own large, well-trained family. He was horrified and shocked at their ill-timed levity. But his daughter pointed to the end of his nose, where he had placed what he took to be court plaster, but

J. Bowers Lane

what was really the ticket of one of the "Coates' Spools," which, in beautiful gilt letters, was "warranted 200 yards," and which, being placed upon the end of a very long nose, seemed to the congregation to be peculiarly applicable. The good Deacon was never able to escape the joke as long as he lived.

Other merchants came to Hillsboro and opened stores, but to follow them in detail would be tedious. Other branches of business, in the meantime, were established in the town. Hotels were built and accommodations for "man and beast" offered to the wayfaring man who came along. We have already alluded to the taverns built by Jackson and Rutledge. Mr. Rountree says of the latter: "His was the first old-fashioned tavern sign we ever saw, embodying, as it did, a large tiger on a white ground, surrounded by his name and occupation. His, as well as Mr. Jackson's, were houses of entertainment, and not houses for the sale of liquors, though they both came under the same law. Any one who kept a grocery for the sale of liquor was compelled to take out a tavern-keeper's license, ranging from $5 to $20, and were under bonds to keep sufficient room and bedding for the entertainment of at least two persons, with sufficient provender and stabling for their horses. It was optional with them whether they sold liquors, and, though they may have kept them for the use of their guests, we cannot remember ever to have heard of them selling otherwise than in a private way." Other taverns were opened by enterprising people in the new town.

Hillsboro flourished in a moderate, old-fogy way, growing slowly but somewhat surely. Merchants, mechanics, etc., came in and gave the town a healthy impetus. Among the earliest citizens were mechanics, who proved excellent citizens. Nussman, the first inhabitant, was a wagon-maker, and also established a distillery in an early day. The distillation of whisky then was not a disreputable business, as it is now; neither was the drinking of it so strongly condemned. Indeed, it was deemed essential in a new country like this was. His distillery was carried on for some time, when it gave place to a tan-yard, a business more honorable, if less profitable. Joseph Miller carried on a tan-yard also, as one of the very early industries of Hillsboro. Jacob Wilson was one of the earliest shoemakers, and used to go from house to house, making up shoes for the entire family. John Slater was another of the pioneer shoemakers. So was Deacon Alexander Scott. The following incident is related of the good Deacon's wife. She survived him some years, and, when near her end, but still able to be around, she had a dream so vivid and life-like that she accepted it as an omen, and prepared herself accordingly. She dreamed that her husband came to her, not as he left her, an old man, but young and handsome as when he visited her as a lover, and told her he wanted them to be married early in October. This she accepted as an omen that she would then depart and be again united to him. She visited her friends for the last time, as she maintained, made all her porparations, and, when all was done, she sickened, and, early in October, she died, having steadily refused all remedies looking to her recovery. This romance was so contrary to her natural disposition that she firmly believed that the spirit of her husband had warned her of her approaching dissolution.

Among the early blacksmiths of Hillsboro were Nathan and Burton Harmon and a Mr. Hutchinson. W. A. Morrison and Kimball Prince were the next blacksmiths, perhaps, who located in the town. Fred Hillsabeck was also an early blacksmith. Another of the early blacksmiths was Ned Gossage, as he was called. He lived in a small log cabin, with no floor but the ground, and his shop was a similar structure. Mr. Wesley Seymour is supposed to be the next wagon-maker to Nussman. John Meisenheimer was also a wagon maker and a carpenter. John Dickerson, David [illegible], Ira Boone and Hudson Berry were the first brick makers of the town. William Brewer established a turning-lathe very early and manufactured furniture, working in wood work generally. Thomas Sturtevant, Alfred Durant, E. B. Hubbell and James Blackman were of the same trade, and followed the business for years.

The first steam mill in the town was built by John Tillson. It was originally started by David B. Jackson as an ox tread-mill for sawing lumber. But Tillson enlarged it, supplied steam and made a flouring and saw mill, which was of great benefit to the town and community. It was burned down about 1840. No town in Central or Southern Illinois is better supplied with mills than Hillsboro is at the present day. That of Glenn Bros. is a very paragon of excellence, while there are several mills in town, quite as good, but of smaller capacity.

Hillsboro has never made any pretentions toward manufactories. A few rather small ones, such as Gunning's, which was burned early in 1873, and the woolen factory in the south end of town, a few small wagon and carriage factories, comprise her manufacturing ventures. She has never aspired to anything beyond being a quiet, retail business town. The grain trade is perhaps the largest business carried on in the town. Since the opening of the I. & St. L. R. R., in 1855, Hillsboro has become the center of a large grain trade. An immense quantity of corn, oats and wheat is annually shipped from this point. Enterprising buyers are always on hand in the grain season, who keep up with the market price and always pay the very best figures. The completion of the railroad gave the town quite an impetus, and from that time it grew more rapidly in population than it ever had before. Persons often wonder, particularly strangers, why the depot is away down under the hill where it is, instead of being east from the court house. The principal reason, we have been informed, was in consequence of a little game of "loggerheads," played between the railroad people and the citizens of the town. The railroad people wanted to run their road through the south end of the town, a route the citizens very rightly objected to. Hence, to gratify a little malice, the railroad people then placed their depot as far off as possible and in the most inconvenient location. But with the depot in an out-of-the-way place and the road down under the hill, it has been the crowning event in the history of Hillsboro, and given her an increase of business, prosperity and importance she had never known before.

The first court house built in Montgomery was in Hillsboro, as the general dissatisfaction of Hamilton as the county seat had prevented the erection of a court house at that place. But when Hillsboro was selected as the future seat of justice, it was believed the selection would remain permanent, and therefore arrangements were at once entered into for the building of a court house. It was of simple architecture and material, but up to the spirit of the times in which it was built. It was twenty-five feet square, a story and a half high, of hewed logs, the cracks well chinked, two glass windows of 8x10 glass, one for the room below and one above. The floors were of plank, as well as the doors, instead of puncheons and clapboards, and the roof was of shingles. Primitive as this building may appear, when compared to Hillsboro's present temple of justice, it was, in that early day, by far the most pretentious building in the embryonic city, and a great improvement on the residences of the people. It was situated on the southeast corner of the square, where it did duty until the next one was built -1836-37. When the log house was finally removed, the logs were used in a small building still standing back of the photograph gallery. The first Clerk's office was also built of logs, and is, or was until recently, standing, a solitary relic of the pioneer period, near the Methodist Church.

The original jail was a log structure, and a very formidable prison for that early period, when criminals were not so smart as they are now, nor so thoroughly educated in crime as they are in this fast age. It was of hewed logs and the walls were of three thicknesses - two horizontal and one perpendicular tier. When torn down to give place to a more modern "bastile," many of the logs were used for street crossings, thus displaying a spirit of economy worthy of imitation in these latter days.

The old log court house faithfully served its day and generation, and was used in other capacities than meting out justice to the offenders of the law. It was used by most of the religious denominations until they built church edifices and for all public meetings. The first term of court held in it was on the 17th and 18th of June, 1824, Judge Thomas Reynolds presiding. Joel Wright was Sheriff; Jarvis Forehand, Coroner, and Hiram Rountree, Clerk. As an item of interest to the present Clerks of the Court, it might be well to state that the fees of Hiram Rountree were $8 for the first year he held the office of Clerk. The following incident related of Mr. Rountree, and the first term of the Circuit Court held in Montgomery County, is given here as illustrative of the primitive days of the county. The first term of the Circuit Court was held at Joseph McAdams,' before the county seat had been located at Hillsboro. Hiram Rountree, with his family, was residing at the house of Joseph McAdams, a cabin of two rooms, and in one of them the court was held, while Mrs. Rountree retired to the other with her two children until court should adjourn. Judge Reynolds very calmly and dignifiedly, it is said, reposed his "judicial honor" on the side of the bed. Mr. Rountree sat in a splint-bottomed chair—the only one in the room, by the side of a walnut table made of puncheons, smoothed off with the ax, both chair and table his own manufacture, and, with a goose-quill pen, kept the records and administered the oaths, etc.

Somewhere about the year 1836 or 1837, a new court house was built, and the old log structure was removed. This second building was a frame, and was a square edifice, two stories high, the lower story the court-room, and the upper story divided into offices. The court-room being below, about two-thirds of the floor was mother earth; the remainder was laid of plank and was two or three feet above the ground, with a railing or banisters around it. And inside of this railing was the Judge's stand, Clerk's desk, lawyers' tables, etc., etc. The spectators and lookers-on remained outside of the railing, where they could spit their tobacco juice in the dust without any lynx-eyed officer "to molest or make them afraid." During the recesses of the court, the hogs occupied the room, and made a bed-chamber under the floor, which, as we have said, was two or three feet above the ground. This small square, frame building, with roof running up to a point in the center, with a small cupola set on top, very much resembling a chicken-coop, was used as a court house until about 1854, when it was displaced by a brick building, at a cost of some $5,000. It was a two-story house, with large columns in front supporting a portico, something in the style of the present academy building. Some years later, a wing was added to it, the upper story of which formed the jail and the lower story the jury-room, etc. This building is still standing and serving the county as a court house, though it has been considerably repaired since the late war. It stood, however, until 1868, without material change, when it was very substantially repaired and transformed into its present magnificence.

The court house as it now stands is but the old one remodeled. As is the case in many other counties in Illinois, there has been quite a contest between Hillsboro and Litchfield in regard to the county seat--on the part of Litchfield to possess it and on that of Hillsboro to hold it. It is said that "possession is nine points in law," and hence Hillsboro holds "nine points" against Litchfield in the contest. When the subject came up, soon after the close of the war, as to the propriety of building a new court house, the question of removal to Litchfield was feared by those opposed to removal, if the project was undertaken to build a new house out and out, and hence it was finally resolved to merely "rejuvenate" the old one, and thereby save the county the expense of erecting a new and costly building. The sequel proved that the improvement of old buildings was not wholly devoid of cost. After deciding upon repairing the old court house, an architect was brought down from Chicago, who drew plans and designs for the work, and from them the present building was made out of the old one, at a cost of something like $120,000 and $15,000 or $20,000 more for finishing the jail. In order to carry out the original design of repairing the old building, some half dozen or so of the old brick were left in the new house, which, notwithstanding all that has been said, or may be said about it, is a handsome and imposing structure and a credit to the county and the people. When we look at the sum expended on it, it appears to be a rather costly edifice, but the difference in the price of material and labor then and now considered, perhaps the cost is not extravagant. It is a comfortable and convenient house, as well as an imposing one. The court-room, which will comfortably seat about 500 persons, is in the second story, together with jury-rooms, consultation-rooms, etc., while the first story is taken up with offices, comprising those of County and Circuit Clerk, County Judge, Recorder, Sheriff and County Superintendent of Schools.

The jail and the Sheriff's residence is in the north end or side of the building, and is quite a convenient part of the designs. The jail is in the top story, while the Sheriff's residence is in the second, the house being three stories high on this side. The prison portion is finished up in the most safe and substantial manner, and is intended to keep an evil-doer, when once incarcerated in it, until he is taken out by the proper authorities.

The court house is situated on the highest ground within the city's limits, and stands as a way-mark to the passing traveler, and is usually the first object observable when approaching the town. From the lofty tower which ascends skyward from the southwest corner, a fine view can be had of the country for miles around. Indeed, one with a good pair of eyes, on a clear morning, may look away to the West, across the States of Missouri and Arkansas, and see the buffalo grazing on the prairies of Texas. Fact! The handsome court house, with its spacious court-room elegantly furnished, conveniently arranged offices, substantial jail and Sheriff's comfortable residence, taken all together, present quite a contrast to the old log buildings of fifty years ago.

Hillsboro was laid out as a village, as we have seen, in 1823. It was incorporated as a town under the State law, and was governed by a Board of Trustees, with the necessary officers for the proper administration of its affairs. It remained under this style of government until 1869, when it was incorporated as a city, by an act of the Legislature approved March 30 of that year. It was, under its charter as a city, divided into four wards, represented by members in a Common Council, of which the Mayor was and is the presiding officer. Since its organization as a city, the following gentlemen have served as Mayor, viz., John T. Maddux, 1869; Fred Noterman, 1870; Paul Walters, 1871; Fred Noterman, 1872; A. H. Brown, 1873; A. H. H. Rountree, 1874; E. S. Burns, 1875; John F. Glenn, 1876; M. M. Walsh, 1877; George H. Blackwelder, 1878; William Conklin, 1879; Charles B. Rhoads, 1880; Ben E. Johnson, 1881; Ben E. Johnson, 1882.

In March, 1882, the city was re-organized under a special State law regulating the municipal government of cities. This order of things necessitated a new division of the city into districts or wards. Hitherto, under the old regime, the city was divided into four wards, but when re-organized and redivided, it was laid off into three wards. Each of these are represented in the Common Council by two members, who, with the Mayor and Clerk, comprise the municipal government. The present Council (1882) is as follows: W. L. Blackburn, J. M. Cress, members from the First Ward; A. H. May, B. Philips, members from the Second Ward; J. M. Truitt W. M. Neff, members from the Third Ward, with Simon Kahn, City Clerk; C. H. Witherspoon, City Treasurer, and Ben E. Johnson, Mayor.

The streets, buildings (residences and business houses) of Hillsboro are as good, if not better, than are to be found in the majority of cities of her size and wealth in the State. It is true that the people generally of Illinois towns and cities do not take as much pains, nor spend as much money in beautifying their streets, parks, etc., as some of the older States farther east. The streets of Hillsboro are beautifully shaded with trees, and, with a little care and taste, might be made exceedingly attractive. Many handsome residences and grounds are an ornament to the city, and show a refinement of taste that should extend to the beautifying of the streets and the purchasing and laying out of a park. Young people require a summer resort and a promenade, and the addition to Hillsboro of a public park would be a judicious investment by the city authorities, and relieve the railroad depot of crowds of idle visitors. The business houses, as a class, are good, of modern style and arrangements, and every class of retail business is represented, from the banking house and first-class store, down to the most ordinary shops, and the annual trade of the city will compare favorably with that of any of its sister cities.

In looking back over the sixty years that have come and gone, we see the few log cabins that stood upon the crest of a hill, grown and expanded into a flourishing little city, instinct with life and the bustle of business. We have traced its growth and development in trade and traffic briefly for the sixty years that have elapsed since it was selected as the seat of justice of Montgomery County. We have seen how its first inhabitants settled down in the proverbial log cabin, and, by honest toil and strict integrity in their daily life and transactions, became prosperous and happy. And now we close the record of its growth, development and business, and, in the chapters succeeding, take up other branches of its history.

CHAPTER IX.*

HILLSBORO—ITS RELIGIOUS HISTORY—THE METHODIST CHURCH—ORGANIZATION, MEMBERS AND PREACHERS—THE PRESBYTERIANS—THEIR CHURCH—OTHER RELIGIOUS ORGANIZATIONS—BENEVOLENT INSTITUTIONS—THE MASONS—ODD FELLOWS, ETC., ETC.

"God attributes to place
No sanctity, if none be thither brought
By men who there frequent.—*Milton.*

THE Rev. N. S. Dickey, in his address upon the semi-centennial of the Presbyterian Church of Hillsboro, said: "The good seed carried by emigrants is usually sufficient to begin the work of raising society to a higher level of civilization, and their transforming power counteracts those demoralizing influences which tend to social degeneration and disruption. These Christian influences are active in their conflicts with evil and attractive in social power; and they usually act as a nucleus around which will gather those influences necessary to carry society onward to a state of comparative perfection. We may see by comparison with the past how much has been done in this respect. The progress and triumph of Christian truth, the superstructure on which every society which approximates perfection must rest, is also made apparent. It is thus seen that no other power but Christian truth can vitalize, expand, harmonize, direct and control the forces which underlie and build up the great fabric of society." This was true of the early settlers of Hillsboro and vicinity. It is much to their credit that they were mostly a Christian people, and laid the foundation of religious organizations in an early period of their occupation of the country. The Methodist circuit-riders, the forerunners of Christianity, as John was of the Master, were the first heralds of the Cross in the wilderness of Illinois. They traveled over the country on horseback, gathering the scattered settlers together, preaching the Gospel to them, and forming them into religious societies. As early as 1820, they made their regular visits to the neighborhood and preached in private houses. Jesse Walker, Peter Cartwright, Samuel Thompson, Charles Holliday, Joshua Barnes and Thomas Randall, pioneer Methodist preachers, were in the county from 1820 to 1823, and preached frequently in the settlers' cabins, and later, Bishops Morris and Ames preached in the old log court house and schoolhouse in Hillsboro. Thus was the introduction of Christianity coeval with the settlement of the country by white people.

The Methodist Church.—The organization of the Methodist Church of Hillsboro dates back to about 1824–25. Says Mr. Rountree: "It worshiped mainly in one old log schoolhouse, while for more general annual worship a camp ground was established on land now owned, and perhaps then, by Wesley Seymour, near his house, but across the road in the brush." Among the regular ministers who preached at at Hillsboro, in that early day, were Revs. John Dew, John Benson, James Mitchell and his brother, John T. Mitchell. Rev. N. S. Bastian, now of the Christian Church, is said to have preached his first sermon on the Hillsboro Circuit. Among the early members of the church were Benjamin and Joseph Miller, Mr. Stout, John Prentice, Hiram Rountree, Samuel Bennett and others of the pioneers of the neighborhood. "Though much zeal was mani-

*By W. H. Perrin.

fested, it was at a much later day before an effort was made to build a church edifice. A frame building was commenced and partially inclosed about 1834–35, on the lot now used as the Methodist parsonage. Being, however, unable to finish it for want of means, at the suggestion of John Tillson, who promised to largely assist them in completing it they moved it to South Hillsboro, on ground known since as the Wyman lot, where it stood in an unfinished state for several years, being only used in summer when the weather was pleasant."*

The great financial panic that swept over the country in 1837–38, so paralyzed the people that this building was never completed. About 1840, a combined effort was made to build a church, and all denominations united together, the result of which was the final completion of the old Methodist Church that stood upon the corner of the square, and which was completed during the administration of Rev. N. S. Bastian. It was informally dedicated by a revival of religion which increased the membership of the church to over one hundred. Following Mr. Bastian, Rev. John Van Cleve came—a man of the highest order of talents and piety, as well as of usefulness in the church. Mr. Rountree gives the following as the manner in which these early preachers were paid for their services as pastor: "It was often amusing to cast up accounts and see how they were paid. For instance, few could pay money—nearly all paid in truck or traffic. One would send, say, twenty-five bushels of corn, at 12½ cents a bushel; another, ten bushels of wheat, at 37½ cents a bushel; another, fifty pounds of side bacon, at 3 cents a pound, or hams at 4 cents; while whole hogs of fresh pork would be at the rate of 1½ to 2 cents a pound. Again, one would furnish clothing, say, jeans, at 50 cents per yard, or linsey, at 25 cents, besides articles, such as gloves, socks, etc., at similar low prices. It was a mystery then, and is still a mystery, how they lived; but they did live, and that, too, when it was fashionable to have large families, and to educate them at their own expense. They did live, and generally within their income, if their pay could be called income.' The problem of how they lived may be solved in the simple statement that the good old fashioned Gospel of that day was not so expensive an article as that served out to us at the present time, by the Beechers, Talmages and other silk-stockinged divines of the country, who proclaim the word from marbled desks to audiences arrayed in silks and broadcloths, who doze away the time in softly-cushioned pews, laid with Brussels carpets."

Rev. John Van Cleve was followed by Rev Robert Blackwell, and he by Rev. Samuel Elliott who, the next year, was succeeded by the Rev D. J. Snow. The Methodists differ from most other denominations, in that they change their ministers every two or three years. Rev. Mr. Elliott is represented as a preacher who won great popularity while pastor of the church at Hillsboro, and was almost unanimously petitioned for again, but from some cause the Conference saw fit not to grant the petition, and sent him elsewhere, which somewhat excited the indignation of the Hillsboro Church, and Rev. Snow found grim visages and sour faces confronting him upon his first appearance. He seemed to comprehend the situation at once, or had had an inkling of how matters stood, and took for his text upon the occasion of preaching his first sermon, the following words from Matthew, xi. 3: "Art thou he that should come, or do we look for another?" The announcement of his text is said to have brought to the countenances of many of his hearers feeble smiles, and the manner in which he handled it, and the application he made, restored all to good humor, and he finally became a popular and beloved pastor. He was succeeded the next year by Rev. S. Shinn, and he by Rev. T. W. Jones. Next came Rev. Preston Wood;

*Rountree Letters.

he was followed by Rev. James Crane, and he by Rev. William Pallet, who died in 1873. Rev. B. C. Wood was the next pastor, succeeded by Rev. D. Bardrick, who remained two years; he was followed by Rev. Green McElfresh, he by Rev. B. Hungerford, and he by Rev. McCaskell, who did not stay, and the place was filled by Rev. W. C. Lacy, followed the next year by Rev. A. C. Vanderwater. Rev. S. S. Meginniss came next, remaining two years, and under his administration the present church was built, and the old one on the corner sold.

Of this building, which was erected in 1863, Mr. Rountree says: "Though money enough was subscribed to nearly pay for its erection, still a debt was created, that with the debt on the parsonage, remained an incubus over the church for ten years, and was paid up in full this year (1873) leaving the church free from debt, with a building worth some $15,000 and a parsonage worth about $3,000, and some one hundred and fifty members with sufficient ability to support a first-class preacher." Since the above was written by Mr. Rountree (in 1873), the church under the pastorate of Rev. Mr. Hoffman, experienced quite a revival and increase of membership. He remained with the church for three years. The present pastor is Rev. Thomas I. Coultiss, a preacher of great ability, a pleasing speaker, and a natural orator. He is now (1882) serving his first year with the church, and his accomplishments as a pastor should endear him to his congregation.

The Methodist Church of Hillsboro, almost from its original organization has maintained a Sunday school. At present it is large and flourishing under the superintendence of Mr. Burns.

The Presbyterian Church.—From a sermon delivered March 10, 1878, upon its semi-centennial anniversary, by Rev. N. S. Dickey, at the time pastor, we compile the following sketch of the Presbyterian Church of Hillsboro: Hillsboro, March 10, 1828.—Rev. John M. Ellis met several people of Hillsboro and vicinity, at the house of John Tillson, Jr., and formed a church, to be known by the name of the "Presbyterian Church of Hillsboro." John Tillson, Jr., was received on certificate, and Mrs. Margaret Seward on examination; John Tillson, Jr., was ordained as Ruling Elder. It thus appears that this church began with two members, one of whom was made Ruling Elder. From the organization, March 10, 1828, to September 28, 1828, Rev. Solomon Hardy occasionally moderated the session and supplied the pulpit, or rather preached in the school-house and the court house, for there was no house of worship nor pulpit in Hillsboro. Four persons were added to the church under these labors, two on examination and two by letter, making a total of six. For more than a year after this there is no record, and report says the church only had occasional preaching from passing clergymen. From April, 1830, to October, 1841, a period of seven years and six months, Rev. Thomas A. Spillman was the stated supply of the church. The first recorded report of the church was made to the Presbytery of Central Illinois, April 2, 1830, a little more than two years after its organization, and was as follows: "Total in communion, per last report, six; added on certificate, one; total now in communion, seven. Funds for Commissioner to General Assembly, $1." In October of the same year, another report was made to the same Presbytery, when the communicants had doubled. October 11, 1830, the records of the church were first presented to the Presbytery, and with slight exceptions were approved. The approval was signed by Rev. Benjamin F. Spillman, Moderator of the Presbytery.

The next report, April 1, 1831, was made to the Presbytery of Sangamon, holding its session at Springfield, when the membership had again doubled, being twenty-eight; $3 was given to the Commissioner's fund. In 1832, the membership was fifty-three, and $3 was contributed for Assembly's fund. According to the report made April. 1837, the membership was sixty-four, $3 was given to the Commissioner's fund, and $41 to education. These $41 are the first given by the church to any benevolent cause, and shows that the fathers were wise in providing for future pupils of the church.

During the ministry of Mr. Spilman, 138 persons were received to the membership, forty on examination, and ninety-nine by certificate; thirty-three died, and sixteen were dismissed. The church under this ministry contributed $215 to missions, $60 for education and $39 for Commissioner's fund. No report of contributions for the last two years of Mr. Spilman's ministry is recorded, though no doubt collections were taken as usual. What was paid for salary and congregational expenses is not recorded. The average yearly additions to the church under his labors were fourteen. Mr. Spilman was a faithful pastor, and did much toward laying a good foundation for building up a successful church. Under his ministry the Sabbath school was a union one, and usually all denominations worshiped with his congregation. The first house of worship was built during this time. Rev. T. E. Spilman, of Butler, and Rev. J. H. Spilman, of Bethel, honored and useful ministers of Jesus Christ, are his sons. During the fall of 1841, and the winter of 1842, Rev. James Stafford, pastor of the Greenville church, is recorded as having moderated the session several times, when twenty-three persons were received into the church. Mr. Stafford supplied the pulpit for a few Sabbaths and held a protracted meeting during this time, when the Spirit was poured out upon the people.

Rev. Archibald C. Allen received a unanimous call to the pastorate of the church, March 24, 1842, at a salary of $500. He was installed pastor by the Kaskaskia Presbytery, June 11, 1842. Rev. James Stafford presided, put the the constitutional questions, and delivered the charges to pastor and people. Rev. Thomas A. Spilman preached the installation sermon. During Mr. Allen's ministry of two years, fifty persons were added to the church, forty-two on examination and eight by letter; fifteen were dismissed and six died. In these years the church gave for benevolent work, $56—$28 per year. The average yearly increase during this pastorate was twenty-five. The church was vacant from May, 1844, until March, 1846. During this time Rev. C. C. Riggs supplied the pulpit a Sabbath or two, and was invited to become pastor. The records for this period, nearly two years, are meager. John Tillson and wife, and five other persons, were dismissed. John Paisley and Margaret W. Paden died, and Benjamin S. McCord was received into the church on profession of his faith in Christ. Rev. Alexander Ewing moderating the session.

February, 21, 1846, Rev. T. W. Hynes, for some time a Professor in Hanover College, Indiana, was unanimously chosen to supply the pulpit at a salary of $400. He accepted and entered upon his work in the spring of 1846. The report to Presbytery from April, 1845, to March, 1846, gives the total in communion as one hundred and one, five having died and nine having been dismissed. Mr. Hynes' name appears upon the records as Moderator of sessions up to August 3, 1851, a period of about five and a half years. During his pastorate, forty-one persons were received into the church and sixteen were dismissed. Robert Paisley Henry Tibbets, William Brown, Joseph T. Eccles, Thomas Sturtevant, were elected and installed Ruling Elders. From September, 1851, to August, 1853, the church seems to have been without a pastor. September 24, 1851, the session was moderated by Rev. J. Smith, D. D., and six persons were received on examination to the fellowship of the church. June 21, 1852, Rev. Mr. Hamilton presided over the session, and two names were enrolled, one by letter and one on examination.

On the 12th of August, 1853, Rev. R. M. Roberts was called to the pastorate of the church, at a salary of $400. He accepted the call, and continued to sustain this relation until it was dissolved at his request, and the church declared vacant, October 30, 1859. Mr. Roberts served the church a little more than six years. During his ministry, one hundred and sixteen persons were received, an average of nineteen per year. Resolutions highly complimentary to Mr. Roberts, and indorsing him as a Christian gentleman, and commending the fidelity of his labors, were passed by the congregation at the time of his withdrawal. November 12, 1859, twenty-one persons were dismissed to form the Hillsboro Congregational Church. Rev. William L. Mitchell acting as Moderator of the session.

On the 20th of December, 1859, Rev. William L. Mitchell was called as pastor of the church, at a salary of $500, and on December 23, 1859, was ordained and installed by the Presbytery of Hillsboro. He continued this relation with acceptance and success, until his lamented death, February 23, 1864—a period of a little more than five years. During this time seventy-one names were added to the roll, forty-six on examination, and twenty-five by letter—an average of fourteen per year; twenty-nine were dismissed. Mr. Mitchell's remains are buried in the city cemetery. After Mr. Mitchell's death, Rev. Julius A. Spencer, of St. Louis, supplied the pulpit for several weeks. March 1, 1865 Rev. J. R. Brown was invited to supply the pulpit. He at once entered upon his labors and continued to serve the church until March 22, 1870, a period of five years. Fifty persons were added to the church during his pastorate, on examination, and sixty-five by letter—a total of one hundred and fifteen—an average of twenty-three per year; twenty-nine persons were dismissed.

From the close of Mr. Brown's labors until the beginning of the next year, about nine months, the church was vacant. August 24' 1870, Rev. J. H. Spilman acted as Moderator of the session, and Mr. and Mrs. Cyrus Davidson were received into the church by letter, and three were dismissed.

Rev. S. A. Whitcomb seems to have commenced his labors about the beginning of the year 1871. He served the church two years, at a salary of $1,000 per year, and free use of the parsonage. Rev. W. W. Williams was, by a unanimous vote of the congregation, April 27, 1873, invited to supply the church for one year, at a salary of $1,000, to be paid quarterly in advance, and also the free use of the parsonage. Mr. Williams worked with energy and acceptance for nearly nine months, directing his efforts to the completion of the audience room of the house of worship. The first services help therein, still in an incompleted state, was the funeral of the pastor. Resolutions of commendation were passed by the congregation, in reference to Mr. Williams, after his death. After this, the church was vacant for several months. In September, 1874, Rev. Charles Fueller was invited to supply the pulpit at a salary of $1,000, and use of the parsonage. He served the church for three years, during which time fifty-nine persons were added. Mr. Fueller labored earnestly to lift the debt off the house of worship. Under his lead furnaces, at a cost of $346, and cushions, at about the same cost, were placed in the church, besides what was done to lift the encumbrance from the building. He ceased to serve the church October 1, 1877, and January 1, following, Rev. N. S. Dickey, entered upon his work as stated supply. At the present writing (1882) the pastor is Rev. S. C. Dickey, a son of the above, and a young man of rare promise.

During the half century just closed, ten ministers have acted as stated supply or pastor. Seven others are recorded as having acted as Moderator, once or oftener, of the session, including those who organized the church. The whole number of members received since the organization is 669—321 on examination, and 348 by letter. This is an average of about fourteen per year, nearly equally divided by letter and on examination.

At a meeting of the congregation, held August 7, 1859, it was resolved to build a new and larger house of worship, taking down the old one and working the material into the new—provided sufficient funds could be raised. Rev. R. M. Roberts was appointed to canvass the congregation and take subscriptions and report at another meeting. Success did not crown this effort, and the old church was used until 1860, when it gave place to the present edifice, the basement being used in the fall of that year. During construction the congregation worshiped in the Unitarian Church, and in Clotfelter's Hall. According to the report of the building committee, made by Judge J. T. Eccles, the cost of the edifice and furnaces was $13,758.31; of this sum the ladies paid $663.43. Furnaces were put in the first year of Mr. Fueller's pastorate, at a cost of $346. Cushioning the seats cost nearly $400 more, so that the whole cost of the house in its present state was about $14.500. For some years a debt rested upon the house of worship. April 25, 1875, Judge Eccles donated $2,602.18, principal and interest due him for money paid upon the building. This noble example stimulated others; Mr. James Paden donated several hundred dollars due him, and under the lead of the pastor, Mr. Fueller, the whole debt was paid except a few hundred dollars, for which the parsonage is held. A united effort and this no doubt could be very easily paid.

October 15, 1857, during the Rev. R. M. Robert's pastorate, at a meeting over which Joseph T. Eccles presided, William Brown, William Witherspoon, D. S. and A. L. Clotfelter, and L. H. Thom were appointed a committee to make estimates of the cost of a parsonage. A lot was bought for $300, and the present house was built at a cost of about $1,200.

The Sabbath school has not been neglected. A number of years before the organization of the church, a school was maintained by the Tillson family, in their residence. In the early years of the church, all denominations represented in the town patronized the school, and, though it was under the supervision of the session, it was carried on as a union school. In later years, the other denominations drew off and established their own schools. According to rules adopted by the church, the Superintendent and Vice Superintendent are to be chosen at a congregational meeting appointed for the purpose, the election to be by ballot, all the members of the church, in good standing, having a right to vote. The Superintendent thus chosen, with the advice and consent of the session, is to appoint the teachers; "keeping always in view Christian character, and aptness to teach." The records of the school, until recently, have not been preserved. The interest for a few months past, has been growing, but many of the officers, and many of the church members, do not attend the school, nor show that interest in it essential to its growth and highest growth and usefulness. Every member of the church, young or old, should, if practicable, be connected with the Sabbath school, as teacher or learner. That church which does not take care of the spiritual interests of the rising race must, in time, fail of success.

In addition to the church Sabbath school, several interesting neighborhood schools, under the supervision of some of our people, have been and are maintained in the country, a few miles from the city.

The Congregational Church.—This church is an offshoot of the Presbyterian Church of Hillsboro, and, as we have seen, was organized by a number of persons, who were dismissed for that purpose. In the fall of 1859, they organized themselves into the Congregational Church of Hillsboro, or became the nucleus of the organization. From Dr. Washburn, who communicated to us the principal facts connected with the history of this church, we learn that there was a large Eastern element here at that time who had not identified themselves with any church, and these, with the twenty-one persons from the Presbyterian Church, formed a membership of about forty. The auspices seemed favorable for building up a large church, and up to the civil war everything in connection with it seemed prosperous. At the call for volunteers, a large proportion of its membership and congregation enlisted. Some never returned from the war; some of the members moved away, and others died. In the meantime, the Old and New School Presbyterians united, a fact familiar to all readers of their history.

At the close of the war, in 1865, the present brick church was built, at a cost of over $7,000. Services were continued and good congregations were kept up for several years. A comfortable parsonage was built in 1878, and the society was free of debt. However, removals, and the death of some of its best members, gradually reduced its strength and its financial ability, and since the beginning of the present year (1882) no services have been held. Its future usefulness and prosperity, at this time, seems somewhat in doubt. "The rapid growth of the town might infuse new life and continue its existence, but at present it would seem as well that they should become associated with the other Protestant churches of the place, rather than drag out a feeble existence." Though no preaching is had now at the church, a Sunday school is maintained.

Lutheran Church.—The early history of the Evangelical Lutheran Church of Hillsboro is somewhat obscure, and the best efforts to obtain the first written records of the society have proved of no avail. They have disappeared from the archives of the church, when or how, no one seems to know, and hence we are obliged to glean its early history from other and, perhaps, less reliable sources. Mr. Springer furnishes us the following of this church:

The Lutheran denomination was particularly strong in North Carolina, whence had come many of the prominent families of Hillsboro and vicinity. It was one of their first acts to provide themselves a church and a pastor in order to continue in the forms of worship familiar and dear to them. The Rev. David Scherer was the father of the Lutheran Church at Hillsboro, and organized it about the spring of 1833. The society worshiped for the first two years in the old log court house, and then commenced the erection of a comfortable frame church building on the sight of the present edifice. "Father Scherer," as he was called, and is now referred to, served the church for six or seven years, and was followed by the Rev. A. A. Trimper, and he, in 1847, by Rev. Francis Springer; he by Rev. J. J. Lovengood, in 1852; he by Rev. George A. Bowen; he by Rev. J. M. Cromer, and he by Rev. C. A. Gelwick, the present pastor.

The congregation, at a meeting held in February, 1856, resolved to build a new house of worship, and $1,700 were at once subscribed. Work was commenced, and the result was the present building, which was finally completed. It is a brick structure, with basement, and auditorium above, and is handsomely finished and furnished within. Among the officers of the church, as Elders and Deacons, in its earlier days, were Jacob W. Scherer, Alfred Miller, Henry Meisenheimer, Caleb T. Sifford, John Ritchie, Simeon Scherer, E. B. Hubbell, Henry Walter, Richard McFarland, Jacob Cress, Sr., Jacob Cress, Jr., and Edmund Miller, about half of whom are yet residents of the county. The church has always been one of great influence for good in the community, having many liberal-hearted workers in its membership, and being favored in general with ministers of energy and high literary attainments. The church has long carried on and supported an interesting Sunday school.

The Unitarians were an early religious organization of Hillsboro. Their old church building is one of the relics of the past, and few of the rising generation, perhaps, know that such a church ever existed in the city. The old building, now occupied by Mr. Cress as an agricultural implement depot, south of the American House on the main street was the temple of worship of the Unitarians thirty or forty years ago. But, as the old and prominent members died off, or moved away, the church diminished in numbers, and eventually became extinct. There has been no Unitarian service in the town, we believe, since the war, but the old church building still stands, a monument to their former zeal and influence.

The Cumberland Presbyterians organized a church in Hillsboro, prior to the late civil war. Rev. Mr. Logan, at the time editor of a religious paper at Alton, was chiefly instrumental in its organization, and was present at the time the church was constituted. A number of persons of the Cumberland Presbyterian faith united with the society here, and for several years the organization was kept up. Meetings were held in the old Unitarian Church building for a time, and arrangements were attempted for the erection of a building of their own, but the movement was unsuccessful. The membership increased but slowly, the effects of the war were experienced, and the "Ship of Zion" was finally abandoned. Some of the members united with the Cumberland Presbyterians at McDavid's Point and at other places, while others cast in their lots with some of the churches in the city, mostly with the Presbyterian Church.

The Baptists have an organized society in Hillsboro, but have no church building. The society was organized a few years ago, and arrangements made for occasional preaching, its limited number of members not admitting of its paying a regular pastor. The organization is still kept up, and administered to now and then by visiting preachers.

The Catholics.—St. Agnes' Roman Catholic Church represents that denomination in Hillsboro. The first Catholic services in the city were held in private houses from about the year 1854 to 1859, by traveling missionaries, especially by Father T. Cusack, now of Shipman, Ill. From 1859 to 1870, the Catholics of Hillsboro were attended from Litchfield. It was not until the latter year that the building of a church in Hillsboro was encouraged, and for that purpose a subscription was commenced by Father L. Hinssen, now of Belleville, Ill. The church was placed under the patronage of St. Agnes, and has since been known as the "St. Agnes' Roman Catholic Church." It was built under the supervision and management of R. H. Stewart, of this city, costing, when completed, about $6,000, and to its construction both Catholics and non-Catholics contributed with equal liberality. The building is 40x60 feet in dimensions, and the membership at present is between fifty and sixty families. The regular pastors of the church have been, since its organization, Rev. Gr. Lohman, from 1871 to 1876, now of Aviston, Clinton County, Ill.; Rev. P. J. Virsink, from 1876 to 1882, now at St. Marie, Jasper County, Ill. Present pastor is Rev. J. Storp, and to him we are indebted for the above facts.

The colored people, of whom there are quite a number in Hillsboro, hold services every Sunday afternoon in the basement of the Lutheran Church. They have no regular pastor, and only enjoy occasional preaching by ministers from abroad.

Secret Orders.—In conclusion of the chapter on the church history of Hillsboro, it is not inappropriate to devote a brief space to those benevolent organizations, which, in their quiet way, exert as widespread influence almost as the church itself. The good accomplished by these institutions cannot be estimated. There is nothing more wonderful in Freemasonry, the most ancient of these honorable and charitable fraternities, than its perpetual youth. Human governments flourish and then disappear, leaving only desolation in the places where their glory used to shine. But the institution of Freemasonry, originating so long ago that the oldest history tells nothing of its beginning, has survived the decay of dynasties, and the revolutions of races, and kept pace with the marvelous march of civilization and Christianity. Freemasonry was established in Hillsboro at an early day by the formation of a lodge of the order, and has existed with more or less zeal ever since.

The first lodge organized here was known as Hillsboro Lodge, No. 33, A., F. & A. M., and was formed under the authority of the Grand Lodge of Missouri, by which grand body its charter was issued, under date of October 9, 1840. Among the charter members were C. B. Blockberger, H. Kingsley, M. Kingsley and M. P. Nickerson. Of these, the first three (in the order named), constituted the first Master and Wardens. The lodge continued to work under the Grand Lodge of Missouri until the formation of the Grand Lodge of Illinois, when it was rechartered and re-organized.

Mount Moriah Lodge, No. 51, A., F. & A. M., was chartered October 4, 1848, and was but a re-organization of the original Hillsboro Lodge, under the Grand Lodge of Illinois. Its charter members were Ira Millard, Ira Boone, Jeremiah Hart, John S. Hillis, J. H. Ralston, M. J. Blockberger, M. Turner, Jacob Lingafelter, and their charter was signed by William Lavely, Grand Master, and William Mitchell, Grand Secretary. The first officers were Ira Millard; Master; Ira Boone, Senior Warden, and Jeremiah Hart Junior Warden. The lodge has a flourishing membership, and is at present officered as follows: M. W. Miller, Master; C. L. Bartlett, Senior Warden; J. B. Atterbury, Junior Warden; J. W. Edwards, Treasurer; Benjamin E. Johnson, Secretary; J. M. Smith, Senior Deacon; J. B. Dreyhur, Junior Deacon, and W. R. Truesdell, Tiler.

The lodge formerly met in the upper story of a building used by Gunning as a blacksmith shop. Afterward, in connection with the Odd Fellows, they built a hall on Main street, near the court house. Finally, they sold out and built their present hall. They own the third story of a large brick building on the Main street, and have it handsomely fitted up and furnished.

Montgomery Chapter, No. 63, Royal Arch Masons, was organized several years ago, by the Grand Royal Arch Chapter of Illinois. For a time it worked zealously, then the members seemed to become lukewarm, meetings were less frequent, and finally ceased altogether. The charter has been surrendered to the Grand Chapter, and Montgomery Chapter is, for the time at least, extinct. "It is not dead, but sleepeth," and may revive again when the companions awake from their present Rip Van Winkle sleep.

Hermon Chapter, No. 46, of the Order of the Eastern Star, was chartered by the Supreme Grand Chapter of Adoptive Masonry of Illinois, January 18, 1871. The first officers were Isaac Shimer, a Master Mason, Worthy Patron; Sister Augusta D. Marshall, Worthy Matron, and Sister Eveline C. Harris, Associate Matron. For several years an active interest was taken by the ladies of Hillsboro in the Order of the Eastern Star, and at one time their chapter was one of the most flourishing in the State. But of late their zeal has flagged, and they have suffered it to become almost entirely dormant.

Montgomery Lodge, No. 40, I. O. O. F., was instituted in Hillsboro May 30, 1848, by William M Parker, of Belleville, Grand Master. The following persons were initiated into the order on that occasion, viz.: David B. Jackson, A. S. Haskell, Hiram Brown, William K. Jackson, John Burnap, George Blackman, George J. Brooks, J. L. Whitmore, and John R. Paisley. The first officers were: Henry Richmond (now of Litchfield). Noble Grand; David B. Jackson, Vice Grand; William K. Jackson, Secretary, and John Burnap, Treasurer. They met regularly in the hall then owned and occupied by the Masonic lodge being the second story of Gunning's blacksmith shop. In 1855, in connection with the Masons, they built the hall already referred to. This was completed and dedicated on the 13th day of June, 1856. Afterward they bought out the Masons and in October, 1867, deemed it advisable to sell their hall and build a new one on the opposite side of the street. The corner-stone of this building was laid on the 23d of October of that year, and the building completed early in 1868, when the lodge moved into it, and still occupies it. The present officers are: Wilbur B. Ralston, Noble Grand; J. L. McHenry, Vice Grand; William K. Jackson, Secretary; C. L. Bartlett, Treasurer; William K. Jackson, District Deputy Grand Master.

The Encampment branch of the order was instituted by Charles Trumbull, of Alton, January 16, 1857, and the following officers elected and installed, viz.: D. B. Jackson, Chief Priest; G. G. Withington, High Priest; William K. Jackson, Senior Warden; J. W. Cassaday, Scribe; A. S. Haskell, Treasurer, and A. H. Brown, Junior Warden. The membership of this body has never been large.

Hillsboro Lodge, No. 265, I. O. G. T., was organized February 11, 1881, with some thirty odd members. The present officers are as follows: A. G. Taylor, W. C. T.; Mrs. Tirzah Depuy, W. V. T.; Jacob Beck, P. W. C. T.; James Lynch, W. S.; Mrs. Mary Johnson, W. F. S.; J. J. Miller, W. T.; C. W. Taylor, W. M.; Mrs. M. H. Johnson, W. D. M.; Libbie Horton, W. A. S.; Dudley Depuy, W. S.; Meda Hanna, R. H. S.; Lucy Robb, L. H. S.; Rev. S. C. Dickey, W. C. The lodge is small in numbers, but stong in faith, and inspired with the lofty aims of the cause in which they are engaged; the members though few, work none the less zealously. That they have accomplished much, none can deny, but the field is still large for the exercise of their good work.

CHAPTER X.

HILLSBORO—EDUCATIONAL INTERESTS—EARLY SCHOOLS AND THE OLD LOG SCHOOLHOUSE—HILLSBORO ACADEMY—ITS COLLEGE CAREER—THE PUBLIC SCHOOLS—NEWSPAPERS—THE FIRST PAPERS OF THE TOWN—UPS AND DOWNS OF THE BUSINESS—THE "NEWS" AND THE "JOURNAL" OF TO-DAY, ETC.

"A little learning is a dangerous thing,
Drink deep, or taste not the Pierian spring."

AMID the various conflicting opinions on moral, political and religious subjects, there is need of charity and forbearance, concession and compromise. Citizenship is of no avail unless we imbibe the liberal spirit of our laws and institutions. Through the medium of the common schools are the rising generation of all nationalities assimilated readily and thoroughly forming the great American people. The common schools are alike open to the rich and the poor, the citizen and the stranger. It is the duty of those to whom the administration of the schools is confided, to discharge it with magnanimous liberality and Christian kindness. Diligent care should be taken by instructors, to impress upon the minds of children and youth committed to their care, the principles of morality and justice, and a sacred regard to truth, love of their country, humanity and universal benevolence, sobriety, industry and frugality, chastity, moderation and temperance, and all other virtues which are the ornaments to society.

The people of Hillsboro displayed an early interest in educating their children, and among the pioneer institutions of the town, may be noted the old log schoolhouse, already frequently mentioned in these pages. Says Mr. Rountree, in his early reminiscences of Hillsboro: "It is a remarkable fact that Hillsboro, like Jacksonville, was a kind of Athens of Illinois. The early citizens, coming as they did from the older States, where education was the rule, the great mass of them were intelligent, well educated men and women. One of the earliest school teachers in Hillsboro was Nancy Crumba, who was a sister of the first wife of David B. Jackson. She taught frequently in Hillsboro, and was a refined, cultivated lady—so much so, that girls and young women were sent from abroad—Vandalia, Carlyle and Edwardsville, to her, that she might put on the finishing to the education that they had received at home."

By W. H. Perrin.

Another of the early teachers of Hillsboro was Rosetta Townsend, who was raised on the place known as Rose Hill. She afterward married Andrew M. Braley, an old sailor and surveyor, and died early, leaving one child, Ann Eliza, who also taught in Hillsboro years after John C. Terret was another early teacher, and the first who taught the classics in a school in the town. Many other good and efficient teachers taught in Hillsboro up to the time of building the academy.

The first schoolhouse ever built in Hillsboro was in the winter of 1825. It was of round logs twenty-five feet square, chinked and daubed with mud; the fire-place occupied nearly one whole side of the house, its jambs of mud, and chimney of sticks covered with the same material. A log was sawed out on two sides of the room, and the long space filled with sash and glass, while on the fourth side was the door,

John T. McDavid, Sen

with shutter made of clapboards. The floor was of puncheons, the benches of split logs, with legs in the round side, and the upper side somewhat smoothed with axes. There was no loft or ceiling; a few shelves on pegs, etc. The roof was of clapboards held to their places with weight-poles. Two writing desks made of puncheons, perhaps a chair, a water "piggin," no andirons except rocks, no tongs, a clapboard shovel, wooden fire-poker, a mud hearth, and a few "peep holes" through the chinks or cracks. This was the first temple of learning with which the youth of Hillsboro became acquainted, and in the unpretending structure, the foundation of the education of some of Illinois' great men were laid. This early schoolhouse stood on the crest of the hill above the natural spring at Rountree's pasture, in the eastern part of what is now the main city. Of the teachers who instructed in this old house, it may be said, that they were men and women of culture, some of whom arose to eminence. Of these we may mention Maj. Campbell, of Carlisle; Maj. John H. Rountree, a prominent politician and legislator; Hon. James M. Bradford, who held various offices, and John Hays, Mr. Springer, W. L. Jenkins, Frank Dickson and many others. There are many of the citizens of the town and county received their education wholly or in part, viz., the Cresses, Rutledges, Blackbergers, Seymours, Boones, Grubbs, Rountrees, etc., etc.; also Revs. R. J. Nall and W. S. Prentice, prominent Methodist preachers; James and Sidney Harkey and Jacob Scherer, of the Lutheran Church, and Gen. Tillson, of Quincy whose part in the late civil war highly distinguished him. Indeed many persons of distinction taught or were taught in that old building, Hillsboro's first schoolhouse.

No doubt the memories connected with it says Mr. Rountree are warm in their hearts but the old house is gone. Other buildings have been erected to take its place. Our [illegible] [illegible] worthy of our pride. The old academy still flourishes. But it is a question if they are more useful in their day than the log houses for similar purposes were in the pioneer days. Of the new brick schoolhouse, it is a comfortable and commodious structure, standing on a beautiful lot north of the court house. It is built after the usual style of architecture of the modern schoolhouses, and is finished and furnished in the latest improved manner.

The Academy.—About the year 1836, the people united together and built the Hillsboro Academy. At the time of its erection it was one of the most magnificent temples of learning in the State. John Tillson was the moving spirit in its construction and endowment, and to him, more than to any other single individual is the community indebted for the high reputation of the institution. Young men and boys came from all the surrounding country to receive academic and collegiate training at Hillsboro Academy, and afterward College. Here the energy of Mr. Tillson shone out. He brought the first Superintendent, Prof. Isaac Wetherill, from the East, and his wife to associate in the female department with Prof. Edward Wyman associate in the male department, and Miss E. F. Hadley, teacher of instrumental music. The first session commenced the first Wednesday in November, 1837, and was liberally patronized for years. It gave Hillsboro so great a reputation for education and morality that no other public school building was erected until the present brick edifice alluded to above.

The Academy was changed to a college and carried on several years as such by the Lutherans, but was abandoned by them in 1852, when they removed their institution to Springfield. The building then became the property of the common schools, and has since been used by the city as the high school department. It has lost nothing in this capacity from the high standard of excellence it occupied, and [illegible] [illegible] ment. It stands in the most pleasant part of the city, near the center of a gently rolling piece of ground, whose rich, grassy carpet is shaded with a profusion of fine old forest trees of a century's growth. In a word, no city of its size and population possesses better facilities than Hillsboro for a good common school education.

The Press.—The newspapers of Hillsboro next claim our attention, and in connection with the educational history their mention is peculiarly appropriate, as the press has always been deemed a zealous friend and advocate of learning. From the "Rountree Letters, so freely quoted from in these pages, we gather the early history of the press of Hillsboro, and no man, perhaps, was more capable than Mr. Rountree of doing the subject justice.

The *Prairie Beacon* was the first paper published in Hillsboro, and was established about the year 1838, by a stock company. It was published in the upper story of Hayward & Holmes' old storehouse, and Aaron Clapp, Esq., was its editor. He is described as a tall, straight, red-haired man, badly cross-eyed, but a fine scholar, fresh from an Eastern college, and a friend and college-mate of Prof. Isaac Wetherill, then Principal of the Hillsboro Academy. The *Prairie Beacon* proved a poor and unprofitable investment, and after struggling on for about a year and a half it ceased publication. The press, type and fixtures were sold to some parties in Platteville, Wis., where it was used in the publication of a paper called *The Northern Badger*. So disastrous was the failure of the *Prairie Beacon* that some years elapsed before another attempt was made to establish a paper at Hillsboro. In 1850, Frank and Cyrus Gilmore established the *Prairie Mirror*, with Rev. Francis Springer as editor. The boys, for they were but boys at the time, did all the office work themselves. In national politics the *Mirror* was Whig, but upon home affairs it advocated "State policy," which by its success staved off the building of a number of other railroads until the building of Hillsboro's road. The Gilmore boys sold out to William K. Jackson in 1851, who became its proprietor, with C. D. Dickerson as editor. In the reconstruction of political parties the *Mirror* became the exponent of the Know-Nothing party. Dickerson bought out Mr. Jackson in 1854, and carried it on himself until 1856, when he changed it to the *Montgomery County Herald*; afterward sold it to James Blackman, Jr. and removed from Hillsboro.

The *Herald* was continued by Mr. Blackman as a Know-Nothing paper until 1858, when he sold out to J. W. Kitchell and F. H. Gilmore, who ran it as an independent paper until the opening of the campaign of 1860. They then sold it to Davis, Turner & Co., who published it through the campaign as a Democratic paper, and late in the season sold it to F. H. Gilmore, who continued it as a Democratic paper. In 1862, he sold it to E. J. Ellis, a refugee from Missouri. Mr. Ellis was an old editor, and after the war returned to Missouri, where, at the last account of him, he was publishing a paper called the *Montgomery Standard*. He sold the *Herald* to Ed. L. Reynolds and Wilbur F. Stoddard. They continued it as a Democratic paper until 1867, when they sold it to William McEwen and John Auginbaugh, who, the next year (1868), sold it to E. J. C. Alexander. Mr. Alexander continued the paper as Democratic, but changed its name to the *Hillsboro Democrat*. "He so run the paper," says Mr. Rountree, "as to make a fortune and elect himself to the State Legislature, where he is now (1873–74) serving his constituents. While it claims to be a Democratic paper, it is only negatively so; and it is in full accord with the 'Farmer movement,' as against both political parties, hanging with the Democrats in their fight with the Republicans." With the issue of April 29, 1874, Mr. Alexander changed the name of the *Democrat* to that of *The Anti-*

Monopolist, and became the zealous exponent of the farmer or grange movement. Still he was not happy, and another change came over his paper. This time he called it the *Hillsboro Blade* and changed its politics to Republican. He then sold it to James L. Slack, who again changed its name, calling it the *Hillsboro [illegible]*. Slack sold it to Charles R. Truitt in 1881, the present editor and publisher. It is a handsome eight-page paper, neatly and tastefully printed, ably edited, and is the Republican organ of Montgomery County.

About the year 1859 or 1860 the *Illinois Free Press* was established in Hillsboro, as the advocate of the views of the Republican party. It was published by a stock company composed of the leading Republicans of Hillsboro and Butler, and Mr. D. W. Munn was its editor. Later it was in charge of J. B. Hutchinson and James Munn. Hutchinson afterward moved to Iowa and Munn was slightly wounded at Donelson, Tenn., when he retired from the army, and finally returned East whence he had come and where he was lost sight of. The *Free Press* was never a financial success, and suspended publication, but was resurrected again in 1863 by John W. Kitchell, and the name changed to the *Union Monitor*. D. W. Munn had become sole proprietor previous to the sale to Mr. Kitchell. It was next bought by Mr. Thomas J. Russell, Mr. Kitchell remaining as editor, until he was drafted into the army in the spring of 1865, when Mr. J. E. Henry, a native of Bond County, a good writer and an able man, became editor. He afterward removed to St. Joseph, Mo. Mr. Alexander, afterward editor and proprietor of the *Democrat*, became, in May, 1867, proprietor of the *Monitor*, as the Republican organ, but becoming a little "tender-footed," as he expressed it, on the negro question, he sold out to B. S. Hood, of Litchfield, a man of fine abilities but not being acquainted with the *modus operandi* of running a newspaper, did not make a fortune out of his investment. It was removed to Litchfield, and for a time was run by a stock company. Messrs. Bangs & Gray finally became the purchasers, who after a little while divided the office, and from this division sprung the *News Letter* of Hillsboro, conducted by C. L. and E. T. Bangs. The remainder was sold to Taylor & Kimball, of Belleville, who conducted the *Monitor* a few months by agents, and then transferred it to Coolidge & Litchfield, and it became what is now the Litchfield *Monitor*.

The *News Letter* was sold to Slack & Tobin, and the name changed to the *Hillsboro Journal*. Mr. Tobin sold out to Slack, who sold to Johnson & Tobin in 1875. Up to this time it had been Republican in politics, but Johnson & Tobin changed its name to *Montgomery News*, and its politics to Democrat. In 1876, Johnson sold his interest to George W. Paisley, and February 6, 1882, Paisley & Tobin sold the paper to Benjamin E. Johnson, who is the present owner and editor. The *News* is the official organ of the Democracy of Montgomery County, and is a large eight-page paper, well edited by Col. Johnson, a man of considerable newspaper ability, experience and enterprise.

The press of Hillsboro at the present time is second to that of no town of its importance in Southern Illinois, and the people should be justly proud of it, and extend to it the support and patronage it so richly merits. No town can prosper without live, enterprising newspapers, and such papers cannot exist without liberal patronage.

CHAPTER XI.

NORTH LITCHFIELD TOWNSHIP—DESCRIPTION AND TOPOGRAPHY—CHARACTER OF SOIL—EARLY SETTLEMENTS—THE BRIGGS FAMILY—OTHER PIONEERS—THE FIRST PREACHERS AND CHURCHES—SCHOOLS AND TEACHERS—PIONEER INCIDENTS—TAX RECEIPTS, ETC.—EARLY DISEASES AND DEATHS—EFFECTS OF THE WAR, ETC., ETC.

THIS township, lying on the west side of the county, is south of Zanesville, west of Butler, and north of South Litchfield. The west fork of Shoal Creek passes from north to south through the east side, and is fringed with timber for nearly a mile on each side. The west two-thirds of the township are prairie. The west and north portions discharge their surplus waters through a branch into the creek, while the southwestern sections send their drainage into the Cahokia, and the southeastern sections lie on Rocky Branch, an affluent of the west fork of Shoal Creek. For three miles the Indianapolis & St. Louis railroad divides it from South Litchfield. The Jacksonville road enters at the northwest corner and leaves it two miles east of the southwest corner. The St. Louis branch of the Wabash, going north, enters the township two miles from the county line and leaves it two miles west of the northeast corner. It thus contains nearly sixteen miles of railroad.

The soil along the creek is white and better for straw grain than for corn. In the prairie the soil is black, glutinous and deep. The surface in the prairie region requires artificial drainage which has been in part supplied by the construction of railroads, and a more careful attention to the location and improvement of ordinary highways. In the farms along the timber rail fences are the rule; in other and more recently cultivated farms board fences [illegible] All the prairie and much of the timber is fenced, and this has led to the adoption of a stock law.

In 1816, Robert Briggs, born east of the Blue Ridge, and emigrating to Ohio en route to Edwardsville, where he dwelt in the fort and where children were born to him, located on Lake Fork in Walshville. He built a cabin and began a farm. Two years later, the land was bought from under him by Government entry, and Mr. Briggs, leaving his cribs filled with corn removed in 1818 to a point nearly a third of a mile east of Martin Ritchie's house and began anew. His old neighbors relieved him of his cribbed corn, and he had no new neighbors in the modern meaning of the word. A few miles to the north, a family settled a little later, and five miles to the south were two or three families. The region abounded in gray wolves, tall, fierce, gaunt fellows and occasionally a black one was seen. Muskrats were numerous in the shallow ponds, and skunks were met everywhere. The few sheep Mr. Briggs owned were penned each night to protect them from beasts of prey, for black bears and panthers were not quite unknown. Grapes grew in the woods and [illegible] yielded their delicious sweets to the pioneer. Wagons were not in use in place of the [illegible] rude ox carts were in general use, frequently made without iron. Cattle were [illegible] exclusively draft animals; horses were employed only under the saddle. [illegible] orchestra. Oxen wrought in the ordinary yoke, but horses had wooden hames on shuck collars made by some neighbors and connected to the whippletree with chains, supported by a strip of raw hide over the horse's back.

The cattle were natives, small and hardy. A fattened animal which weighed dressed half a thousand pounds was a monster. The horses were usually about fifteen hands high, and of light weight. In a few years after Mr. Briggs' settlement, the Archy stock was introduced from North Carolina and was highly esteemed for the saddle. All travel was on horseback and a steed, sure-footed, hardy and with a swift, easy pace, was a possession keenly appreciated. Swine of the baser breed prevailed. They were not inclined to take on flesh, were fleet of foot and insatiable in appetite and pugnacious. The few sheep were kept for the wool. Quail and gray squirrels and wild turkeys, water fowl and herds of deer, made the country a valuable game region. Of song birds the pioneers do not speak; they came in with the cessation of the annual burning of the prairie, and the appearance of orchards and trees around human habitations.

For several years Mr. Briggs grew cotton for home clothing. When picked it was ginned by hand, and then prepared on hand cards in the house for the spinning wheel. Sometimes wool was mingled with the "batts" for spinning. The cotton was carded, spun, wove and dyed at home, and the cloth fashioned into garments by the housewife's shears and needle. Nearly every home contained a spinning wheel and loom and a variety of saddles. The children tasted neither tea nor coffee. Sassafras tea or crust coffee does not tempt a healthy or a capricious thirst. The johnny cake board was as necessary in a well regulated family as knives and forks, and the corn meal was brought from Elm Point or the "Pepper Mill." The meal, wetted with water and salted and baked on a board set sloping before the fire, and eaten with milk was a healthful food, and the children throve on it.

The Briggs family went to Old Ripley, in Bond County, for meal, and their meat was wild game; the forest yielded them grapes and plums: their garden Irish potatoes and sweet ones. The father tanned each year, imperfectly, leather in a trough, and from the product, which had the properties of rawhide, he made shoes for his children. When wet these shoes were a world too wide! When dried on the feet they shrank until they bound like compresses.

The first school his children attended was in a log schoolhouse, two miles and a half east of home, and probably in Butler Grove Township. The second school was taught in the first schoolhouse in the township, a few rods due north of the home of E. K. Austin. Religious meetings were first held at private houses, but, when schools were introduced, the school-room during the week was the church on Sunday. The first sermon, so far as known, was perhaps delivered by Bennett Woods, a Hardshell Baptist, of whom our informant narrates several amusing incidents. The preacher had on one occasion forgotten his glasses, and when he arose to give out the hymn – which it was the custom to "deacon" in consequence of the want of hymn books – he began:

"My eyes are dim; I cannot see,
I've left my specs at home."

The leader of the singing immediately raised the tune and the congregation began to sing! "Stop, stop! That is not the hymn; I meant to say I forgot my spectacles and will not read a hymn this morning.

On another occasion a mother was carrying her wailing infant out of the house to avoid disturbing the congregation. "Sister Sally, if you go out you will not hear the sermon." "Yes I will, I will sit near the house, and will hear every word." In a few moments Mr. Woods went to an open window, and thrusting out his head and shoulders continued his discourse in order that "Sister Sally" should not lose the benefit of it.

The first church in the township was erected near the southeast corner of the west half of the northwest corner of Section 33, or just west of State street and half a mile north of the Indianapolis & St. Louis railroad. It was used jointly by the Lutherans and Presbyterians. This is the popular opinion which has found a place in local histories, but a log church near Honey Bend was built many years earlier, which long since decayed to a ruin, but the site can be identified just over the line in Zanesville Township. Near it several hundred Indians were encamped in huts of pawpaw. The unwelcome visitors were energetically pressed to move on, and their shelters perished by natural decay. This church belonged to the Hardshell Baptist —a sect which believes in unsalaried preachers and in paying their debts. The second religious body was the Williams Society of Methodists near Honey Bend. William Williams the founder, is still spoken of as a godly man, whose piety was ardent and consistent.

Isaiah Hurley was the first school teacher, a mild, inoffensive person. The Wilkinson boys were his special tormentors.

The Briggs family at first ate from pewter plates and drank from gourds or tin cups. The light at evening was the wood fire, or, if there was any grease to be had, a saucer was filled with it, in which a wick floated. Hickory bark or dry branches of trees were used as light wood to illuminate the cabins, and the boys spelled out their bibles or books by their flickering flare. Sometimes buttonwood balls were gathered, and, when dried, soaked in fat and lighted. They afforded good light, but were speedily consumed.

Their earlier neighbors were the Mathews family, living a couple furlongs to the west. That family went west of the river during the "twenties," leaving no representative here, but a remembrance older than the oldest living inhabitant of the township.

About the earliest physician was Dr. Hillis, of Hillsboro, lately deceased. The people did not allow to become ill, and midwives attended to women in labor.

The scenes of Indian warfare are quite all outside the county, but the early settlers had seen their portion of these horrors. Robert Briggs maternal grandfather, living in the Fort at Edwardsville, rescued a daughter from the savages, and, while bearing her home to the fort, began bleeding at the nose and died from loss of blood. Samuel Briggs, the eldest son, born in 1809, was a soldier in the Black Hawk war, and Stephen R., the second son, born in 1812, was for eleven months a ranger.

As late as 1830, only a few families had settled in the township. Mathews had removed; Wilkinson and Lockerman remained, and Williams and the Woods and Ash had located along the Three-Mile Branch.

The polls for the earlier elections were held at "Tennis School-house" in Zanesville Township, and when the west side of the county was divided into three election precincts the polls of Long Branch Precinct, which included North Litchfield, were opened at John A. Crabtree's house in South Litchfield. The poll lists contain few names; from a dozen to twenty votes would be received. As the population of North Litchfield by the last census was outside of the city of Litchfield, only 951 on thirty-four square miles, and contains neither mill nor shop save at Litchfield and Honey Bend, it is credible that the township attracted population slowly. Nearly all the people are of Southern birth or origin.

The elder ones still relate many homely incidents of the early days. When a family arrived and it was understood that they wanted a house, the settlers assembled, and some cut logs and built the walls, while others split shooks for the roof, and others hewed puncheons for a floor and another portion erected the chimney. They did not cease until the house was ready. If the supply of meal gave out, and high water or the state of the trails prevented a journey to Old Ripley, corn was bruised in a hollow block of wood with an iron wedge or a wooden pestle. The finer portions were used for bread, and the coarser part was converted into hominy. Scant time had the settlers for social visits, but when one was paid the party came on horseback, the wife *en croupe* behind her husband.

An annual visit to Mr. Briggs by Mr. Whiteside, the partisan ranger, well known for his prowess in Indian warfare, was the signal for renewed confabs on the incidents of border life. Whiteside, Robert Briggs, Sr., and his son Samuel were the center of the group, and the children would huddle into the corner terrified by their tales. Bits of description in their stories were of high merit for their graphic literalness. What the good wives talked of is beyond conjecture. He is a bold man who will venture an opinion as to the topics in a woman's palaver.

The inquisitorial list of questions in the assessor's blanks, prepared in the early history of the State is inferential evidence as to the condition of the Illinois homes. But we have seen tax receipts of those relatively far-off days, in which the taxes on six hundred acres of land were $2.10, and on eighty acres, 12½ cents, and these receipts were given to early settlers of North Litchfield and its sister township, South Litchfield. The wages of a stout, willing boy were a "bit" a day during the summer, and a good harvest hand was paid as high as half a dollar, or the exact price of a pound of coffee. "Hired girls" had not become a class; in case of illness some young woman would leave home for a few days to care for the afflicted household, but her services were not rendered for the pay she received. The discharge of the sacred duty to care for the sick was the motive, and it was never neglected. The accepted life of a woman was to marry, bear and rear children, prepare the household food, spin, weave and make the garments for the family. Her whole life was the grand simple poem of rugged, toilsome duty bravely and uncomplainingly done. She lived history, and her descendants write and read it with a proud thrill, such as visits the pilgrim when at Arlington he stands at the base of the monument which covers the bones of 4,000 nameless men who gave their blood to preserve their country. Her work lives, but her name is whispered only in a few homes. Holy in death, it is too sacred for open speech.

Some of these cheerful dames still live, and seem to regret the times which will never come again. One of them says the floor of her cabin was so uneven that she placed rude wedges under her table legs to keep it steady, and when a heavy rain fell the water which came down the chimney formed a pool in the depression called a hearth, and she baled out the water with her skillet. Gourds were used for drinking cups, milk pails, dippers and receptacles for lard, some of them held half a bushel. When she became the owner of a stone pitcher, she felt rich, and at the table no person could have a knife and fork; if he had the former, the latter fell to another, and often the same knife answered the table needs of two or three.

Until 1828, the whole county voted at Hillsboro, and there was the post office, store and physician. In 1830, twelve years after its settlement, but seven families had located in the township—Robert Briggs, Thomas Briggs, Aaron Roberts, Mathews, Wilkinson and Lockerman, and possibly T. C. Hughes. A war trail from the timber at the head of the Cahokia to the timber on Shoal Creek ran along the southeastern sections, and the Indian-fighter, Whiteside, and his rangers, pursued a band of warriors along this, and brought on an action near the southeast corner of the southwest quarter of Section 26. Whiteside, years after the battle, pointed out the site. Flint arrow-heads and tomahawks have been found there. Tradition has preserved no details of the fight, save that the savages suffered from the shotguns. Whitesides was a laborious slayer of Indians, but wrote no detailed history of his exploits on the trail. The early settlers lived in fear of Indians, though no incidents are preserved of any outrage here later than 1815.

Bennett Woods settled in the township east of Shoal Creek, and found that in addition to those previously mentioned, Aaron Roberts had preceded him. Of this Mr. Roberts, we can learn only that he was a man of great humor, and was not of kin to John C. or James S. Roberts, long well-known residents of "Roberts' Settlement" the earlier name of Honey Bend. Thomas C. Hughes settled in 1829, on the farm now owned by Martin Ritchie. Thomas Briggs, a brother of Robert Briggs, lived about a mile south of Hughes. The farm afterward passed into the hands of Samuel Kirkpatrick, brother of the famous Sheriff.

When 1830 dawned, the settlers lived at the edge of the timber -Bennett Woods east of the Creek, Aaron Roberts, the third settler, on the creek, and Mr. Hughes and the two Briggs west of it. Mathews had vanished and there is no mention of Lockerman or Wilkinson. There were certainly five families, and possibly seven in the township. Mrs. Bennett Woods died in 1829, and was the first death. The first marriage was Joshua Martin to Sarah Briggs, eldest daughter of Robert Briggs. The first sermon was preached at the house of Bennett Woods, by James Street or Larkin Craig —probably the fromer. They belonged to the Missionary Baptists, and their earliest house of worship was a log chapel, a few rods over the line, on Section 35, in Zanesville—the venerable John Woods is able to fix its location. This decaying in 1865, Little Flock Church was built at Honey Bend. The Cherry Grove Chapel, in Butler Grove, was the primitive church for the Methodists of several townships. Being near the line, the Methodists had no place of worship in this township until 1855, when the Hardinsburgh Chapel was drawn to Litchfield. Some of the early Methodists attended at Asbury Chapel, Raymond; some at Cherry Grove, in Butler Grove, and some at the Hardinsburgh Chapel.

The Baptists first attended the log church near J. Woods,' but by the subdivisions in which that denomination rejoices, there are now four houses for their occupation.

The first burial place was the Bennett Wood's Graveyard. There were laid away Robert Briggs in May, 1857, and his wife in 1850, Mrs Bennett Woods and other pioneers. The Crabtree Graveyard was perhaps the second one, though it is in South Litchfield. We were not curious enough about mortuary matters to seek to know these things in their grim minuteness. The fact that a cemetery was found near each church or regular preaching place, points with great clearness to the fact that no funeral was thought to be properly conducted without a sermon, and the exposure of the face of the dead for a last look by the spectators, though the Baptists—almost the sole religious denomination—discountenanced funeral sermons or mortuary services at a church. The dead were lovingly borne from the house to the place of burial and there left to the awful care of the grave.

The coffin was the handiwork of a home workman; the dead was arrayed in the chill simplicity of a shroud. It was unknown that a dead person was buried in the dress worn in life, or in such a dress as living people wear.

The defense of any custom is its utility, and the records of the pulpit contain little evidence of abiding religious impressions from the funeral sermons. Perhaps they are the Protestant form of praying for the dead.

The diseases were chiefly fever and chills; at times nearly every home contained more or less sick members. We have visited neighborhoods in which every house had its sick inmates. The first physician was Dr. Moore, of Woodboro, and North Litchfield was the home of no physician until 1854.

In 1832, Israel Fogleman occupied his life-long homestead, though he brought no wife to his cabin for six years. Peter Blackwelder had settled half a mile west, and Aaron Kean a couple of miles north. The Striplings were in the north part of the town, and in 1840 the township contained ten or twelve families. Alfred Blackwelder settled south of S. A. Paden's. Some children of the first settlers married and settled near the ancestral home.

The Bandys and Pete Thompson, Jesse and Israel Ash, John C. and James Roberts, Isaac Weaver, Ahart Pierce, C. W. Sapp and Ralph and Jacob Scherer and Elihu Boan came, and, in 1850, there was one schoolhouse, near the site of the brick one, just west of Mr. Austin's. In 1852, the Terre Haute & Alton railroad was located on the south line of the township, and, with the laying out of Litchfield and the opening of a market for grain, and the consequent appreciation of land, a new era dawned. The vacant prairie began to be fenced and brought into tillage. The salient feature of this decade was the creation of the village of Litchfield, with a population of 1,500, many of them of different nationality, and widely differing in manners and customs. The original settlers were conservative in habits and modes of thought. Litchfield was a good place to buy and sell in; it was a convenience; but socially and politically it was looked upon with coldness. If a Litchfield man wanted a county or town office, he failed to secure it.

When the war was in its earlier stages, various parties proposed to resist what they erroneously supposed was in contemplation. Their fears were soon dissipated, and gatherings of armed men at private houses, and armed sentinels around, were omitted. But men did meet at night for instruction in the military art, but they soon became ashamed of their untoward zeal, which had been stimulated by the presence of disloyal refugees from the States in rebellion. The result was an immediate feeling of unquietness, but no one imagined that this spasmodic moment of feeling would glut itself in action. It evaporated in fast riding and loud, boastful talk.

On an evening in February, 1864, three men called at the house of William G. Porter, five miles north of the city, and knocked for admittance. They said they were neighbors on their way home, and had broken their wagon, and desired a hammer and nails to repair the injury. Mr. Porter and his wife were alone and had retired for the night. He went to the door with the nails, when he was seized, and a demand made for his money. Mr. Porter showed fight in his nightdress. One person stood guard and two dealt with Mr. Porter and his wife. He received a slashing blow from a pistol, which laid open a long wound, and was shot in the head, the bullet plowing into the skull, where it remains. Porter made a lively fight, and foiled the robbers. But help was coming, and the robbers fled. No arrest was made, as the assailants were masked. Their purpose was simple robbery, and no political meaning was attached to the affair. But in October of the same year, three persons, about 7:40 P. M., visited the house of John C. Roberts, of Honey Bend, on an errand of plunder. Each had two revolvers, and the family were wholly defenseless. They obtained a gold watch, $150 in money and the family silver. One of the robbers, being lame, walked on the side of his foot, and was tracked to Litchfield. Arrests were made, but as they were refugees from Missouri, a presumptive alibi was made out, and they were released. There was, in the selection of the family and the undoubted character of the robbers, a political element in this crime. Thompson Williams, a half-mile west of Mr. Roberts, was robbed of a gun the same night, but it was afterward found in a field where the robbers had cast it away.

These three events comprise the criminal history of North Litchfield for sixty-four years, for the plundering of chicken roosts and the occasional relief of a smoke-house, were incidents not unknown in all frontier settlements, and were accepted at their real significance.

In 1870, the St. Louis Division of the Wabash road was built, and a station was located at Honey Bend. A town was laid out, and a post office established, J. E. Hickman, Postmaster, who also opened a store there. The place has neither passenger nor freight depot, but the shipments of cattle and grain have been noticed in the decrease of shipments from Litchfield. The village contains a church, schoolhouse and several shops, and about twenty neat dwellings.

The adoption of township organization in 1872, and a judicious road law have wrought marvelous changes in the condition of the highways. The chief roads have been ditched and graded. Safe bridges and culverts were placed at the water courses. Of course taxation increased, and whether the consumption of iron be the test of civilization or not, no one will deny that increase in taxation marks the history of our settlements. With the growth of wants comes a more rapid increase of taxation: and organized and regulated benevolence and administration of law have superseded the action of individuals who took care that no deserving persons suffered for food or shelter, or set at defiance the laws of mine and thine.

There are now five school districts in the township, all with good houses in which schools are maintained for at least eight months in the year. For the convenience of those who had worshiped at Cherry Grove, or Asbury Chapel or Litchfield, Phillips Chapel, about two miles south of Honey Bend, was erected in 1872, and this house and the one in the Bend, are the only religious houses in the township, outside of the city.

A brick-yard is in operation a mile east of State street, and the margin of Shoal Creek affords an abundance of compact, crystalized limestone. Burned into lime it yields a superior article, which has been found especially useful in building the abutments of bridges and culverts.

The pioneers of sixty years ago are represented by gray-haired men and faded-tressed women. The ox cart has utterly perished: the wooden plow, the winning shot, the sheep folds, exist only in imagination. The log cabin has gone, the flax and cotton fields are no longer tilled, the music of the spinning wheel and the beat of the loom are silent; sidesaddles are out of date. And we have written of things which were the familiar sights and sounds of our youth, that those in the morning of life may learn what was only sixty years since.

Our rural friends are incredulous as to the wonders of the telephone, and to the child on our streets to-day, the history we have written will be incredible: but that it is of modern times we have been speaking, he would class us among the weather prophets. Evidence wins assent, but experience commands belief, and we chide not the lad for believing only what is confined to his own experience, when eminent men contemptuously reject whatever their poor reason cannot compress or fathom.

We have tried to bring back to the reader the time which is now purely historical in North Litchfield. The prevailing peace and quiet of the people have been due to their own strong, simple, sturdy, high hearted characters, and to the auspicious fact that the law and the customs of their age were on a level with the average strong working moral quality of the people.

CHAPTER XII.

SOUTH LITCHFIELD TOWNSHIP—ITS DESCRIPTION, BOUNDARIES AND GENERAL TOPOGRAPHY—SETTLEMENT OF WHITE PEOPLE—THEIR EARLY HABITS AND INDUSTRIES—FACTS AND INCIDENTS—EDUCATIONAL AND RELIGIOUS—MISCELLANEOUS TOPICS, ETC., ETC.

THE northeast third of this township was originally well timbered, and forest is found on one or two sections on its south border. The surface is generally well-drained by Long Branch, Shoal Creek, Lake Fork and its three northern affluents. The northwestern sections discharge their surplus waters into the Cahokia. The center and west portions of the township are not as fairly drained as the other divisions, and may be called flat. The soil obeys the general law of change and decrease in depth, as one travels south. The black clinging soil, peculiar to the prairie, loses its northern depth. White soil is more frequently met. But there is as much in the cultivator as in the soil, and farmers in South Litchfield are among the solid men of the county. Brick clay is found near the town and down by Shoal Creek. Stone is quarried along the Creek and down Rocky Branch.

The township is exclusively agricultural. There is no shop or store or mill now nearer than Walshville and the city of Litchfield; and but two churches—a German Lutheran in the south, and a union house in the east. The people are all farmers. Three railroads, the original Terre Haute & Alton, the St. Louis Division of the Wabash, and the Jacksonville & Southeastern—the last one just opened—connect the township with the wide, wide world.

It was originally settled in 1816, by Nicholas Lockerman, who occupied the east half of the southeast quarter of Section 15 now the property of John A. Briggs. The first settlement in the county was at the Clear Spring Church, in Hillsboro Township, about two miles east of South Litchfield, and the early settlers located in the neighborhood, along the West Fork of Shoal Creek. Lockerman was not a desirable neighbor. His life was a scandal. He had a natural, but no legal wife, and Rev. James Street, finding him and the mother of his three children one day in the corn-field, lectured him so sharply and effectively that he coerced him to marry the woman, and the ceremony was performed in the field. It was the first marriage in the county. One of his sons settled on the Davenport place in the city of Litchfield, and another one on or near the Martin Ritchie farm in North Litchfield. He was killed, many years since, at Zanesville, by Andy Nash. The family long ago became extinct in this region. Probably Mr. Street settled at Clear Spring in 1814, as we have seen a tax receipt given him, in this county, dated that year. If this be conclusive as to the date, the settlement of the county must be set back a year or two.

The Indian trail, from the timber on the Cahokia to Shoal Creek, crossed the northwest corner of the county. So well was it used that the path, hard beaten, is still accurately remembered, and flint arrow-heads were frequently found on the prairie, by the older settlers. The existence of "buffalo wallows" seems to indicate the fact, or at least the belief, that buffalo once roamed this region, and an occasional bear or panther was seen by frightened families peering into their homes. The fear of Indians was not unknown, and the trampling of a man's horse around the house has sent the trembling inmates into the loft to shiver in fright until a new day banished their terrors by disclosing the cause.

The political condition of a people depends on the tenure of land. If a settler could call land his. in the sense that a horse or a rifle was his. the region could not be retarded in its development. or such grave embarrassments arise as have been witnessed in older States. The land tenures of the Northwest were perfect, and hence its peace was placed on a solid basis. The sole contingent blemish in the titles is the right of eminent domain. The land in this region was put in market for the benefit of the State by attracting settlements. There were no "land grants" in those days. when the price of land was put up to enrich the seller. The worth of a State is its people and their condition. and it is yet a question whether the people which feed the world or the one which clothes the world , the people who produce or the people who traffic, will. in the long run, be the world's arbiters.

We have been moderately curious as to the motives which set journeying hither so many from the States south of the Ohio. Most of the emigrants had not reached life's meridian. They were young hopeful, courageous, and poor in actual worth, but rich in possibilities. Illinois was a Territory, reposing under the noble provisions of the famous Dane Ordinance of 1787. Not a few of the pioneers have left their record that they sought homes here because the land would not be blemished by negro slavery. and civil and social distinctions would be yielded only to those who owned "niggers." A fat soil ready for the plow, cheap lands and a temperate climate, were not peculiar to Illinois or South Litchfield. For the grand simplicity. the sturdy virtue of their lives. they got recognition and fame as Enoch Arden did- after death. And though few families in South Litchfield are descendants of the pioneers, yet these few retain their pre eminence, and from them are selected with rare assent of unanimity, the guardians of the orphans. the administrators of estates and the servants of the public in township or county offices.

We cannot write history as a blind man goes about the streets. feeling his way with a stick The facts are transparent. and through them we catch gleams of other facts. as the raindrop catches light. and the beholder sees the splendor of a rainbow. We are to speak of common men whose lot was to plant civilization here. and who, in doing it. displayed the virtues which render modern civilization a boast and a blessing. These early times cannot be reproduced by any prose of a historian. They had a thousand years behind them, and in their little space of time they made greater progress than ten centuries had witnessed. Theirs was a full life. The work thirty generations had not done. they did, and the abyss between us of to-day and the men of sixty years ago is wider and more profound than the chasm between 1815 and the battle of Hastings. They did so much that it is hard to recognize the doers. They had a genius for doing great things. That olive leaf in the dove's beak perished as do other leaves. but the story it told is immortal. Of their constancy. one can judge by the fact that not one of them went back to the ancestral South.

The only history worth writing is the history of civilization, of the processes which make a State. For men are but as coral. feeble, insignificant. working out of sight. but they transmit some occult quality or power. upheave society. until from the moral and intellectual plateau rises. as Saul above his fellows. a Shakespeare. a Phidias or a Hamilton. the royal interpreters of the finest sense in poetry, in art and statesmanship. At the last, years color life more than centuries had, as the sun rises in an instant, though he had been hours in hastening to this moment.

As the county, in 1830, contained but 2,953 inhabitants, in 1840, only 4,490, and ten years later 6,277, it will be understood that the border townships, separated from Hillsboro, the political and commercial capital, by the deep valleys of Shoal Creek and its West Fork, must have gained slowly in population. Lockerman's cabin was the nucleus of the earliest settlement. Melchoir Fogleman located south of him just over the line in Walshville, and slowly pioneers planted themselves between their homes.

In 1821, Melchoir Fogleman, John Norton and James Bland, his son-in-law, had their homes in South Litchfield. It is not possible to determine the order of their arrival. It appears plainly that they located about the same time. There could have been only a few days or weeks difference in dates. Fogleman was a blacksmith, and brought from his North Carolina home the remarkable sum of $800 to Illinois, and after a stay of two years in South Litchfield, he removed to the neighborhood of Clear Spring, and in 1824 the Pepper Mill was built, the first water-mill in the region. Norton and Bland disappeared from the local history, leaving only their names. Spartan Grisham and Theodore Jordan lived with Fogleman, and were members of his family. Their descendants are still among us. Thus in 1820, Lockerman's was the sole family in the township, and the population of the county is estimated at 1000—nearly all in Hillsboro, and East Fork Townships. Lockerman lived on the southeast quarter of Section 15, near the spring. In the ten years ending with 1830, six families had settled in the township—four have been named and a Mr. Macaffee had settled where Newton Mill, and Spartan Grisham and Theodore Jordan had modest distilleries near by and made whisky, which passed as a legal tender at 50 cents a gallon. Before the Pepper Mill was built in 1824, the people went to Old Ripley or Edwardsville, to mill, and if those places could not be reached, corn was grated on the lower side of a tin sieve, or it was shaved off by a plane, or rudely crushed in a bowl, burned out in the top of a stump, by means of a wooden pestle, suspended from a spring-pole.

The few families were within two miles of the east line of the township. In 1830, or 1831, John A. Crabtree located on the farm, where he lived in honor and usefulness until his death a few years since. Wholly uneducated in books he possessed the masculine average common sense of his times, and like all other pioneers, was a life-long Democrat.

It has not been possible to determine the date of the arrival of Jesse Horn, but it is possible it was prior to 1830. Several young unmarried men were domiciled with the earlier families. They were sojourners rather than settlers, and a portion of them were but the spume which crested the tide of advancing settlements and having a large region where to choose drifted to other neighborhoods. Some of their names are remembered, but their history has been forgotten.

The James Copeland family appeared in the township about 1832, and the Forehands moved from Clear Spring to the bluff southwest of Truitt's Ford, not earlier than 1830. We can hear of no family here which did not come from south of the Ohio, and the earliest ones were from North Carolina.

About 18[illegible] the first schoolhouse was built a hundred and twenty rods east of J. N. McElvain's. The first teachers are not remembered.

the children attended. If their parents could pay, it was well. If they could not nothing was said about it. Fogleman received about $40 for his school, and after paying his board, had $30. The State had no public school system, and private schools alone were known here. The sessions opened in the morning and continued until night. The pupils were dismissed in season to reach home before dark. The teacher's hours were the same as a farm laborer's—from sunrise to sunset and if the school was not up to the "graded" standard, just consider how much time was of it. People were not afraid their children would injure their health with hard study.

John Corlew moved into the township in 1836. He was a commissioned officer in the Mexican war, and was elected Sheriff in 1848 and again in 1852, and since the adoption of township organization, has been almost continuously Supervisor. William Simpson was an early settler in the southeast part of the township. He was County Treasurer in 1871-73, but with this exception has attended strictly to the care of his farm. He came in 1831. By 1840, the township contained about eight or ten families. This year John Fogleman settled on his present homestead. Lewis McWilliams arrived in 1843, and his brother Thomas in 1849, and a third brother, John M., probably about the same time. Ezra Tyler located within the city limits in 1849.

Newton Street settled on his present farm in 1833, and has restricted himself to agricultural pursuits. About 1852, himself and John M. Paden had a steam saw-mill near his house. He feels the incurable illness of old age, but is still glad in his conversation to live over again the half a century he has been an inhabitant of South Litchfield.

The first burial-ground was the Crabtree Cemetery, now in parts thickly crowded with graves, and there rest the early forefathers. There beneath noticeable monuments lie buried Stephen R. Briggs, long a Judge of the County Commissioners' Court; Israel Fogleman the general guardian and administrator and John A. Crabtree the model of consistent firmness and average working good sense. The cemetery was laid out in 1843 and the first interment was Julia Parmele, wife of John Young. The first church was the Union Church near John Fogleman's in 1852, and a burial-place is near it. The third church was the German Lutheran, near Henry Nemires built about fifteen years since. The Methodist Chapel, at Hardinsburg, was the second one, erected in 1853 or 1854, and subsequently removed to the village of Litchfield.

At the close of this decade, the township may have contained thirty families, chiefly in the east half. The high road from Hillsboro to Alton, ran along the south line of the first six sections and a mile from the county line, the village of Hardinsburg was planned on Section 7. Seventeen blocks, of eight lots each, were laid out and several families had homes there. James Cummings kept the public house and afterward built a store and was appointed Postmaster. It was the only village between Woodboro and Bunker Hill, and was founded before the hope was entertained of a railroad in the vicinity. With the founding of Litchfield, its growth ceased. A part of its buildings were removed to the new town, and in two years the site of Hardinsburg was a plowed field again. In local history it still retains its place as a village, as the town plat has not perhaps been legally vacated. But the passer-by sees nothing to instruct him that this was once designed to be the metropolis of the west side of the county.

Few of the early settlers came direct from the South. The Foglemans, the Streets, the Padens, the Forehands and the Corlews paused near Clear Spring or Woodboro for a few years, before coming west of Shoal Creek. Brokaw and J. N. McElvain, David Lay and

W. Meisenheimer came during Fillmore's administration. Mount Olive, in Macoupin County, a short distance from the county line, was a German settlement, and Germans began to buy lands in South Litchfield. They never sell, but keep adding acre to acre, and to-day are the owners of the southwest part of the township.

The four events which have marked deepest the development of the township are the construction of the Alton & Terre Haute Railroad in 1854; the city of Litchfield; the Free School law, and the road law. The first put the people in easy communication with the river cities; the second afforded a local market; the third ministered to the better worth of the growing citizens, and the last has improved drainage and given safe highways.

The Litchfield coal mine, the oil wells and brickyards, are in the north part of the township, where are also the water works and huge ice houses.

During the war, a few residents proposed to nullify all laws for re-enforcing the army by a conscription. They made furtive visits and urged a neighbor to accept the leadership of the enterprise. They did not desire the draft enforced, as then they might have occasion to see Canada. The neighbor declined their overture, and the scheme was abandoned, and the authors went on voting the same old ticket from the force of habit. Wheat at $3.50 per bushel satisfied their loyalty.

The population of the township outside the city, is nine hundred and forty nearly, and the wide stretches of open land, which only a few years since were numerous, have now been reclaimed, and the last acre of speculators' real estate has passed into the hands of residents.

CHAPTER XIII.*

THE CITY OF LITCHFIELD—ITS FIRST SETTLERS—LAYING OUT A TOWN—GROWTH AND DEVELOPMENT—PUBLIC SALE OF LOTS—CITY IMPROVEMENTS AND INCREASE OF BUSINESS—POPULATION IN 1857—LITCHFIELD'S FIRST CIRCUS—SOME OF THE PIONEER BUSINESS MEN—THE MACHINE SHOP AND MILL OF BEACH—LIFE AND CHARACTER OF THE PEOPLE OF EARLY LITCHFIELD, ETC., ETC.

"A city that is set on an hill cannot be hid."

The city of Litchfield, lying two-thirds in North Litchfield Township and one-third in South Litchfield, and two miles from the west line of the county, is forty-two miles due south of Springfield, and twenty-six miles east, and thirty-four miles north of St. Louis. It is 310 feet above St. Louis, and is popularly held to be the highest point on the railroad between Alton and Terre Haute. Its waters of drainage flow in three cardinal directions and find their way to the Mississippi through Cahokia Creek and the Kaskaskia River. The town site is nearly level, one or two gentle mounds alone breaking the monotonous level.

The first settler within the limits of the town was Isaac Weaver, who in 1842 occupied a cabin at or near the entrance to the public square. But in 1835, Evan Stephenson entered the southwest quarter of Section 4, in South Litchfield, and in 1836, Joseph Gillespie entered the east half of the southeast quarter of the section. In 1838, G. B. [illegible] entered the west half and the south half of the east half of the northwest quarter of the section, and Isaac Ross entered what remained of the northwest quarter and all the northeast quarter, while not until 1849 did John Waldrop and Ezra Tyler enter the west half of the southeast quarter of the section, Tyler taking the south forty acres.

But Weaver's cabin was the first building, though, in 1847, Royal Scherer had a cabin on the southeast slope of the mound now owned by W. S. Palmer. Scherer was unmarried and did not occupy his hut. This year Ezra Tyler settled on his land, and the next year Ahart Pierce moved into his log house, placed on the mound, partly on the street and partly on the grounds of W. H. Fisher. In 1849, Mr. Pierce and Caleb W. Sapp entered the southwest quarter of Section 34, in North Litchfield, the south half, of which became the nucleus of the present city. Weaver's rights of possession were extinguished by purchase, and Sapp and Pierce divided their purchase, the former becoming the owner of the south half, which extended from the Wabash Railroad half a mile east along the Indianapolis and St. Louis Road, with a uniform width of a quarter of a mile. Ezra Tyler had the east half of this tract in September, 1850, which in May, 1861, passed to J. Y. McManus, who also bought the west half. This extinguished Sapp's title, who had built him a house on the south side of the public square, and the remains of his well are still easy to recognize.

In April, 1852, Nelson Cline bought the east forty of the Sapp purchase, and a year later he sold the west six acres to Y. S. Litter, who also purchased the forty acres lying immediately west of them. The same year George

*By H. [illegible]

James H. McPherson

F. Pretlow bought out Etter, and when the initial plat of Litchfield was laid out in the fall of 1853, it covered only Pretlow's forty-six acres and the thirty-four acres recently owned by Cline.

In the summer of 1853, residents of the present city were Alfred Blackwelder, near the site of the Weipert House, burned in 1880; Jacob Scherer, on the mound in the north-western quarter of the city; his brother, Ralph Scherer, a quarter of a mile east of him; Nelson Cline, two doors east of Fred Stahl's; Ahart Pierce, on the schoolhouse mound; J. Y. Etter, between Martin Haney's restaurant and the Wabash Railway; O. M. Roach in a diminutive room in Cummings & McWilliams' addition; Ezra Tyler, in the southeast part of town, and J. W. Andrews on the Davenport estate. The site of the town laid out for building purposes was a corn field, and when Simeon Ryder and Hon. Robert Smith, of Alton, Hon. Joseph Gillespie, of Edwardsville, Philander C. Huggins, of Bunker Hill, Josiah Hunt, Chief Engineer of the Terre Haute & Alton Railway and John B. Kirkham, formed a syndicate to purchase the sites of prospective stations along the line of the road then in process of construction, they bought out Mr. Cline. They agreed to lay out a town on the eighty acres owned by Pretlow and Cline, and after reserving the land needed for streets, public squares, and railroad uses, to reconvey to Pretlow one half the lots and blocks on his forty-six acres in full payment for the remainder. Mr. Kirkham was made the agent of the syndicate, but in a few days he was replaced by P. C. Huggins, who retained his position through successive purchases of additional land to be laid out in village lots until E. B. Litchfield, road was completed no farther than Bunker Hill from the western end, when Thomas A. Gray, County Surveyor, in October, 1853, laid out among the standing corn the original plat of the town. Gillespie was also laid out and Messrs. R. W. O'Bannon, T. W. Elliott, H. E. Appleton, James W. Jefferis and J. P. Bayless, and W. S. Palmer, of Ridgely, Madison County, having decided to remove to a point on the proposed road, drew straws to determine whether to locate at Gillespie or Litchfield. The fates willed in favor of the latter town. Accordingly, in January, 1854, Mr. O'Bannon bought the east half of the block facing on State Street and lying between Ryder and Kirkham streets for $120, on time. Any part of the east front would now be a bargain at that price for a single foot. This was the first purchase in the proposed town. He at once began arrangements to build a store on the southeast corner of his purchase. Mr. Jefferis appears to have been the second purchaser, and Mr. Appleton and Mr. Palmer must have secured lots soon after. Mr. O'Bannon obtained lumber for the frame of his store in the neighborhood, but the other lumber was obtained at Carlinville. His store was completed and occupied April 24, 1854, and Mr. Jefferis had his dwelling, now the south part of the George B. Litchfield House, nearly ready for his family; but Mr. Elliott, by bringing here the material of his home at Ridgely, managed to get his family placed in it May 5, 1854, and thus he was the pioneer settler of the town, though his home was antedated by the Jefferis house. Mr. Jefferis' family came three days later than Mr. Elliott, whose house stood nearly on the ground now occupied by the Parlor Shoe Store. The fourth building was a rude [illegible] on Mr. Southworth's corner. [illegible]

L. Hoffman's bakery, but as Mr. Palmer went to the woods and hewed out the framing timmer, he did not finish his store until fall. The next building was erected by E. Tyler, for a grain warehouse, on the side of the "O. K." Mill.

There was not time to build houses, and rude structures and small buildings were drawn over the slimy prairies on runners from other points. Thus J. P. Bayless brought here on rollers one-half of what had been a blacksmith shop at Hardinsburg. It had no door, floor or window. He placed it on the corner north of Mr. E. Burdett's shop and made it do for a home for several years. Up to this date Mr. Tyler supplied meals and lodging to the men who were founding the town. As to roads, the great highway from Hillsboro to Bunker Hill ran a mile south of the town, and the route from Edwardsville by way of Stanton to Taylorville, entered the town near its present southwest corner, and ran diagonally to the half-section line of Section 34, in North Litchfield. The road was laid out by striking a furrow on one side for several miles and then returning with a furrow on the opposite side. The road lay between these shallow ditches, and marked the route well enough for the few people who were condemned to use it.

Mr. Pretlow dying in the spring of 1854, the lots owned by him were kept out of market for a whole year. Mr. O'Bannon, wishing a quiet home, bought a couple of acres of Mr. Pierce on State street, between Division and Third streets, and built his present home on the gentle swell, during the summer of 1854, and placed his family in it during the fall, while it was unfinished.

Mr. Appleton built a wagon shop just in the rear of Jefferis' blacksmith shop, during the fall, and used the rear portion as a dwelling. Mr. Palmer and Mr. Mayo, his brother-in-law, put a stock of general merchandise in the store just built by the former, and the east end was also his family residence. There had planted themselves here by the latter part of 1854, six families, and the town consisted of about a dozen buildings, of which one was a wagon shop, one a blacksmith shop, and two were stores. By November, 1855, the number of dwelling-houses had increased to eleven, and the town seen under a December sky had an uninviting aspect. The population must have been at least one hundred, for when need comes, folks can be compacted together as close above ground as in it.

By October, the railroad was opened as far as Clyde, and in January the Pretlow estate was sold by his executor. The sale was held in the store of W. T. Elliott (the firm of R. W. O'Bannon and W. T. Elliott was so advertised by a sign over the door) and the day is still widely remembered for the dense rain which prevailed. The embankment for the railroad had formed a dike across State street, and interrupted its drainage. A miniature lake was formed, and it was the policy of parties owning land just west of the town plat, to have the dyke maintained, in order to force the location of the passenger station in their vicinity where, in anticipation of a decision in their favor, a side-track had already been graded. Mr. O'Bannon, Mr. Bayless, and others, cut the dike, and thus averted the location of the passenger house a quarter of a mile to the westward.

The earlier sales of lots on State street had been made at the rate of $30 for sixty-six feet front. The price in May, 1854, was increased to $50. There were no apparent natural advantages for the creation of a prosperous town. It was not known that the railroad shops would be located here. Shoal Creek was a serious barrier to communication with the country to the east; and, on other sides, the prairie still spread, with here and there a settler who was toilsomely breaking, breaking the virgin sod. The site of the plat had been bought in midsummer, 1853, at $8 or $10 per acre, and the plat gave two acres to eight lots and the surrounding streets. At the Pretlow sale one half the lots in the west part of the town were sold by public outcry, and it is instructive to note the purchasers and the prices paid. But few of the buyers have representatives in the city. The terms were one-third down and the balance in one year. The Pretlow estate, after the original plat had been recorded, consisted of Blocks 6, 8, 10, 12, 22, 24, 26, 28, the west half of Block 20, Lots 2 and 3, Block 4, Lot 10, Block 2, and Lots 2, 4, 6 and 8, in Block 33. One familiar with their location will readily understand how sadly the withholding this real estate from sale and improvement delayed the growth of the town. The influence of this was fully seen in the two years immediately following the sale.

PURCHASERS.	LOT.	BLOCK.	PRICE.
W. F. [illegible] & Co.	1	28	$164 00
John S. Stewart	2	28	100 00
James Cumming	3 & 4	28	200 00
T. C. Kirkland	5	28	140 00
J. W. Andrews	6	28	118 00
T. C. Kirkland	7	28	160 00
S. C. Simmons	8	28	1[illegible] 00
S. C. Simmons	1	26	[illegible]6 25
Addison McLain	2	37	37 00
William Holloway	3	37	26 00
David Cobb	4	37	42 00
R. H. Cline	5	37	6[illegible] 25
Peter Shore	6	37	50 00
T. C. Kirkland	7	37	66 00
Peter Shore	8	37	127 25
W. C. Henderson	2	33	100 00
L. Sweet	4	33	57 00
James Cummings	6	33	80 00
L. Sweet	8	33	5[illegible] 00
James Cummings	1	22	92 00
James Cummings	2	22	60 00
T. L. Van Dorn	3	22	42 50
A. McLain	4	22	54 00
Benjamin Hargraves	5	22	77 00
T. L. Van Dorn	6	22	60 00
J. W. Andrews	7	22	67 00
J. W. Andrews	8	22	100 50
John M. McWilliam	3	20	111 00
T. C. Kirkland	4	20	80 00
L. P. McWilliams	5	20	86 00
John S. Roberts	6	20	175 00
J. W. Wa[illegible]	2	4	60 00
P. Shore	3	4	51 00
H. H. Hood	1	12	[illegible]7 00
T. L. Van Dorn	2	12	60 00
John S. Stewart	3	12	41 00
O. P. Jones	4	12	[illegible]5 00
W. M. Bronson	5	12	50 00
W. M. Bronson	6	[illegible]	50 00
H. B. Hood	7	12	137 50
Charles Davis	8	12	83 00
Isaac Baker	1	24	31 00
J. B. Kirkland	2	24	20 00
Peter Thompson	1	6	29 00
John P. Bayles	2	36	36 00
A. J. Thompson	3	36	35 50
J. L. Wallis	4	36	27 00
A. J. Thompson	1	8	[illegible]8 00
R. M. Gamble	2	8	18 50
R. M. Gamble	3	8	17 00
W. H. Fursh[illegible]	1	8	16 75
William Allen	2	24	17 50
J. W. Jefferis	3	24	15 00
Samuel Harr	4	24	17 00
Joseph Davis	5	24	16 50
Joseph Davis	6	2[illegible]	15 00
J. W. Jefferis	7	24	13 50
John C. Hughes	1	10	20 00
R. H. Cline	2	10	20 00
T. D. Whit[illegible]	3	10	20 25
J. P. Bayles	4	10	20 25
Don W[illegible]	5	10	20 50
W. H. Fur[illegible]	6	10	17 75
S. C. Shu[illegible]	7	10	23 25
J. C. Hughes	8	10	38 50

One of the lots would to-day sell for 300 per cent more than the sixty-six did at that sale, which was at least four times greater than the value of half the town site before it was laid out.

In 1854, "Nigger Dan," from Carlinville, built a hotel which is now the east part of the Phœnix House. He was able only to inclose the building, and such as it was, it was the first house of entertainment in the town. The next year, E. W. Litchfield supplied means to finish it. I have not been able to learn his real name or subsequent history. Dr. Gamble was the first physician, and lived on a half-floored house west of the Methodist Church. Dr. H. H. Hood, who first opened an office at Hardinsburg, was the second one, and had his office (in August) at J. M. McWilliams store, which was between the Phœnix House and the Central Hotel. On November 24, of this year, the railroad was opened to Litchfield and the sale of the Pretlow property soon following, the town received an impetus which it has not since lost, though panics, fires, the war, and the removal of the railroad shops, have each given a breathing time to lay wiser plans and build its prosperity on a more stable basis.

By the close of the year, eight or nine families had homes in the city in addition to six or seven families on farm lands when the town was surveyed. We can enumerate R. W. O'Bannon, W. T. Elliott, H. E. Appleton, Jas. Jefferis, J. P. Bayless, W. S. Palmer, "Nigger Dan," and probably G. Evans. T. G. Kessinger came in not much later. In the spring of 1855, Messrs. E. W. Litchfield, E. E. Litchfield, E. S. Litchfield, George H. Hull, and the three Dix brothers, and C. F. How, came from Central or Western New York; all related to E. C. Litchfield, who had become practically the owner of the town site. Several additions to the town were laid out. James Cummings removed his store and contents from Hardinsburg, and placed it just west of the cigar factory on Ryder street. He was the first Postmaster. The original plat of the town which bore the name of Huntsville was never recorded. It was the purpose to have the name of the post office the same as the name of the town, and as there was a post office called Huntsville in Schuyler County, the name of the town was changed to Litchfield in honor of its virtual proprietor. Up to this date, the present townships of North Litchfield and South Litchfield were a part of Long Branch (Election Precinct), and I have heard an early resident say, that a dozen ballots would be cast at an election.

The railroad being open to Alton, Messrs. E. W. Litchfield and C. F. How began timidly the sale of lumber, buying a carload or two at Alton and unloading it where State street crosses the railroad. E. E. Litchfield bought the Tyler grain warehouse, and, removing it to the site of D. Davis' grocery store, converted it into a store and began the sale of dry goods. A year or two later, he went out of dry goods and became a hardware merchant. James and William Macpherson erected a flouring or grist mill and a residence just north of the Planet Mills' office. These were the first buildings south of the railroad. In the fall, ground was broken for the railroad shops, but when S. E. Alden arrived in November, there were but eleven dwellings and a few shops or stores in the place. W. T. Bacon, from Adrian, Mich., had formed a partnership with Messrs. How & Litchfield to deal in lumber, and had projected a planing-mill. The winter of 1855-56 was an open one, and the tide of emigration setting in deep and steady, building went on during the entire season, and a hundred dwellings and other buildings were put up by the close of 1856. The passenger station had been completed and the round-house with thirteen stalls had been inclosed, and the foundation laid for the machine-shops. The town had been incorporated as a village; R. W. O'Bannon, President of the Board of Trustees. The public houses had increased to four; The Montgomery House now the Phœnix, by A. C. Paxson; the Litchfield House, opposite Woodman's lumber-yard, by Mr. Johnson, the nucleus of the Central Hotel, by J. Hawkins, and the beginning of the Palace Hotel, by R. Chism. The Methodist and Presbyterian Churches were built, but not quite completed.

Hood & Bro., and Dr. Grinsted, had drug stores, the first adjoining O'Bannon's store on the north, and the second in the building now occupied by G. B. Litchfield as a restaurant. Bagby & Corrington had succeeded McWilliams & R. N. Paden in the State Street store south of the public square. O'Bannon & Elliott and Palmer & Jefferies, in their own buildings, continued to sell dry goods and clothing; and Henderson, Hull & Hawkins had a store across the street south of Woodman's lumber-yard. Til. Shore sold stoves and hardware in the Harris Building, below Brewer & Grubb's Bank, which he had erected in 1855; E. E. Litchfield was in the same line on his corner; James Cummings & Son were merchants in the Cummings Building, opposite the Central Hotel; John McGinnis sold clothing and groceries where Julius Machler's saloon now is. John P. Bayless had succeeded James Cummings in the post office, which was in O'Bannon's store. There was one saloon open a part of the time where Peter Kane dispensed, and B. C. Beardsly had begun business in Litchfield's store. There were two physicians, Hood and Grinsted, but no lawyer; one schoolmaster, and no resident preacher.

When the railroad was opened as far east as Litchfield, John P. Bayless was appointed the first agent, and his office was among the foundation timbers of the water tank, which stood near the southwest corner of the car works office, while a sister tank stood about on the site of the present one. R. E. Burton was the painter and photographer; John P. Davis & Brothers, the plasterers; William Downey, the brick-layer. Farrar & Sinclair had the livery stable where Griswold's stable is. P. J. Weipert made and sold horse furniture, and C. Hoog made boots and shoes, and J. W. Cassiday was the one sufficient tailor. Mr. Johnson and his sons, with saws and bucks, cut the fuel for the locomotives. G. W. Nelson —"Fiddler George" was the Constable, and L. D. Palmer, the Justice of the Peace. J. L. Hood sold furniture in the Cummings' building for Olcott & Co., of Alton; and W. B. Charles—"Captain Charles" -in his old age had deserted the river steamer, and had a little stock of clothing in the same building. Carpenters were counted by the score, and their wages were high.

The population had, by 1857, risen to six or seven hundred. The earliest residents were chiefly from the slave states, Kentucky or North Carolina. Messrs. Appleton, Grinsted, and Mr. Long, his assistant, and a Mr. Thomas, were of English birth. Messrs. Hoog and Weipert were Germans. A few came from Ohio, and there was a liberal infusion of persons from the State of New York, and the Irish brogue was heard constantly.

The spring of 1857 opened late with rain and cold. The streets were gorged by the depth of black, unctious, tenacious mud. Sidewalks there were none. The second block east of State street was a shallow pond, much visited in the season by water fowl. Drains and sewers were unknown, and the rainfalls skulked and dodged through grass and rubbish to the heads of the water channels which begin half a mile or more distant. A few dwellings boasted more than two rooms. The people stayed here, comforting themselves with hopes of improved futures and release from narrow surroundings. The railroad had been opened to Terre Haute the previous year. Edwin C. Dix had succeeded Mr. Bayless as station agent. And occasionally some merchant would tell that he had, the previous year, shipped several car-loads of grain in sacks to St. Louis. The nominal village organization was kept up, E. C.

Dix being its President. Some ordinances were adopted, but not enforced. The town was the common fighting ground for the surrounding county. A group of bullies would ride into town, fire their courage with whisky, if they could get it, and then gallop through the streets, shouting and carrying clubs or weapons, seeking a fight. On such occasions, "Old Shake," foreseeing their purpose, would usually lock his door, and disappear for the day, under the pretense of hunting or fishing, though a thinner excuse than fishing could not be imagined.

The first circus tent spread here drew not less than five thousand persons to town, people coming as much as forty miles to witness the moral horsemanship, and be astonished at the wit of the clown, and admire the frisky mules. Still the religious impressions of the performances in the ring have not yet been observed, or, if so, have failed of a chronicler, though the town is not wholly ignorant of preachers who thought the noblest passage in the Bible was Job's description of a horse. There have been circuses here since, but not to arouse the excitement of that first one, and men are said to have gone fishing, but no one with so good a purpose as "Old Shake," or equally commendable results. The most noticeable effect observed has been the reputation of the fishermen for accuracy of statement. Had the fish been bigger, their reputation would have acquired the rudiments of a moral quality.

At length—it was in 1855—the domination of bullydom came to inglorious grief. Bullies had paraded the town nearly the entire day putting quiet citizens to great fear of personal violence. At last one of the gang stood up a citizen against Palmer's store and cursed him with Satanic eloquence and energy. He hoped to tempt him to some act of resistance. A crisis was imminent when a preacher of the Christian Church, just risen from a sick bed, came down the street. He comprehended the situation and said it was time to push things. A local preacher of the Methodist's coincided, and, saying he had in his store a basket of fine savory eggs well matured for use in such a case, brought them forward. The eggs were thrown at the bully with malignant precision, the missiles as they crushed on his face and against his person emitted a pungent odor. It was afterward thought the eggs were addled; no one knew; there were none left to experiment with. The gang fled, but the crowd, in anticipation of this had taken possession of a pile of spalls at the railroad crossing, and as the odorous bully and his confederate came up a volley of stones was hurled at them with convincing effect. He never recovered from his injuries, but died a few years later of consumption. One other event completed the subjugation of the rowdy element. In 1867, the same element proposed to "run" the town for a day; the plan—a rough one—prospered until evening; when the shopmen were going home to supper, the opportunity was too rich for county blood; a demonstration was made on a workman, and incontinently, the aggressor, was the worst whipped man in Central Illinois. The victory was complete, the town had conquered a peace. Thenceforward there was amity between town and county rowdy, and no town of the State of equal population since that event shows a better record as to breaches of the peace.

Manufactures.—At the founding of the city the only manufactories of the neighborhood were a blacksmith shop at Hardinsburg, a tread-wheel carding machine near Wilson Meisenheimer's, a steam saw-mill near Newton Street's, a second one near Judge Briggs' home, and perhaps a grain mill at Truitt's ford.

In 1854, James Macpherson, and William, his brother, built a grain mill and residence on the site of the Planet Mill, and these were the first buildings south of the railroad, after the laying-out of the town. The mill would be called a humble affair to-day, but then it was ample for local wants. The next year R. H. Peall and J. M. McWilliams became the owners, and enlarged it and added expensive machinery. McWilliams dying in 1857, the mill, under the operation of law, fell into the hands of Ezra Tyler, who ran it with the aid of his sons until 1860, when he sold it to M. J. Gage. He at once put in a new engine and sets of buhrs, and other needed machinery, fully doubling its size and capacity. Practically, he made the mill a new one. He subsequently admitted his son to a partnership, and when he sold it, in 1866, he had paid his indebtedness and was the possessor of a moderate fortune. Best & Sparks, the purchasers, leased it first to E. A. Cooley and John Best, and then to A. W. Samson. While the latter was the lessee, the owners planned to replace the wooden structure by a brick mill. The main building was erected, when, in 1870, an evening fire destroyed the mill, and the project of replacing it was first deferred and finally abandoned. For ten years, at least it was a flouring-mill, and shipped its goods to Eastern markets.

A second flouring-mill was completed in 1860, half a mile up State street, by John C. Reed and James Macpherson. In the spring of 1863 this, in an unknown manner, was also destroyed by fire. The attempt to connect its destruction with military and political troubles had no sufficient basis. Perhaps some card-playing youths knew more than they told. The mill was not rebuilt.

Wesley Best and David R. Sparks, from Staunton completed a 300-barrel mill, on the railroad a quarter of a mile west of State street The mill was twice enlarged, and its goods achieved a flattering reputation. It, too, was burned, in February, 1879, and arrangements were made to rebuild it in 1881, but when the walls were fairly begun, the property was sold to D. L. Wing & Co., who demolished what had been built, and the barren site is to-day the sole memorial of what was one of the best old style mills in Central Illinois. As long as it stood, the city maintained its pre-eminence as a local market for wheat, and its destruction was a general calamity.

Peter Boxberger, in 1868, built a flouring-mill on the railroad, a quarter of a mile east of State street. Three years later he sold it to Daniel McLenan, in whose charge it was when destroyed by fire in 1873, bringing financial ruin to its owner. About this time, T. G. Kessinger had a custom mill opposite Best & Sparks' mill, but it was not kept up long. In 1871, Mr. Boxberger changed the furniture factory of Whitaker & Rogers into a grist and flouring mill, and held it for two years, when L. G. Hicks and T. G. Kessinger obtained possession of it. They remained in control as long as possible. Whitaker & Rogers ultimately regained it by litigation, and the junior member of the firm still runs it. In 1873, Mr. Boxberger built the flouring-mill near the Indianapolis & St. Louis depot. Becoming embarrassed, he formed a partnership with Julius Maehler, and the firm failed. The mill was sold, and for a year it was operated by L. Whitaker, but in 1881 J. W. Thynne came into control, and it is now run under his management. All the mills used buhr stones, and completed the manufacture of flour in two grindings. Their capacity was limited, and until the opening of the coal mines and the introduction of water works, they struggled under formidable difficulties. But in the spring of 1881, Messrs. D. L. Wing & Co., of Springfield, Mass., began the erection of the Planet Mill, which by reason of its capacity and the new system of converting wheat into flour and the character and completeness of its appointments will bear a rapid description.

The mill building proper is 50x100 feet and five stories high, exclusive of basement and texas. The basement contains shafting and main driving pulley, elevators, fans and wheat sink. The main floor contains seven reduction mills for grinding middlings, and nine sets of smooth and corrugated rolls, fifteen purifiers, six bolting chests and flour chests, packers and cleaning machines. It may be of interest to know that flour-making consists of about thirty operations. A barrel of flour is made every two minutes and a half. The motive power is given by a 300-horse-power engine. The grain elevator has a capacity of 100,000 bushels. There are six buildings belonging to the mill, and the out and the in business is equal to twelve car loads per day. Sixty five men are employed. The cost of the mill was $200,000; W. N. Hewitt Superintendent. The mill went into operation in November, 1881, and the wheat is nearly all obtained from the close neighborhood. The O. K. Mill was put in operation about 1873, and is owned by Perley, Beach & Co. In 1881, Mr. Whitnall opened tile works on the east margin of the city. His wares are for the most part shipped to other counties.

The foundry and machine shop of H. H. Beach & Co. was built in 1857, and operated as a separate interest until 1876, when by sale they were consolidated with the car works. The original concern for years supplied the railroad repair shop with castings, and was largely engaged in the manufacture of engines and mill machinery. The concern worked an average of fifty men. The work is kept up by the new company.

As early as 1856 a planing-mill was running where is now Weigreffe's lumber yard. In a few years it was dismantled, and in 1867, Mr. Weigreffe built his sash, door and blind factory, which was discontinued in 1876, and the machinery removed. L. Hoffman had a brewery where the coal shaft is, and finding the business ruinous abandoned it. J. E. Gay had a carriage factory, working twenty hands. He had no capital, and went into the bankrupt class.

The railroad shops were removed to Mattoon in 1870–71, and the spacious buildings stood tenantless and silent. Those who imagined that the permanent welfare of the city depended on retaining the shops, began to look for the signs of decay. The mystery of cause and effect is insoluble but as a sequence, the city's gift of $50,000 to the Decatur & East St. Louis Railroad was followed closely by the removal of the shops, and when that decision was made public the population had sunk to the lowest point touched in twenty years. It was learned that the shops could be obtained on a long lease for a low sum. They could quickly and cheaply be turned into car works and the scheme was elaborated to organize a stock company to build railway cars and coaches. Parties from the East offered to conduct the business if Litchfield would supply the capital. The proposal was declined without thanks. In the winter of 1871–72, the company was formed and in May work was begun. A year later a fire from the cupola destroyed the foundry and machine shop. This portion of the works was rebuilt. In a few years the company's patronizing roads were unable to meet their engagements and the company obtained an extension on its own paper, and at the appointed dates honored all its obligations. The company reorganized in 1877 with a diminished capital stock, but in effect with enlarged resources, and has been prosperous. Last year the pay-roll bore over 400 names, and the monthly pay sheet exceeded $19,000. The coal mine and the car works employed nearly six hundred and fifty men and the monthly wages were $30,000.

The influence of manufactures on population can be learned from a comparison of the census returns for a series of years, with the condition of our industrial enterprises. For 1870 and 1880, the Federal census is given; for the other years the school census is used:

1869	4036	1875	4160
1870	3750	1876	4135
1871	3837	1877	3730
1872	4289	1878	3685
1873	4432	1879	3959
1874	4358	1880	4343

In 1877 and 1878, the car works were resuming business, and but few workmen were employed. The full consequences of the panic of 1873 had reached the climax. The fluctuations in the census accurately measures the activity in productive industries. In 1881, the population reached 5,250, and over a hundred dwellings were constructed.

We herewith give a statement of the business done in the Litchfield Post Office, during the past five years ending June 30, 1882:

GROSS RECEIPTS.

July 1, 1877, to June 30, 1878	$3,266 88
July 1, 1878, to June 30, 1879	3,496 41
July 1, 1879, to June 30, 1880	3,865 17
July 1, 1880, to June 30, 1881	4,572 69
July 1, 1881, to June 30, 1882	5,279 35

SALES OF DOMESTIC MONEY ORDERS.

July 1, 1877, to June 30, 1878	$2,117 00
July 1, 1878, to June 30, 1879	2,303 00
July 1, 1879, to June 30, 1880	2,683 00
July 1, 1880, to June 30, 1881	3,088 00
July 1, 1881, to June 30, 1882	3,301 00

The sales of international money orders during the past five years amount to $450, and there have been registered in the same period 2,057 letters and parcels against 1,188 for the eight years previous to June 15, 1877.

Perhaps the growth of local or city taxation for school and city purposes may bear on this question of manufactures and growth of the city. For 1859, the taxes given are for the levy of that year; then until 1872, the taxes are the sum called for by the Collector's warrant, which includes the yearly levy and all back takes. Until 1865, the City Council served without pay. Subsequently the members were paid:

Year.	Tax.	Year.	Tax.
1859	$2,187 89	1867	$19,098 94
1861	1,511 93	1868	22,307 23
1862	1,531 59	1869	22 802 63
1863	2,000 19	1870	27,114 62
1864	2,149 39	1871	19,936 75
1865	11,547 91	1872	18 457 29
1866	18.146 53		

The sum of $4.000 should be added to the figures for 1871–72 for interest on railroad bonds which is collected as a part of the State tax.

Until 1873, the city taxes were levied on the assessment made by the City Assessor, and were collected by the City Collector. From that year the taxes for the city were levied by the State authorities in part, by the School Board in part, by the City Council in part, and in part by the citizens of North Litchfield and South Litchfield in town meeting. For five years the School Board and the City Council was the same body, but acting in two capacities.

It appears proper to give a more detailed statement of local taxes from 1873 inclusive, representing only the amounts extended on the tax books, but having nothing to do with the amounts collected, and nothing to do with the expenditures of each year for current purposes.

Year.	Mayor.	Assessments.	Local Taxes.	
1873	W. S. Palmer	$1,4[illegible] 868	City	$9,447 98
			School	7,500 00
			City Bond	3,394 74
			Total	$20,342 72
1874	S. M. Grubbs	12,2[illegible],894	City	$14,[illegible] 70
			School	15,602 29
			City Bond	4,409 12
			Total	$37,716 42
1875	D. Davis	1,1[illegible] 379	City	$14,43[illegible] 18
			School	10,4[illegible]6 74
			Bond	5 [illegible]17 18
			Total	$[illegible] 10
1876	D. Davis	83[illegible],859	City	$11,1[illegible]7 20
			School	[illegible],157 47
			Bond	5,487 89
			Total	$21,[illegible] 56
1877	W. Best	687,[illegible]90	City	$7,21[illegible] 11
			School	4,08[illegible] 34
			Bond	4,7[illegible] 13
			Total	$16,071 78

Year.	Mayor.	Assessments.	Local Taxes.	
1878	P. B. Updike	[illegible]	City	$[illegible] 74
			School	3,534 14
			Bond	4,707 09
			Total	$13,[illegible] 97
1879	D. Davis	[illegible]	City	$4,04[illegible] 64
			School	3,0[illegible] 45
			Bond	4,[illegible]
			Total	$11,[illegible] 18
1880	R. F. Bennett	[illegible]	City	$3,[illegible]14 [illegible]
			School	4,02[illegible] 20
			Bond	3,1[illegible] 17
			Total	[illegible]
1881	E. Southworth	4[illegible],927	City	[illegible] 18
			School	7,170 34
			Bond	3,[illegible]
			Sinking Fund	[illegible]
			Total	$16,[illegible]07 48

During each year the city was in the receipt of a revenue from miscellaneous sources of at least $6,000, which with the taxes collected represent the total yearly expenditure for city purposes. The era of high taxes represents the years of building the new school-house, and the quickly abandoned policy of paying off floating and bonded indebtedness.

We make no attempt to explain the decrease in the assessed valuation of the city, nor the wonderful sums yearly spent under the ambiguous heading of city expenses.

In April, 1857, the first number of the Litchfield *Journal* appeared, of which a fuller account will be found in a subsequent chapter. In March, M. B. Savage, of Brooklyn, N. Y., appeared here to become a partner of E. E. Litchfield; J. W. Haggart succeeded E. C. Dix, as railroad agent. J. L. Childs had, a few weeks earlier, become the successor of E. W. Litchfield in the lumber firm. Mathew Cyrus followed Mr. Paxson in the Montgomery house, and in May or June, H. W. Beach and D. C. Amsden arrived to begin the erection of a foundry and machine shop. This was made the terminal point of the division of the railroad, and work was begun on railroad machine shop. Messrs. O'Bannon, E. W. Litchfield and E. L. Dix opened a lumber yard where the Ballweg elevator stands. The railroad employes abounded, and railroad talk drowned politics. Shore's steam saw-mill, on Rocky Branch, after sawing three cuts had settled down to permanent idleness, and the ruin of its owner. This year the railroad engine house, machine shop and blacksmith shop were built and supplied with machinery, and there was a sudden increase of population—the families of mechanics and laborers in the shops. John S. Miller was the master mechanic. The road was not prosperous only one freight train each way per day, and the train as low as three cars. Pay day was irregular and, with the panic which set in with tremendous severity, and low wages, the profits of labor were scanty. O'Bannon and Litchfield's lumber yard was sold to Perley & Co., a firm consisting only of R. G. Perley. The year went out in gloom and various helps to discouragement. A second saloon had been opened, a billiard table set up, two more physicians had settled here, and a couple of lawyers had an office; of these brief mention should be made, for they were conspicuous persons for a few years.

B. M. Munn, a young man, came here from Charleston. He was a man of untiring industry, a gentleman in dress, temper and manners, ambitious and hospitable. But he was poor and impatient to become rich. He borrowed money and his plans did not prosper. He lost public confidence, went out as a three month's man at the beginning of the war, and drifted to Cairo and ceased to be a member of the county bar.

He had hardly opened his office in the fall, when T. N. Marron, a native of Lewis County N. Y., in some way lounged into town, nearly or quite penniless, and with but an apology for personal baggage. He said he had during the summer been engaged in the survey of railroads in Iowa, and had failed to receive his pay. Mr. Munn tendered him a desk in his office, shared his slender purse with him, and sought to aid him in securing legal business. But Marron was a Bohemian lawyer and no student.

He was, however, dignified and impressive in his manners, and soon was noted for the condensed energy of his conversation. Though quick of resentments, he delighted in festive scenes and noise. Whatever his theory as to the adequacy of statute law and legal precedents as a good substitute for principles founded on Christian morals, he failed to win clients, and in the second year of the war he disappeared, and was afterward seen in Cairo, where former acquaintances deemed it proper not to covet his society. His will acted in whirls and side currents, and he was as poor a friend to himself as he was to others. He was a man of impulses, jealous of others' success, ignobly poor, with tastes which a fortune alone could gratify; he neglected the patient industry indispensible to a lawyer who would rise in his profession.

If the year ended in omens of disaster, judged by the usual but fallacious standards adopted elsewhere, there was no time for despondency. The better wealth of the town lay in the character and temper of its people. Messrs. Hood & Fields, of Michigan, had built and occupied a grocery store on the lot immediately north of Litchfield's hardware store. Burr Robbins, of circus fame, and his brother began a saloon on the next business lot, and the brother dying the property was bought by C. W. Ward, who enlarged the building and carried out the design of the original owners. In May, D. C. Amsden and family arrived from Wisconsin, and the next month was joined by H. H. Beach, his brother-in-law. Mr. Beach brought the engines and equipment for a machine shop and foundry, and running up a huge barn-like structure, put the furnace in blast two months afterward, and then as resident partner and manager of the firm of Williams, Angel & Beach, entered upon a career of brilliant usefulness and prosperity as a mechanic and citizen. He was in the forenoon of life, and fully trained in practical mechanics and railroad work. He may have been worth a thousand dollars in his own right but had a sound, healthy intelligence in his profession. He built his shops for the future, and then awaited the developments of business. He had the only foundry and machine shop between Alton and Terre Haute. Soon after kindling his fires, the dread panic desolated the country, paralyzing enterprise, and bringing financial ruin to many, and hardship to all. For weeks Mr. Beach was on the brink of failure. Only by his popularity and personal influence could he get money to keep his shops open. The age of iron—the badge of power and industrial development—was about to dawn here, and its harbinger was the inevitable train of disaster which preceded the establishment of a radical change in the methods and implements, and machines in the world of production and trade. The hour for an expedient had come. He bought on credit a mill for corn meal, and placing it in the loft over his machine shop. Mr. Amsden to his other incongruous duties added the care of the mill. Corn was abundant and cheap, and meal was high. Each week a shipment to St. Louis brought in money to keep affairs in order, and by spring the crisis in his fortunes was fairly over. The year had tested men. Whoever could see the end from the beginning, could then have predicted the future of the town.

Its history is but the simple monotonous story of the life of a little community, which had no startling or exceptionable incidents. If life here was quiet, it was intense and stern. All commercial and industrial facilities had been made the most of. It was not quite a frontier or pioneer town, but when it was founded the region around was sparsely settled, and large tracts of land were uninclosed and untilled. The people were rich in the prospective appreciation of their lands, but poor in actual wealth. They had clung to the timber along the streams, and the more sanguine had excited the derision of their neighbors by saying that in half a century settlement might advance several miles into the prairie. Wheat sold at Alton for 20 cents a bushel above the incidental expenses of transportation on wagons. The best wealth of the town was the sort of people who gave it tone and character. No one hoped to get on by pulling a neighbor down. The latest arrival was welcomed and helped to make a start. Competing tradesmen were warm personal friends. There was a broad public sentiment which attracted population. There was prompt co-operation in each new enterprise. Each man thought he would best benefit himself by contributing to the common weal. Life was a good, earnest, manly fight with narrow fortunes. It was won by character, intelligence, industry, prudence and courage. And it needed to be so. A greater progress than had cheered the last century was to be crowded into twenty years; the full work of four generations of an earlier day, was now flung on one. A better Thermopylæ was here, but the myriad Helots who died on Persian swords to lend deathless fame to their three hundred masters, had no representatives. Only a few men could do much, but all did what was possible. Through that year and subsequent ones, can be traced like a fairy ring, the example and influence of a few men from the East, who being full of go, sent their fiery energy and daring through the community. Their positive incisive traits were as strong as passions and beautiful as hope. They came to succeed and stay and, believing in themselves, they did.

CHAPTER XIV.

LITCHFIELD—INCREASE OF POPULATION—EARLY POLITICS—POLITICIANS AND POLITICAL QUESTIONS—THE JOURNALS—DOUGLAS AND LINCOLN—INCORPORATION OF LITCHFIELD AS A CITY—THE FIRST MAYOR—SOME OF THE LATER BUSINESS MEN—PHYSICIANS—PRESIDENTIAL ELECTION OF 1860 AND ITS RESULTS—THE CITY DURING THE WAR—FIRES—REMOVAL OF RAILROAD SHOPS—RECAPITULATION, ETC.

"Recollection is the only paradise from which we cannot be turned out."—*Richter.*

BY the beginning of 1858, the population of Litchfield might have been a thousand, nearly all drawn hither from a distance. They were poor, if reckoned by material standards, but young, earnest, pushing, resolute, and able and willing to make favorable circumstances if they could not find them. Their true power and wealth lay in their capacity to work and their skill in their callings, and their readiness to multiply themselves by doing so many unlike things well. They had to succeed. The population was a busy one, and splendidly in earnest. Somehow they tore their way upward. The same man was in the course of the day a coal dealer, superintendent of the foundry, melting three tons at a heat; ran a corn-mill, carrying the corn in the ear on his back to the second story, shelling it and sifting the meal by hand, sacking it for shipment; keeping the books of the firm, taking the time of the workmen, attending to the correspondence, and in the intervals doing the "chores" around the establishment.

Everybody not a railroad man, talked politics, if not with wide knowledge, yet with zeal and earnestness. The Democratic headquarters were at O'Bannon's store, and there on rainy days as well at sundry other times were gathered Thomas C. Hughes, Elihu Boan, Stephen R. Briggs, Israel Fogleman, John A. Crabtree, with "Uncle Dick" as Moderator, smoking amicable pipes and turning over their oft-expressed opinions as to the issues then prominent in Kansas. All these had been born and reared in slave States, and cherished the views peculiar to the South.

They believed as their party believed, and small forbearance had they for any one who uttered to-day what the party would not utter until to-morrow. Next to being an Abolitionist, was the effrontery of believing anything until the party believed it, unless he was in Congress or had owned a "nigger." It was all the force of habit, and an endless diversion.

The Republicans were few but conspicuous. Andrew Miller, H. H. Hood, D. C. Amsden, W. S. Palmer and H. H. Beach could not be overlooked in any community. They held caucuses, voted a straight ticket, and were uniformly beaten. Mr. Miller was suspected of being a train dispatcher on the Underground Railroad. Dr. Hood alone was an Abolitionist, and it was no festive thing to be an Abolitionist where one of your neighbors had been one of the hunters of fugitive slaves—for the lowest motive men dare to acknowledge, and which if good, will even [illegible] Arnold's meditated betrayal of West Point. Politics or self love had no little to do with a

* By H. A. [illegible]

condition of things which ultimately was no disadvantage. For twenty years the town had only forlorn friends beyond its own limits. There was a unanimous discrimination against its citizens in business and matters political, and for a quarter of a century, though Litchfield contained one fifth the population, it saw but one of its citizens elevated to a county office. The public consequence was that no one here was spoiled or made a bench loafer by seeking or holding an office.

In April, 1857, was begun the publication of the Litchfield *Journal*. The office was brought hither from Central New York, on representations and assurances which were coolly repudiated when they had served their purpose. The paper had a small circulation and little other patronage. The publisher did not grow quickly rich, and seven years afterward he sold out and turned his attention to other things. He was so poor that no one would give him credit. He thus kept out of debt, though his subscribers did not, and the statute of limitation long since restored his books to white paper, or something even less valuable.

The spring of 1858 was phenomenal for mud and bad roads. Even good intentions will not pave a prairie road in March. The cars ran ricocheting along the iron rails, and the rain fell dense day after day. Farm work was delayed. In January the highways were hard and dusty, and many a plow was stirring. The frostless nights ushered in delicious days, and winter was side-tracked up North. February brought a change, and it was long ere we saw hard ground or a clear or warm day. Not a few improved the weather by falling ill, and potion glasses were a relief from the drip and mud. We learned in the schools which books patronize the mysteries of a Western winter. During the summer the car shop and the paint shop were built, the Montgomery House enlarged, and the railroad continued its monthly issues of scrip in jocular payment of its employes. The Linder Brothers gave up business; Cummings & Son failed to meet their engagements; Henderson, Hull and Hawkins were embarrassed, and E. E. Litchfield owed more than he could pay. E. W. Litchfield built Empire Hall, and a brass band was formed. Our sorrows came not alone, but in battalions.

Senator Douglas, whose official term was about to expire, was a candidate for re-election. A chasm had opened between him and his party. Illinois had gone Republican at the State election two years before, and he could hope for no aid from the National Administration, and had grounds for anticipating its hostility, whether covert or open. On the Legislature to be chosen in the fall depended his hopes, and if he would not fail, he deemed it essential that he should make a popular canvass. The central counties were the debatable region, and on their political complexion rested the prospect of success. Mr. Lincoln, the Republican candidate opposed to him, gained the initiative before his return from Washington. And soon after Douglas began his popular efforts, the terms of the famous forensic contest between them were settled. Their joint debate reduced to the plainness of axioms the pending issues in the irrepressible conflict. Trumbull also entered the canvass, and in an address at Chicago, spoke of cramming the lie down Douglas' throat. Douglas' readiness and anxiety to meet his accuser on the hustings for a reply to this insult was well understood. The day that Trumbull spoke here, Douglas had an appointment at Gillespie. John M. Palmer was announced to follow Trumbull in the evening, from the Republican stand at the southwest corner of the public square. Several Democrats visited Gillespie to invite

Douglas here to speak in the evening. A rude stand was improvised against the north side of Empire Hall, where there was an open space about fifty feet by one hundred, thickly strewn with brick bats. Douglas came, and proclamation was made that he would speak. When the hour came no one was at the Republican stand, and several hundred persons were at the other one. Trumbull was not in the crowd, but a few rods away, where he could hear. Douglas knowing this, replied to the boast made in Chicago: his remarks were not reported, but it would be a charity to pretend that his language was parliamentary. It was vigorous, and uttered with a fiery vehemence and passion which manifested its earnestness. When he concluded, the Democrats shouted for Dick Merrick, who accompanied Douglas. The Republicans yelled for Palmer. The former claimed the stand; the latter clamored for fair play. They wanted Douglas to draw a crowd for their side. The shouting went on. If there was a lull, it was only to take breath. The brick bats were suggestive. Some of the people laughed at the confusion, and some grew red in the face with anger or excitement. Finally, Judge Weir mounted the stand, and in a few sentences brought the meeting to a close. The Republicans admitted the provocation under which Douglas spoke, and the boisterous display of feeling when he sat down, led to no serious results. A few days later was election, and the total vote of the Litchfield Precinct and the 359 majority for the Douglas candidates for the Legislature, were so unexpected that the legality of the vote was questioned at Springfield in an unofficial way, and the suspicion was removed only by the aggregate of the city election the following spring. During the year the removal of John P. Bayless, Postmaster, was attempted on a charge of virtual Abolitionism. Had the allegation been sustained, his official sin would have been unpardonable. He was invited to reply to the charge, which he accomplished to the satisfaction of the Department, and he was not again molested in his office until Lincoln was seated in the White House.

The village organization had been dissolved, and in November a special charter was drafted, for presentation to the Legislature about to convene for the incorporation of the town as city. At a series of public meetings this draft was submitted to the citizens, and, being approved, B. M. Munn went to the capital to urge its passage. On the 19th of February, 1859, it became a law, and at the first election under it, in April, W. E. Bacon was chosen Mayor, and C. W. Ward City Clerk and James Kellogg Street Commissioner. The next year Mr. Bacon was re-elected.

The new city had an onerous task. An entire code of ordinances was to be framed and adopted, and public opinion to be educated to the knowledge and obedience to wholesome municipal regulations. The Council served with no compensation. The City Clerk received $50 a year; all other officers accepted their fees in full of salaries and sidewalks were laid at the expense of real estate thus improved. The first year a tax of $2 200 was levied for schools and municipal purposes, and at the close of the year the Treasury contained a few hundred dollars to the credit of the next twelve months.

The first stage of the transition period had been reached. The business fever of the day when people were daily arriving with their little accumulations to buy or build homes, was passing, and the hope of the people lay in their daily wages and employments here. Corn in the fall of 1859 sold at 10 cents a bushel, and the railroad continued its payment of "scrip," which was worthless in the city market. Debt was universal; but as frost pulverizes the earth for a future crop, so adversity prepared the people for a sounder prosperity. The class of adventurers, the Jeremy Diddlers, was weeded out. The men who could not pay and would not work, drifted to other places.

A telegraph line had been built, and George H. Smith appointed operator. An effort to secure the location of the County Fair was unsuccessful, through a dishonesty not to be extenuated. The commercial influence of the town was rapidly fostering political importance. A big Democratic majority in Litchfield was something bound to be respected, especially as the party was run by men who three years before were Henry Clay Whigs, and a fervent class not to be moderate in views or zeal.

In 1859, E. Southworth, wearied of failure to gain a livelihood on a farm where some calamity robbed him each year of the expected fruits of his labor, and judging the future by the past, came to the city to become a lawyer. He had crossed the plains on foot to be a miner in California; had taught school and tried farming. Here he read law fifteen hours a day. He preserved the honesty of common life, and circumstances bowed down to his energy. He was an officer at the beginning of the war; has served as Alderman and Mayor, and been State Senator. He rose to the leading position at the city bar, and looks for promotion.

William A. Holmes, formerly of Morrisville, N. Y., but later of Platteville, Wis., came here about the same date, in the vain hope that the milder climate of Central Illinois would stay, if not heal, the pulmonary disease of his invalid wife. A man of social tastes, of warm [illegible]ality, and ardent affections, he never rallied after her death a year after his arrival. For a time he sought legal business, but though a dozen years before distinguished by forensic ability, he shunned the court room and became distinctively an office lawyer, and confined himself to the preparation of court business. In the suspension of litigation which accompanied the war, he failed to improve his fortunes, and sought to dispel the gloom in which his days were shrouded by irregular indulgences. He died on that terrible New Year's day of 1864, in the absence of the early friend who alone here knew the secret of his earlier life, and had been glad and proud of his friendship. By temperament born to suffer, and in his pride strong to keep silence, he lost no friend and made no enemy.

Messrs. D. and O. Quick came here in 1860, and remained but a few months. They did not distinguish themselves at the bar. Litigation was of the simpler kind and afforded but small opportunity for lawyers. Hugh Colton, a young Irishman, needed toning down. He was impulsive, and had not learned that an orator at the bar succeeds quite as surely by being a profound lawyer as by his rhetoric. His stay here was not a long one.

George L. Zink passed from a lawyer's office in Steubenville, Ohio, to a pedagogue's chair in Gillespie, and in 1865, came here to begin the practice of his profession, bringing his political principles from the sanguinary field of Perryville. He had the legal cast of mind, was a hard student and a forcible speaker. When he became associated with R. McWilliams, he entered at once on a lucrative practice. Subsequently, he was a member of the legal firm of Southworth & Zink, and on its dissolution opened an office in his own rooms. In 1868, he was a delegate to the Republican National Convention, and four years later went into the Greeley party, and in 1878 was sent by the Democrats to the Legislature.

Robert McWilliams flitted from Shelbyville to Hillsboro, when J. M. Davis was most intolerant of the presence of a second lawyer in the county. Whether from constitution or abstemiousness, the plan of drinking him out of the county was a failure, and McWilliams had clients and success in the courts. He was a Republican, and the time came when he re-enforced his exhortations by enlisting and raising a company and going into the field. At his own request, he was relieved from service just prior to the battle of Nashville; but his Irish temperament would not let him come home until he fought through that decisive affair. About 1866, he removed to Litchfield, and asserted himself at the bar, in real estate operations and politics. He has just closed a term as a member of the Legislature, and the charity of the reader will not deem this much of a stain on a lawyer. Somebody must go to the Legislature and be misreported.

George A. Talley, who completed his legal studies in McWilliams' office, and on his admission to the bar became his partner, remained a few years, and then removed to Chicago. Though young in his profession, he had earned a high reputation for honesty and thoroughness. He had the aptitude of a student. He learned to know before deciding or giving opinions. He knew the law that others knew, and much that they did not. He cherished an honest judgment, and his departure was sincerely regretted.

There is an inevitable meanness in every grand event, and homeliness of detail in each heroic life which time does not wholly erase. We go a thousand miles away to get the mountain's height, and we are too near the men and things of which we write. The present tense is the fit one for our task. A fine ear would still detect the echoes of the first hammer strokes in the town. The writer was a part of what he writes, and as the sentences grow, the events return in their freshness, and he is moved by his recollections as he was moved by the events themselves, and he cannot compose a history of the city on perspective, and, like a Chinese draughtsman, leave the background and shadow out. Any one can be wise for yesterday, for he has results to guide his judgment. But Litchfield scarcely has a yesterday. Its history still retains the morning freshness of to-day. The incidents of its first years are as freely canvassed as those of the present. Each feeling and prejudice has been nursed to keep it warm.

Dr. Gamble was the first physician. He dwelt in a log cabin half floored, a couple of blocks west of the Methodist Church, and left but a faint record. H. H. Hood transferred his office from Hardinsburg to Litchfield in the summer of 1854. A man of decided opinions, active, persistent and inflexible, he is familiarly known to all. Dr. John Grinsted came in 1856, from Woodburn, and, opening a drug store, practiced as a physician until advancing years compelled his retirement. In 1857, Drs. Strafford and Speers located here from St. Louis. Speers sojourned but a short time, but Dr. Stafford, much reduced in health, remains here. He never gained the position to which, by his skill, he might properly have aspired. Dr. Ash was here a year or two, but the field was too unpromising, and he removed to Brighton. Dr. John Skillman, from Alton, sought employment here, and then returned to Alton, but came back to die. His history is comprised in his Alton life.

Dr. R. F. Bennett located here in 1862, and has gained a large practice, and possesses a modest fortune. He has been twice Mayor, and twice an Alderman. Of Dr. Neff it is proper to say that he is better remembered for his financial transactions than for his professional successes. Dr. Colt, forced by the failure of his health from service in the gunboat fleet, came here in 1863, and has reached an enviable rank in his profession. He loves the science of medicine, and the rod and gun, when he can steal a day with them. Dr. Backwelder went with Sherman to the sea, and finally settled here, and has a large list of patients Dr. Clearwater was for many years the country physician. His practice was enormous, and his fees would have been large had he exacted them. His reputation is built on his success in healing his patients. Dr. James, after serving in Price's army, came here. He lost his health, tried farming, and went to Virginia to die, but regained his health, and now attends to professional duties. Dr. Leach was the first homeopathist, and since his removal, ten or twelve years ago, has not been seen here.

Early in the "sixties," Ben Davis, the "snapping doctor,"made semi-monthly visits. His audience room in the Cummings Building contained several backless benches, on which were seated a score or two of patients, as grave and silent and patient as "mourners" at a religious assembly. Davis circulated about the apartment, snapping his fingers like castanets, and professing to heal diseases by occult magnetic influences imparted from himself. The cures did not follow. His visits have been nearly forgotten, and the burly Ben is dimly remembered.

Only by an effort can the names of several other physicians who tarried here be recalled.

In the long, honorable list but three names have fallen to the ground. Drs. Alexander, Skillman and Grinsted have died. It is the best evidence of their worth and skill that, with the increase of population, the bills of mortality in 1881 were but little larger than in 1857, with only one-eighth of the present population.

In 1860, Litchfield was a microcosm. Not a speech at Washington, not an editorial by Greeley or Medary, or an utterance of the Charleston *Courier*, which was not re-echoed here. Not a general interest could be touched and not affect some business here. Politics was a study for each one. Supreme attention was paid to the presidential canvass, and there was much whistling to keep up a show of courage and hopefulness. Lincoln was elected, and the outlook was toward clouds and darkness. All classes here desired peace, and petitioned for the passage of the Crittenden resolutions.

For some reason as inscrutable as a prize conundrum, a delegate Democratic State Convention was called to meet at Springfield to deliberate on public affairs and offer suggestions. A county convention was accordingly held to appoint delegates. The writer drafted and presented resolutions to the effect that as the Republicans already were in power in the State, and were about to go into power in the nation, and, therefore, would be responsible for the administration of public affairs, it would be time enough for Democrats to give advice when it was asked for; as the Democratic party when in power had not averted the present danger, it was not clear how any advice they could give would now meet it; and hence the county should send no delegates to the proposed State Convention. Every member save Jesse M. Phillips and B. M. Munn, was in favor of peace and a peaceful policy. Those two gentlemen breathed war and battle. The resolutions were adopted and fully met the views of the people —a fact whose significance became apparent within a few years.

The Peace Congress was held, and accomplished nothing it was convened to accomplish, and much that was not anticipated. Wrongs it might have redressed, but it could not change the fixed purpose of the South, which, by dividing the party, had caused the election of Lincoln, and then plead the consequences of its own act as a pretext for the consummation of a policy pursued for years. The Southern members of that Congress did not seek means of pacification. Their solicitude was to learn if the Yankees would fight. The answer covered more than the question. We quote the verbal version of it, as told by a member of the body:

"If, on a summer morning, in the season, you visit the wharf of any of the little seaports near Boston, you will see many little undecked boats newly arrived from the fishing-ground with their night's catch. The owners are marine farmers. They gain their livelihood by fishing. The sea and their boats are their patrimony. Enter into conversation with the fisherman who is tossing his catch on the wharf. Dispute his assertions; call him a liar. 'Mister, I can prove what I say.' Spit in his face, and, as he wipes off the saliva with his brown arm, he will reply: 'Mister, look out!' Abuse his State, and 'Mister, my State supplies your shoes, your clothes and your markets.' You cannot anger him or provoke him to a breach of the peace. You conclude he has no spirit. But touch one of his fish, and in a moment he'll thrash you within an inch of your life." The Southerner stood on the principle of personal honor, a shadowy thing, while the Northerner stood by the rights of property.

The one was a chimera; the other is the foundation of States and the Ægis of civilization. The news of the attack and capture of Fort Sumter was known here dimly on Sunday afternoon. The next morning the daily papers brought the details, and the humiliation of the policy which would not believe or act. A call was at once made for a public meeting in the evening. Empire Hall was packed, and R. W. O'Bannon presided. Several brief, pointed speeches were made. The sentiment was that as war had actually begun, force must be met with force, National supremacy be maintained, National property protected, and the Union preserved. The hour for debate had gone by. Action was the alternative, and forty persons that evening enlisted to tender their services to the General Government. In two days more the ranks were filled, and on the third day the company departed for Camp Yates, at Springfield, to be mustered into service in the first regiment raised in the war.

By association and early residence, this region was friendly to the South. But her conduct startled the people to a comparison of the claims of duty against the glamour of sentiment. Everybody lost his feet, and bowed to the whirlwind of feeling in behalf of the Union. At a later day, a lower set of principles came into prominence, and men gave to party what belonged to the country.

The history of the city during the war belongs in part to a distinct chapter. But as the value of slavery as a preponderating sectional issue flung off disguises which misled no one who did not wish to be misled, and its disappearance, by changing public policy, consigned a proud party to disaster and a minimum of influence, a changed attitude was assumed by not a few. A lodge of the Golden Circle met in the city. Men met by moonlight for military drill. Speeches were made on the main streets, exhorting the people to resist the draft. Men left the station for Ohio to vote for Vallandigham. Others departed for Chicago to co-operate in St. Leger's conspiracy to capture Camp Douglass. Refugees from Slave States led furtive lives here, and used a freedom of speech not permitted at home. The war was denounced, because in camp the "Democrat boys" became

Republicans. Both the Democratic papers in the county were conducted by war-Democrats, and the elements of hostility to the war lacked coherence for want of leadership and public expression. About this time one B. F. Burnett came to town to gain a livelihood by soliciting legal business. His success as a lawyer was not great, but he prated dolorously of the misery of war, the sorrow it brought to uncounted families, and the blessings of peace. He knew some law, and might have been a reputable citizen if he had not. He became a nucleus for disloyal manifestations —a fit office for a loose-tongued scoundrel. Secret organization provoked a rival organization, and in the spring of 1863, a Union League Lodge was established here, meeting in the engine house of the car shops. The League decided to seek control of the city government, and all the measures were quietly made. A messenger was sent on Sunday to Alton to procure ballots, and the printer was taken from church to provide them. The messenger could not return until nearly noon of election day. The Democrats were ignorant of what was devised, and only themselves attended the polls, and few ballots were offered. The Republicans seemed to have lost their interest in civil affairs. The train came in from the west, and with electric quickness the ballots were distributed, and by evening were in the ballot boxes. The result indicated that about half of them had been deposited by former Democrats, and the League ticket had a tremendous majority. The Democrats were dumb with amazement, and the Leaguers, delighted by their success, celebrated the result in a manner which left headaches the next morning. The astounding change in public sentiment was not fruitless. Numerous volunteer associations arose to aid the Sanitary Commission, and in various ways to remember the boys in blue. But here, as in all popular effervescences, the worst elements came uppermost. Efforts were made to hurry the League into measures to gratify personal malignancy, and they were promptly discountenanced and their authors vanished. Rumor magnified the strength and purposes of the League. About the county, measures were concerted for forcible resistance to a draft. A military organization was maintained for the purpose. But it was known that boxes of Ballard rifles had been procured by the Leaguers to preserve the peace and the supremacy of the law. Bounty-jumpers skulked along the streets.

An emissary of the Golden Circle paid a visit to a Leaguer who was his personal friend. He said that he had heard that 5,000 stand of arms were in Litchfield. His friend gave an ambiguous assent. He exhibited to him a Ballard rifle as a sample of half the weapons, and then producing a Henry rifle, or a sixteen shooter, affirmed the second half of the arms were of that pattern. What report was made to the Circle has not been made public, but there was no longer danger that Litchfield would be molested, or the draft resisted.

The town was startled by fires, clearly the result of gross carelessness or incendiarism, and there was a disposition to connect them with political troubles. That pretence was speedily abandoned The disappearance of specie as a circulating medium, the depreciation of greenbacks, and the augmentation of the paper currency, inflamed prices and the city rushed into public improvements. Taxes went up like a rocket. A city hall was built a schoolhouse was built, and the money was in good part borrowed at 15 per cent. The city was drunk on the excellence of its credit. Population rose to 4,300; wheat was $3.50, and corn 95 cents a bushel; sugar, four pounds for $1; muslin, 40 cents a yard, and flour $19 per barrel. Those were good times, but they did not last. The people went wild on railroads. The sum of $50,000 was voted to the stock of a railroad west to Louisiana, Mo.; the same amount to the St. Louis division of the Wabash, and $75,000 to the Springfield & St. Louis road. Fortunately, only the second one was built, and the other subscriptions lapsed. The town gradually adapted itself to the changed conditions prevailing since the war. Population had fallen off, the decadence of prices was established, and the Granger element was about to begin its by-play.

The removal of the railroad shops was completed in 1871, and the leading market for labor was closed. The spacious shops stood silent and tenantless. The city's opportunity had come; difficulty was but a goad to spur it on. Several parties here organized a company to lease the shops for the manufacture of rolling-stock for railways. The stock was eagerly taken, and in 1872 the fires were lighted and the machinery set in motion. The new enterprise soon disclosed that it would do more for the city than railroad shops had done. But within two years a series of fires, not all accidental, perhaps, had raged on State street. The schoolhouse, the pride of the community, had gone down in flame and ruin, and now a conflagration burst forth in the car works. Fortunately, most of the works were saved, but the loss of property and time was still serious. The town was brought face to face with the imperative want of water for industrial and fire purposes.

It is proper to be specific by way of recapitulation. In April, 1867, a fire kindled in the rear of the hardware store near the southwest angle of the public square, had humbled to ashes three stores and most of their contents, bringing financial ruin to two of the owners, and causing a total loss of $25,000. Fires mysteriously appeared in the rear of other business houses, and were discovered in season to avoid damage. In the fall of 1871, the alarm of fire again startled the town. A crown of flame rested on the *Journal* building, and the rear rooms glowed with the yellow radiance of a fire fed by dry pine. Five buildings crumbled to blackness in a couple of hours, and the losses were not light to bear. A year or two later, fire bells summoned the people to witness the conflagration of six business places, from the O'Bannon corner north on State street. The Criterion Mill, in the early morning, went down in smoke and flame, and the Gage Mill on a Sunday afternoon lay under a pillar of smoke. Pale flames traveled through the interior. The blaze broke white through the roof, and for a few moments the people forgot the disaster in the presence of the magnificent spectacle. In 1873, the car works had their baptism of fire. Brick walls and earnest labor checked the flames when their fury was but half glutted. All these fires, most of them compressed into two years, had touched only individuals, and any philosopher can maintain his equanimity in the presence of his neighbor's calamity. The vagueness of each one's personal interest in the general welfare, and it is only personal interest which moves the common mind, provoked only unsubstantial regrets. The losses did not directly touch the purses of the many. In whatever the public undertakes, it is seldom indifferent to its own advantage. It was so in Litchfield. But this complacency at the prevalence of fires was rudely shattered. The spacious schoolhouse, overlooking the city, and in its designs and proportions as beautiful as a poem, was the pride and the object of the personal affection of every citizen. For several days the teachers and their 800 pupils had been choking with the acrid odor of smouldering wood. Like a gangrene, the perfume clung to the rooms. No smoke was seen, no fire discovered. A superficial survey detected no cause for the poison which had insinuated itself throughout the building. It was a Monday evening, about 6:30. A young married woman lay dying in the neighborhood. A lambent flame was seen quivering on the roof near the south chimney. Black smoke crowned the summit. Pale tongues of fire lapped at the woodwork. All the city rushed to the school grounds. The house burned like a flambeau. Nothing could be done to stop its destruction, and the people stood in speechless sorrow and saw the fire crawl downward from floor to floor, and expire in the cellar for want of fuel. Each one knew the fire brought financial loss to him, and that with proper water-works $40,000 would have been saved the city.

The frequent recurring fires, and the extent of the losses, gave emphasis to a desire for protection from further losses of a similar character. Protection was better and cheaper than insurance. There was forced or hurried eagerness to meet this general demand. Various schemes were considered. The cost of providing cisterns and a fire engine was computed, and the annual outlay of the system was found to be 10 per cent on the cost of a different system which would afford greater protection, and in addition produce a revenue from its value to shops, mills and households. In 18[illegible]5, the car works brought water here by railroad. Best & Sparks paid $1,000 to teams to draw water four miles to their mill. The desirability of a water supply was not questioned, and there was a unanimous desire to fling a strong dike across Long Branch, a mile south of the city, and from the capacious reservoir thus created, send water into the heart of the town, under conditions which would meet our varied requirements.

The sort of works demanded was in substance the Holly system, or the system of direct pressure on the mains equal to the maintenance of a column of water 400 feet high, and through 100 feet of hose would project a stream upward of 100 feet into the air. Estimates of the cost of such a system were made to include only the dike, the mains and the pumping machinery, and this estimate was promulgated as a fair statement by experts of the cost of the water-works. We make no excuse for the error in simple multiplication, which affected the cost of the dike 100 per cent. We have no comment on the suppression in the exhibit submitted to the citizens of numerous expensive items of cost, which, in the aggregate, were truly formidable. The facts speak for themselves. A few citizens knew the water-works could not be built within $25,000 of the explained estimates, and their voices were overruled and they reduced to silence. They would, at the proper hour, have appealed to the courts to prohibit the issue of bonds by alleging a want of power to legalize them. They could not be blind to the mendacity or want of rudimentary capacity to make simple calculations on the part of those who held that it was none of the tax payers' business how they run things. Again, it was a matter of law against expediency, as if it can be expedient to do wrong.

People are easily deceived when they want to be deceived. There was no uncertainty as to the value of water-works, none as to the ability of the city to build them, but there was a broad, explicit prohibition of law against going into debt beyond 5 per cent of the last assessed valuation of property, and our municipal debt was at that time within $12,000 of that limit. But the debt was in great part nominal, and not virtual. Since the completion of the Wabash road, in aid of which the debt was created, the assessed valuation of property had increased $800,000, and by the Railroad Aid Law, the State taxes on that amount were appropriated to paying the debt. This tax met annual interest, and left an excess of several thousand dollars as a sinking fund which would quite extinguish the principal at maturity. It was this law which alone induced the city to issue $50,000 in bonds to secure the road. The bonds were against the city, but the State agreed to pay them. This debt then was treated as virtually canceled, and taking this view, and listening to the vehement assurances of men in power that the water-works completed could not cost more than $42,000, or by adopting the higher plan, $55,000, and there was no intention of doing this, the citizens in various ways expressed their enthusiastic approval of the project at an extreme cost of $45,000.

This was the plan approved by the community, under the knowledge that the operation of the Railroad Aid Law released them from liability for the bonds granted to a railroad.

True, in letter, they were bound; but in fact, the debt was to be paid not at their charges. But when, after expending nearly $20,000 on the ground dike and facing walls, the authorities ordered the preparation of bonds for $50,000 additional, framed so as to give full effect to the legal inhibition against their issue, and so as to give the city ground to contest their payment, because issued in violation of law; and the omission in the recital which was to do this was passed over in silence — the thing became too flagrant. Yet at home complaints came too late. Nothing could be done to stop the authorities, and soon there was a wide suspicion that private objects were sought under guise of zeal for public ends. The works were completed by contract, and as well and economically as the public is usually served by contractors. The work was done when labor and material were one-fourth dearer than two or three years later, when by comparison with the reduced prices, men, having their own aggrandizement only in view, bellowed about the town vague accusations of fraud and veritable peculation.

Not one of these fellows could be induced to make and stand to a single specific charge. They proved their statement by numberless repetitions —a sort of evidence better for a certain class than positive proof.

The works cost $77,000 against the $45,000 they were to have been built for. But they stand, and have not in eight years failed in their duty for an hour. They are worth all they cost, and more, and the clamor about them which had no higher origin than a personal difference about matters disconnected with public affairs, would have died away had it not been kept alive by the city's repudiation of her bonds. Noisy advocates for the works refused to pay taxes to meet any part of the indebtedness, and the Council, by resolution, refused the payment of interest. Suit was instituted, and in the court of last resort a decision was obtained that the issue of the bonds was illegal. The vast majority of the citizens desire their payment, and the decision defeats their wishes.

This narrative of our shame had not been written or been true, had not the opinion crept into officers that their delegated powers were a franchise to be exercised according to their caprice. They forgot their representative position, and spurned conference or opinions from a tax payer. They never forgot self, and no offense was so great as the assertion that the people had any rights not vested in them.

In 1870, the population had fallen below three thousand seven hundred. The variance in population is the exact criterion of the industries of the town. In 1880, the total was reported at 4,343, and this was known to be too small. In 1881, the Jacksonville road had been extended to the city, a second coal shaft had been opened, oil had been found, the Planet Mill was in course of construction, the car works were over-crowded with work, and 100 buildings were erected, as the population had risen to 5,250, and the city had again rehearsed the old lesson that the people are the city, and that their future would be what they willed it to be.

CHAPTER XV.

LITCHFIELD—EDUCATIONAL HISTORY—THE CITY SCHOOLS—GRAMMAR SCHOOLS—BOARDS, PRINCIPALS, TEACHERS, ETC.—THE PRESS—ESTABLISHMENT OF THE "JOURNAL"—THE "MONITOR" AND OTHER PAPERS—BANKS AND BANKING—COAL INTERESTS OF LITCHFIELD—THE DIFFERENT SHAFTS AND THEIR EXTENT AND CAPACITY—THE SANITARY CONDITION OF THE CITY.

A SCHOOL fails in its office if its educational value to its pupils is not greater than the wages paid its teacher. If it be true, as the wise affirm, that education is the awakening of the mind to think and reason correctly, rapidly and persistently, to improve the heart and enlarge the understanding, the office of a school has specific limitations. All its instruction should be subordinate to education. Whatever be the amount of knowledge imparted in scholastic studies, it is true that the only positive instruction obtained in a school, which, under all circumstances is available and used precisely as it was learned, is reading and the multiplication table. The lumber of text-book rules becomes in actual life dry and pithless. They teach only to swim on dry land. The man needs the result of scholastic training; the processes are but as the scaffolding to a builder. At last education makes a man more valuable to his community than to himself.

The city north of the railroad was included in School District No. 1, of North Litchfield; the territory south of it belonged to the Crabtree District, in South Litchfield, whose schoolhouse stood a few rods south of the residence of Samuel Stratton. District No. 1 used the Lutheran Church, near the southeast corner of Scherer's Addition, for a schoolroom, and here B. S. Hood, of Jerseyville, taught a school for six months, in the summer of 1854. Lusk Wilson taught there—a winter term in 1854-55 and a summer term of 1855. The Cummings building was erected in 1856, and the west half of the second floor was the schoolroom for several years, and H. A. Wells opened there the winter term of 1856-57. He continued in charge of the public school until 1860. Julia Palmer was first assistant in the Scott & Long building, then standing on the north side of Division street, a few yards east of Jackson. Hannah Skillman was the second assistant in the house two or three doors below the store of Thorp & Leach. For a term of six months. Mr. Wells received $360 and his assistants each $200. This was the first school of the Litchfield School District, created by the city charter, the Council exercising the combined powers of Trustees and Directors.

In the summer of 1860, Mr. Wells suddenly disappeared, leaving his bills uncollected and his few debts unpaid. The next year, he as suddenly re-appeared. In explanation of his flight, he professed forgetfulness of his departure. His life was a blank to him. He had a lucid moment at Niagara Falls and was astonished to find himself there; then he again became unconscious of his movements for an unknown period. When reason returned

*By H. A. Coolidge.

to him, he was in mid-ocean on a vessel bound to England. Friends told him that he sought their party at the Falls; he journeyed with them to Quebec, and when they said they were going to England, he declared that he, too, would go. He was transferred to a homeward bound ship, and came to America. Of his wanderings for a year after he landed on native soil, he gave no clear account. He arrived here in the fall of 1862, coming from the West. He said he had just been discharged from military service. His subsequent conduct throws much doubt on his version of the history of his flight.

In the fall of 1860, the grammar school was opened with two departments. Samuel Taylor, of Terre Haute, was elected Principal, and Sarah G. Perrot, assistant; the three ward schools were conducted by Hannah Skillman, Julia P. Palmer and Mary Gillham. The schools were notoriously insufficient for the instruction of the children in the city. This fact was very widely regretted, and the schools were not distinguished for educational value.

The Litchfield School District had vainly tried to obtain possession of the avails of the levy made in 1857, by District No. 1, to build a schoolhouse on the northwest corner of Block 68, where L. Settlemire's residence stands, the site having been given by E. B. Litchfield for that purpose. The Litchfield School District contained nearly 95 per cent of the property of the present district, and the holder of the school funds—not the Township Treasurer—declined to recognize the legality of the claim. An act of the Legislature was obtained on the joint request of all parties apportioning that building fund to the City School District and District No. 1, in proportion to the amount raised by each, and, after some delay, the parties who had borrowed it liquidated their indebtedness, and the city district used its share to support its schools.

For 1861-62—and the public schools were maintained only six months in the year, the summer schools being private ones — the wages of the Principal were fixed at $45 per month, while his four assistants were allowed $27. George C. Mack was chosen Principal and Mrs. Abby Paxton, now Mrs. H. H. Hood, was his assistant, and two teachers in each ward school. All applicants for positions in the schools were specially examined by Prof. Miller, of Hillsboro, at the request of the School Board, and it was thought Litchfield school officers were becoming particular when the certificate of the County Superintendent was not a sufficient guarantee of pedagogical qualifications. But the board was not content with the learn-as-you-please style of teaching.

Mrs. Paden declining her appointment, Mrs. Stevenson was elected to fill the vacancy. The disbursements during this school year were $1,863.76, which included $780.24 for seats, repairs and payments on grammar school building, and the liabilities amounted to $2,097.71, chiefly for teachers and balance due on house and loans from the general fund. The fiscal statements were made up in March of each year, before the close of the schools and before the receipt of the school tax or the State fund.

For 1862-63, Mr. Mack was again employed as Principal. Miss J. N. Lauder was his assistant and five teachers were employed for the three ward schools: two of the five were termed assistant teachers, and their wages were fixed at $15 per month. Mr. Mack did not complete his term and a Mr. Morrison was appointed in his place. Miss Lauder appears not to have accepted her appointment, as Mrs. Stevenson's name is borne on the rolls as assistant in the grammar school. The disbursement from the school treasury for the year, for school purposes, was $1,622.41, and $511.50 were drawn from it and expended on the streets, and the district liabilities were $2,028.61. Probably the School Board believed the money would do more good on the streets than on schools. Like matrimony, the schools were accepted "for better or worse," and if it was illegal to use school funds to improve streets, no one objected to it.

For 1863-64, eight teachers were employed in the four schools. P. H. Pope, Principal, and Miss Hyde, his assistant. The expenditures were $1,470; liabilities, $1,493, and the treasury showed a balance in its favor of $2,078.24.

The following year, the grammar school was closed and two teachers were placed in each of the three ward schools. Among these were Blanche Keating, now Mrs. D. Davis; Mrs. Elizabeth Burton, now Mrs. G. P. Hanks; Miss Kate Hyde, and Julia P. Palmer, now Mrs. George Stevens, of Jacksonville. The expenditure amounted to $1,547.97; the liabilities were $14.35 and the balance on hand, $591.60. When the average man buys a piano, another farm, or goes to the White Mountains, he finds it necessary to "retrench" by having school only half the time and cutting down teachers' wages.

By the summer of 1865, the population of the city had, from temporary causes, risen to 4,300, money was abundant and the city had no debt. The time had arrived to place the schools on a higher plane. The School Board informally decided to erect a house for a graded school large enough for the present and prospective wants of the district. By several purchases from B. H. Hargraves, Wilder W. Davis and Ahart Pierce, an entire block was obtained on the west slope of Pierce's mound, on which to built the schoolhouse, at a contemplated cost of $15,000, though a proper house should be built even if it cost a third more. In July of this year, Messrs D. R. Sparks, Thomas G. Kessinger and W. S. Palmer, of the School Board, were appointed a committee to select a plan and estimate of the cost of the desired house, for the consideration of the Board and definite action. The committee chose the design prepared by George P. Randall, of Chicago; the board confirmed their selection and the contract was given to W. F. Bushnell, of Mendota, for the building above the stone basement, at the outside figure of $28,000. His contract was $5,500 higher than the architect's estimate, yet did not include seating or heating apparatus.

In September, 1865, six teachers were employed for the three ward schools, half of them at $35 per month and half at $30. The grammar school building did fairly well for the Second Ward, but the other houses were tolerated only for the reason that no better ones could be leased. Not much was expected, and the public expectation was not disappointed.

The expenditures for this fiscal year were $4,526.90, and $1,992.02 were, in effect, loaned to defray the expenses of the city government. Nearly half the disbursements for school objects was applied on the new schoolhouse. The increase of taxation was to meet the demands of the contractor.

In March, 1867, Mr. Bushnell was at his request released from his contract, as it was evident that he could not fulfill it. An expert was employed to examine the work up to date, and his report confirmed the opinion that in all respects it was satisfactory. During the spring and summer, the house was completed and furnished under the direct orders of the board, the price of labor and material being something frightful; the cost of the property was swelled to $48,000; a large debt was incurred, bearing usurious interest.

The School Board containing such men as D. C. Amsden, D. R. Sparks, John L. Hinkley and S. M. Keithly and David Davis, proposed that a new era should dawn on the city with the opening of the graded school. Much anxiety was manifested to secure an accomplished and efficient Principal. Confidential inquiries were made, and Mr. A. J. Blanchard, of the Sycamore Graded School was unanimously selected, at a salary of $1,500 for a term of forty weeks, and he was requested to select his assistants, with a view of securing harmony in the corps of instruction and a fair trial of his system in school. Mr. Blanchard, a man tall, well proportioned, muscular, in the meridian of life and of great intensity of character, began his preparation of re-organizing the school, by approving the selection of such teachers as Misses Fanny E. Tower, Kimberly, Dustin, Lauder, Lyon and Mrs. Abby Paden and Hull. The house he was about to enter was a three-story brick edifice, heated by furnaces and seated in the best manner. The twelve rooms had a seating capacity for 800 pupils. New text-books had been adopted. Six of his eleven assistants were from abroad, and, at the close of the winter session, no more than two home teachers remained in the school. New rules of government and new modes of instruction were introduced, and the teachers had good wages and they earned them. There was a tremendous amount of application to study, and, for the first time in our school history the capacity of the pupil was not underestimated, nor his comprehension of former studies exaggerated. The Principal put double energy and industry into the school, and sought only the educational welfare of his pupils. He made it his chief business to see that each teacher did her utmost for the true benefit of those under her charge. He believed in good teaching; he believed equally well in good study. He handled young men as other teachers handle children: he subjugated the vicious and willful; stimulated the languid and idle; punished the insubordinate and controlled the mischievous.

Of course, this could not be done without raising issues, which, though not forgotten, it is not wise to revive. Mr. Blanchard thought to maintain himself by success in the schoolroom alone. He failed just as others have who relied on the same merit. Outside dissatisfaction, by the close of the winter term, had grown until it was in doubt whether the school must not be closed. At the decisive moment, a county teachers' institute was held in the house, and several of the teachers consented to illustrate the methods of study and teaching pursued in the school by having their classes recite in the presence of the institute. The examples exemplified how lessons were learned and how recited, and the result of the double process, as shown by the rapid advancement of their pupils. The spectators, and among them were not a few of the opinion-makers of the town, were amazed and delighted. They saw what could be done in school with competent teachers and correct methods, and the fate of the Litchfield school, which had been in fearful jeopardy was settled at once and for many years. The entire term was completed and Mr. Blanchard declining a re-engagement, Mr. P. R. Rider, now of the Missouri Normal School, of Cape Girardeau, became his successor. Wages and salary were reduced, and seven home teachers were engaged. Then began the policy of employing teachers because they lived here instead of on account of their success in the schoolroom.

The next year, B. F. Hodges, proposing to take sole charge of the high school, was employed as Principal, but when elected, earnestly solicited an assistant. Mrs. Lockwood, of Alton, was selected. A German department was added. The total enrollment exceeded a thousand. Mr. Hedges remained two years.

In 1871-73, W. C. Catherwood, from Jacksonville, was the Principal—a thorough teacher and hardly an apology for a Superintendent. The tax bills for those years are conclusive as to the existence of a public school. Early in April, 1872, the schoolhouse caught fire in the roof, and, in the presence of thousands, burned like a candle down to the basement. A portion of the seats and the library were saved. The insurance covered two-thirds the loss. This misfortune closed the public school, and private schools were speedily opened in different parts of the city.

Contracts for rebuilding the house were made with John D. Carson, with no avoidable delay, on a modification of the original design. Pending its completion, public schools were resumed in the fall in the several buildings around the public square.

The second schoolhouse was occupied in the fall of 1873, under the superintendency of L. M. Hastings, from Iowa, at a yearly salary of $1,650, for a term of thirty-six weeks. The five assistants who accompanied him from that State were a valuable addition. One of them, Miss Mary Fredericks, is fondly remembered as a teacher of wonderful qualification, aptitude and success. By the failure of her voice near the end of her fifth session, she was compelled to retire for a season from the schoolroom. On her return to her profession in Iowa, the deplorable fret and wear of teaching, lessened her usefulness by inducing a nervous condition of irritability and peevishness. The harmony of the school was sadly violated by the controversy with Mrs. Johnson. The affair is too recent for description, though the district records are voluminous on one side of the trouble. Mr. Hastings' management of the school and the character of the teaching, were in brilliant contrast with the previous five years and the succeeding ones.

J. N. Dewell, of Pike County, was the Principal for 1875-77, and, under his care, there were no complaints of over study or rigid school duties. The first year, a Board of School Inspectors were appointed, but their powers and duties not being clearly settled by usage, the Council soon supplanted them. The Inspectors retired. Thus ingloriously ended this honest attempt to take the school out of politics and favoritism. It was, perhaps, significant, that our Council usually begins its reformatory measures just as a majority are going out of office, and thus leave them to be carried out by their successors.

The school year was reduced to eight months, or thirty-six weeks, and George C. Ross, of Jackson County, remained at the head of the school for a year at a salary of $1,000. An unseemly struggle in the School Board over the election of teachers, during which the value of the applicants in school work was subordinated to personal feeling, was followed by the inevitable result. The school was a general and profound disappointment.

For the last three years, Thomas J. Charles has been the Principal.

The Press.—At the solicitation of E. B. Litchfield, the proprietor of the town site, and on his assurance of a large and profitable line of work—an assurance which was wholly illusory, H. A. Coolidge, in February, 1857, removed his printing office from Cazenovia, N. Y., to Litchfield. Mr. Litchfield, in anticipation of his arrival, erected him an office, on Jackson street, better known as the grammar school building. Here he issued the first number of the Litchfield *Journal*, in April though dated in May. The paper was a four-page, six-column sheet, set in long primer and minion, and, as there were then no "patent insides," the editor and his assistants were busy in the mechanical department. The circulation did not exceed 200, and, during the six years of his control, never rose to 400. The paper was welcomed, but the town was too small and the neighborhood too scanty in population to afford the venture an adequate support. Those were the days of credit, and the payment of subscriptions was frequently omitted. The county was Democratic and intensely pro slavery and the political views of the *Journal* not altogether satisfactory to the arbiters of local opinion. The attitude of men on the "Kansas Question," where the doctrine of popular sovereignty was exemplified by open war and the mockery of political rights, was the crucial test of his party fealty. The *Journal* dared, in May, to announce the views held by Douglas in the following December in the Senate, and, for its temerity in disseminating opinions in advance of an utterance by a party leader, it fell under a suspicion of unsoundness, and there is no forgiveness in politics. Success alone condones offenses, and the *Journal* received late toleration. It supported Douglas for Senator in 1858, and for President two years later.

The panic of 1857 nearly caused its suspension. For sixteen consecutive days in the February following, its total receipts were half a dollar. Somehow the paper lived, and in mechanical appearance has not been excelled in the county. The editor was a Yankee with an odor of books, and to be a Yankee here was to lead no popular life.

Lincoln entered the White House, and in April the war of the rebellion began at Charleston. The evening after the heavy news was received, a public meeting was held at Empire Hall, and the editor briefly urged that the integrity of the Union must be preserved and force be repelled by force. The *Journal*, foreseeing the influence of the war on parties, continued to advocate and sustain the policy of military coercion. Arms had been selected by the South as the arbiter of its pretensions, and the *Journal* accepted the arbitrament. By degrees a large section of the local Democracy first deprecated this policy, and then actively connived to thwart the Union arms and openly "sympathized" with the South. The patrons of the office fell away, income dwindled, and at one time a rush was made to wreck it for alleged "copperheadism." The attempt was defeated by the Union men of the city.

In 1863, the office was leased to a Mr. Cook, and then to John Harris, now of Clyde, and Thomas B. Fuller, of Calhoun. The publishers changed the name to Litchfield *Democrat* and placed its editorial management in the hands of B. F. Burnett, Esq., who well understood the art of writing without saying anything, but week by week in the thick coming news of Union victories, prated dolefully of the horrors of war and the woe of desolated families, and the beauties of peace. He was the perpetual Chairman of the standing committee of dissent. He had principles, but would have been a better citizen if he had not.

The next year Mr. Coolidge sold the office, which for four years had been located in the *Journal* building on State street, to E. J. Ellis, a refugee from Troy, Mo., whose climate had become pernicious to his health since bushwhacking ceased to pay in that region. He called his paper the *Prairie City Advocate*. He toiled assiduously and was repaid for his labor. The war being over, he desired to retire to the congenial wilds of Missouri, and sold, October, 1865, his office to E. J. C. Alexander, from Greenville, who changed the name again to the Litchfield *News*, and declared it a Republican journal. He did not meet with distinguished success.

In April of the following year, the material of the *Union Monitor*, of Hillsboro, was, to evade a seizure by the Sheriff, conveyed to him and the publication of a newspaper in Litchfield was discontinued until the last of 1867. The *News* office was kept open for job work and advertisements, which were sent in type to Hillsboro. The *Monitor* was regularly dated at Hillsboro, T. J. Russell, editor, on the first page, while the third page was headed Litchfield *News*, dated at Litchfield, E. J. C. Alexander, editor.

In a short time the second head disappeared from the third page, but when the Hillsboro editor of the *Monitor* was struck off, the head and date line were changed to Litchfield *News*, and half a dozen quires were printed for the Litchfield folks.

From April, 1866, to December, 1867, no newspaper was printed in the town, with a population four thousand. This was not satisfactory—Alexander was "not the man for Galway." Steps were taken in 1867 to re-establish a home paper, and it became certain that B. S. Hood would be the editor. Money was furnished, and Alexander learning what had been done, and what was contemplated, changed his politics one day while crossing the street, and sold out to Mr. Hood, who began in the basement of Masonic Block the publication of the *Republican Monitor*, which in four months became the Litchfield *Union Monitor*. From these subterranean quarters he removed the office to Ferguson's Hall, enlarged to eight pages with "patent insides," and late in 1870, with more experience than profit from his venture, transferred the office to Messrs. C. L. Bangs and Ed. Gray, of Carlinville, both excellent printers. In the spring of 1871, J. H. C. Irwin was selected as editor and the *Monitor* had in addition C. L. Bangs and Emma Bangs as editorial writers, and B. S. Hood as local editor. Irwin excelled in "memories of the future." Bangs paragraphed on woman's rights, and Hood did the city locals. The paper was too rich for common blood, and in October, 1871, Bangs & Gray disposed of the *Monitor* to Kimball & Taylor, of Belleville. William Fithian, a graduate of the Carlinville *Democrat* office, was put in the office as editor and manager. In a year, the proprietors sunk a couple of thousand dollars and sold out at heavy loss to H. A. Coolidge, who thus found himself again in the editorial chair with the press and much of the printing material he had brought West fifteen years earlier. His absence for eight years from the newspaper world had taught him the value of a journal to the community where it is published. He was now to learn that this value was quite distinct from any value to its publisher.

He admitted G. B. Litchfield as a partner. The office was removed to Empire Hall until the fall of 1874 when it again began its wanderings. Litchfield withdrew, 1874, to begin the *Montgomery County Democrat*, and Coolidge for a year managed to conduct the *Monitor* without the handicap of a partner. In 1876, F. O. Martin became his partner—a good printer—and remained until 1878, when the paper was sold to Charles Walker and B. S. Hood. Walker went out of the concern in three months, and Mr. Hood in the spring of 1881 put in a Campbell press and took in J. G. Campbell as a partner. The circulation under his management rose to 1,100 or nearly double what any predecessor had been able to obtain.

In the fall of 1861, a Union ticket for county officers was presented as a rallying point for such as cared most for the country. To aid the design involved in the ticket, the *Campaigner* was founded by J. P. Bayless, with whom Dr. H. H. Hood was associated. It was intended to maintain it only until the fall election, and was issued from the *Journal* office. Not a copy of it is known to exist.

About May, 1862, the *Illinois Free Press* was removed here from Hillsboro. J. B. Hutchinson, editor. It found a home in the Cummings Building, and after languishing a few weeks, ceased to exist. In June, 1871, Messrs. Kimball & Taylor bought G. B. Litchfield's printing material in the Elliott Building and began the publication of the *Independent*, an eight column quarto sheet, three pages of which came ready printed. H. A. Coolidge was the salaried editor. The paper went up like a rocket. No such prosperity had attended a paper in this region. It began without a subscriber, and on its consolidation, by purchase, with the *Monitor*, had two-thirds its circulation. Only fifteen numbers were issued until it was lost in its ancient neighbor.

Mr. Fithian having ceased to be editor of the *Monitor*, in the late summer of 1872, purchased a newspaper outfit and began the publication of the *Review*. George B. Litchfield, printer. The 5th of the following December, Mr. Litchfield retired from the *Review*, which thereupon suspended, and subsequently, the material was sold to Messrs. Coolidge & Litchfield of the *Monitor*.

In November, 1874, Mr. Litchfield and Robert S. Young issued the first number of the *Montgomery County Democrat* in a room over Beach, Davis & Co.'s Bank. Mr. Young, the editor, owning none of the material, was in a few months out of the editorial chair, and Mr. Litchfield assumed the sole management. For a year, embracing a portion of 1879-80, Col. Ben. E. Johnson, of Hillsboro, was associated with Mr. Litchfield as editor and business manager of the *Democrat*. On his retirement, Mr. Litchfield again became editor and proprietor until August, 1881, when he sold to Charles Tobin, late of the Hillsboro *News*. Mr. Tobin, in March following, enlarged the paper which he renamed the Litchfield *Advocate*, to a six-column folio, and is doing a prosperous business, increasing his list of readers and hurried by job work.

Quite a thousand copies of the *Monitor* and *Advocate* are taken at the home post office. Both attend chiefly to local matters and leave editorials proper to the imagination of their subscribers. The papers are conducted on business principles, and like newspapers generally are more valuable to the town than to their proprietors.

Banking.—In 1862, Haskell, Davis & Co., of Hillsboro, opened a private bank in a wood building, whose site is now occupied by Updike's hardware store, Thomas F. Seymour being clerk or manager. Five years later, the name of the firm was Haskell, Seymour & Co., Mr. Davis being succeeded by Mr. Seymour. Mr. Haskell had removed to Alton, and in December, 1869, his interest appears to have been purchased by Judge Brewer, of Hillsboro, and the firm became Brewer, Seymour & Co., and S. M. Grubbs entered the bank as Teller. The following year the present banking house was built, and for ten years the firm remained unchanged. Then Mr. Seymour's sight failing, he was forced to retire from business, and the firm became Brewer & Grubbs. The house passed through the panic of 1873 with unimpaired credit and resources, as whatever its nominal capital, its virtual capital was twenty times greater. Its solvency was not for a moment in doubt. Its present officers are: S. M.

J. C. Sinclair

Grubbs, Manager, and T. F. Davis, Bookkeeper. The volume of business transacted over its counter must be left to conjecture, as all information on this point is refused.

In 1860-61, John W. Haggart opened a bank in Beardsley's jewelry store, and dealt in exchange and occasional loans. He was not believed to control sufficient capital, and did but a meager business. His "bank" soon ceased, and its funds were easily transferred to a vest pocket, and the "banker" departed to another State.

Under a special charter, the Litchfield Bank, Nathan Kenyon, President, and N. P. B. Wells, Cashier, opened in July, 1870, with a paid-up capital of $20,000. The officers were from Brockport, N. Y., and held half the stock; the balance was held here. Financially, the institution was not fortunate, and ere the first year was over, Kenyon sold his stock and retired from the house. Thirteen of the original stockholders formed a partnership under the name of Beach, Davis & Co., and, dissolving the corporation, continued the business with D. Davis, Manager, and D. Van Deusen, Cashier. The bank was located in Hoog's Building, where Mr. Smith, now is. The new firm began business in their proper name in May, 1871. Two years later, the articles of partnership were revised, three new partners admitted, and the paid-up capital increased quite fourfold. The business had been remarkably prosperous, and the stock was held firmly.

When the panic came, and the balances held in foreign banks became unavailable by reason of closing their doors, a meeting of the partners was held in the bank parlor, and the situation was rapidly considered. A rush on the bank was anticipated, but in a few hours the current funds had been increased threefold, and all paper was met, and no engagement was delayed or abandoned. The bank pays regular dividends.

The Coal Mine.—From 1817 to 1855, wood was the only fuel in use in this county for household and heating purposes. Until 1858, the nearest coal mine was thirty miles to the southwest, and not until the railway was opened for traffic was it expedient to change to coal for shops or mechanical uses. In 1858, there was not a coal-burning locomotive on the railroad. Fitful attempts to find coal in this neighborhood were prosecuted in the mid "50's," and to no purpose.

As early as 1856-57, coal from the Wood River Mine was bought at a cost of $17 freight for a car load, and closed out from the car at 15 cents a bushel, the buyer paying for draying and weighing. Gradually the price fell to eight bushels for the dollar, though if, as not unfrequently happened, the supply ran short, the price leaped up to 18 and 22 cents a bushel. The flouring mills and car shops were large consumers, the annual consumption being estimated at 300,000 bushels per year. If the supply at any time failed, the writer is afraid to recollect the fabulous sum he gladly paid for wood.

In the first part of 1867, Andrew Howard, of Bunker Hill, a practical coal-miner, proposed to Messrs. Beach & Amsden and Best & Sparks, that for a bonus of $2,000 he would sink a coal-shaft 350 feet, and these firms guaranteed its acceptance. Howard's capital consisted chiefly in his skill, energy, hopefulness and a high-shouldered mule. A few acres of land were bought on Rocky Branch, just outside the corporation, and in March, 1867, he began work. Mr. Howard's purse was soon exhausted, but he persevered, being effectually aided by the late M[illegible] Moudy. The bonus was expended and Mr. Moudy was unable to defray the expenses of the work. A few citizens deeply interested in discovering coal here, a[illegible] opening and working a coal mine, were convened, and Mr. Howard requested the formation of a mining company with a capital of $20,000, into which he would enter, putting in the unfinished shaft at $5,000, to continue the work. His request was promptly acceded to, a company was formed and incorporated, officers chosen, with R. W. O'Bannon, President; D. R. Sparks, Treasurer, and H. A. Coolidge, Secretary. The stock was taken by nearly fifteen persons, Amsden & Beach and Best & Sparks subscribing largely and others according to their ability. The shaft went down slowly; the cost was nearly $50 per foot and when, in December, 1868, a thirty-two inch vein of coal was reached at a depth of 416 feet, the entire capital had been consumed, and no one was willing to contribute more capital to open and work the vein. Some debts had been incurred, and in the summer of 1869 the mine was sold at auction to pay debts and was bid in by Warder Cummings, acting in behalf of a new organization inside the mining company. A new company was at once legally organized. The stock of the old one was worth only five per cent, and most of the stockholders did not receive even that pitiful legacy. The capital of the new company was $10,000. Mr. Howard was discharged, and Messrs. Green & Little, of M[illegible], Ill., took the contract to finish sinking the shaft. A third vein of coal was reached at a depth of 500 feet, and then the company learned to their consternation that it costs as much to open a mine as for sinking the shaft. The [illegible] wanted [illegible] wages, $20,000 more, the capital stock was expended, and still the mine was not prepared to put out coal.

In this emergency, Messrs. D. C. Amsden, H. H. Beach, James W. Jefferis, J. Smith Tally, Charles E. Benton and Warder Cummings formed a partnership and leased the mine, and assumed the payment of the debt from the lease money. In 1874, these partners had become possessed of the entire shares of the mining company which was thereupon dissolved, as its predecessor had been, and the Litchfield Coal Company organized, with a nominal capital of $10,000, but with a property which had cost six times that amount. This third company still operates the mines, and by prudent management has reduced the expense of mining so that coal is delivered to local buyers at 10 cents a bushel, and yet satisfactory profits have been gathered. The price of mining was at one time such that miners received upward of $30 a week.

In 1878, a second shaft was sunk at one half the cost of the first one, and the output rose to 5,000 bushels a day in the busy season. At the foot of the second shaft a boring rod was sent down about a hundred and fifty feet, to develop the character of the underlying strata, and coal oil was reached. The astonishment of the miners was unbounded. The news was received with incredulity. But the oil rose to the bottom of the mine and overflowed the floor. A few barrels of it were collected and the well carefully closed in order to the safety of the mine.

Secret Societies.—Whether it be from the disposition of the human mind which would pry into a knowledge of the paintings on the left-hand side of the temple of Paphos, or from the absence of the joys of home, or from a desire to draw closer the ties of brotherhood, or from purposes unrebuked with self-hood, secret societies were early planted in Litchfield, and have flourished in undecayed vigor and influence and usefulness.

The list of secret organizations of a temperance character is long, and the history of each one is brief and uneventful. They were each short lived, and, like the "Murphy movement" have died and left no sign or contingent memorial. Total abstinence organizations are not unknown here but none of them are secret.

Until 1857, the Masonic fraternity had no lodge nearer than Hillsboro. But on the 4th of March in that year, a dispensation was granted to G. G. Withington, W. S. Palmer, W. H. Cummings, R. H. Peall, James Thalls, Samuel Boothe, S. W. McDonald and C. W. Parish, who instituted Charter Oak Lodge in the city and the first regular communication was held on that date. W. S. Palmer, Master. The lodge met in the texas of Cummings' building which was occupied jointly with the Odd Fellows until 1865.

R. H. Peall was the second Master. In 1859, W. H. Cummings was Master and then in succession came J. T. Duff, W. T. Elliott for two years, C. W. Parish, W. T. Elliott and D. C. Amsden. In 1865, the lodge removed to the Elliott corner, State and Kirkham streets. Mr. Amsden was re-elected in December, 1866, and G. M. Longmiller in 1867. James Rogers was chosen Master in 1868 and C. W. Amsden in 1869, and James [illegible] in 1870. G. M. Longmiller was Master 1871, 1872, 1873, 1874 and 1875. But in 1876 [illegible] was Master through 1877, 1878, 1879 and [illegible] G. M. Longmiller was Master. In December, 1881, the annual time of election, J. W. [illegible] was chosen Master. In 1882 the lodge [illegible] the [illegible] of Masonic Block [illegible] streets [illegible].

[illegible] Commandery No. 30, Knights Templar, was organized [illegible] 3, 1868. H. W. Hubbard [illegible] Commander [illegible] assisted by several Knights from Alton. On November 6, 1868, the charter was granted to Sirs George H. Pomeroy, [illegible]

Commander the first year, since which George M. Raymond has continuously filled the office. James Rogers has been the constant secretary and B. C. Beardsley the Treasurer. The Commandery has fifty members.

August 9, 1867, a dispensation was granted to G. M. Raymond, W. E. Bacon, S. D. Kirkpatrick, James W. Davenport, H. C. Watson, C. W. Parish, [illegible] S. Tyler, George A. Stoddard, John B. Hall, N. C. Alexander and Wesley Best for a second lodge here, which was to be called Litchfield Lodge. September 3, 1867, the regular charter was received and G. M. Raymond was chosen Master and re-elected the following year, when he was followed by W. E. Bacon, and he in turn by George A. Stoddard. By years the successive Masters have been: 1871, G. A. Stoddard; 1872, G. M. Raymond; 1873, G. W. Goodell; 1874, G. W. Goodell; 1875, W. E. Bacon; 1876, W. E. Bacon; 1877, [illegible] Keithley; 1878, W. E. Bacon; 1879, [illegible]; 1880, W. E. Bacon; 1881, W. E. Bacon; 1882, [illegible] Keithley.

Of Elliott Chapter, No. 120, no facts have been learned beyond the facts of its existence and that [illegible] W. Amsden has for ten consecutive years been High Priest.

Litchfield Lodge No. 202, of Odd Fellows, was instituted by O. B. Jackson of Hillsboro, March [illegible], 1857, with the following charter members: R. S. Caden, S. W. McDonald, E. R. White, B. W. [illegible] and John P. [illegible]. Mr. [illegible] was the first presiding officer.

Until 1865, the lodge met in the Cummings building. [illegible] years it met [illegible] and since has occupied a hall on the third floor of the Masonic building.

[illegible] Encampment No. 8[illegible], of O. F. [illegible], was instituted by [illegible] B. J[illegible] on July 22, 18[illegible]. The charter members were [illegible] Dilmer, [illegible]

White Cross Lodge, No. 66, Knights of Pythias, was founded April 27, 1876, by W. T. Vandever, of Taylorville. The charter members were Joseph Lawrence, J. R. Blackwell, G. W. Rattenbury, E. C. Thorp, L. G. Tyler, J. W. Steen, T. J. Cox, C. Paullis, Jr., George S. Webb, Ben. C. Best George Kilmer, H. G. Tuttle and A. J. Reubart. Mr. Rattenbury was the chief officer.

February 14, 1875, Augusta Lodge, No. 507, of Odd Fellows, was instituted. This is a German lodge, and the ritual and the proceedings are in that language. They had a separate lodge room here, initiated thirty-eight members, and received eleven by card. Three members here died, and fifteen have terminated their membership by removal or otherwise. The present list contains the names of forty-four members. The lodge has had peace and prosperity within its gates.

Sanitary.—As early as 1854, cholera appeared in South Litchfield, by importation from a river town. Several cases terminated fatally, but the disease did not visit the scanty population of the village.

In 1857 or 1858, a case of small-pox was declared in Litchfield; the patient, a man named Johnson, was removed to a pest house a mile from State street, where he died. A few of the citizens were attacked, but they recovered. In later years, sporadic cases were exhibited. There is no tradition as to their origin. No alarm was manifested; suitable precautions were observed, and no fatal results followed. But in the winter of 1881-82, the loathsome contagion gained here a determined lodgment. It was a sequence of immigration or railroad travel. Notwithstanding the prompt adoption of preventive or remedial measures, the fearful plague continued its insidious advances until forty four persons had been smitten of whom nine died. The mortality might have been less had all the sick refrained from grossly imprudent courses. General vaccination was enforced, and the disease starved out.

In the summer of 1867, five members of a circus company were seized with cholera the same night while at a hotel. The patients rallied enough to be removed to Pana, where it is believed they died. The pestilence spread, and several citizens fell its victims. Seven years later, the conditions were favorable for its re-appearance. The heated term was intense and protracted, and sanitary matters were generously suffered to run themselves. An elderly couple from Tennessee came in on the railroad, ill with cholera. They were removed to a private house, and within twenty-four hours were dead. Other persons were speedily attacked, and in a few hours were moribund. On two occasions, the deaths were four per day. The total number of cases was nearly ninety, and the deaths were reported to be thirty-nine. The stroke was swift. Men in apparent sound health at night would be dead in the morning.

In each visitation of cholera, the disease was plainly of a foreign origin, and if the contagion theory be well-founded, the ravages here have been only such as may be apprehended in any town so placed that careless or infected strangers are constantly on its streets or stopping at its hotels.

The average annual mortality cannot be accurately given. The usual record of interments is of no use here; as for family reasons sepulture is in distant cemeteries, while the city cemeteries are used by town and country alike. It is certain that the ratio of mortality in the city is as low as in the country, and last year did not exceed two per cent. With a population exceeding five thousand, the total deaths were about eighty.

CHAPTER XVI.

TOWNSHIP OF NOKOMIS—POSITION AND BOUNDARIES—SURFACE SOIL, STREAMS, ETC.—FOREST GROWTHS—AGRICULTURAL PRODUCTIONS—EARLY SETTLEMENTS—ROADS—SCHOOLS, CHURCHES, ETC.

"Once o'er all this favored land,
Savage wilds and darkness spread."

NOKOMIS occupies a scope of territory lying in the northeastern part of Montgomery County, west of Audubon and east of Rountree Township. It borders on Christian County on the north. Witt Township on the south, and is admirably located with reference to railroad and other accommodations. Its close proximity to the flourishing towns of Hillsboro, Morrisonville, and other equally good market places, affords many advantages to the citizens which they have not been slow to avail themselves of, as is shown by the increased prosperity of the agricultural interests throughout its territory. The distinguishing characteristics of Nokomis are its fine, undulating prairie lands, which, in point of fertility and productiveness, are unsurpassed by any other similar amount of territory in the State. The northern portion is somewhat flat, and in certain places contains some low, marshy land, but the great majority of its acres are susceptible of a high degree of cultivation, as is attested by the rank which the township takes as an agricultural district. In the southern part, along the several water-courses and among the wooded portions, the surface is more rolling, but in no place is it too broken or uneven for tillage. The soil is generally a fine quality of loam, mixed with clay in certain localities, and sand in the low places along the creeks. The township is sufficiently well watered for agricultural purposes and stock-raising, with several beautiful streams traversing it in different directions, the chief of which is the East Fork of Shoal Creek. This is a stream of considerable size and importance in the southern townships of the county, and has its source in Section 1, from whence it flows in a southwesterly direction through Sections 22, 28 and 33. A small stream flows through the northeastern part of the township, draining that portion, and receiving in its course a number of rivulets which are not designated by any particular names.

Originally, about one-sixth of the township's area consisted of timbered land, the wooded districts lying chiefly in the southern and southwestern parts. The productions of these forests were at one time the source of considerable wealth to those who settled in the timber and made the lumber business a specialty. At the head of these forest products stands the black walnut a tree unequaled in the United States for its many uses in cabinet-making. It is becoming scarce in this part of the country on account of its wide demand, and owing also to the prodigal manner in which much of it was destroyed by many of the pioneer settlers. Next in value is the oak, of which several varieties are to be found growing in the forests of this township. It affords the principal amount of lumber for all practical purposes to the farmers in this section of the country, and considerable quantities of it have been shipped to other localities. Another of the forest monarchs is the elm, which grows to gigantic sizes in the low lands skirting the water-courses. There are several different kinds of maple to

*By G. N. Berry

be seen here, all of which are much used for artificial groves, on account of their hardiness and rapid growth. These species are highly ornamental, delighting the eye of the most careless, and giving a charm to the most uninviting prospect. Hickory is found in certain localities, and is much used in the manufacture of carriages sleighs, and almost all agricultural implements made in the different factories throughout the State. Besides the different varieties already enumerated, there are many trees and shrubs of smaller growth known as underbrush, much of which has been cleared away of late years.

Of the farm products we can speak only in a general way, as no statistical information concerning them was obtained. Agricultural productions of every kind indigenous to this latitude are certain of a rapid growth and large returns. As is shown by the vast wealth that has been drawn from the bosom of the soil during the thirty years that have passed—a wealth that has covered its surface with beautiful homes, and contributed toward feeding the hungry millions of other lands. Wheat is and has been the staple product of Nokomis, to which its soil seems peculiarly adapted, and has been known to yield as high as thirty five and forty bushels per acre in favorable seasons although its average production is much less. Other cereals are raised in the same proportion, particularly oats and rye, which return abundant and well-paying harvests almost every year. As a corn district, this part of the country will compare favorably with any other locality in the county, as the land in the main is sufficiently rolling to render drainage easy. While other townships in the county suffered more or less severely during the drought of 1881, the farmers of Nokomis raised a sufficient amount of corn for home consumption and some for market also. Apple orchards are beginning to be extensively cultivated, and fruits of the finest and hardiest varieties yield abundantly, and are being produced in large quantities, while the already large area of orchards receives yearly additions. This product alone in a few years will form one of the principal articles of sale during its season.

The early settlement of Nokomis is so interwoven with the pioneer settlements of the adjoining townships that their history is, in the main, almost identical. The same difficulties were experienced, the same hardships endured by the pioneers of Nokomis that for years retarded the development and advancement of older municipalities. There were no roads, so to speak no stores nor mills nearer than Grisham and Butler Townships, a distance of twenty or thirty miles; no school buildings except of a very primitive character, and no places of worship except the houses of the pioneers. These and other experiences of a similar character were what the first settlers of Nokomis had to contend with in the days of its infancy but, thanks to the energy and thrift with which the early settlers were characterized, all these difficulties have been successfully overcome, and on every hand are to be seen well-tilled farms elegant private residences, good roads, handsome church edifices, commodious school-buildings, and other evidences of prosperity, which combine to make this part of the county a desirable locality.

The first permanent settler in Nokomis Township, as it is now designated, was one Bluford Shaw, the exact date of whose arrival could not be ascertained, although it is supposed to have been prior to the year 1840. In the year 1843, Hugh Hightower, a name familiar in the northern part of the county, came to Illinois and settled on a piece of land lying in Section 33. Here he erected the first house ever built within the boundaries of the township, traces of which still remain. For the space of three years, Hightower was the only resident in this part of the county, his nearest neighbors living at a distance of at least ten miles away. John

Henry located here in 1846, securing land in Section 26, which he improved quite extensively. After him came John Lower, John Nichols, Mason Jewett and an old man, by name Redden, all of whom located near the site of the present city of Nokomis. In the year 1854, a number of settlers located in the northern part of the township, where they founded quite an extensive community. Among this number can be mentioned the names of Royal N. Lee, John Wetmore, William Bouton, Absalom Van Hooser, William Lee and Andrew Coiner, several of whom are still living on the farms they settled, and numerous descendants are scattered over different parts of the county. The northeastern part of the township was settled principally by an intelligent and thrifty class of Germans, who have improved that locality until it is now one among the very best farmed sections of country in the township, and in point of improvements, as houses, barns, etc., it will compare favorably with any other community within the limits of the county.

It has been asserted, and wisely so, that the avenues of communication are an undoubted evidence of the state of society. The history of this planet from its earliest days furnish indisputable proof of this now universally admitted truth. As civilization progresses, intercommunication increases, and the channels of trade are improved, while the conveyance of products and the movements of armies require an unobstructed highway. Of the Eastern nations who comprehended the truth of this great principle, the chief were the Romans, whose broad highways and ruined arches still survive to remind us of the former power and greatness of those masters of the world. While in the Western Hemisphere Mexican causeways and Peruvian stone roads attest the vigor of a national life centuries departed. But the trails across the prairies and through the forests of this part of the country—ample for the aborigines of Illinois and withal equal to their capacity, have given place in turn to a network of highways, while not comparable to the military roads of the Romans or ancient Mexicans, and perhaps far inferior to the turnpikes to be seen in older States, are at least equal to the requirements of a highly civilized people. The first road established in Nokomis passed through the township in a northeasterly direction, and was known as the Hillsboro and Nokomis road. Its original course has been changed, although it is still one of the important highways in the northern part of the county. A road leading from the town of Nokomis to Irving was laid out and improved in an early day, but does not appear to have been properly established until several years later. One of the most important highways passes through the central part of the township from north to south, and is rather extensively traveled. The greater number of roads which traverse the township in all directions have been established in recent years, and are well improved. Like the highways in all parts of Central and Southern Illinois, these thoroughfares, during certain seasons of the year, become well-nigh impassable, owing to their muddy condition. The porous nature of the soil, however, causes this mud to dry up quite rapidly, and in a comparatively short time after the frost leaves the ground in the spring, the roads improve and remain in good traveling order until the following winter.

Passing through the southeast corner is the Indianapolis & St. Louis Railroad, which has promoted the material interests of the township more than any or all other improvements combined. In its course, it passes through Sections 32, 28, 22, 14 and 12, intersecting the southern boundary at a point about one and one-half miles from the Rountree Township line and the eastern boundary two miles south of Christian County. The city of Nokomis owes much of its prosperity to this road, as does also the township at large.

It is a fact which the splendid educational

institutions of the present make it difficult for us to-day to comprehend, that in the early settlement of the country, one of the greatest disadvantages under which the pioneer labored was the almost entire absence of facilities for the education of his children. When the question of keeping soul and body together had once been solved by the constantly increasing acreage of farm land, and the corn waved over the spot which required toil and perseverance to conquer from its primitive natural state, and bountiful harvests told of no more immediate wants, then the pioneer's attention was called to the necessity of schools, and means of supplying the want were most earnestly sought. A man by the name of Henry Lower, an excellent teacher by the way, is said to have taught the first school in the township, at his private residence, about the year 1848. It was attended by the boys and girls in the new settlement and supported by subscriptions, as were all the early schools in the county. The first house erected for educational purposes was built on Section 27, and is still in use. There are a number of good frame schoolhouses in the township, and the citizens can point with pride to their educational institutions, which, for efficiency and thoroughness of work, are unsurpassed by any in the county. Many facts relating to educational matters of the township, belong properly to the town of Nokomis, and will be spoken of in connection with the history of that place in the next chapter.

One of the first public officials of the township was John J. Wetmore, who was elected Justice of the Peace in an early day, although we are unable to give the date. About the same time, J. W. Hancock was elected Constable, in which capacity he served the township several years. His marriage to Miss Margaret Meratt was the first event of the kind ever solemnized in Nokomis. Several healthy religious organizations, with as many substantial temples of worship, are the most convincing evidence of the existence of high moral principles, and a sense of religious duty on the part of the people. The Methodists organized the first church in the township, and their ministers were the first to find their way to the cabins of the pioneers, and preach the everlasting truths of the Gospel to the early inhabitants. Rev. J. L. Crane conducted the first religious services, and assisted in the organization of several churches of his denomination, in the township and town of Nokomis. The first church edifice was built by the Lutherans, in the town of Nokomis, and will be more particularly spoken of in the chapter devoted to that place. The Lutherans and Methodists have several good societies in the township, whose congregations are in excellent condition, and destined to accomplish a great amount of good in their respective communities. For want of particulars concerning the various churches, the writer is obliged to give them the above very brief notice. For further church history, see the following chapter on city of Nokomis.

CHAPTER XVII.

TOWN OF NOKOMIS—ITS LOCATION AND SETTLEMENT—THE FIRST STORES, MILLS AND OTHER BUSINESS—GRAIN TRADE OF NOKOMIS—MANUFACTURE OF AGRICULTURAL IMPLEMENTS—SCHOOLHOUSES, ETC.—THE PRESS—RELIGIOUS HISTORY—THE DIFFERENT CHURCHES, PREACHERS, ETC., ETC.

"History enriches the mind, gratifies a worthy desire to be informed on past events, and enables us to avail ourselves of the experience of our predecessors."

IT is not expected that the simple narrative of these pages will be anything more than a mere record of events that have occurred within the limits of this quiet little town. To sketch its progress and improvement from the building of the first cabin to its present growth and prosperity is the extent of our aim in this chapter. In the preceding chapter, the history of Nokomis Township has been given by another writer, and hence the village only will occupy our attention. In gathering statistics concerning early settlements, organization of churches, etc., it is sometimes difficult to find records which will give, with certainty and accuracy, the information wanted. While we have taken pains to secure facts, it is possible that in the following pages there are inaccuracies.

The town of Nokomis was settled as a village about the year 1855. It was laid out by T. C. Huggins, of Bunker Hill, Ill., and Capt. Simeon Ryder, of Alton, Ill., and it is beautifully situated on the Indianapolis & St. Louis Railroad, about twenty miles northeast of Hillsboro, the county seat. It was incorporated as a village March 9, 1867, and has since been incorporated as a town under special charter. It is the third town in the county in size of population, and is a place of considerable business, having a large grain trade.

The first store in the village was owned by Oliver Boutwell. He was bought out by H. F. Rood, who built another store in the year 1859. The first hotel was built by a Mr. Hart, and is the same building, which, with recent improvements, is now called the Eureka House, and stands north of the railroad. The second hotel was built by James Bone, in the year 1865, and burned down in 1881. The first physician locating in Nokomis was Dr. James Welch, who came to the place about the year 1859.

A flouring-mill was built in 1857, by Jewett & Wetmore. This mill, as well as the third one, which was built by Mulkey & Gamble, burned down. The second mill built, which is the one now standing, and doing good work, was built by Rhoades & Boxberger. It is now owned and operated by Hobson & Hartsock.

The first schoolhouse in Nokomis was a one-story frame, built in the year 1858, and served the wants of the town for educational purposes until the present handsome brick building, containing seven rooms, was erected in the year 1871. This edifice cost a little over $13,000, and is finished and furnished in the latest improved style.

The Nokomis Post Office was probably opened about the year 1856, and had for Postmaster Oliver Boutwell. In 1858, Mr. H. F. Rood took the position of Postmaster. He was followed about the year 1861 by W. F. Mulkey. Mr. Mulkey held the situation probably something less than a year, when

* By Rev. T. F. Spilman.

the office came again into the hands of Mr. Rood, who conducted it until probably about the year 1864, when it came into the hands of Thomas Judson. The present Postmaster, D. P. Brophy, came into possession of the office in the year 1865, and is a faithful and efficient officer.

The grain trade was commenced in Nokomis probably as early as the year 1860, by H. F. Rood. In 1868, there were four parties buying grain; at the present time there are three. The country in the vicinity of Nokomis is a fine one for agriculture, and the grain market is good.

The oldest dwelling house standing in the town is probably the small building, made of logs, now boarded upon the outside, standing south of the lumber yard.

Nokomis has never been much of a manufacturing town, but has paid most of her attention to grain and merchandise. J. C. Runge & Bro. commenced the manufacture of agricultural implements about the year 1868. Their factory is now worked by a steam engine, of about eighteen-horse power. They do quite a large business.

The Nokomis National Bank had its origin in the year 1872. Its Directors were James Pennington, A. E. McKinney, J. H. Beatty, T. Ernst, Jacob Haller, John Johns and C. W. Townsend. Its President was J. W. Beatty; Vice President, John Johns, and its Cashier, B. F. Culp. It commenced business with a capital of $50,000. It now has a surplus of $10,000. The President of the bank at this time is H. F. Rood; Vice President, George Taylor, and Cashier, Alfred Griffin.

Secret and benevolent institutions are represented in Nokomis by Masons, Odd Fellows and Knights of Honor. The society of Freemasons was organized in the year 1856, the Odd Fellows in 1866, and the Knights of Honor February 6, 1879. These organizations have comfortable halls, and appear to be in a flourishing condition.

Newspapers.—The first newspaper published in Nokomis was the Nokomis *Advertiser*, edited and published by Draper & Henderson. It was established in the year 1868, and had a free circulation. It was devoted largely to the land interest of the country.

About the year 1871, Messrs. Picket & White came to the place and commenced the publication of the *Gazette*. At this time the *Advertiser* was suspended, and the whole field given to the *Gazette*. The expenses of publication being greater than were anticipated, the concern was sold to meet encumbrances. A. H. Draper then, in 1873, commenced the publication of the *Bulletin*. Its career was closed in 1876.

After a time, the publication of the *Bulletin* was resumed, taken up at first by H. F. White, one of its former proprietors, and afterward passed through the hands of several successive publishers.

In 1877, E. M. Hulburt entered upon the publication of the *Free Press*, and in March, 1878, it was consolidated with the *Gazette*, and took the name of the *Free Press-Gazette*, the consolidated paper being edited and published by E. M. Hulburt.

In 1880, H. M. Graden commenced the publication of the Nokomis *Atlas*, which closed its career in 1881.

In December, 1880, E. M. Hulburt began to publish a paper in the German language, called the *Deutsch Amerikaner*.

In the year 1881, Mr. Hulburt purchased, and has now in successful operation, a Campbell cylinder press.

The *Free Press-Gazette*, and the *Deutsch Amerikaner*, under the control of Mr. Hulburt, are the only papers now published in the town of Nokomis.

Churches.—In the year 1855, St. Mark's

Evangelical Lutheran Church was organized at the village of Audubon, seven miles east from the present site of Nokomis. and was called Zion's Evangelical Lutheran Church. Sometime afterward, an organization of the Lutheran Church was formed in Nokomis. A house of worship was built, being the first house of worship erected in Nokomis, the cost being about $4,500. This house was dedicated to the worship of God by the Lutheran Church October 21 1866, the dedicatory sermon being preached by Rev. M. M. Bartholomew. The two churches, the one at Audubon, and the one at Nokomis, were organized into one October 22, 1866, and called St. Mark's Evangelical Lutheran Church. The names of those who signed the Consiitution of this new organization were as follows: Christian Easterday Anna M. Easterday, Daniel Easterday, Jane Easterday, Leonard Leas, Mary Leas, George Culp, Elizabeth Culp, Stephen L. Latimer, Joseph Miller, Isabella Miller, Solomon Miller, Samuel Friend, Martin V. Easterday, J. W. Russell, Martha B. Russell, Isaac F. Strider, Amos W. Easterday, Anna M. Easterday, Hannah M. Easterday, Benjamin F. Culp, Barbara A. Culp, Sophia Graden. The first pastor chosen by this church was Rev. M. M. Bartholomew. His successors have been Revs. John Rugan, M. L. Kunkelman, J. C. Wesner, D. M. Henkle, D. D., and John Booher, the present supply, a student not yet having completed his theological studies.

The first Elders chosen by the church were Leonard Leas and Joseph Miller. The first Deacons were S. L. Latimer and J. W. Russell. The church has a membership at present of fifty, and maintains a good Sunday school.

The Baptist Church of Nokomis was organized in the year 1856, by Rev. Mr. Hutton, at a schoolhouse in what was known as C t tingham's Grove. The following are the names of those who at that time entered into the organization: Mason Jewett, Royal W Lee, Christopher Jewett, Polly Lee Jane Jewett, Melvina Wetmore, Mary Jewett and Marcusia Smith. The house of worship now occupied by this church in the town of Nokomis was built in 1870, and the first service held in it was on the 9th of July of the same year. The following ministers have been supplies of this church: Revs. R. R. Coon, Jacob V. Hopper, E. Jones, J. H. Mize and the present supply, Rev. S. G. Duff. The present membership is probably near fifty.

The Methodist Episcopal Church of Nokomis had an imperfect organization as early as about the year 1857, and appointed as its Class Leader James Watson. In the year 1860, the society was more perfectly organized by Rev. John E. Lindley, at that time supplying the Irving Circuit. About the year 1873, Mr. Lindley was appointed to the Nokomis Circuit, and died while in charge, February 19, 1875. His remains were buried in the cemetery near the town. The first sermon preached in Nokomis Township was by James L. Crane, a Methodist minister, about the year 1848. The house of worship now occupied by the Methodist Church was built in 1869, and dedicated November 14 of the same year.

The pulpit of the Methodist Church has been regularly supplied by the following ministers: Revs. Taylor, Kershner, John E. Lindley P. Honnold, E. E. Copperthwait, S. H. Whitlock, Martin Miller, George Miller J. M. West, T. M. Dillon, L. T. Jones, and the present pastor, J. W. Crane.

The roll of the original members has been imperfectly kept; but the following is probably nearly correct: Mr. Taylor, Jonathan C. Fellers, Margaret Fellers, Nancy Rood, Horace Graves, Ann Graves, Elias P. Baxter,

Elizabeth Baxter, James Watson, Mary Watson, Solomon Smith, Mary F. Bone, Susan Brophy, John Hancock, Margaret Hancock, Alexander Vanhauten, Martha Jane Vanhauten, Stephen B. Waples. The present membership of the church is probably about one hundred and fifteen. A Sunday school is carried on the year round.

The Christian Church of Nokomis was organized by Rev. William Vanhooser in the spring of 1861, with the following members: John Lower, Mrs. Magdalena Lower, Miss Diana Lower, A. B. Vanhooser, Mrs. Mary Vanhooser, Mrs. Mary Swords, F. M. Osborn, Mrs. E. C. Osborn, E. M. Thompson, Mrs. Ann Thompson, Miss Malissa Thompson, Rev. William Vanhooser, Mrs. Jane Vanhooser, W. F. Mulkey, Mrs. M. A. Mulkey, William R. Vanhooser, J. A. Vanhooser, Miss R. A. Vanhooser, Miss N. E. Vanhooser, T. Patterson, Mrs. M. J. Patterson and Mrs. Maria Lant. At the time of organization, the congregation worshiped in the public schoolhouse. The present house of worship, at a cost of about $4,000, was completed and opened for worship in 1863. Rev. A. D. Northcut preached the dedicatory sermon, assisted in the service by Rev. Newton Mulkey.

The following ministers have been regularly employed as Pastors of the church: Revs. William Vanhooser, Abraham Martin, John Friend and James Ament. Rev. William Vanhooser has been re-employed, and is at present the Pastor of the church. Several other brethren have, for a few months at a time, also been supplies of the pulpit. The church has at present a membership of about fifty. Only five of the original members are now residents of the town.

The Presbyterian Church of Nokomis was organized by Rev. Joseph Gordon, in June, 1862, with the following members: Thomas Derr, David Nickey, Wilson Sible, Jane Nickey, Rebecca Matkin, Eglantine Strider, Rebecca Sible, Phœbe D. Derr, Nellie A. Derr, Irene B. Derr, Amanda E. Matkin, Nancy Yarnell. David Nickey was chosen Ruling Elder. Rev. Joseph Gordon was the first regular supply of the pulpit. His successors have been Revs. Gideon C. Clark, C. K. Smoyer, N. Williams, J. P. Mills, James Lafferty, D. L. Gear, and the present supply, T. E. Spilman.

This comprises a brief sketch of the town of Nokomis from its laying-out as a village to the present time. As both time and space were limited, we have confined ourself to a brief statement of facts, avoiding all unnecessary embellishments.

CHAPTER XVIII.

EAST FORK TOWNSHIP—BOUNDARIES—WATER-COURSES—EARLY SETTLERS—MILLS AND CATTLE-RAISING—ROADS—CHURCHES, SCHOOLS AND SECRET SOCIETIES.

"Like the race of leaves is that of human kind.
Upon the ground the winds stir one year's growth,
The sprouting grove puts forth another brood that
Sport and grow in the spring season.
So is it with man,
One generation grows while one decays."—*Iliad.*

IT is difficult to realize as we travel along the highways that traverse this beautiful prairie township, and note the broad, fertile acres of well-tilled soil and the stately farm-houses, where the happy husbandman lives in the midst of plenty and contentment, that scarcely three-quarters of a century ago these luxuriant plains were peopled by a few wandering savages and formed part of a vast, unbroken wild, which gave but little promise of the high state of civilization it has since attained. Instead of the primitive log cabin and diminutive board shanty, we now see dotting the prairie in all directions comfortable and elegantly formed mansions of the latest style of architecture, graceful, substantial and convenient. We see also the bosom of the country decked with church structures of all religious denominations and well-built school-houses at proper intervals. Her fields are laden with the choicest cereals, her pastures all alive with numerous herds of the finest breeds of stock, and everything bespeaks the thrift and prosperity with which the farmer in this fertile division of the county is blessed. East Fork is one of the southern townships of Montgomery County, and is also one of the largest, being ten miles in extent from north to south and six miles from east to west. It contains sixty square miles of land, and is, in many respects, one of the best townships in the county. The northern boundary is Irving; eastern, Fillmore; its southern boundary is La Grange Township, of Bond County. It is bounded on the west by Hillsboro and Grisham Townships. The area embraces one township and a half, the northern part being designated as Township 8 north, Range 3 west, while that division lying south of the dividing line is known as Township 7 north, of Range 3 west. The township is well drained by a number of small creeks and their tributaries, which meander through the prairie in many different directions. The most prominent of these are McDavid's Branch, in the southeastern part and the East Fork of Shoal Creek, near the eastern boundary. The first named rises near the northeastern corner of the township, flows in a zigzag channel toward the southwest to within a mile of the county line, where it empties into Shoal Creek.

East Fork, the largest and most important water-course, flows in a southerly direction through the eastern part of the township, and affords an excellent system of natural drainage, plenty of stock water and is indispensable to the success of the farmer and grazier in this region. Bear Creek is a stream of considerable size in the western portion. It receives many small tributaries, which frequently flood the lands through which they flow during very rainy seasons. Brush Creek flows in a northwesterly direction and intersects the northern boundary at a point about one half mile east of Hillsboro Township. Wolf Pen Branch and Indian Camp Branch are small streams in the western part, but are of no considerable importance. The greater part of the surface of East Fork consists of undulating and gently rolling prairie lands, of the very best and most fertile soil in the county. In the southern and southeastern parts, for about three miles along Bear Creek and McDavid's Branch, the surface is broken and in some places hilly. The soil on these high places differs very materially from that of the prairies, being thinner and more sandy, but nevertheless very productive.

The greater amount of timber is in the southern part of the township, adjacent to the creeks already named. There are also small strips of woodland in the eastern and northeastern parts, but the most of this has been cleared and put in cultivation. Like the timber in the other townships of the county, the varieties consist of elm along the water-courses, hickory, oak and walnut on the uplands. The best of the timber was cut years ago, what is left being merely a new growth, which has made its appearance since the country was settled. On McDavid's Branch, in the western part of the township, is a large, beautiful spring, where the [illegible] Indians in years gone by made their home. Near this spring numerous relics have been found, such as beads, flint spear heads, silver trinkets of various kinds, pipes, stone axes, etc. These Indians did not remain long after the white man made his appearance, but left for parts unknown in the year 1[illegible]. Scattered bands frequently visited the scenes of their former camping-ground year after year, but they never remained for any great length of time. [illegible] disappeared, and no Indians have been seen in East Fork since 1[illegible]. The first settler in this township was William McDavid, who came to Illinois from Tennessee as long ago as the year 1820, and entered a piece of land lying in Section 34, [illegible] now known as McDavid's Point. He came in company with one Jesse Johnson, who stopped at the little settlement in Grisham Township near where the village of Donnellson now stands.

At the time McDavid settled in East Fork, there was no house nearer than five miles, and for several months his neighbors were few and scattering. Time, however, makes great changes and within a few years the little settlement became one of the most thrifty and flourishing communities in the county. McDavid lived in the place where he first settled exactly forty-six years. He died the 14th day of February, 1866. His wife is still living, having reached the ripe old age of eighty-two years. The old homestead is now owned by his son, T. W. McDavid, who has added to it much of the surrounding land. His farm is one of the largest in the county. Another son, W. C. McDavid, lives on the farm adjoining that of his brother. He was the first white person born in the township, and his whole life has been passed within its borders. The next settler of whom anything definite is known was James Card. He found his way into the wilds of East Fork in the year 1821, and located the farm now owned by Daniel Cress in Section 4. Here he erected a cabin and lived one year when his wife died, after which he returned to his former home in Kentucky. In the year 1823 he came back to Illinois and settled in the northern part of East Fork near the Irving Township line, where he remained for two years. He moved from this last place to Hillsboro Township. Card came from the mountains of [illegible] and was in many respects a remarkable man. Daring, enterprising and [illegible], he knew no such word as fail, and all his undertakings were crowned with success. He made the first journey from this township to St. Louis for flour for the settlement, a task attended by no little trouble and inconvenience, as there were no roads in the country. He directed his course across the almost trackless prairies by means of a pocket compass, cut his own roads in the woods through which he was obliged to pass, and [illegible] traveling with his slow ox team. The return trip was made in face of fully as many difficulties, as he was more heavily loaded, and the way was made almost impassable in some places by the heavy rainfall. Several sons of Mr. Card are living in Illinois, one of them being a business man of Hillsboro. A number of settlers located in the southern part of the township between the years 1821 and 1826, among whom were the following: Joseph Williams, John Kirkpatrick E. Guin, Henry Rowe and David Bradford. Williams settled on the farm where Riley Hampton now lives. Kirkpatrick located in the southwest corner of the township near the village of Donnellson. The places on which the other three settled is not known, nor could the dates of their deaths be ascertained. The earliest settler in the northern part of East Fork was Benjamin Rhodes. He came here from Southern Indiana in the year 1826 and located a farm in Section 8, about two and a half miles east of Hillsboro. Aside from the little settlement at McDavid's Point already alluded to, Rhodes' cabin was

he disposed of all his possessions in this State and moved to Arkansas.

He was a man of sterling integrity high moral character and unbounded hospitality. No one was ever allowed to leave his pioneer home in need of anything which his liberal hand could supply. He raised a family of eleven children of whom seven are still living. Andrew J. Williford, one of the sons of Jordan Williford, can be called an early settler, as he came here with his father when but eleven years old, and has been a resident of the township ever since. He is a Baptist preacher and, like his father before him, is a man universally respected by the community in which he has resided. Robert and Joseph Mann, two brothers, were among the first settlers in the northern part of East Fork. Little is known definitely about them, as to where they came from or how long they remained, but they are spoken of as good citizens and were well thought of. Just south of the place where the Mann brothers settled, James Walker located, though how long he remained was not learned. The Allens

Edwardsville and the little mill on Shoal Creek, in Grisham Township, were the only places where breadstuffs could be obtained. The first mill in the township was built by G. W. Traylor in the southeastern part, about the year 1830, as near as could be ascertained. This was a steam mill with saw attached, and was in operation about twenty-five years. Another mill run by steam was that of D. M. Williams, in the southern part. This mill was in operation as early as the year 1840, but at just what date it was erected, and how long it was run, was information which the writer was unable to obtain. A. M. Miller built a mill in 1867, which is still in operation. This is a steam mill with saw attached, and is doing a good business. The Brown Mill was moved into this township about the year 1875, and operated till 1877, when it was torn down, and taken to Fillmore Township, a few miles away, where it is still standing.

C. C. Root has a saw-mill in operation in the southern part of the township, which is doing a large and paying business. There have been several portable mills in the township at various times, but none of them did business on a very extensive scale. They have all been removed, and, at the present time, there are but the two mills already mentioned in operation in this section of the county.

The stock business—breeding, raising and shipping stock, receives considerable attention from the citizens of East Fork, and a number of large farms are to be seen where large herds of fine cattle and sheep are kept.

Prominent among those who make the stock business especially are J. B. McDavid, William H. Wilson and Thomas H. Wilson. McDavid owns one of the most extensive tracts of land in the county, there being in his farm over one hundred and twenty acres of choice land, which is well stocked. Thomas H. Wilson owns some six hundred and forty acres of land in the best part of the township, and has some very fine breeds of cattle and sheep. The first stock-markets were reached by driving the cattle overland to St. Louis, but the presence of railroads in the county brings the market nearer home. The first roads through East Fork were probably better than the early roads in any other part of the county, as there are but few hills to cross and little woods to go through. The township is now well supplied with good roads passing through it or along its boundaries.

The oldest road through the township is the Vandalia and Hillsboro road, which connects those two places, and is one of the most important highways in the county. It intersects the eastern boundary of the township at a point about one mile and a half southeast of Hillsboro, and passes through the township in a southeasterly direction. Its course varies but little till within a couple of miles from the line which separates the township from Fillmore, where it bears southward for a short distance. The Hillsboro and Fillmore road passes through the northern part of the township from east to west, and is one of the early roads of the county. It was laid out in the year 1825, and established in 1827. Among the first roads laid out in the township was the Irving road which runs through the western part from north to south. It intersects the Fillmore and Hillsboro road at right angles about one-half mile from the Irving line and the Vandalia and Hillsboro road at McDavid's Point in the southern part of the township. The Hillsboro and Greenville road runs in a southerly direction from Hillsboro and forms part of the boundary between [illegible]

L. H. Thomas

township in different directions and intersect each other at various points, but they are known by no particular names.

The early pioneers of East Fork were a moral and religious people as is evidenced in the fact of a church being established as far back as the year 1830. The Bethel Regular Baptist Church dates its organization from this year, though there had been religious services held at different places in the township several years previous to that time. The first sermon was preached by Elder James Street, in a private dwelling house. He was assisted in the services by Elder Jordan, and together they organized the church already named some time afterward.

The first meetings of this church were held in private dwellings of the members in cold and inclement weather, and in the groves, "God's first temples," when the weather would admit of out door services. Among the first members of this church were the following: Eleanore Freeman, Mary Goodwin, James Card, Mr. and Mrs. Colbert Blair, not one of whom is now living. James Street was the first pastor, in which capacity he acted for about twenty-five years. He was succeeded by Elder Larkin Craig, of Kentucky who ministered unto the church for a period of about forty years. Craig was a fine pulpit orator and a man of more than ordinary vitality and energy. He would frequently travel twenty-five miles on Saturday, preach Saturday night Sunday morning, afternoon and evening, and be at home in time to do the greater part of a day's work the following Monday. Elder Sears assisted Craig for several years, preaching in the latter's absence.

Willis Dodson had charge of the church for five years. He was succeeded by Elder Peter Long, who preached for the congregation a long time. The present pastor, A. J. Williford, has been preaching for the church during the last twenty years. The house in which the church was organized belonged to Elisha Freeman, and stood in the southeast part of the township. This was the principal place of worship for about ten years. The first church edifice was built of logs and stood one mile north of the place where the church was organized. It served as a place of worship about six years, when the organization was moved farther west and the meeting place changed to a little schoolhouse on Shoal Creek. The congregation met at this place until the year 1855, at which time the building in which they now worship, was erected. This house stands on an acre of ground which was donated the church by Samuel Brockman. The house was remodeled in the year 1880, and is a very pleasant and comfortable house of worship. The church has decreased somewhat in membership through deaths and removals, having at present only about thirty names on the books. The Presbyterians organized a society in the year 1833, under the auspices of Revs. Joel Knight and John Barber. The original membership was about ten or twelve in number, mostly from other churches in the county. Their first building was of logs, and stood on Section 4, in the northern part of the township. For a number of years public services were conducted at this place, but the organization was finally abandoned or moved to some other place. Nothing definite concerning this church could be learned.

The Methodists have an organization in the southern part of the township, where for years a faithful band of Christians have met to worship. This church is no longer the stronghold that it used to be, many of the members having died and many moved to distant places.

The writer was unable to obtain any facts or data concerning this society, and much to his regret was obliged to pass it by with the foregoing brief notice.

The Presbyterians organized a society, known as the McDavid's Point Cumberland Presbyterian Church, in the year 1857. The organization was brought about by the labors of Revs. Joel Knight and Joseph Bone.

The records of the church give the names of ten persons as constituting the original membership, most of them being from the church at Donnellson. We give some of their names as follows: William Linxwiler and wife, J. B. McDavid and wife, Mrs. Elizabeth McDavid. Many of the best citizens from time to time been members of this church. The first building used for a place of worship was the schoolhouse, where the congregation met for almost three years. As the church increased in numbers, a larger house was required, and their present commodious structure was erected in the year 1860. This building is 30x40 feet frame, and will comfortably seat three hundred and fifty persons. It cost the sum of $2,000 and is one of the most comfortable and substantial church edifices in the county. It was dedicated in the year 1861, by Rev. J. B. Logan. A flourishing Sunday school is maintained in connection with the church, and like the congregation, is in splendid working order. Rev. J. B. Logan was the first pastor of the church. He was succeeded by L. P. Dutheridge, who ministered in the congregation for several years, and was in turn succeeded by Rev. T. W. McDavid.

Revs. Daniel Bell, E. R. Jones and E. R. Rogers have preached for the church at different times, though not as regular pastors. At present the congregation is without a pastor. The Walnut Grove Free Methodist Church is located in the southern part of the township, and was organized in the spring of 1880 by F. H. Ashcroft, with a membership of twenty-nine.

For six months after the organization, all the public services of the society were held in the barn and private dwelling of William Neal. The house in which the congregation now worships was built in the fall of 1880. This is a very tastefully arranged little building, and cost about $600. The first sermon was preached in the new house by Rev. E. Outlander. The first pastor of the church was Rev. C. A. Flemming. Present membership, about thirty; services are held every Sabbath; prayer-meetings every Wednesday evening. It is impossible to estimate the great good done by these religious societies, in the communities where they are to be found. They have had a tendency to elevate the morals and strengthen the nobler instincts of life. Many vices have been shunned through their influence, and the result is an abundant harvest of pure lives. May the churches continue their well-begun work until

"All crimes shall cease, and ancient frauds shall fail
Returning justice lift aloft her scale
Peace o'er the world her olive wand extend,
And white-robed innocence from Heaven descend."

The early school history of the township is almost wholly lost in the shadows of the past and many dates and interesting incidents relating thereto, have been forgotten long since hence, we cannot hope to give it with perfect correctness. The first schoolhouse, as near as can be learned, was built in the year 1828, on Section 8. This was a diminutive log cabin of the most primitive kind, no vestige of which remains to show the exact spot where it stood. One of the first schools was taught by Lewis Cass, in the year 1829. The house in which Cass wielded the birch stood near McDavid's Branch, and was similar in many respects to most of the schoolhouses of that day, having neither floor nor chimney. A log removed from the side of the building left a considerable opening, over which greased paper was pasted, thus affording a very fair substitute for a window. Fires were built in one end of the room, the smoke finding its way out through a large opening in the roof the best way it could. The furniture was of the simplest kind, consisting of a few benches made of hewed logs, and a broad writing desk, fastened to the wall by means of several long pins. These early schools were all supported by subscription, and were attended by the children of the settlers from miles around. The first public school was taught by A. J. Williford, in a little house which stood near the county line. This school was taught in 1839, and lasted but three months. Michael Walker was one of the early teachers of East Fork, having taught a school in the western part of the township in the year 1830.

The first frame schoolhouse was built in 1843, on McDavid's Branch. There are now seven good schoolhouses in the township, five of them frame and two brick. The school board is composed of the following gentlemen, viz., John Fath, W. S. Barry, A. C. Williams, Trustees; George Linxwiler, Treasurer.

The East Fork Post Office was established in the year 1873, with S. H. Smith as Postmaster. This office was kept in Smith's store, in the western part of the township. It was discontinued several years since.

The first store in the township was kept by a Mr. Cockerel, whose stock of merchandise consisted of groceries, boots, shoes, dry goods and whisky. His place of business was in the southern part of the township, and was the scene of many knockdowns and riots, occasioned by a too free use of the fire-water. One evening a man stopped here, on his way, as he said, to Kentucky. He drank heavily, and did not take his departure until a late hour in the night. The next morning his dead body was found a short distance below, on which were marks indicating the fact that he had been choked to death. The supposition was that he had been followed, robbed and murdered by some unknown parties who had been on his track for the purpose. No clew to the mystery was ever found. The body was buried near the spot where it was found, according to the law of that day.

A man by name of Rutter was killed near

Wood. It seems that the two had some difficulty, during which Rutter became very abusive, and wanted to fight Wood. The latter tried to get away, and begged to be let alone, as he wanted no trouble. Rutter, however, would not be pacified, but continued to follow Wood up, and finally struck him. Wood returned the blow, and struck Rutter on the neck just below the ear. The blow was fatal. Rutter dropped and died instantly. Nothing was ever done with Wood for the killing.

A part of the village of Donnellson lies in East Fork, though none of the original plat of the town. There is one good store here kept by R. C. Clark, whose stock of merchandise represents a capital of several thousand dollars. M. N. Allen keeps an agricultural store in connection with his blacksmith shop, and is doing a very fair business.

Over Clark's storeroom is a nice, commodious Hall, where Lodge No. 255, A., F. & A. M., holds its meetings. This lodge was established October 8, 1858, by Most Worshipful Master Harrison Dill with a membership of seven. Their names are as follows: William Gordon, M. S. Davenport, J. C. Hanner, P. S. Davenport, Casba Hawkins, Tipton Cox and James H. Moss. The first officers were William Gordon, W. M.; M. S. Davenport, S. W.; J. C. Hanner, J. W. The hall was built in the year 1861. Present officers of the Lodge are: M. N. Allen, W. M.; R. C. Clark, S. W.; F. W. Kunmell, J. W.; J. B. Casy, S. D.; H. S. Hanner, J. D.; B. F. McLain, Sec.; William Williams, Treas.; Henry Walkerlin, Tiler. Present membership, 35. At one time this was one of the strongest lodges in the county, but of late years the membership has decreased to a considerable extent.

Several granges and farmers' clubs have been organized throughout the township, but

CHAPTER XIX.*

FILLMORE TOWNSHIP—BOUNDARIES—FIRST GROWTH—PIONEERS—MILLS—SCHOOLS—CHURCHES, ETC.

"To the West, to the West, there is wealth to be won;
The prairie to break is the work to be done—
We'll try it, we'll [illegible] it, and never despair
While there's light in the sunshine and breath in the air;
The [illegible] independence that labor shall buy
Shall strengthen our hands and forbid us to sigh.
Away, far away, let us hope for the best,
And build up new homes in the land of the West."
—*Mackay.*

THE great rapidity with which certain portions of the Western States have been explored, mapped out and settled, and the numerous changes that have been made by bringing the vast fertile prairies, but a few years ago the roving grounds of savage Indians and vast herds of deer and buffalo, into cultivation, furnishing happy homes for hundreds of the restless population of the South and East, has [illegible] the wonder and admiration of the entire country. Especially is this true of that portion of Montgomery County to which this chapter is devoted; although settled in a very early day, it is, comparatively speaking, a new country. Fillmore is situated in the southeastern part of the [illegible] from Witt Township [illegible] on the south, a[illegible] Shelby and Fayette Counties [illegible] eastern, while East Fork Township [illegible] boundary. It is [illegible] by the East Fork of Shoal Creek, [illegible] flowing in a [illegible] western part. [illegible] importance has its source in Section 10, and flows in a southeasterly direction, draining that part of the township. Hurricane Creek and Dry Fork are the principal water-courses in the southern portion, and along which the first settlements of the county were made. The surface is undulating and gently rolling in the northern half, while along the course of Shoal Creek the land is more broken, being considerably hilly in some localities. The soil like that of the greater part of the county, is a rich, dark loam, sand mixed in certain places near the streams, and very fertile. Clay underlies a great deal of the surface, making it easily drained. Gravel beds and sand banks of considerable extent are found in the vicinity of Shoal Creek and other water-courses, sufficient for building roads and all other practical purposes. The southern part was at one time covered with a dense growth of deciduous timber, among which was a very large proportion of walnut, maple, oak, hickory and other valuable varieties. Much of this was used for rails, and destroyed by the early settlers in clearing their lands, as they then had no adequate idea of its value. Some years since, many thousand feet of black walnut were exported annually, besides immense quantities of oak, maple and sycamore lumber. There is still a good supply left, which, by judicious management, will supply all demands for lumber for many years to come.

The forest productions in Fillmore are not excelled in quantity or quality by any other township in Montgomery County.

*By [illegible]

The principal crops to which the farmer looks for his maintenance are wheat, to which the soil seems peculiarly adapted; corn, rye, oats, hay, vegetables, fruits—in short, all the productions common to Southern Illinois.

The first settlements in what is now known as Fillmore Township were made by a small band of pioneers from the State of Kentucky, as early as the year 1817. The previous year had been spent by them within the present limits of Bond County, although at that time there were no civil divisions, Illinois being a Territory.

Being considerably harassed by Indians, they were compelled to fortify, which they did by building a block-house, where the entire company took refuge. Several attacks were made at different times on this fort but so obstinately was it defended by the brave little garrison that the savages, finding they could accomplish nothing by their hostility, finally withdrew, and gave the settlers no further trouble. Parties from this little settlement passed through the southern part of the present township of Fillmore in one of their hunting excursions, and, being favorably impressed with the appearance of a tract of land on Hurricane Creek, induced the company to locate there, which they did in the spring of 1817. This was the first settlement by white men in Montgomery County. Among this little band of pioneers were Harris Revis, Henry Hill, Levi Casey, Aaron Casey, John Lee, and a number of others whose names have faded from memory. Their little cabins were built in a group around a large spring, from which each family obtained its supply of water. The Indians at that time had undisputed sway, but caused the settlers no annoyance after they located in this locality. Bears and wolves infested the woods in great numbers, proving very destructive to the live stock, which had to be closely watched to insure safety. It required will, nerve and a determined resolution to successfully grapple with the many serious obstacles presented; yet, despite all the hardships and trials through which they were called to pass, the pioneers flourished and were happy. As time passed, the different members of the little community selected the lands destined for their future homes.

Revis located his claim on Dry Fork Creek, near the southeast corner of the township, where he lived until the year 1840, at which time he died. Several grandchildren are living in Fillmore and adjoining townships. Henry Hill entered a piece of land adjoining that on which Revis settled.

Both of these places are now owned by Samuel Hill, a grandson of Henry Hill, and one of the well-to-do citizens of Fillmore.

John Hill improved a farm in the vicinity, which is still in the possession of his descendants.

Levi Casey settled on the place since known as the Briggs farm. He sold the place in 1837, and, with his family moved to Shelby County, where he afterward died.

Aaron Casey, a son-in-law of Revis, settled on a part of the Samuel Hill farm, which was his home for twenty-three years. A portion of this place was improved by John Lee, also, who purchased it about one year after its settlement by Revis. Joseph Wright was one of the little community. The place which was selected for his home is now owned by his son, Jarrett Wright, a prominent citizen of the township. A part of the Wright farm was improved by Henry Piatt, who came to the State in the year 1818. He was an upright honorable man, and one of the leading citizens in the community. He became the possessor of a considerable tract of land, and a number of his grandchildren are now living in the county One of the most prominent pioneers of Fillmore and one who did as much, if not more, than any other man to advance its material interests was Newton Coffee, father of Cleveland S. Coffee. Identified with the early history of the county his life demands more than a mere passing notice. He was born among the hills of Kentucky, where were passed his youth and early manhood in those rugged out door pursuits which so well fitted him for a pioneer. When he came to Illinois, the territory now embraced in Montgomery County was a wilderness, into which but few white men had penetrated. The one small settlement already referred to was the only spot within its borders cheered by the presence of civilization, and of this little community he had no knowledge until nearly one year passed away. He built a little cabin in the timber near the Bond County line, and lived there for several years, with no neighbors nearer than eight miles. This was in the fall of 1817. After leaving his place here he went farther north and entered the land where Hillsboro now stands, twenty acres of which he afterward donated for the county seat. He died in the year 1[illegible]49, at a good old age. The place where he settled lies in Section 18 South Fillmore, and is at present owned by his son, Cleveland S. Coffee. A number of early settlers located in the vicinity of the Coffee farm in 1819 and 1820, among whom were [illegible]ton Whitten, Colbert Blair, Thomas Beck and Stephen Wynne. They were all Kentuckians. Whitten bought a tract of land on Dry Fork, which he improved the year after coming to the State. The place is now in possession of his son, Thomas Whitten. Beck added an eighty-acre tract lying just north of Coffee's farm. This comprises the early settlement of the southern part of the township, as far as we have been able to learn its history. Other early settlers there probably were whose names properly belong to the foregoing list, but in our research we have been unable to obtain any particulars concerning them. The northern part of the township was settled by emigrants from Kentucky, Tennessee and North Carolina, but it was a number of years after the settlements already referred to were made. Among the first to locate and improve farms in North Fillmore were James Card, T. J. Todd, John Alexander and M. Mason.

The oldest settler now living in the county is Cleveland S. Coffey. He was fifteen years of age when his father came to this part of the State, and for sixty-five years has been a resident of Fillmore Township. He is still a vigorous man for his years, and in possession of all his mental faculties. The writer will always remember the pleasant hours passed under the hospitable roof of this stanch old pioneer while gleaning the facts of history contained in these pages.

For many years during the early history of this section of the country, the lives of the pioneers were not enviable ones. Their trials were numerous, and the hardships they were called upon to encounter would discourage the bravest-hearted of the present day. Hard as was the life in the wilderness, it had its seasons of recreation, when the pioneers would meet, recount various incidents, talk over old times, and thus relieve the monotony of their isolated situation. Light hearts, good health and clear consciences made the toilsome hours pass pleasantly, and old men now living whose youth was passed amid the stirring scenes of those times look back with pleasure to the old days as the most enjoyable period of their existence. The nearest market where groceries could be obtained was St. Louis, then but a mere village, fifty-five miles distant. Flour and meal were obtained at Pad's Mill, about ten miles nearer. Many of the early families manufactured their own meal. Cleveland Coffey gives the following description of a primitive hand-mill used by his father: "The top of a solid hickory stump was hollowed out to the depth of about eight or ten inches. Over this was suspended a heavy iron wedge made fast to a pole, after the manner of an old-fashioned well-sweep. By working this up and down with considerable force, the corn in the hollow could be crushed and a very good meal obtained." Wild meat of all kinds was plenty, on which the pioneer's family fared sumptuously. Tanned deer-skins formed the wearing apparel of the men, while the women clothed themselves with a coarse cloth manufactured from cotton, of which each settler raised a goodly patch. The first mill in Fillmore was erected in the year 1825, by John Beck. This was merely a tread-mill, which the proprietor operated with a yoke of oxen, and, although an insignificant affair, it answered the purpose for which it was intended, and for a number of years did all the grinding for the entire neighborhood. New machinery was afterward supplied, and, altogether, the mill was in operation about twenty years. Benjamin Rose built a little horse-mill in Section 18 about the year 1838, and operated it ten years, when he sold it to a man by the name of Austin. Austin kept the machinery running several years, and did a very flourishing business.

The next mill of which we have any knowledge was a steam-mill, built by John Hill, near where the village of Van Burensburg now stands, in 1840. The mill had but one buhr, and was kept running almost constantly in order to supply the increasing demand for its products. It was sold to Harris Wright and James Kirk in 1842, and by them operated until the year 1846. It was torn down a number of years ago. The first lumber manufactured in the county was sawed by hand with a whip-saw, and used in the construction of Newton Coffey's dwelling house. Some of this lumber can still be seen in the kitchen of Cleveland Coffey's residence.

A saw-mill was built by John Fuller, in Fuller's Grove, about four miles west of Van Burensburg, in the year 1840. It was in operation a little more than one year, when it was sold and removed from the township. A steam saw-mill was built on Shoal Creek, near where the Vandalia road crosses that stream, many years ago. It was in operation but a very short time. A great amount of lumber has been sawn in the forests skirting the several creeks, by portable mills, at different times. Several of these mills are in operation at the present time, and the lumber business still continues to be an important industry.

In educational matters, Fillmore is not behind her sister townships in the county. Her citizens have always taken special interest and pride in the public schools, which have been well sustained and patronized. Its school history begins with the year 1825, or with the advent of Mr. Hatchett, the first teacher. This gentleman taught school in a little log house that had formerly been used as a residence by the family of Aaron Casey. It was situated in the southeast corner of the township, on Hurricane Creek.

The following winter, Benjamin Robbins taught school in a cabin that stood on the east bank of Shoal Creek, near the eastern boundary. Josiah Whitten was one of the pioneer teachers of the county, having taught several terms in the southern part of Fillmore, when the early settlements were in the infancy of their existence.

In these early schools, nothing but the simplest elementary instruction was imparted, as many of the first teachers were men of limited intellectual attainments. Reading, writing, spelling, and the rudiments of arithmetic, comprised the sum total of branches taught.

The first schoolhouses were built of round logs, undressed, with chunks in the cracks and daubed with mud. Puncheon at the bottom and split sticks at the top were the chimney material, with pounded dirt jambs and packed mud hearths. No floors were laid; the earth being smoothed off by constant use, became in time very compact.

There were puncheon and plank seats, without backs. A long window around the room, with a rough writing-desk against the wall, complete the picture of one of these primitive college buildings. This may be taken as a sample and general description of the condition of the schoolhouses in this part of the county from the year 1820 to 1845.

The first frame schoolhouse was built about the year 1845, near the little village of Van Burensburg, and was known as the Easley Schoolhouse. The township has a number of good, substantial frame schoolhouses, all well furnished with patent seats and desks, globes, maps, charts, and other necessary requisites to education. The old cramped ideas of instruction have long since been abandoned, and the schools are now enlivened by an invasion of fresh ideas and methods, which have been well received throughout the township. Near the Dry Fork of Hurricane Creek, a burial-ground was staked off in the year 1821. This graveyard is the site of an old battlefield, where at one time, many years before, an encounter took place between a detachment of United States troops and a band of hostile Indians. Many human bones, musket balls, spear-heads, knives, etc., have been brought to the surface at different times, while graves were being digged. The first interment in this cemetery was that of Stephen White, who died in the summer of 1821. The first marriage in what is now Fillmore Township took place in 1822, the contracting parties being John Revis, son of Harris Revis, and Patsey, daughter of Newton Coffey. The ceremony was performed by Squire Levi Casey. A daughter of John Beck was the first white child born in the county. This birth occurred in 1819, the same year that the family came to the State.

As the country increased in population, good roads became a necessity, and many of the old crooked by-ways were abandoned. The Vandalia road, which passes through the township in a southeasterly direction, was the first regularly established highway. A county road was surveyed and established through the southern part of the township in an early day, the exact date of which was not learned. Many other roads were laid out and improved as the settlements increased, but, as none of them were roads of much importance, a further description is unnecessary.

Van Burensburg is a small village, situated near the southwest corner of the township, about fifteen miles from the city of Hillsboro. It was founded by Joshua White, in the year 1842, who kept a store there for several years. There are now one store, post office, blacksmith shop and two churches. The post office was established about the year 1837, with Benjamin Roberts as Postmaster. The second Postmaster was Robert White. It is kept at present by a man by the name of Bookstrock. One of the first stores in the place was kept by a Mr. Eddy, whose stock of merchandise consisted of groceries, a few dry goods and a plentiful supply of whisky. A man by the name of Nathan Harmon was killed at this place shortly after Eddy started his saloon, under the following circumstances: It appears that Harmon was a dissipated, worthless character, and, when under the influence of whisky, very quarrelsome and abusive. Upon the occasion referred to, he had been drinking rather freely, and, seeing a stranger pass the door of the saloon, made some insulting remark to him. To this speech the stranger paid no attention, but kept on his way, whereupon Harmon became very furious, and started in pursuit, for the purpose, he said, of killing the "damned scoundrel." The stranger tried hard to avoid having any difficulty with the drunken man, but Harmon, with many fearful oaths, sprang upon him. Calmly the stranger met him, turned aside his high, wild thrusts, and, in return, struck him several well-directed and crushing blows on the chest and head. Harmon fell, and in a short time expired. The citizens regarded it as a just punishment, and no arrest was made.

The early pioneers were not derelict in their religious duties, as is proved by the fact that devotional exercises were conducted in the little settlement on Hurricane Creek the first year in which it was founded. These social meetings were held as often as circumstances would admit, in the houses of different members of the community, and were led by some one selected on account of his peculiar fitness. The first church established was in 1820 or 1821, by the Regular Baptists, who were more numerous than any other religious denomination. This church was organized under the pastoral labors of Elder James Street, a preacher who figures rather prominently in the early church history of Montgomery County. He was a man of strong powers of intellect, to which were added fair scholastic attainments and a persuasive power of oratory rarely excelled. He assisted in the organization of all the early churches of his sect in the county, and of him it can truly be said, "his life was spent in traveling about doing good."

The first congregation was known as the Hurricane Creek Regular Baptist Church, to which nearly all the early settlers on Dry Fork and Hurricane Creek belonged. For several years, public services were held in private dwelling houses, but in course of time a log church was built, which stood until the year 1862. At that date, a frame edifice was erected, in which the congregation has worshiped until the present time. Among the pastors of this church were the following: Henry Sayers, James Street, — — Prather and Jackson Williford.

The Methodists held meetings at several different places in the township during the early days of its history, as did also the Presbyterians. Among the pioneer preachers of the latter denomination can be named Revs. Knight, Barlow and Finley. The Shiloh Cumberland Presbyterian Church was in existence as early as the year 1837. It was organized by the Rev. William Finley, in the little village of Van Burensburg, with a considerable membership. The first ordained Elders were John Blair, James R. Abell and Benjamin Rose. Since its organization, the church has had seventeen ordained Elders. The church was re organized several years ago, and the place of meeting changed from Van Burensburg to a point about four miles west, where a neat house of worship was erected. The following preachers have ministered to the congregation: Joseph Barlow, Joel Knight, ——— Smith, William Hutchinson, William Turner, J. B. Mitchell, — — Linxwiler, — — Porterfield, ——— Deatheridge, — — Reppito and T. W. McDavid.

The Methodist Church, known as Fuller's Chapel, was organized at Fuller's Grove many years ago. A house of worship stood a little north of the grove. It was burned in the year 1880, and since that time the congregation have met for worship in different places. The Lutherans have an organization in the eastern part of the township, but nothing was learned concerning this church.

The United Baptist Church was organized by Elder Richard Keel, in the year 1860, at the East Fork Schoolhouse. The first members of this congregation were the following: Richard Blackburn and wife, George Blackburn, Cyrus Whitten and wife, Cleveland S. Coffey, Moses Fuller, Malinda Hurd, Anna Whitten and Betsey Evans.

Richard Keel was the first pastor, in which capacity he acted for two years. Richard Gregg succeeded Keel, and preached about eighteen years. He was followed by David Barber, who had charge of the congregation two years. Newton Coffey has preached for the church about six months. Their present church edifice is situated about one mile and a half northeast of Fuller's Grove, and was built in the year 1861.

The Methodist Church at Van Burensburg was organized about the year 1877. They have a good house of worship, which cost about $1,200.

In addition to the churches already enumerated, there are two other organizations in the township, of which no particulars were obtained by the writer.

Fillmore's war record stands out untarnished. She might risk her reputation on the evidences of loyalty she exhibited during those dark hours when the gallant ship of state was almost stranded upon the rugged rocks of disunion. She furnished her full quota of volunteers, and more. Indeed, Fillmore could not have done otherwise, as loyalty is a ruling passion among her sons. But few firesides were unrepresented where age would permit. Those remaining at home contributed freely and generously of their means, whereby they sought to reward the brave boys who donned the blue. We should be pleased to name each volunteer from this township, and point out his destiny, but space forbids. Broken firesides ever remind us that many a brave boy who responded to his country's call, went, but never returned; and, although no towering shaft nor storied urn marks their last resting-place, a grateful Republic and a grateful people will cherish their memory, and the nation's fame and greatness will be their appropriate monument.

"Their swords are rust; their good steeds dust;
Their souls are with the saints we trust."

CHAPTER XX.

BUTLER GROVE TOWNSHIP—BOUNDARIES—SOIL—TIMBER—EARLY SETTLERS—ROADS—EDUCATIONAL AND RELIGIOUS—VILLAGE OF BUTLER—BUSINESS INTERESTS—SECRET SOCIETIES, ETC.

IN obtaining the fragments of history contained in the following pages, we have been obliged to rely largely for much of the information upon persons who have long been residents of the township, and whose lives have been identified with its development. It may be that some of the facts and dates which are given are only approximations to the truth; other facts of interest may be omitted, while others still may not be accurately recorded, yet we believe that the following statements can be relied upon as a brief synopsis of history free from any serious errors.

Butler Grove was one of the first settled townships of Montgomery County, and was surveyed in the year 1819, at which date there was but one white family living within its boundaries. It lies in the central part of the county, with the following townships as boundaries: Raymond on the north, Irving on the east, Hillsboro on the south, and North Litchfield on the west. Like the greater part of the county, Butler Grove is composed of fine, fertile prairie lands, interspersed with numerous groves and thickly wooded mounds. There are no very large hills, although the southern part is somewhat broken. But little of the land, however, is too broken for cultivation. The most extensive wooded districts are in the northern, northeastern and southern parts. There is also a grove of many acres in the central part of the township, known as Ware's Grove, having derived its name from an old settler, who formerly resided there. It is estimated that the woodland of this township comprises about one-tenth of its area, the remainder being rich, rolling prairie, and contains some of the finest farming lands of Southern Illinois. The quality of the soil on the uplands, in the southern part, is rather inferior for agricultural purposes, although, by proper tillage, remunerative crops are often obtained. The timber is composed mainly of the following varieties: Black oak, white oak, hickory, walnut and cottonwood on the upland, while skirting the creeks on either side are large willows and gigantic sycamore. The best timber has disappeared long since, as the lumber business was carried on quite extensively at an early date.

This township is watered and drained by Brush Creek, the Middle Fork of Shoal Creek, and their tributaries. The former has its source in the northern part, and flows in a southwesterly direction, crossing the township line about one mile west of the village of Butler. Shoal Creek flows in a southeasterly direction through the southeast corner of the township, and receives as a tributary the East Fork of Brush Creek about one half mile north of the township line. There is a small creek in the northern part which flows in a northerly direction, but it is an in-

* By G. N. Berry.

significant stream, being dry the greater part of the warm season. Aside from the creeks enumerated, there are no other streams of importance in the township. During very rainy seasons these creeks frequently overflow their banks and do considerable damage to the farms through which they run, often times carrying away many rods of fencing, and sweeping away entire fields of grain.

The early pioneers of this section found no royal pathway to affluence, and have probably witnessed as great changes wrought by the onward march of civilization as any within the limits of the entire State. They came here when Illinois was in its infancy as a State and when the great West, particularly that portion lying west of the Mississippi, was occupied almost wholly by wild Indian tribes. They have heard and seen the dying away of the voyager's song upon our western waters. They have seen proud cities rear their regal heads upon the favorite hunting grounds of the red men, and the iron horse, the modern civilizer, dart with the speed of the hurricane along the paths beaten into the prairie by the hoofs of the buffalo ages before the white man ever dreamed of battling with the wilderness of the unknown West. All these and many other changes have these hardy pioneers witnessed since they first made their appearance in this part of the Mississippi Valley, and opened up its broad acres to the world's traffic.

The first white settler of Butler Township was Jacob Cress, who moved here with his family during the early part of the year 1818, and located the farm known as the "Old Cress Farm," now owned by Jacob Scherer in Section 34. Mr. Cress was from Indiana, but originally from North Carolina, from which State he moved in the year 1816. The journey of this hardy old pioneer to his new home in the West was replete with many interesting incidents and stirring adventures, and many days were required to reach his destination. It was during the hottest part of the year that this journey was made, and the emigrants found it impossible to travel during the day, owing to the excessive heat and the immense swarms of flies, which proved a serious hindrance to the live stock which Mr. Cress brought with him. At that early date there was not a regularly laid out road in the southern part of Illinois, all roads being mere trails or buffalo paths across the prairies: so Mr. Cress had nothing by which to direct his course but these trails and the stars.

Mr. Cress brought a great deal of live stock with him to Illinois, part of which consisted of a large drove of hogs. To keep them from being lost on the prairie, he had bells put upon them, so the loneliness of their night journeyings was relieved somewhat by the tinkling music never before heard in this western country. Mr. Cress died in the year 1865, full of years and ripe with honors. By his industry and many sterling qualities, he did much toward developing the resources of his township and bringing it up to its present high standard of civilization. Of the children of Mr. Cress there are living at this time one son and four daughters, all of whom are residents of Butler Township.

The next settler was Israel Seward, who moved from Hamilton County, Ohio, in the year 1819, and located his home upon what is known as "Seward's Hill," about one half mile south of the village of Butler. Mr. Seward was a noble type of the pioneer, a man of more than ordinary powers of intellect, and a devoted Christian. Though dead, he still lives in the influence which he formerly exerted upon the community that he was instrumental in founding. The exact date of Mr. Seward's death was not obtained. William Seward, a son, was born in Indiana one year before the family moved to Illinois. He was for a number of years mail carrier between the cities of Hillsboro and Jacksonville. His whole life has been identified with the history of the township and he is justly considered one of its most prominent citizens. The original home of Israel Seward is now owned by his son George C. Seward, the first white child born in Butler Grove Township. He was born October 11, 1821, and has resided at the home he now occupies for the last thirty-six years. One incident in the life of Mr. Seward is remembered with interest by his friends. It was his lot in his younger days to carry the mails, as we have stated, between Jacksonville and Hillsboro, and also between Hillsboro and Alton. At one time there came a freshet which raised the waters of Shoal Creek to an immense height. Mr. Seward tried to cross the creek with a two horse conveyance, but a part of the bridge being carried away by the flood, he found that his vehicle could not withstand the force of the current; so driver, carriage and horses were carried a considerable distance down the stream. Mr. Seward got out of the carriage, and, stepping upon one of the horses, caught hold of a small elm tree, which, after becoming thoroughly wet, he succeeded in climbing. The stream at that time was about three fourths of a mile wide, and the current baffled their efforts to reach the tree. The logs which were being carried down by the stream would strike the tree with such force that he found it extremely difficult to maintain his hold on the branches. From his lofty perch he could see and hear his friends, which served to beguile the long, weary hours he was compelled to pass in his airy prison. He remained in his uncomfortable quarters all night, and it was not until 9 o'clock the next day that his friends succeeded in rescuing him by means of long poles and a horse trough.

A daughter of Israel Seward, Mrs McGowan, lives in the village of Butler, where she has resided the greater part of her life. Israel Seward was a cousin of the late William H. Seward, who served as Secretary of State during the administration of President Lincoln, and whose name is among the brightest upon the pages of American history.

Prominent among the early settlers of Butler Grove was Obadiah Ware, who came to Montgomery County in 1823, locating the west half of the northwest quarter, and the west half of the northwest quarter of Section 15, upon which land he resided during a period of fifty one years. The life of this good man demands more than a passing notice in these pages. Mr. Ware was a native of New Hampshire, where he was born in the year 1795. Reared upon a farm, his early life was passed in the usual routine of farm labor, and he grew to rugged manhood amid the bracing airs of his mountain home, where he was taught the dignity and nobility of labor, and those lessons of economy and frugality which so well fitted him to encounter the difficulties incident to the life of a pioneer. In 1821, after his marriage, he and his young bride started for the Far West to secure a home. Across the great States that stretched away in unbroken and uninterrupted grandeur from the Mississippi eastward, they journeyed until they reached the then diminutive city of St. Louis. He located near that city temporarily, remaining two years, where he engaged in farming. Having a determination to remove to a point where land could be entered, he visited Montgomery County, where he entered the land before referred to. At his home, after a long

his life of usefulness, his wife died in the year 1848. Mr. Ware survived her twenty-eight years, dying September 24, 1876. The following testimonial appears in biographical sketches of citizens of Montgomery County, from which many of the above facts have been gleaned. "Mr. Ware has been a leading and influential member of the Lutheran Church for nineteen years, during which time he has given liberally of his means for the dissemination of Gospel truths, and for the building of houses dedicated to the worship of God. Educational matters have also elicited considerable attention from him, and he has ever been active and generous in his assistance to every project looking to the advancement of educational facilities. He placed a proper and very correct estimate upon the value of our common school system, regarding it as invaluable to the State and the surest bulwark of constitutional liberty." A very eloquent funeral oration was delivered over the remains of Mr. Ware by the Rev. John Hamilton, which has been published and extensively circulated. Two daughters and one son of Mr. Ware are still living — Mrs. Hulda Harris, Elizabeth Wescott and Benjamin Ware. The old Ware farm is now owned by William A. Young.

Benjamin Ware, a brother of Obadiah, was also among the early settlers of the township, locating upon land adjoining that of his brother's. Like the former, he was one of the substantial citizens of the county, and left a reputation upon which no one dared cast a single aspersion. A son, Justus Ware, occupies the farm formerly owned by his father.

Many other early settlers, additional to those already mentioned, are entitled to a notice in these pages. Among these were William Townsend, who located in the southern part of the township as early as the year 1824. He remained here as a citizen for a number of years. The exact date of his death could not be ascertained, and none of his children are living in this part of the State.

William H. Cass came to the county in the year 1824, and settled in the northwestern part of the township, on Section 5. Many other names could be added to the list already given, but the dates of their settlement, and the facts concerning their early life have been obscured by the lapse of time.

Thus many of the old pioneers who were prominently identified with the early history of the township have passed away, "as a tale that is told," many being scattered to other lands, but by far the greater number have passed to "that mysterious bourn from which no traveler ever returns." The first improvement of importance to the pioneer after he has erected a shelter for himself and family, is a mill, an industry that always advances with civilization. The early settlers of Montgomery County were obliged to go to St. Louis for their breadstuffs, and several days were often required to complete the journey. As early as the year 1823, a mill was built at Edwardsville, a distance of thirty-five miles from Hillsboro, which continued to be the source of supplies during the following two years. The first mill in the township was built by Jacob Cress, in the year 1825, and was known throughout the entire country as the "horse mill," horses supplying the power by which the machinery was run. This mill was kept running day and night, and supplied flour and meal to the country within a radius of twelve miles around, people often coming much farther and remaining several days in order to get their grinding done. At that early date, the threshing machine was unknown, wheat being tramped out by horses and sifted by hand at the mill through the large seive made for that purpose. The mill was run in this way until 1845, when the old machinery was taken out, the building remodeled, and new machinery put in, run by steam. One year later, a saw was attached. The mill was kept running a great many years, until the machinery was worn out. The engine was removed in the year 1881, and taken to the village of Butler. The old building is still standing, a monument of the days that were. The next mill was built by a Mr. Seward, about one-half mile south of the town of Butler. This was a combination mill also, steam supplying the power. It was erected in the year 1839, but did not prove a financial success, as it was built upon a scale too extensive for the country at that time. In the enterprise, Mr. Seward became financially embarrassed, and the mill was in operation but a short time. Mr. Seward left the mill standing idle, and went to California, where he remained for several years, amassing quite a fortune in the meantime. He afterward returned home, satisfied his creditors, and disposed of the mill, which was torn down and the machinery removed to the village of Butler.

Another flouring-mill was built by Mr. Hoffman west of the town of Butler, but the exact date of its erection could not be ascertained. It was the only mill of its kind in the township for several years, and was torn down in 1881.

At the present writing there is a very extensive mill in process of construction just north of the village of Butler, which, when completed, will be one of the most complete mills in the county. The building is of brick, 23x36 feet, the engine room 40x18 feet, and was erected at a cost of $4,500. This mill will have three run of stone, and a capacity of about thirty-six barrels of flour per day. The aggregate cost of the mill will probably reach $6,000. It is owned by J. S. Emery, late of Ohio, a man who has spent his life in the milling business.

An extensive creamery was built in the town of Butler, in the year 1875, at a cost of $3,500; the apparatus cost $1,600. This factory was owned by a stock company, and was known as the Monte Cabonne Creamery Company. The enterprise proved very remunerative, but was in operation only two years, being completely destroyed by fire in the year 1877. The loss occasioned by this fire aggregated about $6,000. There have been several planing-mills in the township at different times, but none of them did business on a very large scale. D. W. Manners built and operated a planing mill one-half mile west of the town of Butler, but it is not in operation, it having been injured by fire some time since. Aside from the industries referred to, there have been no others deserving of particular mention in the township.

The first roads through Butler Grove were not laid out with any reference to section lines. Each settler took the shortest route across the prairie in order to arrive at his destination as quickly as possible, and, as a result, there are a great many zigzag roads, which have been a source of considerable annoyance to the land-owners through whose farms they pass. Efforts are being made, however, to have the roads properly established, and in time it will be effected. The first road that was extensively traveled in this part of the county was the old Springfield road, which passes through Butler Grove from northeast to southwest. As early as the year 1825, this was one of the principal thoroughfares of Southern Illinois. The Taylorville road runs through the southeast corner of the township, and intersects the St. Louis road at a point not far from the southern township line, near the city of Hillsboro. The St. Louis road forms part of the southern boundary of this township, and is probably the oldest road in the county.

The township in the main is well supplied with good roads, which are kept in good condition, as the citizens are alive to all public improvements. There are no pikes in the township, owing to a scarcity of gravel.

During the early spring seasons many of the roads become well-nigh impassable, especially those which run through the low prairie lands, and there seems to be no way of obviating the difficulty.

There is one railroad that passes through this township, the Indianapolis & St. Louis, which affords ample means for farmers to ship their agricultural products and live stock. This railroad passes through the southern part running northeast to the village of Butler, where it describes a curve, then bears southeast, crossing the southern boundary line at a point near the Shoal Creek bridge. This railroad has aided largely in the development of the township, although it has had a tendency to affect the business interests of the town of Butler in such a way as to discourage business men from locating there, the greater amount of traffic being taken to the cities of Litchfield and Hillsboro.

A great deal of attention is given to the cause of education in this township, and the schools are among the very best in the State. "The opportunities for acquiring an education in the early pioneer times were scarce, and books were limited," although a school was organized as early as the year 1823. This school was taught in a little log cabin, located on Section 31. The length of the term was three months, and the school was supported by subscription. The name of the teacher was Mrs. Mary Townsend. The first schoolhouse was originally a part of the residence of Capt. Thomas Philips, situated on Section 29. Reuben Ross assisted Mr. Philips in fitting it up for school purposes. This was the only schoolhouse in the southwestern part of the township for a number of years. The next schoolhouse was a log cabin built in the year 1839, near where the Montgomery Schoolhouse now stands, on Section 12. The first school taught in this house was by Miss Mary Burnap, the year after it was built. One among the first buildings used for school purposes was part of the residence of Mr. Seward, near the village of Butler. This building was torn down and moved to the town many years ago, and now forms part of the residence of Mr. Crowley.

Butler Grove now has seven schoolhouses, all good, substantial buildings five of them frame and two of them brick. There are six whole districts, and five union districts in the township, and six schools outside of the town of Butler.

The following named gentlemen comprise the present Board of Township Trustees: William A. Young, Isaac Doyle, Charles W. Jenkins and Robt. Bryce the last named being Township Treasurer and Clerk of the Board. The school year begins the first Monday in October, and the average length of the term is about six and one-half months.

The neat little village of Butler is situated in the southern part of the township, on the Indianapolis & St. Louis Railroad, and was at one time one of the most thriving business points in the county. The growing cities of Hillsboro and Litchfield, on either side, and within a few minutes' ride, have affected its business interests to such an extent that its traffic is no longer of any great importance, although there are several firms that are doing a very fair of amount of business. This town derived its name from the fact that a

W. R. Waggoner

great many of its early settlers came from Butler County, Ohio. The village was built upon land formerly belonging to William Seward, and was laid out by him in the year 1853. The first survey of lots was made by James Starr, who surveyed eighty-six lots and within a short time afterward the remaining lots were surveyed and laid out by a Mr. Bayless. The first store was kept by William Wood, who built a very large and substantial brick building upon the east side of the principal street, about one square north of the railroad. Mr. Wood kept a general stock of merchandise in his store, and was for a number of years one of the leading merchants of Montgomery County. This store building was completely destroyed by fire during the conflagration which swept away the greater part of the town, and of which a more extended notice will be given further on in these pages. There were a number of other business houses built and operated successfully, but the writer was unable to obtain any authentic facts concerning them. At one time in the history of this town there was more grain and live stock handled here than there was at any other town in the county outside of the city of Litchfield. The grain trade is still an important industry, and is carried on by the Brown Bros., who own the warehouse, and buy and ship grain during the entire year.

The town was incorporated in the year 1865. The first schoolhouse built in the village was erected in the year 1857, by John McGowan; an addition was put to it eight years after, so that it consisted of two rooms. When there were more pupils than the house could accommodate, the deficiency was met by securing the use of rooms in private dwelling houses. In the year 1863, the present handsome and commodious school building was erected. It is a two-story brick building, containing four large and handsomely furnished school rooms, and is surmounted by a lofty steeple. The location is an eminence on the eastern slope of Seward's Hill, in the southwestern part of the town, and commands an extensive view of the surrounding country. This building was erected at a cost of $11,000, and is one of the finest and most completely furnished schoolhouses in Montgomery County. The first school in the village was taught by Charles Seward, in the year 1857. This school lasted but two months, and was supported by subscription. Among the early teachers were George Paisley, Edmund Keeler, Charles Parks, Jesse Barrett, Rev. Daniel Lee and Rev. —— Mize. The last named was a Baptist preacher of considerable ability, and, in addition to his duties as teacher, he ministered to the Baptist Church during the time that he remained in the village. The schools are, at the present writing, under the efficient management of Prof. Nathan T. Veatch, A. M., assisted by Lucy Stuckey, Josephine Wilson and Grace Bryce. The average attendance during the past year was 135. The citizens of Butler are justly proud of their schools, which, in point of discipline and thoroughness of the work done, will compare favorably with the best conducted schools in the State. The first physician to locate in Butler was Charles Harper, who came to Illinois in company with his early friend, ex-Gov. Bissell, with whom he practiced his profession for a number of years. He is not at present a practicing physician, having retired from the profession several years ago on account of his advanced age and infirmities incident thereto. The date of his location in Butler was the year 1877, and he is still a resident of the village.

The following list comprises the physicians who have practiced medicine in Butler i different times: ——— Sargent, J. B. White, Jesse Stick, C. R. Ross, Daniel Schadron, P. L. Brown, Benjamin Perlee, J. H. Kesler, A. Gifford. The present physician is Dr. M. L. Moyer, of whom a more extended notice will be given in the biographical department of this work.

Henry Richmond was the first Postmaster of the town. The office was established sometime in the year 1856, and was the first post office in the township.

Bryant McReynolds kept the first hotel in the Butler House in the year 1858. This house is still standing, and is kept at present by Henderson Howard, who has been in the hotel business here for a number of years past. The business of Butler is represented by the following parties and firms:

J. W. Weisner, M. D., druggist and dealer in groceries, notions and fancy articles. Dr. Weisner keeps a very complete stock of goods, and reports his business good.

Hoes & Bros., is the leading dry goods house in the town. They also keep a line of boots and shoes, hats and caps, and ready-made clothing. Their business is in a prosperous condition, and their stock represents capital to the amount of several thousand dollars.

H. Boss keeps a shoe-shop and restaurant.

N. J. Rhodes, dealer in dry goods, boots, shoes and groceries.

— Webber, merchant tailor.

Robert Bryce, blacksmith and dealer in agricultural implements.

Brown & Bro., grain buyers and stock dealers. This firm is one of the strongest grain firms in the county, owning warehouses here, and a large elevator in Hillsboro.

Robert Henderson, barber.

J. C. Sammons and Conrad Hentus, blacksmiths.

William N. Brookman, Henry Wilson, Hiram Nail and James White, carpenters.

J. C. Emery, miller.

H. Howard, veterinary surgeon.

The Odd Fellows and the Masonic fraternities both have lodges in Butler. Butler Lodge, No. 617, I. O. O. F., was organized in the year 1865, with the following-named persons as charter members: Henry Richmond, G. W. Brown, Jr., W. B. McReynolds, Samuel Berry, Alexander Gray, William Williamson and George Grassell. The charter was issued October 11, of the above year, by A. S. Barry, G. M. The present officers of this lodge are as follows: Daniel Pope, N. G.; A. D. Washburne, V. G.; George Sharpe, Secretary; George W. Brown, Treasurer: William N. Brookman, Warden: Fred Luddcke, I. G.; R. B. Hough, O. G.: S. M. Stuckey, Conductor: C. O. Brown, R. S. N. G.: W. A. Weisner, L. S. N. G.; James Duke, R. S. V. G.; A. H. Brown, L. S. V. G.; T. S. Hoes, R. S. S.; M. L. Moyer, L. S. S.; W. A. Weisner, M. L. Moyer, Fred Luddcke, F. S. Hoes, R. B. Hough, Trustees. The lodge numbers about forty members, and meets every Saturday night in the hall which they own in connection with the Masonic fraternity.

Butler Lodge, No. 459, A., F. & A. M., was established in 1865, with nine charter members. The first officers of this lodge were Samuel Holmes, W. M.; James Rogers, S. W.; J. A. Roth, J. W.; C. M. Ross, Secretary; William Wood, Treasurer; J. Judd, S. D.; M. Helm, J. D.; G. W. Van Sandt, Tiler. The first petition was presented August 1, 1865, by Thomas T. Eliman. The present officers are: G. W. Brown, Jr., W. M.; M. M. Stuckey, S. W.; Isaac Doyle, J. W.; Charles O. Brown, Secretary; H. S. Stanley, Treasurer; W. G. Diddle, S. D.; William Eliman, J. D.; John Van Dorn,

Tiler. There are about forty five members of this lodge, and it is in good working condition. The hall in which both lodges meet is very nicely furnished, and is situated on the main street of the village. It was built in the year 1866.

Several very destructive fires for so small a place have visited Butler at different periods during its history. In 1866, the large store building occupied by J. R. Roth, near the railroad, and the saloon adjoining it, were totally destroyed by fire, entailing a very heavy loss upon the owners of the property. The planing-mill of D. W. Manners, located in the western part of the town, was burned to the ground in the year 1867. In the spring of 1875, the dwelling belonging to William Van Sandt, in the northern part of the village, adjoining the blacksmith shop of Robert Bryce, took fire, and, before the flames could be checked, the building was almost entirely consumed. The most destructive fire that ever visited Butler was the conflagration of 1877, which swept away an entire block of buildings on the east side of the main street, opposite the Butler House. Concerning this fire we copy the following account from the revised village ordinance of December, 1871. "On the night of the first or the morning of the second day of October, 1877, a fire broke out in the building adjoining Seward's Hall and continued its destructive work until the building and the hall, containing all the village records, papers and other property belonging to the village were consumed by the devouring elements against all the attempts made to save them." Later, in the same year, the creamery was burned, but to this fire we have already referred.

The religious history of this township dates from the first settlement, although there were no churches organized for a number of years later. Religious services were held from house to house, and it was quite a number of years before any of the denominations gained sufficient strength to erect places of public worship. The first regularly organized church, of which there is any authentic record, is the Montgomery Methodist Episcopal Church, about five miles north of Hillsboro, and about the same distance northeast of Butler. This church was organized in the year 1836, and consisted of the following members: James Osborne and wife, Michael Webber, Mrs. Sarah Webber, Henry Nichols, Mrs. Ellen Nichols, Joseph Webber, Mrs. Eunice L. Webber, James Wiley, Mrs. Sarah Wiley, Nicholas Webber, Albert Dryer and Mrs. Eunice Dryer. The church was organized under the ministerial labors of the Rev. — — Hall. For a number of years the congregation worshiped in a schoolhouse near where their church building now stands. The neat and comfortable house in which the congregation now worship was built in the year 1872. The building is frame, 40x60 feet, and was erected at a cost of $2,000. It was dedicated the latter part of the year 1872, by the Rev. C. P. Baldwin. It belongs to the Irving and Butler Circuit, and is at present ministered to by Rev. W. C. Howard, of the latter place. The Cherry Grove Methodist Episcopal Church, situated about three and a half miles northwest of Butler, was established as early as the year 1838, at which time it had a considerable membership, the names of whom were not obtained, as the early records of the church have been lost. From some cause or other, this church so declined that in a few years after its organization there remained of it but a few scattered families. It was re-organized in the year 1851, when the church for the first time elected Trustees, and assumed the name of Cherry Grove Church. The following are the names of those who assumed membership at its re-organization: John Nail, Mrs. Martha Nail, Nathan Nail, Mrs. Sarah Nail, Mrs. Susan Williams, Anderson Walker and wife, Manasseh Camp and wife, William Williams and wife, James Roberts and wife and Mrs. Sarah Baker. The congregation originally worshiped in a private dwelling house, upon the farm now belonging to D. C. Burris. Their present house of worship was erected in the year 1856, at a cost of about $1,600. This church is one of the points on the Butler and Irving Circuit, and is at present enjoying the pastoral labors of Rev. W. C. Howard.

In the year 1856, the Butler Methodist Episcopal Church was organized by Rev. — – Boon. This was the first church established in Butler, and consisted of the following members: Mrs. Alexander Gray, Moses Berry, Mrs. Eliza Berry, Mrs. J. M. Ghaston, Thomas Wood, William Williamson, James Wood and wife and Mrs. Benaiah Kelly. The first preacher who ministered to the congregation was the Rev. J. E. Lindley. Since its organization it has had the services of the following pastors: Revs. — – Aldridge, —— Calric, R. W. Travis, T. S. Johnson, O. E. Orr, J. H. Holloway, W. F. Lowe, M. M. Cooper, J. D. Bodkin, R. M. Beech, J. W. Lapham, F. D. Randall and W. C. Howard. Their house of worsihp is a very neat, substantial frame building, located in the western part of the village, and cost the sum of $2,500. It was built in the year 1867, and dedicated the year following. The present membership of this church is about seventy-five or eighty, a number considerably smaller than it was several years ago, many families who once belonged having removed from the village.

The Presbyterian Church of Butler was organized in the year 1858, in the old school-house, by a committee, consisting of the following persons: Rev. R. M. Roberts, minister; F. W. Washburne, M. D., and J. F. Eckles, Elders. The names of the original members are as follows: Mrs. W. H. Harper, Mrs. Catharine Coudy, Israel Seward, William Seward, Mrs. Mary Cunningham, Mrs. Martha Burnap, Robert Bryce, S. M. Hedges, Mrs. Deliverance Hugg, Mrs. Mary McReynolds, Mrs. Steere and Mrs. Sarah Ware. The first pastor who ministered to the church was Rev. R. W. Roberts. Since then the following ministers have preached for the church: Rev. W. L. Mitchell, – – Todd, Mr. Cornelius V. Canfort, licentiate, Rev. Lougheed, Mr. Moses Paisley, licentiate, and Rev. J. E. Spillman. The last-named minister had charge of the church from 1872 until the year 1881, and was a man of a high order of intellect and a writer of considerable note. The pastor who has charge of the church at present is Rev. A. S. Hughey, a recent graduate from Wabash College, Ind. The membership numbers about sixty-five. The house of worship in which the congregation meets is a beautiful frame building located in the southwestern part of the village. It was built in the year 1864 and was dedicated July 3 of the same year, Rev. T. W. Hynes preaching the dedication sermon, R. M. Robinson assisting in the services. The house cost about $2,200. A Sunday school is maintained the entire year, with an average attendance of 100 scholars.

The Evangelical Lutheran Church, known as Ware's Grove Church, was organized December 24, 1860, by Rev. J. Livingood, with a membership of five persons Jacob W. Scherer, Henry Meisenheimer, Mrs. Rachel Meisenheimer, Mrs. Mary Scherer and Mrs. Rebecca Cress. Their present membership is forty five, among whom are some of the first citizens of the township. The congrega tion built the house in which they now worship, in the year 1862. It was dedicated in December of the same year, the dedication sermon being preached by Rev. George A. Bowers.

A society known as the Farmers' Club was organized in the year 1879, for the purpose of a mutual interchange of views relating to agriculture, stock raising, fruit growing, and all the subjects pertaining to the farmer's occupation. The exercises were frequently varied by a literary programme, music and original essays upon a variety of topics. The meetings were held weekly, to which the public were invited, and any one who so desired could participate in the exercises. The officers consisted of a President, Vice President, Secretary and Treasurer. This society was finally merged into the Grange, a lodge of which was organized at Butler in the year 1871. This lodge ceased to exist several years since, and facts concerning its organization, first officers and length of time it lasted could not be obtained.

Butler Township has a war record of which her citizens feel justly proud, having sent eighty men to the front to do battle for the country during the dark days of the rebellion. Of this number sixty-six returned at the close of the war, twelve having been killed in battle, and two lost, of whom nothing has ever been heard.

There has never been a murder committed in the township, and but one suicide, as far as known. The facts concerning this suicide were related to the writer by Jacob Cress, and are as follows: Mr. Cress, when but a boy, met a man by the name of Stewart in the highway, near the home of the former. Cress had been hunting, and carried a gun, which Stewart asked him for, as he said he wished to look at it. Cress at once handed him the gun; but no sooner had Stewart gotten hold of it than he placed the muzzle to his forehead and tried to discharge it with a long stick. He failed in this attempt to take his life, being foiled by Cress, who tried to take the gun away from him. Finding that he could not succeed in taking his life by shooting himself, he took from his pocket a large, dull knife, and deliberately cut and mangled his throat in such a horrible manner that he died the next morning. It appeared that Stewart was insane, though he regained consciousness before he died.

We have, in the foregoing pages, tried to give a brief and impartial history of Butler Grove Township from its earliest settlement up to the present time. We are indebted for many of the facts and dates to Jacob Cress, Charles Jenkins and Justus Ware, to each of whom the thanks of the writer are due for the courteous and gentlemanly manner in which the desired information was given.

CHAPTER XXV.*

RAYMOND TOWNSHIP—BOUNDARIES—EARLY SETTLEMENT—SCHOOLS—CHURCHES—BUSINESS INTERESTS—THE FIRE—SECRET SOCIETIES.

RECURRENCES to the past, with the recollections and associations which make it pass, in life like review, before our mental vision, will continue to be, as of yore, a source of satisfaction, especially when they connect themselves with incidents reflected back from our own experiences. These reminders vanish with the life of the participants, when no landmarks remain to save us the pictures faintly delineated on the tablets of memory, the impressions of which are only retracings from the modelings of others. To preserve these from forgetfulness before they have lost their distinguishing originality is the work devolved upon the writer of history. History fails in its mission when it fails to preserve the life features of the subjects committed to its trust. Local history, more than any other, commands the most interested attention, for the reason that it is a record of our own, with the experiences of others, who, in times gone by, traveled the thorny pathway of life as our companions, acquaintances, friends and relatives. The township of Raymond, to which this chapter is devoted, is an excellent body of land, composed of thirty-six sections, situated adjoining the county line and Harvel Township on the north, Rountree Township on the east, Butler Grove on the south, and Zanesville Township on the west. It was named in honor of Thomas Raymond, at one time Vice President of the St. Louis Division of the Wabash & Pacific Railroad.

The surface of this township is considerably varied, being rolling, and, in certain places in the southern and western parts, along the different water-courses, broken and somewhat hilly; while in the central and northern portions the land consists of a broad stretch of level prairie, interspersed with numerous small groves, both natural and artificial, at different places. The West Fork of Shoal Creek, with its tributaries, and Blue Grass Creek, are its water-courses, along the banks of which, for considerable distances, the land is covered with a goodly growth of timber, the most prominent varieties being elm, oak, walnut, maple, sycamore, etc. Previous to the year 1830, the country along the southern boundary was in the main a dense forest, containing much valuable timber, the greater part of which has been worked into lumber, rails, etc., and much of it ruthlessly destroyed by the early settlers. The soil, like that found in other parts of the county, differs in different places; near the streams the sandy element predominates; on the high grounds, it is of a clay mixture; while the lower portions and level prairie lands in the central and northern parts is a deep, rich black loam. Generally speaking, it is a choice body of land, very fertile, and capable of producing, in a high degree, all the cereals raised. Fruits of all varieties common to this latitude are grown in abundance, as are also vegetables, small fruits, grass, etc., etc.

The date of settlement by the whites goes back to the year 1830, when the first pioneers came into the township and commenced to improve farms. Pioneer life in all time has been characterized by incidents peculiar either to the locality or the make-up of the pioneers themselves. Western pioneer life has been subjected to conditions common to the experience of all early settlers. The primary elements in the composition of those who have taken their lives in their hands and battled successfully with the privations and hardships incident to settlements in the wilderness, without companions, save their "household gods," away from the echoes of civilization, depending for subsistence upon their own good right arms—were will-power, physical vigor and energy. Thus endowed, the brave pioneer boldly cuts loose from the moorings of civilization, turns his face toward the wild, unknown West, and, after days and weeks, perhaps months, of weary journeying over trackless prairies, tangled woodland, rocky steeps and through rushing torrents, at last determines the spot where his future home shall be, at once makes a start by erecting a little cabin, breaking a small patch of ground. Soon he is joined by others, and the little settlement becomes the foundation of those communities which are to-day the pride and boast of our country. But we are digressing from the more specific part of our subject. The first permanent settler to brave the solitude of nature in Raymond was Butler Seward, who came to Illinois from Ohio in the year 1829, and located near Seward's Grove, in Butler Grove Township, from which place he moved into what is now Raymond the following year. The place where he settled in this township is known as Seward's Point, near the southern part, and is now in possession of Elias Miller. Several descendants of this excellent man still reside in the county, among whom can be named Oscar Seward and John Cass, the oldest living settlers of this township. Shortly after Seward had located and commenced to improve he was joined by Matthew Mitchell, who entered a tract of land in the vicinity on Section 30. Mitchell came from Ohio also, and was a man of prominence in the little community. He sold the land on which he settled to David Scherer, another pioneer, shortly after the first improvements were made, and moved to another locality. The farm is now owned and occupied by Fred Mundhenk. Seward and Scherer having done so well in their new home, others were induced to follow them, and the next year saw several families moving into the little community, among whom were James Baker and a man by the name of Conyer. Baker improved the farm where Oscar Seward now lives, in Section 30, while Conyer selected his home near by, in Section 33, on a place which he afterward sold to John J. Cass. The foregoing were the only permanent settlers in the territory of Raymond up to the year 1833. In that year, John Cass moved into the township and purchased the Conyer farm, on which he resided until the year 1836, at which time he died. He was an industrious, exemplary man, and true Christian, who carried his Christianity into the actions of every day life. Two daughters and one son are living at the present time. The latter, to whom we have already referred, is one of the leading citizens of the township. Oscar Seward, son of Butler Seward, can be called an early settler, as he came here as early as the year 1835, and has been a prominent resident ever since. He purchased the Mitchell farm of David Scherer, which property he still owns. He is the oldest settler now living in Raymond, and has seen many wonderful improvements wrought by the busy hand of time. (For further particulars concerning Seward, we refer the reader to his biography, which appears elsewhere.) John Huffman and family were among the settlers who came in the year 1835, as were also a number of others whose names were not learned by the writer. Huffman settled in the southeast corner of the township, near the Irving boundary line. The prairies in the central and northeastern parts were not taken up until several years had elapsed from the first settlements along the southern border. Among the first settlers on these prairie lands were Thomas Thompson, David Huffman and Brookston Lewis, all three of whom settled on land near the present town of Raymond. Samuel Quinton settled north of Raymond, on the Ishmael McGown farm. Simpson Finley bought the land on the opposite side of the road from where William Bowles now lives, a short distance northwest of Raymond. William Gray was an early settler, having purchased a tract of land near the Chapman farm a short time after it came into market. Among those who came in at an early date and shared in the privations and hardships of pioneer life, but whose dates cannot be correctly ascertained at present, were John W. Guthrie, Lemuel Mays, William Costley, Morgan Costley, R. W. Grimm, John W. Hitchings and Orson Young. One of the prominent settlers near the town of Raymond was William Chapman (see portrait and biography), who bought the place where he now resides about the year 1851. He was one of the chief movers in the organization of the township, and can be classed among her well-to-do and wealthy farmers.

This comprises the early settlement of Raymond Township as far as we have been able to learn its history. The early struggle of the pioneers with hardships, trials and other objects calculated to deter them is but a repetition of those experienced by all other settlers in a new and uninhabited country. Many daring deeds by many unknown heroes have passed into oblivion, and many of nature's great men, who won signal victories in the hard-fought battles with nature in the wilderness, now lie in obscure and unknown graves. The first year was generally the most difficult, as the little stock of provisions frequently gave out, and many hardships were endured in order to obtain the necessaries of life; but after the first crop was harvested, there was generally a sufficiency for home consumption stored away and husbanded with scrupulous care. The deficiencies were procured from older settlements. The forests and prairie generally supplied the meat from the bountiful store of game, in quantity and quality according to demands. As settlers increased in numbers, a common cause was made in meeting the wants of each other, helping for help again. The idea of assisting another for a pecuniary consideration never obtruded itself into the mind of the pioneer in those early days. No greater insult could have been offered than a hint that money was to pay for a neighbor's help. If a cabin was to be raised, all the occasion demanded of the neighbors far and near was a knowledge of the time and place; distance was nothing, and other less pressing engagements had to succumb in order to render the needed assistance. Those old days are gone, buried in the dead past, but with them are gone a world of happy memories. The sentiment expressed in the old ballad, repeated in the writer's hearing by an early pioneer,

> "For I am one of the olden times, and may be thought too slow,
> But give to me those good old days of fifty years ago,"

is the sentiment entertained by all the frosty-headed veterans whose early lives were passed amid the stirring scenes of those early times. The first impulse of the people, upon whom devolved the responsibility of giving form and character to society in primitive Raymond, was to inaugurate a system of education which should in the future insure a safe foundation for permanent prosperity. Hence, schools were established at an early date. well sustained and patronized. The first sessions were held in private dwellings, but, as the population increased, more roomy buildings were required, and a number of log schoolhouses were erected in different localities.

The first term of school was taught by Mrs. Martha J. Cass, mother of John Cass, in a room of her residence, in the year 1835. This school numbered perhaps eight or ten pupils, was supported by subscription, and lasted about two and a half months.

The first building set apart especially for school purposes was a small structure, which stood on Oscar Seward's farm, and had formerly been used by his family as a residence. Seward fitted up the house, furnished and donated it, and for several years it was the only school building in the township. The second schoolhouse, according to the most authentic information, was built a short distance northeast of the town of Raymond. It was built by Ishmael McGown and William Ault but the date of its erection was not ascertained. This was, we believe, the first frame schoolhouse in the township. It is still standing. At present there are a number of good frame schoolhouses in the township, in which schools are taught the greater part of the year. The results of the teaching done in the schools have been immense, and is the pride of the people. There is one large graded school building, two stories high, in the town of Raymond, but of this building and schools taught therein we will speak more fully further on in these pages. Among the early industries of the township were several saw-mills, located at different points on Shoal Creek, which were in operation until nearly all of the best timber was sawn into lumber. These mills have been removed long since, and at the present time there are no mills of any kind in the township outside the town limits of Raymond. The first settlers obtained their flour, meal, etc., from Hillsboro and the mills situated in different parts of the county. There were no early flouring-mills in Raymond.

Amid the toils and privations of pioneer life, the first settlers found time to look after those higher and holier duties which they owed to their Creator. Pure religion and fervent piety flourished in those times in a very marked degree, long before any religious society had an organization, but, as soon as time and means would permit, church edifices were erected and societies of various denominations established, so that all could worship God according to the dictates of their own consciences. The original settlers in the southern part of the township were nearly all members of churches in Butler Grove, Litchfield and Irving Townships, farther south, and it was not until many years afterward that a permanent religious organization was effected in what is now Raymond. The Methodists had a flourishing society about one mile south of the town of Raymond, which was, according to the best information at hand, the first church organization in the township. This was a number of years ago, but, as the early records could not be found, but little satisfaction was obtained in looking up its early history. Public services were held at this place until about eight or ten years ago, when the congregation decided to remove the organization and building to the town of Raymond, which was accordingly done. Previous to its removal, the church was known as Ashery Chapel, and numbered about eighty members. The building was moved and remodeled at a cost of about $800. It is now a handsome edifice, capable of seating 350 persons comfortably, and is valued at $1,500. The following pastors have, at stated times, ministered to the congregation: — — Barrett, John Roberts, E. M. Pitcher, Alkier, A. D. Beckhart and John Slater; present pastor is Elijah Haley. In connection with the church services is a large, flourishing Sunday school, at present under the efficient superintendency of David Colvin, with an average attendance of over one hundred scholars. The church membership at present exceeds one hundred, among whom are some of the best and most highly respected citizens of the town and surrounding country. The United Baptist congregation, known as the Blue Mound Church, was organized in a schoolhouse situated about three miles southeast of Raymond, in the year 1871, Elder John Barbee officiating at the first meeting. The original membership was about twenty, but quite a number of others were added to the church during the meetings which followed its organization. The present edifice which the congregation occupies is situated near the place where the church was organized, in Section 19. It is a frame building, and was erected in the year 1876, at a cost of $1,000. Among the regular pastors and stated supplies of this church may be mentioned Thomas Jones, —— Culp, Hanks. There are now about forty-five names on the church records. George Fry is Superintendent of the Sunday school, which is in good condition and well attended. Rhodes Chapel M. E. Church dates its history from the year 1872. Their house of worship is a neat frame building, situated near the Blue Mound Church, in Section 19, and was built in the year 1876. The church has continued, with varied success, from its organization until the present time, the membership now being about forty. A Sunday school is maintained during the greater part of the year, and is reported in good condition. The present Pastor of the church is Rev. Elijah Haley. The remaining churches of the township are in the town of Raymond, and will be spoken of in connection with the history of that village further on in this chapter. The first ground consecrated to the burial of the dead was laid out on the farm belonging to John Cass, and is still known as the Cass Graveyard. The first interment made in this cemetery was in 1852. The name of the person buried was James Crosse. The St. Louis Division of the Wabash, St. Louis & Pacific Railroad runs through the northwestern corner of the township, intersecting the northern boundary about two miles from the Pitman line and the western boundary at a point near the west central part of the township. This road has been a decided advantage to the farmers of this section of the country, furnishing them an easy means of transportation for their farm products and live stock. The township's development has been very marked since the completion of this road. The town of Raymond is situated on this road, about one mile east of the Zanesville line, in the western part of the township, and is one of the live business places of Montgomery County. Its population is estimated at about nine hundred. The ground on which the principal part of the town stands was formerly owned by Ishmael McGown and Nimrod McElroy, who had it surveyed into lots in the year 1870. The lines were run by an experienced civil engineer by the name of Bass. The first house in the place was a residence erected by James Sanders, shortly after the survey was made. A few weeks later, another house was in process of erection, belonging to Thomas Fahey. A business house was erected the same year, by David Hoffman, and rented to Messrs. Van Dorn & Van Evor, who stocked it with a general assortment of merchandise, and did a large, flourishing trade for three years. This building is at present occupied by the dry goods and grocery store of Brown & Co. In connection with their mercantile business, Van Dorn & Van Ever built a large warehouse near the central part of the village in the fall of 1870, and handled an immense amount of grain during the next two years. Encouraged by the success which attended the business venture of the foregoing, other business men came to the village shortly afterward, and, finding it a safe place for capital, several stores and different kinds of shops were started.

The second store building was erected in the western part of the town, in the spring of 1871, by Charles Davis, who did a good business for four years, when he disposed of the stock to W. P. Carter. The latter continued the business at the same stand for three years, when, meeting with several financial reverses, he concluded to retire from the store, which resolution he put into effect a short time afterward.

In the fall of 1871, a third store was started, by Parrot & Scott. Like other stores in the place, their stock consisted of a general assortment of merchandise. The name of the firm was afterward changed to that of Scott & Nevins. The entire stock was finally purchased by Nimrod McElroy, who for some time conducted a business with a stock representing several thousand dollars. One of the first merchants of the town was A. W. Marshall. The first brick building was erected in the year 1876, by John O'Bannon. This was a large storeroom. A. Henn erected a brick store house the same year, also. D. J. Parrot built the large elevator near the railroad crossing in 1874, and still operates it. This is one of the largest and most extensive elevators on the line of the St. Louis Division of the Wabash road, and many thousand bushels of grain of all kinds are handled and shipped yearly. Another elevator was erected in the year 1880, by E. R. Carter, who sold it soon after.

Frank Hicks was the first physician of the town. He located here shortly after the town was laid out, and is still one of the practicing physicians of the place. Dr. Barton came next. Dr. Hermon was one of the early physicians of the township, where he has a large and lucrative practice. He moved into the town several years since, where he still resides. Drs. Easley, Wheeler and Blevins are located here, all of whom are regularly graduated M. D.'s of the different schools of medicine.

The Raymond Post Office was established in the year 1871, with Charles Davis as Postmaster. The office is now kept in the hardware store of Thomas Kissinger. The first blacksmith to locate in the village was William Develin, who started a shop in the year 1871. W. H. Pepper built the second blacksmith shop the same year. The citizens, realizing that "'tis education that forms the common mind," turned their attention, during the early days of the village, to the necessity of erecting a schoolhouse large enough to meet the demands of the increasing population. A building was erected in the year 1874. It is two stories high, contains four large-sized, comfortable rooms, all of which are well finished and furnished, and the building, as a whole, does credit to the town and township. It is situated in the northeastern part of the town, and surmounted by a large bell-tower, from the top of which an extended view of the surrounding country for many miles can be obtained. The first schools in this building were taught by Misses Hattie Wood and Bettie Street, in 1875. The next year, the schools had so increased in size that a third teacher was required, when they were placed under the able supervision of Prof. James Young, who gave a new impetus to the educational interests of Raymond. Prof. S. A. Moore had charge of the schools during the years 1877 and 1878; George Bowers, in 1880. The present corps of teachers consists of the following: Prof. C. E. Cook, Principal; C. J. Lapp, Louisa Watson and Hetty C. Doer, assistants. The schools have been brought up to a high standard of usefulness under the successful management of the different Principals, and are now enjoying well-earned and well-merited prosperity. The Board of Education is composed of the following gentlemen: William Bowles, President; D. J. Parrott, Vice President; P. J. Hermon, Clerk. The schools last eight months of the year, and have an average attendance of about two hundred pupils.

The Raymond Steam Flouring-Mill was built in the year 1875, by Montgomery Range, and has been operated by him ever since. It has three run of stone, and a capacity of about thirty barrels of flour per day. George H. Hooser built a steam merchant mill in 1880, at a cost of $6,000. This mill has three buhrs, and does a large and lucrative business.

The first hotel in the place was erected by John Brusaw, in 1872, and by him sold to James Sanders six months later. It is known as the Central House, and is at present kept by T. J. Kissinger. B. R. Hubbard built a hotel in 1875. It was purchased by Mrs. Pallard, who kept it about three years, when it was completely destroyed by fire in the general conflagration which visited the town in 1881. The Raymond House was built in 1881, by Louisa Chism, and is at present under the management of her brother, Robert Chism, who keeps one of the best hotels in the county.

A small sheet, the Raymond *Reporter*, was started in the year 1877, by T. M. Snedley, and issued semi-monthly for about six months. The Raymond *Independent*, a weekly newspaper, was established by J. W. Potts in the year 1881. It is conducted with considerable energy and success, and has reached a circulation of over five hundred. The office and composing rooms are the best in the county, and the editor, Mr. Potts, has won many favorable opinions from his brethren of the quill for the fearless and able manner with which he treats the subjects of the day. The paper is in every respect independent, and promises to remain one of the permanent fixtures of the town.

The Raymond Bank was established in 1881, by John Green. It is an individual concern, and, for the amount of capital invested, is doing a flourishing business.

The town was incorporated in 1871. The first officers elected were the following: R. M. Van Dorn, President of the Board; E. A. Hanna, Clerk; and W. P. Carter, Treasurer. The present officers are: William Fitzgerald, President; E. R. Day, Clerk; W. A. Maxey, Treasurer; P. J. Harmon, George Hooser, D. C. Kelley and D. J. Parrott, Trustees.

A most destructive fire visited the town in the month of August, 1881, during the progress of which the best part of the improvements were completely burned to the ground. The fire originated in the livery stable of Noah Moore, on the east side of Main street, from which it spread to the west side, and caught in the butcher-shop of Paul Zink. From this building the flames leaped with lightning-like rapidity from house to house, and, before the fire could be checked, all the buildings in Block 13, with the exception of two small structures situated in the northwest and southwest corners respectively, were a smoldering mass of ruins. Every effort that could be desired was resorted to in order to check the devouring element, but all attempts were futile. The buildings destroyed by the conflagration were the following: Barber shop and family residence of Paul Zink; livery stable belonging to Noah Moore; hotel of Susan Chism; store and restaurant belonging to the Harvel heirs; storeroom and stock of goods of George Zimmerman; Frank Grainer's saddler shop; Zink's meat-shop; Colvin & Son's store; Costley's livery stable; agricultural warehouse of E. R. Day; store building occupied by William Fitzgerald; Maxey & Roberts' grocery store; Anderson's restaurant; Piggot's blacksmith shop; dwelling and ice-house belonging to George Zimmerman; barn belonging to David Huggins; and the store and stock of Deer, Morrison & Co The loss caused by this devouring fire is estimated at $35,000, of which amount $11,000 were realized by insurance. The citizens soon rallied from the effects of this terrible visitation, and many new buildings were pushed rapidly forward. The large and elegant brick buildings situated on the east side of Broad street, and known as the Union Block, were erected the latter part of the year 1881, as was also the fine storeroom belonging to Paul Zink, situated on the opposite side of the street. The present business character of Raymond may be estimated from the following list: There are five dry goods and grocery stores, two hardware stores, one cabinet and furniture store, two drug stores, two stores that make groceries a specialty, two boot and shoe stores, two barber shops, one harness shop, two millinery establishments, one agricultural store, two lumber yards, two blacksmith shops, one cooper shop and one wagon shop.

There are four religious organizations, with as many houses of worship, the oldest of which is the Raymond M. E. Church. Its history we have already given in a previous page.

The Presbyterian Church was organized in the year 1871, by a committee appointed by the Alton Presbytery, of which Rev. Thomas E. Spilman was Chairman. This committee met in the office of Dr. Ira Barton, and the following names were recorded as members. John H. Barton, Mary N. Barton, William P. Hamilton, Mary B. Hamilton, William Kennedy and Dr. Ira Barton. At this meeting, the following Elders were selected: John H. Barton and William P. Hamilton. The first public services were held in the Independent Schoolhouse. The house now in use is a frame building; is the first one erected by the congregation, and will seat about three hundred persons. It is a nicely furnished edifice, and is valued at $1,500. The first minister was Rev. R. Walker. The following ministers have had charge of the church at different times: Revs. E. R. Rankin, A. H. Parks, — Reynolds, Adam Simpson, James Lafferty, Solomon Dickey, and M. C. Butler, the present pastor; present membership, about thirty; Sunday school is under the charge of S. A. Merriwether.

The Raymond Christian Church commenced its history in the year 1874, with a membership of thirty, who assembled at times for worship in the vacant storeroom belonging to W. D. Moore. The organization was effected under the energetic labors of Elder Corwin, of Macoupin County. The first regular Pastor was Elder J. W. Balinger. In the fall of 1874, the congregation bought a lot, and, shortly after, commenced the erection of the present church edifice, which was dedicated in the spring of 1875, the dedicatory sermon being delivered by Elder J. H. Garrison, of St. Louis. The building is frame, and, as it stands, is valued at $2,200. J. W. Balinger labored earnestly for the congregation one year, and was succeeded by L. L. Norton, who exercised a pastorate of five months du ration. H. R. Trickett and S. B. Lindsley were the next pastors. J. J. Cathcart preached one year. Elders Standley and Van Hoosier conducted a series of meetings in the year 1881, during the progress of which twenty one additions were made to the congregation. At present, the church is without a regular pastor, although devotional exercises are conducted each Lord's Day. The membership is about one hundred and fifteen. Their Sunday school is large and well attended, with an average of 120 scholars, and is under the efficient management of D. J. Parrott, Superintendent.

St. Raymond's Roman Catholic Church was organized about the year 1873. It was re-organized in 1880, by Rev. Father Virena, and the present handsome building erected. This edifice is the largest house of worship in the town, and can be ranked among the best in the county. Its dimensions are 34x56 feet; will comfortably seat 400 persons, and cost the sum of $5,000. The number of members is estimated at five hundred. Public services are held every third Sunday, by the pastor, Rev. John Gezenhauser, of Bartholto. There are two flourishing secret societies in the town Masons and Odd Fellows.

Raymond Lodge, No. 692, A., F. & A. M., was established under dispensation in 1871. Their charter was granted in 1872, by De Witt C. Cregier, G. M. On this charter appear the following names: George A. Vannever, Robert M. Van Dorn, J. R. M. Wilder, Samuel S. Peebles, Edward Grimes, William Chapman, S. S. Wertz, James R. Williams, John King, E. A. Hanna, Osman White, D. J. Parrott, P. J. Hermon, Isaac Eldridge, John G. Moore, Alvis Sharpe, C. P. Kerns and John Dowdle. First officers were:

George Vannever, W. M.; Robert Van Dorn, S. W.; J. R. Wilder, J. W.; William Chapman, Treasurer; S. S. Peebles, Secretary; E. A. Hanna, S. D.; O. White, J. D.; Isaac Elledge, Tiler. Present officers: John Kidd, W. M.; John Green, S. W.; F. C. Hitchings, J. W.; Jacob Guller, Treasurer; James A. Bradley, Secretary; Edward Grimes, S. D.; Harrison Sharpe, J. D.; Sylvester Keplinger, Tiler; D. J. Parrott, Chaplain. Membership, at present, thirty-two.

Raymond Lodge, No. 476, I. O. O. F., was organized October 8, 1872, with the following charter members: Norris Crane, Nimrod McElroy, G. W. McAtee, Elias R. Day, George A. Vannever, James N. Guthrie, Walker Gunn, James Sanders. The first officers of the lodge were the following: James Sanders, N. G.; Norris Crane, V. G.; G. A. Vannever, Secretary; Nimrod McElroy, Treasurer. The different offices are filled at present by the following: F. B. Wood, N. G.; J. F. Laller, V. G.; M. G. Sisson, Secretary; W. A. Maxey, Permanent Secretary; R. N. Long, Treasurer; A. H. Johnson, Warden; B. P. Query, Conductor; Corder Jones, Chaplain; W. S. Richie, I. G.; James Norris, O. G.

The hall in which these lodges meet is owned jointly by them. Both organizations are reported in good working order.

The part taken by Raymond in the great war of the rebellion does credit to a township of her population. Scarcely had it been announced that Sumter had been fired upon before the spirit of war commanded the thoughts and actions of her citizens. The response was as ready as the impulse was determined, and the history of the part taken by our brave boys in the various encounters that mark the progress of the war presents a record as creditable, perhaps, as that of any other township in the county. We would gladly give a list of the boys in blue who went from Raymond, but the limits of our space forbids.

For information concerning the early history of the town and township of Raymond the writer is indebted to Ishmael McGowen, Dr. P. J. Hermon, E. R. Carter, William Chapman and John Cass. They have his most sincere thanks for the courteous and gentlemanly manner with which the desired information was given.

CHAPTER XXII.

IRVING TOWNSHIP—BOUNDARIES—SOIL—PIONEER SETTLERS—SCHOOLS—CHURCHES—PHYSICIANS AND MERCHANTS.

It is not claimed that the statements contained in the following pages are in strict harmony with the truth in every particular, as much of the information concerning the early history of this township is a matter of mere conjecture. Traditions are numerous, but are very unsatisfactory sources from which to obtain correct and definite statements. And "perfectly reliable history written from conflicting accounts is an absolute impossibility." No two men who are questioned will give similar accounts of the same transaction or event, thus adding much to the perplexity of the writer or placing the question beyond a correct solution. Seventy years ago, this division of Montgomery County was a wilderness, whose only inhabitants were a few scattered savages and their wild companions, the wolf, deer and buffalo. Occasional hunting parties of white men had passed through it long before any permanent settlement had been made, but its history properly begins with the year 1826, at which time the first pioneer made his appearance and located his humble home in the wilderness. Since then there has been a constant influx of population, until now it is one of the most thickly settled and enterprising townships in the county. Irving consists of thirty-six square miles of territory, lying near the central part of the county, and is designated as Township 9, north of Range 3 west. It lies between Butler Grove and Witt, the former being the western boundary and the latter the eastern. The township lying north is Rountree, while East Fork Township forms the southern boundary. The general character of the land is what might be termed rolling, but in the western part it verges into the broken, some of the higher portions being called hills. The eastern and northern parts exhibit a rolling and undulating surface, possessing a rich, fertile soil, consisting of a dark loam with a clay subsoil. This soil is very rich, and produces abundant crops of grain, vegetables of all kinds, and many fine varieties of fruits. The soil in the western and southwestern parts is not so well adapted to agriculture being somewhat thin, and largely composed of clay and gravel. The best cultivated parts of the township are in the northern and eastern portions, where can be seen some of the finest and best improved farms in the county. The principal streams, by which this region is watered and drained, are the Middle Fork of Shoal Creek, a stream of considerable size and importance, which runs through the western part, from north to south, and Long Branch, a tributary of the former, which flows in a northwesterly direction through the southwest corner. The land along these creeks is composed of a rich, black, mucky soil, and was originally covered with a dense growth of timber. Much of this timber has been cut off, and from the land thus brought into cultivation, some of the largest and best paying crops are produced. About one-half of the area of the township was formerly timbered, much of which has been cleared of late years until now the woodland comprises only about one-third of the area. The timber still standing consists mostly of hickory, elm, oak of several varieties, syca-

G. W. Waggoner

more and walnut. But little of the latter is left, the greater part having been bought up by agents of the Indianapolis Furniture Company, several years ago. Many farmers in the northern and eastern parts of the township are giving considerable attention to the cultivation of artificial groves, and within a few years the timber thus produced will afford a sufficiency for all practical purposes. The early settlement of Irving Township cannot be given with perfect accuracy, as many of the statements concerning the pioneer settlers are vague and unsatisfactory. It is safe to say, however, that the first white settler was one Lawrence Franklin, who moved to Illinois from Kentucky in the year 1826, and settled in the southwestern part of Irving, on the farm now owned by Mr. Hughes, in Section 29. It was here that the first cabin was erected, which stood till a few years ago. Some of the old timbers of which it was composed can still be seen near the spot which it formerly occupied.

A brief description of this primitive domicile may, perhaps, be of interest to some reader whose life has been passed in more comfortable and commodious quarters. The dimensions of the structure were about fifteen by eighteen feet. One room was the sum total of apartments it contained, which answered the four-fold purpose of kitchen, bedroom, dining-room and parlor. The floor was made of split logs, called puncheons. These had been smoothed off with a common chopping-ax until they composed a surface which was tolerably level. A large, open-mouthed fireplace, capable of receiving a log of almost any dimensions, occupied very nearly an entire end of the building. The furniture of the room was of the most primitive kind, and in perfect harmony with the interior of the apartment, as we have described it.

Yet from this humble cabin home no way-worn traveler was permitted to go hungry or sleepy. A place was always allotted the stranger at the frugal board, and a shelter for the night assured him if desired. Hospitality was a trait cultivated to a high degree of perfection by the early pioneer, and a part of his religion was to welcome with open doors any wayfarer who might happen to wander near his little mansion. With Shelly he could say to the stranger,

> "You must come home with me and be my guest,
> You will give joy to me, and I will do
> All that is in my power to honor you."

Mr. Franklin resided upon the farm he settled till the year 1858, when he sold the place to Mr. Hughes, and moved to the city of Hillsboro, where he died the following year. Several sons of Mr. Franklin still reside in the county, all of whom have been prominently identified with the growth and development of the township. Ezra Bastick, another early settler of Irving, came from Illinois to Kentucky some time prior to the year 1824, in company with his two sons-in-law, William and Joel Knight, They stopped for a couple of years in the southern part of the county, near where the little village of Donnellson now stands, in East Fork Township. Mr. Bastick settled in Irving in the year 1826, but at just what place could not be learned. He was an old revolutionary soldier, and many were the thrilling stories he told of that memorable struggle while seated with his grandchildren around the blazing hearth of the little cabin home. He was in nearly all the battles of the war, and received a severe wound in one engagement, which so disabled him that he remained a cripple during the rest of his life.

Joel Knight, who accompanied Bastick to Illinois, located the farm known as the Harmon place, about two and one-half miles northeast of Hillsboro, in Section 29. He was a Presbyterian preacher of considerable ability and assisted in the organization of nearly all the early churches of his denomination throughout the county. He traveled extensively from settlement to settlement, preaching in groves, barns and in private dwellings, and many are the stories told of the wonderful power of his eloquence and logic over the audiences that used to assemble to greet him on his regular preaching tours through the country. In the year 1877, Mr. Knight died at a ripe old age, and was buried in the old Bear Creek Cemetery, near the place where he first settled.

> "An old age, serene and bright,
> And lovely as a Lapland night,
> Led him to an honored grave."

Two brothers, Mark and James M. Rutledge, came into this township some time in the year 1826, and settled in the western part, near the boundary line. The farm on which they built their first house is now owned by Mrs. Hogsett whose husband purchased it the same year in which James died. Mark did not remain a great while in Irving, but moved to Hillsboro Township in 1827, and bought a farm, on which he resided until the year 1858, at which time he disposed of his land and moved to the city of Hillsboro, where he died a few years ago.

John Lipe settled in the northern part of the township as early as the year 1828. He was a stanch old German, well fitted to encounter the many hardships which beset the pioneer settler in a new country. Lipe came to this State from North Carolina in company with quite a number of German families that located in different places throughout the county. The farm on which he first settled is in Section 3, and is at present owned by Trimper Heffley, a relative, who purchased it shortly after Mr. Lipe died. The date of this old pioneer's death was not ascertained, though it occurred a number of years ago. His wife survived him many years. She died in 1881, and was followed to the grave by over four hundred descendants and relatives probably the largest number of relations that ever attended the funeral of any one person in the State. James Kelly was one among the earliest settlers, and located on Section 27 in the year 1829.

Just how long Mr. Kelly lived in the township is not known, though it can be said that he lived long enough to see the wilderness where he first located his humble home changed to a very garden. Six sons of Kelly are now living, five of them in this State and one in Utah.

Andrew King was prominent among the first settlers of Irving, but in what year he came into the township is not known, though we may be safe in saying that it was prior to the year 1830. He came from Tennessee, from whence came many of the early settlers of Southern Illinois, and located on Locust Fork, about one and a half miles northwest of the town of Irving, in Section 16. The land on which King settled was prairie, covered with a thick growth of sedge grass. This grass furnished the material out of which the first brooms used by the early settlers were made. King died in the year 1862. His descendants living are two sons, S. F. and William T., both of whom reside in the village of Irving. The Berrys are also an old family of this township, and were among the first settlers of Montgomery County. James M. Berry moved here in 1829, and improved the farm in Section 16, now owned by Thomas Black. He owned the greater part of the land where the town of Irving now stands, and was one of the principal projectors of that village, which he helped to lay out in the year 1856. He moved into the town a number of years ago, where he has since resided. He is one of the oldest citizens of the township. His brother, William S. Berry, though not an actual settler in Irving, was among the first pioneers of the county, having settled in Hillsboro when it was but a mere niche in the surrounding forest. He moved to this township a number of years ago, and purchased a fine tract of land. His son is one of the leading business men of the town of Irving.

John Christian was also an old settler, who emigrated from Kentucky, and settled in Irving Township in the year 1830. The original homestead of Christian is at present owned by a Mr. Mitz. Christian was one of the first Baptist preachers in this part of the State. He assisted in the first religious services ever conducted in the township, and was instrumental in founding several churches of his denomination in the county.

In 1830, John Grantham also appeared, and purchased a farm in the southwestern part of the township. This farm now belongs to Seth Washburne.

Grantham was a Methodist preacher, and for a number of years supplied the pulpit of the Hopewell Church, of which he was an original member. He died in the year 1842. Three sons are still living in the township, all of whom are prominent members of the Methodist Church of Irving.

Many other early settlers of this township might be mentioned in connection with those already named, but the date of their settlement and facts connected therewith have been forgotten, and they have long since passed into that silent palace of the dead whose doors open not outward. To the energy and perseverance of these sturdy strong-handed pioneers is the township indebted for much of its present prosperity.

The early settlers in this township, like the first settlers in many other parts of the county, were obliged to go long distances to obtain flour and meal. The nearest mill for several years was the little rude affair in the southern part of the county known as Fogleman's pepper-mill. This mill ground so slow that many went by it to Edwardsville, a distance of thirty-five or forty miles. A mill was built in Butler Grove Township, in an early day, by Jacob Cress. This mill was extensively patronized by the first settlers of Irving till one was erected nearer home. James T. Paden built a mill in the year 1831, about three and a half miles southwest of the village of Irving, on the Hillsboro road. The machinery of this mill was operated by horse power, ground both corn and wheat and was patronized by the citizens of this and the adjoining townships of Witt and East Fork. This mill was purchased by Ezekiel Grantham, after it had been run about eight years remodeled and supplied new machinery. The machinery was removed a short time afterward to the town of Irving, and used in the construction of a mill at that place. The old building was torn down and hauled away about two years ago.

A saw-mill was built in the southwestern part of the township, in an early day, by a Mr. Hickman. It was situated on Shoal Creek, from which it received the power that operated it. This mill was run but a very short time, and does not appear to have done a very extensive business. The first steam mill was built by Kelly & Harris in the year 1864, at a place two miles southwest of the town of Irving. They sold it in the following year to a man by name of Stevens, who in turn disposed of it to H. M. Kelly two years afterward. Kelly moved the mill to the town of Irving, and operated it several years. The machinery was finally taken out and used in the construction of another mill at that place, of which we will speak more fully further on. The old building was purchased by S. F. King, who moved it on his lot, where it answers the purpose of a barn.

Schools were opened in Montgomery County in an early day, and the necessity of educating the pioneer children forced itself upon the minds of the first settlers, and many schools were at once established. The first building used for school purposes in this township was a small cabin in the southern part, built as early as the year 1827. It was used as a meeting-house also. The room was furnished with a few rough benches made of small logs split once, and hewed smooth with a common chopping ax. These rested upon a dirt floor that required no sweeping. A broad board extended around the apartment next to the wall, and served the purpose of a writing desk during certain hours of the day. A large fireplace occupied the greater part of one end of the building, in the construction of which neither brick nor stone were used; a bank of earth being merely thrown up against the logs to keep them from taking fire. A small rough stand was provided for the teacher near the center of the room, from which he could issue his decrees, give his commands or mete out condign punishment to any juvenile offender who had the temerity to violate any of the iron-clad rules of the school.

The first pedagogue who wielded the birch in this primitive college was Joseph McEntire, an old man of three-score and fifteen years though possessed of a wonderful amount of vitality and strength, as many unruly urchins learned to their sorrow. In those days, it required muscle as well as brain to conduct a school successfully, and Mr. McEntire seems to have given universal satisfaction, as he could strike as hard a blow as many younger brethren of the profession. This school was supported by voluntary subscription, and lasted but three months. The teacher "boarded around," as was the custom of that day and received $1.50 per scholar for his compensation. Among the first schools in the township was one taught by John Grantham in the Hopewell Church house, shortly after the building had been erected. No preparation had been made for this school in the way of fitting up the room, and there were neither desks nor seats for the pupils. No floor had been laid, nor fireplace built. The room was warmed by a fire in the center of the dirt floor, around which the scholars seated themselves upon the sleepers of the building. In the spring the house was abandoned for a grove, where the school was continued during fair weather. When it rained, the exercises were conducted in a large tent which Mr. Grantham had prepared for that purpose.

The first frame schoolhouse was built in 1848, on Locust Fork, near the place where the residence of Mr. Ault now stands. This house is still standing in the town of Irving, where it was moved in 1860. It is still used for school purposes.

The first public school of the township was taught in this building by William F. King, in the years 1848 and 1849. As time passed, the number of schoolhouses increased. The little log cabins disappeared, or were replaced by the more comfortable and commodious brick and frame buildings. There are at present seven schools in the township outside of the town of Irving. The schoolhouses are all well built, and furnished with latest improved furniture and fixtures. Four of these houses are frame, and three brick. The present school board is composed of the following gentlemen: Joseph Platte, W. W. Webber and J. E. Knight, Trustees; A. J. Huestis, Township Treasurer and Clerk of the Board. The schools last about seven months in the year.

One of the first essentials of civilization is a well-defined roadway. The first roads through this section were mere trails over the prairies, or winding byways among the hills and through the woods. These zig-zag roads were laid out with a view to benefit the greatest number of settlers with the smallest amount of inconvenience. The first road of any importance in this township was the Hillsboro and Shelbyville road, which was established in the year 1830. It passes through the township from east to west, and is extensively traveled. Another road was established about the same time, known as the Hillsboro and Nokomis road. This was one of the first roads laid out in the eastern part of the county, and is still the principal thoroughfare between those two cities. It intersects the eastern boundary line at a point about one-half mile north of the Indianapolis &

St. Louis Railroad, in Section 1, runs west three miles, where its course is abruptly changed southward. Within half a mile of Irving, the course is again changed to the west. It intersects the western boundary of the township near the Middle Fork bridge. One of the first roads established in Irving was the old north road, which ran through the northern part of the township from east to west. The east road in the eastern part is also an old road, and one of the most important highways in the township. A number of roads intersect each other at various places throughout the township, but are not designated by any particular names.

The Indianapolis & St. Louis Railroad passes through Irving in a northeasterly direction. It makes one small curve in the southern part; the remainder of its course is very straight. In all there are about ten miles of this road in the township. It has been a great benefit to the country through which it passes, and has done more than anything else toward the development of the township. The town of Irving dates its origin from the year in which this road was completed.

The early church history of Irving is involved in considerable obscurity, and many dates and interesting facts relating thereto have faded away from the memory of the oldest inhabitants. The early settlers were members of different denominations, and held their public services from house to house for several years. At these early meetings, all met on a common level, and left their denominational peculiarities at home. The Presbyterian, Methodist, Baptist and Lutheran all united in these meetings without regard to creed or doctrine, and worshiped together the same God in unison and harmony. Many of the early itinerant preachers were men singularly gifted with a powerful eloquence which fired the hearts of the pioneers, and many converts were gathered into the different churches. It is not positively known who preached the first sermon in the township, but, as near as can be ascertained, it was a Baptist preacher by the name of Jordan. He conducted a series of meetings in a grove near the southwest corner of the township in the year 1829, but nothing definite could be learned concerning him.

The first church organized in the township was the Hopewell Methodist Episcopal Church. The organization was effected in the year 1829, by Revs. Benson and Bastian, two itinerant preachers who came into the county several years before.

Among the original members of this church were the following: John Grantham, Thomas Christian, Elizabeth Grantham, James Grantham and wife, Isaiah Grantham and wife, Silas Kelly and wife, Madison Berry and wife. Madison Berry is the only one of the original members now living. John Grantham was a local preacher. Thomas Christian was the first class leader. The first pastor who had charge of the church was Rev. Lowry, who preached for the congregation two years. He was succeeded by Rev. John Dew, the exact length of whose pastorate was not learned, as the early records of the church could not be found. For two years, the congregation held their public services in groves, private dwelling houses and barns. These meetings were attended by all from miles around. In the year 1830, a house of worship was erected on Locust Fork, in the western part of the township, and was named the Hopewell Church. Here the congregation worshiped till the year 1856, at which time the organization was moved to a place about one mile northeast of the village of Irving. For twelve years the exercises of the church were conducted at this place. In the year 1868, it was decided by the congregation to move the church into the town of Irving, which was accordingly done. A reorganization was effected the same year, and the name of the church changed. It has since been known as the Irving Methodist Episcopal Church. In the year 1860, the propriety of erecting a new house of worship was discussed by the congregation, and it was decided to begin the building at once. Work was commenced on the new house in the spring of 1861, and it was completed the following autumn. This building is frame, dimensions about 36 by 56 feet, and will comfortably seat three hundred and fifty persons. It represents a capital of about $3,000. It was dedicated by Rev. J. H. Aldridge in the year 1861. Since the reorganization of the church, the following pastors have preached for the congregation: William Taylor, —— Hutchinson, J. E. Lindlay, James Calric, J. F. Holloway, W. F. Lowe, A. E. Orr, —— Rhodes, D. H. Stubblefield, J. W. Lapham, —— Schwartz, William Birks, —— Hamill and W. R. Howard, present pastor. The membership will number at present about two hundred and sixty, one hundred of whom were added to the church during a great revival, conducted by Rev. J. W. Lapham, while he was pastor.

A good Sunday school is supported, and the church is reported in excellent working order.

The Presbyterians were prominent among the pioneer churches, and had a flourishing organization at a very early day. This church was organized by Rev. Joel Knight, who was the only preacher for a number of years. The old organization was maintained for a considerable length of time, but owing to deaths, removals and other causes, it was finally abandoned. In the year 1866, the society known as the United Congregation of the Cumberland Presbyterian Church was organized in the town of Irving with about fifty members. The first pastor was Rev. L. P. Deatheridge, a man of brilliant attainments and wonderful eloquence. He did as much if not more than any other man toward establishing the church upon the firm footing that it at present maintains. He was succeeded by Rev. Joel Knight, one of the pioneer preachers of the county, and founder of the congregation of 1830. He was followed by Rev. Mr. Barber, who labored with the congregation for several years. Revs. W. J. McDavid and T. W. McDavid have also preached for the church at stated intervals. The congregation worshiped for three years in the Lutheran Church of Irving. The house in which the church now worships was built in the year 1869, at a cost of $5,000. It is a brick building and contains the largest audience room in the township.

A Sunday school is maintained in connection with the church, with an average attendance of 100 scholars. The St. John's Lutheran Church was organized in the year 1842, and has a present membership of about sixty-five. Rev. Daniel Trimper was the first preacher, and it was under his labors that the church was organized. The following names appear on the old church records as original members: Henry Carriker, Mary Carriker, Tillman Hetfley, —— Hetfley, Nancy Lipe, John Lipe, Rachel Lipe. Rev. Trimper was a man of remarkable force of character, and under his administration the church grew to be a power for good in the community. The first house used by the congregation for public worship was built in 1845. Twenty-seven years afterward, their present edifice was erected. This is a frame building, 28x30 feet, and was built at a cost of $1,200. It was dedicated in the year 1872 by Rev. George Bowers. Rev. J. Livingood, Rev. —. Scherer, Rev. —. Schwartz, Rev. John Cromer and Rev. George Hammer have been pastors of this church.

The Irving Lutheran Church is an offshoot of the East Fork Church, one of the oldest organizations in the county. The Irving Church was organized in the year 1858, by Rev. Isaac Short, who was its first pastor. The records, now in possession of David Gregory, show the following names of original members: H. M. Neisler, Isaac Lewey, George File, Reuben Lingle, Elizabeth Neisler, David

Gregory, Susan File, Catherine Lewey Rebecca Gregory, William Newcomb, Samuel T. Bartlett, Mary Newcomb and Patsy Bartlett. Since its organization, the church has been administered to by the following pastors in the order named: J. B. Cromer, Martin Miller, Hiram Gregory, Francis Springer, L. C. Groseclose, George Hammer, and J. M. Lingle, present pastor. The congregation continued to meet with the East Fork Church till 1860, when their neat, comfortable building was erected. The building is frame, the aggregate cost of which was about $1,500. Their Sunday school has an average attendance of about sixty, and is superintended by E. P. Cromer. Public services are held every alternate Lord's day, and prayer meeting every Wednesday evening. Is one of the aggressive churches of the town.

The Christian Church of Irving was organized about the year 1856, by Elders J. G. Ward and J. M. Taulbee. For several years, this church was in flourishing circumstances, but just previous to the war the members became scattered, and the organization was finally abandoned. It was reorganized in the year of 1876, by Elders J. M. Taulbee and B. R. Gilbert. The first pastor was Elder L. M. Linn. The following pastors have had charge of the church at stated intervals: L. Wood, — Muman, — Price, A. C. Layman and J. M. Taulbee. The congregation held their public services, during the year 1876, in the room beneath Masonic Hall. The handsome house in which they now meet was built in 1877. This building is frame, and is one of the neatest and most comfortable houses of worship in the town. It cost about $1,400.

The membership of the church is now about sixty.

The town of Irving is situated in the southeastern part of this township, on the I. & St. L. R. R., and is one of the growing towns of the county. The first house erected here was a store building. It was built by William S Berry and T. G. Black in the year 1846. This was the first store in the township, and represented a capital of several hundred dollars. One year later, another store house was erected by Edwards & Petrie. Both of these stores did a very flourishing business for several years, and as the population of the village increased, their trade increased also, until more room was required, hence their buildings were enlarged. Quite a number of families moved into the village and built houses, in the years 1846 and 1847. The first dwelling house was built by J. M. Taulbee. The town dates its growth from the year 1856, at which time it was laid off into lots by Messrs. Huggins & Rider. The survey was made by J. M. Taulbee. Huggins & Rider sold out to R. W. Davis and Madison Berry the year following, who at once commenced to improve the town. The first brick store-building was built in 1856, by H. J. Huestis. This building stands just north of the depot, and is at present occupied by the store of Knight & McDavid.

Among the first buildings erected was the blacksmith shop of — Sanford, which was built in the year 1856. This was the first shop of the kind in the township. It was sold to Jacob Bird, two years after it was built, who continued to work at the trade till within a very recent date. The first school in the village was taught by a Mr. Frink, in the old Hopewell meeting-house, which had been moved to the town in the latter part of the year 1856. The next school was taught by J. W. King. John Franklin and George Baker were among the first teachers in the village. The little frame building was the only schoolhouse in the town for several years. When there were more pupils than it could accommodate, rooms in private dwelling houses were fitted up for the surplus scholars. In the year 1866, the present school building was erected at a cost of $2,000. This house is of brick, two stories high, and contains two large-sized school rooms. These rooms are not sufficiently large to accommodate all the pupils of the schools, and the propriety of enlarging the building is being discussed.

The schools are at present under the superintendency of Prof. M. T. Miller, assisted by W. C. Hobson, Miss Means and Miss Hogshett. The first post office was established in the year 1856, with W. W. Wiley as Postmaster. The office was kept in the building now used by Berry & Grantham as a restaurant. A steam flouring-mill was erected in 1856, by Kelly & Wiley. Part of the machinery used in the construction of this mill was taken from the old Kelly mill, which formerly stood in the western part of the township, near Shoal Creek. A mill was built in 1868, by Hanners & Williams. This was a steam mill, also. It burned down in the year 1870, but has since been rebuilt, and at present is the only mill in the town. It has two run of buhrs and a capacity of about twenty-five barrels of flour per day. Two large elevators were built in the town in the years 1870 and 1871, only one of which is now operated. The large hotel which stands in the eastern part of the town was erected in the year 1868, by W. J. McClure, at a cost of $7,000.

Dr. J. H. Spears was the first physician who practiced medicine in Irving. He came here in the year 1858 and remained till 1863. Since 1858, the following physicians have been located here: W. F. Linn, Elias Petre, J. P. Murphy, W. H. Hobson, B. F. Burries, — Hart, - Tuck, — Nicholby J. F. Whitten, — Sweet W. B. Sprinkle, Joseph Cobb, Vincent Parkhill, J. W. Parkhill, A. B. Ault and Isaac Short. The best growth of the town has been since the year 1878. The large brick building occupied by the stores of Kelly & Berry, Thomas H. Padgett and A. W. Kelly, was built in the year 1880, as was also the brick building in which the stores of James McDavid and S. D. Bartlett are kept. Bartol Leon built the large house which he and his son occupy as a place of business in the year 1881. Several fine dwelling houses have been erected during the past two years, and quite a number of others are in process of erection at the present time. The town was incorporated in the year 1868, under a special charter. In 1873, it came in under the general law, when the ordinances were all revised by S. F. King and published. The present officers of the town are the following: John T. McDavid, President of the Board; Augustus McDavid, Clerk; M. D. L. Cannon, George Rarer, James M. Taulbee, Hiram J. Huestis, W. S. Berry, Jr., Trustees. An Odd Fellows Lodge was organized in the town at an early day, but of late years has not met. Nothing concerning the organization could be ascertained. Irving Lodge, No. 455, A. F. & A. M., was instituted in the year 1865, with the following charter members: B. F. Barnes, E. B. Randle, W. B. Van Horn, B. F. Pitts, H. J. Huestis, William M. Cox, George M. Davenport, Bartol Leon, John E. Lindley, Ryland Tuck and John B. Cox. The first officers of the lodge were Benjamin F. Barnes, W. M.; Edward B. Randle, S. W.; George M. Davenport, J. W. The present officers are the following: John T. Carriker, W. M.; Thomas Padgett, S. W.; H. J. Bowtell, J. W.; William S. Berry, Treasurer; A. A. Rinehart, Secretary; D. H. Luther, S. D.; Palmer Yemens, J. D.; B. T. McClure, Tiler. The membership is about thirty-two. The hall in which the lodge holds its meetings was built in the year 1868. It is owned by the organization.

A temperance organization known as the Royal Templars of Temperance was established here in the year 1879. The meetings are held semi-monthly. This organization is secret, and has the following officers: Select Councilor Vice Councilor, Past Councilor, Secretary, Treasurer, Herald, Guard, Sentinel and Deputy Herald.

The Irving Coal Company was recently incorporated with a capital of several thousand dollars. They have erected machinery in the western part of the town, where they are prospecting for coal and oil. We conclude this article on Irving with the following list of business men and the particular business in which they are engaged:

Kelly & Berry keep a large dry goods store, also an extensive line of ready-made clothing, boots, shoes and groceries. They represent a capital of perhaps $7,000, and are doing a flourishing business.

S. F. King makes groceries a specialty.

S. T. Bartlett & Son, James McDavid and Knight & McDavid also keep stores whose stocks consist of a general assortment.

Berry & Grantham, restaurant and bakery.

James M. Taulbee, feed and provision store.

Mrs. A. E. Newberry, milliner.

Williams Sisters, milliners.

There are three drug stores kept by the following persons: Thomas H. Padgett Sprinkle & Brother, Bartol, Leon & Son. D. D. Boutlett & Co., hardware; D. H. Luther, A. M. Edwards and J. Scherer, blacksmiths; George Rarer, wagon-maker: M. D. L. Cannon, cabinet-maker and undertaker; C. B. Wiley, livery stable; J. T. Maulbee, Jr., and I. G. Dawson, barbers.

CHAPTER XXIII.*

ZANESVILLE TOWNSHIP—POSITION—BOUNDARIES, ETC.—SOIL AND PRODUCTIONS—CREEKS AND TIMBER—PIONEER SETTLEMENTS—ROADS AND MILLS—FIRST ELECTION AND FIRST BIRTH—EARLY SCHOOLS—CHURCHES—VILLAGE OF ZANESVILLE—ITS GROWTH AND DECAY—INCIDENTS, ETC.

THE original Zanesville Precinct included within its area the townships of Pitman and Bois D'Arc, and was reduced to its present dimensions as an independent division in the year 1873, when the township organizations throughout the county were called into effect. It lies in the western part of the county, south of Pitman, north of North Litchfield and west of Raymond Township, with Macoupin County as its western boundary, and contains a fraction over thirty-four sections of choice tillable land, which, in point of fertility and productiveness, is second to none in this part of the State. Topographically, the country may be described as principally of an even face, in the central and northern portions, with occasional undulation of a somewhat irregular character in the southern part, while in the southeast corner the land is more uneven, though in no place is it too rolling for farming purposes. The soil is similar to that of the surrounding townships, being the rich black prairie loam common to this part of the country and everywhere noted for its fertility. This township lies in the great wheat belt of Illinois, and that cereal is the principal staple, although corn, rye, oats, flax, barley, together with the root crops usually found growing in this part of the State, are raised here in abundance, while nowhere in Montgomery County is there better encouragement offered to the fruit-grower. A soil of peculiar adaptability and a climate equally favorable, insure a large yield almost every year, facts of which many of the citizens have taken advantage, as is evinced by the numerous orchards to be seen in different parts of the township. The country is sufficiently well watered and drained for farming purposes by several streams that wind throughout the township and numerous small tributaries flowing into them from many points. The largest of these water-courses is the West Fork of Shoal Creek, which has its rise in Section 30, from whence it takes a devious course, flowing in a northeasterly direction about one mile, and then a southeasterly direction, passing through Sections 28, 27, 26, 35 and 36 before leaving the township. There is a small creek in the northern part, flowing through Sections 7 and 8, which affords stock water and drainage to that locality the greater part of the year. During the early spring months, these streams are hardly sufficient to carry off the immense quantities of water which spread over certain parts of the country, and from mere rivulets they become raging torrents, overflowing their banks for considerable distances on either side, and sometimes doing a great deal of injury to the farms through which they pass. From the head of Shoal Creek to the southern boundary of the township are several strips of timber of the varieties usually found in

*By G. N. Berry.

the woods of Central Illinois—walnut, hickory, elm, sycamore, maple and oak predominating. The original timber has disappeared long since before the ax of the lumberman, a character who made his appearance coeval with the first settler, and that which is now standing is, comparatively speaking, of recent growth. Much attention is given to the growing of timber and many farmers have surrounding their dwellings and outbuildings groves of considerable magnitude, which, in a few years, will furnish them not only with lumber for all practical purposes, but with fuel as well. That this part of the county was at one time in the dim and remote past inhabited by a prehistoric race possessed of many of the attributes of what we term a high degree of enlightenment, is probable, from the existence of several mounds at different places throughout its territory and numerous strange relics that have been unearthed in several localities. Who were these strange people? Whence came they? Whither did they go? These questions must forever remain to form a melancholy interest in the wondrous past, and a mystery which neither time nor circumstance, nor science, nor the more wondrous future, may reveal. But since their time, another race, mighty in numbers, has come and gone from their ancient homes and favorite hunting-grounds, though yet not quite extinct. When the white man made his first appearance in what is now the territory of Zanesville, it was a favorite hunting-ground and retreat of several tribes of savages, notably among which were the Kickapoos and Pottawatomies. Their camping-grounds were usually selected near the source of Shoal Creek and in the timber skirting Macoupin Creek, a small stream just across the line in the adjoining county. When the white settlers began to increase in numbers, these Indians moved farther west, though at different intervals for several years re-visited the scenes of their former camping-places, but never to do any mischief.

These visits were discontinued about the year 1830, and since that period no Indians have been seen in the northern part of Montgomery County. We have no data from which to give an exact statement, as to either the time the first settlement of the township was made or the individuals who made it. It is known, however, that a man by the name of Robert Palmer settled near the site of the present village of Zanesville, where he kept a hotel as early as the year 1824. His place was a stopping-point for travelers, on the road leading from Springfield to Vandalia, being one of the first public houses in the county. Palmer proved to be a notorious gambler, blackleg and a very bad character generally. His house was a rendezvous of a gang of thieves and rowdies as bad as himself, and the place became noted throughout the country as a dangerous locality. Several daring robberies having been committed in the neighboring towns and settlements, and the evidence being very plain against Palmer as the perpetrator, he left the country rather unceremoniously and fled for parts unknown. It was afterward ascertained that he went to Iowa, where he was arrested for complicity in a brutal murder, convicted and hanged. So much for the first pioneer of Zanesville. Several transient settlers located in the vicinity of Palmer's tavern shortly after it was erected, but none of them appear to have taken up land or in any way improve the country. The next actual settler of whom we could learn anything definite was one George Brewer, who entered the land where Zanesville Village now stands, which he laid off into town lots about the year 1828. Through his efforts, a post office was established, which, together with the town, was called Leesburg, after Robert E. Lee, a wholesale merchant of St. Louis, in whose name the land was entered. Brewer appears to have been a man of considerable public spirit, and, seeing an opportunity, as he supposed, of making a fortune in the town which could not help but grow, expended quite an amount of money in various improvements, among which was a good-sized store building. This building was stocked with a miscellaneous assortment of merchandise, purchased at the house of Lee in St. Louis, from which place it was transported in wagons, a distance of about seventy-five miles. Soon other parties, attracted by the promising opening which the village presented, or by the fertile lands in the vicinity, came in, and, by the year 1830, there was a thrifty and enterprising community on the high road to prosperity. The town grew apace; lots were sold rapidly at good round sums; shops of various kinds were established; a school was organized, other storerooms erected, and business of all kinds increased to such an extent that the village at one time was considered the second place of importance in the county. In the year 1829, a settlement was made in the southwest corner of the township by immigrants from the South, among whom can be named Isaac Bailey, James Crawford, Thomas Williams and Zebedee Williams. These were all men of consequence in the early settlement of the township, and left the impress of their characters on their descendants, many of whom still reside in the community which their ancestors founded.

A prominent settler in the same locality was Robert Allen, who came in a little later, and who, for a number of years, appears to have been a leading and respected citizen of the township. Between the years 1835 and 1840, Beatty Burke George Burroughs, Dores D. Shumway and a man by the name of Chastine entered and improved lands near the village of Zanesville. Those early pioneers are all dead or have moved to other localities, as the writer was unable to learn any facts concerning them in his canvass for information among the old settlers of the township. From 1840 to 1848, a settlement was made around the head of Shoal Creek and a number of farms improved. The principal men connected with this settlement were Walker Williams, Elgin Smith, Jeff Parrott and Moses Martin, all of whom had formerly resided in the South. Among other prominent settlers were Joseph Vignos, a Frenchman, who located near the central part of the township; Dr. Caldwell, one of the earliest physicians of Zanesville, and S. Smitherman, a noted farmer and stock raiser, who purchased land near the village, all three of whom are still living. The northeastern portion of the township has been settled more recently, yet in point of progress and improvements it is behind no other locality, and, in many respects, is far superior to some. Since the year 1848, the settlements in different parts of the township have been so simultaneous that a mention of names of early settlers entitled to a notice in these pages would transcend the limits of our space. Suffice it to say, however, that they are justly entitled to all the honors accorded them as founders of a community which occupies a prominent place in the galaxy of townships forming Montgomery County. There was a regularly laid out road through Zanesville Township as early as the year 1830, known as the Jacksonville & Vandalia road, as it connected those two places. It is still traveled, and its direction, though slightly devious, is on the whole pretty direct, the general course being northwest and southeast, and differing but little from the original route. Another early road which was pretty generally traveled was the one leading from Carlinville to Taylorville. Its course through this township was from northeast to southwest, though its direction has been greatly changed of late years, and it is no longer the important thoroughfare that it was during the early days of the county. Among other early established highways were the St. Louis road, which passed through the township in a northwesterly direction; the Girard road, which crossed through the western part of the township, from north to south, and the Zanesville & Litchfield road, connecting these two points and running in a southeasterly direction from the former place. There are many other roads traversing the township and intersecting each other at different points, but, like other roads of the county, are deserving of no particular description. Among the pioneer industries of Zanesville was the little horse mill erected by Edward Crawford, in the western part, about the year 1838. This primitive mill was the only one aside from the present mill at the town of Zanesville ever erected in the township, and, for a number of years, was operated almost constantly in order to supply the demands of the neighbors for flour and meal. It was torn down several years ago, and at present there remains no vestige to mark the spot it formerly occupied. The Zanesville Mill was built in the year 1869, by Messrs. Sharpe, Johnson & Berry, at a cost of $15,000. It is operated by steam, has three run of buhrs, and, when kept running all the time, can grind about 100 barrels of flour per day. From 1869 to 1872, it did an enormous amount of custom and merchant work, and returned to the proprietors a large per cent on the capital invested. Johnson sold his interest to Samuel Caldwell in 1872, who in turn disposed of the same to Sharpe & Berry the same year. The latter parties becoming financially embarrassed on account of various speculations, sold the mill to S. Smitherman and Clark Sinclair, in the year 1873, and since that time from some cause unknown to the writer, the machinery has stood idle, much to the regret of the farmers of the surrounding country.

The first election in the township, of which we have any reliable record, was held in the year 1835, when George Brewer and James Crawford were chosen Justices of the Peace, offices which they held uninterruptedly for several consecutive years. Stephen Crawford, son of James Crawford, was the first white child born in Zanesville, the date of his birth being the 13th of November, 1831, the same night of the great meteoric display known as the falling stars. The early educational history of the township is somewhat vague and disjointed, although sufficient information has been gleaned to warrant the assumption that schools were not established until several years had elapsed from the date of the first settlements. We of the present day with our pleasantly located common schools, normal institutes and colleges, can scarce realize the vast difference, when even scenes depicted in that popular and much-perused work, "The Hoosier Schoolmaster," would have been looked upon as a wonderful advancement toward what might now be termed the extravagances of a higher education. For several years after the advance guard of the early pioneers who made Zanesville what it is to-day, first came into this part of the country, schools and intellectual training were thought of only as adjuncts of that civilization which they had left behind—things to be desired but hardly to be hoped for. It was for some time simply a question of keeping body and soul together by laborious toil, and the hardships endured in procuring the bare necessities of life, precluded the possibility of looking far for intellectual improvement. But as the farm lands broadened, the little settlements grew more numerous, and the labors of the inhabitants had, by the favor of a kind Providence, placed them beyond immediate want, they bethought themselves of their duty to their little ones, and schools were established. The names of the early teachers cannot be given with that accuracy which we term reliable, although it is generally conceded that the first pedagogue was Henry Mayer, who taught in the southern part of the township about the year 1833.

This school was attended by about fifteen children, and, like all early schools, was supported by subscription, the teacher being compelled to collect the tuition fees. The first schoolhouse was built by Edward Crawford and others in the southwest corner of the township. The land on which the building stood was afterward entered and the house lost before it was occupied as designated. Another house was built of logs the same year, on Section 26, in which the school already mentioned was taught. The second term was taught near the village of Zanesville by a teacher whose name was not learned. In educational matters at present, Zanesville is not behind her sister townships of the county, as is proved by the presence of six neat frame schoolhouses, furnished with all the modern improvements. Teachers skilled in their profession are the only ones employed by the efficient School Board. The term lasts eight months of the year, and generally begins the first Monday in October.

Among the early pioneers of Zanesville were many persons in whom the fear of God was a predominant element and their religious duties were at no time neglected. The first public services were conducted by the veteran pioneer preacher, Elder James Street, at the residence of Jacob Baker, about the year 1830. The first church was a society of the United Baptists, which was organized at the head of Shoal Creek, where the organization is still maintained. They have a substantial temple of worship, a progressive membership and are doing much good in the community where the church is located. The disciples or Christians organized a church a number of years ago, which is still a prominent society, numbering among its members some of the leading and substantial citizens of the country. A very handsome and commodious house, situated in the southeastern part of the township, serves the congregation as a place of worship. The Methodists maintained a flourishing organization at the village of Zanesville for a number of years, but the society was finally merged into churches at other points, and at present there is no class at that place. The village of Zanesville, to which we have already referred in the opening of this chapter, is situated in the northwest corner of the township, about two and a half miles east of the county line, and is but a mere shadow of its former self. During the early years of the county, it was a prominent business point, a reputation it sustained until the year 1869, at which time there were four large stores, all doing a good business, one grocery three blacksmith shops, two wagon shops, two hotels, cooper shop and two plague spots in the shape of whisky saloons. Among the merchants who did business here at different times were the following: Harvey Madison, Joseph Vignos, —— Sharpe, William Street, Joseph Booth, James Little, John McNiel, John Hamilton & Son and Emert & Son. The earliest physicians in the place were George Mayfield, J. W. Wheeler and G. W. Caldwell, the last named being still in the village. Strong efforts were made by the citizens of the village and surrounding country to induce the Wabash

Railway Company to run their road through the town, but without avail. The road was built two and a half miles west, and, together with the growing town of Litchfield, proved a death blow to the business interest of Zanesville, as it began to wane from that time. The merchants moved their stores to more eligible places, shops were closed, mechanics sought more remunerative fields of labor and a general decay fastened itself upon the once prosperous village. The post office was taken away in the year 1881. George Hamilton was the last Postmaster.

The business of the place at present is represented by one small grocery store and a blacksmith shop. What few buildings remain are old, time-worn and present a very dejected appearance, and the time is not far in the future when the village is destined to disappear entirely. Several incidents of tragic nature have transpired at this town at different times during its history, two of which are worthy of mention. In the year 1853, Andrew Nash and a man by the name of Lockerman had an altercation brought on by the too free use of whisky, during which the former stabbed the latter in a very brutal manner. Lockerman died immediately, and Nash, becoming alarmed, fled the country. Detectives were placed on his track, and succeeded, after several weeks' diligent search, in finding him in Arkansas, where he was arrested, brought back to Carlinville, tried and sentenced to be hanged. A petition was put in circulation by his friends, praying the Governor to commute the sentence to imprisonment for life, which was accordingly done, but before the prisoner was made aware of this step in his behalf, a mob, or rather the appearance of a mob, gathered about the jail one night, which so frightened the poor fellow, that, rather than fall in to their hands, he hanged himself with a sheet, which had been twisted into a rope and made fast to a beam overhead.

Dr. Mayfield and a man by the name of Hardy had been enemies for a number of years, and the former took occasion to insult the latter whenever they chanced to be thrown together. They met one day in the highroad, and, as usual, Mayfield threw out some of his taunts, which provoked several spirited replies from Hardy, whereupon the former alighted from his buggy and gave Hardy a sound horse-whipping. A few days afterward, while the latter was passing the hotel, Mayfield came out of the house and commanded him to halt: he was told to mind his own business, which answer so exasperated the Doctor that he drew a revolver and fired, some say directly at Hardy, while others contend that the shot was only for the purpose of frightening him. Hardy stepped around a corner of the building, drew out an old-fashioned horse pistol, with which he had armed himself, came back and fired directly at his enemy, the shot taking effect in his side. Mayfield returned the fire with two shots, neither of which took effect, and then fell. He was carried into the hotel, where he expired within a very short time. Hardy was arrested, tried and acquitted on the ground of self-defense. This occurred in the year 1854.

CHAPTER XXIV.

WALSHVILLE TOWNSHIP—TERRITORY EMBRACED—SOIL AND TIMBER—CROPS—FIRST SETTLEMENTS—SCHOOLS—ELECTIONS—FIRST MARRIAGE—RELIGION, ETC.

"The verdant fields are covered o'er with growing
grain,
And white men till the soil, the soil
Where once the red man used to reign."

WALSHVILLE is situated in the richest and best portion of Montgomery County, and was one of the first townships settled by white men.

Its territory was formerly embraced by Bond County, from which it was separated when the division was made in 18—. It is bounded on the north by South Litchfield Township, on the east by Grisham Township and a part of Bond County, on the south by Bond County and Silver Creek Township of Madison County, and on the west by Staunton Township of Macoupin County. Its length and breadth are each about six miles, and it contains thirty-six square miles of territory, or 23,040 acres. Its principal system of drainage is through one of the forks of Shoal Creek, which flows along its eastern boundary and into which many streams of minor importance, having their sources within the township, empty.

The configuration is good, being, in the greater part a beautiful prairie land, sufficiently undulating to present a very pleasing appearance. Numerous groves are to be seen at intervals which relieve the monotony of the prairie to such an extent that many persons, on seeing it for the first time, do not hesitate in pronouncing Walshville the most beautiful part of the entire county. The soil is rich, deep and fertile, and in places where it has been cultivated for at least sixty years, is still very productive. When first seen by the white man, the surface was clothed with a luxurious growth of tall, waving prairie grass which afforded rich pasturage for numerous herds of deer, buffalo and antelope. There were, also, thick growths of timber in certain localities consisting principally of cottonwood, hickory elm, walnut, maple, oak and other varieties indigenous to the southern part of Illinois.

Among the timber was a luxuriant growth of underbrush and vines of various kinds that rendered traveling through the wooded portions extremely difficult. The majority of the first settlers located in the timber skirting the various water-courses and in time the greater part of the woodland disappeared before the pioneer's ax. The dense undergrowth has also been cleared away, and the woods that now remain present a striking contrast to the forests of long ago, as the space among the trees is beautifully sodded over in many places with a thick covering of blue grass. The best wooded districts are in the eastern and southern parts. Stretching away from Shoal Creek westward, is a broad expanse of prairie dotted here and there with artificial groves of more recent growth.

These groves, owing to the genial atmosphere and rich soil, grow very rapidly, and within a few years after setting out, the trees are sufficiently large to be sawn into timber or used for fuel.

The leading occupation of this section is agriculture although considerable attention is given by certain parties to stock raising, and in the near future this industry promises to be

By G. N. B[illegible]

William Watson

quite extensive, as certain localities seem peculiarly adapted to it, there being plenty of rich pasturage and stock water in abundance.

At present, however, it is to the different crops that the majority of the people look for their chief support. The soil appears to be particularly adapted to corn and wheat, although all the other cereals, common to this latitude, are here raised in abundance. Fruit, many varieties and excellent flavor, are to be found growing in almost every orchard. The pioneer's attention was early called to fruit culture, and many old orchards, that have been bearing for years, are to be seen in various parts of the township.

The first line of settlements in the southern part of the county extended from the western limits of Walshville, eastward through Grisham to the central part of East Fork, all of which were made about the same time, or with a few years intervening.

Single families at first came, then in groups of three or four, locating at different places in the same locality, until soon the prairie was thickly dotted with pioneer dwellings. Soon schoolhouses were built, churches organized, mills erected, in fact the foundation of that civilization which makes this part of the State noted abroad was laid. This remarkable development has been brought about within a comparatively short time, for looking back through the vista of sixty years, these broad, fertile prairies and productive fields were the grazing-places of numerous herds of the wild denizens of the plains and the camping-ground of the hostile savage. Now the rich soil is everywhere broken, woods have fallen, pleasant drives, well-tilled fields, beautiful orchards and delightful homes checker the view, speaking volumes for the enterprise and energy which characterizes the citizens of this township. The first white inhabitants of Walshville were Nicholas Voiles and family. Voiles moved here from his home in North Carolina in the year 1818, and built his log cabin on the farm now owned by George Webster, about one and a half miles northeast of the village of Walshville. He improved this place and made it his home until the year 1826, when he sold it and moved to Schuyler County.

About the same time, Melcher Fogleman, a strong-handed, warm-hearted German, made his appearance and entered the piece of land adjoining that on which Voiles settled. His house was erected close to a large spring among the hills skirting Shoal Creek. This spring was the nucleus around which several other families clustered, and for a number of years was the only water supply for the little community.

Fogleman was a blacksmith, and it was here that the first shop in the township was erected. A son was born while the family resided in this locality. This was the first birth in the township and one of the first in the county. This son is still living, near Litchfield, and is one of the highly respected citizens of the community in which he resides. The next family of which we have any knowledge was that of William Stevens, a son-in-law of Voiles. He came from North Carolina, also, but did not purchase or enter land in the township, being but a temporary resident for about two years, when he moved to Shelby County. Elias Baker took a claim in Section 25 in the fall of 1819. His son, James, came with him and assisted in opening the farm for cultivation.

In about one year the old gentleman became dissatisfied with the new country, and went back to the hills of his native Georgia, where he died two years later.

James resided on the place his father settled for a number of years, an honored and respected citizen. The place is at present owned by John Kirkland, who has made it one of the best farms in the township. Austin Grisham came to the State when it was a territory, and settled in what is now Bond County in 1816. Four years later, he moved farther north and entered a piece of land where his son, James Grisham, now lives, in Walshville Township. This place is in Section 24, near the southern part. Here his family lived for a number of years, with no neighbors nearer than four miles. The country surrounding their little home was a wilderness infested by wolves, which proved very destructive to their stock.

Different members of the family took their turns in watching the pig-pens at night, but despite all their precautions, many a fat porker was killed, and several calves more or less injured by these gaunt scourges of the prairie. The Pottawatomie Indians had a camping-place in what is now known as Kirkland's Grove, near Grisham's residence, which they visited every year for the purpose of hunting. These Indians were not troublesome, although they would carry off a pig occasionally, when a favorable opportunity presented itself. They discontinued their incursions into this part of the county a few years after the first settlements were made, and save a few scattered bands, none have been seen since 1825. Grisham died in 1852 at the advanced age of eighty-two years. His son, James, of whom a biography appears elsewhere in this work, is the oldest settler living in the township.

Prominent among the early settlers of Walshville who came prior to the year 1821 was James Jordan, a Baptist preacher. He moved here from Indiana in 1820, and entered a tract of land in Section 28, which he at once began to improve. He was one of the first preachers of the county, and a most exemplary man. It was at his residence that the first religious services in the township were held, shortly after he came into the little settlement. He sold his land to Jonathan Voiles, in 1825, and moved into what is now Grisham Township. The place is now owned by Jacob Lindley. Several representatives of the Jordan family reside in Grisham Township, and are justly considered among the best citizens in the community where they live. J. W. Garrison was also an early settler of Walshville, locating on what is known as Miller's Tract, Section 25, about the year 1826. Thomas Evans came the same year and settled on the Robb Mound, two miles south of the village of Walshville. Joseph Dokes became a resident of the township some time previous to the year 1826, but at what place he settled was not learned. Among the early settlers can be named John Evans, Joseph Evans, both of whom came in 1826. Robert Kirkland settled on Section 15 a couple of years afterward. No permanent residents settled in the northern part of the township until the year 1840. At that date, John Simpson and John King bought and improved farms near where Walshville now stands. Since that time, the population of the township has steadily increased, and to give a notice of each family that came, up to the year 1842 would transcend the limits of our space. Probably no division of the county was settled by a more worthy set of pioneers than Walshville as they were with but few exceptions men of piety and sterling integrity. Such lives were not harvests of regrets, but grand realities, and by imitating their many virtues we may become better men and more worthy citizens.

Like the early settlers in all new countries, the pioneers of this township were compelled to brave many difficulties and hardships. While it is true that there were no hostile Indians to encounter, nor any very ferocious wild animals to guard against, yet the new condition of the country made it very difficult to obtain wearing apparel, groceries, breadstuffs and other articles necessary to convenience and comfort. The greater amount of trading during the early days was done at Edwardsville and St. Louis, as they were the nearest market places. Flour and meal were obtained at those places in the summer time, but during the winter seasons many families manufactured their own meal by hand, crushing the grain with pestle and mortar, a slow process, but withal a very sure one.

Corn was the most practical staple. The early families, in fact, had to subsist in the main upon this product, variously prepared, and yet aside from this chief edible they feasted often upon prairie chicken, turkey, deer and other wild game that thronged the woods and prairie, fish that filled the streams and honey that could be obtained in great quantities from large trees in the forests.

Several small mills were erected in the adjoining townships at an early day, which served as a source of supplies to the citizens of the locality, and until within a comparatively recent period there were no mills of any kind at Walshville.

Very fair roads intersect all parts of the township, as is the case with almost all other parts of the county. The first roads have all been changed somewhat and improved. Some of them were crooked and irregular having been abandoned altogether. During certain seasons of the year, especially in the early spring, these roads became almost impassable in some places owing to the depth of the mud.

The first road that was regularly established was the one leading from Hillsboro to St. Louis. It passed through the township in a southwesterly direction. The Alton & St. Louis road was laid out in an early day also and at one time was one of the most extensively traveled highways in the southern part of the county. Intersecting this road near the southern boundary is the East Fork road, extending through the township from east to west. Traces of other early roads are still to be seen in various places, but none of them appear to have been roads of much importance. Many of the first pioneers of Walshville were men of culture and education received considerable attention at a very early date. Emil Clowsen was one of the first teachers in the southern part of the county but of him nothing is known save that he taught a little school in 1842. The house in which the school was taught was a little log structure that had formerly been occupied by the family of some "squatter." It was situated in the southwest corner of Section 23.

The second house used for school purposes built on the place where George Hoisington now lives, near the central part of the township. Among the early teachers at this place were Winfield Hicks and Henry Havens, but when and how long they taught are facts which the writer was unable to obtain. The first frame schoolhouse was built in the village of Walshville in 1850. There are now seven good frame schoolhouses in the township well provided with apparatus, in which school is taught from six to eight months in the year. The schools are in progress at the present time and all doing well.

One of the first elections in the township was for Justice of the Peace, held about the year 1850. At this election, Irwin Cory received very nearly the unanimous vote. He held the office several consecutive terms. The first Constable was elected at the same time. The honors of the office settled upon the head of William Towell, who wore them with becoming dignity. In the year 1825, James Jordan, son of John Jordan, was married to Elizabeth, daughter of Austin Grisham, at the latter's residence. This was the first marriage that took place in Walshville as well as one of the earliest in the county. A burial ground was laid out on the farm of John Kirkland, in the southern part of the township, in a very early day, and is now known as the Kirkland Graveyard. Among the first interments here were Peggy Garrison and a child of John Woods. It is not known with any degree of certainty which of the above deaths occurred first, some contending for the one and some for the other. There were several graves here previous to this time, as different parties had been brought here for burial from the little settlement farther south in Bond County.

But limited satisfaction has been derived in tracing up the early church history of Walshville Township. The first sermon was preached by Elder James Jordan at his residence, but to this we have already referred. The first religious organization of which we have any knowledge was a society of Methodists organized by the noted pioneer preacher, Peter Cartwright, at the residence of Elias Baker, in the year 1824.

This society increased in numbers as the years went by, until it became one of the Methodist strongholds in this part of the county. The residence of Baker was used as a place of worship until he moved from the neighborhood, when the dwelling of Jacob Holbrook was tendered the congregation.

The congregation was finally separated; part of the members organized the congregation known as the Dry Fork Church, in Bond County, and a portion united with the congregation that worshiped at Mount Carmel Church in Grisham Township. The Walshville Baptist Church was organized at the residence of William Kline, about two miles southeast of the place now occupied by the village of Walshville, in the year 1836, by Rev. William Burge. Among the first members of this congregation were the following: William Kline and wife, Reuben Kline and wife, George Varner, Henry Bryant and wife, James Bryant and James Simpson, the greater number of whom have long since left the scenes of their earthly labors to enjoy the fruits of well-spent lives in the "church triumphant above."

The public services of the church during the first eight years of its history were held in private dwellings of the different members. A little log building was erected in 1846, which served the congregation until the year 1862, when it was decided to remove the organization to the village of Walshville, and there build a more suitable temple of worship. A neat frame house was built and dedicated the following year. This building stood but four years, when from some unknown cause it took fire and burned to the ground.

In 1869, their present house was erected at a cost of $1,000. There are upon the records the names of forty-five members in good standing. At present, the church is without a pastor, but efforts are being made to secure one. We will speak of the other churches of Walshville in connection with the history of that village a little farther on. Near the central part of the township is a German Missionary Baptist Church, which dates its organization from the year 1879. The church is small in numbers, but has a very neat and comfortable building, which was erected and dedicated in the year 1880. We were unable to learn any particulars concerning the congregation, and will be obliged to pass it by with above very brief notice.

The beautiful little town of Walshville is situated in the northern part of the township, about two and a half miles from the northern boundary. It is surrounded by an excellent farming country, and its inhabitants are energetic and intelligent.

The first building was erected here in 1850. It was a storeroom built by L. D. Smith, who did a good business for three years, when he sold his stock to a Mr. Bowers. Bowers sold to Chapman & Kennedy, who in turn sold to Michael Walsh in the year 1855. Walsh laid out the village in 1855, and gave it the name by which it is at present known. It was from him, also, that the township derives the name Walshville. One of the first houses was the residence of John King, which was put up about the same year in which the store building of L. D. Smith was erected. I. Irwin had charge of a store about three years. Seymour & Kline built a brick storeroom and stocked it with goods in the year 1855. They conducted the business as partners but six months, when Kline sold his interest to Eli De Shane, who shortly afterward purchased the entire stock, and for several years did a flourishing business. Michael Walsh was one among the first business men of the place, having sold goods in the residence of John King when there were but two or three houses in the place. Hodges & Sanders, Blevins & Denny, Hodges & Boyd, are the names of firms that have sold goods in Walshville at different times during its history.

The first physician was a Dr. Green, who located in the vicinity in the year 1848, and practiced his profession for about two years. Dr. William Williams located here a short time afterward, and for several years was the only physician in the county south of Hillsboro. Samuel Denney, John Wadkins, L. C. Stoddard, Nathan Jayne, Dr. String, E. F. Newberry, have at different intervals practiced medicine in the village. The present physicians are Ambrose Barcroft, John T. Koen, M. S. Davenport and V. B. Barcroft.

A post office was established here in 1846, with John King as Postmaster. It was kept at King's residence for several years. Allison Corlew was the second Postmaster. The office is at present kept by Samuel H. Henderson, at his place of business.

A. J. Sitten erected a neat little hotel in the year 1867, which was extensively patronized by the traveling public. It is now run by William Shurtleff. John G. Hawkins keeps a hotel in the town also. The Walshville mill was built in the year 1853, by Messrs. Grisham & Simpson. This was a steam mill with three run of stone, and for nine years was kept running almost constantly, doing an immense business for a mill of its capacity. It was completely destroyed by fire in the year 1862, entailing a loss of at least $13,000 on the proprietors.

A steam saw-mill was erected in the village in 1855, by Nicholas Price, who operated it about five years, and then sold it to Isaac Parish. It was by him moved from the town to Shoal Creek, shortly after he made the purchase.

John Rud built a steam flouring-mill in 1863, which he operated for two years. It was sold to F. C. Kirkland for the sum of $7,000, and afterward purchased by McCracken & Lilly, who ran it at intervals until the present time. It is not now in operation. There are four neat church buildings and five religious organizations in the town, of which the following is a brief history. The Walshville Methodist Episcopal Church was organized in 1850, with a membership of twelve. Their names, as recorded on the church book, are as follows: Joseph Price and wife, Anna Price, Edwin Brown and wife, James Whitesides and wife, Martha J. Whitesides, Caroline Whitesides, Maria Clark, William M. Towell and wife. The most of these had been members of previous organizations elsewhere. The church owes much of its success to the labors of Rev. Rogers, the first pastor and principal mover in the organization. The first preaching place was the village schoolhouse, which was used until the Baptist meeting-house was completed, when they were allowed the use of it every alternate Sabbath. Up to this time the church had so increased in numbers that it was decided to erect a house of worship in harmony with its growing strength. The building was erected and dedicated in the year 1866. It is a substantial edifice 40x56 feet, and, with improvements recently added, is valued at $3,300. The following is a list of the pastors who have had charge of the church since its organization: — — Moore, Asa Snell, George Compton, C. J. F. Tolle, David Stubblefield, —— Walker, S. P. Groves, L. C. English and William Van Cleve. Sixty members comprise the strength of the church at present. Their first Sunday school was organized in 1867, William M. Towell was the first Superintendent. The school is now one of the best in the village, and is superintended by T. T. Smith. The Cumberland Presbyterian Church of Walshville is one of the live religious organizations of the township. The original congregation from which this society sprung was known as the Mount Pleasant Church, and met for worship in Grisham Township. From this congregation two churches were organized, the one at Pleasant Branch in Bond County and the other at Walshville. The dates of these different organizations were not ascertained, though we may be safe in saying that the latter was organized about the year 1868. Thirty-five names were enrolled at the first meeting, the most of whom had previously belonged to the old Mount Pleasant congregation. The schoolhouse supplied the wants of the society as a place of meeting about one year, after which their public services were held in the Methodist Church until their present house of worship was built. This edifice is situated in the eastern part of the town, and was erected in the year 1871. It cost the sum of $2,000. C. G. Keon preached for the church two years; D. R. Bell two years. For several years the church was without a regular pastor, the pulpit being supplied occasionally by ministers from neighboring churches.

Rev. R. H. McHenry, the present pastor, commenced his labors in the year 1879, and was shortly afterward regularly called as pastor.

A Sabbath school has been conducted in connection with the church ever since its organization.

The Christian Church was organized in the year 1874, by Elder A. D. Northcut. The original membership numbered ten. With little influence in society, few in numbers, without a house of worship, and all these disadvantages under the shadow of the three other strong organizations this little band of disciples, protected and blessed by Him "who doeth all things well," began to increase in numbers rapidly until within a short time it was the strongest church in the place. L. M. Linn, the first pastor, preached two years, and did much toward making the church what it is to-day He was succeeded in the pastorate by Elder J. H. Garrison, of St. Louis, one of the most gifted pulpit orators of his church in the West, and editor of one of its leading periodicals.

He remained about three years, and was followed by Elder J. H. Smart, who preached nearly or quite two years. H. P. Tandy preached one year; L. F. Wood six months. Elder Vance, the present pastor, has been with the church since 1881.

For several years the Baptist Church was placed at the disposal of the congregation, who used the same until 1878.

A new house of worship was then erected, which, in point of neatness and finish, is one of the best church edifices in the county. It was dedicated the same year in which it was built by J. H. Garrison. The membership is at present about eighty-five. J. T. Koen is Superintendent of the large, flourishing Sunday school. A society known as Free Methodists was organized in 1880, by Rev. F. H. Ashcroft. At the time of organization the society consisted of fifteen members, which has since increased to thirty. Their meetings are held in the vacant storeroom belonging to Mr. Blevins. The present officers of this organization are J. D Tiffin and N. Neal, Stewards; H. S. Henderson, Class Leader; Miss Norah Neal, Superintendent of Sunday school. Public services every Sunday.

In 1865, the Walshville Lodge, No. 475, A F. & A. M., was established. The first meetings were held in an unfinished room in the school building, which was afterward fitted up for a hall. The following names were copied from the charter: Isaac Sturges, W. A. Kingston, L. Baily, F. D. Whitesides, William M. Towell, Peter L. Davenport, John J. Miller and M. S. Davenport.

The different offices are filled by the following persons, viz.: A. T. Strange, W. M.; John T. Koen, S. W.; E. M. Root, J. W.; Thomas Greenwood, Treasurer; A. B. Copeland, Secretary; J. J. Davenport, Tiler.

The township of Walshville bore a commendable share in the gallant and patriotic work of putting down the great rebellion. She gave of her sons and citizens with their blood and treasure without stint until the flag of beauty and glory waved in triumph over a united country. It would be invidious to make comparisons between this and other townships, as they all did their duty willingly, fearlessly, well, and their whole duty.

Soldiers from Walshville did service and partook of the dangers and glory of every battle of any considerable note. We would give a list of all the soldiers the township sent to the front were it practicable, but it would far transcend the limits of our space. May the country never need their services more in the dread business which carries fire and sword among mankind; and leaves widespread desolation and blackened ruins where all was smiling plenty. Those who went but never returned—who laid down their lives to avenge the honor of an insulted flag—will never be forgotten. It is the verdict of the loyal heart of Walshville, expressed not without a tinge of regret, that she can well afford to spare her noble dead. May they rest in peace. Let not the flowers that spring from the mold above them be trodden down by soldier nor war-horse.

CHAPTER XXV.*

WITT TOWNSHIP—SOIL, TIMBER AND CONFIGURATION—SCHOOLS, PAST AND PRESENT—THE CIRCUIT RIDER—CHURCHES AND SUNDAY SCHOOLS—MILLS AND OTHER INDUSTRIES.

THE greater share of Witt Township consists of a beautiful, undulating surface of prairie land. Its western and southern parts, though not exactly level, are not so broken as much of the land of East Fork and Fillmore Townships lying farther south. The principal and only stream of note is the East Fork of Shoal Creek, which flows through the township from north to the southwest. In its course it passes through the following sections of land, viz.: 5, 8, 17, 19, 30 and 31. Its bed and banks are very muddy, and the stream, through an unknown period of years, has cut several channels in the soil at different places. The flow of the current is characterized by a sluggishness in some places and by great rapidity in others. The territory through which it passes in this township is nearer level than the land lying adjacent to it in the township of East Fork. During the warmer months of dry seasons, the waters of this creek are very low, and sometimes becomes almost or quite dry, but in ordinary years the stream remains quite full, and sometimes during heavy rains, the current becomes a rushing torrent, which overflows the banks on either side for several hundred yards. The higher portions of land which skirt this creek in the southern part form a very pleasing contrast to the broad stretch of monotonous prairie, and are covered with thick growths of walnut oak and hickory trees. The largest and best of these trees have been cut down and sawn into lumber years ago, although there are still standing many good sized trees of more recent growth. Among these higher portions of the township are to be seen a number of springs of pure clear water, where the Indians had their camping grounds many years ago and around which many interesting and curious relics have been found. A small stream in the southeast part drains that portion of the township, and flows into Fillmore from Section 16. Another small creek rises near the south central part and takes a northwesterly course, flowing into East Fork Creek, near the line which separates Witt from East Fork Township. The surface soil of this section of the county is largely a black loam, very fertile, rendering tillage easy, and, in an agricultural point of view, this township is one of the best in the county. In the low flat lands along the creeks the soil contains much decayed vegetable matter, and when properly drained and cultivated produces immense crops of corn and grass. Among the broken and hilly portions in the southern part, the soil is largely sand, mingled in some places with clay in sufficient quantities to make the land very productive and valuable. There is, perhaps, as little waste land in this region as there is in any other township in the county, but very little, if any, being too broken or wet for tillage.

Witt lies in the eastern part of the county with the following boundaries: Nokomis Township on the north, Irving on the west, Fillmore on the south. The eastern boundaries are Audubon Township and Hurricane Township, of Fayette County. It is exactly six miles square, and contains thirty-six sections of land. Forty-six years ago, the area embraced in Witt was comparatively an unbroken wild. The settlers were few and far between, and it was only

* By G. N. Berry.

after a ride of several miles across the trackless prairies, and through the scraggy forests, that the traveler might find evidence of advancing civilization in the presence of a log cabin planted near a spring, or some small stream, or an insignificant board shanty near the edge of a small plowed field on the prairie. Broad expanses of prairie lay around him without the sight of a human habitation, while the woods along the creeks as yet furnished but few signs that they had been penetrated by the white man, and these signs were principally the blazed paths, made by cutting through bark of the trees, a sign scarcely distinguishable after twilight set in. Here and there corners had been staked out by county surveyors, and they were always a welcome sight to the luckless one who found himself lost on the wide, trackless plains. But the scene has changed marvelously since then, and the wilds of Witt now blossom and bloom like the rose. Her broad, fertile prairies are now divided off into well-tilled farms, on which are many fine and elegant residences, evidences of the prosperity with which the farmer is surrounded and blessed. The iron horse dashes through the verdant fields, and its white plume curls over the smiling land, where peace, plenty and intelligence combine to render the well-to-do and hospitable citizens contented and happy. Witt was not settled as early as some of the neighboring townships of the county—that is, by permanent settlers. A number of squatters entered the township several years prior to the first permanent settlement, but just when they made their appearance cannot be known with any degree of certainty. It is well known, however, that when the first permanent settlers who were owners of the land appeared, there were living in the township, along the creeks, several of these transient settlers, none of whom appear to have made much improvement in the way of tilling the soil or clearing the woodland. The remains of several small cabins are the only vestiges left of these squatters, who packed up their effects and moved on farther west as the country became more thickly populated. The first permanent settlers of the township were two brothers, James and David Brown, who came to Illinois in the year 1831, and located on East Fork Creek, in Section 17. Their two places lay on opposite sides of the stream. David settled on the west side, on the farm now owned by a Mr. Thumb, of Irving, and James located the farm on which a Mr. Blipsen now resides. For two or three years, these two families were the only settlers in the township; north and east of them was an unsettled prairie of many miles in extent, while south and southwest were no houses for the distance of four or five miles. About the year 1833, Martin Harkey came into the township, and located a farm in the southwest quarter of Section 17. He came here from Iredell County, N. C., and settled in Hillsboro when it was but a mere hamlet. From Hillsboro he moved to the place in Witt already named, where he resided until the year 1857. Another early settler on Section 17 was Christopher Armantrout. He appeared a short time after the Browns, and settled close to their places, on an eighty acres of school land, which he purchased. He afterward purchased other tracts of land, which are now the property of his descendants. When Armantrout first arrived, his family lived for some time in a little hut built on the piece of land we have already described. In 1837, he bought the farm on which Martin Harkey settled, and erected thereon a more comfortable and permanent residence, which is still standing. Armantrout died in the year 1856, after a long and useful life. By his industry and frugality he became the possessor of a great deal of very fine land, which is still in possession of his widow and family. Two sons are now living in the township—George W. and John L., both of whom are in affluent circumstances, and prominent members of the Prairie View Methodist Church. In the spring of 1839, Joshua Seckler came to the township, and settled in Section 9, on the farm now owned by Christian Balsley. He was a young man of energy, and soon had his new place fitted up with a neat cabin, into which he introduced a helpmate one year later. His brother, M. W. Seckler, followed him to the new country about the year 1840, and settled on the same section, where he resided for a number of years. A daughter of the latter, Mrs. Carriker, still lives on the old place. They were both Carolinians, and men of influence in the community where they resided. In the early part of the year 1841, Williams Lights, from Virginia, arrived in Witt built a rude dwelling, and began making improvements. Lights located on Section 8, where he resided about one year, after which he sold the place to Alfred Borer, and moved to Iowa. By this time, the township was quite well populated, especially along the creek, and improvements were pushed rapidly forward. The rich, fertile soil allured many from the more thickly settled portions of the southern part of the county, and the prairies were soon dotted with dwellings. Lands at that time were remarkably cheap, and many men in moderate circumstances availed themselves of the opportunity, and purchased good tracts of land which in after years became very valuable. It is a noted fact in this, as in many other townships of the county, that the first settlers invariably selected the lands among the hills, or lying adjacent to the streams, for their homes, thus leaving the richer and more valuable prairie to be taken up by the more fortunate settler, who came in later years. These prairies were looked upon with much misgiving by the pioneers from the mountains of Carolina and Virginia and were avoided for the more broken and less valuable land which more nearly resembled their old homes. The early settlers of Witt found it somewhat difficult to travel from one place to another for the lack of good roads. Everybody had his own thoroughfare, and for some years the township was considerably cut up by these random roadways, but, in the course of several years, they were straightened somewhat and properly established. The first thoroughfare laid out through what is now Witt was the old Shelbyville and Hillsboro road, which connected those two places. This was in the early days a route extensively traveled, and was the only highway of any importance between the two cities. The original course has been changed considerably, and it now passes through the township in a southwesterly direction, and is nearer straight than formerly. The second road through the township was laid out about the year 1838 and was known as the Nokomis road. This road enters the township between Sections 3 and 4, and crosses it in a southerly direction, and intersects the Shelbyville road in Section 16. Other roads were planned and laid out to suit various neighborhoods, and after being traveled several years, were finally established and improved. The roads of Witt will compare very favorably with the highways of any other township in the county.

The first school in Witt was taught in the southwest part, near East Fork Creek, in a little log house that had been built by a squatter, and was probably the first building erected in the township. The house was about seventeen feet square, and the first teacher was a man by the name of Gay. The first term was taught in 1836, and, after that date, there were several schools taught in the same place.

There were several schools started shortly afterward at various places in the township, some of which were taught in private dwellings that could accommodate the greatest number of pupils. John Wheat was among the early teachers. He taught the second school in the township in a little cabin about the size of the one already mentioned, which stood on the west bank of East Fork Creek, in the southwest corner. The second school in this place was taught by Benjamin Norman about the year 1839. All of these early schools were supported by subscription, and, at stated times, the teachers were accustomed to make their regular tours through the neighborhoods for the purpose of collecting their bills for tuition. The first frame schoolhouse was probably the one known as the Prairie Valley Schoolhouse, which was built in the year 1849, and is still standing.

Here the first public school in the township was taught the same year in which the building was completed. The next frame building was erected the following year, and goes by the name of Maxey's Schoolhouse. Since 1850, there have been several good houses built, all of which are well furnished and in good repair.

There are now seven school buildings in the township, and the schools are maintained during seven months of the year.

The first ministers to preach the Gospel in Witt were circuit-riders of the Methodist Church, who preached in the township adjoining on the west. Several meetings were held at different places before any permanent organization was effected. The first society was organized at or near the place where James Brown settled on East Fork Creek, by Rev. Aldridge, who preached for the little congregation for several years.

Their meetings were held in a neighboring schoolhouse until the year 1855, when a house of worship was erected. This house became famous throughout the country for its great revivals.

The organization was moved farther south several years afterward, and the place of meeting again changed to a schoolhouse in the neighborhood. The old building was torn away some time since, and a reorganization of the society effected. Among those who assumed the responsibility of membership at the reorganization were the following: Christian Balsley and wife, George Hightower and wife, Alfred Borer and wife, Mrs. Ellegood, James Hall, J. W. Smith, Mrs. Elizabeth Armantrout, Sarah Armantrout and J. F. Armantrout. The schoolhouse was used as a place of worship until the year 1870, when the present church edifice was erected. This is a neat frame structure, and cost the sum of $900. It was dedicated in 1871, by Rev. W. S. Hooper, of Hillsboro. Rev. George Miller was the first pastor, and to his efforts is the church largely due for its reorganization. Rev. S. H. Whitlock succeeded Miller, and preached from 1871 to 1873. J. E. Lindlay had charge of the church from 1873 until the time of his death in 1875. The unexpired year was completed by Rev. E. E. Cowperthwaite. J. W. West ministered to the congregation from 1875 to 1876; F. M. Dillman from 1876 to 1879; L. T. Janes, son of Bishop Janes, from 1879 to 1880. The present pastor, J. W. Crane, has been with the church since 1880. The membership will number about forty. A good Sunday school is in progress under the superintendency of George W. Hightower. A society known as the Protestant Methodist was organized in the eastern part of the township in the year 1872. They have a good frame building, but the church is not in a very flourishing condition. At present they have no regular services and no pastor. The Sandy Bend Union Church building was built in the year 1880, by the Christian Union and Methodist organizations, which hold services in the house alternately. This Methodist church is one of the points on the Irving Circuit, and was organized a number of years ago, though at what date we were unable to learn. Nothing definite concerning these two organizations was ascertained, though it can be said that they are in a flourishing condition, and are doing good work for the Master.

The next church which claims our attention is the Witt Methodist Episcopal Church. The circumstances which led to the organization of this society are worthy of mention in these pages. William L. Updike and wife moved into the village of Witt in the year 1869. At that time, there was no organization in the place, nor nearer than five miles. The first Sunday after moving to the place, Mrs. Updike took a ride through the country, and seeing quite a number of people at work in the fields as usual, conceived the idea of organizing a Sunday school. Word was circulated throughout the neighborhood to that effect and the following Sunday saw eight children and a few grown persons at her house. These she organized into a school, and an hour was spent in religious exercises. The next Sunday, the school had increased to eighteen. It continued to grow in numbers each week, until her house would not contain the crowds.

Encouraged by the success of her Sunday school venture, she determined to have a church organized, and accordingly went to work to that end. Rev. John R. Chapman was invited to preach in her house, a room of which was fitted up for that purpose. He accepted the invitation, and a two weeks' meeting was held, which resulted in several conversions. After this meeting, Updike and family moved into another house and fitted up their old residence for a place of worship. Another protracted meeting was held the same winter for about six weeks, during which about thirty persons professed conversion, and the church was accordingly organized. Prominent among the first members were the following: A. Duncan and wife, William Updike and wife, Samuel Williams and wife, J. R. Chapman and wife, John Deer and wife A. F. Duncan and wife, Samuel H. Wiley and wife, George McClure, Theresa Chapman, Andrew Chapman, Mrs. George McClure, John Lohr and wife, William Lohr and many others.

The congregation continued to meet in the residence of Updike until the spring, when the place of worship was changed to the warehouse of William Woods. Their church building was erected in the year 1876. Its dimensions are 32x40 feet, seating capacity about two hundred and seventy-five. The first regular pastor of the church was Rev. J. B. Rhodes, who preached one year. Hazen preached one year; Stubblefield, two years. George Campton preached a short time; E. Randall, one year. The following pastors have had charge of the church at different periods: J. W. Lapham, — Brooks, — Cunningham, — Hamill, — Muhler, and C. R. Howard, present pastor. The church has declined considerably in numbers during the last four years. The exact membership was not ascertained.

The Witt Cumberland Presbyterian Church was organized in 1873, by William McDavid, with a membership of about thirty The following were some of the original members: J. Lohr and wife, Mary Lohr, W. Updike, Eugene Updike, William Lohr and wife, Christian Marks and wife, Maggie Marks, James B. Marks and wife, Alice Marks. The public services were conducted in a vacant dwelling house, which stands in the rear of Wubker's store. This building served the congregation until the year 1875, at which time the beautiful edifice in which the congregation now worships was erected. This is a frame building, dimensions 30x38 feet, and cost about $1,300. Rev. T. W. McDavid preached for the church two years. He was succeeded by W. C. McDavid, who ministered to the congregation for four years, and was in turn followed by Rev. William Turner, who preached but a short time. — McHenry preached for one year, and was succeeded by Rev. — Baker, present pastor. Officers of the church—William P. Strain, Adam Bolt, C. Marks—Elders; James Barton, N. Bentz—Deacons; John Schooping, Superintendent of Sunday school.

The first mill in the township was a small affair in the southwest corner, on the farm of David Gregory. The machinery was run by horse-power and ground nothing but corn during certain days of the week. Gregory afterward built a carding machine on his place, which was also run by horse-power. A saw was attached, and in addition to carding wool, he managed to saw some lumber. This machinery was in operation but a short time. This was the only mill, with the exception of the one at Witt, ever erected in the township. The village of Witt is situated in the northwest corner of the township, on the Indianapolis & St. Louis Railroad, and dates its growth from the year 1869, at which time the first building was erected by William Woods. This was a storehouse and was stocked with a general assortment of goods by Keys & Bartlett. They conducted a business here for one year, at the end of which time they became financially embarrassed and were compelled to dispose of their stock. Another store was started the following year by Lee Hall, who had charge of the railroad office also, which was established the same year.

Hall had charge of this store two years. The next store in the place was started by Antonio Leon, who run it for a short time and then traded it to Christian Marks for a farm. Marks sold out to Lewy & Leon in the year 1876, who did a good business for ten months. Henry Wubker purchased their stock of goods in the year 1878, and has been in business here ever since. In addition to his stock of general merchandise, he has also a good drug store and deals extensively in agricultural implements. His combined stock will probably represent a value of $7,000, and his business is one of the best in the county.

The Witt post office was established in the year 1869, with a man by name of Keys as Postmaster. The office at present is kept by James S. Vermillion. The first physician to locate in Witt was Doctor Melrath, who came to the place in 1870. D. Luther started the first blacksmith shop in the town, which he worked two years.

N. Bentz erected a large steam elevator and mill in the year 1876. This elevator is said to be one of the best on the Indianapolis & St. Louis Railroad between Indianapolis and St. Louis. The mill has two runs of stone and a capacity of about fifteen barrels of flour per day. The population of the village will not exceed seventy-five, but the citizens are all wide awake and energetic, and the town promises to become a place of considerable importance in the near future.

CHAPTER XXVI.*

HARVEL TOWNSHIP—POSITION AND BOUNDARIES—TOPOGRAPHY—PHYSICAL FEATURES—PRODUCTIONS—EARLY SETTLEMENTS—SCHOOLS—VILLAGE OF HARVEL—ITS EARLY HISTORY—INDUSTRIES, ETC.—VILLAGE CHURCHES—SECRET SOCIETIES.

"We cross the prairies, as of old
The pilgrims crossed the sea,
To make the West, as they the East
The homestead of the free."

HARVEL TOWNSHIP is situated in the northeastern part of Montgomery County, and has the following boundaries: Bois D'Arc Township on the north, Raymond on the south, Christian County on the east, and Pitman Township on the west. It originally included the territory of Pitman, from which it was separated in the year 1878, upon petition of the citizens living in the eastern part of the township. The surface is generally speaking, level in appearance, especially in the northern half, where, in certain localities, the ground is low, flat and marshy, rendering agriculture exceedingly difficult. Many of these low, wet places have been drained by a successful system of tiling, and much fertile soil has been reclaimed, from which abundant and well-paying crops are produced. In the southern portion of the township, the land is more rolling, although there are no undulations sufficiently high to be termed hills. Prior to its settlement by the whites, and before there were any roads, travelers had no difficulty in crossing the territory of this township in any direction as there were no streams, ravines, hills, woods or any natural obstacles to impede their progress.

The soil in all parts of Harvel is the fine, black, rich loam, so common in the Western prairie States, and which has given to this part of the country its peculiar advantages as an agricultural district. In many places, it is mixed with sand, drift and rests upon a stratum of clay, thus making artificial drainage comparatively easy where sufficient outlets can be obtained. There is but one stream of any considerable importance within the limits of Harvel, the West Fork of Shoal Creek, into which a number of small streams and rivulets empty. This creek has its source in the western part of Pitman Township, and flows in a southeasterly direction through the southern part of Harvel crossing the township line at a point in Section 31, about one mile and a half from the western boundary.

This division of the county is almost entirely bare of native timber, there being but few scattering trees skirting the banks of the creek already named, while in the northern part of the township at the time of its settlement there was but one large tree standing alone on the wide prairie.

This tree still stands, and is known as the lone elm. It can be seen for several miles, and in former years was an object of almost veneration to the red men, who held their councils, concocted their hunting schemes, planned their forays against their enemies, and made their treaties while seated under its wide-spreading branches.

Artificial timber-growing is everywhere encouraged, and several groves of considerable magnitude are to be seen at various places in the township. The principal occupation of the people is agriculture, and as a farming country this section ranks among the best in the

* By [illegible]

county. The prairies, clothed only by natural processes, presents its own testimony to the richness of the soil, which, when properly cultivated, returns a rich yield of grain of all kinds. Corn has been one of the principal crops in this township ever since its first settlement, and it matures well and yields abundantly almost every season. The average yield of wheat for the last five years exclusive of 1881, which was an unusually dry season, was about fifteen bushels per acre. The oats grown here are generally heavy, and contain an unusual proprotion of nutritious constituents. Rye yields a good average; barley, timothy, clover, flax, grow here abundantly, while the wild prairie grasses are famous for the nourishment they contain. Garden vegetables, root crops of all kinds, and the different fruits are produced in great variety. The richness and abundance of the native grasses naturally attracted the attention of cattle-growers at an early day, and stock-raising is now an important industry of this part of the county. It was found that pasturage frequently continued fair until nearly winter time, and in the spring grass made its appearance very early, and grew so rapidly that the feeding season was comparatively of short duration. This fact has led several parties to engage in stock-raising, and the business has already assumed considerable magnitude, involving in the aggregate a good proportion of capital. Harvel was one of the most recently settled townships of Montgomery County although its lands were surveyed and sold many years before any permanent improvements were made. The early settlers were nearly all Germans and French, fresh from their native lands, who came to this country with a goodly stock of that energy and perseverance, so necessary to the success of the pioneer in a new and uninhabited country. According to the most reliable information within the writer's reach Herman Poggenpahl led the van of civilization in the township of Harvel. He came to Illinois from Germany in the year 1854, and located on the northeast quarter of Section 30, near the central part of the township, where he still resides. Interested in all movements calculated to develop the township's resources he is justly looked upon as one of its leading and influential citizens. C. Courcier, an early settler, made his appearance in the latter part of the year 1851, and purchased land near where Poggenpahl settled, in Section 20. Courcier came from France and was a man of more than ordinary intellectual culture and refinement. After residing on his place until the year 1866, he sold the land to Joseph Vincent and with his family went to Texas, where he has since accumulated a vast property, and is now a very wealthy man. The farm is at present owned and occupied by Adolphus Aull. Nicholas Hankinson was among the first settlers in the township having made his appearance a short time after the arrivial of Poggenpahl and Courcier, in the year 1854. The land on which he made his first improvements lies near the central part of the township, directly north of the Poggenpahl place in section 29. It was sold to William Bail several years ago, who at present occupies it. Several decendants of Hankinson still live in this part of the county all of whom have been identified with the history and growth of Harvel. The Jordan family were among the prominent settlers in Western Harvel and Pitman Townships, where they came early in 1855. William P. Jordan purchased the southwest quarter of Section 7, and the southwest quarter of Section 8 on the latter of which he at present lives. A. C. Jordan located in the northwest corner of the township, on Section 6, while C. H. Jordan purchased land lying adjacent to the western boundary line in Section 19.

A Frenchman, by name of Jean Baptiste Millett came to the township in an early day, purchased land and made improvements in the southwestern part about two miles north of the village of Harvel, in Section 28. The date of Millett's arrival was the spring of 1855. The place on which he settled is at present occupied by the farm of William Bockenwitz. In connection with the township's early history can be mentioned the name of John Munsterman, a stanch old German, who located near the northern boundary, on farm now owned by Conrad Weller, in the summer of 1855. He was a person in whom were combined many of these elements necessary to the successful career and all movements calculated to develop the township's material interest received his hearty and willing support.

Several representatives of this family are living in the township and various places throughout the county. A list of Harvel's early pioneers would be incomplete without the name of B. Tulpin, a Frenchman, who passed over nearly every acre of its territory about the time the first settlements were made. He is now a leading business man in the village of Harvel, where he is operating a store with a stock representing a capital of several thousand dollars. Since the year 1860, the population has steadily increased until now the township is thickly settled with a class of industrious, thrifty and intelligent people, and it can be said without the slightest tinge of prejudice in favor of Harvel, that it is destined at no very distant day to become one of the leading townships in Montgomery County.

The first roads across the prairies of Harvel were mere paths or Indian trails, which after being changed and improved somewhat, in time became regularly established thoroughfares. There are no really good roads in the township, especially during the early spring months, when they become so muddy that they are only accessible to horsemen. Considerable attention is given to grading and otherwise improving the highways, but the absence of gravel and stone for piking purposes will always cause them to remain in poor condition during certain seasons of the year. The Wabash, St. Louis & Pacific R. R. runs through the southeast corner of the township. This road is a great advantage to the citizens of the township, especially to those living in the town of Harvel and vicinity, as it affords ample means of shipping the large amount of corn, wheat and other crops produced in this region. The educational history of Harvel cannot be given with accuracy, although it is evident that schools were established as soon as there were children enough to start them. It is not known who taught the first school, nor could it be ascertained where the first school building was located. Among the first teachers, if not the first was one John Hitchings, who taught in a small frame building known as the Munsterman Schoolhouse, situated near the central part of the township. This school was taught at some period prior to the year 1860. The second school building was erected about the year 1862, and is known as the Lone Elm Schoolhouse. The first term in this house was taught by William Moore, one of the foremost instructors in the county. There are at present three good frame school buildings in the township, outside of the town of Harvel, which supports a graded school, of which we will speak more fully further on. The schools last seven months in the year, and are at present taught by William Moore, Logan Slater and Mr. Ash. The educational interests are looked after by W. D. Matney, Harmon Hendricks and James Braden, Township Board of Trustees.

The live little town of Harvel is situated in the southeast corner of the township, on both sides of the line which separates Montgomery and Christian Counties a small part of the village being in the latter. It was laid off by John Harvel, after whom it was named, in the year 1869, at which time there was not a single house standing in the locality. The survey was made by Col. Monroe, a civil engineer, who had been an officer in the rebel army, from

which he deserted and came to this part of the State, during the last year of the rebellion. The first sale of real estate in the new town was made to William Van Sandt who purchased a lot on which he erected a residence and storeroom in the year 1870. He stocked this room with a general assortment of merchandise, and soon had a large, flourishing trade, which was well sustained for a year and a half, when the store was sold to other parties. A second store building was erected in 1870, by B. Tulpin, whose stock of goods consisted of dry goods, groceries, boots and shoes, clothing and drugs. This store has become a permanent fixture in the town, and the proprietor is deserving of the success which has attended his efforts in building up his large and increasing business. The Harvel Post Office was established in the year 1870, with George Van Sandt as Postmaster. It is at present kept by George Ramsey. Nestor De Moline built the first blacksmith shop in the fall of 1870, which he operated several years. A large elevator was erected by Ira Nelson and D. O. Settlemire in the year 1873. It is now controlled by Settlemire alone, who handles many thousand bushels of wheat and corn annually. Finding that one elevator was not sufficient to receive all the grain handled here for market, Henry Niehaus built a second and larger one about the year 1876. This is one of the most capacious warerooms on the line of the railroad, and is second to none in the amount of business transacted yearly. Niehaus sold the elevator to H. C. Millot in the year 1879, who at present operates it, doing a flourishing business. A flouring-mill was moved from Litchfield to Harvel in the year 1871, by George Slater. The venture proved a success in every particular, as the mill has been extensively patronized by the citizens of this and adjoining townships for many miles around. The mill is built of brick operated by steam, and has a grinding capacity of perhaps forty-five barrels of flour per day.

Henry Bennett was the first physician to practice the healing art in Harvel, having located here and built a small office the same year in which the town was laid out. There are now in the village three disciples of Esculapius—John W. Petrie, F. M. Cox and W D. Matney all of whom are graduates of first-class medical colleges. The legal profession is represented by G. W. Slater and L. L. Slater, attorneys at law and Notaries Public. The village schoolhouse is situated just over the line in Christian County, but as almost the entire town lies in Harvel Township, we think it proper to give the school history in connection with the history of the village.

The first school in the town was taught in Leonard May's hotel, by Miss Effie Kinser, about the year 1871. The present building was erected one year later, and cost the sum of $1,200. It is a brick house containing two commodious and well-furnished schoolrooms, in which schools are sustained during the greater part of the year. The first pedagogue to wield to birch in the building was Samuel Nelson, who taught in the years 1873-74. The present teachers are Misses Ida Clark and ——— Clauson. The first hotel in the place was built by Leonard May, about the year 1870, and kept by him for several years. The large brick hotel, situated opposite the depot, and kept by Henry Hauptman, was built in the year 1878, and cost about $3,000.

The growth of the village during the last five years has been steady, many neat residences having been erected and several new stores established. The business interests of the town presents the following exhibit: William Vasel, dealer in groceries and general merchandise; B. Tulpin, keeps a good line of ready-made clothing, drugs, groceries, etc.; Henry Hauptman, makes groceries a specialty; George Van Sandt, Hendricks Bros., John Rogers and H. Tomlinson, keep general assortments of goods, and all report their business good.

In addition to the stores already enumerated there is a hardware and drug store kept by George Ramsey & Bro.; Philip Mangers, boot and shoe maker; Henry Beesman, harness maker; William Putney and Jefferson Davis, blacksmiths; Oscar Young, wagon-maker; John Rogers, barber; Adams & Nelson, dealers in lumber. In a religious point of view, the village is up with the times, as there are two good churches, both well sustained. The Harvel Methodist Episcopal Church was organized in the winter of 1874, under the labors of Rev. John Cumings. The first public services were held in the district schoolhouse, and it was not until the year 1879 that a house of worship was erected. The original members of this society were eight in number. Their names appear on the church records as follows: George Van Sandt Isabella Van Sandt, Moses Wright Mrs. Wright E. B. Young, Orson Young, Mrs. Orson Young and Mrs. John Hawkins. From this small beginning the church steadily increased, until now the congregation numbers more than forty members and is in excellent condition. Rev. Cumings preached for the church one year, on a salary of $35, but being a man full of zeal in the cause of his Master, did not hesitate on account of small pay, but put forth all the energies at his command toward building up the congregation, and was soon gratified to note a large increase, both in members and influence. He was succeeded by Rev. W. Roberts, who filled the pulpit for one year and was in turn followed by Rev. John Beckhart. The latter had charge of the congregation one year, also. Rev. ——— Slater preached acceptably for the church one year. The present pastor, Elijah Haley, is on his second year's pastorate, and is working in harmony with his congregation, which is considered one of the strong organizations in Raymond Circuit. The present church edifice was built in 1879. It is a neat frame structure and cost the sum of $2,000.

The St. Jacob's Evangelical German Lutheran dates its history from the year 1879, at which time a small organization was effected by Rev. Lewey Sahn of Nokomis, in the Liberty Schoolhouse. At the first meeting ten persons enrolled their names as members. The schoolhouse was used as a place of worship until the spring of 1880, when a very commodious frame building was erected, which is one of the chief ornaments of the village. This house cost the congregation about $3,000, and will comfortably seat 350 persons. The first pastor was Rev. L. Miller, who taught school in the village; served the congregation until the year 1881. The present pastor is Rev. Fred Berger. A denominational school was established in connection with this church in 1880, with an attendance of fifty pupils. It is, at present, under the management of the pastor, and is held in the neat little school building which was erected for the purpose in the fall of 1881. The school is well attended at present, and much good promises to grow out of it.

Harvel Lodge, No. 706, I. O. O. F., was instituted on the 23d day of March, 1882, by J. F. Harvel, P. G. of Lodge 413, as Deputy Grand Master for the occasion. The dispensation was granted by Alonzo Elwood, Grand Master of the State of Illinois. The charter members were John W. Petrie, P. G.; Andrew J. Nash, Taylor Boyce, Reuben Rambo, J. M. Williams, Leonard Nash, Newton Corn, C. C. Young and J. J. Carey. First officers elected: Reuben Rambo, N. G.: A. J. Nash, V. G.; Taylor Boyce, Secy; Newton Corn, Permanent Secy; L. Nash, Treasurer. The membership at present is thirteen, and the organization is reported in good working order.

CHAPTER XXVII.

ROUNTREE TOWNSHIP—SOIL, DRAINAGE AND TIMBER—THE FIRST WHITE MAN—PIONEERS—SCHOOLS—ROADS—THE VARIOUS RELIGIOUS DENOMINATIONS.

FIFTY years ago, the territory now known as Rountree Township was a wide, unsettled expanse, wild in every sense of the word—inhabited by wild men and infested by wild beasts. In this year, it is in every part an exhibitor of the highest civilization. Where the cereals and fine fruits of all varieties now grow in abundance, tall prairie grass and rank weeds covered a soil of wealth unknown. Blooded herd and flock now loll and graze where, less than three score years ago, the timid deer fled from its crouching foe, the panther, only to be pursued by the gaunt hungry wolf.

Fields, now jocund with the merry song of the contented farmer, were once lurid unto the glare of the Indian camp-fires, or made hideous by the discordant yells of the savage war dance.

But the deep prairie soil held abundant food for civilization, and it needed but stout hearts, strong wills and sinewy hands to set it free. They, in time, came, and stout hearts they were both from necessity and from nature. Rountree is one of the northern townships of Montgomery County, and possesses a pleasant diversity of surface and soil. Large tracts of rolling and undulating prairie occupy the southern portion, which form a striking contrast to the level surface of the country farther north. The only water-course of any note in the township is the Middle Fork of Shoal Creek, which flows in a southerly direction through the western part, receiving in its course several smaller streams not designated by any particular names. These streams afford an excellent system of drainage, and to the stock raiser are a necessity that could not be dispensed with. A good growth of timber once covered that part of the territory through which these creeks and rivulets run consisting mostly of walnut, sycamore, maple elm, and the different varieties of oak common to this part of the State. Forty years have served to change the appearance of this wooded district, the greater part of the timber having been cut and sawn into lumber by the early settlers along the creeks. The attention of the pioneer was early called to the necessity of supplying himself with a means of procuring timber for his necessities, and a number of large artificial groves were set out, from which the owners now obtain both lumber and fuel.

The soil of the township is a strong, deep, rich loam, with a slight mixture of sand along the streams, and clay on the more elevated portions. Rountree is noted chiefly for its farming interests, and for that purpose it was sought by the early settlers; and, taken as a whole, its territory presents as fine a tract of farm land as there is to be found in the county. The boundary lines of Rountree are Christian County on the north, Nokomis Township on the east, Irving on the south, and Raymond on the west. The township was named in honor of Judge Rountree, one of the earliest and most prominent citizens of Montgomery County. The name is a fitting tribute to the memory of that most excellent man, who did as much, if not more than any other person toward the development of the county.

From the most authentic sources within the

*By G. N. Berry.

writer's reach, John Nusman was the first white man who fixed his residence within the limits of Rountree. He had been a resident of the county several years prior to moving into the township, having settled in the town of Hillsboro when it consisted of but two or three insignificant cabins. From Hillsboro he moved his family to Rountree in the year 1830, and cleared a small patch of ground lying near Shoal Creek, where he lived for a number of years, the only white man in the county north of Irving Township. At that time, the country was wild, game of all kinds plenty, and the family fared sumptuously on venison, turkey, partridge and honey, which was also found in large quantities in the woods.

Elizabeth Nusman says that when they first came to the country the deer were so plenty that her father would stand in the door of his cabin and shoot two or three of them as they sported about near the house; and as for turkeys, they were almost as numerous then as chickens are now. Near Nusman's residence was a camping place of the Kickapoo Indians, who came into the country once a year for the purpose of hunting. They were not at all troublesome, but on the contrary seemed to take a great deal of interest in the welfare of the family, making them presents of many small trinkets and trading them deer skins and venison for ammunition and bacon. Many were the visits they paid to the family, during which the most profound decorum was observed. Their arms were always left outside the gate, a mark of the greatest respect and when leaving they would evince their satisfaction by a series of bows, grunts and grimaces that would often cause the younger members of the family to laugh outright. Mrs. Nusman manufactured all the wearing apparel for the family with her own hands. This consisted of thick, heavy jeans, linsey, and a coarse cloth made from cotton grown on the place.

Nusman lived on the place he entered until the year 1852, at which time he died. The place is now owned by his son, Henry Nusman, one of the oldest settlers in the township. One daughter, Elizabeth Nusman, lives here also, and it is to her the writer is indebted for many of the facts concerning the early history of Rountree.

In 1833, John Dryer came into this part of the county from Tennessee and settled on the farm now owned by Augustus Carriker, in Section 30. When he first came, he brought his family with him; and as they had no house to move into, they hastily constructed a rude temporary lodge of poles to live in while building their cabin.

The latter edifice was erected in due time, and like all the early houses of that day consisted of parlor, bed-room, dining-room, etc., all combined in one apartment. The floor was of puncheon, as there were no saw-mills, and had there been the pioneers were seldom able, either from want of money or time, or owing to distance and absence of good roads, to procure lumber.

No other settlement was made in what is now Rountree until the year 1840, when William Heffley made his appearance and entered a piece of land in the southern part, which he sold to Wiley Lipe four years later. In 1842, came Wilson Carriker. He settled the farm where Jacob Miller now lives. Two years later, William Tanner and John Ridenour located in the little settlement and figured prominently as early settlers. Tanner purchased a tract of land in the northern part of the township, where he lived until the year 1872. Ridenour pitched his tent a little farther east, on the place where Martin Lingle now lives. The following year, Nicholas Ridenour, a brother of the preceding, came into the township and settled the place where his widow still resides.

These were all men of sterling integrity, and are spoken of by those who knew them as men well calculated to successfully overcome the many privations and trials through which the pioneer is called to pass. Again we glean the following who came prior to the year 1846: George Carriker, Alfred Carriker and Allen Lipe. These have been still followed by a long catalogue of others, the names of whom we were unable to learn. Will only name a few of the more active and prominent ones who still remain to speak for themselves: Wiley Lipe, Henry Nusman and Noah Lipe. Space forbids a further enumeration. The first frame house in the township was built by Allen Lipe, in the year 1842, which is still standing, though not in use as a dwelling-house.

In an attempt to learn the early school history of this township but limited satisfaction has been derived. Evidently the first session of school was held in a log building near the southwest corner, sustained by subscriptions and taught by Wesley King. This house was erected in the year 1847, and was used jointly for school and church purposes. It was at this place that the first religious services of the township were held by itinerant ministers of the Methodist Church. King was a man of good acquirements and splendid tact as a teacher. He taught in various localities, and everywhere left his impress. While teaching in Rountree, he made his home in Irving Township, a distance of at least six miles from the scene of his labors. This distance was traversed every day, and during the period of his first school not an hour was missed from his work nor was he tardy a single minute. According to the best evidence we have at hand, the first structure erected especially for school purposes was situated in the southwest corner of the township, on the farm of Noah Lipe. Lipe took the contract to build and furnish the house for the sum of $75. It was built of hewed logs nicely fitted together, well furnished, and for a number of years was the best schoolhouse in the township. We have not been able to learn the exact year in which this building was erected, though it is thought to have been in 1846 or 1847. Wesley King taught in this house for about six consecutive years.

One of the earliest schools in the township was taught in a little log cabin on the farm of Tillman Hefley, by a Mr. Miller, sometime between the years 1847 and 1850. The first frame schoolhouse was built in the year 1861. It is still standing and is known as the Hazel Hill Schoolhouse. There are at present five good frame school buildings in the township, all of which are good substantial structures, well furnished.

The earliest birth in Rountree of which we have any definite knowledge was Laura Dryer, a daughter of John Dryer, born in the year 1836, just two years after the family settled in the township. The earliest marriage traceable was that of Peter Cress to Catherine Nusman, in the latter part of the year 1836. William Marks, a Justice of the Peace, from the city of Hillsboro, officiated at the ceremony. The first resident of the township to be summoned away by the death angel was Catherine Nusman, wife of John Nusman. Her death occurred in the year 1846, after having lived in the township fourteen years. The early roads of Rountree, like the first roads in most parts of the county, traversed the country in almost every direction, and every man had his own highway. The first road of any importance was the one which runs from Rountree to the village of Irving, although it has not been very extensively traveled of late years.

The Taylorville road was laid out through the township in an early day, and was for many years the most important highway in the northern part of the county. Its course through the township was from northwest to southeast. The most important roads at the present time are the roads running east and west on the boundary between Rountree and Irving Townships and one passing through the central part of the township from north to south. The last named intersects the former in the southern part of Section 33.

Almost all the roads traversing the township are regularly established on the proper section lines, and are in good condition. The first Justice of the Peace was Henry Freedmeyer, who was appointed in the year 1845 and continued in the office about twelve years. Dr. Elias Petril was the first soother of the sick to locate in the township. He came here in 1850, and for several years made his home with the family of Henry Nusman. Seventeen years later, Dr. Marion Osborne became a resident of Rountree and practiced his profession until the year 1880, when he sold out and went to Nebraska. There were no very early mills in this part of the county. The first settlers obtained their flour and breadstuffs from the Cress Mill in Butler Grove Township, and the Fogleman Mill situated south of Hillsboro. A small horse mill was erected by George Carriker on his farm near Shoal Creek in the year 1842, operated about eight years. During that time, he did a very flourishing business, and was extensively patronized by the neighbors for several miles around. Carriker sold this mill to Nelson Lipe in 1850, who removed it to his farm farther east, where it is still standing. The bolting apparatus has been taken out and no flour has been made for a number of years. Meal of a superior quality is still ground by the old machinery, and the mill is at the liberty of any one who wishes to use it. Noah and Allen Lipe bought and operated a couple of portable steam saw-mills as early as the year 1848. They were located in the southwestern part on the creek, and for several years sawed an immense amount of lumber. Messrs. Robertson & Southworth purchased these mills several years since and moved them to Fillmore Township, where they are still in operation.

Religion has flourished in the township ever since its first settlement, as is proven by the many church-going people now residing within its borders. Probably the first minister was the celebrated Peter Cartwright of the Methodist denomination. At the time he came, in 1842, there were no church buildings in the country, so he was obliged to hold public services in private dwelling-houses and groves. A society was organized in the year 1843, mainly through the efforts of Peter Cartwright, and met for worship in a little log cabin situated in Section 30. Revs. Wiley, Wildman, Frost and Trotter were among the early pastors of this church. Unwritten history tells us that this church maintained its organization until the year 1874, when it was abandoned by mutual consent of the members, a portion of them uniting with Montgomery Church in Butler Township, while those who lived farther north cast their lots with the congregation that met for worship at Burk's Chapel. The old church building where the congregation held their meetings for a long number of years has disappeared, and nothing remains to mark the spot where the first church edifice in the township stood. The next religious organization of which we have any definite knowledge, is the Mount Zion Evangelical Lutheran Church. This church dates its history from the year 1868, although there had been religious services held in the neighborhood two or three years previous, in private dwellings and schoolhouses. In the year 1868, a meeting of the few scattered Christians in the vicinity was convened at the Shoal Creek Schoolhouse for the purpose of discussing the propriety of organizing a church. The meeting was presided over by Rev. J. B. Cromer, and a constitution adopted to which were appended the following names: Martin L. Walcher, Julia M. Walcher, George C. Carriker, Arvina Carriker, James W. Huffman, Esther Huffman, Mary J. Carriker, Daniel Carriker, Jr., and Leah Walcher. To this list were added at the next meeting the names of M. F. Pollard, Thomas Sorrels and Amanda J. Sinds. A meeting of several days followed the first services conducted mainly by the Pastor, J. B. Cromer, during which many members were received into fellowship with the church. The congregation used the schoolhouse as a place of worship until the year 1872, at which time the beautiful building in which they now worship was erected. This building is frame, and will seat about three hundred persons. It was dedicated the latter part of the year 1872. Since its organization, the church has been ministered to by the following pastors, viz.: J. B. Livingood —— Shaver, L. C. Groselose, G. W. Hammer, M. L. Walcher and Ephraim Kitch. The first member to leave the church militant for the church triumphant was sister Leah Walcher, who passed over the river May 1, 1869. In point of numbers, the congregation is not as strong as formerly, quite a number having withdrawn and joined the Free Methodists, a society recently organized in the community. Others have died or moved to distant places, yet the remnant left is in a healthy condition, and are doing a good work in the service of the Master. The present membership numbers about thirty-five. The Sunday school is a flourishing one, and is under the efficient management of Winfield Walcher, Superintendent.

Burk's Chapel Methodist Episcopal Church was organized by Rev. John Chapman in the year 1868 at the Shoal Creek Schoolhouse with a membership of ten. The society worshiped in the schoolhouse until the year 1872, when they were allowed the use of the Lutheran Church building. They met in this house at intervals for five years, when they commenced the erection of a new frame house of worship south of the Lutheran Church about two miles. This building was completed in the year 1880, and cost $600. The following list comprises the ministers that have been pastors of the church since its organization: R. B. Rhodes preached two years, James Stubblefield one year; J. W. Lapham, one year; —— Schwartz, one year; E. H. Hammill, one year. C. R. Howard, present pastor, has been with the church since 1880. Like the Lutheran Church, many members of this congregation have been absorbed by the Free Methodists, and the church cannot be spoken of as in good condition.

Of the society of Free Methodists, recently organized, we were unable to learn any particulars, yet we may be safe in saying that it is in a flourishing condition. The growth in numbers has been steady, and among its members are to be found many of the substantial citizens of the community. What its future may be is, of course, hidden from us, but there certainly seems to be a great work for it to do, and we only hope that he who writes a more elaborate history of it hereafter, may tell of many scores of souls which it has prepared for the better life in the Paradise of God.

CHAPTER XXVIII.

BOIS D'ARC TOWNSHIP--BOUNDARIES AND TOPOGRARHY—ITS EARLY SETTLEMENTS—FIRST DEATHS-EARLY ROADS, CHURCHES, SCHOOLS, ETC, ETC.

IN folk lore there is the story told of a man who became tired of the patient cultivation of the soil, and who desired to become rich without the drudgery of labor. The lack of wealth had made life become stale, flat and unprofitable. He dreamed three nights in succession that there was a rich treasure hid somewhere under the earth in his old orchard. Three is the regular number that makes a dream true, and so in an ecstasy of excitement he imparted the good news to his wife, and together they at once began to dig for the hidden gold. Round one tree they dug a mound of earth, and around another until there was not gnarled trunk about whose roots he had not let in the vitalizing air, but the treasure was not found. Of course he became angry over his wasted labors, and a sorry time he had of it when his neighbors passed by and laughed at him for his folly. Springtime, however, came, and the trees were full of blossom. Autumn followed, and they were loaded down with luscious fruit. Years rolled by and the orchard was the source of a rich revenue to the old man, who realized that there was indeed a golden treasure hidden in the soil which only needed proper exertion to bring it to the light. In the fertile region of Central and Southern Illinois, we can see the moral of the foregoing story practically demonstrated in the presence of richly cultivated farms, handsome and costly private residences, commodious barns, numerous flocks of live stock and other evidences of that wealth which has been wrung from the generous bosom of mother earth by the strong arms of the successful husbandmen. Especially is this true of that division of country to which the present chapter is devoted, where broad fertile prairies were looked upon with much suspicion, and carefully shunned by the early pioneers of Montgomery County. Bois D'Arc is one of the largest townships in the county, lying in the extreme northwestern part, and embracing in its area 34,560 acres of land, all of which is well adapted to agricultural purposes. Its boundaries on the northeast and west respectively are the counties of Sangamon, Christian and Macoupin. Its southern boundary is the township of Pitman, with which it was formerly united as a part of the Zanesville Precinct. Bois D'Arc was reduced to its present limits and formed into an independent body principally through the efforts of one of its prominent citizens, Lewis H. Thomas, who gave it the name by which it is at present designated. In physical features and general topography it resembles Pitman Township, which has already been described, with the exception of the entire absence of native timber, the surface being exclusively prairie. At the time of its settlement by the whites, years ago, there were but a few dozen small, scrubby trees to be seen in the entire township, the prairie being then clothed by a rank covering of native grass, which attested the fertile quality of the soil beneath—a soil which to-day is regarded as the richest and most productive to be found anywhere in the entire county. Several small streams flow through different parts of the township, the largest of which is Macoupin Creek, which rises near the southwest

*By G. N. Berry.

corner from whence it takes a southerly course, and receives several smaller streams as tributaries before intersecting the boundary line. Bois D'Arc is pre-eminently an agricultural, and is considered in this respect the banner, township of the county, an honor to which it is justly entitled. Compared in population with other divisions of the county, there are, among its inhabitants, a greater number of comfortably situated owners of the soil they till, than in any other section we have visited; while among its large farms are some which in point of improvements, such as hedging, elegant residences, barns outbuildings etc., will compare favorably with the best improved farms in any other part of the State. Indeed, we will be doing nothing more than justice to Bois D'Arc when we say, as hundreds have already said, and as a gold medal awarded by the State Agricultural Society fully proves, that it has the best tilled farm and most complete and costly farm residence to be found in Illinois.

The first settlement in the territory of this township was made about the year 1825, at the head of Macoupin Creek, near the southern part, by a certain John Henderson. He was followed shortly afterward by a Mr. Hendershot, who built the first house in the township. For a number of years, these two families were the only inhabitants of the broad stretch of prairie lying between what is now Zanesville Township and Sangamon County. They moved away some time prior to the year 1835, and nothing has been heard of them since. In 1835, a man by the name of Woods made his way into the northern part of the county and entered a piece of land at a place known as Macoupin's Point, on the old Springfield & Hillsboro road, where he built a hotel which was a favorite stopping place for travelers passing through this part of the country. A post office was established here also, which for a number of years was kept by Mr. Wood in his hotel. It was discontinued about the year 1855, since which time there has been no post-office in the township.

The place where Wood formerly lived is at present owned and occupied by Lewis Seedentop. In the year 1850, two brothers, Lewis H. and Samuel R. Thomas, passed through this part of the country, and being favorably impressed with the fertile appearance of the prairie, determined to select sites for their future homes, a resolution which they put into effect the latter part of the same year, although they did not move unto their respective claims until the spring of 1852. The farms they located lie in the northern part of the township, bordering on the Sangamon County line in Sections 2 and 3. Here their first house was built from lumber which had been hauled from Greene County for the purpose, and was occupied temporarily during the summer season while their first crops were being tended. To the energy and public spirit of these two men is this section of the county largely indebted for its present prosperity and prominence as an agriculturel district.

Their farms are models in every respect and among the wealthy real estate owners of the county take no second rank. Concerning the improvements made by Lewis H. Thomas (whose portrait appears elsewhere), we copy the following from the "Historical Atlas Map" of Montgomery County, published several years ago. "Mr. Thomas entered 970 acres of land lying in the northern part of the township which was the fourth and by far the most important entry. Here the second land-breaking was done for a hedge row in the spring of 1851. On entering the land Mr. Thomas went to work and hedged the entire tract. This extensive hedging was considered a rash experiment, as the Osage or Bois D'Arc was looked upon with considerable suspicion by the cautious farmer. The result surpassed the expectation of all and others soon followed his example, and soon several farms were inclosed by hedges. Thus the first successful hedging in the county was accomplished in this township. From this fact the name Bois D'Arc, upon the petition of Mr. Thomas, was given this township. On this hedging Mr. Thomas has taken two diplomas, accompanied by two medals. These were the first gold medals ever awarded by the State Agricultural Society. Mr. Thomas has given considerable attention to the growing of artificial groves. The first grove was a ten-acre lot planted in locust timber in the year 1852. Another lot of fifteen acres was put out in the spring of 1854. In eleven years from the first planting the cuttings from fifteen acres furnished enough wood to burn 300,000 bricks. An ornamental grove was put out in 1855 near where the family residence was afterward erected. This grove comprises fifteen acres and includes about every variety of timber indigenous to the United States.

"This beautiful grove drew, in 1858, a gold medal from the society from which the other medals were obtained, given for the best grove of cultivated timber. This medal was one of the first granted in the State for that particular industry." The foregoing extract may be taken as illustrative of the energy of this prominent citizen in all his undertakings. It is to his farm the writer referred in a preceding page as the prize medal farm of the State. (See biography.) A prominent settler who came into the township the same year with the Thomas brothers, was Absalom Clark. He entered the north half of Section 7 and the south half of Section 8 in the northern part of the township, which he improved extensively and still owns.

From 1852 to 1856, aside from those already mentioned, there settled in the northern, central and western parts of Bois D'Arc, Pryor Witt, John Jones, William Smith, Joseph Smith, Anthony Almond, John Ward, Frank Dunkley, Mark Risley Hiram Young, William Evarts and father, all of whom entered and improved lands in their respective localities. Joseph Evarts settted in the southeastern part in the year 1855. George Rice entered land in the western part of the township, which he afterward improved about the same time.

The first permanent settlement made in East Bois D'Arc was by an Irishman by name of McConnell, about the year 1850. The place he entered and improved lies in Section 7, and had been occupied temporarily by a German by name of Sedgwick a few years previous. Sanford Clow Peter Christopher and his brother Joseph were among the first actual settlers of east Bois D'Arc, having settled in Section 4 in the spring of 1854. During the next five years, Albert Clayton, John Price and James Woodward made their appearance and settled in different places throughout the township. A little later came William Garrison, Henry Weston, Henry Hathaway, William King and Michael Samison, all of whom located farms in east Bois D'Arc. Two brothers, George and Cornelius Lyman, settled in the southeastern part of the township about the same time that the Christopher family located in the northern part.

The names enumerated comprised the earliest settlers of Bois D'Arc, as far as we have been able to learn. Other names there no doubt were that properly belong to the foregoing list, but the writer, in his canvas for information, did not learn them. The first person of this township to be summoned away by death was Mrs. Hendershot, wife of the second settler, whose death occurred about the year 1828. The second event of the kind transpired in east Bois D'Arc September 25, 1856, when John Christopher, son of Peter and Elizabeth Christopher, died. The first road leading through Bois D'Arc was the old Springfield & Hillsboro highway, which passed through the township from northeast to southwest, and was, during the early history of the county, an important thoroughfare.

The State road, which passes through the township in a southerly direction, was surveyed by L. H. Thomas, and through the intercession of Mr. Woodson, a member of the State Legislature, was properly established in the year 1854. The old road had been traveled considerably by parties living north of Bois D'Arc, directly through the farm of Mr. Thomas, causing him no little annoyance, who, in order to induce them to take the new route, plowed a furrow for a considerable distance on the line, along which he traveled back and forth for several miles with a loaded wagon, thus making the road visible.

Another early road was laid out parallel to the Springfield road by way of Pawnee, in Sangamon County. The roads of Bois D'Arc at present are all properly established, intersect each other at right angles, and are in very fair condition. The first marriage in the township was that of Andrew Armstrong to Miss Martha J. Evarts, the date of which was not ascertained. The second marriage was solemnized in the year 1862, at the residence of Joseph Christopher in east Bois D'Arc, the contracting parties being John Murray and Mary Williamson; the ceremony was performed by Rev. John Nicodemus.

Hiram J. Young was the first Justice of the Peace appointed in the year 1862. Jasper Witt was appointed Constable at the same time, an office which he filled acceptably for several consecutive terms.

Jackson Boyles built the first blacksmith shop, near the central part of the township, which is still in use.

Religious services were held in Bois D'Arc during the early days of its history by itinerant ministers of the Methodist Church, and an organization effected in the year 1862 which does not appear to be in existence at the present time. A church was organized in east Bois D'Arc by Rev. Samuel Lily, about the year 1863, at the Prairie Dell Schoolhouse. A church edifice was afterward erected, and a flourishing society is still maintained. A Baptist Church was organized at the Thomas Schoolhouse in the year 1865, by Rev. T. B. Jones. The original membership of this church was nine, which has since increased until now there are sixty names on the records. Their house of worship is situated in Section 3, west Bois D'Arc, and is in many respects the finest and most completely finished country church building in the county. It is tastefully furnished throughout, and represents a capital of about $3,500. The present pastor is Rev. John Barbee.

The Catholics have a strong church in the southern part of the township, with a membership of perhaps 150. Their building is a commodious frame structure, capable of seating 400 persons comfortably, and was erected at a cost of $4,000. In matters of education, the citizens of Bois D'Arc early took an interest, and her schools to-day are among the foremost in the county. The first school building in west Bois D'Arc was built in Section 3; is still standing, and known as the Thomas Schoolhouse: the name of the first teacher at this place was not learned. The second schoolhouse was a small log structure, situated in Section 4, east Bois D'Arc, and went by the name of Prairie Dell. The first school in this building was taught by Miss Sallie Goodrich. It was afterward occupied by the following teachers: Samuel Laird, Sarah Gale, Mary Harlan and Charles Walters. The old house, after being used for school purposes a number of years, was finally sold to private parties, and replaced by a more commodious frame building, erected near by at a place called White Oak. The first teacher to occupy the new building was Miss Mary Harlan, a lady who appears to have been prominently connected with the early schools of Bois D'Arc. The present school buildings of the township are all frame, well furnished, and in point of architectural finish, among the best in the county, as the majority of them have been erected quite recently. In several of these district schools are taught, additional to the common course of study prescribed, some of the higher branches of education usually belonging to the high school or academy, and nobody but first-class instructors are employed. Next to the agricultural interest of Bois D'Arc, the rearing of stock is the most important industry in this section of the country, a business in which a number of parties have engaged quite extensively. The richness of her pastures, the presence of plenty of stock water, and the peculiar suitability of her native grasses for beef-making, won for this township an enviable reputation, and her stock-farms are the largest in the county. The first introduction of improved cattle into this part of the county is due to the enterprise of L. H. and S. R. Thomas, who have upon their extensive farms a number of Short-Horns and other superior breeds, brought here at great expense. Among others who made stock-raising a specialty is a man by name of Willis, living in the northern part of the township, who, in addition to his large herds of cattle, pays considerable attention to other live stock, especially sheep, of which he is one of the most extensive breeders in the county.

CHAPTER XXIX.*

GRISHAM TOWNSHIP—LOCATION—SOIL AND DRAINAGE—EARLY SETTLERS—RELIGIOUS—SECRET SOCIETIES, ETC.

GRISHAM TOWNSHIP, to which this chapter is devoted, is situated in the extreme southern part of Montgomery County, with the following boundaries: On the north by Hillsboro Township, on the east by the southern part of East Fork, on the south by Bond County and on the west by the northern part of Walshville Township. The greater part of the area of this division is rough and somewhat broken, though in the north and east there is considerable fine rolling prairie land. The western part, though far from being level, is not so broken and irregular as that portion lying in the central part of the township. The southern part and all the land lying adjacent to the numerous creeks by which the township is traversed, is cut, divided and subdivided into innumerable bluffs and hills of all shapes, sizes and altitudes. Many deep ravines wind around these hills and knolls toward the several streams which flow among them. On account of the broken surface of the central and southern parts of the township, the land was not considered of very great value by the early settlers, who passed it for the more desirable prairie lands of the northern and eastern parts. A number of people have located among these hills during the last five years, and much of the broken land has been cleared and put in cultivation. Fully one-half of the surface was originally timber land, much of which has been cut off and improved. There are large tracts of territory still covered with forests in the southern part, which have never been improved. Lying adjacent to Shoal Creek, in the western part, are several extensive scopes of woodland, as there are, also, skirting Bear Creek in the eastern half of the township. The timber is composed principally of the following varieties: Black oak, post oak, hickory, ash, walnut and elm. The oak is by far the most numerous and valuable. The greater part of the walnut has been cut away many years ago. Some of the recent settlers in the central part of the township derive the greater amount of their incomes from the sale of cord wood, which they cut and haul to Hillsboro, where they always find a ready market and good prices. The soil of the township is considerably diversified. The eastern and northern portions are inclined toward a rich black loam, in some parts more fertile than in others. This land is very easily tilled and produces abundant crops of wheat, corn and oats. It is also well adapted to fruit growing, and many fine varieties of apples and peaches are raised by the farmers in this section.

The soil along the creeks, though flat and wet, is very rich with decaying vegetable matter and gives promise of great fertility when the sun's rays can be unchecked by the removal of the dense foliage by which it is shaded. The high portions of the central part are not so well adapted to agriculture, as the soil is composed too largely of clay and gravel to be very fertile.

The most important water-course is Shoal

*By G. N. Berry.

Creek, which enters the township from the north about two miles east of the western boundary line, and passes in a zigzag course to within half a mile of the Bond County line, thence flows east, leaving the township about three miles east of the southwest corner. The valley through which this stream flows varies in width from a few rods to a mile or more the greater part of which is in cultivation. It was formerly covered with a thick growth of elms and underbrush. This land, when the season is not too wet, is very valuable and produces abundantly, but when the season is rainy, the crops are almost always ruined by the overflowing of the creek.

The hills skirting the lowlands are in some places very high and rugged, and can only be used for grazing. Numerous small streams enter Shoal Creek, among which are Parish Branch, Lick Branch and Lake Fork. The last is the largest tributary. It flows in a northeasterly direction and empties into Shoal Creek at a point about one mile north of the county line. Bear Creek is another stream of considerable size, which runs through the township in an irregular channel from northeast to southwest. It receives a number of small tributaries, also, the principal of which is Town Fork. This creek empties into the former about two miles northwest of the village of Donnellson. The lands lying adjacent to these creeks is in many respects similar to that through which Shoal Creek runs, being high and broken, and, in many places, too rough for cultivation. In an early day, there were several mills built along these streams from which they received the power that operated them. Among the very first settlements in Grisham Township made by white men was that by Spartan Grisham, in the year 1819. He settled on a tract of land in the southern part and improved a farm which is now owned by a Mr. Atterbury. He came to Illinois from Tennessee and was a man of character and influence. Just how long he remained in the township is not known, nor could the date of his death be ascertained. Several descendants of Mr. Grisham still live in the county, all of whom are upright and intelligent citizens. When a name was wanted for the township, it was suggested that Grisham was the most appropriate, not because he was the first settler, but from the fact that he did as much, if not more, than any other man toward its development. James Fogleman came to the township some time during the latter part of the same year in which Grisham came, and settled near the central part on Shoal Creek, where he built the first mill that was ever erected in the county. Of this mill we will speak more fully further on in these pages. He was also a Tennessean by birth, and brought with him to this county a stock of vitality and independence which he had acquired amid the genial airs of his mountain home. Two sons of this sturdy old pioneer are still living in the county—one in Walshville Township and one in Litchfield. They are both prominent citizens and are in affluent circumstances. The next settler of whom we have any definite record was Jesse Johnson, who located the farm now owned by Thomas Atterbury, in the southern part of the township, in the year 1820. He came to Illinois from Tennessee, in company with William McDavid, who went farther east and settled in East Fork Township at a place which has since been known as McDavid's Point. Uncle Jesse, as he was called, was a true type of the pioneer, and loved nothing better than the excitement incident to the life of an early settler in a new country. He lived on the place where he settled until the year 1840, when, finding the houses were becoming too numerous to suit his pioneer tastes, he sold his farm to a

Mr. Trabul, turned his face toward the West and took his departure for the then almost unknown State of Iowa He lived in Iowa for a number of years, till, becoming restive under the increasing civilization of that State, he again started West, determined not to stop this time till he had reached the Pacific coast which he did in 1850. He died in Oregon, and was buried among the mountains near the spot which he called his home. He is remembered by the early settlers of Grisham as a very eccentric and adventurous character, whose greatest pleasure was in hunting or in riding in fierce gallops over the prairie. It was about this time that Nathan Irving came into the wilderness of Grisham and built his little cabin upon a piece of land near the southern boundary, now known as the Lewey farm. The residence of Lewey stands near the site of the orignial cabin, and thus keeps in memory the location of one of the first houses built by the hands of the white man in Grisham. Irving came from North Carolina, but had lived in a number of States before he settled in Illinois. He left this State and went to Missouri a number of years ago, since which nothing has been heard of him. In the year 1820, James Street, a Baptist preacher, settled on Shoal Creek near the Fogleman Mill, where he built a cabin and lived for a number of years. He had lived in the county a year before he came to this township, but this was his first permanent residence. He preached the first sermon that was ever preached in the county in a little log house, situated just south of the city of Hillsboro, in the year 1819. He was a most excellent man, of unblemished character, and was considered quite a noted preacher in his day. 'Tis true that his oratory was not what would now be termed classical, nor were his scholastic acquirements of that profound type which is considered so essential to the success of the modern divine; yet he was endowed with a strong practical mind, which was well stored with plain, unvarnished facts. He preached the Gospel of Christ with but few of the adornments of rhetoric, and was untiring in his efforts and zeal to establish the cause of his Master in the sparsely settled localities of the new country.

Several churches were established through his instrumentality, both in Grisham and East Fork Townships, for which he preached a number of years. Goldsmith's beautiful lines descriptive of the village preacher can be appropriately applied to this pioneer evangelist of the West:

"At church, with meek and unaffected grace,
His looks adorn the venerable place,
Truth from his lips prevailed with double sway,
And fools who came to scoff remained to pray

The date of this good man's death could not be learned, but it is supposed that he died about twelve or thirteen years ago.

The same year that saw Street settle in Grisham witnessed the coming of William Griffith, who located on a piece of land near the old Baptist burying-ground, in the central part of the township. He was from the South as were many of the early settlers of Montgomery County, and was one who probably did as much in a humble and unpretentious way to advance the township's material interests as any man within its borders. Two sons are living in the county—one in Hillsboro Township and one in the city of Hillsboro. Another early settler in Grisham was Thomas Edwards, who came to Illinois from Kentucky in the year 1826, and improved a farm on Bear Creek Prairie, in the northeastern part of the township. The farm is now owned by his son, C. H. Edwards, and has been in the family ever since it was settled.

In company with Edwards came John Elder, who bought the piece of land now owned by John Price, lying about one-half mile west of Edwards' Chapel M. E. Church. Robert McCullough settled on the piece of land adjoining the farm of Elder the following year. These three men died long since, but the influence of their examples will always live, as they were men noted for piety and high Christian character. They were untiring in their efforts to advance every interest essential to the stability and improvement of the society of their section of the community.

Another name deserving of mention in connection with the early history of this township is that of Rev. C. C. Aydelott, a Methodist preacher, who came here from East Fork, where he settled in the year 1827. He located in Grisham in 1828, on the farm now owned by his son, G. R. Aydelott. He was a soldier in the Black Hawk war and met with many stirring adventures during that struggle with the Indians. Mr. Aydelott was a devoted Christian, and assisted in the organization of the first Methodist Church in the township. He died in the year 1865, at the age of sixty years. His wife is still living, having reached the advanced age of seventy-five years. To her the writer is indebted for many of the facts connected with the early settlement of the township.

William Young, a brother-in-law of the preceding, was also an early settler of Grisham. He came to the township in the year 1828, and located on the farm now owned by Henry Hickman, on Section 2. This place was his home for two years, when he sold the farm to a brother, James Young, moved to the southern part of the township and bought the tract of land on which Mr. Rhodes now resides. Here he lived till the year 1880, at which time he disposed of the place and moved to Hillsboro, where he has since resided. He is the only one of the original settlers of Grisham now living.

He relates the following incident: "James Wilson, a great practical joker, and William Crisp, a neighbor from Bond County, were at one time out hunting among the hills lying along Shoal Creek, when night overtook them in the woods and they decided to camp till morning. Wilson told Crisp that he would go farther up the creek to see if he could find a more suitable place where to pass the night. When he got out of Crisp's sight, he rode his horse across the stream and up and down the muddy banks several times till the water was considerably stirred up. Then riding hastily back to where he left Crisp, he told him in a very excited manner that a band of hostile savages had just crossed the creek and were bent on mischief. Crisp, who was at heart a great coward, would not credit the story until he saw the tracks and muddy water, when he betook himself to the woods and passed the long dreary night in an agony of fear. Wilson found him the next morning and undeceived him, but was never forgiven for the cruel and heartless joke." Many other prominent settlers of this township are entitled to a mention in these pages, among whom are William Paisley, Robert Paisley, Spartan Jordan, Jacob Holbrook, William Rogers, but the limits of this chapter forbid a more extended notice.

To travel over a country with any degree of comfort or satisfaction, roads are necessary. The first roads were laid out without any regard to section lines, each person taking the shortest route to reach the place where he was going. As a result of this indiscriminate way of traveling, the township is traversed by many zigzag and crooked roadways. One of the first roads established was the old Sangamon road, which ran through the township in

a northwesterly direction and intersected the southern boundary at a point about one half mile west of the village of Donnellson. Its course has since been changed and it is no longer a thoroughfare of any importance. The Greenville & Hillsboro road was another of the early roads, not only of this township, but one of the first in the county. It connects the cities of Greenville and Hillsboro, and passes through the richest and best settled part of Grisham. Part of the way it forms the boundary between Grisham and East Fork Townships. This is still an important roadway, and is very extensively traveled. A road was laid out in an early day through Bear Creek Prairie, in the northern part of the township, and is still traveled, although the original course has been considerably changed. It runs in a zigzag course toward the southwestern part of the township where it branches off into several small and unimportant byways.

In addition to those already named, Grisham, like all other townships of Montgomery County, is traversed by many very fair roads, which pass through it in all directions.

The Toledo, Cincinnati & St. Louis Narrow Gauge Railroad will, when completed, pass through the southern part of the township from east to west, about one half mile north of the line which separates Bond and Montgomery Counties.

At present writing, the work is being rapidly pushed toward completion, the greater part of the grading being done and many of the bridges built. This road will prove a great benefit to the country through which it runs and will afford ample shipping facilities for the farmers in the southern part of the county. One of the great sources of anxiety to the pioneer in a new country is the procuring of bread. When the first white settlers came into this country, they found none of the conveniences of life by which the citizens of to-day are surrounded. No improvements, such as mills, bridges or roads, greeted his eye, but instead he saw nothing but unbroken solitudes of thick woods and monotonous prairies. In face of nature's wild deformities and all the annoyances which beset them, the pioneers went to work manfully and bravely, erected their humble cabin homes, broke the stubborn soil with their primitive plows and began that hard struggle for life which only the early settler has experienced. Mills were few and far between, and many miles of rough and almost impassable roads had to be traversed by the early settlers in order to obtain flour and meal—articles of food essential to their existence. These journeys consumed much precious time, as every moment was as gold to the pioneer. A small mill was built in a very early day by a Mr. Fogleman, on Shoal Creek, near the central part of the township. It received the power by which the machinery was run from a couple of small springs, situated at the foot of a hill near by. A small race conducted the water to the little overshot wheel. This mill was a very rude affair and was called the old Pepper mill. It had but one buhr and ground very slow. It was in operation but a few years. The old race way can still be seen, and some of the old timbers still remain to mark the place where the first mill in the township was built.

One of the first mills in the county was built by a man named Nicholson, on Shoal Creek, a little south of the place where the old pepper mill stood. This was a water mill, also, and was operated by the water of the creek. It was extensively patronized by the neighborhood, and for several years did a very good business. It was torn down many years ago and replaced by a steam mill, built by McPherson & Lewis. This was a combination mill, sawed lumber and ground both wheat and corn. It was torn away several years since, and has never been rebuilt. Prior to the erection of the above, there had been a saw-mill built on Shoal Creek by William Ross, in the year 1845, which was the first mill of its kind ever built in the township. No vestige of this mill remains, and it is difficult to tell exactly where it stood, though it is supposed to have occupied a spot near where the long bridge crosses the creek in the southern part of the township. Among the first industries of the township was the woolen factory built by James Street in the year 1828. It was operated by a small stream which was fed by a number of springs. The water, after leaving the mill, was discharged into Shoal Creek. It was operated by Mr. Street for a number of years, and, at his death, passed into the hands of his sons, who continued to run it until the machinery was worn out. It did a very paying business and supplied much of the wearing apparel used by the early settlers. At the present time, there are no mills or factories of any kind in the township.

Some attention has been given to stock-raising by the farmers of this township and a number of good farms are to be found within its limits. C. C. Root and C. H. Edwards were among the first to make stock-raising a specialty, and many fine cattle and sheep are to be seen upon their farms. While stock has received considerable attention, agriculture is the principal occupation of the people, and promises to be for years to come.

The subject of education has always held a high place in the estimation of citizens of Grisham, as is manifest by the interest taken in their public schools, which are as ably conducted as those of any other township in the county. The first schoolhouses were small cabins built of post-oak poles, without either floor or windows. Light was allowed to enter the room through a long opening in the wall into which greased paper was fitted in lieu of glass.

The seats and desks were of the simplest kind, but answered the purpose for which they were intended in the absence of better furniture. Books were scarce and limited to the few who were able to purchase them. These schools were conducted upon the principle that silence was not at all necessary and all studying was done orally. One of the first schools of the township was taught by Clement C. Aydelott in a diminutive little hut which stood a short distance east of the place where Edwards' Chapel now stands. Like all of the early schools, it was supported by subscription and lasted but three months. As time passed, these small and inconvenient buildings gradually gave place to more comfortable and commodious structures, until no the township has five good substantial schoolhouses. The schools last about seven months in the year. The term generally begins the first Monday in October.

It is difficult to determine with accuracy where the first religious services were held in Grisham, or under what circumstances. Many of the early settlers were devoted members of churches before they came to the new country, and did not abandon Christian worship after they arrived. Public services were often held in private dwellings during the early days, and were principally conducted by some person whose gift of speech was more fluent than that of his neighbors, or by any traveling preacher that might happen along. The first church organization of which we have any definite knowledge is the Presbyterian Church of Donnellson, or, as it was formerly called, Bear Creek, of which the following is a brief history.

The Donnellson Cumberland Presbyterian Church was organized by a few families from the church of Kentucky and Tennessee. This was in response to a proposition made by Mr. Rice, and the organization took place at the house of William Robertson, a Presbyterian, who lived about two miles north of Greenville, Bond County. The names of the original members of this organization are given as follows: Robert Paisley, Elizabeth Paisley, Jonathan Berry, Polly Berry, William Young and Phenly Young. The date of the permanent organization is not given in the old records, but the name Bear Creek was given the church at the organization of the first Presbytery of the State, which took place at the residence of John Kirkpatrick, in Montgomery County, May, 1823. The first Elders of the church were Robert Paisley, Jonathan Berry and John Kirkpatrick. Mr. Paisley and Mr. Berry were from churches in Kentucky, and Mr. Kirkpatrick was from Sugg's congregation, Tennessee. Joseph McDavid was ordained Ruling Elder in the congregation in May, 1822, while the church was still in Bond County, and was the first Elder ordained by the church. The present Board of Elders consists of four. In all, the church has had thirty Ruling Elders up to the year 1881. The church has had many Acting Deacons, but it never had but five ordained Deacons. The present membership is about 130. The first pastor of the church was Rev. Green B. Price who preached for the congregation four years. He was succeeded by Rev Joel Knight, who had control of the church for an unknown but long time. A. M Wilson was the pastor one year; Joseph Gordon, for one year; J. M. Bone, fourteen years; B. H. Blackwell, nearly one year; J. W. Blosser, six months; Dr. Bell, one year; E. R. Rogers, for a short time; J. H. Hendricks, two years; E. M. Johnson, two years, and William Frieze, the present pastor, who has been with the church three years. Some of the most influential churches of the county are offshoots of this congregation, among which are McDavid's Point, Pleasant Prairie, Goshen and many others. Many of the congregations in the far West have found that their best workers were from the membership of this church.

For a number of years, the congregation held their public services in private dwelling-houses. The first church edifice was built in Grisham Township about two miles northwest of the village of Donnellson, where the first cemetery in the southern part of the county was laid out. This was a frame building and served the congregation as a place of worship till the year 1856, at which time their present edifice was erected. This house is the largest church building in the township, and cost about $3,000. A flourishing Sunday school is kept up during the year, which is at present under the superintendency of D. F. Davis. The present Board of Elders consists of the following members: Henry Hawkins, Milton Ross, James Johnson and Michael Hampton.

Edwards' Chapel, the oldest Methodist Church in the county south of Hillsboro, was organized in the year 1829, with membership of twelve persons, whose names are as follows: Thomas Edwards and wife, C. C. Aydelott and wife, Thomas Grady and wife, John Hammond and wife. The organization was effected in a little log cabin, which stood in the southern part of the township, near the East Fork boundary line.

For many years, the little congregation had no house of worship and held their public services, protracted and quarterly meetings in groves, private dwelling-houses and barns.

> "No silver saints, by dying misers given,
> Here bribed the rage of ill-requited heaven;
> But such plain roofs as piety could raise,
> And only vocal with the Maker's praise."

These meetings were attended by all from miles around and did much toward bringing the remote settlements into social contact. Among the first pastors of the church were Revs. Holiday, Ames, Walker and Dew. These were all able men and to their efforts are many of the Methodist Churches of the county indebted for their success. In the year 1850, a house of worship was erected near the residence of Thomas Edwards an old settler in the northeast part of the township, on Section 11.

The house was dedicated the following year by the celebrated Peter Cartwright. The occasion was one of unusual interest, and the vast crowd assembled to hear the famous man, who preached a sermon, which, for force of logic, eloquence and wit, could hardly be surpassed. The building was of frame and served the congregation till the year 1872, when the present neat structure was erected. This building is frame, and cost the sum of $1,800. It is one of the best audience rooms in the county and will comfortably seat at least 300 persons. It stands directly west of the spot where the old building stood.

The present membership of the church is about eighty-five, among whom are some of the best and most substantial citizens of the community. A large and flourishing Sunday school is maintained throughout the year, and is at present under the superintendency of W. H. Edwards.

A Baptist Church was organized by Elder James Street many years ago, and a house of worship erected, but of this society we could learn nothing, as it was abandoned a long time since and no efforts have been made to revive it. The burying ground near which the old meeting house stood was one of the first graveyards laid out in the county.

Another Methodist Church, Mt Carmel, was organized at an early day in the western part of the township, but at just what date the organization was effected could not be learned, as the original records were taken away a number of years ago and never returned. It was, however, one of the first Methodist Churches organized in the county, and has been in progress for at least fifty years. At one time, this church was very strong in numbers, but of late years the membership has fallen off considerably, through death and removals. There are at present about forty members belonging to the church, and it is in good working condition. The first building in which the congregation worshiped was a little log cabin, situated in the southwestern part of the township, near the Bond County line. It served the congregation for about twenty years. The building in which the church now meets was erected about twenty five or thirty years ago. It has been remodeled several times and is still a very comfortable and neat house of worship. The membership will number probably thirty. The pastor who has charge of the church now is the Rev. William Van Cleve.

The Waveland Presbyterian Church, of the Presbytery of Alton, is situated in the northern part of the township, about five miles south and one half mile west of Hillsboro. The Rev. A. Cameron Allen met a part of the members of the Presbyterian Church, of Hillsboro, at the house of W. P. Brown, in the year 1843, and organized them into a society called the Waveland Presbyterian Church. A sermon was preached upon the occasion by Rev. Allen and the following names recorded as original members: John Brown, Sarah Brown, Levi Brown, Newton G. Brown, William P. Brown, Elizabeth Brown, Nancy Brown, Eliza Brown, Rufus Brown, Jr., Margaret Craig, Jesse D. Wood, Minerva J. Wood, Sarah D. Blackwood, Emeline

Blackwood, Levi H. Thorn, Margaret Thorn, George Nicholson, George S. Clodfelter, Elizabeth Barry, Joseph McLean, Abigail McLean, Enos Clodfelter and Elizabeth Brown. The first Ruling Elders were John Brown, Levi H. Thorn and Dr. Jesse L. Wood. Mrs. Elizabeth Brown was the first of the members to be summoned away by death. She died August 1, 1843, just one month after the church was organized. After its organization, the church was for a number of years a sort of outpost of the Hillsboro church, of which it is an offshoot, and was supplied by the ministers of that church till the year 1846. The first pastors who ministered to the congregation were Rev. Cameron Allen and Rev. Thomas H. Hynes, who preached at stated intervals till the year 1859. Since then the following pastors have preached for the church: Robert M. Roberts, from 1851 to 1859; William Hamilton, 1859 to 1861; John S. Howell, 1861 to 1866; James H. Spillman, 1869 to 1871; H. Hynes in the year 1876; W. P. Baker, Willis Patchen and W. S. Rodgers have also had charge of the church since the year 1876. For many years, the congregation had no house of worship, and, during that time, held their public services in a grove in pleasant weather and in the private dwellings of William Brown, Levi Brown, Joseph McLean and Dr. Brown when the weather would not admit of outdoor meetings. On the 5th of October, 1847, the church obtained by gift from John Brown and his brother, Maj. William Brown, a deed for six acres of land, on which they erected a plain, though comfortable, house of worship. The times were hard, and, the majority of the people being very poor, the building was erected mainly by days' work, contributed by the members. Very little money was donated or needed. This house was used by the congregation for about twenty years, when the church concluded to replace it by a more commodious structure. In the summer of 1872, the present handsome building was erected at a cost of $1,600, the whole amount of which, it may be said with credit, was raised at home without drawing upon the general funds of the church for aid. When the second house was built, the congregation was still without large numbers or much wealth, but they took hold of the work earnestly, and their efforts were crowned with success. While some contributed liberally, none were impoverished or seriously embarrassed by their liberality. The pastor, Rev. J. H. Spillman, was most active and zealous in pushing the work forward, and to his energy is the church largely indebted for its success. In the summer of 1848 the church established a parochial school and sustained it for three years. It was taught in the old meeting-house, first, by Mary F. Wait, of Vermont, and afterward by Miss Elvira M. Powers. It was successful and useful beyond expectation of the congregation and all its friends. It was distinctly Christian, rather than sectarian, and accomplished much good among the youth of the church and neighborhood, giving at the same time both literary work and religious instruction. A neat parsonage was built in the spring of 1881, just south of the church edifice, which cost the congregation the sum of $600. The present officers of the church are the following: G. W. Mansfield, D. H. Clodfelter and W. F. Hickman, Elders; I. N. Moss, James Brown, George McGhee, Deacons; G. N. McFail, Jesse Seibert, Monroe Holmes and I. N. Moss, Trustees. A flourishing Sunday school is maintained, which is now superintended by G. W. Mansfield. Fifty-one Christians from other places have here been associated for the worship of God, and 102 have come out from the world and cast their lot with the church. Twenty five have died and quite a number have been dismissed to other congregations. The present membership numbers about sixty-five.

Connected with each of these churches is a cemetery, where one may read much of the history of the early settlers. The oldest cemetery is Bear Creek, and among the first ones buried there was Robert Paisley, of whom we spoke in a previous page. "The moss-covered slabs tell of the sweep of Time's scythe more truly than could be written by our feeble pen, and the little mounds, with the short records and dates tell to the wanderer through these silent resting-places of the recklessness with which death marked as his own the old and the young indiscriminately."

The village of Donnellson is situated in the southeast corner of Grisham, and was laid off into lots in the year 1860 by James Hutchinson, who built the first house. Mr. Hutchinson kept the first store in the township; his first stock of goods was kept in the kitchen of his old residence. He was also the first Postmaster of the village, having been appointed when the office was established in the year 1860. Several dwelling-houses were erected in the years 1861 and 1862, though since that time the growth of the village has been somewhat slow. A good hotel was built in the year 1881, by Michael Hampton, at a cost of $1,500. There are two blacksmith shops, a wagon shop, one good store, an ax-handle factory and a paint shop in the town, all of which are doing a good business. The first physician who located in the place was Baxter Haines; he practiced his profession here for a number of years. The present physician is Dr. J. B. Carey. The future of this village is promising, as it is one of the points on the Toledo, Cincinnati & St. Louis Narrow Gauge Railroad. There is no town nearer than Hillsboro, a distance of twelve miles. Many lots are being brought up and improved, and the place promises to become at no very distant day one of the best shipping points in the county.

CHAPTER XXX.

PITMAN TOWNSHIP—POSITION AND BOUNDARIES—PHYSICAL FEATURES—PRODUCTIONS—SETTLEMENT OF THE WHITES—EARLY MILLS—SCHOOLS AND CHURCHES—SECRET SOCIETIES—ROBBERY, ETC.

PITMAN was originally included in the territory of Harvel Township, from which it was separated and formed into a distinct division in the year 18 . Lying in the northwestern part of Montgomery, it is surrounded on the east, north and south by the townships of Harvel, Bois D'Arc and Zanesville respectively, while Macoupin County forms its western boundary. It was named in honor of J. H. Pitman, a prominent citizen and one of the chief movers in its organization. Viewed from a topographical, geological or agricultural standpoint, it is so very similar to other townships already described as to render it unnecessary to enter into minute details. The surface in the main consists of fine prairie land, sufficiently undulating to present a very pleasing prospect to the observer, while the soil is of the black loamy nature, common to this part of the State, and noted for its richness, depth and fertility.

The tributaries of Macoupin Creek, a stream which flows along the western boundary in the adjoining county, are the only water-courses in the township. But little native timber is left standing, although at one time there were several strips of woodland in the southern and southwestern parts.

Realizing the necessity of timber, the settlers, as soon as their farms were broken, turned their attention to its cultivation, and in many places throughout the township are now to be seen artificial groves of considerable extent and beauty. The varieties of timber most commonly found growing in these groves, are the different species of maple, ash, walnut, hickory and cottonwood, all of which grow rapidly, and attain to considerable size in a few years after planting. The agricultural productions of Pitman, like those in all parts of Montgomery County, comprise the cereals usually grown in this latitude—corn, flax, vegetables of all kinds and varieties, while the cultivation of fruits receives great attention and has acquired considerable importance as an industry. The early history of Pitman is similar to that of many other townships of the county, and its experience has been the experience of all early settlements, with all the exciting scenes and deprivations of pioneer life, and the gradual unfolding and development of a community complete in its organization, and rich in the high elements of domestic, social and religious life.

The pioneer moves into the new country with his few household goods around him, and rises a king and conqueror. Here he erects his altar, builds his house, breaks the prairie or levels the forest; calls down the sunlight to thrill with life the sleeping soil and adorn its surface with the bloom of vegetable life, while Nature in her loveliness matures and yields to him her ripening fruit, the richest treasures of her bosom. Here is laid the keystone in the arch of a new social structure, above which are to cluster and unfold all the elements of a high civilization. Hence we see the importance of collecting in successive order all the scenes and events of a communi-

By G. N. Berry.

ty's growth, from its earliest settlement—its first germ—to its full organization, and its most recent form, together with the influences, local characteristics, and other combinations that may have modified or directed its development. Thus we are enabled to grasp the science that underlies and governs its life—a science that should be perpetuated in imperishable records to our children and our children's children.

The earliest settler in Pitman of whom we have any record was a man by the name of Denton, who made the first entry of land in the year 1822, on the farm now owned and occupied by John Husband. He lived in this place until the year 1830, at which time he died, his death being the first that occurred in the township. John Haines came here about the same time that Denton made his appearance, and entered land in the western part of the township, near the Macoupin County line. The above are the only settlers of Pitman of whom any account could be obtained prior to the year 1829, although there are vestiges of several old buildings to be seen which afforded shelter and temporary homes for a number of squatters who moved farther west as the country became more thickly populated. John L. Rogers was one of the first permanent settlers of Pittman having come to this part of the State about the year 1829, and entered a tract of land in the western part of the township, in Section 30. His enterprise was here auspicious, not only in fitting land for cultivation but also in erecting a small grist mill on his place near the county line, thus becoming a pioneer in mill building as well as in farming. Rogers died in the year 1852, having reached the good old age of seventy-two years. He had three sons and two daughters, all of whom are living in the State. The old Rogers farm is at present owned by Theodore Rogers, a son of the preceding, and a prominent Methodist preacher of Central Illinois.

Davis Bagby was a resident of Pitman as early as the year 1832, having come here in company with his father-in-law, Miller Woods, both of whom located in the south west corner of the township. The place where Woods first settled is now owned by William Hackney. Bagby subsequently purchased a piece of land in Section 19, where he lived until the year 1865, when he died, lamented by all who knew him. He was a soldier in the war of 1812, having served his country faithfully throughout that memorable struggle. Another prominent pioneer was D. G. Whitehorn, at present the oldest living settler in Pitman Township. The date of his arrival in this part of the State was the year 1831. He located a farm in Section 18, where for fifty-one years he has lived a prominent and upright citizen. In the year 1834, he was married to Catharine Bagby, daughter of Davis Bagby being the first marriage that took place in the township.

George Wagoner was prominently connected with the early history of the Township, and can be named among its pioneer settlers. He moved here from Kentucky about the year 18—, and secured a piece of land in Section 29 which is still in the possession of his family. His death occurred in the year 1864. Frederick Hamilton was an early settler also, having entered land in the western part of the township about the year 1833. His death, which occurred two years later, is the second event of that kind that transpired in Pitman.

Subsequently there appear the names of Zadok Leach, William King, Tazewell Brown, Flower Husband, William Hamilton and L. C. Richardson, all of whom came from States farther south and settled in the territory of Pitman between the years 1837 and 1840. The place where Leach settled is at present in possession of the Wagoner heirs. King sold his farm to a man by the name of Young, and moved to Christian County, where he died several years ago. Brown entered land lying in the west-central part of the township, where his widow still lives. L. C. Richardson, who, next to Whitehorn, is the oldest resident of Pitman, selected as his home a piece of land lying in Section 30, on which he still resides, surrounded by the comforts and conveniences which he has accumulated by a life of industry and economy.

There are other names connected with the early history of the township aside from those already enumerated, which we were unable to learn. In the old burying ground at Sulphur Springs, where the hardy and energetic pioneers are sleeping in their last resting-place, can be seen many of the names mentioned in these pages, while others, who were as prominently identified with the township's history, lie in graves unmarked by the simplest epitaph. Those early pioneers were men of sterling integrity, high moral worth, and eminent in all those virtues which make men great. Though their bodies have moldered back to Mother Earth, they are not dead. The body may die; a good example will live forever. They have gone to

"Join the choir invisible, of those immortal dead
who live again
In minds made better by their presence; live
In pulses stirred to generosity;
In deeds of daring rectitude; in scorn
Of miserable aims that end with self,
In thoughts that pierce the night like stars,
And with their mild persistence urge men's minds
To better issues."

The inconveniences of the first settlers, though probably not comparable with those experienced by pioneers in older sections of the country, were still of such magnitude that we of the present can form but an approximate idea of their realities. A very great inconvenience felt among them was the want of a mill to grind their corn and grain, the nearest being in Butler Grove and Hillsboro Townships. During the winter season, when the deep snows precluded the possibility of traveling over the trackless prairies, the settlers manufactured their own meal by grinding or rather cracking corn in common coffee mills. Other contrivances were improvised. One method very much in vogue was to make a rude mortar by hollowing out the top of a stump. Sometimes this was done by boring or chiseling, but it was frequently burned out and the cavity scraped with a knife or other instrument until all the charred spots were removed. In this cavity the corn was placed and pounded with a heavy, rude pestle attached to a swing-pole overhead. The bruised corn was known by the name of "samp," and when pounded was made into "johnny cake," the coarser part being boiled into "mush." The first mill in the township was erected by J. L. Rogers for his individual use. It was a very primitive affair, operated by horse power, and ground very slowly, but made a fair article of meal. It was much used in after years by the settlers in grinding corn for horse feed. A second mill was built by Flower Husband on his farm about one-half a mile south of the Rogers place, in the year 1840. This mill was operated by horse-power also, and it seems to have done a very good business, as it was kept running quite extensively for ten years. David Plane built and operated a little mill just across the line in Macoupin County about the year 1850, and for several years supplied breadstuffs to the people of the adjoining townships.

A number of the first settlers had been men of influence and education in their old homes, and did not neglect the intellectual culture of their children after locating in the new country, and schools were at once established. The first schools were kept across the line in the little settlement in Macoupin County, and were attended by the youth of this township for several years. The first school in Pitman was taught by William McIver in a little frame building erected for the purpose and known as the Friendship Schoolhouse. The date of this school was about the year 1854. The second school was taught by Bluford Pillsbury the following year. William King, Edwin Rogers and a Miss Harris were among the early teachers of the township. The first house in which a public school was taught is situated in the west-central part of the township, and is still used for educational purposes. The first public school was taught by a Mr. Ware about the year 1858, as near as could be ascertained. Generally speaking, the progress of the public schools here as elsewhere throughout the country has been of a most remarkable and satisfactory character. The primitive, ill-ventilated and unhealthy log shanties have given place to neat and commodious frame structures, while the former teachers, of whom many were possessed of but indifferent scholastic attainments, and would now be considered far from competent, have been supplanted through the means of the normal institutes and model schools, which the liberal-mindedness of our law-makers has given us with those who are a credit to the present system and the State which supports it.

John L. Rogers was the first Justice of the Peace elected in Pitman, an office he filled with ability for two years. He was elected in the year 1840; John Snow was chosen Constable at the same election. The Justices of the Peace, at present, are William Woods and —— Richards. The first birth mentioned as having occurred in the township was that of Mary Rogers, daughter of John L. Rogers, who was born in the year 1832. The first cemetery was laid out near the Providence M. E. Church in the year 1862, and the first person interred therein was a man by the name of Newell, who died the same year. The early pioneers of Pitman found ample time amid their other duties to discharge those higher and holier obligations which they owed their Creator, the majority of them being devoted church members and sincere Christians. The Methodists had a flourishing church at a place called Sulphur Springs in Macoupin County, as early as the year 1840, which was attended by the residents of western Pitman for a number of years. The organization was moved into this township in the year 1851, and the name changed to the Providence M. E. Church. The Friendship Schoolhouse was used as a place of worship by the congregation until the year 1864, when the present church edifice was built. This building cost the sum of $1,500, is of frame, and will comfortably seat 275 persons. At the time the organization was moved from Macoupin County, it was presided over by Rev. James Hutchinson, and numbered fifty members. Since then, the number has decreased somewhat, there being at present but forty names on the church records. Among the pastors of this society can be named the following: —— Sample, David Bardrick, George Craig, Henry Wilson, Adam Wagoner, L. L. Harlan, —— Prettyman, O. H. P. Ash, James West, A. T. Orr and —— Sloan. The present incumbent is the Rev. A. D. Beckhart. Their Sunday school, which is in good condition and well attended, is under the superintendency of S. R. Rice. This church is one of the points in the Millwood Circuit.

The Missionary Baptists have a strong organization near the central part of the township on Section 28, known as the Prairie Grove Church, though at what time it was organized was not learned. Their building, which is the finest church edifice in the township was erected in the year 1880 at a cost of about $2,500. The present membership of this church is about fifty.

The Prairie Chapel M. E. Church is situated near the northeast corner of the township in Section 12, and was organized in the year 1879. Their house of worship, a neat frame building, was erected the same year, and cost in the neighborhood of $2,200. There are now on the church books the names of about fifty members, and the congregation is reported in a flourishing condition. It is a point in the Raymond Circuit, and is at present ministered to by Rev. A. D. Beckhart.

At one time there were several granges of the Patrons of Husbandry in successful operation in this township, only one of which is in existence at present. Washington Grange, No. 970, was instituted in the spring of 1874, with a membership of twenty-seven. The present membership is about seventy, among whom are many of the foremost farmers of the township. Their meetings are held in the East Union Schoolhouse, situated in Section 19. The officers of this lodge at present are R. N. Long, W. M.; S. R. Rice, W. O.; William Howland Steward; Edwin Grimes, Gate-Keeper; H. G. Wagoner, Treasurer; Jasper Street, Secretary; Mollie Howland, Ceres; Mollie Bowman, Assistant Steward; Miss Street, Flora. We will conclude this brief sketch of Pitman with the following account of a very daring robbery, which took place in the year 1881, at the residence of Enoch Perrine, who lives in the northwestern part of the township. Perrine is a prominent stock-dealer, and is known to have carried large sums of money on his person. Shortly after making a heavy sale of stock, his house was visited one night by a party of three masked men, who forced an entrance into the same, and, after tying and gagging the different members of the family, searched the premises, and carried away about $7,000, which Perrine had that day received. The members of the family were left tied, and in this helpless condition they remained till nearly morning, when one of them succeeded in freeing himself. The rest were soon liberated, an alarm given and soon detectives were on the tracks of the robbers, one of whom was overhauled in St. Louis, and the other two were captured shortly afterward in Chicago. They were brought to Hillsboro, tried, convicted and sentenced to a long term of imprisonment in the penitentiary.

CHAPTER XXXI.

AUDUBON TOWNSHIP—TOPOGRAPHY AND DESCRIPTION—PHYSICAL FEATURES—WATER COURSES —EARLY SETTLEMENT—FIRST BIRTH, DEATH AND MARRIAGE—THE LITTLES—EARLY CHURCHES AND SCHOOLS—THE OLD TOWN OF AUDUBON, ETC.

THE township of Audubon lies in the northeast corner of Montgomery County, and consists of two parts commonly known as North and South Audubon. North Audubon is made up of thirty-six sections, while the portion known as South Audubon is a fractional township, containing only eighteen sections. It is bounded by Christian County on the north, by Shelby County on the east, by Fayette County on the south, and on the west by the townships of Witt and Nokomis. Most of the surface is level prairie land, though along the streams it is somewhat rough and broken. Originally, about one-fifth of the township was covered with timber, consisting of oak, ash, walnut, elm, hickory etc. Much of this original timber has, however, been cleared away. Throughout the township are numerous small watercourses among the most important of which is Ramsey Creek rising in the northeast corner of county, and, flowing in a southerly direction, unites with Elliott Creek in the northwest corner of Section 14 in South Audubon. Carter's Branch has its source in a small lake in the southern part of Section 1, in South Audubon and, flowing almost due south, unite with Otter Branch and together, empty into Elliott Creek. Hooker's Branch rises in the northwest corner of Section 5, in South Audubon, and winds its tortuous course, first in a southeasterly direction, and then almost directly east, until after it has become a stream of considerable size. It is given the name of Elliott Creek, and leaves the township at the southwest corner of Section 14. Caesar Creek flows through the western part of South Audubon. The soil is of average futility, producing good crops of corn, wheat oats, rye etc. Considerable fruit is also raised in this section.

Among the first white people who ventured to settle in this portion of Montgomery County was Thomas Hill. He came in about the year 1832 and located in the eastern part of the township. About the same time, Basil Hill and Joseph Davis came in and located a little west of Thomas Hill, near the central part of the township. James Card came in about 1833 and settled in the central part. In 1834, the most important settlement was made by a colony of emigrants who came from the State of Massachusetts. They laid off the town of Audubon a short time after their arrival. Prominent among these were Isaac Hinkley, Robert Little, Otis Little and William Pike who entered large tracts of land, and for some time farmed very extensively. They all have descendants living here at present, and Robert Little is now the largest land-owner in Audubon Township. The first settler in what is known as North Audubon, was Thomas Price, who came in in 1831 and located on Section 36. The first white child born in North Audubon was John Henry Price, son of Thomas Price, who was born in 1832 and Amanda Price, daughter of Thomas Price, who died about this time (1832), was the first death. The first Justice of the Peace in North Audubon was M. S. Cushman, who was elected in 1836, and about the same time William H. Russell was elected Constable. Radford Virden came in 1832, and settled in the south-

By T. J. Riley

eastern corner of the township. George Cottingham, another early settler, came about 1835, and located in the southwestern corner. He was soon after, in 1836, followed by Bailey Osborn William Craig and William Cottingham, who located in the same neighborhood. Shipton Estes settled in the northeastern corner of South Audubon in 1843, and during the same year, William Orear, James Smith and William T. Slater located near him. At quite an early date, a number of wealthy settlers came in from Massachusetts, and entered large tracts of land. They built magnificent residences and farmed extensively, but after remaining a short time grew discouraged and sold out, disposing of their land at a price ranging from 30 to 60 cents an acre. The fine houses built by them, partially remain, and though they have gone very much to decay, they still bear signs of their former grandeur. A part of one of these farms is that known at present as the "Old Blue Farm."

In 1846, William T. Slater was elected the first Justice of the Peace in South Audubon, and Elias Pearce the first Constable. The first two marriages occurred in 1845; John Slater to Miss Julia Coy, and Miss Isabel Slater promised to "love, honor and obey" Dr. A. S. Vandeveer. The first birth was that of Sarah J., daughter of William and Elizabeth Orear, in 1843, and the first death was a daughter of Shipton and Margaret Estes.

Of the early schools of this township, but little can be said. They were of the usual primitive character, and the buildings were the ordinary log structures so common at an early day. The first house for school purposes was erected on Section 12 in South Audubon, in 1849, and was a log building, with a large fireplace and a stick chimney. The first teacher was Charles Turner, and his school was taught

The first church erected in this township was by the Unitarian denomination. The church was organized by the Rev. Mr. Huntington, and a house of worship was built in the spring of 1839. The second church in South Audubon was of the Baptist denomination. It was organized by Elder Samuel Rogers a Baptist preacher, and the first church edifice was built in 1850.

The only village in this township is that of Audubon. As stated, it was laid out by a colony of emigrants from Massachusetts, in 1834. For some years after its settlement, it gave promise of becoming a town of considerable importance, and, at one time, competed with Hillsboro for the county seat. Hiram Holmes built and kept the first hotel. He also built the first mill, which at that time was considered a very extensive affair. M. S. Cushman and Samuel Patch were the first merchants. Isaac Hinkley was the first land agent and also the first Postmaster. Not long after the settlement of Audubon, a party of Eastern capitalists came in and built a magnificent hotel. They were compelled to haul all of the material from St Louis, and their poor facilities made it a very expensive undertaking. It was operated without success for several years, and was finally torn down and a farm house made of it. A court house was also erected here in an early day, but Hillsboro being chosen as the county seat it was very little used and was finally sold to the Methodist denomination for a church, and is at present used as such. After a few short years of prosperity, the town gradually began to die. Merchants moved their business to other places, and the extensive town plat was slowly changed into farming land, until at present only three or four houses, a few ruins and numerous old wells remain to mark the place where the town once stood.

PART II.

BIOGRAPHICAL DEPARTMENT

PART II.

BIOGRAPHICAL SKETCHES.

GREENVILLE CITY AND PRECINCT.

DR. WILLIAM A. ALLEN, one of the most prominent physicians of Greenville, was born in Jacksonville, Morgan Co., Ill., son of William and Mary (Killingsworth) Allen; he a farmer, born at Knoxville, Tenn., in 1799, and dying in Hillsboro, Ill., in 1862; she also a native of Knoxville, born in 1824, and still living; they were the parents of eleven children. Our subject, Dr. Allen, after his primary education was completed commenced the study of medicine, finishing the same at the St. Louis Medical College, from which institution he graduated, when he began the practice of his profession at Greenville in 1855, where he has continued in active and successful practice. He has filled the position of member of City Council of Greenville, and member of the Board of Health, and served two years during the late war for the Union as Assistant Surgeon of the Ninth Illinois Infantry. In 1860, he married Miss Mill[illegible] N. Blanchard, born in Greenville, daughter of Mr. L. Blanchard, of Stoughton, Mass., who came West about 1822; three children have been born to them—Victoria, J[illegible] and Ethel. He is a Congregationalist, a Mason, an A. O. U. W. and a Democrat.

LEMUEL ADAMS, Postmaster, Greenville, was born in Dayton, Montgomery Co., Ohio, in 1831, son of John and Mary (Bacon) Adams, he born in Kentucky in 1802, by occupation a cooper, and dying in 1877; she, a native of Allegany County, N. Y., born in 1804, and died in Greenville, Ill., in 1877; they had six children. Our subject, after obtaining an education afforded by the common schools of Indiana and Illinois, learned the blacksmith's and wagon-maker's trades, and has chiefly followed those trades and merchandising until his appointment as Postmaster of Greenville, in the winter of 1881-82. In April, 1861, he entered the military service, and was elected Lieutenant of Company D, Twenty-Second Illinois Volunteer Infantry, and was wounded at the battle of Belmont, Mo., in November, 1861, coming home in 1862 on account of disability from wounds. In 1862, in Greenville, he married Miss Julia Ellen Birge, a native of Bond County, born in 1839, daughter of Ansel and Millicent (Twiss) Birge, both natives of Vermont, he born in 1788 and she in 1808. Three children have been born to Mr. Adams—L[illegible], Edgar and Cora Alice. Mrs. Adams died in 1874. May 4, 1882, he married Miss A[illegible] Morris, of Milton, Ind. Mr. Adams [illegible] to Bond County in 1852. Is independent in his religious views; is a Mason, an Odd Fellow, and a Republican.

GEORGE F. BERRY, merchant, Greenville, of the well-known general merchandising firm of Berry & Davis, is a native of Bond County, and was born in 1844. His father, from whom our subject takes his name, was a farmer by occupation, and was born in Rockingham County, Va., A. D., 1819, moved to Christian Co., Ky., thence to Bond County in 1827. He took as his wife Miss Louise Enloe, the fruits of this alliance being three sons and four daughters. He departed this life in 1867. George F., Jr., received his early education in the common schools of Bond County, and closed his studies with a special academic course. He received his first business experience as a salesman in a store and in 1869 established the business with which he is now connected. October 10, 1871, he married Miss Eliza J. Henry, daughter of Judge A. G. Henry, a prominent and successful politician and a pioneer of Bond County. Mrs. Berry was born in Bond County in 1852. They have four children—Mary N., Nousie, Ellen and Henry. Mr. Berry is counted among the successful business men of Bond County, and has represented his [the Forty second] district in the Thirtieth General Assembly of Illinois. He has also served one term as Clerk of the city of Greenville, is a member of the Christian Church, and of the Ancient Order of United Workmen. His grandfather, David Berry, was a native of Delaware, born in 1767, removed when a young man to Rockingham County, Va., where he married. Here all but two of their eight children were born. In 1811, he removed to Christian County, Ky., where they resided until 1827, when he came with his family to Greenville, Bond County. Here he resided until his death, which occurred in September, A. D. 1842. But two of his children are now living.

HENRY BASS, Greenville. In a [illegible] of some of the most prominent agri[illegible]lturists and self-made men of Bond County, the name of Henry Bass, of Greenville City, occupies a prominent place. He was born in F[illegible]ette County, Ill., April 22, 1833, and [illegible] the sixth child of the family of twelve children of Guilford and Mary Ann (Proc[illegible]) Bass. Guilford Bass was a native of North C[illegible]rolina, and removed from there to Kentuc[illegible] for a time, thence to Tennessee, thence [illegible] Fayette County in 1832, locating northe[illegible] Vandalia about twelve miles. There he r[illegible]ained until his death, in 1845. His wife s[illegible]rvived until 1872, when she also departed t[illegible] life, leaving ten sons and two daughters [illegible] mourn her departure. But two of these, William and our subject, are now resident [illegible] Bond County. Henry left home at t[illegible] [illegible] of fourteen. He came to Bond Coun[illegible] [illegible]ught and found employment on a farm, receiving only $7 for a hard month's work, an[illegible] saved sufficient means to make part paym[illegible] [illegible] his first purchase of 100 acres of B[illegible] County land, in Beaver Creek Precinct. In August, 1856, he made a second purchase of 1[illegible] acres, which he still owns, and to which he has since added, owning at one time 1[illegible] acres. Mr. Bass married Nancy Goodso[illegible] [illegible]ughter of Spencer Goodson, a native of K[illegible]cky, a farmer and blacksmith, and came [illegible] Illinois when a young man. With the ex[illegible]ion of a four years' stay in Missouri, he h[illegible] been a resident of Illinois, and now [illegible] [illegible]stian County. Mr. Bass is the sixth chil[illegible] They have six sons and two daughters—William H., Abbie, George, Edward, Wal[illegible]r, Louis, Leoni and Leonard. Abbie is n[illegible] Mrs. C. C. Squires, of Beaver Creek Towns[illegible]p. Mr. and Mrs. Bass are members of the [illegible]aptist Church of Smith Grove. Their h[illegible] is in

Beaver Creek Precinct, Town 4, Section 20. Guilford and Charles S. are deceased. Guilford died November 14, 1856, and Charles S. August 31, 1866, at one year and eighteen days old.

C. R. BENNETT, one of the most prominent and successful drug merchants of Southern Illinois. Commenced business in Greenville, in the fall of 1861, at the corner of Second and Main streets, where he continued until the following February. He then removed to west side of public square, where he conducted a most successful business, and in 1869 purchased his present location, whereupon he erected a substantial brick block, fronting twenty six feet on Third street and and seventy-five feet on College avenue. This is one of the most substantial and attractive blocks in the city of Greenville, is two stories in height and has a roomy basement. The upper floor is occupied with business offices. The first floor and basement are stocked with a complete line of drugs, medicines, paints, oils and varnish, toilet goods, trusses, pocket books and porte-monnaies and pocket cutlery, tobacco, cigars and confectionery, etc. Mr. Bennett also carries a full line of sugars teas, coffees, spices and fancy groceries. Mr. Bennett is a native of Ohio, and was born at Xenia, Greene County. His father, Mr. E. Bennett is a native of New Jersey, and a pioneer druggist of the Buckeye State, and C. R.'s marked success as a druggist is largely due to his early and life-long experience, as well as the fact that his goods are always bought and sold at prices made upon the cash basis. The stock of his establishment is always well selected and complete. Mr. Bennett gives his personal and undivided attention to his business, and makes a point to supply all the demands of the trade, and the sales of the establishment are annually increasing.

WILLIAMSON BARKER, a farmer and a native of Bond County, is very properly classed among the pioneers, having been born near Old Ripley March 5, 1835, although he has not continously lived in the county since that time. He is distinguished in his vicinity as having driven an ox team more miles than any other man in the county. The feat of driving a yoke of horned animals from Illinois to San Francisco, Cal., is one worthy of record, especially when accomplished by a backwoods country lad, such as was Mr. Barker in 1854. Williamson's father, Jordan Barker, was a native of Randolph County, N. C., a farmer by occupation, and emigrated to Illinois in the year 1817, and located near Old Ripley, on a tract of 240 acres of land, a portion of which he entered. He was a fearless and aggressive pioneer, came to stay and did stay, developing a farm, taking part in all public enterprises for the advancement of civilization; was an under officer in the Black Hawk war, and took part in other minor Indian engagements. He raised a family of ten children, Williamson being the third and the only one now living. Williamson's mother was one Nancy Pruitt, and a member of one of the early pioneer families of Bond County. Our subject received the educational advantage of county schools of Old Ripley, and at nineteen years of age took an overland journey to California, where he spent in all about twenty-four years of his life, making the trip three times. He there spent his time in gold mining with moderate results; returned to permanently remain in Greenville in 1878, and is now independently retired on a fertile farm of 274 acres near the city.

LEVI BORROR, farmer, P. O. Smithboro. The Borror family came originally from Germany, and settled in Hardin County, Va. The father of our subject was Solomon who emigrated from Virginia to Franklin

County, Ohio, about the close of the war of 1812; the family consisted of the grandparents of Levi. The names of the children were Absalom, Solomon, Jacob, Isaac, Christina and Martin, all of whom settled near Columbus. Levi was born January 14, 1834, in Franklin County; is of the third generation of those who came to Ohio; his brothers and sisters were Elizabeth, Ichabod, William C. and Gilbert L. Elizabeth married Wesley Titus, and resides in Litchfield, Montgomery County; Gilbert L., in Marshall County, Ind.; William C., died in the army; Levi, came to Bond County February 28, 1868, and located in Town 5, Range 2, in Greenville Precinct, where he has since lived. His farm consists of 270 acres. He has been twice married, and had children by both wives, both now deceased. His first marriage was March 1, 1859, to Catharine C., —— who bore him two children—William alone now living. His second wife was Elizabeth Roach, born in Pickaway County, Ohio, daughter of Charles Roach. Mr. Borror had by last wife five children—Benjamin F., Walter W., Albert J., Mary P. and Marion R. Mr. Borror is a member of the Baptist Church; his father of the Christian Church.

THOMAS M. BROWN, farmer, P. O. Pocahontas, was born in Belmont County, Ohio, April 12, 1828; son of Simon Brown, born in Virginia in 1783, a millwright and farmer by occupation, who died in December, 1864; his wife, Martha (Williams) Brown, dying in 1860. They were the parents of eleven children, six boys and five girls. Our subject has been engaged in farming all his life; has served as School Director eight years, also Road Supervisor. During the war, he served in Company F, One Hundred and Thirty-fifth Illinois Volunteer Infantry, Capt. Macadams. He owns 120 acres of excellent land, and is a Democrat and an Odd Fellow. In this county, November 5, 1849, he married Mary E. File, born September 13, 1828, daughter of George and Mary A. File, by which union there were born seven children—Lafayette, Emma M., Marcella, Samuel M., Mary M., Sylvester and Benjamin.

SAMUEL M. BROWN, son of the above, Thomas M. Brown, was born in Ripley Township January 24, 1857. He received his education in the schools of the county, and has followed farming his entire life. January 6, 1881, he married Frances R. Dixon, born in Greenville Township October 8, 1861, daughter of J. M. Dixon, a farmer, and one son has been born to them—Jesse M.; is a Democrat.

L. S. BROOKS, P. O. Greenville, farmer and stock-raiser, is the owner and proprietor of "Prospect View" farm. He was born April 13, 1853, in Penfield, Monroe Co., N. Y.; son of Garry Brooks, who was born July 5, 1806, near Middletown in the State of Connecticut, and was married to Emma Chauncey, the mother of L. S. She was a daughter of John and Amelia (Goodridge) Chauncey. The paternal grandsire of L. S. was Samuel Brooks, a native of Scotland, who emigrated to the Eastern States prior to the year 1800. Garry Brooks is a resident of Fairport, in Monroe County. In his early life, he was engaged in farming pursuits and became wealthy, and has since retired from active business life. He had but three children—Fannie L., L. S. and Emma J. Our subject had good school advantages, and was brought up to farming pursuits. Having heard glowing accounts of the West, and the beauties of the prairies of Illinois State, he resolved to cast his lot there, and in the spring of 1877 he came west to this county, and the year following purchased the farm he now owns, on which he has since built a large and handsome residence and two large barns, the residence being located on a beautiful eminence which overlooks the entire township. He has the best improved farm in Bond County, and is one of the young and progressive farmers of the township. His wife was Mary McMillan, daughter of James McMillan and Susan Harmon. This union has been crowned with four children—Chauncey G., Fannie F., Jesse L. and Emma S. He is a member of the Presbyterian Church.

OTIS B. COLCORD, blooded stock raiser Greenville. Mr. Colcord is a native of Yarmouth, Me., and was born March 16, 1818. His father, Daniel Colcord, was a native of Exeter, N. H., and by trade a potter. He had a family of five children, of whom our subject was the third. All of these are now living, and residents of Illinois. Otis B. received his schooling in the public schools of his native place, and came West in the year 1837 on a prospecting tour into Indiana. Returning East the following year, he repeated his journey as far as Bond County in the year 1839. The following eighteen years of his life he spent in the employ of the reaper and mower manufacturing company of D. M. Osborne & Co., of Auburn, N. Y., as their Western agent, with headquarters at St. Louis, and at the same time conducting a farm of his own, making a specialty of Mambrino stock. Among some of his finest specimens of horse flesh are Mambrino Athlete, Leno Mambrino, Lady Harris, Rockey, Lady Plant, Lady Cooper, Membrino Queen, Grape Shot, Maid of the Mist, Marshal, et al.

J. J. CLARKSON, merchant, Greenville, is a native of England, born in 1845; son of James and Elizabeth B. (Douglas) Clarkson, both natives of England, but she of Scotch descent, and at present residing at Alton, Ill. Our subject, in addition to the ordinary common school education, took a course at Jones' Commercial College, St. Louis, and began life as a farmer, but has been in the express business, and at present is merchandising. In Carlisle, Ill., in 1870, he married Elizabeth McDowell, of Scotch nativity. Mr. Clarkson served his adopted country during the late war, as a member of the One Hundred and Thirty third and One Hundred and Forty-fourth Illinois Volunteer Infantry. He is a Presbyterian, a member of the I. O. G. T., the A. O. U. W., the I. O. M. A. and is a Republican. Mr. Clarkson is at the head of the well-known firm of J. J. Clarkson & Co., who do an extensive business in their line. They carry a full line of hardware, and are agents for various agricultural implements, being one of the most reliable concerns in Southern Illinois.

GEORGE DONNELL (deceased). Among those men whose personal history is inseparably interwoven with the pioneer history of Bond County, was the lamented George Donnell. He was a man possessed of all the essential qualifications for a most successful pioneer, and came to Bond County at a time when men of his type were most needed. Of his forefathers, this much only can be said: They were of Scotch nativity, and at the time when religious persecution prevailed in Scotland, they fled to the North of Ireland. George Donnell's grandfather, Thomas Donnell, was constrained to leave Ireland because of the unsettled state of religious affairs there, and in 1731 came to America with seven brothers and two sisters, and settled near Philadelphia, Penn. Of his immediate family or personal life little is known, except that he lived to a good old age, and that a son of his, Maj. John Donnell, emigrated to Guilford County, N. C., engaged in agriculture, and there raised a family of fifteen children. Maj. John Donnell was an earnest and zealous advocate for the principles of free government, and fought nobly for the independ ence of America in the Revolutionary struggle, where he gained his military title. He was twice married. First, to Hannah Meeks, and by her had three daughters and two sons. For his second wife he took one Betsey Denny, and by her had five daughters and five sons, George, our subject, being his father's eleventh child, or his mother's sixth. He was born in Guilford County, N. C., July 1, 1793. His parents were both Christian people, and early in life he imbibed the truths and teachings of the Holy Bible, and connected himself with the Presbyterian Church of Buffalo, N. C., where they for many years resided. May 30, 1815, he married Miss Anna McLean, also a native of Guilford County, and born June 18, 1795. Her father was Joseph McLean, a North Carolina pioneer who married one Peggy Mabin, and Anna was their sixth child, and the second youngest of the family. She grew to be a woman of great strength of character, possessing unfaltering energy, and has been to her chosen companion a most faithful wife, to her offspring a loving and devoted mother. This union was blessed with a family of thirteen children, namely, Joseph M., John D., Polly E., William N., James M., Betsey A., Thomas S., George W., Mary J., Robert L., Levi S., Henry C. and Emily R. all born in Bond County except the two first named. Three, Betsey A., Polly and James M., died in infancy. George W., Henry C. and James are in the West. Joseph M., William N., John D. (deceased), and Thomas S. (deceased), all settled on farms in Bond County. Robert, Mary and Levi are deceased, and Emily, the youngest, married Col. [illegible] McCord, of Greenville. George Donnell emigrated to Bond County in the year 1819, and first settled near the forks of Shoal Creek, where he lived for several years. He sold his property there and bought one quarter section of land about three miles north west of Greenville. This land he improved, erected upon it good buildings, making for his family a comfortable home, and not unfrequently the weary traveler a welcome stopping place. To his landed estate he from time to time added, so that as his children came of age he gave each a farm of 160 acres. To the education of his family he devoted no little time and means, and for a time took up his residence at Hillsboro that they might have the best of school advantages. As a religious man, Mr. Donnell was always prominent. At once, when coming to Bond County, he identified himself with the people of God, and united with the Shoal Creek Presbyterian Church, the second of the order in Southern Illinois. He, with others, organized the first Sabbath school in Southern Illinois, and believed by many to be the first in the State. This school held sessions on Saturdays and Sundays, reading, writing and arithmetic being in the Saturday programmes. The advantages of this school were improved by whole pioneer families, who came from long distances to attend. Mr. Donnell was one of the organizers of the Presbyterian Church of Greenville, and aided with much time and money in erecting their first church edifice in the city, in 1827. In March, 1828, he was elected and ordained a Ruling Elder, which office he filled with great fidelity until 1875. As he advanced in years he sold most of his farming lands, and afterward secured a comfortable home in Greenville, and from that time until his death lived a comparatively retired life, devoting much of his leisure time to social and religious duties. Mr. Donnell was a man of positive traits of character, but realizing man's liability to err, he was always open to conviction, and anxious to repair an injury. Old age crept upon him, disease was found lurking in his system, and a stroke of paralysis in 1864 ensued.

Fr[illegible] this he gradually recovered. A second and [illegible] severe stroke, however, seized upon him, [illegible] resulted in his death Monday, April 16, 1877, at the residence of Col. George C. M[illegible]d, surrounded by his children and friends who lovingly administered to his every [illegible]. Mrs. Anna Donnell, for more than [illegible] years his devoted wife, still survives [illegible] and lives with her son-in-law, and youngest child, Ellen, Mr. and Mrs. McCord. She [illegible] over eighty-seven years of age, but still enjoys the use of her mental faculties, [illegible] than average good health. A full [illegible] portrait of the late stalwart pioneer appe[illegible] this volume.

W. S. DANN & CO. The mercantile house of W. S. Dann & Co. justly deserves notice in a history of Bond County, as standing at the [illegible] of the mercantile trade of Southern Illinois. The business was first established in 187[illegible] Mr. W. S. Dann and a brother, Mr. [illegible] Dann, who opened a general stock in th[illegible] number of the present establishment. Mr. E. L. Dann continued until 1875, wh[illegible] retired, and W. S. Dann remained alon[illegible] Mr. F. P. Joy, the present junior partn[illegible] manager, became associated with hi[illegible] business increased so rapidly that m[illegible] was demanded. An adjoining lot [illegible], and the store enlarged and refitt[illegible] making it roomy and well lighted. It [illegible] a frontage of fifty-one feet on C[illegible] avenue, and extends fifty seven feet on [illegible] street, and comprises two floors and [illegible] basement. The basement is used for the [illegible] of surplus stock, and second floor for [illegible] of carpets mattings, etc., and w[illegible] of ladies' cloaks and shawls. The [illegible] is the general salesroom. It has [illegible] double front entrances on College avenue [illegible] conveniently arranged on the department[illegible] the stocks or different lines of goods [illegible] assorted and displayed in their respective departments. The stocks of these departments embrace complete lines of dry goods, including dress goods, silks and trimmings, embroideries, white goods, ladies' and gents' furnishing goods and notions, extensive line of boots and shoes of standard makes, hats and caps, and a fine assortment of staple and fancy groceries. The departments and stocks are presided over by Mr. Joy and his corps of seven efficient salesmen and one saleslady. Each clerk is an experienced stock keeper, and is responsible for its condition. It must be in good order, every article or piece marked with price in plain figures. They also keep stock memoranda of goods to be purchased, and from time to time buy or order what the market demands, with the sanction or suggestions of the manager. Goods are all bought, marked and sold upon a cash basis, doing a general produce exchange business. The general clearing-out sales of unseasonable and remnant stock are a taking feature of the institution, and the entire establishment is conducted upon modern business principles. Business discipline, not so rigid as to become impracticable, is also a noticeable feature of the establishment This house carries a stock of about $28,000, and does an annual business of nearly $100,000. Mr. W. S. Dann not being able to devote his personal time and attention to the business, spends much of his time abroad, and Mr. Joy assumes entire charge, and is always during business hours found at his store.

WILLIAM H. DAWDY, lawyer, was born in Shelby County, Ill., January 1, 1845; son of John H. and Nancy (Frazier) Dawdy, he [illegible] resident of Pana, Ill., a lawyer by profession of twenty years' practice, and was for[illegible] a merchant; has been Associate Judge of Christian County, and held other minor offices; i[illegible] Police Magistrate of Pana; his wife is a native of Kentucky. They had two childre[illegible]

William H. being the oldest. Our subject attended the seminary at Shelbyville about five years, afterward at Walton Academy, Pana, and later at Eureka College, Illinois, one year. After leaving school he began the study of law with Henry and Ross, and was admitted to practice July 1, 1865. Located at Pana, two years, Vandalia, one year, and came to Greenville August 14, 1868, where he has remained since, having obtained a lucrative practice, and being regarded as one of the ablest and most successful lawyers of Bond County. He has held the position of City Attorney of Pana, City Attorney of Greenville, Justice of the Peace, and State's Attorney of Bond County from 1872 to 1880. July 7, 1872, in La Crosse County, Wis., he married Miss Amelia A. Tripp, born in Trumbull County, Ohio; daughter of Almer Tripp, a native of Vermont. One child has been born to Mr. Dawdy—Clarence A.; is a member of the Christian Church, of the Odd Fellows, Workingmen, Good Templars and the Democratic party.

MICHAEL V. DENNY, cashier in bank, Greenville, born August 31, 1833, in Bond County, the only child now living of Samuel W. and Catharine (Finley) Denny, he born in North Carolina in 1805, a farmer by occupation, and died in 1841. His wife was born in Tennessee in 1808, and is still living. Our subject received his education in the academy at Sullivan, Moultrie Co., Ill., where, in 1860, September 6, he married Margaret S. Perryman, who was born in Shelbyville, Ill., April 26, 1838. Her parents were John and Ann S. Perryman, he of North Carolina and she of Ireland. To Mr. and Mrs. Denny was born a family, of whom three daughters are now living—Annie L., Katie M. and Lizzie S. Mr. Denny was in the mercantile business ten years, bank cashier thirteen years, County Superintendent of Schools five years, Township Treasurer about ten years, and Treasurer of Greenville City for several terms. His politics, Democratic; his religion, Christian; is a member of the I. O. O. F. and A. O. U. W. His grandfather, James Denny, came West with his family from North Carolina and located at McCord, now Cottonwood, where he was engaged in farming.

NATHANIEL DRESSOR, banker and farmer, P. O. Greenville, was born June 24, 1825, in the State of Maine; son of Rufus and Tamer Dressor, both natives of New England. His father emigrated to Bond County in October, 1837, and was there engaged in farming and milling. The subject was the fourth child of a family of five sons and two daughters; his education was received in the common schools; he was a very successful farmer and a shrewd financier, being President of the First National Bank of Greenville. He married Elizabeth S. McFarlan, daughter of Robert McFarlan, a farmer. They had five children—Alenia, now Mrs. John W. McCord, of Milan, Ill.; Charlotte, deceased at the age of twenty-five, was an accomplished, thoroughly educated lady, being a graduate of McKendree College; Edwin, a farmer, near Greenville; Roxanna, deceased 1878; Julia, deceased 1880, was the wife of William A. Northcott, present State's Attorney of Bond County; and Winnie, now in school. Is a member of the old Republican party, and always a strong Union man.

EDWIN W. DRESSOR, farmer, P. O. Greenville, is the only son of Nathaniel Dressor. He was born in Cottonwood Grove, on the homestead farm, December 12, 1854; he was raised to farming and trading pursuits, and remained under the parental roof until his marriage, March 7, 1877, when he cast his lot in a matrimonial way with Mary M. Kirkland, a native of Walshville Township, Montgomery County, this State; she was a daughter of T. C. Kirkland, one of the prominent farmers and business men of Montomery County. Immediately after his marriage he located on the farm he now occupies, in this township, where he has since been engaged in farming and stock-trading, being one of the largest dealers of his age in the county. He has had two children born him; but one living Edith Mabel, born Aug. 11, 1880.

WILLIAM M. EVANS was born in Bath County, Ky., March 12, 1819; son of Thomas and Anna (Martin) Evans, he a native of Kentucky, born in Bath County May 27, 1799, and died August 19, 1870; she, a native of Virginia, was born March 6, 1798, and died September 15, 1847; they had eleven children, all of whom lived to maturity, William M. being the eldest. Our subject came to Illinois in 1845, from Indiana, settling in Bureau County, and, in 1855, came to Greenville and commenced the cabinet business, in which he continued until the war broke out, when he sold his business, and, in 1864, entered the 100-day service in the Union army, remaining four months. In 1856, Mr. Evans was one of the prime movers in the organization of the Republican party in Bond County; was a delegate to the Convention in 1858, that nominated Abraham Lincoln for Congress; in 1860, member of State Convention at Decatur, Ill., and went from there to Chicago to labor in the interest of Mr. Lincoln; was member of State Convention in 1862; in 1880, was a delegate to State Convention at Springfield; in 1876, he was elected to represent his (Forty second) district in the Lower Branch of the General Assembly of the State. After leaving the army, he commenced merchandising, in which he continued until 1877. On August 11, 1840, Mr. Evans married Miss Lovica Young, born in Virginia October 12, 1819; daughter of Charles Young, who died in 1851, leaving two children. December 28, 1852, he married Mary C. Hubbard, born in Bond County Ill., January 12, 1822; daughter of Peter Hubbard, of Hennepin, Putnam Co., Ill. His oldest son Daniel B., is clerk in First National Bank, and his other son, Woodford P., is a farmer in Iowa. The father of Mr. Evans moved to Iowa in 1854, where he died.

MOSES W. ELAM, farmer, P. O. Smithboro, is the third child born and eldest son of Moses Elam, of Town 6, Range 2. Moses W. was born March 3, 1853, on the homestead near Mulberry Grove. He was brought up on the farm, and made his father's house his home until maturity. He was married when twenty years of age. His nuptials were celebrated December, 1873; his wife was Cypha Morey, born in Knox County, Ohio daughter of Lucius Morey and Ruth Ann Cumston. Lucius was born 1828, in Knox County; son of David Morey, a native of Vermont, who emigrated to Knox County, and there settled as a pioneer. Ruth Ann was born in Pennsylvania, daughter of Benjamin Cumston. Mrs. Elam came to Fayette County with her parents in 1865. Her mother died in 1868, leaving two children— Mrs. Elam, and Inez, who married Thomas, the brother of her husband. After Mr. Elam's marriage, he removed to Fayette County, living there five years, then returned to this county, where they have since lived, locating on their farm in the fall of 1880. Said farm consists of 160 acres on the northeast quarter of Section 5. He has three children Wilbur, Rose and Daisey. He and wife are members of the Christian Church.

JOEL ELAM, manufacturer, Greenville, was born in North Carolina, December 9, 1817; son of Edward and Letitia (Clayton) Elam, he a native of Virginia and a Cla smith by trade; they had a family of fifteen children, Joel being the youngest. Our subject, after receiving an ordinary education, learned the blacksmith's trade, in Greenville, and at present is engaged in that business and saw milling with his sons, Thomas and John, under the firm name of Elam & Sons. Mr. Elam has been married four times: first in 1843, to Nancy Clay, in Menard County, Ill.; she died the first year of her marriage; second, Sarah E. Smith, in 1845, who died the same year, leaving one child—Charles Edward, now deceased; third, Sarah McCormick, of Greenville, she had two sons—William and Thomas; fourth, Sarah White, of Greenville, who has three daughters and one son—Ellen, Sarah, Miriam and John. Mr. Elam is a Presbyterian and Republican.

GEORGE B. ENLOE, farmer, P. O. Greenville; born Aug. 7, 1848, on the homestead situated in Town 6, Range 2, where his father, Ezekiel Enloe, settled and remained until his death. The mother of George B. was Charlotte White, who was born in North Carolina, daughter of Richard White. Eight children were born to Ezekiel Enloe and wife. The eldest was Marshall, then in order of birth came Claybourne, Thomas, William Edward, Mary E., Benjamin and George B., who was the youngest one of the family. He married Susan E. Foster, a native of this State, daughter of William Foster. Four children, Johnnie, William, Della and Ezekiel, are the issue of this marriage. In 1873, he located on his farm, where he now resides, having about 120 acres, selected on the south half of Section 31. He has one brother, Edward, in this township, and William in Town 6, Range 3. Mary E. married D. H. Kingsbury, and resides in Greenville. Mr. E. had two brothers in the late war.

CHARLES W. FLOYD, farmer, P. O. Greenville, is a native of Kentucky, Todd County. He was born in 1822, and was a resident of his native State until 1833, when he came with his parents to Bond County. His father's name was John W., a Kentuckian by birth, and was a son of Charles Floyd, of Old Virginia. John W. Floyd married Betsy Johnson, a native of Indiana. To Mr. Floyd was born a family of ten children, viz., Ella married P. G. Vowter; Nancy became the wife of William Harlin; Polly, Mrs. W. Blackwell, George; Jane, Mrs. D. P. Hagee; Charles W.; William J.; Sarah, Mrs. W. D. Henry; John S., and Thomas W., who was a physician. In February, 1844, he married Eliza Henry, daughter of John Henry, a Kentuckian. After his marriage, he located in the edge of Clinton County. In 1849, he entered land in this county, one mile east of Wisetown. Moving on the same, he began improving it. In 1852, he moved south to Texas, and purchased land in Grayson County, and engaged in farming and stock raising, remaining here until 1866, when he located on the farm he now owns, on Section 33, Town 6, Range 3, in Greenville Precinct. He has a fine location, one of the best in the precinct; he is a good farmer and has been successful in his business; his wife died June 22, 1877; he has four children—Jane, the eldest, and is the wife of E. D. Wallace; George A., Mary and Charles H. The father of our subject was for many years a member of the Methodist Episcopal Church; and served in the war of 1812, and died in 1846; and during his his life was affiliated with the old Whig party.

JAMES P. FILE, farmer, P. O. Greenville, born in Bond County, Ill., March 5, 1850. He was the son of George and Mary (Lyttaker) File, he a farmer and distiller, died in 1858, and she in Bond County, Ill. Our subject received part of his education in New Douglas, Madison County, and part in Bond County, Ill., where, in 1870,

January 6, he married Ella E. Bolton, daughter of John and Sarah Bolton, natives of Ohio. To Mr. and Mrs. File were born five children—Charles H., Louella B., Edwin N. (deceased), George J. P. and Alberta J. Mr. File has always been a farmer. He was School Director for three years; his political views are with the Democrats; he is also a member of the Masonic order. He is a young man, thirty-two years of age; he has an excellent farm, which by his energy and industry, he has rendered very valuable.

DR. JAMES GORDON, Greenville, for eighteen years a practicing physician of Bond County, is a native of Huntsville, Ala., and was born on the 17th of January, 1818. Is a son of Hugh Gordon and Martha Jane, née J[illegible], his wife. His father, a native of South Carolina, born in 1788, settled in Alabama in 1816, and though a slaveholder, was a Whig in politics, and advocated emancipation. He died December 3, 1851; his mother, also a native of South Carolina, was born in Chester District in 1798, died January 3, 1849. James received his early education in the common schools of his native place, and in his youth imbibed those habits of industry that have characterized his busy life. He united with the Methodist Episcopal Church at an early age and spent three years studying with a view to entering the ministry, but his mind gradually inclined to the study of the science of medicine and he abandoned his purpose and entered the Memphis Medical College. After completing his studies, he entered upon the practice of his profession in Mississippi, and continued it there and in Arkansas until 1864, when he became a resident of Jamestown, Clinton Co., Ill. Practicing there till February, 1870, he removed to Greenville, where he has built up an extensive practice. In the spring of 1875, the Missouri Medical College conferred upon him the *ad eundem* degree. In early life, he became a member of the Masonic fraternity and has advanced to the Royal Arch degree. Dr. Gordon has been twice married, first in Huntsville, Ala., December 22, 1835, to Miss Mary Ann Sanderson, of Madison County, Ala., born September 22, 1819, daughter of James and Elizabeth (Bell) Sanderson, the former born in 1789, died February 5, 1853, the latter born in Chester District, South Carolina, in 1793, died in 1862. She died in 1860, leaving twelve children—Mary E., Hugh D., James B., John H., William P., Jerry T., Sarah F., Martha J., Robert W., Rufus B. and two others who died without names. He again married in the month of June, 1860, to Mary Jane Marshall, born in Johnson County, Ark., August 26, 1837, daughter of Joseph N. and Annis R. (Neeley) Marshall, the former still living, born in Tennessee in 1800, the latter also born the same year, died January 6, 1858. By the second marriage he has had ten children. Of the twenty-two, ten are now living—Madison D., Margaret A., Ferdinand R., Katie L., Emma H., Hattie M., Thomas F., James M. and two others who died without names. Five of this number are married and are parents of his thirty grandchildren; two of his children have died after having married. Dr. Madison D. is the only one now of age not married. Of his family seven sons have become practicing physicians, and four of those now living, including Madison D., his present partner, are in active practice. Dr. Gordon is a Republican in politics, but does not take active part in political contests. He is independent in thought, social and genial in his manner and inflexible in purpose. He has attained success in his profession and life by close application and a strict adherence to principles of Justice.

A. J. GULLICK, Sheriff of Bond County and insurance, Greenville, was born in Mad i[illegible]n County, Ill., October 27, 1827, son of Beniah and Elizabeth (Ginglis) Gullick, he a native of North Carolina, a wagon-maker by trade, now deceased; she of same State, also deceased. They had five children, only two of whom are now living, our subject being the eldest. He was educated in the common schools of his native county, and for some years followed peddling, being so successful as to accumulate enough to purchase a farm. He came to Bond County in 1852, locating at Mulberry Grove. Mr. Gullick was elected Sheriff of Bond County in 1872, and served three terms of two years each. In 1880, he was again elected to the shrievalty, and is now serving in that office, which he fills admirably, acceptably, and with a faithfulness to duty and the rights of his fellow citizens that will make his retirement from the position a matter of regret among all classes. September 20, 1857, he married Miss Eliza A. Dudley, daughter of Mr. Alfred Dudley, a pioneer and farmer of Bond County, and the following children have been born to them: Seward A., Mason E., Harris A., Ruda E., Nellie E., Walter A., Pearl D., and an infant son unnamed. Mr. Gullick is a Freemason, an Odd Fellow, member of the A. O. U. W., and a Republican.

ULRICH GAFFNER, farmer, P. O. Greenville. Of the representatives of this township none are more deserving than the above gentleman, who has made himself what he is to-day all by honest industry and rigid economy. He was born in Switzerland, August 22, 18[illegible]; son of Ulrich, who was born in Canton Bern in 1801; his wife was Mary Smocher, daughter of John Smocher, a native of Switzerland. The father of our subject was a farmer, which vocation our subject was early taught in life, in company with his brothers, who are yet at home in Switzerland, and engaged in farming on their own possessions, except one of the brothers, Godfrey, who emigrated to this State in 1857, and is now a prominent farmer in Christian County, this State. Ulrich, having heard very favorable accounts of America, and the advantages afforded the laboring man here, which so far surpassed those at home, that he determined to emigrate to this country, which he did, arriving here in May, 1860. He began working out by the month and saving his earnings, until he acquired sufficient means to enable him to make a purchase of land on his own account. His farm consists of 13[illegible] acres; the greater portion he bought of [illegible] H. Ko[illegible]mee, situated on Section 31. He was married in 1864, to Sarah Sahnert, born in Hesse-Darmstadt, daughter of Peter and Elizabeth (Wyandt) Sahnert. To Mr. Gaffner have been born five children—Lizzie A., William, Mollie A., Lois and Edward—who have crowned this union. Mr. Gaffner is a man that has a high regard for right and justice, and has no desire to do injury to any one, but to live an honest and upright life, and he is a good citizen in the community. He is a member of the Lutheran Church, as well as a stanch, worthy citizen of the community.

ANDREW G. HENRY, Greenville, County Judge of Bond County, and son of John and Betsey Henry, was born February 28, 182[illegible], near Paris, Bourbon Co., Ky. His parents removed to Illinois in 1827, and settled in the north part of Clinton County, where they resided a few years, and then removed to near Beaver Creek Post Office in Bond County, where they resided until Mr. Henry reached his majority. He secured as good an education as the limited school facilities of the county at that time afforded, the studies consisting only of the common English branches. Securing such books as he could for study and general reading, he pursued his studies at home working on the farm and at the carpenter's trade. In 1851, he was married to his present wife, Mary A. Hull, daughter of the late Benjamin Hull, of Bond County. In 1853, he began the study of law, and in 1854 he removed to Greenville, the county seat of Bond County, and was admitted to the practice of the law at the bar, and has practiced in Bond and adjoining counties ever since, devoting himself largely to that department of law belonging to real estate. Upon the organization of the Republican party he warmly espoused its cause, and attended its first State convention, which met at Decatur, Ill., in 1856. He was a warm supporter of Abraham Lincoln for President, and after his inauguration as President, was an earnest supporter of all the war measures of the administration, and from that time has indorsed all the leading measures and the general policy of his party, taking an active part in all its campaigns. In 1872, he was elected to the Lower House of the Legislature, and re-elected again in 1874, serving with marked ability and to the entire satisfaction of his constituents. In 1877, he was elected County Judge of Bond County, which office he now holds. Mr. Henry was one of the originators of what is now the Vandalia Line Railroad, being a large subscriber to the stock of the original company, and through the efforts of himself and a few other prominent citizens of Greenville, Bond County is indebted for that railroad. Mr. Henry has held a [illegible] as Director in the company ever since its organization. Mr. Henry's family consists of himself, wife and two daughters, one of whom is the wife of George F. Berry, of Greenville; the other is still at home. Mr. Henry is always benevolent, aiding every worthy cause, and is kind and courteous to all. Being a man of strong convictions of right, and earnest in maintaining them, he is a man with strong personal friends and followers, and as would necessarily follow, occasionally he makes an enemy; but at home among his neighbors, and wherever he is known, no man stands higher than does the Hon. A. G. Henry, the subject of this sketch.

CHARLES DOUGLAS HOILES, banker, Greenville, was born in Greenville, December 1, 1844, son of Charles and Elizabeth S. (Morse) Hoiles, he a native of New Jersey, born in 1819, and for many years a prominent and successful business man of Bond County; she a native of Lowell, Mass.; they had two children—Charles D., our subject, and Stephen M. Mr. Hoiles received his early education in Greenville, later at Mount Union, and still later at Shurtleff College, Upper Alton, Ill., but mostly at select schools in Greenville, under Prof. S. W. Marston. He commenced his business life in the mercantile business with his father, which lasted five years, when they entered the banking business under the firm name of Hoiles & Son. S. M. Hoiles, the brother of our subject, was admitted to the firm in 1872, which changed it to Hoiles & Sons. The father retired from the business in 1881. Mr. C. D. Hoiles was a member of the Twenty-eighth Official General Assembly of the State of Illinois in 1872; delegate to the National Democratic Convention at Baltimore, which nominated Horace Greeley; twice a member of the Democratic Central Committee; once a member for the State at large; candidate for nomination before the Democratic Congressional Convention, to represent the Sixteenth Congressional District in the National Legislature. The convention held sessions for three days and adjourned without making a choice. He is now serving his second term as Mayor of the city of Greenville. He was first married to Miss Sarah F. Weir, daughter of Dr. John Weir, of Edwardsville, Ill.; she died June 30

1874, leaving one son, Charles W., and one daughter, Ione. He again married in June, 1876, Miss Juliette P. White, daughter of Prof. John B. White, long connected with the educational interests of Bond County. From this last marriage, have been born a son, Guy B., and a daughter, Anna L.

STEPHEN M. HOILES, banker, is a brother of the gentleman whose sketch appears above, and was also born in Greenville, on the 8th of April, 1853. He is a member (as stated above) of the banking house of Hoiles & Sons, and, like his brother, is one of the best business men of the county. December 20, 1871, he married Miss Welma C. Stoughtenberry, daughter of Jacob S. Stoughtenberry, deceased, who was a resident and capitalist of Madison County, Ill. They have three children—Stephen D., Clarence E. and Sarah Bell. Stephen M., like his brother, is a Democrat.

T. S. HUBBARD, farmer, P. O. Greenville, was born March 9, 1815, in Madison County, this State, eldest son of Peter Hubbard, a native of South Carolina, born February 23, 1782, and emigrated to Randolph County, this State, in 1809, remaining but a short time, when he removed to Madison County prior to the war of 1812, in which he participated. In March, 1817, he located in what is now Bond County, on Section 1, Town 5, Range 3, where he remained until his death, which occurred November 25, 1868, his wife preceded him to the grave in 1854. They raised a family of eight children—T. S., being the eldest that grew up, George W., Lewellyn B., Mary A., William C., Isom G., John T. and Margaret J. were the others in order of birth. The Hubbard family are of Welsh ancestry, both the father, grand and great grandfather of our subject bore the old Bible name of Peter. The mother of T. S. was Martha, daughter of Thomas Gillham. Thomas S. was reared to farm labor, and was educated at the common schools of his neighborhood. He was but two years of age when he came to this county. In early manhood, he was appointed to teach his district school of this township, now No. 2, in the year 1848, by subscription, being the first teacher who taught there. He liked mathematics, and learned surveying, which he put into practice for some time as Deputy Surveyor of the county. In this county, February 3, 1843, he married Anna E., daughter of Asa L. and Ann E. (Wright) Saunders. In 1841, he purchased land where he now resides, then raw and unimproved. After his marriage, located on the same, has since continued a constant resident, and is one of the stanch and substantial citizens of the county. Since 1843, he has been a consistent member of the Congregational Church, serving as Deacon and Trustee of the same much of the time. In business, he has been successful, having (before he divided out among his children) about 700 acres of land. In educational matters, he has taken an active part in his neighborhood. His children are Lewis S., Julian S., Harriet L., Henry A., George C., Alfred C. and Mary J. Julian S., in Kansas; George C., in Iowa; others are settled in this county.

HENRY HILL, farmer, P. O. Greenville, born May 29, 1814, in Seneca County, N. Y., the eldest son and third child born to Henry Hill, his father, who was born November 26, 1790, in one of the Eastern States. November 16, 1809, he married Abigail Shutz, who was born April 5, 1791. To them were born the following children, the old family Bible tells the following tale: Nancy M., born October 30, 1810; Sally, May 30, 1812; Henry, May 29, 1814; Theodosia, March 15, 1816; Rosana, April 29, 1818; Polly, August 1, 1820; Ruann, August 7, 1822; William, April 19, 1825; Melinda, November 2, 1827; Jonathan, July

10, 1830; Clarissa, November, 1832. The father died January 16, 1852, his wife April 17, 1844. When five years of age, our subject removed with his parents to Montgomery County, Ohio, remaining there until 1842, when they came to this State, locating in Madison County. In 1868, he came to Bond County, locating on the northwest quarter of Section 31; here he has since lived. He has 272 acres of land. He began poor, had nothing but his lands and a willing mind to battle with the times in which he was surrounded, yet by diligence and rigid economy, he has acquired a home and competence by hard labor and patient industry. March 11, 1849, he married Mrs. Nancy Glenn, born in this county, daughter of Daniel Moore, who was born February 6, 1792, in Rutherford County, N. C., son of Philip Moore, from Virginia; he (Philip) married Phebe Elam, of North Carolina. Daniel Moore married Jane Stewart, who was born in North Carolina, April 13, 1804, daughter of Robert Stewart and Jane Turntine. Robert was a son of Alexander Stewart an Irishman by birth. Daniel Moore and family came to Bond County in 1818, making first settlement on Section 19, Town 5, Range 2. Mr. Hill has had eleven children born to him, five living: Daniel, George, James, Lemuel and Samuel. Belle died September 18, 1881, aged twenty-two years. She married Smith Long; by him had two children—Charlie and Marion.

[illegible] W. HILL, retired, P. O. Greenville, was born in New Milford, Litchfield Co., Conn., on June 6, 1821. His father, Roswell Hill, born July 12, 1788, died October 16, 1844, also a native of New England, was a school teacher and emigrated West about 1827. His mother, Frances (Buckingham), born April 16, 1791, died January 27, 1864, was also a New Englander. They were the parents of six sons and two daughters, the subject being the third son. He got his education in a common school in Ross County, Ohio, and commenced life as an apprentice to William Gilmore, tailor, Ohio, at the age of fifteen. He moved to this county in 1840, and with the exception of eight months in 1844, when he lived in Hillsboro, Montgomery County, he has been a resident and business man in Greenville, and up to 1867 was a prominent and prosperous merchant. In Edwardsville, Madison Co., Ill., on August 25, 1847, he married Elizabeth Barnes Plant, born, October 28, 1828, in Pocahontas, Bond Co., Ill., daughter of Williamson and Martha (Sugg) Plant, he born in Anson County, N. C., May 6, 1799, died May 12, 1833; she, born in North Carolina, died November 21, 1834. Subject has gained his position as one of the most frugal, thrifty and just-minded citizens of Bond County, by pursuing a straightforward course, doing business on business principles and making most of his time and opportunities.

W. McLIN HUNTER, Greenville, was born in Bond County March 17, 1827; son of Joseph and Elizabeth (Mabin) Hunter, he born in 1795, she in 1793, and both dying within one week of each other, in 1851. They were the parents of seven children, four boys and three girls. Our subject received a very limited education in the schools of his native county, and has always been a farmer. He has served as School Director and Road Supervisor, but has generally avoided politics and the seeker after office. November 28, 1850, in Zion Precinct, he married Nancy R. Glenn, born in Zion November 11, 1832, daughter of Alexander and Frances Glenn, and eleven children have gladdened his household. Joseph F., Alexander K., Robert M., John R., Francis E., Betsey A., Mary J., Sophia E., Susan E., Laura B. and Finis E. Mr. Hunter and family are Cumberland Presbyterians, and he is a Democrat. The Hunters were among the earliest settlers of this section, and McLin Hunter now lives upon and owns the old homestead property, consisting of 280 acres, in Section 24.

MARSHALL HUNTER, farmer, P. O. Pocahontas, was born in Bond County March 1, 1820, son of Joseph and Elizabeth (Mabin) Hunter, he born in Tennessee in 1795, a farmer, dying in 1851; she, a native of N. Carolina, and dying one week succeeding her husband, leaving seven children, four boys and three girls. Our subject received his education in the subscription schools of his native county, and began life as a farmer, in which occupation he has continued throughout his entire life. He has served as Road Supervisor several years, and is very highly esteemed as a man and a farmer. His farm comprises 244½ acres of excellent land, which is under a high state of cultivation. In Zion Precinct, October 1, 1846, he married Miss Elizabeth M. Glenn, born July 25, 1826, a daughter of Alexander and Frances Glenn, and which union has resulted in seven children—Frances E., Armina, Emily J., Mary E., Sarah E., Joseph W. and Ida A. Mr. Hunter is a member of the Cumberland Presbyterian Church and a Democrat.

SOLOMON HARKEY, farmer, P. O. Greenville, was born July 28, 1852, in the northern part of Bond County, Ill.; son of William Harkey, a farmer, who was born in North Carolina April 29, 1811, and came to Illinois at an early date. His mother, Nancy (Thacker) Harkey, was born in Kentucky January 1, 1814. The subject is the youngest of a family of nine, eight of whom are still living. He received a common school education at La Grange Precinct. He followed farming about fifteen years; later, he went into the restaurant business at Hillsboro, Montgomery Co., Ill., and still later was in the grocery business. He was married February 19, 1874, in Bond County, to Caroline Prater, daughter of John and Sallie (Hunt) Prater. His wife dying, he again, December 9, 1874, married Laura Wright, daughter of George W. and Emily (Able) Wright. He had three children—William L., Hattie V. and Minnie A. The latter is by his second wife. He was a Republican in politics.

JOHN W. JETT, farmer, P. O. Greenville, was born December 11, 1820, in Culpepper County, Va., and emigrated to this State in 1836, and located in Bond County with his parents, where he has since resided. The family first located on Jett Prairie in Town 6, Range 2. In September, 1842, he married Miss Sophia B. Blanchard who was born June 30, 1825, in East Stoughton, Mass.; daughter of Lemuel Blanchard and Sibyl Packard, both natives of the Bay State. The same year of his marriage, he located in the northwest corner of this township and engaged in farming, where he remained until 1866, when he purchased a farm in the southwest part of the same township, on Section 31, where he located and has since resided, having 240 acres; has but one son living, Warren, who was born January 22, 1853, and October 31, 1877, he married Mollie Smith, born in this county, daughter of Theodore and Margaret (Allen) Smith. Mr. Jett is a member of the Regular Baptist Church, and a Republican. Our subject was a son of Francis Jett, who was born 1792, in Culpepper County, Va. He served as a soldier in the war of 1812. He married Elizabeth Wood, a native of Fauquier Co., Va., daughter of Dickinson Wood, who married a Miss Weather. Francis Jett died in this county in 1859; his wife survived him until 1877. Daniel, Gabriel, John H., James and William were the children born to them; all are now deceased except John H., the subject of these remarks. The children of our subject are Helen C., Eunice A., Mary E., Warren, Edward, Harry Lee and Frances W.

E. P. JUSTICE, merchant, Greenville, one of the most prosperous business men of the thriving little city of Greenville, was born January 5, 1840, in Clinton County, Ill. His father, J. J. Justice, a retired farmer of Carlisle, same county, is a native of Georgia; came to Illinois when about nine years of age. Of his four children, our subject is the only one now living. He lived on his father's farm in Clinton County most of his life previous to coming to Greenville. In November, 1876, he opened his present business, with an entire new stock of groceries, provisions, hardware, willow-ware, etc. The first year's business was one beset with the difficulties that must attend the efforts of a young man with a small capital in establishing a trade; but since that time, by close application, and strict adherence to business principles, his business has steadily increased, and he now controls a fine trade. Mr. Justice first married Miss Mary Crocker, of Clinton County, Ill., in 1862. She died in 1874, leaving two children. One, Alice E., is now living. He again married, July 6, 1879, to Miss Mary E. Curlee, of Greenville, and a native of Bond County.

DR. N. H. JACKSON, surgeon dentist, Greenville, Ill., was born in Warren County, Ky., May 20, 1853. He is a son of C. C. Jackson, born in 1820, who was a native of Virginia, and by occupation a farmer. C. C. Jackson was one of the pioneers of Kentucky, in which State he spent most of his life, and there died in 1861, at forty-one years of age. His wife, Sarah Jackson, *nee* Hendrick, was born in 1830, and now of Bowling Green, Ky., is a native of Warren County, that State, and daughter of John R. Hendrick (deceased), who was a Cumberland Presbyterian clergyman. Dr. Jackson is the second of a family of five children, four of whom are living. He received his rudimental eduaction at Bristow, Ky., his native home. He after studied the higher branches at Bowling Green, and when but a youth apprenticed himself to an uncle, Dr. J. F. Hendrick, an eminently successful dentist of Bowling Green, Ky., and under his tuition gained a thorough and practical mastery of the dental profession. September 29, 1878, Dr. Jackson married Miss Ida A. Gracey, born September 27, 1861, in Macoupin County, Ill., daughter of W. C. and Sarah J. (McGahey) Gracey. Her father is a well-known farmer of Pleasant Prairie, Bond County. In November, 1880, the Doctor permanently located in Greenville, where he has built up a lucrative and steadily increasing practice. Mr. Jackson's success is entirely due to his thorough knowledge of his profession and ability to do first-class work. He has commodious rooms in the Coverdale Block.

JOHN C. JACKSON, farmer, P. O. Greenville, was born in Tennessee December 28, 1826; son of Larkin and Anna (Parker) Jackson, he a native of North Carolina, a farmer by occupation, dying in 1869, his consort having preceded him to their last resting-place in 1864. They were the parents of sixteen children, ten boys and six girls. Our subject attended the schools of Lawrenceburg, Tenn., and began life as a farmer, in which occupation he has continued since, being one of the most successful farmers of Bond County. He is highly respected, is energetic and foremost in all that may redound to the good of his community and the welfare of the public generally. He has served as School Director and Road Supervisor several terms. He is a Republican. In Greenville Precinct, October 4, 1848, he married Miss Eleanor Jane Nelson, daughter of Calvin and Mary F. Nelson, natives of Virginia, and three children have been the fruit of the union Mary M., William Calvin (deceased), and John.

C. H. KOONCE, farmer, P. O. Greenville. The Koonce family emigrated to the Sucker State in the year 1840. They were natives of the Old Dominion, Jefferson County, near Harper's Ferry, where our subject was born January 31, 1825; son of Nicholas Koonce, whose birthplace was Loudoun County; son of Henry Koonce, who was likewise of Virginia birth. The mother of our subject was Elizabeth, a native of Loudoun, daughter of Christopher Schriver, who was a native of Germany. Ten children were born to Nicholas Koonce, seven sons and three daughters. Nicholas Koonce was a farmer and mechanic; he worked several years in the arsenal at Harper's Ferry; also in a mill, and turned his attention readily to anything of a mechanical nature. Our subject emigrated West with his parents when he was about fourteen years of age. His father rented land some time east of Greenville, finally located on Section 31, in this township, and remained until his death, which occurred several years prior to the late civil war. His wife still survives him, being nearly ninety years of age. The family born them are as follows: David, Sarah, George, John, Jacob, Christopher H., Elizabeth, Nicholas, Joseph and Mary. But two are living in this township, C. H. and Elizabeth, wife of J. C. Lovett. Joseph resides in township adjoining. In October, 1850, our subject married Jane Wait, of Alexandria, Va., daughter of William Wait. Mr. Koonce resides on the farm he entered and improved, consisting of 225 acres; has six children, viz.: Charles, Josiah, Lucy, Angie, George and Hattie. His brother, Nicholas, resides in the south part of the State, a short distance above Cairo. The remaining brothers living are now residents of Virginia, having returned there to spend their remaining life in the land that gave birth to their progenitors.

JOHN KINGSBURY, attorney at law, Greenville, was born February 7, 1837, in Hamilton County, Ind. He was the son of Ira and Hannah (Fierce) Kingsbury; he was a surveyor and farmer, born in Vermont and died on his homestead in 1872, October 26. His wife Hannah was born in Hamilton County, Ind. Our subject was their fifth child. He received his education in the common schools of the county, and also attended the Greenville Academy, in 1859-60. In 1873, September 25, at Hagarstown, Ill. he married Sarah J. Jay, who was born in Bond County, Ill. She was the daughter of Joseph A. and Nancy A. (Rhea) Jay. Joseph A. was born December 19, 1826, in North Carolina, and Nancy A., his wife, July 1, 1831, in Tennessee. Subject had a family of four—John M., Mary G., Anna G. C. and Lucy N. Mr. Kingsbury remained at home and worked the farm, supporting his aged father, and when thirty six years of age began studying law with D. H. Kingsbury, at Greenville, and was admitted to practice in the courts of this State in 1870, which he continued until he was elected County Surveyor, at which he is now serving his third term. His religion was that of a Baptist, his politics Democratic, and was a member of the A. O. U. W. and I. O. M. A. orders. His father, Ira Kingsbury, came to Bond County, Ill., in June, 1844, and at the time of his death he owned 320 acres of land. His mother died at Mt. Carmel, Ill., November 28, 1843.

WILLIAM KOCH, Treasurer-elect of the city of Greenville, is a native of Germany, and came to America in the year 1849; landed at New Orleans, sailed up the Mississippi River to St. Louis, thence into Illinois overland to Vandalia, Fayette County, and entered farming about ten miles north of that place. His success as a farmer soon enabled him to purchase a second farm about two and one-half miles northwest of Vandalia. He moved on to the latter purchase, and there remained until 1869, when he sold and removed to Greenville, and entered the lumber trade with Mr. J. C. Gerrichs as his partner. He closed out his interest in 1882, and retired from business. He has the esteem and confidence of his fellow-citizens, and was elected to the office of Treasurer of the city of Greenville in the spring of that same year.

JOHN C. LOVETT, farmer, P. O. Greenville, first saw the light of day August 29, 1825, in Tolland County, Conn.; son of John G. Lovett, born in same county and State October 30, 1780, son of James, of English descent and was a soldier in the Revolutionary war. The mother of our subject was Roxana Chapman. Her father was Hosea, of English descent. The family trace their ancestry back several hundred years. The Lovett family emigrated to this State in 1837, arriving here in the fall of the same year, and for four years lived in Town 5, Range 3; afterward moved southwest on a farm now owned by Smiley Denney. While here he entered the land upon which he afterward settled in 1846, and remained on the same until his death July, 1854. His wife survived him until April, 1864. He was for many years a member of the Congregational Church. He was a strong Whig, and advocated its principles. He had born him the following children: Christiana, Juliana, Orestes H., Delia, John C., Francis M. Of this number but two are living Orestes, who has resided in Washington Territory since 1849, and John C., who was brought up under the care of his parents receiving good school advantages and before coming of age began teaching, which he continued for several years. [illegible] located on the homestead and since lived there. He has four children Julia Adelaide, Christiana Louise, Charlotte Alberta, Francis Jacob. Since 1839, he has been a member of the Congregational Church. He has [illegible] acres of excellent land.

JAMES M. McADAMS, County Treasurer, Greenville, was born June 13, 1828, in Greenville Precinct, son of Samuel G. and Priscilla (Smith) McAdams, he born near Nashville, Tenn., December 8, 1813, and was killed December 13, 1864, while arresting deserters in Bond County; she, born in Indiana, and died in 1844; they had five children. Our subject was raised to farming, and followed stock raising for a number of years; was elected County Treasurer and Assessor in 1879. In 1861, he enlisted in the Twenty-second Illinois Infantry, as a private, and the same year was elected Second Lieutenant; next year promoted to First Lieutenant, and was honorably discharged in 1864. February 16, 1865, he married Miss Fannie Smith, born in Clark County, Ohio, March [illegible], 1845, daughter of Samuel Smith, a native of the eastern shore of Maryland, and two children have blessed the union Samuel S. and Nellie M. Mr. McAdams is a Republican and an enterprising, go-ahead man for the times, and makes a popular and efficient officer. The father of Mr. McAdams was in the Mexican war, a Captain the Twenty-second Illinois Volunteer Infantry for three years, and afterward Captain in the One Hundred and Thirty-fifth Regiment. His only brother was a member of the Third Illinois Volunteer Cavalry during the rebellion.

T. P. MOREY, Circuit Clerk and Recorder of Bond County, was born September 2[illegible], 184[illegible], at Mulberry Grove, Bond County; [illegible]

ing on his homestead at Mulberry Grove: she, a native of Tennessee, born May 4, 1827, and died August 25, 1875. They had ten children. In addition to the ordinary common school education, our subject attended McKendree College. In 1867, he commenced teaching school, which he continued for six years. In 1876, he was elected to the positions he now so ably fills—Circuit Clerk and Recorder of Bond County. September 27, 1873, at Mulberry Grove, he married Miss Ollie Borror, born in Franklin County, Ohio, December 26, 1848, daughter of Mr. Isaac Borror. The people of Bond County have shown their appreciation of a capable and faithful official in retaining Mr. Morey so many years in the responsible positions he occupies, and when he retires from them, it will be with the regret of his many friends, both inside and outside of his party.

GEORGE C. McCORD, Greenville, Deputy United States Marshal. Mr. McCord was born November 15, 1835, at Nashville, Washington Co., Ill. His father, Charles A. McCord, was a Methodist preacher of Southern Illinois, and was a native of Christian County Ky. His mother was one Mary Patterson, daughter of Joseph Patterson, a farmer of the State of Georgia, which was the State of her birth, and she died in 1844, at thirty-six years of age. Charles A. McCord had eight children; six lived to maturity. He entered the ministry at twenty-two years of age, and continued his ministerial labors until his death June 24, 1861. He was a second time married to Mrs. Jane Lemon, of Washington County, Ill., and two of his eight children were by his last wife. George C. received his rudimental education in the public schools of Washington County, Ill., and closed his school days with a brief course at the Nashville Academy. He entered farming and stock raising in Bond County, and made that his business until 1875. October 11, 1862, Mr. McCord was commissioned Second Lieutenant of Company B, One Hundred and Eleventh Illinois Volunteer Infantry, by Gov. Yates. This regiment served three years in the war. March 2, 1863, he was made a First Lieutenant. In 1867, Mr. McCord was appointed Deputy United States Marshal by United States Marshal E. R. Rose, and was re-appointed in 1880. During his term of office he has made 470 arrests. July 29, 1881, Gov. S. M. Cullom, having special confidence in his ability, patriotism and valor, appointed him his aid-de-camp, and commissioned him Commander in Chief of the Illinois State troops in the Sixteenth Congressional District, with a rank as Colonel. It is needless to say that Col. McCord makes a very acceptable and efficient officer. Col. McCord first married, November 1, 1856, to Miss Altha A. Means, daughter of Josiah Means, a farmer of Christian County, Ill. She died March 22, 1861, leaving one daughter, Rosa B., now an efficient teacher in the graded schools of Greenville, and one son, Charles R., present Assistant Surgeon in the Illinois State Prison, at Chester. Mr. McCord again married, March 8, 1863, to Miss Ella R. Donnell, youngest daughter of the lamented George Donnell, one of Bond County's most respected pioneers. They have three children living —Ella, George A. and Emma H. Emily died in infancy.

ABE McNEILL, banker, Greenville, is a native of Clinton County, Ill., son of Neilly and Minerva (Mills) McNeill, he born in Ireland, and she in Kentucky. They had nine children, seven of whom are now living. Our subject received his education in Bond County, and began life as a farmer and dealer in stock. He has been a resident of Greenville for about fifteen years, in which time he has proven himself to be a thoroughly practical and successful business man, having been identified with many of the business and public enterprises of Bond County, notably the First National Bank of Greenville, as the President of that institution for several years. In 1853, Mr. McNeill married Miss Elizabeth Etzler, daughter of John Etzler, a native of Virginia, and five children have been born to them -Alice J,, Horace M., William A., Mary and Martha.

J. B. McADOW, farmer, P. O. Greenville, was born September 22, 1839, in Greenville Precinct, Bond County, Ill.; son of Samuel N. and Jane (Paisley) McAdow. His father was born in Tennessee September 10, 1807, and was a pioneer farmer of Bond County, and died in November, 1873; he was twice married; his first wife (Jane Paisley), by whom he had nine children, our subject being one, was born at Elm Point, Ill., July 14, 1817, and died September 3, 1844. His second wife, by whom he had five children, was Betsey Brewster. Our subject, who is an extensive reader and a well-informed man, received a fair education and adopted the occupation of a farmer. At Alton, Ill., October 6, 1867, he married Miss Clough, born in Alton, Ill., April, 1847, daughter of Samuel and Lucy (Brooks) Clough. Samuel Clough, who was a carpenter by trade, was born in Portland, Me., in March, 1805, and died in April, 1874. His wife, who is still living, was born in Lowell, Mass., in December, 1809, and is now a resident of Madison County, Ill. Mr. and Mrs. McAdow are the parents of five children--Anna Clay, Lillie Jane, Samuel Guy, Fred Clough and William Henry. Mr. McAdow has been a School Director for several years; his brother, William P. McAdow, served in the One Hundred and Thirtieth Illinois Infantry from the autumn of 1862 to the close of the war, participating in the engagements at Vicksburg, and several other important battles during the war. Our subject is a member of the Cumberland Presbyterian, and his wife of the M. E. Church. His father was a Presbyterian minister, and one of the founders of the Cumberland Presbyterian Church in the United States. Mr. McAdow served as a Judge of Bond County about nine years, being first elected to fill the unexpired term of Judge Draper, in 1855.

ROBERT MACKAY, farmer, P. O. Greenville, was born February 14, 1829, in Greenville Precinct, Bond County; son of Alexander C. and Mary (Carson) Mackay, he a native of Kentucky, who emigrated to Bond in an early day; she a native of Tennessee, who died in 1844, leaving four sons and one daughter. Mr. Mackay owned 240 acres of land at the time of his death, which occurred July 8, 1856. Our subject, after receiving the education usually accorded to the sons of farmers, began life in the same occupation as his father, at which he has continued throughout life. In November, 1853, he married Miss Margaret Sugg, a native of Bond County, and daughter of Noah A. Sugg, a pioneer, by whom he has had the following children: Mary A., now Mrs. J. T. Corrie, of Kansas; George; Eleanor J., Emily R., Sarah E., Henry, William, Alvin, Ollie and Walter, all of whom are now living. There is one dead, Mattie, who died at the age of eighteen months. Mr. Mackay is a Republican.

ROBERT MERRY, Greenville, was born in Kentucky, near the Mammoth Cave, February 8, 1828. He is one of twelve children born to David W. and Isabella (McLonehon) Merry. His father, David W., a farmer by occupation, was born in Virginia in 1801; came to Bond County about 1830, and died in 1852. The mother of our subject was born in Kentucky in 1802, and died January, 1871. Robert received his education, which was such as the common schools of that day afforded, in Madison County, Ill. In Bond County, November 18, 1849, he married Mary E. Clouse, born in Bond County September 28, 1834, daughter of William and Sallie (Sags) Clouse, the former born in Nashville, Tenn., September, 1818; was a farmer by occupation. During the Black Hawk war, he served as Major, having previously been promoted from the rank of Captain, and died May 20, 1871. The latter, a native of Alabama, died in March, 1838. Mr. and Mrs. Merry are the parents of six children: Charles W., thirty years; Robert A., twenty-seven years; Sallie C., twenty-five years; James W., twenty-two years; Emily E., nineteen years; and Ella, sixteen years of age. Charles W. is married, and follows the mining business in Colorado; Sallie is now Mrs. C. H. Ma[illegible], of Greenville, and Emily C. is Mrs. [illegible], wife of a farmer of Cottonwood Precinct, Bond County. Mr. Merry was formerly a farmer, but abandoned that business, and removed in the autumn of 1881 to Greenville, where he engaged in the livery business. He has ten good outfits, and is doing a good paying business. He is one of the prominent men of Bond County.

ANDREW B. MERRY, farmer, P. O. Greenville, is one of the good farmers of Town [illegible], Range 3. He was born in Madison County, this State, November 28, 1840, and [illegible] brought to this county with his parents [illegible] a babe. He was the sixth son of [illegible] Merry, who first settled in Town [illegible], Range [illegible], and came to the township [illegible] the year 1848, and died in 1852, January [illegible]. Andrew B. was then brought up under [illegible] fostering care of his mother, with whom he [illegible] until her death, January 31, 187[illegible]. [illegible] 27, 1879, he married Keturah [illegible], born in Ohio, daughter of Daniel [illegible]

1878, and located in Town 7, Range 2. Mr. Merry has but one child, Gertie. He has 169 acres of land, and is a neat and judicious farmer, and successful withal. His farm is located in the northeast quarter of Section 31, in Town 6, Range 3, in Greenville Precinct.

McLAIN & CO., millinery and fancy goods, Greenville. The business of this house was first established in 1870, by J. M. Miller, who conducted it alone until the year 1874, when Mr. William A. McLain purchased a one-half interest, and the house then took its present title. In 1875, Mr. Miller sold his interest to Miss Ella E. Hull. Julia E. Locke succeeded to Miss Hull's interest in 1878, and still holds her interest in the business. This house holds a position at the head of the millinery and fancy goods trade of Bond County, and in those lines aim to have their stock always complete and fresh. A stock of books, stationery and notions occupy a portion of their salesroom, which is also kept well assorted. They enjoy the confidence of the business and buying public, and have a liberal and steadily increasing patronage.

ISAAC NORMAN, merchant, Greenville, was born in Parke County, Ind., February 22, 1841, son of Wesley and Elizabeth (McGelvery) Norman, he a native of Kentucky, born in 1816, a retired farmer now living at Eureka Springs, Ark.; she a native of Indiana; they are the parents of five children. Our subject began his business life as a clerk at Martinsville, Ind.; afterward at Vandalia, Ill., and later at Greenville. In 1864, at Vandalia, Ill., he married Lydia E. Walker, daughter of L[illegible] Walker, a jeweler of Vandalia. Four children have been born to them: Louis V., Minnie R., Laverne and Roy T. Is a Methodist, a Mason and a Republican. Mr. Norman is a member of the well-known furniture firm of Gerichs & Norman, the representative firm in its lines of Bond County. The business was first organized by Mr. J. C. Gerichs in 1875. Mr. Norman has conducted the business for him from that time until 1880, and then took a half-interest in the business. Under his management they have built up a large and growing trade. Their stock is always full and complete, and the extended popularity of this firm is largely due to that fact and the inducements they offer their customers in the way of low prices.

S. [illegible] PHELPS, lawyer, Greenville, was born June 2, 1817, in Otsego Co., N. Y., son of Joshua and Elizabeth (Pick) Phelps, of Connecticut, who emigrated to the then far West, Otsego County, N. Y., in 1799. The subject was [illegible] family of nine, being the youngest of [illegible] mother's own children. He attended the common school of Otsego County, and afterward entered Union College, Schenectady, N. Y., [illegible] the full course, and graduating in [illegible]. He first commenced the practice of his [illegible] in Mississippi, at Woodville, in [illegible], and continued there until coming to [illegible] County in 1844. During the first two years he farmed near Greenville. In 1844 [illegible] married Anna Bulkley, of New York, and [illegible] 1856 came to Greenville and practiced [illegible]. His wife died in 1843, and in 184[illegible] married her sister Caroline. Have two [illegible] Alfred and George; the former is [illegible] at Denver, Colo.; went out as a private [illegible] the 100-days' service in the One Hundred and Thirtieth Illinois [illegible] served three years and returned; [illegible] was State's Attorney of Bond County [illegible] the office, and opened practice [illegible], Colo. Philo is a Presbyterian minister of Livermore, Cal.; Charles [illegible]. The subject was a member of the Presbyterian Church. As a politician he [illegible]

ture in 1862, and received a majority of 200 in his own county; Madison County turned the majority against him. From 1858 to 1865, he was one of the most active Republicans. During the war he was the one to deliver stump speeches throughout Bond County on the political issues of the day. He is the oldest practicing lawyer in Greenville or Bond County; he has his office over the post office.

JAMES PLANT, deceased, was born in Dixon County, Tennessee, on the 9th day of April, 1808, and was a son of Williamson Plant, a native of North Carolina, and was a tailor by trade, and who married Frances Walts. They had five sons and five daughters, James being the second youngest. The subject commenced life as a farmer, and received his education chiefly in Pocahontas, having come to this county in 1818. He was married on the 13th day of April, 1837, to Miss Angeline Chappell, a daughter of Robert Chappell, who was a native of North Carolina, and died in Tennessee. Angeline came here with her mother, who had seven children, four of whom are living, Angeline being the second. The subject has three children — Nancy I., now Mrs. D. F. Hunter; Sarah E. (third child), and George F., a farmer of Greenville, who was born October 28, 1845, and married on the 3d day of March, 1872, Miss Orrie A. White, a daughter of Wesley White, one of the oldest settlers in Bond County. They have three children — Oscar, Sarah J. and Hattie. The subject was Methodist; in politics, a Democrat, and owned 160 acres of land. His first wife was Elizabeth Watson, by whom he had three children. He died on the 22d day of March, 1850.

JOHN W. PLANT, farmer, P. O. Greenville, was born in Humphrey County, Tenn., March 12, 1817. He was one of a family [illegible]

John was born in South Carolina in 1785; was a farmer by occupation, and died in Tennessee in 1865. Mary, his wife, came to her death by being struck by lightning, in 1830; What little education our subject obtained was in the subscription schools of Tennessee. He learned the molder's trade with his brother, William Plant, in Tennessee, where, at Palmyra, July 30, 1845, he married Ann F. Williamson, who was born there in 1826. Her parents were Burwell and Evanna Williamson, of South Carolina. To Mr. and Mrs. J. W. Plant were born thirteen children, three of whom are dead--Robert, Mary C., Cornelia, Cave J., Samuel W., William A., Perry F., Edward, Margaret A., Laura, Martha, John B and Lizzie. Mr. Plant followed his trade seventeen or eighteen years, and since then has farmed here twenty-eight years. He is a Methodist, and his political views are with the Republicans. By hard work, economy and industry, Mr. Plant now owns 662 acres of as good land as can be found in Bond County.

COL. JOHN B. REID, retired, Greenville, was born in Ireland August 8, 1830; son of James and Isabella (Barclay) Reid, who came to America in 1831, bringing a family of eight children, John B. then being only one year old. Alexander Reid, the grandfather of our subject, was a soap and tallow chandler in Ireland, and his son James, the father of our subject, learned the business of his father, but abandoned it for music, which he made the profession of his life. When he came to America, he made Nova Scotia his home for several years, and finally, in 1863, died in New Brunswick, his wife dying the year previous. They left six sons and four daughters, John B. being the youngest son. He was educated partly in New Brunswick, and partly in New York, and afterward learned the shoemakers trade, in which he continued until 1860, having come to Greenville from Boston in 1854. From 1856 to 1861, he was Postmaster at Greenville, and was Clerk of the Circuit Court from 1860 to 1868. In 1862, he enlisted in the One Hundred and Thirtieth Illinois Volunteer Infantry, and was elected Captain, but was commissioned as Major on the organization of the regiment; was afterward promoted to Lieutenant Colonel, and later, Colonel. While in the army, he was elected to the Clerkship of the Circuit Court, and the Government being appealed to, it was decided that he could hold the civil as well as the military office at the same time. He served about three years, having been wounded in the shoulder by a Minie-ball, and was taken prisoner and confined for a couple of months, when he was paroled. His wife was Miss Emma T. Holden, of Woburn, Mass.; has five sons and five daughters; two oldest sons married and in business. Col. Reid is a member of the Baptist Church, being a Deacon in the same; is Master of Masonic Lodge, No. 245; is an Odd Fellow, an A. O. U. W., a temperance man and a Democrat.

ROBINSON & REID, general loan and insurance agents. This enterprising business firm, composed of William E. Robinson and J. Ward Reid, is one of the most wide-awake and prosperous in its line in Bond County. In one sense, this copartnership may be said to have existed longer than any other in Bond County, as Will and Ward were both born in the same neighborhood, and in youth attended the same school. In 1876, they graduated at the Greenville High School, under Prof. Inglis. Mr. Robinson then taught school one year, and Mr. Reid entered upon a course of study at the Illinois State University, at Champaign, and his schoolmate naturally enough came the next year. They each spent two years at Champaign, during which time the possibilities of a bright and prosperous business future became a favorite topic for conversation and discussion between them, which talk finally led to the abandonment of their studies. Mr. Robinson entered the Circuit Clerk's office, at Greenville, and during his nineteen months' connection with that office, he made a business trip to Colorado. During this time Mr. Reid clerked in H. T. Powell's drug store, Greenville. In the fall of 1880, they entered an abstract and insurance office at Mt. Vernon, Ill., where they obtained practical ideas of their business. They formed their copartnership September, 1881, and Mr. Reid immediately commenced work upon a set of abstract books, which are now the most complete in the county and in fact the only ones, since all others are but indexes of the county records. Much time and labor have been bestowed upon these books, and Robinson & Reid have now the only complete set of abstract books in Bond County. These valuable records enable this firm to furnish to applicants abstracts of titles on much shorter notice and in less time than any others. They are also making a specialty of fire and tornado insurance, and represent the Liverpool, London, and Globe; Continental, of New York, American, of Newark, N. J., the German, of Freeport, Ill., California, of San Francisco, and the Manhattan, of New York. The first mentioned is the largest fire insurance company in the world, and the others are equally safe, and each has its desirable features for the insurance of different classes of property. Mr. Robinson returned to Greenville in December, having, during the past summer, written up a complete set of abstracts of the records of Platte County, Neb. Since that time this young and enterprising firm have been building up a business which shows the confidence the people have in them as men of business and reliability.

JOHN RIEDLINGER, saloon-keeper, Greenville, was born in Highland, Ill., March 11, 1854; son of Martin and Margaret (Rude) Riedlinger. He was a shoemaker by trade, and died in 1873; his wife is still living. They were the parents of four boys and four girls. Our subject learned the tinner's trade with Mr. Theodore Ruger, in Highland, and afterward tended bar for Mr. Schotte, in Greenville. In Greenville, April 28, 1875, he married Miss Mary Ellen Huessey, born October 7, 1854, daughter of Jacob and Annie Huessey, and three children have been born to them—Louis F., Lela M. and Ida A. Is a German Protestant, a member of the Mutual Aid Association, and a Republican. The father of Mr. Riedlinger removed from Germany, his fatherland, to Switzerland, and from there came to America, his wife accompanying him in his travels. He was a man much respected in his own country as well as this.

JOHN J. SMITH, deceased, was born in Harrison County, Ind., April 10, 1813; son of James and Sarah (Long) Smith, he a native of Virginia, a farmer, shoemaker and blacksmith; she, a native of Kentucky. They had ten children, John J. being the eldest. The father of James, and great grandfather of the seven sons of John J., was Edwin Smith, one of three brothers who came to America during the Revolution, as British soldiers, but Edwin's heart not being in that unjust struggle against the weak but determined colonies, he left the army of England and settled in Virginia, afterward removing to Kentucky, where he died. John J., our subject, only received a common school education, but was a well-informed man. He followed farming all his life, and was a man highly respected for his many qualities of mind and heart. He left each of his sons 200 acres of land, and such was his systematic methods of doing business that it cost only $225 to settle his estate. He was fifty-seven years of age when he joined the Baptist Church of Smith Grove (named for him). He was a Democrat in his political views, but always conservative in sentiment. July 15, 1840, he married Eliza Hubbard, born in Tennessee June 30, 1822, daughter of Philip and Emily (Smithwick) Hubbard, he a Bond County pioneer, and she a native of North Carolina, and eight sons were born to Mr. Smith, one of whom, David D., died from the bite of a snake in 1854; the other seven are all residing in this county, and a short sketch of each one we give as follows:

CYRUS J. SMITH, farmer, P. O. Greenville, was born January 17, 1842; is a thorough going farmer, and has 287 acres of land, all well improved. He is a Democrat. He has been married twice: first, June 16, 1867, to Miss Catharine Watson, daughter of James Watson, a native of Tennessee. She died December 17, 1876, leaving one daughter, Annie. August 2, 1877, he married Hannah Orme, daughter of Thomas Orme, a resident of this State up to the time of his death November 10, 1879, he being a native of England and emigrating to this country in 1838; was a shoemaker and farmer, and had four children, Mrs. Smith being the youngest. The [illegible] are John T., Walter L. and Lawrence E. Mrs. Smith's mother was Ann H[illegible], of English birth.

N[illegible] P. SMITH, a farmer, was born April 2[illegible]. September 14, 1864, he married in Beaver Creek Precinct, Emeline Castle, who was born in Ohio February 27, 1841, daughter of John P. Castle, a farmer, and native of the State of Ohio, who came to Bond County about 1845. Mrs. Smith was the oldest child. Mr. Smith is an enterprising farmer, and owns 227 acres of excellent land, on Section 28, Township 4, Range 5, and twenty-three acres on another section. He is a Democrat; he has seven children—William N., Arthur D., Robert M., Rhoda L., Lois L., Emeline and Lillie M.

JAMES M. SMITH, farmer, was born December 25, 1844, and was, like his brothers, raised to a life of farming. He was married May 1, 1870, to Miss Martha Castle, daughter of John Castle, and they have one child, Grace, born in November, 1878.

J. FRANK SMITH, farmer, was born September 26, 1854, on the old Smith homestead, in Greenville. He has 195 acres of good land, which came to him from his father's estate. February 10, 1876, he married Ellen McCulley, a native of Bond County, born March 28, 1856, daughter of Frank McCulley and Mary (McCaslin) McCulley, he a native of Tennessee. Mr. Smith has three children—Mollie, Dora and Harry. Is a Democrat.

CHARLES C. SMITH, farmer, was born in Greenville Precinct, on the old homestead, March 28, 1857, and was married March 10, 1878, to Miss Anna M. Goad, born April 16, 1860, daughter of William and Amanda (Allen) Goad. Mr. Goad has been a resident of Bond County for about seven years, and has three children, Mrs. Smith being the oldest. One child has been born to Mr. Smith, Pearl, born December 6, 1879. He owns 210 acres of good land, and is a Democrat.

PHILIP SMITH, at home on the homestead, was born December 8, 1858, and married Miss Frances Hunter March 12, 1882.

PETER L. SMITH was born December 12, 1859, is unmarried, and lives on the homestead with his mother, he being, like his six brothers, a farmer.

H. H. SMITH, trader, railroad agent and

Postmaster of Smithboro, Greenville Precinct, is the founder and chief proprietor of Henderson, which is situated four miles east of Greenville, on the Vandalia & Terra Haute Railroad. The subject of these lines was born in C[illegible] County, Ohio, Feb. 19, 1833; son of Samuel Smith, a Marylander, son of William, who emigrated with his family and settled in Clark County, Ohio, when it was a wilderness. The [illegible] of our subject was Anna, daughter of [illegible] Hedrick, who was likewise an early settler in Clark County, Ohio. Hiram H. had good common school advantages, completing the same at Delaware, Ohio; came to Illinois in 1854, to Greenville; his father came [illegible] years later. When Mr. Smith came [illegible] the county, he purchased 800 acres in T[illegible] 5, Range 2, and engaged in farming and [illegible] raising, came to this place in 1870, and [illegible] the exception of two years spent in Gr[illegible], he has been a resident of this township, and has done much toward encouraging [illegible] growth and improvement of the t[illegible] founded the town soon after he ca[illegible], and since 1871 has been Postmaster [illegible] being named in honor of him. H[illegible] railroad agent here, and does a g[illegible] business, and is a thorough-[illegible] energetic business man. In 1868, he w[illegible] ried to Eleanor C. Culver, born in Her[illegible] County, N. Y., daughter of Andrew C[illegible]. Mr. Smith has no children; has a[illegible] hundred acres of land; is a mem[illegible] M. E. Church, and a strong and [illegible] temperance man.

W[illegible] S. SMITH, merchant [illegible] Greenville, was born in Hamp[illegible] Co[illegible] County, Va., son of Middleton a[illegible] (Williams) Smith, both natives of V[illegible], he a farmer by occupation, born in [illegible] County December 27, 1786, died December 30, 1784, also died in Greenville December 22, 1845. She was the mother of nine children: William S., Thomas W., John A., Isaac M., Samuel, Jane M., now wife of John S. Hall, a farmer near Greenville, Ill.; Mary A., Ellen and Joshua M. Subject began the business of life at fourteen years of age as a clerk in a mercantile house, and has since been engaged in mercantile business and banking. At the age of twenty three, he removed from Virginia and located in Greenville, in which place he has ever since resided. He is one of the founders of the First National Bank of Greenville, of which he was President for several years, and at the present time a Director; has filled the offices of School Commissioner and County Assessor and is at the present time City Alderman of the Third Ward, Greenville. During the years 1846 47, he was Representative in the Legislature. He has been twice married. His first wife, whom he married near Greenville, was Amanda M. Hall, second daughter of Joshua and Charlotte Hall, of Jefferson County, Va. She died January 21, 18[illegible], leaving seven children: Tiffin A., Sarah A., William S., Jr., Charlotte L., Ellen E., Mary H. and Joshua S. He was married the second time at Stony Point, Crittenden Co., Ky., to Elizabeth W. Greathouse, daughter of J[illegible] S. Greathouse, attorney at law, of Shelbyville, Shelby Co., Ky., who married Lucy M. Cl[illegible] of Anderson County, Ky. From this second union [illegible] children have been born: Ed[illegible] T., Lucy F., Alice G., Elizabeth L., Lucretia G. and Clark S. Mr. Smith was an old-time Whig, is now a Republican, and is a member of the I. O. O. F.

DR. R. C. SPRAGUE, physician and surgeon, Greenville, was born in Washington County, Ohio, on the 10th day of June, 1828 died July 9, 1856. His mother, Susannah Sprague, a native of Fort Waterford (first garrison in Ohio), was born April 2, 1793, and died December 9, 1857. They were married in Washington County, Ohio, in 1806. The subject's father was a farmer, and held the office of Justice of the Peace for several years, and moved to Franklin County, Ohio, in 1832. The family were long and well known as active and zealous members of the Christian Church. They had nine children, five sons and four daughters. Dr. Sprague's first schooling was in the district schools of Franklin County, Ohio, near Columbus; afterward he attended the academy at Reynoldsburg, in the same county. He commenced his college career at the Eclectic Medical Institute, Cincinnati, Ohio, where he graduated in 1857. He also took a course in the Eclectic Medical College of New York City, in 1866. He came to Greenville with a brother, Dr. Anson Sprague, in 1852. In 1854, at Vandalia, Ill., July 6, Dr. Sprague married Miss Martha J. Johnson, born in Bond County, Ill., May 15, 1832, daughter of Duncan Johnson, who was born in Tennessee January 11, 1803, and died December 12, 1867. Polly Johnston, *née* Powers, Mrs. Sprague's mother, was born in Tennessee August 5, 1807, and died January 22, 1852. They were married May 27, 1824, and moved from Tennessee soon after, locating in this county. Mr. Johnson was a farmer, and held the office of Justice of the Peace for many years. He was prominently connected with the milling interest of this and Fayette County, and was a zealous worker in the Methodist Church, all his family belonging to the same denomination. Dr. Sprague has been a member of the City Council for many years, and is the father of seven children, four living—Clara Ellen, now Mrs. John, of Greenville; Sarah Maud, now Mrs. W. H. McIntyre, of Rushville; Romulus D. and Ruby B., now in school. The children deceased are Mary Irene, Beverly J. and Hattie Mabel. The Doctor is a member of the Christian Church, an A. O. U. W., and a Republican.

WILLIAM B. SYBERT, farmer, P. O. Greenville, was born in Ohio February 13, 1822; son of Henry and Sarah Sybert both of whom are dead, he departing this life in 1864, and she in 1866. He was a farmer by occupation, and left eleven children, seven girls and four boys. Our subject attended school in Madison County, Ind., and commenced the life of a farmer in Greenville Precinct, in which occupation he has continued, owning at the present time 227 acres of the best land in the State, and being highly respected as a farmer and a man. He has filled the position of School Director, and is a Methodist and a Republican. October 3, 1844, in Greenville Precinct, he married Miss Malinda E. Edwards, daughter of John Edwards, and seven children have been born to them—James F., John H., Harriet M., Lemuel, Albert, Morgan L. and Betsey E.

REINHOLD SUESSENBACH, farmer, P. O. Greenville, was born in Prussia March 19, 1838. He was the son of Christian Wilhelm and Renate (Taesler) Suessenbach, both dying in Germany, he in 1859, and she in 1840. Our subject was one of a family of three. He was educated in Prussia, where the law requires them to attend school for eight years. In Bond County, in June, 1875, he married Mary Schmollinger, daughter of Christopf and Frederika Schmollinger. Subject had a family of three—Amanda Bertha, Conrad Gustav and Heinrich Oscar. In Germany, he learned the brick and stone-mason and plasterer's trade, and has worked at it a good deal, but is farming at present. He is a Republican.

D. D. THOMSON, farmer, P. O. Greenville, Greenville Precinct. Among the enterprising farmers in this township is Mr. Thomson, who was born October 2, 1846, in Hendricks County, Ind. He is a son of John R. Thomson, a Kentuckian by birth, and emigrated to Indiana about the year 1842. He was a farmer and stock-trader, and was prominently identified with that country as a business man. He died August 5, 1862. He was a member of the Presbyterian Church. His wife survives him. Nine children were born to them; seven are now living. Their names are as follows—Nelson C., David D., Sarah E., Samuel E., Arthur R., Ollie D., John R. and Ella D. All reside in Indiana except David D., who was raised a farmer, and remained with his father until he became of age. September 26, 1867, he married Lavinia S. Hendrix, born in Hendricks County, Ind., daughter of Jesse Hendrix, of that place. In the fall of 1871, he came to this county, and after buying and locating on several different farms in the county, March 31, 1881, he purchased the Samuel Colcord farm, comprising 272 acres, where he now resides. He has four children living Amos D., Cordia N., Bertha and an infant unnamed. Mr. Thomson is a member of the German Baptist Church.

CAPT. S. M. TABOR, livery, Greenville, was born in Madison County, Ill., October 29, 1833, son of Isham and Phoebe (Adams) Tabor, he a native of Tennessee, a farmer, who died about 1837; she also of Tennessee, dying in 1841. They were the parents of five children, four sons and one daughter, Capt. S. M. being the third in order of birth. After receiving an ordinary education, young Tabor began his business life as a farmer; but in 1877, he entered the livery business in Greenville. In 1862, November 20, he married Miss Sarah A. Jett, daughter of Daniel Jett, a pioneer of Bond County, and six children have been born to them—Lizzie, May, Flora, Hattie and Josie; Edwin, an only son, died in 1874, aged one year. Capt. Tabor was Deputy Sheriff of Bond County from 1868 to 1878, and has held the office of Constable for about thirteen years, and his present term will not expire until 1885. In 1861, he entered the service of his country as a private in the Third Illinois Cavalry; was promoted to a Second Lieutenancy in 1864, and to Captain in 1865, giving four of the best years of his life in battling for the preservation of the Union—a record to look back upon with feelings of genuine pride. He was in thirty-two engagements, and being slightly wounded three times. Self and family are members of the Christian Church, and he is an I. O. O. F., A. O. U. W., a Good Templar and a Republican.

HON. WILLIAM S. WAIT, deceased. The subject of this sketch was born in Portland, Me., March 5, 1789, and was the second of a family of nine children, three of whom died in childhood, and six living an advanced age. Of his ancestors we have no extended record. His father, Thomas Baker Wait, born August 4, 1762, was of Welsh descent, an only child, and by occupation a printer, publisher and book-seller. He was a man of firm character and delighted in literary pursuits. The mother, whose maiden name was Elizabeth Smith, was born October 25, 1760, and was loved and blessed by all who knew her, and died January 1, 1845. William S. received his rudimental schooling in the public schools of his native town, and when a youth entered the book publishing house of his father, continuing with him, who was at times associated with others in the business, until over thirty years of age. Their business was at different times conducted in Portland, Me., and Boston, Mass., and extended over all parts of the Eastern, Middle and Southern States. When a mere boy, William S. and a brother two years older for a time did all of the labor, mechanical, editorial, and otherwise necessary to publish a weekly newspaper. In June, 1817, he started on a journey to the west, through the States of New York, Pennsylvania, Maryland, Ohio, Indiana, Illinois, and Missouri. This he accomplished, arriving at St. Louis, Mo., January 3, 1818. He returned into Illinois, reaching Old Ripley, Bond County, February 14, following. There he made his first land entry February 17. He started on his tedious return in the month of April, and reached Boston July 11, 1818, having traveled more than five thousand eight hundred miles, mostly in the saddle. With the keen fore-sight of an old time pioneer, Mr. Wait made note of the wonderful advantages that the Great West afforded the man of energy and nerve. June 27, 1819, he started out on a second prolonged business trip in the interests of his house, to Virginia, via New York City, Philadelphia and Washington, making a canvass of the last-named State for some of their publications, riding about six thousand miles, and returning to Boston in April, 1820. In May 1820, he married Sarah Newhall, of Salem, Mass. She was born January 31, 1797, and was the sixth child of a family of eight. Her parents, Thomas and Mehitable (Cheever) Newhall, were born 1754 and 1762, and died January 1, 1852 and January 12, 1830, respectively. They were both natives of Massachusetts, and have extensive family relations. Of their children none but Sarah ever married. Soon after their marriage they started on his second trip to Illinois. The journey was a tedious one, and attended with the perils of a long drive with horses and light wagon through a dense, unbroken wilderness. It was, however, safely accomplished, and the bride and groom arrived at Old Ripley late in the summer of 1820 [illegible]

In 1821, he became interested in a mill. He lived at Ripley until the summer of 1824, when he returned East with his wife and child, on a visit to their parents. Mr. Wait's previous business relations had given him a thorough knowledge of the country and an extended acquaintance with its people which in future years were of much avail to him in his business. The winter of 1824-25 was spent in traveling for a publishing house through the Middle States and Illinois, and early in April, 1825, he was for a third time at Old Ripley, his wife and two children joining him in the following November. They returned to Boston, Mass., in February, 1827, however, and until the spring of 1835, he was there actively engaged in publishing, when he again returned to Illinois, and made a permanent stay, settled near Greenville engaged extensively in farming. A prominent feature of Mr. Wait's enterprise as a farmer was the planting of one of the largest apple orchards in Illinois. William S. Wait was always foremost in any local undertaking that was calculated to advance the interests of the community, and was ever ready with his pen or good words to assist in State or National enterprises. His readiness and ability as a local statesman had won for him the personal acquaintance and esteem of all of the Illinois Governors from 1818 to 1865, and with many he was on intimate terms. He was known as a man who could not be bought and sold, was never backward to form and express plainly his views on any important subject. With political tricksters and wire-pullers, he was not a special [illegible]. He was not an office-seeker, and had [illegible] gains to drive [illegible] allowed them to go their own way. October 14, 1845, he presided as Chairman of the National Industrial Convention in New York, on which occasion he delivered an [illegible]

Congress, held at Philadelphia, representing the various National Reform Associations of the United States, nominated Gerrit Smith as their candidate for President of the United States, and William S. Wait for Vice President, which candidacy Mr. Wait respectfully declined. To make mention of the numerous conventions and meetings, political, agricultural, railroad, etc., in which Mr. Wait took a prominent part, would necessitate the addition of an extra chapter. We will further state, however, that he took a deep interest in the formation of the laws of Illinois, wrote many letters and newspaper articles regarding them. Many articles or parts of the Constitution of 1878 were from his pen, as also the first drafts of many of the acts of the Illinois State Legislature. He took prominent parts in County and State Agricultural Societies; was the prime mover in the projection of the Mississippi & Atlantic (now Vandalia line) Railroad and in its interest spent a great part of his time from 1846 to 1865. (See history of Vandalia Line and general history of the county in this volume.) He was also one of the incorporators of the St. Louis & Illinois Bridge Company. Mr. Wait always kept well-informed on all matters of improvement, whether pertaining to county, State or Nation. He was an investigator of all new subjects, a close student, and a clear and voluminous writer on political, educational, agricultural and reformatory subjects, a constant correspondent with many of the best minds of the age, and a frequent contributor to the press. He died July 17, 1865, and she who had been his faithful helpmeet and loving wife for more than forty-five years, departed the following 14th day of September. Of their eight children, two died in infancy; one when just budding into womanhood. One is a resident of Tulare County, Cal., and four are residents of Bond.

T. B. WOOD, harness and saddlery, Greenville, for several years a thriving citizen and business man of Greenville, was born in Highland County, Ohio, August 9, 1838. His father, Thomas J. Wood, also a native of the Buckeye State, was a hatter by trade, which he followed until after middle life, and then entered the retail grocery business. He took for his wife one Evelyn Hardy, a native of Massachusetts. Our subject received in youth only the advantages of a common school education in the rural districts of Highland County, Ohio, and at about fifteen years of age learned the harness-maker's trade at Mt. Sterling, Ohio. After remaining in Mt. Sterling two years, he went to Washington, Fayette Co. Ohio, for about the same length of time, and came to Greenville, Bond County. In the spring of 1861, he entered the Twenty-second Illinois Infantry, taking up arms in defense of the Union. After six months' service, he was discharged on account of disability. Returning to Greenville, he re-enlisted in the One Hundred and Thirtieth Illinois Infantry, after a respite of about six months. He remained in the service until the close of the war, having served about three years. He was at the battle of Vicksburg, also in the heat of the battle of Mansfield, where he received a severe wound, and was captured by the enemy. After confinement in a hospital for about three months, he was paroled, and later exchanged, and closed his term of service on the Gulf of Mexico. In 1865, he returned to Greenville, entered his present business, in which he has been successful. He manufactures everything in the harness line, and carries in his stock a complete stock of saddles, etc. His store is located on the east side of the public square, where he can always be found ready to meet his customers.

EDWIN B. WISE, merchant, Greenville, was born in Hebron, N. H., December 2–

1836. He was one of twelve children born to David and Elizabeth (Hoyt) Wise; he, a native of New Hampshire, a farmer by occupation; came to Illinois in October, 1854, with his family. He died May 30, 1864. His wife was the daughter of Abram Hoyt, a native of New Hampshire, and a pioneer of this State. Our subject received a common school education in New Hampshire, and at Greenville. Mr. Wise was twice married; first, on February 7, 1862, to Lestina D. Corbin, daughter of Ephraim Corbin, who was a native of England, and by occupation a lumber merchant of Hannibal, Mo. She died April 20, 1871, leaving three children— Alonzo D., John L. and Katie, the latter having died; second, August 24, 1871, he married Kate M. Miller, daughter of George Miller, of Clinton County, Ill., a carpenter by occupation, and a native of Perry County, Penn. She is the mother of two children— Ernest and an infant now deceased. Mr. Wise was in the mercantile business at Wisetown, Beaver Creek Precinct, Bond County, a thriving little trading post, which he established himself, remaining there until February 1, 1882, when he purchased one-half interest in the stock and business of the well-known New York clothing house of Lewis Kaufman, and the connection of Mr. Wise with this establishment is a sufficient guarantee to the buying public that the New York clothing house has become a safe and profitable place to exchange money for merchandise. Mr. Wise enlisted in Company C, Twenty-sixth Illinois Infantry as Sergeant August 19, 1861, and was at the siege of Corinth, Miss., in 1862, and in the battle at Farmington. He was promoted to Second Lieutenant, and afterward discharged on account of disability. In politics, he is a Republican; is a member of the A., F. & A. M. and A. O. U. W. Mr. Wise is a very successful merchant, and is highly esteemed.

WILLIAM H. WATSON, grocer, Greenville, was born in Newport, Bond County, July 31, 1849; son of Andrew W. and Cynthia A. (Diamond) Watson, he born in Cleveland County, N. C., in 1812, and died June 6, 1881. He was a farmer and merchant, and came to Bond County in 1820, locating in Zion Precinct. He merchandized for twenty years in the town of Newport. His wife was a native of Tennessee, and died in 1856, leaving four children. In 1858, he married Cornelia J. Daniels, and by her had seven children, five of whom are living. Andrew W. Watson served one year in the Black Hawk war. Our subject attended the schools in Newport, and was raised on his father's farm, and worked in his father's store. May 1, 1880, he married, in Greenville, Louisa A. Jett, daughter of Mr. Gabriel Jett, a pioneer of Bond, who died in 1860. Mr. Watson is of the firm of Watson & Jett, grocers, who commenced business together in 1880. They carry a fine stock of goods, and do an extensive trade; also, a general produce and exchange business. Mr. Watson is an Odd Fellow and a Republican.

THOMAS WAFER, miller, Greenville, was born about twleve miles northwest of Greenville, in Cottonwood Grove Precinct, and is a son of the late James and Sarah (Elder) Wafer, he born on Bullock Creek, within seven or eight miles of King's Mountain, District of York, in the State of South Carolina, on the 28th day of September, 1785, and died on the 8th day of February, 1873, at his home in Bond County, where he had resided for fifty-three years; she, born in Livingston (now Crittenden) County, Ky., May 22, 1795, died July 11, 1847. The subject's grandfather, named Francis, was born in

South Carolina about 1750, and died in Kentucky in the year 1823, and his great-grandfather, also named Francis Wafer, was born in Ireland about the year 1706. The parents of the subject had eight children, and he began life as a farmer, and married at the residence of the bride's parents Mary Agnes Davidson McLain, daughter of John A. McLain, who was born in Bedford County, Tenn., June 17, 1826. The subject is a member of the well-known firm of Plant & Wafer, millers. He has one son, Charles Louis, and one daughter, Orrey E., who married Robert Thacker. In religion, Mr. Wafer is a Presbyterian, and in politics a Republican. He is one of the earliest pioneers of Bond County, and one of its most substantial citizens.

JOHN B. WHITE, deceased, was a farmer and one of the early settlers of Bond County. He was born in Rutherford County, N. C., January 20, 1790; son of Thomas White, a school teacher, who is said to have taught the first school in Bond County, near Greenville. He was of North Carolina birth, and his wife, a Miss Torrence, was also of the same State. They had two daughters and five sons, John B., our subject, being the oldest, who died June 28, 1873; his wife preceded him February 18, 1848.

ELIJAH H. WHITE, son of the above, was born in Bond County October 6, 1835; is a farmer by occupation. February 22, 1863, he married Miss Harriet A. Goodsen, by whom he has four children—Ida E., John B., Hattie A. and George W. Is a Presbyterian and a Republican.

S. [illegible] WHITE is another son of John B. White and was also born in Bond County; is, and has always been, a farmer. In April, 1857, he married Miss Martha Goodsen, and has three children—William T., Maggie E. and Fannie M. He is a Republican.

SPRAGUE WHITE, Justice of the Peace, Greenville, was born February 19, 1813, at Greenville, Bond Co., Ill. He was the son of James White, who was the third child of Thomas White, and the only child now living, and Mary (Denny) White, daughter of James Denny, a pioneer of Bond County, Ill. Subject was one of a family of seven, four of whom are still living. He was educated in Bond County, having attended the academy at Greenville. In 1877, he married Virginia A. Corrie, daughter of Joseph Corrie, a farmer an old settler of Bond County. Subject had one son—Roy Sprague White. Our subject began teaching school when but a youth. He taught about twenty years in Jersey County, Ill.; then, in 1875, he taught in Texas, and has since been a resident of Greenville, where, in the fall of 1881, he was elected Justice of the Peace. Mr. Sprague White is regarded as one of the best informed men on general topics, having devoted his entire life to reading and studying of a general character. He is an Old-School Presbyterian and a Whig-Republican. His grandfather was the son of John White, who was of English and Irish descent, and emigrated to this country about 1740.

DAVID WILKINS, physician and surgeon, Greenville, was born March 28, 1829, in Merom, Sullivan Co., Ind.; son of David W. and Frances (Balthas) Wilkins. David W. was born in Virginia in 1778; removed to Indiana about the year 1820, and died in 1848. His wife, also a native of Virginia, was born in 1782, and died in 1847. Our subject, the youngest of a family of five sons and five daughters, attended school in Sullivan County, Ind., and, having chosen the medical profession, took his course in the Medical Department of Michigan University, graduating in 1853. He began the practice of his profession in Mulberry Grove, Bond Co., Ill., and removed to Greenville in the autumn of 1859. At Medarysville, Ind., May 29, 1853, he married Maria M. Gwinn, born in Michigan City, Ind., May 27, 1836, daughter of Andrew and Mary Ann (Fultz) Gwinn. Andrew Gwinn was a native of Londonderry, Ireland; was born in 1788, and died in 1848. His wife was born in Baltimore, Md., in 1804, and died in 1863. Mrs. Wilkins bore her husband four children—David R., Lillian G., Corwin and Harry E. Our subject entered the One Hundred and Thirtieth Illinois Volunteer Infantry as Surgeon in 1862, and was discharged in 1865. He is a skillful physician, and has a large practice. In politics, he is a Republican, and formerly belonged to the old Whig party. Mrs. Wilkins is a member of the Baptist Church.

RIPLEY PRECINCT.

ANNA MARY ARNOLD, hotel keeper, Old Ripley, was born in Franco-Germany December 31, 1834, the daughter of Peter and Catharine (Molter) Kloster. They were born in Germany, he in 1807, and died in 1849; she was born at the same place November 22, 1811, and is still living. They had six children, four daughters and two sons. Subject went to school in Germany, and was married to George Arnold in 1849, at St Louis, who was born in Alsace, Germany, April 24, 1812. He was the son of John and Annie (Assolt) Arnold. Subject had eleven children — Edward, Jacob, Annie, Clotilda, Emil, Rosa, Birdie, Julia, Lizzie George and Charlie. Subject kept Strasburg Hotel, St. Louis, and since then has kept a hotel here. Mrs. Arnold is a Catholic.

JOHN W. COX (deceased) was born in Bath County, Va., December 15, 1845. He was the son of John and Charity Ann Cox. John was a dentist, and died at Carrollton, Ill.; his wife died in 1868. They had a family of eleven. Subject received most of his schooling in Marine, Ill. At Mexico, Mo., October 5, 1871, he married Mary J. West, who was born there on February 3, 1851. Her parents were J. J. and Zelophia West, he of Tennessee, and she of Kentucky. By this union subject had a family of five — George W. (deceased), Berthold, Corwin, Josie (deceased) and Nellie. Mr. Cox was a miller at Troy, Ill.; afterward built a mill at Chillicothe, Mo. He died February 11, 1882, and was buried in the old Brown Cemetery at New Berlin. He was a Methodist a Democrat, and a member of K. P. order. Mr. Cox was an excellent business man, public spirited, of strong character, and loved and esteemed by all who knew him.

J. W. CLANTON, hotel keeper, Old Ripley, was born in Bond County, Ill., June 16, 1850; the son of Wesley and Nancy (Brewer) Clanton. Wesley was born in North Carolina, 1811; was a farmer, and died in 1872. Mrs. Clanton is still living. They had a family of four boys and four girls. Subject's opportunities for receiving a good education were limited, having only attended school a few years in Bond County, Ill., where, January 19, 1873, he married Mary E. Long, who was born in Bond County October 17 1853. She is the daughter of I. N. and Nancy Long. By this union they had three children John W., Lula A. (deceased) and Wayne A. Mr. Clanton is a Baptist and a Democrat He is at present engaged in the hotel business at New Berlin, Ill.

FRANK H. DALHAUS, farmer, P. O. Old Ripley, was born in Prussia, Germany, February 22, 1830; son of Aberhardt and Margaret Dalhaus, both born in Germany. He died in Germany in 1854, and she one year later. They had seven children, five girls and two boys. Subject attended school in Germany, for seven years, and after this worked at brick making there. He was married in St. Louis, April 11, 1874, to Christina Urich, born there June 22, 1852. She is the daughter of Henry and Neberga Urich, natives of Germany. Subject has one child - Henry G. During the war, Mr. Dalhaus served in Company D, Third Illinois Regiment, under Captains Davis and McLain He kept [illegible] in New Berlin, Ill., twelve years, and since then has farmed. He is a Catholic and a Republican.

JOHN N. FILE, farmer, P. O. Pocahontas, was born July 21, 1828, in Ripley Precinct His parents were Moses File, born in North Carolina, in 1804; was a farmer, and died August 27, 1865, and Elizabeth (Lyttaker) File, born in Tennessee July 1, 1811. They had thirteen children, of whom our subject is the oldest. He received but little education, and that in this precinct. Mr. J. N. File was twice married; first, on December 24, 1851, at Pocahontas, to Mary A. Stallard, and second, on January 6, 1856, at Pleasant Prairie, to Julia A. Cruthis, who was born there April 9, 1831. Her parents were John and Millberry (Redfearn) Cruthis, both born in North Carolina. Subject had a family of nine Elizabeth Millberry, John J., Thomas A., Mary E., Martha A., Ida M., William M., Henry W. and Edward R. Mr. File has always been a farmer, and worked hard to clear the wilderness, and now owns 697½ acres of as good land as can be found in Bond County. He is a Methodist, and his political views are with the Republican party.

THOMAS B. FILE, farmer, P. O. Pocahontas, was born in Ripley Precinct March 14, 1830; is the son of Moses and Mary E. (Lyttaker) File. Moses File, a farmer, was born in North Carolina in 1803, and died August 26, 1865. His wife was born in Tennessee in 1811, and died in 1869. Subject was one of a family of thirteen. His education, which was but scant, was received in Ripley Precinct. At Greenville, Bond County, October 2[illegible], 1856, he married Mary E. Gillespie born in Clinton County, Ill., February 6, 18[illegible], daughter of John and Mary Gillespie, the former a native of Tennessee the latter born in Madison County February 5, 1814. By this union they had six children

Frederick S., John W., Benjamin M., Thomas Elmer, Augusta, Martha A. (deceased). Mr. File has always farmed in this precinct, and owns 638¾ acres of the best land in Bond County. He made the first road across the Bond County prairies. Mr. File was School Trustee for twelve years, Road Supervisor four terms, and is at present Overseer of the Poor. He is a Methodist and a Republican; also belongs to the Masonic and A. O. U. W. orders.

JOHN F. FILE, farmer, P. O. Greenville, was born in Ripley Precinct July 13, 1832. His parents were George File, born in North Carolina; a farmer, and died in February, 1877, and Mary (Lyttaker) File born in Tennessee, and died in March, 1878. They had thirteen children. The subject received his education in Ripley Precinct, where he was married March 17, 1853, to Miss Willie, who was born in Pocahontas in 1837. Her parents, Wilson and Fannie Willie, were natives of Tennessee By this union they had nine children—Columbus (deceased), Mary F., George W., Carrie F., Emma L., Lemuel, John F., Henry and Lulie. During the war, Mr. File served eighteen months under Capt. McLain and Col. Carnahan, in Company E, Third Illinois Cavalry. He began business as blacksmith with his grandfather, Peter Lyttaker; has also been a Constable and Deputy Sheriff of Bond County. In politics, he is with the Republican party. He now owns eighty acres of land on the Alton road, and is at present a farmer.

JOHN C. FLECK, farmer, P. O. Old Ripley, was born in Baden, Germany, February 29, 1845; son of Jacob and Jacobina (Aalzgeber) Fleck, both natives of Baden, Germany, he born December 14, 1818, she in 1825. They are both still living, and had a family of nine with but one daughter. Subject went to school in Baden for eight years; after this he learned the blacksmith's trade with his father, who was a blacksmith at Baden, Germany. In St. Louis, May 7, 1872, he married Mary Neifahrt, born in New Berlin, Ill., January 6, 1858, the daughter of Jacob and Sybilla Neifahrt. Subject has three children—John L., Ida E. and Charles F. Mr. Fleck was a blacksmith in St. Louis, Mo., in Pleasant Hill, Mo., Pekin, Ill., again in St. Louis, in Pocahontas, and lastly in this place. For the last three years he has farmed here, is a Justice of the Peace for Ripley Precinct, a Republican, and a member in good standing of the A., F. & A. M., and I. O. O. F.

FREDERICK W. FRITZ, carpenter, Old Ripley, was born at St. Louis, Mo., April 21, 1862, a son of Jacob L. and Catharine (Withmer) Fritz, natives of Bavaria, South Germany: he, born March 15, 1832, a painter, and she, born February 15, 1840; both are still living. Our subject is one of a family of three; attended school in Ripley, and was successful in his studies. He taught school at the Union Schoolhouse, in Ripley, for awhile, but has since followed the carpenter's trade, which he learned during his apprenticeship with William Boldt. Mr. Fritz is a Republican.

REV. THOMAS W. HYNES, farmer and preacher, Old Ripley, was born at Bardstown, Nelson Co., Ky., October 5, 1815; was the son of William R. and Barbara (Chenault) Hynes. William R. was born in Washington County Md., January 27, 1771; was a merchant and farmer in Kentucky, and died at Bardstown, Ky, April 10, 1837. Barbara, his wife, was born in Essex County, Va., March 13, 1793, and died at Greenville, Ill., June 1, 1856. Subject's father was married twice; by his first wife he had seven children, and by his last he had twelve, of which our subject is one. He first attended his uncle, Stephen Chenault's, school, at Bardstown; then for two or three years attended a Roman Catholic college, called St. Joseph's College, at the same place; then entered the Hanover College, Indiana, and lastly the Theological Seminary at Hanover, Ind. He taught mathematics six or seven years in Hanover College; then became a Presbyterian minister. At Hanover, Ind., October 1, 1839, he married his first wife, Nancy J. Dunn, born at Hanover, Ind., November 22, 1820. He married Elizabeth Wafer, who was born in Bond County, Ill., March 30, 1825. She was the daughter of James and Sarah (Elder) Wafer, he born in York County, N. C., September 28, 1775; she born in Livingston County, Ky., May 22, 1795. Subject had a family of eleven, five of whom are still living—William D., who is route agent for the Vandalia Railroad, living at Indianapolis, Ind.; Samuel B. is General Agent for A., T. & S. F. Railroad at Chicago, Ill.; Ella M., Charles H. and Walter B. Mr. Hynes was County Superintendent of Schools in Bond County for nearly twenty years. He is a Republican.

W. H. HARRIS, physician, Old Ripley, was born in Fillmore Township, Montgomery County, Ill., September 10, 1858. He was the son of Samuel and Emma (Allen) Harris, both natives of England, he a blacksmith, born February 4, 1834, and died July 26, 1867, and she, born January 23, 1836, and died May 1, 1870. Our subject was one of a family of seven. He was educated in the common schools of Fillmore Township, and attended the College of Physicians and Surgeons at Keokuk, Iowa, and the American Medical College at St. Louis, Mo. In Montgomery County, Ill., April 14, 1882, he married Katie E. Moody, who was born in Fillmore Township February 16, 1859. She was the daughter of James S. and Eliza (Bliss) Moody, he a native of Indiana, and she a native of Vermont. Dr. Harris is a practicing physician at present, and is doing well, and his efforts to assist and lighten the sufferings of humanity are being appreciated more and more every day. He is a Republican.

AUGUST HUHN, farmer, P. O. Greenville, was born in Prussia March 18, 1823; a son of C. C. and Mary (Thasler) Huhn, both natives of Prussia, he, a coal miner, died in 1865; she in 1830. Our subject was of a family of three boys and two girls, and was educated in the land of his birth. In 1859, in Lake County, Ind., he married Sophia Riabe, also a native of Prussia. They had seven children—Otila, Amanda, Mary, Selma, Emma and two died in infancy. Subject's second wife, Anna Mary Anders, is a native of Austria. Mr. Huhn was a coal miner in Prussia for twelve years, and came to this country when he was thirty years old. He is now a farmer, and owns 160 acres of land; is a Lutheran, a Republican, holds the office of School Director, and has been Road Supervisor several terms.

LEMUEL B. LONG, farmer, P. O. Old Ripley, was born in Ripley Precinct July 22, 1833. He is the son of Peter and Betsey S. (Vincent) Long. He was born in Washington County, Ky., August 9, 1804; was a farmer, and is still living. His wife was born in North Carolina July 31, 1807, and died September 3, 1839. Subject was of a family of seven—four boys and three girls. What little education he got was in the common schools of Ripley Precinct, and a short time at Greenville, where, on January 16, 1862, he married Sarah G. Smith, born in this county October 7, 1831. She was the daughter of Aaron and Mary (Laughlin) Smith. Aaron was born February 4, 1789, in Spartansburg District, N. C.; died October 12, 1854, and his wife was born in Pendleton District, S. C., January 26, 1796, and died April 12, 1879. Subject had a family of six—James E., Paul W., Peter L., Mary C., Sarah E. and Lemuel S. Mr. Long was a printer, farmer and merchant; was Postmaster in Old Ripley for twelve years, and Justice of the Peace at Ripley Precinct for some time. He has been engaged merchandising in New Berlin, Ill., for sixteen years. His religion is that of a Bapist, his politics Republican, and is a member of the Masonic and A. O. U. W. orders.

E. J. MUNSON, physician, Old Ripley, was born in Licking County, Ohio, March 24, 1834. He is the son of Dr. George and Emily (Bliss) Munson, he born in Ohio in 1808; was a physician, she, born in January, 1817, is still living. They had twelve children, three boys and nine girls. Subject first attended school in Jeffersonville, Ind.; then about six years at New London, Iowa, where he studied medicine with his father. He was married three times, and each time in Bond County. First time, February 5, 1863, to Adeline M. Watson, daughter of Wilson Watson; second time to Jeannette Gunn, daughter of Seal Gunn, an old resident here, and third time to Martha E. West, daughter of Thomas West another old settler. Subject had four children die in infancy and has a son living, Lorenzo F., eight years old. Dr. Munson served ten months in Company I, Fifty-seventh Illinois, under Capt. W. B. Guthrie. The Doctor is a Republican, and commenced his professional career as a physician in New London under his father's supervision. The Doctor is a writer of considerable ability; has written several able lectures, and has now manuscript ready for publication of several important lectures.

JOSEPH J. MUELLER, blacksmith, Old Ripley, was born in Wabasha County, Minn., July 7, 1858. His father, Anton J. Mueller, was a saddler and harness-maker. He died February 17, 1868. His mother, Magdalena

(Botschart) Mueller, is still living. They had two sons and one daughter. Subject attended school about four years at Greenville. Here, on February 23, 1882, he married Frances E. Hunter, who was born in Bond County April 28, 1857, and daughter of Wm. McLin and Na[illegible] (Glenn) Hunter. Mr. Mueller is a blacksmith, and has run a shop at New Berlin for two years, with his custom increasing every day. He is a member of the Cumberland Presbyterian Church, and a Democrat.

JOSEPH NEATHAMMER, farmer, P. O. Pocahontas, was born in Bond County April 20, [illegible], son of John Neathammer (whose biography appears in this work) and Catharine (Pandermann) Neathammer, born in Germany, and died November, 1878. They had a family of four girls and one boy. Subject was educated at Mt. Vernon School, Bond County, and two years at Highland, after which he went on the farm. He married October [illegible], 1876, in Greenville, Isabella Zeller, born in Madison County December 20, 1857, and is a daughter of Sebastian and Margaret Zeller. They have four children—Catherine M., Isabella O., Joseph A. and Ro[illegible]. Subject held the office of Road Supervisor in 1880, is a Republican, a member of the I. O. O. F. and A. O. U. W. societies, and owns 138 acres of fine land.

JOHN H. PAINE, farmer, P. O. Greenville, was born in Ripley Township, Bond County, January 12, 1836, son of Elisha and N[illegible] A. (Fenton) Paine, he a farmer, born in North Carolina; died July, 1871; she died in 1877. Subject is one of a family of twelve, and was educated in this county, where, June 3, 1858, he married Elizabeth Bean, born in Tennessee in 1840, and daughter of William and Margaret Bean. Subject had eight children, two of whom died in their infancy. Th[illegible] living are Mary, Margaret A., John H., Lewis A., George and Albert. At the time of the war, Mr. Paine joined Company B, Sixty-second Illinois Regiment, under Capt. Jourdon. He is a Baptist, a Democrat, has always been a farmer, has held the offices of School Director and Road Supervisor, and owns ninety acres of land.

JAMES WHITE was born in Rutherford County, N. C., in the year 1794, and emigrated to Illinois in company with his father, Thomas White, and family, in the fall of 1816. They came by wagon, the only means of transportation at that time, James being the driver of a five-horse team, carrying the household goods of the family over a route, the greater portion of which traversed as hilly, mountainous and rugged a country as can be found in the United States east of the Mississippi River. They crossed the Blue Ridge and the Cumberland Mountains over roads that would now be called impassable. In going down the steep, rocky mountain sides, in addition to having both the hind wheels of the wagon locked, it was often necessary to cut down small trees and fasten them by the top end to the hind part of the wagon, in order to prevent its going too fast and becoming unmanagable. The crossings of the mountain creeks and rivers were equally hazardous; but in the face of every obstacle they persevered until, being ferried over the Ohio River in a flat boat pushed along with poles, they landed in Illinois, the land of beautiful prairies, which, to mountaineers, as they were, appeared surprisingly level. Continuing their northwestern course from where they crossed the Ohio, near Golconda, they came to a halt, and settled in Section 9, Town 5 north, Range 3 west, one and a half miles west of where Greenville now stands. The country was then a wilderness, without roads, bridges, mills, schools, churches, or any other appurtenances of civilization. The wild beasts usually found in this region, and the

Indians who hunted them, roamed at will over the vast domain. The forests were rich with the stores of the wild bee, and the streams abounded with fish. The prairies were covered with a rank growth of grass, as tall as a man, and in many places much taller, while the timbered lands, in many localities, produced a luxuriant growth called by the settlers "wild pea-vine," which was equally as tall, and through which it was almost impossible to pass, either on foot or on horseback. All this afforded ample pasturage for the few cattle and horses that were in the country. All supplies for the settlers had to be procured at St. Louis, then a small trading-post, and were exchanged mostly for furs, venison hams, honey, etc., and Mr. White, having had ample experience as a teamster, was engaged much of the time during the first years of his residence here in hauling to and from St. Louis, for the different traders scattered over a wide extent of country. The only means of crossing the Mississippi then was by what was called a horse-boat—that is, a boat propelled by horse-power. When the people wished to go to mill, or when they needed a physician they had to go to Edwardsville, there being none nearer. The subject of this sketch was married in August, 1823, to Miss Mary Denny, whose family emigrated to Bond County in 1819, from Lincoln County, N. C. He settled on a tract of land in Section 9, above named, where he resided until the death of his wife, which occurred in 1852, she having been his faithful consort during twenty-nine years of the toils and hardships incident to frontier life. They raised a family of six children, five of whom are yet living. Since his wife's death, he has resided most of the time with his youngest son, near Jerseyville, Ill., and, although eighty-eight years of age, is in the enjoyment of excellent health and spirits, and bids fair to live many years longer. He has been a consistent member of the Presbyterian Church for over sixty years, and has never been addicted to intemperate habits of any kind. His recollection of the scenes and incidents connected with the early history of this country is remarkably good, and he delights to tell of the ups and downs of frontier life in Illinois.

ROBERT WILLEFORD, farmer, P. O. Old Ripley, was born in Rutherford County, Tenn., June 6, 1818. His parents were James and Sallie (Price) Willeford. James was born in Southampton County, Va., in 1791; was a farmer, and died in 1862. His wife was born in Franklin County, Va., and died in 1824. They had a family of two boys and two girls. Our subject attended a subscription school in Tennessee about two months, and for a short time in Bond County, where, on January 3, 1849, he married Malinda E. File, who was born in this county in 1830. Her parents were Daniel and Martha (James) File. By this marriage they had one son, Edward L., who married Lucy Davenport in 1869, and has five children. Mr. Willeford served twelve months in the Mexican war under Capt. Benjamin Sellers and Col. Ferris Foreman. Subject has always been a farmer and stock-raiser; has held the offices of School Director, County Commissioner and Township Trustee. He is a Regular Baptist, his political views are Democratic, and he owns 515 acres of the best land in Ripley Precinct.

WILLIS WILLEFORD, farmer, P. O. Old Ripley, was born in Ripley Precinct January 30, 1832; was the son of James and Nancy (Price) Willeford, natives of Virginia. James was born November 30, 1791; was a farmer by occupation, and died April 25, 1862. Nancy, his wife, was born February 6, 1801, and is still living with her son Willis, the subject of our sketch, who is one of her family of eight. He never went to school much; what little education he received was in subscription schools. He married in Bond County February 22, 1855, Polly A. Long, who was born in Madison May 15, 1836. She was the daughter of Peter and Elizabeth (Vincent) Long. Subject has six children—John, Elizabeth, James L., Martha E. (all married), William and Mary. Mr. Willeford is a farmer and stock-raiser. He was Justice of the Peace in 1864, Road Supervisor in 1855 and is at the present time Township Trustee. He is a Regular Baptist and a Democrat. Mr. Willeford is one of the most thrifty and successful farmers in Bond County, and now owns nearly fourteen hundred acres of land.

MULBERRY GROVE PRECINCT.

M. F. BOOK, farmer, P. O. Mulberry Grove, is a native of Lawrence County, Penn.; was born January 21, 1841, the second son born to his parents, who were John C. and Mary W. (Dick) Book. She was born February 18, 1821, in Mercer County, Penn. He was born in the same county and State October 16, 1816, son of Michael Book, of Washington County, Penn., a soldier in the war of 1812, and died in Pennsylvania. John C. Book emigrated west to this State in 1874, and died August, 1878. Our subject was brought up to farm labor, working for his father on the home estate. August 27, 1861, he volunteered his services in the defense of his country, was enrolled with Company D, One Hundredth Regiment of Pennsylvania Volunteer Infantry. He participated in many hard fought and bloody battles, some of which were James Island, N. C., Bull Run, Chantilly, South Mountain, Antietam, Fredericksburg, Jackson, Miss., siege of Knoxville, battle of the Wilderness, Spottsylvania, North Anna and Cold Harbor, where he was three times wounded and from the effects of said wounds he was discharged in February, 1865, and returned home to his family. May 16, 1861, he became the husband of Elizabeth A. Davis, born in Mercer County, Penn., daughter of Daniel and Sarah Davis. In November, 1871, he emigrated to this county and purchased land where he now resides, having about one hundred acres. He is a member of the M. E. Church, and a stanch Republican.

G. C. BRUNSON, farmer, P. O. Mulberry Grove, was born in the Empire State, in Chautauqua County, December 15, 1818; is the sixth child and fourth son born to Abel Brunson, a native of Oneida County. The mother of our subject was Sallie Love, daughter of John Love. The subject of these lines was reared under the paternal roof until of age, and in fact he remained with him until he attained his thirty fifth year, at which time he determined to cast his fortunes with the Buckeye State, locating in Ashtabula County, on the Western Reserve. Here he remained until the fall of 1863, when he came to this State, purchasing eighty acres in this township, and twenty acres in Fayette County. He has since been a constant resident of this township and associated with its interests. He has now 190 acres of land, and has improved the same, and brought it to its present state of progress, having a new house, good fences, and the surroundings are in keeping with the average of improvements in the county. While in Ashtabula County, he married Mrs. Bugby, a native of that State. Her maiden name was Betsey Whittaker. By this marriage he has one child, Dwight W., who resides with his parents on the farm, and has the principal charge of the same. It may be said of Mr. Brunson that he is a self made man. He received nothing from his parents by way of legacy or endowment, and started out in the world upon his own foundation, and by close application to his business, he has at length secured a competence for himself and family, having given his attention to farming as a business. He is a member of the Christian Church.

CHARLES E. DEE, miller, Mulberry

Grove, is the pioneer miller in the town of Mulberry Grove, and a truly self made man. He is a native of Vermont, born in 1837, near the [illegible] of Georgia; son of Hiram and Mary (W[illegible]) Dee. The Dee family are of Scotch and German ancestry. Hiram Dee was born in V[illegible]ont October 17, 1812; son of Washington Dee and Lucy Cooley. Hiram Dee w[illegible]rried in Vermont May 7, 18[illegible]5, to M[illegible]ria Walker, who was also a Vermonter, bor[illegible] 12, 1813, daughter of Lewis Walk[illegible] Mary Potter, who raised a family of t[illegible]ldren, Mary being the ninth in order [illegible]. Our subject removed in the fall of 18[illegible] [illegible]th his parents to Des Moines County, Iowa, [illegible]hin nine miles of Burlington. Here the[illegible] remained seven years. Then they m[illegible] this State and located at St. Jacobs, in [illegible]dison County. While here Mr. Dee died March 5, 1863, from disease contracted wh[illegible] the army. He was for many years a [illegible] of the Methodist Church, and was a[illegible] Whig, and later a stanch Republic[illegible]. His wife yet survives him and resides w[illegible]arles E., who took his father's place as [illegible] of the family, and had charge of th[illegible]. After coming to maturity he enga[illegible]arming, and subsequently accumulat[illegible]gh means to enable him to purchase a t[illegible]ng machine, which he run for twelve y[illegible] connection with his farming. In 186[illegible] came to Mulberry Grove. His first [illegible] was to build a saw mill. In 1870, h[illegible] the flouring-mill, and for several y[illegible]n the saw machinery in connection w[illegible] grist part. He was first associated in [illegible]ership with E. W. Dee. This lasted u[illegible]873, when our subject purchased his p[illegible] interest, and since has run the same o[illegible]n account, and is doing an excellent bus[illegible]. August 4, 1870, he married Sarah B. [illegible]ughter of William Riley, of this township. He is a member of the M. E. Church, and has two children George E., born November 7, 1873, and Charlie, born April 8, 1881.

CAPT. ISAAC N. ENLOE, farmer, P. O. Mulberry Grove, is a son of James Enloe, one of the old settlers in Bond County. He was born on the homestead on Section 3, March 7, 1836, the second son, and oldest one now living. Capt. Enloe has always been a resident of the township where he was born, remaining at home until he commenced doing business for himself. November 12, 1857, he married Sophronia V., daughter of Rep. Joseph Hensley, of Mercer County, whose wife was Elizabeth McGuire. The year following his marriage, he located on the farm he now owns, consisting of 124 acres in Section 4, all of which he improved. August 13, 1861, he volunteered as private in Company C, Twenty-sixth Illinois Volunteer Infantry; first promoted to Fourth Corporal, then to First Duty Sergeant, afterward to Orderly Sergeant, and finally was commissioned Captain of the Company, which he had charge of until July 29, 1865. During his service he was engaged in New Madrid, the advance on Corinth, Jackson, Miss., Resaca and all the battles in which his command was engaged until August 15, 1864, when he was wounded, being shot by a sharp-shooter, and was disabled until January, 1865, when he joined his command, and remained in the service until discharged July 29, 1865, since which time he has been engaged in farming. In politics, a Republican of the stanchest sort; he cast the first Republican vote in Mulberry voting precinct. He is a member of the Christian Church at Greenville. He has five children Alice wife of George Berryman, of Greenville; Solon A., James S., Lois and J[illegible] Foy.

JAMES ENLOE, retired farmer, P. O. Mulberry Grove, has been a resident of the

State since 1816, and of Bond County from 1818 to 1882. He was a son of Asahel Enloe, who was a native of York District of South Carolina, where our subject was born October 27, 1803. The grandsire was Isaac Enloe, of Scotch parentage, and served in the war of the revolution. Our subject came to Madison County, Ill., with his father in 1816, the next year making a crop there, and in 1818 came to what is now Bond County. Asahel (his father) purchased land where Greenville now stands. The cemetery now embraces a portion of said purchase. He was a scholarly man for his time, and taught school for many years, and was appointed Surveyor of the county by Gov. Bond, and held his office well on to forty years. He was for many years a member of the Presbyterian Church, being a Clerk and Chorister for years. He was a valued member of the community, esteemed by all who knew him as an upright man and Christian gentleman. His remains now repose in the cemetery in Greenville on the grounds that he first purchased. His wife was Sarah Stewart, a native of Ireland. She bore him ten children, five sons and five daughters– Mary, Violet, Cynthia, Ezekial, James, Hannah, Louisa, Enoch, Nathaniel and Isaac. James, our subject, made his father's house his home in his early manhood, and in 1825, began for himself, and worked out by the month and job. January 1, 1829, he married Sarah Bradford, sister of Judge Bradford, of Greenville. She was born in Kentucky March 19, 1816, and died November 22, 1871, having born twelve children. Eleven of the number lived to be grown— Nancy Ann, Mary E., William B., Isaac N., Violet R., Samuel G., Emery L., Harriet N., Louisa I., James S., Cynthia E. and Zontonia E. In 1832, Mr Enloe located on the farm he now owns, and has since remained; has 240 acres of land. Since 1835, he has been a member of the Presbyterian Church. He has always been a true Republican, and never missed an election.

SAMUEL G. ENLOE, farmer, P. O. Mulberry Grove. One of the Commissioners of Bond County, elected November, 1881, is S. G. Enloe, who was born on the homestead March 30, 1840. He is the second son of James and Sarah (Bradford) Enloe. Samuel received the advantages afforded by the schools of his neighborhood. At the outbreak of the war, he donned the blue, enlisting as private in May, 1861, in Company D, Twenty-second Regiment Illinois Volunteer Infantry. Soon after he was transferred to Company F, One Hundredth and Thirtieth Regiment, with which he served until April, 1865, when he was commissioned as First Lieutenant in Company B, in the same Regiment, in which capacity he served until the close of the war. He was mustered out in August, 1865, and returned home in September of the same year. During his association with the army, he participated in the following engagements: Fort Gibson, Miss., Champion Hills, Black River Bridge, Siege of Vicksburg, Siege of Mobile, and after his transfer to New Orleans he served in all the battles in which his regiment was engaged in Louisiana, and on Cane River. Upon his return home he began improving his farm, upon which he located after his marriage November 30, 1871, to Elizabeth V. Martin, born in Rockingham County, N. C., daughter of J. H. Martin and Rachel Proctor, now of Montgomery County, this State. In politics, Mr. Enloe is a Republican, and in November, 1881, he was elected County Commissioner. His farm consists of 115 acres. He has one child, Ernest R.

MOSES ELAM, farmer, P. O. Mulberry Grove. Among the substantial citizens of Bond County none are more highly respected than the above. He was born October 25,

1821, in Rutherford County, N. C., and emigrated to Fayette County with his parents when a mere lad. Here he remained about fifteen years. December 23, 1841, he married Martha F. Elam, who was born Jan. 12, 1827, a native of Virginia, daughter of Daniel Elam and Mary Graves, who emigrated from Virginia to Maury County, Tenn, about the year 1828, where they remained until the year 1831, when they removed to Bond County, stopping near Greenville, but remained a short time, and located permanently in Fayette County, where they remained until their death. Their deaths occurred in 1862 and 1854 respectively. They raised a family of six children, four of whom are now living, of whom Thomas resides in Arkansas: Mary J., Mrs Elisha Matthews, of this county. Susan became the wife of William Cheeseman, of Henry County, Mo. After Mr. Elam's marriage he remained in Fayette County three years, and then moved across the line into Mulberry Grove, and engaged in merchandising, continuing twelve years. October, 1856, he located on the farm he now owns, situated in Section 26, and has since been engaged in farming, and has been successful, having nearly six hundred acres of land, 320 here, and 242 in Fayette, and besides assisted his children in making a start in life. He has five children Moses, Thomas E., Melvina, Jenkins and Richard, all residents of this county. Melvina married Rev. Thomas [illegible], of the Christian Church. The father of our subject was William Elam, born and married in Virginia, and son of Alexander Elam, a native of Virginia, and of English descent. The mother of our subject was Patience, daughter of Philip Hunt, who removed from Virginia to North Carolina, where they remained sixteen years. Mr Elam is a member of the Christian Church.

E. V. GASKINS, farmer and stock raiser, P. O. Mulberry Grove. "Son," as he is best known, was born in Greenville November 29, 1841. He is the only son and sole heir of Judge Enrico Gaskins, a native of Norfolk, Va., born June 14, 1812, and son of Spencer Gaskins. Enrico, the father of "Son," was a hatter by trade, and came West to Greenville in 1835, where he set up in business, continuing the same for several years, and afterward became prominently identified with its business interests. He was Clerk of the Court about twenty years, and eight years County Judge. He was a thorough and correct business man. In 1859, he entered land in Town 6, Range 2, and purchased other lands adjoining the same, which land is now owned and occupied by E. V. Mr. Gaskin was a prominent member of the Masonic fraternity; also of the Independent Order of Odd Fellows. In politics he was a stanch Republican, and in every sense of the word a representative man and valued member of the commonwealth. His marriage with Mrs. Sarah Conn, relict of Dr. Conn, was crowned with the birth of three children; but one of the number is now living, E. V. He located on the farm in 1872. His death occurred February 18, 1879. Mrs. Gaskin's maiden name was Hall, daughter of Joshua and Charlotte (Strider) Hall. She was born June 18, 1814, in Jefferson County, Va., and came West with her parents to this county in 1833. E. V. has been located on the farm since his father's location here in 1872. In 1863, he married Charlotte, born in this county, daughter of John S. Hall. He has one daughter, Lena, aged sixteen. For four years Mr. E. V. Gaskin was a resident of Mulberry Grove, being engaged while here in merchandising. Since his location here on the farm, he has been engaged in farming, and is giving his attention to the breeding of fine cattle and horses, of which he has the best stock. He has 600 acres of land, located on Section 23, with a new house and comfortable surroundings.

J. J. HARPER, farmer, P. O. Mulberry Grove. The Harper family rank among the pioneer families in Town 5, Range 2. They were natives of Tennessee, and located where J. M. Harper now resides. The subject of these lines is a descendant of this family. He was born May 28, 1838, on the farm he now owns on Section 22. He is the second son of Thomas Harper, who was born in Maury County, Tenn., and emigrated to this county in the year 1829. The mother of our subject was Priscilla Segraves, daughter of Bennett Segraves, likewise one of the earliest settlers in this township. But two children were born to Thomas Harper and wife, whose names were Robert and Jefferson J. The latter was young when his father died. His mother died in 1867. J. J. succeeded his father on the homestead, where he has since lived. February 10, 1859, he married Milley E. Brown, born in Fayette County, daughter of James and Dorcas Brown, both natives of Tennessee. Mr. Harper has a farm of 170 acres. He has two children—James T. and Alice.

J. P. LILLIGH, farmer, P. O. Mulberry Grove. Clarion County, Penn., sent some good farmers and citizens to Bond County, among whom is the above, who was born in February, 1841, being the eldest son of Jacob Lilligh and Catharine Mahle. Jacob Lilligh was born in Lancaster County, Penn.; son of Jacob, a native of Germany. The family emigrated West to this locality in the spring of 1865. J. P. married in Pennsylvania Hannah Cornish in 1854. She was a daughter of Henry Cornish. She died in 1872, leaving two children—Addison and Kate. His last marriage was to Miss Nancy Buchannon, a native of this county. She was a daughter of John Buchannon, who was one of the early settlers of the county. When Mr. Lilligh first came here he purchased eighty acres of land, and has since added to the same until he has now 500 acres. For twenty years he has been a member of the German Baptist Church, with which his parents have long been identified. He has by his last marriage two children living—Minnie and Grace. He has improved the farm greatly since his location here, having built all the substantial improvements on the same.

HENRY LILLIGH, farmer, P. O. Woburn, is the second son of Jacob Lilligh. Henry was born May 1, 1849, and emigrated to this county with the family in 1865. In 1872, he married Harriet Morey, daughter of Hiram Morey, one of the old time settlers in this county. After his marriage, he located in Mulberry Grove, where he engaged in the mercantile business, where he continued until 1875, when he located on the farm he now owns. He is an excellent farmer, and has been successful. He has 280 acres of land, forty of which is timber. His farm is well improved, and is very productive. He is a member of the German Baptist Church and has recently been promoted to the rank of minister in his church. He has four children—Ida Marian, Mary Louisa, Emmet Wilburn and Edward Earl.

J. MATTINLY, physician, Mulberry Grove, specialist of the eye and ear, also of the treatment and cure of cancers, who first saw the light of day July 7, 1813, in Lincoln County, Tenn.; son of Rollin, born March 10, 1788, in North Carolina, who was a son of Richard Mattinly, whose children were David, James, John, Rollin and Waring. The mother, Nancy Luttrell, was born March 31, 1793, and died May 13, 1881; she was the daughter of Michael Luttrell, a Revolutionary soldier, and who lived to be almost a centenarian, the family being remarkable for their longevity. Our subject removed with his father to Alabama, in Jackson County, when he was a lad of tender years, where they resided until the year 1830, when they came to Marion County, this State, where his father died September 6, 1866. Very much credit is due the subject of our sketch, as he was thrown upon his own resources at an early age, leaving home without shoes or sufficient clothing to shield him from the inclement weather, and unable to read the simplest sentence in a newspaper. He hired out at $6 per month, and assisted in maintaining the family in the meantime. For five years he drove stage, and during that time he made use of his spare time in improving his mind, being resolved, that as his temporal affairs were being advanced, that his mind should receive its share also. He came to this township in 1839, and was married the same year to Mary A. Hubbard, who died in 1840, leaving one son, David Rollin. His second and last wife was Sarah Tate, born in Stokes County, N. C., September 9, 1809, daughter of Samuel Tate, born in Stokes County, N. C., in 1776, and died April 23, 1842, and Sarah (Faulkner) Tate, born in Wake County, N. C., in 1775, and died in 1853. She bore him three children, two of whom are living —Lizzie, wife of John T. Buchannon, Annie and Sarah E. Soon after he came to this place, he entered a piece of land and began farming, which he continued until 1860. In the meantime he was reading scientific works, medicine being his favorite. February, 1861, he began practice in Greenville. Since April 10, 1862, he has been located here in Mulberry Grove, giving especial attention to the treatment of the eye and ear, as well as cancer, treating them with success. He has 200 acres of land, and considerable town property. The Doctor has done much to impress upon the minds of the people the necessity of the knowledge of phrenology and sexual science among the people.

E. W. OLIVER, physician, Mulberry Grove, is a North Carolinian by birth, born in Rockingham County February 10, 1844; son of Elijah Oliver, born in Rockingham County, N. C., about 1805, and died January 5, 1881, whose father was Peter, who was a resident of North Carolina at the time of the battle of Bunker Hill. The mother of the Doctor was Annie, daughter of Enoch Axton, born in Rockingham County, N. C., about 1805, and died in 1863. In 1861, he left North Carolina for Indiana, where he remained a short time; then came to Charleston, Coles Co., this State, where he remained some length of time. He was, early in life, left to his own resources, with a limited education, in North Carolina. The nearest school from his father's house was three miles and a half; hence his advantages for schooling were not encouraging. After his coming to Illinois, he, by close application to his studies, succeeded in acquiring such qualifications that enabled him to teach the district school of the neighborhood, which he did for several terms. During this time he took up the study of medicine. In 1870, he gave the subject his earnest attention. He continued the same until his graduation, receiving his diploma at Keokuk, Iowa, February 17, 1874, in the College of Physicians and Surgeons, at which time he came to Woburn, Town 6, Range 2, and engaged in the practice of his profession, where he remained until September, 1881, when he came to Mulberry Grove, where he has since been identified, and is having a liberal patronage of the people. He was educated to the old-school system, but he ignores to some extent some of the medicine commonly used in that system, calomel, for instance, and in its stead makes use of other remedies equally as effective. In 1871, he married Virginia A. Jett, born in Montgomery County, Ill., July 8, 1850, daughter of Washington A. Jett, who died about 1856, and Sarah Wright. By her he had five children the first still born, Albert W., William E. (dead), Essie W. and Harry J. He is a member of the Christian Church and of the Masonic order. He has but two sisters living—Sarah and Rachel, the former of Virginia, the latter in Rockingham County, N. C.

JAMES C. PINNEO, farmer and stock-raiser, P. O. Smithboro, is a native of Newark, N. J., and was born July 17, 1839. He is the youngest of the family. His father is James B. Pinneo, one of the prominent and well-known business men of that locality (New Jersey). He was born in Milford, in the State of Connecticut; son of Bezaleel Pinneo, a Presbyterian minister. Our subject is a near relative of the grammarian, whose works are so well known in the Eastern States. Eliza, the mother of James C., was a daughter of Samuel Lyman, of Goshen, Conn., of Puritanical stock. The family of Bezaleel, consisted of seven children, four sons and three daughters, of whom James B. was the eldest. The subject of these lines received good school advantages, and of a good business education. He first came West in October, 1861, and for some time was in Government employ, being connected with the Quartermaster's Department and afterward engaged in trading and in commercial pursuits in St. Louis and elsewhere. In 1869, he made the purchase of the farm he now owns, situated on Section 9, and moved on his property the following year. His residence is built upon a gentle eminence which he has improved by planting shrubbery and evergreens, and on either side of the drive are beautiful maples, which give the place a refined appearance. Mr. Pinneo has put all the improvements on the farm that now appear, in the way of building, and very much of the fencing, and has spent much labor and money executing his designs, and has an excellent farm, which is adjacent to Smithboro Post Office and Henderson Station, and four miles from the county seat. June 9, 1870, he married Miss Minnie Gray, born in Stamford, Conn., daughter of William E. Gray and Sarah Adams, the latter a sister of Stonewall Adams. The parents of Mrs. Gray emigrated West in 1858. Her father was a prominent builder and contractor in the West and North. Mr. Pinneo has one child—Saida L. He is a member of the Presbyterian Church.

JOHN RILEY, farmer, P. O. Mulberry Grove, was born December 1, 1828, in Town 5, Range 3, in Bond County, and in 1835 removed with his parents to Town 6, where he lived until about the year 1868, when he removed to this township, where he has since lived. The father of our subject was named Barnabas Riley, who was born in Georgia, and emigrated North to this State in this county in 1818. He stayed one year, when he went South to Kentucky, but returned to this county the following year, where he remained until his death, which occurred in 1849. His wife survived him until 1876. He was a soldier in the war of 1812, and was for many years a member of the M. E. Church for many a long term of years and leading light in the same, being Class-Leader and Steward for many years. John, our subject, was raised to agricultural pursuits, his father being a farmer. He worked as carpenter and builder, but gave his attention to farming principally. He raised a family of nine children, whose names were James, William, John, Elizabeth, Minerva, Samuel M., Barnabas, Sarah and Mary. March, 1850, he married Jane C. Steele, a native of this State, and daughter of Andrew Steele. She died in 1866, leaving one child, which died young. His present wife was Mrs. Elizabeth J. Kingsbury, daughter of Richard Withers, of Collinsville, this State. Mr. Wither's wife was Eliza Johnson, her father being Mr. Johnson, one of the first settlers in Madison County. By his last wife Mr. Riley has three children—Vahlue S., Anna E. and John E. Mr. Riley is a Republican, and filled the office of County Commissioner one term, and since 1846 has been a member of the M. E. Church. He has 155 acres of land. His brother William served in the late war, and was a member of the Twenty-second Illinois, and was badly wounded, and is now on the pension list.

J. H. SPRADLING, farmer and merchant, P. O. Mulberry Grove, was born August 1, 1828 in Maury County, Tenn.; son of James Spradling, who was born in Tennessee April 9, 1796, and died April 11, 1867, who served in the war of 1812, and married Frances T. Oliver, who was born in Virginia March 25, 1789, and died December 7, 1869, and by her raised a family of three children. The eldest was Amarantha P.; J. H. and Frances J. were the other two. Amarantha is now the wife of James Riley, and Frances J. married John Segrest, both of this township. Our subject emigrated to this locality with his parents when he was quite young, his father making a purchase on Section 25, Town 6, Range 2 west. He entered the land from the Government, and engaged in farming, and spent the remainder of his days on the farm. He was a stanch Democrat, and highly esteemed by his fellow-citizens, and was affiliated with the Methodist Church, and lived a life in harmony with his profession. His death occurred in April, 1866, having attained one year over his "threescore and ten." J. H. having attained the years of manhood, succeeded his father as a husbandman. December 30, 1849, he wedded Cynthia A., his wife who was born in Hancock County, Ind., February 20, 1832, daughter of William, born in North Carolina September 1, 1807, and Eliza (Snodgrass) Jackson, he being a native of North Carolina, and she of Indiana, daughter of James Snodgrass. John Jackson, the paternal grandfather of Mrs. Spradling, was for many years a resident of Carolina and removed with his family to Indiana. His son, William Jackson, removed to this county locating in Town 5, Range 2, near Fairview when the county was partially settled Mrs. Spradling being about ten years of age when she came with her father. The family consisted of her father, three brothers and herself. The mother died in Indiana. Since Mr. Spradling's marriage, he has been a resident of the township. Since 1870, he has been a resident of the Grove, and been engaged in merchandising, his stock consisting of hardware, grass seed and agricultural implements. He has about three hundred and twenty-six acres, eighty-six being in the county adjoining, and all of which he yet carries on. He has seven children—John F., Eliza P., Mrs. Joseph Call; William H. who resides in Pocahontas; Albert M., George L. Laura B. and Harry W. Mr. Spradling is a good Republican, and a member of the Christian Church.

L. J. SEGRAVES, farmer, P. O. Pleasant Mound, is the oldest living settler in the township, having been a constant resident here since the spring of 1828. He was born March 11, 1816, in Maury County, Tenn., and emigrated to this locality, as stated above. His father was Bennett Segraves, a native of Georgia, born July 21, 1791, and when a young man moved to Tennessee, where he married Margaret Lockhart, who was born December 25, 1797, in Davidson County, Tenn., and died September 22, 1844, daughter of

Thomas and Martha Lockhart. He (Bennett) died July 29, 1868. The paternal grandfather of our subject was Jacob Segraves, of Scotch descent, a Revolutionary soldier. He remained and raised a large family, among whom were Vincent, Bennett, Daniel, Isaac and Sarah, who were his offspring by his first wife. By his second wife he had Jacob, William, Henry Jackson, John, Jane, Polly and Malinda, none of whom are living. Bennett Segraves was in the war of 1812, and a Democrat all his life, and a substantial member of the community, and passed to his rest July 7, 1868, having raised to maturity the following children: Priscilla, who married Thomas L. Hooper, Lockhart J., Sarah J. E., wife of James Widger; Nancy D., wife of John George; Martha, Mrs. William Henninger; Love married Mr. Steele; Mary H., wife of Wilson T. Hays; Rebecca never married; Nelson B.; Margaret C., Mrs. Booker; Lucinda P., Mrs. John Whitley. Of those living are Sarah, Margaret, Lucinda, Mary, Lockhart J., who was married January 6, 1843, to Diana, born in Tioga County, Penn. March 10, 1826, daughter of Gilbert, born October 12, 1793, and Lucinda (Ives) Vangorden, born October 22, 1797, and died April 5, 1867. He was a native of New York, and she of Pennsylvania. They came West to Michigan in 1836, and to this county in 1840. Mr. Segraves has but one child, John Bird, who married Letta Johnson. He resides on a portion of the homestead farm. He has three daughters—Lillie E., Lucinda G. and Della. Mr. Segraves has 207½ acres of land, and is a member of the I. O. O. F. Mrs. Segraves is a member of the Baptist Church. The children born them deceased are—Maria Lucinda, who died July 7, 1871, aged twenty-three years, eleven months and nine days; Mary Eveline died in 1852, aged fourteen months.

JOHN WATTS, farmer, P. O. Mulberry Grove, takes first rank among the su[illegible]tial farmers and stanch men of Bond [illegible]. He began in the world poor, having [illegible] his father until twenty-four years of [illegible] him the entire benefit of his labor [illegible] ings in the meanwhile. He [illegible] ruary 17, 1808, in York State; [illegible] William Watts, a native of Mas[illegible]. His wife was Susanna Hodge, wh[illegible] ten children, eight of whom grew [illegible] a lad of eight years, our subject re[illegible] his parents to Franklin County [illegible] remaining there until after attaining [illegible] hood, when he removed to Madis[illegible] where he lived until the fall [illegible] he came to Illinois and located i[illegible] ship, and purchased 205 acres, fift[illegible] were somewhat improved. Since tha[illegible] has been a constant resident of the [illegible] and been identified with its temporal [illegible] religious interests, having joined the M. E. Church soon after his location here [illegible] a consistent member of the same. In [illegible] poral matters, he has been successful, having acquired and owned at one time about six hundred acres of land, a large porti[illegible] of which he has since sold and divided out among his children, reserving 265 [illegible] for himself. After leaving his father [illegible] twenty-four years of age he was married t[illegible] Babcock, a native of Pennsylvania, [illegible] of Nathaniel Babcock and Rache[illegible]. Of a family of seven children born [illegible] six grew up—Susanna, Catharine, Li[illegible] Lucy J. and Rosilla. Susanna is [illegible] William Goff, of this township; Lin[illegible] in Town 5, Range 2, and is the wife [illegible] Walker; Catharine married John S[illegible] and moved to Kansas City; Jasper [illegible] this county; Rosilla and Lucy J. [illegible] ried and raised families, but have [illegible] ceased.

POCAHONTAS PRECINCT.

JACOB CRICHFIELD, deceased. The grandfather of the above was an Englishman by birth. His given name was Robert, and he served on board of a British man-of-war. When near the Massachusetts coast he with several others premeditated their departure, got permission to go out rowing in the jolly boat, and while out made good their escape. Soon after landing, they met a Quaker, who, judging them to be deserters, said to them, "Thee must change thy clothes and thy names, or thee will be caught." Acting upon this piece of useful information, Robert (it is not known what his surname was) changed his to Crichfield. He had three sons born him, whose names were Benjamin, Absalom and William, all of whom served in the war of the Revolution, after which Benjamin settled in R[illegible], Va., William in Somerset County, Penn. Absalom never married. He was a musician; the others were farmers. The descendants who came here to Illinois were children of William, who settled in Pennsylvania. He had a family of twelve children, all of whom came to maturity. Among this number were Joseph and Jacob, who came to this county. Joseph emigrated to this region of country at the time of the war of 1812. His wife was among the number who sought refuge in the old fort which stood in this township, of which history gives an account. Jacob, his brother, came West to Bond County, arriving here April 4, 1839, fixing his location on Section 25, in Town 4, Range 4, in Mulberry Grove Precinct, where he remained until his death June 8, 1846. His wife's maiden name prior to her marriage was Johanna Jellison, daughter of Robert Jellison, an Englishman. She died in 1850. Mr. Crichfield was a member of the M. E. Church, and his house was the home for the ministers. Four children were born him: Edith E., Hannah S., William M. and Freeborn. Of the number Edith died unmarried. Hannah married J. H. Gilmore, and settled in Greenville. She died in 187[illegible]. William M. and Freeborn both served in the war as true and valiant soldiers. William M. enlisted in June, 1861, in Company F, Twenty-second Regiment, and served three years, and participated in all the battles in which his company took part. F. G. enlisted in August, 1862, in Company E, One Hundred and Thirtieth Regiment Illinois Volunteer Infantry. He also served three years. April 11, 1865, William M. married Emma Wilds, who was born in Hamilton, Ohio, daughter of Ralph Wilds and [illegible] Jackson. He has three children: Lil[illegible], Dale S. and Grace E.

TOBIAS FILE, farmer, P. O. Bade[illegible], came to Bond County with his parents in 18[illegible], and located with them in Old Ripley Precinct. He was born March 20, 1810, in Cabarras County, on Rock River, N. C. His father was Henry File, and his mother's maiden name was Rupp. To Henry File was born the following family: George, Daniel, Moses, Tobias and Sallie. Sallie resides in Litchfield, and is the wife of Isaac Bilyew. She and Tobias are the only ones [illegible] of the family. All of the above settled in Bond County and have descendants. Tobias [illegible] remained with his father until [illegible]. His boyhood was spent on the farm, [illegible] assisted his father in clearing up the land. His school advantages were of the most limited character, and he has had to plod his way through life without having any substantial school benefits. In January, 1830, he married Sarah Gillespie, a native of Tennessee, daughter of John Gillespie and Nancy McFerron. Mr. File located in Millersburg Precinct, where he now resides, in 1837, and has since remained. His wife died in 1850, having borne him seven children, six of whom are living—Samuel, William, Nancy J., Tobias, Jacob and George. He married Fannie Cook for his second wife, who died leaving no issue. His third and last wife was Mrs. Hannah Baker. Mr. File has 400 acres of land, and since 1832 has been a member of the M. E. Church, and has always been one of the substantial citizens of the commonwealth.

JOHN H. GORDON, physician, Pocahontas, is among the worthy and successful practitioners of medicine in Bond County. He was born October 29, 1842, in Huntsville, Ala.; is of a family of seven sons, all of whom were doctors, sons of Dr. James and Mary (Sanderson) Gordon. When a babe, he removed with his parents to Spring Hill, Miss., and left there prior to 1850. He was educated at the best schools at Russellville, Ark., and began the study of his profession before seventeen, and began practice ere he attained his majority. In 1864, he received the benefits of the St. Louis Medical College. His practice was attended with the most favorable encouragement, which kept him busy, and his graduation at the Missouri Medical College was not completed until 1874. He began practice in Millersburg, this township, in 1864, and two years later he came to Pocahontas, where he has since lived, and been engaged in his profession. At the time he came here there were eight physicians, including himself, in a town not exceeding five hundred inhabitants. In 1868, he associated with his brother, J. T. Gordon, under the firm name of J. H. Gordon & Brother, which copartnership lasted until 1870. He then purchased his brother's interest, and continued alone until 1873, at which time he took in as partner his brother W. P., and continued together until 1878, when he subsequently associated with Dr. A. R. Clinton, January, 1878, which partnership was dissolved in the summer of 1879. Since this time he has been running it alone and has an excellent practice. December 15, 1861, he married Emily Torrence, born in North Carolina, but raised in Arkansas. She is a daughter of John T. Torrence and Jane Linch. The Doctor has eleven children born to him, five of whom are living—William E., Charles C., Lewis L., Kate and George D. The others died in infancy, except Nancy J., who died December 3, 1877, aged ten years. The Doctor has been a member of the M. E. Church since he was fifteen years of age. He is a member of the A., F. & A. M., of this place. He makes a specialty of female complaints, in the treatment of which he is successful.

JOHN W. HARNED, farmer, P. O. Pocahontas, was born in Red River County Tex., January 26, 1819; son of William and Hannah (Boyer) Harned, he born in 1792, a Methodist preacher, left the Yuba River, Cal., October 8, 1850, and was never afterward heard of. His wife was born in Pennsylvania, in 1792, and died in November, 1850. They were the parents of eleven children, seven boys and four girls. The only education our subject ever had was received in a log cabin, in the Red River bottoms, where he attended school for a short time. He first worked on the farm of Williamson Plant, Bond County, and has been in the farming business ever since. In Bond County February 2, 1842, he married Mary M. Nelson, born in Bond County August 16, 1820, daughter of William and Mary (McLean) Nelson. He has nine children William C., Henry C., Joseph, Nelson, Melvina, John B., Eda R., Louis, James M. and Jennie. Mr. Harned is a member of the Methodist Church, and his wife has been connected with the old "Gilead" Cumberland Presbyterian Church for forty-five years. He spent the first ten years of his life in what is now Texas, but which was then part of Mexico, and owing to his constant association with neighboring Indian tribes, he could speak the Choctaw language much better than English. His father was bitterly opposed to slavery: and, during his residence in the South, suffered many persecutions on account of his abolitionist principles. He stood by the side of Lovejoy when he was shot. He built a hotel in Alton, Ill., in 1833, where our subject met Lincoln, Douglas, and many others of the noted men in the early history of our country. Mr. Harned was well acquainted with the famous Black Hawk, chief of the Fox Indians.

JAMES S. JOHNSTON, farmer, P. O. Pocahontas. The above gentleman first beheld th light of day July 20, 1827, in Cincinnati, Ohio: second son of Campbell Johnson, a native of Londonderry, Ireland, where he was born about the year 1793, and came to America in 1808, in company with his brother James, with whom he worked several years as carpenters. Prior to the war of 1812, they engaged in the manufacture of nails at Pittsburgh, and shipped their products down the river on flat-boats, and were en route for the Lower Mississippi at the time of the battle of New Orleans. About the year 1818, he went to Cincinnati and engaged in a general mercantile business, remaining here until the year 1832, when he moved to Clermont County, Ohio, and purchased a farm, upon which he died in 1842. He was a Presbyterian, and a stanch Jackson Democrat. His wife's maiden name was Jerusha Sandford, who died in 1852, having borne five children who came to maturity John, James S., Nancy C., Hannah H. and Robert A. John served in the Mexican war, and is now a lawyer in Cincinnati. Nancy C. resides in the same place, and is the wife of Thomas Sherlock. Hannah H. never married. Robert A. also resides in Cincinnati, and is now serving his second term as Common Pleas Judge. James remained at home until his marriage, when he attained twenty two years of age. His wife was Melvina Simpkins, of Clermont County, daughter of David Simpkins, also an Ohioan. After the marriage of our subject, he engaged in merchandising at Belfast, Ohio, where he continued until the spring of 1857, when he came to Bond County, locating where he now resides, on Section 33, in Ripley Township, Town 4, Range 5, where he has been engaged in agricultural pursuits. He has about four hundred acres of land, and has given considerable attention to sheep raising, and particularly to fruit culture, having one of the largest and finest orchards in the county, embracing nearly sixty acres. He has a good knowledge of law, and does considerable local practice. He is a Democrat, and in the affairs of his county and township he bears his proportionate part. He has six children Mary, Nancy C., Cora, Campbell D., Lucinda and Hattie.

HENRY H. METCALF, Greenville, is a descendant of one of the early settlers, whose name was Baalam Metcalf, who was born in April, 1806, in Jackson County, Ga. He emigrated to Bond County in the spring of 1829, making his first location on the north east quarter of Section 14, in Beaver Creek Township, Town 4, Range 3. He afterward removed to Greenville, where he remained some time, then came to this township, and remained from 1854 until his death December 15, 187[illegible]. He was a staunch old Whig, and after the formation of the Republican party he became affiliated with it, and was true to its principles as long as he exercised his right of suffrage. He took a deal of interest in the affairs of his county, and for several years was Justice of the Peace, and meted out justice to the settlers to their satisfaction. His wife's maiden name was Emeline Brown, daughter of Thomas, whose wife was a Hill; both families came from the Carolinas. Henry H. was the only son, and has always been a resident of Bond County, except the time spent in the army, which he entered at the age of seventeen, enlisting in the spring of 1861 in Company E, Twenty-second Illinois Infantry, and served until July, 1864, and took part in many of the prominent engagements in which his regiment was in, some of which were Charleston, Mo., Stone River, Resaca, Corinth, Mission Ridge and Chickamauga. September, 1866, he married Ellen Hilliard, daughter of J. C. Hilliard and Jane Dewey. For several years, Mr. Metcalf was engaged in teaching. He located on his farm in 18[illegible], and has 150 acres. He has five children—[illegible] L., Ralph E., Jennie E., Hugh and M[illegible]. He is a member of the M. E. Church. He was elected Justice of the Peace in the fall of 1881.

JOHN NEATHAMMER, farmer, P. O. Pocahontas, was born in Bond County, February 2[illegible], 1847, son of John and Mary (Heek[illegible]) Neathammer, he born in Wurtemberg, Germany, in 1808. He followed the occupation of farmer, and died in 1859. His wife was [illegible] Tennessee, and died in 1851. [illegible] County, in 1870, he married Ollie Seafeldt, born in St. Louis in 1850, daughter of Julius and Mina Seafeldt, of Pocahontas. Mr. Neathammer is in politics a Republican, and is a member of the A. O. U. W. During the war, he served two years in Company E, Third Illinois Cavalry (Capt. McLane), and took part in the engagements at Memphis and Nashville. He has three children—Mary, Mina and Julius.

LEARNER BLACKMAN PLANT, Pocahontas. Contemporaneous with the earliest settlement of Bond County was the coming of the Plant family to Pocahontas Township, whose advent to this locality was shortly after the war of 1812. The subject of these lines was born in this township April 12, 1819; is the eldest son of Robert Plant and Nancy Patterson, to whom three children were raised to maturity, L. B. being the eldest; Elizabeth, who married George Patterson, and America, wife of Henry Eppstine. Robert Plant died in 1852, highly esteemed by his friends and neighbors. Learner B. remained with his father until he married, which was in December 5, 1839, to Rebecca Duncan, a native of Madison County, daughter of Joseph. After his marriage, he moved where Stubblefield Station now is, and engaged in farming. In 1858, he located on the farm he now owns in the northwest part of the township. Before dividing among his children, he had over four hundred acres of land, reserving the larger portion, upon which he lives. He has five children—Joseph, I. D., Sarah C., Henry C. and Mary A.

JAMES S. RIDGWAY, Pocahontas, was born in Scioto County, Ohio, August 27, 1831, eldest son of William Ridgway, born [illegible] j[illegible] came to this county with his father in t[illegible] 1841, and settled in Ripley Town s[illegible] He remained here about five years, and th[illegible] settled on Section 29; remained there u[illegible] his death, December 11, 1868. In early d[illegible] a Democrat, and in 1856 a Republican. H[illegible] to maturity a family of four children: [illegible] S., William, Mary and George W[illegible] this number James S. is the only [illegible] in this county. William died in [illegible] Mary became the wife of W. S. W[illegible] W. resides in Kansas. James S[illegible] with his father until his marriage. [illegible] twice married, and by his [illegible] has four children: Nancy, Benjamin, William and Ralph. He began improving the farm in 1855, locating on it after his marriage in 1860, and has since remained. H[illegible] about four hundred acres of land i[illegible] 27, and is quite extensively engaged in general farming. He is Demo[illegible] [illegible]ities. His wife is a member of the Methodist Episcopal Church.

GEORGE L. SCHNEIDER, farmer, Pocahontas, was born in Darmstadt, Germany, August 23, 1829; son of Lewis and M[illegible] Schneider, he a carpenter and [illegible] by trade. He died in Germany, and also his wife. They were the parents of five children, three boys and two girls. Our subject attended school in Darmstadt until he arrived at his sixteenth year, when he chose the trade of his father, and [illegible] with him. In Bond County, in August, [illegible] he married Anna Brown, born [illegible] 25, 1829, daughter of John and [illegible] Brown. Mr. Schneider has followed the occupation of a farmer, and has [illegible] at his trade in Bond County. He [illegible] the office of School Director for [illegible] and is at present County Commissioner. He is a member of the German [illegible] Church, and is connected with the

Masonic fraternity. In politics, he is a Republican. His farm of 160 acres is one of the best in Pocahontas Precinct. He has seven children—John L., Nancy Ann, Henry M., William C., Benjamin F., Simon L. and Martha S.

JOHN LEWIS SEHNERT, hotel, saloon and general business, Pierron. Among the principal business men of Oakdale is John L. Sehnert. He was born June 23, 1850, in Hesse Darmstadt, and is the third child of a family of five. His father, Peter Sehnert, was married to the mother of John in the Fatherland. Her maiden name, prior to her marriage, was Anna E. Weischant. Peter Sehnert was born in Hesse-Darmstadt September 20, 1820, and died in 1881. His wife yet survives him. John Lewis was but a babe when his parents emigrated to America. Their first place of living, soon after their arrival, was in Bloomington, McLean County, where the family remained two or three years, and in 1857 came to Greenville, where he lived about ten years, when he located in Madison County, where he spent the remainder of his days. He raised a family of four children. The eldest was Mary, who married Ulrich Gaffner, and lives in Town 5, Range 2. Lizzie, the second daughter, married Michael Maugers. John L. and John Peter are the sons. John Lewis was raised a farmer, and has learned the machinist's trade and has had much practical experience in running machinery. November 10, 1874, he married Miss Franciska Spengel, a native of Madison County, daughter of Sebastian Spengel. Mr. Sehnert removed to Pierron in February, 1881, and engaged in business. He is proprietor of the Oakdale House, and provides amply for the entertainment of both man and beast. He farms some, and has a steam thresher (road engine) which he [illegible] has three children born him—George, Sebastian and Margaret. George and Sebastian are still living.

W. S. WAIT, farmer, P. O. Pocahontas, was born in 1828, in Cambridge, Mass., the eldest son of William S. and Sarah (Newhall) Wait. He came with his parents to this county when a lad of few years, being about the year 1834 or 1835, and since that time has been a constant resident of the county. In 1854, he began running a saw-mill near Greenville, which he moved to this place in 1857, to which he added a grist-mill, being the first permanent mill of the kind ever run in the place. He engaged in the stock business, buying and selling, which he carries on in conjunction with his farming. He has been twice married. First, in 1859, to Mary Ridgway, who died soon after, leaving no living issue. In May, 1877, he married Adele Ravold, a native of France, who has borne him three children. Mr. Wait has been successful in business. He has about seven hundred acres of land. He is not a member of any church organization, but is affiliated with the I. O. O. F. of this place.

BEAVER CREEK PRECINCT.

HENRY BASS. In a list of some of the most prominent agriculturists and self-made men of Bond County, the name of Henry Bass, of Greenville City, occupies a prominent place. He was born in Fayette County, Ill., April 22, 1833, and was the sixth child of the family of twelve children of Guilford and Mary Ann (Proctor) Bass. Guilford Bass was a native of North Carolina, and removed from there to Kentucky for a time, thence to Tennessee, thence to Fayette County in 1832, locating northeast of Vandalia about twelve miles. There he remained until his death, in 1845. His wife survived until 1872, when she also departed this life, leaving ten sons and two daughters to mourn her departure. But two of these, William and our subject, are now residents of Bond County. Henry left home at the age of fourteen. He came to Bond County, sought and found employment on a farm, receiving only $7 for a hard month's work, and saved sufficient means to make a part payment on his first purchase of 100 acres of Bond County land, in Beaver Creek Precinct. In August, 1856, he made a second purchase of 100 acres, which he still owns, and to which he has since added, owning at one time 1,500 acres. Mr. Bass married Nancy Goodson, daughter of Spencer Goodson, a native of Kentucky, a farmer and blacksmith, and came to Illinois when a young man. With the exception of a four years' stay in Missouri, he has been a resident of Illinois, and now of Christian County. They have six sons and two daughters—William H., Abbie, George, Edward, Walter, Louis, Leoni and Leonard. Abbie is now Mrs. C. C. Squires, of Beaver Creek Township. Mr. and Mrs. Bass are members of the Baptist Church of Smith Grove. Their home is in Beaver Creek Precinct, Town 4, Section 20. Guilford and Charles S. are deceased. Guilford died November 14, 1856, and Charles S. August 31, 1866, at one year and eighteen days old.

REV J. J. BLIZZARD, farmer, P. O. Dudleyville, is a descendant and grandson of James Blizzard, one of the earliest settlers in the township. James Blizzard was born in Scotland, and emigrated to Kentucky at an early day, where he remained until the winter of 1817 and 1818, when he came to what is now Bond County, locating in this township, on Section 3, one-fourth of a mile west of Dudleyville, and remained there as long as he lived. He was an upright, Christian man and his house was used for church purpurposes as early as 1820. Here the pioneer preachers were entertained, and the hardy settlers worshiped under his roof until a more suitable place could be obtained. His son James succeeded him; he was born in 1801 August 4, and was but a lad of sixteen when his father came here. He remained with him until October 9, 1823, when he married Fannie McCord, daughter of Robert McCord, one of the pioneers of Bond County. Shortly after his marriage, he located on Section 4, where he settled and raised a family of six children—William M., Mary J., Anna D., J. J., Robert B. and Harriet A. Of this number, but three are living—William M., J. J., and Harriet A., who resides in Saline County, Mo., wife of James W. Gower. William M. and J. J. reside in this township. James Blizzard died October 2, 1861. They were for many years members of the M. E. Church, and were highly esteemed by all who knew them

heads this sketch, was born November 8, 1829, on the northeast quarter of Section 4, where he was reared to manhood, and received a common school education. May 29, 1851, he married Catharine McAdam, born in this county, daughter of Jesse McAdams and Elizabeth Williamson, which couple came to this locality from Logan County, Ky., in 1828. In the fall of 18[illegible] Mr. Bizzard located where he now [illegible] and has been engaged in farming pursuits, having 260 acres of land. He has served as Justice of the Peace for several years; was elected in 1859, and is now acting as justice to the people in this part of the township. At [illegible] years of age, he was converted, and since has been an effective worker in the M. E. Church, both as a layman and minister, in which capacity he has officiated for over a score of years. He has eight children: James [illegible] Lucy E., H. W., Sarah E., John J., Jr., Jesse W., Mary C., Edward S., Fannie A. and L[illegible] S.

ROLLIN C. DEWEY, deceased. The Dewey family came to Bond County about the year 1837. Nelson, the father of the above, married Lois Scribner, and emigrated from Vermont with his family to Bond County, [illegible] in the northwest part of Beaver Creek Township, and remained there the remainder of his days. His death occurred January, [illegible] his wife August, 1847. Rollin, the eldest [illegible] born in Vermont April 8, 1827. His brothers and sisters were Clay, Jonathan, Judson, [illegible] Thomas, Hinton, Mary C., Ann, [illegible] Jane and Artie, all of whom lived to be grown except Thomas. January 8, 1852, he married Elmira C. Skelton, a native [illegible]

Frederick M., Mary E., Henry A., Virginia Rose, Lois A. and Katie A. The other died young. Of the above, Mary E. is the wife of W. F. Taylor. The estate consists of 4[illegible] acres, upon which the family live, the farm being conducted by the elder brother, Frederick M.

HENRY GERKE, farmer, P. O. Beaver Creek. Among the German representatives of Bond County, none are more deserving of credit than Mr. Gerke. He came to this township in 1856. His earthly possessions were wrapped up in a handkerchief, which he carried under his arm as he walked across the prairie from St. Louis, where he landed upon his coming from his native home in Hanover, now Prussia, where he was born November 23, 1836, being the eldest son of his parents, Henry and Maria C. (Dorr[illegible]) Gerke, whom he left in the old country at the age of twenty, and embarked for the land of the free and the home of the workingman. When Mr. Gerke came to this locality he had nothing to commence with but his hands. At first he worked out by the month for two years, and saved enough money to buy him a team and such things necessary to go to farming, and for four years he rented land and saved money enough to purchase forty acres where he now resides, and he has since added to the same until he now has 200 acres. He was among the number who assisted in building the German Methodist Church in this township, and was one of the first Trustees. February 5, 1867, he married Catharine, born November 4, 18[illegible], in St. Gall[illegible], Switzerland, daughter of Ma[illegible] of F. Utlaut. Mr. Gerke has three children: Edward Lincoln, born November 10, ... Ward, born November 22, 1872, Annie, ... 1875.

CAPT. U. B. HARRIS, retired farmer, P. O. Beaver Creek. Among the representative men of Bond County is Capt. U. B. Harris, who was born on Section 27, in this township. He ... the light of day February 10, 1833, ... youngest of a family of seven children. ... father's name was John Harris, a native of ... County, Ky., son of Rev. William Harris, ... of the pioneer ministers of the Cumberland Presbyterian Church of that locality. ... Harris family are of Irish extraction. ... Harris, the father of our subject, came to ... county in the fall of 1824 with the ... family. He first settled on Government land and afterward purchased of the ... and remained a citizen of the county ... his death, July 4, 1832, about seven ... prior to the birth of his last child, Urban. The mother of our subject was Nancy ... born in Kentucky, daughter of William and Sarah (Maxey) Goodman. The names of the brothers and sisters of our subject were ... Rice E., both ministers of the Cumberland Presbyterian Church; Amanda J., wife of William Murray; Nancy E., wife of Harvey Field; Sarah A. and John A. The ... died at an early age. All of the ... are now deceased except Rev. Rice E., ... went out as Chaplain in the Thirty-fifth ... Volunteer Infantry. He has not been heard from since 1876. Urban B. remained with his mother until twelve years of age, ... left home to do for himself. He had ... to rely upon but himself. He obtained a common-school education, and for ... years was engaged in teaching. In ... he raised a company of men, and was commissioned Captain of Company F, One ... when on account of impaired health he was mustered out February, 1864, at New Orleans, and returned home. During his term of service he participated in all the principal battles in which his command was engaged. His principal engagements were Magnolia, ... Champion Hills, Black River Bridge, Siege of Vicksburg, Jackson (Miss.) and afterward was with Banks' division on Red River. Upon his return home he located at Millersburg, where he purchased a farm and engaged in agricultural pursuits, where he remained until March, 1867, when he came to Beaver Creek and embarked in the mercantile business under the firm name of Goodson & Harris. After a partnership of two years he purchased his partner's interest and continued the business himself until 1880, when he gave up the business to his son, who is now conducting the same. February 1, 1853, he married Elizabeth A. Gregory, daughter of John and Sarah Gregory. This marriage has been crowned with the birth of seven children, four of whom are living: Margaret, wife of Thomas J. Hull; Luther J., John ... and Shaw L. The others died in infancy. He has been Township Treasurer for sixteen years. In 1867, he was elected County Commissioner and served four years. In 1876 he was again elected, and re-elected in 187..., and has since filled that position with credit to himself and to the satisfaction of his friends. He is a member of the I. O. O. F., and of the Cumberland Presbyterian Church and Elder of the same, of which body his parents were also members. His father was a Whig ..., having since the party came into existence been affiliated with the Republican party ... is a stanch supporter of the same.

S. J. HUNTER, farmer and stock raiser, P. O. Pocahontas. Samuel Jefferson Hunter was born in Bond County. He first beheld the light of nature March 15, 1827, in Greenville in Davidson County, Tenn., son of John Hunter, an Irishman by birth, who immigrated from his native country to Tennessee and raised a family and emigrated to Bond County about the year 1824, and settled near Shoal Creek, and remained here until his death. He raised a family of seven sons, all of whom came to man's estate, viz.: William, Thomas, John, Joseph, James, Samuel and David, all of whom settled in Bond County. David Hunter, the father of S. J., was married in Tennessee to Elizabeth Copeland, and removed to this county about two years prior to his father's coming. He remained in the county until his death, which occurred in the winter of 1875, his wife in 1855. Seven children were born to them, who were John B., Samuel J., Thomas N., Rebecca I., Susan A., George W. and Joseph J., all living at the present date, save George W. and Susan A. The father of the above was a Democrat all his life; a soldier in the Black Hawk war, and was for years a member of the Methodist Church. Samuel J., the only one of the name in this township, was brought up on the farm, where he lived until his marriage, which occurred January 30, 1850, to Sarah Young, a native of Bond County, daughter of William Young. After Mr. Hunter's marriage, he located near Greenville and engaged in farming, and has since been a resident of the county. He located on the farm he now owns, consisting of 510 acres, in 1857. He has children, viz.: Laura F., Hattie A., William R., Harry A., Benjamin A., Hugh E., Archie A. and Pearl. He has been a member of the Methodist Episcopal Church since about 1862.

D. B. HAWLEY, farmer, P. O. Dudleyville. Of the enterprising farmers in Bond County, Mr. Hawley ranks among the first. He was born February 2, 1831, in Trumbull County, Ohio; is the second son and third child born to his father, Milton Hawley, who was born 1802, in Western New York. His ancestors were of English stock. Milton Hawley came West to Trumbull County, and there married Mary Taft, and removed to Madison County in 1836, and remained there until 1843, when he came to Okaw Township, and entered 1,800 acres of land. He was a man of energy and was well read in law, and had excellent business qualifications. In politics, he was formerly a Whig; but, later in life, he came out with the Republican party and was a strong anti-slavery man, and withal generous and kind-hearted. His death occurred 1867; his wife 1865. He raised a family of ten children, seven sons and three daughters. Celia, the eldest, married J. G. Wright, and resides in this township; Luther C., eldest son, resides in California; Delevan, Bement Roman M., Virginia, Julius A., Victoria A. and John H. and D. B., the subject of these lines, who remained under the parental roof until March 9, 1854, when he married Susan Steele, born in Madison County, daughter of John W. Steele and Catharine Russell. She was a daughter of Hezekiah Russell. Mr. Hawley came to this farm in 1862, and has since resided there. He has nearly 200 acres of excellent land, which he farms in a neat and tasty manner. He has put all the principal improvements on the same, and keeps his fences and buildings in excellent repair. Has the following children: Catharine A., Mrs. Samuel Anderson; Harriet L., in California, wife of J. M. Reeves; Lucy A., Susan E., Laura A., Edwin B., John M., William W. and Patience V.

JOHN H. HESTON, P. O. Dudleyville, born May 30, 1812, in Bucks County, Penn., being the eldest of eight children. His father was Amos Heston, who was likewise a Pennsylvanian, born about the year 1774, and died in 1869, aged ninety-six. His father's name was Samuel Heston, whose ancestors came with William Penn, and settled in Pennsylvania. Samuel served in the Revolutionary war. His wife was a Price, prior to her marriage. Amos, being the fruit of this marriage; he, Amos married Letitia Hagerman, daughter of Barnett

Hagerman, who also served in the Revolution. His wife's maiden name was Groom. The Hestons and Hagermans are both of Quaker stock. None of either family came West, save J. H. and his uncle David, who came to this county as early as 1815, and remained here until 1834, when he moved to Leavenworth, Kan. Our subject came West to Muskingum County, Ohio, during his minority, afterward went to Franklin County. On April 17, 1834, he enlisted in the regular army as private, and served through the Florida and Mexican wars, and served until November, 1848, when he resigned with rank of Captain. July, 1849, he married Catharine Rarey, born in Franklin County, Ohio, daughter of Rev. Charles Rarey and Mary Kramer. Charles Rarey was a pioneer of Franklin County, and cut timber where the city of Columbus now stands. He was a son of John Rarey, a native of Germany. Mr. Heston came to Bond County in the spring of 1852, and settled where he now resides. He has put nearly all the improvements thereon. He has since been engaged in farming pursuits, and been a large wheat raiser. Has 300 acres of land, and well improved. He has seven children—Joseph S., Sarah and Mary (twins), De Witt and twin that died, Hattie M., Steve A. D. and John C.; Sarah, wife of Wallace E. Smith; Mary, wife of L. Meabeimer; Joseph S. in Kansas. Mr. Heston is self-made; his brothers and sisters were Jesse G., Morris, Mary A., Jenks S., Sarah, Samuel and Watson. Jenks and Samuel were killed in the late war.

WILLIAM G. McCASLIN, farmer, P. O. Dudleyville. Cotemporaneous with the early history of Bond County, was the advent of the McCaslin family to this township. The head of the family was James McCaslin, a native of the Emerald Isle. He emigrated to North Carolina at a very early day. While here he married a Scotch lady, and subsequently removed to Caldwell County, Ky., where eight children were born to him. According to the order of their birth, were as follows: Hugh, James, Gray, John O., Jane, Martha, Mary and Rachel. With this family, he came to Bond County and settled in Beaver Creek Township, on Section 11. Of this number mentioned, but one is now living—Hugh, who was the eldest, and he resides in Montgomery County. John Oliver the father of our subject was born about the year 1807, and married Mary Mills, daughter of William Mills and Mary Plant. Both families were early settlers in the county. This marriage was blessed with the birth of the following children, viz., William G., Elizabeth, Mary J., James W., John W., George W. Ellen and Rebecca were the ones that grew to manhood and womanhood. The father died September, 1859. He was a Whig, and a Presbyterian in faith. The mother was a Methodist. She died August, 1879. William Gray was born on the farm where he now lives July 13, 1829, and where he was reared to manhood. In March, 1852, he married Mary J. Steele, born in Morgan County, this State. She was a daughter of John Walker Steele and Catharine Russell, both of old and substantial families in old Morgan County. To Mr. and Mrs. McCaslin have been born twelve children, eleven of them now survive, whose names are John Walker, Catharine I., Clara A., James A., Harriet M., Loretta C. B., Warren E., William H., Mary F., Alonzo O., Hezekiah C. Catharine, wife of Samuel Floyd, resides in Okaw; Clara resides in Clinton County, wife of J. E. Wise; Harriet resides in Okaw, wife of Jackson Huff. Mr. McCaslin has spent his life in farming pursuits, having 280 acres of land. He is agent for Sharp's Stump and Grub Puller, a very desirable and useful implement to farmers having stumpy land to till.

FELIX G. POTTS, farmer, P. O. Greenville. Of the early settlers of Bond County, Stranger or "Stringer" Potts was among those who came in during the winter of 1830. He was born about the year 1797, in Rutherford County, Tenn., son of Daniel Potts. "Stringer" ran away from his father when a lad, and joined Gen. Jackson's command, and participated in the battle of New Orleans. He married Anna, daughter of Amos Winset, and by this union twelve children were born, viz.: Daniel, Zephaniah, Henry, [illegible], Amos, John W., Millie, Robert, Loranda, Felix G., William and Stranger. Of this number nine of the eldest were born in Tennessee. [illegible] this number are living: Daniel and W[illegible] reside in California; Henry, in Highland, Madison Co.; Amos resides in Clinton County; Millie in Moultrie County (wife of M. Miller). Stranger Potts emigrated to Bond County, locating in Pocahontas Township, in the winter of 1830, but soon after came to this township and remained here until his death, which occurred in February 1836, his wife dying the year previous. Felix G. was born April 18, 1829, and was left fatherless at an early age. He went to live with Andrew Mills of this township, and remained with him until grown; he then hired out, and then laid the foundation of his present possessions. He had a very limited education, yet he worked hard and patiently. In August, 1852, he married Margaret A. Brown, daughter of James Brown, from Tennessee. Mr. Potts has nine children—Louisa Jane, Mary, James, Henry, Martha Ellen, Nancy Henrietta, Millie and Marion. He has 540 acres, all accumulated by his own industry.

JOHN THOMEN, farmer, P. O. Beaver Creek, has been identified with Bond County since September, 1843. He was born Feb. 5, 1829, in Canton Basel, Switzerland, son of John and Ursilla (Dedwiler) Thomen. The family left the old country in May, 1843, and, after a long voyage on the ocean, they reached the American shore, and, in September of the same year they located in Bond County. His father entered land on Section 27, in Beaver Creek Township and resided on the same until his [illegible] viz.: Elizabeth (wife of George Bernride), John and Anna B. (who married Edward Fr[illegible]). Our subject remained with his parents u[illegible] after he attained his manhood. October 2[illegible], 1855, he married Susan E. Dizerens, a n[illegible] Switzerland. Mr. Thomen has been a me[illegible] of the German Methodist Church since [illegible]ganization, and was one of the first m[illegible] that assisted and was comprised in the [illegible]ganization. He has 80 acres of land; his [res]idence is located on the northwest qu[illegible] Section 27.

MARTIN L. ULMER, farmer, P. O. [illegible] Baden, is the eldest son of George Ulmer [and] Priscilla Tishhouser. George Ulmer was [born] March 14, 1823, in Canton Graupenten, [Swit]zerland, son of Martin and Anna Ulmer, [who] came to Bond County with his son Geor[ge in] 1839, locating in the west part of the tow[nship]. His children were George, Lena, Martha, [illegible] Casper and Paul, all dead except George, [Cas]per and Lena. None of the name are no[w re]siding in the township except Martin L., [who] was born here February 25, 1853, and was [mar]ried February 29, 1876, to Sarah A. Stub[ble]field, daughter of William Stubblefield [and] Susan Bray. After he married, he locate[d on] the homestead. He came to this farm in [illegible] and built the residence he now occupies; [he] has 130 acres. He has two children: [Il]a Ellen and Edward Clyde; Ida Ma[illegible], infant, died in 1877. To George Ulmer, [the] father, were born Anna E. (wife of C. Gaf[illegible]), M. L., Rosa L. (wife of William Daggett), Edward and George F. In 1876, George [Ul]mer, father of Martin L., removed to St[illegible] County and there resides. William St[ubble]field, father of Mrs. Ulmer, was born in Ma[d]ison County, March 15, 1806, son of Willi[am] Stubblefield; he died March 7, 1873. William Jr. married Susan Bray, who was born F[ebru]ary 7, 18[illegible], in Randolph County, [illegible]

Mr. Ulmer. The family came here in the spring of 1829, and settled east of Greenville To William Stubblefield, Jr., were born eleven children; six were raised, four of whom went into the army- James Henry, Samuel and Fielden; James and Henry died there. The Stubblefield family are likewise among the early settlers of Bond County. Mr. Ulmer is a Baptist

AUGUST H. UTLAUT, farmer, P. O. Baden Baden, was born February 18 1853, near Edwardsville in Madison County. His father, Eberhart Utlaut was born January 2 1798, in Europe, and came to Madison County in the fall of 1852 and six years later, came to this county, locating in Beaver Creek Township, and purchased 150 acres of land, and has since remained and is living, being now in his eighty sixth year. August being the only child (now living), has always remained with his father and lived on the homestead. He was married October 17 1872 to Anne Gerke, who was born January 1, 1852 only daughter of her parents and sister of Henry Gerke, of this township. Mr. Utlaut has now 200 acres of land; has two children Minnie Julia and Frederick William; is a member of the M. E. Church.

DR. J. A. WARREN P. O. Beaver Creek, ranks among the substantial and successful practitioners of materia medica in Bond County. He was born, December 5, 1836 in Marion County, this State, and was raised in Randolph County where he removed with his parents when small. His father was Alfred Warren, who emigrated from Tennessee to Marion County in 1817 with his father John Warren, a native of the Carolinas. John Warren's wife was [illegible] S. Nelson, born in Virginia daughter [illegible] Ezekiel Nelson. Both were Virginia families and moved first to Tennessee, thence [illegible] Illinois during its early settlement and there became identified with its interests as farmers and agriculturists. The subject of these lines was raised to farm labor, attending school during the winter and applied himself to the farm in the summer and finally engaged in teaching, which vocation he followed for several years still alternating upon [illegible] farm In 1865, he began the study of [illegible] cine his father dying the following year. 1868 he commenced the practice of his profession at Keysport and came to this place 1870 and has since continued. He received [illegible] diploma at Cincinnati in 1873. He has a [illegible] practice and has been uniformly successful and has the confidence of his patrons. In 186[illegible] married Jennie A. [illegible] born in Randolph County this State, daughter of Maj. A. M. Wilson [illegible] Susan Young. Is a member of the A., F. & A.

SAMUEL G. WHITE, farmer, P. O. Beaver Creek is a native of Bond County, where [illegible] was born September 1 1833, being the [illegible] son and sixth child that was born to his [illegible] Samuel White, a native of North Carolina, Irish extraction, born 1794 and when twenty-two years of age he came to what is now Greenville, and remained in the county until his death. He was a tanner by trade and built the first institution of the kind ever made in Greenville. He was also a farmer, and followed [illegible] vocation up to the time of his death. He [illegible] family of eight children the eldest being Ma[illegible] E. who married John [illegible] Shields, now of K[illegible] [illegible] E. B., in Greenville. John, now deceased. Letitia J., married William Donnell; [illegible] Barr; Samuel G. James was drowned at Bat[illegible]ville in 1862, on the Arkansas River. William C., the youngest. Samuel G. remained at home under the parental roof, until he attained [illegible] several years past his manhood. He was [illegible] in 1862, to Martha J. Hull daughter of [illegible] Hull. After Mr. White's marriage [illegible] in the vicinity of Greenville and engaged [illegible] farming. In 1878 he came to Beaver Creek and purchased a farm of 120 acres in the [illegible] east corner of Section 36, where he now resides having lived all his life in Bond, save two years spent in Clinton County Mo. His [illegible] was a Whig and Presbyterian in belief and practice. Samuel G. is a good farmer and is partial to good stock; has three children—Carrie C., Benjamin and Ida.

WARREN E. WISE, farmer, P. O. Beaver Creek, is the eldest son born to D. W. Wise by his marriage to Evaline Blaze. Warren E. was born January 22, 1856, in Wise Town, and was raised to farming pursuits. March 4, 1877, he married Mary Myatt, born in this township, daughter of Wesley Myatt and Mildred McNeil. Soon after his marriage, he located in this township, and has since lived here. He removed to the farm he now owns in the fall of 1881. His farm consists of 240 acres on Section 19; has two children—Mildred E. and Edward L.

D. W. WISE, deceased, was one of the prominent business men of Bond County, and during his life was a valuable factor in the representative business interests of Bond County. He was born January 15, 1816, at Hebron, in New Hampshire, son of David Wise and Eliza Hoyt. In 1842, Mr. Wise came West to Illinois, locating first in St. Clair County, where he lived until 1848, when he came to Bond County, where he remained until his death. He was four times married. His first wife was a Barnes; his second wife was Mary McCracken; third wife was Harriet Stewart, who bore him two children—Joseph and James. The former was killed by lightning. James resides in Okaw, and is engaged in farming. He married his last and fourth wife in 1855 (March); she was Evaline Blaze, born in Botetourt County, Va., daughter of William Blaze and Catharine Inglehart, who came West in 1842, and located in Clinton County, and to Bond in 1845. Mr. Wise laid out Beaver Creek, and for several years was engaged in merchandising there and was a very successful business man, and was identified with the religious interests of the county. At first was a member of the Baptist Church; later in life was a Methodist. His death occurred January 17, 1871, having 1,300 acres of land at his death. In politics, he was liberal, and was early a representative business man of Bond County, and highly esteemed by all who knew him or had any business relations with him. By his last wife he had seven children—Warren, George, Catharine, Mary, Grant, Della, and David. Mrs. Wise has in her own right 280 acres of land. She is the only one living of her brothers and sisters, seven of them, she being the youngest.

GEORGE W. WISE, farmer, P. O. Beaver Creek, is the second son of D. W. Wise by his last marriage. He was born on the homestead March 3, 1858, where he remained until he embarked upon his own responsibility to do for himself. He was united by marriage in September, 1880, to Miss Maggie Wren, born in Bond County, daughter of Dr. Edward Wren. Since his marriage he has been a resident of the farm he now owns, consisting of 150 acres on the northeast quarter of Section 27, where he has built a new residence, and is well situated in life, and has bright prospects for the future. He has one child—George.

FAIRVIEW PRECINCT.

JOSIAH BAITS, farmer, P. O. Pleasant Mound, has been identified with Bond County since 1840. He was born September 26, 1826, in Cincinnati, Ohio, the youngest child of his parents. His father was Daniel Baits, a native of Vermont a soldier in the war of 1812, and married Hannah Jewett, a native of Connecticut, a daughter of Benjamin Jewett, who served in the French and Indian war and Revolution. The paternal grandfather of our subject was David, who served as an officer in the Revolution. The subject of these lines is one of the self-made men of Bond County. By the death of his father he was thrown upon his own resources, and had the care of the family upon his hands for several years. He left Cincinnati when young, assisting in digging the Miami Canal, and for a time assisted the Engineer Corps in their labors. When the canal was completed, he drove horses on the tow-path and afterward worked on the boat as served as steersman, and otherwise made himself useful. About the age of sixteen, he commenced learning the boat and ship carpenter's trade and continued at the same about four years. In 1840, he came to this township, where he has since lived, except three years spent in Minnesota prior to his marriage. October 1847, he married Amanda M. Edwards, born December 1, 1825, of Scioto County, Ohio, daughter of Charles Edwards, born July 26, 1806 in Mercer County, Penn., and emigrated to Ohio when thirteen years of age. He was a son of David Edwards, whose wife was Catharine George, daughter of Jacob George, of Germany. Charles Edwards married Margaret Buffington, who was born in Meigs County, Ohio April 14, 1806, daughter of Joseph Buffington, of Pennsylvania. His wife was Chloe Harvey from Indiana. The Edwards family came West in December, 1841, and located in this township. Charles Edwards died July 19, 1875. In 1848 Mr. Baits located forty acres he had purchased on Section 35, northeast quarter, for which he paid $2.25. Upon this he located and remained on the same until January 1881, when he located where he now resides having 334 acres in all, 294 in this township, the remainder, forty acres, is located in Fayette County. To Mr. and Mrs. Baits have been born eight children, five sons and three daughters—Winfield S. (now a minister of the Cumberland Presbyterian Church), Harriet L. (wife of William L. Wells, of Jewett County, Kan. Margaret B. (married Marcus L. Whiteworth) Anson Z., Amanda M., Charles D., Josiah J. and Eli B. Since 1867, he has been a member of the M. E. Church.

IRA BEANBLOSSOM, farmer, P. O. Pleasant Mound; is the only surviving male member in this township of the Beanblossom family. The above was born in Miami County, Ohio, November 1, 1847, and emigrated to this county with his parents in April, 1856, who located on Section 23, where they lived until 1859, when they moved to southwest quarter of Section 34. His father was Peter Beanblossom, who was born in July 1822, son of John, who was born December 18, 1792, in Rowan County, N. C., and emigrated to this county in 1856, remaining here two years, then returned to Miami County, but stayed a short time and returned again to Bond County, where he abode until 1865. He returned then to Miami County, where he is yet living, now ninety years of age. He had a brother, George B[illegible] blossom who came to this county in 1830, locating in this township. He was a minister of the German Baptist Church, and one of the first members of that order and church in this township. He remained here until 1858, when he moved to Macoupin County, where he died about 1867. The mother of our subject was Barbara Brandt, born in Perry County, Penn., December 16, 1822, but raised in Ohio; she was a daughter of Abraham Brandt. The father of our subject was a millwright and carpenter, which vocation he followed to some extent after he became identified with this county. He also was engaged in farming. He met with accidental death in February, 1862, while repairing a wheel in Mr. Bourner's mill, his head coming in contact with some of the machinery which crushed him in such a manner that he lived but a few hours after. He was a member of the German Baptist Church. He had the following children born to him: Ira, Levi, Simon, Martin, Abraham and Martha. Levi resides in Norton County, Kan.; Simon in Jewett County, same State. Martin also a resident of that State; Abe, in Montgomery County, Ohio. Martha married John Sapp, of this county. January 1, 1869, our subject married Sarah E. Kellogg, a native of Crawford County, daughter of Oliver and Mary (Welch) Kellogg. He located in this township in 1873. He was of English extraction. To Ira Beamblossom have been born five children—Ira, Edwin, Frances, Addie, John C. and Ella May. Is a member of the German Baptist Church.

WILLIAM DAVIS, Jr., farmer, P. O. Pleasant Mound, first saw the light of day January 19, 1830, at Old Ripley, now New Berlin, in Bond County. He was the eldest son of William Davis, a native of New Hampshire, born April 1, 1796, son of Jonas Davis. William Davis was married in Massachusetts, to Lucy Mayo, daughter of Thomas and Amy Mayo, and emigrated to Bond County in November, 1829, locating at Old Ripley where he remained one year, and moved to Greenville, making this his place of residence until the spring of 1838, when he located on the northwest quarter of Section 23. About the year 1853, he returned to Greenville, where he spent the remainder of his days. His death occurred September 13, 1881. For years he was identified with the New School Presbyterian Church. Politically, he was a Whig; later, Republican. Ten children were born to him, seven of whom came to the years of maturity, viz., William, Mary A., Caroline, Adelaide, George, Amy and John. William, our subject, was married May 1, 1851, to Margaret S. Taylor, born in Vandalia, Ill., daughter of John H. Taylor. She died 1879, having borne nine children; five are living, viz., Lucy M., wife of A. Cable; Hannah, a teacher; Mary E., wife of Alvin H. Jackson; John T. and Amy, at home. Farming has been the business of his life. His farm consists of eighty acres. Since the spring of 1866, he has been a member of the Presbyterian Church, and is an official member.

BENJAMIN F. MAYO, farmer, P. O. Greenville, is among the substantial citizens of Bond County. He was born July 5, 1810, in Boston, Mass., and emigrated to Bond County, in the year 1834, arriving at Greenville in August the same year, and since that date has been a constant resident of this county. He is a descendant of an English family, he being of the tenth generation descended therefrom. His father was Thomas Mayo, who died when B. F. was a mere lad. He was the son of Joseph Mayo, who was a Revolutionary soldier. Thomas Mayo married Amy Davis who was born in Roxbury, Mass. She, too, came from Puritanical stock. By the death of his father our subject was early in life thrown upon his own individual resources, but being energetic and imbibing that spirit inherent to Yankeedom, his course was soon marked out. He first laid the foundation for a sure thing in point of trades, and he spent seven years in learning three trades—painter and glazier, carriage making and trimming. He also became familiar with the use of carpenter's tools. Thus armed with three trades he felt sure that he could always get employment at one or the other. About this time the West presented to him advantages which induced him to remove thither, which he did, starting with $600 in money, but taking very sick at Smithland, on the Ohio River, on his way here, part of his money was spent: but he came on, and upon his arrival in Greenville he made himself useful in the practice of his trades. In 1838 he married Lavinia Jewett, who died 1853. The same year of his marriage he located on the north half of Section 15. He purchased a squatter's claim and then entered the land. He remained on the farm until 1874, when he sold out and located on Section 22 where he now resides. In his farming he has been successful, having acquired a competence for himself and good farms for his sons. Seven children were born to him by his first wife, four of whom are living—Eugenia E., wife of Mr. A. Clump, in Jefferson County, Mo.; Alonzo J., in Mount Vernon County, same State; Henry and Edwin, at home. In 1854, Mr. Mayo married Elizabeth Deitch, a native of Bedford County, Penn., daughter of Daniel and Christina (Houser) Deitch, who came West to Wayne County Ind., in 1820, remaining here until 1852, when they removed to Fayette County, this State. They raised a family of six children, five of the number living—John and Alexander reside in Wayne County Ind., Catharine married Zenas Evans, and resides in Kansas; Susan resides in Thayer County, Neb., wife of Joseph Matchett. Mr. Mayo has always stood aloof from any association with lodges or church organizations, having never associated himself with any, yet is not hostile toward any sect of people or denomination, but has lived a life that has been conducive to morality and worthy of imitation.

JOHN RENCH, farmer P. O. Pleasant Mound, one of the members of the early families is Mr. Rench, who was born November 5, 1824, in Darke County, Ohio. He is a son of Joseph Rench, who was born in Lancaster County, Penn., July 13, 1785. When a lad he removed with his father to Ohio, where he was afterward married, August 21, 1811, to Rhoda Coates, born December 29, 1789. To them were born twelve children—Delilah, William, Peter, Mary, Catharine, Daniel, Joseph, John, David, Rhoda, Jacob and Aaron. All of whom lived to be grown and married before there was a death in the family. Joseph Rench moved with his family from Ohio in the spring of 1837, and entered land in the northeast quarter of Section 26; also entered other lands in the township near by and resided on the same until his death which occurred September 7, 1856. He was one of the early members of the German Baptist Church, and helped to organize the same. His wife died February 12, 1877. Of the children born to them are Daniel, who lives in Virden, Macoupin County; Catharine, now Mrs. Abe Waggoner, of Keokuk, Iowa; David and Peter, in Fairview and Rhoda (Mrs. Sutton), the others deceased. Our subject was raised on the farm and remained with his father until his marriage, November 26, 1849, to Mary F. Dixon, born October 25, 1829, in Madison County Tenn., daughter of Alexander and Sallie Stallings, both natives of North Carolina. He died in Texas. Mrs. Rench came with her mother to Fayette, in 1836. After marriage he located on the farm on which he now lives. Ten children crowned this union, seven of whom are living—Thomas J., Eveline Almira, Nancy, John L., Martha E. and Ida M. Eveline is the wife of John Hunter in Greenville, Deputy Sheriff of this county. The subject of this sketch is a member of the German Baptist Church, and a respected member of the community in which he resides.

LA GRANGE PRECINCT.

CAPT. THOMAS M. DAVIS, farmer, P. O. Greenville, born in Trigg County, Ky., the fifth child who grew up that was born to Jonathan Davis, a Virginian, of Albemarle County. Jonathan came to Trigg County when a young man, and married, in Bryan County, Margaret McLean, of Pennsylvania, daughter of Thomas McLean. The father of our subject was an early settler in this county: he came in 1817, to what is now Old Ripley; here he lived four years. He was a millwright by occupation, and built the first mill in the precinct, and perhaps was the first in the county. The site is now known as Brown's Mill. Jonathan died here in 1821, and his remains now lie interred in the Brown Graveyard, he being the second one buried in it—the first was Dr. Baker. After the death of his father, our subject returned with his mother to Kentucky, where he remained until 1835, when he returned to this State; went fist to Montgomery County, where he married Jane Williams, who died in 1840, leaving no children. He came to this county in 1837, where he has since remained. His second wife was Mrs. Jane Smith, born in Trigg County, Ky., daughter of Samuel Scott; she died in 1876, leaving but one child—William D., who resides with his father on the farm. In August 1861 Mr. Davis raised a company, which was lettered D, Third Illinois Cavalry, and served two years. In the battle of Pea Ridge he had his horse shot from under him, yet himself escaped uninjured. After his return home, he resumed farming. Since 1839, he has been a member of the Cumberland Presbyterian Church, and was made Elder at the time of the organization of the Maple Grove Society here. His wife died in 1876. He has about 400 acres of land, and is a thorough and energetic farmer. His son William D. was born in 1842, and married Gabriella, daughter of Rev. William Hamilton and Phebe Stahl, of Kentucky, who came to this State about the year 1846. To William D. have been born seven children, but there are but three living—Horace E., Luella A. and Orra M. In the winter of 1881–82, they lost three children by that dire disease, diphtheria, all within the short space of eleven days. William G. was aged fifteen, John T. aged twelve, and George W nearly two years of age. Capt. Davis had one brother—James—who emigrated to this State very early, and was for many years prominently identified with the county. He first taught school for several years, and for a time carried on a store here in the township, and afterward in Greenville. Subsequently, he was appointed, under Taylor's administration, to the office of Register of the Land Office at Vandalia. He was elected as a member of the Constitutional Convention. He afterward located at Hillsboro and engaged in the practice of law; was elected to the Legislature, and afterward to the State Senate and died in 1868.

JOHN S. DENNY, farmer, P. O. Greenville, was born in this township, on Section 33, Town 6, Range 3, August 13, 1827, son of John Denny, who was born in Lincoln County, N. C., about the year 1793, and of Irish descent. He emigrated to this locality in 1817, before it became a State. He was married about the year 1820, to Sarah Moore, a Virginian, born near Wheeling, daughter of Samuel Moore, an early settler, who married a lady by the name of Shepherd. John Denny, the father of our subject, settled first in Town 7, Range 3, and cleared up a farm and remained on the same until 1851, when he removed to his son's and died in Greenville, in November 1870; his wife died about the year 1868. He was an excellent citizen, and for many years was a member of the Presbyterian Church, and an Elder in the the same. In politics he was a Whig; after the dissolution of that party he became a Republican, which he remained until his death. The eldest child born to him was James, who died at twenty-two; William at the age of seventeen, Zimriporter in infancy; next in order came John S.; Alfred N.; Shepherd died in 1878 in this county. Alfred was a minister of the Presbyterian Church; he left no issue. John S. received good school advantages and afterward graduated at McKendree College, in the scientific course in 1854. He began teaching at the age of twenty, and continued as a teacher of the young idea for quite a term of years. In 1859, he was brought out as a candidate by the Republican party for County Treasurer, then moved to Greenfield in 1860, and was twice re-elected. In 1865, he was elected County Clerk, and served twelve years in this capacity. In 1877, he returned to his farm and was elected County Commissioner, and served as such three years making in all twenty-one years in public service. In 1854, he married Marietta Mears, of Morgan County, daughter of James and Mary (McCord) Mears. By this marriage seven children were born, but two are living—Charles Irving and Effie May. His last wife was Dorcas, born in Missouri, daughter of James Rosebrough. He has been a member of the Presbyterian Church for thirty-six years. His farm consists of 230 acres situated on Section 28; residence on the northwest quarter of the section.

GEORGE H. DONNELL, school teacher, Greenville, son of Thomas S. and Catharine J. (Paisley) Donnell; was born in Bond County, December 7, 1853. His father, who was a farmer, was born in Greenville, Bond County. His mother, who is still living, is a native of Montgomery County. Our subject, one of a family of five, received his early training in the school at Greenville, Ill., finishing at the Northern Indiana Normal and Business College. He also pursued his studies at Hillsboro for a year. Mr. Donnell chose for himself the profession of a teacher, his first charge being the school at Cherry Grove in La Grange Precinct. He has followed the profession ever since, and is at present teacher of the common school in New Berlin. He is a member of the Presbyterian Church. In politics, a Republican.

NEWTON A. HUGHEY, farmer, P. O. Greenville; is a native of Missouri. He was born October 8, 1838, in Perry County. His father was Milus Hughey, born March 5, 1811, in Rowan County, N. C., and was married November 2, 1837, to Staty Regina Parks, born November, 1818, daughter of Joseph Parks, of North Carolina. Milus removed with his father Henry Hughey, to Perry County, Mo., about the year 1825, when a lad. Here the family settled. Henry Hughey was born May 25, 1785. He married Elizabeth Gillen, born January 20, 1788. The fruits of this union were John, Stanhope, Newton A., Jane, Mary and Milus, all of whom attained to man and womanhood, and settled in Missouri. Henry Hughey died December 25, 1831; his wife, January 26, 1845. Milus Hughey was a farmer, and for many years was a member of the Presbyterian Church, and a Ruling Elder of the same. He died January 29, 1867; his wife 1844. But two children were born them—Newton A. and Susan E. The latter married Henry Bimpage; she is now deceased. In April, 1861, Newton A. Hughey married Julia A. Stevenson, born November 2, 1840, in Cape Girardeau Co., Mo., daughter of A. K. Stevenson, of North Carolina. He was a son of James Stevenson and Jane Fleming. They raised a family of three children. Mr. A. K. Stevenson died November 9, 1881; his wife in 1844. Mr. Hughey came to

Bond County in 1864, locating where he now resides. He has 210 acres, and has put nearly all the improvements on the same. Has four children—Emery G. Linley J., Pearl E. and Roxana. Two died when infants. Mr. Hughey is a member and elder of the Presbyterian Church. Mrs. Hughey's brother Linley was a soldier in the late war; member of Company B, Twenty-ninth Missouri Infantry. He died October, 1862, in the hospital at St. Louis.

JAMES M. JETT, P. O. Elm Point, was born, June 1, 1812, in Fauquier County, Va. He is the eldest son of John Jett, a Virginian who was born in 1787, son of William Jett, to whom was born the following children: James, John William, Thomas, Washington and Jefferson. James M., the grandson of William, above mentioned, removed, with his parents, when a lad, to Greene County, Tenn., afterward to Knox County. His father was a farmer, yet a mason by trade, which he followed when convenience was consulted. In the fall of 1829, he, with trowel in hand, walked from Tennessee to this county, to look out a home for his family. Having no money, he defrayed his expenses going to and from by the aid of his trowel, occasionally putting up a chimney for the pioneers as he passed through. He selected a place on Section 4, Township 6, Range 3, and moved his family out in the fall of 1831. Here he settled, and remained until his death, which took place October 31, 1867. The farm is now owned by his son, B. F. Jett. But two of his brothers ever came to Bond County. They were John William and Thomas. The brothers and sisters of J. M. were William, John, Washington, Jacob, Jefferson, Benjamin F., Marion and Henry. Of this number J. M., William, Jacob and Jefferson are in this county and precinct. Washington moved to Wisconsin. Marion and Henry to Kansas. The sisters were Susan, Polly [illegible] Sallie Jett, daughter of Humphrey Jett, the pioneer. She died, leaving three children—William C., Mary and Humphrey. In 1846, he married Mrs. Eliza Pentecost, whose maiden name was Edwards, daughter of John Edwards, who came to Bond County in 1819. In the fall of 1837, Mr. Jett located where he now resides. He first entered sixty-seven acres, to which he has added at different times, until he now has about three hundred acres. He has been hard working and industrious, and what he has is mainly the fruits of his own accumulation. He for several years, has been a member of the Cumberland Presbyterian Church. By his last wife he has the following children: Samuel A., Martha, John, Margaret, Henry, Linda and Finesse. John resides in Kansas; Margaret in Missouri, wife of Lafayette Bently.

JAMES W. JETT, farmer, P. O. Greenville, son of William B. and Carisa Parker Jett. James W. was born December 27, 1824, in Oldham County, Ky., and came here, with his parents, in 1834. The grandfather of J. W. was William. The father of J. W. was a farmer. He purchased land about the year 1838 and settled on the same, and remained in the county as long as he lived. He died, aged fifty-five, in 1844. He raised a family of seven children, the eldest of whom was Elizabeth; next in order came James W., then in rotation, Thomas J., George W., Ann E., Frances, Louisa J., Henry C. and Owen, who married Nancy Laws, by her had one daughter—Cora. Thomas J. served in the Mexican war, and there died. Henry served three years in the late war. After the death of his father, J. W. lived with his mother. At the age of twenty-three, he married a Miss Smith, who was born in Caldwell County, Ky., daughter of Thomas Smith. Since his marriage, he has been a constant resident of the township. He began with nothing, and from this small commencement he now has nearly two hundred and

He is a member of the Christian Church; has seven children—Mary J., wife of James M. Jones of Montgomery County; Louisa married Abe [illegible]; Agnes is the wife of William Smith. The remaining are George, Henry B., Ida and Isaac N.

B. F. JETT, farmer, P. O. Elm Point, is the seventh son and tenth child. His parents were John Jett and Elizabeth Hittle. B. F., or "Doc" as he is called, was born in December, 1831, on the farm he now owns, his birth occurring the same year of his father's location in Bond County. Benjamin F. was raised to farming pursuits, and remained under the home roof until he attained his manhood. May 11, 1857, he married Mrs. Nancy Thatcher, a native of Bond County. She was a daughter of James Shelton and Edith Bently. Mrs. Jett is a granddaughter of Col. Richard Bently, an early settler [illegible] Bond County; came here about the year [illegible], and settled in Cottonwood Precinct, near [illegible]thel. He was a prominent man in his day. [illegible] was identified with the Baptist Church in [illegible] organization, and a Democrat. He was [illegible] elected to the Legislature, and in all his [illegible]ions with his friends and neighbors he [illegible] high regard and esteem of all. He [illegible] a ripe old age, lived to see his [illegible] grandchildren. After the marriage [illegible] removed to Jefferson County in 18[illegible] and remained here about two years, and re[illegible] the homestead farm and has since been [illegible] resident of the same. He has eighty acres of land; has eight children—Edwin, Shel[illegible] Logan, Frank, James E., Edith O., Ric[illegible] and Lizzie. [illegible] is a member of the Christian Church at Hopewell.

S. [illegible] KENAGA, farmer, P. O. Elm Point, is one of the substantial farmers of La Grange Precinct. He was born October 18, 1841, in Mifflin County, Penn., the youngest son of his father, John Kenaga, whose father was Jacob, a native of Holland. The mother of our subject was Sarah Byler. Prior to her marriage to John Kenaga, who died when S. B. was a lad, he removed with his mother to Lawrence County when eight years of age. Here he lived until eighteen years of age, when he came to Logan County, Ohio, where he lived until 1868, at which time he came to Bond, and located where he now resides, on Section 8, in La Grange Precinct. February, 1864, he married Mary Yoder, a native of Huntingdon County, Penn., born 1841, and came to Logan County with her parents in 1845. Her parents were Daniel Yoder and Mattie Hooley, to whom were born five children, three sons and two daughters. Mr. Kenaga is a successful farmer, and principally a self-made man. He has 200 acres of land, is a substantial citizen of the community, and a member of the Christian Church since 1873. His children are Sarah J., Anthony J., Walter O., Lewis J. and Emma M.

WILLIAM R. McCASLIN, farmer, P. O. Donnellson. The McCaslin family came to Bond County in 1831, where they have since been identified. The pioneer was Thomas G. McCaslin, who was born February 16, 1795, in Tennessee, son of James McCaslin, of Scotch-Irish parentage. November 10, 1818, he married Sallie Robinson, born in the same State May 18, 1794, daughter of Samuel Robinson. Subsequent to their marriage, they removed to Caldwell County, Ky.; here William R. was born January 6, 1825, being the eldest son and fourth child of his parents. He removed with them at the time of their coming; the family spent one year south of Greenville six miles, where they made one crop. Coming north in the spring of 1832, his father located 400 acres in Town 7, Range 3, in the extreme north part of the county; said lands were embraced in Sections 27, 28 and 29. Here the family settled, and have since been associated with the county and its interests. His father Thomas G. died about the year 1844; his companion survived him until 1869. Seven children were born them, who were Elizabeth J., C[illegible] dilla A., Isabella C., William R., Mary M., James W. and Sarah R.; of the above who married and settled in this county, were Elizabeth (married Isaac G. Barr); Cindilla, William Smith, of Bethel; Isabella, Robert Frame; Mary M., William Laws, of Montgomery County, and Sarah Allen Thacker, of the same county; all the rest settled in this county and are living, except James, who died young. William R. remained with his parents until he attained his majority. He was first married in 1846 to Lucinda McIntyre, who died, leaving two children—Sarah E. (now wife of B. F. McLain) and Thomas C.; his second wife was Mary H. Denny, daughter of George Denny, the pioneer; she died, leaving three children—Elizabeth M. (wife of George Lewis), Emery and Henry B. His present wife was Nancy A. Roper, a Kentuckian, who bore him one daughter—Hattie M. All of his children except the last are married and settled in this county and are doing well. Since he was first married, he has been a resident of the farm he now owns, having some 300 acres of land, all of which he has improved. For twenty-five years he has been a member of the Old School Presbyterian Church.

JOSEPH McCULLEY, farmer, P. O. Greenville. Of the self-made men and substantial farmers Mr. McCulley ranks among this list. He was born November 11, 1821, in Rockbridge County, near Lexington, Va. He was the eldest son and second child born to his parents. His father was Frederick McCulley, a native of County Derry, Ireland. He married Margaret Irving, and, in 1819, emigrated to Virginia, where he located, and remained until the year 1838, when he removed with his family to Lauderdale County, Ala. Here he abode until the spring of 1841, when the family started in wagon for Illinois, and $50 in money, having $25 when they reached Montgomery County. There was a family of eight children. A cow was purchased for $10 and a plow for $8, leaving $7 to buy such things as their necessities required. The family was poor, and had no means to purchase land; but they began work in earnest. Joseph, being the eldest son, he took the lead of the work. In 1843, he came to Bond County, and selected a place for the family, and purchased eighty acres of land at $3 per acre. There were twenty acres partially cleared and a small cabin on the same. Here his parents died. They raised a family of six children: Elizabeth, now of Kansas, wife of Calvin [illegible]; Joseph; Margaret, married Jerry McC[illegible]; Martha, married S. W. R. Hull, and James, all of Kansas. Joseph maintained the family and worked for them, bringing into the [illegible] the fruits of his labor. He remained a bachelor until April, 1876, when he married Martha [illegible] Mitchell, a native of Cape Girardeau County, Mo. He has one daughter—Margaret Lunett. Mr. McCulley is a member of the Presbyterian Church. He has 400 acres. The McCulleys were of Scotch descent.

R. C. PAISLEY, farmer, P. O. Greenville, is a native of Bond County, and was born June 21, 1830, on Section 6 in this township. His father, William Paisley, was a native of Guilford County, N. C., born June 8, 1795; his wife was a native of the same State; her maiden name was Nancy Nelson, born May [illegible], 1795, and they were married August 13, 1816, and emigrated to this State two years later, locating on Section 6 in this township, and remained a constant resident. He died August 29, 1870; his wife preceded him August 3, 1847. He served in the Black Hawk war, and was a man of quiet and reserved manner, yet withal a worthy and respected citizen. He married Catharine Denny, who yet survives him; she bore him no children. The children born to him by his first wife were Malinda, who married J. Potter, and resides in Lincoln, this State; John W., the second child, resides in Lee County, Iowa; Joel B. resides in Lincoln, in the dry goods; William F. resides in this township,

Mary E. married Clemons Boyd, and also resides in Lincoln. Robert C., after coming to his manhood's years, gave his attention to farming. In 1852, he went the overland route to California, and spent three years mining in El Dorado County, and returned to this county in 1855. April 20, 1858 he married Lydia Libby, born Oct. 21, 1835 in Pawlet, Vermont, daughter of Isaac T. Libby, born 1812, in Vermont, who married Nancy Frisbee. In 1850, he located on the farm he now owns which he has improved, having now 476 acres. Mr. Paisley served one year in the late war was a member of Company B, Fifty-ninth Illinois. He has three children—Anna M., Frank N. and Horace. His grandfather, Paisley, was named John, and of Scotch descent, and had a family of twelve children born to him. Mr. P. and wife are members of the Cumberland Presbyterian Church.

CHARLES WOOD, deceased, was one of the pioneers of Bond County. He was born January 9, 1798 in Darlington District, South Carolina, son of Thomas and Jane (Jenkins) Wood. The subject of these lines emigrated to this county in the fall of 1826; he made one crop on the farm of William Paisley, and the following year he located on Section 29, in Town 7, Range 3 La Grange Precinct; here he settled and cleared up his land and remained a constant resident of the township until his death, January, 1867. His wife's maiden name was Sarah McCormick, a native of Scotland, who bore him eight children. Mr. Wood was truly a representative man. While in Carolina, he obtained a good education for that time, and for several years taught school prior to his coming West. He was an industrious and thoroughgoing business man; he was often consulted by his neighbors to make mathematical calculations, and settled affairs too complicated for his rural associates, who always found in him a valuable and safe adviser. As a neighbor, he was kind and obliging, and ever stood ready to lend them a hand or do them a kindness. He was a hospitable man; no stranger or wayworn traveler was ever denied food or shelter under his roof, neither was he ever known to make a charge or a bill for his hospitality. He was not a member of any church or society, but never opposed those who were, but aimed to abide by the golden rule as near as he knew how. He left land and property for each of his children, although he had nothing himself when he settled in this county. His children were as follows: Caroline, Eli, Ezra, Nancy J., David, John, Sarah A. and Ira, all of whom lived to be grown, except David, who died young, all of whom married and settled in this county, except John, who never married, yet has remained in the county and since the death of his parents has resided with his brother Ezra. John served three years in the late war, and was a true and faithful soldier. He was a member of Company B, One Hundred and Seventeenth Illinois Volunteer Infantry and participated in many hard-fought battles and came home unscathed. Ira, also was a soldier; he served in the cavalry department and died since the close of the war. Six of the family, three brothers and three sisters, reside near each other, all doing well and have good homes.

ZION PRECINCT.

J. M. BINGHAM, farmer, P. O. Woburn, is a Carolinian by birth, born March 19, 1828, in Lincoln County, N. C. His parents were Samuel Bingham and Barbara Carpenter, both natives of the same State. His maternal grandfather was Jacob Carpenter. Samuel Bingham was a farmer by occupation, and raised a family of ten children, viz., Susan, William, Elizabeth, Jacob, Christopher, Anna, Samuel, Martin, Peter and Joseph M., who is the youngest of the family; his father died when he was fifteen; he then remained with his mother until he attained his majority, at which time, in 1849, he came to Macoupin County, where he engaged to work by the month. Having no means left him by father he had to "paddle his own canoe," and depend solely upon his own exertions. In August, 1860, he came to Bond County, and the same year he married Narcissa V. Grigg, a native of this county, daughter of Frederick Grigg. By this marriage five children were born, viz: John F., William E., Lizzie R., Carroll S. and Emma J. After his marriage he located in Town 6, Range 2, where he remained until the spring of 1863, when he moved to Town 7, Range 2, and located where he now resides, purchasing at first eighty acres on Section 32; he has since added to the same, [illegible] he now has 190 acres; he has put all the substantial improvements on the same; has a good location and a pleasant home, all of which he has acquired by his industry and frugal economy. Of his brothers and sisters the following settled in North Carolinia: William, [illegible], Elizabeth, Jacob and Christopher. Jacob finally removed to Iowa, and settled in Marion County. Samuel settled in Lucas [illegible] having married John Lackey. Since 1867, Mr. Bingham has been identified with the United Baptist Church, and an efficient member of the same.

JOHN T. BUCHANAN, farming and insurance, P. O. Mulberry Grove, is a descendent of one of the early settlers. He was born March 31, 1842, in this township, on the southwest quarter of Section 35; his father was John Buchanan, born February 17, 1797, and in 1828, July 31, he married Eleanor Long, who was born November 18, 1809. Ten children were born of this marriage, of whom eight lived to be grown —James L., Mary A., Nathaniel W., Sarah J., Martha E., Priscilla J., John S., Nancy E., George P. Deceased are Martha, Priscilla, Nathanial W. John Buchanan died March 13, 1880; he was for many years a member of the Baptist Church. In his early life he followed the shoemaker's trade, but later he took up farming. His widow yet survives him. Our subject was raised to farm labor. April 9, 1862, he enlisted in Company I, Sixty-fifth Regiment of Illinois Volunteer Infantry, and served in this command until the close of the war; was in Miles' surrender at Harper's Ferry, and taken prisoner here. He came through the war without wounds or receiving serious injury. In 1866, he married Lizzie R. Mattinly, daughter of Dr. Mattinly, of this county. After marriage he lived at the Grove some time; came here in February, 1879, locating on Section 15, where he purchased eighty acres and is engaged in farming. In addition to his farming he is interested in protecting his neighbors and friends against loss by fire, and gives them a reliable indemnity in such companies as the Rockford,

ities Mr. Buchanan is Republican; has three children—Jesse E., born October 15, 1867; Sallie J., born August 22, 1869; and Annie B., March 15, 1876.

M. W. CRUTCHLEY, farmer, P. O. Mulberry Grove, born February 13, 1829, in Jefferson County, Va., fifth son of John Crutchley and Ann Chambers. The family emigrated west to Saline County, Mo., in 1839, and the following May came to this county; father died 1841, mother two years later. But three children now living—Samuel and M. W. of this township and county, and George a physician in Carroll County. Our subject started in life on his own merits and for seven years and five months he worked continuously for John S. Hall on his farm of Town 5, Range 2; during this time he saved some money which he invested in land. November, 1856, he married Elizabeth Miller, born in this county, daughter of John Miller. The same year of his marriage he located on the farm he now owns, which land he entered. In politics he has been Democratic and stanch in the principles of his party. His brother, Frank, was accidentally killed on an adjoining farm in 1869. He has [illegible] acres on southwest quarter section 33, where he resides, and since his location here has given his attention mainly to farming. March [illegible] 1881, the partner of his bosom and mother of his children was borne away to the spirit land, leaving eight children to mourn her loss, whose names in order of their birth are George N., Anna E., Mary F., Thomas S., [illegible] A., Albert W., Elizabeth G. and Silas W.

JAMES S. CORNISH, farmer, P. O. Smithboro. Among the young farmers of this township, who have been here less than a score of years is the above who was born October [illegible] 1847, in Clarion County, Penn., son of Henry Cornish, who was born September 26, [illegible], in Massachusetts, son of Andrew Cornish. His mother's maiden name was Susan, daughter of Andrew, who was a son of Mark Noble, of Massachusetts. The family first settled in Venango County; afterward, in 1847, located in Clarion County, where James S. took his first observations. Father died in his sixty-eighth year; he was for many years a member of the German Baptist Church, and minister of the same. The children born to Henry Cornish and wife are Rosanna, Henry, Mark, Susan, Sarah, John, James and Aurilla. James received but a common school education. His early manhood was spent in the lumber woods yet at the age of twenty he began doing business on his own account. In 1874, January 1, he married Susan McDowell, born in Clarion County, May 1, 1848, daughter of James McDowell. In the spring of 1876, he emigrated to this State, locating in Bond County. His first purchase was forty acres on Section 21; soon after he added twenty more. In the spring of 1879, he sold out, and purchased eighty acres on Section 28, where he has since lived, having added to the same until he now has 120 acres. He began upon his own resources, and had nothing donated to him, but by industry and frugality he has secured his present possessions solely upon his own individual merits.

THOMAS K. CLINE, farmer, P. O. Woburn, was born on the farm where he now lives, Sept. 28, 1842. Is the youngest son of Thomas Clme, the pioneer, who was born July 15, 1800, in Lancaster County, son of Henry Cline, from Germany, with whom he emigrated from Pennsylvania to North Carolina when young. He had several brothers and sisters, who were Amos, Martin (Thomas) and Mary. October 18, 1825, Thomas Cline was married to Sarah Mitchem. She was born June 12, 1807, in Lincoln County, N. C., daughter of Nathaniel and Mollie (Tucker) Mitchem. After marriage they raised one crop, and made a sale that fall which amounted in all to $109.25, which they could not then collect. The same fall, they came to this county with one old blind mare. During that winter, Mr. Cline went to Vandalia where he was allowed to enter eighty acres and pay for the same when he could command the money: he after entered eighty more. This land is now owned by his son Thomas, on Section 29. It was a wilderness then: but two houses between his home and Greenville at that time. He died June 24, 1868 and for many years was identified with the Presbyterian Church, but before his death a few years joined the Methodist Episcopal Church, there being no church here at that time. Eight children were born to him who grew up Mary, William, Nancy, Lizzie, Jennie, John, Sarah and Thomas; the two latter are residents of this township. Thomas was raised a farmer. February, 1864, he enlisted in the Third Illinois Cavalry, Company G, and served until the fall of 1865, when he was mustered out having participated in all the battles in which his command was engaged. In 1867 he married Sallie, born in Fayette County daughter of Frank Doyle. Has six children Lucy, Willie, Jennie, Frank, Josie and Peter. In 1879, he moved to the farm he now owns, where he has recently erected a new house. He has a very fine spring on his farm, which feeds a large fish pond, which is being stocked with many varieties of fish. His mother is yet living, and is like a shock of corn, fully ripe for her Master's use. She is a member of the Free Methodist Episcopal Church.

PHILIBERT DECHENNE, farmer, P. O. Woburn. The old countries have furnished no better husbandmen and citizens than Mr. Dechenne, who hails from Valdajal, Lorraine, France, where he was born February 2, 1813, son of Nicholas Dechenne, a farmer, whose wife was Marianna Bolmont, who bore him Isadore, Corinne, Philibert, Virginia, Julian, Francis, Mary, Gilbert all of whom, except Isadore, emigrated to America in 1837, coming direct [illegible] called French Village. The father of our subject was a farmer, and owned considerable property in France, but being largely in debt he resolved to sell out and pay his creditors, and emigrated to the United States and cast his lot with those of his family. When he arrived at St. Louis, he had but about $200. He located at French Village, where he died October, 1844, aged sixty-two: his wife died 18[illegible]. Philibert, at the age of eighteen, learned the blacksmith trade which he followed at French Village for several years working on the farm a portion of the time. In 1850, he went to California, where he spent two years at his [illegible]. Upon his return to this State he located at Rich Prairie, St. Clair County where he [illegible] until 1858, when he came to this county [illegible] fall of the same year and purchased [illegible] acres in this township, where he has since remained, having now 170 acres. In 1847, April 14, he married Agatha Royer, born 1829 in Lagarde, Lorraine France daughter of Francis Royer, who emigrated to St. Clair County with his family in 1846: he died two years after. His children were Francis, Jacob, Celestine, Agatha, Mary and Matilda. Francis and Jacob are deceased. Matilda resides in Jasper County, Celeste and Mary in California. Mr. Dechenne has nine children—Jules, Delphine, Eugene, Leonora, Theodore, Victor, Henry, Edward and Millie. Delphine is the wife of Jacob Metcalf and resides near the homestead. Mr. Dechenne has one brother in Pocahontas, this county. Has one brother, Frank, in California, and one sister in New Orleans. Member of the Catholic Church.

FREDERICK DURR, farmer, P. O. Wo[illegible] a thrifty farmer in Town 7, Range 2, son of John Durr, a native of Germany, who came to America, and when a young man cast his fortunes with Bond County, when it was but partially improved. For several years he worked out by the month and earned sufficient means to enable him to purchase a home in this [illegible] ship. He married Malinda Kimbro, a native of North Carolina, daughter of Frederick Kimbro, which family were likewise very early settlers in this part of the county. Mr. Durr and wife had born them the following —John H., Mary E., Frederick, George, Isley, Jonathan, Martha A. and William. Of the above John H., Martha A. and Jonathan are deceased. Mr. Durr died November 15, 1860, Frederick, his successor, was born February 12, 1844, on Section 28, Town 7, Range 2, on the homestead upon which he lived as his home until his marriage. In March, 1865, he enlisted in Company K, Third Illinois Cavalry, in which he served until the fall of the same year; his range of observation during this time extended from Davenport, Miss., to St Paul, Minn.; received his discharge October 19. December 3, 1868, he married Julia S. Roberts, born in this township, daughter of R. S. D. Roberts, an old and highly respected resident of the county. By this union he has four children Keturah E., John R., Samuel T. and Illinois Maude. Mr. Durr has 360 acres; located on the farm he now owns in 1868; after his marriage sold his farm on the south half of Section 32, Town 7, Range 2. He and wife are members of the United Baptist Church.

F. M. ELAM, farmer, P. O. Woburn. One of the largest land-holders and most successful farmers in Town 6, Range 2, is Francis Marion Elam, known among his friends as "General," not that he earned the title from his association with gory battle-fields or valorous deeds in martial array, but his father dubbed him with this handle to his name when a youth, which name he has since borne. This gentleman was born in Rutherford County, N. C., April 18, 1826, the eldest son and fifth child born to his parents, who were Thomas and Elizabeth Elam, the latter a daughter of Edward Elam. The paternal grandsire of Francis M. was Alexander, a native of Virginia, who emigrated to North Carolina. In 1827, the family moved to Sumner County, Tenn., where they remained until 1833, when they came to Fayette County, this State; here Thomas Elam died in 1854, his wife dying in 1877; he and wife were members of the United Baptist Church. Twelve children were born to them, nine of the number lived to be grown, viz. Susan, Nancy, Cicely F. M., Thomas A., Sabra C., Lovincia, Sarah and Edward. Francis M remained at home until he reached his majority In 1846, he married Nancy, born in Sangamon County, this State, daughter of Richard Walker, a Kentuckian by birth. When Mr. Elam was married he moved to this township; he had a small commencement in the way of this world's goods; had one yoke of young steers, three cows and a three year-old filley. His outfit for keeping house was bought for $5; he worked hard during the day and at night he made such furniture as they most needed; with a cheerful heart and willing hand he pushed ahead, and as fast as he made money he invested it in land. In 1849, he located where he now resides. Before he divided up his land among his sons he owned 1,200 acres; he has now about 700. He has been a zealous member of the United Baptist Church for many years. Liberty Church, of which he is an officer, stands upon the land he deeded for that purpose. Of the following eight children born to him but five are living Mary E., James F., John S., A. J., Daniel E., Sarah, Samuel D. and Joel A.

EUGENE ENLOE, merchant and P. M., is the eldest son of Thomas B. Enloe, born in this county in Town 6, Range 3, August 1830, son of Ezekiel Enloe, of North Carolina. The wife of Ezekiel was Charlotte White, daughter of Richard White, of North Carolina. In 1858, May 1, Thomas B. was married; his wife was Sarah Cline, daughter of Thomas and Sarah (Mitchem) Cline. After the marriage of Mr. Enloe, he moved to the old homestead, where he died November 20, 1864. Four children were born to him—Eugene, Henry, Ellen and Thomas B. To Ezekiel Enloe were born ten children; eight grew up, viz., Marshall, Clayburn, Thomas B., William, Edward, Mary, Benjamin and George; five are now living; Thomas Marshall and Clayburn are deceased. Eugene, whose name heads this sketch, was born April 24, 1859; he was raised on the farm. April 30, 1879, he married Clara M. Moss, daughter of L. S. Moss; has two children—E. M. and baby unnamed; is now running a store at Woburn. November 15, 1881, he was commissioned Postmaster.

LEWIS S. HUBBARD, farmer, P. O. Smithboro. This gentleman is a grandson of one of the earliest settlers of this part of the county and son of T. S. Hubbard, and Ann E. Saunders. Lewis S. was born on the homestead farm, situated in the northwest corner of Town 5 Range 2. He first saw the light of day January 11 1845. His father, T. S. Hubbard, being a farmer, his sons were brought up with the same education. While in his nineteenth year, he volunteered his services to put down the rebellion, enlisting in January, 1864, in the Third Illinois Cavalry. The first six months of his service he with his company E, acted as an escort to Gen. Steele, after which, he with his company joined the regiment, and started in pursuit of Hood, on his march in the rear of Sherman. He participated in all the principal battles in which his company was engaged, and escaped without wounds but during his exposure he contracted rheumatism, which is now a source of considerable annoyance to him. After the close of the war, he and his command were sent North into Minnesota, to look after the Indians, and he did not receive his release from the army until the fall of 1865, after which he returned home and resumed labor on the home farm. September 17, 1873, he married Frances Seaman, daughter of Jonathan and Mary Ann (Miller) Seaman. Since his marriage, he has been a resident of the farm he now owns situated on the southwest quarter of Section 33, which farm he began improving in 1876. He has 120 acres, and his wife sixty. He has one son, Earl S.

WILLIAM A. JETT, farmer, P. O. Greenville, born January 15, 1819, in Fauquier County, Virginia, second child and son of Thomas and Elizabeth (Rogers) Jett. When ten years of age, he went with his parents to Tennessee and from there they removed to this county about the year 1831, his father making his location in Zion Precinct. William A. remained with his father until several years past his majority; in fact, he made his father's house his home until he was married, which was August 28, 1856. His wife was Emma S. Davis, native of La Grange Precinct. Her parents were William and Lucy A. (Nance) Davis. William Davis was a native of Trigg County, Kentucky, son of Rev. John T. Davis, a Baptist minister. Lucy A. Nance was born in Versailles, Woodford Co. Ky. Mr. Davis removed with his family to Bond County, locating in La Grange Precinct on Section 9, about 1836-'7, where the Foster brothers reside. Mr. Davis died April, 1857; Mrs. Davis, August 1875. To them nine children were born; of this number the following are living: Robert Dale, traveling salesman; Amanda, wife of Samuel Plant, of Greenville Precinct; Margaret resides in Fayette County, wife of Henry Casey; Lucy A., wife of James Saunderson, same precinct; also Laura, who married Addison Thompson. Mr. Jett located on the farm he now owns shortly after his marriage; he has 160 acres. His family consists of six children: Sarah M., the eldest, is the wife of James W. Reed, of Greenville; Flora married John H. Booher, and resides in La Grange Precinct; those at home are Stephen A. D., William L., L. Virginia, and James Arthur Dale. Mr. Jett is not a member of any church society; Mrs. Jett of the Christian Church.

STEPHEN JACKSON JETT, farmer, P. O.

Greenville, is a representative of Jett Prairie Born June 12, 1827, in Fauquier County, Va., and emigrated to this State, with his parents, when only eighteen months old. They located on Section 6, Town 6, Range 2; here he was reared, and has since been a constant resident. His father's name was Thomas Jett, a native of the Old Dominion, son of William Jett, a Revolutionary soldier. When Thomas Jett came here, he entered about two hundred and sixty acres of land which he cleared, and remained on the same until his death, which occurred June 29, 1854, at Pocahontas, of cholera, while on his way from St. Louis. He was a Whig and a member of the Christian Church. His wife died 1859. To them ten children were born, all of whom grew to manhood and womanhood—James H., William A., Alexander W., Thomas J., Stephen J., Wesley, Susana, Mary J., Eliza and Sarah. Stephen J. and William reside on farms adjoining. Our subject was married, in February, 1849, to Nancy, born in this State, daughter of John Booher. She died 1866, leaving four children—John W., William E., Thomas M. and Stephen. Mrs. Jett died May 9, 1866. His second marriage was to Eliza Bull, of Morgan County, daughter of Moses Bull, and four children were born to them—Solomon, Oscar, Nancy and Charles. Mr. Jett has 210 acres of land.

L. S. MOSS, farmer and stock-raiser, P. O. Woburn, is the eldest son of W. W. Moss and Drusilla Scoggin, daughter of Lemuel Scoggin. The former was born in North Carolina, 1787, son of Henry Moss, a Revolutionary soldier. The Moss family are of English stock. Three brothers emigrated from England, one of whom settled in Virginia, another in North Carolina, and the third in the Eastern States. The subject of these lines came West with his parents and grandfather in 1830. They located first in Madison County, and about five years later his father came to Bond County and bought a claim; he died 1861; his wife, one year previous. The number of children born were L. S., James H., Henry J., Martin V., Edward A., W. Preach and Mary; but two of the above are in this county—L. S. and James H. L. S., not liking the way matters were being "run" about the parental roof, he ran off at the age of sixteen and began to scratch for himself, and hiring out at $6 per month, he thus continued on, and well knows what is to "paddle his own craft," and in this time saw much of the workings of human nature and the cold side of humanity. At the age of eighteen, he went to Wisconsin, remained here some time. While in this State cast his first vote for Gen. Pierce, and has since been a Democrat, and voted his sentiments as well as talked them. From Wisconsin he settled here permanently in this county, where he has since been identified, not only in farming, but in trading and commercial pursuits. W[illegible] for several years engaged in running a store [illegible] Woburn, also a mill in company with his brother J. H. In 1850, he married Sarah, daughter of Lewis Kerr and Selma Watson, both families from North Carolina. Seven children have been born him, viz.: America, Josephine, Clara Dolera, George L., James H. and Edith H. He has 370 acres of land adjoining Woburn; has forty-eight acres set in orchard; raises stock and grain. Is a member of the A. F. & A. M.

JAMES H. MOSS, farmer, P. O. Greenville, born February 11, 1833, in Madison County, this State, is the second son born to his parents who were William Moss and Drusilla Scoggin. J. H. remained with his parents until he attained his majority, or nearly [illegible] home at the age of twenty. In 1856, he married Elizabeth Jay, born near Shelbyville, this State, daughter of Edward Jay. The mother of James was Jane, daughter of Burril Gregg. After his marriage, he first located on the Kinn place, and from 1854 to 1858 he was interested in running a saw-mill. Afterward he moved to the Cross Roads (Woburn), where he and his brother, L. S., were for some time engaged in the mercantile business, also in running the steam saw and grist mill. In 1868, he located on the farm now owned by Lemuel S., which he improved, where he lived until 1874, when he located on the farm he now owns, containing 680 acres on Section 30. Of a family of ten children born to him, six are living—William W., Rose E., Amy L., Della A., Lena E. and babe unnamed. Since 1859, he has been a member of the Methodist Episcopal Church; more recently has been associated with the Free Methodist Church, as well as an official member of the same.

HENRY H. MULL, farmer, P. O. Woburn, is a thriving farmer of Pennsylvania origin, born September 20, 1840, in Venango County; son of Abraham Mull, who was born in Berks County, 1812, and married Hannah Gilger, who was a native of Lancaster County, same State, daughter of James Gilger. This marriage was crowned by the birth of nine children, of whom Sarah was the eldest. In order of birth came the following: Margaret E., Henry H., Samuel E., Jonas L., Catharine J., Charles W., David E. and Oliver G., all of whom are living in Pennsylvania, in Venango and Clarion Counties. Father died in 1862; mother yet survives him. Henry H. received a good common school education and early in manhood learned the carpenter's trade of his father. In June, 1862, he volunteered to serve three years in the defense of his country's flag, joining Company A, of the One Hundred and Twenty-first Regiment, which command he continued with until the close of the war, serving in all the hotly contested battles from that of Antietam on. At the battle of Gettysburg, he was taken prisoner, but joined his command two months after. He returned home at the end of the war unscathed. In 1866, he cast his lot and his fortunes with the good people of Bond County, arriving in this township April 18, and immediately engaged at his trade, which he followed regularly until 1873, having, three years previous, located where he now resides, and has improved the place very materially since his occupation. The forty acres occupied by the house was given his wife by her father, when she married, in January, 1870; her name is Priscilla, born in Clarion County, Penn., daughter of Jacob Lilligh. Mr. Mull has added to the forty acres given his wife 180 more, all of which he has earned by his industry and management, having received but about $200 from his father's estate. Has three children—Charles O., John W. and babe not named.

A. W. MAHLE, farmer, P. O. Woburn. This gentleman was born June 19, 1812, in Hesse-Cassel, and emigrated to Lancaster County, Penn., with his parents in 1819; three years later they moved west, to what is now Clarion County. Here his parents died, having had to them born twelve children, ten of whom grew up, three of whom are now living. The mother of our subject was Maria Strichenberger. Mr. Mahle was first married to Catharine Sickworth, who bore him seven children, of whom Edward, Sarah and Maria are in Pennsylvania, Louisa and Emanuel in Arkansas. John resides in this county, a druggist in Mulberry Grove. Mr. Mahle married for his second wife Sarah Shaner, a native of Pennsylvania; by her has three children—Elizabeth, Marietta and Clemons. She was born March 16, 1827, daughter of Henry Shaner and Elizabeth Rapp, the former a native of Lehigh, she of Berks County. To them were born six children, Mrs. Mahle being the eldest of the number. Mr. Mahle purchased land in this township in the spring of 1865, on Section 21, where he lived until 1882; in March located near Woburn, where he has improved a home. Since 1847, he has been identified with the German Baptist Church, and was mainly instrumental in getting the church built in this township. His farm he now rents, he being in a manner retired from active business associations.

E. P. POINDEXTER, physician, Woburn, takes rank among the first physicians in the county. He is a representative of an Old Virginian family. He was born August 10, 1838, in Patrick County, in the Old Dominion, a son of Joseph S. Poindexter, a native of Campbell County and of French descent, born Oct. 5, 1802, son of John Poindexter. His mother's maiden name was Martha Frasier, who was born and raised in Rockingham County, in North Carolina, near the Yadkin River, daughter of Thomas, an Englishman, a man noted for his large size and physical development, being six feet and seven inches in height, and weighed 240 pounds, and a giant in strength; he moved to Jackson County, Ohio, in 1837, and died in 1845. John Poindexter, the paternal grandsire of our subject, was a large slave-owner, owned nearly 300 slaves in Virginia. He married Elizabeth Chilton, and by her had seven children. Joseph S., the father of our subject was the eldest who emigrated with his family West to Saline County, Mo., where he died July 3, 1863, leaving four children, three sons and one daughter. The subject of these lines, by the force of circumstances, was thrown upon his own resources when a young man; he received the advantages afforded by the common schools, and in 1858 he entered McKee College, but the war broke out, preventing a further prosecution of his studies at that time. Dr. H. B. Redmon was his first preceptor. In the spring of 1861, he joined Capt. Brown's company (Capt. Brown was a son of Sam Brown, who fought Cassius M. Clay), after, in Col. Brown's regiment, in Parson's division, Price's army. The Doctor served through the entire war. He at one time raised a company and served as Lieutenant under Capt. Gullet; he was wounded but once. In the battle of Pea Ridge he was gunner in one of the batteries and did effective work. He followed the fortunes of Price's army all through the war, serving in various localities and in different positions, enduring much hardship and exposure. Returning to his former residence after the war, the feeling being so strong against him on account of his advocacy of the Southern cause that he came away, and cast his fortunes in the Sucker State, where he has since lived. In 1867 he began the study of medicine at Charlestown, in Coles County, under Drs. Silverthorn & Trower, continuing his studies, graduating in the spring of 1874 in St. Louis Medical College. His course was a slow, yet a thorough one; he borrowed the money to enable him to prosecute his studies to completion. April 16, 1870, he came to Woburn, Bond County, and has since been in the practice of his profession, and he has been very successful, having the entire confidence of the people. In his practice has given the poor the benefit of his skill without fee or reward, and did it cheerfully. September 17, 1873, he married Tabitha J. Goodrich, born in Salem, Marion County, daughter of Chauncy and Ruth (Coburn) Goodrich, of Masssachusetts. The Doctor has three children—Don Victor, Annie and Della Maude. In religious matters, he is a free-thinker.

JOHN W. PRATER, farmer, P. O. Greenville. The Prater family were about the first settlers in this part of the county. The pioneer was Halliday, born January 23, 1777; he married Anni Adair, who was born May 1, 1776. The family emigrated from the Carolinas to Kentucky in the early part of the century, but remained here but a few years; finally came to this locality before it was a State, making his settlement on Section 31, Town 7, Range 2; here he remained until his death in 1846, November 28; his wife the same year, August 30. The father of John W. was Samuel Prater, born March 31, 1800, in South Carolinia; he married Nancy Walker, daughter of James Walker, of Virginia. Five children were the issue of this marriage, who were in order of birth as follows: Tabitha, John W., Michael H., Martha Ann and Mary. Tabitha married William Beard and settled in Madison County. Michael never married, but remained with his mother; Martha A., married James M. Brown; Mary. Willis Sands, all of whom reside in this locality; father died February 26, 1852. John W. was married March 12, 1846, to Sarah Hunt, born in 1827, in Warren County Ky., daughter of John Hunt and Elizabeth Wright, who raised a large family of children, a dozen or more. Mrs. Prater's parents never came here; she came with her uncle, Joseph Wright, who settled here in Illinois. In the spring of 1848, our subject located on the farm he now owns; first lived in a cabin, but a few rods from his present residence, which he built in 1871. His farm consists of 266 acres: has had seven children — James, William, John Thomas, Caroline, Samuel, Sissie and Jessie K. Mr. Prater was born on his farm December 5, 1824; since been a constant resident of the township. He drinks neither tea, coffee, whisky nor uses tobacco.

R. S. D. ROBERTS, farmer, P. O. Woburn, was born in Kentucky, Henry County, September 15, 1822, and came to Bond County with his parents when three months old, remaining here about two years, when he went with the family to Montgomery County, where he came to manhood's years. He was married in July, 1843, to Mary R. White, a native of Loudoun County, Va., daughter of James and Mary (Vernando) White, who came to this State about the year 1839. Shortly after his marriage he came to this county, locating in Town 6, Range 2, purchased land, and has since been identified with this township and been engaged in farming pursuits. He has been successful in his business, having 272 acres of land. Had eight children—four sons and four daughters—six living. Mary is the wife of Hardin Elmore; James H. resides in Fayette County; Julia is the wife of Frederick Deen; Elizabeth married Fred. Kimbro, now deceased; George deceased; Harriet, wife of J. F. Elam and Richard at home. Stephen. Mr. Roberts has been a member of the United Baptist Church many years, having joined the church at Liberty soon after its organization. Mr. Roberts served in the Mexican war under Col. Foreman: was a member of Company E, Third Regiment, and has been a Jackson Democrat of the first order, and has always since he cast his first vote been a warm supporter of Jeffersonian principles. The father of our subject was a son of Capt. Benjamin Roberts; he died in Kentucky. Roberts died 1847. he was one among the first school teachers in Montgomery County. He married the mother of R. S. D.; her maiden name was Sarah Simmons, daughter of Samuel Simmons, a Revolutionary soldier of seven years' service; he lived to be one hundred and fifteen years old. His wife died at the age of one hundred and seven of cancer. Our subject had one brother, Henry, who served in the Black Hawk war, and was out with the Rangers, and also in the Florida war, and one brother, Marcus S., who was in the Mexican war; he is now in Colorado.

COTTONWOOD GROVE PRECINCT.

JOHN D. ALEXANDER, retired farmer, Cottonwood Precinct, is one of the oldest pioneers in Bond County, having been here since May, 1820, a constant resident. He was born October 21, 1793, in Mecklenburg County, N. C., son of Jedediah and Betsey Alexander. Jedediah was born 1757, son of Francis, who was born 1730. The Alexander family are of Scotch-Irish descent. John D. lived in North Carolina until twenty-three years of age. September, 1816, moved to Maury County, Tenn., where he lived until May 1, 1820, when he came to Bond County, and located three miles southwest of Bethel Church on the William Cruthis farm, where he lived until 1832, when he located on Section 12, in this precinct, where he has since lived. He joined the Sugar Creek society of the Presbyterian order, at the age of seventeen, when in North Carolina, and has since been a member of that organization, and was one of the first members at the time of the organization of the Bethel Church, September 15, 1825, and of sixty-two members he is one of three now living. His wife was Mary Scott McCord, whom he married on December 10, 1819. She died January 8, 1837, having borne the following children: William F., James H., Robert W., Demas W., John L., Amelia and Melanthon Hill. None lived to be married except Amelia J., wife of J. V. McFarland, Melanthon and Demas M. Robert went to California in 1850, and was killed by the Indians. Demas M. served through the late war, and one year after in the regular army. He was first commissioned as Captain and came out as Brevet Major; he went out from Kansas, where he had gone in 1856. He was prominent and well known in that locality. He served as Justice of the Peace and was twice elected Representative from Douglas County. He died in 1871, highly esteemed by all who knew him. Melanthon H. was born June 12, 1828, on the Cruthis farm, and moved with his father to the place he now owns, where he has since lived. January 1, 1860, he married Caroline V. Foster, born 1841, near the Hudson River, in Dutchess County, daughter of Rev. Aaron Foster, whose wife was a Sloan. He is a minister of the Methodist Episcopal Church, now located in Vermillion County, where he came from New York in 1843. Mrs. Alexander has one brother, John L., now of Vermillion County. Mr. Alexander has four children living—Leroy E., Mary, Percy and Clarence. Walter died, aged ten years, in 1875. Mr. A. is a member of the Presbyterian Church and has 310 acres.

J. V. McFARLAND, farmer, P. O. Cottonwood Grove, born May 15, 1833, in Cape Girardeau Co., Mo., son of Robert S. and Agnes (Cummings) McFarland. Robert S. was born in North Carolina, in 1799, son of Jacob McFarland, a native of Scotland. In the spring of 1818 the father of our subject came to what is now Bond County, and made a crop on the site of ground where Greenville now stands. He remained there however, but a short time after, when he moved South to Tennessee, afterward removed to Missouri, when he returned to this county with his family in 1837, and located in Cottonwood Precinct and remained here until his death, March 15, 1863; his wife survived him until May 12, 1865. They were both members of the Presbyterian Church. Of seven children born to them but two are living—H. Columbus and John V., who remained under the parental roof until his marriage. He was married April 26, 18[illegible]

Amelia J. Alexander, born in this county, daughter of John D. Alexander, and Mary S. McCord, both old and highly respected families in the county. Since his marriage he has been a resident of the farm he now owns, having 174 acres and good improvements, which were of his own establishment. He has no children. He has served as County Commissioner one term, also Overseer of the Poor. Is not a member of any church yet not an opposer of religion but a friend to the same and maintenance of good morals.

WILLIAM P. PAISLEY, farmer, P. O. Elm Point born November 24, 1856, on the homestead of the old Pioneer, William Paisley, situated in Town 6, Range 2, in Cottonwood Grove Precinct He is the youngest son of his father, and remained with him until his death. November 24, 1880, he married Alice Hendrick, a native of Alabama daughter of Robert and Julia (Philips) Hendrick she moved to Bond County with her parents in 1875. Mr. Paisley has been a resident of the homestead since his marriage having 235 acres of land. He is a member of the Cumberland Presbyterian Church, having his membership at Donnellson. Has one child Lucretia, born September 21, 1881.

JAMES REDFEARN farmer, P. O. Greenville. The Redfearn and Carroll family are contemporaneous with the early settlement of Bond County. James Redfearn was born in North Carolina, September 8 1813, son of Isaac who moved with his family to Bond County about the year 1825 and settled at Round Prairie, this county. Isaac had the following-named children, of whom James was the eldest the others in order of birth were John, Jane, Isaac Mulberry Jemina, Martha, Ruth, Lydia and Ira. James Redfearn, whose name heads this sketch, was brought up to hard labor, raised on a farm and had little or no school advantages. In March 1, 1842, he married Nancy Carroll, who was born May 15, 1822, in Virginia, daughter of Mac Carroll and Elizabeth Baron, who were Virginians. The family first removed from Virginia to Tennessee, and from there they came to Bond County, about the year 1827, and settled with the Redfearn family on Round Prairie. Eleven children were born to them, viz.: Ambrose, Jackson, Nancy, Caroline Rhoda, Tillman, Robert Mary, Elizabeth, Berdine and Susan, all of whom lived to be grown and raise families except Elizabeth. After the marriage of Mr. and Mrs. Redfearn they settled near Bethel, where they remained until they came to this farm in 1851. Of ten children born to them, nine are living —John T James P., Lydia M., Mary F., Nancy E., Jemima E. McClellan, Millie J. and G. M.; Isaac deceased. Lydia married E. B. Dagget Mary F. married John Sibert Nancy, Wilson File Jemina Charles B. File all residents of this county. Of Mrs. Redfearn's brothers and sisters, living are: Tillman, Robert and Berdine they reside in Linneus, Linn Co., Mo.; Rhoda of Sioux City, Iowa, wife of Henry Jandt a prominent business man. Susan resides in Round Prairie, wife of James Sauer; Mary married John Hochdorfer, and lives in this county. Mr. Redfearn has 960 acres of land Mrs. R. is a member of the United Bap. Church, and a thoroughgoing business woman.

JAMES W. ROBINSON farmer, P. O. Cottonwood Grove was born in North Carolina March 14, 1800, son of Alexander and Betsey (White) Robinson, both natives of North Carolina, who came to Montgomery about 1812, he a harness maker by trade, and dying October 10, 1853, the wife having died many years previous. Seven children were born to them our subject being the eldest, who was raised to a life of farming, afterward carrying on milling both grain and saw milling. In 1831, he married Catharine Hess, who died July 11, 1833, leaving one son, Alexander S. February 12, 1835, he married Mary Ann Armstrong, daughter of John and Polly (Dudley) Armstrong, he of Georgia, and she of North Carolina. Alexander S., the eldest son of our subject, entered the Union service, enlisting in Company B, Illinois Volunteer Infantry, Twenty-second Regiment, and was captured at Chickamauga, dying in Libby Prison, Richmond, January 20, 1864. Mr. Robinson has had born to him four daughters and two sons. Two of the daughters are living—Mary E., Mrs. J. N. Roseborough, and Alvira R., Mr.s H. M. Ferguson. Sarah was Mrs. Rev. F. G. Strange, who died leaving two sons. Lemuel F. Robinson died July 20, 1854.

JOHN M. ROSS, farmer, P. O. Cottonwood Grove, was born in Maury County, Tenn., June 7, 1823, son of Thomas Ross, a farmer born in Georgia in 1786, and died in Montgomery County, in 1835 whither he had moved in the spring of 1829, locating in Town 7, Range 4. Our subject's mother was Sally (Armstrong) Ross, a native of Tennessee. John Ross came to Bond County when a mere child of five years, and received his first schooling in the pioneer schoolhouse, just over the north line of this county. At Cottonwood Grove he learned the blacksmith's trade with Reuben Morrell, and followed this trade about fifteen years. July 13, 1847, at Pleasant Prairie, this county, he was married to Ruth N. Jones, a native of the same county as her husband, daughter of Pleasant and Sallie (Osborn) Jones, the former from Virginia, the latter from North Carolina. The father of Thomas Ross was one Andrew Ross, a native of Scotland, and, like his grandson, learned the trade of blacksmith, and was known to have made swords and bayonets for use in the Revolutionary war. He was buried in North Carolina. Thomas was his only son. Our subject has five children living—Albert D., S. Jeanette, J. Warren, Sprague D., L. Shoeman; one, Louis J. is dead. Thomas Ross' family consisted of six children, four sons and two daughters, three of whom are now living: two residents of Bond and one of Montgomery County; all farmers. Our subject bought his first twenty acres about 1845, and has since added until he has now 276.84 of which he entered June 22, 1853.

JAMES M. VOLLENTINE, farmer, P. O. New Douglas. Prominent among the early settlers and representative men of Bond County was William Bigford Vollentine, a native of North Carolina, son of Hardy Vollentine. William B. emigrated from North Carolina to Tennessee, where he married Fannie Plant. While here he served in the war of 1812, and participated in the battle of New Orleans. He emigrated to what is now Bond County when it was a Territory. When he first came here, he remained for a time where Pocahontas Township now is, and finally located in Town 6, Range 4, on Section 18, where he remained until his death, which occurred in 1869. He was thrice married. His first wife bore him the following children—George W., now of Christian County, Hardy of Wisconsin, Mrs. Elizabeth Condiff of Montgomery County, Mrs. Nancy Brown, now of Minnesota. His second wife was Sophia Suggs, a native of Tennessee, daughter of Josiah Suggs. This union was crowned with eleven children, those living are: James M., John J., Rebecca, Letta and Christopher C. J. M. and C. C. reside in this township, Letta, wife of James Ridgeway, of Pocahontas Precinct. His third marriage was to Elsie Preckett, a native of Kentucky; she bore him five children—Jennette, Lois, Charles J., Margaret Jennette and Douglass. William B. Vollentine was one of the prominent men of the county, he became a large landholder, and owned at one time 2,000 acres. He was a stanch Democrat and took a lively interest in the affairs of his county, he served some time as Justice of the Peace was County Commissioner and Associate Judge, and for many years was a leader in the Methodist Episcopal Church, during the early part of his life. He was generally known all over the country, being a thorough business man trading largely in stock, and farmed quite extensively was a man of great energy and perseverance, and a successful financier, and the father of twenty-three children; of this number J. M. was of the second set. He was born February 4, 1828 on the homestead, where he remained until his majority, after which he attended school two years. In the spring of 1852 he went to California, where he spent seven years in Nevada County, where he was engaged in trading and freighting, and had a varied experience. He returned here to this township in 1859, and since remained. He, for a time run a store in New Douglas, and in 1866 he located on the farm he now owns, which place was settled by William Carson. In August 7, 1860, he married Louisa J. Jernigan, born in Christian County, daughter of Lewis H. and Sallie (Curry) Jernigan. Lewis H. was born in Tennessee, son of Jesse. Lewis H. was a very early settler in Christian County. Gabriel Jernigan, son of Jesse was Sheriff of his county two terms, and represented his county in the Legislature. Mr. Vollentine has one brother, Napoleon B., he is a liveryman in New Douglas. Lizzie, a sister who resides in Marion County, Kan., wife of Ben Nesbitt, and Emma Mrs. William Connor, of same county. Mr. Vollentine has a good farm of several hundred acres, and is a thorough and progressive farmer, and one of the best in the township. He is a member of the Methodist Church, and has been a class leader and Steward for several years, and a great Sunday school worker, at Corrington Chapel. Had three children born to him, two are living—James P. and William Lewis. His only daughter, Sallie Sophia, was removed by death, August 16, 1876, aged nine years.

E. J. VOLLENTINE, farmer, P. O. New Douglas, is a descendant of one of the early settlers. He was born February 3, 1837, on the homestead farm which is now owned by W. B. Vollentine. He is the second son and third child of Jackson O. Vollentine, whose wife was an Armstrong. Jackson died about the year 1852, March 30. He served in the Black Hawk war, and for years was a member of the Methodist Episcopal Church. He had four children born to him, viz.: William D., E. J., Alonzo and Thomas. E. J. was married in 1860 to Mary Smith. She died 1870, leaving two children—Ellis T. and Jackson O. He has 260 acres and is a member of the Methodist Episcopal Church.

OKAW PRECINCT.

JACOB BARTH, farmer and stock-raiser, P. O. Heilsburg. Among the prominent farmers and self-made men of this portion of the county is Jacob Barth, who was born October 9, 1826, in Hesse-Darmstadt, son of George and Barvell (Mann) Barth. Jacob, when a lad, learned the glazier's trade in the old country, and at the age of nineteen bid good-bye to the land of his nativity and cast his fortunes with America's freedom. He left home with nothing, his father's only endowment was a whipping, which he gave Jacob before leaving. Jacob came first to St. Louis, and sought employment at his trade which was at the time unprofitable here; he then learned the wagon-maker's trade and worked at journey work for several years, and traveled over several States. In the fall of 1850 he came to Bond County and made a purchase in the locality where he now resides, and engaged in farming, and has since lived here, and became one of the leading farmers in his township. He has nearly 600 acres of land, which he farms very successfully. In 1850 he married Elizabeth Gertner, a native Wurtemberg, who has borne him six children—Edward, Theresa E., Matilda E., Henry G., Jacob and George. The daughters are married to two brothers, James and John Gunn, and reside in this township.

ALEXANDER MYATT, deceased. Prominent among the early settlers of this precinct is the Myatt family, of whom the above was the head and father. He was born February 9, 1802, in Tennessee, son of Wiley Myatt, and came to Bond County in the year 1831, locating first in Beaver Creek Township, and removed to this township, locating on the west half of Section 33, in the year 1836, and remained here until his death, September 4, 1865. For many years he was a member of the Methodist Church, his house being used in early time as a place for holding meetings, and the pioneer minister ever found under his roof a hospitable welcome. He was a man of quiet and unpretentious habits; yet, withal he was a man of substantial worth and merit. He was twice married; first to Mary Chiseuhall, of Tennessee, who bore him six children, viz., Emily, Martha, Perneeia, Wiley, Wesley and Mary. His second and last wife was Mrs. Murphy Wilmerth, whose maiden name was Sugg, by whom he had six children as follows: William C., Josiah, Alexander B., Nancy E., Sarah S. and Murphy L., all of whom were born in this county. Of this number William C. and Alexander B. reside on farms adjoining. Alexander Barnes' sons reside upon and own the homestead farm here; he was born April 17, 1837, and was married June 30, 1858, to Caroline Powell, who was born February 18, 1836, in Montgomery County, Tenn., daughter of Benjamin and Nellie (Cossie) Powell; he was a son of Eaton Powell; she was born in Kentucky, daughter of Robert Cossie. Mrs. Myatt was the second of a family of six children, but two of the number living, herself and Catharine, who reside in California, wife of Alfred Louis. The Powell family came to Illinois in 1844, and were Methodists. To Mr. and Mrs. Myatt have been born four children, but two living, Fannie E. and Roxcillana. The entire family being members of the Methodist Episcopal Church. Mr. Myatt has 265 acres, and with the exception of about four years spent in Greenville educating his daughters, he has remained a constant resident of the farm.

MONTGOMERY COUNTY PIOGRAPHIES.

HILLSBORO CITY AND TOWNSHIP.

LIEUT. JESSE K. ALLEN, deceased, was born in Kingston, Tenn., September 5, A. D. 1828, and, at an early day, came with his parents to Hillsboro, Ill., which was about the time of the location of the county seat of Montgomery County at that point, and when there were but very few houses in the town. William Allen, the father of the subject, was born in Roane County, Tenn., January 15, 1799, and was married to Mary K. Killingsworth, the mother of Jesse K. Allen, to whom were born eleven children—first, the subject of this sketch; second, William A. Allen, for many years a prominent physician in Greenville, Ill.; third, Margaret Allen, now intermarried with Theodore Smith, of Greenville, Ill.; fourth, Aaron Allen, now deceased; fifth, Rufus S. Allen, now a physician, employed the General Government in doctoring the Indians; sixth, John H. Allen, now in Kansas; seventh, Emily E., now wife of Charles L. Bartlett, a merchant of Hillsboro, Ill.; eighth, Mollie, now married to Dr. Perkins, of Fredonia, Kan.; ninth, Frank F. Allen, also a physician, Neodesha, Kan.; and tenth, Laura Allen, now deceased; and Charles F. Allen, now at Mattoon, Ill. William Allen, the ancestor, was a man in very moderate circumstances, and consequently, his son, Jesse K., was denied many of the advantages enjoyed by his youthful companions. In his youth, he attended such schools as opportunity afforded, in the town of Hillsboro, and later, when what was then known as the Hillsboro Academy was built, in 1836, Jesse attended such academy as far as means could be afforded him, and it was here he gave promise of the future man. He was here noted for his industry and untiring energy in his efforts to acquire an education. He particularly excelled in mathematics and those studies which called more particularly for the exercise of the reasoning faculties. He was held in very high esteem by the Faculty of the Hillsboro Academy, which was at that period second to none in the State. Lieut. Allen, having finished the school course at the academy, looked about him for something to do. At this time, there happened to be a vacancy in the cadetship from his Congressional District, and, through Gen. Shields and his friends in Hillsboro, and the then Representative in Congress, the appointment to West Point was secured to him, and in 1851 he entered as a cadet to West Point. He remained at the Military Academy for the usual course of four years, and in 1855 graduated with honor and distinction. In this Military School, as in the academy at home, he excelled in the study of mathematics, and he also acquired distinction in civil engineering. After he graduated, he entered the army, being at that time in the meridian of life and vigor of manhood. He was full of ambition, and entered the army with a high resolve to win for himself a name and fame as a soldier. He was appointed Lieutenant in Company B of the Ninth Infantry, and in this capacity served the Government in active service for three years. He had the entire confidence of his superior officers, and was often intrusted with services which called forth special judgment and nerve. In the winter of 1856, he was intrusted with $3,500 in specie, to be carried from Washington Territory to some point in Vancouver's Island, in command of fifteen men. They were overtaken in a very severe snow storm, and all his men deserted him but two, and it was supposed he was lost, but in a few days, he, with his two remaining men, came riding into camp, with the funds all safe. Whether as citizen or soldier, he was always reliable, and never disappointed the expectation of his friends. It seemed at this time that a life of activity and usefulness was open before him, and he was surely prepared to enter upon it: but the end came before it could reasonably be expected. About 3 o'clock on the morning of the 15th of August, 1858, in the moment of accomplishing a successful surprise on a camp of Indians, he was shot down, and thus, in his early manhood, and while the dew of youth was on his brow, he was called upon to die the death of a soldier. He died as he had lived in the line of duty. The following letter was written at the time by his superior officer:

HEADQUARTERS YAKIMA EXPEDITION,
CAMP ON THE UPPER YAKIMA RIVER,
August 15, 1858.

MAJOR: It has become my painful duty to communicate to you for Gen. Clarke's information, and through him the Adjutant General of the army, the sad intelligence of the death of Second Lieut. Jesse K. Allen, of the Ninth Infantry, who expired at this camp at about 2 o'clock to-day. Lieut. Allen [illegible]

He [illegible] this morning at the moment of accomplishing a [illegible] surprise of a camp of [illegible] Indians [illegible]ally by one of his own men in the darkness of the hour.

I must be permitted here to express my own sorrow for the untimely end of this young officer, and to offer this officially my tribute to his worth. He was an officer of rare energy and zeal, and an acquaintance with our army of seventeen years' duration, warrants me in uttering the conviction that his place will not again be readily filled in our service. His loss to this command can scarcely be overestimated.

His remains will be taken back to-night to Fort Simcoe by his company commander and personal friend, Capt. Frazer Ninth Infantry, who will take the charge of his effects, required by the regulations. It is perhaps proper to report in this connection that Lieut. Allen's party (fifteen mounted men) captured in this sad affair twenty one men, about fifty women and children, seventy head of horses, and fifteen head of cattle, besides considerable of the Indian property.

Three of the men having been recognized as participants in the attack on the miners were shot in compliance with my general instructions on this subject.

I am sir, very respectfully your obedient servant,

Signed, R. S. GARNETT,
Major Ninth Infantry Commanding.

MAJOR W. H. MACKALL,
Assistant Adjutant General U. S. A.
Fort Vancouver, W. T.

The remains of Lieut. Allen were brought to Hillsboro by his parents and relatives, and were interred in Oak Grove Cemetery, near his childhood home. Had his life been spared until the commencement of our late civil war, he would have been found battling for the Union, and doubtless, with his energy and courage, would have attained high rank as an officer in our army.

J. C. BARKLEY, grocer, Hillsboro, was born in North Carolina December 15, 1850; son of John C. and Elizabeth (Morrison) Barkley, natives of North Carolina. John C., who is a farmer, was born in 1815. His wife died April 14, 1851. Our subject, the second son of a family of five sons and two daughters, [illegible]

Hillsboro, and at Freehold, N. J. He came to Hillsboro when seventeen years old, without money or education, and but few clothes. He first worked on a farm, then in a brickyard. He traveled for a wholesale house in St. Louis (Udell, Schmieding & Co., dealers in wood and willow ware), and finally engaged in the grocery business on his own account in Hillsboro, where, by push and energy, he has acquired a lucrative trade. He was in the hotel business in Hillsboro for about eighteen months, and was one of the [illegible] citizens who lost heavily by the failure of the banking firm of Haskell, Harris & Co., of Hillsboro. He married in Hillsboro, November 4, 1875, Emma A. Slack, born in Ohio October 18, 1857, daughter of Daniel Slack, [illegible] of New Jersey, who died in Ohio in [illegible]. There have been born to them one [illegible] Edward Daniel, and one daughter, Maggie Elizabeth. Mr. Barkley is a member of [illegible] Methodist Church, and was Assistant Superintendent of the Sunday school in Hillsboro [illegible] two years. In politics he supports the Republican party.

[illegible]HARLES L. BARTLETT, grocer, Hillsboro, was born in Montgomery County December 20, 1839; son of Samuel T. and M[illegible] (Maxey) Bartlett. Samuel T. was born in Henry County, Ky., in 1818. He removed to Illinois about the year 1835, and is now living at Irving, where he owns and manages a large farm and a general store. [illegible], who is still living, was born near Bowling Green, Ky., in 1819. Our subject is the second son of a family of seven sons and two daughters. He received his education chiefly at Irving, Ill., and began life as a [illegible], but, after being three years in that occupation, he abandoned it and engaged in the mercantile business in Irving, where he remained four years. He left Irving in 1872 and came to Hillsboro, where he has since been engaged in the grocery business. He started in business with but small capital, but by his tact and enterprise, he has built up and is now enjoying a lucrative trade. In Hillsboro, in 1868, he married Emily E. Allen, born in Hillsboro in 1839, daughter of William and Mary K. (Killingsworth) Allen, the former born in Tennessee, and died in Hillsboro in 1863; the latter, still living, was also born in Tennessee, in 1812. Mr. and Mrs. Bartlett are the parents of two children, Charles William and Nellie; Carry Bell, their first child, died in infancy. Mr. Bartlett has filled the offices of Deputy Sheriff and Jailer of Montgomery County for two years. In politics he is a Democrat. He is a member of the Masonic fraternity and the I. O. O. F. They are members of the Presbyterian Church.

JACOB BECK, gun-smithing and cancer doctor, Hillsboro, was born in Franklin County, Penn. November 30, 1820. He was taken to Virginia when about nine months old by his parents, and there raised. Christian Beck, born in Lancaster County, Penn., on June 17, 1785, was a gun-smith by occupation, and died in Oregon on July 15, 1862. Mother was Lena Ahl, born February 6, 1790, in Cumberland County, Penn, and died September 5, 1821, in Williamsport, Md., while en route to Virginian with her husband and family. Parents had seven sons, subject the youngest. Subject was educated at Martinsburg, Va., common schools. Began life as a gun-smith, an occupation he has kept up through life. In 1860, subject began the practice of cancer doctoring with a remedy he had come into possession of some two years previous, and had experimented with it sufficiently to satisfy himself of its merits. From that time to the present time he has treated large numbers of cases successfully, having never lost a single case that came to him before cancer had been cut. Subject was Commander in Chief of the Anti-Mormon forces of Hancock County, Ill., in 1845-46, and forced them into the city of Nauvoo from all parts of the county and surrounding counties, and there they submitted to a compromise to the effect that they (the Mormons) be allowed sufficient time to send a committee West and seek a suitable location and return and report which they did during the summer of 1846, and left that fall for St. Joseph, Mo., where they wintered, leaving twelve men behind at Nauvoo to dispose of their property and settle up their business. Immediately after the settling of the Mormon difficulties, subject enlisted for the Mexican war, or rather bought the place of another young man in a company that was already organized, paying the young man $27 for his position. It was Company A, First Illinois Volunteers, called the Quincy Riflemen, commanded by Col. John J. Hardin, James D. Morgan, Captain. He participated in the battle of Buena Vista. In politics he is a Democrat. Self and family are all members of the Lutheran Church. He was married at Indianapolis, Ind., February 10, 1848, to Phebe Ringer, who was born in Frederick County, Md., March 5, 1821, and was the daughter of Jacob and Maria Magadalena (Darr) Ringer, he a native of Washington County, Md, and was born March 15, 1791, and died April 22, 1859; she also a native of Washington County, Md., was born February 22, 1790, and died in the year 1824. They have had four children born to them: Julia Agnes, born November 2, 1848, and died in 1856; Virginia Magadalena, born November 9, 1853; Luther Melanchthon, born September 4, 1856, and Clara Belle, born June 1, 1859. Subject belongs to the Masonic order, and also to the Good Templars.

ADAM H. BELL, farmer, P. O. Hillsboro, was born in New York September 26, 1831. Frederick Bell, his father, was born in New York, in the town of Warren, Herkimer County, October 10, 1800; was a tanner and currier by occupation, and emigrated to this State in 1856, and went to farming in this township. He died February 15, 1880. Elizabeth Voorhies, his mother, was born in German Flat, Herkimer Co., N. Y., March 31, 1802. She died in this State in 1878, and was the mother of three children, the subject being the youngest of the family. He was raised in the town of Chaumont, Jefferson County; was educated in an academy of his native state, and at the age of twenty years, he commenced civil engineering, which he followed successfully in different parts of the United States until 1856. He came to Montgomery County, Ill., and commenced farming, his first purchase of land being eighty acres, and has added to that until he has accumulated 300 acres of good, tillable land. He has quite a neat cottage, and good barn with all necessary outbuildings and was married in New York, March 12, 1857, to Miss Lana Fox. Levi M. Fox, her father, was born in Chester, Washington Co., N. Y., May 7, 1809. Her mother, Cynthia M. (Jerome) Fox, was born in Paris, Oneida Co., N. Y., February 6, 1804. The wife of subject was born January 22, 1832, and she has a family of four children. The names are as follows: Franklin J., born July 9, 1858; Frederick Meade, born August 12, 1860; Harry, born March 17, 1870; Cora Grace, born November 5, 1871. He is a member of the Masonic order, and is quite a public spirited man, encouraging all public improvements that he thinks best for the county at large. He has held the office of County Surveyor one term, 1860-61. He gave general satisfaction, but found it did not pay to neglect his farm for the benefit he received from the office.

W. L. BLACKBURN, dry goods, groceries, boots and shoes, etc., Hillsboro, was born in Clark County, Ohio, January 16, 1847; son of Robert B. and Sarah Ann (Fuller) Blackburn. Robert B., a farmer by occupation, was born near Harper's Ferry, Va., March 3, 18 . About the year 1836, he moved to Ohio, thence to Illinois in 1850. His wife was born in Ohio; our subject was their only child. He received a liberal education at Hillsboro, and began life on the farm. In 1872, he left the farm, and came to Hillsboro, where he worked at the carpenter's trade for about two years. He then engaged in the mercantile business in partnership with C. L. B. In 1877, this partnership was dissolved, and he has since carried on the whole business himself. He does a brisk business, and employs seven or eight clerks. He owns a commodious frame house in Hillsboro, where he resides. He married in Hillsboro, November 11, 1875, Mattie J. Stewart, born in Hillsboro November 12, 1857, daughter of J R. Stewart. From this union two children have been born to them Wallace Stewart and Blanche Ittel. Mr. Blackburn is a supporter of the Republican party, and a member of the Masonic fraternity. His wife is a member of the Methodist Church.

CHARLES W. BLISS, attorney, Hillsboro, was born in Montgomery County, January 8, 1846, to Rev. Alfred Bliss of the Methodist Episcopal Church, a native of Bradford, Vt., where he was born in 1811, to Seth Bliss, a farmer, who died in Vermont. The son came early to this county, and engaged in farming, but subsequently entered the ministry. The maiden name of the mother of our subject was Jerusha Strong. She is the mother of eight children, five of whom are now living—Eliza A., wife of James I. Moody, a farmer of Fillmore Township; Celesta J., wife of E. C. Devore, a lawyer at Seymour, Ind.; George A., a hardware merchant at Nokomis; Alice, deceased, wife of Lyman C. Allen, a farmer of Fillmore Township. She left three children—Charles W., Nellie J., wife of John C. White, a lawyer at Effingham, Ill. Our subject worked on the farm and attended the common schools, and graduated from McKendree College, at Lebanon, in June, 1869. He then taught school and read law with Irwin & Krone, of Edwardsville, Ill. He was admitted in the fall of 1871, and located in Hillsboro, where he has become one of the leading young attorneys at the Montgomery County bar. He was married, October 15, 1872, to Elizabeth W. Phillips, a neice of Judge J. J. Phillips, and daughter of Burrel Phillips, a stock dealer of Montgomery County. By her he has two children—Noi Celesta and Clinton. He has been City Attorney several terms, and his political tenets Republican. He is a Royal Arch Mason, in which fraternity he has held numerous offices, and with his family belongs to the Methodist Episcopal Church.

WILLIAM BREWER, retired, Hillsboro, is the third son of William Brewer, a Carolinian of Welsh extraction, and the youngest of three brothers. Daniel and George, eldest of that number, left Carolina at an early date, and settled in Tennessee. The family of William, Sr., was John J. and Jesse, who died in Carolina; our subject, and Thomas, who died near Evansville, Ind. The daughters were Candis, who married a Mr Williams, settled and died in Iowa; Keziah, wife of a Mr. Alder, near Hopkinsville, Ky., and Annie died young. The mother of these was Millie West, a Carolinian. The subject of this sketch was born in Chatham County, N. C., June 18, 1803; removed to Christian County, Ky., and settled near Hopkinsville, with his parents, in 1807, and where they died, and where he was raised and married to Miss Delilah Hough, a native of Loudoun County, Va., where she was born October 1, 1807, to Samuel and Azuba (Skinner) Hough, natives of Virginia. Her grandfather Hough was an Englishman by birth, and came early to this country with two brothers, who settled in Vermont; he in Virginia. With this lady he lived happily for forty-four years, and until her death, August 26, 1869, when she left him with three surviving children of nine born to them: William H., now of Hillsboro; Mary, wife of S. M. Grubbs, of Litchfield; and Ellen, wife of Alfred A. G. Sawyer, of Hillsboro. Mr. Brewer removed with his family to Illinois in November, 1834, and settled at Palestine, Crawford County, where he remained until the spring of 1839, when he removed to Hillsboro, his present place of residence. In 1843, he was elected County Judge, the first Whig ever elected in Montgomery County. He was re-elected in 1845, and again in 1847, thus serving three consecutive terms. In 1850, he was elected to represent the counties of Montgomery, Bond and Clinton in the State Legislature, and served two sessions, but positively refused to suffer his name to be used for that honor longer, although often and strongly solicited. In 1853, he was elected Justice of the Peace, in which capacity he acted until 1869, when he refused to act longer. While in this office he did a very large business, and decided more cases than any other officer in the county, and what is still more remarkable, never had any of his decisions reversed. He has been an eminent example of a self-made man, who, unaided, has arisen from a humble station in life to wealth, honor and influence. From boyhood he took the side of morality and piety, and thus gained the public confidence. As a member of the Methodist Church of sixty-three years' standing, he has had a large share in building up the morals and character of the people of his community. He still, although in the [illegible] autumn of life, stands a monument of [illegible] energies rightly directed, with a large [illegible] ence, large acquaintance, large exp[illegible] and large means and usefulness. Mr. Br[illegible] was married the second time, to Mrs. R[illegible] of Elkton, Ky., and is quietly enjoy[illegible] well earned honor and reputation in the [illegible] of a people whose growth has been [illegible] his own eye. His only living son, Wi[illegible] H. Brewer, was born January 4, 18[illegible] Trigg County, Ky., and in 1827 r[illegible] with his parents to Todd County, Ky. [illegible] remained with his father during his boyh[illegible] receiving limited advantages for educ[illegible] and in manhood has been connected wit[illegible] father in his business interests. He al[illegible] been twice married. First, on the 1[illegible] November, 1857, to Miss Permesia Ph[illegible] daughter of Capt. Thomas Phillips. B[illegible] he had four children, all of whom [illegible] young, the mother following them [illegible] grave July 27, 1867, in her thirty-[illegible] year. His second marriage occurred [illegible] 14, 1875, to Mrs. Mary J. Brown, wid[illegible] William W. Brown. By her he has th[illegible] children: Mary, Dwight and Raymond. [illegible] her first husband she has two children: Ell[illegible] and John T. Mr. Brewer is a stanch Rep[illegible] lican, and with his family belongs t[illegible] Methodist Episcopal Church.

JAMES A. BROWN, station agent [illegible] Indianapolis & St. Louis Railroad, Hillsb[illegible] was born in Montgomery County, Ill., Ma[illegible] 23, 1848; son of George W. and Sarah [illegible] (Jenkins) Brown, he a farmer, born in G[illegible] sey County, Ohio, July 9, 1819, mov[illegible] Illinois in 1837, and settled in this cou[illegible] where he still lives; she born in Darlin[illegible] Village, S. C., June 30, 1819, and is still [illegible] ing. Subject is the third son of a family [illegible] five sons and one daughter; educated in H[illegible] boro Academy, where he received a good, thorough course, such as was taught in that school, and began life here in town as a newsboy, then telegraph operator, taking charge of an office at Pana, afterward at Paris, Kan., Litchfield, Mattoon, in the General Superintendent's office, St. Louis, and was then appointed to this place, at the age of eighteen years, December 4, 1866. He has also been a coal dealer in this town for about ten years; been in the grain business for a short time. He has been Alderman for two terms, and was defeated in 1876 by a small majority for Circuit Clerk, owing to being a Republican, and the county being Democratic by about eight hundred majority at the time. A change of sixty votes would have elected him. At Litchfield, Montgomery County, September 20, 1871, he married Margaret S. Evans, born in Montgomery County July 1, 1853, daughter of James D. and Elzira (Eames) Evans, he born in Virginia in November, 1823, and died July 23, 1855; she born in Kentucky January 4, 1832, and died at Litchfield October 21, 1873. From this union five children have been born to them—Frederic G., Herbert (deceased), Ethel M., Sarah Eleanor (deceased), and Horace E. Mr. Brown is a Methodist, and has been connected with the official board of that church as Trustee and Steward for ten or twelve years; is a member of the Chapter of the Masonic fraternity, and has been Master of his lodge in Hillsboro for a year, besides filling other subordinate offices therein. He owns a two-story frame residence in Hillsboro.

THOMAS B. BROWN, Postmaster, Hillsboro, was born in this county July 10, 1857. His father was Newton G. Brown, born in Hillsboro, N. C., April 26, 1822, and died September 4, 1879. He was a hotel proprietor by occupation, and when about thirteen years of age emigrated to Illinois with his parents, and settled in Montgomery County, and on August 16, 1849, was married to Euphemia J. Grantham, daughter of William and Susannah (Mann) Grantham. She was born in this county July 11, 1832. Parents had six children born to them, two sons dying in infancy. There are living one son (subject) and three daughters, viz.: Medora F., now the wife of C. A. Freeland; Lucy and Ollie G. Subject was educated at the Hillsboro High School and Academy. He began business as a dry goods clerk, in 1871, in this town, where he continued until February 7, 1881, at which date subject was commissioned Postmaster at this place, a position he still holds. In politics, he is a Republican. Subject belongs to the Methodist Church at Hillsboro; his mother and sister Lucy are members of the Congregational Church. The father, Newton G. Brown, when he first came to this State, settled in this county on a farm, and pursued that avocation for a few years, and then moved to Missouri; remained there about one year, and then returned to this county and settled in Hillsboro about 1856, and engaged in teaming, and also run a meat market, the only one then in town, for quite a number of years, perhaps until about 1863. He then purchased the American House. In the fall (October) of 1869, Mr. B. sold out, having run the hotel from the time he purchased it in 1863 until the above date, and moved to St. Louis, where he soon was taken sick, and remained until the following spring, engaged in keeping boarding house, and then returned again to Hillsboro and resumed the hotel business, this time at the City Hotel, where he continued until the time of his death. Since that time, our subject being the only son, assumed the principal responsibility of the family.

EDWARD S. BURNS, Deputy Circuit

Clerk, Hillsboro, was born at Harper's Ferry, Va., January 1, 1832, and moved to Ohio with his parents in 1836, and came to Illinois in 1852; the son of Philip and Catharine B. (Blackburn) Burns, he born in 1774, was a teacher, and died in Ohio in 1846; she born in Loudoun County, Va., in 1808, and died at Hillsboro, Ill, in 1856. Subject is the oldest of a family of six. He received an education in the subscription schools of Ohio. In this county, September 27, 1855, he married Rachel C. Mann, who was born here September 14, 1834, the daughter of John and Euphemia (Hancock) Mann, he born in North Carolina July 24, 1800, and died in this county January 24, 1838; she born in Kentucky in 1805, and died in 1867. Of the Mann family there were four sons—Samuel, Henry, Robert and William, and three daughters—Margaret, Mary and Rachel, the latter being the wife of our subject. Mr. Burns has seven children—William T., Charles H., John T., Eddie, Mary E., Emma C. and Minnie B. He taught school about four years in Illinois, then manufactured brick for two or three years, and from 1866 to 1875 was engaged in the mercantile business in Hillsboro, at which time he was appointed Deputy Sheriff of Montgomery County, served two years and was then appointed Deputy Circuit Clerk, which position he still holds. During the war, he was drafted, but furnished a substitute and remained at home to care for a wife and two or three little children. Mr. and Mrs. Burns are Methodists, and he is a member of the Masonic and the I. O. O. F. orders, a Democrat, and owns a very comfortable frame residence, with Lots Nos. 12, 13, 21 and 40. Subject's father was married in Virginia and moved to Ohio when he (subject) was about three years old, and he was only fourteen years old when his father died. At the age of twenty one, he, with his mother, two brothers and three sisters moved to Illinois, all of whom married, and whose families now live in this county, with the exception of the oldest sister, who lives in Neosho County, Kan. Subject's wife's parents were married in Kentucky, and emigrated to Montgomery County, Ill., in October, 1827.

WILLIAM O. BONE, Deputy Sheriff Hillsboro, was born in Ohio September 18, 1852, and came to Nokomis, this county, with his parents in 1862; son of James S. and Mary (Miller) Bone, he a farmer and hotel proprietor, born in Ohio in 1815, and is now living at Nokomis, where he owns 320 acres of land; she born in Ohio, and died there in 1854. Subject is the youngest son of a family of two sons and two daughters. He received his education principally in Illinois, and commenced life as a farmer. He clerked in a mercantile house for some time, railroading several years, and was Constable of Nokomis for four years; from that he was appointed Deputy Sheriff, an office he has filled two years, and is now a candidate for Sheriff. Mr. Bone is a Democrat.

REV. THOMAS I. COULTAS, pastor of the Methodist Episcopal Church, Hillsboro, is a son of George and Eliza (Wilson) Coultas, natives of Yorkshire, England. George, with three of his brothers, sailed for America and landed at New York April 14, 1830. They went from there to Rochester, N. Y., where they remained for a few months. From there they went by boat to Cleveland, Ohio, and from there to Jacksonville, Ill., by the way of Cincinnati, Ohio, Louisville, Ky., and St. Louis, Mo., living for a brief time in each of these places. Near Jacksonville, Ill., he formed the acquaintance of Eliza Wilson, also a native of Yorkshire, England, and who preceded him a few years to this country. Their acquaintance ripened into a greater intimacy, and on July 8, 1835, they were married. Shortly after this, Mr. Coultas purchased from the Government a tract of land near Winchester, then in Morgan, now the county seat of Scott County, Ill. Here he lived, following agricultural pursuits to the time of his death, June 10, 1859. Mrs. Coultas, Sr., died October 26, 1875. Thomas I. is the youngest of a family of five sons and two daughters, and was born May 5, 1853. He lived on the farm until he was sixteen years of age, spending most of the time in school, first in the country schoolhouse, afterward in the high school in Winchester. In September, 1869, when he was but a few months past sixteen years of age, he was regularly licensed as a minister, and received into the traveling connection in the Illinois Conference of the Methodist Episcopal Church, perhaps the youngest man ever thus received and put into the regular work. After serving churches in Sangamon and Champaign Counties respectively for two years, he left the regular pastorate to further prosecute his studies. In September, 1871, he entered the Illinois Wesleyan University, of Bloomington, Ill., and was graduated from that institution in June, 1875. While a student, Mr. Coultas distinguished himself and brought honor to his alma mater by representing this institution in an inter college contest in oratory, where eight of the leading colleges of the State contested in original oration, the judges declaring him to be the champion. By virtue of his success, he represented the State of Illinois in an inter-State contest in oratory, held at Indanapolis., Ind., in May, 1875, where the champions of six States, which had held similar contests, met, and here also Mr. Coultas won the gold medal over all his competitors. After his graduation he entered immediately upon the work of the ministry. After serving the church at Barry, Pike County, for four months as a supply, he was re-admitted into the Conference, and returned to this church for two years in succession. After this pastorate he very acceptably served the church in Pittsfield, the county seat of Pike County. From this church he was sent by his Conference to the Trinity Church, Quincy, Ill. Here he was largely instrumental in removing from this church a heavy debt, which for years hung as a shadow over it. The church in other respects greatly prospered under his pastorate. In September, 1881, he was made pastor of the church in Hillsboro, and, although he has been here but a short time, he is held in high esteem by his congregation and the community. Mr. Coultas was married, November 23, 1875, to Miss Angie Morrison, the daughter of Henry B. and Caroline (Sears) Morrison, then of Bloomington, now of Monticello, Ill., and the neice of Washington Sears, of Scott County, and Rev. Hiram Sears, of East St. Louis, one prominent as a legislator, and the other as a minister and educator. Mrs. Coultas was also educated at the Illinois Wesleyan University. There have been born unto them Aldo Bliss Coultas, March 10, 1877, and Edna Bernice Coultas, March 16, 1879. Mr. Coultas is a Republican in politics. He belongs to the I. O. O. F., and is also a member of Union Chapter, No. 10, A., F. & A. M.

CLARENCE E. COLE, insurance agent, Hillsboro, was born in Sussex County, N. J., April 30, 1848; son of John S. and Elizabeth (Paddock) Cole, he a farmer, born in Sussex County, N. J., October 6, 1806, and came to this State with his family in 1849, and died August 30, 1880; she born in Sussex County, N. J., about 1813, and died in this county November 13, 1877. They had one son and three daughters. Subject was educated at Hillsboro Academy, began life as a farmer, continued as such for fifteen years, commenced the insurance business in 1875, and now enjoys a very fair business. He married at Nokomis, October 10, 1871, Fannie E. Ellis, daughter of D. B. Ellis, a Virginian, born at Princeton, Ill., February 24, 1850, and died August 13, 1878. The result of this union was Gracie E., born August 25, 1872; John E., born January 16, 1874, and Floy A., born September 15, 1876. Mr. Cole's second marriage took place at St. Louis April 21, 1880, when he married Miss Eunice E. Garrettson, born at Marion, Linn Co., Iowa, February 24, 1860, and daughter of G. W. Garrettson, of Marion, Iowa. Mr. Cole is a Republican, and enlisted in the Federal army in April, 1864, as drummer of Company H, One Hundred and Forty-third Illinois Volunteer Infantry, and served six months under Col. Dudley C. Smith, of Shelbyville, Ill.

GEORGE R. COOPER, attorney and teacher, Hillsboro, was born July 25, 1855, at Greencastle, Ind.; came to this county with his parents in 1858; son of Jacob R. and Eliza (Robinson) Cooper, he a carpenter, born in Fleming County, Ky., on November 16, 1816, and went to Indiana in 1841, where he remained until 1858, and died in November, 1877; she born in Kentucky in 1820, and is now living in East Fork Township, Montgomery County. Subject is the second son of a family of three sons and three daughters; received his education at Hillsboro Academy; worked on the farm until he was seventeen years of age, and at the age of eighteen began teaching school, which he has followed for seven years, and on April 1, 1880, he began reading law with Rice & Miller; then went to the office of Judge E. Lane, with whom he still reads, and will make application for admission to the bar this fall. This young man deserves great credit, as he has by his own efforts educated himself; his parents being of limited circumstances, could not give him such an education as he desired. He taught school for six years in Fillmore, Fillmore Township; is a Republican and a member of the Masonic fraternity.

EDMUND DOUGLAS, physician and druggist, Hillsboro, was born near Chillicothe, Livingston Co., Mo., February 1[illegible], 18[illegible], to William and Parmelia (Strawn) Douglas. He was born in New Gallaway, Scotland, March 9, 1817, and still living in Pike County, Ill. He was a son of John and Jannette (Morey) Douglas, natives of Scotland. He came to America in 1836, was a carpenter and one of the contractors on the State University at Columbia, Mo., where he was married, and in after life engaged in farming. His wife is a native of Guilford County, N. C., where she was born August 25, 1823, and came to the West in 1830 with her parents, Edmund and Dorcas (Morton) Strawn, natives of North Carolina. Our subject is the third of twelve children, seven of whom are living—Andrew, a farmer; Mary, Edmund, John, a farmer; Churchwell, a farmer; William W., a physician, and James, a farmer. All are in Pike County but our subject, who received a district and high school education, and graduated at Bryant & Stratton's Commercial College, at St. Louis. In 1867, he engaged in a general business at Milton, Ill., and in 1872, at the same place, entered into the drug business, where he continued until in 1873, when he came to Hillsboro, where he has since continued. He studied medicine in connection with his business pursuits, and attended lectures at the St. Louis College of Physicians and Surgeons, from whence he graduated February 28, 1881, and practices in connection with his business. He was married October 15, 1875, to Illinois Phillips, daughter of Burrill Phillips, and neice of Gen. [illegible] J. Phillips. By her he has two living children

--Noi Elizabeth and Mary Jannette. He is a member of the Masonic Lodge and Chapter, and, in his political belief, Democratic.

JOSEPH T. ECCLES, retired merchant, Hillsboro, was born in Mercer County, Ky., January 7, 1807; son of Henry and Polly (Gaunt) Eccles. Henry [illegible] native of Berkeley County, Va., was born Ma[illegible] 4, 1781, and when about eighteen years old he moved to Kentucky and settled in Mercer County, where he married August 15, 1805. In the autumn of 1830, he removed to Vandalia, Ill., and shortly afterward located on a farm about four miles from that town, where he remained until 1837, when he removed to Coles County, Ill., where he died September 21, 1851, aged seventy years, four months and seventeen days. His wife, Polly Gaunt, was born at Watson's Station, Mercer Co., Ky., March 15, 1783, and died at Vandalia, Ill., September 21, 1835. Our subject, who began the business of life as a teacher, received his education chiefly in Harrodsburg, Ky. He taught school at Vandalia, Ill., for about two seasons, after which he clerked in a store about a year, and then engaged in the mercantile business in Vandalia on his own account for five or six years; then, abandoning the business of a merchant, he located on a farm about five miles from Vandalia. He followed farming about nine years, but gave it up and removed to Hillsboro, Montgomery County, where he again engaged in mercantile business, and, being successful, retired a short time ago. He owns some fine property in Hillsboro, consisting of his residence, a brick store, town lots, etc. In Todd County, Ky., August 12, 1829, he married Jane L. Anderson, born in Green County, Ky., May 23, 1809, daughter of Pearney and Nancy (Lynch) Anderson. Pearney Anderson, a native of Virginia, died in Todd County, Ky., June 6, 1837; his wife was also a native of Virginia. Mr. Eccles has filled the office of Justice of the Peace at Vandalia, Ill., and also in Hillsboro for several years. He was a delegate to the Constitutional Convention, held at Springfield, Ill., in 1847. He has also been Assistant Assessor and Deputy United States Revenue Collector. During the war, he was a recruiting officer [illegible] Hillsboro, and while acting in th[illegible] [illegible] in thirty new recruits. He al[illegible] [illegible] and returned to the army twe[illegible] seven deserters. He served in the Black [illegible] war in 1832. He nominated Richard Y[illegible] for Governor at Decatur, Ill., in 1860. [illegible] are Old-School Presbyterians. He is [illegible] member of the Sons of Temperance. In politics, he was originally an old Cla[illegible] [illegible] now supports the Republican par[illegible]

JOHN W. EDWARDS, lumber merchant, Hillsboro, was born in Tennessee [illegible] 1821; son of John and Elizabeth (Dunca[illegible]) Edwards. John, who was a farmer, was born in North Carolina in 1777; removed to Tennessee about the year 1800, and left there [illegible] 1828, afterward residing in Pike County, Jefferson County and Upper Alton. He died in the latter place about the year 1852; his wife was born in North Carolina in 17[illegible], and died in Hillsboro about the year 1868. Our subject, the fifth son of a family of eight sons and three daughters, received a limited education in Tennessee. He removed from that State with his parents in 1828, and settled in Pike County, where he remained two years; then removed to Jefferson County. Up to this time he had worked on his father's farm. After remaining in Jefferson County two years, he moved to Upper Alton, where he stayed until 18[illegible], engaged in mercantile business. From Upper Alton he removed to Hillsboro, where he engaged in the mercantile and grain business five years, the[illegible] in [illegible] nine years, then in the [illegible] nine years. In 1878, he gave [illegible] drug business, and returned to his old occupation of dealing in lumber, which business he is now engaged in. He is the owner of a comfortable frame residence in Hillsboro, with about three acres attached. In Hillsboro, in 1848, he married Joanna Meade, born in Ohio in 1825. From this union there have been born to them eight children, six of whom are living: David A.; William A., physician at Winchester, Ill.; John M., now residing in Kansas; Albert N., a harness-maker in Hillsboro; Frederick W. and Sarah Isabel King. Mr. Edwards and his wife are members of the Methodist Church, of which he has been Steward, and is now Trustee. He is a member of the A., F. & A. M. and I. O. O. F., in which orders he has held all the offices from the lowest to the highest. In politics, he supports the Republican party.

LEONARD G. FATH, Sheriff, Hillsboro, born in Perryville, Mo., November 20, 1847; son of Leonard and Miss (Barkman) Fath, both natives of Germany; he, a farmer by occupation, came to the United States about the year 1840, and now resides in Montgomery County; she came to America with her parents, married in Perryville, Mo., where she died in 1848. Subject, the second son of a family of two sons and one daughter, received his education in the common schools in Missouri, and at the age of fourteen years was taken from school and placed in a blacksmith shop to learn the trade. In 1864, he came to Montgomery County with his parents, and engaged in the agricultural implement and grocery business in Hillsboro, for two years, then giving up mercantile business, he worked at his trade for two years; then removed to Nokomis in 1873, and followed his trade there till the fall of 1876, when he was elected Sheriff, an office which he held for two years, but was, at the end of that time, defeated by a small majority in the convention. He then traveled through the country for nearly a year, selling agricultural implements. At the convention held May 24, 1879, he was again elected Sheriff, an office which he now holds. During the summer of 1879, he spent much of his time in devising a patent plow sulky attachment which he patented November 30, 1880. His invention is meeting with success among the farmers, and promises to prove remunerative to the inventor. In Montgomery County February 23, 1871, he married Laura A. Marshall, born in Ohio in 1853, daughter of John L. and Harriet (Lattimore) Marshall from this union two children have been born one son, Leo G., living, and one daughter deceased. Mr. Fath owns a house and lot in Hillsboro; he is a Democrat.

I. W. FINK, physician, Hillsboro, was born at Jonesboro, Ill., August 24, 1824 to John and Sophia (Lingle) Fink, both of whom were natives of North Carolina he born November 12, 1797, and came to Illinois in 1817, his parents dying in his childhood; he settled in Union County, where he carried on tanning and farming until his death, which occurred November 6, 1858; his wife was born August 1, 1800, and died January 11, 1866; she came to the State early in life from Hamilton County, Ohio, whither she had gone, with her parents, from her native State. Their children were I. W. Henry J., born March 2, 1828; Mary A. March 21, 1832, wife of John Miller; John M., deceased, without issue; George W. born October 19, 1838; Levi A., Jan. 30, 1845. All are farming in Union County, Ill. except the subject of this sketch, who received a common school education, with the addition of two years at the Hillsboro Academy. In 1850, he began the study of medicine with Dr. A. S. Haskill, of Hillsboro, where he remained, including his attendance upon lectures, three years, and graduated from the St. Louis Medical College in 1854, when he began the practice at Hillsboro, where he has since been located (except one year at Shelbyville), and has built up a large and remunerative practice. He is a member of the National, State, District and County Medical Societies, the latter of which he organized and held the office of President. He was married, April 24, 1855, to Miss Emeline M. Burnap, born in Montgomery County May 26, 1835, and died January 8, 1857; she was a daughter of George and Maria (Seward) Burnap, the latter related to the noted Secretary Seward; by her he had one child—Mary M. D.; he was again married Oct. 2, 1858, to Sarah C. Sawyer, born in Boston, Mass., November 7, 1834; by her he has three children—Juliet K., John W. and Hugh K. He is a member of the Masonic order and of the Democratic party, and with his family belongs to the Congregational Church.

ENOCH JAMES FILE, Hillsboro, born in Bond County, Ill., October 19, 1832; son of Daniel and Elizabeth (James) File. Daniel, who was a farmer, was born in North Carolina in 1801, and in company with his father, Jacob File, who died in 1842 came to Illinois in 1816, when it was a Territory; died in 1851; his wife, born in Middle Tennessee, in 1811, died in 1845. Our subject, the second son of a family of six sons and six daughters, received very little education, his school life being limited to four months that he attended in Bond County. He began life on the farm, then learned the carpenter's trade, which he followed eight years, then served as clerk, then in the hardware business on his own account for seven years. At the end of that time he sold out his business to the firm of Challacombe & Ramsey, for whom he now clerks. In 1861, he enlisted as private in the Federal army, Company D, Twenty-Second Illinois Infantry, and during his time of service was promoted from time to time, until he received command of a company. He participated in the engagements at Belmont, Mo., Stone River and Chickamauga, Tenn., Atlanta, etc.; was wounded three times—in skull, side and hand. In 1853, in Hillsboro Township, he married Mary Ann Brown, born in North Carolina in 1829, died in 1856. Her parents were William and Elizabeth (Craig) Brown; the former born in North Carolina September 5, 1791, came to Illinois in 1835, where he died in 1866; the latter, born February 12, 1807, died August 4, 1848. Mr. File was again married November 25, 1870, to Virginia C. Brown, sister of his first wife, born September 26, 1842, and from this union there has been born to him two daughters—Leva and Anna; his first wife bore him one daughter—May. He is a supporter of the Republican party, and a member of the Masonic fraternity.

JAMES ROBINSON GLENN, miller, farmer and stock raiser, P. O. Hillsboro, born in Ireland, August 16, 1834; came with his parents, one brother, John F., and one sister, Catharine J., to the United States in 1837, and lived in Louisville, Ky., about five years. His mother's name was Catharine Jane Robinson. Her father was born in Fintona, Ireland; built a Methodist Church in that town with his own money. In 1839, he chartered a ship, and, with his second wife and one son and seven daughters, went to Australia, settled in Melbourne, where he purchased property, and lived there the balance of his life. He purchased a cattle ranch in Australia, 6x15 miles, and died there at the age of ninety years. Grandfather Robinson's grandfather went from England with William, Prince of Orange, was in the battle of the Boyne and the siege of Londonderry. Subject's father, Thomas S. Glenn, born in Ireland about 1807, is still living in this county; his grandparents were born in Ireland; his great-grandfather was born in Scotland and was a mechanic. Mr. Glenn began life by buying grain in Litchfield, came to Hillsboro in 1858 and started the first grocery; was married in Macoupin County in 1860 to Miss Sarah V. Love, born in Cabell County, W. Va., in 1840, daughter of Louis L. and Emily (Eastham) Love. The result of this union is three daughters—Nora, Laura and Wilmina. Mr. Glenn is a member of the Lutheran Church, a Republican, a Freemason and a member of the Council. After going out of the grocery business in Hillsboro, he built a mill, in 1866, which he has operated continually since its erection. Himself and brothers were the prime movers in starting the bank at Hillsboro in 1870, known as the Montgomery County Loan and Trust Company, subject having been elected President on its organization, and holds the office at the present time. The Glenn Bros. also own a farm near Hillsboro, containing 1,0[illegible]0 acres, and about 15,000 acres in Texas.

REV. C. A. GELWICKS, Lutheran minister, Hillsboro, a native of Pennsylvania, and was born January 7, 1835, and son of John Gelwicks, a farmer, and also a native of Pennsylvania, and was born March 16, 1811, and is still living. His wife, Magdalena Wolf, was also a native of the same State, and was born December, 1812. She is also living in her native State. The parents had six children born to them, but only three raised to maturity—two sons (C. A. being the eldest) and one daughter. Our subject was educated at Gettysburg, Penn., at the Pennsylvania College, where he took a classical course, but was called away just three months before he would have graduated, and then went to the Theological Seminary at Springfield, Ohio, where he graduated in 1858, and took charge of a church at Strasburg, Penn., immediately after leaving the Seminary. He has devoted his entire life, up to the present, in the profession of his choice. Our subject was a volunteer in the sanitary department of the federal army during the war, and was at Mechanicsburg at the time that town was surrendered to the Rebel forces in 1864, which occurred a few days prior to the battle of Gettysburg. Subject is now and has always been a Republican in politics, and has been a member of the Good Templars for a number of years. He was married at Springfield, Ohio, on the 24th of June, 1858, the same day that he graduated and took charge of his first church. His wife was Mary Isabell Wilson, a daughter of Elon Wilson, of Springfield, and she was born December 26, 1836. Her father was born March 31, 1801, and died in October, 1864. Her mother, Mary Wilson, was born in March, 1810, and is now living at Ida Grove, Iowa. Subject has had six children born to him, but four living, one son, Wilson Gelwicks, and three daughters, viz.: Jennie, Belle and Lena. Himself, wife and eldest daughter are members of the Lutheran Church. Our subject has been a successful minister, as is proven by the few moves he has made. In twenty-four years' service he now has his fifth charge. He certainly has reason to feel proud of his ministerial career.

DAVID S. GILMORE, millwright, Hillsboro, was born in Hardin County, Ky., April 13, 1832; son of Alexander Gilmore, born in Virginia about 1805. When quite young he came to Kentucky with his parents and settled in Hardin County, where he died about 1850. He was also a millwright by trade. His wife was Millie Mudd, who was also a native of Virginia. They raised three chil dren, two sons (David S. being the eldest), and one daughter. Our subject came to this State in 1859, and first located in Macoupin County where he remained probably some three years, thence to this county, where he has since lived, in different parts of the county but for the past sixteen years has resided in Hillsboro. He received a common school education in Kentucky. He began business for himself when only eighteen years of age, as millwright, which he has followed through life, in connection with his other business, such as wagon-making, stocking plows and other such work as is done by any first-class mechanic, such as our subject is justly entitled to be called. He is Democratic in politics; also a member of the Masonic order. He was married in Grayson County, Ky., on August 12, 1847, to Rachael Watkins daughter of Isaiah Watkins and Catharine (Thomas) Watkins. Subject has three sons viz.: James D., Robert Lee, Jesse, and four daughters, Nancy A., wife of Duncan Cole; Lurena, Libbie May, Sarah E. Our subject owns a comfortable little residence in East Hillsboro. He has worked at his trade through different parts of this State, Missouri and Kentucky.

SOLOMON HARKEY, Hillsboro, was born in Iredell County, N. C., December 26, 1806; son of Martin and Christina (Mensinger) Harkey. Martin, who was a farmer by occupation, was born in North Carolina February 24, 1771, where he married October 9, 1794 In 1830, he left North Carolina and came to Hillsboro, where he died February 16, 1846. His wife, a native of North Carolina, was born February 12, 17[illegible] and died at her son's (subject's) home in Hillsboro, September 17, 1850. Subject, the fourth of a family of eleven, received but very little education, the schools of that day being very inferior to those of to day. The school which he attended was a log cabin with an earthen floor, and the books studied were Dilworth's Spelling Book and Pike's Arithmetic, the Bible being the only reader. He began life as a tanner, and followed that business from April, 1829, to March 1833, in Edwardsville, Ill.; thence he removed to Hillsboro, where he followed the tanning business for ten years, when he abandoned it and became a farmer. He owns a fine farm of 653 acres in Hillsboro Township, a fine two-story frame residence, and five lots and five acres of land in the town of Hillsboro, besides about 200 acres in Wisconsin. He has been a noted horseman in his day, and has handled many fine ones. He made a specialty of draught horses. In Hillsboro Township, March 31, 1831, he married Sophia Cress, born in North Carolina March 26, 1809, daughter of Jacob and Catharine (Bost) Cress, both natives of North Carolina. She (Sophia) came to Illinois with her parents about the year 1817, and died December 21, 1878. Mr. Harkey was again married October 30, 1879, to Mrs. Eleanor T. (McHenry) Evans, born July 11, 1826, daughter of George McHenry He has had nine children, four of whom are dead—William P., now in Yuba City, Cal.; Jacob M., Solomon S., Sarah C., wife of Benjamin Wilton; Virginia T., Laura L. (deceased), Martha J. (deceased), Mary S. (deceased), and Daniel L. (deceased). During his business career he met with many reverses; in 1861, he lost $2,060 by the failure of a New York bank; in 1878, he lost $2.700 by the Farmers Mechanics' Bank, of Hillsboro; and in December, 1881, he lost about $2,700 by the failure of Haskell Bros. & Co., of Hillsboro. He and his wife are members of the Methodist Church; he is a member of the I. O. O. F.; in politics he supports the Republican party.

THOMAS E. HARRIS, County Superintendent, Hillsboro, was born in Massachusetts in 1815; son of Thomas and Abigail (Chapin) Harris, he born in Massachusetts, died in Vermont, and she, the mother of five sons and three daughters, was born in Vermont. Our subject is the second son; received a good education at the Public Schools; commenced life as a clerk in a wholesale dry goods establishment in New York; went to England, lived in Manchester for three years, came from there to this State and commenced farming, which business he still follows. He has been Township Trustee for about twenty years; Supervisor of Butler Township three years, and was elected County Superintendent of Public Schools in December, 1877, an office he has filled acceptably to the present time. Mr. Harris was married in this county about 1842, to Hulda Ware, a native of this county, and a daughter of Obediah and Electa (Post) Ware. They have one daughter, Julia, wife of Michael Robertson, of this county, and who now lives in Butler. Although Montgomery has a Democratic majority of 500 or 600, yet our subject is a Republican, and has no trouble in getting the position he now holds, such is an evidence of his qualifications and popularity. He owns 200 acres of land in Butler Township.

A. HARTLINE, boots and shoes, Hillsboro, born in North Carolina October 3, 1845; his parents are natives of North Carolina; his father, who was a farmer and a blacksmith by trade, died there in 1874; his mother, who is now about seventy-five years of age, is still living in her native State. Our subject, the fifth of a family of seven sons, received a limited education in Iredell County, N. C., and remained with his father on the farm and in the blacksmith-shop till he was seventeen years old; he then learned the shoe making trade, which he has since followed. Beginning without any means, he has, by industry and economy, worked up a good trade in custom work, and in addition carries a good stock of ready made goods; he owns a neat store and a comfortable two-story brick residence in Hillsboro. He married, in Hillsboro, October 5, 1870, Mary Ann Sharp, born in North Carolina, daughter of William Sharp, a native of that State, who died near Hillsboro. Mr. and Mrs. Hartline are the parents of five children: George, Flora, Jessie, Bertie and Grace. He enlisted, in 1864, in Company E, North Carolina Infantry, and served under Gen. McCray till 1865, when he was captured near Petersburg, Va., and kept a prisoner till the close of the war. He and his wife are Methodists; in politics, he is a Democrat.

JAMES HAYNES, County Treasurer, Hillsboro, born in Morgan County, Ill., September 25, 1843; son of John and (Harriet) Seymour. John, who was a farmer by occupation, was born in Indiana about the year 1815; he lived in Kentucky, principally, till he was fourteen years old, when he moved to Illinois, and settled in Cass County for a few years; thence he removed to Morgan County, thence to Montgomery County, where he settled permanently in 1854; his wife was born in North Carolina about the year 1819; she came to Illinois with her parents when quite young, and is still living. James, who is the eldest of a family of five sons and two daughters, attended school in Montgomery County, and afterward at McKendree College, at Lebanon, and the Soldiers' College at Fulton, Ill. He followed farming till 1877, when he was elected County Treasurer, an office which he still holds. In 1862 he enlisted as private in the Federal army, Company F, One Hundred and Twenty-second Illinois Infantry. In the battle of Tupelo, Miss., July 14, 1864, he lost his right arm;

he was captured next day and held a prisoner till the close of the war, during which time he was imprisoned in the following places: Mobile, two weeks; Cahaba, Ala., four months; Macon, Ga., two and a half months; Andersonville, one month; Selma, Ala.; Meridian, Miss.; Vicksburg and St Louis. From St. Louis, he was released, and having reported at Springfield, Ill., was discharged in the spring of 1865. He is a Methodist; in politics, he supports the Democratic party.

GEORGE B. KING, lumber merchant, etc., Hillsboro, born in Rowan County, N. C., September 21, 1824; came to this county in 1867; son of James King, born in Surrey County, N. C., in 1798; farmer; served last two years in the war of 1812; was in nine months in the same war, in the early part, as a substitute for another party, when only about sixteen years of age; he served also in the regular army some time after the close of this war. Subject has now in his possession a white vest that was made by a French lady for his father, at St. Louis, during the war; he died in North Carolina, December 26, 1825. Elizabeth (Barringer) King, subject's mother, born in Cabarrus County, N. C., January 27, 1799, and died in Hillsboro, Ill., August 7, 1870. Subject's parents raised one son and two daughters. He was educated in North Carolina and Virginia; farmed and taught school for a start in life; although he learned no trade, yet he possessed sufficient natural genius to adapt himself to almost any kind of work; was in the habit of making his own shoes, harness, lay brick, build chimneys, etc. When he first came to this place, in 1867, he taught school and worked at the carpenter's trade at intervals, and finally in August, 1872, he began in the lumber business, which he still follows. Subject was conscripted in the Confederate service, in March, 1863, remained there till the following June, when he was taken sick and sent to the hospital; after becoming able, he was sent on to rejoin the army, took a different route and came to Ohio; remained about one year, and then came on to this State. Republican now in politics. Member of the I. O. O. F. Was married in Hillsboro, Ill., March 29, 1872, to Miss Lydia A. Dilworth, born in Grant County, Ky., June 5, 1849; a daughter of Absalom H. Dilworth, born in Guilford County, N. C., July 25, 1815; lived several years in Kentucky, and then came to this State, where he still lives. He (Mr. Dilworth) married Elizabeth Work, born in Guilford County, N. C., December 13, 1823 was brought to Kentucky, when only nine years old, by her parents, and settled in Grant County, where she died August 15, 1861. Subject has one son—Charlie D., born March 26, 1879, and one daughter—Nellie D., born June 22, 1881. Subject is a member of the Lutheran Church. Owns six lots in town, two lumber yards, nice two-story frame residence, etc.

HENRY H. KEITHLEY, Deputy County Clerk, Hillsboro, born in Indiana, November 26, 1844; came to Litchfield, Ill., in 1857; son of Seth M. and Anna Theresa (Miller) Keithley, he, a mechanic, born in Kentucky, October 18, 1812, went to Indiana, with his parents, when quite young; moved to Litchfield in 1857, where he still lives and owns twenty acres within the limits of that town; she, born in Maryland November 13, 1808, died at Litchfield, Ill., November 22, 1869. Subject is the oldest son of a family of two sons and three daughters; got his education at Litchfield and Springfield; was a printer for four years, Deputy Postmaster at Litchfield for two years, clerked in a drug store there for two years; moved from there to Hillsboro in December, 1873, when he was appointed Deputy County Clerk, by George M. Raymond, County Clerk, an office he still fills satisfactorily. Mr. Keithley was married in Hillsboro, September 8, 1875, to Miss Camilla Brown, born June 7, 1853, who has borne him one child—Amy R. Subject enlisted September 3, 1864, in the Federal army, and served as private and Corporal until the end of the war. He is a Methodist, a Republican, is a member of the Masonic fraternity, and owns a nice residence in East Hillsboro.

JUDGE EDWARD LANE, attorney, Hillsboro, is a native Ohioan and was born in Cleveland March 27, 1842, to John, born April 15, 1803, and Catharine (Berry) Lane, who were also natives of Ohio, and died in the "Forest City" about 1850, at about the same time, the father having been a merchant of that city. Both families were of Irish extraction, and possessed of a marked shrewdness and energy. The orphaned family consisted of two sons, the eldest of whom died at about eighteen years of age, being four years the senior of Edward, who came to Hillsboro in the spring of 1858, and engaged in work upon a brick yard, at which he continued about three years, then began going to school, working at the same time for his subsistence. In the fall of 1863, he began reading law in connection with school-teaching, and was admitted to the bar in the fall of 18[illegible]. He immediately began the practice of his profession in Hillsboro, where he has built up a large and remunerative practice, and stands in the front rank of the legal profession of Montgomery County. In 1869, he was elected for a term of four years to the office of County Judge. In 1870, October 3, he was married to Miss Tucie Miller, born June 19, 1848, a native of Lawrenceville, Ill., and daughter of Samuel K. and Margaret Miller. By her he had two children—Bessie and Guy C. He is a member of the Masonic order, and with his family, belong to the Lutheran Church. In his political sentiment, he is Democratic.

E. F. LEAK, miller, Hillsboro, was born in Philadelphia, Penn., July 22, 1847, son of Thomas and Mary (Walker) Leak. Thomas Leak was born in England in 1806; emigrated to America while quite young, and died in Newark, Del., in 1872; he was a painter, a sailor, and finally a farmer. His wife was born in England in 1817, and died in Jerseyville, Ill., in 1873. Our subject is the third son of a family of five sons and one daughter. He received a common school education in Delaware, and learned the milling business, in which occupation he is still engaged. He began the business with very moderate resources, but has been successful, and now owns a comfortable frame cottage in Hillsboro. He married, in Philadelphia, in April, 1873, Esther Comly, a native of Delaware, daughter of Samuel and Miss (Sanders) Comly. Samuel Comly whose parents were Quakers, was born in Pennsylvania. Mr. and Mrs. Leak are the parents of three children—Edward, Della and Bertha. He is a supporter of the Republican party, and a member of the Knights of Pythias.

JOHN J. McLEAN, Circuit Clerk and Recorder, Hillsboro, was born at Metuchin, Middlesex Co., N. J., April 1, 1849, and came to this State when fourteen years old, with his parents. He was the son of Martin and Mary (Cary) McLean. Martin was born in Ireland in November, 1819, and came to the United States in 1847, and located in New Jersey, remaining till 1862, and moved with his family to this county, where he still lives. He is a farmer, and owns 500 acres of as good land as is in the county. Mary Cary, his wife, was born in Ireland in 1812; was married there; came to the United

States one year prior to her husband, and died July 9, 1879. Our subject is the oldest of a family of three; received his education partly in the East and partly in St. Louis, where he graduated from Bryant & Stratton's Commercial College. He also took a classical course at the Christian Brothers' College, St. Louis, but did not graduate. In Bois D'Arc Township, Montgomery County, Oct. 10, 1877, he married A. Amanda Thomas, who was born [illegible] October 10, 1855, daughter of Samuel R. and [illegible] E. (Dayton) Thomas. He was born in [illegible] County, Ill., May 2, 1829; is still living; she was born in 1831 at the same place; still living. Subject has two sons: William R[illegible], born July 17, 1879, and Edgar M., born March 21, 1881. Mr. McLean taught school for a year, and was afterward elected County Treasurer of Montgomery County, and served two years. He next engaged in real estate and abstract business from 1875 to [illegible], when he was elected Circuit Clerk, an office he still holds. He owns a nice two-story [illegible] residence in Hillsboro, besides [illegible] acres of land in Montgomery County, and a valuable set of abstract books worth, probably, $10,000. He is also an inventor, having patented what is known as McLean's File Cabinet for court papers. This is an invention that promises to be very valuable to the patentee.

GEORGE W. MICHAEL, hotel proprietor and [illegible], Hillsboro, was born in North Carolina, [illegible] 30, 1827, son of Jacob and Annie [illegible] Michael, both natives of North Carolina. Jacob was born about the year 1798. He is a farmer by occupation and still living in his native State. His wife died in Indiana about the year 1872. They were the parents of twelve children, nine sons and three daughters, six of the sons deceased. Our subject received but a limited education in North Carolina. He learned the house carpenter's trade, and has followed it the greater part of his life. He came to Illinois March 18, 1881, and settled in Hillsboro, where he has conducted a hotel since that time. He married, in North Carolina, October 20, 1857, Belzora Hedick, a native of that State, born July 5, 1833, daughter of John and Barbara (Causler) Hedick. John Hedick, who is a farmer, was born in North Carolina, March 30, 1795. His wife, also a native of North Carolina, was born February 12, 1804. Mr. and Mrs. Michael have had six children, four of whom are living: Thomas J., who married Miss Teenie Nichols, of Hillsboro; John T., Jennie, wife of John Goodman, and Emma H. During the war, Mr. Michael served in the Confederate army, Company E, Fourth Cavalry, Deering's Brigade, Stewart's Cavalry, participating in the battles of Manassas and others of less importance near Petersburg, Richmond, etc. On one occasion, he and a comrade, by coolness and strategy, succeeded in capturing nine federal soldiers. Seeing the importance of a good education, Mr. Michael has endeavored to give his children all the advantages in that direction within the reach of his ability. He and his family are Lutherans. He is a member of the Masonic fraternity; in politics, he is supporter of the Democratic party.

SAMUEL H. McLEAN, physician, Hillsboro, is a native of Montgomery County, where he was born, near Hillsboro, April 12, 1849, to Robison and Emily (Barry) McLean, he a native of Greensboro, N. C., and came to Montgomery County at about twenty-one years of age, or in about the year 181[illegible]. Here he engaged in stock-raising and farming, which he followed until his death, which occurred in January, 1876. Emily, the mother of our subject, was born in Barren County, Ky., and came with her parents when but a child to Montgomery County. She is still living at an advanced age. Our subject is the second of seven living children. He received the meager advantages of the district schools until seventeen years of age, when he spent two years at the acadamy at Hillsboro, and the years 1871-72 were spent at the University at Lincoln, Ill. In the fall of 1872, he entered the Eclectic Medical Institute at Cincinnati, graduating therefrom in the spring of 1874. He immediately commenced practice at Donnellson, Montgomery County, where he remained three years. In the spring of 1877, he came to Hillsboro, where he has since resided, in the practice of his profession, and built up a large and lucrative practice. Since his professional career in the county, he has held the offices of Secretary, President and Vice President of the County Medical Society, and has been twice appointed as delegate to the State Medical Association, of which he is a member. He was married, September 19, 1876, to Miss Tena Kerr, a native of Ohio, and daughter of Robert Kerr, now of Montgomery County. He is Republican in political sentiment, and with his family, belongs to the Methodist Church.

WARREN M. NEFF, blacksmith, Hillsboro, was born in Clark County, Ohio, in 1848; son of William H. C. and Susan (Huffman) Neff. William H. C. was a farmer, and was born in Clark County, Ohio, in 1825; removed to Montgomery County in 1854, where he died the following year. His wife was born in Ohio, in 1830; she married twice, the second husband being James White, of Montgomery County. Warren, our subject, has two sisters and three half-brothers. He received his education, chiefly, in Hillsboro, and worked on the farm till he was twenty years old, when he learned the blacksmith's trade, which he has followed ever since. He began life with little or no means, but by industry and economy, and strict attention to business, he has built up an extensive trade, and is the owner of considerable property. He owns a blacksmith shop and lot adjoining, a house and lot in the south end of Hillsboro, and eighty-three acres of land in East Fork and Fillmore Townships. In Hillsboro, November 17, 1875, he married Elmira A. Stout, born in Indiana, in 1855 and died in Hillsboro, December 4, 1880. Mr. Neff is a Republican, and a member of the I. O. O. F. and the A. F. & A. M.

GEORGE WILLIAM PAISLEY, attorney, Hillsboro, was born in this county, in 1838; son of Joseph Paisley, born in North Carolina in 1797, and emigrated to this State in 1822, and spent first two years in Bond County, thence to this county, where he spent the remainder of his life. He died on his farm here in 1857. In 1837, he was married to Martha A. Allan, a native of Kentucky, born near Lexington in 1815, and is still living with her son, subject, in this county. Parents raised but one son, subject, he being by the second wife. There are two half-sisters living by first wife. Our subject was educated at the Hillsboro Academy. He was admitted to the bar in 1870, having read law off and on some several years previous. He began life as a farmer, at the death of his father, which he followed for four or five years. He was next County Surveyor, being elected in 1865, an office he filled for two years. He next engaged in mercantile business, some two years. He held the office of Master in Chancery from 1868 to 1869, was elected to the State Legislature in 1880, position he now holds; enlisted in 1862, in the One Hundred and Twenty-second Illinois Infantry as a private, and was afterward elected Orderly Sergeant, and served three years; participated in the battle at Nashville, Tupelo, storm and capture of the works of

Blakely, at Mobile, Ala., besides several minor engagements; was never captured nor wounded during the war; belonged to the command that followed Price through Missouri and a portion of Kansas, in 1864, a distance of about 600 miles; left Jefferson Barracks on the 2d of October and got back to St. Louis on the 18th of November; Democrat in politics. He was married in Macoupin County, this State, on the 5th of June, 1872, to Maggie M. Middleton. She was the daughter of Rev. John and Sibilla (Galbreath) Middleton; wife was born in 1846. Our subject has five children, all daughters, viz.: Anna, Ethel, Georgia, Maggie and Susie. His wife is a member of the Reformed Presbyterian Church, commonly called Covenanter, her father being a minister of that church. Subject owns about 1,000 acres of land in this county.

SAMUEL PAISLEY, farmer, P. O. Hillsboro, was born in North Carolina in the year 1811, on the 6th of July. John Paisley, his father, was born in Pennsylvania, on the 10th of August, 1763, and was taken to North Carolina in infancy and remained there until sixty-four years of age, and was a farmer by occupation. He emigrated to Illinois in 1828 and settled in Montgomery County, and commenced farming. He entered 160 of land and bought 120 acres of unimproved land, on which he put all necessary improvements, and raised a large family of children. He married in North Carolina in the year 1791, to Miss Jane (Rankin) Paisley. She was born in North Carolina in the year 1771, and of Scotch-Irish descent, and was the mother of twelve children, our subject being the eleventh child, and was raised on the farm and assisted his father in his boyhood days. He was educated in the common schools of the county, and by observation and energy has a good practical education. He commenced business for himself as a farmer; went into the Black Hawk war, at the age of twenty-one years, and served three months; came back to this county and purchased forty acres of land with the money he received for his services, and has added to it until he has reached the handsome estate of 414 acres, the most of which is good tillable land, with all necessary improvements. He was married September 1, 1842, in this county, to Miss Clarissa Fuller; was born in Clark County, Ohio, January 11, 1821. Moses Fuller, her father, was born in New Brunswick, in 1787, and died November, 1879. Elizabeth Prillam, her mother, was born in Virginia, in the year 1778, and was mother of nine children, eight living. The wife of subject was the seventh child, and she is the mother of five children, one deceased. Their names are as follows: Moses F., in the war three years, was in several battles, entering the service at seventeen years of age; Lucinda C., Nettie, William C., Laura J., deceased. They are members of the Presbyterian Church. Identified with the Republican party. William Paisley, his paternal grandfather, was in the Revolutionary war, and was wounded at Guilford through the wrist. Mrs. Paisley, the mother of Rev. Samuel Paisley, said that she had no recollection of her parents, they having been killed by the Indians, and her mother died soon after. She never spoke of her captivity at all.

JOSEPH POLLARD, hotel proprietor, Hillsboro, was born in St. Louis January 2[illegible], 1856; son of Daniel and Mary (Phalan) Pollard. Daniel Pollard was born in Ireland and emigrated to America at the age of twenty-two. He settled first in New Orleans, but afterward moved to St. Louis, where he was married August 15, 1850. He followed steamboating for several years, and was afterward employed on the police force in St.

Louis. He died at Little Rock, Ark., in 1867. Of his seven children, three sons died prior to his death, and were buried in St. Louis. Since his death, one son and one daughter have died, and been buried in Litchfield, Ill. The remaining two are Joseph (our subject) and Margaret. His wife, Mary Phalan, was born in Ireland in 1826. She came to America with some friends, when she was seventeen years of age, and stopped for a time in New Orleans, then moved to St. Louis. Since the death of her husband, she and her son, the subject of this sketch, have been engaged in the hotel business. They first kept hotel in Butler, where they stayed nine years; thence they moved to Raymond, remaining there four years, and finally located in Hillsboro, in June, 1879. Here they ran the old American Hotel for two years and a half, after which they moved to their present house, the City Hotel, where they have met with an extensive patronage. Our subject, his mother, and sister, are Catholics. He is a supporter of the Democratic party.

JUDGE EDWARD YOUNG RICE, attorney, Springfield, was born in Logan County, Ky., February 8, 1820. In his native State he remained until about fifteen years of age, when he came with his parents to Macoupin County, Ill. His father, Francis Rice, was a native of Caswell County, N. C. He was engaged in a ministerial life, and identified with agricultural and mercantile pursuits. His death occurred in August, 1837, aged about sixty-three years. His wife was Mary Gooch, also a native of Caswell County, N. C., and a daughter of William and Mrs. (Carr) Gooch. Both were among the prominent families of North Carolina. The parents of our subject had seven sons and four daughters, of whom two sons and one daughter are now living, of whom the Judge is the youngest. [illegible]

County, and Susan, widow of Robert Andrews, of the above county. The Judge received a limited education in the common schools, with the addition of about two years at Shurtleff College. He then taught school and studied law with Gov. Palmer, at Carlinville, from which place he was admitted to the bar in February, 1844. In September of the following year he came to Hillsboro, where he practiced his profession until in October, 1881, when he entered into partnership with Judge A. N. J. Crook, at Springfield, Ill. While engaged in the practice of his profession, he has always been honored with a large and lucrative practice. In 1847, he was elected to the office of Recorder of Deeds of Montgomery County. In November, 1848, he was honored with an election to the Lower House of the Illinois Legislature, [illegible] session carrying him to the year 1851. In that year he was elected to the office of County Judge to fill the unexpired term caused by the resignation of Jos. Johnston, and during the years 1853 to 1857 he was Master in Chancery. In August, 1857, he was elected to the office of Circuit Judge for a term of four years, but by the formation of a new circuit, composed of Sangamon, Macoupin, Montgomery and Christian Counties, he was re-elected for a term of six years, and in 1867 for a term of six years longer, but before the term expired he resigned his office to accept the nomination for Congress from the "old Tenth District." In that position he served until in March, 1873, and it was during his term that the State was re-districted. He was a member of the Constitutional Convention which assembled in December, 1869, and completed its work in May, 1870. In that convention he served upon many important committees. In the early part of 1871, [illegible]

Miller, opened their present law office in Hillsboro, now under the firm name of Rice Miller & McDavid. He was married November 29, 1849, to Mrs. Susan R. (Allen) Condy, a native of Clark County, Ky. She had one child—Isabella, wife of F. C. Bolton, a railroad operator in Indianapolis. By this marriage, the Judge has two children living—Mary, wife of Amos Miller, and James E. V., who is attending Blackburn University. He is a Democrat in political tenets, and, with his wife, belongs to the Presbyterian Church.

GEORGE M. RAYMOND, County Clerk, Hillsboro, is a native of Woodstock, Windsor Co., Vt., where he was born September 8, 1832, to George G. and Judith Hix (Phillips) Raymond, both natives of the above county, where they both died. She was a daughter of Shadrach Phillips. George G. is a son of George and Phebe (Cobb) Raymond. The parents of our subject had four children, of whom he was the oldest. The others were Edna L., widow of James E. L. Southgate, who, at the time of his death, was Assistant Cashier of the Winnebago National Bank; at that place his family now resides. Sarah S., a maiden, residing with her widowed sister; Elwyn P. died November 11, 1881, aged thirty-eight years, at Shellmound, Le Flore Co., Miss., where he had been for a considerable time in the capacity of book-keeper. Our subject received his education at the district school and at the Green Mountain Liberal Institute in his native town, after which he begun life as a farmer. In 1853, September 12, he came to Rockford, Ill., where he engaged in mercantile business, remaining two years. In 1856, he went to Alton and engaged in the marble business, which he carried on until in 1860, when on the 17th of July of that year he was married to Jennette Burdett, a native of Lowell, Mass., of English-Scotch descent, and daughter of Emmons and Margaret (Carr) Burdett, he wheelright and machinist now residing with his family in Litchfield. By this marriage there were two children, both of whom died in childhood. In February, 1861, he moved to Litchfield, and there formed a partnership in mercantile business under the firm name of Stoddard & Raymond, which they continued on for twelve years, when by the dissolution of the firm, he entered upon the duties of book keeper for the banking firm of B[illegible] Davis & Co. During his residence at Litchfield, he held the following city offices: Alderman, two terms, City Treasurer, two terms, and City Clerk, one term. In December, 1873, he took upon himself the duties of the office of County Clerk, having been previously elected upon the Granger ticket, the county being nearly six hundred Democratic majority. He was re-elected on the Republican ticket in a square political contest, and by virtue of an amendment to the Constitution, another year was added to his term, so that, in December, 1882, he will have served the people in this office nine years. He is a member of the Masons at Litchfield, in which order he has for several years been commanding officer. He and wife are members of the Methodist Episcopal Church, and highly esteemed citizens of Hillsboro.

FRANCIS ROOT, local preacher and farmer, born in Massachusetts, raised principally in New Jersey. He was married to Mrs. Marandis D. Holmes (widow of J[illegible] Holmes, deceased) April 2, 1873. Her first husband, Mr. Holmes, son of Daniel and Mercy (Day) Holmes, was born in [illegible], Me., April 3, 1813, and married Mar[illegible] D. Bennett, of Wilbraham, Mass., October 3, 1843. Mrs. Holmes was born December 29, 1826. Their children, all born in Hillsboro, Ill., have been Mary M., Morrill D., J[illegible] F., Lucy N., Edward and Alice A. M[illegible]

Holmes, deceased, was a piano-maker in New York City for a number of years, and after coming to Illinois, he worked at the carpenter's trade. He died on his farm, five miles south of Hillsboro, on April 5, 1870. His son, Frank, ran the farm after his father's death, for several years, and on account of his health failing, he was obliged to quit the farm, and his brother Morrill then took charge of the farm and still continues to run the same. He, the father, was not connected with any church, but was a Methodist in belief, and shortly before his death, he professed religion, and died happy. He was a highly esteemed citizen of high moral character, very benevolent all through life, and perhaps had as few enemies as any man in his country, at the time of his death. He was a Republican in politics. Left considerable estate consisting principally of lands. He left several hundred acres to his family, besides other means. His widow (now Mrs. Root) and three children Frank, Morrill and Mary M., wife of Joseph F. Hughes, still living. Mr. Root, second husband, was born in Massachusetts, February 14, 1809. Left there when six years old and went to New Jersey with his parents, where he was educated: left there when about twenty five years old and went to Ohio; remained there about two years; from there to Richmond, Ind.; remained there about twenty-five years in the woolen factory business, hotel, grocery, etc; from there to Greenville, Ill., remained there six or seven years, farming principally, and from there to this county, five miles south of Hillsboro; moved to Hillsboro in May, 1881, where he now lives. Began preaching, as a local preacher, in the Methodist Episcopal Church, about twenty years ago, and still preaches occasionally. Was married first in New Jersey, in 1831, to Mary B. Brown. She died in 1869. His second marriage was on April 2, 1873, to Mrs. Marandis D. Holmes. Mr. Root has five living children, all by his first wife—James, William and Francis C., and two daughters Sarah and Julia A. Republican, politically Was one of the first Abolitionists in Indiana; was driven out of the church on this account.

CHARLES A. RAMSEY, hardware, Hillsboro, born in Pennsylvania January 8, 1845, son of William H. and Mary (Rarer) Ramsey. William H. was born in Pennsylvania, in 1820, and is a contractor and builder by occupation. His wife, also a native of Pennsylvania, was born in 1825. They are both still living. Charles A., the eldest son of a a family of five sons and three daughters, received a good education at Pine Grove Seminary and Academy, and also at the Pennsylvania State Agricultural College. He began life as a clerk; afterward taught school; studied medicine for about two years, but gave it up and engaged in the drug business in Irving, Ill. In 1877, he gave up the drug business in Irving, and came to Hillsboro, where he engaged in his present business, hardware and agricultural implements. He has filled the office of Township Supervisor. In 1862, he enlisted in the Army of the Potomac, as private, and served under Gen. Miles and others, and was promoted to the rank of Sergeant Major, and afterward to Adjutant. He served till the close of the war, and participated in many hot engagements. In Shelby County, Ill., in 1870, he married Elizabeth Corley, born in Shelby County, July 2, 1849, daughter of B. W. and Lois (Wakefield) Corley, natives of that county. From this marriage, they have one daughter Mary. Mr. Ramsey is a Republican, and a member of the Masonic fraternity. His wife is a member of the Presbyterian Church.

FRED A. RANDLE, attorney, Hillsboro, was born at Bunker Hill, Ill., January 21,

1874, to E. B. and Mary E. (Powers) Randle. She a graduate of Oberlin College, Ohio, and sister to A. G. Powers, deceased, the artist, and cousin to Hiram Powers, the sculptor; she was born in Otto, Cattaraugus Co., N. Y., in 1826, and was the youngest daughter of a family of seven sons and four daughters; her death occurred October 10, 1857, when the subject of this sketch was about four years of age; she was a very intelligent lady and a kind and loving mother. E. B. Randle was born at Bellville, Ill., September 8, 1826, and is now engaged in the hardware and drug business at Bethalto, Ill.; he was one of a company who went to California in 1849, locating near Sacramento City, where he engaged in mining, and was quite successful; on his return home in 1851, by way of the Pacific and Gulf of Mexico, where upon the latter sea he was shipwrecked, and, when in a perishing condition, he was picked up by a friendly vessel, and returned home and engaged in mercantile pursuits. He married his second wife, Marietta Nelson, of Gillespie, Ill., January 6, 1859, by whom he has two living children—Mattie and Mary E., who was married, June 13, 1880, to W. F. Nutter, of Bethalto, Ill., by whom she has had one child, Lottie E.; he is engaged in business with his father-in-law, who is a son of Rev. Richard Randle, one of the pioneer preachers of the State, a native of Georgia, and still living, at eighty-three years of age. Our subject was the only child by his father's first marriage; he lived upon the farm and attended district school in winter. In 1874, he entered the Preparatory Department of McKendree College, at Lebanon, Ill.; there he worked for his board, and surmounted the many obstacles in the way of a youth educational advancement, until completing his Junior year, having passed by examination the course of Freshman; during the Junior year, he also took the first year in the Law Department, and, in the year 1879, graduated from that institution, and came to Hillsboro, where, in July of that year, began the practice of his profession, in which he has to the present time met with flattering success. In May, 1881, he was elected for a term of four years to the office of Justice of the Peace, which position he is filling to the satisfaction of his constituency. He is a member of the M. E. Church, and is a young man of good moral and religious habits.

JOHN A. RALSTON, boarding-house keeper, Hillsboro, born in Mifflin County, Penn., August 30, 1818, came to this State in 1843 and stopped in Hillsboro; the son of William and Anna (Black) Ralston; he a tanner, born in the North of Ireland in 17[illegible], came to the United States when quite young; settled in Philadelphia, Penn.; was a soldier of the war of 1812, but the war was brought to a close before he was called into active service and died December 25, 1862; she born in Carlisle, Penn., in 1782, and died in June, 1873. Our subject is the second son of a family of four sons and two daughters; educated in the common schools of Perryville, Penn., and was married, in 1852, near Taylorville, Ill., to Ann Elizabeth Ladd, born in Stonington, Conn., in 1826, who came to Illinois in the spring of 1849 with her mother and family, and settled six miles north of Taylorville; she is the daughter of Noyes, born in Franklin County, Conn., in 17[illegible], died 1838, and Harriet L. (Williams) Ladd, born in Stonington, Conn., died June, 187[illegible]. Our subject has four children—William Curtis, Hattie E., Eleanora and Florence A. He went to Missouri in 1844; remained there about ten months, then went to Vandalia, Ill., for two years; then back to Pennsylvania for six months; returned to Taylorville, Ill., for three years, then to Hillsboro in 1853, where he now resides. Our subject is a tailor, and has followed that business for thirty years; was in the Federal army from 1862 to 1865; enlisted as a private; promoted to Second Sergeant and was at the fall of Vicksburg, but was not called into action. He is a Republican, and his son, William Curtis, is a graduate of the public school at Hillsboro; read law with Hon. George W. Paisley, of this place; went to Iowa, located in Pocahontas Center; admitted to the bar there in the fall of 1881, and now has a fair practice in connection with the real estate business.

CHARLES W. SPRINGER, abstracts and real estate, Hillsboro, born in Springfield, Ill., October 5, 1846, son of Francis and Mary (Kreigh) Springer; he, born in Maryland in 1810, came to this place in 1838; established Hillsboro College; was President of same till 1852; moved to Springfield, where the college was opened; served again as President for several years; afterward elected Superintendent of City Schools; came back here in 1874; was Superintendent of County Schools for several years, and again returned to Springfield in 1880, where he now is; he is a pastor in the Lutheran Church; has been a preacher all his life, and graduated at Gettysburg College, Gettysburg, Penn.; she, born at Hagerstown, Md., in 1815, is still living. Our subject was educated principally at the university, Springfield, Ill.; began life in the dry goods business, in which he continued about three years; taught in the academy, Hillsboro, under his father, as Principal, for a term of one year, and then began his present business; enlisted in the Federal army (100-days' service) in the summer of 1864, when he was only in his teens, and was the whole time at Rock Island in charge of the prisoners. His parents have seven living children, subject being the third son, and now Public Administrator of Montgomery County. He made a trip to Utah in 1871; spent six months there; been a law student for several years; expects to be admitted to the bar next winter, and will make law his profession. His brother, Phil M Springer, is an agricultural writer, and publishes annually the American Berkshire Record at Springfield. Another brother, John [illegible] was Quartermaster of the Tenth Cavalry during the war, and is now United States Internal Revenue Gauger of the Springfield District and served in the same office in Arkansas for ten years.

GEORGE W. SCOTT, lawyer, Hillsboro, born in Putnam County, Ill., July [illegible] 18[illegible]; came to this county September, 187[illegible]; [illegible] George and Harriet B. (Phillips) Scott; he, born in Virginia March 10, 181[illegible]; [illegible] St. Charles, Mo., with his parents in 1820; his father, Phelix Scott, was Lieutenant Governor of Missouri in 1827-28, and his father, Col. Charles Scott, was Colonel in the Revolutionary army; she, a daughter of [illegible] Thomas Phillips, of Hillsboro, was born in Livingston County, Ky., in 1823. Our subject is the youngest son of a family of three sons and one daughter; attended the high school at Henry, Ill.; graduated at the Northwestern University at Chicago in 1872; commenced reading law, in the summer of 1874, with his uncle, Judge Phillips; began practicing in 1876; went West February 25, 1879, and returned August 20, 1881, having visited Colorado, New Mexico, Old Mexico, Arizona, California, again to Arizona, [illegible] home. He was admitted to the bar in Colorado, and practiced there ten months. Our subject was married, in Hillsboro, December 29, 1875, to Jennie Russell, born at Greenville June 6, 1857, daughter of Thomas [illegible] and Mary (Buchanan) Russell, he born at Harper's Ferry, Va., in 1833, still lives here, w[illegible] she was born in Greenville, Ill. The result of this union is one daughter, Pearl, born January 30, 1877. Our subject is a Democrat, a member of the Masonic fraternity, and was married by Rev. James Woolard, who had officiated at his wife's father's and mother's marriage, and also at his wife's grandfather's and grandmother's marriage.

J. P. SPANGLER, saddler, Hillsboro, was born in Pennsylvania April 8, 1846; father was George Spangler; he was also a native of Pennsylvania; was a blacksmith by trade, but, in after life, followed the vocation of farming; he died in Pennsylvania about 1852; mother's name was Nancy Myers; she was also a native of Pennsylvania, where she now lives; parents raised three sons and two daughters; subject is the second son, and was educated at the common schools of his native State; began life by working on the farm, and, at about the age of seventeen years he began to learn the saddler's trade, which business he has followed the principal part of his time since, except he traveled about two years in commercial business. He worked at his trade about three years in Memphis, and the next place he located was at Hillsboro, Ill., in the spring of 1874, where he still continues. Our subject is engaged here by a company known as the Montgomery County Co-operative Association, and is manager of their business. Subject was married, in this town, October 18, 1877, to Miss Tillie Holderead, daughter of Anthony Holderead, who died at this place about 1880. Subject has one child, Mamie Adell, born September 25, 1878. Subject owns a commodious two-story brick residence in town. Republican in politics. Member of the Masonic order at this place; self and wife are members of the Methodist Church.

ALFRED A. K. SAWYER, dry goods and farming, Hillsboro, was born in Boston August 8, 1832, and came to Illinois in 1840. His father, Amos Sawyer, a native of Ireland, had four children, two boys and two girls, our subject being the eldest, who was educated partly in Hillsboro and partly in St. Louis, and began life farming, after which he traveled awhile, clerking on steamboats and on levee; was also in business in Chicago about two years; has been in the dry goods trade and farming in Montgomery for about sixteen years; he owns a fine farm of 250 acres; has one residence with thirteen acres attached, and another on Main street, has a fine trade, usually employing from three to five clerks. In 1860, in Hillsboro, he married Ella Bremer, a native of Kentucky, whose father was a North Carolinian, and her mother a Virginia woman; he is living in Hillsboro, but his wife is dead. Mr. Sawyer has had five children born to him—Amos, Edgar, Hubert, Augustus and Ella. One son, William, is dead. Is a Methodist, and a member of the Masonic and Granger fraternities; has also filled the position of Justice of the Peace.

THOMAS D. WASHBURN, physician, Hillsboro, was born in Greenfield, Mass., upon the 25th of April, 1819; he is the eldest and only son of Dr. Seth and Asenath (Dickman) Washburn, both of whom were natives of the above State, she, born about 1800, died in 1840, a daughter of Thomas Dickman, a printer and book-seller at Springfield, Mass., and a man of considerable prominence in his business; he, born at Leicester about 1790, died February, 1825. The only sister of our subject is Ruth W., widow of William G. Bancroft, of the firm of Barnes, Bancroft & Co., one of the oldest, wealthiest and most prominent wholesale and retail dry goods houses in Buffalo, N. Y. Dr. Washburn, in his boyhood, pursued, in the different academies and colleges of New England, the languages, sciences, mathematics and classics, obtaining a valuable and practical knowledge in the special course which he selected. At the age of twenty-one years, he began the study of medicine under Dr. Ralph Severance, at Saxon's River, Vt., then with Dr. James Dean, and from his tutelage he entered the intermediate school of Bowditch, Cole & Shattuck, at Boston; after remaining for a time at this school, his health failing, he went to the State of Georgia, where he taught a private school for three years, and then entered the University of New York, from which he graduated in the spring of 1846, and then began the practice of his profession at Syracuse, N. Y., where he remained three years. He was married, at Oswego, N. Y., May 25, 1846, to Roxanna M. Joslin, born at Easton, N. Y., April 25, 1819, daughter of Peter and Hannah (Rounds) Joslin, he born in 1784, died in 1858, she born at Easton in 1787, died in 1862. From Syracuse he removed to Grayville, Ill., thence to Lawrenceville, and, in 1856, settled in Hillsboro, where he has since resided and enjoyed a large practice in his profession. In 1874, he held the office of President of the Æsculapian, which is the oldest society in the State, and the same year delivered the valedictory address before that society; he has also held the office of President of the State Medical Society, and at the present time fills that position in the Montgomery County Medical Society, and Vice President of the Inter-State Medical Society. His contributions to medical literature have been numerous and of great value to the medical profession throughout the country. He served three years as Assistant Surgeon of the One Hundred and Twenty-Sixth Illinois Volunteer Infantry the last eighteen months of the time being spent as Post Surgeon at Little Rock, Ark. By his marriage, there were born the following: Seth Emory and Daniel W., living; John and Edward, dead. The family are members of the Congregational Church, in which the Doctor has held for a number of years the offices of Deacon and Trustee. He is a Republican in his political tenets; a man of prominence, and highly esteemed by the citizens of the county; he is a nephew of Emory Washburn, ex-Governor of Massachusetts, and late Professor in the Harvard Law School.

M. M. WALSH, furniture, etc., Hillsboro, born in County Wexford, Ireland, in December, 1841; his parents, James and Mary (Redmond) Walsh, were natives of County Wexford, Ireland, and lied there. He is the second son of a family of two sons and two daughters; he received an ordinary education in Ireland, and emigrated to America in 1854, and settled in Montreal, Canada, where he remained till 1856, when he came to the United States. He learned the trade of a wagon-maker in Potsdam, St. Lawrence Co., N. Y., and at the end of his apprenticeship, in 1859, moved to Stamford, Conn., where he worked at his trade until 1861. In 1863, he went to Philadelphia, where he worked about a year stocking rifles for the Government; thence he went to Pittsburgh, Penn.; worked at his trade there one year; thence to Cincinnati, Ohio, worked six months, and then returned to Pittsburgh; from Pittsburgh he went to St. Louis, and thence to Hillsboro, where he arrived April 9, 1867; here he worked at his trade till 1869, then engaged in the hardware business till 1873, when he sold out his hardware stock and engaged in his present line—furniture, coffins, sewing machines, etc. In Hillsboro, December 15, 1870, he married Minerva M. Hanson, born at Tribe's Hill, Montgomery Co., N. Y., June 25, 1846, daughter of John A. and Susan (Lingenfelter) Hanson, both natives of Tribe's

Hill, N. Y., the former born October 11, 1811; the latter, still living, was born February 29, 1806. Mr. and Mrs. Walsh are the parents of two children—Ada Irene, born September 3, 1873, and Mina M., born July 5, 1878. He enlisted, in New York City, April 16, 1861, in the Federal service, Fifth New York Volunteer Infantry, better known as Duryea's Zouaves; was commissioned Lieutenant early in 1863, and remained with the army during its term of service. He was taken prisoner during the seven days' fight around Richmond, Va., and confined in the tobacco factory prison on Carey street, Richmond, for twenty-six days, when he was paroled and exchanged; he took part in the battle of Fredericksburg. He is a supporter of the Republican party.

PAUL WALTER, livery business, Hillsboro, was born in North Carolina, Cabarras County, October 2, 1821. Nicholas Walter was born in Pennsylvania about 1790, and moved to North Carolina about 1809, and married Catharine Goodman, of that State. The father, Nicholas Walter, was in the war of 1812, and served during the war; participated in the memorable battle of New Orleans; he was a farmer and millwright, and died in North Carolina in 1825; parents raised four sons (subject, youngest son) and three daughters. Subject was educated at the common schools of North Carolina; began life as a farmer in this State in 1839, that being the year of his emigration; has followed farming and stock-trading the principal part of his time since till the last few years; went to California in 1850, in search of gold; was there about six years in all, and came home about $45,000 winner. Being a liberal-hearted, whole-souled fellow, he indorsed freely for his friends, and was caught for upward of $40,000, which amount he paid by selling his own property, never waiting for an officer to settle any of his transactions. This loss, coupled with some unprofitable investments, reduced our subject again to moderate circumstances, as he had begun. In the late war, he volunteered in the First Illinois Cavalry, in Company E; subject was Captain of the company, under Col. Marshall; was captured at Lexington, Mo., by Gen. Price; was paroled and exchanged, and again entered the service, but was discharged by the Government on account of a violation of their oath, having taken the oath to enter the service no more during the rebellion; after the battle of Lexington, subject was offered the position of Major, an office he refused to accept, preferring to stay with his company; he is a Democrat now in politics; member of the Masonic order; has taken all the degrees from Entered Apprentice to Knight Templar. Subject married, in this county, February 1, 1844, to Emeline Scott, who was born in North Carolina in 1827, but came to this State when quite young, in 1833, with her parents; she was a daughter of Alexander and Elizabeth (Wood) Scott. Subject has eight children, four sons—George, Scott, Miller and James; and four daughters, Marcilla, Illinois, Susan and Estella; wife is a member of the Methodist Church; eldest son, George, was educated for a Presbyterian minister, but, on account of his health failing, was obliged to give it up.

E. L. WAGGONER, Hillsboro. E. L. Waggoner, the youngest son of Milton R. Waggoner; Sarah R. McCollough, his mother, was born in Montgomery County, Ill., September 28, 1863. His boyhood days were spent principally in attending the country school; at sixteen years of age, he attended the school of Valparaiso, Ind., one year, and two years at Blackburn University; he then came to Hillsboro, Ill., and commenced in the mercantile business as a clerk, as he intends to make that his avocation through life. He and his brother have a very fine property in this county, and our subject stands as high as any young man in the county, socially, and for his integrity and industry, and manly principles, he has no superior.

CITY OF LITCHFIELD AND NORTH AND SOUTH LITCHFIELD TOWNSHIPS.

DANIEL CUTTING AMSDEN, manufacturer and Secretary of the Litchfield Coal Company, born in Southington, Conn., January [illegible], 1814, was, when three years old, removed to Manlius Square, N. Y. Here his father remained a winter, and, in the spring, removed to the site of the present village of Homer. After a brief residence of three years he went to Cato, Cayuga County, and became a contractor on public works. When he was twelve years of age, his parents located in Erie County, and young Amsden was reared to farm labor, which, in character and severity of toil, is inappreciable to the pioneers of the prairie region. Before attaining his majority, he drove stage into Buffalo, then little more than a hamlet, and also tried the rude hardships of a lumberman. Prior to his marriage, in 1841, to Miss Mary Beach, he had leased a hotel at Gowanda, Cattaraugus County, which pursuit he afterward exchanged for shop-keeping, and then farming. He was an ardent politician; held several offices; declined to be Sheriff; and made money only to see it slip away in the financial reverses which shook the credit of States and the nation, as well as the fortunes of individuals. In 1854, he removed to Berlin, Wis., and for three years was interested in regular mercantile pursuits, and did not improve his present fortunes. In May, 1857, he arrived in Litchfield, then a little village, with its few cheap houses, located as if sown by the wind, and of a general appearance to dissipate day-dreams or poetic fancies. Here he entered the employ of the foundry and machine shop company as book-keeper and general utility man. Until he came to Litchfield, his life had been a wide preparation for the success which has since dogged his steps. He had looked on fortune's smiles, and felt her frowns. His schemes had successively turned to ashes, and, past life's meridian, he came here, poor but resolute, to repair previous disappointments. For ten years, he spared himself no toil or economy. Tall — he is six feet two in his stockings — thin, with joints of strength and great muscular powers, he made himself indispensable to his employers. In 1865, he became by purchase, an equal partner in the foundry and machine shop, the firm being H. H. Beach & Co. The affairs of the firm were prosperous. Their shop was crowded with orders, and prices were good. In 1867, he was elected Mayor of the city, and his firm made the advances of money and credit which caused the opening of the coal mine at the eastern limits of the city — the solid foundation of its subsequent prosperity. He was, in 1871, one of the original stockholders of the Litchfield Bank, and the next year was a heavy subscriber to the stock of the Car Works, and the same year was the Republican candidate for State Senator, and was not elected — an adverse majority of 1,200 was too great a barrier to be scaled. In 1875, the foundry and machine shop were sold to the Car Works Company, and Mr. Amsden gave his chief attention to coal-mining. He now has a large and valuable interest in the mine here, [illegible] several mines in the famous block coal region of Indiana, and is a member of the firm of J. ach, Davis & Co., bankers. He owns a comfortable interest in the Car Works and the Litchfield Coal Oil and Pipe Line Company, and has bonds and a goodly balance to his credit at the bank. There has been no accident in his prosperity. If one would put money into ventures which should benefit himself while enriching the community, he must be able to bias public opinion in their favor and direct currents of business. If the former prospers, it will be for the reason that success is as much of the man as of the circumstances. The following children have been born to Mr. Amsden: George W., Helen A. and John B. W. Mr. Amsden has become widely known as a man of influence in local affairs. Every politician of his faith seeks his counsel or co-operation. Himself seeking no office, he is a vigorous, racy specimen of a man grown wealthy by the homely arts possible to all; of decision, industry and economy.

EDWIN K. AUSTIN, Litchfield, was born in the town of Becket, Berkshire Co., Mass., August 8, 1814; he received an academical education in his native State, and at the age of eighteen went to Kentucky, where he sold clocks for two years. From Kentucky he removed to West Tennessee, near Memphis, where he taught school, and also engaged in merchandising seven years, then removed to Northern Mississippi, where he taught private schools till 1861. He then moved North to Illinois, and settled on 120 acres of land in Montgomery County, near the eastern border of North Litchfield Township, and afterward added 120 acres more, which he farmed till 1866; in that year he sold out, with the intention of removing to the Southern States, but, owing to the changed relation of the races after the war, he abandoned the idea, and, in 1868, purchased 186 acres of land, on which he resides. In Fayette County, Tenn., July 20, 1845, he married Marian W. Hawley, a native of New York, born February 25, 1821; they have two children—Edwin M. and Laura T. Mr. Austin has taught school nearly seventeen years, which has seriously impaired his health.

ABRAM D. ATTERBURY was born in Grayson County, Ky., February 26, 1827; passed his youth on the farm, and, at the age of twenty was apprenticed to the blacksmith's trade in Harlan County, Ky. In 1850, he came to Illinois, alone, and has ever since lived in the vicinity of Litchfield, where, in the above year, he entered a quarter-section of land, at $1.25 per acre. He afterward engaged in breaking prairie land, where Litchfield now stands, for two years, with an ox team; farmed one year, then worked at his trade at Zanesville two years, and at Litchfield two years: bought out Jeffries, and he and H. Kessinger, now of Raymond, were the two blacksmiths of the place. In 1857, he settled on the quarter section of land that he had first entered, where he has since resided, and by the year 1862, had the entire 160 acres under cultivation. He has engaged largely in wheat-raising, with good success, and has added to his original purchase of land, until he now has 550 acres in this county, which he has acquired by his own efforts. In 1853, he married Mrs. Julia Ogle, of St. Clair County, Ill., widow of the late Joseph T. Ogle by whom she had one child, Joseph T. Ogle, Jr., now a resident of this county. Mr. and Mrs. Atterbury are the parents of three sons—George W., James H. and Charles M. He is a member of the Methodist Church, of which he is District Steward and Trustee.

S. E. ALDEN was born in Hartford, Conn., December 15, 1819, and, when nine years old, moved with his parents to Madison County, N. Y. When fourteen years of age, he began learning the carpenter and joiner's trade with his father, and remained in Cazenovia, Madison Co., N. Y., till he was twenty-one years old. In 1843, he went to New York, where he worked as a journeyman until 1851, when he took the Panama route to California, where he worked for a mining company as machinist and pattern-maker; he also prospected for a time, and afterward engaged as contractor and builder in San Francisco and Marysville, Cal., where he remained in business thirteen months, at the end of which time he returned to Cazenovia, N. Y. In 1855, he left Cazenovia and came West to Litchfield, Ill. His first work in Litchfield was on the buildings of the Terre Haute & Alton R. R., on which he worked two years, during which time the present depot was erected; he then went into business on his own account as a contractor and builder, and constructed many of the first buildings of Litchfield; he carried on business in the city and county principally until 1878, when he became foreman carpenter for the Wabash, St. Louis & Pacific Railroad, and remained in that position three and a half years; he built the Montgomery County Court House in 1865, and a Methodist Episcopal Church at Hillsboro some time before. In Cazenovia, N. Y., in 1842, he married Cynthia H. Russell, born in Connecticut July 6, 1824, third daughter of Jesse and Mary (Andrus) Russell, natives of Connecticut, of Puritan stock, and parents of four sons and five daughters, all living save one; the Russells were for many generations strict Presbyterians and stanch Whigs; Jesse Russell, father of Mrs. Alden, a blacksmith, and very skillful in his trade, was a fifer in the war of 1812, under Gen. Jackson; in 1825, he made a trip to Western New York, purchased a farm and sowed some grain, but became discouraged and returned to his old home in Connecticut; in 1828, however, he returned with his family and settled at Cazenovia, N. Y. Mr. and Mrs. Alden have four daughters. Mr. Alden is a descendant of one of the Pilgrim fathers; three brothers came over in the Mayflower by the name of Alden—John, Ezra, and one, name unknown, who died soon after landing; Ezra, the grandfather of our subject, was a well-to-do farmer, and lived at Greenwich, Mass.; he had six sons and three daughters; his second son, Samuel, the father of subject, was born near Greenwich, Mass., in August, 1793; he was a carpenter and joiner by trade, and worked at it at Hartford, Conn., until 1828, when he moved to Cazenovia, N. Y., where he died in January, 1854; his wife, Fanny Andrus, born in 1791, died December 1, 1874; they were the parents of three sons and three daughters, of whom our subject, Samuel E., is the eldest. The Aldens were Presbyterians and Whigs.

LOUIS ALLEN, attorney at law, Litchfield, was born in Clinton County, Ill., in 1852; he passed his youth on a farm in his native county. At the age of twenty-one years, he entered the McKendree College at Lebanon, Ill., and spent two years there. After teaching one term of school, he entered the Union College of Law at Chicago, Ill., in the fall of 1874, and graduated from it in June, 1876. In the fall of the following year, he located for practice at Litchfield, and has practiced in the courts of this county ever since; for two years he was City Attorney of Litchfield. In 1879, he married Miss Sophie Bond, of Clinton County.

HENRY E. APPLETON, Vice President Litchfield Coal Company, Litchfield, was born in Hampshire, England, in 1828; he was raised on a farm, and, at the age of fourteen years, learned the trade of wagon-making near Southampton, England. He came to the United States in 1851, and located in Madison County, Ill., where he worked at carriage and wagon making until April, 1854, when he came to Litchfield with "Uncle Dick" O'Bannon, and here started the first carriage and wagon shop of the city, his place of business being the site of the market house. He carried on this manufacture until about 1867, he executing the wood work and Mr. Jefferis the blacksmithing. Mr. Appleton was connected with the engineer's department on the construction of the Wabash Railroad while it was building. He became time-keeper for Jefferis, Amsden, Benton & Co., at the coal mines, in about 1870, and, some time later, became a member of the Litchfield Coal and Mining Company; since the organization of that company, he has held in it some official position, being several times its Assistant Superintendent, and now being its Vice President; for the last eleven years he has given the coal mines his close attention. He is a member and also Vice President of the Litchfield Oil and Pipe Line Company. In 1853, at Ridgely, Ill., he married Miss Herndon, of Madison County, Ill.; her death occurred in 1857. In 1874, he married a second time, the lady being Miss Alice Butt, of Litchfield, of English birth.

ALFRED BLACKWELDER, whose portrait appears in this work, was born in Cabarrus County, N. C., near Concord, July 17, 18[illegible]. He started from his home, October 4, 1834, on horseback, and came through to Illinois, reaching Union County in twenty-one days, where a sister lived, and he remained there until April, 1835, when he came to Hillsboro, where he found the Circuit Court in session in a log house. (He has helped to build three court houses since that time.) His earthly possessions, when he arrived here, were a small sorrel horse and $10 in money; he worked for $10 per month for three years, working first for Judge Rountree, who held all the county offices, office-holding patriots being scarcer in those good old days than at present. He married, April 19, 1837, Miss Joanna Scherer, daughter of Frederick Scherer, of North Carolina, who came to this State about 1833. Mr. Blackwelder rented land until about 1840, when he bought eighty acres at $5 per acre, unimproved, in South Litchfield Township; he built on it a small frame house, and lived there about sixteen years, when he sold his farm to secure a larger tract for his growing boys, and, by exchange and purchase, secured 240 acres in the same locality, farmed it six years, and made great improvements upon it; when the Indianapolis & St. Louis Railroad was built, E. B. Litchfield, through his agent, Maj. Huggins, bought this land at $20 per acre, and part of it became a portion of the town site of Litchfield. Mr. Blackwelder then bought of James Turner 180 acres, and of John C. Reed 240 acres, and these two tracts comprise the 420-acre farm of our subject, inclusive of his 100 acres of excellent timber. Very little or no improvements were made upon his land when Mr. Blackwelder purchased it, but he has so persistently and intelligently managed his possessions that it is at present in a high state of cultivation, and every acre is inclosed with fences. Since 1878, Mr. Blackwelder has relinquished the active management of his farm to his three sons; he has eight children living and married; four died when young; those living are Daniel Monroe, William Riley, Minerva C. (now Mrs. Robert Morrison), Jacob Francis, David Alexander, John Martin, Harriet Louisa (now Mrs. Gideon Davis), Samuel Richard. All Mr. Blackwelder's sons are residents of Montgomery County, and all of them farmers; both sons-in-law are also residents of Montgomery County, and farmers. Mr. Blackwelder is a member of the Lutheran Church, and filled for twenty years the office of Deacon, or Elder, holding membership with his denomination for over fifty years. Mr. Blackwelder has always been a Democrat, casting his first Presidential vote for Van Buren. His wife died January 31, 1876, being in her sixtieth year; they had been married almost forty years. The old gentleman says that when the State road was laid out from Edwardsville to Taylorville, they plowed two furrows all the way through. Mr. Blackwelder has always been in favor of anything that would redound to the credit of his county, and is a man who has won and retained the respect of all.

JAMES F. BLACKWELDER, physician, Litchfield. The Blackwelders were originally from Germany, and settled in North Carolina some time before the Revolutionary war. The family name signifies "black forest." Peter Blackwelder was born near Concord, Cabarrus County, N. C., in 1810, and came to Illinois in [illegible], accompanied by a cousin, Alfred Blackwelder; they settled in Hillsboro, and came all the way on horseback. They purchased land, and Peter at one time owned a half-section in North Litchfield Township; by trade he was a carpenter, and, in addition to this, was engaged in farming. He was a Lutheran, and was the first Superintendent of the Sunday school organized at the Long Branch Schoolhouse. This was long before the city of Litchfield was planned and laid out. He was a quiet, unassuming, worthy man, and, politically, was a Free-Soil Democrat. He married Mrs. Nellie Wagoner, daughter of Frederick Scherer, of this county; she bore him four sons and three daughters, all of whom are living except the youngest daughter, who died in infancy. Peter Blackwelder died in 1855, and his wife in 1853. They were the parents of our subject, Dr. James F. Blackwelder, who was born in Montgomery County, Ill., in what is now North Litchfield Township, on August 2, 1841; he was educated in the Lutheran College building, which was then known as Hillsboro Academy. In 1861, he began the study of medicine under Dr. I. W. Fink, of Hillsboro, where he read until he entered the St. Louis Medical College, taking his first course in 1863. The following year, he entered the Cincinnati College of Medicine and Surgery, from which he graduated in June, 1864. A few days later, he entered the army of Gen. Sherman, and was assigned to duty at Marietta, Ga., as Acting Assistant Surgeon in hospital service, and for four months served there and at Atlanta, Ga. He was next Assistant Surgeon for the Thirty-second Illinois Infantry, and followed its fortunes on the memorable march to the sea; he continued until mustered out, at Washington, D. C., in 1865. On his return from the army he practiced at Hillsboro, Ill., for some three years, and at Moro, Madison County, for about the same length of time. In June, 1871, he located permanently at Litchfield where he has built up a large and lucrative practice. He is a member of the Montgomery County Medical Society, of which he has been Secretary, and has also a membership in the District Medical Society. The Doctor has two sons.

DANIEL M. BLACKWELDER was born in Montgomery County, near Hillsboro, February 27, 1839, and was raised to a life of farming, attending, in the meantime, the schools in his section. At twenty-one years of age, he began farming for himself. In 1861, he married Miss Helena Cress, a native of North Carolina. He bought ten acres of timber land, and lived for nine years on the homestead, during which time he added to the original purchase until his tract contained 125 acres. Mr. Blackwelder has of late years paid considerable attention to fine stock raising, principally sheep and hogs

He has served nine years as School Director, and seven years as Commissioner of Highways; takes much interest in all improvements and in educational matters; he has two sons.

HENRY HARRISON BEACH, manufacturer, Litchfield, of Connecticut ancestry, is a native of Otsego County N. Y., whence he was removed by his parents in his early childhood, to Erie County, same State. At the age of fourteen years, he entered a machine shop as apprentice, and, at a general shop at Rochester, completed his training. Continuing three years in the machine shops, he then ran an engine on the New York Central Railroad, and a construction train on the Great Western Railroad of Canada, and then became foreman of the shops of the Michigan Southern & Northern Indiana road. In 1854, when twenty-five years old, he was appointed Assistant Master Mechanic of the Michigan Southern shops at Adrian. Three years later, Dyer Williams, the Master Mechanic, and Henry A. Angel, the owner of a foundry, together with our subject, visited the village of Litchfield, where they decided to build a foundry and machine shop. Mr. Beach to be the manager, and resident, and business partner. Mr. Beach, at this time, had become an accurate and accomplished machinist; he possessed a social disposition, good health, courage and hopefulness. These qualities constituted almost his entire capital. In August, 1857, the foundry was put in blast, and his machine shop, containing a few pieces of second-hand machinery and lathe engines, was ready for business. At this hour, the panic began; his venture appeared about to collapse; for, in a sparsely inhabited region, where the people were wedded to rustic implements and the soil, he was obliged to create a demand for his wares and labor; he had no rival shop between Alton and Terre Haute; various small loans made on the "street" delayed a catastrophe, and, when ruin seemed only a few days away, he bought, on credit, a portable mill for grinding corn, and, placing it in the loft of his machine shop, began the manufacture of Indian meal for the St. Louis market; by the profits of this humble enterprise, he tided over the first winter and spring, until the complete removal to this point of the railroad shops created an active demand on the resources of his shop and foundry. In 1860, Mr. Angel retired from the firm, and a couple of mill engines had established Mr. Beach's reputation as a builder of steam engines. In 1865, Mr Williams ceased to be a partner, and a third interest in the concern was sold to H. C. Amsden, on the usual terms of payment, and the firm was thenceforward H. H. Beach & Co. Mr. Beach was married, in 1866, Elizabeth Gage; he has been blessed with one child, Estelle H. At length, the private and industrial welfare of the city demanded cheap fuel at its doors, and in 1867 his firm bought real estate, and, with Bess & Sparks, millers, guaranteed a large bonus for sinking a coal shaft. The experiment of seeking for coal at this point was a bold one, as no coal-field was known to exist nearer than twenty miles; the prospector failed, and a coal company, with a capital of $20,000, was formed, his firm being the largest stockholders; the company collapsed when its capital was exhausted, and the mine was not ready to raise coal; a second one, with a capital of $10,000, was organized, to continue the work, and again his firm was its chief supporter. When this company, burdened with a debt of $22,000, was unable to put the mine in working order, his firm, with a few individuals, assumed the debt, and advanced the funds to develop the mine. Three years' work and $50,000 were required to open it The coal company, of which he is the head, has disbursed in wages three-quarters of a million, and reduced the price of fuel to two-thirds the previous price. Mr. Beach was active in measures to secure the Wabash Railroad, a railroad to Louisiana, Mo., and one to Springfield, Ill.; these two are not yet built, but the Jacksonville road, to which he also contributed, is in operation. In 1868, he became a member of the firm of Hagar & Seath, of Terre Haute, who desired to build a foundry and car works in that city; Mr. Beach was the banker, and, when the investment became profitable, he retired; by his aid, Mr. Seath now writes himself one of the solid men of Terre Haute. In 1871, he took one-third of the stock of the Litchfield Bank, which, proving a better thing for its officers than for its owners, he aided to close out their interests, and founded on its site the banking house of Beach, Davis & Co., whose success was its own, and whose misfortunes were a result of the panic of 1873, which, however, passed with no loss of stability or public confidence. The removal of the car shops left vacant a series of buildings well adapted for car works. Mr. Beach and others conceived the design of forming a company to build cars. Two Eastern gentlemen offered to supply the skill to operate the company, if other parties would supply the money; their offer was declined, and a home company organized, Mr. Beach subscribing one-seventh of the stock. The company nominally failed in a few years, paying only 85 cents on the dollar. Again his aid was implored, and, by his personal assurances and engagements, the creditors were appeased; he also advanced thousands to J. B. L. Keating, the brilliant grain merchant, who, paying out a couple of millions for grain, failed—as men trading on borrowed capital usually do. In 1875, his firm sold their plant to the car works, and the securities taken shrank to half their former value. He was called on to meet a vast amount of accommodation paper, and this, with other losses, scaled his fortune down to one-third its value in 1870; but he was an officer of the car works and the coal company with a comfortable salary; he became the proprietor of a flouring mill and elevator; he invested in the Indiana coal mines; he is the foremost man in the Oil and Pipe Line Company. Although Mr. Beach began life without means or business connections, the enterprises which are indebted to him for existence, or for their prosperity, have at times disbursed wages at the rate of a third of a million a year. His agency in securing water works for the city is treated of more fully elsewhere in this work.

R. F. BENNETT, physician and surgeon, and Mayor of Litchfield, was born in Shelby County, Ill., on October 2, 1839; he resided there until he was nineteen years of age; he received a good education from the Moultrie County Seminary at Sullivan, Ill.; he left school at seventeen and began teaching, continuing two years. At the age of nineteen years, he began the study of medicine with Dr. Henry, of Paradise, Coles County, where he continued two years, in the meantime attending two sessions at the Cincinnati Eclectic Medical College, from which he graduated in 1861, and, in the spring of the following year, he located in Litchfield for the practice of his profession, in which he has since been actively engaged. In January, 1881, he formed a partnership with Dr. J. H. Tilden, and the firm has a large and lucrative practice. September 1, 1861, our subject married Miss Lizzie Storm, of Shelby County, Ill. He is now serving his second term in the Montgomery County Eclectic Medical Society as its President; he was also President of the State Eclectic Medical Society, and is now its Treasurer. In politics, he is a Republican. During 1880 and 1881, he was Mayor of Litchfield, and now serves his third term, being elected this third time by a large majority. Dr. Bennett is esteemed as a citizen, popular in politics and valued as a physician. Dr. Bennett has been blessed with two children—Harry, born June 12, 1871, and Mary, born May 10, 1876.

JOSEPHUS BARRY, deceased, was born in this county March 2, 1835, and married, December 29, 1858, Miss Mary M. McAdams, settling on a farm of 160 acres, afterward buying at different times, until he owned, at his death, 240 acres of land; his death occurred January 8, 1877, his wife having passed over to the land of the hereafter July 4, 1868, leaving an only son, Charles Barry, who was born March 23, 1860, who took charge of the homestead on reaching his majority, and who married, February 25, 1880, Lucy J. Corlew, daughter of John Corlew, of Montgomery County.

ISAAC N. BARRY, farmer, was born in Hillsboro Township, Montgomery County, December 19, 1837, and, after receiving a fair education, began farming on eighty acres of land, with sixty acres in timber, which his father purchased for him in 1859-60; it was partly broken, and he has so added to his farm that he has at present 200 acres, principally in grain and for grazing. In 1868, he married Miss Margaret A. McAdams, daughter of Thomas McAdams, of this county, but of Kentucky nativity; he has one son and two daughters living, and one son and one daughter dead. Father John Barry was born in Barren County, Ky., in July, 1806; his wife was Elizabeth Robinson, who had one son, Wilson, who came to Montgomery County in 1830, locating five miles southwest of Hillsboro, where he passed his days; he served as Justice of the Peace two terms; he was an Old School Baptist and a Democrat; he was for many years owner of the Pepper Grist-Mills, which stood on part of his estate; he died March 6, 1876, in his seventieth year; his wife died June 8, 18[illegible]; they had a family of nine children, all of whom grew to maturity except one: they w[illegible] Wilson, Susan J., Elizabeth A., Jos[illegible] Isaac Newton, John Robinson, William [illegible] Palmyra C. and Sarah A.

STEPHEN R. BRIGGS, deceased, was born near Zanesville, Ohio, in 1812, [illegible] when twelve months old, his father [illegible] Illinois, making his home at Edwards[illegible] over two years, when he moved to the terr[illegible]tory of this county in the spring of 18[illegible]. Our subject lived in this county until [illegible] death, on May 13, 1872; he entered sev[illegible] tracts of land in North Litchfield; his or[illegible]nal home was eighty acres three and a half miles from the present city of Litchfield. [illegible] was in the ranger service, and crossed [illegible] Western plains, being over sixty days on the way, and a portion of that time was [illegible] half rations. At one time, Mr. Brig[illegible] the owner of 500 acres of land; he w[illegible] sidered a very successful farmer, bein[illegible] fortunate only in giving his name to friends as surety, and in consequence being obli[illegible] to liquidate the debts of others during [illegible] latter part of his life. For eleven years [illegible] was Associate Judge of this county [illegible] with the Democratic party until the war [illegible] he joined the Republican ranks, holdin[illegible] the Democratic party had drifted away from him. In 1839, he married Miss Paul[illegible] Wood, daughter of James Wood, of Sa[illegible]mon County, Ill.; she was born in Virg[illegible] in 1823, and died on May 18, 1881; [illegible] a family of ten children, seven of wh[illegible] living. James M. Briggs is the oldest [illegible] child, born in Montgomery County, Ill., October 1, 1842; he obtained a fair common school education by attending school in winters, after the corn was gathered in. On attaining his majority, he began farming on the homestead, and, after the war, owned land in that vicinity. In 1876, he came to his present place, and here engaged in the ice trade, erecting in that year a building with a capacity of 2,000 tons, being eighty four by sixty feet, twenty feet high, and located on the reservoir; this ice building is to be connected by a side track with the Wabash, St. Louis & Pacific Railroad. Since his commencement, he has done an excellent retail business in the city of Litchfield. In 1877, he married Miss Crilla Brandle, who bore him one son.

ROBERT BRIGGS was born May 10, 1824, on the place now belonging to Green Bandy's heirs, in this township, son of Robert and Polly (Lockhart) Briggs. Robert Briggs, Sr., was born in Pennsylvania, and emigrated to Ohio at a very early day, finally coming to Illinois. During the troublous Indian times, he took refuge in a fort at Edwardsville, and there joined old Capt. Sam Whitesides in excursions against the red devils at Rock Island; the Indians, according to the old gentleman, seemed to be as thick as the grass on the prairies. They remained in the fort about two years—mother and three children—the husband going out to hunt with others for provisions. The grandfather of our subject was also in the fort, and was a great hunter and Indian fighter. Robert, on leaving the fort, about 1814, settled on Lake Fork, near where Walshville now stands, but a man named Baker entered the land over Robert's head, thereby dispossessing him of all the improvements he had put on the land; he then settled on land now belonging to Bluford Bandy's heirs, upon which he built a cabin and commenced raising corn; he sold his crops in St. Louis. He raised ten children. Robert, our subject, remained at home until he was twenty-six years of age, when he married, October [illegible], 1849, Miss Penelope Petty, of Tennessee. Having entered forty acres of land near where Raymond now stands, he lived there a few years, when, his parents becoming old and feeble, he went to take care of them, all the other children having left home to do for themselves. Mr. Briggs moved to his present place March 4, 1861, and has since lived there. He has two children, and one dead. Pleasant and Burd, his two sons, are at home.

H. L. LENIPE, proprietor Phoenix Hotel, Litchfield, was born in New Philadelphia, Ohio, in 1834, but was raised in Wayne County, where he lived, receiving his education in St. Joseph College, in Somerset, Ohio. In 1858, he came West and settled in Columbia, Boone Co., Mo., where he engaged in the manufacture of plows and wagons, and the livery business, until 1874, during part of that period constructing large contract—macadamized streets in the city of Columbia. He next came to Litchfield and bought his present hotel, naming it the Phoenix, after having renovated and repaired it from top to bottom; he has conducted it ever since, except during a period of fourteen months, when he rented it to look after other interests; he has the only three story hotel in the city, and his house contains thirty five rooms and three sample rooms; he is located near the Indianapolis & St. Louis depot, and runs a free omnibus to all the railroad depots; an obliging landlord and a good house make the Phoenix a hotel a fair reputation.

CHARLES BALLWEG, dealer in liquors, Litchfield, was born in Baden, Germany, February 15, 1843, and came to the United States with his parents when he was six years old; in the summer of 1852, his parents located in Adams County, Penn., where he received his education in the Abbott [illegible]

Penn., schools; in the spring of 1863, he came to Minnesota, and was a dealer in liquors; he kept a restaurant in St. Paul in 1864 and 1865; he went thence to Winona and represented a wholesale liquor house of that city, traveling in the Western States two years, when he located in Rochester, Minn., where he remained until the fall of 1872, being a dealer in liquors and keeping a billiard hall. In 1873, he came to Litchfield and engaged in his present business, which is the wholesale and retail sale of liquors; he carries on business on the corner of State and Ryder streets, and does a prosperous business. He was a dealer in grain in the firm of Ballweg & Gilmore, and had the mill elevator from 1875 to the summer of 1876, when Gilmore retired, and our subject continued in the business for several years. In politics, he is a prominent Democrat, having been a member of the Central Committee of the county, and of the Congressional Committee; several times he has been a delegate to the Congressional and State conventions.

J. R. BLACKWELL, grocer, Litchfield, was born in Fayette County, Ill., in February, 1844, the city of his birth being Vandalia, the old capital of the State, where he lived about ten years, when he moved thence to Hillsboro, Ill., at which place he lived with his uncle, the Hon. J. T. Eccles; in June, 1861, at the age of sixteen years he enlisted in the Eighth Illinois Volunteer Infantry, under Col. Richard J. Oglesby, his company being B, under Capt. Sturgis; under the call for three-months' volunteers, he served three months, during which time the regiment was quartered at Cairo, Ill.; on July 5, 1862, he re-enlisted, at Hillsboro, in the One Hundred and Seventeenth Illinois Volunteer Infantry, in Company B, under Capt. R. McWilliams; he participated in the campaign from Vicksburg to Meridian, Miss., in the Red River campaign, in Arkansas and Tennessee, in the Nashville and Fort Blakely campaigns, the Tupelo and Price campaigns, in the campaign against Hood in Middle Tennessee, and in the Mobile campaign; thence to Montgomery, Ala., where the regiment was at the close of the war; in all, his regiment marched 2,487 miles, traveled by rail 778 miles, and by water 6,19[illegible] miles; they captured two stand of colors and 442 prisoners of war; Mr. Blackwell never was wounded, taken prisoner, off duty, nor in the hospital; he was mustered out on July 5, 1865, and would have veteranized if the war had continued; on his return from the army he studied law with Maj. McWilliams, of Litchfield, where he located for practice, being admitted to the bar in 1867; he practiced his profession here four years; from 1869 to 1877, he served as Postmaster of Litchfield, and went out under the general order of President Hayes that no re-appointments be made when there was a contest and the incumbent had served eight years; the largest number of names ever signed to a petition was sent to the department from this place, indorsing him and asking for his re-appointment; the petition contained the indorsement of Senator R. J. Oglesby, Gov. Beveridge and Congressman Gen. J. S. Martin, the petitioners numbering 1,500. He was Alderman from the Second Ward two years, and was defeated for Mayor in 1878 by a small majority; in that year, he engaged in mercantile business at Benton, Ill., continuing about two years when he returned to Litchfield and here engaged in the grocery business; he has now a model grocery, on Kirkham street, called the "Wabash Store," and is doing a leading business. In 1866, he married Miss Hattie, daughter of Rev. P. P. Hamilton, of Litchfield; she died in 1878; to them were born three children, two girls and one boy. He remarried, in 1879, Miss Alice, daughter of Rev. Hugh Corrington. Robert Blackwell the father of our subject, was born near Shelbyville, Ky., in 1802; he learned the trade of printing at Hopkinsville, Ky., and, when a young man, came to Illinois, locating at Kaskaskia in 1815, at which place he became editor of the first paper ever printed in the State; it had been established shortly before the time of his arrival, by Mathew Duncan, who was also from Shelbyville, Ky.; the paper was styled the *Illinois Intelligencer*. Mr. Blackwell became public printer of the new State, and was at one time State Auditor; he was twice elected to the State Senate from that district in Illinois. When the capital was removed from Kaskaskia to Vandalia, he removed there, and resided there thirty years, during which time he was engaged in mercantile business, being a long time the partner of William H. Browning, late of Chicago; he died in 1870, leaving one son and two daughters by his second marriage, their mother being a sister of Hon. J. T. Eccles, of Hillsboro. He was three times married, his first wife, who bore him no children, being a sister of Dr. Stapp, of Decatur, Ill.; his widow, née Miss Mary Slusser, from Ohio, lives at Vandalia; his demise leaves a vacancy felt by the public, and one not easily filled.

WILLIAM M. BEINDORF, manufacturer, Litchfield, was born in Prussia, Germany, in the city of Essen, on January 24, 1838. When but ten years of age, he came to the United States with his mother and settled in La Fayette, Ind. In his seventeenth year, he began to learn the machinist's trade in the shop of Joseph Habler, where he served three years' apprenticeship and one year as journeyman; he then entered the employ of the La Fayette & Indianapolis Railroad Company, in the machine department, where he remained two years, removing thence to Fort Wayne, Ind., where he worked two years for the Wabash, St. Louis & Pacific Railroad Company. In 1863, he came to Litchfield, where he worked in the railroad shops seven years, and afterward engaged his services to H. H. Beach & Co., remaining with them two years. After the organization of the Litchfield Car Manufacturing Company, he worked for them a year. In 1875, he opened his present machine shop in Litchfield, which has been in active operation ever since; he employs five hands in the manufacture of threshing engines and wagons of superior quality, and in doing a general repairing business. In Fort Wayne, Ind., in 1863, he married Miss Kate D. Myers, who is the mother of his three children.

JAMES W. BUTTS, plasterer, Litchfield, was born in Greenbrier County, Va., now West Virginia, in 1844, and lived in that place until 1862. His first service was in the Fiftieth Virginia Infantry Regiment, White's division, under Joe Johnston; he was sixteen years old when he enlisted, and in the regiment mentioned he served eighteen months; he fought in the Confederate army in the battles of Fort Donelson, Five Oaks, Williamsburg, Malvern Hill and Gaines' Mill; he was captured by the Illinois troops in the seven-days' fight at Malvern Hill, and taken to Washington, D. C., whence he was sent to Camp Chase, where he took the oath, in August, 1862, and enlisted in the Forty-fourth Ohio Volunteer Infantry in November, same year; his regiment was assigned to duty in Kentucky, and he fought in the battles of Somerset, Ky., Knoxville, Tenn., and in other minor engagements, until June 29, 1863, when he was honorably discharged on account of disability. He then located in Columbus, Ohio, where he recovered, and he again enlisted, this time in the Thirteenth Ohio Volunteer Cavalry, in July, 1864, and joined the

Army of the Potomac, and participated in the battle of Harper's Ferry, the siege of Richmond, and in all battles up to the surrender of Lee; he was in the Third Brigade of the Second Division of Sheridan's Thirteenth Cavalry Corps, and was mustered out at Columbus, Ohio, July 21, 1865. Among his many engagements were the battle of Boyden's Plank Road, Stony Creek, Five Forks, Farmersville and Appomattox; he was wounded in the arm at Dinwiddie Court House on March 31, 1865, by a pistol ball. After the war, he began business as clerk in the wood-yard of Lane & Early, and remained with them six months. He removed to Iroquois County, Ill., and settled on a farm near Onarga, where he engaged in farming until 1869, when he came to Montgomery County, Ill., and lived at Butler and at Hillsboro, working at various employments until 1873, when he located in Litchfield and learned the plasterer's trade, working one year with G. W. Jackson and two years with John K. Milnor. Completing his trade, he worked as partner of Mr. Milnor two years; since that, he has been a contractor for himself, working from two to three other men, with good success. In 1873, Mr. Butts married Miss Jennie Allen, of Litchfield.

WILLIAM E. BACON, real estate agent, Litchfield, was born in March, 1821, in Onondaga County, N. Y., where he lived until he was thirteen years of age, when he spent two years in Michigan, at a branch school of Michigan University, of Monroe, going thence to New York State again, where he acted as clerk in Cazenovia for a time, and then went into mercantile business at Fabius, in his native county, as the partner of Elisha C. Lichfield, a relative of his, who was a Director of the Michigan Southern Railroad, and through him obtained the position of Paymaster on the railroad, which he held five years, after which he became Chief Clerk in the Superintendent's office, under General Superintendent Samuel Brown. In 1856, he resigned, in order to come here, where he learned the shops of the Terre Haute, Alton & St. Louis Railroad were to be located, his informant being Mr. Litchfield, who was one of the originators and builders of the road, and the man for whom the city was named. Mr. Bacon came to Litchfield in October, 1856, and established the first lumber-yard and planing mills, conducting a prosperous business two years. Selling out, he became the real estate agent for Mr. Litchfield, disposing of property at this point, at Gillespie and at Pana; he also prepared the first abstract of titles for this city. In 1872, he became Secretary of the Litchfield Car Manufacturing Company, which position he retained until August, 1880, when he devoted his entire attention to real estate. Mr. Bacon is a practical surveyor; he has taken an active interest in the affairs of the city since its organization, having been its first Mayor, and re-elected to that position, since which time he has served as Alderman. The father of our subject was a native of Vermont, and a distinguished physician and surgeon, who died in New York. William E. Bacon is the youngest son.

JOHN CALDWELL, farmer, P. O. Litchfield, was born in County Derry, Ireland, on March 16, 1837, and came to the United States with his parents in the following year; they settled on a farm near Staunton, Macoupin Co., Ill. Our subject was raised on a farm, and in his boyhood attended a few terms of subscription school in the schoolhouses of the primitive sort. Until 1868, he worked the old homestead of his father, and then came to Litchfield, where he purchased twenty six acres of land, on which he built a substantial brick building; his purchase lies in the northeastern corner of the city limits, in Burr's Addition; in addition to this property, he owns and operates several other tracts of [illegible] lands in the vicinity. He married Miss Amelia S. Aughinbaugh in 1861; they have had six children, all of whom died when quite young. Mr. Caldwell is a Presbyterian. The father of our subject, Mr. Hugh Caldwell, was born in Ireland in 1805, and came to the United States in 1838, farming in Macoupin County, Ill., until the close of the war. From 1866 to 1882 he served as Postmaster at Staunton, Ill. During the war, he was Deputy Provost Marshal.

[illegible] J. CHARLES, Superintendent of Schools, Litchfield, was born in San Francisco, Cal., May 9, 1855, and, when [illegible] years [illegible] came to Litchfield, where, in the public schools, he prepared for college; in 18[illegible]3, he entered Westminster College at Fulton, M[illegible], and took a three years' elective course. In 1876, he began teaching in the public schools of this county, continuing two years, when he became teacher of the high school department of the Litchfield schools, holding that position one year, at the expiration of which time he was elected Superintendent of the Schools, which position he still retains. The city schools include twelve departments and over 825 pupils.

WILLIAM CAMPBELL, Postmaster, Litchfield, was born March 17, 1843, in the county of Monaghan, Ireland, his parents being Scotch Protestants. He was but four years old when he came to the United States with his widowed mother and her six other children. She resided seven years in New York City, where she acted as dressmaker and forewoman of a large manufacturing establishment; she died in 186[illegible] [illegible] 185[illegible]. Mr. Campbell came to Illinois, being then thirteen years old; he made his home with Philo Judson, of Evanston, the S[illegible] [illegible] one year. In 1857, he went to Carlinville, where he engaged his services as clerk [illegible] G. W. Woods; he continued a year, [illegible] removed to Franklin, Morgan Co., Ill., where he lived three years with Abram C. Woods, and clerked in the store two years of that period, the remainder of the time working on the farm. In July, 1862, he enlisted in the One Hundred and First Illinois Infantry, Company H, for three years, and served his entire time; his regiment was assigned to the Army of the Mississippi, and, during 1863, the company to which he belonged was assigned to marine duty on the gunboat La Fayette, which ran the blockade at [illegible] of Vicksburg and silenced the [illegible] Grand Gulf; late in 1863, they were transferred to the Army of the Cumberland, and their battles were the midnight [illegible] Lookout Valley, Missionary Ridge, Lookout Mountain and Sherman's march to the [illegible] the first battle at Resaca, Ga., Mr. Campbell was wounded in the neck by a Minie [illegible], on May 14, 1864; passing beneath the jugular vein, it lodged in the tissues of the [illegible] and was removed on the following day; [illegible] sent to Jeffersonville, Ind., where the [illegible] which had been badly neglected, [illegible] rapidly that in June he went on d[illegible] hospital nurse. He left the hosp[illegible] from choice, and, on July 10, st[illegible] to join his regiment, which he did [illegible] and, two days later, engaged in th[illegible] Peach Tree Creek, where he was wounded twice early in the fight by some [illegible] which struck his ankle, crushi[illegible] bone, and produced a flesh wound [illegible] [illegible] ing out; he was consequently [illegible] and lay in the hospital until July 18[illegible] he was discharged. He returned to [illegible]ville and entered school for the winter [illegible] the spring of 1866, he became a clerk [illegible] old employer, G. W. Woods, at C[illegible]

Ill., where he remained until March, 1873, when he came to Litchfield and took charge of the ticket and express office of the Indianapolis & St. Louis Railroad, under Mr. Keeler, continuing three and a half years; he then entered the employ of the Litchfield Car Company as assistant book keeper, holding that position a year, when, learning that none of the applicants for the post office were successful in receiving appointment to the same, he made application for it, and, fifteen days later, was appointed by President Hayes, his term beginning on June 15, 1877; in January, 1882, he was re-appointed for four years, after a severe contest for the position. In 1869, he married Miss Sarah J. Orcutt, of Carlinville; they have had four children - Lelia Rose, Essie Orcutt, Lucy and Grace. Mr. Campbell is an efficient and obliging Postmaster and an estimable citizen.

F. W. CROUCH, druggist, Litchfield, came to Litchfield in March, 1881, and formed a partnership with Dr. J. B. Adelsberger, and, under the firm name of Adelsberger & Crouch, bought the drug store of J. W. Steen, and they have since conducted a prosperous business on State street. In June, 1881, they opened a branch store at Mt. Olive, and enlarged it, in September of the same year, by purchasing and adding to it the drug house of Flint Bros. He was appointed a member of the School Board in June, 1881. Mr. Crouch was born in Washington County, Tenn., on January 1, 1846, and in 1857 came with his father to Greene County, Ill., where he lived a short time, and, in 1858, moved to Macoupin County, where he received his education during the winter months, and did farm work the remainder of the time, until 1866, when he entered a select school at Scottville, under Prof. J. H. Woodel, continuing three summer terms, and teaching during the winters of the same years; after this, he adopted teaching as a profession, and followed it in the county until 1877, when he was elected by popular majority the Superintendent of Schools for Macoupin County, serving until June 16, 1881, resigning a few months before the expiration of his term, in order to engage in mercantile pursuits. He has been an active member of the County Normal since 1872.

JOHN A. CRABTREE, deceased, born in Kentucky May 9, 1809; the youngest child of John and Mrs. (Harkins) Crabtree. His mother died when he was three years old. When eleven years of age he came to Illinois with his sister, Mrs William Jordan, and her husband. With this sister he lived until his marriage, in 1831, to Ann Griffith, a native of Montgomery County, who bore him twelve children, viz., William (deceased), Margaret (deceased), James (deceased), Nancy, Francis, Job, Phœbe (deceased), John, Louisa, Mary, and Charles and Isaac (twins). He worked at farm labor for others prior to his marriage, after which he entered a tract of land in South Litchfield, on which was a small cabin. During his life, he put about 360 acres of wild prairie land under cultivation, and had acquired in all over seven hundred acres of land by hard work and unceasing industry. He made most of his estate before the war by raising grain and stock for the St. Louis market; he served in the Black Hawk war; donated the land to what is now known as the Crabtree Grave yard. He died March 15, 1874. Although uneducated, Mr. Crabtree had one of the brightest intellects of his county. In business, he was shrewd and successful; in social life, generous and hospitable. He was an adherent of the Democratic party.

JOHN CORLEW was born in Rockcastle County, Ky., in January, 1813, son of Philip and Anna (Kincaid) Corlew, he, a native of

North Carolina, came to Kentucky when a lad; followed farming during his life: he and his wife died a few years previous to the breaking-out of the late war, aged respectively eighty and sixty-eight years; they were the parents of nine children, only four of whom are living, viz.: John, David, W. M. and Jane (now Mrs. Israel Fogleman). The subject of this sketch removed to Missouri with his parents in the spring of 1817, who, after a short sojourn in St. Louis, moved to St. Charles, and remained in Missouri until 1819, when they moved to Madison County, Ill.; here his father took a lease in timber land on Mississippi River bottoms, cleared the place and raised four small crops; in the winter of 1822-23, moved to Montgomery County with his wife and family of seven children, and located in what is now Hillsboro Township on the place now occupied by C. H. Missimore, entering eighty acres on the edge of the timber. John's first teacher was Peter Long, who is still living in Bond County; the school which he attended was about one and a half miles from his home, the schoolhouse being a split log building, 14x14, with stick chimney, puncheon seats and floor, a long crack in the wall covered with greased paper serving the purpose of a window. After attending one term at this school, he went to the Clear Spring Baptist Church School, two miles distant from his home. He enlisted in Capt. Hiram Rountree's company and went out in the campaign of 1832, serving in the Black Hawk war. About the year 1835, he, with his brother Lindsey, who died soon afterward, made his first entry of 160 acres of land where he now resides; he worked on his farm till the opening of the Mexican war, when he enlisted in Company C, Third Illinois Infantry, under Capt. McAdams, and participated in the battles of Vera Cruz and Cerro Gordo; was promoted to the rank of Second Lieutenant, and returned home in 1847 and resumed farming. In 1850, he was elected Sheriff of Montgomery County; served two years, and, after an interim of two years, was re-elected, and again served a two-years' term. He has steadily acquired property until he now owns about two thousand acres in Montgomery County, one-third of which is under cultivation; he has bought and sold largely in real estate. In 1856, he married Mrs. Eliza J. Jett, widow of Wesley Jett; from this union five children were born, still living, viz.: Alice, wife of Douglass Simpson; John Martin, who lives near San Francisco, Cal.; Lucy J., wife of Charles Barry; E. R. and Rosanna, at home. Mr. Corlew is a Democrat; was elected Sheriff by that party; he has held several positions of trust in his township.

JACOB CLEARWATER, physician, Litchfield, was born in December, 1821, in Highland County, Ohio, and, at the age of two years, with his parents, left his native home, and lived successively in several different counties of Indiana until 1831, when they removed to McLean County, Ill., where our subject was raised and educated. At the age of sixteen years, he began reading medicine with Dr. Moran, then of Leroy, but afterward a distinguished physician of Springfield. He finished his medical studies with Dr. Zera Wakefield, of De Witt County, Ill., after which, for a period of four years, he practiced with Dr. James A. Lemon, of De Witt; he located then at Mt. Pleasant, now Farmers' City, De Witt County, and there practiced eight years. In 1854, he came to Macoupin County, and at Clyde and Gillespie practiced his chosen profession until 1861, when he came to Litchfield, at which place he had had patients as early as 1854. Dr. Clearwater has built up a large and lucrative practice, in the eclectic school, in this place; he is a member of the Medical Association of Montgomery County and of the State Medical Association: he has been Treasurer and Vice President of the former.

JOHN D. COLT, physician, Litchfield, was born in 1839, in Mahoning County, Ohio, at Berlin, where he passed his youth and received his early education; he attended an academy at Ellsworth, Ohio, and, at the age of seventeen years, began the study of medicine with Dr. George W. Brooke, of Ellsworth; he subsequently continued his studies with Joseph Wagner, of Deerfield, Portage Co., Ohio, to which place his parents had removed in the meantime. He entered upon a course of study in the Western Reserve College (now the Medical Department of Western Reserve University), and was at the same time under the private direction of Dr. Proctor Thayer until 1861, when he joined the United States Navy as able-bodied seaman, and was assigned to gunboat service; he was on the Ohio River for a time, but was finally transferred to Admiral Porter's command. Soon after entering the navy, he ceased to do sea service, and was employed as Assistant Surgeon, and, after an examination by the Fleet Surgeon in 1862, was transferred to the hospital boat Red River; he acted in this capacity without commission until 1863, when he was taken sick, and, in July, returned home. He attended a second session of the Western Reserve Medical College, and graduated in the spring of 1864, and at once came to Litchfield, where he has since enjoyed an excellent practice. He has a membership in the Montgomery Medical Society, and one also in the State Medical Society.

BARNARD W. COOPER, machinist, Litchfield, is the son of William and Jemima (Kellaud) Cooper, the former of whom was a Sergeant in the Royal Marine Artillery, and died in Barbadoes, West Indies, on January 1, 1862, and was there buried. Barnard W. Cooper was born in Portsmouth, England, on January 27, 1857; he was educated in the Royal Naval School at Greenwich. At the age of fifteen years, he began to learn the machinist's trade, serving two years' apprenticeship. He came to the United States, reaching Litchfield in June, 1874, where he worked at various employments until August, 1875, when he entered the employ of the Litchfield Car Manufacturing Company, and there completed his trade in three years; he has continued in their employ ever since, except for a period of six months, when he engaged his services at Elkhart, Ind., as machinist in the shops of the Lake Shore & Michigan Southern Railroad. On January 1, 1882, he became foreman of the machine shops of the Litchfield Car and Machine Company, a position he still holds; his department has in its employ twenty-two men.

JOSEPH J. DOLLAR, Litchfield, was born in Baden, Germany, in the town of Portsheim, in December, 1853, and came to the United States when eighteen months old, with his parents, who settled in Marion County, Ohio, on a farm, where he lived until 1865, in which year he moved to Terre Haute, Ind., where he began the blacksmith's trade at the age of eighteen years, with Seith & Hagar, car-builders, serving three years' apprenticeship, and continuing with them seven years as journeyman. He spent the next eighteen months in the M., K. & T. R. R. shops at Parsons, Kan.; the following year he spent in farming. He returned to Terre Haute and worked for Seith & Hagar three months, at the expiration of which period he came to Litchfield, Ill., and worked in the forge department of the car and machine shops about eighteen months. In the fall of 1880, he was made foreman of the blacksmith department, of which he has had charge ever since; in busy seasons, it employs thirty-five hands. In 1870, at Terre Haute, Ind., he married Miss Susannah M. Garner, who died on August 9, 1871, leaving one daughter. In the fall of 1872, he married Miss Martha J. Mulligan, of Terre Haute; of this marriage, there are three children.

DAVID DAVIS, grocer and banker, Litchfield. David Davis, deceased, the father of our subject, was born in 1785, of Welsh parentage, near Genoa, Italy, and, at the age of fourteen years, came to the United States. In New York City he learned the baker's trade, and from that city moved to St. Louis, Mo., when it was but a French village; he was in the regular army five years; he participated in the war of 1812, and was wounded in the battle of Queenstown, with a saber, which enabled the enemy to take him prisoner, which they did, carrying him on flat boats to Boston, Mass., where he was confined and compelled to endure many privations. He lived in St. Louis, Mo., until about 1840, when he removed to Madison County, Ill., where he engaged in farming sixteen years or thereabout, coming to Litchfield in 1856. After coming to Litchfield, he was the business partner of his son, the subject of this sketch, until 1872, in which year he died, in his eighty-seventh year, having lived a life of honor. David Davis was born in Madison County, Ill., in December, 1838; he received his education in his native county, and, at the age of sixteen years, came with his parents to Litchfield, Ill., where, until 1858, he successively engaged his services as clerk and book keeper in several business houses of the city. In September, 1858, he engaged in the grocery trade, being one of the first grocers of Litchfield; he opened his line of groceries in the building now occupied by Mr. Hoog as a sack depot. In 1871, Mr. Davis erected his present building, on the same block, but located on the corner of State and Edward streets, where he has since conducted a flourishing wholesale and retail business. In 1870, he became a stockholder in the Litchfield Bank, and, the following year, was elected its President. Shortly after this election, they re-organized the bank as a private bank, under the firm name of Beach, Davis & Co.; of the new departure Mr. Davis is one of the managing partners. That he is an estimable citizen is evident from the fact that he has been three times elected Mayor of Litchfield, the elections being made by the Independents; he served in 1875, 1876 and 1879; in 1866 and 1867, he was elected Alderman. December 23, 1868, he married Miss Blanche Keating, of Rockbridge, Greene Co., Ill., and has four living children, two being deceased.

WILLIAM G. DAVIS, liveryman, Litchfield, was born near Meadville, Crawford Co., Penn., in 1842, and, until he was ten years old, was raised on a farm; his parents then removed to Hartstown, Penn., and he attended an academy there, finally becoming a teacher in the same school. In the summer of 1860, he came to Litchfield, Ill., where he engaged in the sale of lime and plasterers' and bricklayers' furnishings for a period of three years, during which time, in the winters, he taught three terms. He next engaged in the fancy groceries and restaurant business, with good success, for about four years. He was six months in the army, serving half the time in the Seventh Illinois Volunteer Infantry, under Capt. Munn, and the remainder of the time in the Eighty-fourth Ohio Regiment. In the fall of 1872, he engaged in the livery business, and has since continued, enlarging his trade from year to year. In 1881, he built a large brick addition to his original business house, and this consisted of two stories, with an elevator; the present dimensions are 115x132 feet, covering almost two lots. Mr. Davis does a large livery, feed and sale business, having on hand a full line of vehicles, and a stable furnishing capacity for from seventy-five to one hundred horses. In 1875, he married Miss Susan Aughinbaugh, of Hillsboro.

WILLIAM T. ELLIOTT, deceased, a native of Franklin County, Ky., was left an orphan at an early age. In his twelfth year, becoming justly dissatisfied with his treatment and condition in his uncle's household, he, in 1838, was informally adopted by R. W. O'Bannon; for thirteen years he was a member of his estimable family; with no ties of blood to bind the lad to his foster parent, they were, in esteem and affection, as father and son; he shared Mr. O'Bannon's fortunes, removing successively to Missouri and Madison County in this State. In 1849, he married Miss Adeline Swett, of that county, and, forming a brief partnership with a blacksmith at Ridgely, he wrought for several months at wagon making. Turning from this, he began mercantile life with his foster parent; successful in this line, he, in May, 1854, removed his family to Litchfield, which then consisted of his store and dwelling, and one other dwelling, not occupied. He was by three days the pioneer settler, James W. Jefferis being the second householder. With Mr. O'Bannon as a partner, he opened the store of W. T. Elliott on the corner now covered by the banking house of Beach, Davis & Co. April 24, 1854; the name of the firm was twice changed in the ensuing twelve years, and fortune smiled on his venture. In 1866, he retired from commercial life, and, in connection with P. B. Updike, engaged in the sale of agricultural implements. He took the tide at its flood, and it bore him to wealth. The little house on "cheap corner" was exchanged for a commodious home a quarter of a mile north, on State street. No reverses swept across his path. His eye was not yet dim, nor his natural force abated. But pulmonary disease appeared, and, after a few months of hoping against hope, and dissolving his partnership with Mr. Updike, he died, March 24, 1868, to the profound regret and grief of the city. Mr. Elliott was a charter member of the Charter Oak Lodge of Masons, and an Odd Fellow; for several terms he presided over the lodges of both fraternities; in graceful recognition of his zeal and efficiency in works meet for a true and accomplished brother of the mystic tie, the chapter bears his name. He greatly aided in the erection of a new church for the Christian society. He was equally estimable in what he did and for what he was. He was of medium stature, spare, but sinewy, he was of courteous bearing, diligent in business, upright in his dealings, discreet in speech, without concealments or the need of them, and true to his party, which was a bar to no personal friendships, and never limited his readiness to assist others. Leading a spotless life, losing no friend and making no enemy in the dolorous years when a difference of opinion meant hatred and all uncharitableness, he blushed only at his own praises. Three of his six children still survive. William Lewis, his eldest son, at twenty-two a Knight Templar, and the youngest one in this section, died in 1876, in his twenty-sixth year; his second daughter, Lillie, "went home" the following year; one died in infancy Minnie.

ISRAEL FOGLEMAN, deceased. Melchoir Fogleman was born in Cabarrus County, N. C., in 1779, and was educated in both English and German, afterward learning the trade of blacksmith. March 4, 1811, he was married to Elizabeth Meisenheimer, and, on the 17th day of June, 1812, a son was born to them, he being our subject, Israel Fogleman, who was baptized March 4, 1813. In the autumn of 1813, Melchoir and family set out for the West, first landing in Indiana, but, not being satisfied with the country, removed to Illinois, reaching the vicinity of what is now Walshville on the 6th of June, 1818, and for several months, the family, consisting of father, mother, the son and two daughters, subsisted chiefly on venison and honey, of which there was an abundance; Melchoir afterward (about 1820) removed to the West Fork, where he lived till 1824, then he moved to the Clear Spring Branch and built the grist mill known as the old "Pepper Mill." They had two sons and one daughter born in Montgomery County, in addition to the children born before arriving there. Melchoir died February 10, 1827, and his widow remained at the mill. In 1832, Israel bought out James Parrish, and commenced improving a farm near where Litchfield now is, building a house and removing his mother and the children into it in 1841. He enlisted in the Black Hawk war in 1832, being Sergeant in Capt. Boone's company. Receiving a land warrant for services in the war, he entered another eighty acres, to which he added until he had 350 acres of land. In November, 1838, he married Miss Jane, daughter of Philip and Anna (Kincaid) Corlew, who was born January 27, 1821. Mr. Fogleman had borne all the vicissitudes of pioneer life, and was a man highly respected and trusted. It is said that he acted more frequently as administrator and executor of estates and guardian for minors than any other man in the county; he served as Commissioner, Justice of the Peace and School Treasurer; was a Democrat, and cast his first Presidential vote for "Old Hickory." He died June 17, 1876. He was the father of fourteen children, but six of whom are now living; of those dead, two died in infancy and three grew to maturity; those living are Amanda E, wife of William R. Blackwelder; John W., merchant in Miller County, Mo.; Sarah L., wife of W. Frank Rainey, of Montgomery County; Alida M., Joel M. and William D. are at home.

JOEL M. FOGLEMAN was born April 7, 1826; is a son of Melchoir and Elizabeth (Meisenheimer) Fogleman. He lived with his mother near the old mill till he was fifteen years of age, and attended school in the old Clear Springs Baptist Church. In 1841, his mother, with her family, moved to what is now North Litchfield, and settled near her eldest son, Israel Fogleman. Joel M. worked and improved his present place—a quarter of School Section 16, which had been purchased for him about the year 1843, till 1846, when he enlisted in Company C, Third Illinois Infantry, under Col. Forman and Gen. Shields, and served in the Mexican war from June to November, but was taken sick and sent home from Matamoras, Mexico. He married, December 30, 1847, Nancy Jane Crabtree, born in Edwards County, Ill., daughter of John Crabtree, a native of Kentucky and an old Revolutionary soldier, who died about 1837, and who had twenty-two children, Mrs. Fogleman being the twentieth child. Mr. and Mrs. Fogleman are the parents of seven children, of whom two daughters died; those living are Henrietta, now Mrs. David A Blackwelder; Eliza, now Mrs. Charles Rose, of Montgomery County; John F.; Lizzie, now Mrs. Milton C. Ash; and William J. Mr. Fogleman moved to his present place in 1848, having built a frame house, which is still standing, at the rear of his present residence; he has ever since remained on the same place, which is all under cultivation. His mother, who was born February 4, 1788, died April 27, 1850; her children are Israel, born June 17, 1812; Sarah, now Mrs. Dillard

Duff; Catharine, now Mrs. George Forehand; John, living in South Litchfield; Peter, died in infancy; Mary A., died in 1857; and Joel M., our subject. Mr. Fogleman is a Democrat; he and his wife are members of the United Baptist Church.

JOHN FOGLEMAN, son of Melchoir and Elizabeth (Meisenheimer) Fogleman, was born in Montgomery County, Ill., one mile east of where Walshville now stands, on Easter Sunday, April 11, 1819, and was the first white child born in Walshville Township, and is now perhaps the oldest native resident of Montgomery County. Melchoir Fogleman, the father of our subject, started a mill where the "Pepper Mill" now stands, in 1824, the wheel of which was overshot, the water being brought from one-half to three-quarters of a mile, in oak troughs placed on the hillside, connected with springs of water; the mill, which had a capacity of 100 bushels in twenty-four hours in flood time, did a good business, drawing the patronage of all the early settlement; the buhrs were of native stone, taken from the prairie. Melchoir Fogleman died in 1827; his widow held the mill until 1843, when she sold it to John Kirkpatrick. Our subject attended school principally at Clear Springs Church; his last school term (in 1835); he attended the school a mile west of Hillsboro, taught by J. Grantham, now a sub-clerk in the United States Treasury at Washington, D. C. In his early days, John worked in his father's mill, and was familiar with all the heads of the families in the county at that time. In 1840, he bought eighty acres of land of John Corlew, forty prairie land and forty acres in timber, and April 23 of that year moved into a small cabin on the border of the prairie, and the first year tilled six acres, which he had cleared in the timber, but his crop was nearly all taken by squirrels and raccoons, which infested the woods; he soon added twenty acres to his original purchase, and, from 1866, steadily increased his property, till he is now the owner of 300 acres in this township and 200 acres elsewhere. He married, April 19, 1840, Elizabeth Kirkland, daughter of Robert and Jane (Long) Kirkland, and from this union ten children have been born, of whom six died in childhood; those living are Daniel M., Israel P., Mary E. U. and Francis M. Mr. Fogleman cast his first vote for Van Buren in 1840, and has since been a stanch supporter of the Democratic party; he invariably filled the office of Clerk for township and county elections; has been Township Trustee or Treasurer for a great many terms, and has acted on county and township committees; he was elected Sheriff of Montgomery County in 1860, and served one term.

FRANCIS MARION FOGLEMAN, farmer, P. O. Litchfield, was born on the place of his father, John Fogleman, on July 15, 1858. He was raised a farmer, and still follows that occupation with his father, on whose place he has resided since his marriage, on March 2, 1881, to Miss Nancy E. Z., daughter of David Corlew. He is a young man of enterprise and industry.

WILLIAM H. FISHER was born in Middlesex County, N. J., October 15, 1829, where he lived until six years old, when his parents moved to Ohio, residing at Mt. Vernon for eight years. In 1845, his parents came to Illinois and settled on a farm in Jersey County, where William H. lived ten years. In 1856, he married Elizabeth Ivens, of Dayton, Ohio, and, the same year, bought forty acres of land three miles from Litchfield, adjoining the county line of Macoupin County, and in ten years he acquired 480 acres of valuable land, which he sold in 1865, and moved to Litchfield, and, a short time thereafter bought 160 a[illegible]s within the corporate limits of the town wh[illegible] he has since lived and been engaged in farming near the city, possessing about four hundred acres, the larger portion of which is [illegible] Montgomery County. The father of our s[illegible]ct, William B. Fisher, was a native of N[illegible] Jersey, and a farmer in that State, but k[illegible]ing a hotel after moving to Ohio. After m[illegible]ing to Illinois in 1845, Mr. Fisher, Sr., r[illegible]ed farming, which he continued until [illegible] death, some ten years later; he was the [illegible] of ten children, nine of whom are liv[illegible], William H., our subject, being the sec[illegible]; the mother is still living, aged sev[illegible]ty-seven years. Our subject has three c[illegible]dren; is a member of the Baptist Church.

HENRY K. GARDNER was born in Will[illegible] County, Tenn., November 24, 1807; w[illegible] reared on a farm in Maury County, Tenn., [illegible] worked in a distillery during the winter. H[illegible]me to Illinois in 1833, stayed one year [illegible] Mulberry Grove, Bond County, then [illegible] to the eastern part of Montgomery C[illegible], where he entered eighty acres of land, [illegible] which he worked five years, and improved the greater portion of the farm; he then re[illegible] to Fayette County, where he worked a f[illegible] for sixteen years, then, in 1855, bought h[illegible] present place of 120 acres of prairie land, which at that time had a small patch of ground broken, and on which stood a small ca[illegible]. Since he came to Montgomery County, M[illegible] Gardner has been chiefly engaged in f[illegible]ng, but has also worked at the brick and s[illegible] mason's trade, which he learned from [illegible] father, though he never served any regu[illegible] apprenticeship. In Tennessee, in October, 1[illegible], he married Winnefred Wollard, born O[illegible] 1, 1807, who bore him three sons and t[illegible] daughters (all living), and died in Fay[illegible] County in April, 1854. October 12, 1[illegible], he married his second wife, Mrs. A[illegible]nda Jane Jones, widow of Lewis Charlton Jones and daughter of Alexander McWilliams, one of the pioneers of Montgomery County; she was born in that county April 29, 1826; from this second marriage two children have been born—one son and one daughter, both living; Mrs. Gardner had four children (all living) by her first husband, Mr. Jones. Mr. Gardner has had fair success as a farmer, and is now owner of 254 acres of land, though he began without capital; he has always been a Democrat; has been a member of the Old-School Baptist Church for about forty years.

FRANK H. GILMORE, Master in Chancery, Litchfield, was born in Greenville, Bond Co., Ill., on January 3, 1833. Here he passed his early youth, except a few years spent in Northern Illinois. His father, James Gilmore, died when he was twelve years old, and, two years later, he entered the printing office of the *Protestant Monitor*, which was the first paper of Greenville, and finished his trade in the office of its successor. In 1851, he came to Hillsboro, Ill., and there started the *Prairie Mirror*, of which Dr. Francis Springer was editor; he conducted that and other papers as publisher at the same place until 1862, excepting two years. In August, 1862, he enlisted in Company B of the One Hundred and Seventeenth Illinois Volunteer Infantry, and served until the close of the war; at the organization of the company, he was elected Second Lieutenant, and came home its Captain. At Memphis, Tenn., our subject was detached, and was a depot ordnance officer for the Army of Tennessee from Chattanooga to Atlanta; he joined his company, and, just after the battle of Nashville, led his command in the battles attending the capture of Mobile, Ala., and in other engagements, till the close of the war. He returned home, and, in 1866, was elected Sheriff and Collector of Montgomery County, serving one term—at that time the full limit; after those two years, he engaged in the real estate business with John D. Maddux, at Hillsboro, continuing until 1874, when he came to Litchfield and engaged in the purchase and shipment of grain, the firm name being Ballweg & Gilmore; he continued at that but one and a half years. In November, 1880, he was appointed, by Judge Zane, Master in Chancery of this county; he is also Director and Secretary of the Litchfield Oil and Pipe Line Company, and has been since its organization. November 16, 1858, he married Mary S., daughter of Col. Robert Blackwell, of Vandalia, Ill.; they have had the following children: Angelina E., James R. and Frank P. (both deceased), Henry E., May V., Sarah E. (deceased) and Mary E. A. He was raised a Whig, but voted for Stephen A. Douglas, since which time he has acted with the Democratic party, being conservative in his views. His father was a native of East Tennessee, and his mother of Virginia; they emigrated here from Hardin County, Ky., about 1828, and settled in Greenville; his father was a carpenter and builder, and died June 13, 1844; his Grandfather Gilmore was for many years Probate Judge of Bond County.

CAPT. EPHRAIM M. GILMORE, retired, Litchfield, was born in Christian, now Todd County Ky., January 15, 1811. Seven years later, he was brought by his parents to Bond County, Ill., who settled within four miles of Greenville, where he grew up and learned the elements of an English education. There he married, January 19, 1832, Miss Mary W. Harris, a native of Tennessee, after which he moved to Greene County, Ill., where he farmed until 1861, in October of which year he raised a company of cavalry, and, by permit of Gov. Yates, it was attached to Col. Logan's Thirty-second Illinois Volunteer Infantry, and went into Camp Butler for the winter, and in December, it was detached from the Thirty-second; in February, 1862, it was ordered to Quincy, and, in the last days of February, it was Company F, in the Twelfth Illinois Cavalry, and ordered back to Camp Butler until July, 1862, when they were ordered to Martinsburg, Va.; there Capt. Gilmore was forced to resign because of poor health. In April, 1832, he was out forty-seven and one-half days in the Black Hawk war. In December, 1862, he came to Litchfield, and has resided here ever since. For some years, he engaged in the grocery business, but is now passing his time in retirement. He has always been a Democrat; in 1868, he was elected to the Legislature in Montgomery County by the Democratic party, he became a member of the State Board of Equalization in 1876, and served four years; he was also a member of the Land Committee. In 1866, he was elected Mayor of Litchfield, and is now Assessor of North Litchfield Township. Capt. Gilmore has had the following children: Lucinda Isabella, John H., Harvey M., Harriet Elvira, Rachel Eleanor, William Persis, James Polk, Louis Barr, Nancy Mitter, Mary Murphy. He lived in Bond County till 1834, when he moved to Macoupin County, and lived there until the spring of 1852, when he moved to Greenfield, Ill., where he was a merchant and farmer for ten years. His father, John Gilmore, was appointed Justice of the Peace by the first Legislature of Illinois, at Vandalia, and held that office for many years; for [illegible] years he held the office of Probate Judge of Bond County.

SAMUEL M. GRUBBS, banker, Litchfield, was born in Hillsboro, Montgomery Co., Ill., in 1835, where he was educated in the public schools. At the age of twenty-two, he engaged in general merchandising in the town of his birth, and continued with fair success until the close of the war, when he sold his stock and came to Litchfield, where, in partnership with R. H. Peall, he engaged in mercantile pursuits, they having bought the business of J. W. Jefferis; the firm afterward became Jefferis & Grubbs. Our subject sold to Mr. Jefferis in 1868, and became a partner in the private banking house of Brewer, Seymour & Co., which became the firm of Brewer & Grubbs in 1880. Since January, 1869, Mr. Grubbs has given exclusive attention to banking. In 1857, he married Miss Mary, daughter of William Brewer, whose sketch appears elsewhere. In 1874, Mr. Grubbs, by an independent ticket, was elected Mayor of Litchfield; prior to this, he was City Treasurer. He is a Steward and Trustee of the Methodist Episcopal Church. The father of our subject was Moody Grubbs, a native of Virginia, who moved to Todd County, Ky., when a young man. He married Miss Cynthia Boone, of Bowling Green, Ky.; she was a great-niece of Daniel Boone. Moody Grubbs came to Hillsboro, Ill., in about 1833, and died four years later; he was a brick-mason by trade; his wife still survives, in her eighty-eighth year.

S. H. GEROW, D. D. S., Litchfield, was born in St. John, New Brunswick, in 1850, and there was educated in the grammar schools. In October, 1879, he entered the Dental Department of the University of Michigan at Ann Arbor, from which he graduated in March, 1881, with the degree of D. D. S. In July, 1881, he came to Litchfield to locate for the practice of his profession, and has since been actively engaged, having pleasant dental rooms on State street, where he performs both mechanical and operative dentistry. Although he has been here but a short time, he has been very successful in the practice of his profession.

CONSTANTINE HOOG, dealer in boots and shoes, Litchfield, was born in Baden, Germany in 1825. At the age of nineteen, he began learning the shoemaker's trade, and completed it in two years. In 1850, he came to the United States with his parents, and in that and the year following, worked as journeyman in Alton, Ill., where he opened a shop of his own and carried on his business until 1856. In that place, he married Miss Charlotte Niemann in 1854. In April, 1856, he came to Litchfield, and lived in a small shanty just east of the dwelling now owned and occupied by William Wiegreffe; here he put out a sign and made shoes during the summer; then he bought the site of his present home, it being Lot 3 in Block 29, and occupied a little frame building which stood on it until 1859, in the fall of which year he built the present two-story brick residence, moving into it the same year. He conducted a shop for the manufacture of custom work from 1856 to 1873, when he began selling Eastern work. Two years later, he sold his store, and, for three years, ran a hide house and sack depot. In 1878, he re-opened his present shoe store, and has since conducted a good business in boots and shoes. He was the second shoemaker of Litchfield, and, from his humble beginnings, he has steadily gained a prominent place among the business men of this city. He has always been a Democrat, and was Alderman from the Second Ward in 1869. Mr. Hoog's wife died in 1874. He has one son and four daughters living.

VALENTINE HOFFMAN, merchant, Litchfield, was born in Bavaria on May 14, 1833, and came to the United States in 1842 with his parents, who settled in Columbus, Ohio, shortly after removing to a farm near Reynoldsburg, Franklin Co., Ohio, where our subject grew up and received an English education in the public schools. At the age of sixteen, he learned the trade of iron molding at Gill's Foundry, at Columbus, serving five years as apprentice and journeyman; he then traveled two years as journeyman, working in St. Louis and Indianapolis. In 1856, he came to Macoupin County Ill., where he married Miss Martha Turner January 15, 1857, and, the following year, came to Montgomery County, Ill.; here he entered the employ of H. H. Beach & Co., as molder, and continued until the war broke out. He first enlisted for three months in the Seventh Illinois Regiment, and served his time out. He then returned to his old place with H. H. Beach & Co., and remained until September, 1862, when he again enlisted, this time in the Ninety-first Illinois Regiment, as private soldier; he was mustered in as Orderly Sergeant, and his first engagement was at Elizabethtown, Ky., where he and the entire command were taken prisoners. During his confinement, he was made Second Lieutenant at Benton Barracks; he was retained a prisoner from January 1, 1863, to June 3, 1863, and was then exchanged, when he joined the Thirteenth Army Corps in their first engagement at Morganza, La. He went into quarters at Carrollton, above New Orleans, and, in December, 1863, he went with Banks' expedition across the Gulf to Texas, where, for seven months, he experienced continual skirmishing. In March, 1865, he left Texas, and took part in the capture of Mobile, Fort Blakely and Spanish Fort. At Fort Blakely, Capt Hoffman was wounded in the wrist by a Minie ball while on the skirmish line, March 26, 1865. In 1864, he was promoted to Captain of Company A, Ninety-first Illinois Regiment. After his wound, he was sent home on leave of absence, and was honorably discharged, being mustered out at Camp Butler, Ill., in September, 1865. The following year, he engaged in mercantile pursuits at Litchfield, at first having bu[illegible] small stock; he has won success by his i[illegible]dustry and perseverance, and for nine [illegible] has been located on Jefferson stre[illegible] he has built up a large trade in gr[illegible] queensware, boots, shoes, etc.; h[illegible] four persons in his store. He cast his [illegible] vote for Fremont, and has always been [illegible]publican. He has ever taken an active in[illegible]est in city affairs and all matters of [illegible] interest. He served one term in [illegible] Council. Mr. Hoffman, true to his [illegible] birth, is fond of music, and creates i[illegible]ious musical instruments.

MRS. MARTHA HOFFMAN, Lit[illegible] daughter of James and Catharine [illegible] Turner, was born in Westmoreland C[illegible] Penn.; she received a common school [illegible]cation in Ohio, to which Stat[illegible] her [illegible] moved, settling in Licking County, when [illegible] was eleven years old; after living in O[illegible] about seven years, they moved to Ma[illegible] County, Ill., where her father engage[illegible] farming; he now resides in Litchfield, [illegible] in his eightieth year; her mother di[illegible]teen years ago. Our subject married C[illegible] V. Hoffman in Macoupin County; [illegible] marriage, six children have been b[illegible] three of whom are living, the others having died in infancy; those living are, namely, Ella Nora, the oldest daughter, who was born in Litchfield on February 1, 1861, [illegible] received her education in the public sch[illegible] of this city, in addition to a fine musical [illegible]cation; on May 3, 1882, in Litchfield, she married George Andrew Beeler, of Hamil[illegible] Ohio; the second daughter, Ida, was b[illegible] September 15, 1872; and the third living child, a son, Walter R., was born Mar[illegible] 1876. Mrs. Hoffman is one of a famil[illegible] nine children, five of whom are deceased.

JOHN C. HUGHES, deceased. The [illegible]

of our subject, Thomas C. Hughes, was born in Knox County, Tenn., in about 1804. He was raised on a farm, and was married, in his native county, to Miss Mary Godsey. In 1828, he came with his family to this county and first settled in the Gray neighborhood, afterward moving to the place now owned by John Cover; he moved thence to the Crawford neighborhood, and thence to where Martin A. Ritchie now lives; here he lived several years, and each one of the previous places he improved and sold at an advance. After leaving the Ritchie place, he moved to the head of Shoal Creek; thence to Litchfield, where he traded largely in town property, at the time of the building up of the city; here he lived until after the war, when he moved to Section 22. In all, he owned about four hundred and sixty acres of land, and was remarkably successful in almost every undertaking. Mr. Hughes was Justice of the Peace in North Litchfield Township four years; he was a member of the Methodist Church for many years. He was the father of four sons and three daughters, all of whom are living except John C. Hughes, his oldest son, whose sketch appears in another paragraph. Thomas C. Hughes died November 14, 1871, and his wife in 1866. John C. Hughes was born in Knox County, Tenn., on December 17, 1823, and came to Montgomery County, Ill., with his parents when in his sixth year; he was fortunate in obtaining a common-school education superior to that of most farmer boys, and was the school-mate of Gen. Jesse Phillips. He was ingenious with tools, and picked up the carpenter's trade, building several barns and houses in the country when not engaged in farm labor. On November 26, 1846, he married Miss Susan E. Roberts, daughter of Josiah and Susan (Hart) Roberts. He bought a Mexican land warrant about three years after he had settled here, on vacant land, and by it became the owner of 160 acres in 1849. He engaged in farming here until 1852, when he went by ox team from St. Joseph, Mo., to California, the journey continuing over one hundred days. After spending about eighteen months in the mines, he returned by the Panama route in 1854, and lived on his farm until his death, on November 17, 1879. At the time of his demise, he owned 200 acres of land, all of which was acquired by his own labor; he was a hard-working, shrewd and enterprising farmer. He had five sons and one daughter, one son died at the age of six weeks; his children are William H., born June 23, 1849, a stock dealer in Colorado; Hiram J., born February 27, 1855; John C., Jr., born June 23, 1857; Mary J., born October 15, 1862, the wife of John Gundy, of this county; and George B., born April 19, 1864. Three sons are still living at the homestead.

ESQUIRE WILLIAM C. HENDERSON, real estate agent, was born in Columbus, Miss., on January 25, 1817. When about ten years old, his parents removed to Illinois, first settling in Clinton County, where they lived on a farm until 1835, in which year they moved to Macoupin County, settling near Gillespie. In 1838, our subject married Miss Martha Caulk and settled near Mt. Olive, Macoupin County, where he farmed twenty years with good success. He came to Litchfield in 1858. In April, 1876, he was elected Justice of the Peace, and since that time has filled the office of magistrate. He is now engaged in the real estate and collecting business. Politically Mr. Henderson is a Democrat, and always has been such. In 1859, he married a second time, the lady being Mary A. Green, of this county; of this marriage there are no children, but of his first there are six living.

H. H. HOOD, Litchfield, was born September 19, 1823, in the city of Philadelphia; his father was Lambert Hood, born near Camden, N. J., April 16, 1792, and died July 27, 1850; the mother of our subject was Sarah (Hughes) Hood, who was born in Wales January 25, 1793, and died July 20, 1844. Mr. H. H. Hood was married, first in Jerseyville, Ill., June 11, 1855, to Matilda W. Jackson, born in Philadelphia August 23, 1829, daughter of Charles S. Jackson, of Philadelphia. His second marriage was at Taylorville, Ill., July 7, 1869, to Abigail E. Torrey, born September 10, 1833, daughter of Joseph Torrey, of Woodstock, Conn. The following children have been born to Mr. Hood: Charles L., who died in infancy; George P., Sarah Frances, Annie H., Oliver, Harold H. and Abigail Louise.

WILLIAM W. HEWITT, Superintendent of Planet Mills, Litchfield, was born in Shropshire, England, in April, 1849, and was brought to the United States in the fall of 1851 by his parents, who settled in Terre Haute, Ind., and there raised and educated him. He was successively book-keeper and manager of a yard and freight department of the Vandalia Railroad at Terre Haute from 1869 to 1875; since 1875, he has been in the lumber, grain and milling business, first with McKeen Bros., of Terre Haute, with whom he continued until October, 1881, when he entered the employ of D. L. Wing & Co. as Superintendent of the Planet Mills, which were erected in Litchfield in 1881.

JOSEPH E. HICKMAN, Honey Bend, was born in Crittenden County, Ky., June 1, 1851, son of William B. and Eliza A. (Witherspoon) Hickman, who were the parents of eight children, all living. William B. removed from Kentucky in 1851 and settled on a farm near Hillsboro, Ill., where he died in March, 1857; his wife removed to Butler, Ill., with her family, and died November 9, 1869. Joseph E. received his education in Hillsboro and in Butler, and left school at the age of sixteen and entered the store of Hedge & Bro. as clerk, and remained with them and their successors, McGowan & Watkins, for seven years. He spent the year 1872 in Nebraska, then returned to Butler and worked on the farm one year, and from that time until 1878 he ran a steam threshing machine during the summer season, and taught school in winter. In January, 1878, he came to Honey Bend, which at that time consisted of a post office and blacksmith shop, with no railway facilities except a side-track for passing trains; there were but two houses in the town; he was appointed station agent and Postmaster in March, 1878, which positions he has since held, in addition to which he is now agent of the Pacific Express Company; he also engaged in mercantile business with his brother, under the firm name of Hickman Bros.; they do a fine trade; besides general merchandise, they also deal in coal and lumber. Mr. Hickman married, January 20, 1881, Ida L. Hart, born in St. Clair County, Ill., December 20, 1861, daughter of Joseph and Mary (Hilt) Hart; they have one child, Ida May.

JAMES B. HUTCHISON was born in Trigg County, Ky., November 8, 1830, and received his education in Cumberland College, at Princeton, Caldwell Co., Ky. He came to Montgomery County in August, 1848, having preceded his parents, who followed in November; they bought land in Bond County, where they died. Our subject taught school three terms at Walnut Grove, in the southern part of the county, and one term at Lazy Neck. In the spring of 1849, he married Miss Sarah J., daughter of Capt. James Black, an early pioneer; he spent some time in Marshall County about 1852–53, but returned to Montgomery in 1854 and engaged in mercantile business at Donnellson until

1857, during which time he, in conjunction with T. C. Donnell, laid out the town named. Selling out his business, he traveled for some time in the nursery business. In 1865, he purchased seven acres, which he has since increased to twenty-two acres, and follows the nursery and market gardening business; he has about ten thousand apple and fifteen hundred peach trees, in addition to other fruits and shrubs. He has four sons and three daughters living. The father of our subject, Rev. William T. Hutchison, was a minister of the Cumberland Presbyterian Church, and was born in Montgomery County, Tenn., in December, 1799. He traveled in Missouri when it was a Territory. His wife was Miss Mary Clay Davison, a native of Bourbon County, Ky., and by her had ten sons and two daughters, subject being the second son; he died on his farm near Greenville in September, 1868, having preached in this State twenty years; his wife died in 1864.

THE HOOD FAMILY. Of the ten children born to Lambert and Sarah Hood, seven grew to mature years, and the four still surviving live in Litchfield. The family on the father's side were for several generations residents of the city of Philadelphia, where the four surviving children were all born; their mother was Welsh, coming in childhood with her parents to this country. The father was poor, and was able to support his family only by the constant labor of his hands, united with the strictest economy, and aided by his wife and older sons. In 1837, the parents, with four of the children (of whom H. H. and B. S. alone survive), removed to Alton, Ill., and afterward to Otter Creek Prairie, then in Greene, now in Jersey County. Their stay in the West was only for about eighteen months, at the end of which time they returned to Philadelphia. The mother died in 1844, and the father in 1850. Ann Hughes Hood the eldest child, was for twenty years a teacher in the schools of Philadelphia; in 1857, she resigned her position as Principal of one of the secondary schools to accompany her brother (with whom she still lives) to Litchfield; she has been a member of the M. E. Church since her childhood. Joseph Lybrand Hood, second child, was born August 22, 1819. In 1845, he was married to Miss Rebecca Shapley, who died nine years later. Four children were born to them, of whom one died in infancy and two in womanhood; those who attained maturity were Herbert Shapley (still living), Sarah Hughes and Edith Prizer. In 1856, he left Philadelphia, and, with B. S. Hood, engaged in the sale of drugs and books, under the style of Hood & Brother; the successors of this firm, Hood & Son (Joseph L. and Herbert S.), are still in business. He united with the M. E. Church about forty years ago, and has been an active worker in church and Sunday school during most of that time. Humphrey Hughes Hood, the fourth child, was born September 19, 1823. In 1848, after reading with a tutor, he entered Jefferson Medical College, Philadelphia, and was graduated in the spring of 1851. In the following autumn, he removed to Jersey County, Ill., where he had lived a short time during his boyhood. After teaching a winter school and having charge of a drug store in Jerseyville for one year, he removed to Hardinsburg, a village then about two miles southwest of the present site of Litchfield, and engaged in the practice of his profession. Late in the following autumn, Litchfield was laid out, and, in the summer of 1854, he removed his office to the new town. In June, 1855, he was married to Miss Matilda Woodhouse, eldest daughter of Charles S. Jackson, of Jerseyville, who died January 2, 1867; by this union he had five children, of whom three survive, namely

George Perry, Sarah Frances and Annie Hughes. In September, 1862, he entered the army, with the appointment of Assistant Surgeon of the One Hundred and Seventeenth Illinois Volunteer Infantry, and, after one year, was appointed Surgeon of the Third United States Heavy Artillery, with quarters at Fort Pickering, Memphis, Tenn., holding that position three years, during a part of which time he was on the staff of Gen. John E. Smith as Surgeon-in-Chief of the District of West Tennessee. In July, 1869, he was married to Mrs. Abigail Elvira Paden, daughter of the late Joseph Torrey, of Springfield, Ill.; two children, both living, were the fruits of this marriage--Harold Humphrey and Abigail Louise. Dr. Hood has been three times elected Alderman of the city of Litchfield, and once Supervisor of the town of North Litchfield; the discharge of his official duties have invariably been with the most thorough and conscientious exactness, always making himself familiar with the business before him and the best method of disposing of it for the public good, before committing himself. The same traits, together with a warm fidelity to the interests of his friends, have characterized his conduct in private life. In politics, he and his brothers were originally Free-Soilers, and, since the organization of the Republican party, close adherents of the latter. Benjamin Smith Hood, eighth child, was born October 24, 1832; was educated in the public schools of Philadelphia; came West in April, 1852; taught school the following summer in Madison County, Ind., and afterward, till the spring of 1856, in Illinois, principally near Jerseyville, but, in the summer of 1854, in the old Lutheran Church, which stood on what is now Scherer's Addition to Litchfield. In April, 1856, he, with J. L. Hood, engaged in the drug business, from which he retired in January, 1867. Since that time, he has been a Notary Public and insurance agent. In April, 1859, he was married to Miss Mary Tanner, second daughter of Charles S. Jackson, of Jerseyville, who died December 25, 1866; three children were born to them, of whom Mary, Louise and Charles are still living. In December, 1867, he bought the offices of the *Union Monitor*, of Hillsboro, and the Litchfield *News*, and consolidated the two under the name of the Litchfield *Monitor*. He sold this business in January, 1870, but again bought it in January, 1878, and has since conducted it the last year in partnership with Mr. John G. Campbell. He was Village Clerk in 1857, and at different times has filled the office of City Clerk for nine and a half years. In 1861, he served three months as private in Company D of the Seventh Illinois Volunteer Infantry.

P. T. JAMES, physician, was born in Franklin County, Va., January 5, 1828, and passed his youth in the village of Rocky Mount and vicinity; was educated at Emory and Henry College, in Washington County, Va., from which he graduated in 1846, when he began the study of medicine, reading a preliminary course with Dr. William L. T. Hopkins, of his native place; entered the Medical Department of the University of Virginia in 1848, and graduated from that institution in March, 1850. He began practice at Elamsville, Va., but only remained a short time, when he returned to his native county. In 1855, he went to Missouri and practiced until the war broke out, when he entered the First Missouri Cavalry Regiment, under Col. William Brown, afterward becoming Regimental Surgeon of the First, and then Acting Division Surgeon under Gen. Sterling Price, serving until the latter part of 1863, when he was captured by Missouri Federals, held two months, and finally released on bond. Setional feeling becoming so bitter at that time and the Doctor feeling that his property was in jeopardy, he removed to Illinois in 1861 and located at Litchfield, where he has since been engaged in the practice of his profession, with good success. In addition to his previous preparation for the intelligent and thorough understanding of his profession, the Doctor attended a regular course of lectures at the St. Louis Medical College, from which he received the degree of M. D.; he also received the degree *ad eundem* from the Missouri Medical College. In December, 1850, he married Miss Emily R. Woods, of Franklin County, Va., a relative of Gen. Jubal Early. His paternal ancestor was Welsh, and his mother, whose maiden name was Elizabeth Thompson, was of English parentage, both of whose families settled in the Old Dominion before the Revolution, the Joneses being amongst the first colonists at Jamestown; he has seven children living. The Doctor received the nomination for Coroner of Montgomery County at the hands of the Democratic convention in June 1882.

GEORGE W. JONES, City Clerk and attorney at law, Litchfield, was born on April 14, 1846, in Macoupin County, Ill., near Bunker Hill, he is the son of Simeon and Dorothea (Starkey) Jones, who were natives of Madison County, Ill., both being born near Bethalto. His father was born in 181[illegible], and was raised to the occupation of farming. The grandfather of our subject was Rev. William Jones, one of the first Baptist preachers in the State; he was sometimes called the "fighting preacher." Simeon Jones came to Bunker Hill in 1828, having just married and settled on a farm one mile west of that place, and resided there until his death, in 1852. By his efforts he acquired a handsome property. He was a prominent man in his county and [illegible] of his township. In religious matters, he entertained the Baptist doctrine. He was the father of nine children, six of whom grew to maturity and are still living. Our subject was raised on the farm, and educated in the common schools and in Bunker Hill Academy. He began reading law with Woodson & Walker, of Carlinville, Ill., in the spring of 1866, and was admitted to the bar in September, 1867. He began the practice of his chosen profession as the law partner of George P. Fowler, in Litchfield, in the spring of 1868; the partnership was dissolved in the fall of the same year, and he has practiced in this city ever since. He was elected City Attorney in 1869, and served one year; he was first elected City Clerk in 1878, and is now serving his fifth term; in the spring of 1882, he was elected City Attorney, and is also serving in that capacity. He is Director of the Public Library, and Secretary of its board. On October 26, 1870, he married Miss Eugenia A., youngest daughter of J. V. Hopper, of Bunker Hill.

WILLIAM A. LEACH, grocer, Litchfield, was born October 11, 1833, in Philadelphia, Penn., and, at the age of one year, was taken to Salem, N. J., thence two years later, to Wilmington, Del., where he grew up, and, at the age of sixteen, apprenticed himself to the molder's trade, serving his time under Bush & Lobdell, in their foundry, working also two years as journeyman. He went to Atlanta, Ga., in 1859, and worked four years in a foundry there, and at Macon, Ga., was foreman for one year in the Macon & Western Railroad shops. In December, 1864, he came to Litchfield, where he has since resided. He worked as molder here in the railroad shops ten years for Mr. H. H. Beach. In about 1875, he bought a farm in South Litchfield Township of 206 acres, and conducted it [illegible]

In January, 1880, he engaged in the grocery trade with Mr. Thorpe, and since has conducted a prosperous business under the firm name of Thorpe & Leach, on Jackson street. In 1862, he was married to a widow lady, Mrs. Jones, née Miss Temperance Fowler, at Atlanta, Ga.

BENNETT P. LEWRIGHT was born near Winchester, Frederick Co., Va., May 4, 1813, son of Robert and Elizabeth (Price) Lewright; Robert was at one time wealthy, but became involved through security debts. Bennett P. received a good English education at Upperville, Va.; went to Ohio when twenty-one years of age and taught school there three years; went to Missouri about the year 1837, and taught school three years in Franklin County, that State, where he afterward farmed till 1856, then moved to Miller County, Mo., where he remained nine years engaged in farming. In 1865, he came to Montgomery County, Ill., having exchanged 555 acres of land in Missouri with Mr. Bowen for 172 acres near Litchfield; here he lived about two years, then moved to his present place, consisting of ninety-six acres, to the cultivation of which he devotes his time. In Ohio, in 1838, he married Narcissa Soofbourow, a native of Fayette County, Ohio, who has borne him twelve children, viz.: Edmund M., Maria S., Alphonso J., Robert W. (deceased), Marium F., Corinne P., Robert, William L., Harley B., Jennie R. (deceased), Frances E. (deceased) and James S. Mr. Lewright is a stanch Democrat; he has been a member of the United Baptist Church forty years.

EGBERT S. LITCHFIELD, real estate, New York City, was born in Onondaga County N. Y., in 1836, and, when a mere child, was removed to Cazenovia, where he was educated in a seminary. He came to Litchfield in the fall of 1855, with his brother, E. E. Litchfield, and they engaged in mercantile business, opening a general store on the site of D. Davis & Co.'s present grocery building, continuing four years, when our subject went out of the business and returned to his home in New York. In 1860, he returned to Litchfield and remained a year, when he went to East Saginaw, Mich., where he engaged in the manufacture of salt for a period of four years; retaining an interest in real estate, he has frequently visited the place since. He lived five years in St. Paul, Minn., when he went to New York, where he engaged in the real estate business.

JOHN LANGE, Superintendent Car and Machine Company, Litchfield, was born in Oldenburg six miles from Bremen, Germany, in August, 1832. In his fifteenth year, he left school and became a seaman on a merchant vessel; he shipped as boy, and, after sailing four years, became ship carpenter, in which capacity he served four years; he was on the sea from 1845 to 1853, and sailed on the Atlantic and Pacific Oceans, Mediterranean, North and Baltic Seas in his travels; he rounded Cape Horn and Cape of Good Hope, visited Australia, the Indies and South America; he made several trips between Europe and the United States. Leaving the sea, he came, via New Orleans, La., to Alton, Ill., in the fall of 1853, and there became car-builder for the Terre Haute & Alton Railroad; he remained at Alton until the shops were moved to Litchfield, in 1858, when he came also, and worked in the car department, where he rose to the position of Master Car-Builder; when the shops were removed to Mattoon, Mr. Lange went there for six months to aid in starting them in operation. He became a charter member, and also a Director, of the Litchfield Car Manufacturing Company; at the opening of that company's shops, he became Superintendent of refitting shops for manufacturing purposes, and was the first

Superintendent of the shops, which position he virtually has held ever since, at various times having been elected to other offices in the company. At the re-organization of the Litchfield Car and Machine Company, he became a stockholder and Director; he has been Superintendent and Vice President of the present company. Since 1858, he has been in the shops continually, except the six months at Mattoon. In Alton, Ill., on December 18, 1853, he married Miss Fanny Bohnens, a native of Hanover, Germany. His father's name was Charles Lange, a carpenter.

GEORGE B. LITCHFIELD, restaurant, Litchfield, was born in Syracuse, N. Y., in 1842, and came West in 1856, with his parents, locating in Litchfield. At the age of sixteen, he began his apprenticeship in the office of H. A. Coolidge, publisher of the Litchfield *Journal*. In 1863, he formed a partnership with E. J. C. Alexander and ran a job office here for a year, when he formed a partnership with B. S. Hood and published the Litchfield *Monitor* for a period of two years; then, selling his interest in that paper, he bought a job office, and, during that year, printed a paper for the Fithian Brothers of Carlinville. He next sold the job office to Kimball & Taylor, who established the *Independent*, and he then became manager of its office, continuing about one year, when he started the *Montgomery Democrat*, which afterward became the Litchfield *Democrat*. For the first year, he took in R. S. Young as editor, after which he conducted it in his own name until September, 1881, when he sold it to Mr. Charles T. Tobin, and engaged in the restaurant business on State street. His father, Elisha W. Litchfield, was born in Litchfield, Conn., in 1819, and moved to Syracuse, N. Y., at which place, in 1839, he married Mary E. Johnson. At that place he was a large wholesale grocer and last manufacturer. After coming to Litchfield, he engaged in the lumber trade, and subsequently in the grocery business, at which he continued until his death, on April 28, 1862; his wife and son died in the same year. He was the second Mayor of the town, and held that office two years.

ELI LEE, grocer, Litchfield, was born in Greene County, Ill., where he lived until December, 1829. He entered a grocery in Carrollton, where he conducted business until he came to Litchfield, in 1863, and opened a grocery and provision store on the site he now occupies, at No. 67 State street, where he has carried on that business ever since, except a period of about three years, during which he was engaged in the agricultural implement business. Mr. Lee has taken an active interest in public affairs of the city and county, and has served several terms in the City Council; he is now a member of the Township Democratic Committee. In 1859, he married a daughter of Capt. E. M. Gilmore. The father of our subject is Archibald Lee, who was born in Huntsville, Ala., in 1804, and came to this State in 1814, with his parents, who settled in White County and lived there until 1832, when he removed to Greene County, where he has since resided; he now lives in Greenfield, Greene County, in his seventy-seventh year. He served in both campaigns of the Black Hawk war. He married Miss Jane Upton, of White County, in 1822, and raised a family of fourteen children, twelve of whom are living.

GEORGE A. MATTHEWS, merchant and contractor, Litchfield, was born in Caroline County, Md., in 1830, and, when four years old, left his native State. He was raised in Muskingum County, Ohio, and, at the age of eighteen, began to learn the brick-mason's trade, and also brick-making; he served three years' apprenticeship in Zanesville, Ohio. In 1857, he came to Illinois to build the railroad shops at Litchfield, and acted as foreman of the men on brick and stone work during 1857 and 1858; he was foreman when the shops were remodeled for the Litchfield Car Manufacturing Company, and also rebuilt them after the fire of 1872; he was a contractor and builder in partnership with his brother, W. T. Matthews, under the firm name of Matthews & Bro., until the close of the war, after which the firm name was Matthews & Chamberlain, his business career in this direction extending over a period of twenty-five years, during which time they put up the major portion of the brick structures of the city. In 1865, he formed a partnership with Mr. Kessinger, the firm name being Kessinger, Matthews & Co., and engaged in the grain and merchandising business, continuing about three years, when Mr. Matthews sold his interest to Kessinger & Baker. In addition to the brick yard and brick-laying, he afterward engaged in the manufacture of candies and in the bakery business for two years, when he again devoted his entire time and attention to brick work. In October, 1877, he bought out the store of L. Cramp, and continued business in the frame building on the corner of State and Madison streets, which he replaced with a handsome two-story brick building in 1881, in October of which year he sold his old stock. In January, 1882, he formed a partnership with Theodore Hart, under the firm name of G. A. Matthews & Co., and opened a new stock of groceries in his new building on the old site, where they are conducting a good and lucrative business. He has built ten dwelling houses for himself, and two storerooms, and has given employment to from eight to twenty men for a large portion of each year. Mr. Matthews is a stanch Republican. In 1866, he was married to Miss Temperance Jones, of Litchfield. In 1859, he married Miss Hattie Carlo, of Zanesville, Ohio, and removed to Wyandotte, Kan., where he lived three months, when his wife and child died, in September, 1860. His present wife, née Miss Jones, has one daughter, Jessie, born on May 30, 1879. The father of our subject was a ship carpenter, and his wife, Mr. Matthews' mother, was of Quaker parentage was Sarah Vain; she died at the age of seventy-eight. Their children, with the exception of our subject and another son, are residents of Ohio.

JACOB MOCK was born in Alsace, France about twenty miles from Strasbourg, in 1826, and came to the United States with his parents when two years old. They settled in Montgomery County, Penn., where our subject spent his youth, and, at seventeen, went to learn the carpenter's trade, serving two years and three months, after which he worked as a journeyman; also worked one year under instructions in Philadelphia. He then went to Cincinnati, New Orleans and St. Louis, then to Madison County, Ill., where he and his brother worked, taking wild land in payment, thus becoming owners of 140 acres of land; he worked at his trade for some years, and, in the meantime, improved his land. In 1863, he sold his farm and came to Litchfield, and has worked at car-building ever since, with the exception of six years at mill wrighting. February 17, 1853, he married Miss Lucinda Wetmore, daughter of Reuben and Martha (Olmstead) Wetmore, of Madison County. They have had the following children: Charles J., George W., Martha Arnetta, Jessie Bell and Orris C.; those living are Edward M., William F. and Mabel M. Mr. Mock was originally a Whig, but is now a Republican; is also a member of the Free Methodist Church. The father of our subject, John Mock, was a cooper. His mother died when he was eleven years old, and he was raised by a Dunkard named John Crater, of Pennsylvania.

JOHN H. McMANUS, photographer, Litchfield, was born in Macoupin County, Ill., near Palmyra, December 2, 1843; son of G. F. and Em[illegible]ine McManus, he, a native of Tennessee and she of Kentucky. In addition to the ordinary common-school education, young McManus attended the high school at Carlinville, Ill. He removed with his father to Athens, Henderson Co., Tenn., in 1855, where he lived three years, dividing his time between going to school and assisting his father in his cabinet-shop. His father removed to Texas in 1858, and our subject worked with him till the latter part of 1860, when he erected a large mill, in which he was engaged till January 8, 1862, when he enlisted in a company which ultimately became a part of the Twenty-second Texas Volunteer Infantry, and attached to the Trans-Mississippi Department of the Army of the Confederate States. In June, 1862, he became snare drummer and remained till July, when he was transferred to a brass band, J. B. Norman, leader, and remained in it until the close of the war, in 1864-65, playing the leading instrument. In May, 1865, the army disbanding, Mr. McManus returned to Mt. Pleasant, Texas, where he attended a select school for some time, after which he accompanied his father to Dallas, where they took charge of the Osceola Flouring-Mills, where the son worked as engineer. In 1866, he came to Macoupin County and obtained the position of engineer at the woolen factory, which he shortly gave up, and worked at carpentering till the fall; the following winter he spent as a student in a private school, taught by Mr. [illegible], and, June 7, 1867, he entered the photograph gallery of D. C. Bacon, spending three months under instructions; then to Macoupin County, farming, going to school in the winter; continued farming in 1868, and worked at building with his father. During a portion of 1870, he assisted Mr. Bacon in his gallery. In January, 1871, he bought his present gallery, in Litchfield, which he has since conducted with marked success, and turning out work equal in chemical effect and artistic execution to the best work done in the cities. Mr. McManus, having made a study of his present profession, is able to cope with the best artists anywhere, as he thoroughly understands the chemistry of photography, as well as that very important accompaniment of good portraiture artistic effect.

THOMAS McWILLIAMS, deceased, son of Alexander and Nancy (Kirkpatrick) McWilliams, was born in Hillsboro Township, Montgomery County, in July, 1822. He received an ordinary education, and learned the wagon-maker's trade. He served in the Mexican war under Capt. McAdams, and for his services received a land warrant of 160 acres, in addition to which he entered, in 1848, the land on which his widow now resides. He married, in 1850, Susan Jane Barry, daughter of John Barry, and from this union eight children were born, of whom two sons and four daughters are living. The names of the eight children are as follows: Sarah E. (died at two years of age), John Newton, Nancy P., Amanda J., Mary Alice A., William Henry (died at eighteen years of age), Franklin W. and Minnie. Previous to his marriage, he had erected a log cabin on his land, had broken a few acres and fenced a small tract; he afterward built a shop near his residence, where he worked at his trade, principally on repairing; he also worked at the carpenter's trade, and assisted in the erection of his own residence and outbuildings; he, however, devoted his time chiefly to farming, and owned at his death 452 acres of land, which he had accumulated chiefly by his own labor, although his health was broken down by his army services; the homestead farm of 280 acres he kept in a good state of cultivation. He was a supporter of the Democratic party.

JAMES N. McELVAIN was born in Simpson County, Ky., five miles from the Tennessee line, May 17, 1818, son of William and Jane (Neely) McElvain. William, the father of our subject, born in Cumberland County, Penn., in October, 1783, went to Virginia when seven years of age, thence to Kentucky when twenty-two, and to Illinois in 1850; lived in Sangamon County for some years, and died in Macoupin County January 12, 1864; his wife, a native of Orange County, N. Y., died February 1, 1849; they were the parents of fifteen children—ten sons and five daughters, subject being the fifth child; of this family, six sons and one daughter are living. James N. received his education in the subscription schools of Kentucky, and began farming in his native county. In 1841, he married A. A. Hamilton, of Scott County, Mo., who has borne him six children, of whom four are living, viz.: Andrew J., William H., James N. and Mary A. In the fall of 1847, he moved from Kentucky with his family and settled in Montgomery County, Ill., on 160 acres of land which he purchased of Benjamin Hathaway, who had entered it some years previous, and had broken about twenty acres. Mr. McElvain has since resided on the place, of which 120 acres are under cultivation, the remaining forty acres being timber land; he also owns various tracts of land elsewhere. He has given particular attention to stock-raising, for which his farm is well adapted, and raises cattle of a good grade; before the late war, he raised horses and mules. In the fall of 1870, he was elected to the State Legislature from Montgomery County, and served during the sessions of 1871–72; he acted on the Committees on Banks and Corporations; was elected Justice of the Peace in 1852, in which office he served four years. He was a Whig until 1852, and has since been an adherent of the Democratic party.

SYLVESTER MURPHY was born in Macoupin County, Ill., June 10, 1845; is the only living child of Hiram and Sarah (Huff) Murphy. Hiram Murphy, born in Clermont County, Ohio, December 8, 1816, came West with his parents in 1828 and settled near Carrollton, in Greene County, Ill., where he lived four years, then moved to Macoupin County, Ill., with his parents, where he has lived for half a century; he has been a successful farmer; beginning with nothing, he now owns 600 acres of improved land. His wife, whom he married about 1843, was of German descent. Sylvester received his primary education in the district schools of Macoupin County, and finished at the high school in Carlinville. He came to Montgomery County about the year 1868; lived on the farm there two years then moved to the city of Litchfield, and carried on farming in North Litchfield Township, raising good crops of corn and wheat; he served as Town Clerk of South Litchfield in 1880. The great-grandfather of our subject was a native of Ireland; his wife was a native of Germany, named Hess, and bore him seven sons; he started to return to the old country, but was never afterward heard of, and is supposed to have been lost at sea. John Murphy, subject's grandfather, was born in Jefferson County, Ky., January 26, 1791; he served in the war of 1812, and afterward located in Ohio; he engaged in flat-boating to New Orleans on the Ohio and Mississippi Rivers; was married three times, and had eleven children by the first two marriages; he was the youngest of seven sons, all of whom were in the war of 1812, after which they became scattered.

ALEXANDER McWILLIAMS, deceased, was born in Virginia, and removed with his parents to Madison County, Ky., when seven years of age, where he afterward married Nancy Kirkpatrick, who bore him thirteen children—six sons and seven daughters; of this family, three were born in Kentucky; three are now living, viz.: Lewis, Mrs. Vandaver and Mrs. Gardner. About the year 1816, he came to Montgomery County and settled on a quarter-section (160 acres) of land where William Atterbury now lives, near the Truitt Bridge; at that time, there were but five families in Montgomery County, the nearest mill being that of Edwardsville. He built a log cabin on his place and began farming, in which occupation he met with success, having at his death about five hundred acres of land. He was a Democrat, and, though not a member of any church, favored the belief of the Old-School Baptists. Lewis McWilliams, the son of our subject, was born on the farm now occupied by William Atterbury, in Montgomery County, April 12, 1820, and attended school at Clear Springs Church, two miles from his home, during the winter season, till he was a large boy. In 1842, his father entered for him eighty acres of land, on which he made, hauled and put up 7,000 rails during the winter of 1842-43. In March, 1843, he married Martha Jones, daughter of David Jones, of Montgomery County, and from this union five children were born—four sons and one daughter—of whom two are deceased. After his marriage, he settled on the eighty acres which had been entered for him, on which he now resides, and which he has since increased to 400 acres, which is chiefly under cultivation; he has handled and fed stock quite extensively. His grandfather, Hugh Kirkpatrick, in the early days of the county, built a horse-mill near where Woodbury now stands.

JACOB T. MILES, deceased, was born near Brighton, Macoupin Co., Ill., May 21, 1833. His paternal ancestors were from the Carolinas, emigrating thence to Logan County, Ky., early in the present century. Mr. Miles' father entertained strong anti-slavery convictions, which, in 1833, induced him to seek a home in a free State, settling near Brighton. He was a farmer and merchant until the last fifteen years of his life, during which he was in the ministry of the Protestant Methodist Church. He died in 1865, the father of twelve children, of whom Jacob was the first born in Illinois, and the tenth son. One brother and one sister survive. The latter is the wife of the Rev. John Friend, a Christian preacher, lately of this city, but now of Iowa. Col. Jonathan R. Miles, of Miles' Station, Macoupin County, and George W. and F. M. Miles, formerly of this city, and Samuel Stratton, were cousins of the deceased, and Mr. John R. Simmons, formerly a farmer of South Litchfield, now near Brighton, was his nephew. The family removed to Missouri in 1839, and returned in 1844, living in Madison and Macoupin Counties. At the age of eighteen years, Jacob began to learn the trade of carpenter in Alton and worked thereat in that and various neighboring towns till the spring of 1856, when he removed to Litchfield. Here he carried on the business of a carpenter and builder until 1873. During part of this time, he was in partnership, first, with Lewis Whitaker; some years afterward, with John D. Carson; and still later, with R. A. George. In 1873, he was elected Justice of the Peace, and since then has united the duties of that office with the business of insurance and real estate. In 1859, he was elected Alderman of the Third

Ward of this city, and filled that position two years. In April, 1861, he enlisted, as a private in Company D, Seventh Illinois Infantry, and served three months. Mr. Miles was three times married, having become twice a widower. The ladies were the Misses Elizabeth, Susan and Lou Linder, sisters of the late Mr. Emmett Linder, well known in this city. His first marriage took place in 1858. He died at his home, in Litchfield, Ill., about 5 o'clock P. M., on Saturday, April 29, 1882, in the forty ninth year of his age. His demise was sudden and unexpected, and the news of it filled the townspeople with grief, for he had been esteemed by all. He leaves a family well provided for, consisting of his wife and seven children --two grown daughters and five sons --Stella F., Alice M., William T., James L., Benjamin L., Arthur M., and Perley, the youngest, being four years old. He is greatly missed in the community, and his departure leaves a place vacant none other can fill.

MARK M. MARTIN, Vice President of the Litchfield Car and Machine Company, Litchfield, was born in Onondaga County, N. Y., on May 31, 1831. He learned the trade of car-building at Syracuse, N. Y., beginning at the age of eighteen; he plied his trade there and at Adrian, Mich., being foreman of the Michigan Southern shops from 1853 to 1858, in September of which year he came to Litchfield, Ill., and entered into the employ of the Indianapolis & St. Louis Railroad Company (then the Terre Haute, Alton & St. Louis Railroad). He superintended the erection of its shops here, and at their completion became master car builder, continuing to hold that position until 1864, when he removed and became master car builder for the Ohio & Mississippi Railroad Company, having charge of their shops from 1864 to 1872. He then was Superintendent of the Cincinnati Division of the Cincinnati, Hamilton & Dayton Railroad, and in 1873 returned to this place, where, the railroad shops being removed, he became a member of the Litchfield Car and Machine Company, who leased the present building. He was at that time elected Superintendent and has held an office in the new company ever since, except for a period of three years, during which he was master car-builder of the Cincinnati, St. Louis & New Orleans Railroad, being located at McComb City, Miss. On his return, he was Superintendent of the works two years, when he was elected to the office of Vice President, which he creditably fills.

JULIUS C. MACHLER, of German parentage, was born in April, 1844, in New York City, and educated in its public schools. In the fall of 1862, filled with the adventurous enthusiasm of youth, he enlisted as drummer boy in the One Hundred and Third Regiment New York Volunteer Infantry. The regiment joined the army at Fortress Monroe, and served in Burnside's expedition to open the coast of North Carolina, and was stationed at Newbern. Here young Machler was detailed as Orderly or Interpreter to the General Director or Medical Officer of the Volunteer Hospital, and remained nearly two years. Under this officer he saw service at the battles of Goldsboro and Kingston, and was present at the surrender of Joe Johnston. Mustered out in April, 1865, he returned home, and for six years was in a shop for the manufacture of ladies' hats. In 1871, he came to Litchfield, where he has since been interested in business. Politically, a Democrat; he is now serving his third term in the City Council, and is deemed a careful, painstaking and industrious officer. He married, in 1875, Miss Mary McGinnis, and has four children.

MICHAEL MORRISON, dealer in wines,

liquors and tobacco, Litchfield, was born in County Mayo, Ireland, on November 2, 1850, and came to the United States in 1851, with his parents, who settled in New York State, at Dundee, moving thence in a short time to Illinois, where they settled on Rock River, near Elgin, where our subject lived until he was five or six years old. The family then moved to Beaver Dam, Wis., where they lived two years on a farm. Next they lived in La Crescent, Minn., for about one year, and then moved to Freeborn County, same State; that county was then but sparsely settled, and they remained about two years, when the father died, and, in consequence of that sad event, the family broke up, and our subject first found employment as water-carrier on the railroad, going to school at Rochester, Minn., during the winters, until 1864–65, when he took a commercial course with Hurd & Belknap, following them from Rochester to Winona, Minn., and completing his course in the spring of 1866; he found employment as clerk in a furniture store at Rochester, Minn., for one summer, and the following winter he pursued his studies in a private school there. In June, 1867, he was employed by O'Rourke & Woods in their grocery and liquor store, continuing until December, when he removed to Austin, Minn., where he clerked in a dry goods house until the fall of 1868, when he returned to the old firm which had changed from the grocery to the dry goods business, and stayed with them until February, 1869, when he went to Dodge Center and worked in W. A. Higgins' general store until July, same year, and then returned to Rochester and worked in the same business for John Chute, having charge of a branch house at Eyota, Minn., one year. On September 8, 1870, he began work for Charles Ballweg, at Rochester, Minn., from which place they removed to New Ulm, Minn., in 1872, and remained until May, 1873, when they came to Litchfield, Ill., subject remaining with him here until September, 1881, except six months (from March to September, 1878), when he acted as Deputy County Treasurer in Hillsboro, and another period of three months (in the winter of 1877–78), during which time he was on a Western tour. In September, 1881, he leased a building on the corner of State and Ryder streets, where he opened a retail liquor and tobacco store, which employs three persons.

RICHARD McMAHON, Roadmaster, Indianapolis & St. Louis Railroad, Litchfield, was born in County Kerry, Ireland, in November, 1845. He received a good academic education in his native country, and, in 1864 at the age of nineteen years, came to the United States, locating in Elmira, N. Y., where he worked two years on repairs of the New York & Erie Railroad. He moved to Mattoon, Ill., in 1866, and there worked two years as laborer on the track of the Indianapolis & St. Louis Railroad. From 1868 to 1871, he was Road Clerk in the General Roadmaster's office at Mattoon; the following year, he acted as section foreman on the track of the same road, at Sunnyside, Ind. From 1872 to 1876, he was again Clerk in the General Roadmaster's office at Mattoon, and, during that time, was Roadmaster of a branch road called the Sullivan & Decatur Railroad. In August, 1876, he was promoted to the position of Roadmaster of the Middle Division of the Indianapolis & St. Louis Railroad, his division consisting of seventy-five miles. He presided over this until 1880, when the Roadmaster of the East Division resigned, and our subject was transferred to it. He had this division, which consisted of 110 miles, until July 14, 1881, when the road was redistricted in two divisions, and he was transferred to the West Division, extending from Mattoon to East St. Louis, a distance of 137 miles. He has since filled that position, having headquarters at Litchfield. November 28, 1872, he married Honora, daughter of D. O'Sullivan, of Mattoon, Ill. The names of their children are as follows: Mary Ann, Denis Joseph, Brian Augustin, Terrence Patrick, Margaret Teresa.

BENJAMIN McHUGH, merchant, Litchfield, was born in the town of Cornwallis, Nova Scotia, on March 1, 1833, and came to the United States in 1845, settling forty miles west of Milwaukee, Wis. His father, James McHugh, died just before the son's emigration, in which he was accompanied by his mother and grandfather. After living four years on the farm on which they first settled, our subject returned to Nova Scotia on a visit; he then sailed on a schooner from Cornwallis to St. John, New Brunswick, with his brother-in-law, continuing one season. The following season, he worked his brother-in-law's farm on shares, and went to New York as supercargo to sell his farm products, returning to Wisconsin. In the spring of 1853, he started across the plains to Oregon, with Dr. Knight, of Dogtown, Mo., traveling seven months by ox team. His destination was Chahalam Valley, Ore., where lived a cousin, with whom he stopped about two months, and then, via steamer, went to California, landing at San Francisco, from which point he went north to Port Orford and entered the Rogue River Mines at Gold Beach, where he entered the diggings and worked about two months, when his employer was killed. He had located about fifty claims, and sold over $700 worth in the next two months. He next became the proprietor of the Elk River Ferry, north of Port Orford a distance of five miles, by agreement with the Indians, and conducted it with an eating house and provision trade, for three months, with good success. During this time, the Coquel Indians had an outbreak, and Mr. McHugh was cook for the garrison two weeks, when they subsided. Mr. McHugh then left the ferry and returned to Portland, Ore., where he took up a land claim and improved it to some extent, then removed to Jacksonville, Ore., and worked in the mines for a short time. He went thence to Yreka, Cal., and mined during the winter of 1854-55. Then he joined his brother at Kelsey's Diggings, in El Dorado County, Cal., remaining about a year, after which he worked six months in a tunnel at Goodyear's Bar, which place he left, next locating at Cold Springs, in El Dorado County, until the fall of 1857, working in the diggings. He returned via steamer Central America, Panama route, reaching New York City and going thence, via Niagara Falls, to Walworth County, Wis., where he worked at farming one year, and then came to Pike County, Ill., where he took a contract to chop 500 cords of wood, for the accomplishing of which he employed men during the winter of 1858-59. In the spring, he took a trip through Kansas, and, on his return, came via St. Louis, Mo., to Bond County, Ill. Here he taught a four-months' summer school at Millersburg, and, during the winter of 1859-60, taught near Ripley. In the spring of 1860, he married Miss Emily C. Bilyew of Pocahontas, Ill. For ten years after his marriage, he farmed in the summers and taught school in the winters, in Bond County. After the war, he bought a farm of 173 acres near Pocahontas, and conducted it about ten years, when he traded it for town property and a stock of goods in Millersburg, where he merchandized about one year, and then traded it for land near Irving, Montgomery County. This farm he conducted for about two years, and then traded it for a stock of goods at East Fork, where he conducted a store and post office for two years. He then returned to Irving with his stock of goods, and continued merchandising one and a half years. He moved to Litchfield in September, 1881, and has been engaged since in merchandising on Jackson street, carrying on a good trade. In April, 1882, Mr. McHugh was elected Town Clerk of South Litchfield Township. The names of his children are as follows: Frank M., Mary F., Annie E., Cresada A., Charles W., Thomas N., Nellie B., Lewis A., Daisy M. and Cora E.

RICHARD W. O'BANNON, the first settler in the city of Litchfield, is the great-grandson of a Mr. O'Bannon who came to this country from Ireland before the Revolutionary war, and eventually settled in Virginia. The father of our subject, Isham O'Bannon, a native of Fauquier County, Va., whose wife, Mary Winn, was also a native of Virginia, and connected with the family of Stonewall Jackson, being an aunt of that famous Confederate General. Isham O'Bannon was Captain of a company of Virginia militia, and in that capacity served his country in the war of 1812. Their youngest child but two was Richard W. O'Bannon, who was born on November 1, 1808, in Fauquier County, Va., near the town of Salem. There he passed the early years of his life, and there he lost his mother, who died when he was but four years old. In the year 1816, he removed with his father to Shelby County, Ky. Here his father became a successful farmer, working twenty-five hands and owning thirty-five servants, and here our subject grew to manhood. At the age of nineteen, he began his life-long employment of merchant, in the store of Graham & Standford, of Shelbyville, Ky., where he remained three years. July 29, 1830, he was married to Miss Matilda Dorsey, of Jefferson County, Ky. Subsequent to his marriage, he engaged in mercantile pursuits on his own account, in Oldham County, Ky. Those were the days of the stage coach, when Louisville and Cincinnati were not as great marts of trade, and when the merchants of Kentucky went to Philadelphia and cities farther east for their supplies—journeys involving more of time and money than journeys to Europe at this day. Mr. O'Bannon made many such journeys, adding to his stock of knowledge and experience in the ways of men. About the 1st of September, 1842, he came to Illinois, having left Kentucky some time previously, and living in the meantime in the State of Missouri. There fortune had not favored him, and he came to Illinois to begin anew the battle of life. Settling upon a quarter-section of uncultivated prairie, near to the present hamlet of Ridgely, in Madison County, they proceeded to transform it into the most highly cultivated farm in all that region. Mr. O'Bannon proved himself as good a farmer as merchant, which avocation he also found time to pursue. Here he lived and prospered for twelve years, gathering about him hosts of friends, and here Mrs. O'Bannon organized a Christian Church and built for it a house of worship. In January, 1854, he came to Montgomery County on a tour of inspection. It cannot be said that he came to Litchfield, for then Litchfield was not. But he visited the site of the future town, then bristling with the remains of the last year's corn crop, and, with good judgment, selected and bought of Maj. P. C. Huggins, for $120, the east half of Block No. 21, which now includes the principal business houses of the city. The ground to-day, exclusive of all buildings on it, is worth $30,000. During the winter, on this purchase he built a one-story frame store, 22x36 feet, the site of which, still owned by him, is covered by the banking house of Beach, Davis & Co.

This was the first house built in the place, and, at the time of its erection, the Terre Haute & Alton Railroad had not reached the site of the town, and all building material, as well as goods, had to be delivered in wagons. In March of the same year, he placed in this store $6,000 worth of a general assortment of merchandise, and commenced business, with William T. Elliott as his partner. In the year 1854, the firm sold $42,000 worth of goods. During this year, the Ridgely Colony moved to Litchfield. It consisted of R. W. O'Bannon, his wife, two sons, Samuel and Joshua; Miss Sue Elsberry; John P. Bayless and wife and two daughters, Matilda and Martha; W. S. Palmer; W. T. Elliott and wife and son, William, and daughter, Maria; Henry E. Appleton and wife; James W. Jefferis and wife, and Charles M. Davis. Soon after coming to Litchfield, Mr. O'Bannon bought the property where he now lives, building the house the first summer. In the history of our country, 1854 was a fateful year—the year of the Kansas-Nebraska struggle. Mr. O'Bannon had been a Whig of the Henry Clay school, but, in the issue of 1854, he arrayed himself with the Democracy, with which party he has ever since affiliated. He was a Douglas Democrat and, in 1861, presided over the first Union meeting held in this city after the commencement of the war. He also subscribed liberally in aid of the families of the volunteer soldiers. Mr. O'Bannon continued in active business with W. T. Elliott for twelve years, doing a very large and profitable business. In 1859, they erected the store now occupied by Frank R. Milnor, and which continues the property of Mr. O'Bannon, to which they removed their business, and where they continued until 1866, when Mr. Elliott retired from the firm, the business being conducted by Mr. O'Bannon and sons till the completion of the Decatur & East St. Louis Railroad, to the construction of which Mr. O'Bannon largely contributed, when it was transferred to the new town of Raymond. This town is on the Wabash & Pacific Railroad, then known as the Decatur & East St. Louis Railroad. In Raymond, Mr. O'Bannon had large interests, being one of the company by whom the town was laid out; consequently, he moved to it, and resided there one year, with his son Joshua, who carried on the business. After that, he moved to his large farm in Zanesville Township, about nine miles from this city, where he lived with his son Samuel. This was in the years 1872 and 1873. About this time a friend for whom he was bound, failed in business, and by unanimous consent he was put forward as the assignee of the unfortunate merchant. Mr. O'Bannon was himself a large creditor, and, to recover in a measure what he had lost, he took the stock and once more engaged in business. In this he associated with himself his oldest son, and for several years O'Bannon & Son have held a front place among the business men of Litchfield with eminent success. The churches, the railroads, the coal mines, the car-shops and the great mill have all been helped forward by him. His familiar form is identified with every stage in the history of the town.

JOHN MILTON PADEN, contractor and builder, Litchfield, son of James and Margaret (McElvain) Paden, was born in Todd County, Ky., August 31 1821. He was in his fifteenth year when he came to this county in 1835, with his parents. He received part of his education in the private schools of Kentucky, and finished his schooling in the old Hillsboro Academy, which he left in 1840. He learned carpentering with Hamilton Hughes, of Hillsboro, serving two years, when he began taking contracts, which were principally in the neighborhood of his old home. He continued at this until 1852, when he bought a saw-mill, which he conducted two years, one mile east of Litchfield. In 1854, he purchased, in South Litchfield Township, a farm of 175 acres, on which he lived until the spring of 1882, when he moved to Litchfield. He engaged in contracting and building in the vicinity of Litchfield, in addition to his agricultural pursuits, for twenty-five years. He has been a member of the Presbyterian Church of Litchfield since its organization, and helped to erect that church building. He has been Trustee and Deacon for many years. In politics, Mr. Paden is a Democrat. He served as Deputy Sheriff of this part of the county four years, and also one term as Deputy Assessor for the western part of the county. In April, 1843, he married Miss Martha Street, daughter of James Street, and raised a family of four sons and three daughters, one son dying at the age of twenty six years.

ROBERT N. PADEN was born in Todd County, Ky., in 1830. James Paden, the father of subject, was born near Charleston, S. C., in October, 1777, and lived on his native place till he attained his majority. His father died when a young man. His mother was a lady of Celtic descent. James, when he reached the years of manhood, moved to Virginia, where, in Adair County, he married Margaret McElvain, and, about the beginning of this century, moved to Todd County, Ky., where he farmed till 1835. He then came to Montgomery County, Ill., bought 120, and entered eighty, acres of prairie and timber land, four miles southwest of Hillsboro, where a few families had previously settled; here he resided until his death, in 1845; he was a Deacon in the Presbyterian Church, and assisted in the erection of the first church at Hillsboro. The subject of this sketch, who is the seventh son of a family of ten children, came to Montgomery County with his parents in 1835. He received his rudimentary education in the Clear Springs Baptist Church, a log structure covered with clapboards, and having puncheon floors and seats; he completed his studies at the Lutheran College, then at Hillsboro, now of Springfield. In 1851, he engaged as clerk in Hillsboro, and continued in that occupation until 1855, when he opened a furniture store there, in which business he remained one year. In February, 1856, he came to Litchfield and opened a general store in partnership with J. M. McWilliams, but after a year sold out his interest in the business and returned to Hillsboro, where he engaged in the lumber business till 1860. In that year, he became Deputy Circuit Clerk under Benjamin Sammons, which office he held for two years, then returned to Litchfield, and was appointed Deputy United States Collector and Assessor of Internal Revenue in District 10, which position he held till 1868. He then removed to Southern Minnesota and engaged in general merchandising and drug business in Rochester and Austin, that State, until 1878, then returned to Litchfield, where he has since resided, engaged in real estate business. He married October 17, 1855, Illinois E. Blackwell, who died May 16, 1881; she was a daughter of Col. Robert Blackwell, of Vandalia, Ill. Mr. Paden is Director, Secretary and Superintendent of the McWilliams Oil and Mining Company, which began operations in January, 1882; was elected Mayor of Litchfield without opposition in 1865, and, during his administration, built the City Hall, and contracted for the first public schoolhouse. He was appointed one of the Trustees of the Illinois Industrial University of Champaign for six years, by Gov. Cullom, in 1881. He was formerly a Whig, and is now a Republican.

AHARTE PIERCE, deceased, was born

Wythe County, Va., on May 22, 1808, and removed with his parents to Johnson County, Ind., when a young man. About 1842, he came to Illinois, and first settled in Macoupin County. In 1848, he entered 160 acres of land, with another party, on which the city of Litchfield now stands. In September, same year, he rented a house on the mound where Mr. W. S. Palmer now lives. In the fall of 1849, he built a small log house on the site where W. H. Fisher now resides, and, when the town was laid out, the east side of the house extended into Madison street. He farmed his land, which was all raw prairie, until the laying-out of the town, by which time he had it all under cultivation, and stood above debt, for it and its improvements. He sold fifteen acres, to be platted at that time, to Wesley Andrews and Benjamin Hargraves. The remainder was laid out by Mr. Pierce himself, and it reached five additions; it is now all included in the corporation limits, and the lots, excepting two, on which his son Granville resides, are all sold. Before the war, he purchased another farm of eighty acres near the city, and lived on it three years during the war excitement. He passed the remainder of his days near his first settlement, and lived a retired life in his latter years. His first marriage was in Indiana, to Polly Brown, who bore him one child. His wife died in Macoupin County, Ill. In 1847, Mr. Pierce married Mrs. Brown, daughter of David Jones, a Virginian, who settled in what is now South Litchfield in about 1833. The first coal-shaft of this city was sunk on a part of his original purchase. Mr. Pierce gave several lots to various benevolent enterprises of the city, including schoolhouse and various church lots. Politically, he was a Democrat, and was the first Assessor elected after the city's organization. He died June 15, 1878; his widow has three children by her last marriage. One son, Granville F. Pierce, was born in Macoupin County, Ill., October 27, 1845; he received an education in the Litchfield schools, and in 1862 left the farm and became a clerk in a clothing house, continuing for some years; he afterward engaged in the grocery business for about four years; he then began clerking, and has been for nine years with the present grocery house of G. A. Stoddard, as salesman. In January, 31, 1877, he married Miss Dora A. Ware, of this county, and has two children—Essie May and Gracie A.

CHARLES PAULLIS, Jr., foreman painter, Litchfield, was born in Buffalo, N. Y., in October, 1853, and lived there five years, after which he lived in Dunkirk, same State, seven years, and then moved with his parents to Zaleski, Ohio, where he began learning his trade. He was fourteen years of age when the family came to Litchfield, and he at once began the furtherance of his mechanical studies in the Indianapolis & St. Louis Railroad shops, then the St. Louis, Alton & Terre Haute Railroad shops, where he worked at painting four years. When the Litchfield Car Manufacturing Company organized, he entered their employ as journeyman, and for the last six years has been foreman of the paint department of the shops, the company changing, in the meanwhile, to the Litchfield Car and Machine Company. His department employs from fifteen to twenty-five men. Mr. Paullis has been an earnest worker, and has made steady and rapid progress since he began his trade. He was married, in June, 1878, to Miss Fannie, daughter of B. W. Arnold. The father of our subject, Charles Paullis, Sr., was born in Prussia, and came to the United States when a child, his parents settling in New York, where he followed the trade of painting. He is engaged in the same occupation, as contractor, in Litchfield.

W. H. PHILLIPS, Litchfield, only child of Samuel and Mary B. (Webster) Phillips, was born in Jersey County, Ill., March 11, 1856; lived in Macoupin County four years, and came to Montgomery County with his step-father, Samuel Stratton, in 1860. In the Litchfield Public Schools he secured an education, which he furthered at McKendree College and at the Industrial University at Champaign, Ill. In 1876, he engaged in the grocery business at Miles' Station, remaining almost a year; he then, in the spring of 1877, came to Litchfield and engaged in the same business here two years. In January, 1880, he became agent of the Pacific Express Company, and, a year later, became also agent for the United States Express Company, both of which agencies he has since conducted with great care and ability. On December 20, 1877, he married Amanda B., daughter of Dr. J. S. Hillis, of Hillsboro; they have two children—Claude and Stanley H. The father of our subject was born near Lebanon, St. Clair Co., Ill., March 28, 1821; he was a farmer, and was one of the most successful land-tillers of Macoupin and Jersey Counties, in both of which he left large landed estates; he died in 1859. The Websters were originally from Tennessee.

LOUGHLIN QUEALY, foreman molder, Litchfield, was born in County Kilkenny, Ireland, in July, 1830, and came to the United States in June, 1845, his parents having died in his native country. He served three years' apprenticeship in the foundry of Edwin Davis at Andover, Mass., learning molding. He moved farther west in 1848, and lived in Columbus, also Zanesville, Ohio, plying his trade as journeyman. In 1855, he went to Chicago, Ill., where he followed his trade for two years. His brother, William J. Quealy, was a heavy railroad contractor, and our subject had charge of his works at Sheboygan, Wis., for a time; he was afterward contractor on the Fox River Railroad, in Kenosha County, Wis. In 1858, he returned to Zanesville, Ohio, where, two years later, he married Miss Anna E. Coyle. In November, 1860, he moved to Clay County, near Kansas City, Mo., for the purpose of becoming a railroad contractor, but the breaking out of the war put a stop to the business; he therefore entered a large foundry of his brother's at Hanover, Mo., remaining from 1861 to 1875, being Superintendent of it except the first two years. He took charge of the Ohio Falls Car Company's foundry, in Jeffersonville, Ind., in 1877, continuing two years. In August, 1881, he came to Litchfield, where he since has been foreman of the Litchfield Car and Machine Company's foundry, which melts thirty-six tons of iron per day, and employs in this department from sixty to sixty-five men.

JAMES ROGERS, miller, proprietor Eureka Mills, Litchfield, was born in Decatur County, Ind., April 5, 1835, where he lived until 1857, receiving his education in the public schools. At the age of seventeen, he apprenticed to the carpenter's trade, which he followed until 1858. In March, 1857, he came to Walshville, this county, and, the following year, engaged at merchandising, continuing until 1861, when he came to Litchfield and kept a grocery eighteen years, during which time he was associated in mercantile business with Mr. F. M. Miles and Mr. J. F. Setzer. Miles & Co. added to their interests the milling business, and ran the present mill two years, when Mr. Lewis Whittaker and our subject bought it, in 1877, the firm name becoming Whittaker & Rogers; this continued two years, when Mr. Rogers became sole proprietor, previously having sold his interest in his store; he has run the mill since, doing a large custom business, with a capacity of twenty barrels per twelve hours: he retains the old process; has two run of buhrs and employs three men; his mills are called Eureka Mills. Mr. Rogers has been Township Collector, and has served as a member of the Litchfield School Board; he is a member of the Masonic fraternity, and a charter member of the St. Omar Commandery, No. 30; he has been Recorder of the Commandery ever since its organization. Mr. Rogers was married, October 8, 1857, in Walshville, to Martha J. Deshane, born in Montgomery County January 15, 1838, daughter of Eli Deshane; they have had the following children: Laura I., Charlie and Mabel– Laura and Mabel being deceased.

FREDERICK W. REESE, deceased, was born in Hanover, Germany, on August 1, 1824; his home was in the country, and, at the age of five years he was an orphan; he learned the trade of cabinet-making in his native town, and afterward traveled as journeyman cabinet-maker, working but a few years in any one place; he occupied his time in this manner until he was twenty-eight years old. In 1854, he came to the United States: his boat freezing in the Mississippi River necessitated his walking to St. Louis, where he found employment, but, when the summer came on, he left the city on account of the cholera epidemic, and located at Redbud, Randolph Co., Ill., where he married, in January of the following year, Miss Christiana Gever, a native of Saxony, Germany, who proved a helpmeet by working industriously, shoulder to shoulder, with him, almost day and night, at first, in order to help him get a good start in life, her part of the work being the varnishing and sand-papering of the furniture he made. After his marriage, he worked at carpentering, and in the winter at cabinet-making. He came to Litchfield in 1860, and worked for awhile for Mr. Whittaker at cabinet-making, managing his business while that gentleman was absent. In about 1862, he opened a shop of his own for the manufacture of furniture, engaging in the sale of it and in the undertaking business; he at first started on Ryder street, but the rapid and steady increase of his business caused him to move to State street, where he built a large brick store, occupying it until his death, on July 24, 1880; he had no capital when he came, and, in twenty years, made, by his own labor and careful management, a handsome competency. He was a Master Mason in politics, he was a Republican; he had six children, who are living. When he died, Litchfield lost a worthy citizen.

JOHN W. RITCHIE, Litchfield, was born in Cabarrus County N. C., August 14, 18[illegible]4, son of John and Sela (Blackwelder) Ritchie, natives of Cabarrus County, N. C., he born in 1798, died September 25, 1854; she born in 1808, died October 23, 1854. Subject came to Hillsboro, Ill., in December, 1855, where he and his brother, Martin A., bought a quarter-section of land, which they farmed together till after the war; on this place Martin A. still resides. John W. married May 20, 1856, Rachel S. Cress, a native of Cabarrus County, N. C., born January 23, 18[illegible], daughter of G. Henry and Elizabeth (Fogleman) Cress, both natives of Cabarrus County, N. C., he born April 11, 1811, died in March 1844; she born July 26, 1813. Mr. and Mrs. Ritchie are the parents of eleven children, viz.: George A., James M., Laura J., Mary E., Sarah E., Joel E., Charles A., Flora R., Alice A., Prestin and Albert L. In 1861, he returned to North Carolina, and remained there till 1864, then returned to Montgomery County and bought 150 acres of land, on which he has since resided, engaged in farming and stock raising; he at present owns 260 acres of land, of which 230 is prairie and thirty timber land. Mr. Ritchie is a Democrat, and is a member of the Evangelical Lutheran Church.

MARTIN A. RITCHIE was born in Cabarrus County, N. C., August 11, 1829; he worked in his father's mill for two years, but left that and began farming for himself in 1853, and, the same year, married his first wife, who died in 1854. On December 24, 1855, he arrived at Hillsboro, Ill., and, February 13 following, he bought 217½ acres of land, where he now resides, and moved onto it in the latter part of same month; he has ever since lived on the place; raises grain principally, and for many years raised and handled a goodly number of horses and cattle. His second wife is Martha Cress, whom he married in North Carolina; of his twelve children, only four are living. He has held the office of Township Assessor three years—1879-81; been Township Treasurer since 1872; served as Collector of this township during 1874 and 1875; is an Elder of the Lutheran Church at Litchfield; has been a member of that church since he was eighteen years of age; he is an adherent of the Democratic party; he now owns 320 acres of prairie and twenty five of timber land.

JACOB RAUSCH, grocer, Litchfield, was born in Province Coblenz, Prussia, on the River Rhine, in September, 1832. At the age of sixteen years, he began to learn the hardware and grocery business, and served five years' apprenticeship. In November, 1854, he came to the United States, and first located in Philadelphia, Penn., where for five years he clerked in a wholesale French confectionery store; the next five years he spent in the State of New York, acting as clerk in hardware stores of Lockport and Buffalo. He went to California in 1862, by the way of New York, Aspinwall and San Francisco, and lived in Marysville, doing hardware business one year, after which, for a period of four years, he engaged in the drug business in San Francisco. He returned to New York by water in 1867, and located in Oswego, where he remained until 1872, acting as clerk in a book store. In May, 1872, he came to Litchfield, Ill., and was at that time broken down in health; in July of the same year, he purchased his present site and erected storeroom and dwelling, and opened a grocery and provision store on Jackson and Martin streets, where he has since done a prosperous business. In Oswego, N. Y., he married Miss Marian Collys, a native of Alsace, France, their union occurring in 1867; they have two daughters.

WILLIAM SIMPSON was born in Lincoln County, N. C., September 21, 1812, son of Samuel and Elizabeth (Brown) Simpson. Samuel, subject's father, came to Illinois with his family in 1831, and lived, during their first summer in the State, near where Staunton, in Macoupin County, now stands; he settled on the land where subject now resides, earning the money to enter the first forty acres by hauling sand for the building of the first frame court house in Montgomery County; at his death, which occurred in March, 1848, he owned 160 acres of land, which he had accumulated by his own labor and industry; his wife survived him about twelve years, and was about eighty-four years of age when she died. The subject of this sketch began working by the month about a year at brick making for Judge Hiram Rountree, and at farm labor for $13 per month, which at that time was considered high wages. In 1835, he began learning the blacksmith's trade with Thomas Tarrantine, of Hillsboro, with whom he worked about twenty [illegible]. He married, November 17, 1836, Elizabeth A. Beck, daughter of Paul Beck, of Fayette County, Ill., and from this union six children have been born, still living, viz.: Elizabeth J., wife of Fletcher Gamble, died in 1862, leaving two children; William M., a farmer in Montgomery County; Eveline, wife of James C. Holloway, of Litchfield; Emily, wife of Robert Ferguson, of Montgomery County; John W., of Montgomery County; Alonzo Douglas, a farmer, also of Montgomery County; and Laura, at home. After his marriage, Mr. Simpson purchased forty acres near his father's place, which he farmed until his father's death, when he took charge of the homestead and managed it for his mother until her death, when he bought the claims of the other heirs and became sole owner of the homestead, on which he has since lived, engaged in farming; he now owns about four hundred and eighty acres of land. In 1871, he was elected Assessor and Treasurer of Montgomery County, which position he held for two years; he has also filled various other positions of trust; he is a Democrat of the Jackson school.

DAVID O. SETTLEMIRE, President of Car and Machine Company, Litchfield, was born in Cape Girardeau County, Mo., in 1827, and the year following his parents emigrated to Greene County, Ill., settling ten miles from Alton. Mr. Settlemire was raised at Brighton, Ill., on a farm, and his education was limited to six months' attendance at a log schoolhouse of the primitive kind, having slab seats, and the marked lack of school comforts characteristic of the school buildings of the frontier. In his seventeenth year, he left home to serve an apprenticeship to the cabinet maker's trade at Carlinville, Ill., where he worked three years; he then gave up that trade and commenced carpentering, at which he continued until 1858, at Brighton, Bunker Hill and Gillespie, as contractor; his last work was a large flouring-mill at Gillespie, Ill., and he ran it until 1861, when he sold the mill to J. D. Martin, and engaged in the grain business, in connection with merchandising, at that place, until the fall of 1866, when he purchased property in Litchfield, and, the following year, erected his present homestead, and the grain elevator now known as the O. K. Mills and Elevator, it being the first regular grain house kept in operation here throughout the year. In that year he brought his family here, and has since been a resident of this city. In 1870, he closed out the mills to J. B. L. Keating. Mr. Settlemire built the Wabash Elevator, and furnished it with a "dump" and corresponding machinery for handling, unloading, shelling and cleaning corn, it being the first one used in the State; consequently, it attracted much attention and admiration, and succeeded in revolutionizing the methods of handling grain. In 1871, he built the Harvel Elevator, and, with Maj. R. McWilliams, laid out the town. In 1873, he rebuilt the elevator at Mt. Olive, and, six years later, bought and remodeled the elevator at Morrisonville, which he is still running. On March 20, 1876, Mr. Settlemire was elected President of the Litchfield Car Manufacturing Company, which had made an assignment, on March 3, to Mr. M. M. Martin, as assignee, for whom our subject ran the business until August, 1877, when he purchased the property of the car manufacturing company, and then organized the Litchfield Car and Machine Company, of which H. H. Beach was elected first President. On August 14, 1878, Mr. Settlemire was elected President of the company, and ever since has been annually re-elected to that position. By careful management and shrewd judgment, Mr. Settlemire has greatly increased its value, and the product in 1881 was about $1,000,000. Mr. Settlemire's marriage occurred November 29, 1849, the lady being Sarah J. Adams, daughter of John Adams, a native of Massachusetts; their children are George L., Iola E., the son being married.

F. W. STAHL, Secretary and Treasurer of Car and Machine Company, Litchfield, was born in Prussia, Germany, in the province of Posen, on August 3, 1833. At the age of fourteen years, he began learning coppersmithing in his native town of Chodziesin, where he served four years' apprenticeship, and, in 1852, sailed for the United States, landing in New York City; he worked two years in Albany, N. Y., then one year in New York City, after which he went to Texas, remaining a short time. After this, he worked three months at New Orleans, when he came to Illinois, via St. Louis, and settled in Bloomington, where he worked five years in the Chicago & Alton Railroad shops. In February, 1860, he went to Alabama and engaged in the stove and tinware business, but, the war coming on, he returned in August to Litchfield, Ill., and here found employment in the railroad shops for eighteen months, and, at the expiration of that period, he bought out the stove and tinware business of John Fowler, and conducted with it extensive trade in hardware and agricultural implements, with good success, until 1875; he then disposed of the hardware branch of his business, and for two years dealt in agricultural implements alone; he then settled up his business, and became a stockholder in the Litchfield Car and Machine Company in 1879. In August, 1880, he became a Director of the company; in March, 1881, was made Treasurer; and in August, 1881, he was elected Secretary and Treasurer, a position he still holds. Mr. Stahl is also a stockholder in the McWilliams Oil and Mining Company. In 1857, at Bloomington, Ill., he married Miss Margaret J. Waldron, a native of New York State.

HON. ELIZUR SOUTHWORTH, lawyer, Litchfield, was born in West Fairlee, Vt., September 22, 1826; his parents were also natives of the same State; on the paternal side, of English extraction, and on the maternal side, his ancestry was of Irish birth. His education was acquired at the academy in Bradford, Vt., in the high school at Post Mills, and in the Thelford High School, at one time a famous educational establishment. He was the youngest of a family of five, and, at a very early age, was compelled to rely upon his own exertions to secure a livelihood. At the age of eighteen, he commenced teaching school, a calling which he pursued in Vermont, Massachusetts and in New Hampshire, thus securing, while instructing his pupils, a fair and varied education. In 1847, he removed to Illinois, where he continued to teach in several counties during the ensuing three years. In 1850, he went to California, crossing the plains on foot, and driving an ox team from St. Joe to Sacramento. Upon arriving at his destination, having experienced many hardships on the road thither, he engaged in mining for about fifteen months; he then returned to the East, to Bradford, Vt., where he became the proprietor by purchase of a newspaper establishment, which he conducted one year, until his business was destroyed by fire. In the spring of 1854, he again removed to Illinois, and settled in Montgomery County, where he engaged in farming and agricultural pursuits, continuing thus employed during the succeeding four years. Having applied himself to the study of law while teaching school, he was admitted to the bar in 1859, and, in January of that year, entered upon the practice of his profession in Litchfield, where he has since permanently resided, engrossed in professional labors, his practice being very extensive and lucrative. Politically, he was originally a Democrat, but in 1856 he cast his vote for John C. Fremont, and was eventually one of the original Republicans of the State; after that time, he voted with the Republican party until 1872, when he cast his vote in favor of Horace Greeley, and has since acted with the Democrats; in 1869, he was nominated by his party for County Judge, but failed to secure an election, the county having been always governed by Democratic views, although on this occasion he reduced a 600 majority to thirty six. Starting out in life young, poor and friendless, he has been truly the architect of his own fortune, and has won his present enviable position as a legal practitioner and as an esteemed citizen solely through his own abilities and tireless energy. In 1876 and 1878, he was elected to the State Legislature from Montgomery and Christian Counties, and served four years; he was elected Mayor of Litchfield in 1881, and served one term; he served in the State Senate from 1878 to 1880.

JAMES A. SMITH, ice-dealer, St. Louis, Mo., was born in London, England, in 1823, and was a lighterman on the River Thames. He came to the United States in 1857, and first located in Chicago, Ill., where he dealt in grain three years, and went thence to St. Louis, Mo., where he began dealing in ice in a wholesale and retail way, the trade at that time being but small everywhere. In connection with ice, he was engaged in wrecking on the Upper and Lower Mississippi River during the war, his work being the raising of sunken boats. At the close of the war, he began extending the ice business from year to year, until he has now thirty houses scattered through the States of Illinois, Missouri, Iowa and Minnesota, which have an aggregate capacity of 150,000 tons, which is shipped by barge and railroad to the Mississippi Valley as far south as Texas, during the cutting season, he employs from five hundred to seven hundred men, and in the shipping season has from fifty to eighty men. In the spring of 1880, James A. Smith & Son purchased five acres of land, lying between the Wabash, St. Louis & Pacific Railroad and the Litchfield reservoir, and leased the ice privilege of about three-fourths of the reservoir for twenty years, and, in November, 1880, they began the construction of an ice-house which cost $28,000, being 160x160 feet, thirty-six feet high, with a self-supporting roof, and three-feet walls filled with saw-dust, the whole having a capacity of 21,500 tons; this house is filled by the Knickerbocker endless chain hoisting machinery, which has a capacity of 1,200 tons per day; the present firm is James A., Sr., and James A., Jr. The Litchfield building was erected under the supervision of Mr. Arthur Smith, who is the youngest son of our subject, and who has had charge of this and the Oakland, Iowa, department, which latter consists of three houses. Mr. Smith's general office is at No. 817 North Seventh street, St. Louis, Mo.

WILLIAM S. LEA, grocer, Litchfield, was born in Yorkshire, England, in February, 1830, and came to the United States in 1848; he learned the trade of stone-cutter and mason at Spofforth, England, beginning at the age of thirteen years and serving nearly six years' apprenticeship. In the United States he was contractor and bridge-builder on several railroads until 1859, first working on the Des Moines Canal, in Iowa and Missouri, and afterward on the Alton & Chicago Railroad with his two brothers, building the masonry from Alton to Carlinville; on the Pacific Railroad he constructed the bridge across the Des Pres River; he was employed on the masonry of the Illinois Central Railroad bridge spanning the Little Wabash, and the Iron Mountain bridge across the Merrinake River; in 1857, he took contract for grading and masonry of five miles on the West Branch of the Pacific Railroad, at the completion of which, in 1859, he settled on a farm in Macoupin County, Ill., which he operated until 1866, when he removed to Litchfield, Ill., and for two years was a contractor on the North Missouri Railroad. In 1868, he embarked in the grocery business in Litchfield, continuing until 1876, when a fire destroyed the entire stock and building, covered by only partial insurance; from that period until 1881, he managed his farm and other interests, and in the latter year again opened a grocery on State street, in which he is still doing a good business. Samuel Lea, the father of William S., was a surveyor and civil engineer, and came to Illinois in 1850, and for two years resided in Alton, then removed to Centralia, where both parents died in 1857, of milk sickness. Our subject married, April 30, 1852, Miss Caroline Barrett, youngest daughter of Elisha Barrett, one of the early settlers of Greene County, Ill. Elisha Barrett was born in the State of Virginia, of Scotch-Irish parentage, somewhere about the year 1779; he came to Kentucky when small, with his parents, who settled near Lexington, where, on reaching manhood, he married Mary Jenkins, an English lady, by whom he had twelve children, five of whom are still living; he became the owner of a large landed estate in Oldham County, Ky., on which he farmed until about 1836, when he was dispossessed of his property by a prior French claim, and sought a home in the West, settling in Greene County, this State, where he resided until his death, in January, 1845; his widow, left with a large family, subsequently removed to Alton, Ill., where she died in 1851. Mr. and Mrs. Lea are the parents of eight children, three of whom died in infancy, and four are living—Edwin, a farmer of this county; Charlie; Harry, who died at the age of seventeen; Jennie and Sammy.

PRESTON SHEPHERD, farmer, P. O. Litchfield, was born in Kentucky on November 7, 1832. When an infant, he was brought to Illinois by his parents, who settled east of Hillsboro, Montgomery County, but, after a few years, removed to Section 15, North Litchfield Township; his father owned 120 acres of timber land there, and died on the farm where Bluford Bandy now lives, leaving a wife and four children, two of whom are deceased. Hiram Shepherd, the only brother of our subject, lives in the eastern part of Montgomery County. The widowed mother, Mrs. Anna (Brown) Shepherd, died in 1846, leaving our subject at the age of fourteen, an orphan without means; she had been previously married to Mr. Henry Hill, and had two children of that marriage. When thrown upon his own resources at so early an age, Mr. Shepherd worked by the month, doing different kinds of work; he was frugal, and, with his savings, purchased his brothers' and sisters' interests in their father's estate; having gotten that in his possession, he farmed it until 1862, when he exchanged it for his present farm in Section 16, of 120 acres, to which he since has added largely. Mr. Shepherd has lived here just twenty years, during which period he has been very successful raising grain; he has now 330 acres of land, all earned by his own labor and perseverance, except the one-fourth interest bequeathed him of his father's farm of 120 acres. In 1857, he married Miss Sarah A. Thompson, daughter of Peter Thompson, a farmer of this county; he is the father of eight children, three of whom are deceased.

JOSEPH STREHLE, retired, Litchfield, was born in the town of Aeflingen, Wurtemberg, Germany, on June 10, 1835; he attended school until he attained the age of fourteen, years, and then served three years' apprenticeship to the trade of wood-turning. In 1854, he came to the United States, locating in New York City, where he entered a bakery, remaining one year; the following year, he came to Alton, Ill., and conducted a confectionery and restaurant business there until 1866, when he came to Litchfield, Ill.; here he established a bakery, which he conducted until 1880 with fair success, and then sold out on account of feeble health. At Alton, in 1860, he married Miss Mary Eiter, who died five years later, leaving two daughters. He married Miss Minnie Weipert, of Litchfield, in 1868, which union has been blessed with one son. His father, John Strehle, was a farmer and baker, and died when our subject was but nine years old; his mother's maiden name was Barbara Menne; he has two brothers living in Wurtemberg.

EDWARD SUMMERFIELD, merchant tailor and clothier, Litchfield, was born in Posen, Prussia, on August 5, 1829; his ancestors for several generations were merchants. He received his education in the common schools of Posen, and from private instruction in his father's home, which, at the age of sixteen years, he left, and traveled in England, selling merchandise until 1856, when he came to the United States, landing in New York in September. From there by ocean route he went to New Orleans, thence to St. Louis, Mo., which place he reached in March, 1857, with small means; he traveled thence into Illinois for one year, with merchandise, and, during that period, decided to locate here, which he did on March 13, 1858; he opened a stock of clothing, and was the first regular clothier to locate here; his first stock cost $850, and his business has grown steadily from year to year; by close attention to buisness, he has built up a large trade; for several years he conducted the business personally, until it largely increased, and, since 1870, has admitted some of his employes into partnership, and at the marriage of his daughter, in 1880, the present firm, Summerfield & Co., consisting of Mr. Summerfield and his son-in-law, I. L. Mosler, formerly of Indianapolis, Ind., was formed. Among his twenty-four years' experience here he has educated a goodly number of young men in the clothing trade, many of whom are now very successful business men; in 186[illegible] he added a merchant tailoring department, and now occupies two large business rooms for his business and manufacturing departments; he employs twenty men. In 1880, Mr. Summerfield began the manufacture of gas for the purpose of lighting his business rooms which are illuminated by fifty-four jets; his stock has grown with consecutive years of active labor and constantly increasing sales from $850 to $50,000 per year.

C. R. STEVENSON, passenger and freight agent of the Wabash, St. Louis & Pacific Railroad, Litchfield, was born in Lawrenceburg, Ind., July 6, 1856; when quite young, he went with his parents to Indianapolis, Ind., where he lived until he was nine years old; the family then removed to New York City, where they lived until 1878. Mr. Stevenson was educated in the public schools of New York City, and in private schools in New England. In the spring of 1871, he went to Europe, where he attended a preparatory school at Dresden one year, and another at Munich, Bavaria, for the same length of time, after which he spent three years there in the study of engineering in the Polytechnic Institute. In July, 1876, he returned, and worked on the architecture of the Coney Island and Manhattan Beach Hotel, where for a time he remained as clerk. In January, 1878, he was made a clerk in the general freight office of the Wabash Railroad at Toledo,

Ohio, remaining one and a half years. He then came to Litchfield, in July, 1879, where he since has been passenger and freight agent of the Wabash, St. Louis & Pacific Railroad. His father, Columbus S. Stevenson, was born in New Orleans, La., in 1817, but moved to Kentucky when young, and lived in that State and in Indiana until after the late war, in which he served, being Paymaster; later, he was Cashier of the State National Bank of Indiana, at Indianapolis; he is now Inspector of the Manhattan Elevated Railroad. He married, in New York City, Miss Julia Ellis, a native of that city.

F. M. STRATTON, physician Litchfield, was born in Jefferson County, Ind., September 22, 1829, and, being left an orphan at an early age, he began, when nine years old, to earn a living and secure an education for himself; he was employed in a drug store at that place for a period of one and a half years; at the age of thirteen, he removed to Jefferson County, Ky., thence to Henry County, Ky., where, at the age of seventeen, he began to learn the trade of carpentering, at which he hoped to earn means to pay for an education; he served as apprentice three years, and then began taking contracts. In the evening, after his work by the firelight he studied medicine, being without a tutor; his early education was obtained through many difficulties, and all his spare hours were devoted to earnest study of the profession he has since adopted and now practices with marked success. At the age of twenty-two years, he married, in Kentucky, and in 1852, removed to Morgan County, Ind., taking some large contracts at Morgantown, which he completed with good success. In August of the following year, he returned to Kentucky, and there his wife died in June, 1854. In the fall of that year, he entered the Medical Department of Michigan University at Ann Arbor, taking a six-months course, at the close of which he entered the office of Dr. O. B. Payne, at Columbus, Adams Co., Ill. In the fall of 1855, he entered the Iowa University at Keokuk, and graduated in medicine in March, 1856. He located at Ashland, Iowa, where he practiced a short time; he then removed to Mill River, Mass., and practiced among the old Berkshire hills eighteen months, and again, in 1858, removed to Fort Madison, Iowa, where he practiced three years, leaving, in May, 1861, for Louisville, Ky., where, with his brother, he engaged in the drug business. The war coming on and cutting off Southern trade made it expedient for them to sell out their stock of drugs, which they did in less than a year, and the following winter, he took a partial course of lectures in the University of Louisville. In May, 1862, he landed in Hillsboro, Ill., and there became the medical partner of Dr. Owen; here he continued two years, and, in April, 1864, he started overland for Montana Territory, in search of adventure, gold and health; he spent nearly two years in the mines, and returned to Illinois in July, 1866, locating permanently in Litchfield, where he has practiced ever since, except during a portion of the years 1877 and 1878, which he spent in Kentucky and Texas. Mr. Stratton's children are John A., Owen T. and Francis M. Dr. Owen was for over seventeen years in the same office with our subject.

MOSES B. SAVAGE, merchant, Litchfield, was born in Granville, Washington Co., N. Y., on June 8, 1803, and, at the age of one year, was removed by his parents to Onondaga County; he received a good common school education, and remained with his father until he was thirty years of age, assisting him on the farm and in his mills and shops. He was married, at Delphi, N. Y., in February, 1828, to a Miss Clark, who died

March 12, 1830. October 23, 1835, he married Mrs. Sophia Cobb, a native of Greenville, N. Y., daughter of Aaron and Rebecca (Tuttle) Lake. Mr. Savage had the following children: Lucia M., deceased, Marcia Adeline, Sophia Lake and Moses. In 1833, he went to Michigan, and lived in Monroe eleven years, engaged in mercantile business; he then went back to New York, and was two years in Onondaga County; he hoped thus to regain his health, which became impaired in Michigan. In 1847, he went to New York City; residing in Brooklyn, he was Superintendent of a large manufacturing establishment for a period of ten years. He came to Litchfield in March, 1857, and formed a partnership with E. E. Litchfield in the hardware business, continuing two years; he next engaged in the dry goods business, and continued two years, after which he was a partner in mercantile business with Mr. Palmer, with whom, under the firm name of Palmer & Co., he was connected from 1869 to 1879, since which time he has been salesman for Mr. Towey. Mr. Savage has been in active business for nearly fifty years; he was the third Mayor of the city of Litchfield; politically, he was a Whig, and is a Republican.

WILLIAM B. SCHOEN, merchant, Litchfield, was born in Bavaria, Germany, on October 13, 1843. He was in his fifth year when he came with his parents to the United States; they settled in Franklin County, Mo., and his father carried on a shoe-shop there until 1853, when they removed to Baltimore, Md.; there our subject lived with them until 1857, when he came to St. Louis, Mo., and lived with an uncle, entering his employ in a gun and jewelry store, and continuing until the war broke out, when his uncle became a Sutler, attached to the Fifteenth Army Corps, and Mr. Schoen became its manager, acting as such until 1864, when he was employed in Little Rock, Ark., for a year, as clerk; he next opened a dry goods and clothing house in Mattoon, Ill., and conducted business therein until March, 1866, when he engaged in the clothing and gents' furnishing business in Kansas City, Mo., until October, 1868, when he went to Omaha, Neb., remaining until 1870, in the clothing trade. In February, 1870, he came to Litchfield, Ill., and here became a member of the firm Levy & Schoen, J. Levy being the senior partner in the house until September 1, 1875, when he sold to his brother, S. Levy, and the new firm continued under the same name until February 18, 1878, when it was dissolved, and Mr. Schoen has since continued the business in his own name. He located at No. 45 State street, and there does a prosperous business in dry goods, millinery and fancy goods; he employs six persons, exclusive of the dress-making department, which employs from ten to fifteen ladies. Mr. Schoen was married, in Baltimore, Md., December 4, 1873, to Rose Mandelbaum, a native of Winchester, Va., born February 4, 1856; they have one child, Ira D.

EZRA TYLER, deceased, was born in Boston, Mass., in 1793, and lived near his birthplace during his youth, receiving a good common-school education, after which he engaged his services as clerk until he reached manhood, when he came West to Indiana and settled on a farm near Michigan City, where he married Miss Maria Connaway; in a few years, he removed to Aurora, Ind., and there conducted a farm until 1846, when he sold out and came to Montgomery County, Ill., where he bought a farm of about five hundred acres in different sections in South Litchfield Township, about one hundred and sixty acres of which comprised that part of Litchfield City south of the Indianapolis & St. Louis Railroad. This portion of the county was but sparsely settled when he came, and he was obliged to find market and trading points at Hillsboro, Carlinville and St. Louis. He erected a log cabin near the southeast corner of the city limits, now known as Tyler's Third Addition, where he lived five years, and then built the house now occupied by his son, Larkin, whose sketch is hereunto appended. Until the completion of the Indianapolis & St. Louis Railroad, he devoted his attention to farming, and afterward, in addition to his farming interests, he bought and enlarged a steam flouring-mill, located on the site of the present Planet Mills, and ran it several years; he then engaged in the manufacture of brick, and sold to different parties tracts of land, out of which three additions were made to the city. In politics, he was a Whig, and subsequently a Republican, and took an active part in public affairs. He died in the fall of 1872. He was the father of twelve children, all but one born in Indiana; but three are deceased; those living are, viz.: Mrs. James Parmlee, now near Los Angelos, Cal.; Jesse, John and Shelby, residents of Kansas; Mrs. Ed C. Thorne and Mrs. James Thalls. Those who reside in this county are Miss Almira Tyler, William and Larkin G. Larkin G. Tyler was born near Aurora, Ind., in October, 1845, and was but one year old when his parents moved to this county, where he has since resided, receiving his education here in the public schools. At the age of fifteen years, he engaged his services as clerk in the clothing house of A. R. Monforte, continuing his services one year, when the firm of Ludden & Forrester came here, and he engaged his services to them; the firm afterward became Ludden & Taylor; he remained in that house some three years. In 1866, he engaged in the grocery business on Jackson street, and for eight years conducted business there. In June, 1877, he became Assistant Postmaster, serving for a short time, when he became agent for the American and the United States Express Companies, which agencies he retained until the latter was superseded by the Pacific Express Company, since which time he has conducted the agency of the American Express Company exclusively. He represents several fire insurance companies. He is a stanch Republican, and served as Alderman of Litchfield. In 1873, he married Miss Lytle, of Carlinville.

LUKE TERRY was born in 1833, in Harrison County, Old Virginia (now West Virginia). He received a fair education in the schools of his native State, which he improved by his own personal efforts. On attaining his majority, he engaged in merchandising, and speculating in various enterprises. In the fall of 1865, he came to Illinois, and purchased 190 acres of land in North Litchfield Township where he has since resided, engaged in farming and the raising of stock of a fine grade; he has a fine orchard on his farm. In 1857, he married Ann Eliza McKinney, a native of West Virginia, who bore him seven sons, of whom five are living. Mr. Terry lived near the West Virginia oil region, and, previous to and during the war, operated in oil and oil lands; he also dealt in horses.

J. W. THYNNE was born in Dublin, Ireland, in 1842; his parents were of Scotch descent. He received his education in a parochial school about seventeen miles south of Dublin, having moved from the city when nine years old; left school at the age of fifteen and worked at farming; clerked in a store for a time, and also followed the occupation of a fisherman. In 1862, he emigrated to the United States, and came to St. Louis, Mo., in November of that year, where he lived with his step-father, a merchant tailor of that city, until August 3, 1863, when he enlisted in Company K, Eleventh Missouri

Cavalry, and served until the close of the war, in Third Brigade, Second Division of the Seventh Corps, which operated in Arkansas until they were ordered to New Orleans, La., where they were mustered out in 1865; he first served as private; was promoted to a Sergeancy, and afterward commissioned Second Lieutenant of his company. At the close of the war, he returned to St. Louis and engaged in tailoring with his step-father until 1868, studying, meanwhile, in his spare hours, at the Rohrer Commercial College of St Louis, from which he graduated; he held the position of clerk in the office of the Chief Commissary of the Military Division of Missouri for thirteen months; was engaged as clerk and book-keeper in Alton, Ill., and Cleveland, Ohio, for twenty months; he was employed as book-keeper with George S. Shryock & Co., tobacco manufacturers, three years, and afterward at Victoria, Ark., as clerk, for nearly a year; he then returned to St. Louis, where he held the position of book-keeper for the Home Bitters Company six years; afterward, book-keeper in the office of the Atlantic Milling Company from February, 1881, until August of the same year, when he came to Litchfield and bought the B. B. B. Mills, which he has since conducted under the firm name of J. W. Thynne & Co. Mr. Thynne married, in Litchfield, in 1878, Emma, daughter of Peter Boxberger, of Litchfield; the mills (old process) are situated on the Bee Line; they have a capacity of about eighty barrels a day, and do a good custom and merchant business.

CHARLES T. TOBIN was born in New Orleans, La., August 25, 1849. His father, who was a grocer, moved to St. Louis when subject was two years old, and remained there three years, during which time four of subject's brothers died of cholera. The family then removed to Peoria County, Ill., in 1854, where the father died about four years afterward, leaving five small children, Charles T. being the second son living. The mother then moved with her family to Brimfield, Peoria County, where the boys worked at anything they could find to do for the support of the family. Charles T. worked on a farm in summer and attended the town school in winter. At the age of seventeen, he entered the office of the Carlinville *Democrat*, where he remained four years, and thoroughly mastered the business in its various branches; he then obtained a position as foreman on the Cape Girardeau *News*; stayed about a year, and came to Hillsboro, Ill., in March, 1870; became foreman of the Hillsboro *News Letter*, working half time in the office, attending the remainder of the day the Hillsboro Academy, and pursuing his studies at night; he purchased the *News Letter* September 11, 1874, and, in partnership with James L. Slack, published the Hillsboro *Journal*, the successor of the *News Letter*. After six months, he sold out his interest in the paper to Mr. Slack, and became foreman of the *Illinois Sentinel*, of Jacksonville, remaining in that position three months. He then went to Springfield, Mo., where he had been engaged as foreman in the office of the Springfield *Leader*. There he remained six months; was afterward foreman of the Shelbyville *Leader* for a short time, and, July 30, 1875, purchased the Hillsboro *Journal*, changed the name to that of the *Montgomery News*, and, after eight months, sold a half interest in the paper to Ben A. Johnson. After this firm had published the paper a year, George W. Paisley, on August 11, 1876, bought out Johnson's interest in the business; this new firm then managed the paper till February 23, 1882, when they sold out to Col. Johnson. Paisley & Tobin then purchased the Litchfield *Democrat*, changed the name to the Litchfield

Advocate, and have since conducted it under that name.

JAMES TOBIN, foreman machinery department car and machine shops, Litchfield, a native of County Clare, Ireland, was born in 1838. Coming alone to America in 1850, he was for a year a student in Burr Seminary, Vermont, and then went to sea, sailing to Cadiz via New Orleans, and then making several voyages between New York and Liverpool, going next around the Horn to San Francisco; on the return voyage, he visited Callao and Lima, and then the Chincha Islands; doubling Cape Horn, he sailed to England, and then on order to New York. After six years of seafaring, and reaching the position of Second Mate, he abandoned nautical life and entered a machine shop under instruction. In December, 1857, he began work here for the Terre Haute & Alton Railroad, first as a fireman, then as clerk in the storeroom, and then for ten years as timetaker in the shops, until, in 1870, they were removed to Mattoon. When the Litchfield Car Works were opened, in 1872, he entered their service, and, in March, 1881, was foreman of the machinery department. He married, in May, 1859, Miss Eliza Moon, a daughter of his native isle.

JOHN H. TILDEN, M. D., Litchfield. Joseph G. Tilden was born in Norwich, Windsor Co., Vt., on May 19, 1810; he was the son of John Tilden, a New Hampshire farmer; his mother's maiden name was Grace Goodrich, of Vermont, where John Tilden ultimately settled and raised his family, consisting of five boys and one girl. Joseph G. began his education in the common schools of Vermont, and, in that State and in Massachusetts, he taught school, at the same time pursuing his medical studies; he attended lectures in the medical schools of Castleton and Woodstock, graduating at the University of Norwich. Following this, he pursued his post graduate studies, in connection with school teaching, for eight years. At Highland, Ill., he began the practice of his profession, and for two years taught the schools of that place. He removed to Van Burensburg, Montgomery County, in 1843, that place being then one of the best business points in the county; he practiced his profession there, in conjunction with the drug and general merchandise business, until 1871, when he removed to Raymond, Ill., where he now lives. He was one of the first practitioners of this county; when he located here, he found Drs. Hillis and Herrick practicing in Hillsboro, and Dr. Lane at Fillmore; they were the only regular doctors here, he thinks, and there may have been a few irregular. In that early day, the country was rough and wild, the doctors being obliged to travel mostly on horseback, and, owing to the sparsely settled country, their rides were long and tiresome; he rode twenty miles, his practice extending to near where Ramsey, Nokomis and Irving are now located, and also into Fayette and Bond Counties; to-day, he is the only surviving physician who practiced in Montgomery County when he settled here. Joseph G. was married to Ann W. Hill, daughter of John and Sarah (Casey) Hill, who was born in this county in 1819, her parents being among the early emigrants here from Kentucky. From that marriage have been born nine children: three daughters died in early infancy; the six remaining are Joseph, a locomotive engineer, living in Mississippi; John H., subject; Scott S., druggist, of Raymond; Seth H., now studying medicine with his father; Ruth E., wife of H. C. Coleman, commission merchant of St. Louis; and George A., who is drug clerk for his brother Scott. Dr. John H Tilden, subject of this sketch, was born in

Montgomery County, Ill., on January 21, 1851, and was educated in the public schools of Litchfield. He left home at the age of seventeen to labor for his own support and education. He began the study of medicine with his father, and, at the age of seventeen, had finished reading several works on medicine. In September, 1869, he entered the office of Dr. J. Fellows, of Nokomis, Ill., and read two years, when he entered the Eclectic Medical Institute of Cincinnati, Ohio, attending lectures there two sessions, and graduating on May, 21, 1872. He began practice in Nokomis, Ill., continuing eight years; in the meantime, during the spring of 1877, taking a post graduate course in the American Medical College at St. Louis, Mo. In August, 1879, he left Nokomis, and for two sessions was connected with the American Medical College as lecturer in anatomy and physiology, residing in St. Louis until June, 1881, when he came to Litchfield and formed a partnership with Dr. R. F. Bennett, with whom, under the firm name of Bennett & Tilden, he enjoys a large and lucrative practice; he is a member of the State and county medical societies, and was elected Adjunct Professor of Anatomy in the American Medical College in June, 1872. In September, 1873, he married Miss Rebecca Maddux, of Hillsboro, Ill., and by their union there are two children living, namely, Edna and Elsie.

EDWIN C. THORP, grocer Litchfield, was born at Upper Alton, Ill., May 21, 1843. At the age of five years, he accompanied his parents to Springfield, and, after living there three years, moved to Woodburn, Ill., where he remained until 1862, and engaged in farming. In August, 1862, he enlisted in Capt. Carr's company at Upper Alton, and served two years, he was ten months in the Eightieth Illinois Volunteer Infantry and assigned to the Army of the Cumberland, his regiment passed through twenty-three hard fought engagements, besides skirmishes; he was in all the active engagements of his regiment, and was only off duty three days from sickness; he was taken prisoner on Sand Mountain in 1863, while on a raid in Georgia: Col. Streights' brigade were all captured, and were only in the hands of the enemy fourteen days, when they were paroled. Mr. Thorp was mustered out at the close of the war, and came to Litchfield in July, 1865; here he engaged in the fruit and grocery business on State street, continuing for a period of five months; after selling off his stock, he was successively an employe in the business houses of Smith & Tuttle, J. Levy, L. Levy and Valentine Hoffman: Mr. Hoffman sold his interest to Ezra Tyler, and our subject continued for a time with the new firm; he afterward entered the employ of Mr. Stetson, continuing eighteen months, when he went into business for himself, buying out William Edwards in December, 1872, but in a few months sold his stock at auction. After spending five months as shipping clerk in a sash and blind factory in Chicago, Ill., he returned to Litchfield and engaged his services to Mr. Hoffman again; after continuing five years, he became the partner of Mr. Leach, and established a grocery and boot and shoe business on Jackson street, near the Catholic Church; here they have built up a large and flourishing trade; in 1881, they enlarged and improved their store. Mr. Thorp was married, on May 23, 1867, to Miss Rachel L. Tyler, daughter of Ezra Tyler, of Litchfield; they have six children—Addison C., William T., Fran[illegible] Edwin, an infant child which died unnamed and Bertha.

JAMES THALLS, undertaker, Litchfield, was born in Preble County, Ohio, near Eaton, on June 27, 1825, and lived there until 1852. At the age of twenty years he learned the carpenter's trade, which he followed, in connection with farming, in Ohio, and moved to this (Montgomery) county in the fall of 1852, settling on a farm of eighty acres, which now is included in the southwestern part of the city of Litchfield. In 1853, he sold his farm, and until 1860 devoted his attention to his trade, putting up many of the early buildings of this city, among others the Presbyterian Church, and also took several contracts in the county. In 1860, he bought another farm, west of the city, and conducted it, at the same time plying his trade; this farm he owned twenty years. Mr. Thalls has been a contractor here for almost thirty years. In 1882, he engaged in the undertaking business on Barnes street, with Edward Greene. In 1848, he married Miss Hester D. Whitlock, in Eaton, Ohio; she died in 1868, leaving six children, all of whom are now living. In 1870, he married Mrs. Maria Shore, daughter of Ezra Tyler; he has one son by the last marriage. Mr. Thalls is a consistent member of the Methodist Episcopal Church.

D. A. TINKLEPAUGH, engineer, Litchfield, was born in Poughkeepsie, N. Y., in 1839, and came West in 185[illegible] with his parents, who settled in Livingston County, Ill., removing thence to Iroquois County, where his father died in 1864. Five years after that event, our subject went to Chicago, Ill., and there entered upon an apprenticeship in the machine shop of Mason & McArthur, serving three years, after which he worked for a short time as journeyman in that city. He soon began running an engine, and, at the close of the war, went to Milwaukee, Wis., where he acted as engineer for Hunter & Bros. in their large mills for a period of about four years, at the expiration of which he went to Minneapolis, Minn., where for ten years he was chief engineer in the large lumber mills of William H. Eldred; he went thence to Sauk Center, Minn., as engineer in the flouring-mills of Harmon Holmes & Co., continuing until February, 1882, on the 20th of which month he came to Litchfield and became chief engineer in the Planet Mills of D. L. Wing & Co., which responsible position he holds still. His parents were natives of Dutchess County, N. Y., and his father was a farmer.

MOTHER URSULA, Superior of Ursuline Community at Litchfield, was born in Elberfield, Prussia, where she lived until she was twelve years of age, when she came with her parents to the United States, in 1848. They located in Cincinnati, Ohio, where she continued her education with the Sisters of Notre Dame for a period of two years. They then removed to St. Louis, Mo., where she was further educated by the Sisters of the Sacred Heart until 1852. Two years later, she entered the community of the Ursulines at St. Louis, Mo., and, in 1856, took the vows of that order. She was assigned to the work of teaching, and taught in St. Louis until 1859, when they established a community of Ursulines at Alton, Ill., and she was one of the seven sisters who took charge of the work of teaching there, continuing until 1880, in September of which year she was sent to preside as Superior of the community of Ursulines at Litchfield, Ill.; she at present has charge of the academy.

COL. DELOS VAN DEUSEN, Litchfield, banker, was born in Jamestown, N. Y., in December, 1823, and there received a good academic education. He came West in 1846, and located in Dayton, Ohio, until 1857, being connected with the boot, shoe and leather business, and moved thence to Illinois, locating in Litchfield in July, 1858. After the war broke out, he raised a company of volunteer infantry for three years, and was elected its Captain; this company was the first raised in this section of the country for three years, as the call for three year volunteers had but recently been made; he raised this company at that time when Missouri was in danger of being taken by the Confederate soldiers, and when even her Governor was favoring the rebellion; this made the demand for Union soldiers in Missouri greater than the supply, and our subject, with his company, through a desire to enlist their services where there was greatest need, went immediately, June 16, 1862, and joined the Sixth Missouri Infantry in defense of the United States Arsenal at St. Louis; their company, with the regiment, served as guard to Pilot Knob and Iron Mountain, and in November, went to join Fremont in the march on Springfield; returning, they went into camp at Otterville during the winter. In May, 1862, they joined Gen. Grant at Pittsburg Landing, becoming a part of the First Brigade, Second Division, Fifteenth Army Corps, under command of Gen. W. T. Sherman, and served with his army until the close of the war, participating in the siege of Vicksburg, Mission Ridge, the capture of Atlanta, the march to the sea, through Georgia and the Carolinas. Our subject commanded his company (H) in the Sixth Missouri Regiment until March, 1864, when, the regiment having reenlisted, he succeeded to the command of the regiment, and advanced to the rank of Lieutenant Colonel, and commanded the Veteran Sixth Missouri Volunteer Infantry until the close of the war, being mustered out of service at St. Louis, with his regiment, in September, 1865 After his return to Litchfield, the Colonel served four years as City Magistrate, and, at the expiration of that period, became Cashier of the bank of Beach, Davis & Co , which position he still creditably fills; he is at present City Treasurer, which office he has held six years.

DANIEL P WOODMAN, lumber-dealer, Litchfield, was born in Newbury, Essex Co., Mass., September 11, 1834, and at the age of seventeen, went to St. Louis and became a clerk in a wholesale fancy dry goods house on Main street; here he remained four years, when he removed to Louisville, Ky., there pursuing the same vocation for another period of four years. In July, 1861, he came to Litchfield, where, with his uncle, he was engaged for over a year in the cattle business. In June, 1863, he became a partner in the firm Perley & Woodman, at Alton and at Litchfield, the business being lumber-dealing, in which he engaged until the death of Mr. Perley, in 1879, since which time Mr. Woodman has conducted the business in his own name, being recognized by all as a prompt and efficient business man. Mr. Woodman was married, at Bunker Hill, Ill., to Miss Knowlton, daughter of Samuel and Elizabeth (Woodward) Knowlton, both natives of Connecticut. Mr. Woodman had one child who died August 17, 1872, and has one living, Mary Perley, born December 6, 1879.

JOHN WIEGERS, grocer, Litchfield, son of Bernard and Elizabeth (Konnig) Wiegers, was born in town of Lugde, Prussia, on August 10, 1831. He left school at the age of fourteen years and entered upon an apprenticeship to the blacksmith's trade in the town of Pirmont, continuing three years, after which he worked three and a half years in Hanover. He came to the United States in 1853, leaving the seaport of Bracke, Wurtemberg, on May 27, and sailing seven weeks, landing at New York, stopping three days in the city; on his arrival, he had $600. Leaving New York City, he came direct to Chicago, Ill., remaining two days; thence to St. Louis, Mo., remaining four days, going thence to Edwardsville, Ill., where he worked at his trade a year, his remuneration being $14 per month; after this, he went to Alton, where he stayed four months, during which time he acted as waiter in the Franklin House. He next removed to Manchester, Mo., where he worked nine months at blacksmithing, going thence to Iowa, where he worked four months at farming; here he met with an accident with a threshing machine, resulting in a broken leg, which disabled him for thirty-three weeks, at the end of which time he was in debt for $37. As soon as he was able to do so he commenced as waiter in a hotel, continuing eight months, and then returned to Edwardsville, Ill., where he drove a mill team two months, and subsequently, in his twenty-seventh year, entered a cooper-shop there for the purpose of learning the trade; he served eight months' apprenticeship, during which time he gained the ability to do good work and receive full wages. He next removed to Staunton, Ill., and pursued the practice of this trade for fourteen months. In the spring of 1860 he came to Walshville, Montgomery County, with a capital of $240, which enabled him to open the first cooper-shop for himself, which he conducted about a year, when he removed to Staunton, being in the cooper business for himself until March, 1864, when he came to Litchfield, Ill., on the 27th day of the month, having accumulated a capital of $[illegible]00. On coming to this city, he purchased, for $400, a barn of Perley & Co., which he turned into a cooper-shop on the site of his present store and residence; the first year he employed fourteen men, and afterward as many as twenty-six men; from the first he had the confidence of all, and his credit was always good. He continued with good success until 1873, when his shop and stock burned, with a loss of $4,000; the property was insured for $1,600, but $1,000 being paid. He immediately began to rebuild the shops and continued in the cooper business until 1881, when he gave his entire attention instead, to mercantile pursuits. In the spring of 1879, he changed into storerooms his two-story brick building, which had been used as his cooper-shop, and, with Mr. Joseph Bartman, under the firm name of Wiegers & Co., he engaged in the grocery and liquor business, at which he still continues, with good success. Mr. Wiegers was married, in Staunton, Ill., on August 28, 1862, to Miss Spovleder, of that place; they have five children living, namely, John, Frederick, Lisse, Christ and Anna.

REV. M. WEIS, priest, Litchfield, was born in Bavaria, in Franconia, on June 8, 1838, and came to the United States in 1852, at the age of fourteen years, with his parents, who settled in Montgomery County, N. Y. in the vicinity of Amsterdam, and remained there five years. He came to Illinois in 1857, settling in Effingham County, in Teutopolis (called German City), and two years later began teaching in a primary school, continuing one year, when he came to Edwardsville, Ill., and there for two years taught a parochial school. During that time he studied, preparatory to entering St. Joseph's College at Teutopolis, which he did in the fall of 1862. He studied there three years, completing classics and philosophy, and in the summer of 1865, he started for Montreal, Canada, where he entered upon the study of theology, in the Grand Seminary there, in charge of the Sulpician Fathers, where he received holy orders. He was ordained to priesthood at the Alton, Ill., Cathedral, by the late Bishop Younger, in the spring of 1868. He began his pastoral work by taking charge of the Catholic Church at Vandalia, Ill., having also missions at Ramsey, Oconee, Sandoval and at Vandalia. After a year and a half he was transferred to Marine, Madison Co., Ill., where he remained two years. In

September, 1871, he was removed to Effingham, and was pastor there five years, during which time he built a large church, costing over $36,000, and a hospital for the Sisters of St. Francis. Being broken down in health, he started in the spring of 1876 for California, and returned to Minnesota in June, where he took charge of two congregations in the diocese of St. Paul, called respectively Hoka and La Crescent, near La Crosse, continuing three months. He was then recalled to the diocese of Alton and appointed Secretary and Chancellor to the Bishop, which important and laborsome position he held until 1880. He was sent thence to Saline, Madison Co., Ill., where he enlarged and finished a church and built a schoolhouse, filling that pastorate until he came to Litchfield in October, 1881, when he was transferred to the Church of the Assumption of the Blessed Virgin Mary, at Litchfield, Ill.

EDWARD WHITMER, tile manufacturer, Litchfield. Henry M. Whitmer was born in Juniata County, Penn, in 1833, and was raised among the Alleghany Mountains, on a farm. He came to Peoria, Ill., just before the war, and there engaged in the carpenter trade for a year, then removed to Decatur, Ill., where he became a large contractor and builder. For the past eighteen years he has been a large manufacturer of brick, and of late years has manufactured tile. He married in Snyder County, Penn., Miss Anna A. App, by whom he has five children living. He started in life with limited means, and by hard work has gained for himself a handsome competency. He established the Litchfield Tile Works in May, 1881, for which purpose he purchased eight acres at the eastern limits of Litchfield, on the Indianapolis & St. Louis Railroad, choosing that locality because of the superior quality of the clay which stands every test necessary to make drain tiling. He erected two dry sheds 200x20 feet, with two round, down-draft kilns, and a Tiffany improved auger machine, with an average capacity of 5,000 feet per day of ten hours. The tile works employ about twelve hands, the products of the works (consisting of tile of all the various sizes), supplying a large local demand, and there are shipments made by railroad to other points in the State. Edward Whitmer, the oldest son of H. M. Whitmer, and the subject of these lines, is Superintendent and Manager. They have on the same premises a yard for the manufacture of brick, which was established the same year of the tile works. The yard employs about fifteen hands.

DANIEL WALLWORK (deceased) was born in Newtown, Lancashire, England January 9, 1829. At the early age of eight years, he went into the mines of Pendlebury, in Lancashire, and worked there as a miner until 1856, when he came to the United States, where, for a period of about eight months, he worked in the mines of Pennsylvania. In 1857, he came to Alton, Ill., thence to Brighton, and thence to Moro, where he was Superintendent of the mines, and in the latter part of 1869 he came to Litchfield and here became Superintendent of the mines of the Litchfield Coal Company, a position which he held until his death, which occurred on February 14, 1880. He was a man of great industry, a successful miner, and was loved by his employes. He was a practical engineer and surveyor, and drew all the maps of the mines, etc. In May, 1847, he married Miss Sarah Greenhalgh, and ten children were born to them, but two of whom are living John Wallwork, now Superintendent of the mines, and a daughter. John Wallwork was born in Newtown, England, in 1847, and came to the United States with his parents in 1856. His first mining was done at Alton, Ill., when he was twelve years of age. He was Assistant Superintendent of the mines of Litchfield under his father, and still holds that position under Mr. Amsden. On April 4, 1882, he married Miss Violet Tinnell, of Litchfield.

M. C. WHIPPLE, druggist, Litchfield, was born in Canton, Stark Co., Ohio, in 1838. At the age of seventeen years, he entered a drug store at Massillon, Ohio, and learned the business. He afterward clerked in a drug store at Wooster, Ohio. In 1856, he engaged in the wholesale grocery business at Massillon, Ohio, continuing three years. In April, 1861, at the first call for volunteers, he enlisted in the Thirteenth Ohio Volunteer Infantry, and served until December, under Gen. Rosecrans, in West Virginia, and after that in the Army of the Ohio and Army of the Cumberland, under Gens. Buell, Rosecrans and Thomas. He was mostly on detached duty in the medical department of the army. His time having expired, he was mustered out June 26, 1864. After the war, he went to Tennessee, where he engaged in various pursuits, among which were the drug business and real estate, until 1873, when he came here and opened a drug store, and is yet in the same business, and also manages a farm near the city. In March, 188[illegible], he formed a partnership with Joseph B[illegible]rger, his former clerk for eight years. Mr. Whipple was married in October, 187[illegible], to Miss Julia L., second daughter of the Hon. [illegible] Cummings, one of the pioneers of [illegible] County, Ill.

WILLIAM WIEGREFFE, lumber dealer, Litchfield, was born in Hanover, Germany, on February 13, 1828. His father was [illegible]ler, and taught him the trade wh[illegible] This he followed until he came to the United States, in 1850. He landed in New Orleans [illegible]

[illegible] on a farm in Jersey County, Ill. He then came to Montgomery County, and bought a farm of 160 acres of raw prairie land near Zanesville. He still owns it, and lived on the place until 1868, when he came to Litchfield, Ill., and started in the lumber business. The same year he built a planing-mill, which he ran until 1877. Until 1872, he was associated with Mr. A. Perley, the firm name being Perley, Wiegreffe & Co., and afterward with his brother; but since 1877, Mr. Wiegreffe has conducted the business in his own name. He came to this country without capital, and has gained all he possesses through the merits of his own efforts. In 1861 he married Miss Eva Sen, at Carlinville, Ill. They have six children. From 1874 to 1876, he was Alderman from the Second Ward. His business includes lumber and building material, sash, doors, etc. He employs from two to five hands.

FREDERICK WEBER, manufacturer of soda and mineral waters, Litchfield, was born in Bavaria, Germany, near the River Rhine, in that portion called Pfalz, in the town of Zeiskam, on January 1, 1838. Until fourteen years old, he attended school, and then spent two years' apprenticeship in a bakery in his native town. In 1856, he came to the United States, and located first in St. Louis, where he worked at his trade until the breaking out of the war, when he enlisted, becoming a member of the Convalescent Corps, acting as pastry cook. He served eighteen months in the Good Samaritan Hospital, at St. Louis, and, being then discharged, he joined the Forty-seventh Indiana Infantry, being pastry cook for them for six months, at Helena, Ark. [illegible] 1865, he married Miss Elizabeth [illegible], at St. Louis, a native of Germany, and located in Cairo, Ill., where he [illegible] a bakery one year. He then returned [illegible] St. [illegible] the old country, returning in April of the following year, after which he farmed for a short time near St. Genevieve, Mo., and in the fall of 1865, discontinued it in order to establish a bakery in St. Louis. This he did, but at the end of one year sold his bakery and moved to Litchfield, Ill., where he worked for Mr. William Roth, in a bakery, for eight months. In June, 1867, he started a factory for the manufacture of soda and seltzer waters, to which he still devotes his attention. In 1881, he manufactured during the season an average of one hundred dozen of bottles per day, and these were shipped to various points in the State. These waters have become very popular as a healthful beverage, and, in consequence, the demand has steadily increased from year to year. For the past two years, Mr. Weber has run a steam cider press with good success. During the busy season, his business requires the services of eight active men. The following children have been born to Mr. Weber: Lizzie, Louise, Anne, Rosa, Kate, Mary and Frederick William.

WILLIAM G. WARDEN, carpenter, Litchfield, was born in Allen County, Ky., on May 2, 1832. He lived on a farm in his native State until October, 1850, when he came to Illinois. His father died when he was small, and he came to this State unaccompanied, arriving on a foggy Sunday, being obliged to climb the sign-posts to see the directions. He first stopped with his sister, Mrs. Young, with whom he lived, south of Hillsboro and worked until the summer of 1851. Then he returned to Kentucky, but in the fall of the same year came back to this State with a brother, with whom he lived two years, helping on the farm. He again returned to Kentucky, and in the fall of 1853 brought his mother to this State. She settled here permanently in 1854, the memorable "famine year." Our subject lived with her four years. Previous to this time he had learned carpentering with his brother, and in 1855-56, he worked with Robert Frame on contracts in the northern part of Montgomery County. In 1857, Mr. Warden began taking contracts alone, working in the southern part of this county until 1865, when he moved to Litchfield, where he has been engaged in carpentering ever since. During 1866-67, he also ran a wagon shop. For a period of one year he worked on the bridge work of the Indianapolis & St. Louis Railroad. When the Wabash Railroad was built, he was one of the first to begin work, and after working on the bridges, he superintended a company of men in the construction of the depot and freight building, etc., from Warder to Decatur. Since then he has engaged in carpentering and building. Mr. Warden is a Democrat, and has taken an active interest in politics. He was Justice of the Peace for five years, beginning at the time the township system was adopted. After that he was Town Clerk four years. In the spring of 1882, he was elected Assessor of South Litchfield Township. He acted one term as Alderman of the First Ward of Litchfield City in 1877. In 1860, he married Miss Anna E., daughter of A. C. Atwood, of Allen County, Ky. Their children are as follows: Alonzo W., born August 1, 1861, and died October 27, 1866; William J., born June 30, 1864; Ivy, born July 24, 1880; and all born in Montgomery County.

IRVING WELLS, farmer, P. O. Litchfield, was born in Rowan, now Davie County, N. C., November 13, 1825, and with his parents came to Illinois by team, in the fall of 1830, the journey lasting eight weeks. They stopped in Madison County until the spring of 1831, when they went to Greene County, where his parents resided until their death.

His father, John Wells, Sr., was born on April 27, 1795, in North Carolina, and died April 17, 1873. He was the father of seven children, and when he came to Greene County his means were limited to 31¼ cents. He was a member of the United Baptist Church. Our subject began teaching in 1847 in Greene County, and continued until 1858, in the meantime working on a farm. He came to Walshville Township, Montgomery County, in 1858, having purchased a land warrant, eight years previous, for eighty acres. On coming here he engaged in farming, and taught school five winters, living upon his original purchase until 1867, when he removed to his present place of 160 acres, where he since has engaged in raising grain and stock. February 6, 1860, he married Miss Lucetta, daughter of Edwin Brown, a Methodist preacher of Walshville. Twelve children were born to them, but seven of whom are living Julia, deceased; Oscar A. deceased; Washington L., deceased; John F.; David E.; Matta, deceased; Clara J., Albert S., Cora O., Ollie M., Myrtle, and Effa, deceased. Mr. Wells started in life without capital, and worked at first for $8 a month. Politically, he is a Democrat. His mother's maiden name was Matilda Irwin; she was from North Carolina. Although the father of our subject met many discouragements, he persevered in earnest, faithful labor, and made for himself an estate worth about $12,-000. He was twice married, and was the father of thirteen children, eleven of whom grew to maturity, and ten of whom still live, nine being of his last marriage.

LEWIS WHITAKER, Litchfield, was born in Deerfield Township, Cumberland County, N. J., September 2, 1835, and obtained his education in his native State. At the age of seventeen years, in 1852, he came to Carlinville, Ill., where he began learning the carpenter's trade, continuing one year, when he removed to Alton, Ill., there completing his trade. He spent the winter of 1854-55 in Mississippi and Louisana. He came to Litchfield, Ill., on October 8, 1855, and, after spending six weeks at his trade here, he went to his old home in New Jersey, where he spent the winter of 1855-56. In July, 1856, he returned to Litchfield, and worked as contractor and builder two years, when he went into the furniture and undertaking business, at which he continued about fifteen years, meeting with and meriting excellent success. His first furniture store was located where Boepple's bakery now is, and he afterward did business on the lot now occupied by Mr. Enniger. He next built the block where the *Regulator* is at present. In January, 1874, he retired from the furniture business, and in April of the same year he was elected City Marshal, which office he held one year. He then became a member of the firm of Whitaker & Rogers, in the milling business, continuing about two years. He next leased the Boxberger Mill, and took in as a partner Mr. Roth, for two years continuing in the milling and grain business, with very excellent success. Mr. Whitaker is a member of the McWilliams Oil and Mining Company, which began operations in this county in January, 1882. He has been a member of the City Council. On December 25, 1861, he married Mary E. Shore, sister of Tilman Shore. Mr. Whitaker is at present a member of the Litchfield Board of Education. In politics, he is a Republican.

GEORGE L. ZINK, was born in Steubenville, Ohio, September 19, 1841. He received an academic education in Jefferson County, Ohio, and devoted his own personal efforts in the study of the languages after leaving school. He began the study of law at seventeen years of age, with J. H. S. Trainer, of

Steubenville, Ohio, and was admitted to the bar at Pomeroy, Ohio, in 1864. In 1862, he enlisted in the Fifty second Ohio Volunteer Infantry, and participated in the battle of Perryville, Ky., and went as far South as Bowling Green, Ky., where he lay sick until December, 1862, and afterward in the hospital at Louisville; went out on duty again at post headquarters until July, 1863, when he was discharged. He then returned home, taught school for a time, and completed his law studies. In May, 1864, he enlisted for 100 days, and was stationed at Fort Delaware until the expiration of his time of service. He came to Illinois in 1865, and for eight months taught school at Gillespie, and in May, 1866, located in Litchfield, where he has ever since practiced his profession successfully, being admitted to the bar in this State in 1866, and in 1867 was admitted to practice in the Federal Courts. Mr. Zink was a Republican until 1872, when he joined the liberal movement, and was Presidential Elector for the old Sixteenth District on the Greeley ticket. In 1878, he was nominated and elected by the Democrats as Representative to the Illinois Legislature, from the Thirty fourth District, composed of Montgomery and Christian Counties.

WALSHVILLE TOWNSHIP.

DR. A. BARCROFT, physician, Walshville, was born in New Jersey in 1829; son of Ambrose and Ann (Wolverton) Barcroft. Ambrose Barcroft was born in 1793. He was for many years Captain of an ocean vessel, but finally quit the seafaring life and became a farmer. He died in York County, Penn., in 1881. His wife was born in New Jersey in 1795, and is now a resident of Washington, D. C. Our subject, the fourth child of a family of six, attended school at Pennington, N. J., from 1844 to 1847; at Baltimore College from 1854 to 1856, and, having chosen the medical profession, entered the National College at Washington, D. C., from which he graduated in 1862. He first began life as a clerk in a drug store. After graduating at Washington, he practiced in the Armory Hospital in that city from 1863 to 1864. He is now practicing his profession in Walshville. In Armstrong County, Penn., in 1853, he married Charlotte D. Woodward, a native of that county, born in 1835, daughter of John S. and Caroline (Barkley) Woodward. From this union there have been born to them six children, two of whom died in infancy. The four living are Ellis W., Victor B., Anna C. and Ambrose. Dr. Barcroft is a Republican, and a member of the A., F. & A. M.

V. B. BARCROFT, physician, Walshville, was born in Armstrong County, Penn., in 1857, son of Dr. A. and Charlotte (Woodward) Barcroft. The Doctor, whose sketch also appears in this work, was born in New Jersey in 1829, and has successfully followed the practice of his profession for many years. His wife was born in Armstrong County, Penn., in 1835. Our subject, the second of a family of six children, began his education at Lincoln, Logan Co., Ill., and, having chosen his father's profession, entered the Missouri Medical College at St. Louis, from which he graduated in 1879. He is now practicing medicine with his father in Walshville. He formerly taught school in Bond and Montgomery Counties.

JESSE BOYD, farmer, P. O. Walshville, was born in Franklin County, Va., August 22, 1810; son of Henry and Ellender (Woods) Boyd. Henry Boyd was born in Franklin County, Va., in 1789, and died in Montgomery County, Ill., March 25, 1877. His wife, a native of Virginia, was born in 1789, and died in Montgomery County in 1872. Our subject, the second of a family of nine children, received his education in Warren County, Ky. He also attended school at Staunton, Macoupin Co., Ill. He has followed the occupation of a farmer in Macoupin and Montgomery Counties for the last fifty years. In Macoupin County, Ill., in 1832, he married Matilda Voyles, born in Pendleton County, N. C., in 1811, daughter of Robert and Hester (Morris) Voyles. From this union they have had twelve children, six of whom died in infancy. Those living are Hester R., William J., Ellender M., Martha A., Robert H. and Jessie S. Mr. Boyd is a member of the Methodist Episcopal Church, and of the A., F. & A. M. He is a Republican in politics.

WILLIAM BURKE, farmer, P. O, Walshville, was born in Kentucky February 6

1817; son of John and Catharine (Barlow) Burke, he born in Virginia in 1785, and died in Montgomery County, Ill., in 1846; she, born in Virginia, and died in this county in 1836. Our subject is the seventh child of a family of eleven, and received his education in the common schools of this county. In 1840, he married Temperance Holiday, born in this county in 1820, and died here in 1860, and daughter of Elliott Holiday. His second wife was Mrs. Sarah Brown, born in Kentucky, and died in this county in 1870, and his third wife, Mrs. Sarah M. Dukes, was born in Livingston County, Ky., October 18, 1823. He has had twelve children, ten of whom are living: John B., Martha J., Joe A., Mary E., William R., Sina L., Alice E., Adda B., Edna C. and Katie A. Mr. Burke has always been a farmer; having farmed in this county for fifty years, and is known as one of the leading farmers in the district. He is a Presbyterian, a Democrat, an A., F. & A. M., and an I. O. O. F.

ANTONY BUERGER, farmer, P. O. Mt. Olive, Macoupin County, whose parents, John and Mary C. (Fastlabend) Buerger, were natives of Germany, was born in that country September 2, 1822. John Buerger, who was a farmer, died in Madison County, Ill., October 18, 1846. His wife died in the same county in 1872. Antony, who was the eldest of a family of ten, received his education in Germany, and engaged in farming, which occupation he has always followed. He married in St. Louis, Mo., May 13, 1853, Louisa Bartman, born in Germany in 1830, daughter of John Bartman. From this union seven children have been born to them: Joseph, John F., Mary, Matilda, Henry, Louisa and Leonora. Mr. Buerger is a member of the Roman Catholic Church, and in politics a Democrat.

MRS. SARAH D. CURRY, farmer, P. O. Walshville, was born in Morgan County, Ill., in 1834, daughter of William and Tabitha (Bell) Elledge, he born in Kentucky, and died in Morgan County, Ill., in [illegible]; she, born in Kentucky, and died in Pike County, Ill., in 1874. Subject was the sixth child of a family of seven, and was educated in Morgan and Pike Counties, Ill. She was married in Pike County, Ill., in 184[illegible], to Riley J. Curry, a farmer born in Kentucky, and died in this county August 13, 187[illegible], son of Nicholas Curry, a native of Ireland, who came to this country in an early day, and died in Morgan County, Ill., about the year 1850. Our subject is the mother of ten children, namely: James A., Tabitha E., George F., William R., Charles B., John F., Winefred L., Elbert G., Edwin H., Esther B. Mrs. Curry is a member of the Christian Church.

DR. MARTIN S. DAVENPORT, son of Jack S. and Lucy S. (Lewis) Davenport, was born in the State of Virginia, Charlotte County, November 1, 1818. His father was born in Charlotte County, Va., in 1780. His mother was also a native of Charlotte County, Va., was born in 1784, and died in October, 1860. The family moved from the Old Dominion to Kentucky, where his father died in May, 1834. Left in orphanage, Mr. Davenport, in connection with a younger brother, undertook the support of the widowed mother and family, and nobly did they work to this end. Naturally of an inquiring and literary cast of mind, and deprived to a great extent of school facilities, he commenced when quite young the work of his own education by the light afforded from burning fagots and pine knots. In this manner he acquired a fair English education. In Christian County, Ky., in April, 1841, he married Miss Lucy S. Lewis, born in Charlotte County, Va., in December, 1813, daughter of Edgecome and

Anna (Davenport) Lewis, both natives of Charlotte County, Va., the former born in 1780, and died in March, 1843; the latter born 1793, and died in July, 1847. Immediately after his marriage he commenced the study of medicine, to which profession he had manifested a proclivity from the seventeenth year of his age. He received a medical diploma from Dr. Curtis in 1848, and graduated at the Physio-Medical College, Cincinnati, Ohio, in 1870. Mr. Davenport moved into Montgomery in 1848, and located in the town of Walshville in 1864. He has had a constant practice in his community for over twenty-six years, and is now regarded as one of the most successful practitioners in the county. Though now in his fifty-fifth year, he is hale, hearty and energetic, and in physique does not appear more than forty years old. This may be accounted for in part from his strictly temperate habits, never having during his life been under the influence of intoxicating liquor in the least degree. The Davenports are English in descent, and were among the first settlers in this country. Richard Davenport, the Doctor's grandfather, held the office of Captain in the Revolutionary war, and was present and participated in the battle of Yorktown. At the close of the war, he settled in the State of Virginia, Charlotte County. He raised quite a family—Glover (deceased), of Norfolk, Va.; Martin W., a wholesale merchant of Lynchburg, Va.; Ballard (deceased), one of the pioneers of Kentucky; Mary (deceased), wife of John Franklin, of Virginia, and grandson of Benjamin Franklin, illustrious patriot, statesman and philosopher; Martha, wife of Barnet Edwards, of Kentucky; Mrs. Sarah (John) Mathews; and Mrs. Catharine (Putnam) North, both of Virginia, are some of the names handed down. Jack S., Dr. Davenport's father, was a Lieutenant in the war of 1812. He served under Gen. Jackson. Glover was a Colonel in the same war. The Doctor has the following children: George W., John J. and Peter W., druggists, all of Walshville. George and Peter served as soldiers in the late rebellion. We believe they were both veterans of the Union service. Dr. Davenport has good cause to feel proud in the contemplation of his family record. Not one of the numerous and long family line was ever arraigned before the courts under a criminal charge, and they have always espoused the cause of patriotism, from the Revolution against English tyranny to the suppression of treason during the late war of the Southern States. They are a family noted for public spirit, literature and Christian morality.

PETER EGELHOFF, farmer, P. O. Walshville, was born in Germany October 12, 1830; son of William and Mary (Schroth) Egelhoff. William, who was a native of Germany, was born in 1806, and died in Jerseyville, Jersey Co., Ill., September 19, 1879, where his wife, born in Germany, in 1810, also died, March 23, 1866. Peter, the eldest of a family of seven children, received his education in Germany, and worked at the blacksmith's trade for some time. About twenty years ago, he moved to his present place, which, at that time was rough and unimproved; but, by incessant labor and economy, he has made it one of the finest farms in Montgomery County. He has a fine, large barn, granary, stock scales, etc. In Montgomery County, in 1856, he married Mary A. Ostermeyer, born in Germany September 22, 1830, daughter of Frederick Ostermeyer, a native of that country, and there have been born to them nine children—William F., John C., Louisa, George, Otto, Mary, Peter J. and two others who died unnamed. Mr. Egelhoff, who is a Democrat, is one of the substantial men of Walshville Township.

DICK ENGELMANN, farmer, P. O. Mt. Olive, Macoupin County, was born in Germany, November 5, 1840. His parents, Henry and T[illegible]a (Gosmann) Engelmann, are natives of Germany, and are now living in Ostfriesland, Kingdom of Hanover. Henry was born November 13, 1820. Richard is the eldest of a family of four children, and received his education in Germany. He has always been engaged in farming and stock raising. He has been Highway Commissioner in Walshville Township for some time. Mr. Engelmann has been twice married. First, in Madison County, Ill., November 8, 1878, he married Lizzie E. Engelmann, born in Germany in 1844, and died in Montgomery County March 5, 1879. She was the daughter of Minke Engelmann. His second wife, whom he married at Hillsboro, Montgomery County, in January, 1880, is Gretchen Arkebauer, born in Germany in 1845. Mr. Engelmann has four children—Henry, George, Michael and Tine. He is a member of the Lutheran Church, and in politics is a Democrat.

I. F. FOGELMAN, farmer, P. O. Walshville, son of John and Elizabeth (Kirkland) Fogelman, was born in Montgomery County August 29, 1844. His parents were both born in Montgomery County, and still reside there. His father was born April 8, 1819; his mother was born in 1819 or 1820. Our subject, who is the fourth of a family of ten children, received his education in the schools of Montgomery County, and engaged in farming, which occupation he has always followed. He is Assessor of Walshville Township, which office he has held for six years. During the war, he served in Company A, Ninety-first Illinois Infantry; was captured at Elizabethtown in 1862, by John Morgan, and released on parole. Returning to service in July, 1863, he took part in the engagements at Vicksburg, New Orleans and Spanish Fort, on Mobile Bay, receiving his discharge at the latter place in 1865. In Montgomery County, in 1865, he married M. M. McPhail, born in Montgomery County October 12, 1841, daughter of Macon and Elizabeth (Beedels) McPhail. There have been born to them two children—Willis M. and J. W. M., the latter dying October 18, 1871. Mr. Foglemar is in politics a Democrat.

JAMES GRISHAM, farmer, P. O. Walshville, was born in Dixon County, Tenn., January 14, 1811, son of Austin and Fanny (Powers) Grisham, he born in Guilford County, N. C., March 10, 1771, and died in Montgomery County March 9, 1853; she born in Virginia October 10, 1775, and died in Montgomery County May 10, 1851. James, the fourth child of a family of five, finished his education in Montgomery County in 1829, and began life as a farmer, which occupation he has ever since followed. He is one of the first settlers of Montgomery County, having entered the land he now lives on in 1820. He took part in the Black Hawk war, in 1832. In Montgomery County, January 8, 1830, he married Martha R. Garrison, born December 22, 1813, and died September 29, 1843. She was a daughter of John Garrison, who died in Tennessee. In Montgomery County, November 30, 1845, he married his second wife, Pamelia Cannon, born in Illinois in April, 1828, daughter of William and Catharine (Lovings) Cannon, he born in Kentucky, and died in 1880; she, also a native of Kentucky, is still living. Mr. Grisham has a family of seventeen children—John A., William S., Amanda C., Fanny M., Thomas K., Polly P., Melissa R., Martha R., Mary F., Margaret M., Alfred F., Elias E., Charles S., Henry R., Baby, Ulysses C. and Allen A. He is a member of the Missionary Baptist Church, and a supporter of the Republican party.

MRS. E. R. HODGES, Walshville, was

born in Montgomery County, Ill., in 1834, the daughter of James and Mary (Barlow) Bostic, he a farmer, who died in this county in 1842; she born in Tennessee, and also died in this county in 1838. Subject is the third child of a family of four. She was educated in this county, and married in 1860 to Mr. Hodges, born in Tennessee in 1814, a son of H[illegible] Hodges, a Virginian by birth, who moved to Tennessee and died there. Mrs. Hodges has had six children—Alice G., Mary E., [illegible] F., Julia, Jessie C., and one dead. The late Mr. Hodges was engaged in farming in his early life, but for many years before his death was a prominent merchant of Walshville, where he died May 13, 1876.

JOHN B. JOHNSON, farmer, P. O. Mt. Olive, Macoupin County, was born in Germany, January 1, 1830; son of Bornn Johnson, who was a native of Germany, and a farmer by occupation, died in Madison County, Ill., in [illegible]. His wife, also a native of Germany, who is now a resident of this county, was born in 1799. Of a family of six children, our subject was the third. He received his education in Germany, and emigrated to this country in 1851. He first settled in Madison County, Ill., for a short time; then removed to Macoupin County, Ill., where he remained eight years, after which he removed to Montgomery County and permanently settled on his present place. Mr. Johnson has followed the occupation of a farmer all his days, and now owns a fine farm near Mt. Olive. In Macoupin County, Ill., in March, 1857, he married Miss Rosmuller, born in Germany in [illegible]828, daughter of Fried Rosmuller. From this union they have had the following children: John, Mary, Margaret, Friede, Ida and F[illegible]de. Mr. Johnson is a Republican, and a member of the Lutheran Church.

H[illegible] KEISER, farmer, P. O. Mt. Olive, Macoupin County, was born in Germany October 8, 1839; son of John and Gerke (Heien) Keiser. John Keiser, who was a farmer, was born in Germany in 1816, and died in Macoupin County, Ill., September 6, 1855. His wife, also a native of Germany, and who now resides in Montgomery County, was born in 1810. Our subject, the eldest of six children, received his education in Germany, and, having emigrated to America in 1854, settled down to farming with his father in Macoupin County, Ill. He has been a farmer all his days. From Macoupin County he removed to his present place in Montgomery County. In 1874, he was elected Secretary of the Mt. Olive Coal Company, which office he held until 1881, when he was elected to his present position of Superintendent of the company. He has also held the office of Supervisor of Walshville Township. In Macoupin County, Ill., July 11, 1863, he married Mary (Kerren) Keiser, born in Germany October 18, 1845, daughter of John and Folkea (Vesser) Kerren. From this union there have been born to them nine children—Annie G., John, Henry W., Hermann J., Katie H., Sophia W., Hannah M., Lydia E., Edward A. Mr. Keiser is widely and favorably known as a worthy citizen. In politics, he is a Republican. He is a member of the German Methodist Church.

ANDREW KEISER, miller, Mt. Olive, Macoupin County, was born in Hanover, Germany, September 28, 1845; son of John H. and Gerke (Heien) Keiser, both natives of Germany. John H., who was a farmer, was born in 1816, and died in Macoupin County, Ill., September 6, 1855; his wife, who is now a resident of Montgomery County, was born in 1810. Our subject, who is the third of a family of six children, received his education in Germany, and has followed farming and milling since he came to this country with his parents. He has been twice married.

His first wife, Annie Ross, born in Madison County, Ill., daughter of Gird and Mary (Arkabauer) Ross, and died in Montgomery County September 28, 1875, leaving three children: Annie G., John and Mary. In Macoupin County, March 29, 1879, Mr. Keiser married his second wife, Frances Ross, born in Madison County, Ill., March 9, 1855, daughter of John and Mary (Arkabauer) Ross. Mr. Keiser has held the offices of Assessor and Collector in Walshville Township. He is a Republican in politics, and a member of the Lutheran Church.

T. C. KIRKLAND, farmer, Walshville, was born in St. Louis County, Mo., July 26, 1823; son of Isaac and Melinda (Mann) Kirkland, he born in Mercer County, Ky., December 25, 1796, a tanner by trade, and afterward a farmer, and died in Litchfield, Montgomery County, April 5, 1881; she, also a native of Mercer County, Ky., born November 16, 1799, and died in Jersey County, Ill., October 7, 1853. Our subject, the third of a family of four children, received a fair education in Jersey County, Ill., and began life as a farmer. In 1865, he moved to his present place, which is one of the finest farms in Montgomery County. He is a prominent member of the community, and has held the offices of Supervisor, School Director and Trustee for a number of years. In Jersey County, February 18, 1847, he married Edith Irwin, born in Iredell County, N. C., March 1 1823, daughter of Abijah and Elizabeth (Eaton) Irwin, he born in North Carolina February 1, 1791, and died May 15, 1863; she, also a native of North Carolina, born January 27, 1791, and died September 8, 1827. Mr. and Mrs. Kirkland are the parents of five children: Matilda Ellen, Sarah Elizabeth, Ann Eliza, John Harden and Mary Melinda. He is a Methodist, a supporter of the Republican party, and a member of the A., F. & A. M.

CHARLES KEUNE, farmer, P. O. Walshville, was born in Germany July 7, 1837; son of Christine and Mary (Kalthammer) Keune, he a farmer, born in Germany, and died there in 1852; she, also born in Germany, and died there the same year. Our subject was the fifth child of a family of eight; was educated at Brunswick, Germany, and came to this country in 1856, located at St. Louis, Mo., and came to this county in 1881. He married Minnie Schueffe, in St. Clair County, Ill., in 1867, born in Germany in 1844, daughter of William and Joanna Reni... Schueffe. Subject has six children: Andrew W., Arnold H., Charles, Emma S., Amelia and Minnie S. Mr. Keune is independent in politics.

GEORGE McPHERSON, farmer, P. O. Walshville, was born in Scott County, Ill., in 1852; son of James H. and Elizabeth (Johnson) McPherson. James H., who was a farmer, was born in North Carolina, and died in Scott County, Ill., in 1879. His wife, a native of North Carolina, also died in Scott County, Ill., in 1846. Subject, who is the eldest of a family of seven children, received his education in the common schools of Montgomery County, finishing at Litchfield. He began the business of life as a farmer, and has ever since been in the same occupation, and is Road Commissioner at present. In Hillsboro, Montgomery County, in 1878, he married Alice Kirkwood, born in Jersey County, Ill., in 1850, daughter of David and Elizabeth (Cowen) Kirkwood. He is a Republican, and a member of the Christian Church.

FRED NIEMANN, farmer, P. O. Mt. Olive, Macoupin County, was born in Germany February 11, 1823, son of Casper and

Anna (Witte) Niemann. Casper Niemann was a native of Germany, and a farmer by occupation. He died in Germany in January, 1847. His wife, Anna, also a native of Germany, died there the same year as her husband, leaving eight children, of whom our subject was the second. The subject of this sketch began life as a farmer in his native land. In 1847, he emigrated to America, and located in Macoupin County, Ill., where he lived for twelve years; thence he removed to Montgomery County, where he purchased a tract of land, which, by push and industry, he has made a first-class farm. In Germany, September 6, 1850, he married Anna Shrodar, a native of that country, born in 1833, daughter of Henry and Mary Shrodar. From this union there have been born to them five children—William H., Julius L., Frederick W., Hannah H. C. and Anna. Mr. Niemann is a member of the Lutheran Church. In politics, he is a Republican.

B. C. NEAL, plasterer, Walshville, was born in Logan County, Ky., December 28, 1824; son of Benjamin and Mary (Hayden) Neal. Benjamin Neal, who was a farmer, was born in Virginia, and died in Logan County, Ky., September 22, 1856. His wife, who was a native of North Carolina, was born in 1792, and also died in Logan County, Ky., in 1872. Our subject, the ninth of a family of ten children, received his education in his native county. He followed the occupation of farmer for many years, but since learned the plastering trade, which business he now follows. In Allen County, Ky., in 1847, he married Susan F. Warden, a native of that county, born August 17, 1829, daughter of James and Rebecca (Kelley) Warden. She died in Montgomery County April 5, 1870, leaving five children—Virgil S., Eloise, Martha P., Elnora C. and William S. Mr. Neal is a member of the Christian Church. He is in politics a Greenbacker.

ALBERT SCHON, farmer, P. O. Mt Olive, Macoupin County, is a native of Hanover, Germany, was born May 17, 1833. His parents, Hiram and Folka (Tiden) Schon, were both natives of Germany, and died in that country. Hiram Schon, a farmer by occupation, was born in 1801, and died in 18?? His wife, born in 1804, died in 1879. Albert, our subject, the third of a family of eight children, emigrated to America in 1854, and located in Madison County, Ill., where he remained for about ten years. He then removed to Montgomery County, where he purchased his present property. He has always been a farmer, and is one of the influential men of Walshville Township. He married in Madison County, Ill., October 18, 1854, Miss A. Arkebauer, born in Germany, February 15, 1837, daughter of Jordan and Frances (Wauhoff) Arkebauer, and there have been born to them eleven children—Hiram, George, Mary, Frances, John, Willie, Zena, M. A., Annie, Lida, and one deceased (unnamed). Mr. Schon is a Republican, and a member of the Lutheran Church.

T. T. SMITH, farmer, P. O. Walshville, was born in Madison County, Ill., April 29, 1838, son of Jonathan Green and Elizabeth (Tindall) Smith. Jonathan Green Smith was born in Pittsfield, N. H., July 9, 1814, and died in New Mexico February 26, 1848. His wife was born in Madison County, Ill., December 11, 1820, and died there in September, 1844. Our subject, the eldest of a family of four, received his education in the common schools of Madison County, Ill. He married in Montgomery County February 2?, 1861, Susan Sackett, born in Madison County, Ill., December 25, 1842, daughter of Elisha and Elizabeth (Voyles) Sackett. Elisha

Sackett, a native of South Carolina, was born about the year 1812, and died in February, 1849. His wife, born in 1816, died September 24, 1854. Mr. and Mrs. Smith are the parents of four children—Mary Lorett, Edgar Leighton, John Elvin and Bert (deceased). Mr. Smith has always been a farmer, and is one of the substantial men of Walshville Township. He has held the offices of Supervisor, School Trustee and Highway Commissioner. Both he and his wife are members of the Methodist Episcopal Church. In politics he is a Republican.

W. J. WHITESIDE, retired farmer, P. O. Walshville, was born in Chester County, S. C., in 1801; son of Abraham and Janet (Hannan) Whiteside. Abraham was born in South Carolina July 4, 1775, and died in Montgomery County August 24, 1857. His wife, born in North Carolina, died February 6, 1829. Our subject, the eldest of a family of five children, received a fair education in Maury County, Tenn., and learned the cabinet-making trade, which he engaged in for forty years. He has also been a farmer for many years; was one of the early settlers of Montgomery County. He married in Tennessee, in 1824, Mary G. Bingham, born in Guilford County, N. C., November 7, 180[illegible], daughter of Robert and Martha (Reed) Bingham. From this union there have been born ten children—Martha J., Tennessee [illegible], Zianna, John M., Sarah P., Thomas [illegible] M. E., Margaret A., Robert L. and William Newton. Mr. Whiteside is a Methodist and a Democrat. Robert L., the ninth child of the family, was born in Hickman County, Tenn., in 1842; received his education at Walshville, and engaged in farming, which occupation he still follows. He is a Democrat.

GRISHAM TOWNSHIP.

G. R. AYDELOTT, farmer, P. O. Donnellson, was born in Montgomery County, Ill., in 1844; son of C. C. and Levina (Young) Aydelott; he born in Tennessee in 1806, died in Montgomery County, Ill., in 1865; she, a native of Kentucky, moved to that county in 1829. The subject of this sketch who is the eleventh child of a family of thirteen, received his education in the schools of his native county, and began life as a farmer, his father having left him one of the finest farms in Montgomery County. He married in Montgomery County in 1866, Aurilla Brooks, born in Warren County Tenn., daughter of Loyal Brooks, a native of Cheshire, Conn. Mr. Aydelott served two terms as Tax Collector of Grisham Township; has been Supervisor for many years, and was re-elected to that office in the spring of 1882; is a Methodist a member of the Masonic fraternity; has always been a staunch Democrat.

CHRISTIAN A. [illegible]NGERSTINE, farmer, P. O. Donnellson, was born in Hanover, Germany, in 1825 son of Henry and Christina (Kalals) Angerstine, both of whom were natives of Germany and died there, he in 1852 she in 1879; subject is the youngest of a family of five children. He received his education in his native land, and began the business of life as a farm hand. In 1854, he emigrated to the United States, and has been living in Montgomery County for twenty five years, during which time he has been engaged in farming. In St. Louis, Mo., in 1855, he married Wilhelmine Bramer, a native of Germany, daughter of Hender Bramer, also a native of that country. From this union three children have been born, viz. [illegible] is a member of the Lutheran Church at [illegible]boro, Ill.; he is a Republican.

REV. W. P. BAKER, farmer, P. O. [illegible]boro; born in Macon County, Ill., in 18[illegible]5, son of W. D. and Marilla (Martin) Baker, [illegible] present reside in Macon County, Ill. His [illegible] W. D. Baker, was born in Lincoln County, N. C., in 1800, and follows the occupation of a farmer. The subject of this sketch is the [illegible] child of a family of seven. He received his education in his native county, and engaged in farming, but has spent the greater part of his life as a minister of the Presbytarian Church[illegible] has preached for nineteen years in Southern Illinois, and is at present pastor of M[illegible]'s Point Church in East Fork Township. Mr Baker has been married twice first in Macon County, Ill., in 1857, and the last time in Montgomery County, Ill., in 1864. The maiden names of his wives were Mary Wilson and Margaret McLane. His children are Ora [illegible] Joseph M. Mary J. and William C.

R. H. BOYD, framer, P. O. Walshvi[illegible] in Macoupin County, Ill., in 1846; son of [illegible] and Matilda (Morris) Boyd; he born in [illegible] lin County, Va August 22 1810; [illegible] the eight child of a family of twel[illegible] received his education in Montgomery County and at Staunton, Macoupin County. [illegible] Montgomery County in 1866, he married Am[illegible] Whiteside, born in that county in 1851, daughter of Thomas D. and Minerva J. Whiteside. [illegible] ject has five children—Thomas D., Je[illegible] M. Jessie J., Hattie E. and Frederick R. [illegible] Republican; is a Northern Methodist [illegible] been a farmer all his days.

Wilson and Mary Ann (Chilton) Cary was born in Bond County, Ill., December 29, 1843; his father was a farmer, born in Virginia and died in Bond County, Ill.; his mother was a native of East Tennessee. Our subject was the sixth of a family of twelve children; he graduated from the Hillsboro Academy in 1862; he was married in Lee County, Iowa, June 4, 1869, to Laura M. Donnell, a of native Iowa, born February 25, 1848; daughter of William A. Donnell, who was born in Guilford County, N. C., and of Callista (Hamilton) Donnell, a native of New York State. Our subject has been blessed with the following children: Flora C., Ada J., deceased, Alvin P. and Katie A. After graduating from the academy, he read medicine under Dr. Hills, and has practiced in this county for eighteen years. During the late war, he served under Gen. J. J. Phillips, of Hillsboro, in Company H, Ninth Illinois Regiment. The family are Presbyterian, and Mr. Cary is a member of the Masonic fraternity, Lodge No. 55, Donnellson.

P. L. DAVENPORT, farmer, P. O. Walshville, was born in Charlotte County, Va., son of Jack S. and Lucy S. (Lewis) Davenport. His father was a farmer, born in the same county in Virginia and died in Logan County, Ky., in 1836; his mother was also a native of Virginia, died in Trigg County, Ky., in 1860. They had four children, of whom our subject was the youngest; he received his education in the common schools of Virginia, and began life as a carpenter; he has worked at his trade and carried on farming in this county for a period of thirty years. He was married in Trigg County, Ky., in 1844, to Frances Elizabeth Roper, a native of that county; she died in this county in 1857. Her parents were Henry C. and Nancy (Lewis) Roper, both natives of Campbell County, Va. Mr. Davenport it at present Assessor of this township, and has held the office of School Director for many years. He has been three times married, his second wife being Mrs. Martha Brown, a native of Fayette County, Ill., and the third, Mrs. Frances Bishop, of this county. He has been blessed with the following children: Eliza C., Lucy S., Ann E., Louisa F., Sarah M., Ruth J., Martin S., Ulysses J., John J., Essa O. Tipton C., Thomas R. and Francis J. His religious connection is with the Christian Church, and his political sympathies are with the Republican party.

CHARLES H. EDWARDS, farmer, P. O. Hillsboro, was born in Montgomery County, Ill., August 20, 1835, son of Thomas and Nellie (Brown) Edwards, natives of Iredell County, N. C. Thomas Edwards, a farmer and also a miller, moved to Montgomery County, Ill., in 1827, where he died in 1857, and where his wife also died in February, 1837. Charles H., the subject of this sketch, is the tenth of a family of thirteen children. He received his education in Montgomery County, and began life as a farmer, which occupation he still follows; has been Justice of the Peace and School Trustee for many years. In 1861, he enlisted in Company A, Twenty-sixth Missouri Infantry, and was discharged in 1864. He married in Montgomery in 1858, Nora E. Cannon, a native of that county, daughter of William Cannon, born in Mercer County, Ky., in 1807, died in 1878: from this marriage nine children have been born, viz., Mary E., William H., Eddie C., Clara J., Thomas C., Charles M., James A., Jessie F. and Minnie B. Mr. Edwards is a Methodist; has always been a Democrat; is a member of Grange No. 917, at Mansfield.

WALKER F. HICKMAN, farmer, P. O. Hillsboro, the fourth of a family of nine children, was born in Crittenden County, Ky., in 1838, and moved to this county in 1852. His parents were William and Eliza (Witherspoon) Hickman, the former born in Bourbon County, Ky., in 1803, a farmer by occupation, and died in this county in 1857; the latter born in Crittenden County, Ky., and died in this county in

1867. Our subject was educated at Hillsboro Academy, and his occupation is that of a farmer. In 1862, he was married to Melissa McClain, who was born in this county in 1836, daughter of Joseph and Abigail (Paisley) McClain, the former born in Guilford County, N. C., in 1800, and the latter a native of the same county. Mr. Hickman has in addition to his farm labors, filled the office of School Director for many years; he was in the late war, a member of Company B. One Hundred and Seventeenth Illinois Regiment, having enlisted at Hillsboro, Ill., in August, 1862. His children are as follows: Alma M., Ellert M., Frank C. Eva O., Carl C. and Ethel E. Mr. Hickman is a Cumberland Presbyterian, and politically a Republican.

FRED HELFERS, farmer, P. O. Donnellson, was born in Hanover, Germany, in 1849, son of John and Louisa Helfers, both natives of Germany, and at present residents of Montgomery County, he born in 1821, and she in 1825. Fred Helfers is the eldest child of a family of three; he was educated partly in Germany and partly in the common schools of St. Clair County, Ill.; he is a farmer, and has by his industry bought his present home. In St Clair County, Ill., he married Margaret Schaumleffel, who was born there in 1847 she is the daughter of Adam Schaumleffel, a native of Germany; subject has two children Charles F. and Leonard.

ROBERT LOGSDON, farmer, P. O. Walshville, was born in Hart County, Ky., in 1828, son of William K. and Maria (Remus) Logsdon, he born in Hart County, Ky., where he died in 1832; was a farmer; she, born in North Carlinia in 1808 died in Montgomery County in 1879; subject is the second child of a family of four his education was obtained in Hart County, Ky., where in 1852, he married Mary E. Johnsey, who was born there in 1831: she is the daughter of George B. and Jane (Simms) Johnsey; subject has the following children: John W. George, Marietta, Martha Ann, Celesta, Ida, Lucy M., Robert E., Lee and Ervin. Mr. Logsdon is a practical farmer, and has one of the most highly cultivated farms in Montgomery County. He is one of the oldest settlers: himself and wife are Methodists; he is a strong Democrat

JOHN W. LOGSDON, farmer, P. O. Walshville; born in Hart County, Ky., in 1853, son of Robert and Mary E. (Johnsey) Logsdon, both natives of that county, he a farmer by occupation, born in 1828; she in 1831. John W is the eldest of a family of twelve children; he received his education in the schools of Montgomery County, and engaged in farming, which occupation he still pursues. In Howard County, Ind., in 1876, he married Amy C. Beeler, daughter of William and Margaret (Burk) Beeler, he born in Pennsylvania in 1817, now resides in Adams County, Ind.; she a native of Ohio. From this marriage two children have been born Bertia and Hattie. Mr. Logsdon is a Democrat.

J. H. McPHERSON, farmer, P. O. Walshville, whose portrait appears in this work, was born in Muhlenburg County, Ky., December 13, 1826, and was raised upon a farm. He was brought to St. Clair County Ill., by his parents when he was but an infant where they ramained about seven years, then removed to Morgan, now Scott County, Ill., near Winchester. He was there educated in the common schools, remaining in that county until nineteen years of age, when he embarked in the sawmill business, a business he has followed a good many years He commenced business without a dollar, and has had many trials and disappointments, but by energy and perseverance has overcome them, and now owns 645 acres of good bottom land, well improved and in an excellent state of cultivation. He and his brother built the first flouring mill in Litchfield, where the noted steam mill now stands, but sold it in 1856, and then engaged in a machine shop until 1863, when he took an overland trip to California but believing he could do better at home, returned within six months, and engaged in his old business, saw-milling. This he followed until December, 1878, since which time he has been engaged in farming. He was married in Scott County, November 19, 1851, to Miss Rebecca J. Ash, also a native of Kentucky, and who was born February 9, 1830. She was the mother of six children, and died May 13 1870. Jesse Ash, her father, was born in Kentucky, also her mother. His second wife, Margaret Missmore, was born in Hillsboro, Ill., February 3, 1833; her father was from North Carolina, and her mother a native of Tennessee. James McPherson, the father of our subject, was born in North Carolina January 28, 1796, and was a farmer. He emigrated to Kentucky, and from that State to Illinois in 1827 where he bought land, and raised a large family of children, who grew up useful men and women. He was in the war of 1812, though he served but three months; he was in the battle of New Orleans; he died in October, 1879. His wife, Elizabeth Johnson, was a native of North Carolina; was born January 29, 1799, and was the mother of thirteen children, of whom our subject was the fifth.

MRS. H. E. McCULLOCH, farmer, P. O. Donnellson, was born in Montgomery County, Ill., in 1838, daughter of William and Jane E. (Paisley) Young, he a farmer by occupation, born in Tennessee in 1810, now residing near Hillsboro, Montgomery Co., Ill., where his wife, a native of North Carolina, died in 1852. Subject who is the fourth child of a family of nine, was educated in the schools of Montgomery County where, in 1864, she was married to W. J. McCulloch, a native of that county, who died there in 1876. Their children are Samuel R. and Jennie. Her husband was a farmer, and for many years filled the office of Supervisor in Montgomery County; he was a Democrat. Mrs. McCulloch is a member of the Cumberland Presbyterian Church.

JOHN PRICE, farmer, P. O. Hillsboro, born in Wayne County, Ky., in 1816, son of Richard and Mary (Johnson) Price, natives of Virginia. Richard Price was a farmer by occupation; subject the fifth child of a family of six, received the foundation of his education in the common schools of Montgomery County, and finished at Hillsboro in that county. He has always been a farmer; has been School Director for some time. In Montgomery County in 1841, he married Ellen Nora Lovrin, born in Simpson County Ky., in 1824 daughter of William and Keziah (Morgan) Lovrin, natives of Virginia. From this union there have been born the following children, viz.: George W., John E., Thomas J., Mary C., Isaac K., James F., Joseph A., M. C., William H., Julia A., Sarah E. and Harriet L. Mr. Price is one of the leading men of Grisham Township; has been a member and class leader in the Methodist Church for thirty years his membership being at Edwards Chapel in the above township. He is a Republican and a member of the A., F. & A. M.

ASA SWAIN, farmer, P. O. Walshville, was born in Washington County, N. C., December 22, 1811, son of Stephen and Priscilla (Phelps) Swain, both natives of North Carolinia; the former died in Macoupin County, this State, in 1846, the latter also dying in the same county. They had nine children, of whom Asa was the fourth, and received his education in his native county. He early learned the cooper's trade and has followed farming in this and Madison County for half a century. He has been twice married, and has had the following children—Maria J., Stephen H., Clarissa E., Martha C., Snowden S., Sarah M., Asa F. and three who died unnamed. Mr. Swain is a leading farmer and an early settler, and highly respected citizen. His religious connection is with the Christian Church; his politics Democratic.

MARTIN VOGAL, farmer, P. O. Walshville, born in Baden, Germany, in 1826. His parents, Martin and Margaret (Bowen) Vogal, were both natives of Germany; his father, who was a farmer, died there; subject, the third child of a family of eight children, received his education in his native town, and worked out for many years as a farm hand, and has been farming on his own account in Montgomery County for a long period. He has been twice married, at Belleville, St. Clair Co., Ill., and at St. Louis, Mo. Mrs. Vogal, whose maiden name was Kala, was born in Hanover, Germany; her parents, Henry and Mary (Myer) Kala, were natives of that country. Mr. Vogal has four children—Martin, Mary, Fred and George. He is a Republican, and a member of the Lutheran Church.

JOSEPH S. WHITESIDE, farmer, P. O. Walshville, was born Bond County, Ill., [illegible] 1837, son of Thomas D. and Eliza (Bruce) Whiteside. Thomas D., a native of North Carolina, now resides at Litchfield, Montgomery County; his wife died in Bond County, Ill.; subject is the third child of a family of thirteen. He received his education in Bond and Montgomery Counties, and began life as a farmer, which occupation he still follows. In Montgomery County in 1859 he married Mary J. Barlow, daughter of Joseph and Harriet (Smith) Barlow, natives of Tennessee. From this union three children have been born, viz., Harriet E., Laura B. and Eva F. Mr. Whiteside is a member of the Presbyterian Church; he is a Republican.

BUTLER GROVE TOWNSHIP.

GEORGE W. BROWN, Jr., grain dealer, Butler, was born in Montgomery County, Ill., May 30, 1843; son of George W. and Sarah A. (Jenkins) Brown, he born in Ohio July 9, 1819, a farmer by occupation, and coming to Illinois in 1836; she, a native of South Carolina, born June 30, 1819. They were the parents of six children. Our subject received his education in Hillsboro Academy. He came to Butler in 1865, and was employed as salesman by Joe Baum & Co. for two years, and in April, 1867, commenced business as a grocer, in the building known as Haywood's old stand. In a few months he and his brother, Charles O. Brown, entered into partnership, constituting the firm of Brown & Bro. In the early part of the year 1869, they purchased the Haywood Building, and continued to do business in it until 1873. In 1871, they added to their stock dry goods and boots and shoes. In May, 1873, they purchased the McReynolds property, and moved their goods to this building, adding to their stock ready made clothing, where they continued until April, 1881, when they sold their stock of goods to Hoes & Bro. In July, 1879, they commenced buying grain, to which business they now devote their entire attention. They have increased in business, and prospered greatly since their small beginning, until they now own 280 acres of excellent land, besides houses and lots in Butler, and an elevator at Hillsboro. They do a very extensive business, having handled in 1880 81 over 120,000 bushels of grain. January 4, 1865, Mr. Brown was married to Miss Henrietta M. Judson, born in Newark, N. J., November 15, 1844, daughter of James P. and Elizabeth F. (Gale) Judson, natives of New Jersey. Six children have been born to Mr. Brown — James Park, Winnie Pauline, Charles Judson, Frank Harold, Louis Sylvester and Roland Otis.

GEORGE W. BURRIS, farmer, P. O. Butler, was born in Montgomery County, Ill., February 22, 1850. He received his education in the common schools of the county, and entered upon his career in life as a farmer, and remained upon the old homestead until the death of his father, when he assumed all the cares and responsibilities of the family and farm. He was married in Montgomery County, November 3, 1881, to Miss Fannie V. Harris, who was born March 7, 1861, to John and Elvira Harris. Dewitt C. Burris, the father of George, was born in Jackson County, Ohio; was one of the early settlers of Montgomery County. He was an energetic and enterprising man, and a practical farmer, and, perhaps, no man has done more for public improvements and for the advancement of agricultural interests in the county than Mr. Burris. His death occurred January 4, 1879, at the age of fifty three. He was a man of prominence in the township, and his loss will long be felt. His wife, Roseline Mack, was born in New Hampshire. She is still living, and is the mother of eight children — George, Emma J., wife of John Wallace, Hattie Ellen, Carrie A., Elzina, William O., Charles D. and Wesley C., all of whom are living on the old homestead, except Emma, who, with her husband, is living in Butler

Township. George, the subject, is identified with the Democratic party. He devotes his time to growing the usual crops and raising stock. The farm consists of about nine hundred acres of choice farm land, which he keeps in a high state of cultivation.

JOHN BURNAP, farmer, P. O. Butler, was born in Montgomery County, Ill., October 2, 1854, son of Joseph S. and Sarah (Hugg) Burnap, he born in Ohio September 21, 1821, a farmer by occupation; she born in New Jersey December 25, 1833. They had five children, John being the eldest child. Our subject, after attending the common schools of his county, began farming which he has followed through life, being in charge at present of his father's fine farm of 340 acres of choice land, his father having removed to Texas where he owns a large tract of land, and upon which he expects to locate permanently. March 6, 1878, he married Rosa Nail, born in Montgomery County September 21, 1856, daughter of Hiram and Susan (Williams) Nail, he born in Indiana December 22, 1833; she in Montgomery County December 7, 1834. Three children have blessed the household of Mr. Burnap Earle, Tessie and Ina. They are members of the Presbyterian Church. He is a Republican.

JACOB CRESS, farmer, P. O. Hillsboro, was born in Harrisburg, Washington Co., Ind., May 5, 1818, son of Jacob and Catharine (Bost) Cress natives of North Carolina, he born December 26, 1779, a cabinet maker by occupation and dying November 10, 1865; she, born August 28, 1786, and dying February 1, 1859. They had ten children. Our subject, after receiving an ordinary education, began life as a farmer, which he has continued to the present time. When but a few weeks old, the parents of Mr. Cress moved to Montgomery County, and located a mile northwest of Hillsboro, on what is known as the Cress Mill farm, but on the 5th of May, 1840, Jacob removed to the farm he now owns, and upon which he resides, two miles east of Butler. It contains 784 acres of land, and is highly improved, having fine buildings, etc. He also owns 200 acres in Kansas, eighty acres in Franklin County, and eighty acres in Missouri. December 23, 1840, he married Miss Helena Scherer, born in Pendleton County, Va., October 8, 1818, daughter of Rev. Daniel Scherer, a native of North Carolina, and eleven children have blessed the union Alexander A., John M., Jacob D., William S., Samuel E., Benjamin L., Sophia Lucretia, Joseph E., James H. (deceased), Mary Illinois (deceased) and Thomas J. Mr. Cress has served as Road Commissioner six or seven years, is a member of the Lutheran Church, and a Democrat.

MARY BASSETT CLINESMITH, farmer, P. O. Butler, was born in Middlesex, Yates Co., N. Y., September 18, 1828, daughter of Ira and Louisa (Cleaveland) Bassett, he an architect by profession, born April 10, 1788, and dying July 29, 1844; she, born August 26, 1798, and dying February 2, 1873, being a native of Massachusetts. They were the parents of nine children. Mrs. Clinesmith was educated in Rushville, Yates Co., N. Y., and married March 1, 1861, in Athens, Mo., John Clinesmith, a native of Pittsburgh, born December 18, 1812, and died January 20, 1876, leaving one child, Orville H., born May 27, 1862. When eighteen years of age, Mrs. Clinesmith, then Miss Mary Bassett, who had adopted the profession of school teaching, and which she followed afterward for sixteen years, went to Warren County, Penn., where she remained one year, after which she spent one year in Geauga County, Ohio, when she removed to Fond du Lac, Wis., where she resided ten years, after which she removed to Lee County, Iowa, and remained there two years. After her marriage with Mr. Clinesmith, she removed with her husband to Montgomery County, where he settled on a farm in Butler Township, and where he died.

S. [illegible] CRESS, farmer, P. O. Butler, was born in Montgomery County November 8, 1847, son of Absalom Cress, who was a native of North Carolina, and a farmer by occupation. He had eight children born to him, all of whom are living. Our subject, after receiving an education in the schools of his native county, began the life of a farmer, and in connection with this has followed milling about eight years. He has a fine farm of 200 acres of land in Montgomery County, and fifteen acres in Litchfield. Mr. Cress married, in January, 1868, Miss Jennie Clodfelter, born in 1847, daughter of William and Susan (Sherer) Clodfelter, he a native of North Carolina. Mr. Cress has four children living. He is a Democrat.

ISAAC DOYLE, farmer, P. O. Butler, was born in Greene County, Ill., June 14, 1842; son of Thomas and Mary (Cress) Doyle, both natives of Kentucky, who emigrated to Greene County in 1832. They were the parents of eight children, Isaac being the sixth in order of birth. Our subject received an ordinary education in the common schools of his native county, and commenced life as a farmer, in which he has continued, owning at the present time 160 acres of well-improved land, three miles northeast of Butler. September 17, [illegible] he married Miss Mary Mitts, born in Sangamon County, Ill., March 15, 1845, daughter of Jesse and Zerilda (Shelton) Mitts. Two children have been born to them: John L. and [illegible] F. Mr. Doyle has served as School Director, is a Mason and a Democrat.

JOHN [illegible] GRASSEL, farmer, P. O. Butler, was born January 14, 18[illegible]; son of George C. and Kathrine (Esperi) Grassel, both natives of Bavaria. They had ten children, our subject being the second child. Shortly after their marriage, the parents removed to this country, first settling in Ohio, and afterward in this State, where, in Montgomery County, he owns 800 acres of land, upon which the son, our subject, has a fine residence with all suitable outbuildings. After receiving an ordinary education, he adopted the life of a farmer, in which he has continued. In April, 18[illegible], he married Miss Mollie Lewey, born in this county in 1853, daughter of Oliver and [illegible] (Stevenson) Lewey, and the union has been productive of one child, Harry Lewey. Mr. Grassel has served as School Director two years, and is a Republican. His wife is a Presbyterian.

C. H. HOES, merchant, Butler, was born in Washington County, Md., September 15, 1845; son of Hartman and Elizabeth (Knobley) Hoes, he a native of Germany, a tailor by trade, who emigrated to America in 1837, dying in 1864; she, a native of Maryland, born January 1, 1814. They were the parents of nine children, eight boys and one girl. Our subject received his education in the common schools of his county, and commenced life as a farmer, which he followed for eight years. In 1859, he went to California, where he remained two years, and then returned to Butler and went into merchandising, in which he is still engaged, the firm being known as Hoes Bros. Mr. Hoes was in the late war for the preservation of the Union, having been a member of an Illinois regiment. April 7, 1865, he was married in Montgomery County to Miss Mary A. Rush, born in Kentucky in 1847, daughter of Isaac Rush, a native of Pennsylvania. Three children have been born to Mr. Hoes: Lillian, Lucretia and George E. He is a Republican.

L. SCOTT HOES, merchant, Butler, was born in Hancock, Ind., September 6, 1853;

son of Hartman and Elizabeth (Knobler) Hoes, he a native of Germany, a tailor by trade who emigrated to America in 1837, dying in 1864; she, a native of Maryland, born January 1, 1814. They were the parents of nine children, eight boys and one girl. At the age of three years, our subject was taken to Freeport, Ill. and at four years to a farm near Butler, where he lived until 1877, during which time he followed threshing for about ten years, and farming. In 1877, he took a trip to California for the purpose of going into mining with his brother. After working several months without turning up a dollar's worth of the shining metal, he at last "struck it rich," and to such an extent as to justify the erection of a ten stamp mill, which proved profitable, paying large dividends. He remained in California until the fall of 1880, when he returned to Butler, leaving his brothers to control the mining interests, and in the spring of 1881, engaged with his brother Charles in merchandising. September 14, 1881, Mr. Hoes married Miss Ida L. Wheelock, born June 21, 1861, in Decatur, Ill., daughter of Thomas and Mary Wheelock, he a native of New Hampshire born November 29, 1830; she, born February 9, 1860. Mr. Hoes is a Republican.

THOMAS F. HODGES, farmer, was born in Jersey County, Ill., September 29, 1851, son of E. M. and Nancy (Davis) Hodges, he born in Missouri in 1820, and died in 1875; she born in Kentucky in 1821. They had nine children, Thomas F. being the fourth child in order of birth. Our subject was raised to the life of a farmer, and attended the common schools, receiving such an education as they afforded. In 1872, he removed from Greene County to his present place. He owns two shares in 370 acres of fine land, which belongs to the heirs of his father's estate. In September, 1875, he married Miss Mary Sherer, born in 1857, daughter of John and Nancy (Peters) Sherer, all natives of this State. Three children have been born to them —Arthur, Gracie and Walter. His wife is a member of the Methodist Episcopal Church, and he is a Democrat.

MATTHEW McMURTRY, farmer, P. O. Butler, was born in Doagh, County Antrim, Ireland, December 12, 1807; son of Ezekiel Sinnn and Jane (McAllister) McMurtry of Thorndyke, Ballyclose, Antrim, Ireland. At the age of fourteen, our subject went to Belfast to learn the trade of millwright, and the first steam flouring-mill built in Belfast was built during his apprenticeship, by his uncle. Matthew was afterward employed at millwrighting in this mill until he came to America in 1831. Arriving at New Orleans, he went to Nashville, Tenn., where he remained about one year; then went to Cincinnati, Ohio, and from there to Covington, Ky., where he lived many years. In 1855, he went to St. Louis, and other points, prosecuting his business, and in 1858 moved with his family to this county, and settled on the farm which has been his home ever since. He has dealt in grain, also, to some extent, in Butler. October 9, 1827, at Strandtown, County Down, Ireland, he was married to Elizabeth Smyth, born in 1804, daughter of Robert and Janet (Laird) Smyth, resident of County Down, Ireland, and by this union they have had the following children: Jane, born July 24, 1828, at Belfast, Ireland, and died November 2, 1834, at Covington, Ky.; Sarah, wife of Robert Bryce, born November 9, 1830, at Belfast, Ireland; Elizabeth, born February 22, 1833, near Nashville, Tenn., and died October 27, 1837, at Covington, Ky.; Mary Ann, born December 26, 1834, at Covington, Ky., and died August 2, 1855, at St. Louis, Mo.; Ezekiel James, born August 17, 1837, at Covington, Ky., and died November

1, 1837, at Covington, Ky.; Jane Elizabeth, wife of James S. McMurtry, of St. Louis, Mo., born November 13, 1838, at Covington, Ky.; Susanna Esther, born February 10, 1841, at Covington, Ky.; James Matthew, born April 20, 1843, at Covington, Ky., and died September 17, 1877, at Davidson, Colo.; Abigail Emma Simm, born March 12, 1847, at Covington, Ky., and died April 16, 1861, near Butler, Ill. Mr. McMurtry is a member of the Seceder Church.

M. L. MOYER, physician, Butler, was born in Iredell County, N. C., March 19, 1850, son of J. M. and M. A. (Kimball) Moyer, he a farmer, born in Cabarrus County, N. C., April 7, 1820; she, also born in North Carolina, April 7, 1825. They had four children, two of whom are dead. Our subject received his primary education in the schools of Hillsboro, and commenced his business career as a carpenter, afterward trading in stock, dealing principally in the far South. In 1876, he began the study of medicine and attended the Medical College at Keokuk, Iowa, from which institution he graduated in 1880. He immediately located in Butler, where he has worked into a fine practice. The Doctor is an able and conscientious practitioner, having been and still is a hard student, leaving no modes or processes untouched that may increase his skill in his profession. He is a genial gentleman, and highly respected in the community where he has made his home. He has been for sixteen years a member of the Lutheran Church, and is an Odd Fellow and a Democrat.

FRANCIS PHILLIPS, farmer, P. O. Butler, was born in Randolph County, Ill., February 14, 1827. His education was limited to such as could be obtained in the old log cabin schools at that early day. He commenced his career in life as a farmer. He purchased his first land in Butler Township, the farm containing 200 acres of land, only a part of which was improved, and on which the only building was a log cabin. He remained on the property for about seven years, when he sold it and bought the property he now resides upon. He has made all the improvements himself, but had the misfortune to have his buildings all destroyed by fire in 1872; but, being possessed with a stout heart and an energetic spirit, he at once erected a new residence, and the appearance of his property denotes Mr. Phillips to be a practical farmer and a man who labors for public improvements, and for the advancement of the agricultural interests of the county. He has endured the hardships of a trip to the gold regions of California, where he remained about one year, and returned to his native State, the recollections of which trip are still fresh in his memory. He was married on February 1, 1826, to Miss Sarah Jane Scherer, who was born in North Carolina, and brought to this State while yet a child. She is the mother of two children living—Harriet Virginia and David. The father of Francis was Burrell Phillips, a native of one of the Southern States, but sought a home in the far West, and settled in Randolph County, Ill. He was a prominent farmer in an early day. His death occurred in 1832. His wife, Harriet Brown, was the mother of four children, of whom Francis was the youngest. Politically, his sympathies are with the Republican party. Religiously, himself and wife are connected with the Lutheran Church. He has been a prominent member of the Odd Fellows order for a number of years.

MICHAEL REMENSNIDER, farmer, P. O. Butler, was born in Germany in 1826, son of Andrew Remensnider, he a native of Germany, and a farmer by occupation, born in 1798, and died about the year 1863. Subject, who is the youngest of a family of four children, received a fair education in the common schools in Germany, and began life as a farmer. When he was twenty-six years old, he emigrated to America; landed in New York, where he remained ten months; removed to Indiana, and lived there seventeen years, and in 1870 came to Sangamon County, Ill., where he stayed six years, and finally removed to Montgomery County, where he now resides on a farm of 155 acres of fine, improved land. In Indiana, in 1856, he married Miss Recilla Shear, born in Ohio in 1839, and died in 1861, leaving two children Elizabeth and Alain. Her father, Christian Shear, was a native of Germany; her mother of Pennsylvania. Mr. Remensnider's second wife, Noretta Reed, born in Ohio September 24, 1838, daughter of James Reed, a native of Pennsylvania, who died leaving seven children. His third wife is Eliza Brown, born in Illinois December 15, 1841, daughter of Samuel Brown, a native of Kentucky; she is the mother of one child, Henry. Mr. Remensnider is a Democrat and member of Charter Oak Lodge, No. 232, A., F. & A. M., Litchfield, Ill. His son, Alain, an energetic young man who has just begun farming on his own account, owns a farm adjoining his father's, and bids fare to be one of the leading agriculturists of the county.

JOSEPH STICKEL, farmer, P. O. Butler, was born in York County, Penn., August 26, 1814; son of John and Mary (Benzly) Stickel, he a farmer, born about 1791, and dying in 1869; she, born about 1791, and dying in 1862; both natives of York County, Penn. They were the parents of nine children, Joseph, our subject, being the eldest. After receiving the education obtainable in the common schools of his native county, Joseph began his business life as a farmer and carpenter. After following for three years the businesses named, he entered into merchandising, after which he went into milling and farming, in which he has continued since, in the meantime filling the position of School Trustee and Director of his township. He owns a fine farm of 308 acres of land, which is highly improved. Mr. Stickel has been married three times; first, in Pennsylvania, and twice in Illinois. The first wife was named Susanna Shelly, the second, Catharine Smith, and the third, who is living, was Sarah Scott, born in Kentucky October 9, 1828, their marriage occurring November 8, 1855. Mr. Stickel has been blessed with eight children, three deceased Francis M., Susanna M., Fletcher A., Nancy A., John A., Alexander W., James H. and Ellie C. He is a member of the Methodist Episcopal Church, and he is a Republican.

JOHN M. TUMES, farmer, P. O. Butler, was born in Hillsboro, Montgomery Co., Ill., April 27, 1848, son of Thomas and Theresa (Allen) Tumes, he a native of Ireland, she of Illinois. They had eight children, John M. being the second in order of birth. Our subject received his education in the Hillsboro Academy, and commenced life teaming and farming, in which latter occupation he has been engaged to the present time. October 26, 1876, he married Mrs. Fannie M. (Chapell) Harkey, whose husband, Daniel Lee Harkey, died in 1875, leaving two children Ida Sophia and Ella Lee. Mrs. Tumes is the daughter of George and Rebecca Chapell, the latter having departed this life in 1862. One child, Mattie H., has been born to Mr. and Mrs. Tumes. He is an Odd Fellow and a Democrat.

JUSTUS H. WARE, farmer, P. O. Butler, was born at Ware's Grove, near Butler, Montgomery Co., Ill., July 11, 1834; son of Benjamin and Sarah (Slayback) Ware, he born at Gilsum, Cheshire Co., N. H., May 27, 1796, a farmer by occupation, and dying

July 31, 1855; she, born near Lexington, Ky., September 13, 1805, and still living. They had two children born to them, our subject being the second. Mr. Ware, after attending the schools of his county, began life as a farmer, and at present owns a farm of 280 acres of excellent land, which is under a high state of cultivation and with good improvements thereon. He was married in Keene, N. H., September 26, 1860, to Miss Lucelia A. Brigham, born at East Alstead, N. H., August 25, 1836, daughter of Aaron and Susan (Pecor) Brigham, and the following children have been born to them: Mary Flora, born November 29, 1862; Carrie Susan, born May 5, 1864, and died December 1, 1866; George Vincent, born September 5, 1867; Amy Lillian, born April 24, 1873. Mr. Ware has served as School Director of his township, is a member of the Lutheran Church and a Republican.

DR. W. A. WESNER, druggist, Butler, was born in Indiana February 27, 1851, and emigrated to Montgomery County in 1874. His father was Jacob Wesner, born in North Carolina in 1800, and died in 1860; his mother, Elizabeth (Killian) Wesner, born in 1806, and dying in 1857. They had eleven children. Our subject, after his education in the schools of his county, went to farming, and then in the restaurant business. In 1872-'73, he attended medical lectures at Indianapolis, and, after finishing his course, located first at Nokomis, Montgomery Co., Ill., and remained one year practicing medicine, and in drug business. He moved to Butler in 1878, where he has a large and remunerative business in the drug line, it being the only establishment of its kind in that town. March 29, 1876, he married Mary J. Phillips, born in Montgomery County, Ill., in 1856, and three children have been born to them—Glen Allen, Donard Clayton and Iva Leena. He is a member of the Lutheran Church, an Odd Fellow and a Democrat.

HENRY WARE, farmer, P. O. Butler, was born in Butler Grove Township May 4, 1845; son of Obadiah and Electa (Post) Ware, he born in Gilsum, Cheshire Co., N. H., January 2, 1795, a farmer by occupation, and dying September 24, 1876, she born in Addison County, Vt., July 15, 1800, and dying November 15, 1859. Our subject was educated in the common schools of his county, and began life as a farmer, in which he has been and still is engaged, owning at the present time a fine farm of 240 acres of well-improved land, lying on the cross road running from Springfield to Hillsboro. In addition to general farming, Mr. Ware makes a specialty of raising fine sheep, having a large flock always in his fields. In Lee County, Iowa, January 24, 1867, he married Miss Louisa H. Morrison, born March 14, 1846, daughter of Joseph and Miriam (Baugh) Morrison, he a native of Tennessee, and she of Kentucky.

WILLIAM WATSON, farmer, P. O. Hillsboro. Among the prominent families of Butler Grove Township is that of him whose name heads this sketch. Mr. Watson, whose portrait appears in this volume, was born in Machery Knappen, parish of Refo, County Donegal, Ireland, January 14, 1800; his father, James Watson, was a native of Ireland, and was born about the year 1755; he married Margaret McClary, a native of Ireland; they had four children, of whom the subject was the eldest; he died in 1825. Our subject was educated in the schools of the country, and emigrated to America, arriving at Albany, N. Y., when he was eighteen years of age; he went from there to Geneva, N. Y., where he remained ten years, then removed to Genesee County and lived there ten years, when, on the 26th of November, 1839, he came to Montgomery County, Ill., and settled on the farm where he now resides, five miles north of Hillsboro. He was married, August 4, 1834, in New York, to Miss Mary Taft, who was born December 10, 1815, and is a daughter of William and Elizabeth (Davidson) Taft, all of Ireland; Mr. and Mrs. Watson have had born to them the following children: William, Aaron, Margaret, John, James, an infant (died without name), George W., Anna, Augusta, James, Eliza and Isabella. Mr. Watson is one of the staunch farmers of the county who settled in it more than forty years ago; has grown up with it, advanced in prosperity, and has grown in wealth and importance; has become identified with it in its growth and development, and is a part of its history; he has never sought office nor political preferment, but has always been an energetic friend of education, and a determined advocate of all public improvements calculated to promote the welfare of his adopted county. Politically, he is a Democrat and socially, a warm friend and pleasing companion. His wife is a woman of intelligence, a helpmeet to her husband, and a zealous member of the Presbyterian Church. William Watson, Jr., deceased, the eldest son of the above, died from the accidental discharge of a pistol in his own hand, March 20, 1882; he was born in Genesee County, N. Y., November 20, 1835, and came with his parents to Illinois in 1839; he was never married, but owned a fine farm some five miles north of Hillsboro, and his brother John, and sister Margaret (likewise unmarried), lived with him; he was a dutiful son and, to the day of his untimely death, never undertook any enterprise without consulting his parents, whose advice and more mature judgment he always heeded; he left to mourn his sad fate his aged parents and his brothers and sisters—Aaron, Margaret, John, George, James, Eliza and Isabella; though not a member of any church, he was a moral man and a constant reader of the Bible; he never swore an oath, was temperate in all his habits, and a firm believer in Christianity; he lived nobly, prospered in wealth, won the confidence of all, and died an honest and upright man. Aaron Watson, the second son, was born also in New York, February 7, 1837, and brought by his parents to Illinois in 1839; he was reared on the farm, and received his education in the common schools of the county, and began life for himself as a farmer; owns forty acres of excellent land, in a fine state of cultivation, and which joins the old homestead; politically he is a Democrat, and socially he is unmarried. John Watson, Jr., was born in Montgomery County, Ill., January 28, 1840, and is the third son of William Watson, Sr.; he was brought up on the farm, and received such educational advantages as the common schools afforded; he began life as a farmer, and purchased eighty acres of land, to which he has added since until he now owns an excellent farm in Butler Grove Township. He is an energetic and industrious farmer, and like his father, is a good Democrat. George W. Watson, the fourth son, was born in Montgomery County July 8, 1842; he attended the common schools, and afterward took a regular commercial course in a business college at Poughkeepsie, N. Y., from which he graduated in 1865; he then entered the telegraph office there, in the employ of the Hudson River Railroad, remaining two years when his health gave way and he was obliged to return home, since which time he has engaged in farming; he lives in Rountree Township (this county), where he owns a farm of 360 acres of well-improved land. On the 23d of December, 1869, he was married to Miss Lucy A. Peck, a daughter of William H. Peck, of Montgomery County; they have three children living, viz., Estella, Lenna and Rolla; also have three children dead. Mr. Watson is Treasurer of Rountree Township. James Watson, the youngest son, was born on the homestead, in Montgomery County, in 1849; he was brought up on the farm; educated in the common schools of the neighborhood, finishing his education at Hillsboro Academy; he commenced his business career as a farmer and stock raiser, which business he has successfully followed to the present time; his first purchase of land was twenty-three acres, to which he has since added until he now owns 188 acres of as fine land as any in Butler Grove Township; he makes a specialty of raising and handling cattle, but gives more or less attention to all kinds of stock; he is liberal in his views upon all matters of public enterprise, and contributes freely of his means to promote the prosperity and welfare of his town and county; he has always been identified with the Democratic party, believing its principles to be the foundation stone of our free institutions; he still lives with his parents, and takes care of them in their old age, thereby winning the respect and approval of his neighbors and friends. The Watson family own about two thousand acres of land, well improved and well cultivated; they are noted far and wide for their enterprise, public spirit and generous hospitality.

RAYMOND TOWNSHIP.

DANIEL E. ADAMS, baker and grocer, Raymond, was born in Macoupin County, October 13, 1840. His early childhood was spent in attending the common schools of his native county, and in assisting his father upon the homestead farm. At the age of twenty years, he embarked upon his career in life as a farmer, in Macoupin County, where he remained two years, and then removed to Montgomery County, and purchased forty acres of wild prairie land, which he improved and eventually sold. He then moved to Zanesville Township and rented a farm, upon which he remained three years. He then returned to the same section where his last farm was located, and purchased sixty acres of prairie land, which was partly improved. Soon after he sold it, and purchased 110 acres near by, and lived upon it three years, at the end of which time he sold out again and returned to Zanesville Township, and bought eighty acres. He continued in the occupation of a farmer until 1880, when he again sold out and removed to Raymond, where he purchased twenty-eight acres of village property, and entered into a grocery, at which business he was more than ordinarily successful, and by his energy, business habits, and the pleasing manner in which he attended to the wants of his customers, he built up a large trade. He eventually sold his interest and entered into partnership in a general mercantile business with W. H. Wilbanks, with whom he continued about one year, when he bought his partner's interest and continued in the business by himself. In January, 1882, he sold his business, and at present is engaged in conducting a bakery, grocery and restaurant, where, for the short time he has been in the trade, he has succeeded in building up a large and steadily increasing trade. He was married, October 24, 1860, to Elizabeth Jane Wagner, who was born in Washington County, Ill., November 14, 1840. She is the mother of eight children—Emma Elnora, born in Macoupin County, August 19, 1861, wife of P. B. Burgo, now living in Nebraska; Anna Nevada, born August 2, 1863; Jacob L., born January 20, 1867; Charles W., born March 16, 1871; William H., born February 23, 1874; Viola Jane, born March 16, 1879, and two infants, deceased. Mrs. Adams is a daughter of Jacob D. and Lucinda (McDonald) Adams, he born in Illinois, and one of the early settlers of Macoupin County and still living; she, born in Tennessee, deceased. William C. Adams, the father of our subject, was born in West Virginia; moved from there to Tennessee, but eventually to Macoupin County, in 1827, a farmer by occupation. His death occurred January 21 1853. His wife, Margaret Ward, was a native of Tennessee, and is still living. She is the mother of twelve children, of whom Daniel was the ninth child. He was elected Constable in 1873, and served one year. In 1874, he was elected a Highway Commissioner of Zanesville Township, and served three years. He has been an active member of the I. O. O. F. order for a number of years. Politically, his sympathies are with the Democratic party. Religiously, himself and wife are connected with the Christian Church.

PETER BERRIE, retired farmer, P. O. Raymond, is a son of Thomas Berrie, who was born in Pennsylvania, of English descent. He was a farmer by occupation. His wife, Susan, Lark, was also a native of Pennsylvania; she died in 1823. The result of their union was twelve children, of whom Peter, the subject of this sketch, was the [illegible] child. As educational privileges were very much limited at that early day, his education was necessarily limited. His early life was spent in assisting his father in his agricultural pursuits. He remained at home until he reached the age of nineteen years, when he entered upon the battle of life with all the energy of a young man bound to make his way in the world. He engaged as a farm hand near home receiving but a small compensation for his labor. He soon tired of that occupation, and tried river life for a few months but soon concluded that a farm life was preferable, and he again took upon himself the duties of a farm life, following in that occupation in different localities, and eventually came to Montgomery County, Ill., where he has since resided. In 1841, he purchased his first real estate, consisting of eighty acres of unimproved prairie land, to which he has continually added, until his farm now consists of about two hundred and twenty-five acres of choice farm and timber land. He has made all the improvements necessary for comfort and convenience, and has placed his farm in a high state of cultivation, and it will compare with any of the best improved farms in the county, and he is proud of the fact that, having started upon his career a poor boy, his present possessions represent the dollars earned by himself. He was married, December 15, 1841, to Mary J. Cass, who was born January 27, 1821, and died November 13, 1865. She bore him eight children, viz.: Adolphus, born May 26, 1843, and died July 15, 1864; Aurelius, born August 14, 1845, and died November 11, 1871; Isabelle, born July 7, 1848, and died February 25, 1853; Clarence, born November 17, 1850, and is still living; Florence, born March 8, 1853, and died January 26, 1875; Lockwood, born September 23, 1855, and died November [illegible], 1868; Mary, born May 14, 1859, and died in infancy; Chester, born December 17, 1861, and is still living. Mr. Berrie was married again June 22, 1869, to Mary J. Guthrie, who was born in Charleston, Coles Co., Ill., November 16, 18[illegible]. She is the mother of one child, Fannie, born November 11, 1870, and died July 4, 1871. Mrs. Berrie was a daughter of Green J. and Mary J. (Van Deren) Guthrie, natives of Kentucky. He died in 1850; was a prominent merchant of Charleston, Ill.; she still living, at the age of sixty-one. She is the mother of five children, of whom Mrs. Berrie was the second child. She is a lady possessing all the womanly graces. Mr. Berrie is not a politician, but has always been identified with the Republican party. Although possessing all the energy and enterprise that has characterized all his efforts, he has retired from farm life, and is now enjoying the fruits of a well-spent life.

IRA BARTON, physician, Raymond, was born in Grant County, Wis., April 17, 1844, where he received his early education, the foundation of his subsequent learning. The years between fourteen and twenty-one were employed in assisting his father in his agricultural pursuits. He then entered the service in Company I, One Hundred and Fifty-second Illinois Volunteer Infantry, with Capt. J. W. Brown; regiment commanded by Col. Stephenson. He remained in the service about seven months, and soon after his discharge he began the study of medicine, reading with Dr. A. B. Penniman, at Woodburn,

Macoupin County. He attended three courses of lectures in the Medical Department of the University of Michigan, from which institution he graduated in 1869, receiving his diploma as an M. D. He did not enter regularly upon the duties of his profession until June of the following year, when he located at Raymond, where he has since been engaged in the practice of his profession, with the exception of one year, when he took the place and practice of his old preceptor, at Woodburn. He has, by his thorough knowledge of, and strict attention to, the duties of his calling, succeeded in building up a reasonably good practice which is steadily on the increase, and socially has gained the highest esteem of the community. He was married, December 17, 1871, to Miss Mary H. Scott who was born in Steuben County, Ind., August 15, 1845. She is the mother of three children, viz.: John H., Sarah and infant the latter dying in early infancy. Mrs. Barton was a daughter of Joseph H. and Mercy (Kinsman) Scott, natives of New York, he living, she deceased. John H. Barton, the father of our subject, was born in Massachusetts in October, 1805, and is still living. At the age of twenty one, he sought a home in the then far West, and located near Jacksonville, Ill., where he remained several years, but eventually resided in Wisconsin and Minnesota, and has engaged in several occupations during his life, such as lead mining, farming, merchandising, etc and now, at an advanced age, he is enjoying the fruits of a well-spent life. His wife, Mary N. Reid, was born in Lexington, Ky., in 1812, and is also living. They have lived together as man and wife fifty three years, and the result of their union was seven children, three of whom have reached manhood and womanhood, viz.: Sarah, wife of A. B. Penniman; Mary, wife of William P. Hamilton, and Ira, the subject of this sketch. He has always been identified with the Republican party. Religiously, he is in connection with the Presbyterian Church, and was one of the six members who organized the church at Raymond; has always taken a prominent part in all temperance movements.

A. BRYAN, lumber dealer, Raymond, was born in Arkansas March 20, 1850; received his education principally in the common schools of that State; came to Montgomery County Ill., in 1864. His first enterprise for himself was school teaching, but eventually took upon himself the duties of a farm life. Since 1873, he has been working at the carpenter ring and joiner trade, and in January 1882, bought the lumber yard and business of D. J. Parratt & Co., located at Raymond. On the 29th of March, he entered into partnership with D. C. Kelley, in the same business. They are enterprising and energetic business men, and have built up a large and steadily increasing trade. Mr. Bryan has just completed a fine frame residence on one of the principal streets of Raymond. He has done most of the work himself, and the house does honor to the town and to Mr. Bryan as a competent workman. He was married in Pulaski County Ark., February 18, 1872, to Miss Matilda Powers, daughter of Oliver and Margaret (Hustin) Powers. They have three children living viz.: Letha, William and Claudie May. Ira died in infancy. The father of the subject, Darius Bryan, was a native of North Carolina, and was one of the early settlers of Arkansas. He was a farmer by occupation; his death occurred in 1876. His wife, Susan Elizabeth Hamilton, was a native of Illinois, and died on the same day as her husband, and both of small-pox. He is a Democrat

WILLIAM L. BATEMAN, lawyer, Raymond, was born in Knox County, Ohio, October 13, 1858; son of Luther and Mary Jane (Shurtliff) Bateman. Luther, born in the same house in which his son William L. was born, June 7, 1833; is a farmer by occupation. He moved to Montgomery County in March, 1867, and located on a farm near Raymond, where he remained until the spring of 1870, when he moved to Walshville, and there engaged in the carriage and wagon painting business. In the spring of 1873, he left Walshville and moved to Litchfield, where he continued the same business; also doing house painting and sign writing; left Litchfield in 1877, and returned to Walshville, where he remained but a short time; then moved to Hillsboro, where, in addition to painting, he carried on the manufacture of carriages and wagons. In 1880, he removed to Raymond, where he carried on business until 1882, when he sold out to Isaac Dudson, and is now engaged as traveling salesman for J. S. Culver, Taylorville, Christian Co., Ill. His wife, born in Hebron, N. Y., October 20, 1835, is the mother of two children Nettie and William L. Subject attended school in his native town, in Knox County, Ohio, and finished at Litchfield, Ill. After the completion of his education, he commenced the study of law under the instruction of Judge Jesse J. Phillips; was admitted to the bar at Mt. Vernon, Ill., in February, 1880, and entered upon the practice of his profession at Raymond. He is a supporter of the Republican party, and is correspondent for a number of newspapers.

WINFIELD P. CARTER, stock dealer, Raymond, was born in Madison County, Ill., November 11, 1843. His father, Henry T. Carter, was born at Knoxville, Tenn., in 1811. He remained in his native State until he was eighteen years of age, when he entered upon his career in life, and sought a home in the then far West, locating at Alton, Ill., and entered 320 acres of wild prairie land, a large portion of which he eventually improved and resided upon until his death, which occurred July 21, 1844. He was married in 1832, in Madison County, to Miss Hannah Davis, who was born at Trenton, N. J., July 12, 1815, who was brought to Illinois by her parents when but seven years of age. She was the mother of five children, viz.: Harriett, wife of J. H. Stahl, of Madison County; Louisa, wife of Edward Sanders, of Macoupin County; Henry D., now living on the old homestead; Julia A., wife of M. V. McKinney, of Madison County, and Winfield, the subject of this sketch, all of whom were small children at the death of their father. Mrs. Carter continued upon the farm, which was managed by herself until the children were able to take the duties upon themselves, and to assist in the support of the family. She is still living and resides upon the homestead with her son Henry. Winfield remained at home until he was seventeen years of age, assisting in the labor of the farm, and attending the common schools, to which his educational privileges were limited. In 1862, when he left home, he entered into the service in Company B, Eightieth Illinois Volunteer Infantry, with Capt. A. F. Rogers, in the regiment commanded by Col. Allen. He remained in the service twenty-two months, receiving his discharge on account of injuries received from a bayonet, and being otherwise injured while removing a battery; was taken a prisoner by John Morgan, but was paroled soon after. Upon his return home, he again took upon himself the duties of a farm life, remaining at home about one year, at the end of which time, in company with two others, he turned his face westward, to try his fortune in California, where he engaged in mining and farming. At the expiration of two years, he returned to his native State, and continued in the occupation of a farmer. On January 25, 1868, he was married to Miss Anna H. Mayhew, who was born at Shiloh, N. J., September 26, 1849. They have five children, viz.: Philip Henry, born October 25, 1869; Mary Louisa, born June 1, 1871; Edward B., born September 20, 1872; Maud E., born August 1, 1874; Ernest M., born June 25, 1876, and died June 3, 1877; Clyde W., born August 6, 1878. Mrs. Carter is a daughter of James and Sarah (Howe) Mayhew, natives of New Jersey. He was a farmer by occupation, born at Shiloh, N. J., in 1809, and died in 1858; she born in 1814, and is still living. Mr. Carter remained in Madison County, upon the farm, until 1870, when he removed to Raymond and opened a lumber yard, which was the first enterprise of the kind in the town. He continued in the business until the fall of 1872, when he sold out and entered into partnership with C. M. Davis in a general merchandising store. Two years later, he purchased his partner's interest, and continued in the business until 1878, when he disposed of his stock, since which time he has been engaged more or less extensively in dealing in stock. He has a small tract of land in the outskirts of the town of Raymond, upon which he has erected a fine dwelling, surrounded by a fine grove of maple trees, planted by himself. The prospects for Mr. Carter's residence becoming the finest place in Raymond are very flattering. Mr. Carter has taken a great interest in the growth and prosperity of the town, and to him is ascribed the honor of having been the first Treasurer. He has also served upon the Town Board two years, and was Deputy Postmaster for about six years, at an early date in the town history. Politically, Mr. Carter has always been an exponent of the Democratic party. He is an energetic and enterprising business man, and socially enjoys the highest esteem of the community. Upon his return from California, his trip was anything but pleasant, as he was called upon to pass through several perils. He purchased a ticket from San Francisco to New York, upon the steamer Daniel Webster; but, before sailing, met a friend about to sail upon the steamer Moses Taylor. He disposed of his ticket, and took passage upon the Moses Taylor. Both steamers left the wharf the same day, and were caught in a storm in which the Daniel Webster was lost with all on board. The Moses Taylor, however, reached San Juan del Norte although badly damaged. They crossed Lake Nicaragua in a terrible storm, and, while passing down Nicaragua River, ran on a shoal. The steamer then had to be abandoned, and, after being exposed eleven days to storms and hardships, with a scarcity of food, part of the time walking and part of the time in skiffs, reached Greytown, on the Atlantic shore, from which place he embarked upon the Santiago de Cuba, for New York; but again they were doomed to pass through a storm, which disabled the steamer, which was towed into port at Charleston, S. C. Having passed safely through the perils of the deep, he determined to finish his journey by rail, and the train upon which he was carried, while running at a high rate of speed, was thrown from the track, killing four persons. Having escaped injury in all of these misfortunes, he at last arrived home safely, after forty-nine days dangerous travel, the recollections of which trip are still fresh in his memory.

ROBERT CHISM, proprietor of the Raymond House, Raymond, was born in Grayson County, Ky., June 24, 1831, and was brought to Macoupin County, Ill., when one and a half years of age, and his education was received in the common schools of that county.

mained six months, and then returned to Montgomery County, and followed hunting until 1863, when he married, purchased the farm he now resides upon, and spent the winter in getting out rails for fencing, and in the spring of 1864, moved upon the farm where he has since remained, engaged in agricultural pursuits. He is now the owner of 120 acres of prairie land, under cultivation, and twenty acres of timber land. November 12, 1863, he was married to Miss Cordelia Cass, a native of Montgomery County, born December 25, 1832, and died November 24, 1868. She was the mother of three children, one of whom is living, viz., Abbie, born September 22, 1864. Politically, Mr. Crane is a Republican. His brother, Norris, was the sixth child of Norris and Elizabeth Crane, and was born at Hamilton, Ohio, October 2, 1834. He received the principal part of his education in his native county. His early life was spent in assisting his father upon the farm, and his first business for himself was teaming upon the Quincy & St. Louis Railroad, where he remained one year. He then engaged as a farm hand and followed in that occupation several years. He was elected by the people as Constable, the duties of which office he performed about fifteen years. He clerked in a merchandising store at Butler one year, and was the first person to sell goods at Raymond, where he was engaged with Van Ever & Van Darren as clerk. He remained with them something over a year, since which time he has been engaged in farming, in connection with his brother. He has served the people as Deputy Sheriff one term, and has been an active member of the I. O. O. F. order for a number of years. Politically, his sympathies are with the Democratic party.

MORGAN COSTLEY, farmer, P. O. Raymond, was born in Greene County, Ill., July 31, 1836, and received his education in his native county, where his early life was spent upon the homestead farm. He came to Montgomery County in 1856, and purchased 144 acres of wild prairie land, which he improved, and upon which he remained until 1878, when he removed to his present place of residence, where he has 200 acres of as well cultivated land as can be found in Raymond Township. He has accumulated a large amount of this world's goods, and has at one time had in his possession about five hundred acres of land. The high state of cultivation under which he keeps his farm shows him to be a practical farmer, and well worthy of the high esteem in which he is held by the community. He has also been a prominent dealer in and feeder of stock, chiefly cattle and hogs. Although he grows all the crops usually raised upon a well-regulated farm, he makes a specialty of grain. He was married in Montgomery County in 1859, to Miss Melvina McGown, who was born in Greene County to Alexander and Louisa (McNeal) McGown. She has borne him six children, viz., William A., John P., Della, Charles, Alta L. and Perry, the latter of whom died in infancy. William Costley, the father of Morgan, was a native of Kentucky, a farmer by occupation, and died in 1869. His wife, Elizabeth Mathis, was a native of Illinois; she died at Raymond in 1875. She was the mother of thirteen children, of whom Morgan was the fifth child. Politically, he is identified with the Democratic party. His wife is a member of the Baptist Church.

EDWIN R. CARTER, grain and coal dealer, Raymond, was born in Tuscarawas County, Ohio, December 2, 1842; son of Daniel W. Carter, a native of Maryland, born in 1811; a farmer; died in the spring of 1865. Jane Tinkler, his wife, was born in New York in 1819, and is still living with subject, who left Ohio when ten years of age, and lived in Indiana until the fall of 1869, when he removed to Pana, Ill., and eventually to Raymond. His first enterprise for himself was farming. On his arrival at Raymond he engaged in the coal and grain business, at which he still continues; built his elevator in the fall of 1879; commenced without any available means, and is a self-made man, and his business ability and enterprise have added largely to the growth and prosperity of Raymond. He was married at Reynolds White Co., Ind., February 25, 1866, to Miss Mary Cartmell, who was born in Clark County, Ohio, April 3, 1845. They have four boys and two girls living, viz.: Bruce, Charles, Benjamin F. Asbury L., Ruth and Naomi; two boys died in infancy. He has served as Township Clerk, Collector, Assessor, and Police Justice, or Magistrate, for several years; was Sergeant in Company K, Eighty-sixth Indiana Volunteer Infantry, with Capt. J. Southard, regiment commanded by Col. Hamilton; in service three years; is a Republican; has been a member of I. O. O. F. several years. Himself and family are Methodists. His father's family consisted of four children, viz.: Jesse, died in 1864 aged twenty eight years; William, of Logansport Ind.; Ferguson, in San Francisco, clerk in State House, and Edwin R., subject of sketch.

PROF. CHARLES E. COOK, Principal of schools, Raymond, was born in Fillmore, Putnam Co., Ind., July 12, 1857; son of William H. and Elizabeth (Robinson) Cook, he born in Kentucky March 27, 1833, a physician by profession, and practicing at East Fork, Montgomery County; she, born in Indiana October 1, 1835, the mother of four children, still living, viz.: Ella, Melville and Charles, William R. having died in infancy. The education of our subject was commenced in the common schools, from which he advanced to the academy at Hillsboro, where he remained several terms, teaching part of the time. He entered the Normal School at Valparaiso, Ind., in the fall of 1878, where he graduated the following year, his academic education having fitted him for the advanced classes which he entered. After receiving his diploma, he entered upon the duties of his profession at Fillmore, but eventually became Principal of the public schools of Raymond, where he is still engaged, and in connection with these duties is engaged in the study of the law with the intention of fitting himself for and entering upon the practice of that profession. In Hillsboro, September 14, 1881, he was married to Miss Jennie B. Shimer, born April 10, 1860, daughter of Isaac and Jane (Gunning) Shimer, natives of Ohio. Mr. Cook has served as County Assessor one year, and is a Democrat.

JOSEPH R. CHAPMAN, farmer, P. O. Raymond, was born August 1, 1843; son of William Chapman (see history), and was raised to a life of farming. April 25, 1867, he married Miss Catharine Hendrickson, born May 18, 1844, who died July 22, 1878, leaving three children: Robert, Gideon P. and Samuel Byron. July 29, 1880, he married Miss Isabel Rogers, born April 18, 1856, daughter of William Rogers, of Macoupin County. By this union Mr. Chapman has one child, Grace Reynolds. Mr. Chapman served during the late war as a member of Company H, One Hundred and Forty third Illinois Infantry, under Capt. James P. Stewart. He is a Methodist, and a Republican. His wife is a member of the Christian Church.

ALBERT ESTABROOK, farmer, P. O. Raymond, was born in Madison County, Ill., September 13, 1820. The father of this gentleman, John Estabrook, was born in Boston, Mass., in March, 1799, and in 1818 settled in Madison County, where he engaged

living—Etta, Harry and William Ross; all at home. He is a Democrat.

JOHN C. GREENE, banker, Raymond. The grandfather of our subject was a native of Kentucky. In 1819, he sought a home in the then far West and became a resident of Greene County, Ill. In many ways he will be long remembered as one who helped materially toward making Greene County one of the most flourishing counties in the State, and which was named in honor of himself and his brother John. His death occurred in 1828. He was the father of five children, of whom Nelson, the father of our subject, was the fourth child. He was born in the year 1822, and grew up to be a stout and vigorous boy, early becoming inured to the hard work of a farm. He was married in 1847, to Ann E. Gano, a daughter of John S. Gano, a Virginian. In his own language—"I borrowed the clothes I wore to the marriage" and subsequently borrowed many of the household utensils that formed the simple furniture of his cabin; but he worked hard, and thus paved the way for future success. He is the owner of 120 acres of land in one of the best townships of Greene County; is a whole souled, liberal gentleman, and enjoys the confidence of his many friends. He was twice elected Justice of the Peace serving eight years. He is the father of eight children, namely: Emily, wife of N. M. Perry, Jr., at Olathe, Kan.; Mary, wife of Luther Snell, of Carlinville, Ill.; Sarah, wife of Scott Greene, of Tallula, Ill., a prominent farmer and stock raiser; Nancy, Herschel, Robert, Clarence and John, the subject of this sketch, who was born on the old farm homestead April 15, 1847, receiving a liberal education from the common schools of his native place. His first venture in business was made with Mr. N. M. Perry, in the town designated as Old Kane, where a general merchandising business was done. Subsequently, Mr. Greene purchased the interest of Mr. Perry, and conducted a successful business for a number of years. In September, 1880, he opened a general banking business at Raymond, and, in addition to the duties of this business, he is Township Collector, elected by the Democratic ticket. He was married August 31, 1870, to Miss Emma F. Perry, who was born in Greene County December 26, 1846. They have two children—Mabel, born August 18, 1871, and Morrison, born December 26, 1877. Mrs. Greene was a daughter of Col. N. M. and Eliza (Hill) Perry. He was born in Orange County, Va., November 30, 1806, and was the sixth child of James and Ann Perry, who were of English descent. In 1864, he was nominated and elected as a candidate of the Democratic party to a seat in the Legislature of Illinois, and in that responsible position acquitted himself with honor. His death occurred in 1875, and that of his wife in 1861. Mr. Greene is a prominent member of the Masonic fraternity, Blue Lodge, Chapter and Commandery. He is a man of unsullied reputation, and well worthy of the high esteem in which he is held by the community at large.

GEORGE W. GREENAWALT, farmer, P. O. Raymond, was born in Sangamon County, Ill., February 24, 1831. As educational privileges were limited in the country at that early day his education was also limited to such as could be obtained in the common schools. He remained upon the homestead, assisting his father upon the farm until he reached the age of twenty-one years, when he entered on the battle of life in reality, rented a farm, and continued in the occupation of a farmer; at the end of three years, he had accumulated enough funds to enable him to purchase land, which he did in his native county, the farm consisting o

148 acres of unimproved prairie land, upon which he erected a residence and all other buildings necessary for comfort and convenience, and also placed his farm in a high state of cultivation. At the end of sixteen years, he disposed of the property and removed to Macoupin County, where he remained five or six years, but, during two years of the time, carried on farming in Montgomery County. In March, 1874, he removed to Raymond and retired from active labor, but, being of an energetic nature, he is continually adding improvements to his already beautiful place. He was married, at Springfield, Ill., February 2, 1854, to Miss Louisa Holloway, who was born in Kentucky November 3, 1832, to George W. and Harriet (Tade) Holloway, natives of Kentucky, he living, she deceased. Jacob Greenawalt, the father of George, was born in Kentucky; was a farmer by occupation; he died February 24, 1863, aged fifty-nine years; his wife, Mary Bradley, was also a native of Kentucky, and is still living, at the age of seventy-two years; she is the mother of eight children, of whom George was the third child. He has now in his possession about four hundred acres of choice prairie land in Bois d'Arc Township, which is now rented, but all of which is under cultivation. Mr. Greenawalt has been an active member of the order of A., F. & A. M. about sixteen years, and has attained the degree of Master Mason. Although possessing all the energy and enterprise of a thorough business man, his health has been impaired for a number of years, necessitating his retirement from active life. Politically, his sympathies are with the Democratic party.

EDWARD GRIMES, farmer, P. O. Raymond, born in Jersey County, Ill., May 24, 1843, son of Jarratt T. and Charity (Brown) Rogers. Jarratt, a native of Jersey County, was born January 29, 1820; he is a prominent farmer and stock-raiser, and has been identified with the growth and prosperity of his native county; his wife was a daughter of Joseph Brown, who was a native of Virginia, and one of the early settlers of St. Charles, Mo., where she was born May 7, 1820; she died July 21, 1876, leaving nine children, of whom subject was the third. His education was commenced in his native county, and completed at Shurtleff College, Madison County, Ill.; he began the business of life as a farmer, on the farm where he now lives. He came to Montgomery County in 1867, and, at Butler, in that county, October 7, 1868, married Emma E. Sammons, born in Lewis County, N. Y., January 4, 1850, daughter of John C. and Elizabeth (Bedell) Sammons, natives of Lewis County, N. Y.; he born August 18, 1821, follows the blacksmith's trade at Butler; she born September 1, 1827, died January 19, 1882; of her six children, three are now living, viz.: Emma (Mrs. Grimes), Estella and Leonard E. Mr. and Mrs. Grimes are the parents of five children—Eugene F., born August 18, 1869; Charles C., born October 15, 1871; Frankie, born May 16, 1873, died September 3, 1873; Ernest Robert, born August 17, 1874; and Leroy, born January 5, 1878. He owns 280 acres of fine farm land, which he keeps in a high state of cultivation; his house was built in the year that he came to Montgomery County; he is a Democrat; a prominent member of the Masonic fraternity since 1868; has served as Township Supervisor for two terms; his wife has been for a number of years a member of the Presbyterian Church at Butler.

JOHN P. HITCHINGS, farmer, P. O. Raymond, was born in Onondaga County, N. Y., May 20, 1810, to John and Lydia (Ramsdell) Hitchings. John Hitchings was born at Malden, Mass., July 8, 1773; he was a farmer; he removed to Otsego County, N. Y., in about

living, viz.: James F., William Henry, Belle and Frederick. Politically, Mr. Hartwick is identified with the Democratic party; is an active member of the order of A., F. & A. M. at Raymond. His father was born in New Jersey in 1811; is a farmer by occupation, and resides in Macoupin County; his mother was also born in New Jersey, in 1810, and is still living. They are the parents of seven children, of whom our subject is the fourth child. He is the owner of one of the finest horses in Montgomery County, called "Independence, Jr.," and is of St. Lawrence and Eagle stock; Mr. Hartwick is also a breeder of Short Horn stock.

JACOB HAUSER, farmer, P. O. Raymond, was born in Germany August 11, 1842. At the age of twenty two years, he emigrated to America and settled in Pennsylvania, but soon after joined a German army corps and entered the service, where he remained six months, and then went to Greene County, Ill., where he remained ten years, and came to Montgomery County, and soon after purchased the farm he now lives upon; he has made nearly all the improvements himself, and his surroundings show Mr. Hauser to be an energetic and enterprising man; his farm consists of eighty acres of choice farm land, situated near Raymond, and which, as a practical farmer, he keeps in a high state of cultivation, and which denotes his interest in public improvements and advancement of agricultural interests in the county. He received a very good education in Germany, and has always performed the duties of a farmer. He was married, in Montgomery County, July 4, 1875, to Dora Reeser, who was born in Germany and came to America when twenty one years of age; she is the mother of two children, viz.: Mena and Anna. Politically Mr. Hauser is independent; devotes his time to growing the usual farm crops and raising stock. Socially, he enjoys the highest esteem of the entire community.

GEORGE HENRY HOOSER, miller, Raymond; first business for himself was that of carpenter and joiner, which he followed sixteen years, when he turned his attention to farming, and which he followed ten years; he then built a grist mill at Raymond and engaged in a general milling business, in which he has been successful and built up a large trade; had nothing but his hands with which to enter upon the battle of life, but, being possessed with an energetic spirit, determined to make his way in the world. His education was limited to the common schools. He was born in Todd County, Ky., August 27, 1827; his father, William Hooser, was a native of North Carolina, and was taken by his parents to Kentucky, at a very early day, and when there were but a few settlers in that State; he was a farmer, miller and distiller by occupation; his death occurred in March, 1880. His wife was Purety Faulk, also a native of North Carolina, and grew to maturity in Tennessee; her death occurred in 1879; she was the mother of seven children, of whom George was the third. He was married, in St. Louis, in 1858, to Lucy Cheney, who was born in New York, daughter of Louis Cheney; by her he had two children; she died in 1862, and he was again married, in 1864, to Martha Pettyjohn, of North Carolina, by whom he has six children; his children are William, Dora, Ralph, Mary, Margaret, James, Frank and Lewis. Mr. Hooser is a Republican, and is a prominent member of the Masonic order.

CORDER JONES, Police Magistrate, real estate and collecting agent, Raymond, was born in Macoupin County, Ill., July 12, 1848; his education was limited to such as could be obtained in the common schools. When seventeen years of age, he came to Montgomery County and engaged in farming in Litchfield Township. In 1878, he located at Raymond, and worked at the carpenter and joiner's trade, but eventually took up the trade of a painter, which he still follows. In 1880, he was elected on the people's ticket to fill the office of Police Magistrate, the duties of which he has filled with marked zeal and integrity, and to the full satisfaction of the citizens of the village. In addition to his other duties, he is engaged in dealing in real estate and as collecting agent. He was married, in Montgomery County, December 20, 1872, to Leonora A. Gore who was born in St. Louis, Mo., August 4, 1856; she is the mother of two children, viz.: Olive W., born August 20, 1874; and Orion N., born August 8, 1878. Mrs. Jones was a daughter of John P. and Martha (Hardy) Gore, he born in Illinois, she in Kentucky. The father of the subject, Isaac N. Jones, was born in Illinois, a farmer by occupation, and is also a Justice of the Peace in North Litchfield Township; his wife, Keturah Stone, is a native of Tennessee; she is the mother of six children, of whom Corder, our subject, is the third. Politically, he is identified with the Democratic party; he is also a prominent member of the I. O. O. F. order at Raymond. Religiously, himself and wife are connected with the Baptist denomination at Honey Bend; is an advocate for the advancement of the cause of temperance.

JOEL JONES, farmer, P. O. Raymond, born near Bunker Hill, Macoupin Co., Ill., April 11, 1836, son of Simeon and Dorothy (Starkey) Jones. Simeon, a farmer, and Treasurer of Bunker Hill Township, Macoupin County, for fifteen years, was born in Madison County, Ill., February 2, 1811, and was identified with the growth of the county up to the time of his death, which occurred December 30, 1850; his wife, also a native of Madison County, born June 27, 1812, is now living with her son Joel, the subject of this sketch; of her ten children, of whom Joel was the third, six are living. Subject received such education as the country schools of that day afforded, and entered upon the business of life as a farmer, and has, by his energy and industry, accumulated 180 acres of fine land near Raymond, which he, as a practical farmer, keeps highly cultivated; he has lately erected a large and commodious frame residence. He married, in Montgomery County, April 13, 1871, Mary C. Blackwelder, born in Cabarrus County, N. C., September 5, 1843, daughter of Martin and Malinda (Ovenshine) Blackwelder, both natives of Cabarrus County, N. C., and both deceased. Mr. and Mrs. Jones are the parents of five children—Alva W., Jesse V., Charles E., Eugene D. and Emily A. He formerly was a Democrat, but is now a Greenbacker; is a member of the Baptist Church.

JOHN KING, farmer, P. O. Raymond, was born in Bourbon County, Ky., September 10, 1826; his education was limited to such as could be obtained in the old log schoolhouses of that early day; however, by observation and encounters with the world, he has attained a very good practical education. At the age of fifteen, he went with his parents to Indiana, and located in Shelby County, where he remained fourteen years, employed on a farm as farm hand. He entered upon the battle of life a poor boy, but, being possessed with a stout heart and an energetic spirit, he determined to make his way in the world. He came to Illinois in 1854, and permanently located in Montgomery County in October, 1859, and rented the property he now owns; by his industry and economy, he soon was able to purchase eighty acres of land, which he has continued to increase until it now

ISHMAEL McGOWN, farmer, P. O. Raymond, was born in Johnson County, Ill., June 14, 1821. He was removed by his parents to Greene County in 1830, where he received his education, and where he remained with his parents, assisting in tilling the soil of his father's farm. At the age of twenty years, he left the homestead and entered upon his career in life as a farmer; in 1850, he entered eighty acres of wild prairie land in Montgomery County, and, in the year following, removed with his family to their new home, and where he still resides; he made all the improvements himself, such as building fences, orchards and all other improvements necessary for comfort, and which are found upon all well-regulated farms; by his energy and economy, he continued to add to his original purchase, and at one time had in his possession 200 acres, and at the present owns 160 acres of fine farm land, which, as a practical farmer, he keeps in a high state of cultivation, which denotes him to be one of the successful farmers of the county. He was married, in Greene County, August 4, 1840, to Clarinda Jackson, who was born in Greene County March 10, 1823; she is the mother of eight children, three of whom are living, viz.: Shadrach, William A. and Anderson Monroe. Mrs. McGown was a daughter of Shadrach Jackson a native of North Carolina, and one of the early settlers of Greene County; his death occurred in Texas, in May, 1879; his wife Prudence Finley, was born in Madison County; she died December 31, 1855; the result of their union was eight children, of whom only three are now living. Samuel McGown, the father of our subject, was born in Tennessee, and was one of the early settlers of Greene County, where he followed the occupation of a farmer for a number of years; his death occurred in 1861. The mother of our subject, Nancy Westbrooks, was born in North Carolina, but raised in West Virginia; she died in the spring of 1852; they were the parents of eight children, four of whom are still living, and of whom Ishmael is the third child. Politically, he is identified with the Democratic party. Religiously, himself and wife have been connected with the Christian Church for a number of years. Although Mr. McGown grows all of the usual farm crops, he makes grain his principal crop. He is a public-spirited man, and has always taken an interest in the growth and prosperity of the county, and, when Raymond was first laid out, furnished a large portion of the land now covered by the village, and perhaps no man has taken more interest and done more for the prosperity of the town than Mr. McGown.

WILLIAM A. MAXEY, merchant, senior member of the firm of Maxey & Starr, grocers, Raymond, was born in Montgomery County, Ill., August 27, 1856, and received a common-school education; he remained upon the homestead until he attained the age of twenty years, when he entered into the mercantile business as clerk at Hillsboro; he followed in that occupation at different places until November, 1880, when he entered into business for himself at Raymond; he was very successful in his new enterprise, but, at the time Raymond was destroyed by fire, he was one of the sufferers, his stock being nearly all destroyed; he did not despair, however, but immediately secured a new room and continued the business, which gradually assumed larger proportions, and now, in connection with his partner, Mr. Starr, has the satisfaction of conducting a large and steadily increasing trade, the result of a thorough business knowledge, energy and enterprise; their store is centrally located on the principal street of Raymond, and any one may feel sure of a welcome and receiving kind attentions from the gentlemanly proprietors. Wilson M. Maxey, the father of our subject, was born in Kentucky, and was one of the early settlers of Montgomery County; is a farmer by occupation, and still living upon the place of his original purchase; his wife, Eliza Newcomb, was a native of Virginia; she died in about 1864; was the mother of seven children, of whom William was the third child. Politically, his sympathies are with the Democratic party; he was elected by the people of Raymond, in the spring of 1882, to fill the office of City Clerk, which office he still holds; he also holds the office of Secretary in the I. O. O. F. order at Raymond, of which he has been an active member for about two years.

I. G. MOORE, farmer, P. O. Raymond, was born in Holmes County, Ohio, in 1828, the son of a farmer, who moved to Missouri in an early day (1842), when there were no railroads, but when land could be bought for $1.25 per acre; they settled in Gasconade County, and began operations in true pioneer style, making their own plows and living in the simplest manner; they broke the land up, however, burned timber out for a clearing, and finally had excellent farms; the necessaries of life were hard to get hold of, and all groceries had to be obtained in St. Louis, a hundred miles away. Mr. Moore married in 1852. During the war, he was engaged buying horses and mules for the Government, but lost a good deal of property in consequence of military raids through the section where he resided. In 1865, he moved to Montgomery, where he has since followed farming; he has had quite an eventful life; has seen many ups and downs; has made and lost a great deal of money, but, thanks to his energy and economy, is now comfortable in this world's goods.

HEZEKIAH MOORE, farmer, P. O. Raymond, born in Holmes County, Ohio, November 7, 1833; son of Thomas Moore, born in Ohio, a stone-mason by trade, who moved to Missouri in 1840, and was one of the first settlers of Gasconade County; his death occurred in July, 1852. Catharine Best, wife of Thomas and mother of subject, born in Ohio, died in March, 1872; she was the mother of twelve children, of whom Hezekiah was the sixth. His education was limited to such as could be obtained in the common schools in the country at that day. He commenced his career in life as a farmer, remaining in Missouri until 1868, when he removed to Montgomery County and purchased the farm on which he now lives, and made all the improvements; the surroundings and state of cultivation show Mr. Moore to be a practical farmer; since his advent into the county, he has been identified with its growth and prosperity, particularly with its agricultural interests. He was married, in Missouri, May 9, 1860, to Rose Ann Coleman, who was born in Missouri January 9, 1841; they have four children, viz.: John, Emma, Thomas and Lillie; and have lost three, viz.: Hattie, Nettie and Willie, all of whom died in infancy. Mrs. Moore is a daughter of Ephraim Coleman, a native of Ohio, a farmer by occupation, and now living with the subject of this sketch. Nancy Best, a native of Ohio, died in December, 1879. Mr. Moore has served the people as Road Commissioner several years; entered the service in Company M, Fifty Iowa Cavalry, with Capt. D. A. Waters, regiment commanded by Col. W. W. Lowe; remained in the service three years. Politically, his sympathies are with the Republican party; he has been a member of the Masonic fraternity for several years; before the war, he was connected with the [illegible] at Linn, Mo., but, during the war, the order gave up its charter. He owns [illegible] of choice farm land, on which he [illegible] siderable stock, besides the usual crops; has also 150 acres of land southeast of Raymond, and twenty-eight acres of improved town property in Raymond. He and his wife are connected with the Methodist Church.

MILLARD F. MAY, Clerk of township and village, and carpenter and joiner by occupation, Raymond, was born at Girard, Macoupin Co., Ill., March 15, 1860, son of Jesse W. and Mary (Kitzmiller) May, he a prominent stock dealer, born in Tennessee in 1830, who came to Illinois in 1855; she, also of Tennessee, born in 1835; they had five children Florence, wife of J. A. Bradley; Millard F., Mary, Dora and Jessie; the latter died when four years of age. Our subject, after receiving an education in the schools of his native county, learned the carpenter and joiner's trade, and has assisted in building some of the principal business blocks of Raymond; he is at present (1882) engaged in building a residence for himself on one of the principal streets of Raymond. October 31, 1881, he married Miss Belle Miller, born in Montgomery County April 21, 1862, daughter of Lemuel G. and Lucinda (Lee) Miller, both of Greene County, Ill. Mr. May is a Freemason and a Democrat.

JOSEPH W. POTTS. Joseph W. Potts, the subject of this sketch, was born on a farm near Chapman's Point, in the north part of Macoupin County, Ill., on the 19th of September, A. D. 1841, where his parents remained until the year 1852, when they moved to near the head of Bear Creek, in same county, where they carried on the business of agriculture for five years, at the end of which time his father purchased a large tract of land at and near Pleasant Hill, Montgomery Co., Ill., to which place they moved in the fall of 1857. Joseph W. remained on the farm working with his parents until his marriage on the 12th day of March, A. D. 1862, with Miss Mary J. Miller, daughter of Lemuel G. Miller, one of the then leading farmers and stock-raisers of Montgomery County, Ill. William B. Potts, father of Joseph W. Potts, was born in Frankfort, Ky., on the 22d day of February, A. D. 1814, where he resided until the year A. D. 1829, when he emigrated to Illinois with his father, Richard F. Potts, and his brother and sister, Jessie Potts and Millie Potts, and settled in Morgan County, near Old Berlin. After his father was comfortably situated, he hired himself as a farm hand to Jacob Strawn, the great cattle king of Illinois, for whom he worked constantly until his marriage with Miss Rhoda A Richards, of Macoupin County, Ill.; the issue of this marriage was twelve children— six boys and six girls. Joseph W., the subject of this article, was the fifth in order of birth. Richard F. Potts, grandfather of Joseph W., was born on the 4th day of July, 1776, near the present site of Bentonville, N. C., where he resided until he was four years old, when his father, Washington A. Potts, moved to Kentucky, near Munfordsville, where he erected a water-mill on one of the tributaries of Green River; after many days of arduous labor and great privation, having to work by day and watch the prowling red man by night, the mill was built; but the thinly settled country necessarily brought him poor returns for the money and labor invested; finally, on Christmas night, in the year 1786, a prowling band of Indians burned the mill and tomahawked the whole family, consisting of sixteen, with the exception of Richard F., who made his escape across the hills to the celebrated Mammoth Cave, where he subsisted for several days on the blind fish that inhabit its waters; he was finally rescued by a party of hunters, consisting of Daniel Boone and others, and taken to Boonesboro, where he was kindly cared for in the family of Boone until his uncle, Christopher A. Potts, commander of a British man-of-war cruising off the coast of South Carolina, was notified of his safety and whereabouts, ordered him to be sent to Charleston, S. C., where he met him and took him on board his ship, where he served in the capacity of midshipman for several years in Her Majesty's service. At the age of eighteen, he returned to Owensboro, Ky., where he resided until his marriage with Miss Elizabeth Cummings, when he located on a farm near what is known as the Yellow Banks, on the Kentucky River, where he remained until he emigrated to Illinois. Washington A. Potts, commander of the British man-of-war, as before mentioned, received orders from Commodore Downie, commander of the British fleet near Quebec, to proceed to Quebec, near the mouth of the St. Lawrence River; his ship was caught in a storm and wrecked, with the loss of the entire crew, and among them Washington A. Potts perished, in the year A. D. 1814. Ezekiel E. Potts, brother of the deceased, ordered the remains to be returned to North Hampton, England, the home of the family, where they were sepultured in the family cemetery; a beautiful monument marks the family resting place; he who passes that way can read the monumental inscription; it is as follows: "Here resteth Solomon Q. Potts, father of Ezekiel and Washington A. Potts; also his son Ezekiel, who lost his life in Her Majesty's service (Queen Anne) in foreign lands. May they rest in the hope of a glorious resurrection." We will deal no more with the ancestors of the subject of our sketch; suffice it to say they are of pure Norman origin. We will now return to Joseph W. Potts. After his marriage, in 1862, he settled on a farm near Pleasant Hill, in Montgomery County, where he resided for eleven years, at the expiration of which time, he, becoming wearied with farm life, entered into the mercantile business in Raymond, Ill., a town which sprang up as if by magic on the Wabash Railroad in the year 1871, where he has since constantly resided. During his residence in Raymond, Ill., he has been engaged in various pursuits of life, filling many offices of trust and is now editor and proprietor of the Raymond *Independent*, a weekly newspaper of large circulation and unlimited influence wherever circulated. Joseph W. Potts is now forty-one years old, hale and hearty, and bids fair to live long and enjoy the rewards of a well-regulated life, and the blessings of his wife and their two sons, Lemuel L. Potts and Roy A. Potts.

JOHN C. REBHAN, farmer, P. O. Raymond, was born in Germany December 6, 1843, and brought to New Orleans by his parents when he was quite young; his father is living in St. Clair County, this State, where he owns and cultivates a fine farm. Our subject was educated partly in New Orleans and partly in St. Clair County, and, when a youth, learned the saddle and harness-making business, but eventually became a farmer. May 10, 1870, in St. Clair County, he married Miss Emma F. Sandick, a native of that county, born April 2, 1847, and from which union has resulted four children—James L., William Charles, Edward A. and Emma Virginia. Mr. Rebhan held a position in the railway postal service for ten years, after which he came to Raymond and purchased the farm on which he now lives, a fine tract highly improved, of 160 acres of land; is a member of the Masonic fraternity, Blue Lodge, Chapter and Commandery, and is a Republican.

WILLIAM SCHMIDT, farmer, P. O. Raymond, was born in Germany August 21, 1821, where he received his education in his mother tongue, and assisted his father upon the old homestead farm until he was fifteen years of age, when he engaged as a farm hand, receiving but a very small compensation for his labor; he followed this occupation for about three years, when he concluded to try his fortunes in the New World, and emigrated to America, where he found himself a stranger in a strange land; but, being possessed with a stout heart and the energy necessary to make his own way in a strange country, he set to work with a will, and rented a farm in Morgan County, Ill., where he remained eight years, and, by his energy and industry, succeeded in laying up enough funds to enable him to make a purchase of land for himself; he purchased a part of the property he now owns, and removed with his family to Montgomery County, where he has continued to add to his possessions until he now owns 200 acres of as fine land as can be found in Raymond Township, and which he has improved by way of buildings, orchards, fences, etc., until it will compare with any of the well-improved farms of the county, and places Mr. Schmidt in the list of practical farmers. His father, Henrick Schmidt, was a native of Germany, and was a farmer by occupation; he died in 1862, leaving his wife and five children to mourn his loss; his wife, Louisa Pascher, survived him two years. William was the youngest child. He was married, in Morgan County, March 15, 1858, to Hannah Schelp, who was born in Germany in November, 1843, and brought to America when but eleven years of age; she is the mother of six boys and six girls, viz.: Jennettie, wife of Henry Weber; Christ William, George Henry, Louisa Rachel, wife of Aug Beder; Emma Anna, Carolina Louisa, John Henry, Harmon, Minnie Anna, Dora Gusta, Edward Martin, Henry Phillip all of whom are still living. Mrs. Schmidt is a daughter of Philip Schelp, a native of Germany and a prominent farmer of Morgan County, where his death occurred November 29, 1863; his wife, Rachael Lakers, was also a native of Germany, and is still living in Morgan County, and is the mother of five children, three of whom are still living, viz.: William, a wagon-maker in Morgan County; George, a farmer in same county; and Hannah, the wife of Mr. Schmidt. Mr. Schmidt has a brother and sister living in this county, viz.: Chris. and Henrietta, widow of W. Ganoeft. Politically, Mr. Schmidt is a Democrat, and religiously, himself and wife are connected with the Lutheran Church.

D. WILL STARR, merchant, Raymond, of the firm of Maxey & Starr, was born in Greensboro, Guilford Co., N. C., November 17, 1853, where his early childhood was spent in assisting his father upon the homestead farm and in attending the common schools of his native county. At the age of ten years, he left home and attended an academic school two years, at the end of which time he began learning the painter's trade, and followed in that occupation about fourteen years in different localities, he then purchased a livery stable at Raymond, Ill., but sold his interest in a few months, and, on March 15, 1882 became one of the firm of Maxey & Starr, dealers in groceries, at which business they have become more than ordinarily successful, owing to their strict attention to business and the pleasing manner in which they attend to the wants of their many customers; in business, they are energetic and enterprising, and socially, enjoy the highest esteem of the community at large. Mr. Starr, the junior member of the firm, sought a home in the North when he was about twenty-two years of age, and eventually located at Raymond. He was married, at Palmer, Christian County, December 25, 1881, to Miss Maggie Lee, who was born December 25, 1857, daughter of

Capt. E. T. and Mary A. (Hill) Lee, he a native of Virginia, one of the early settlers of Bear Creek, Christian County, a very prominent farmer and stock-dealer, at which business he has become very wealthy; his wife, Mary, is a native of Kentucky, and still living. Daniel M. Starr, the father of our subject, is a native of North Carolina, and still living in his native State, engaged in farming and fruit raising; his wife, Sarah M. Low, is also a native of North Carolina, and is still living; she is the mother of eleven children, of whom D. Will is the fourth child. Although he does not take much interest in politics, he is identified with the Republican party.

DAVID Y. SCHERER, farmer, P. O. Raymond, was born in Montgomery County February 3, 1842; received a common school education and entered upon his career as a farmer, and the land he first owned is still in the possession of the family; purchased his present property in 1869, and has made all of the improvements himself, and the surroundings show him to be an energetic and enterprising man and a practical farmer; his farm consists of 160 acres of choice farm land, which he keeps in a high state of cultivation; he devotes his time to growing the usual farm crops and raising stock of all kinds; he has taken an active part in public improvements, and in the advancement of agricultural interests in his neighborhood, and in the educational privileges he also takes a leading part. He was married, in Montgomery County, December 11, 1862, to Louisa Morrell, who was born in Ohio; they have six children, viz.: Mary E., William J., Robert A., Oliver F., Alice R. and May L. Mrs. Scherer was a daughter of Robert and Rebecca (Spangler) Morrell. David Scherer, the father of the subject, was a native of North Carolina, a farmer by occupation; he died in 1860; his wife, Mary Elizabeth Waggoner, is also a native of North Carolina, still living, in Butler Township; she was the mother of fourteen children, of whom David is the eleventh; has been School Director; is a Republican; himself and wife are members of the Lutheran Church.

SCOTT S. TILDEN, druggist, Raymond, was born in Montgomery County, Ill., October 18, 1855, son of Dr. Joseph G. and Ann W. (Hill) Tilden; he born in Vermont and came to Illinois in 1837, settling in Montgomery County, and still living in Raymond; she born in Kentucky, still living, and the mother of nine children; those living are Joseph, Jr., living in Alabama; John H., physician at Litchfield; Scott S., our subject; Emeline, wife of H. C. Coleman, of St. Louis; Seth H., living in Raymond; and George A., at home. Our subject, after receiving an education in the common schools, entered a drug store at Nokomis as clerk, where he remained one and a half years, then moved to Kansas City, where he remained two years, and then returned to Raymond and worked for his father eight years, and entered into business for himself in September, 1880, in Raymond, where he conducts the drug, oil, paint, lead, wall paper and fancy goods business; he has lately moved into a new and commodious room, fitted up especially for his business. In Montgomery County, January 1, 1879, he married Mary A. Neal, born March 4, 1862, and one child has blessed the union, Anna May, born March 4, 1881; his wife is a member of the Methodist Church.

GILBERT H. WHITEHEAD, farmer, P. O. Raymond, is a native of Louisiana, having been born in that State December 18, 1846, and came to Illinois in 1867, first settling in Jersey County, whence he came to Montgomery County one year later. His father, Wyatt J. Whitehead, was a native of

South Carolina, a farmer by occupation, who married Miss Adeline Zeigler, of Mississippi, and who was the mother of five children, Gilbert H. being the second; the father died in 1873, and the mother followed her husband the next year. Mr. Whitehead, our subject, married, in Montgomery County, in 1875, March 11, Miss Fanny Devasier, a native of Montgomery County, born March 26, 1853; four children have been born of this marriage—Rosa Lee, Samuel, Nancy and Zenora. He owns 131 acres of choice land, and affiliates with the Democratic party.

SAMUEL H. YOUNG, farmer, P. O. Raymond, was born in Clermont County, Ohio, December 12, 1852, son of Orson and Sarah (Hall) Young, he a farmer and mechanic, born in New York State; she a native of Ireland—both of whom are living, in the township of Harvel, Montgomery County, this State; they are the parents of six children, Samuel H. being the second, who, like his father, is a farmer. Our subject married, in Montgomery County, December 31, 1871, Mary Amanda Grummon, born in Madison County May 29, 1857, daughter of John L. Grummon, of St. Clair County, Ill., from which union have been born four children—John O., Samuel L., S. Catharine and Irene; Minnie died in infancy. Mr. and Mrs. Young are members of the Methodist Church, and he is a Greenbacker in politics.

ZANESVILLE TOWNSHIP.

WILLIAM A. BEATTY, farmer, P. O. Raymond, born in Grayson County, Ky., January 29, 1847; received his education from the common schools of his native county. He remained with his parents in Kentucky until 1864, when he enlisted in the Federal army. Twenty-sixth Kentucky Volunteers, commanded by Burbridge, afterward by Maxwell, last by Col. Farley; served about thirteen months; mustered out in July, 1865; in 1866, removed to Montgomery County, where he commenced by working as a farm hand, continuing the same until 1872, when he rented a farm of 160 acres and worked it until 1876, when he bought 100 acres, and has since added 100 to it, now having 200 acres. In 1876, January 27, in Montgomery Conuty, he married Sarah A. Bowles, a native of Greene County, Ill., born in 1857. When he commenced on his farm, there were no improvements; upon his farm he has a good residence; wheat, corn, oats, cattle and hogs of good stock; father was Joseph Beatty, born in Grayson County, Ky., in 1823; now lives near Raymond; mother, Sarah Akres, born in Kentucky; she died in 1847, aged about twenty-one years; parents had one child, our subject. Subject has had four children, three living--Oliver M., William A. (dead), Orrie, Bessie. Politically, Republican.

R. B. BOWSHER, farming and livery stable, P. O. Barrett. Jesse, the father of this gentleman, was born in Wyandot County, Ohio, in 1812; during his life, followed the occupation of a farmer, and died February 20, 1856. His wife, and mother of our subject; was Elizabeth Clayton; she was born in Wyandot County in 1814, and died in February, 1850; they were blessed with five children, R. B. Bowsher being the second child. He was born in Upper Sandusky, Wyandot Co., Ohio, May 19, 1837; his early life was spent in receiving such an education as the common schools of his native county afforded, and assisted his father in tilling the soil of his farm until 1856, when he removed to Macoupin County, Ill., where he engaged in agricultural pursuits on his own account; he remained in Macoupin County until the spring of 1882, when he removed to Montgomery County, where, in connection with his farming, he is engaged in the livery business, and has a good stable, well stocked with fine horses, buggies, etc., and, in fact, everything to complete a first-class livery stable. He was married, in Macoupin County, in 1861, to Miss Mary Range, a native of Macoupin County, Ill., and the daughter of Allen and Agnes (Crouch) Range; they have five children Columbus, Baker, Leon, Nellie and Maud. Mr. Bowsher is a progressive and energetic business man, a kind neighbor and a good citizen; he is one of those men who add to the prosperity of the county; he is an active member of the order of A., F. & A. M., Lodge No. 171, at Girard; in politics, is identified with the Democratic party.

JAMES W. CLINE, farmer, P. O. Raymond, was born in Montgomery County February 27 1837, to Reuben H. and Nellie (Smith) Cline. Mr. Cline's early days were spent in receiving an education and assisting in tilling the soil of his father's farm; he re mained with his father to the time of his death, and for a few years previous to his death, took the entire management of the same; in 1855, removed to Bond County and hired out as a farm hand, and continued working by the month until 1862, and married and removed to the southwest corner of Montgomery County, where he rented a farm of eighty acres, and in 1863, returned to Bond County, and in 1865 removed to Madison County, where he bought a farm, in 1867, of 120 acres, and remained until 1869, when he sold it and moved to the Bluffs, near St. Louis, and again rented, and in 1870 again removed to Madison County, and bought a farm in Rountree Township of 165 acres and continued on that farm and added to it until he had 220 acres; he remained there until the fall of 1879, when he removed to his present residence and has now 440 acres of land, and one of the best farms of Montgomery County, upon which he has a fine residence, barn, with wind-mill and everything for use on a good farm; makes stock raising and trading in stock a specialty. In October, 1862, in Montgomery County, he married Miss Mary E. Thompson, a native of Licking County, Ohio, born in 1844; they have had four children, all of whom are living—Leighton W., Susan C., Alex C., James S. In 1861, he enlisted in the Federal army, under Col. Marshall, and was taken prisoner by Gen. Price, and was discharged in October, and was again discharged in July 1862. Himself and family are members of M. E. Church; Republican in politics; member of A. F. & A. M., No. 692 at Raymond. Commenced life a poor man; has now a good property; parents had eleven children, subject being the oldest child.

WILLIAM COLEMAN, farmer, P. O. Raymond, was born in Crawford County, Mo., August 25, 1842, to Ephraim Coleman and Nancy (Best); father was born in Muskingum County, Ohio, in 1812; during his life, followed farming, and now resides in Montgomery County, Ill., with his children; mother was born in Muskingum County, Ohio, in 1813; she died in 1877, in Missouri; parents had eleven children, eight of whom are living—four boys and four girls, subject was third child. He received his education from the neighborhood schools of Fayette County, Ind., at the time living with his uncle, Thomas Coleman; commenced life by trading in stock in Missouri in [illegible], and continued until 1870; shipped to St. Louis, where he engaged as brakeman on the Missouri & Pacific road, at the end of a year, was given a train, and acted as conductor until 1875, when he commenced farming in Osage County, Mo., by renting; in 1877, he bought a farm of 105 acres in same county, where he continued until 1881, when he sold out and removed to his present residence and is now the owner of eighty acres of well improved land, upon which he has a good residence, good barns, etc.; he intends to make stock raising a specialty. In 1878 he married, in Missouri, Miss Susan Phelps, a native of Osage County, Mo., born in 1842, daughter of Charles Phelps of Missouri; they have no children; wife is a member of Christian Church; in politics, is a Democrat; he gave up railroading because he disliked it.

JOHN J. CLARKSON, farmer, P. O. Atwater, was born in Walker County, Ga., June 30, 1845, to J. P. and Lavina (Massa) Clarkson; father was born in Georgia October 9, 1822, and died December 24, 1844, in Georgia; his life was spent in Georgia, engaged in agricultural pursuits; mother was born in Lawrence County, S. C., February 25, 1826, and now lives with her only child, our subject. Mr. Clarkson came to Montgomery County in 1850 with his mother, and, in the fall of 1851, removed to Macoupin County, where he received his education in the Union School; in 1867, began farming on his own account, and continued the same in Macoupin County until the spring of 1884, when he removed to his present residence, where he has a farm of ninety two acres: wheat, oats and corn; some stock. In 1867, in Macoupin County, he married Mrs. Mary E. Bevers, a native of Tennessee, daughter of T. W. and Elizabeth Whitfield, by whom he has had two children—Charley and an infant girl; in politics, unites with the Democratic party. The father of Mr. Clarkson died when John J. was an infant.

JAMES DEULEN, farmer, P. O. Atwater, was born in Greene County, Ill., October 30, 18.., to Kelen and Sarah (Dawson) Deulen; father was born in Greene County; was a farmer, and died in January, 1875, aged about fifty five years: mother was born in Hamilton County, Ohio, and now lives in Iowa; she had nine children, subject being the second child; received his education from the common schools of Greene County, and, at the age of sixteen, with his parents, removed to Wayne County, Iowa, where he also attended school. In 1869, he returned to Greene County and began business for himself as a farm hand; in 1870, returned to Iowa, and in 1871, returned again to Greene, where he rented a farm for one year, and again hired out as a farm hand for four years. In 1874, he married and removed to Montgomery County, and rented a farm, and in 1873 bought the farm upon which he now resides, having ninety acres of land, and is also renting about sixty acres. In 1874, he was married, in Montgomery County, to Lucy Rummons, a native of Warren County, Mo., and the daughter of John and Juliett Rummons; they have two children—Charley and Edna. In politics, he votes with the Republican party.

WILLIAM FOOKS, deceased, was born in London, England, in 1815; he was educated in London; married and came to Bunker Hill, Macoupin Co., Ill., in about 1845; his wife died soon after he settled in Illinois. In 1860, at Bunker Hill, he married Jane Taggart, his second wife. In 1864, he with his family, removed to her present residence, and, during his life, accumulated in Montgomery County about two hundred and twenty five acres; was a very successful farmer, and also very industrious; he was a member of the Presbyterian Church; he was a Republican; a man who believed in doing right in every respect; he died in 1875; his children by his first wife were three, all now dead; his children by his last marriage were four, three living—George, Fanny and Jane—all at home, George being the one who carries on the farm; family are members of the Presbyterian Church. Mr. Fooks took great interest in making his home comfortable and caring for the happiness of his family.

W. C. GALBRAITH, farmer, P. O. Atwater, was born in Wayne County, Tenn., June 11, 1834, to Alexander and Margaret (Snodgrass) Galbraith; father was born in Shelby County, Tenn., in 1808; was a farmer; he died in December, 1871, in Johnson County, Ill., where he had resided for ten years previous to his death. In an early day, he took great interest in politics; was Justice of the Peace of Wayne County, Tenn., for a term of twelve years; was an Old Time Whig; he was son of Thomas Galbraith, a native of North Carolina, son of John Galbraith, a native of Scotland. Subject's mother was born in North Carolina in 1810, and died in 1854, in Macoupin County, Ill. Parents had one girl and four boys, subject being third child. Subject lived in Wayne County, Tenn. until he was fourteen years of age, and there attended school; in 1848, with his parents, removed to Henderson County, Ill.; in 1850, removed to Macoupin County, where he received the most of his education from the neighborhood schools. In 1855, he hired out as farm hand; in 1856, rented a piece of land until 1859, when he bought land in Montgomery County and removed to this county and settled in what is now known as Pitman Township, where he remained until the spring of 1864, when he sold out and bought land in Zanesville Township, and in six months, sold out and bought another farm adjoining the land he now owns; in 1867, bought his present residence and farm, and has made all the improvements on it, there was not even a house there; he built a comfortable farm residence, and upon his place has a pair of stock scales, and everything for a first-class farmer, and now is the owner of 120 acres, making wheat a specialty, and trades some in stock. In 1857, in Macoupin County, he married Miss Lydia Ann Gray, a native of Macoupin County, born in 1837, a daughter of John Gray, a native of Tennessee; four children—Alzirah, Antoinette, William J. and Anna J., at home; Alzirah is now the wife of A. C. McPherson, and now lives in Kansas. Member of order of A., F. & A. M., No. 692, at Raymond; self and wife are members of the Methodist Church for about twenty-five years; politically, a Republican; was nominated and elected Justice of the Peace in 1878; held office for three years, filling vacancy; in 1881, was re-elected for same office for a term of four years. Mr. Galbraith commenced life a poor man; when he left his parental home, he had only 25 cents in his possession, and, by his honesty, industry and economy, has succeeded in gaining a good property, and a name and reputation which is beyond reproach.

FRANCIS McGOWN, farmer, P. O. Raymond, was born in Johnson County, Ill., July 10, 1830, to Samuel and Nancy (Westbrook) McGown; father was born in Warren County, Ky.; he was a farmer; came to Johnson County, Ill., being among the early settlers; and, in the fall of 1830, removed to Greene County, and in the spring of 1851 removed to Montgomery County, where he died in 1861, aged seventy-seven years. Mother was born in Kentucky, and died in Montgomery County in 1852, aged sixty-three. They had six children, subject being the youngest. He was taken to Greene County when an infant, by his parents, where he received his education from the common schools; he remained with his father to the time of his death, assisting him in farming, and, for years previous to his death, took the management of the farm. In the fall of 1850, he removed to Montgomery County; settled on same farm he now occupies; bought ninety-five acres, and is now the owner of 120 acres, and continued to till the soil of the same until 1875, when he was compelled to give up work on account of rheumatic affliction; at the present time, is unable to do any work; the farm is now carried on by his son and son-in-law. In 1854, in Greene County, he married Miss Elizabeth Banning, a native of Greene County, born in 1835; they have had thirteen children, and now have three living—Edward A., Nancy E., Julia; self and wife are members of the United Baptist Church; Democrat.

GEORGE A. NORVELL, farmer, P. O. Raymond, was born in Sumner County, Tenn., November 28, 1813, to William and Mary (Payne) Norvell; father was born in Frederick County, Va., August 4, 1771; he was a farmer; was in the war of 1812; removed from Virginia to Tennessee in 1800; in 1828, removed to Macoupin County, Ill., where he died January 24, 1833; mother, born in Botetourt County, Va., March 10, 1775, and died May 10, 1872, in her ninety-eighth year;

they were married in 1800; they had twelve children--six boys and six girls George A. being the seventh child. Subject received some of his education in Tennessee and some in Macoupin County, Ill. He came to Macoupin County with his parents in 1828. He began life by farming upon his father's farm, and continued until 1853, when he removed to his present residence, where he has since remained, engaged in farming and is now the owner of a large tract of land. In 1852, in Macoupin County, he married Miss Mary Ann King, a native of Jefferson County, Ky., born October 10, 1834; they have eleven children living--William J., James P., John S., Charles H., Mary A., Edward E., Jennie B., Nathaniel F., Erastus W., Effie S. and Helen E.; and two dead--George A. and Ruth S. Mr. Norvell has held the position of Justice of the Peace in Macoupin County, and was formerly an Old-Line Whig, but is now a Greenbacker; his wife is a member of the Methodist Church, and he is a member of the A., F. & A. M., at Girard, Ill. Mr. Norvell is one of the first settlers of Macoupin County, and was there before it was organized as a county.

DANIEL P. ROGERS, farmer, P. O. Litchfield. That there is no "royal road to success" is well illustrated in the history of Mr. Rogers. In 1861, he entered 160 acres of land near where Butler now stands: this land was entered with the proceeds of an interest in a wheat crop raised on his father's farm. April 12, 1854, he married Miss Lavina C., daughter of James and Rebecca (Parks) Sinclair. In 1855, he sold out his land near Butler and bought 120 acres of fine land in Zanesville Township, where he now resides: the same season, he "broke out" forty acres; when this land was broken, the prairie grass, then several feet in height, appeared as a wall surrounding it on every side; the next season, a small frame house was erected, into which he moved. He has continued to improve and add to his farm until it now amounts to about three hundred and eighty acres of good land 320 in cultivation; this land is very rich and well drained. The Rogers family descended from German ancestry, who came to the United States when they were dependent colonies. Capt. Henry Rogers, Mr. Rogers' grandfather, won his epaulets as a Revolutionary soldier; he distinguished himself at the battle of Trenton, and the sword which he took from a Hessian officer is now in the possession of the grandson, the subject of this sketch. Henry Rogers, after the close of the war, settled in New Jersey, where William H., Mr. Rogers, father, was born. William raised the following family by his wife, formerly Miss Catharine Perrine: Henry, of Monmouth County, N. J.; Robert, who died in California; Daniel P. and Charles A., of Montgomery County; Mrs. Elizabeth Wood, deceased; Mrs. Catherine (Cornelius) Dey, of Macoupin County; Mrs. Sarah (Edward) Atkinson, of St. Louis, Mo.; Mrs. Margaret (Capt. Charles) Borden, deceased, of Fall River, Mass.; and Mrs. Jane (William) Pitman, of Jerseyville, Ill. Mr. Rogers is not only represented in the war giving birth and being to our liberties, through his immediate paternal ancestry, but also can boast of another grandfather, Robert Perrine, his mother's father, who served in the Revolutionary war as a Captain; his sword is also handed down, and is now in the possession of Mr. Charles Rogers, of Zanesville Township. Mrs. Rogers also had two grandfathers who were Revolutionary soldiers Grandfather Sinclair, on her father's side, and John Parks, of her mother's lineage Mr. and Mrs. Rogers have the following children: William Pitman, Robert P., and Misses Lizzie A. and Jennie A.; one son,

Tolbert A., died September 12, 1858. Mr. Rogers' chances of an education were rather poor, never getting the opportunity to attend school during his school days more than two months in a year; he has nevertheless secured a fair business education; he certainly has a strong intellect and keen discrimination. He forms a part of the County Court as Supervisor for his township, and well does he fill the position; and many of his friends expect him to fill still higher positions in the gift of the people. Mrs. Rogers is one of those whole-souled, excellent Christian women whom we think it would be hard to praise too much. Mr. Rogers and wife are members of the Baptist Church, and enjoy the friendship, confidence and esteem of all good people where they are known. With the greatest of pleasure we introduce them to the good people of Montgomery County, and shall ever regard the privilege as one of the most agreeable duties connected with a long, and, we hope, a lasting friendship.

OSCAR RUMMONS, farmer, P. O. Atwater, was born in Warren County, Mo., July 6, 1849, to John and Juliett (Pringle) Rummons; father born in Madison, Ky., in 1810; during his life, was a farmer, and died in Montgomery County, Ill., in 1874, where he had resided, engaged in farming, since 1868; mother born in Litchfield, Conn., in 1811, and died in 1865; parents had three children who grew to maturity—one daughter and two boys; subject youngest child. Subject received his education in Warren County, Mo., and came to Montgomery County with parents in 1868, and remained with parents to the time of their death. He now has a farm of 140 acres of well improved land, making wheat and corn a specialty, also stock. In 1876, he was married, in Montgomery County, to Julia B. Mitchell, a native of Cooper County, Mo., born in 1857, daughter of Thomas C. Mitchell; two children—Hattie May, Maggie Laura; member of order of A., F. & A. M., No. 692, at Raymond; politically, Democrat.

J. C. SINCLAIR, farmer, P. O. Litchfield, was born in Greene County, Ill., in 1837, to James and Rebecca (Parks) Sinclair; father was born in Tennessee; was a farmer, and died in 1850; mother was born in Tennessee, and died in 1850; parents had nine children, subject being the fifth child; at the age of thirteen left Greene County with his parents, and settled in Macoupin County, where he principally received his education; at the age of twenty left Macoupin County and removed to Montgomery County, and settled upon the place where he now resides, and where he has ever since been engaged in tilling the soil of his beautiful farm of 1,300 acres; he rents the largest portion of the farm, having retired from active labor in 1881. In September, 1863, he married Elizabeth Jones, a native of Macoupin County, Ill., and the daughter of Lodowick Jones, from which union there have been born four children—James C., C. A., Eva M. and Vesta; in politics, unites with the Democratic party; subject's father was in the war of 1812.

EZRA STARKEY, farmer, was born in Madison County, Ill., March 21, 1833, to David and Mary (Jones) Starkey; father was born in Virginia in 1802; was taken to Madison County by his parents when quite a child; he remained in Madison County to the time of his death, which occurred in 1869; he was a farmer; he was the son of Russell Starkey, a native of Virginia; mother was born in Madison County in 1809, and died in June, 1877; she was the daughter of William Jones, a native of Tennessee, who was a Baptist preacher; parents had eleven children, our subject being the third child. He remained with his parents, receiving an education, and assisted in tilling the soil of his father's farm until 1861, when he bought the farm upon which he now resides. In 1861, in Madison County, he married Mary S. Deck, a native of Madison County, born January 7, 1836, daughter of Nicholas and Elizabeth (Dugger) Deck, first a native of Virginia, and the latter of Tennessee. Mr. and Mrs. Starkey have had eight children, five of whom are living—Eliza J., Virginia, Charles, Forest and Tilden. He is a Democrat. Mrs. Starkey's grandfather, Michael Deck, was in the Revolutionary war.

JOSEPH VIGNOS, farmer, P. O. Raymond, was born in the eastern part of France, December 1, 1817, to Claud and Margaret (Barquin) Vignos; his father was born in France, where he followed the occupation of farming during his life; he died in 1858, aged sixty-two years. His mother was also a native of France; she died in 1862, aged seventy-two years. They were the parents of nine children, Joseph Vignos being the oldest child. His early life was spent in receiving such an education as the common schools of France afforded, and assisting in tilling the soil of his father's farm, and, for two years previous to his departure from home, taught school. In December, 1845, he bade his parents and native place farewell, and emigrated to America, where he followed the dyeing business in New York City for nearly two years, and then traveled through Pennsylvania, Cincinnati, Louisville, New Orleans and St. Louis, and, when he first came to Montgomery County, was a peddler of notions. While staying overnight at Zanesville, the citizens persuaded him to embark in the mercantile business at that place, at which he was successful until 1854, when he bought the same farm that he is now residing on and commenced giving his attention to agricultural pursuits; he is now one of the representative farmers of Zanesville Township, and is the owner of a large tract of land. In 1846, he married Miss Sarah J. Allen, a daughter of Robert Allen; she died in May, 1852. In 1853, on January 6, he married a second time, Miss Harriet E. Baydy. By his first marriage he has two children—Agnes, who is married and living in Kansas; and Francis A., who is now in Texas. By his second marriage he has six children, viz.: Joseph, Claud M., Jerome, Josephine, Mary and Susan. He and family are members of the Christian Church. As a business man, no man stands higher then Mr. Vignos; his word is regarded in everything equal to his bond; hence he has the esteem and confidence of all well-disposed citizens.

WILLIAM WHITE, farmer, was born in Italy, near Venice, April 24, 1816, to John and Ellen (Murry) White, who were also natives of Italy; was educated as a seaman, and was on the ocean from the time he was five years old, and made his last trip in 1837, when he followed steamboating on the Mississippi and Ohio Rivers. In 1846, he came to Jefferson County, Ill.; farmed in summer, and was on the river in winter, in 1851, he removed to Morgan County, where he followed only farming—being compelled to give up navigation on account of an accident in dislocating his shoulder—where he remained until the spring of 1865, when he came to his present residence, where he has since remained, engaged in farming; when he came here, he bought 100 acres of land; there were but few improvements, and only a small house; he now has a large house, which shows that he is as well adapted to farming as he was to navigation. He was married, in 1855, in Arkansas, to Delia Thompson, a native of Cincinnati, Ohio, born in 1828; she died in 1881; she bore him four daughters and three sons; his son, John H. White, was in the Federal army, under Gen. Sherman, as a member of a regiment from this State; he was wounded, and died sixteen months after he returned home. Mr. White has been selected for office at different times, but has uniformly declined all such honors; self and family are members of the Methodist Church, he having held connection with that church since 1850; is an Odd Fellow, and helped to get a charter for the lodge located at Mt Vernon; is a Republican.

FREDERICK WIEGREFFE, farmer, P. O. Atwater, was born in the Kingdom of Hanover, Germany, April 26, 1835, to Frederick and Henrietta (Pereol) Wiegreffe; father was born in Germany in 1797; was a miller; emigrated to America and settled in Jersey County, Ill., in 1852 and in 1855 removed to Montgomery County, where he died in the same year – fall of 1855; mother was German, born in 1799, and now resides in Litchfield, Ill., with her son William; parents had six children; subject fourth child. He was educated from the common schools of Germany, and, in 1852, emigrated to America and settled in Jersey County, and commenced farming with his brothers; in 1855, removed to Montgomery County with his parents, where he has since remained, engaged in farming, having accumulated a large tract of land of 240 acre; makes wheat and corn a specialty. In 1869, in Montgomery County, he married Mary Kuhne, a native of Germany, born in 1848; they have had four children George, Anna, Flora and Bessie; self and family are members of the Lutheran Church, and he is a Republican; commenced life a poor man, and made all his property by hard work.

E. F. WOODMAN farmer, P. O. Raymond, was born near Carrollton, Ill., January 8, 1841, son of Nelson and Zerelda (Boiles) Woodman, he born in Vermont July 12, 1815, she born near Lexington, Ky., in 1825. Nelson Woodman came to Greene County in 1821, being one of the earliest settlers of that section, and where he now lives; he had twelve children—eight boys and four girls, E. F. being the second. Our subject came to Montgomery County in the fall of 1843 with his parents, and remained with them till seventeen years of age, when he commenced as teamster and breaking prairie, going to school between times, receiving the education that he has after leaving home. In 1859, he rented a farm of forty acres, and in 1860, bought forty acres, and is now the owner of 700 acres, principally located in Montgomery and Macoupin Counties, this State, and in Nebraska. December 28, 1871, in Litchfield, Ill., he married Miss Annie Shaw, born in Lyons, N. Y., February 15, 1854, daughter of Joseph and Betty M. (Woodruff) Shaw, both of New York State; two children, both boys, have blessed the household of Mr. Woodman Loy Legrand Woodman and Commodore Beacher Woodman. In 1861, Mr. Woodman went across the plains and remained in Colorado about four years, accumulating considerable property, merchandising, contracting, etc. He is a Blue Lodge Mason, a Royal Arch and a Knight Templar, always "governing himself accordingly;" also a Democrat.

DEXTER WADSWORTH, farmer, P. O. Litchfield, was born in Westboro County, Mass., December 27, 1822, to John and Percis (Kimbrough) Wadsworth. He was born in Grafton, Mass.; during his life, followed the occupation of a farmer, and died in his native State. She was born in Massachusetts, and died in Scott County, Ill. They were the parents of nine children, Dexter Wadsworth, our subject, being the eighth child. He was educated in the common schools of his native State, and, at an early age, apprenticed himself at the shoemaker's trade, at which he continued to work until 1857, when he removed to Scott County, Ill., where he engaged in farming, and continued the same until 1859, when he removed to Montgomery County, where he has since remained, engaged in farming. He served in the Federal army for about one year, in the Twentieth Illinois Regiment, Company A. In 1881, he erected, by his own design, a handsome residence upon his farm. In Massachusetts, in 1843, he married Miss Mary J. Miller, a native of Massachusetts, born in 1825, and died in 1858. Mr. Wadsworth has three children, viz.: Ellen, Mary E. (wife of F. C. Webster) and Warren W. In politics, he is identified with the Republican party.

HARVEL TOWNSHIP.

W. W. ADAMS, retired farmer, P. O. Harvel, was born in Macoupin County, Ill., September 28, 1836, to Giles M. and Elizabeth (Taylor) Adams. His early life was spent in receiving such an education as the common schools of his native county afforded, and assisting in tilling the soil of his father's farm. He embarked on his career in life as a farmer in his native county, where he remained until the spring of 1861, when he removed to Montgomery County, where he bought 240 acres of wild prairie, which he improved; also 160 acres more which he bought soon afterward. By business ability and energy he succeeded in accumulating a good property, and the social esteem of all well-disposed citizens. He has been a prominent farmer and stock-raiser. In 1880, he rented his farms, it being his desire to retire from active labor. Father was born in Halifax County, Va., in the year 1801; removed to Tennessee, and subsequently settled in Illinois, where he became one of the successful farmers of the State. He died in 1870, in Montgomery County. His wife, and mother of our subject, was born in Greenville, S. C., in 1809, and is now residing with her son, our subject, and enjoying good health. She is the mother of five children, three of whom are living—our subject, F. M Adams and Nancy A. Dilliard, residents of Macoupin County. Of the five children born to his parents, W. W. Adams was the fourth child. He has held the office of Supervisor of the township. In politics, he is identified with the Democratic party.

CLAYTON H. ADAMS, lumber, coal and agricultural implement dealer, Harvel, was born April 19, 1839, in Summit County, Ohio, to John and Sarah (Kelsey) Adams. He was brought to near Brighton, Macoupin County, in 1845, by his parents, when but six years of age, and from there removed to Gillespie, of the same county, in 1849, where they located permanently. He received his education from McKendree College, Lebanon, Ill., and high school at Hillsboro, and remained with his parents to the age of twenty-one, and then made a trip West to the Rocky Mountains, where he engaged in mining for two years, and at the expiration of that time returned home to Macoupin County, Ill., where he engaged in farming, and continued the same until 1866, when he engaged in grain and agricultural implement business at Gillespie, and in 1868 a milling business in connection with his other business. He continued the same until the spring of 1870, when he removed to Oregon, and there again resumed the occupation of a farmer, and on January 1, 1875, removed to Harvel, where he engaged in the lumber, coal and agricultural business, and by his energy and attentive business qualities, soon procured a good trade, and has since been steadily increasing until it extends far into Christian and Montgomery Counties. He has also a branch business at Morrisonville, under the management of S. S. Whitner, being under the firm name of Adams & Nelson. His partner is Mr. E. S. Nelson. On January 22, 1878, in Litchfield, he married Miss Mary E. Willis, a native of Carmi, Ill., but raised in Missouri, born November 20, 1846, daughter of James E. Willis, a native of Kentucky, born July 23, 1820, came to White County, Ill., with his parents when a boy. In 1841, he went to Cape Girardeau, Mo., and in September, 1845, was married to Miss J. Rosanna Short, a native of North Carolina. Father of our subject was born in New Hampshire, in 1802, and died in November, 1867. He was a prominent farmer and stock raiser of Macoupin County. He was a Republican, and a very resolute man in all of his business undertakings. Mother was born in 1805, in New Hampshire, and is now enjoying good health in Sheldon, Iowa. She is the mother of six children, four daughters and two boys, subject being the fifth child. He is an active member of the A., F. & A. M. order; has been a member since 1863. Politically, he is identified with the Republican party. Mr. and Mrs. Adams have had two children, one of whom is living. Charley Willis died in infancy; Florence Rosana was born April 5, 1851.

HENRY AULL, retired farmer, Harvel, was born in St. Clair County, Ill., December 2, 1838, to Frederick and Elizabeth (Schrag) Aull. His education was limited to such as the common schools afforded. He remained at home to the age of twenty, when he left his home, at that time in Bond County, and returned to his native county, where he embarked on his career in life as a farm hand, but eventually settled in Montgomery County in May, 1862, and settled in Pittman Township. By his industry and business habits, he succeeded in gaining a good property. His first purchase of land in Montgomery County was forty acres, and has at the present time about three hundred acres. Father was born in Germany in 1813, and during his life followed the occupation of a farmer; he died in 1858. His wife, and mother of subject, was born in Germany in 1819, and died in 1857. She was the mother of eleven children, subject being the second child. Politically, independent.

FRANCIS M. COX, M. D., Harvel, was born in Montgomery County, Ill., November 18, 1853. His father, Tipton Cox, was born in Monroe County, Tenn., April 24, 1825. He was a farmer by occupation; came to Montgomery County in 1852, and settled near Donnellson, where his death occurred February 12, 1880. He was in the Mexican war, and held a prominent position among the practical farmers of the county. His wife, Eliza Wilson, was also a native of Tennessee, born in 1827, and died in 1869. She was the mother of eight children, of whom Francis was the second child. His early education was received in the common schools of the county, and while out of school, he assisted his father upon the farm, where he remained until of age, when he began farming for himself, following in that occupation about five years, and two years of which, in addition to the duties of farming, he read medicine, and at the end of which time he entered the American Medical College, at St. Louis, where he graduated June 2, 1881, and received his degree as M. D. He located at Walshville, where he immediately entered upon the practice of his profession, and where he was very successful, and had a large ride. Six months later, he disposed of his practice, and located at Harvel, where he is successor to Dr. Matney, and where he is highly respected, not on account of his professional abilities alone, but owing to social qualities. He was married in his native county, January 28, 1875, to Miss Malissa Buzan, who was born in the same county December 4, 1854. She has borne him two children, viz.: Norma D. and Walter E. Mrs. Cox is a daughter of Thomas and Mary A. (Moss) Buzan; he deceased in 1851; she li-ing. The Doctor has held the office of Township Clerk of Grisham Township. Politically, he is identified with the Republican party.

HENRY HAUPTMANN, hotel keeper and merchant, Harvel, was born in Germany April 3, 1833. He remained in Germany with his parents, receiving such an education as the common schools afforded, and learned the trade of a tailor with his father. In 1854, he emigrated to America and settled in New Orleans for a period of eight months; worked at his trade, and then removed to St. Louis, where he worked at his trade for one year and a half, and then removed to Morgan County, Ill., at Jacksonville, and there worked as a farm hand for three years, and then rented a farm and gave his attention to agricultural pursuits on his own account, and after renting there for seven years removed to Montgomery County in 1864, where he bought a farm of eighty acres of wild prairie, and by his energy and business habits, succeeded in accumulating over three hundred acres, and has been the owner of five different large tracts of land, being one of the men who has done much for the improvement of the county. In the fall of 1878, he started a hotel at Harvel, which he still continues in connection with his grain dealing, merchandising and meat market. In 1880, he sold out his land, his business in Harvel increasing to such proportions that he was compelled to retire from farming. In 1880, he built the large and commodious hotel he now occupies. In 1853, in Germany, he married Louisa Hilgenbaeumer; she died in 1873, aged fifty six years. She bore him four children—Mary, Henry, George and Lizzie. In March, 1876, in Montgomery County, he married Mrs. Sophia Kalkhorst, born November 12, 1845; she has borne him three children—Lena, Charlie and Nettie. Father was Henry Hauptmann, born in Germany in 1812, and during his life followed tailoring, and died about 1864. Mother died when he was only two weeks old. They were the parents of two children; subject the youngest child. Self and wife are religiously connected with the Lutheran Church. Politically, he is a Democrat.

WILLIAM F. JORDAN, farmer, P. O. Harvel, was born in Maryland September 1, 1825, and when ten years of age his parents went to Trumbull County, Ohio, where he received his education, and assisted his father upon the homestead until he was twenty-one years of age, when he came to Greene County, and eight years later removed to Montgomery County, and settled upon the farm where he now resides, and which was at that time unbroken prairie, and the house built at that time was the first in that portion of the county. He has since made all the improvements necessary for comfort, and which are usually found upon a well-regulated farm. His father, William Jordan, was born in Maryland April 11, 1796, and died May 23, 1870. His wife, Catharine Rummel, was also a native of Maryland, born April 6, 1797, and is still living. She is the mother of ten children, viz.: William F., our subject; Hiram W., born February 3, 1827, and died August 5, 1831; Mary A., born December 9, 1828; Elizabeth J., born February 1, 1830, and died November 8, 1854; Cyrus H., born August 3, 1831; Lewis W., born April 28, 1833; Catharine E., born June 28, 1834; Montgomery P., born October 11, 1836, and died November 15, 1838; Alpheus C., born January 10, 1841; Emily A., born November 20, 1842, and died August 3, 1864. William, the eldest son, was married May 24, 1860, to Weltha Winn, who was born in Greene County, Ill., in 1840, in April. She is the mother of nine children living, viz.: Josephine, Henry, William, Charles,

Marion, Cora, Birdie, George and Hardan. Politically, Mr. J. has been identified with the Republican party, but now his sympathies are with the Greenback party. Although he grows all the crops usually raised upon a farm, he makes a specialty of grain.

JOHN R. LEIGH, farmer, P. O. Raymond, was born in Hunterdon County, N. J., January 28, 1846, to Samuel and Annie (Case) Leigh. He received his education from the common schools of his native county. His early days were spent upon the homestead farm. At the age of nineteen he left his home and removed to Jersey County, Ill., where he embarked on his career in life as a farm hand, and continued the same in that county for a period of seven years. In 1872, he bought 160 acres of unimproved land in Montgomery County, and removed to the same in the spring of 1873, where he has since remained engaged in agricultural pursuits. He has, by his studied economy and business habits, succeeded in accumulating 240 acres of land, all of which are under a high state of cultivation. Mr. Leigh commenced his life very poor, and, by his hard work, succeeded in accumulating a good property, and a name and reputation which is beyond reproach. He was married in 1869, in Jersey County, to Miss Carrie M. Davis a daughter of Wilson Davis, a native of North Carolina, and among the first settlers of Jersey County. Mrs. Leigh was born in Jersey County, Ill., June 5, 1849. Subject's father was born in Hunterdon County, N. J., in 1804, and is now residing in New Jersey, where he has always been engaged as farmer and drover. His wife, and mother of our subject, was born in New Jersey in 1806, and died April 16, 1882. She was the mother of six children, subject being the youngest child. He has held the offices of Road Commissioner and School Trustee. Politically, he is like his father, his sympathies being with the Democratic party. His wife is a member of the Methodist Church. Mr. Leigh is worthy of much credit for the interest he takes in all public improvements. He has met all the ups and downs of a business career, and now stands high in the estimation of his friends. Upon his farm he makes raising grain and hogs a specialty.

WILLIAM D. MATNEY, M. D. Harvel, was born in Shelby County, Ill., January 26, 1840. His early life was spent in assisting upon the homestead farm in the summer, and in winter attending the common schools of the county, where he received the foundation of his subsequent learning. He remained at home until twenty one years of age when he entered the service at the commencement of the rebellion, in Company K, Fifty-fourth Illinois Volunteer Infantry, with Capt. T. C. Rodrig: regiment commanded by Col. Harris. He remained in the service until the close of the war, when he again took upon himself the duties of a farm life, following in that occupation about two years, when he began the study of medicine, and shortly after entered a drug store at Oconee Shelby County, where, in addition to the duties of the store he continued the study of his profession. He remained in the drug business about five years, practicing a portion of the time. In August, 1875, he located at Harvel, Montgomery County; went before the State Board of Health, where he successfully passed examination and received a license. Owing to his perfect knowledge of and the thorough manner in which he attended to his calling, he has been very successful and built up a large practice, the duties of which would fall heavily upon the shoulders of a man many years his senior. He has been twice married. His first marriage occurred in 1867, in Shelby County, to Sarah E. Lowe who was born in Johnson County, Ind,, January 28, 1840. Her death occurred October 16, 1876, at Harvel. She was the mother of six children, all deceased except the oldest child, viz., Mary Ellen, born August 2, 1867. The Doctor was again married September 30, 1878, to Miss Drucilla C. Scott, who was born at Portsmouth, Ohio, April 23, 1854, to Jeremiah and Sarah (Davis) Scott, he deceased, she still living. The father of William D., our subject, Leonard Matney, was a native of Tennessee, born in 1811, a farmer by occupation, and was in the Mexican war. He died in September, 1847. His wife, Mary Burris, was a native of Kentucky, born in March, 1821, and still living, and is the mother of six children, of whom William D. was the second and the oldest living. He has held the office of Postmaster at Oconee for five years, and is the present Clerk of Harvel. Politically, his sympathies are with the Republican party; has been an active member of the Masonic order at Oconee for a number of years. The Doctor has also become a successful inventor, and at present holds a patent upon a burglar alarm, which is operated by means of electricity.

H. C. MILLOT, grain dealer, Harvel, was born in France September 13, 1850, to Peter F. and Justine (Cary) Millot. He was brought to this country by his parents when but about four years of age. His parents first settled in the northern part of New York, in Jefferson County, where he received his common-school education. In 1864, he came with his parents to Montgomery County. Here he attended the Blackburn University, at Carlinville, and afterward the Illinois Industrial University, at Champaign, and Fort Edward Collegiate Institute, at Fort Edward, N. Y. Here he graduated in 1872, and then returned to the Blackburn University, where he attended for two terms, and left in 1874. In the fall of 1875, he entered upon his career in life by embarking in the grain business, in partnership with Mr. Henry Niehaus, and conducted a successful business in the copartnership until 1879, when he bought out the interest of his partner, and has since conducted it alone. Although large at first, his business has steadily increased until the present time. It assumed large proportions, extending far into Christian and Montgomery Counties. They found markets at St Louis and Toledo, and for the last few years at the latter place. In 1876, in Montgomery County, he married Miss Margaret Martindale, born March 1, 1858, a native of Indiana. They have two children—Henry F. and Roy. In politics, he is independent. His father was born in France, in 1809, and is now a resident of Harvel. He has during his life followed the occupation of a farmer. His wife, also, was a native of France, born in 1815, and is the mother of three children, two of whom are living. Stephen is a prominent farmer of Christian County, and Augustus, who was murdered in 1868 by the Indians; served through the last rebellion, and entered as a volunteer soldier, and was mustered out as Second Lieutenant at the close of and in the year of 1868 removed to Kansas, where he was murdered by the Indians, in the same year. Our subject expects to remodel his large elevator, and embark in the milling business. Subject's father came first to America in 1830, and settled in Northern New York for two years, and then returned to France; married and came back to America in 1854.

ANDREW J. NASH, farmer and Justice of the Peace, was born in Edmonson County, Ky., February 29, 1832, to Lewis C. and Millie (Oller) Nash. He was born in Pulaski County, Ky., in April, 1807, and died in Harvel, Ill., February 17, 1881. He was by occupation a blacksmith. She was born in Illinois in 1814, and is now a resident of Harvel. They were the parents of thirteen children, of whom Andrew J. was the second child. His early life was spent in receiving an education and assisting his father in the blacksmith shop. In 1848, with his parents, removed to Grayson County, Ky. In 1849, he embarked on his career in life as a farmer. In the fall of 1851, removed to Wayne County, Ill.; in June, 1854, removed to Macoupin County, Ill.; in 1869, removed to Christian County, and there remained engaged in agricultural pursuits until February 1879, when he removed to his present residence, where he has since remained engaged in farming in connection with his official duties. In Christian County, in May, 1877, he was elected Constable, and at the same time was appointed Deputy Sheriff, which offices he held for two years. In Harvel he is now holding the office of Justice of the Peace, in connection with several minor offices. In Grayson County, Ky., April 4, 1849, he married Miss Sarah Haynes, a native of the same county, born March 1, 1830. They are the parents of nine children, three of whom are now living George W., born July 22, 1851, and died August 18, 1874; Paradine, now the wife of John A. Tosh, and residing near Grayville, Ill.; Lucinda, now the wife of Charles A. Varner, and residing in the county; Franklin E., at home; and Millie J., James M., Mary E., Arthur B. and Herchel, who are dead. Mr. Nash is an active member of the I. O. O. F., at Harvel Lodge, No. 607 In politics, he is identified with the Democrat party. Mr. Nash is regarded as an honest, fair minded, liberal in his views, genial and gentlemanly in his social relations and an industrious, public spirited citizen.

ROBERT S. NELSON, grain and produce dealer, Harvel, was born near Brighton, Macoupin Co., Ill., March 9, 1837, to Robert S. and E. (Kelsey) Nelson. He was a native of New Hampshire, and was one of the early settlers of Macoupin County, having settled there long before a railroad intersected that part of the State. His death occurred in 1857. She was also a native of New Hampshire. Her death occurred in 1857. She was the mother of six children, of whom Robert S., our subject, was the youngest child. He spent his boyhood days in assisting his father in farming, and receiving such an education as the common schools of the neighborhood afforded. His first enterprise for himself was at Irving, Ill., where he entered upon his business career in the grain and agricultural business. He remained there two years, and then sold his interest to William Chamberlin and removed to Litchfield, where he engaged in the same business, but remained only one year, when he removed to Harvel and erected a large grain elevator, and continued as a grain and produce dealer. His business, although large at the start, has been steadily increasing until now it has assumed very large proportions, and his custom extends far into Montgomery and Christian Counties. In 1879, he entered into partnership in the agricultural implement business with Mr. C. H. Adams, which he continues in connection with his other business. Mr. Nelson was married in Litchfield, Ill., April 4, 1872, to Miss Harriet A. Jones, who was born in Carrollton, Greene Co., Ill., May 23, 1850. They have but one child, R. S. Kent Nelson. Mr. Nelson in social life is one of the most genial of men, liberal in his views, and gentlemanly in his social relations. As a citizen, he is enterprising and public-spirited, and has ever taken a leading part in all matters calculated to advance the material interests of his town and county

HENRY NIEHAUS, retired farmer, P. O. Harvel, was born in Germany in April, 1814. Henry Niehaus, the father of this gentleman, was also born in Germany, in 1776, and died in 1836. During his life, he followed the occupation of a farmer. His wife, and mother of Henry, was named Miss Slater. She was born in Germany in 1799, and died in 1854. They were the parents of ten children, of whom Henry Niehaus was the second child. He received his education from the common schools of his native country, and began life by working as a farm hand in Germany, which he there continued until 1855, when he emigrated to America, and first settled at St. Louis, Mo., for a period of three months, and then removed to Morgan County, Ill., rented a farm, and began farming on his own account, and continued the same for eight years. In 1863, he removed to Montgomery County, where he bought a small farm. By his energy and business habits, he succeeded in accumulating over seven hundred and sixty acres of land, upon which he made all necessary improvements. In 1877, in connection with his farm duties, built a large elevator at Harvel, and embarked in the grain business in partnership with Mr. Millot but in the year 1879 sold out to his partner and retired from active labor, he having disposed of all his real estate at that time. In 1839, in Germany, he married Miss Katharine Hieselman. She died in 1868, aged sixty years. The result of this union was three children, of whom Mena and Katharine are living, and residents of Montgomery County. Mr. Niehaus has lived a blameless life, and, as he sits down at nightfall, around the domestic hearth, he has the proud consciousness of knowing that he has wronged no one (at least intentionally), and that his peace is made with the Great King of kings beyond the shores of time. Thus does he live, and thus he awaits the last great change, which his locks, now whitened by the frosts of nearly seventy winters, indicate is not far distant.

JOHN W. PETRIE, M. D., Harvel, was born in North Carolina November 7, 1832. His early life was spent upon his father's farm and in receiving his early education, the foundation of his subsequent learning. At the age of twenty-two years, he began the study of medicine, but soon after entered upon an extended tour through Central America, Great Britain, New Mexico, and eventually located in California, where he remained about five years, engaged at different times in mining, surveying, and upon a ranch. In the fall of 1860, he came to Montgomery County, Ill., near Hillsboro, where he entered upon the practice of his profession four years later, having spent most of the time in study at the Eclectic Medical College, at Cincinnati, Ohio, where he graduated in 1866 and received his diploma. In February, 1866, he went to Taylorville, remained two years and then removed to Palmer, where he entered upon the practice of his profession, and remained twelve years, and during the time was very successful, having built up a large practice, the result of his knowledge of and his close attention to his calling. In the fall of 1881, he removed to Harvel, where his success has followed him, and where he has gained the highest esteem, socially, of the people, and professionally the good-will of all. His father, John Petrie, was a native of North Carolina, where he was born in the year 1778, and where he followed the occupation of blacksmithing and farming to the time of his death, which occurred April 4, 1872. His wife, Elizabeth Jordan, was also a native of North Carolina, born May 1, 1792, and died in 1861. They were the parents of eight children, of whom John W. was the seventh child. He was married in Montgomery County June 16, 1861, to Miss Mournen Franklin, who died in 1863. She was the mother of one child, who died in infancy. The Doctor was married again in October, 1869, to Anna O'Rourke, a native of Ireland, and who has borne him seven children, viz., Ulysses S., David A., Henderson C., Scott T., Libry E., Margaret E. and Albert R., all of whom are living. The Doctor has been a member of the I. O. O. F., and the Encampment and Grand Lodge.

HERMAN POGGENPOHL, farmer, P. O. Harvel, was born in Prussia, Germany, March 7, 1843, where his early life was spent in attending the common schools of his native country and assisting his father upon the farm. At the age of eighteen, his father sent him to America to view the New World. His expectations were more than realized, and two years later his parents followed him and entered 160 acres of land in Montgomery County, where they were among the first to break and improve the wild prairie. Francis Poggenpohl, the father of Harmon, was born in Prussia, Germany, and died soon after his arrival in America. His wife, Maggie Gurke, was also a native of Germany, and died in 1874. She was the mother of six children, of whom Herman was the oldest child. After the death of his father, he bought the interests of the balance of the family, and entered upon his career in life as a farmer, at which he has since continued, and at which he has been more than ordinarily successful, making all the improvements himself and has by his energy and industry accumulated about seven hundred acres of land, nearly all under cultivation. All the surroundings on Mr. Poggenpohl's property show him to be a practical farmer, and well worthy of the high esteem in which he is held by the community socially. In 1873, he returned to his native country upon a visit, remaining there two months. In 1855, he was married to Dena Brokamp, who was born in Germany and brought to America when a child. She died in 1872, leaving to his care six children, viz., Henry, deceased at the age of eighteen years; Mary, wife of L. Young; John, at home; Lizzie, at home; Tony, at home; Maggie, at home. Mr. P. was again married in 1871 to Ragena Musshafer, also a native of Germany, born June 7, 1852. She has borne him six children, viz., Frankie, Christina, Lena, Anna, Kattie and Charles. Politically, Mr. P. is identified with the Democratic party. Himself and family are connected with the Catholic Church.

GEORGE J. RAMSEY, druggist and hardware, Harvel. William Hamilton Ramsey, the father of this gentleman, was a native of Pennsylvania. During his life has been engaged in agricultural pursuits; is now a resident of Milroy, Penn. His wife, and mother of George J., was Mary Rarer, a native of Pennsylvania; she is the mother of nine children, of whom George J. Ramsey is the fourth child. He was born in Pennsylvania September 17, 1849. He was raised upon a farm, and remained upon the old homestead with his parents during his school days. At the age of twenty five, he entered a drug store at Irving, Ill., as clerk, where he remained two years, and then removed to Harvel and engaged in the same business on his own account, and has by his energy and close attention to business succeeded in building up a large and increasing trade. In 1880, he added to his business a full line of hardware and agricultural implements, taking into partnership a year later Mr. Clisby Sims, in the agricultural department. Mr. Ramsey has a thorough knowledge of business, and possesses the faculty of making himself agreeable to the public, and socially enjoys the highest esteem of the community at large. He was married in Montgomery County November 5, 1878, to Miss Laura T. Austin, a native of Mississippi, born July 22, 1856. They have one child living, Charles Earle Ramsey, who was born January 19, 1881, and one dead. Politically, Mr. Ramsey is identified with the Republican party. He has served as Township Clerk for a term of three years, and was appointed Postmaster in 1877, which position he still holds. He is identified with the growth and prosperity of the town by way of public improvements and educational privileges.

CLISBY SIMS, farmer and agricultural implement dealer, Harvel, was born in Madison County, Ill., February 10, 1824. His early life was spent in attending the common schools of his native county, and in assisting his father upon the homestead farm. At the age of nineteen he left home and began his career in life in a saw-mill, in Missouri, where he remained eighteen months, at the end of which time he purchased a farm in Missouri, consisting of eighty acres of unbroken prairie and ten acres of timber land, upon which he made all improvements. He remained in Missouri eight years, and then removed to Macoupin County, Ill., and rented a farm and continued in that occupation there about three years. He then moved to Shaw's Point, same county, where he remained six years, and then removed to Montgomery County, where he has improved three farms, and in addition to attending to the duties of his farming interests he has been engaged about four years in mercantile business, three years of the time at Harvel. At present he owns a farm of 100 acres of well-improved land in Missouri, and town property at Harvel. In January, 1882, he entered into partnership with George J. Ramsey, in dealing in agricultural implements, at Harvel, and where they have succeeded in building up a fair trade for the time they have been engaged in the business. Mr. Sims is a thorough business man and a practical farmer, and socially enjoys the highest esteem of the entire community. His marriage occurred in 1843, in Morgan County, to Elizabeth J. Masters, who was born in Morgan March 9, 1824. She has borne him eight children, viz., Thomas Q., Nancy Ellen, Malissa Ann, James B., William, Benjamin, Jane and Emma Isabell, the two latter of whom are deceased. Mrs. Sims is a daughter of Irving Masters, born in Kentucky, and died at the age of forty-nine, and Mary Jones, born in Morgan County, and died in 1836. The father of our subject, James Sims, was a native of Kentucky, born in 1810, a farmer by occupation, and one of the early settlers of Madison County, Ill., and still living in Macoupin County. His wife, Margaret Robinson, was a native of North Carolina, and died in 1865 at the age of sixty years. The result of their union was six children, of whom Clisby, our subject, was the oldest child. He served the people of the county as Justice of the Peace four years. Politically, his sympathies are with the Democratic party. Religiously, himself and wife have been members of the Baptist Church for several years.

GEORGE W. SLATER, lawyer and farmer, Harvel, Ill., was born in Lawrence County, Ill., July 14, 1832, to William and Jane (Wilson) Slater, he being a native of England, and she of Kentucky. The early education of George W. Slater was very limited, owing to the fact that no schools were near his native place. His time was fully employed upon his father's farm. In 1843, he removed with his parents to Montgomery County; here his parents settled upon an unbroken timber farm near Audubon. At the age of fourteen, his father died, and he lived with his older brother for about one year, and then engaged as a farm hand, and entered upon his career in life, which has been more or less varied. He continued in the occupation of a farmer until 1863, when he went to Litchfield and ran two wood saws by horse power, in the employ of a railroad company, with whom he remained over four years, at the end of which time he again took upon himself the duties of a farm life, at which he remained one year, and then went to milling, and continued the same for over four years. While in Litchfield Mr. Slater was elected to fill the office of Street Commissioner, and was appointed Deputy Sheriff. He has, since his residence at Harvel, served the people in the different offices of Constable and Justice of the Peace, and is now a member of the Town Board. He has obtained more than ordinary education by his observation and study. He has been practicing law in the Justice's Court about seven years in connection with his other duties. He was married, August 19, 1851, to Sarah Matthews, who was born in Christian County March 16, 1832. She is the mother of eleven children, five of whom are now living, viz., Elie, Lewis L., Serene A., James E. and Sarah E. Mr. Slater is an active member of the A., F. & A. M.

ANDREW JACKSON THOMASON, merchant, Harvel, was born in Carrollton, Greene Co., Ill., February 16, 1843. His educational privileges were limited to the common schools of his native county. His early life was spent on the homestead farm, but at the age of eighteen he entered the service during the rebellion in Company G, of the Sixty-first Illinois Infantry, with Capt. J. B. Nelton, his regiment being commanded by Gen. Jacob Fry. He remained in the service a period of three years, and, after his discharge, he took upon himself the duties of a farm life, locating in Greene County, where he remained three years, and then removed to Montgomery County, where he continued the same occupation five years, at the end of which time the town of Harvel had just been incorporated, and he erected the third store in the town, and opened a grocery store having at that time disposed of his farming interests. By his energy, courteous manners, and strict attention to business, he soon built up a large and steadily increasing trade, which demanded an increase of stock, until now he is engaged in a general merchandising business, and has also enlarged his storeroom in order to make room for his increasing stock, and to better facilitate his business. He has always been identified with the growth and prosperity of the town, and held a prominent position in the advancement of public improvements and educational privileges of the town and county, having held the different offices of School Director, Village Trustee, President of the Board of Trustees, Trustee of the Methodist Episcopal Church, and President of the Coal Company. He was married in Carrollton, Greene County, September 7, 1879, to Miss Mary Jane Swires, who was born in New Jersey February 7, 1849. By this union they have had seven children, viz., Alice, Freddie, Frankie, Bertie, Roy, Flora and Nellie. Mrs. Thomason is a daughter of James and Elizabeth (Lisles) Swires, who were natives of England; they are both living. The parents of Mr. Thomason, Spencer and Mary (Stone) Thomason, were natives of North Carolina, and early settlers of Greene County, having emigrated to that county in 1830. He was a farmer, and died in 1847; she died in 1861. They were the parents of seven children, of whom Andrew J., our subject, was the fifth child. He is a member of the A., F. & A. M. at Raymond, and also a member of the Royal Arch Chapter at Litchfield. In politics, he is a Democrat. Mr. Thomason has, by his own unaided endeavors, made life-work thus far more than ordinarily successful, and is entitled to a place among the substantial men of Montgomery County.

JOHN H. TODT, farmer, P. O. Harvel, was born in Germany October 21, 1834. His early life was spent in receiving such an education as the common schools of his native country afforded, and in working as a hired hand upon a farm. At the age of seventeen, he left his native country and sailed for America, when he settled in Greene County, Ill. Here he embarked on his career in life as a hired hand upon a farm for three months, and then removed to Jersey County, where he remained two years engaged in the same occupation, when he spent two years in Montgomery and Macoupin Counties, working summers in the former, and winters with his own people in the latter place. In 1857, he had, by his energy and business habits, accumulated enough funds to enable him to make a small purchase of land, which he did in Macoupin County, a tract of 120 acres of unimproved timber land. Here he remained for a period of eight years; during the time he improved this tract. In 1865, he sold his farm and removed to Montgomery County, where he first bought 160 acres of mostly wild prairie. Here he has since remained, and by his own endeavors has succeeded in accumulating a large tract of land, all of which is under a high state of cultivation. He is now the owner of 480 acres, upon which he built a fine residence, by his own design, in 1879. He has also built large barns, etc., and everything about his place denotes the home of a first class farmer. Much credit is due to Mr. Todt for the interest he has taken in improving surroundings, all of which show toward the welfare of the county. In 1857, in Madison County, he married Miss Maria Poggenpol, a native of Germany, born April 15, 1835. She is the mother of nine children, five of whom are living, viz., William, Herman, Frank, Elizabeth and Margaret; all are at home. Father of subject was Joseph Todt, who was born in Germany; during his life followed farming; joined the army when but seventeen years of age, and fought bravely under Napoleon Bonaparte I. He died in 1835, aged about forty-seven years. His wife, and mother of our subject, was Elizabeth Miller. She was born in Germany in 1801; came to America with her son in 1851; she died in April, 1873. She was the mother of seven children, John H. being the fourth child. He was appointed Postmaster in 1866, and held the office about three years. He has also held the office of Road Commissioner, and has been holding the office of School Trustee for eighteen years. He is also serving the people as County Supervisor to the satisfaction of all. He was elected in 1881. Religiously, self and family are connected with the Catholic Church. Politically, his sympathies are with the Democratic party. When he first came to the county to live, it was but thinly settled, between his place and L. H. Thomas', of Bois D'Arc, there was no settlement a distance of thirteen miles.

B. TULPIN, merchant, Harvel, was born in France April 5, 1836, where he received his education. On August 14, 1855, when nineteen years of age, he was married, and on the day following, emigrated to America with his bride, and landed in Virden, Ill., where he did his first day's manual labor for Mr. John Morrell. He remained near Virden and Girard about three years, working by the month. From there he went to Assumption, Christian County, and commenced farming. He followed that occupation two years in that county, and three years in Montgomery County, at the end of which time he entered upon a mercantile business at which he has since continued. In 1865 or 1866, he erected a store building about half a mile south of where Harvel is now located, and between the surveys of two proposed railroads. His was the first store, and he the first to engage in an enterprise of this nature. His facilities for doing business were somewhat limited, and his stock necessarily small, but being energetic and enterprising in business, and possessing the faculty of making himself agreeable to the public, he was soon enabled to increase his stock. His principal draw back was in speaking the English language, which, during his business career, he has mastered. In 1870, his stock and business had increased until it demanded more room, and he erected the building he now occupies, and where he has the satisfaction of conducting a large and increasing trade, the result of a successful business career; and, perhaps, no man has done more for public improvements and for the growth and prosperity of Harvel than Mr. Tulpin. He is always first in all enterprises, and socially enjoys the highest esteem of the entire community. He has at different times held town offices but usually declines the honors which would otherwise be bestowed upon him. Aside from his business relations, he has added materially to the growth of the town by way of erecting several dwellings. He received his naturalization papers October 8, 1868, and has since been identified with the Republican party. His family consists of his wife and five boys, four of whom are living at home, Arthur, the oldest being married, but assisting his father in the store. Mr. Tulpin has had the misfortune to lose five children, four girls and one boy, all of whom died quite young. He has been a prominent member of the Masonic fraternity for several years. Although usually able to oversee his business, his health has been impaired to such an extent that he is at times obliged to remain at home. His children are Arthur Victor, Hector Maxamillian, Frank Octave Charles Albert and Maurice Emmanuel, five boys, all living.

GEORGE W. VAN SANDT, carpenter and joiner, Harvel, was born in Fleming County, Ky., December 14, 1817, where he received a common school education, and where his childhood days were spent upon the old homestead farm with his father. During the winter season, his time was employed in working at and learning the millwright and carpenter's trade, and at which he still followed when, at the age of twenty-one years, he left his home and entered upon his career in life. He remained in his native State until he was forty-five years of age, when his politics as a Whig did not make it pleasant for him at the breaking-out of the war, and, not being willing to take the oath to not oppose the Confederacy, he removed to Aberdeen, Ohio where he remained two years, and then came to Montgomery County, Ill., and located in Butler Township, and there worked at his trade for about five years. In January, 1870 he removed to Harvel, his present residence, which was then just laid out and was surrounded by wild prairie. He built the first house which was erected at Harvel, and has also built many others, several of which belonged to him, which he rented to others. To him is due much of the credit for making Harvel the prosperous town it now is. For one year he was engaged in the mercantile business, but eventually returned to his trade. He was married in Lewis County, Ky., July 2, 1840, to Miss Isabella A. Cooper, who was born March 15, 1819, to Murdock and Elizabeth (Parker) Cooper, natives of Kentucky

She died January 2, 1875, leaving five children, viz., Allen Jerome, George B., Eliza Bell, James C. and Nelson M. Mr. Van Sandt was married again in Montgomery County Ill., January 1, 1878, to Miss Mary A. B., who was born in Buffalo, N. Y., in March, 1842; she has borne him one child, Hattie. Mr. Van Sandt has been an active member of the Masonic order for about thirty years. Politically, he is identified with the Republican party. Religiously, he and wife are connected with the Methodist Church at Harvel. His father, William Van Sandt, was born in Kentucky in 1794; during his life, followed the occupation of a millwright and farmer. He lived to the advanced age of eighty-four years. His wife, and mother of our subject, was Margaret Williams: she was also a native of Kentucky, and lived to be about sixty years of age, and raised a family of nine children, all of whom grew to man and womanhood.

CONRAD WILLAR, farmer, P. O. Raymond, was born in Germany December 17, 1840. He received such an education as the common schools of his native country afforded, and in tilling the soil of his father's farm. At the age of fifteen, he left his home and began working as a farm hand, continuing the same until he was twenty five years of age, and then, in the year 1865, came to America, making his first stop at St. Louis, where, at the end of a month, he was compelled to leave, not being able to obtain employment. He then went to Butler, Montgomery County, and hired out as a farm hand, continuing thus for four years. In 1869, he married, and bought 240 acres of the farm upon which he now resides, and began farming on his own account. By his energy and business habits, he succeeded in paying for this tract, and in 1871 bought eighty acres more, which makes his farm consist of 320 acres, and it is as fine land as any in the State. January 13, 1869, in Montgomery County, he was married to Miss Elizabeth Munsterman, born in Germany, daughter of Henry and Margaret (Wucherbfennig), both natives of Germany, from which union has been born five children, four of whom are living—Minnie, Henry, Joseph C. and Elizabeth K., all of whom are at home. The father and mother of our subject were both natives of Germany, and the parents of six children, two girls and four boys, Conrad being the third child. Mr. Willar and wife are members of the Catholic Church, and he is a Democrat.

W. W. WHITLOW, farmer, P. O. Harvel, was born in Greene County, Ill., April 1, 1834; son of Daniel and Fanny (Ray) Whitlow. The early life of our subject was spent on his father's farm, and, at the age of nineteen, hired out as a farm hand. In 1854, with his brother, he took charge of his father's farm and in 1856, went to Macoupin County, where he contracted in breaking prairie. In the fall of 1857, he rented a farm at Macoupin Point, and remained there one year, when he returned to Macoupin County; then six years more in Macoupin County. In 1865, he removed to Montgomery County and settled upon a portion of the farm upon which he now resides, which at that time consisted of 240 acres of land, most of which has been improved by Mr. Whitlow, and to which he has added until he has 560 acres. In 1881, he erected from his own designs a fine residence upon his farm, which, with barns, windmill, stock scales, etc., make the surroundings complete. In 1858, in Greene County, he married Miss Fannie Thomason, a native of Greene, born September 16, 1835, who has borne him ten children, six of whom are living—Mary A., born September 25, 1860; Flora A., May 31, 1862; George E., September 1, 1863; William A., March 21, 1865; John W., January 26, 1867; Sarah T., September 10, 1868, dead; Eva E., March 26, 1871; Olive, March 20, 1874, dead; Oscar, March 20, 1874, dead; Herbert, December 1, 1875, dead. Mr. Whitlow is a Patron of Husbandry, and a Democrat; has held the position of Commissioner of Highways for ten years. The father of our subject was a native of Kentucky, a farmer, and died in 1878; the mother a native of North Carolina, and died in 1867. They had three children, subject being the oldest.

JOHN P. YOUNG, farmer, P. O. Harvel, was born in Germany May 19, 1839. His father was Vincent Young, who was born in Germany in 1799; during his life, followed rafting on the River Rhine, acting as steersman. He died October 25, 1851. Mother was Katharina (Glaser) Young, was born in Germany in 1803, and died in 1865. She was the mother of ten children, of whom John P., our subject, was the ninth child. His education was limited to such as the common schools of his native country afforded. His early life was spent at home. At the age of eighteen, he left his home to see the New World. His first settlement in America was in Jersey County, Ill., where he began life as a hired hand upon a farm; he remained here one year. In 1858, he removed to New Orleans, where he worked unloading cars for one winter, when he returned to Jersey County for one year, following farming again. In 1859, he removed to Wisconsin, where he followed farming and other different kinds of work. In the spring of 1860 he returned to Illinois and settled in Montgomery County, where he rented a farm for three years. In the fall of 1863, he removed to Macon County, Ill., where he also rented a farm. In 1865, he removed to Decatur and engaged in meat market business for one year. In 1866, he returned to Montgomery County, where he again took upon himself the duties of a farm life, where he has since remained. By his energy and business habits he succeeded in saving enough funds to buy him a place of eighty acres, all of which has been improved by Mr. Young. He commenced life a poor man, and by his own unaided efforts he has succeeded in gaining a good property and a name and reputation which is beyond reproach, being well worthy of the esteem in which he is held by his neighbors. He was married in 1867, in Decatur, to Miss Stefania Fehr, a native of Germany, born in December, 1843. She is the mother of seven children, six of whom are now living, viz., Frank, Mary E., Annie K., Mena, Sophia K., John P.; Frederick G. is dead. Mr. Young is now holding the office of School Director. Religiously, himself and family are connected with the Catholic Church. Politically, his sympathies are with the Democratic party.

ORSON YOUNG, mechanic, Harvel, was born in August, 1810, in Otsego County, N. Y., to Elam and Irene (Eaton) Young. His father was born near Ballston Springs, N. Y., and during his life followed his profession in the practice of medicine. He served through the war of 1812. He died in Oregon, several years ago. His wife, and mother of our subject, was born in Otsego County, N. Y., and died in Oregon; she has also been dead many years. They were the parents of eight children, six boys and two girls, Orson Young being the oldest child. He was brought to Clermont County, Ohio, by his parents when but six years of age. Here he received such an education as the common schools afforded. At the age of fifteen, he apprenticed himself at the trade of cloth dressing in the factory of Timothy Sprague and remained three years, but, being more adapted to mechanical tools, gave up his trade and followed that of a carpenter. In the summer of 1853, he removed to Montgomery County, Ill., and entered 320 acres of wild prairie, he being among the early settlers of that county. In 1877, he removed from his farm to the town of Harvel, his present residence, where he is engaged in wagon-making. From 1853 until 1877, in Montgomery County, he worked at the carpenter's trade, and was the builder of many pioneer churches and dwellings. He is a man of good moral habits, and has the esteem of all well-disposed citizens of the community. In 1878, he was elected to the Board of Trustees, which office he filled to the entire satisfaction of the community. He has been twice married. The first time in Clermont County, Ohio, to Miss Hannah Burnett, April 28, 1833. She was born in Clermont County, Ohio, April 13, 1810, and died in 1846. The second time, he married Miss Sarah Hall, May 31, 1846, a native of Ireland; she was born in 1824. By his first marriage he had five children, Elizabeth A., residing now in Ohio; Sarah E., now a resident of Indiana; Mary J., Irene and William B., who are dead. By his second marriage he has had six children, Samuel H., a resident of Montgomery County; Edmond B. and George D., of Iowa, and Matilda, of Montana. John and James O., who are dead. Mr. and Mrs. Young are members of the Methodist Church, he having been a member for forty five years.

PITTMAN TOWNSHIP.

ALBERT BURNET, retired farmer, Raymond, was born in New York City May 17, 1812, to William and Catharine (Hutchingson) Burnet. He was born in New Jersey in 1787; during his former life, worked at the trade of a carpenter, and for several years previous to his death followed the occupation of a farmer; he died in 1849, in his native State; he was of English descent. She was born in Scotland in 1791, and died in 1856; she was the mother of seven children, of whom Albert was the fifth child. He remained with his parents till the age of sixteen years, receiving such an education as the common schools of his native State afforded; when he left home, he apprenticed himself at the blacksmith's trade in a small town where now is the city of Newark; here he remained until 1851, when he removed to Jersey County, Ill., where he worked at his trade for one year and six months; he then removed to Alton, Madison Co. Ill.; again worked at his trade for one year and a half; he then, in the spring of 1854, removed to Montgomery County and entered 160 acres of wild prairie; here he has since remained, engaged in agricultural pursuits; by his energy and business, he succeeded in accumulating a good property and a name and reputation which are beyond reproach; he is now the owner of 240 acres. In 1835, in New York City, he was married to Miss Sarah A. Cook, a native of New Jersey; she was born in 1815, May 1, to Samuel and Mary (King) Cook. Mrs. Burnet is the mother of eight children, five of whom are living, viz.: Sarah C., now the wife of W. S. Palmer and residing in Litchfield; James M., now a resident of Pitman Township, Montgomery County; Jane Elizabeth, at home; Henry Cory, at home; Oswald Joseph, at home. Mr. Burnet has held office of School Commissioner. Mr. Burnet and family are religiously connected with the M. E. Church, he having joined the church in 1828; politically, is identified with the Republican party.

REV. JOHN R. BARBEE, clergyman, Girard, son of John and Mary (Ray) Barbee, was born in Green County, Ky., December 26, 1828, where also he was raised, educated and married. His marriage to Miss Nannie, daughter of John and Hila (Rogers) Bottom, was celebrated November 21, 1852, in Taylor County, Ky. In the fall of 1864, Mr. Barbee moved into Pitman Township, Montgomery Co., Ill., where about the same time, he bought a farm, comprising 103 acres of very rich land, well drained, and containing an abundant supply of stock water; he has quite recently erected on these premises a fine two-story frame dwelling house. Mr. Barbee has a family of six children: Mary Ray, the wife of William Howland, residents of Montgomery County; Hila, the wife of Paris Howland, residents of Pike County; Joseph Eller, John Waller, Elias William and Lilla May. Mr. Barbee was ordained to the ministry of the Baptist Church about 1858, while residing in Kentucky; he is regarded by the public as devoted, talented and pious; to this sentiment we give approbation, and add, as an opinion of our own, that he is one of the most industrious workers to be found in his denomination. Mr. Barbee has a family record of which he has a right to feel proud; the relationship has been patriotically represented in every war of the nation from the Revolution to the late civil war of the great rebellion; his grandfather, Elias Barbee, a seventh son, and six of his brothers, were soldiers in the war which gave independence to the American colonies and freedom to the world; Joshua and Thomas are the only names of these brothers handed down. Elias raised four sons—John, Elias, William and Thomas. Of these, John, Mr. Barbee's father, with his uncle, Col. Joshua Barbee, were soldiers in the war of 1812; John was in the engagement in which the celebrated Indian chief, Tecumseh, fell. John Barbee, Mr. Barbee's immediate ancestor, raised a family of nine children—Mrs. Lucy (Benjamin) Thurman, of La Rue County, Ky.; Catharine; Mrs. Elizabeth (David) Mears, of Green County, Ky.; Mrs. Julia (Thomas) Lendrum, of Mc Lean County, Ky.; Mary; Mrs. Lydia (John) Robinson, of Taylor County, Ky.; Elias, deceased; Joseph, of California; and John R., of this sketch. Elias was a soldier in the Mexican war, and was wounded in the battle of Buena Vista, in the same charge in which the brave Col. John J. Hardin was killed. Mr. Barbee himself was a Chaplain during our late civil strife, for the Thirteenth Kentucky Infantry, and was in the siege of Knoxville. The writer of this history has known this family for a number of years, and takes pleasure here to testify to their excellent standing and character, and heartily wishes that the old friendship and strong ties of sympathy may continue.

CHARLES H. BURTON, farmer, P. O. McVey, was born in Greene County, Ill., near Greenfield, to William L. and Rachael (Davidson) Burton, July 25, 1833; he was born in Virginia July 3, 1797; emigrated to Kentucky, and subsequently removed to Illinois about the year 1825, and settled in Greene County, Ill., near White Hall, in 1829 or 1830; here he remained until about 1858, when he removed to Montgomery County and resided with his son, our subject, to the time of his death, which occurred October 5, 1862; during his life, followed the occupation of a farmer; it is supposed he was of German descent; his wife, and mother of our subject, was born in Maryland January 9, 1798, and died January 21, 1852; they were the parents of ten children—five boys and five girls, viz.: Henry James D. (dead), Mary Jane (widow of Nathan T. Maxfield), Elizabeth C. (wife of William F. Carrico, of Kansas), David Parker (dead), Martha A. (first wife of William Carrico—dead), Margaret K. (second wife of Volentine Caswell; she is now dead), John F. (dead), Charles H. (our subject), Sarah M. (dead), William A. (dead). Charles H. Burton received his education at Greenfield, from the common schools and the Greenfield Academy; he remained with his parents to the age of twenty-one, assisting in tilling the soil of his father's farm; he then embarked on his career in life as a school-teacher, in Montgomery County, where he removed when he left his home; he taught during the winters of 1855 and 1856; in the summer of 1857, bought a farm of eighty acres and began farming; his farm was located in Section 16 of Pitman Township; here he remained until February, 1859, when he bought a farm adjoining his present residence, where he resided until the spring of 1863, when he removed to his present place, where he has since remained, engaged in agricultural pursuits; he is now the owner of 100 acres of well-improved land, and under a high state of cultivation. On October 15, 1856, in Montgomery, he married Samantha Rogers; she was born in Macoupin County, Ill., April 18, 1835, to Benjamin and Lydia (Snow) Rogers, who were natives of Kentucky. Mr. and Mrs. Burton have had seven children, six of whom are now living: James O., born November 5, 1857; Lydia Estella, December 9, 1858; Rosa, July 9, 1860; George E., January 26, 1862; John A., April 6, 1863, died September 10, 1864; William W., October 25, 1867; Benjamin R., June 28, 1872. Self and family are religiously connected with the M. E. Church. Mr. Burton was elected County Supervisor in 1877, and served three years; School Treasurer since 1869, and still holds office; Highway Commissioner at present; politically, a Republican; he is a member of Grange Lodge, No. 970, in Pitman Township, and called Washington Lodge. But three of Mr. Burton's children are at home.

CHARLES GILLMAN, farmer and stock-raiser, P. O. Girard, was born in Germany, July 17, 1835, to Charles and Hannah Gillman. His early life was spent in receiving a common-school education; at the age of fourteen, he was hired out to work on a farm by his father, as a shepherd, tending sheep; at the age of twenty-one, he bade his home farewell and emigrated to America; he made his first settlement in Sangamon County, Ill., and was under the employ of Charles Hoppin for over five years; by his close attention to business and his economy, he was able, at the end of that time, to buy 330 acres of land in Pitman Township, Montgomery County; here he commenced farming in 1863 on his own account; by his energy and business habits, he has succeeded in accumulating about nine hundred and thirty acres of land, all lying in one tract in Pitman Township, with the exception of ten acres of timber; he is now principally engaged in stock-raising, making cattle and hogs a specialty, although he raises large quantities of all other kinds of stock; he is now the owner of over two hundred head of cattle; in about 1872, he enlarged his residence making it very large and commodious. In 1862, in Sangamon County, Ill., he married Miss Anna Hantla; she was born in 1846 in Germany; she is the mother of nine children, eight of whom are now living—Frank, Willie, Anna, Henry, Carrie, George Emma and John. He has served the people as School Director. Himself and wife are religiously connected with the Lutheran Church. Mr. Gillman is strongly in favor of the Republican party.

WILLIAM R. HOUCK, farmer, P. O. Raymond. The father of this gentleman was Ross Houck; he was born March 4, 1804, in Pennsylvania; here he received a limited common-school education; he remained with his parents to the age of sixteen, assisting in tilling the soil of his father's farm. At the age of sixteen, he left his home, with a pack on his back, with only 25 cents in his pocket, to embark on his career in life, it being his intention to settle in the far West; he first stopped at Cincinnati, Ohio, and worked at the trade of a carpenter, which he had partially learned before he left his home; here he remained for one year, when he engaged with Virgil Hickox, at a salary of $50 per month and expenses paid, selling books; he remained in the employ of this gentleman for about two years, during the time, by his economy and business habits, succeeding in accumulating enough funds to enable him to start in the same business on his own account, which he did in the State of Illinois, where he continued successfully for a term of five years, during the time, he had accumulated about $5,000, with which he entered land in Madison County, improved land, bought stock, and also opened a general merchandising store; he remained in Madison County for several years, but finally removed to [illegible], where he filled official offices, which took the most of his time; in 1843, he entered 160 acres in Macoupin County, which he improved, and removed his family to the same in 1845; he added to this tract until he owned 380 acres in that county; in about 1850, he entered 840 acres in Montgomery, which he had improved, but at the time made his home in Macoupin County; at the time of his death, he had accumulated 1,140 acres of land; his death occurred December 24, 1868; he was one of Macoupin County's most successful farmers and business men. His wife and mother of our subject, was Lucinda Ann (Huntsman) Houck; she was a native of Kentucky, born November 27, 1811, and is now residing in Macoupin County upon the homestead farm; she is the mother of seven children, all of whom are alive, William R. being the oldest child; he was born in Edwardsville, Madison Co., Ill., January 21, 1833; he received his education from the common schools of Alton, Woodburn, and the McKendree College at Lebanon. At the age of nineteen, he left his home, went to Bunker Hill, Ill., and embarked on his career in life as a clerk in a store; he remained here until 1854, when he started a general merchandising store at Edwardsville, Ill., on his own account, in partnership with Mr. John Prickett; in 1856, he sold his interest to his partner, when he returned to Bunker Hill, and, with Mr. James Rider, bought out the interest of his old employer, T. J. Van Dorn; here he remained for a period of twelve years, during which time he had purchased the interest of his partner; in 1862, he purchased a flouring mill, which he ran in partnership with P. C. Huggins until about the close of the war, when he took an interest in a store at Vicksburg; he remained here about one year, when he returned to Bunker Hill and engaged in farming on the old homestead; in 1870, he removed to Montgomery County and settled on a farm of eighty acres, where he has since remained, engaged in agricultural pursuits; by his energy and business, he has succeeded in accumulating 200 acres of land, all of which is under a high state of cultivation. In Macoupin County October 8, 1855, he married Miss Lucinda A. Allard, a native of Cape Cod, she born June 3, 1836; she is the mother of nine children, seven of whom are living—Carrie L. July 18, 1856; Edward R., March 28, 1858; William A., July 8, 1859; Elmira L., November 4, 1861; Mary E., February 24, 1864; Henrietta V. D. and Thomas V. D. (twins), April 17, 1866; Ross, July 4, 1868; Jessie M., May 12, 1870; Elmira L. and Jessie M. are dead. He is a member of the A., F. & A. M. Lodge No. 151, at Bunker Hill; in politics is identified with the Democratic party; self and family are connected with the Methodist Church.

JOHN HAYNES, retired farmer, Atwater, was born in Harrison County, Ind., May 6, 1816, to William and Ann (Toty) Haynes; he was born in Person County, N. C., July 28, 1790; he was a farmer by occupation; from North Carolina he went to Kentucky, where he remained until after he was married, and then removed to Indiana, where he remained about three years, at the end of which time he returned to Kentucky, remaining only about three years, when he again returned West, and located in a portion of Morgan County which is now Cass County, Ill., where his death occurred the following year, May 25, 1820; his wife was also a native of North Carolina, born in 1791, November 27; died May 4, 1868; she was the mother of twelve children, all of whom, with one exception, grew to manhood and womanhood, and of whom John, the subject of this sketch, was the fifth child. His early boyhood was spent in assisting his father in his agricultural pursuits, owing to the limited school privileges at that early day, his education was [illegible] ily limited; but he has succeeded, by [illegible] vation and by contact with the world, in receiving more than an ordinary practical education. At the death of his father, he assisted his mother in the management of the [illegible] and in the support of the family; he [illegible] with mother about [illegible] which time he apprenticed [illegible] the brick maker's and brick [illegible] which he followed [illegible] he [illegible] land in [illegible] which he sold [illegible] purchased 120 acres of the land [illegible] which he has since resided, and to which he has continually added, until he now has [illegible] isfaction of managing a farm consisting of [illegible] acres of fine farm land which [illegible] compare with any of the best [illegible] the township and places Mr. H[illegible] the list of practical farmers; at present he is retired from active labor, but still remains upon the homestead, overseeing the cultivation of his land and enjoying the fruits of a well [illegible] successful career. He was married in Morgan County, [illegible] 18[illegible], to Miss Harriet Seymour, who was born in North Carolina October 7, 18[illegible]; [illegible] mother of nine children, viz.: [illegible] September 25, 1843; Sarah Ann, born [illegible] 8, 1844, deceased; [illegible] tember 7, 18[illegible]; Mary Jane, born [illegible] 18[illegible]; Alexander, born [illegible] 18[illegible]; Charles, born November [illegible]; [illegible] born November 9, 18[illegible], deceased; [illegible] born July 12, 1857; John, born November 8, 18[illegible], the latter of whom is now at home with his parents. Mrs. H[illegible] was the daughter of James P. and Levina (L[illegible]) [illegible], natives of North Carolina, both deceased. Mr. Haynes is not much interested in politics, and may be said to be independent in politics, and, as he says, votes for men and principles

WILLIAM HACKNEY, retired farmer, Athens, born in New York City June 20, 18[illegible], to William and Margaret (S[illegible]) Hackney; he was born in [illegible], N. Y., July [illegible], 1789; [illegible] born, during his life [illegible] a [illegible] and was [illegible] [illegible] Delhi, [illegible] he followed the occupation of [illegible].

[illegible] he died November 9, [illegible] his wife and mother [illegible] N. Y., [illegible] December [illegible], 18[illegible] [illegible] of nine children [illegible] was the second third, of whom [illegible] William Hackney was removed to [illegible] N. Y. [illegible] his parents in 18[illegible] [illegible] his education from the [illegible] at the age of thir[illegible] he began his [illegible] by working as a [illegible] upon the [illegible] in 1830, with his parents removed to Illinois and settled in Jersey County [illegible] lowed life on the river [illegible] about nine [illegible] farming in J[illegible] where he [illegible] in 186[illegible] where he [illegible] bought 250 acres, a part of which [illegible] timber and part prairie, lying in [illegible] and Morgan Counties [illegible] [illegible] which [illegible] of about three hundred and twenty-five acres [illegible] and has all the [illegible] and [illegible] in Jersey County, he married [illegible] Wilkins, a native of Greene County, [illegible] February 8, 1824; she is a daughter of John and Elizabeth (Lurton) Wilkins, who were natives of Kentucky, and among the first settlers of Greene County. Mr. and Mrs. Hackney were the parents of nine children, two of whom are dead—Margaret E., Sarah T., Joseph, Matthew, John W., Carey O., Henry D., Udolpho and Katie G. Mr. Hackney is an active member of the fraternity of A., F. & A. M., No. 692, at Raymond. In politics, his sympathies are with the Democratic party.

JEDUTHUN B. NEWELL, retired farmer, P. O. Girard, son of Asahel and Elizabeth (Bushnell) Newell, was born in Rome, Oneida Co., N. Y., April 13, 1811; the family came to Greene County, Ill., in 1832; they moved to Calhoun in 1834, where they remained about ten years, during which time the mother died; after the death of his wife, Mr. Newell's father lived among his children during the remainder of his life; he died December 8, 1877; they both lived to a good old age, he dying in his eighty-fourth year, and she in her sixty-fifth; they were members of the church, and each had the reputation of being a devoted Christian. Mr. Newell bought his first land in Calhoun County, a tract of ninety-eight acres, lying on the banks of the Illinois River. November 27, 1834, he married Miss Eunice, daughter of Chuza and Sarah (Bacon) Bushnell, by whom he had four children—William and Sarah, died in infancy; Ira B., died at forty years of age; and Alonzo C. His second wife, Lucinda Underwood, was born in Harrison County, Ky., February 5, 1817, daughter of Francis and Margaret (Jarvis) Underwood, he a native of Shropshire, England, died in 1853; she, born in Fayette County, Ky., in 1784, died in 1857; from this second marriage, four children have been born to them—Moses A., a teacher by profession; and Mrs. Mary A. Hoovebeck, both of Harvel Township, Montgomery County; Lucy E. and William R. died in infancy. In 1844, Mr. Newell sold his farm in Calhoun County, and bought another farm in Greene County about five miles southwest of Carrollton, on which he moved, and where he resided till 1852, at which time he came to Montgomery County, Pitman Township, buying a farm of 280 acres of land where he now lives; this farm is well improved, and has a fine, rich, productive soil. Mr. Newell and wife are both members of the Methodist Church, in which denomination they have good standing; as citizens, they rank high. Mr. Newell has been, and is yet, rather a prominent man in society, and whose judgment is revered; he served three terms as Justice of the Peace while in Calhoun County, and three terms since in Montgomery County; in fact, he held the office as long as he would have it at all; his judgments were generally sustained in higher courts. The Newells are supposed to be of English origin; it is not now definitely known when they came to this country; they were here, however, before our independence as a nation. Mr. Newell's grandfather, Solomon Newell, lived and died in the State of Connecticut. March 4, 1781, Asahel, Mr. Newell's father, emigrated, after his marriage, to Oneida County, N. Y., about 1807; he raised a family of seven children—Isaac, Jeduthun, Mrs. Elizabeth (Alonson) Twitchell, Asahel, Mrs. Clarissa (Thomas) Reynolds, Mrs. Louisa (Charles) Thurp and Mrs. Ruth (Solomon) Despain; Isaac died when about twenty-three years old; three of these children are now living—Jeduthun, Mrs. Reynolds, of Macoupin County, and Mrs. Despain, of Granite City, U. T.

JOSEPH H. PITMAN, retired farmer, Raymond, was born in New Jersey in 1822, October 19, to Samuel and Fannie (Phillips) Pitman; he was born in New Jersey in 1795; during his former life, followed the trade of a weaver, but, during the latter years of his life, followed farming; he removed to the State of Illinois in 1839, and settled in Jersey County, which was at that time Greene County; here he remained to the time of his death, which occurred in 1855; she was born in New Jersey in about 1797, and died in her native State in 1829; she was the mother of seven children, Joseph H. being the fourth child; his school education was very limited, and only such as the common schools afforded; he has received the most of his learning by observation and study by himself; he remained with his father, assisting in managing the farm, to the time of his death, and remained upon the farm ten years after his father's death, supporting and caring for his father's family. In the spring of 1866, he removed to Montgomery County and settled upon his tract of 160 acres of uncultivated prairie land, which he had bought several years previous; here he has since remained, and made all necessary improvements upon his farm, until now it is in a high state of cultivation; in 1879, he rented his land, it being his desire to retire from active labor, having, by his energy and business, accumulated a good property, and a name and reputation which stand beyond reproach. Mr. Pitman has filled many township offices, and has been serving the people as County Supervisor for eight years, to the entire satisfaction of all well-disposed citizens. In politics, his sympathies are with the Republican party. The township of Pitman, of which he is a resident, was named from Mr. Joseph H. Pitman.

DANIEL C. RICHARDS, farmer, P. O. Raymond. The father of this gentleman was Samuel S. Richards; he was born in Lima, Livingston Co., N. Y., February 22, 1818, where he was educated and brought up on a farm. In 1836, he removed to Illinois, settled at Rockford, Winnebago County, where he has been engaged in farming and merchandising, giving his attention principally to the former; he is the owner of 160 acres of land at the present time, he having accumulated, during his life, a large tract of land, all of which he improved; he is a son of Daniel Richards, a native of New York. The mother of our subject was Sarah Brown, who was born in North Carolina February 19, 1818; she was brought to Illinois by her uncle, Aaron Felts, in 1836, and settled in Winnebago County, Ill.; she remained with her uncle, Aaron Felts, and her brother, William Brown, to the time of her marriage, which occurred in 1837; she is the mother of fourteen children, three of whom are now living

Daniel C., our subject; Oscar L., of Rockford, a farmer; Clara M., now at home. Mrs. Richards, the mother of our subject, is the daughter of Daniel Brown, who was a native of North Carolina, and was of German descent. D. C. Richards was born in Harrison Township, Winnebago Co., Ill., August 11, 1838; his early life was spent in receiving such education as the common schools of his native county afforded, and assisting in tilling the soil of his father's farm, which at that time was very wild and unimproved. At the age of twenty-one, he left home and moved to Michigan, where he embarked on his career in life as a farm hand, and, during the two years' stay in Michigan, his time was divided in farming, teaching school and attending a select school taught by a Miss Brown; the opportunity afforded him a chance to complete his education, which he improved. In the summer of 1861, he returned to his home, and taught school the following winter, when he entered the Durand Academy, at Durand, in his native county, for a period of four months, and, on the 5th of July, in 1862, he enlisted in the

Seventy first Illinois Infantry, under command of Col. Gilbert; he served in this regiment for three months, at the expiration of which time he returned home. After the battle of Stony River, he was engaged as clerk in the Quartermaster's Department, and remained in the employ of Quartermaster's Department at Murfreesboro, Nashville and Clarksville, Tenn., until about the 1st of April, [illegible], he then returned to St. Louis, and subsequently to Pitman Township, Montgomery County, and settled on his present residence June 1, 1865; he remained here for about one month, and returned to his home in Winnebago County, where he remained until fall of the same year, when he located permanently on his place October 3, 1865; here he has since remained, engaged in stock raising and farming; in stock raising he has been engaged quite extensively, at times keeping about two hundred head. He is now the owner of eighty acres of land, but generally works about three hundred; his farm is well improved and under a high state of cultivation. [illegible] St. Louis, October 25, 1864, he married Miss Hannah P. Houck, a native of Macoupin County, Ill., who was born June 14, 185[illegible]; she is the daughter of Ross and Lucinda A. (Counterman) Houck; he was a native of Pennsylvania; she was of Kentucky. Mr. and Mrs. Richards are the parents of one child, Frank Claud; he was born March 9, 188[illegible]. Mr. Richards is now serving the people on his second term as Justice of the Peace; he also has been School Director for a number of years. Mr. Richards is a member of the fraternity of A., F. & A. M., No. 166, at Rockford; of the Grangers' Lodge, Maple Grove Grange, at Pitman Township; was Master of the same for several years, and Secretary of County Council for several years; in politics, is identified with the Republican party; he and wife are religiously connected with the Baptist Church; he has been Clerk of the Baptist Church for about nine years, since its organization. Mr. Richards has been actively engaged in Sunday school work and temperance work.

JAMES ROGERS, farmer, P. O. McVey, was born in Macoupin County, Ill., January 11, 18[illegible]; his early life was spent in receiving such an education as the common schools of his native county afforded, and assisting in tilling the soil of his father's farm. At the age of fourteen years, he was brought to Montgomery County by his parents, who settled on the same farm he is now residing on; he remained with his parents to the age of twenty four, when he married and entered upon his career in life as a farmer, at which he still continues, having, by his industry and business habits, succeeded in accumulating [illegible] five acres of land, all of which (eighty five improved and ten acres of timber) is under a high state of cultivation; in 18[illegible] upon his farm he erected, by his own design, a handsome frame cottage; upon his farm he makes stock raising and all general crops a specialty. His farm is located mostly in Montgomery County, his timber land being in Macoupin County. The father of this gentleman, Benjamin K. Rogers, was born in Greene County, Ky., January 30, 181[illegible]; emigrated with his parents to Montgomery County, Ill., in the fall of 1830; his life was spent in following the occupation of farming; was a man who stood high in the estimation of his fellow men. At the time of his death, he was holding the office of School Treasurer, and, in Macoupin County, served several terms as Justice of the Peace, and as many terms in Montgomery County; he joined the M. E. Church in 18[illegible]0, and, at the time of his death, was a faithful member; he lived to see all his children but one in the church; his death occurred December 11, 1868; dur ing his life, he succeeded in accumulating a good farm, all of which he improved; his wife, and mother of our subject, was Lydia Snow, who was born in Simpson County, Ky., May 26, 1816, and died January 19, 1850; she was the mother of eight children, seven of whom are now living, James Rogers being the third child. He was married, in Greenfield, Greene County, November 13, 1861, to Eglantine, the daughter of Valentine and Louisa (Madison) Caswell; Mrs. Rogers was born in Greene County, Ill., December 29, 1843; her father was born in Shawneetown, Ill., June 12, 1820; he has, during his life, been engaged in farming, but is now retired, and residing in Greenfield, Ill.; his wife was born in Ohio June 8, 1824, and died March 7, 1875. Mr. and Mrs. Rogers are the parents of four children: Hollie B. is now the wife of Edgar Massa, of Macoupin County; Dora M., Frederick O., Grant V., at home. Mr. Rogers is now serving the people as School Director of the township; self and family are members of the Methodist Church; politically, he is identified with the Republicans.

JOHN D. STREET, retired farmer, Girard, was born in Shelby County, Ky., August 10, 1820, to David and Catharine (Duncan) Street; his early life was spent in receiving a common school education and assisting in tilling the soil of his father's farm; he was brought to Illinois, Macoupin County, by his parents, in 1831; in 1841, he left home and embarked on his career in life as a hired hand; in 1842, he moved to Iowa, where he remained four years, and, while there, experienced many hardships, such as are found in a pioneer life; one instance he remembers of going sixty miles to a mill to get his corn ground, and, after making the trip, found it impossible to get his grist, as the water was so high as to prevent the running of the mill; he returned, and, to keep from starving, used a coffee-mill to grind corn enough to live on. In 1847, he returned to Macoupin County and engaged in farming, which he followed for about one year, after which he again worked by the month, or day, at carpentering, and, in fact, at anything he could find to do and receive a compensation for his labors. In 1856, he went to Texas, where he followed hunting; while there, he bought 600 acres of land, but was defrauded out of it by the last rebellion; he returned to Montgomery County, Ill., in 1857, and, in 1861, bought 120 acres of unimproved land in Pitman Township, upon which he removed his family in 1862; here he has since remained, engaged principally in raising stock; his farm now consists of 231 acres of land, all of which is under a high state of cultivation. Mr. Street commenced life a poor man; by his honesty, industry and economy, he has succeeded in accumulating a good property; now, in the later years of his life, he is surrounded with those comforts and enjoying those pleasures that are ever the result of honesty, industry and economy. Mr. Street was married, April 3, 1862, to Mary E. Benning; she was born in Illinois in 1838; she was the mother of seven children, of whom six are now living: Andrew T., Sarah C., John W., Jennie A., Charles M., Antoinette G. and Bessie Lula, all of whom are at home. The father of Mr. Street was born in Virginia in 1785, and died in 1855; he was a farmer and stone mason; he was among the early settlers of Kentucky, and also of Illinois; his wife and mother of J. D. Street, was born in Virginia August 26, 1788; was brought to Kentucky by her parents when quite a small child; she died November 1, 1836; she was the mother of eleven children, of whom our subject was the sixth child. In politics, Mr. Street is a Republican; is a member of Washington

Grange. Lodge No. 970, of Pitman Township; in the lodge, he has acted as Treasurer; he and wife are members of the Christian Church.

PETER STUMP, farmer, P. O. Girard, was born in Hocking County, Ohio, June 1, 1819, to John and Catharine (Pouster) Stump; he was born in Pennsylvania in 1797; was brought to Hocking County, Ohio, by his parents when a child; here he remained until 1857, when he removed to Illinois; during his life, followed the occupation of a farmer, and died in Montgomery County in 1872; was of German parentage; she was born in Pennsylvania in 1807; her parents were natives of Germany; she died in 1852. They were the parents of twelve children--six boys and six girls--of whom Peter was the third child. His early life was spent in receiving such an education as the common schools of Hocking County, Ohio, afforded, and assisting in tilling the soil of his father's farm; he remained at home until he was twenty-five years of age, when he embarked on his career in life as a hired hand in a saw-mill. In 1852, he removed to Knox County, Ill., where he remained two years, following farming and working in a saw-mill; in 1854, he removed to Macoupin County, where he commenced farming on rented property; by his honesty industry and economy, he succeeded in saving some money, with which, in 1862, he bought 160 acres of partially improved land; here he has since remained, engaged in agricultural pursuits; he is now the owner of 240 acres of land, all of which is under a high state of cultivation. In 1845, in Hocking County, Ohio, he married Miss Samaney Busby, a native of Ohio; she died in 1857; she was the mother of four children--John, married, living in Missouri; Daniel, married, near Harvel, Ill.; Catharine, wife of Rutledge Fox, of Pitman; Luelza, dead. In 1860, he married Mrs. Nancy Mays; she was born in Greene County, Ill.; she is the mother of one child, Lydia Ann, now at home. Politically, he is a Democrat; himself and wife are religiously connected with the Methodist Church. When he first commenced life as a hired hand in the saw-mill, he worked three years and only missed seven days; worked a portion of the nights; he worked very hard to make a living.

GEORGE W. WAGGONER, deceased, was born in Hardin County, Ky., October 8, 1826, to Adam and Mary Ann (Terry) Waggoner, natives of Kentucky. The Waggoner family is of German extraction, but came to America before the war of the Revolution; in the struggle, they espoused the patriot cause, and bore their part in the struggle to throw off the yoke of British oppression. David, Adam Waggoner's father, was a soldier in the war, and he was the fortunate father of a family who have ever been loyal to the calls of their country. Adam Waggoner was born January 30, 1800, and died August 8, 1860; his wife was born August 11, 1800, and died January 26, 1874; she was the daughter of Jasper and Sarah Terry; this family is of English descent, and has a history running back to the period of the earliest settlements of this country. George Waggoner was brought to Jersey County, Ill., in 1830, by his parents, who were among the first to enter upon pioneer life in the then far West; his early life was spent upon the homestead farm, assisting in improvements and in all the agricultural pursuits incident to early pioneer industries; his educational privileges were limited to the common schools at that early day. In 1849, he entered 480 acres of wild prairie land in Montgomery County, which he eventually increased until he had in his possession about eight hundred acres of land, nearly all of which he improved, and hich, as a practical farmer, he kept in a high ate of cultivation. Mr. Waggoner was one the few men possessing all the energy and nterprise of a man bound to make his mark the world; he entered upon his career in fe comparatively a poor man, and his subse nent possessions represented the dollars arned by himself, and through the result of is good management and thorough and pracical business ability; he was a public-spirited an, always interested in all public improvements and enterprises, and generous in his nations for the advancement of educational nd church privileges; he was for a number years prior to his death an active member the Baptist Church, and, in his daily walk life, emulated the principles of Christiany. He was married, in Macoupin County, l., December 2, 1851, to Elizabeth J. Mc-llough, and, during the fifteen years of arried life, Mr. Waggoner proved himself be a kind father and devoted husband; his eath occurred September 29, 1866; he was e father of four children, viz.: Horace G., eorge B., Henry Q. and John M., all of hom have grown to maturity Mrs. Wagoner was born in Rockingham County, Va.; March 22, 1827; at the death of her husband, e was left with a family of small children, e oldest of whom was but eleven years of ge; she took upon herself the management the property and support of her children; ne is a lady possessing all the womanly races, combined with energy and enterprise, nd she also has the faculty of managing bus ess affairs with a shrewdness and ability hich but few women possess, whether thrown pon their own resources through misfortune r otherwise; she has added to the property, ft by her husband, about twelve hundred cres of land, and most of which is now rented, ut all of which has been under her own management; she is now surrounded by her children, in the declining days of her life, which to her is a comfort and a blessing; the farm lands now consist of about twenty-two hundred acres of land, which Mrs. Waggoner and her sons have mutually decided to divide the property without the assistance of administrators or otherwise. Mrs. Waggoner was a daughter of John and Sarah (McCrea) McCollough; he was a native of Belfast, Ireland, born September 24, 1791, and was one of the early settlers of Macoupin County; he was a farmer by occupation; his death occurred August 30, 1844; his wife was born in Pendleton County, Va., March 27, 1799; she died April 30, 1851; she was the mother of eight children, of whom Mrs. Waggoner was the second child; she was educated in the common schools of Macoupin County. Mrs. Waggoner may well be proud of her family of boys, all of whom are steady and industrious, following business in a manner like their father; her father was in the war of 1812.

WINTER P. WAGGONER, stock raiser, P. O. Decatur, was born in Pitman Township, Montgomery Co., Ill., April 8, 1861, to William R. and Sarah R. (McCollough) Waggoner; he was born in Jersey County, Ill., September 9, 1833, where he received his education; he remained in his native county with his parents, assisting in tilling the soil of his father's farm until he was twenty one years of age, when he removed to Pitman Township, Montgomery County, and entered a small tract of land; here he remained, engaged in farming and stock-raising, during his life, and succeeded in accumulating 1,300 acres of land, all of which he improved and put under a high state of cultivation; in connection with his farming and stock raising, he shipped a great deal of stock, finding a market in St. Louis for the same; for about five years previous to his death, which occurred January 20, 1871, he followed the latter business alone; was a member of the Baptist Church; his father was Adam Waggoner, who was of German descent; his mother, was Mary A. (Terry) Waggoner, who was of English descent. Adam Waggoner served through the Black Hawk war as Captain; in the possession of our subject is a rifle used by his grandfather. Adam Waggoner came from Kentucky, his native place. William Waggoner was married, in Macoupin County, April 16, 1857, to Sarah R. McCollough; she was born in Virginia December 3, 1832, and died June 2, 1866; she was the mother of four children, two of whom died in infancy; our subject, Winter P., and E. Leroy, are now living; E. Leroy was born September 23, 1863, is now clerking in dry goods store of W. C. Miller & Co., of Hillsboro. In 1867, in Greene County, Mr. Waggoner married a second time, Susan C. Race, a native of Virginia; she died in 1880, aged thirty-eight years; she was the mother of one child, S. Colfax Waggoner, who is following the occupation of a farmer. Adam Waggoner was born January 30, 1800, in Hardin County, Ky.; emigrated to Illinois in the year 1830; he died August 8, 1860; he was a farmer; his wife, and grandmother of our subject, was Mary A. (Terry) Waggoner, born August 11, 1800, in Virginia; she died in January, 1871; they had seven children, of whom Winter was the third child. Our subject received his education at Valparaiso, Ind., at the Northern Normal School, and the Blackburn University, at Carlinville, in connection with his common-school education; his father died when he was ten years old, when he made his home with William Seward, and remained there four years, when he made his home in Pitman Township. In the fall of 1879, he commenced farming, and continued the same until the fall of 1881, when he removed to Decatur, where he has since remained, enjoying himself. He was married, March 7, 1880, in Carlinville, to Miss Cora B. Renshaw, a native of Decatur, Ill.; she was born January 20, 1861; is the daughter of Lucius and Martha J. (Walker) Renshaw, he born in Nashville, Tenn., October 27, 1824, died December 27, 1862; he was a contractor, and was the owner of about four hundred acres of land near Decatur; she was born October 22, 1838, in Carlinville, Ill.; she is now residing in Decatur, and is now the wife of William Taggart. Mr. and Mrs. Waggoner are the parents of one child, Winter Preston, Jr.; he was born January 7, 1881; in politics, is identified with the Republican party. Mr. Waggoner is the owner of 540 acres of land, lying principally in Pitman and Zanesville Townships, it being one of the finest farms of the townships; upon his farm he has all modern improvements, and it is under a high state of cultivation, upon which he intends to remove in the spring of 1883, and engage in stock-raising; he and wife expect to spend the summer at Eureka Springs, in Arkansas.

WILLIAM B. WOOD, farmer, P. O. McVey. The father of this gentleman, Alfred Wood, was born in Tennessee in about 1817; emigrated to Montgomery County with his parents in about 1820; during his life, he followed the occupation of a farmer; he died in about 1847; his wife, and mother of our subject, was Malinda Baker; she was born in Arkansas in about 1812, and died in about 1852; she was the mother of seven children, of whom William B. Wood was the oldest child. He was born in Montgomery County April 2, 1842; his early life was spent in receiving such an education as the common schools of his native county afforded, and in assisting in tilling the soil of his father's farm; he remained at home to the age of nineteen, when he embarked on his career in life as a farm hand; he continued as a hired hand until he was twenty years of age, when he rented a farm of forty acres in Pitman Township, where he commenced farming on his own account; he remained here about six months, and removed to Honey Bend and commenced farming on the old homestead farm; in 1862, he bought thirty five acres in Pitman Township, of timber land; upon this farm he remained only about one year, when he sold out and bought forty acres of the same farm he is now residing on; here he has since remained, engaged in farming. In 1862, February 27, he married Miss Mary E. Miller; she was born in Montgomery County March 18, 1845 and died June 11, 1864. She was the mother of one child, Julia A.; she was born August 16, 1863; is at home. On March 15, 1866, he married Miss Hiley A. Rogers; she was born in Macoupin County September 15, 18[illegible]; she is the mother of four children: Nancy M., born May 4, 1867; Alfred B., born October 15, 1869; William E., born February 24, 1872; Nettie, born February 10, 1876. Mr. Wood is now serving the people in his third term as Justice of the Peace, himself and wife are members of the Methodist Church; politically, is identified with the Republican party. In 1865, he enlisted in Company A, One Hundred and Forty-ninth Regiment Illinois Volunteer Infantry; he served one year and twelve days.

BOIS D'ARC TOWNSHIP.

GEORGE H. BROWNING, farmer, P. O. Girard, was born in Greene County, Ill., April 22, 1834; his education was obtained in the common schools of his native county, where his early life was spent in assisting his grandfather upon a farm. At the age of eighteen, he returned home and took upon himself the support of his mother and her family, which duties he performed until he reached the age of twenty-five years, when he embarked upon his career in life as a farmer, and has followed that occupation up to the present time; his first purchase of real estate was in Greene County, and consisted of forty acres of land, which he improved, added to and eventually sold; in 1866, he purchased the property he now owns, and has built most of the buildings and made all other improvements which are usually found upon a well-regulated farm, and everything about the premises confirms the reputation Mr. Browning bears as being a successful and enterprising farmer; he has, by his energy and industry, accumulated a large property, and now owns 200 acres of choice prairie farm land, all of which, as a practical farmer, he keeps in a high state of cultivation, and upon which he grows all of the usual farm crops; he also raises all the stock he handles upon his place. He was married, in Greene County, December 20, 1860, to Louisa E. Adcock, who was born in Greene County April 15, 1838; she has borne him twelve children, viz.: Maxie J. (wife of George Simon), Edward M., William A., Cora L. (deceased), George C., Lena L., John W., Jacob O., Sarah E., Aquilla E., Perry L., Myrtle (an infant). Mrs. Browning was a daughter of Issau and Rachael (Stinnet) Adcock, natives of Kentucky, he deceased, she still living. Matiac Browning, the father of George, was a native of Kentucky, and was one of the early settlers of Greene County; he was a preacher by profession; his death occurred in 1842; his wife, Maxie Wood, was also a native of Kentucky; she died in 1860; she was the mother of nine children, of whom George, our subject, was the fourth. Politically, he is identified with the Democratic party. Mrs. Browning is connected with the Baptist Church.

WILLIAM EVANS, farmer, P. O. Virden, was born in Pittsburgh, Penn., February 12, 1828, and was brought to Illinois when but nine years of age; his father, Henry Evans, settled in Alton when there were but three log houses in the town; he remained there about twenty years, engaged in blacksmithing, and his was the first shop in the town; he was a native of Ireland, and, when twenty-four years of age, emigrated to America with his wife and one child; he died in 1861, aged sixty-five years; his wife, Isabella Gordon, was also a native of Ireland; she died in 1854, aged fifty-seven years; she was the mother of nine children, of whom William was the second child. He assisted his father in his shop until he was nineteen years of age, when the family removed from Alton and settled upon a farm, where the father of our subject remained, engaged in agricultural pursuits up to the time of his death. William remained upon the farm until he reached the age of twenty-three years, when he entered upon his career in life, following in the footsteps of his father, as a blacksmith; he continued in that occupation at Otter Creek, Jersey County, about twenty years, at the end of which time he again took upon himself the duties of a farm life, purchased the property upon which he now resides, and upon which he has made all the improvements, which denote his energy and enterprise as a man, and show him to be a practical farmer; his farm consists of 160 acres of choice land, all of which is under cultivation; although he grows all of the usual farm crops, he makes a specialty of grain. He was married, in Jersey County, April 7, 1847, to Miss Louisiana Noble, who was born in Mississippi July 4, 1829; she has borne him eight children, viz.: Henry (deceased), Isabella, Martha Ann, Albert, Kate, Benjamin, Hattie, William (deceased). Mrs. Evans was a daughter of Solomon and Louisiana (Sojourner) Noble, natives of Mississippi. Mr. Evans has served the people as Supervisor two years; was once elected Justice of the Peace, but declined to serve; politically, he is identified with the Republican party; he has been a member of the I. O. O. F. for a number of years, and is also an active member of the A., F. & A. M. at Virden. Socially, he ranks high in the community, and in him are found the elements which, combined, make a man a good neighbor, a kind husband and an indulgent father.

CHARLES T. HOPPIN, farmer, P. O. White Oak, was born in Madison County, N. Y., June 8, 1817, where he received his education in the common schools, and assisted his father upon the old homestead until he was twenty-five years of age, when he married and engaged in farming for himself. He remained in New York three years, and then concluded to try the pioneer life in the then far West, and settled in Sangamon County, Ill., where he began handling sheep upon the prairies, and was at one time one of the largest sheep and wool dealers in the State; by his energy, he also accumulated a large amount of land in Sangamon and Montgomery Counties, which he improved and cultivated himself, and held a position as one of the practical farmers of the day. He was married, in 1842, to Eliza McConnell, who bore him three children, who grew to manhood and womanhood; she died in 1853, and, two years later, he was again married, to Phinett Parmeter, who is still living, and is the mother of eight children, all of whom are living, and all at home. Politically, Mr. Hoppin is a Republican.

WILLIAM A. KNOCK, farmer, P. O. Virden, was born in Fulton County, Ill., August 27, 1833; his education was limited to such as could be obtained in the common schools of his native county; during his school days, and up to the time he was twenty-nine years of age, assisted his father upon the old homestead; at the breaking-out of the war, he entered the service in Company F, Eighty fourth Illinois Infantry, with Capt. C. B. Cox, his regiment commanded by Col. Waters; he remained in the service until the close of the war, and then purchased the property he now owns, and once again took upon himself the duties of a farm life; he erected a fine farm dwelling, which does honor to the county and to Mr. Knock as an architect; he has also made all the other improvements that are necessary on a well-regulated farm, such as outbuildings, orchards, fences, etc.; his farm consists of 120 acres of fine farm land, which, as a practical farmer, he keeps in a high state of cultivation, and which denotes his energy and enterprise, and makes him worthy of the position he holds as one of the leading agriculturists of the county; he has always taken a leading part in all public improvements and in educational privileges; so cially, he enjoys the highest esteem of the entire community. His father, D. C. Knock, is a native of Delaware, and was one of the first to enter upon pioneer life in Fulton County, Ill., where he is still living, enjoying the fruits of a well spent life, with his wife, Phebe Easley, who was born in Freeport Ohio; she is the mother of thirteen children, of whom William is the second child. He was married, in Morgan County, August 21, 1867, to Sarah J. (Kinnett) Miller, who was born in Hamilton County Ohio, March 2[illegible], 1838; they have two children, viz.: Laetta and Sarah Phebe, both of whom are at home and attending school. Mrs. Knock was a daughter of W. [illegible] and Ann (Brown) Kinnett, natives of Ohio and still living. Mr. Knock has held several town offices; is also a prominent member of the Grange; politically, he is identified with the Republican party.

MARTIN McLEAN, farmer, P. O. Girard, was born in Ireland in 1819; his education was limited, owing to the fact that his early life was spent in assisting his father upon his farm, and that the facilities for gaining an education were also limited; at the age of twenty-six, he embarked upon his career in life as a farmer upon his own account. In 1845 he emigrated to America and remained in New York seven months, and in New Jersey about fifteen years, engaged as a farm hand, at the end of which time he removed to Montgomery County and purchased 160 acres of prairie land, upon which he has made all the improvements necessary for comfort and which are found only upon the best regulated and cultivated farms; by his energy, industry and economy, he has continued to add to his possessions until now he has the satisfaction of overseeing the cultivation of 180 acres of as choice prairie farm land as can be found in Montgomery County, and to him are due all honors that can be paid any man who has begun the battle of life as a poor boy, and has, by energy and enterprise, worked his way through the world until he is now known and recognized as one of the most successful and practical farmers of the county; although he grows all the usual farm crops, he makes a specialty of grain, and raises nearly all the stock handled upon his farm; he is a man who ranks high in the estimation of the community, and of which he is well worthy; he is a public-spirited man, and has long been identified with the growth and prosperity of Bois D'Arc Township, and especially in gaining the position it has attained as being one of the best townships in the county; although he takes no leading part in politics, he is identified with the Democratic party. In 1847, he married Mary Carey, who was born in Kings County, Ireland, and emigrated to America when she was twenty-seven years of age; she is the mother of two boys and one girl, viz.: John James, William Henry and Margaret, all of whom are still living. John is Circuit Clerk at Hillsboro; William H., married and living on the homestead farm; Margaret, living at home. James McLean, the father of Martin, was a native of Ireland, a farmer by occupation; he died in 1868; his wife, Julia Quinland, was also a native of Ireland; she died in 1866; she was the mother of thirteen children, of whom Martin was the seventh child; himself and family are connected with the Catholic Church. St. Martin's Cemetery is located upon Mr. McLean's farm, the property being donated by him to the society, and the cemetery named St. Martin in honor of Mr. McLean.

ABEL S. RANDOLPH, farmer, P. O. Virden, was born in New Jersey August 5, 1831; his father, Louis Randolph, was also a native of New Jersey, but moved to Jacksonville, Ill., in 1835, and remained there one year, and then removed to Jersey County, where he is still living; he was one of the early settlers of the county, and holds a prominent position among the agriculturists of the county; his wife, Mary Compton, was also a native of New Jersey, and is still living; she is the mother of seven children, of whom Abel was the second child; he received his education in the common schools of Jersey County, and assisted his father upon the old homestead until he was thirty years of age, when he came to Montgomery County and continued his occupation as a farmer for himself; he erected his dwelling and made all other improvements on the farm himself, and has now in his possession 200 acres of choice farm land, well fenced, well stocked, and which he keeps in a high state of cultivation; the surroundings on Mr Randolph's farm denote energy and enterprise, and show him to be a practical farmer, and well worthy of the position he holds as one of the leading agriculturists of the county; he devotes time to growing the usual crops, and raises all the stock he handles; politically, his sympathies are with the Republican party. He was married, in Jersey County, June 9, 1869, to Minerva Edwards, who was born in Ohio October 2, 1838; she has borne him one child, Henry, born April 21, 1870. Mrs. Randolph was a daughter of Andrew and Mary (Darlington) Edwards, natives of Ohio. Mrs. Randolph is connected with the Methodist Church at Wesley Chapel.

LEWIS H. THOMAS, son of Samuel and Elizabeth (Isley) Thomas, was born May 24, 1827, in Greene County, Ill., where he was raised; after receiving, in the district schools, an education, he commenced the study of surveying, completing the latter at Carrollton Academy; in the spring of 1851, Mr. Thomas entered 970 acres of land in Township 12 north, Range 5 west, Montgomery County, the entry being the fourth and by far the largest up to that time, in the township; after entering the land, Mr. Thomas put a hedge around the entire tract, which was so successful that the name of the plant, Osage Orange, or Bois D'Arc, was given to the township; he also planted groves of timber, and it is a remarkable fact that, in eleven years from the time of planting a fifteen-acre lot, he cut wood enough from it to burn 300,000 brick, with which he built one of the finest mansions in the State. Mr. Thomas is one of the most progressive men in the State, and is always making improvements on his fine estate; he has been a stock dealer since his boyhood, having inherited the business from his father; he is opening a ranch in Kansas, where he has considerable land inclosed with fences, for convenience in handling high grade stock. Mr. Thomas has been twice married, each time to a daughter of Isham and Sarah Linder, of Greene County; the first marriage, to Miss Minerva C. Linder, occurred May 23, 1851, but she only lived ten days after the birth of a son, who also died a few months after his beloved mother "fell asleep in Jesus." Mr. Thomas, November 11, 1863, married Miss Sarah A. Linder, who has blessed her husband with seven children, five of whom are living—Ettie, John L., William H., Mary L. and Samuel; an infant son and daughter, Harry and Matilda, are dead. The Thomas family are of Welsh extraction, and the father of our subject, Samuel Thomas, was one of the early pioneers of this section, having come to Greene County in 1818, and there he lived until his death, which occurred December 23, 1873; the wife of Samuel, and mother of Mr. L. H. Thomas, was Miss Elizabeth Isley, daughter of Rev. William Jones, a Baptist minister.

SAMUEL R. THOMAS, farmer, P. O. Virden, son of Samuel and Elizabeth (Isley) Thomas, was born May 2, 1829, in Greene

County, Ill., where he was raised and educated; in his education he had only such advantages as were common to district schools; he nevertheless made an extraordinary advancement in literature and science, considering his surroundings, mastering not only the ordinary branches of an English education, but philosophy, higher mathematics, surveying and navigation: these branches were studied without the assistance of a teacher; his mind, by a kind of natural intuition, reveled in mathematical calculation; and in leisure hours he wrote down Colman's Treatise on Algebra; to give an idea of his aptitude in calculation, we mention the fact that, when in his thirteenth year, he mastered all the problems in Smith's Arithmetic in a thirty-days' study; he also, at an early age, familiarized himself with the science of astronomy; he kept his father's books from the time he was thirteen till he commenced business for himself; in connection with his brother Lewis, he managed, for some time, the business of his father's farm, buying, selling and shipping; he was, in truth, a kind of confidential adviser. When in the twenty-first year of his age, he entered a section and a half of land in Township 12 north, Range 5 west; his entry was made in the fall of 1850, and in 1851 he broke a hedge-row, inclosing this entire tract; this was a part of the first prairie breaking done in the township. December 29, 1851 he married Miss Elizabeth M., daughter of Matthew and Margaret (Taylor) Dayton, of Greene County, Ill.; the Daytons also were old pioneers of this section of the State; Mrs. Thomas' grandfather, Thomas Dayton, with four of his sons, Abraham, Isaac, Jacob and Matthew, were soldiers in the war of 1812, and took part in the battle of Plattsburg, next to the last engagement of any consequence of that war; the family are descended from Wales and settled in the United States of America prior to their independence of the mother country; Mrs. Thomas' aunt on her father's side, Betsey Ann Jacobs, of Vermont, when in her seventieth year, cut a new set of teeth, and was re-endowed with an eyesight equal to that of her youth; this fact is mentioned as confirming the theory that nature, in its primitive state, had the power of recuperation and renewal. Mrs. Thomas is of a good family, well educated and intelligent; in fact, during her school days like her husband, she was considered the prime student of her school; before she was married, she taught one or two terms. Mr. Thomas remained some two years in his native county after his marriage, and then came to Montgomery County and occupied his farm; here he has since resided, adding improvements to his lands, and engaged in the stock business, and is the heaviest stock-grower in the county; his farm now consists of three sections of land, as fine as are to be found within the county or State, in a very high state of cultivation; the residence is a handsome and commodious frame building, possessing all the conveniences and apartments adapting it to the wants and requirements of a country seat; a cistern is placed in the attic story, from which the water is conveyed to every room of the house; instead of a cellar, an attachment is made, which consists of a room formed of double walls, and floor some two feet below the grade of the earth's surface; this attachment joins onto the kitchen, and keeps vegetables and fruits as well as a cellar, and does not add a mold to butter and other articles; we advise any one contemplating building to take a look through Mr. Thomas' house first; we are satisfied that it would pay. Mr. Thomas contemplates another improvement which is worthy of notice. A wind-mill and corn-sheller stand at a convenient distance from his house; he meditates putting a large cistern in the tower part of this building, and then running pipe to supply his bath room and a fountain in the yard; two other wind-wheels run as many pumps at convenient points on the farm; from one of these the water is conveyed 120 rods, to supply feed lots; we believe now that every 160-acre tract is well supplied with stock water; he has also on his farm a very nice grove of cultivated timber, consisting of about twenty-five acres. Mr. Thomas' family consists of the following children: Henry Matthew, who married Miss Lydia Ann Baird September 25, 1878, daughter of Zebulon Baird, of Harvel Township; Ann Amanda, Elizabeth Jane, Catharine, Samuel Dayton and Mary Lenora. The parents have spared neither means nor care in educating their children, and have been rewarded with both gratitude and success.

CLAUD J. WILLIS, farmer, P. O. White Oak, was born in England April 19, 1842; he obtained the principal part of his education in his native country, under the instruction of his mother and a governess; at the age of thirteen years, he was brought to America by his parents, who settled in Jacksonville, Ill. Charles Willis, the father of Claud, was a parliamentary lawyer in England, but his health failed him, and he came to America and traveled for his health; his death occurred in 1856; his wife, Ann C. Row, who is also a native of England, and is still living, at Jacksonville; she is the mother of two children, viz.: Charles and Claud. The latter, at the age of twenty years, took upon himself the duties of a farm life, and followed that occupation in Scott County a few years, when he gave up his farming interests and engaged for about ten years in the stock trade, with John Alexander and several other men of Morgan County, who are known as large and extensive operators in nearly all markets. In 1878, he came to the place he now resides upon, and again turned his attention to farming; the farm had been rented for several years before Mr. Willis took charge of it, and had been very badly cultivated, but, owing to the energy and enterprise of Mr. Willis, it will now compare with any of the best-improved farms of the county, and places Mr. Willis in the list of practical farmers, and he is also the largest stock-dealer in the township at the present day. He was married in Greene County, December 23, 1881, to Miss Jane E. Eldred, who was born October 24, 1839, to Elon and Jane (Stuart) Eldred; he was one of the very early settlers of Greene County, and also at an early day one of the first to enter and improve land in Montgomery County, and became very noted as a land-holder, having accumulated at different places about three thousand acres of land, all under cultivation, and managed by himself personally; to him is due all the credit of the early improvements made upon the place now occupied by the subject of this sketch, and his death occurred in 1871, while on the way to make a visit to his Montgomery farm, having expressed a wish to see the "White Oak" farm again—the farm so named from a white oak tree, which is located on the corner of the farm, and being at one time the only tree standing for many miles around, and which served as a landmark and guide to travelers in crossing the prairie before settlement; his wife survived him five years; she was the mother of three sons and three daughters, all of whom are living, with one exception, viz., the oldest son, William; they are all residents of Greene County; Lucius, a leading hardware merchant at Carrollton; and Charles, a prominent farmer and stock-dealer; Louisa, wife of L. F. Wheeler, retired merchant, living at Carrollton; and Julia, wife of R. Pearson, banker at the above place. Mr. Willis is identified with the Republican party; religiously, himself and wife are connected with the Presbyterian Church.

R

ROUNTREE TOWNSHIP.

NOAH LIPE, farmer, P. O. Hillsboro. The grandparents of our subject, Godfrey and Barbara (House) Lipe, were natives of Pennsylvania, and were of German descent their parents having emigrated to America at an early date in this country's history. Godfrey Lipe and wife emigrated to Cabarrus County N. C., and he was noted grain-grower, and withal one of the most practical farmers of the State, and it has been said of him that he drove the best team of horses from Cabarrus County to Charleston, S. C. They were the parents of four boys and three daughters, all of whom grew to maturity, viz., John, Henry Moses, Daniel, Sarah, Catharine and Eula all of whom married in North Carolina, and of whom John and Daniel were the only ones that ever left their native State. John, the father of our subject, was born in Cabarrus County, N. C., in 1789. His early life was spent upon the homestead farm, and eventually he became the owner of land, married and raised a family of eleven children, with whom, in November, 1831, he emigrated to then distant wilds of Illinois, and located in Irving Township, where he entered a tract of wild prairie, which he eventually improved, and by his energy and industry accumulated a large amount of this world's goods, and at one time owned about 500 acres of choice land; although he had but a practical education, he was considered a good business man, and a practical farmer; he lived to see his youngest child married and a mother, and could say he never saw one of his family die. His death occurred in November, 1857. His wife, Rachael Blackwelder, was also a native of Cabarrus County, N. C., born in 1793. She was a kind parent, a true, sincere and consistent Christian woman; she died November 30, 1881, and which is something remarkable, was at the time of her death the mother of thirteen children 131 grand-children, 243 great grandchildren, and 21 great-great-grandchildren making a grand total of 408 descendants, of which at the time of her death, there were living 304. Her own children were, viz., Barbara, was married in North Carolina to Michael Hefly, and moved to Illinois in company with her parents, and settled in Irving Township, died about 1872; Nelson, also married in North Carolina, and came to Illinois with his parents, and settled near the homestead, died November, 1879; Allen, married in Illinois, was the third settler in Rountree Township, died in 1856; Ella, wife of Daniel Bost, died about 1862; Noah, our subject; Delila wife of Michael Walcher, living in Irving; Wiley, living in Rountree; Elizabeth, resident of Irving, wife of Milton Nisler; Helena, married Moses M. Sickles, located in Witt Township, died about 1874; John G., living in Rountree Township; Martin, died in 1879; Catharine, wife of James Morram, Irving Township; Crissa Diana, wife of James T. Fite, Zanesville Township. Noah was the fifth child, and was born in Cabarrus County, N. C., January 20, 1818, where his early childhood was spent in assisting his father in his agricultural pursuits upon the homestead farm. At the age of fifteen, he was removed to Montgomery County, Ill., by his parents, and remained with them until he reached the age of twenty-four, and assisted his father in improving and cultivating the farm upon which he settled. At that early day there were no schools, but eventually a subscription school was started, which he attended about one month; he has, however, obtained more than an ordinary education by close observation and close study at home. He was married in Montgomery County, May 12, 1842, to Miss Elizabeth Weller, who was born in Ohio April 11, 1822, and came to Illinois with her parents when she was about eighteen years of age. She has borne him eleven children, viz., Columbus J., born December 16, 1843, a prominent merchant of Vincennes, Ind.; Martha Jane, born March 18, 1845, died September 13, 1845; John W., born March 6, 1847, died August 3, 1863; Lorenzo Dow, born September 17, 1849, a prominent farmer living near the homestead; Mary M., born May 17, 1851, wife of John Kerr, living in Rountree; Kittie R., born December 5, 1852, wife of Erastus Shere, living in Rountree; Charles E., born February 3, 1855, farmer living near here; Angelia born December 28, 1856, wife of James Simms, living in Rountree; Alice, born April 8, 1859, at home; Etta, born December 11, 1860, at home; Nettie, born February 14, 1863, died April 27, 1864. Mrs. Lipe was a daughter of John and Mally (Lingenfelter) Weller, a native of Stark County, Ohio. He died in 1843; she is still living in Rountree Township with her son Jacob, a wealthy farmer. At the age of twenty-four years Mr. Lipe left home, and entered upon his career in life as a farmer, locating in Rountree Township, where he began life in a small way; built a small log cabin, having a sod chimney (the largest farm in the township was surrounded by a sod fence, containing sixty acres). He has gradually added to his possessions until at one time he had the satisfaction of conducting a farm consisting of 500 acres which represented the dollars earned by himself, the result of energy, enterprise and good management. He has a farm now under a high state of cultivation and is improved by buildings and all the necessary appliances for comfort and convenience. He has given all his children a good education, realizing from his own limited privileges how important a good education is to the rising generation. He has held the offices of School Director and Trustee in the township. Himself and wife are connected with the Methodist Episcopal Church. He has been a member of a Christian Church about forty-two years. His uncle Dan came to Illinois and settled upon a tract of land adjoining that of our subject, in the year 1839, where he lived until 1869, and where he raised a large family; he is now located in Whiteside County. Two of his sons are Lutheran preachers; all the balance of his family held prominent positions.

ELI NUSMAN, farmer, P. O. Irving, was born in Hillsboro, Montgomery Co., Ill., April 9, 1824. His father, John Nusman, was born in Cabarrus County, N. C. He was a farmer by occupation, came to Hillsboro, Montgomery County, in about 1820, where he remained about ten years, and then removed his family to Rountree Township, where he was one of the first settlers, and where he remained, engaged in agricultural pursuits, up to the time of his death, which occurred May 27, 1852 aged about seventy-five years. His wife, Catharine Fogleman, was also a native of Cabarrus County, N. C., born in 1791; she died August 13, 1846. She was the mother of eleven children, of whom Eli, the subject of this sketch was next to the youngest child. As school privileges were very limited at that early day, he was unable to receive such an education as he would have liked; however, by contact with the world, and by observation, he has accumulated more than an ordinarily practical education. His early childhood was employed upon his father's farm, in assisting him in improving the place, and at the death of his parents remained upon the homestead, which he has never left, and which he has at the present time in a high state of cultivation. Mr. Nusman is considered one of the most popular men in the township, and also ranks with the practical farmers of the County. He was married in Montgomery County, May 6, 1858, to Sarah Elizabeth Liticker, who was born in Cabarrus Co., N. C.,

April 6, 1840. They have six children, viz.: Harriet Catharine, born April 15, 1859; Peter, born March 19, 1861; Mary Emiline, born March 16, 1863, Clara Henrietta, born January 12, 1866; Nellie Jane, born March 27, 1868; Elizabeth Nora, born December 12, 1869; all of whom are living. Mrs. Nusman is a daughter of Arba and Mary Ann (McCoy) Liticker, natives of North Carolina, both still living in Montgomery County. Mr. Nusman has in his possession about three hundred acres of choice farm land, upon which he grows the usual farm crops and raises all kinds of stock usually found upon a well-regulated farm. Although not much interested in politics, Mr. Nusman is identified with the Democratic party. He is a man who ranks very high socially, and now in his declining days he is enjoying the fruits of an energetic and prosperous career, surrounded by his family of children, all of whom are living at home. Elizabeth Nusman, a sister of Mr. Nusman, is also one of the household, they having always lived together since childhood. There are but two others of the original family living, viz., John L., at Ramsey, and Sarah, wife of J. Kennedy, living in Missouri. At an early time in his life, Mr. Nusman was considered a great hunter, and while still a small boy he shot and killed two deer, in the morning before breakfast, and has since killed four in one day. Mr. N. is the oldest living first settler in township.

JOSEPH WALERS, farmer, P. O. Morrisonville, was born in the Parish of Christ Church, South Wales, Great Britain, March 18, 1835, where he received a common school education, and at the age of sixteen years was apprenticed to learn the trade of boiler-making, at which occupation he was engaged about four years. Arnold Walers, the father of our subject, was also a native of South Wales, and was a railroad and turnpike contractor by occupation. His death occurred in about 1843, aged fifty-three years. His wife, Mary Pierson, was also a native of South Wales. She died March 5, 1855, aged about fifty-five years. The result of this union was five children, viz.: Henry, a contractor by occupation, and was assisting in constructing the railroad across the Isthmus of Panama, when he was taken sick with the yellow fever, and died in 1863; John, an attache of the British Navy, supposed to be still living; Maria, wife of John Green, now living in South Wales; Ann, wife of William Bailey, living in South Wales. Joseph, the subject of this sketch, at the age of twenty years, emigrated to America, and eventually went to New Jersey, where his brother Henry was at that time engaged in constructing turnpikes; Joseph also engaged in the same occupation, at which he remained about four years, at the end of which time he turned his face toward the setting sun, and eventually located in Jersey County, Ill., where he took upon himself the duties of a farm life. In the fall of 1866, he purchased the property upon which he now resides, and removed with his family to their future home in Rountree Township, where he has since remained engaged in agricultural pursuits. His original purchase consisted of ninety acres, to which he has continued to add until now he has the satisfaction of conducting a farm consisting of about one hundred and seventy-five acres of as choice and well-cultivated farm land as can be found in Rountree Township, the result of energy, enterprise and thorough business habits; being a progressive man himself, he is fully alive to all progressive movements favoring the prosperity of the county, and for the advancement of religious and educational privileges. He is now filling the office of Justice of the Peace, the duties of which office he has performed two terms previous to the present, and which duties he has performed with honesty and integrity, and in a manner approved by all the people. He was married in New Jersey, to Delilah Connovar, who was born in New Jersey to Peter

Connovar, native of New Jersey, deceased, in August, 1835. She is the mother of three children, viz.: Mary, wife of Frank McNorton, living in Rountree Township; Emma, wife of John McCallum, living near the homestead; Hattie, single, living at home. Mr. Walers is identified with the Democratic party, and is always interested in the political issues of the times.

IRVING TOWNSHIP.

SAMUEL T. BARTLETT, dry goods, drug store and farmer, P. O. Irving; born in Henry County, Ky., in 1819. He is the second son of a family of eight, born to Samuel and Elizabeth (Owens) Bartlett, natives of Virginia. Samuel was born about the year 1777; came to Kentucky when a young man, and settled in Henry County, where he farmed and taught school. In 1833, came to Illinois, where he died April 29, 1835. His wife Elizabeth was born about the year 1786, and died in Illinois in 1858. Subject received his education principally in Illinois in the common schools. In Montgomery County, October 2, 1838, he married Martha Maxey, who was born in Warren County, Ky., about the year 1820. She is the daughter of Edward and Elizabeth (Berry) Maxey. He was a Virginian by birth, removed to Kentucky, then came to Illinois, where he died in 1860. His wife was a native of Kentucky, and also died in Illinois in 1837. To Mr. and Mrs. Bartlett have been born nine children, seven now living—John, Charles L., Edward, Henry, Hiram, Douglas and Mary; George and Jane, deceased. Mr. Bartlett still carries on farming, in connection with his other business of dry goods, drugs, etc., in which he has been engaged since 1869. He has held the offices of Township Treasurer and Deputy Sheriff for eight years. Mr. Bartlett and wife are Methodists. He is a Democrat, and a member of the I. O. O. F. He owns about seven hundred acres of good prairie land, nearly all of which is under cultivation, besides town property, consisting of five dwellings and one business house. His son Henry assists him in the dry goods department, and his son Douglas in the drug department of his business.

THOMAS G. BLACK, farmer and grain dealer, P. O. Irving, was born in Kentucky February 21, 1828, son of James B. and Mary G. (McCaslin) Black, he, a farmer, born in Kentucky October 7, 1799, died about the year 1876; she, born July 3, 1793, died September 14, 1836. Subject, the second child of a family of four children, came to Illinois with his parents when three years of age, and stayed one year in Bond County; then moved to Montgomery County, where he received his education in the common schools. He assisted his father on the farm till he was twenty-one years of age, then engaged in the tanning business, which, not proving satisfactory, he abandoned, and began farming. He bought a farm in 1853, but sold it in 1854, and moved to the town of Irving, where he and James N. Berry built the first business house in the place in 1855, and engaged in the mercantile and grain trade, which he followed for twenty years, when he bought the place where he now lives, about a half mile from Irving, and engaged in his present occupation of farming and stock trading, which he carries on successfully. In 1852, he married Nancy A. Whitlidge, a native of Illinois, who died February 21, 1857; her parents were natives of Kentucky. From this union three children were born, one only now living, viz., Mary M. His second wife, Sarah E. Berry, was born February 18, 1838; her parents were natives of Kentucky. She has borne him ten children, of whom eight are living. Mr. Black served in the army three months in 1862, as Lieutenant of Company C, Seventieth Illinois Volunteers, principally on guard duty; has been Supervisor of Irving Township for two terms, was Chairman of the Committee of the Poor Farm, and has done much toward the improvement of the town. He is a Republican, and a member of the Masonic fraternity.

W. MILTON BERRY, of the firm of Kelly & Berry, dealers in general merchandise, was born in Woodford County, Ill., in 1850, and came to this place in 1870. His father, William S. Berry, Sr., was born in Virginia in 1807, but was raised in Kentucky. Came to Illinois when a young man, and settled first in this county, afterward in Woodford County, thence to Wisconsin, whence he returned to this place, where he now resides. The maiden name of his wife, the mother of our subject, was Catharine Johnson, born in Ohio in 1808; both parents are still living and in good health. They had four sons and three daughters. Our subject studied at Eureka, Ill., taking a classical course at Christian College, though leaving a year before the time for graduation. He followed teaching for seven years, five years being spent at Irving. He was married in this place, May 9, 1876, to Kansie L. Kelly, who was born in this county in 1856. His wife's father was James Kelly, a native of Kentucky, who came to this State when a young man. Mr. Berry began at his present business of general merchandising in 1876, and now has a fine trade, carrying a large stock of goods for a small town. He has been Treasurer of the town for the past three years. He owns a good two-story frame residence, one of the prettiest in town, recently built, and has a farm two miles south of town, containing 136 acres of good land, with a hedge fence around nearly the whole of it, and has a half-interest in the stock and business of the firm of Kelly & Berry. He has one daughter, Eunice Ray. Himself and wife are members of the Christian Church, and he is a Republican.

MONROE BOST was born in North Carolina in 1833, and came to Macoupin County, Ill., when twenty-seven years of age, and remained one year; he then moved to Montgomery County and bought the place he now owns, in Irving Township, his first purchase being sixty acres, and has added to that until he now owns 140 acres of good tillable land, on which he has erected a good dwelling and barn, and all necessary outbuildings, and was married, in this State, the 20th of December, 1860, to Miss Rebecca Lipe, she being the mother of eight children, and died December 3, 1877; Wilson Lipe, her father, was born in North Carolina; occupation, farmer; and died in 1881; Nancy Lipe, her mother, was also a native of North Carolina, and still living in this county. Levi Bost, his father, was born in North Carolina about 1806; occupation, farmer; Catharine Raymer Bost, his mother, was also born in same State, about 1812; she was the mother of ten children, the subject being the third child. His second wife, Elizabeth Easterdy, was born in this State April 27, 1852; wife is a member of Lutheran Church, and he is a member of Presbyterian Church; he is a Republican.

NATHAN CANNON was born in North Carolina in the year 1815, and worked on the farm during his minority, following that occupation eight years, when he learned the carpenter's trade, which he followed in connection with farming, and sold out his place in North Carolina and moved to Alabama, where he remained a number of years engaged in farming, and moved from there to Arkansas, and was engaged in cotton speculation and farming; he remained a few years, and came to Hillsboro, Montgomery County, and was a grain and stock dealer, and moved to the town of Butler in 1865, and engaged in lumber and carpenter business, where he remained four years, and was also in mercantile business one year; in 1870, moved to the town of Irving; went into the mercantile, lumber and grain business with his sons; they carried on the business for six years, and has been in the grain and farming business up to the present time, and has bought several tracts, until he has reached the handsome estate of 239 acres, all in Section 15, Irving Township, and has it all in a good state of cultivation. He was married, in North Carolina, in 1834, to Miss Anna M. Slough; she was a native of North Carolina, born in the year 1819; her parents were natives of the same State. William Cannon, the father of subject, was born in North Carolina in 1783; his occupation was farming; died in 1819; Keziah L. Cannon was born in Virginia in 1785, and was the mother of seven children, the subject being the sixth child, and he has a family of eight children, four of whom are dead; those living are as follows: Marquis De L., Robert E., William S., Louisana. He and family are members of the M. E. Church; he has been Deacon since 1855; politically, conservative; he is a Mason, belonging to Irving Lodge, No. 455; he has always been prominent in the advancement of public improvements and agricultural interests, and has been moderately successful in all of his business transactions.

JULIUS CARRIKER was born in this county in 1856, August 8, and assisted his father on the farm until twenty-one years of age; was educated in common schools of country, and entered on his business career as a farmer and running a threshing machine; has always remained on the old homestead, and is now in full possession, having bought out his father; he has a beautiful home, with all necessary buildings and modern improvements to make agriculture a success; he has the name of being an energetic and enterprising young farmer; married, in this county, in 1877, to Miss Lizzie Moraine; she was born in this county in 1858, and is the mother of two children, Pearla and Stella; James Moraine, her father, was born in Madison County, Ohio, February 24, 1828, and is a farmer by occupation; was brought to this State at ten years of age by his parents, and has been a very successful farmer, accumulating a large tract of land; her mother, Sarah (Lipe) Moraine, was born in this county January 10, 1832; her parents were natives of North Carolina, and are all large land-owners. His father, John Carriker, was born in North Carolina, and has accumulated a large landed estate, which he has divided among his children, and retired to a comfortable home in the town of Irving, and is doing a small nursery business; his mother is also a native of North Carolina, and is the mother of nine children, the subject being the sixth child. They are blessed with a beautiful home and two lovely children; are members of Lutheran Church; he is a Democrat.

DOLPHAS CARR, farmer, P. O. Irving, was born in North Carolina February 9, 1852, and came to this State when fifteen years of age; was partially educated in North Carolina; finished in this State, in common school of country, and worked on the farm by day labor until he bought the place on which he now resides, containing 100 acres of well-improved land, with good, comfortable buildings; married, September 19, 1878, to Miss Alice Cline; she was born in this county September 9, 1862; Nelson Cline, her father, was born in North Carolina; her mother was also a native of same State, born about 1815, still living. John Carr, his father, and also his mother, were born in North Carolina; she was the mother of the one child, and he has only one child, Charlie Carr; are members of Lutheran Church; politically, Republican.

GEORGE H. FILE was born in North Carolina June 12, 1828; was brought to this county when three years old, by his parents, and worked on the farm until he became of age, and bought a piece of land near his father's, containing 190 acres; he made the first payment by raising castor beans, which he sold for $1.25 per bushel, hauled to St. Louis, seventy-five miles, which was the only market at that day; the yield was about eight bushels per acre, the most paying crop at that time—in fact, the only crop at that early day that brought the cash. Mr. File was married, in Montgomery County, in 1852, to Miss Susanna L. Cress, daughter of Absalom Cress. At the time of his marriage, he had improved about thirty acres and built a small frame house, which he occupied the first year without plastering; in one year after, he sold that place for $7.50 per acre, and purchased his present home, containing 180 acres of land, with sixty acres improved, and the only building being a log cabin, and afterward added to his first purchase seventy-six acres, on which he has built all necessary improvements, at considerable cost, and has his place under fine cultivation; he has turned his attention to fine cattle, and is making his preparations to go into the stock business. Jacob File was born in North Carolina, Cabarrus County; Caroline Cress, his mother, was also born in same State and county; she was the mother of nine children, our subject being the second child; his wife's father was born in North Carolina; also mother. The subject has had nine children, five of whom are living--Mary Frances Drew, Clara M., Lawrence A., William H., Francis L.; members of Lutheran Church, which they joined while quite young; he has always been identified with the Democratic party.

THOMAS GRANTHAM, restaurant, born in Montgomery County, Ill., April 12, 1841, son of Ezekiel and Eleanor (Wiley) Grantham, he a native of Kentucky, she the mother of fourteen children, Thomas the twelfth child. Our subject was educated in the common schools of Montgomery County, and worked on his father's farm till he arrived at the years of manhood, when he enlisted in Company F, One Hundred and Twenty-sixth Infantry, under Capt. J. H. Cabrick; was detailed on the bakery department, and on guard duty; served three years, and was honorably discharged. Returning to Irving, he engaged in the grocery business about a year, then ran a threshing-mill, and worked out by the day; engaged in the dairy business about thirteen months, and then in the bakery business, and now owns an interest in a restaurant in Irving, doing a good business. In Montgomery County, Ill., October 11, 1866, he married Miss A. L. Saylor, born in Ohio in 1847, who has borne him six children, viz.: Jay V., Lola V., Laura J., Alvee C., Theresa M. and Harry V. The parents of Mrs. Grantham were natives of Ohio, and died in Marion County, Ill. Mr. Grantham and wife are members of the M. E. Church; he is a Republican.

I. L. GREGORY, farmer, P. O. Irving, was born in Montgomery County, Ill., April 22, 1851, son of David E. and Rebecca (Cress) Gregory, natives of North Carolina, he, a farmer and wheelwright, born December 1, 1809; she, born February 12, 1812; they are now residents of the town of Irving, are hale and hearty, and enjoying the comforts of their snug home, having retired from active life, leaving their son on the farm; of their six children, Irvin, our subject, is the fifth child; he received a rudimentary education in the common schools of the county; afterward attended Carthage College a year, and finished at Hillsboro, Ill.; he assisted his father on the farm until twenty-six years of age, when he began farming on his own account, on the homestead place, where he is doing well. In Montgomery County, he married Helen Thumb, a native of that county, born in 1859, who has borne him five interesting children, viz.: Ethel, Marvin, Iva, Rolland and Rosa.

The parents of Mrs. Gregory were born in New York; her father, Marion Thumb, was a farmer by occupation. Mr. Gregory is a Democrat; his wife is a member of the Lutheran Church.

SAMUEL F. KING, farmer and lawyer, Irving, was born in Lincoln County, Tenn., in 1825, son of Andrew and Hannah (Guttis) King; he, a farmer by occupation, born in North Carolina, died in 1856; she, born in Orange County, N. C., died in 1853; she was the mother of eleven children, subject being the tenth child. He came to Illinois with his parents when six years old, and settled near Irving; received a rudimentary education in the common schools of Montgomery County; also attended the high school at Hillsboro, Ill.; after finishing at Hillsboro, he taught school and devoted himself to the study of law; in 1865, he returned to Irving, where he carries on farming in addition to the practice of the legal profession; he was also engaged in the produce business, but sold out quite recently. In Shelby County, Ill., in 1851, he married Narcissus E. Bivins, who died of cholera in 1855; of her two children, one is living. His second wife, Zenobia Kershner, has born him six children, of whom one died. Mr. King served in the Mexican war five months in 1846. he is a Democrat, and a member of the Free M. E. Church.

ISAAC LEWEY, farmer, P. O. Irving, was born in North Carolina November 5, 1822, and came to Montgomery County in June, 1843, and was in the Mexican war in 1846 and 1847; was discharged on account of ill health, came back to Irving Township, and commenced farming on land he received for his services in the war, and has added to that until he now owns 400 acres of good tillable land, on which he has erected a very good in dwelling and very fine barn, and everything in proportion. He married Miss Brown in 1847, in this county, her parents being natives of Tennessee; three children were the result of this union; she, the mother, died March 12, 1855, and his second wife, Miss Elizabeth Griffith, was born in this State in 1831; John Griffith, her father, was born in Tennessee in March, 1808; occupation, farming; Harriet (Pyatt) Griffith, her mother, was born in 1811, in Tennessee, and she was the mother of ten children. The father of our subject, John Lewey, was born in North Carolina; occupation, farming, and died about 1863; and his mother was also born in same State November 5, 1842, and she was the mother of fourteen children, the subject being the eighth child. He has a family of four children, and owns a nice home in the town of Irving, where he now resides and has it handsomely improved; members of Lutheran Church; politically, a Republican.

GEORGE W. LEWEY, farmer, P. O. Irving, was born in Montgomery County December 23, 1853, son of Isaac Lewey, a native of North Carolina. Subject received his early education in the common schools of Montgomery County, and finished at Carthage College; he also took a business course at the commercial College, Poughkeepsie, N. Y.; from Poughkeepsie he returned home and remained till he was twenty one years old, assisting his father on the farm; he then began his business career as a merchant in Nokomis, Ill., in partnership with T. H. Lane; at the end of a year, they moved their business to Witt, where they stayed nine months; then removed to Raymond, where they carried on their business successfully for three years; Mr. Lewey then sold out his share in the business, and bought a livery stable in Raymond; but, after being in the livery business nine months, he sold out and returned to the homestead farm, of which he has full charge and control, his father having retired from active life and moved to the town of Irving; the farm, which is an excellent one, has all the modern improvements. In Montgomery County, in October, 1877, he married Augusta F. Lane, a native of that county, born in March, 1857, daughter of J. B. and Susan (Bost) Lane, natives of North Carolina. Mr. Lewey is a Republican; his wife is a member of the Old Presbyterian Church.

JOHN T. McDAVID, Sr., farmer, P. O. Irving, born in Montgomery County, Ill., February 8, 1824, son of William McDavid, a native of Virginia, whose wife's maiden name was Johnson, she having been born in Tennessee September 20, 1800. Our subject was raised on a farm; received such an education as was afforded by the common schools of that early day, and began life for himself as a farmer in East Fork Township, his first purchase being eighty acres of land, which he traded for horses, on which he realized such a profit as to enable him to buy 123 acres in the year 1850, on which he resided for seven years; he then sold out and bought an adjoining farm of 175 acres, where he lived several years, also buying sixty acres near Hillsboro, on which he realized a handsome profit in a short time; he next sold his farm and bought 760 acres of good tillable land, and erected a fine dwelling, barn and other buildings; in 1881, he again sold out, and bought, in Shelby County, 175 acres of good farm land, north of Shelbyville, and he also has 266 acres in Irving Township, as well as eighty acres in East Fork; he has also helped all his six sons to start well in life. Mr. McDavid was married, in Montgomery County, in 1845, to Edna J. Knight, who was born in this county July 26, 1826, daughter of William Knight, of Kentucky, who was born in 1798, and died December 6, 1862; her mother's maiden name was Barsheba Bostick, born in Kentucky in 1800, and died February 9, 1860; Mrs. McDavid became the mother of six children, and died March 6, 1870. On August 6, 1871, he was married to Linda Snell, who was born and grew up in Macoupin County, Ill., where she received a good education; they have one son by this marriage, Frank Lee, born August 20, 1877. In addition to his other property, Mr. McDavid owns a house and lot in the town of Irving, where he resides, comfortably situated, and highly esteemed for his social worth and public enterprise; the children by his first marriage were Albin B., William J., John T., Jr., Joel K., Augustus B. and James L. Mr. McDavid was elected Sheriff in 1868, and served two years; he was also Deputy Sheriff four or five years; also Assessor; his family are members of the Presbyterian Church.

JAMES McDOWELL, merchant, Irving, was born in Adair County, Ky., February 14, 1842; came to Illinois in 1860 and settled in Montgomery County; his parents, John and Lucinda (Rippetoe) McDowell, were natives of Adair County, Ky., he, a farmer, was born in 1809, and died about the year 1850; she, born in 1811, died at her son's (subject's) residence in 1878; of their four sons, James is the youngest; he received his education in the common schools of Kentucky and began life as a teacher, and taught eighteen terms, he followed the trade of a house painter for a few years, and, in 1873, began mercantile business in Irving; he carries a good stock of goods, does an extensive trade, and is one of the leading merchants of Irving; he was Town Clerk of Irving Township for twelve months. At Beardstown, Cass Co., Ill., April 5, 1865, he married Caroline Wubker, born at Jacksonville, Morgan Co., Ill., March 20, 1845, who has borne him five children, viz.: Walter H., Lena L., Edward H., Albert L. and Clarence M.; her father, William Wubker, born in Minden, Prussia, February 10, 1816, came to the United States when but a small boy; her mother, Helena Maas, still living, was born in Hanover City, Hanover, Germany, August 21, 1818. Mr. McDowell owns a residence and business house in Irving; he is a Democrat; his wife is a member of the Cumberland Presbyterian Church.

ALEXANDER B. ROSS, farmer, P. O. Irving, was born in Center County, Penn., September 4, 1837, and was educated in the common schools of country, and was thrown on his own resources at the early age of fourteen years; his father sold him half-interest in stock and farm, and charged him 6 per cent interest on the investment; he went to work with energy, and, in the short space of three years, he was sole owner of the stock, and in six years he owned the entire interest. He went into the army in 1862, in Company G, One Hundred and Forty-eighth Regiment Ohio Volunteers, and was at the battle of Chancellorsville, where he received a flesh wound in the neck, and was in several battles afterward, and received a wound in the shoulder, which disabled him for a short time; he served in the Commissary Department; greatly to his chagrin, they would not let him go into active service again; he was mustered out, and went to his old home, and married, January 6, 1866, in Pennsylvania, Miss Anna M. Rhinehart; she was born in Pennsylvania February 23, 1841; her father, John Rhinehart, was also a native of Pennsylvania. Robert Ross was born in Pennsylvania in the year 1813, a farmer by occupation, and died July 6, 1863; Sarah McMitt Ross was born in Pennsylvania in the year 1820, and was the mother of eleven children, the subject being the eldest; he has a family of eight children, named as follows: Agnes was born June 10, 1867; Minerva B. was born July 25, 1868; Sarah J was born May 2, 1870; Harriet E. was born December 6, 1871; Thomas was born May 27, 1873; John Alfred was born June 4, 1875; Robert was born June 18, 1878; Penelope Frank, born December 3, 1881. He came to Montgomery County in 1875 and located in the town of Irving, where he remained only one year; in 1866, he bought his present home, and deserves great credit for the manner in which he has succeeded in getting his place in such fine state of cultivation; is a Republican politically; he sold a farm of 175 acres, when he emigrated to this place, at $60 per acre.

A. A. RHINEHART, farmer, P. O Irving, was born in Pennsylvania in 1839, April 10; raised in town, and educated at Potter's Bank, Penn.; remained with his father until eighteen years of age, when he commenced business for himself as a carpenter, which trade he followed two years; enlisted, in 1862, in Company D, One Hundred and Forty-eighth Regiment Pennsylvania Volunteer Infantry; was in several hard-fought battles; was wounded twice at the battle of Chancellorsville, only flesh wounds, however, which disabled him only a short time; at Five Forks he received a wound in the foot which disabled him for several months, and which gives him trouble at the present time if he does much walking on uneven ground; he went out as Sergeant; was promoted to Second Lieutenant in six months, and afterward to Captain of a company, which rank he held during the remainder of the service. He came to Illinois in 1866, and bought sixty acres of land, to which he has since added sixty acres more, making 120 acres of good farm land. He was married, in Pennsylvania, in 1862, to Miss Penelope McAlister, who was born in Bellefonte, Penn., in 1838; John McAlister, her father, was born about the year 1817, and died about the year 1859; Hannah (Thomas) McAlister, her mother, was born in Pennsylvania about the year 1825, and died in 1880. John Rhinehart, the father of subject, was born in Pennsylvania in 1817, and is now residing in Montgomery County; Rebecca (Taylor) Rhinehart, subject's mother, was born in Pennsylvania in 1820, also residing in Montgomery County, and is the mother of thirteen children, subject being the eldest of family. He has no children; he has raised a boy from eight years to twenty, and now has two little nieces whom he is raising. He and wife are members of the M. E. Church; he is a Republican, and is a member of the Masonic fraternity.

J. M. TAULBEE, dealer in provisions, and minister, Irving, born in Wilkes County, N. C., December 23, 1815; son of William H. and Nancy Taulbee, he, a farmer by occupation, born in Stokes County, N. C., October 21, 1791, died October 22, 1842; she, born in Rowan County, N. C., May 9, 1789, died August 14, 1837. Subject, the second child of a family of ten, spent his early days in assisting his father on the farm; he received his education in the schools of Kentucky, whither his parents had moved in 1817; in the fall of 1836, he removed to Fayette County, Ill., where he bought a farm, which he sold in 1853; he then came to Irving Township, Montgomery Co., Ill., where he followed farming during 1855 and 1856; he then moved to what is now the town of Irving, he being the first resident of the place. In Perry County, Ky., June 30, 1836, he married Ann Damrul, born in Morgan County, Ky., April 9, 1817, died June 28, 1853, in Fayette County, Ill., leaving six children; her father, Joseph Damrul, a native of Shenandoah County, Va., died October 15, 1840; her mother, Elizabeth (Dykes) Damrul, born in Floyd County, Ky., March 14, 1798, died October 24, 1839. Mr. Taulbee's second wife, Mrs. Prudence Carriker, whose parents were natives of North Carolina, was born in Tennessee in 1817; she is the mother of four children, two of whom are by her first husband. Mr. Taulbee was ordained a minister of the Gospel in 1851, since which time he has preached; he has now charge of three churches; he is a Republican; has filled the office of Justice of the Peace for twenty-two years, giving general satisfaction to all; he now owns a produce and feed store in the town of Irving, and does a good business; his children are Joseph E., Mary J., Levi L., William, Sarah A. and James P.; two of his sons were in the army during the war; the elder, who served four years, was wounded at the battle of Shiloh, came home and recruited in health, and returned to do battle for his country; the younger served three years.

WILLIAM W. WEBER, farmer and miller, Irving, was born in New York August 23, 1835; educated in common school of country; came to Montgomery County with his parents at eight years of age; settled in Butler Township, and worked on the farm until he arrived at his majority; commenced business saw-milling, and still keeps up that, with farming in connection; in 1862, he purchased 120 acres, to which he has added forty; he has built all the improvements, as it was all wild prairie when he settled; he first located his mill south of Irving two and a half miles, and ran six months, and then moved it to its present location, half a mile west of his present home; was married, in Montgomery County, to Miss Elizabeth Osborn, January 7, 1857; she was born in this county Dec. 30, 1835. The father of subject, Joseph Weber, was born in New York about 1803; occupation, farmer; died May 3, 1853; Eunice (Johnson) Weber, his mother, was born in New York in 1802, and was the mother of ten children, the subject being the sixth child, and he has a family of three children, one dead—William P., George E., Olive J.; one died in infancy. He was Road Commissioner six years, and was School Director for eight years, and now Trustee; member of M. E. Church; is a Republican; member of Odd Fellows.

SAMUEL R. WILEY, farmer, P. O. Irving, was born in Montgomery County, Ill., February 13, 1837, son of Zachariah and Elizabeth (Mann) Wiley; Zachariah Wiley, a farmer by occupation, was born in Virginia March 2, 1804; came to Montgomery County, Ill., in 1820, with his father, and took up a farm, where he died in 1842; his wife, who was the mother of six children, subject being the third child, was born January 11, 1806, and died in 1868. The subject of this sketch was educated in the common schools of Montgomery County; after his father's death, he took charge of the homestead farm, and managed it for his mother till he was twenty-eight years of age, when he began business for himself by purchasing a farm of 120 acres of land, to which he has since added 160 acres more, on which, at the time of purchase, was a small house, the farm, with the exception of thirty acres, being unbroken prairie; by industry and perseverance, he now has his farm in a fine state of cultivation, with comfortable dwelling, fine barn, and all necessary outbuildings; he raises quite a number of Short-Horn cattle, as well as horses and mules; has all the latest improved farm machinery. In Montgomery County, Ill., in 1862, he married Sophia A. Carriker, born in North Carolina in 1844, daughter of John and Mary L. Carriker, he, a farmer, born in North Carolina, is now living in the town of Irving; she, also a native of North Carolina, is the mother of seven children, all of whom are living. Mr. and Mrs. Wiley are members of the M. E. Church; they have six children. Mr. Wiley has been School Director for twenty years, and still holds that position; he is a Democrat.

EAST FORK TOWNSHIP.

JOHN P. BECK, farmer, P. O. Hillsboro, was born in Montgomery County, Ill., March 6, 1837, to John and Nancy (Blair) Beck, he a native of North Caorlina, and was one of the first to enter upon pioneer life in Montgomery County, where he engaged in milling, blacksmithing, coopering, distilling and farming at different times. He entered land in Town 7, Fillmore, Range 2, but at the time of his death had land also in Range 3. His death occurred in 1845. His wife, Nancy, was also a native of North Carolina, and died in 1851. She was the mother of ten children, of whom John, our subject, was the youngest child. His early childhood was spent upon the farm and in attending school at the neighboring log schoolhouse, to which his educational privileges were limited. At the death of his mother, which occurred when he was fourteen years of age, he left the homestead and engaged as a farm hand. At the age of twenty three, he had succeeded in accumulating enough funds to enable him to purchase twenty acres of timber land, and soon after purchased forty acres of prairie, upon which he made all the improvements himself, and to which he has continued to add, and now has in his possession 160 acres of choice farm land, all under a high state of cultivation. He grows all the usual crops, but makes a specialty of grain. He was married in Montgomery County, February 26, 1861, to Miss Nancy J. Brown, who was born in the same county November 15, 1839. She is the mother of five children, viz., Emma J., Mary C., George M., Nina and Laura L., the two oldest of whom died in infancy. Mrs. Beck was a daughter of Harrison Brown. Mr. and Mrs. Beck are connected with the Cumberland Presbyterian Church. Politically, he was formerly a Democrat, but now is considered independent in politics.

WILLIAM S. BARRY, farmer, P. O. Hillsboro, was born in Montgomery County September 18, 1841, to John and Elizabeth (Robinson) Barry. He was born in Barren County, Ky., in 1806. In 1834 or 1835 he emigrated to Montgomery County in Hillsboro Township, where he bought a small tract of improved land. He remained in Montgomery County to the time of his death, which occurred March 15, 18[illegible]6. He was of Irish descent. His wife and mother of our subject, was born in Warren County, Ky., in 1809, and died in Montgomery County, Ill., in 1868. She was the mother of nine children, of whom William S. Barry was the seventh child. His early life was spent in receiving such an education as the common schools of his day afforded, and assisting in tilling the soil of his father's farm. At the age of twenty two, he left home and embarked on his career in life by farming on his own account, on a farm of 140 acres of partially improved land, situated in Section 23, of East Fork Township. Here he has since remained, and by honesty, industry and economy, he has succeeded in accumulating 200 acres of land, all of which is under a high state of cultivation. Besides raising all the principal farm crops, he makes wheat a specialty. Mr. Barry was married in Montgomery County April 2, 1863, to Charity C., daughter of Jabez and Polly Ann (Lewey) Wheeler. Mrs.

Barry was born in Montgomery County, Ill., August 17, 1843. She is the mother of five children, four of whom are now living, viz., Minnie V., wife of Frederick Coffeen, of East Fork Township; Robert F., at home; Hattie, died August 28, 1867; Ina M., home; Fred, at home. Wife, of Cumberland Presbyterian Church. Mr. Barry has served as Highway Commissioner. Politically, he is independent.

GUSTAVUS F COFFEEN, farmer, P. O. Hillsboro, was born in Watertown, Jefferson Co., N. Y., June 19, 1820, to Frederick and Eleena (Hubbard) Coffeen, he born in Schuyler, Oneida Co., N. Y., about 1795, a farmer by occupation, and at one time was a hotel keeper, and dying about 1860. His wife, Eleena, was born in Jefferson County, N. Y., in 1798, and died about 1876. She was the mother of six children, four of whom are now living, and of whom Gustavus is the oldest child living. His paternal grandfather, Henry Coffeen, was the first settler in Watertown, N. Y., having penetrated from Lowville through the woods with his goods and family, drawn by an ox-team. He erected his hut on the ground just west of Iron Block. He was a very prominent merchant and speculator in land. Gustavus, the subject of this sketch, received a common school education in his native town, and spent his early childhood in assisting his father in his agricultural pursuits. At the age or eighteen years, he entered a hotel in Jefferson County with his father, where he remained about fifteen years, at the end of which time he turned his attention to railroading, which occupation he followed about two years in New York, and then came to Illinois, and continued in the same business about two years more, when he turned his attention to farming, and in the spring of 1855, purchased 1,140 acres of wild prairie land. He remained upon the same about eighteen months, and improved about one hundred acres. He then disposed of his property and purchased 160 acres of improved and forty acres of timber land in East Fork Township, where he has since carried on farming more or less extensively. Grows all the usual farm crops, and raising and dealing in stock. His farm now consists of 640 acres of choice farm and timber land. In 1862–63, he served a term in the House of Representatives from Montgomery and Christian Counties; has also served as Supervisor. He was married, November 9, 1846, to Miss Mary Adelia Bell, born in Herkimer County, N. Y., February 2, 1827. She is the mother of three children, viz., Frederick H.; Mary, wife of John McLean, living in East Fork Township; Clotilda Bell, wife of Dr. J. T. Hendrix, deceased. (See history.) Mrs. Coffeen is connected with the Presbyterian Church.

GEORGE C. CAMPBELL, farmer, P. O. Hillsboro, was born in Perry County, Mo., August 13, 1824, to Samuel and Margaret (Cowan) Campbell, he born in North Carolina, in Lincoln County, June 17, 1793, was a tanner by trade, but in 1819 emigrated to Missouri, and engaged in farming up to the time of his death, which occurred October 1, 1864. His wife, Margaret was also a native of North Carolina, born in Rowan County May 25, 1795, and is still living in Kansas, and is the mother of nine children, of whom George, our subject, was the third child; received his education in the common schools of Missouri. He remained upon the homestead until he was twenty four years of age, and entered upon his career in life as a farmer, in Perry County, Mo. In March, 1864, he removed to Montgomery County, and purchased 100 acres of land, which he disposed of five years later, and removed to his present place of residence, where he has about one hundred and twenty acres of choice farm land under cultivation. He was married in Missouri, October 31, 1849, to Miss Mary E. Smith, who was born in Cape Girardeau County, Mo., February 9, 1825. They have four living children, viz., Margaret J., Catharine E., Lamirah, Amanda M. and two infants deceased. Mrs. Campbell is a daughter of Matthew and Margaret (Wallace) Smith, natives of North Carolina, both deceased. Religiously, Mr. and Mrs. Campbell are connected with the Cumberland Presbyterian Church. Politically, Mr. C. was formerly a Republican, but now considers himself independent. Entered the service during the rebellion with Capt. A. C. Bishop, in Company H, of the Eighth Illinois Volunteer Infantry; remained in service about one year, and was in the engagement at Mobile.

HARDY F. JONES, farmer, P. O. Hillsboro, was born in South Carolina April 24, 1815, to James and Elizabeth (Toles) Jones. he, James, was born in America, but was of English descent. He died in 1816, aged sixty-four years. During his life he followed the occupation of a farmer. He served through the war of 1812. His wife, the mother of our subject, was born in Georgia in 1801, and died in 1854; she was of Scotch descent. She was the mother of eight children, of whom Hardy Jones was the sixth child. His early life was spent in receiving such an education as the log schoolhouse of his day afforded, and assisting in tilling the soil of the homestead farm. At the age of three years he was brought to Adair County, Ky., his father having died on the way before reaching their new home. At the age of twenty-one he left home and removed to Greene County, Ind., where he embarked on his career in life as a farm hand, by the month. In April, 1832, he removed to Montgomery County, Ill., and settled in East Fork Township, two miles east of his present residence; there entered eighty acres of land, forty in timber and forty in prairie. He remained upon this tract of land, making all necessary improvements and raising all usual farm crops, until March, 1877, when he bought his present residence and farm, and removed to the same, where he is still engaged in farming. By his honesty, industry and economy he has succeeded in accumulating 360 acres of land, most of which is under a high state of cultivation. In 1832, he married Matilda Nicholson, who was born in Kentucky, and died in 1863, aged fifty-two years. She was the mother of eight children, six of whom are now living—William, James, Joseph, Tabitha, Mary Ann and Rebecca In 1869, he married Mary C. Ragland; she was born in Virginia in October, 1832. She is the mother of two children, viz., Wilson S. and Eugenia. Politically, Mr. Jones is identified with the Democratic party. Mr. Jones remembers of hearing the first preacher deliver a sermon; his name was old Jimmie Street.

HENRY M. LUDEWICK, farmer, P. O. Hillsboro, was born in Montgomery County July 14, 1837, to Daniel F. and Nancy (Cress) Ludewick He was born in Cabarrus County, N. C., December 2, 1800. He emigrated to the State of Illinois, and settled in East Fork in 1831. During his life, he was engaged in farming, and at the time of his death had succeeded in accumulating eight hundred acres of land, most of which he entered, and made all improvements on the same. His death occurred May 4, 1849. He was of German descent. The mother of our subject was born in Cabarrus County, N. C., October 25, 1806, and died October 12, 1852; was of German descent. She was the mother of thirteen children, ten of whom lived to manhood and womanhood. Of the thirteen children our subject was the seventh child. His early life was spent in receiving such an education as the common schools of his day afforded, and in assisting in tilling the soil of his father's farm. He left home at the age of twenty-one, and embarked on his career in life as a farmer, upon eighty acres of prairie and forty acres of timber. His farm is located in Section 11, and by his energy and business habits he has succeeded in accumulating 340 acres of land. In 1862, on the 21st of February, in Montgomery County, he married Cynthia Williamson. She was born in Montgomery County in 1845. She is the daughter of John D. and Nancy G. (Card) Williamson. Mr. and Mrs. Ludewick have had five children, three of whom are now living, viz., Ina O., the wife of Henry H. Whitten, of Fillmore Township; Lowell W., at home; Olive Maud, at home; Robert Grant and Walter, dead. Member of the order of A., F. & A. M., at Irving, No. 455. Wife is a member of the Lutheran Church. Politically, he is identified with the Republican party.

WILLIAM C. McDAVID, farmer, P. O. Hillsboro, was born in Montgomery County, Ill., March 1, 1820, to William and Elizabeth (Johnson) McDavid. He was born in Scott County, Va., in September, 1790; when a boy, was taken to Missouri by his brother, and afterward went to Tennessee, where he joined the Seminole war, and also served through the war of 1812, under Jackson. During his life, followed the occupation of a farmer. In 1832, served six months in the Black Hawk war. In January, 1820, he emigrated from Tennessee to Montgomery County, and settled in East Fork Township, on the same farm that Thomas W., his son, is now residing on. His death occurred February 14, 1866. His marriage took place in Tennessee in 1819. His wife, and mother of our subject, was born in Tennessee September 15, 1800, and is now residing on the same farm where, with her husband, she settled in 1820; she is now enjoying good health. She is the mother of nine children, of whom William C. is the oldest child. His early life was spent in receiving such an education as the log schoolhouses of his day afforded, at that time having to walk four miles to school. He remained with his parents, assisting in tilling the soil of the old homestead farm until he was twenty-one years of age, when he embarked on his career in life as a hired hand upon a farm, and, in fact, doing all kinds of work. He continued in this way until he was about twenty-six years of age, when, with the savings of his meagre earnings, he was able to enter forty acres of prairie land; a portion of this same farm he is now residing on, and, by his economy and business habits, he succeeded in accumulating about four hundred acres of land, all of which he placed under a high state of cultivation. His farm now consists of 190 acres, he having divided his land among his children. On September 2, 1847, in Montgomery County, he married Lydia C. Wilson, a native of Harrison County, Ind., born April 11, 1826. She is the daughter of John and Ruth (Wilburn) Wilson, natives of North Carolina. Mr. and Mrs. McDavid are the parents of six children, four of whom are living—James S., Thomas J., Emily E. and John L. Mr. McDavid has held the office of Justice of the Peace in his township for twenty-eight years, and has never had a judgment reversed, and but few cases of appeal to higher courts. He is an active member of the A., F. & A. M. of Hillsboro. In politics, he is identified with the Democratic party. Self and wife are members of the Cumberland Presbyterian Church.

JAMES B. McDAVID, farmer, P. O. Hillsboro, was born in Montgomery County, Ill., March 31, 1821, to William and Elizabeth (Johnson) McDavid (see history J. T. McDavid), and his early childhood was employed in assisting his parents upon the homestead farm, and in attending the neighboring log schoolhouse common at that early day, and to which his educational privileges were limited; but he has, however, by observation, and in contact with the world, succeeded in obtaining a practical education, that is, perhaps, above the average. He remained upon the homestead farm until he was about twenty-seven years of age, when he married and entered upon his own career in life as a farmer, and moved upon the place upon which he has since resided, engaged more or less extensively in farming. His first real estate consisted of eighty acres of land, to which he has continually added, until he now has in his possession about one thousand and twenty five acres, the greater portion of which is under good cultivation. Although he grows all the usual farm crops, he has, during the last few years, made a specialty of grain, and has also been engaged quite extensively in handling stock. At present, however, he is, to a certain extent, retired from active labor and given place to younger men, who may do well to follow the example Mr. McDavid's life will afford. Mr. McDavid has held several of the county offices having served as County Assessor for a term of ten years, before the township organization. He is the present Township Assessor, the duties of which office he has filled for two terms before the present. He has also served the people as Justice of the Peace about one year, which position he resigned at the end of that time. He was married in Montgomery County February 29, 1848, to Miss Mary A. Burk, who was born in Smith County, Tenn., December 26, 1827, and was brought to Illinois by her parents when she was about two years of age. She is the mother of one child, William A., who was born April 23, 1854, and is now a prominent young farmer living near the homestead. Mrs. McDavid is a daughter of Andrew and Rachel (Burnette) Burk, natives of Tennessee, both deceased. Mr. McDavid served in the Mexican war about nine months, and was discharged on account of sickness. He has always taken a lively interest in the political issues of the day, and has always been identified with the Democratic party. Himself and wife are connected with the Presbyterian Church. He has also been a member of the A., F. & A. M., at Hillsboro, for a number of years.

T. W. McDAVID, preacher and farmer, P. O. Hillsboro, was born in Montgomery County, Ill., September 6, 1833, to William and Elizabeth (Johnson) McDavid. His early life was spent upon the homestead farm assisting in tilling the soil of his father's farm, and receiving such an education as the common schools of his native county afforded, and a few months at the Hillsboro Academy. At the age of twenty-three, he commenced teaching school, following the same in the winter, and during the summer he followed the occupation of a farmer. He followed teaching in the winter season for about six years. He became a candidate for the ministry in 1865, and was ordained in September, 1867, by the Vandalia Presbytery. His first charge was at home and Maple Grove, and held the former for seven and a half years, and the latter for six years. Since, he has served as pastor in the following churches, viz.: Mt. Tabor; Witt Church, four years; Cross Roads; at present, he is pastor Irving Church, C. P., Maple Grove. In connection with his pastoral duties, Mr. McDavid is extensively engaged in farming upon his farm of about four hundred acres; with the exception of eighty-four of timber, it is all under a high state of cultivation. In June, 1860, in Montgomery County, he married Louisa J., daughter of Richard and Tabitha (Vicars) Blackburn. Mrs. McDavid was born September 19, 1841, in Montgomery County, Ill. She is the mother of thirteen children, eleven of whom are now living — Emma D., Lizzie J., Frank M., Ella, Margaret, Annie, Albert C., James E., Minnie, Lester T. and Hattie. Family are all connected with his church, the Cumberland Presbyterian. He is a member of the A., F. & A. M., Hillsboro Lodge. Politically, is identified with the Democratic party.

WILLIAM A. McDAVID, farmer, P. O. Hillsboro, was born in Montgomery County, Ill., April 23, 1854, to James B. and Mary A. McDavid. (See history.) His early childhood was employed in assisting his father in his agricultural pursuits upon the homestead farm, and in attending the common schools of the neighborhood, where he received the foundation of his education. At the age of fifteen he entered the McGee College, at College Mound, Macon Co., Mo., where he remained two years, and then spent two years in Lincoln University, Lincoln, Logan Co., Ill. While at McGee he graduated in book-keeping. At the age of twenty-one years he left the homestead farm, and entered upon his career in life as a farmer, at which occupation he has since continued. In connection with his father he has farm lands numbering about one thousand seven hundred acres, the principal part of which is under cultivation. His residence is located about five miles east of Hillsboro, in East Fork Township, and is surrounded by all improvements necessary for comfort and convenience, and which shows Mr. McDavid to be a practical farmer. His farmhouse was built after his own design, and does honor to him as an architect, and his residence is spoken of as one of the finest in the township. He was married in Montgomery County, April 29, 1874, to Miss Martha J. Wilson, who was born in Montgomery County March 14, 1857. She is the mother of one child, Joseph C., born February 8, 1875. Mrs. McDavid is a daughter of Joshua H. and Sarah (Hutchison) Wilson, natives of Illinois, both deceased. Mrs. McDavid is connected with the Cumberland Presbyterian Church. Politically, Mr. McDavid's sympathies are with the Democratic party.

HIRAM SHEPHERD, farmer, P. O. Hillsboro, was born in Montgomery County, Ill., August 18, 1830, to Pleasant and Anna (Brown) Shepherd. He was born in North Carolina in 1803. When quite a young man he emigrated to Kentucky after a period of seven years; there married and removed to Illinois, and settled in Fillmore Township, Montgomery County. During his life he followed the occupation of a farmer. In the fall of 1832, he sold his property in Montgomery County, and returned to Kentucky, Adair County, and in the spring of 1833, returned to Montgomery County and settled in North Litchfield Township. Here he remained to the time of his death, which occurred April 10, 1834; at the time of his death he owned a farm of 120 acres. His wife, and mother of our subject, was born in Virginia in 1804, and died in 1848. She was the mother of eight children, Hiram Shepherd being the fifth child. His early life was spent in receiving such an education as the common schools of his day afforded, and in assisting in tilling the soil of his father's farm. In his eighteenth year he was left an orphan, and at that age embarked on his career in life as a hired hand, which he followed for one year, when he worked a farm on shares. In 1852, he went to California, and there followed gold mining. In 1854, he returned to Montgomery County, Ill., and embarked in a saw-mill business, near Litchfield. In 1856, he bought eighty acres of land, but soon traded the same for a 100-acre tract of partially improved prairie. He remained upon his farm about three years, when he sold out and bought 100 acres of the same farm he is now residing on. By his energy and business habits, he has succeeded in accumulating 200 acres of well-improved land, upon which he raises all farm products, but makes wheat, corn and oats a specialty, and aims to keep his farm well stocked. On October 21, 1857, in Montgomery County, he married Miss Nancy A., daughter of James and Sarah (Beer) Williams. Mrs. Shepherd was born in Washington County, Ill., December 10, 1832. She is the mother of nine children, viz., Anna E., Sarah E., Martha J., John P., Rosa A., Lillie L., Charles H., Hiram F. and Edward E. Politically, Mr. Shepherd is identified with the Democratic party.

JOEL C. TRAYLOR, farmer, P. O. Hillsboro, was born in Shelby County, Ky., October 6, 1814, to James and Nancy (Cardwell) Traylor, natives of Virginia. He died about 1850, aged about sixty-five; was a farmer by occupation. She died about 1822, aged about thirty years. She was the mother of four children, two of whom are still living, viz., William and Joel. The subject was educated in the common schools of his native State. When ten years of age, he engaged to learn the trade of harness-making; came to Montgomery County in 1844, and settled upon his present place of residence, and has been engaged in merchandising. His farm consists of about three hundred acres, which are worked by his children under his management. In 1874, he was appointed Postmaster, the office being in his house, and known as Ester Post Office. He was married in Kentucky to Julia Gibbs, a native of Kentucky, who died in 1845. His second marriage occurred April 3, 1846, to Sarah A. Ohmart, born in Ohio February 18, 1828. She is the mother of thirteen children, viz., Andrew J., George, Margaret, Joel C., Jr., Harriet, Mahlon, Jacob L., Robert J., Elva A., Bunyan H., Mary F., Clement A., infant son deceased. Seven of these children are now living. Mr. Traylor has served the people as Justice of the Peace about thirty years, and as Township Treasurer about twenty years. Politically, he is a Democrat; religiously, he is a Universalist.

AARON C. WILLIAMS, music teacher and farmer, P. O. Hillsboro, was born in Orange, Essex Co., N. J., August 13, 1830, to Ebenezer and Abigail (Crane) Williams. This family is of Welsh descent, amd emigrated to America early in the sixteenth century. Matthew Williams, the first, was born in 1651; supposed to have been born at Branford, Conn.; died in 1732. His wife, Ruth, died July 27, 1724, aged sixty-seven years. Matthew, the second, was born in Newark, N. J., in 1694, and died in 1772. His wife was Abby Brown, daughter of Thomas Brown. Isaac Williams was the oldest son of their six children, born November 6, 1722, and was the paternal great-grandfather of our subject. His wife was Eunice Pierson; they had eight children; Aaron was the fifth child; he was born July 5, 1759; married Mary Dodd, by whom he had five children, three of whom lived to be over eighty years of age. Ebenezer, the father of our subject, was the second son, born January 7, 1792. He was a carpenter by occupation, and served his apprenticeship in the city of New York. He died February 14, 1874. Two brothers and one sister of his were born, and lived to a good old age, and eventually died in the same house. His wife, Abigail B. Crane, was born in 1795, and is still living. She is the mother of nine children, only four of whom are now living, and of whom Aaron, the subject of this sketch, is next to the youngest child living. His early childhood was employed in attending the public schools of his native county, and in working with his father at his trade. At the age of eighteen he commenced the study of music, and soon after began to teach the same in the city of New York, where he remained until ill health compelled him to give up that occupation. In 1854, he turned his face toward the setting sun, and located in Jacksonville, Ill., where he again began to teach music, at which occupation he continued until 1871, in many of the principal cities of the East and West, viz., New York, Chicago, St. Louis, Quincy, Springfield and Jacksonville. In the spring of 1871, he went to Montgomery, Ill., where he purchased 160 acres of land, and in connection with the duties of his profession, he engaged in farming. He has now in his possession a farm consisting of [illegible] acres of choice farm land, located about two miles east of Hillsboro. In the spring of 1882, he erected a large and commodious farm residence, which is an honor to him as an architect, and is spoken of as one of the finest farmhouses in the county. He was married in Hillsboro, November 25, 1864, to Miss J[illegible] Elizabeth Brown, a native of Montgomery County, born January 8, 1837. They have four children living, viz., Edward E., Margaret A., Mary G., Alfred A. and Elizabeth Jeanette, who died in infancy. Mrs. Williams was a daughter of Maj. William and Elizabeth (Craig) Brown, natives of North Carolina, both deceased. Mr. and Mrs. Williams are members of the Presbyterian Church. Politically Mr. Williams is identified with the Republican party. He is one of those men who always take part in all progressive movements favoring the improvement of the county, and especially in the advancement of religious and educational privileges, and is a warm advocate of the cause of temperance.

ROBERT A. WILLIAMSON, farmer, P. O. Hillsboro, was born in Montgomery County, Ill., March 12, 1837. This family are of Irish descent, and emigrated to America at a very early day in this country's history. The paternal grandfather of our subject was born in Virginia, where he carried on farming, and raised a family of nine children, with whom he removed to Montgomery County, Ill., in the year 1835, where he died September 20, 1861, aged about seventy years. His wife, Jane Davidson, is of Welsh descent, and was born March 15, 1797, and is still living, enjoying as good, if not better, health, than persons usually do who have attained her age. Of her once large family six are still living, and of whom John, the father of our subject, was the eldest child, and was born December 15, 1814, and since he came to Montgomery County with his parents he has continued in the county, engaged more or less extensively in farming, and was at one time considered one of the leading men of the county, but has, to a certain extent, retired from active labor and given way to younger men, who may never be able to display more energy, enterprise and general activity than has Mr. Williamson, who, at the present time, is enjoying good health, and bids fair to live still many years, surrounded by his children, and enjoying the fruits of a well-spent life and successful career. His wife, Nancy G. Card, was born in Kentucky February 14, 1819, is still living, and is also hale and hearty. She is the mother of eleven children, of whom five are still living, viz.,

Robert A., our subject; Otis M. (see history); Cynthia J., wife of H. M. Ludewick; William C., a farmer living in Butler Township; Arra E., wife of W. C. Woodward, living on the homestead. Robert A., the oldest child and subject of this sketch, remained upon the homestead farm until he reached the age of twenty years, assisting his father in his agricultural pursuits, and in attending school in the neighboring log schoolhouse, to which his educational privileges were limited. He has, however, by contact with the world, close observation and reading, succeeded in obtaining more than an ordinary practical education. He entered upon his career in life as a house builder, comparatively a poor man; but, having a stout heart and an energetic spirit, he determined to make his own way in the world. He remained engaged in house building in different localities for about twelve years, and then went to Colorado, where he remained two years engaged in mining. He then entered the service during the rebellion in Company H, One Hundred and Forty-third Illinois Volunteer Infantry, with Capt. James G. Seward; regiment commanded by Col. D. C. Smith. He remained in the service until the close of the war, when he returned home, and took upon himself the duties of a farm life, at which he has since remained engaged. He has sixty-nine acres of choice farm and timber land under a high state of cultivation, which shows Mr. Williamson to be a practical farmer. Although he grows all the usual farm crops, he makes a specialty of grain, and raising stock in a small way. He was married in Montgomery County, September 20, 1866, to Mary E. (Cross) Ludewick, who was born August 18, 1848. She is the mother of two living children, viz., Della Reed and Katy Hays; four children died in infancy. Mrs. Williamson is a daughter of Absalom C. and and Katy (Fogleman) Cross, natives of North Carolina, deceased. Religiously, Mr. and Mrs. Williamson are connected with the Lutheran Church. He is also a member of the A., F. & A. M. at Irving. Politically, he is identified with the Republican party. He is an energetic and enterprising man, and socially enjoys the highest esteem of the entire community. He is a public spirited man, always interested in any county or public enterprise, and for the advancement of religious and educational privileges.

FILLMORE TOWNSHIP.

JOSEPH T. ALEXANDER, farmer, P. O. Fillmore, was born in this county September 17, 1834, and was raised to a life of farming; was educated in the common schools of the county, and commenced business for himself as a farmer, and inherited sixty acres of land, unimproved, on which he built all necessary improvements, and remained there sixteen years, and added to that forty acres, making one hundred acres in the tract; sold, and bought the place on which he now resides, and has erected a very elegant dwelling with all the necessary outbuildings, and has a beautiful location, the land being rolling enough to drain well, which makes it valuable, and was married in Fayette, May 3, 1859, to Miss Irene Wright. She was born in this State July 23, 1839, to Joseph Wright. Her father was born in Kentucky in 1813; was a farmer by occupation, and died November 27, 1873. Rebecca Kirk, her mother, was born in Tennessee in the year 1810, and died in the year 1876. They reared a family of six children, all living. Richard Alexander, the father of subject, was born in Tennessee January 10, 1810, and was a farmer by occupation. He came to this State when quite a boy, and enlisted in a company of rangers against the Indians, and lived and died on the place now owned by subject. His death occurred about May 12, 1874. Sarah Whitten was the mother of six children, the subject being the oldest child, and he has a family of four children, whose names are as follows: Eveline C., Easton W., Sarah R. and Homer L.; was elected Assessor and served one year, and has been Commissioner six years, and filled other offices of township. He belongs to the Masonic fraternity, and is identified with the Democratic party.

LYMAN C. ALLEN, Fillmore, was born in New Hampshire in the year 1836; worked with his parents until twenty-one years of age, and entered on his business career as a school teacher, and followed that profession for several years. He went to Minnesota in 1860, and pre-empted 160 acres of land, improved it, and remained there five years, at the expiration of which time he came back to Montgomery County, Ill., and settled on the farm on which he now resides, on which he has erected a good dwelling and barn, with all other buildings necessary for comfort and convenience. His farm contains 330 acres of good, tillable land; he also owns 400 acres of good farming and stock land in Minnesota. He married in Montgomery County in 1864, Miss Alice D. Bliss. She was born in this State in March, 1843, and was the mother of four children; she died in June, 1879. Her father, a native of Vermont, her mother born in New Hampshire are now living in this State. His second wife, Emeline Russell, was born in this State in February, 1846; was married in January, 1881. Her father, William Russell, was a farmer by occupation; her mother is still living in Montgomery County. Winslow Allen, the father of subject, was born in New Hampshire in the year 1800; was a farmer by occupation, and died in 1859. His wife, Nancy (Grout) Allen, was also born in New Hampshire in the year 1803, and died in 1856. She was the mother of eleven children, the subject being the sixth child, and he has a family of three children (one deceased), named as follows: Ned B., Jesse A. and Carlos E. Mr. Allen has been Supervisor for two years; he is a Democrat. His wife is a member of the Lutheran Church.

AARON G. BUTLER, farmer, P. O. Fillmore, was born in Tennessee January 1, 1838; was raised on a farm; educated in the common schools of the country, and remained with his father until twenty-one years of age. He began business for himself as a farmer, in this State, in 1860, with an uncle in Fayette County, with whom he remained about two years; then came to Montgomery County, and settled on the farm on which he now lives, which contains about six hundred and forty acres of land, four hundred of which are under cultivation, and has all necessary improvements. He also owns seventy acres of land in Fayette County, also improved. He married in Montgomery County in 1863, Miss Jane Casey, born in that county in the year 1847. Her father, John Casey, born in Kentucky November 26, 1825, a farmer by occupation, died August 5, 1863. His wife, Louisa McCaslin, was born in Tennessee November 29, 1825, and died in September, 1868. Calvin J. Butler, the father of subject, a farmer, born in Tennessee, died about 1872. Martha J. Hix, subject's mother, also a native of Tennessee, died about the year 1868. She was the mother of eight children, the subject being the second child, and he has a family of three children, viz., Charlie L., Ora and J. L. S. Mr. Butler was elected Sheriff in 1878, and served one term; has also been Supervisor two terms. He is a hospitable, genial and accommodating gentleman, and has a high social standing in his community. He is a Democrat, and a member of the A., F. & A. M. His wife is a Methodist.

LEVI HILL, farmer, P. O. Fillmore, was born in this county and State in the year 1825, and commenced life as a farmer. His father gave him 100 acres of land, and he has added to that until he has reached the handsome estate of 290 acres, on which he has erected a good and comfortable dwelling and barn, with all necessary improvements, and was married in this county in the year 1848, to Miss Wilmoth (Landers) Hill. She was born in this State in the year 1831. Henry Landers, her father, was born in Kentucky, and died in 1842. Elizabeth Hinton, her mother, was born in North Carolina, and died about 1868. She was the mother of six children, one deceased. Henry Hill emigrated to this State from Kentucky in 1816; he was a farmer by occupation; he entered quite a large tract of land; died April 5, 1855. Mary Prater, his mother, was born November 6, 1803; she died April 16, 1842. She was the mother of twelve children, the subject being the third of the family, and he has a family of seven children, three deceased; names as follows: Mary Hill, December 8, 1849; Henry E. Hill, July 11, 1851; Simeon M., December 15, 1852; Martha, January 22, 1857; Sarah, June 23, 1858; Orlena, February 10, 1860; Illinois, November 17, 1861; Layfayette, August 21, 1863; Celeste, July 9, 1868; Theodore Hill, born August 13, 1869.

SQUIRE HILL, farmer, P. O. Fillmore, was born in Montgomery County, Ill., January 17, 1844, and inherited 160 acres of land, located in Fillmore Township, on which were no improvements. This he sold and bought a place containing 160 acres of unimproved land, which he improved and lived upon about four years; sold out and bought the place on which he now resides, which contains 160 acres of good, fertile land, on which he has erected a fine dwelling and barn, with all necessary outbuildings. The farm is lo cated on Section 33, Town 8, Range 2, about twelve miles east and south of Hillsboro. He was married in Fayette County October 22, 1868, to Miss Mary L. Bost, born in Fayette County in 1849. Her father, Henry Bost, was born in North Carolina about 1826; was a farmer by occupation, and died in 1876. Her mother, Elizabeth (Harris) Bost, was born in Illinois. Henry Gill, the father of subject, was born in Kentucky; his wife was born in North Carolina. She was the mother of six children, the subject being the youngest child. He has a family of three children, one deceased, named as follows: Ollie O., born September 5, 1869; Henry C., born October [illegible], 1873; Anna E., deceased, born February 28, 1876, died August 26, 1876; Mary E. was born April 19, 1878. He has been Supervisor of this township for two terms. He enlisted in Company L, First Illinois Cavalry, in 1862, Capt. Paul Walters; principally on escort duty, and served a short time. He has been always identified with the Democratic party; has taken great interest in public improvements and the advancement of agricultural interest.

DR. JOHN A. HENDRIX, Fillmore, was born in Tennessee in 1845. Harrison Hendrix, his father, a merchant, was born in Tennessee. Elitha Taylor, his mother, was a descendant of President Taylor, and was the mother of four children, the subject being the second child. He was raised near Elizabethton, Tenn., and remained with his father until sixteen years of age. He then entered the Confederate army, in Company C, First Regiment Tennessee Artillery; was taken prisoner at the siege of Vicksburg; had taken part in several previous engagements; was sent to St. Louis prison, but, through the influence of President Johnson, was released in a short time. He remained in St. Louis six months after being released from prison; then came to Montgomery County, and settled in East Fork Township. He was married in 1865 to Miss Clotilda B. Coffeen, born in Jefferson County, N. Y., in the year 1850. She was the mother of five children, all living. She died March 9, 1875. His second wife, Dorcas F. Bost, was born in Illinois in the year 1857. Her father, Martin Bost, born in North Carolina, died about the year 1872. Hannah J. Bost, her mother, born in New Hampshire, is still living. Subject commenced the study of medicine in 1873, with Drs. Hayes & Washburn, of Hillsboro; remained with them three years; then attended Medical College in St. Louis, Mo., in 1877, and graduated at Keokuk, Iowa, in 1878. He first settled at Fairview, in June, 1879, and remained there until October; then removed to the place where he now resides, and bought fifteen acres of land, and has it well improved with all conveniences necessary. He is highly esteemed as a man, as well as a physician; has a good practice.

G. W. ISBELL, farmer, P. O. Hurricane, was born in Fayette County in the year 1855, and has a good practical education. He commenced business as a farmer, and took charge of his father's farm at the age of fifteen years (his father being an invalid), and remained in charge until twenty-three years of age; he then married and moved to Montgomery County, where he now resides. His first purchase of land was sixty acres, which were partially improved, to which he has added until he has reached the handsome estate of 235 acres of good, tillable land, on which he has erected a fine house, barn and outbuildings. It is considered one among the best improved places in the vicinity. He also owns, in Fayette County, 140 acres of land, the most of which is in a good state of cultivation. He was married in

Fayette County, in 1856, to Miss Mahala Hill. She was born in Kentucky; is the mother of six children four of whom are living. She died in May, 1873. Her mother, a native of Kentucky, is still living in Fayette County, Ill. His second wife, Theresa (Elam) (Mason) Isbell was born in Bond County, Ill., in 1848; married in Bond County in 1873. Her parents were natives of North Carolina, and both are now living in Bond County. James Elam, her father, is a minister of the Gospel. Paschal Isbell, the father of subject, was born in Kentucky in 1807, a farmer by occupation, and emigrated to this State in 1828 or 1829; settled in Fayette County, Ill., and died there in April, 1879. Clarissa (Seers) Elam, the mother of subject, was born in Kentucky in 1809, and is the mother of fourteen children, the subject being the fourth child. He has a family of seven children, five living, viz.: Diana, Melvina, William Jackson, Lewis, Jasper (deceased), Jennie (one died in infancy). His wife is a member of the Baptist Church; he is a Democrat. He has always been an advocate in favor of public improvements and agricultural interests. He started out to battle with the world without anything, but, being possessed of a stout heart and an indomitable energy, he has accumulated quite a fortune.

JOHN H. KNOWLES, farmer, P. O. Fillmore, born in Piermont, Grafton Co., N. H., March 16, 1822; raised on the farm. His boyhood days were spent in assisting his father; educated in the common schools of the country; entered on his business career as a farmer; brought to this county by his parents in 1838; settled near Fillmore Township, his father having bought land there, when subject commenced farming; stayed about three years; sold out and went to Vera; bought a half-interest in a mill, and operated that four years; sold out and bought a farm about a mile from the mill, containing 280 acres of land; remained there two years, and bought the place where he now lives containing 260 acres of land. He has all necessary improvements on the farm, and which is in a good state of cultivation. Subject was married at Vandalia, Ill., December 27, 1843, to Miss Sarah A. Casebeer, born in New Philadelphia, Ohio, March 1, 1827. Her father, Christian Casebeer, a farmer and millwright, born in Somerset County, Penn., February 1, 1803, and died October 8, 1849. His wife, Rosanna (Willson) Casebeer, still living, was born near Pittsburgh, Penn., May 17, 1807. The father of subject, Joseph Knowles, born in New Hampshire April 1, 1783, a farmer by occupation, died February 15, 1860. His mother, Hannah (Haines) Knowles, also a native of New Hampshire, born July 12, 1787, died October 31, 1865, was the mother of eight children, the subject being the fifth child. He has a family of four children, Dianna J., Lillie C. and Adel G., and one child deceased. He has been Deputy Sheriff and Constable for five years; also School Trustee for a number of years. Is a member of the Methodist Episcopal Church, a Mason and a Democrat; grandfather was in the Revolutionary war.

ALBERT LIVINGSTONE, farmer, P. O. Fillmore, was born in Amsterdam, Montgomery Co., N. Y., April 16, 1821; assisted his father in the tanning and coloring business in his boyhood days; was educated in the common schools of the country, commenced business for himself as a farmer, in this State, at twenty-two years of age; bought 80 acres of land, his first purchase, which was slightly improved, a log cabin being the only dwelling, and four or five acres of land broken. He has added to his first purchase until he now has 355 acres of good, tillable land, on which he has all necessary buildings

He gave his children 200 acres, north of the home tract, 160 of which is improved. He was married in Fayette County Febuary 26, 1846, to Ann Elizabeth Barringer, born June 17, 1824, in Cabarrus County, N. C., and died August 2, 1862, leaving nine children. She was the daughter of John M. and Crissey M. (Pitts) Barringer, he born in 1803, and died August 4, 1854; she born in 1805, and died in February, 1849. Jane Gatewood, his second wife, was born in Ohio, in the year 1832, and is the mother of four children. Her father, a native of Ohio, died in January, 1879. Her mother, a native of Virginia, is still living. Timothy Livingstone, the father of subject, was born in Massachusetts October 19, 1777, and died in 1861. His wife, Mary (Guran) Livingstone, born April 29, 1786, in Massachusetts, and died April 5, 1821, leaving nine children, of whom subject is the youngest. He has been Highway Commissioner for several years: also School Director for a number of years; has done all he could toward public improvements and agricultural interests; has always been identified with the Republican party. His children are Mary, born December 14, 1846; Joseph P., born June 9, 1848; Adeline, born February 25, 1850; Timothy A., born May 21, 1851; Catharine E., born February 4, 1853; Charles E., born April 2, 1855; George Albert, born September 3, 1857, and Alfred W., born February 22, 1861.

J. BOWERS LANE, farmer and merchant, Fillmore, born in Cheshire County, N. H., September 10, 1826. His father, Timothy L. Lane, was born in Marlboro, N. H., September 1, 1800; was educated at Groton, Mass.; afterward attended Medical College at Hanover, N. H., where he graduated in 1824; commenced the practice of his profession at Sullivan, N. H.; moved to Lunenburg, Vt., in 1832, and remained there two years, at the expiration of which time he located at Gilsum, N. H., where he remained until 1838; thence to Daysville, Ill., practicing his profession there until 1840; then removed to Fillmore Township, and continued his practice until his death, which occurred September 1, 1849. Roxana (Harvey) Lane, the mother of subject, was born in Marlboro, N. H., August 2, 1802, and died January 1, 1849; was the mother of four children, two of whom are living. The subject, the eldest of the family, was raised in town; was educated in the common schools of the country; entered on his business career as a farmer, his first purchase being ninety acres of land, to which he has added from time to time, until he has now a handsome estate of 650 acres of fine farming land. He has given his children 200 acres from that tract, and now has 450 acres on his home place, on which he has all necessary buildings conducive to the health and comfort of man and beast. He has also had a store on his farm since 1861, and is doing a good business: has been Postmaster for a number of years. His place was mostly raw prairie, and he has made all the improvements; was elected Associate Judge in 1869, and served four years, acquitting himself with honor. He is a stanch Republican. He married, February 3, 1852, Rachel G. Bost, born in North Carolina March 22, 1830, daughter of Jacob and Margaret (Cress) Bost, he born in Pennsylvania April 4, 1794; she born in North Carolina February 26, 1797, and died in May, 1853. From this union eight children have been born to them Timothy L., Margaret R., Torrance H., Augusta F., Ora E., Carrie M., Elsie V. and Ella L.

ASA PRATER, farmer, P. O. Fillmore, was born in Bond County December 10, 1829. Alexander Prater, his father, was born in Tennessee October 17, 1807. He was brought to this State by his father in 1818. Halloway Prater, the grandfather of subject, was born in North Carolina in 1777, of Scotch descent; was a farmer and wheelwright by occupation, and died in November, 1846. His grandmother, Anna Adair, was born in North Carolina about 1779. She was the mother of eight children; the father of subject was the fifth child, and married Mary Sears, the mother of subject. She was born in Kentucky about 1809, and was the mother of four children, one deceased, our subject being the second child; was educated in the common schools of the country, but has, by observation and application, a good practical education. He entered 120 acres of Government land which was slightly improved, paying $100 for the improved part, and has added to his first purchase 120 acres more, making 240 acres of good, tillable land, on which he has erected a fine house and barn, with all necessary improvements, and also owns about forty-three acres of timber. He married in this county Artemisia Brown Prater, who was born in this county November 10, 1830. She died June 9, 1857. As his second wife he married, in 1861, Sarah H. Brown, born December 1, 1836, and she is the mother of four children, all living; the names as follows: Horatio L., born February 13, 1862; Flora B., born August 13, 1864; Lillie May, born May 7, 1868; John H., born April 21, 1871. He was Town Clerk one year, in 1873. Members of Primitive Baptist Church; he is also a member of the Masonic fraternity; is identified with the Democratic party, and extremely liberal in his views. His grandfather was in the war of 1812; his father was in the Black Hawk war; has always been an advocate of public improvements, taking great interest in agriculture.

GIDEON RICHMOND, farmer, P. O. Fillmore, born in Licking County, Ohio, September 14, 1820; raised on a farm, and assisted his father until twenty years of age; was educated in the common schools of the country, and began his business career as a farmer, his first purchase of land being fifty acres, partially improved, on which he remained only two years; sold out and moved to Montgomery County, Ill., and bought 100 acres of land; has increased his property to 500 acres of good farming land. He has given his son eighty acres recently; has erected a fine dwelling and barn, with all necessary outbuildings, and his farm is in a high state of cultivation. He was married first in Ohio, to Miss Lois Ames, who died, and he then married Miss Cynthia Dota, also of Ohio, who died, leaving one child; her parents were natives of New Jersey. His third wife, Harriet A. Knowles, whom he married March 14, 1847, was born in New Hampshire August 11, 1830; her father, Joseph Knowles, was born in New Hampshire April 1, 1784; was a farmer by occupation, and died February 16, 1860. Her mother, Hannah (Haines) Knowles, was also born in New Hampshire June 29, 1788, and died October 31, 1845. Mrs. Richmond is the mother of four children. The father of subject, Henry W. Richmond, was born in Adams County, Mass., December 5, 1798; was a farmer by occupation, and died May 4, 1874. His wife, Eliza Cubberly, was born near Trenton, N. J., April 11, 1800, and is still living. She is the mother of three children, the subject being the eldest child. Mr. Richmond has by energy and economy accumulated a handsome property, and he and wife seem to be enjoying the fruits of their labor in their old age; is a good citizen and useful to the community in which he resides. His children are Henry F., Hiram F., George A., Dora L. and Ernest H.

G. A. RICHMOND, Fillmore, was born in Fillmore, Montgomery County, October 8, 1851; worked on the farm with his father until of age, and was educated in the common schools of the country. He commenced life as a farmer, and settled on the old home place of his fathers, beginning on eighty acres of land that his father had given him, to which he has added forty acres of good land, and has erected a good dwelling and barn, and all necessary outbuildings. He was married, September 18, 1877, at Irving, Ill., to Miss Addie Bost, born in Fillmore August 8, 1858, daughter of John J. and Rebecca M. (Sanders) Bost, he a farmer by occupation, born in Cabarrus County, N. C., January 4, 1836, and is still living; she, also living, born in Montgomery County, Ill., January 16, 1839. Gideon Richmond, subject's father, was born in Ohio in 1820, a farmer by occupation. His wife, Harriet Knowles, was born in New Hampshire in August, 1830, and is the mother of four children, the subject being the oldest of the family, and he has but one child, Nellie V., two and one-half years of age. Is a Democrat.

HIRAM S. SHORT, physician, Fillmore, was born in Randolph County, N. C., May 4, 1840. The main part of his early childhood was spent in attending the common schools, where he received the foundation of his subsequent learning. In January, 1854, he was removed by his parents to Fayette County, Ill., where they remained three years, and then removed to Shelby County. Lemuel Short, the father of our subject, a native of Guilford County, N. C., was born February 24, 1814, and from the time he reached maturity followed teaching until the time of his death, which occurred May 6, 1858. His wife, Mary Haskett, was also a native of North Carolina, born November 21, 1816, and is still living, the wife of John H. Buckmaster, residing five miles north of Vandalia. By her first husband she gave birth to eleven children, nine of whom are still living, and of whom Hiram S. was the second child. After reaching Illinois with his parents, he continued to attend the common schools for a short time, and then entered the Quaker High School of Westfield, Ind., where he remained one year and then returned home and taught school a large portion of the following four years, and a portion of which time, in connection with his other duties each year, he read medicine with Dr. J. C. Jones, of Ramsey, with whom he continued from 1865 to 1869, at the end of which time he entered upon the practice of his profession, and, after attending the Cincinnati Medical College two terms, he successfully passed the rigid examination necessary to become an M. D.; received his diploma May 19, 1873, and continued in his practice at Fillmore, where he first located. He removed to Ramsey in September, 1875, and remained until October, 1878, when he returned to Fillmore. His farm consists of eighty acres of choice farm land, which he now rents out and devotes his time to his calling. By his prompt attention to and thorough knowledge of his profession, he succeeded in building up a large and steadily increasing practice, the duties of which would fall heavy upon the shoulders of a man many years his senior, and is the result of a good education, energy and business ability, and qualifications necessary to gain the esteem of all. July 3, 1861, he entered the service in Company C, Thirty-fifth Illinois Volunteer Infantry, with Capt. James Williams, regiment commanded by Col. G. A. Smith. He received his discharge September 27, 1864. While in the service, he took part in several notable engagements, among which are Pea Ridge, Ark., Perryville, Ky., Stone River, Tenn.;

was also upon duty at the evacuation of Corinth, Miss.; also at the battle of Chickamauga, and in Sherman's campaign in Georgia. He was married, October 31, 1871, at Ramsey, Fayette Co., Ill., to Miss Sarah M. Stokes, who was born October 25, 1851. She is the mother of five children, viz., William T., born July 27, 1872; Mary L., born March 12, 1874; Emma E., born October 31, 1876; Ulysses S., born February 25, 1878; Walter C., born March 30, 1880. Mrs. Short is a daughter of Bird and Margaret J. (Casey) Stokes, he a native of Tennessee, born December 25, 1817, and died November 16, 1877; she of Fayette County, Ill., born July 16, 1832, and still living. Although a man not very much interested in politics his sympathies are with the Republican party. He is an active member of the order of A., F. & A. M., of Fillmore Lodge; has been a member of the Montgomery County Eclectic Society since its organization in May, 1870; has also been a member of the State Society since June, 1880.

S. P. TROUTMAN, Fillmore, was born in Cabarrus County, N. C., October 3, 1822, and has a good, practical education. He commenced business for himself as a farmer; coming to Montgomery County at eighteen years of age, stayed there two and a half years, working on the farm, and then returned to North Carolina, where he remained until 1847. He served about eighteen months in the Mexican war, having enlisted under Gen. Zachary Taylor; went back to North Carolina; remained there until August, 1849, when he returned to Montgomery County, Ill., and worked on the farm one month, and at different other occupations until 1852, when he entered 120 acres of raw prairie land on which there were no improvements of any kind. He has since added eighty acres, making 200 acres of good, tillable land, on which he has erected a good and substantial dwelling, with all necessary outbuildings. He also owns ninety-two acres of land one and a half miles west of his home place, Section 30. He was married in Montgomery County in the year 1852, to Miss Sarah Hill, a native of that county, who died in 1853. She was the mother of one child, dead. His second wife, Mary A. Sheppard, a native of Illinois; died in 1865. She was the mother of eight children, only five of whom are living. Christina L. Cruse, his third wife, was born in Union County, Ill., in 1822. Henry Cruse, her father, was born in North Carolina, and was a farmer by occupation. Her mother was also a native of North Carolina. Jacob Troutman, subject's father, was born in North Carolina; served in the war of 1812; was a farmer by occupation, and died about 1829. Christina Walker, subject's mother, was born in North Carolina, and died in 1850; was the mother of eight children, the subject being the third child. He has an elder brother living in North Carolina. He is a member of the Lutheran Church. He is independent in regard to the political issues of the day; has always done his utmost in aid of public improvements, and the advancement of agricultural interests.

JARET WRIGHT, farmer, P. O. Fillmore, was born in Montgomery County in the year 1819, and was raised on the farm and assisted his father in his boyhood days; was educated in the common schools of the country, and entered on his business career as a farmer; went into the Mexican war in 1846, under Capt. McAdams, Company C, Infantry; was at the battle of Cerro Gordo, at the taking of Vera Cruz; was in the service a year, at the expiration of which he came back to Montgomery County, and settled on the land he received for his services in the war, which was 160 acres of slightly improved land, and remained on it for several years, and sold that and moved to the place on which he now resides, consisting of 530 acres, the most of which is good, tillable land, and has it well improved with a good, comfortable house and barn, with all necessary outbuildings, and was married in this county November 8, 1849, to Miss Mary Whitten. She was born in this county in 1821. Easton Whitten, her father, was born in South Carolina; was a farmer by occupation, and died in this State in 1855. Her mother was born in South Carolina, and died in this county in 1851, and was the mother of eight children, wife of subject being next youngest. Joseph Wright, the father of subject, was born in South Carolina, and his mother, Sarah Revis, was born also in the same State; she died in 1855, and was the mother of ten children, the subject being the fifth child, and he has a family of five children living. The names are as follows: Araminda, born July 17, 1851; Emora, born May 8, 1853; Ezra, born July 17, 1855; Esta, born November 17, 1858; Elbert, born October 8, 1861. John Ambler Johnson, the grandfather of subject's wife, was in the Revolutionary war; Democrat all his life. He being one of the old settlers, has done as much as any man, according to means, toward the advancement of agricultural and public improvements.

ELIJAH WRIGHT, farmer, P. O. Hurricane, was born in Fillmore Precinct, Montgomery County, November 24, 1824. Joseph Wright, his father, was born in Kentucky, April 20, 1780. He emigrated to this State in 1814, and entered a large tract of land besides what he purchased; was one among the prominent men of the day; was a farmer and blacksmith by occupation, and died October 1, 1844, after having raised a large and useful family of children, who are among the best citizens of the county at the present day. He married in Kentucky about 1802, Miss Sarah Revis, who was the mother of eleven children, four of whom are living, our subject being the eighth child; was educated in the common schools of the country, and commenced business for himself as a farmer, his first purchase being a tract of eighty acres, and he has added to it until he has reached the handsome estate of 500 acres, 300 of which he has given to his children, and has erected on his home place a fine dwelling and barn, with all necessary outbuildings, and has his farm in a high state of cultivation. He was married in Montgomery Co., Nov. 13, 1851, to Miss Drucilla Lynn, born in Kentucky December 1, 1833. Her father, Jefferson Lynn, was born in Kentucky; Elizabeth Casey, her mother, was also a native of Kentucky; her father was a farmer; they both died in this county. Her mother had seven children, all living except one. She is the oldest of the family, and is the mother of seven children, two deceased. Camallia, born in 1853; Celestina, born in 1855; Joseph Jefferson, born in 1858; Sarah E., born in 1861; Emmerson, born December 14, 1870. Mary Rosetta born in 1860, and died in 1864, and two infants died without name. He is identified with the Democratic party, and has always been instrumental in helping on the agricultural interests and public improvements—a man who stands high where he is known.

EASTON WHITTEN, farmer, P. O. Best Hill, was born in Warren County, Ky., May 22, 1827, and when four years of age was brought to Montgomery County, Ill., by his parents, where his early childhood was employed upon the homestead farm assisting his father in his agricultural pursuits. When he reached the age of twenty-two, he left the paternal roof, purchased eighty acres of wild prairie land which he improved and eventually sold, with the intention of trying his fortune in the gold region of California, where he remained about two years, and succeeded in laying up enough money to enable him to make a start in the world with a good footing. Upon his return home, he again took upon himself the duties of a farm life, at which he has since remained engaged, and has, by his energy, industry and economy, accumulated 580 acres of land near the line between Fillmore and East Fork, the greater portion of which he has under a state of cultivation which shows Mr. Whitten to be a practical farmer. He grows all the usual farm crops, and is also a breeder of stock having now in his stable as fine a stallion as can be found in the county, and which is of Black Hawk Morgan and Arabian stock. Mr. Whitten was married February 6, 1849, to Miss Elizabeth Sanders, who was born in Montgomery County March 7, 1831. They have two living children, Thomas T. and Henry H. Mrs. Whitten is a daughter of John and Elizabeth (Powell) Sanders, natives of Kentucky, he born in the year 1799, and died February 12, 1864; she living, born November 19, 1802. Austin Whitten, the father of our subject, was born in South Carolina November 29, 1802, a farmer by occupation; located in East Fork Township, Montgomery County, in 1831, where his death occurred May 12, 1869. His wife, Keziah Casey, also a native of South Carolican. Being a progressive man himself, he is always in favor of any enterprise that will in any way tend to the advantage of the county, and especially for the advancement of religious and educational privileges.

OTIS M. WILLIAMSON, farmer, P. O. Bost Hill, was born in Montgomery County, Ill., November 19, 1840, to John and Nancy G. (Card) Williamson (see history), and passed his early childhood in the manner common with the children of that day, in attending the common schools, and in assisting his father in his agricultural pursuits. Owing to the limited school privileges, his education was necessarily limited to such as could be obtained in the common schools at that early day. He has, however, continued to add to the foundation laid in the log school house, and now considers his education to be one, if not above the average, a practical education, and realizing from his own meager opportunities the value education gives one at the present time, he has spared no means to provide such a one for his children, and in return they have taken advantage of the privileges allowed them, and bear a reputation as scholars of which they, as well as their parents, may well feel justly proud. At the age of twenty-one years, Mr. Williamson left his paternal roof with nothing but his hands with which to enter upon the battle of life, but possessed with all the energy and enterprise of a man who considers that the world owes him a living and sets out fully determined to make his own way.

sively. During the years of 1862-63, he was in Colorado engaged in mining, and, in connection with the duties of his farm, he has traveled in several of the States where his stock dealing may have called him. He was married in Montgomery County, Ill., February 28, 1864, to Melvina Jane Cress, who was born September 12, 1843. She is the mother of four children, viz., Peter P., born May 12, 1868; Hattie A., born January 27, 1871; Walter A., born February 5, 1875; Torney, born December 16, 1865, and died March 27, 1867. Mrs. Williamson is a daughter of Peter and Katy (Nusman) Cress; he living, she deceased. Mr. Williamson is an active member of the order of A., F. & A. M., Fillmore Lodge, No. 670. He served as Assessor during the first term after township organization, and is the present Supervisor. He is a man that takes a deep interest in all the political issues of the day, and also in all progressive movements favoring the growth and prosperity of the county, and especially in the advancement of religious and educational privileges.

GEORGE O. WOLCOTT, farmer, P. O. Fillmore, was born in Worcester County, Mass., October 26, 1831. William Wolcott, subject's father, was born in Massachusetts in the year 1801; is a farmer by occupation, and a resident of Montgomery County. His wife, Lucy Fairbank, was born in New Hampshire about 1813; she is also a resident of Montgomery County. She is the mother of six children, the subject being the second child. He was educated in the common schools of the country, and entered on his business career as a farmer. He married in Montgomery County May 11, 1857, Miss Jane Mack, born in New Hampshire in 1835. He is the father of seven children, viz., William O., Alice J., George E., Charles W., Illinois, James F. and Frederick. Mr. Wolcott has 240 acres of good farming land, with all necessary improvements, in Fillmore Township, where he now resides, and also twenty acres in Fayette County. He commenced with eighty acres of land, and has by his economy and energy amassed a large and handsome property. He has always been identified with the Democratic party.

WITT TOWNSHIP.

P. C. ABELL, farmer, P. O. Nokomis, born in Sangamon County, Ill., May 15, 1834, son of James H. and Adeline (Durley) Abell; the former, a farmer by occupation, was born in Adair County, Ky., February 12, 1801, and died in Bond County, Ill., April 25, 1863; the latter, born in Tennessee, died in Bond County, Ill., in 1880. The subject of this sketch is the second of a family of fourteen children, and received his education in Bond County, Ill.; he removed from Bond County to Montgomery County in 1867, where he now owns a fine farm of 300 acres; he has filled the offices of Justice of the Peace and Supervisor; has been School Trustee for thirteen years, and is at present candidate for County Treasurer, subject to the action of the Democratic party; during the war, he served in Company D, Forty-seventh Illinois Infantry. In Montgomery County, June 14, 1855, he married Penny M. Lynn, born in Fayette County, Ill., May 31, 1839, daughter of Jefferson and Elizabeth (Casey) Lynn, and there have been born to them three children—Albert J., Zedic McClelland and Mary R. B. Politically, Mr. Abell is a Democrat; he is a member of the Christian Union Church, and of the A., F. & A. M.

J. T. ARMENTROUT, farmer, P. O. Witt, born in Montgomery County May 9, 1849, son of Christopher H. and Elizabeth (Borror) Armentrout, natives of Hardy County, Va.; Christopher H., who was a farmer, was born September 5, 1797, and died in Montgomery County April 2, 1856, where his wife, who was born October 20, 1813, now resides. J. T., who is the fifth of a family of six children, was educated in the county schools, and engaged in farming, which occupation he still follows; has filled the offices of Town Clerk, Tax Collector and Supervisor of Witt Township. He married, September 14, 1871, in Witt Township, Rebecca Vermillion, born in Edgar County, Ill., September 14, 1852, daughter of James S. and Elizabeth (Curnett) Vermillion; their children are Clarence L. Elvira V., Augusta M., Ida G. and Lee; Howard E. died August 13, 1881. Mr. Armentrout is a Methodist, and a Republican.

GEORGE W. ARMENTROUT, farmer, P. O. Witt, born in Montgomery County August 8, 1855, son of Christopher H. and Elizabeth (Borror) Armentrout, natives of Hardy County, Va., he, a farmer by occupation, born September 5, 1797, died in Montgomery County, April 2, 1856, where his wife, who was born October 20, 1813, now resides. Subject, who is the youngest of a family of six children, received his education in the county schools, and engaged in farming, which occupation he has always followed; was Tax Collector of Witt Township in 1880 and 1881. He married, in Witt Township, January 1, 1880, Ella Tucker, born in Walworth County, Wis., February 28, 1858, daughter of James and Eliza (Tratt) Tucker. Mr. Armentrout is a member of the Methodist Church, and a supporter of the Republican party.

T. S. BATTLES, farmer, P. O. Nokomis born in Philadelphia, Penn., January 19, 1803, only child of Nathaniel and Ellen (Stephenson) Battles; he, a sea Captain, born in New England, was lost at sea about the year

1802; his wife, born in Aberdeen, Scotland, died in Philadelphia, Penn. Subject was educated in his native city, and began life as a farmer, which occupation he has always followed. He has been twice married; his first wife, whom he married in Philadelphia, was Susan Snowden, a native of that city; she died in Wayne County, Ohio, leaving four children—Rachel, William S., Johnson G. and Thomas. In Wayne County, Ohio, March 10, 1842, he married his second wife, Ann E. Bright, born in Perry County, Penn., May 20, 1815, daughter of George E. and Barbara (Bruner) Bright; the children born from the second marriage are Philip M., Susan, Barbara E., Ursula, Hannah O. and Anna. Mr. Battles is a Republican, and a member of the Methodist Church.

JAMES R. BROWN, farmer, P. O. Nokomis, born in Witt Township Montgomery County, January 28, 1832, son of David D. and Catharine (Cress) Brown, both of whom died in Montgomery County; David D., a farmer by occupation, born in Tennessee about the year 1805, died in 1847; his wife, born in North Carolina about the year 1805, died about the year 1862. James R. is the eldest of a family of ten children; was educated in the schools of Montgomery County; has always been a farmer; has filled the offices of School Director and Road Commissioner. In Hillsboro Township, Montgomery County, May 10, 1855, he married Nancy J. Sanders born in that county February 5, 1835, daughter of John and Elizabeth (Powell) Sanders, and there have been born to them eleven chil [illegible]

Brown, he, a farmer, born in Tennessee January 8, 1802, died in Montgomery County July 30, 1846; she, also a native of Tennessee, born December 8, 1809, now a resident of Irving Township. Thomas J., the tenth of a family of eleven children, received his education in Montgomery County, and has always been engaged in farming. He has been twice married, in Montgomery County; his first wife, whom he married November 11, 1866, was Virginia E. McCamant, born in Brooke County, W. Va., about the year 1846, daughter of John J. McCamant; she died February 3, 1872, leaving three children—Charles Lee, Carrie J. and Clara. He married, April 2, 1872, his second wife, Rhoda C. Lipe, born in Montgomery County July 23, 1852, daughter of Allen and Leah (Nusman) Lipe; from this second union five children have been born to them James W., Wade Hampton, Tora G., Eva M. and Thomas H. Mr. Brown is a stanch Democrat, and has been elected a delegate to the Democratic Congressional Convention of this district.

WILLIAM BERRY, farmer, P. O. Witt, born in Montgomery County, Ill., March 10, 1856, son of David and Margaret (Martin) Berry, natives of Hamilton County, Ohio, and at the present time residents of Butler Township, Montgomery County: the former was born December 15, 1827, and follows the occupation of a farmer, the latter, born July 11, 1832. Our subject, the eldest of eight children, received his education in the common schools, finishing at Butler, Montgom [illegible] in politics, he is a Republican; he is a member of the I. O. O. F.

E. H. DONALDSON, farmer, P. O. Nokomis, was born in Fayette County, Ill., November 10, 1836; his parents were natives of Carroll County, Tenn.; his father— who had at one time been engaged in mercantile business, but who was engaged in farming at his death— was born February 27, 1816, and died in Fayette County, Ill., October 4, 1872; his wife, whose maiden name was Elvina Hicks, was born December 7, 1816, and is now residing in Fayette County, Ill. Our subject, who was the eldest of a family of eight, received his education in Fayette and Montgomery Counties; first engaged in business as a merchant in Fayette County, Ill.; in 1861, he moved to Montgomery County and located on his present property of 200 acres, and, by devoting all his energies to its improvement, he has now one of the finest improved farms in the township. In Fayette County, Ill., January 3, 1856, he married Mary A. Rhodes, born in Fayette County Ill., October 4, 1837, daughter of Thomas Rhodes, from which union five children have been born William A., Mary E., Aaron B., James McC. and Selena J. Mr. Donaldson is a member of the Christian Union Church, and of the A., F. & A. M.; politically, he is a Democrat.

ROBERT DIXON, grain-dealer and miller, Witt, was born in Coles County, Ill., in 1844; his father, William Dixon, was a farmer, and native of Illinois, and died in Coles County, Ill., about the year 1848. Our subject, the eldest of three children, began life as a farmer, and, on the opening of the war, enlisted in Company B, Fifty-fifth Illinois Infantry, participating in the engagements at Shiloh, Tenn., April 6 and 7, 1862, Arkansas Post, Corinth, Vicksburg, and Jackson, Miss. At the close of the war, he resumed farming till the year 1881, then entered the grain and milling business as a partner in the firm of Dixon & Houck, operating a mill and grain elevator at Witt, Montgomery County. He married, in Montgomery County, April 23, 1870, Lucinda Houck, born in Michigan in 1846, daughter of Daniel Houck, from which union there has been born to them one child, Lula M. In politics, Mr. Dixon is a Republican.

DANIEL GRANTHAM, farmer, P. O. Irving, son of James and Francy (Sights) Grantham, both born in North Carolina about the year 1800. Our subject is the eighth child of a family of twelve, and was born in Montgomery County December 3, 1832; he received a fair education in Irving Township, Montgomery County: has followed the occupation of a farmer all his life, and has held the office of School Trustee for twenty years. In Irving Township, Montgomery County, October 21, 1858, he married Malinda Irvin, born in Casey County, Ky., November 15, 1836, daughter of Perry and Mary (Osborn) Irvin; from this union there have been born six children: Mary H., Henry H., Theodora L., Maggie J., Urilla M. and Rosa M. A. Mr. Grantham is politically a Republican; his wife is a member of the M. E. Church.

JOSEPH HAND, farmer, P. O. Nokomis, born in Staffordshire, England, December 23, 1820, son of Joseph and Sarah (Shipton) Hand, natives of Devonshire, England; he, a farmer by occupation, born in 1787, died in Macoupin County, Ill., August 19, 1860; she, born about the year 1789, died on the voyage to the United States, February 23, 1845. Subject, the third of a family of seven children, received his education in his native shire, and began the business of life as a farmer. In 1845, he emigrated with his parents to America, landed at New Orleans, and proceeded to Paddock Grove, Madison Co., Ill., where he remained six years, thence moved to Macoupin County, where he lived twenty years, and finally removed to Montgomery County, bought a tract of land in its native state, which he has cultivated and improved, and now has 670 acres of fine farming land. In Staffordshire, England, July 8, 1842, he married Mary Wilson, born in Newboro, England, July 21, 1822, daughter of George and Sarah (Hadkins) Wilson, and there have been born to them ten children—George W., Jane E., William, Ann, Sarah, John, Irene M., Libbie L., Joseph W. and Emma J. Mr. Hand is a member of the Episcopal Church, and a Republican.

WILLIAM HOLMES, farmer, P. O. Nokomis, was born in Leeds, Yorkshire, England, April 30, 1815, son of John and Teresia (Parvin) Holmes; the former, born in Lancashire, England, died in Yorkshire, England, about the year 1819; the latter, born in Skipton, England, about the year 1785, died in Yorkshire, England, in 1817, leaving four children, William being the third. The subject of this sketch began life as a clerk in a dry goods store. He emigrated to America and settled in Cincinnati, Ohio, where he learned the trade of coach painting; worked at that trade in Cincinnati fourteen years, when he moved to Indiana, and thence to Illinois. Mr. Holmes has been twice married; his first wife was Ann Richardson, born in Yorkshire, England, in 1819, daughter of Joseph Richardson, a native of England; they were married in Dearborn County, Ind., where Mrs. Holmes died August 5, 1849, leaving five children—Ellen, Emma, Sarah E., Mary B. and William L. In Dearborn County, Ind., December 24, 1850, Mr. Holmes married his second wife, Amanda Rawling, born in Dearborn County, Ind., December 20, 1819, daughter of William and Laura (Lewis) Rawling; by her he has had six children—John R., Thomas P., Laura B., Richard, Louis E. and James F. Mr. Holmes is a member of the I. O. O. F.; in politics, he is a Republican.

F. J. HOLMES, Witt, was born in Hillsboro, Montgomery County, January 1, 1850, son of Joel D. and Marandis D. (Bennett) Holmes, he, a native of Alfred, York Co., Me., who died April 5, 1870; she, still living, the wife of Francis Root. Subject has been twice married; first, in Hillsboro, March 28, 1872, to Lucinda J. Atterbury, daughter of George M. Atterbury, of Kentucky; Mrs. Holmes dying, Mr. Holmes, September 2, 1877, married Florence May Hubbard, of Colusa, Ill., daughter of Martin M. Hubbard, a native of Tennessee. Mr. Holmes has two children—Stella Marandis, born September 2, 1878; and Myrtle Keneston, born November 20, 1880.

ANDREW HOEHN, farmer, P. O. Nokomis, born in Germany July 3, 1834, son of Ambrose and Agatha (Rieder) Hoehn, he, a farmer by occupation, born in Germany in April, 1805, died in Clinton County, Ill., March 8, 1856; she, also a native of Germany, born December 25, 1806, is now residing in Montgomery County. Subject emigrated to America with his parents in 1847; landed in New Orleans, thence moved to St. Louis, where he remained a few months, then moved to Clinton County, Ill., where he lived twenty nine years, after which he removed to his present place; he received a fair education in the schools of Germany and of Clinton County, Ill., and began life as a farmer, in which occupation he is still engaged; has been Tax Collector of Witt Township. In Clinton County, Ill., November 12, 1860, he married Bettie Oberle, born in Germany in 1843, daughter of Andon and Elizabeth

(Blaese) Oberle; from this union there have been born to them eight children—Charles, Catharine, Henry, Isabel, John A., Emma M., Ambrose and Elizabeth B. Mr. Hoehn is a member of the Catholic Church, and is a Republican.

WILSON M. MAXEY, farmer, P. O. Witt, born in Barren County, Ky., February 15, 1829, son of Edward and Nancy (Barry) Maxey. Edward Maxey, who was a cooper by trade, but in latter life a farmer, was born in Halifax County, Va., in 1783; died in Montgomery County November 7, 1859, where his wife, also a native of Virginia, born in 1789, died October 20, 1843. Subject, the eighth child of a family of nine, received a fair education in Montgomery County; has always been a farmer; has been School Trustee for fifteen years. He has been twice married; his first wife, whom he married January 1, 1852, was Louisa J. Newcomb, born in Virginia April 4, 1833, daughter of William A. and Mary A. Newcomb, died in Montgomery County September 27, 1864, leaving seven children—Mary A., Alice L., William A., James H., Flora F., Sarah A. and Louisa J. In Litchfield, Montgomery County, November 30, 1865, he married his second wife, Mrs. Sarah A. Greiner, born in Augusta County, Va., September 5, 1836, daughter of Jonathan and Nancy (Gray) Batsley; their children are Cora D., Charles W., John S. and Jessie M. Mr. Maxey is one of the old settlers of Montgomery County; he is a stanch Democrat; is Chairman of the Democratic Committee of Witt Township, and a delegate to the State convention of that party; he is a member of the Methodist Church.

JOHN M. NEISLER, farmer, P. O. Irving, son of Henry M. and Elizabeth (Lipe) Neisler, natives of North Carolina; Henry M., a farmer and stock dealer, born November 19, 1816, died in Irving Township, Montgomery County, in 1881; his wife, born January 10, 1823, is now a resident of that township, in which, also, subject, the second child of a family of fifteen, was born December 4, 1841; he received a fair education in the schools of Montgomery County, and began life as a farmer; when twenty-two years of age, his father gave him the farm on which he now lives; previous to that time, however, he worked a farm, which he had rented, for two years; has filled the office of Clerk of Witt Township for four years. In Montgomery County November 14, 1861, he married Esther Barringer, born in that county April 14, 1838, daughter of Daniel and Polly (Cress) Barringer, and from this union the following children have been born to them—Melvern E., Ethlen V., Helen E., Florence D., Arthur A. and Herbert F. Mr. Neisler is a Democrat, and a member of the Lutheran Church.

W. L. OPDYCKE, farmer, P. O. Witt, son of Andrew S. and Judith A. (Lanning) Opdycke; the former, born in Bucks County, Penn., July 3, 1803, died in Witt Township, Montgomery County, August 11, 1874; the latter, born in Hunterdon County, N. J., about the year 1810, died at Milford, in that State, in July, 1831. Our subject, the elder of two children, was born in Milford, N. J., April 7, 1830; he received a fair education in Macoupin County, Ill., and began the business of life as a farmer, which occupation he has ever since followed. In September, 1864, he enlisted in Company D, One Hundred and Forty-fourth Illinois Infantry, at Alton, Ill., and was discharged in September, 1865. He was married at Woodboro, Ill., March 28, 1854, to Julia T. Wood, born in Montgomery County July 19, 18[illegible], daughter of William and Rebecca (McWilliams) Wood; the former, born in Darlington District, S. C. [illegible] tober 21, 1808, died May 29, 1873; the latter, born near Lexington, Ky., December 18, 1815, died February 14, 1857. Mr. and Mrs. Opdycke are the parents of nine children—Delia A., H. Eugene, James M., Emma F. R., William D., Carrie J., Ethelbert Lanning, Clinton W. and Hettie H. In politics, Mr. Opdycke is a Republican; he is a member of the Presbyterian and his wife of the Methodist Church.

JOHN STURGEON, farmer, P. O. Irving, is a son of David and Mary (McCarty) Sturgeon; the former, a farmer, was born in Indiana, and died in Montgomery County in 1851; the latter, born in Indiana, and died in Jasper County, Ill., in 1840. Our subject, the eldest of six children, received his education in Montgomery County, and began life as a farmer, which occupation he has followed ever since. He married, in Montgomery County, April 16, 1846, Charity Cindoff, born in Kentucky, who died in Montgomery County February 14, 1851. In Montgomery County, April 2, 1854, he married his second wife, Sarah J. Davis, born in Montgomery County Feb. 27, 1831, daughter of Thomas and Nancy (Martin) Davis. Mr. Sturgeon has eleven children—Austin W., John H., E. H., David B., M. F., Robert Lee, William M., W. R., Mary E., Charles E., Savilla F. and his step-son, William T. He is a member of the Presbyterian Church, and in politics is a Democrat.

FREDERICK F. TATCH, farmer, P. O. Witt, son of John N. and Emeline (Sweet) Tatch; the former, who was Captain of a whaling vessel, was born in Germany October 22, 1813, and died in Macoupin County, Ill., September 14, 1859; the latter was born in Vermont November 22, 1820, and died in Macoupin County, Ill., June 20, 1871. Our subject, who is the third of a family of seven children, was born in Fair Haven, Mass., November 7, 1846; he received a fair education in Macoupin County, Ill.; has been a farmer all his life. He was married, in Hillsboro, Montgomery County, November 13, 1873, to Miss L. F. May, born in Roane County, Tenn., July 31, 1857, daughter of Robert C. and Alvira (Hall) May; from this union six children have been born—William H., Bertie, Vira Estella, Myra Lucilla, Charles M. and Hervey O. Mr. Tatch served in Company I, One Hundred and Twenty-seventh Illinois Infantry, during the war, participating in the engagements at Nashville, Tenn. He is a member of the Presbyterian Church, and of the A., F. & A. M.; in politics, he is a Republican.

JOHN TRATT, farmer, P. O. Witt, was born in Somersetshire, England, March 3, 1830; his parents, Thomas and Betsy (Watts) Tratt, were natives of England; the former, born in Somersetshire in 1796, was a farmer; emigrated to America, and died at Palmyra, Jefferson Co., Wis., January 30, 1874; the latter died at the same place in March, 1876; they were the parents of five children, John being the third. He follows the business of farming and trading in stock. In Jefferson County, Wis., February 23, 1851, he married Sarah Hooper, born in Cornwall, England, September 2, 1830, daughter of John Hooper; from this union six children have been born to them—Joseph, Rosepha J., Lillie M., Thomas H., Jennie and Stella B. Mr. Tratt is politically a Democrat; his wife is a member of the Methodist Church.

HENRY WUBKER, merchant, Witt, was born in Jacksonville, Ill., August 21, 1844, son of William and Lena (Maas) Wubker; the former, born near Minden, Prussia, February 10, 1816; the latter, in Hanover City, Hanover, Germany, August 21, 1818. Our subject, the eldest of six children, received the foundation of his education at Jacksonville, Ill.; he also attended school near Virginia, in Cass County, Ill., and, in 1871 and 1872, attended Chicago University, Chicago, Ill., where he finished his education. Mr. Wubker was engaged in farming and in teaching school till the year 1873; in that year, he removed to Irving, Montgomery County, and engaged in the mercantile business there until 1878, when he removed to Witt, and there carries on an extensive business in dry goods, drugs and agricultural implements. At Irving, Montgomery County, May 3, 1876, he married Lucy A. Cowell, born in Staunton, Macoupin Co., Ill., September 27, 1854, daughter of John and Caroline (Truitt) Cowell; there have been born to them two children—Hubert L., who died July 5, 1881; and Henry T. Mr. Wubker is a man of fine business abilities; in politics, he is a Democrat; he is a member of the A., F. & A. M., and Knights of Honor.

NOKOMIS TOWNSHIP.

D. P. BROPHY, Postmaster, Nokomis, son of Dennis and Julia (Galvin) Brophy, was born in New York City March 3, 1832; he lived in the city till about fourteen years of age, receiving, during this time, the rudiments of a common course of education; upon the death of his mother, in 1846, he went to the city of Philadelphia and engaged in the type-foundry business; after about eighteen months, he went to the city of Baltimore and engaged in the same occupation with Edwin Starr, of the *Sun* building; in about nine months, he engaged on the Pittsburgh & Baltimore Railroad as assistant baggagemaster; this position he held about nine months, when he went back to New York City and engaged in the type-foundry business for a number of years; his health failing, he abandoned this business and engaged in market gardening near the city of Boston, for James Young. In the fall of 1856, he came West, and first stopped at Litchfield and worked for Galvin Howe some six months, and then came to Nokomis. At the beginning of the late rebellion, he responded to the call for troops; volunteered in the One Hundred and Twenty-sixth Illinois Infantry Company F, during this time acting as Postmaster till the close of the war, after which he came back to Nokomis, and was appointed Postmaster, which position he still holds, having been in the employ of the Government for twenty years. September 17, 1858, he married Miss Susan, daughter of Thomas S. and Ann (Oldroyd) Battles, by whom he has had two children — Nathaniel B. and Julia A., both dead. Mr. Brophy traces his ancestry back to an Irish origin through both his father and mother; his great-grandfather settled in New York in an early day, and the Brophys are scattered over the States; Mr. Brophy's father raised two children — our subject, and Hannah, who died in New York City at the age of twenty-three; Mr. Brophy's father died before he was born, and, many years after, his widow, and mother of our subject, married John Roberts and raised two children, a son and a daughter, the daughter marrying James Jackson, a custom house officer in New York City. Mr. and Mrs. Brophy are members of the Baptist Church, and are respected by all who know them.

WILLIAM M. BLUE, farmer and stock-dealer, P. O. Nokomis, born in Franklin County, Ohio, April 26, 1826, son of Peter Blue, a farmer, who was born in Virginia in 1792, married in Ohio in 1823, and died there in 1855, from the effects of a rattle-snake bite, in eight days after being bitten; subject's mother, Nancy (Crabb) Blue, born in Virginia in 1797, is now living at Nokomis, in the eighty-fifth year of her age; they had six children — Letitia, wife of Thomas F. Wilson; William M., our subject; Thomas C., who died at the age of twenty-five; Nancy C., wife of the late N. Brown; Peter, who died at the age of thirty-three; and Susan E., who died at the age of thirty. Subject was married, in Franklin County, Ohio, in 1844, to Rachel E. Marshall, born in that county in 1828, died in Montgomery County April 4, 1869, and a daughter of John and Hannah (Cain) Marshall; by this union, subject had a family of nine—Rebecca J., Alice

A., Francis P. (deceased), Augusta M., William P. (attending law school at Bloomington, Ill.), Ella, Ada, and twins, both dead. Mr. Blue began farming at the age of twenty, and has followed his vocation successfully; besides farming, he is a well-known stock raiser; owns 320 acres of land in this county, and 320 acres in Madison County, Neb.; he began life with a limited capital, but, by hard work and close attention to business, he now ranks among the wealthy men of Nokomis. Mr. Blue is a Democrat; is well and favorably known in his district, and has made, in his busy life, a host of friends.

GEORGE CULP, furniture, Nokomis, born in Jefferson County, Ohio, November 28, 1821, son of Adam and Nancy (Wright) Culp, he, a farmer, born in Pennsylvania July 5, 1795, moved to Ohio about 1812, where he raised fourteen children by two wives, and died there October 20, 1865; she, born in Jefferson County, Ohio, September 20, 1795, died there March 15, 1837. Subject received a common school education; worked at the carpenter's trade and furniture business; has continued to manufacture furniture since his arrival in Nokomis in 1855, and keeps in stock a full line of superior goods. He was married, in Jefferson County, Ohio, September 12, 1844, to Elizabeth Easterday, born in Jefferson County, Ohio, April 27, 1823, daughter of Christian and Ann Marie (Stemple) Easterday, he, born October 18, 1789, in Frederick County, Md., died September 29, 1875; she, born in Morgan County, Va., March 7, 1791, died July 6, 1875. Subject had nine children, seven now living—Benjamin F., Barbara (now wife of C. F. Tindall), Loretta K. (deceased), Adam C., Amos L., James A., Leora E., Lillie M. and Martin William (deceased). Mr. Culp is a member of the Lutheran Church; a Democrat, and is a strong advocate of temperance. The name Culp was of German origin, and was originally spelled Kalb, then changed to Kolp, and afterward to Culp. Baron De Kalb, of Revolutionary notoriety, was of the same genealogy. Baltza Culp, grandfather of subject, came to the United States from Germany about the close of the Revolutionary war.

MARTIN HARKEY, farmer, P. O. Nokomis, who came with his parents from North Carolina and settled at Hillsboro, Montgomery Co., Ill., when there were only eight log cabins (1830); he was born in North Carolina in 1813, and is the son of Martin and Christina (Meusinger) Harkey, who were natives of Pennsylvania, from where they emigrated to North Carolina in an early day; they both died in this county at a ripe old age, and were both respected citizens, and members of the Lutheran Church. Our subject's boyhood days were spent at Hillsboro, and working on a farm; he received a common school education, and began life for himself at the age of twenty-two, by farming, which occupation has ever been his vocation. In 1835, he married Mary, daughter of Jacob and Catharine (Bost) Cress; she was born in North Carolina in 1815, and came with her parents to this county in 1818; they settled close to Hillsboro, and followed farming; father was born in 1779, and died in this county in 1865; his wife was born in 1786, and died in 1859; they were both members of the Lutheran Church. Mr. Harkey, by hard work and economy, has secured a good farm of 300 acres, and a good property in Nokomis. To Mr. and Mrs. Harkey have been born nine children—six sons and three daughters—Sophia C., dead; Harriet R., dead; Henry L., in California; Jane E., wife of E. Brightman, in California; George W., dead; Jacob M., Thomas P., James M., and one dying in infancy. Mr. and Mrs. Harkey are members of the Presbyterian Church and strong advocates of the temperance cause, and, in fact, everything that pertains to good and the promotion of society.

THOMAS G. HOBSON, miller, Nokomis, born in Yorkshire, England, May 10, 1840, son of Robert and Elizabeth (Leaming) Hobson. Robert Hobson, subject's father, a native of England and miller by trade, came to America in 1843; followed his trade in different parts of the United States, and died in Litchfield, Ill., January 25, 1877, aged seventy-three years; his wife, also a native of England, is still living; they had ten children, of whom our subject is the eighth; he received a common school education; at the age of seventeen, learned the miller's trade, and, in 1873, formed a partnership with L. M. Hartsock at Nokomis, where he has since resided. At Staunton, Ill., December 8, 1867, he married Elizabeth Cowell, born at or near Staunton, Ill., September 20, 1847, daughter of James R. and Lucinda (Camp) Cowell; she died May 18, 1870, leaving one child, Gracie May, born May 2, 1870. He was married the second time, at Lincoln, Logan Co., Ill., January 23, 1879, to Matilda F. Snell, born in Staunton, Macoupin Co., Ill. December 4, 1851, daughter of Selby and Sarah Jane (Dees) Snell, he, born May 8, 1811, died February 17, 1872; she, born at Staunton, Macoupin Co., Ill., April 11, 1831, still living. Mr. Hobson is a Democrat, and a member of the Masonic fraternity. Messrs. Hobson & Hartsock have a mill, 60x40, engine room 30x16, and boiler room 30x16; the four run of stones are run by a sixty horse power engine, the mill was built by Rhoader in 1866; the shipments of flour annually average 15,000 barrels; the shipments in 1881 were 20,000 barrels.

L. M. HARTSOCK, miller, Nokomis, born near Johnsville, Frederick Co., Md., November 9, 1841, son of Nicholas and Sarah Hartsock, he, a stone and brick mason, died when our subject was thirteen years old; she died when subject was but four years old; they had two children, L. M. and Maggie E. Subject was raised among strangers, and received a common-school education; at the age of eighteen, he began learning the miller's trade at Little Pipe Creek, near Middleburg, Md., and has followed his trade ever since. At Waterloo, Ill., January 9, 1869, he married Frances A. Cooley, a native of Indiana, born September 6, 1844, her father, Lorin Cooley, dying when she was quite young; her mother, Mary Bowers, is now Mrs. J. D. Jones. Mr. Hartsock has a family of four—Maggie E., Arthur L., Robert L. and Ethel. In 1873, subject went in partnership with Thomas G. Hobson in the milling business, owning a half interest in the Nokomis large mill, a description of which is given in Mr. Hobson's biography, published in this book. Subject is a Republican, a Freemason, and a member of the Knights of Honor. Mr. Hartsock is a fine example of American pluck; starting out in life without a cent, he has, by patience, perseverance and indomitable will, made a name for himself which the ravages of time cannot efface.

CHARLES L. HENKEL, druggist, Nokomis, was born in Virginia, son of Rev. D. M. and Susan (Eger) Henkel, his father being a Lutheran clergyman, as his forefathers were for nine generations back; both parents were natives of Virginia, his mother being a sister of Havemeyer, the great sugar refiner of New York. Our subject received a good classical education; made chemistry a study, and, early in life, engaged in his present vocation as clerk in a drug store at Richmond, Va., and elsewhere; he began in the drug business in Nokomis in 1876, and is considered an excellent pharmacist, having spent the greater part of his early life in familiarizing himself with the details of his profession. He was married, in 1879, to Belle Leas, born in Jefferson County, Ohio, daughter of Leonard Leas, Esq., a native of Adams County, Penn., where he was born March 20, 1811, being now a resident of Nokomis.

F. O. PADDOCK, lumber-dealer, Nokomis, was born in Argyle, Wis., December 16, 1853, son of Oscar H. and Ann (Threadgold) Paddock, he, born in Woodstock, Vt., June 12, 1830, came to Illinois at an early day, and is now in the lumber business at Pana, Ill., and with his son (subject) at Nokomis; she, a native of Yorkshire, England, was born December 12, 1836. Subject received a good business education, and engaged in business at Pana, Ill., where he dealt in lumber and building material; thence he moved to Nokomis, where he carries on the same business; he has the largest stock of any dealer in his line in Montgomery County, and does an extensive trade. At St. Joseph, Mo., August 28, 1877, he married Ada Platt, born in Brooklyn, N. Y., April 8, 1855, daughter of Rudolphus T. and Mary (Nares) Platt, he, born in Clifton Park, N. Y., August 1, 1832, died in May, 1876; she, a native of Geneva, N. Y., born November 8, 1834; from this union, one child, Jessie F., now three years old, has been born. Mr. Paddock is of old Revolutionary stock; his great-grandfather and grand-uncles were Revolutionary soldiers, and he is an honor to the stock from whence he springs.

M. P. PUFELES, merchant, Nokomis, born in Austria in 1852, and came to America in 1868; he was the son of Sigmund and Rosa (Hirschstin) Pufeles. Our subject received a good common school education. In 1879, he married Dora W[illegible] [illegible] born in Austria; they have [illegible] children. [illegible]

New York City; came to Nokomis in 1879, and joined in partnership with Lessel & Bro. for one year; after that, in 1880, went in business for himself, and now does a first-class business in dry goods and general merchandise; sells for cash, and pays cash for his goods, which enables him to sell cheap. Mr. Pufeles is a member of the Masonic fraternity, and a credit to the business community at Nokomis.

H. F. ROOD, banker, Nokomis, President of the Nokomis National Bank, and one of the first settlers of Nokomis, was born in Massachusetts in 1818; he is the third son of Ashael and Asenath (Fuller) Rood, who were also of Massachusetts; father born in 1772, and by occupation was a farmer in his native State, where he died in 1852; his wife was born in 1789, and died in 1828. Our subject spent his boyhood days on a farm, and received a common-school education. In 1843, he married Nancy Londen, a lady of rare attainments, and daughter of Joshua and Nancy Hines Londen. Mrs. Rood has been to her husband ever an efficient co-worker, sharing with him all his trials and sustaining him by earnest co-operation in all his plans; she is an active member of the M. E. Church. Mr. Rood began life by engaging in the hotel business in his native State, and then followed the same business both in Connecticut and New York. In 1850, he removed to Crawford County, Penn., and in 1857, by the solicitation of friends, he removed to Montgomery County, where he embarked in the mercantile business, occupying for his store the first plastered house in Nokomis. By close attention to business and honest [illegible] [illegible] with his customers he soon gained [illegible] [illegible] of the community [illegible] [illegible] merchant [illegible] [illegible] of Nokomis, which position he still retains. To Mr. and Mrs. Reed were born four children—Florence A., dying in infancy; Clarence E., express agent at St. Louis; Horace E., with his brother; and Maude, a promising young lady, and beloved by all who knew her, died in the nineteenth year of her age.

J. W. RUSSELL, merchant, Nokomis, was born in Montgomery County, Ill., in 1839; he is the oldest of a family of eight children that were born to William H. and Catharine (Todd) Russell. William Russell was born in Kentucky in 1818, and came to Montgomery County, Ill., with his father, John Russell, a native of North Carolina, in or about 1823, settling on land entered by them; they followed agricultural pursuits till their death, which occurred in the year 1880. William Russell, the father of our subject, married in this county, about the year 1838; his wife, daughter of Benjamin and Mary Todd, was born in about 1816; is still a resident of Montgomery County. Our subject spent his early days on his father's farm, and received such a common-school education as the advantages permitted in those days. In 1860, he began life for himself by engaging at farming, and in 1871 he embarked in the general mercantile business at Nokomis, and, by honest dealing and a close attention to business, he has not only been successful financially, but has gained the confidence of his many customers. He is a member of the Lutheran Church, Masonic fraternity and Knights of Honor. In 1863, he married Miss Mattie D. Strader, daughter of John and Elizabeth (Avis) Strader; she was born in Jefferson County, Va., in 1842, and died in 1880, leaving one child, Charlie D. In 1881, Mr. Russell married again—Annie Strader.

H. S. STRAIN, physician, Nokomis, born in Highland County, Ohio, June 13, 1837, son of Andrew Miller and Rebecca A. (Patton) Strain; he, a farmer, born near Abingdon, S. C., March 23, 1800, died July 3, 1859; she, born near Lexington, Bourbon Co., Ky., March 29, 1808, died July 31, 1872, their family consisted of seven sons and three daughters. Dr. Strain received a rudimentary education in the common schools of Highland County, Ohio, but afterward attended and graduated at the Worcester University, Cleveland, Ohio. In September, 1861, he enlisted in Company C, Eighty-first Regiment Ohio Infantry, and was detailed as Assistant Surgeon of the regiment, filling that position until 1862. On September 13, 1866, near Greenfield, Highland Co., Ohio, the Doctor was married to Miss Mary A. Walker, by the Rev. McKnight Williamson; she was born March 22, 1840, near Hillsboro, Highland Co., Ohio, and is a daughter of John H. and Margaret B. (Elliott) Walker, he, born in Rockbridge County, Va., in 1806, died November 3, 1875; she, born in Rockbridge County, Va., in January, 1809, is still living in Hillsboro, Ohio. The Doctor has five children living—Maggie H., born February 23, 1869; Annie Kate, born June 22, 1872; John W., born March 13, 1875; Stanley M., born March 24, 1877; and Andrew N. ("Scottie"), born July 22, 1867, died June 26, 1872. In 1865, the Doctor was appointed Surgeon of the One Hundred and Ninety-fifth Regiment of Ohio Infantry, and served until the end of the war. Dr. and Mrs. Strain are Presbyterians; in politics, he is a Republican, and known in his district as an able physician. Samuel Strain, the Doctor's grandfather, was an Irishman; came to America before the Revolutionary war; was a soldier for seven years, and fought under Gen. Green; in one battle, another soldier and himself were the only two who escaped; he had been married four times, raised twenty-two children, and died at the age of eighty-five.

WILLIAM STEINRAUF, M. D., Nokomis, born in Hesse-Darmstadt, Germany, September 18, 1850, son of John and Catharine (Stengel) Steinrauf, he a native of Hesse-Darmstadt, born in 1827, died at St. Louis, Mo., in September, 1872; was a stone mason, and served two years in the United States Army; she, still living in St. Louis, was born in Kurkessen, Germany, November 8, 1822. Subject received a good classical education at St. Louis and Washington, Mo., and graduated, in 1876, from the St. Louis College, Missouri. He was married, at Belvidere, Ill., in March, 1878, to Miss Carolina Kuppler, born at Rock Island, Ill., June 19, 1860, and a daughter of John and Anna Maria (Lepla) Kuppler; he, born in Wurtemberg, Germany, died in 1877; and she, born in Bavaria, Germany. The result of this union is one son, Albert, now four years old. Subject practiced medicine in Jefferson City, Mo., and moved to Nokomis in 1880, where he soon gained a host of friends and an enviable reputation. He is a strict member of the Lutheran Church, and is always on hand when duty calls.

GEORGE M. STEVENS, attorney, Nokomis, born in Canada in 1846, son of John M. and Sibyl (Goddard) Stevens, he a farmer, born in St. John, New Brunswick, now of Shelby County, Ill.; she, also a native of Canada, is still living. Subject received a rudimentary education at the public schools in Canada; afterward attended the high school at Springfield, Ill., graduated at the law school of Ann Arbor, Mich., in 1872, and began the practice of law in Nokomis in 1873. Mr. Stevens was married, at Nokomis, in 1875, to Jennie Blue, a daughter of William M. Blue (a biographical sketch of this family will be found in this work). The subject is a Royal Arch Mason, and a Democrat; has been Attorney for Nokomis for six years and is temperate in all things.

THOMAS TWOHEY, railroad, Nokomis, was born in Ireland in 1832, is the son of Thomas and Ann Twohey. Mr. Twohey came to America in 1848 with the intention of making for himself a home; he located in Massachusetts, where he followed farming for four years; then in Putnam County Ind., and at St. Mary's, Vigo County; then he attended the water tank at Tower Hill for the railroad company for six years, and, after spending one year in Missouri in the employ of a railroad company there, he came to Nokomis and took charge of a section for the Indianapolis & St. Louis Railroad, and has held that position for eighteen years. He married, in 1852, Sarah Bolton, a native of Ireland; five children have been born to them—Mary, wife of N. Singer; John M., Train Dispatcher at Mattoon, Ill.; Patrick, also an operator; Thomas and Michael. Mr. Twohey and family are members of the Catholic Church.

THOMAS J. WHITTEN, M. D., Nokomis, was born in Montgomery County, Ill., February 21, 1844, son of Austin and Keziah (Casey) Whitten, he, born in Newberry District, S. C., November 29, 1802, came to Illinois at an early day, where he followed farming until his death, which occurred May 12, 1869; she, also a native of South Carolina, born March 15, 1799, died in Montgomery County, Ill., October 1, 1856. Subject began the study of medicine in 1856, and graduated at the Jefferson Medical College of Philadelphia, Penn., in 1867; he began the practice of his profession at Hillsboro in 1867, remaining there till 1880, when he came to Nokomis; he now ranks as one of the leading physicians of Montgomery County. He served as Hospital Steward at Fort Prickren from 1862 till the close of the war. At Hillsboro, Ill., January 2, 1868, he married Sophia C. Harkey, born in Montgomery County February 3, 1843, daughter of George and Martha S. (Masters) Harkey, natives of North Carolina, he, born April 5, 1804, died October 29, 1856; she, born June 7, 1803, died August 13, 1852. From this marriage four children have been born, viz.: Harry Hood, George Ernest, Lelia Grace and Lester Cook. The Doctor is a member of the Lutheran Church, a member of the Masonic fraternity, and an Odd Fellow; is Secretary of the County Medical Society, and has officiated as President of the Central Illinois District Society.

D. H. ZEPP, attorney, Nokomis, born in Carroll County, Md., in 1845, the son of Samuel and Caroline C. (Zimmerman) Zepp; he, a farmer, born in Maryland in 1822, was married in 1843, and is still living there; she, born in Maryland, is still living; they had nine children—five sons and four daughters—of whom our subject is the oldest; he received a good common-school education, and, by working on a farm for $6 per month, he was enabled to continue his studies; at the age of eighteen, he began teaching school, and, after having taught school in the county for one year, he became Principal of the Westminster, in Maryland. He was married, in 1874, to Ella Beaver, daughter of Jacob and Sarah (Hammett) Beaver. Mr. Zepp was elected to the Thirtieth General Assembly, and received the second largest majority of any member in the House. He began reading law with Judge John E. Smith, of Maryland, in 1866; admitted to the bar in 1868, and came West in 1869; he was Principal of the Public School at Hillsboro one year, and at Nokomis two years. Mr. Zepp is a Republican, a Knight Templar, and a self-made man; not only has he been successful as an educator, but also as a financier, now owning 400 acres of land near Tower Hill, as well as property in Nokomis.

AUDUBON TOWNSHIP.

CAPT. M. OHLMAN, farmer, P. O. Ohlman, was born near Strasbourg, Germany; his father, Michael Ohlman, was born in France, emigrated to America in 1832; worked on the White House, Washington, where he earned sufficient money to carry him to St. Louis, Mo., where he removed in 1835; his wife, Gertrude Zahn, was born in France, and died in St. Louis in 1853, leaving six children, of whom our subject was the eldest. Our subject first worked on a Mississippi River flat boat; at the age of seventeen was promoted to the post of pilot, which position he held for ten years, when he became Captain and owner of the Star of the West, formerly known as the Polar Star; he was also Master of the D. A. January. In 1861, he gave up steamboating, and became a farmer, and has now a fine farm of 660 acres, together with other land and property, all of which he has accumulated by his own thrift and industry; he has realized as high as $12,000 on his stock at a single sale. In 1851, he married Miss Burbank, born in Cincinnati, Ohio, daughter of Benedick and Elizabeth (Straub) Burbank; there have been born to them an interesting family of six children, all of whom have been given a good education. Capt. Ohlman is a member of the Roman Catholic Church; in politics, he recognizes no party, but polls his vote for the man whom he thinks will best advance the interests of his country; in him all measures for the advancement of education, and all public enterprises, find a liberal supporter. His father, who was a wagon maker by trade, died in California in 1851.

ADDENDA.

Biographies too Late for Insertion in Proper Place.

GREENVILLE—Bond County.

MAJOR P. F. HOLCOMB, retired army officer. A sketch of the eventful life of this war veteran of Bond County furnishes interesting and instructive reading. The following brief outline of the life of Maj. Holcomb, the only retired army officer of Bond County, and one of the most gallant soldiers of our late war, speaks for itself:

He was born January 13, 1824, at Cincinnati, Ohio. His father, P. J. Holcomb, was a native of Vergennes, Vt., a merchant and a mill owner, and came West at an early date, and was one of the earliest and most active pioneers of the Buckeye State. He was of English descent, and married Miss Ruth A. Francisco, of Corsican lineage.

Our subject was the third child of a family of six children. When about seven years of age, his father removed from Ohio to Bond County, located upon a tract of land and began farming. Our subject received his primary education in the public schools of his native town and afterward attended school at Greenville, and at a comparatively early age entered the law office of Judge Ruet of Edwardsville, Ill. Under his tuition he read law, and was admitted to practice in the courts of the State. Maj. Holcomb never practiced his profession, however, but proceeded almost directly to Cincinnati and enlisted in the United States Army for general service in the Mexican war, and joined Company E, Third Artillery, Bragg's Battery.

The gallant services of this battery at Monterey and Buena Vista have made it famous in history. At the first named battle, Maj. Holcomb received a musket ball wound in his right arm. He figured in the Mexican war until August, 1848, when his regiment disbanded.

At the opening of the rebellion, in 1861, Maj. Holcomb was the first in his county to come to the rescue, and immediately set about recruiting a company of soldiers, to defend again the Stars and Stripes. This he accomplished with his usual success, his being the first drilled company to enter the conflict from Bond County. He remained with the company until the latter part of June, 1861, when he received orders to report to Fort Preble at Portland, Me., reaching there in July, and from Fort Preble he was detailed on recruiting expeditions. March 22, 1862, he was ordered to take command of the Second Battery Vermont Light Artillery. He acted as Captain of this battery until they were mustered out of the service in August, 1863. August 20, 1863, he was commissioned Major of the First Texas Union Cavalry. He served with his regiment in that State and Louisiana, a portion of the time as Brigade Commander of the Nineteenth Corps. October 5, 1864, he was ordered, and accordingly reported, to his regiment at Fort Preble, and was soon after detailed to Fort La Fayette, New York Harbor, where he was placed in charge of prisoners, under Col. Burke. In the winter of 1866, Maj. Holcomb was ordered to Texas. He served in regulating the hostiles in that State until January 30, 1867, when, on account of disability and for gallant and meritorious service, he was retired from the service, with a salary sufficient to support him in independence during his declining years.

Maj. Holcomb, it will be seen, served his country continuously for over twenty years. During that time he took active part in over 100 engagements, and many times in the very heat of the most important ones. Eighteen different times shots have pierced through his uniform, but in most instances his person has escaped harm.

April 3, 1856, he was married to Miss Bell Blanchard, daughter of Seth Blanchard, one of Bond County's earliest and most active pioneers, and a native of Stoughton, Mass. They have one son, James E., born September 26, 1874.

PROF. S. M. INGLIS was born in Marietta, Penn., August 15, 1838, son of Rev. George S. and Keziah R. (Martin) Inglis, he is a native of Baltimore, Md., a minister who labored largely in the cause of African Colonization; she a native of Lancaster County, Penn. They were the parents of six children, two boys and four girls. Our subject was compelled, through force of circumstances, to educate himself, but by hard struggling completed a course of study in Mendota Collegiate Institute, located in Mendota, La Salle County, being valedictorian in a class of nine at his graduation. He adopted the profession of a public instructor, and has given nearly all his time to that calling. He enlisted in the One Hundred and Fourth Illinois Volunteer Infantry, but after three months of camp duty was discharged in consequence of disability. He has been a member of the Presbyterian Church since he was fifteen years of age and filled the [illegible] Elder in the same; [illegible] in Sunday school work, being superintendent; Trustee of Southern Illinois Normal University through appointment [illegible] Cullom; also First Lieutenant [illegible] of Illinois State Militia. Prof. [illegible] been for fourteen years [illegible] public schools of Greenville, [illegible] to be the father of the school system [illegible] that city which is the pride of the county and would reflect credit upon any section of the country. In habit, the Professor is industrious and persevering, and benevolent to a fault, always assisting with his means every worthy enterprise and person, being especially the friend of struggling students. He is, and has been since the [illegible] party in 1856, a Republican, and holds membership with the Ancient Order of United Workmen.

WILLIAMSON PLANT, son of [illegible] D. Plant, and grandson of Williamson Plant, was born near Pocahontas, Bond County, Ill., December 19, 1827. The first fourteen years were spent on the farm upon which he was born, and from a near schoolhouse received a common school education for that day, one term of eight months having been spent at school at the academy in Hillsboro, in the winter of 1839-40, in which Mr. Edward W[illegible] man was teacher. He was in partnership in a store in Greenville with his father from 1848 to 1851, and has served three [illegible] terms as Sheriff and Collector of the county, and three other years had [illegible] office, making nine years in [illegible] He has been Secretary of the St. Louis, Vandalia & Terre Haute Railroad Company [illegible] its organization, November 22, 1865. He is engaged in farming, and is one of the proprietors of the "Greenville City Mills." Mr. Plant has been twice married, first on May 3, 1848, to Susan G. Grover, by which marriage he had one son, Emery D. Mrs. Plant died March 15, 1852. He was married to his present wife formerly Sarah Jane Wafer, March 31, 1853. Six children have been born from last marriage: Emma J., Willie W., Ida I., Lillie E., Sallie E. and Ada J., and all living. Mr. Plant has resided at Greenville continuously since December, 1852.

HILLSBORO—Montgomery County.

ARIUS N. KINGSBURY, County Judge, whose portrait appears in this work, was born in Athens, Ohio, February 5, 1830, and is a son of Ira and Hannah (Price) Kingsbury, the latter a native of Ohio and the former of Vermont, where he followed farming. He came to Illinois in 1841, and died in Bond County in 1872; his wife died at Mt. Carmel, Ill., in 1842. Seven children were born to them, of whom the subject of this sketch is the second. He was educated principally in the common and academical schools of the State; studied law at Greenville, Ill., where he was admitted to practice in 1855, and in 1857 came to Hillsboro and entered upon the practice of his profession. In 1873, he was a candidate for Supreme Judge, receiving 1,700 majority in Montgomery County, 1,300 in Macoupin County, and carrying Shelby and Richland Counties. The year previous, he had been a candidate for State Senator in the district composed of Montgomery and Christian Counties, receiving a majority of the delegates, but being defeated in the convention. He was elected County Judge in November, 1873, and has served in that position ever since, giving general satisfaction. No estate has ever lost a cent on account of bonds being insufficient; he is always at his office during business hours, and attends strictly to his official duties. He has been renominated for the office of County Judge at the ensuing November election (1882), by the Democratic party of Montgomery County. He was married, April 29, 1859, to Miss Celeste Hazard, who was born in Alton, Ill., and is a daughter of Evan M. and Jane Hazard, the latter a native of Huntsville, Ala., and the former of Rhode Island. Judge and Mrs. Kingsbury have four children: Mary Evelyn, Jessie C., Willie N. and Rose. Judge Kingsbury is not a member of any particular church organization, but a patron of all; his wife is a member of the Episcopal Church.

HON. JESSE J. PHILLIPS, Circuit Judge. Prominent among the historical names of Illinois is that of the subject of this sketch. Few, if any, of the gallant officers who won their way to distinction, and, by their valor in the field, shed luster upon our army in the great war against the rebellion, can show a record as replete with deeds of daring as that of Gen. Jesse J. Phillips, of Hillsboro. Nor is he lacking in any of those essential elements in the character of the civilian which when properly concentrated and applied, render their possessor a peer among the more prominent of his fellow citizens. Gifted by nature with abilities of a high order, he has, by arduous study, acquired fine attainments as a scholar, and ranks among the foremost

in which he took part was at Shiloh, on the 6th of April, 1862. In this battle the Ninth Regiment went into the fight with 570 men, and of this number sixty-one were killed on the field, 287 wounded and ten taken prisoners. One commissioned officer was killed and nineteen wounded; only four commissioned officers were left unhurt. Among the mortally wounded was a brother, Sidney B. Phillips. The horse ridden by Col. Phillips in this action received three musket shots and one grape shot before he fell, and the Colonel himself was shot through the hand and twice through the right thigh. In March, 1862, the Colonel of the Ninth Regiment was severely wounded, and in consequence the command of the regiment devolved upon Lieut. Col. Phillips, who was retained in this position until the close of the term of service of the regiment.

Upon recovering from the effects of the wounds received at Shiloh, he was ordered to Northern Alabama, and was stationed at Athens, in that State, for several months. This being the extreme outpost, both to the South and West of the Union forces stationed in that locality, made it a point of great danger, and required constant activity and caution during the period the regiment remained there. His command was at this time mounted for scouting purposes, at his request. About the 1st of February, 1863, he with his command engaged in some ten or twelve cavalry fights in one of which, near Florence, Ala., a desperate charge with sabers was made, in which he received a severe injury, by his horse falling after he had broken through the enemy's column. He had made a charge upon seventy men with a detachment of his own regiment numbering but thirty three men, and succeeded in capturing thirty-four of the enemy. The only person hurt during the charge was a rebel, cut down by a saber stroke from Col. Phillips, and that sustained by the latter, as above stated. In connection with, and as a part of, the command of Col. Cornyn, commanding a cavalry brigade, Col. Phillips, on the 15th of April, 1863, had a skirmish with rebel cavalry, at Cherokee, Ala., and on the same day another skirmish at Lundy's. In these two skirmishes the enemy lost, in killed and wounded, fifty men, with twenty-three taken prisoners. The Union loss was five wounded and fifty-nine captured. On the 17th another skirmish occurred at Cherokee, in which the Union forces captured thirteen of the enemy, the former sustaining no loss. Another skirmish took place at Crane Creek, Ala., on the 27th. On the 4th of May, Col. Phillips and his command participated in the fight at Tupelo, Miss., and on the 28th had a skirmish at Florence, Ala., in which a number of the enemy were captured. In this action, Col. Phillips, with his regiment, charged the rebel guns, and by the artillery firing at the rebel guns, one of our men was wounded by the Union guns. On the 31st of May, our forces again skirmished with the enemy in Tennessee. On the 19th of June, 1863, he was in command of about six hundred men, his own and parts of two other regiments, with two guns, and while reconnoitering in Mississippi, was attacked by about three thousand men under Gen. Ruggles, at Mud Creek Swamp, and a severe battle ensued, the fight lasting from 8 A. M. to 3 P. M. Col. Phillips being eighty miles from any support, wisely determined to retreat, but in so doing, to contest every inch of the ground. By securing advantageous positions, and by his tactics and skillful maneuvering, he punished the enemy quite severely on the retreat, and the rebel forces were ordered to discontinue the advance. The rebel loss, as was afterward admitted by them, was 200 in killed and wounded. The Union loss was five killed and eighteen wounded. This contest is referred to in the official reports as having been conducted in a gallant and masterly manner by Col. Phillips, notwithstanding the fact that he was pursued by a force nearly four times as great as his own, he marched forty miles in an orderly manner, over a swampy country, swam his command over two rivers (the Tallahatchie and Hatchie) and brought his artillery through in safety and with comparatively little loss. On the 13th of July, his command, forming a part of a brigade under Col. Hatch, was engaged in a sharp fight with rebel cavalry, capturing about seventy men. Union loss, seven. In August, 1863, he, in command of about sixteen hundred men, raided through Mississippi. At Grenada, they captured and destroyed sixty locomotives, 450 cars of all kinds, and a large amount of stores. At this point the command of Col. Phillips met and drove back a force of 1,500 rebels under Col. Slemmer. He again skirmished with the enemy on Forked Deer River, in Tennessee, October 3, 1863. A short time thereafter, whilst scouting in Mississippi with 500 men and two guns, he found himself in the front of a force of about three thousand rebel cavalry. Surmising that their object was to cut the railroad, and thereby prevent re-enforcements being sent toward Chattanooga from Memphis (as was being done by Gen. Sherman), Col. Phillips dispatched couriers from his command to several points on the railroad, requesting re-enforcements to be sent to him near Salem, as the indications were that he would have to attack the enemy near that place. On the 8th of October, at 11 A. M., with his small force, he attacked the enemy vigorously, and, after fighting two hours, was re-enforced by 800 men under Col. McCrillis; and with this force he continued the fight until dark, when, owing to the disadvantages under which he had to maintain the conflict, he retreated. The loss of the Union forces was thirty killed and wounded. Three days later the rebels attacked Collierville, and on the same day Col. Phillips, in command of a brigade, forming part of a division under Col. Hatch, followed in pursuit, marching upward of seventy five miles, fighting at Graham's Mills and at Wyall, Miss. In the last engagement he had a horse shot under him.

At Florence, Ala., November 30, 1863, he, with 200 men, attacked a force of the enemy, charging them with sabers and capturing thirty four men. At Decatur, Ala., where his command was next ordered, he remained from January, 1864, until the 1st of May, following, during which time he was engaged in frequent reconnoissances and skirmishes. Among the more important of the latter was the action near Moulton, Ala. With 350 men, he was ordered to reconnoiter, and find the locality and strength of an infantry force of the enemy, understood to be in that neighborhood. His instructions were to "*develop the strength of that infantry.*" He accordingly attacked, at Somerville, Ala., a force of about one hundred and twenty five rebel cavalry under Maj. Williams, and after a short skirmish drove them to Danville, where they were re-enforced by an additional force of seventy-five men under Capt. Doan. From Danville the rebels were driven to Moulton, where they were re-enforced by 350 men under Maj. Morehead. Here a sharp fight ensued, and the entire rebel force, 550 strong, who by this time had learned the invincible troops, against whom they were arrayed, were driven three miles beyond the town, where Col. Philips, as he afterward remarked, "developed" the rebel infantry, two or three regiments strong. Ten minutes after the latter "development," he ordered a retreat.

rear, he made a stand against the cavalry that were in pursuit of him, and checked and drove them back until the infantry again came up. During this fight his horse was [illegible] Gen. [illegible] columns, [illegible] Col. Phillips [illegible] his loss was twenty men killed [illegible] prisoners. The rebel loss was [illegible] killed and wounded [illegible]. About the [illegible] day [illegible] which [illegible] preparing [illegible] With the [illegible] were placed [illegible] while Col. Phillips [illegible] ordered to [illegible] Chattanooga [illegible] with a train of [illegible] hundred and fifty wagons, [illegible] miles in the rear. On [illegible] order for him [illegible] the front which [illegible] and the [illegible] morning he [illegible] his command [illegible] the Tennessee [illegible] with [illegible] through [illegible] rebel cavalry force [illegible]

rebel cavalry force under Gen. Wheeler, of rebel cavalry fame. Col. Phillips' force was driven back after a sharp fight of about two hours, during which time he had his horse shot and [illegible] and received a wound by a [illegible] the [illegible] his ankle which was quite painful, and rendered him unfit for service until [illegible] the [illegible] he again assumed [illegible] regiment and took [illegible] before Atlanta [illegible] on active [illegible] placed upon the staff of Gen. [illegible] mention of the [illegible] his official report. On the night of the 22d of July, he was placed in command of a brigade of infantry and bore a prominent part in the battle of the 28th of July, materially aiding the heroic Gen. [illegible] who on that day sustained the brunt of the battle. About the [illegible] of August 1864 he was again appointed [illegible] Gen. Dodge's staff, where he remained [illegible] the capture of Atlanta, when he resigned, his resignation being accepted upon the 1st of September, 1864. On returning to his home at Hillsboro, in 1864, he resumed the practice of law, which he has since continued with great success. He was commissioned as Brevet Colonel, to take rank from the 13th of March, 1865, for gallant and meritorious services during the war, and was commissioned at the same time Brevet Brigadier General, by brevet, for distinguished services, [illegible] taking rank from the [illegible] of March, 1865. Thoroughly Democratic in his political views, Gen. Phillips [illegible] prominence among the leaders of his party in the State [illegible] a well stored and [illegible] balanced [illegible] with intellectual and [illegible] of a high order, he [illegible] brought forward by the party as a candidate for the office of State Treasurer; his first candidacy for that office being in 1866, when he made a thorough and vigorous canvass of the State, speaking at more than sixty different places. He was again nominated in 1868, but the Democracy being largely in the minority, he was again defeated. In social life Gen. Phillips is one of the most genial of men. As a citizen, he is enterprising and public-spirited, ever taking a leading part in all matters calculated to advance the material interests of his city and county. He is at present Circuit Judge of this district, a position he fills with ability.

LITCHFIELD—Montgomery County.

MRS. JULIA MACHLER, née Maurer, is a native of Konigsburg, in the Empire of Prussia. Her father, Casper Maurer, was a Bavarian, and an officer in the household of Queen Lisett (Elizabeth) of Prussia. Her mother, Helena Long, was a personal attendant on the Queen. After his marriage, Mr. Maurer returned to Bavaria and served Queen Caroline, the mother of Lisett. He dying in 1836, his widow remained a pensioner in the royal household until her death, in 1868. Julia, the third child, accompanied an uncle to the United States in 1845, and the following year was married, in New York City, to Peter Machler, fifteen years her senior. He was a native of Crisnacht, Prussia; had been a soldier for six years, and then wrought at his calling. Coming to New York in 1841, he toiled as a journeyman for two years, and then opening a shop of his own, conducted business until his death, in 1857. Mrs. Machler then asserted her character, and, in order to provide for her three children, went into a new line of business, with success. In 1870, she located here in order that her boys might grow up with the town, and was speedily looked upon as one of the "solid" class. A cheerful, home-staying woman, true to her friends, diligent in business, generous, charitable in judgment, she illustrates in her walk of life the virtues which make home happy.

ERRATA.

The biography of William S. Lea, of Litchfield, Montgomery County, is not in alphabetical order, being among the S's, in Litchfield.

www.ingramcontent.com/pod-product-compliance
Lightning Source LLC
LaVergne TN
LVHW012230050325
805252LV00003B/33
9781016072519